OXFORD Learner's Spanish Dictionary

Project management
Nicholas Rollin
Joanna Brough

Editors
Ximena Castillo
Jane Horwood
Amanda Leigh
Meic Haines
Stephanie Parker

Consultant
Isabel Sudea

OXFORD
UNIVERSITY PRESS

OXFORD
UNIVERSITY PRESS

Great Clarendon Street, Oxford OX2 6DP

Oxford University Press is a department of the University of Oxford.
It furthers the University's objective of excellence in research, scholarship,
and education by publishing worldwide in

Oxford New York

Auckland Cape Town Dar es Salaam Hong Kong Karachi
Kuala Lumpur Madrid Melbourne Mexico City Nairobi
New Delhi Shanghai Taipei Toronto

With offices in

Argentina Austria Brazil Chile Czech Republic France Greece
Guatemala Hungary Italy Japan Poland Portugal Singapore
South Korea Switzerland Thailand Turkey Ukraine Vietnam

First published 2006

British Library Cataloguing in Publication Data

Data available

ISBN 978-0-19-911646-1
ISBN OCR edition 978-0-19-918097-4

1 3 5 7 9 10 8 6 4 2

Printed in Singapore by KHL Printing Co. Pte Ltd.

Contents

Introduction

This bilingual dictionary has been specifically written for students of Spanish – from those just starting out all the way up to those preparing for exams. It presents essential information in a format designed to be clear and easy to consult. There are two main sections: Spanish-English and English-Spanish. These sections are divided by a central section in full colour.

TIP To help you find words quickly, the first word on each page is printed top left and the last word on the page is printed top right.

Spanish-English

Look up Spanish words – listed alphabetically – to find their meaning in English. When a word has more than one meaning, make sure you choose the one that is most relevant.

TIP Look at the number after a verb you look up and find that number in the verb tables: it shows the endings for that verb.

English-Spanish

Look up English words – listed alphabetically – to find out how to say them in Spanish. When you find the Spanish word, the entry will tell you whether it is masculine (*masc*) or feminine (*fem*). To choose the right word and use it properly, make sure you read through the examples provided.

TIP To find out more about the Spanish translation that you are given, look it up on the Spanish-English side of the dictionary afterwards.

Colour section

In the colour section you will find reference material such as: verb tables for regular verbs and the most common irregular verbs, key vocabulary (grouped by theme to help you in your oral exam: Leisure and holiday, Career and future plans, etc.), classroom language, useful phrases (e.g. days, months, dates, time); sample letters with key opening and closing phrases; email and text messaging vocabulary; a sample CV and hints for job applications.

Get to know your dictionary

User-friendly layout

- **Two-colour layout**
  Headwords (words you are looking up) are in blue for easy identification.
- **Easy to navigate**
  The alphabet runs down the side of each page indicating what letter you are looking at, and whether you are on the Spanish-English or English-Spanish side of the dictionary:

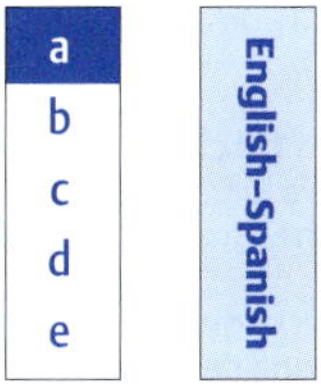

- **The key symbol**
  The key symbol is explained along the bottom of every other page.

  ⚷ indicates key words

Clear entries

- **Parts of speech written out in full**
  Noun, verb, adjective, adverb, conjunction, preposition or *determiner* are all written out clearly after the headword:

  to **baptize** *verb*
  bautizar [22]

- **Gender of nouns and adjectives**
  Both the definite (or if appropriate, the indefinite) article and the abbreviations *masc* and *fem* are used on both sides of the dictionary to make it clear whether a word is masculine or feminine.

  ⚷ **balcony** *noun*
  el **balcón** *masc*

  creased *adjective*
  arrugado *masc*, **arrugada** *fem*

Abbreviations used are:

masc	masculine	*fem*	feminine
pl	plural	*adj*	adjective
adv	adverb	*prep*	preposition
conj	conjunction	*excl*	exclamation

- **All variants shown**
  Normally the masculine and feminine singular forms of adjectives, nouns, and pronouns are given. Where relevant the plural forms are also given.

⚷ el **cual** *masc pronoun*, la **cual** *fem pron*, los **cuales** *masc plural*, las **cuales** *fem plural*

- **Pointers to other parts of speech**
  Where a word can do more than one job (be a noun *and* a verb, for example), a helpful pointer reminds students to check other parts of speech:

⚷ **back** *adjective* ▷ **see back** *adv, noun, verb*
1 (*wheel, seat*) **trasero** *masc*, **trasera** *fem*
the back seat of the car el asiento trasero del coche
2 **the back garden** el jardín de atrás
the back gate la verja de atrás

Extra help with verbs

- **Heavy-duty verbs**
  Common verbs are given special treatment in tinted panels:

> ⚷ **hacer** *verb* **[7]**
> 1 **to make**
> **hacer un ruido** to make a noise
> **hacer un pastel** to make a cake
> **hacer la cama** to make the bed

- **Verb tables in centre section** (*see* **Introduction**)
  The centre section contains full conjugations for regular *-ar*, *-er* and *-ir* verbs plus the most common irregular verbs.
- **Links to verb tables**
  On both sides of the dictionary, each Spanish verb is followed by a number linking it to the central verb tables:

to **baptize** *verb*
bautizar [22]

cuchichear *verb* **[17]**
to whisper

- **Use of *to* before a verb**
  On the English-Spanish side of the dictionary, English verbs are preceded by *to* (see above).

- **Irregular forms of verbs**
  If you look up past participles and non-infinitive forms of a verb, you are cross-referenced to the relevant headword:

cuelga, **cuelgo**, **etc** *verb* ▷ **colgar**

Extra help with difficult points of Spanish

- **Extra help with grammar and spelling**
  'Word tips' give extra help with tricky grammatical points and reminders on how Spanish spelling is different from English:

  WORD TIP Adjectives and nouns for nationality, regional origin and language do not have capital letters in Spanish.

- **Typical problem areas**
  Extra help is given with traditionally problem areas, such as talking about jobs and professions:

  ♪ **a** *determiner*

  4 (*saying what you do*) **She's a doctor.** Es médica.
  I'm a student. Soy estudiante.

  WORD TIP *a* is not translated into Spanish when you say your profession.

- **False friends**
  False friends are shown on the Spanish-English side of the dictionary:

  WORD TIP *actual* in Spanish does not mean *actual* in English; for the meaning of *actual* ▷ **verdadero**

Language in context – example sentences

- **Thousands of example sentences**
  Thousands of examples of 'real language' are given at an appropriate level for the age group, progressing from simpler to more complex sentences:

  el **cine** *masc noun*
  cinema
  ir al cine to go to the cinema
  Vámonos al cine. Let's go to the cinema.
  ¿Qué ponen en el cine? What's on at the cinema?
  • **el cine de barrio** local cinema

- **World Spanish**
  Both European and Latin American Spanish are represented on both sides of the dictionary:

  ♪ **car** *noun*
  el **coche** *masc*, (*Latin America*) el **carro** *masc*
  a car crash un accidente de coche
  He parked the car. Aparcó el coche.
  We're going by car. Vamos en coche.

- **Correctly punctuated**
  All example sentences are correctly punctuated with capital letters and full stops (see above).

Additional features

- **Core vocabulary highlighted**

  The dictionary includes all the key curriculum words secondary school pupils need and a key symbol highlights the key words you must know to prepare for your exams.

  🔑 el **balcón** *masc noun*
  balcony

- **Colour section**

  The full colour central section will help you communicate in both written and spoken Spanish.

- **Mini-infos**

  Boxed notes provide quirky and interesting cultural information throughout the A–Z text:

> **mini-info palabras**
>
> Muchas palabras usadas en la vida diaria son de origen árabe . Se identifican porque comienzan con las letras al-, ar-, az-; por ejemplo alfombra, arroz, azúcar. También hay muchos nombres como el río *Guadalquivir* o la *Alhambra*.

- **Language functions covered**

  Exam syllabus language functions, such as requests and demands, are covered within example sentences:

  🔑 el **café** *masc noun*
  1 **cafe** (*place*)
  2 **coffee**
  ¿Quieres un café? Do you want a cup of coffee?
  - el **café con leche** white coffee
  - el **café cortado** coffee with a dash of milk
  - el **café descafeinado** decaffeinated coffee
  - el **café solo** black coffee

A a

♪ **a** *preposition*

1 (*showing movement*) **to**
Voy al mercado. I'm going to the market.
Iremos al cine. We'll go to cinema.
Gira a la derecha. Turn right.

WORD TIP *a* + *el* becomes *al*.

2 (*with words of giving, sending, talking, etc*) **to**
Se lo di a Laura. I gave it to Laura.
Le mandé un regalo a mi madre. I sent a present to my mother.
Le da clases de piano a mi hermana. She gives my sister piano lessons.

3 (*showing where something is*) **Está a la izquierda.** It's on the left.
Están sentados a la mesa. They are sitting at the table.
Siéntate al sol. Sit in the sun.
Estaban a mi lado. They were beside me.
Está a diez kilómetros de aquí. It's ten kilometres from here.
La vi a lo lejos. I saw her in the distance.

4 (*showing time*) **at**
a las diez at ten o'clock
a medianoche at midnight
Se casó a los veinte años. She married at twenty.
¿A qué hora termina? What time does it end?

5 (*with dates*) **Estamos a dos de febrero.** It's the second of February.

6 (*saying how often, how much, etc*) **dos veces al día** twice a day
a tres euros el kilo three euros a kilo
a ochenta kilómetros por hora at eighty kilometres an hour

7 (*showing method*) **ir a pie** to go on foot
hecho a mano handmade
escrito a mano handwritten
a lápiz in pencil

8 (*showing intention*) **Voy a hacer los deberes.** I'm going to do my homework.
Nos fuimos a dormir. We went to sleep.
Se han ido a nadar. They've gone swimming.
Salimos a pasear. We went out for a walk.

9 (*in commands*) **¡A dormir!** Go to sleep!
¡A comer! Come and eat!

10 (*with a person object*) **Vi a tu padre.** I saw your father.
Llamé a tu hermano. I rang your brother.

WORD TIP *padre* and *hermano* are the person objects. *a* is not translated in English.

la **abadía** *fem noun*
abbey

♪ **abajo** *adverb*

1 **aquí abajo** down here
allí abajo down there

2 **downstairs**
Están abajo. They're downstairs.
Ven abajo. Come downstairs.

3 **de abajo** below, down below
el piso de abajo the flat below

abalanzarse *reflexive verb* **[22]**
abalanzarse sobre alguien to leap on somebody
Se abalanzaron a la ventana. They rushed to the window.

abandonado *masc adjective*, **abandonada** *fem*

1 **deserted**
una casa abandonada a deserted house

2 **abandoned**
un coche abandonado an abandoned car

3 **neglected**
sentirse abandonado to feel neglected

abandonar *verb* **[17]**

1 **to leave**
En verano la gente abandona la ciudad para irse a la playa. In summer people leave the city to go to the seaside.

2 **to abandon**
Abandonó a su familia. He left his family.

el **abanico** *masc noun*
fan

abarcar *verb* **[31]**

1 **to cover**
Abarca el periodo entre 2000 y 2005. It covers the period between 2000 and 2005.

2 **to see**
Desde aquí se puede abarcar toda la ciudad. From here you can see the whole city.

abarrotado *masc adjective*, **abarrotada** *fem*
packed
un bar abarrotado de gente a bar packed with people

el **abecedario** *masc noun*
alphabet

el **abedul** *masc noun*
birch

la **abeja** *fem noun*
bee

el **abejorro** *masc noun*
bumblebee

la **abertura** *fem noun*
1 **opening**
2 **hole**

el **abeto** *masc noun*
fir tree

♪ **abierto** *masc adjective*, **abierta** *fem*
1 **open**
abierto al público open to the public
La puerta está abierta. The door's open.
El grifo está abierto. The tap's running.
2 **open-minded**
Mis padres son muy abiertos. My parents are very open-minded.

abochornado *masc adjective*, **abochornada** *fem*
embarrassed

el **abogado** *masc noun*, la **abogada** *fem*
1 **lawyer**
2 **solicitor**

abolir *verb* **[19]**
to abolish

la **abolladura** *fem noun*
dent

abollar *verb* **[17]**
to dent

abollarse *reflexive verb* **[17]**
to get dented

abonar *verb* **[17]**
1 **to pay** (*a bill*)
2 **to fertilize** (*a field or plant*)

abonarse *reflexive verb* **[17]**
1 **to subscribe**
abonarse a una revista to subscribe to a magazine
2 **to buy a season ticket**

el **abono** *masc noun*
1 **fertilizer**
2 **season ticket**
sacar un abono para la piscina to buy a season ticket for the swimming pool

abordar *verb* **[17]**
1 **to tackle** (*a problem*)
2 **to raise** (*a subject*)

aborrecer *verb* **[35]**
to detest
Aborrezco los callos. I hate tripe.

el **aborto** *masc noun*
1 **abortion**
2 **miscarriage**

abotonarse *reflexive verb* **[17]**
to do your buttons up
Abotónate la chaqueta. Do your jacket up.

abrasado *masc adjective*, **abrasada** *fem*
1 **burnt**
Murieron abrasados por las llamas. They burned to death.
2 **boiling hot**

abrasador *masc adjective*, **abrasadora** *fem*
burning hot (*the weather*)
Hacía un calor abrasador. It was burning hot.

abrasar *verb* **[17]**
to burn
El sol abrasaba. The sun was burning hot.

abrazar *verb* **[22]**
to hug

abrazarse *reflexive verb* **[22]**
to hug each other

♪ el **abrazo** *masc noun*
hug
un fuerte abrazo all the best (*at the end of a letter*)

el **abrebotellas** *masc noun*, *pl:* los **abrebotellas**
bottle opener

el **abrelatas** *masc noun*, *pl:* los **abrelatas**
tin opener

la **abreviatura** *fem noun*
abbreviation

el **abridor** *masc noun*
1 **bottle opener**
2 **tin opener**

abrigar *verb* **[28]**
to be warm (*jumper, coat*)

abrigarse *reflexive verb* **[28]**
to wrap up warmly

♪ el **abrigo** *masc noun*
1 **coat**
ropa de abrigo warm clothes
2 **shelter**
al abrigo de los árboles in the shelter of the trees

♪ **abril** *masc noun*
April
en abril in April
el 5 de abril on 5 April

WORD TIP Names of months and days start with small letters in Spanish.

♪ **abrir** *verb* **[46]**
1 **to open**
Abre la ventana. Open the window.
Abrió la boca para hablar. He opened his mouth to speak.
abrir algo de par en par to open something wide
2 **to turn on** (*a tap*)
abrir el agua to turn the water on

abrirse *reflexive verb* **[46]**
to open
La puerta se abrió. The door opened.
¿Cómo se abre? How do you open it?

abrocharse *reflexive verb* **[17]**
1 **to do up your buttons**
Abróchate la chaqueta. Do your jacket up.
2 **to fasten** (*a seat belt*)
Abróchense los cinturones. Fasten your seat belts.

absoluto *masc adjective*, **absoluta** *fem*
1 **absolute**
2 **en absoluto** not at all
'¿Te importa?'—'En absoluto.' 'Do you mind?'—'Not at all.'

absorbente *masc & fem adjective*
absorbent

absorber *verb* **[18]**
to absorb

abstemio *masc adjective*, **abstemia** *fem*
teetotal
Es abstemio. He's teetotal.

abstracto *masc adjective*, **abstracta** *fem*
abstract

absurdo *masc adjective*, **absurda** *fem*
absurd

abuchear *verb* **[17]**
to boo
El público abucheó al árbitro. The crowd booed the referee.

♪ el **abuelo** *masc noun*, la **abuela** *fem*
1 **grandfather**
2 **grandmother**
3 **mis abuelos** my grandparents

♪ **aburrido** *masc adjective*, **aburrida** *fem*
1 **boring**
ser aburrido, *fem* **aburrida** to be boring
Sus clases son muy aburridas. His lessons are really boring.
2 **bored**
estar aburrido, *fem* **aburrida** to be bored
Siempre está aburrida. She is always bored.

♪ el **aburrimiento** *masc noun*
boredom
¡Qué aburrimiento! How boring!

♪ **aburrirse** *reflexive verb* **[19]**
to get bored

abusar *verb* **[17]**
1 **abusar (de)** to take too much (*alcohol, etc*), to take too many (*pills, etc*)
2 **abusar de** to take advantage of
Están abusando de tu amabilidad. They are taking advantage of your kindness.

abusivo *masc adjective*, **abusiva** *fem*
1 **excessive** (*price*)
2 **unfair** (*rule, law*)

el **abuso** *masc noun*
1 **abuse**
2 **outrage**
¡Esto es un verdadero abuso! This is really outrageous!
• el **abuso del alcohol** alcohol abuse

aC *abbreviation*
(*= antes de Cristo*) **BC, before Christ**

acá *adverb*
here
¡Ven acá! Come here!

acabado *masc adjective*, **acabada** *fem*
finished

♪ **acabar** *verb* **[17]**
1 **to finish**
La fiesta acabó muy tarde. The party finished very late.
¿Has acabado con el abrelatas? Have you finished with the tin opener?
2 **to end**
La palabra acaba en 'r'. The word ends in 'r'.
La historia acaba bien. The story has a happy ending.
3 **acabar de hacer algo** to have just done something
4 **Acaba de salir.** He's just gone out.
Acabo de hablar con él. I've just spoken to him.
Acabamos de llegar. We've just arrived.
Acabábamos de terminar. We had just finished.

WORD TIP *acabar de* in the present tense is translated by *have -ed* in English. In the imperfect tense, it is translated by *had -ed* in English.

acabarse *reflexive verb* **[17]**
1 **to be over** (*parties, films, etc*)
Cuando se acabó la película. When the film was over.
2 **to run out** (*money, food, drinks*)
Se ha acabado el pan. The bread's run out.
Se me acabó el dinero. I ran out of money.

la **academia** *fem noun*
school
• la **academia de idiomas** language school

académico *masc adjective*, **académica** *fem*
academic

la **acampada** *fem noun*
camping
ir de acampada to go camping

acampar *verb* **[17]**
to camp

el **acantilado** *masc noun*
cliff

acariciar *verb* **[17]**
1 **to caress** (*a person*)
2 **to stroke** (*a cat, a dog*)

acaso *adverb*
por si acaso just in case

acatarrado *masc adjective*, **acatarrada** *fem*
estar acatarrado to have a cold

acatarrarse *reflexive verb* **[17]**
to catch a cold

acceder *verb* **[18]**
1 **acceder a algo** to agree to something
Accedió a verla. He agreed to see her.
2 **to access** (*information, computer files*)

accesible *masc & fem adjective*
1 **accessible** (*place*)
2 **affordable**
a precios accesibles at affordable prices

los **accesorios** *plural masc noun*
accessories

accidental *masc & fem adjective*
accidental

el **accidente** *masc noun*
accident
tener un accidente to have an accident
• el **accidente de circulación** road accident

la **acción** *fem noun*
1 **act**
una buena acción a good deed
2 **share** (*in a company*)

el **acebo** *masc noun*
holly

el **aceite** *masc noun*
oil
• el **aceite de oliva** olive oil

aceitoso *masc adjective*, **aceitosa** *fem*
oily

la **aceituna** *fem noun*
olive

el **acelerador** *masc noun*
accelerator
pisar el acelerador to put your foot down (*to accelerate*)

acelerar *verb* **[17]**
to accelerate

el **acento** *masc noun*
1 **accent**
tener acento andaluz to have an Andalusian accent
Casi no tienes acento. You have hardly any accent.
2 **accent** (*on a letter in written Spanish*)
• el **acento agudo** acute accent

acentuarse *reflexive verb* **[20]**
to have an accent
Se acentúa en la última sílaba. It has an accent on the last syllable.

aceptable *masc & fem adjective*
acceptable

aceptar *verb* **[17]**
1 **to accept** (*an invitation, an apology*)
2 **aceptar hacer algo** to agree to do something
Aceptaron dejármelo. They agreed to lend it to me.

la **acera** *fem noun*
pavement

acerca de *preposition*
about

acercar *verb* **[31]**
1 **to move closer**
Acerqué la silla a la ventana. I moved the chair nearer the window.
Acércame un poco la lámpara. Bring the lamp closer to me.
2 **to pass**
Acércame ese libro. Pass me that book.
3 **acercar a alguien a un lugar** to give somebody a lift somewhere
Me acercó a la oficina. She gave me a lift to the office.

acercarse *reflexive verb* **[31]**
1 **to come close**
Acércate más. Come closer., Get closer.
2 **to get close to**
Se acercó a la ventana. She got close to the window.

♪ el **acero** *masc noun*
steel

acertado *masc adjective*, **acertada** *fem*
right (*decision or answer*)

♪ **acertar** *verb* **[29]**
1 **to be right**
¡Has acertado! You've got it right!
2 **acertar algo** to get something right
Acertó todas las respuestas. She got all the answers right.
3 **acertar en el blanco** to hit the target

el **ácido** *masc noun*
acid

el **acierto** *masc noun*
1 **correct answer**
2 **good decision**
Ese regalo fue un acierto. That present was a good idea.

la **aclaración** *fem noun*
explanation

aclarar *verb* **[17]**
to make clear

aclararse *reflexive verb* **[17]**
to understand
Aún no me aclaro. I still don't understand.

el **acné** *masc noun*
acne

acoger *verb* **[3]**
1 **to receive** (*some news, a proposal*)
2 **to take in** (*a refugee, an orphan*)
3 **to welcome** (*a visitor*)

♪ **acompañar** *verb* **[17]**
1 **to go with**
La acompañé al dentista. I went with her to the dentist's.
Te acompaño a tu casa. I'll see you home.
2 **to keep company**
El perro me acompaña mucho. The dog keeps me company a lot.

aconsejar *verb* **[17]**
to advise

el **acontecimiento** *masc noun*
event

♪ **acordarse** *reflexive verb* **[24]**
to remember
No me acuerdo. I don't remember
acordarse de algo to remember something
Acuérdate de traer dinero. Remember to bring money.
¿Te acuerdas de él? Do you remember him?

el **acorde** *masc noun*
chord

el **acordeón** *masc noun*
accordion

acortar *verb* **[17]**
to shorten

♪ **acostarse** *reflexive verb* **[24]**
1 **to go to bed**
¿A qué hora te acuestas? What time do you go to bed?
Normalmente me acuesto a las diez y media. I usually go to bed at half past ten.
2 **acostarse con alguien** to sleep with somebody

acostumbrado *masc adjective*, **acostumbrada** *fem*
estar acostumbrado, *fem* **acostumbrada a algo** to be used to something
Está acostumbrada a levantarse temprano. She's used to getting up early.

acostumbrarse *reflexive verb* **[17]**
acostumbrarse a algo to get used to something
No se acostumbra al nuevo horario. She can't get used to the new timetable.

el & la **acróbata** *masc & fem noun*
acrobat

la **actitud** *fem noun*
attitude

♪ la **actividad** *fem noun*
activity

activo *masc adjective*, **activa** *fem*
active

el **acto** *masc noun*
1 **act**
2 **en el acto** immediately

el **actor** *masc noun*
actor

la **actriz** *fem noun*
actress

la **actuación** *fem noun*
performance (*in a play or film*)

Spanish–English

actual *masc & fem adjective*
present, **current**
la situación actual the present situation
el actual presidente the current president

WORD TIP *actual* in Spanish does not mean *actual* in English; for the meaning of *actual* ▷ **verdadero**

la **actualidad** *fem noun*
1 **en la actualidad** at present, at the moment
En la actualidad viven en Madrid. At present they're living in Madrid.
2 **nowadays**
En la actualidad es más fácil viajar. Nowadays it's easier to travel.

actualmente *adverb*
1 **at present**
Actualmente trabaja en un banco. At present he's working in a bank.
2 **nowadays**
Actualmente se fabrica con máquinas. Nowadays it's made by machine.

WORD TIP *actualmente* in Spanish does not mean *actually* in English; for the meaning of *actually* see *en realidad.* ▷ **realidad**

actuar *verb* **[20]**
to act

la **acuarela** *fem noun*
watercolour

el **acuario** *masc noun* ▷ see **acuario** *masc & fem noun*
aquarium

acuario *masc & fem noun*
▷ see **acuario** *noun*
Aquarius
Soy acuario. I'm an Aquarius.

WORD TIP Use a small letter in Spanish to say *I am Aquarius*, etc with star signs.

Acuario *masc noun*
Aquarius

acudir *verb* **[19]**
acudir a algo to attend something

el **acuerdo** *masc noun*
1 **agreement**
Llegaron a un acuerdo. They reached an agreement.
2 **estar de acuerdo (en algo)** to agree (on something)
Están de acuerdo en la fecha. They agree on the date.
No estoy de acuerdo. I don't agree.
ponerse de acuerdo to come to an agreement
3 **¡De acuerdo!** Okay!

la **acusación** *fem noun*
accusation

acusar *verb* **[17]**
to accuse
acusar a alguien de algo to accuse somebody of something
Me acusó de mentir. He accused me of lying.

la **acústica** *fem noun*
acoustics

el **adaptador** *masc noun*
adaptor

adaptar *verb* **[17]**
to adapt

adaptarse *reflexive verb* **[17]**
adaptarse a algo to adapt to something

a. de C. *abbreviation*
(= *antes de Cristo*) **BC** (*before Christ*)

adecuado *masc adjective*, **adecuada** *fem*
1 **suitable**
ser adecuado para algo to be suitable for something
2 **appropriate**, **right**
El momento no es adecuado. It's not the right moment.

adelantado *masc adjective*, **adelantada** *fem*
1 **advanced**
2 **fast** (*when talking about clocks, watches*)
Tu reloj va adelantado. Your watch is fast.
3 **pagar por adelantado** to pay in advance

el **adelantamiento** *masc noun*
overtaking

adelantar *verb* **[17]**
1 **to bring forward** (*a date or trip*)
2 **to overtake** (*when driving*)
3 **to put forward** (*a clock or watch*)

adelante *adverb*
1 **forward**
más adelante further on
ir hacia adelante to go forward
Hay que seguir adelante hasta llegar al semáforo. You must go on until you reach the lights.
2 (*in expressions*)
más adelante: Hablaremos sobre ello más adelante. We'll talk about it later on.
¡Adelante! Come in!

adelgazar *verb* **[22]**
to lose weight
He adelgazado tres kilos. I've lost three kilos.

a b c d e f g h i j k l m n ñ o p q r s t u v w x y z

♪ **además** *adverb*
1 **además de** as well as
Además de hacerlos los diseña. He designs as well as makes them.
Son tres, además de la madre. There are three, not counting the mother.
2 **besides** (*when you add to what you've already said*)
Además, no es mi problema. Besides, it's not my problem.
No ayuda y además se queja. He doesn't help and he complains as well.

♪ **adentro** *adverb*
inside
Ven adentro. Come inside.
Todos pasaron adentro. They all went inside.

adicto *masc noun*, **adicta** *fem*
addict

♪ **adiós** *exclamation*
1 **bye!**
2 **hello!** (*when you meet somebody in the street*)

el **aditivo** *masc noun*
additive

la **adivinanza** *fem noun*
riddle

adivinar *verb* [17]
to guess

el **adivino** *masc noun*, la **adivina** *fem*
fortune-teller

el **adjetivo** *masc noun*
adjective

adjuntar *verb* [17]
1 **to enclose** (*a document*)
2 **to attach** (*to an e-mail*)

adjunto *masc adjective*, **adjunta** *fem*
enclosed

la **administración** *fem noun*
administration
• la **administración pública** civil service

admirable *masc & fem adjective*
admirable

la **admiración** *fem noun*
1 **admiration**
sentir admiración por alguien to admire someone
2 (*in punctuation*) **un signo de admiración** an exclamation mark

el **admirador** *masc noun*, la **admiradora** *fem*
admirer

admirar *verb* [17]
to admire

admitir *verb* [19]
1 **to admit**
Admitió su responsabilidad. She admitted her responsibility.
2 **'No se admiten perros'** 'No dogs allowed'
'No se admiten devoluciones' 'No Returns' (*sign in a shop*)

el & la **adolescente** *masc & fem noun*
adolescent

♪ **adonde** *adverb* ▷ see **adónde** *adv*
where
La ciudad adonde vamos. The city where we're going.

♪ **adónde** *adverb* ▷ see **adonde** *adv*
where
¿Adónde vas? Where are you going?
'Me voy de viaje.'—'¿Adónde?' 'I'm going away.'—'Where?'

adoptar *verb* [17]
to adopt

adoptivo *masc adjective*, **adoptiva** *fem*
1 **adoptive** (*parents*)
2 **adopted** (*child*)

adorar *verb* [17]
to adore

adosado *masc adjective*, **adosada** *fem*
attached (*housing*)

el **adorno** *masc noun*
ornament
• los **adornos de Navidad** Christmas decorations

adquirir *verb* [47]
to acquire

adrede *adverb*
on purpose

♪ la **aduana** *fem noun*
customs
pasar por la aduana to go through customs
libre de derechos de aduana duty-free

♪ **adulto** *masc adjective*, **adulta** *fem*
▷ see **adulto** *noun*
adult

♪ el **adulto** *masc noun*, la **adulta** *fem*
▷ see **adulto** *adj*
adult

el **adverbio** *masc noun*
adverb

la **advertencia** *fem noun*
warning

Spanish–English

advertir *verb* **[14]**
to warn
Quedas advertido. You've been warned.
Le advertí que no llegase tarde otra vez. I warned him not to be late again.

aéreo *masc adjective*, **aérea** *fem*
air (*traffic*)

el **aerobic** *masc noun*
aerobics

el **aeromozo** *masc noun*, la **aeromoza** *fem* (*Latin America*) **flight attendant**

el **aeropuerto** *masc noun*
airport

el **aerosol** *masc noun*
aerosol

el **afán** *masc noun*
eagerness
Tienen afán de aprender. They are eager to learn.

afectar *verb* **[17]**
to affect

el **afecto** *masc noun*
affection
tenerle afecto a alguien to be fond of somebody

afectuoso *masc adjective*, **afectuosa** *fem*
affectionate (*person*)
Recibe un afectuoso saludo. With best wishes. (*friendly letter ending*)

afeitarse *reflexive verb* **[17]**
1 **to shave**
Hoy no me he afeitado. I haven't shaved today.
2 **to shave off** (*a beard, moustache*)
Se ha afeitado la barba. He's shaved his beard off.

la **afición** *fem noun*
interest
hobby
¿Qué aficiones tienes? What are your interests?
Mi afición principal es la fotografía. My main interest is photography.
Lo hago por afición. I do it as a hobby.

aficionado *masc adjective*, **aficionada** *fem*
▷ see **aficionado** *noun*
1 **ser aficionado, aficionada a algo** to be keen on something
Soy muy aficionada al ski. I'm a very keen skier (*girl speaking*).
Soy muy aficionado a los deportes. I'm very keen on sport (*boy speaking*).
2 **amateur**
un equipo aficionado an amateur team

el **aficionado** *masc noun*, la **aficionada** *fem* ▷ see **aficionado** *adj*
1 **fan**
un aficionado al jazz a jazz fan
un aficionado al rugby a rugby fan
para los aficionados a la cocina for those who like cooking
2 **amateur**
un grupo de aficionados a group of amateurs

aficionarse *reflexive verb* **[17]**
aficionarse a algo to get keen on something

afilar *verb* **[17]**
to sharpen

afinar *verb* **[17]**
to tune (*an instrument*)

la **afirmación** *fem noun*
statement

afirmar *verb* **[17]**
1 **to state**
Afirmó que era de su familia. He stated that it belonged to his family.
2 **afirmar con la cabeza** to nod one's agreement

afirmativo *masc adjective*, **afirmativa** *fem*
affirmative

aflojar *verb* **[17]**
1 **to loosen**
2 **aflojar la marcha** to slow down

afónico *masc adjective*, **afónica** *fem*
estar afónico to have lost your voice
Está afónica. She's lost her voice.

afortunadamente *adverb*
fortunately

afortunado *masc adjective*, **afortunada** *fem*
fortunate

África *fem noun*
Africa
Soy de África. I'm from Africa.

africano *masc adjective & noun*, **africana** *fem adjective & noun*
1 **African**
2 **un africano, una africana** African

WORD TIP Adjectives and nouns for nationality and regional origin do not have capital letters in Spanish.

afuera *adverb*
outside, out
Salimos afuera. We went outside.

las **afueras** *plural fem noun*
las afueras the outskirts
las afueras de Valencia the outskirts of Valencia

agachar *verb* [17]
agachar la cabeza to lower your head

agacharse *reflexive verb* [17]
1 **to bend down**
2 **to duck**

agarrar *verb* [17]
to grab

agarrarse *reflexive verb* [17]
to hold on
Se agarró a la barandilla. She held on to the handrail.

la **agencia** *fem noun*
agency
- la **agencia de viajes** travel agency
- la **agencia inmobiliaria** estate agent's

la **agenda** *fem noun*
1 **diary**
2 **agenda**

el & la **agente** *masc & fem noun*
agent
- el & la **agente de policía** police officer
- el & la **agente inmobiliario** estate agent

agitar *verb* [17]
to shake

agosto *masc noun*
August
en agosto in August
el 12 de agosto on 12 August

WORD TIP Names of months and days start with small letters in Spanish.

agotado *masc adjective*, **agotada** *fem*
1 **worn out**
Estoy agotado. I'm worn out.
2 **sold out** (*goods in a shop*)
3 **flat** (*battery*)

agotador *masc adjective*, **agotadora** *fem*
exhausting

agotarse *reflexive verb* [17]
1 **to wear yourself out**
2 **to sell out** (*goods*)
3 **to go flat** (*batteries*)
4 **to run out** (*reserves or supplies*)
5 Se me está agotando la paciencia. My patience is running out.

agradable *masc & fem adjective*
pleasant

agradecer *verb* [35]
1 agradecerle algo a alguien to be grateful to somebody for something
Te agradezco tu ayuda. I'm grateful to you for your help.
2 **to thank**
Te lo agradezco. Thank you.
Nos agradecieron el regalo. They thanked us for the present.
¡Y así nos lo agradeces! And that's the thanks we get from you!

agradecido *masc adjective*, **agradecida** *fem*
grateful
Le estoy muy agradecido. I'm very grateful to you. (*using the polite form*)

el **agradecimiento** *masc noun*
gratitude

la **agresión** *fem noun*
aggression

agresivo *masc adjective*, **agresiva** *fem*
aggressive

agrícola *masc & fem adjective*
agricultural
productos agrícolas farm products

el **agricultor** *masc noun*, la **agricultora** *fem*
farmer

la **agricultura** *fem noun*
1 **agriculture**
2 **farming**
- la **agricultura biológica** organic farming

agridulce *masc & fem adjective*
bittersweet

agringado *masc adjective*, **agringada** *fem*
(*Latin America*) **having American ways**

agrio *masc adjective*, **agria** *fem*
sour

el **agua** *fem noun*
water
un vaso de agua a glass of water
El agua está fría. The water is cold.
¿Quieres agua? Would you like some water?

WORD TIP *agua* takes *el* or *un* in the singular even though it is feminine.

- el **agua corriente** running water
- el **agua de colonia** eau de cologne
- el **agua mineral con gas** sparkling mineral water ⏩

- el **agua mineral sin gas** still mineral water
- el **agua potable** drinking water

el **aguacate** *masc noun*
avocado

el **aguacero** *masc noun*
downpour

el & la **aguafiestas** *masc & fem noun, pl,* **aguafiestas**
spoilsport

la **aguanieve** *fem noun*
sleet

aguantar *verb* **[17]**
1 **to bear** (*pain or heat*)
No aguanto este calor. I can't bear this heat.
2 **to take**
No aguanto más. I can't take any more.
3 **aguantar la respiración** to hold your breath
aguantar la risa to stop yourself laughing
4 **to hold** (*an object*)
Aguanta esta caja un momento. Hold this box for a minute.

aguantarse *reflexive verb* **[17]**
Tendrás que aguantarte. You'll have to put up with it.

agudo *masc adjective*, **aguda** *fem*
1 **acute** (*pain*)
2 **acute** (*accent*)
3 **high-pitched** (*voice or sound*)
4 **stressed on the last syllable** (*word*)

el **aguijón** *masc noun*
sting

el **águila** *fem noun*
eagle
Vimos un águila. We saw an eagle.

WORD TIP *águila* takes *el* or *un* in the singular even though it is feminine.

la **aguja** *fem noun*
1 **needle** (*for sewing or knitting*)
2 **hand** (*of a watch or clock*)

el **agujero** *masc noun*
hole

las **agujetas** *plural fem noun*
stiffness (*from exercise*)
Tengo muchas agujetas. I'm really stiff.

♪ **ahí** *adverb*
1 **there**
Ahí están. There they are.
Ponlo ahí. Put it there.
2 **Tenemos que ir por ahí.** We have to go that way.
Dejó las llaves por ahí. She left the keys somewhere.
Había unas doscientas personas o por ahí. There were about two hundred people there.

el **ahijado** *masc noun*, la **ahijada** *fem*
1 **godson**
2 **goddaughter**
3 **mis ahijados** my godchildren

ahogado *masc adjective*, **ahogada** *fem*
1 **morir ahogado** to drown
2 **morir ahogado** to suffocate

ahogarse *reflexive verb* **[28]**
1 **to drown**
Se ahogó en el río. He drowned in the river.
2 **to suffocate**

♪ **ahora** *adverb*
1 **now**
Ahora vamos a trabajar. Now we're going to work.
¿Qué vas a hacer ahora? What are you going to do now?
ahora mismo right now
Ahora mismo lo traigo. I'll bring it right away.
2 **in a moment, shortly**
Ahora viene. She'll come shortly.
Ahora vuelvo. I'll be back in a moment.
Ahora lo hago. I'll do it in a moment.
3 (*in expressions*) **de ahora en adelante** from now on
por ahora for the time being
¡Hasta ahora! See you soon!

ahorcar *verb* **[31]**
to hang (*in executions*)

ahorcarse *reflexive verb* **[31]**
to hang yourself

ahorita *adverb*
(*Latin America*)
1 **just now**
2 **right now**

♪ **ahorrar** *verb* **[17]**
to save

los **ahorros** *plural masc noun*
savings
todos mis ahorros all my savings

ahumado *masc adjective*, **ahumada** *fem*
smoked

♪ el **aire** *masc noun*
1 **air**
al aire libre in the open air
teatro al aire libre open-air theatre
salir a tomar el aire to go out for some fresh air

En verano disfrutamos la vida al aire libre. In summer we enjoy life in the open air.

2 **wind**
Hace mucho aire. It's very windy.

3 **appearance**
Tiene un aire interesante. It looks interesting.
Llegó con aire preocupado. She arrived looking worried.

- el **aire acondicionado** air conditioning

aislado *masc adjective*, **aislada** *fem*
isolated

♪ el **ajedrez** *masc noun*
chess
jugar al ajedrez to play chess

el **ajillo** *masc noun*
al ajillo with garlic
gambas al ajillo garlic prawns

♪ el **ajo** *masc noun*
garlic
un diente de ajo a clove of garlic
una cabeza de ajo a head of garlic

ajustar *verb* **[17]**
1 **to adjust** (*a seat, a safety belt*)
2 **to fit**

♪ **al** *preposition + determiner*
1 **to the**
Fuimos al colegio. We went to school.
Se lo di al camarero. I gave it to the waiter.

2 (*with verb infinitives*) **as, when**
Al salir nos encontramos con Marta. As we were leaving we met Marta.
Tengan cuidado al bajar del autobús. Be careful when leaving the bus.

WORD TIP *al* is formed by *a* + *el*; see *a* for more examples.

el **ala** *fem noun*
1 **wing**
el ala del avión the plane's wing
El pájaro bate las alas. The bird beats its wings.
El hospital tiene dos alas. The hospital has two wings

2 **wing, winger** (*in sports*)

WORD TIP *ala* takes *el* or *un* in the singular even though it is feminine.

la **alabanza** *fem noun*
praise

alabar *verb* **[17]**
to praise

el **alambre** *masc noun*
wire

- el **alambre de púas** barbed wire

el **álamo** *masc noun*
poplar tree

el **alargador** *masc noun*
extension lead

alargar *verb* **[28]**
1 **to lengthen**
Voy a alargar esta falda un poco. I'm going to lengthen this skirt a bit.

2 **to extend** (*a visit, a holiday*)
Queremos alargar la vacaciones. We want to extend our holidays.

3 **to stretch out** (*an arm*)
Alargué el brazo para alcanzarlo. I stretched out my arm to reach it.

alargarse *reflexive verb* **[28]**
1 **to get longer**
Los días se van alargando. The days are getting longer.

2 **to go on**
La conferencia se alargó mucho. The conference went on for a long time.

la **alarma** *fem noun*
alarm

- la **alarma contra incendios** fire alarm

alarmante *masc & fem adjective*
alarming

el **albañil** *masc noun*
1 **builder**
2 **bricklayer**

el **albaricoque** *masc noun*
apricot

♪ el **albergue** *masc noun*
1 **hostel**
2 **refuge** (*in the mountains*)

- el **albergue juvenil** youth hostel

la **albóndiga** *fem noun*
meatball

el **albornoz** *masc noun*
bathrobe

alborotar *verb* **[17]**
alborotar a los niños to get the children excited

alborotarse *reflexive verb* **[17]**
to get excited

el **alboroto** *masc noun*
racket
¡Qué alboroto! What a racket!

el **álbum** *masc noun*
album
el mejor álbum del grupo the group's best album
- **el álbum de fotografías** photograph album

la **alcachofa** *fem noun*
artichoke

el **alcalde** *masc noun*, la **alcaldesa** *fem*
1 **mayor**
2 **mayoress**

el **alcázar** *masc noun*
1 **fortress**
2 **palace** (*especially a Moorish one*)

alcanzar *verb* [22]
1 **to reach**
No alcanzo a la ventana. I can't reach the window.
La temperatura alcanzó los treinta grados. The temperature reached thirty.
2 **to catch up with**
Nos alcanzó en el último momento. He caught up with us at the last muinute.
No pude alcanzar al resto del grupo. I couldn't catch up with the rest of the group.
3 **alcanzarle algo a alguien** to pass somebody something
¿Me alcanzas las tijeras? Can you pass me the scissors?
4 **to be enough**
Veinte euros nos alcanzan. Twenty euros will be enough.
No alcanzan los vasos. There aren't enough glasses.

el **alcohol** *masc noun*
alcohol

alcohólico *masc adjective*, **alcohólica** *fem*
▷ see **alcohólico** *noun*
alcoholic

el **alcohólico** *masc noun*, la **alcohólica** *fem*
▷ see **alcohólico** *adj*
alcoholic

el **alcoholismo** *masc noun*
alcoholism

la **aldaba** *fem noun*
knocker

la **aldea** *fem noun*
village

el **aldeano** *masc noun*, la **aldeana** *fem*
villager

alegrar *verb* [17]
to cheer up
Verla les alegró mucho. Seeing her really cheered them up.
Me alegra saberlo. I'm glad to hear it.

alegrarse *reflexive verb* [17]
1 **to be happy, to be glad**
Me alegro de verte. I'm glad to see you.
¡Cuánto me alegro! I'm so happy!
Se alegró de venir. He was glad to come.
Me alegro mucho por ellos. I'm very happy for them.
Me alegro de haberte llamado. I'm glad I phoned you.
2 (*as a reply*) **Me alegro.** That's good.

alegre *masc & fem adjective*
1 **happy**
una cara alegre a happy face
2 **cheerful**
Soy una persona muy alegre. I'm a cheerful kind of person.
3 **bright** (*colour*)

la **alegría** *fem noun*
happiness
¡Qué alegría veros! It's great to see you!
¡Qué alegría me das! That makes me really happy!
saltar de alegría to jump for joy

alejar *verb* [17]
alejar algo de alguien to move something away from somebody

alejarse *reflexive verb* [17]
to move away
¡Aléjate del fuego! Move away from the fire!

alemán *masc adjective & noun*, **alemana** *fem adjective & noun*
1 **German**
2 (*person*) **un alemán, una alemana** German
el alemán German (*the language*)

WORD TIP Adjectives and nouns for nationality, regional origin, and language do not have capital letters in Spanish.

Alemania *fem noun*
Germany
Soy de Alemania. I'm from Germany.

la **alergia** *fem noun*
allergy
tener alergia a algo to be allergic to something
- **la alergia al polen** hayfever

alerta *masc & fem adjective*
▷ see **alerta** *noun*
alert

la **alerta** *fem noun* ▷ see **alerta** *adj*
estar alerta por algo to be on the alert for something
Hay que estar alerta por los carteristas. Be on the alert for pickpockets.

alfabético *masc adjective*, **alfabética** *fem*
alphabetical
por orden alfabético **in alphabetical order**

el **alfabeto** *masc noun*
alphabet

la **alfarería** *fem noun*
pottery

el **alféizar** *masc noun*
sill
el alféizar de la ventana the windowsill

el **alfiler** *masc noun*
pin

⚷ la **alfombra** *fem noun*
1 **rug**
2 (*Latin America*) **carpet**

la **alfombrilla** *fem noun*
mat
- la **alfombrilla de baño** bath mat

el **alga** *fem noun*
seaweed

WORD TIP *alga* takes *el* or *un* in the singular even though it is feminine.

⚷ **algo** *pronoun* ▷ see **algo** *adv*
1 **something**
Tienes que beber algo. You must drink something.
algo así something like that
Su padre es director be banco, o algo así. Her father's a bank manager, or something like that.
2 **anything**
¿Te pasa algo? Is there anything the matter with you?
¿Has tomado algo de aquí? Have you taken anything from here?
3 **some**, **any**
algo de ... some ..., any ...
Queda algo de pan. There's some bread left.
¿Tienes algo de leche? Do you have any milk?

⚷ **algo** *adverb* ▷ see **algo** *pron*
(*with an adjective*) **a bit**
Estoy algo cansado. I'm a bit tired.

⚷ el **algodón** *masc noun*
cotton
una camisa de algodón a cotton shirt

⚷ **alguien** *pronoun*
1 **somebody**, **someone**
Hay alguien en la puerta. There's someone at the door.
2 **anybody**, **anyone**
¿Has hablado con alguien? Have you spoken to anybody?
Si pregunta alguien, di que sí. If anyone asks, say yes.

⚷ **algún** *adjective* ▷ **alguno, alguna**

⚷ **alguno** *masc adjective*, **alguna** *fem* ▷ see **alguno** *pron*
1 **some**
Tiene que ser algún niño. It must be some kid.
Compré algunas cosas. I bought some things.
Nos hicieron algunas preguntas. They asked us some questions.
Algunos participantes no sabían las reglas. Some participants didn't know the rules.
2 (*in questions or with si*) **any**
¿Tienes alguna razón para no ir? Do you have any reason for not going?
¿Tienes algún problema? Have you got any problems?
Si tiene alguna pregunta, no dude en llamarnos. If you have a question, don't hesitate to call us. (*polite form*)
3 (*in expressions*) **en algún lugar** somewhere
en algún momento sometime
alguna vez sometimes, ever
Alguna vez lo he pensado. I've thought about it sometimes.
¿Has estado alguna vez en España? Have you ever been to Spain?

WORD TIP *alguno* becomes *algún* before a masculine singular noun.

⚷ **alguno** *masc pronoun*, **alguna** *fem pronoun* ▷ see **alguno** *adj*
1 (*singular*) **one**
alguno de vosotros one of you
para alguna de sus hijas for one of her daughters
Tiene que haber alguno aquí. There must be one here.
2 (*plural*) **some**
Algunos de ellos no fueron. Some of them didn't go.
Faltan algunas. There are some missing.
3 (*in questions or with si*) **any**
Me sobran entradas, ¿quieres alguna? I've got tickets to spare, do you want any?
Si alguno te interesa, cómpralo. If you're interested in any of them, buy it.

Spanish-English

aliado *masc adjective*, **aliada** *fem*
▷ see **aliado** *noun*
allied

el **aliado** *masc noun*, la **aliada** *fem*
▷ see **aliado** *adj*
ally

la **alianza** *fem noun*
1 **alliance**
2 **wedding ring**

los **alicates** *plural masc noun*
1 **pliers**
2 **nail clippers**

el **aliento** *masc noun*
breath
estar sin aliento to be out of breath
recuperar el aliento to get your breath back
Tiene mal aliento She's got bad breath.

la **alimentación** *fem noun*
diet
una alimentación equilibrada a balanced diet

alimentar *verb* **[17]**
1 **to feed**
2 **to be nutritious**
Las lentejas alimentan mucho. Lentils are very nutritious.

alimentarse *reflexive verb* **[17]**
to feed
Se alimentan de insectos. They feed on insects.

alimenticio *masc adjective*, **alimenticia** *fem*
1 **food**
la industria alimenticia the food industry
productos alimenticios foodstuffs
2 **nutritious**
Ese plato es muy alimenticio. That dish is very nutritious.

el **alimento** *masc noun*
food
El arroz es su alimento básico. Rice is their staple food.
Las lentejas son un bueno alimento. Lentils are a good food.

la **alineación** *fem noun*
line-up (*in a team*)

aliñar *verb* **[17]**
1 **to dress** (*a salad*)
2 **to season**

el **aliño** *masc noun*
1 **salad dressing**
2 **seasoning**

el **alioli** *masc noun*
garlic mayonnaise

alistarse *reflexive verb* **[17]**
to join up
alistarse en el ejército to join the army

aliviar *verb* **[17]**
to relieve (*pain*)

allá *adverb*
1 **there, over there**
allá abajo down there
¡Allá voy! Here I come!, I'm on my way!
Ahora vamos para allá. We're on our way.
2 **más allá** further away
Está más allá de la estación. It's beyond the station.
3 (*in time*) **back**
allá en los años noventa back in the nineties

allí *adverb*
there
allí arriba up there
Lo puso por allí. She put it somewhere around there.
Se fueron por allí. They went that way.

el **alma** *fem noun*
soul

WORD TIP *alma* takes *el* or *un* in the singular even though it is feminine.

el **almacén** *masc noun*
warehouse

almacenar *verb* **[17]**
to store (*goods*)

los **almacenes** *plural masc noun*
department store
abrir unos almacenes to open a department store

la **almeja** *fem noun*
clam (*the shellfish*)

la **almendra** *fem noun*
almond

el **almíbar** *masc noun*
syrup

el **almidón** *masc noun*
starch

la **almohada** *fem noun*
pillow
una funda de almohada a pillowcase
• la **almohada de plumas** feather pillow

el **almohadón** *masc noun*
cushion

a b c d e f g h i j k l m n ñ o p q r s t u v w x y z

almorzar *verb* [26]
1 **to have lunch**
Almorzamos a las doce y media. We have lunch at 12.30.
2 **to have for lunch**
Almorzamos sopa y tortilla. We had soup and omelette for lunch.
3 **to have a mid-morning snack** (*in some areas of Spain*)

el **almuerzo** *masc noun*
1 **lunch**
2 **mid-morning snack** (*in some areas of Spain*)

el **alojamiento** *masc noun*
accommodation

alojarse *reflexive verb* [17]
to stay
Se alojaron en un hotel de cinco estrellas. They stayed in a five-star hotel.

la **alondra** *fem noun*
lark (*the bird*)

los **Alpes** *plural masc noun*
los Alpes the Alps

el **alpinismo** *masc noun*
mountaineering

el & la **alpinista** *masc & fem noun*
mountaineer

alquilar *verb* [17]
1 **to rent**
Hemos alquilado un apartamento en la playa. We've rented an apartment at the seaside.
2 **to hire** (*cars, bicycles, etc*)
alquilar una bicicleta to hire a bike
3 **to let** (*a house, flat, room*)
Se aquila la casa. The house is to let.
4 **to hire out** (*equipment*)
Allí alquilan botas de esquiar. They hire out ski boots there.

alquilarse *reflexive verb* [17]
to let, **to rent**
'Se alquila' 'To let' (*on a sign*)
Se alquilan coches. Cars for hire.

el **alquiler** *masc noun*
1 **rent** (*for a flat, house, etc*)
una casa de alquiler a rented house
una casa en alquiler a house to let
2 **hire charge** (*for cars or equipment*)
coches de alquiler hire cars

el **alquitrán** *masc noun*
tar

alrededor *adverb*
1 **around**
mirar alrededor to look around
a nuestro alrededor around us
un jardín con un muro alrededor a garden with a wall around it
2 **alrededor de algo** around something
Se sentaron alrededor de la mesa. They sat around the table.
Cuesta alrededor de veinte euros. It costs around twenty euros.
Su padre tiene alrededor de cuarenta años. Her father is about forty (years old).

los **alrededores** *plural masc noun*
1 **outskirts** (*of a town or city*)
en los alrededores de Valencia on the outskirts of Valencia
2 **surrounding area** (*of an airport or building*)
en los alrededores del puerto in the port area

el **alta** *fem noun*
1 **darse de alta** to sign on, to join
Me di de alta en el club de tenis. I joined the tennis club.
2 **dar de alta a alguien** to discharge someone (*from hospital*)
Le dieron de alta después de dos días. She was discharged after two days.

WORD TIP *alta* takes *el* or *un* in the singular even though it is feminine.

el **altavoz** *masc noun*, los *pl:* **altavoces**
1 **loudspeaker**
2 **megaphone**

alternar *verb* [17]
to alternate

alternarse *reflexive verb* [17]
to take turns
Nos alternábamos para hacer la comida. We took turns to cook.

la **alternativa** *fem noun*
▷ see **alternativo** *adj*
alternative
No hay otra alternativa. There's no alternative.

alternativo *masc adjective*, **alternativa** *fem* ▷ see **alternativa** *noun*
alternative

la **altitud** *fem noun*
altitude

altivo *masc adjective*, **altiva** *fem*
arrogant

alto *masc adjective*, **alta** *fem*
▷ see **alto** *noun, adv*
1 **high**
una habitación de techo alto a room with a high ceiling
en lo alto de la torre at the top of the tower
La montaña más alta de España. The highest mountain in Spain.
Los precios están muy altos. Prices are very high.
Sacó la nota más alta. He got the highest mark.
2 **tall**
Todos sus hijos son muy altos. All their children are very tall.
Ella es más alta que él. She's taller than he is.
3 **loud**
en voz alta in a loud voice
No pongas la radio tan alta. Don't put the radio on so loud.

el **alto** *masc noun* ▷ see **alto** *adj, adv*
de alto high
un muro de dos metros de alto a two-metre high wall

alto *adverb* ▷ see **alto** *adj, noun*
1 **loud**
Habla un poco más alto, por favor. Speak a little louder, please.
2 **high**
volar alto to fly high

la **altura** *fem noun*
1 **height**
a la misma altura at the same height
¿Qué altura tiene? How high is it?
2 **altitude**
Volábamos a una altura de 10.000m. We were flying at an altitude of 10,000 metres.
3 **a estas alturas** at this stage
A estas alturas no importa. It doesn't matter at this stage.

la **alubia** *fem noun*
haricot bean

la **alucinación** *fem noun*
hallucination

alucinado *masc adjective*, **alucinada** *fem*
(*informal*) **estar alucinado,** *fem* **alucinada** to be stunned
Nos quedamos alucinados. We were stunned.

alucinante *masc & fem adjective*
(*informal*) **amazing**
Es un espectáculo alucinante. It's an amazing spectacle.

alucinar *verb* **[17]** (*informal*)
1 **to amaze**
Me alucina. It amazes me.
2 **alucinar con algo** to be amazed by something
Con esta grabación alucinas. You'll be amazed by this recording.

el **alud** *masc noun*
1 **avalanche**
2 **landslide**

el **aluminio** *masc noun*
aluminium

el **alumno** *masc noun*, la **alumna** *fem*
1 **pupil**
¿Cuántos alumnos hay en tu colegio? How many pupils are there in your school?

la **alusión** *fem noun*
allusion

el **ama de casa** *fem noun*
housewife
un ama de casa a housewife

WORD TIP *ama* takes *el* or *un* in the singular even though it is feminine.

la **amabilidad** *fem noun*
kindness
Tuvieron la amabilidad de ayudarme. They were kind enough to help me.

amable *masc & fem adjective*
kind
¿Sería tan amable de sujetar esto? Would you be so kind as to hold this?

amaestrar *verb* **[17]**
to train (*a dog, a horse, etc*)

el **amanecer** *masc noun*
▷ see **amanecer** *verb*
dawn
al amanecer at dawn

amanecer *verb* **[35]**
▷ see **amanecer** *noun*
1 **to get light**
¿A qué hora amanece? What time does it get light?
2 **to wake up**
Amanece tarde. She gets up late.

amante *masc & fem adjective*
▷ see **amante** *noun*
ser amante de algo to be fond of something

Son grandes amantes del cine. They're great cinema fans.

el & la **amante** *masc & fem noun* ▷ see **amante** *adj*
lover

la **amapola** *fem noun*
poppy

amar *verb* [17]
to love

amargo *masc adjective*, **amarga** *fem*
bitter

♪ **amarillo** *masc adjective*, **amarilla** *fem* ▷ see **amarillo** *noun*
yellow
una cinta amarilla a yellow ribbon

♪ el **amarillo** *masc noun* ▷ see **amarillo** *adj*
yellow

amarrar *verb* [1]
(*Latin America*) **to tie**

amarrarse *reflexive verb*
(*Latin America*) **to tie up**
amarrarse los zapatos to tie up your shoe laces

amasar *verb* [17]
to knead (*dough*)

el **Amazonas** *masc noun*
the (River) Amazon

la **ambición** *fem noun*
ambition

ambicioso *masc adjective*, **ambiciosa** *fem*
ambitious

el **ambientador** *masc noun*
air freshener

ambiental *masc & fem adjective*
environmental

el **ambiente** *masc noun*
1 **environment**
la contaminación del ambiente the pollution of the environment
2 **atmosphere** (*at a party, a match*)
Había muy buen ambiente. There was a good atmosphere.

ambiguo *masc adjective*, **ambigua** *fem*
ambiguous

♪ **ambos** *plural masc adjective & pronoun*, **ambas** *plural fem adj & pron*
both
ambas ciudades both cities
ambos hermanos both brothers
Ambas se quedaron. Both of them stayed behind (*girls*).
Ambos vinieron. Both of them came (*boys*).

la **ambulancia** *fem noun*
ambulance

ambulante *masc & fem adjective*
travelling
un grupo de teatro ambulante a travelling theatre group
una biblioteca ambulante a mobile library

el **ambulatorio** *masc noun*
outpatients' department

el **amén** *masc noun*
amen

la **amenaza** *fem noun*
threat

amenazador *masc adjective*, **amenazadora** *fem*
threatening

amenazar *verb* [22]
to threaten
Amenazó con despedirme. He threatened to fire me.
amenazar de muerte a alguien to threaten to kill somebody

♪ **América** *fem noun*
America
Soy de América. I'm from America.
- **América Central** Central America
- **América del Sur** South America
- **América Latina** Latin America

♪ la **americana** *fem noun*
jacket

♪ **americano** *masc adjective*, **americana** *fem* ▷ see **americano** *noun*
1 **American** (*from the USA*)
2 **Latin American**

♪ un **americano** *masc noun*, una **americana** *fem* ▷ see **americano** *adj*
1 **American** (*from the USA*)
2 **Latin American**

WORD TIP Adjectives and nouns for nationality and regional origin do not have capital letters in Spanish.

la **ametralladora** *fem noun*
machine gun

♪ **amigo** *masc adjective*, **amiga** *fem* ▷ see **amigo** *noun*
hacerse amigos to become friends
Son muy amigos. They are very good friends.

el **amigo** *masc noun*, la **amiga** *fem*
▷ see **amigo** *adj*
friend
un amigo nuestro a friend of ours
un amigo de Carmen a friend of Carmen's
Son amigos íntimos. They are very close friends.
mi amigo del alma my best friend
- el **amigo por correspondencia**, la **amiga por correspondencia** *fem* penfriend

la **amistad** *fem noun*
1 **friendship**
2 las amistades friends
Tiene muchas amistades. She has a lot of friends.

amistoso *masc adjective*, **amistosa** *fem*
friendly
un partido amistoso a friendly match

el **amo** *masc noun*, el **ama** *fem*
owner
el amo del perro the owner of the dog

amontonar *verb* [17]
to pile up

amontonarse *reflexive verb* [17]
to pile up

el **amor** *masc noun*
love
amor mío my love
- el **amor a primera vista** love at first sight
- el **amor propio** self-esteem

amoroso *masc adjective*, **amorosa** *fem*
to do with love
las relaciones amorosas love relationships

ampliar *verb* [32]
1 **to enlarge** (*a photograph*)
2 **to extend** (*a road or building*)
3 **to increase** (*your vocabulary, knowledge*)

el **amplificador** *masc noun*
amplifier

amplio *masc adjective*, **amplia** *fem*
1 **wide** (*road*)
2 **spacious** (*room*)
3 **loose-fitting** (*clothes*)

la **amplitud** *fem noun*
1 **width** (*of a road*)
2 **spaciousness** (*of a room*)

la **ampolla** *fem noun*
blister
Me han salido ampollas en las manos. I've got blisters on my hands.

amueblado *masc adjective*, **amueblada** *fem*
furnished
un piso amueblado a furnished flat

amueblar *verb* [17]
to furnish (*a house or room*)

analfabeto *masc adjective*, **analfabeta** *fem*
illiterate

el **analgésico** *masc noun*
painkiller

el **análisis** *masc noun*
analysis

analizar *verb* [22]
to analyse

la **anatomía** *fem noun*
anatomy

ancho *masc adjective*, **ancha** *fem*
▷ see **ancho** *noun*
1 **wide**
una carretera muy ancha a very wide road
2 **broad**
ser ancho de espaldas to have broad shoulders
3 **loose-fitting** (*clothes*)
Te está muy ancho. It's too loose for you.

el **ancho** *masc noun* ▷ see **ancho** *adj*
width
¿Cuánto tiene de ancho? How wide is it?
Tiene dos metros de ancho. It's two metres wide.

la **anchoa** *fem noun*
anchovy

la **anchura** *fem noun*
width
¿Qué anchura tiene? How wide is it?
Tiene una anchura de cinco metros. It's five metres wide.

anciano *masc adjective*, **anciana** *fem*
▷ see **anciano** *noun*
elderly
un hombre muy anciano a very elderly man

el **anciano** *masc noun*, la **anciana** *fem*
▷ see **anciano** *adj*
1 **old man**
2 **old woman**

el **ancla** *fem noun*
anchor
echar anclas to drop anchor

WORD TIP *ancla* takes *el* or *un* in the singular even though it is feminine.

Andalucía *fem noun*
Andalusia (*the southernmost province of Spain*)

andaluz *masc adjective & noun*, **andaluza** *fem adjective & noun*
1 **Andalusian**
2 (*person*) **un andaluz, una andaluza** Andalusian

WORD TIP Adjectives and nouns for nationality and regional origin do not have capital letters in Spanish.

el **andamio** *masc noun*
scaffolding

♪ **andar** *verb* **[21]**
1 **to walk**
¿Has venido andando? Did you walk here?
Casi no podía andar. I could hardly walk.
2 (*saying how things are*) **andar bien** to go well
andar mal to go badly
¿Cómo andas? How are you?
¿Cómo andas de dinero? How are you doing for money?
3 **to work**
Mi coche no anda. My car's not going well.
4 (*expressing surprise*) **¡Anda! si es Pedro.** Well, if it isn't Pedro!
5 (*telling somebody to do something*) **Anda, date prisa.** Come on, hurry up.

♪ el **andén** *masc noun*
platform

los **Andes** *plural masc noun*
los Andes the Andes

mini-info **Andes**
Los Andes es la cordillera más larga del mundo, extendiéndose desde Colombia hasta Tierra del Fuego por 6.400 km.

el **andinismo** *masc noun*
(*Latin America*) **mountain climbing**

el & la **andinista** *masc & fem noun*
(*Latin America*) **mountain climber**

Andorra *fem noun*
Andorra

el **andrajo** *masc noun*
rag
Iba vestido de andrajos. He was dressed in rags.

la **anécdota** *fem noun*
anecdote

la **anestesia** *fem noun*
1 **anaesthesia**
2 **anaesthetic**

el **anfitrión** *masc noun* la **anfitriona** *fem*
1 **host**
2 **hostess**

el **ángel** *masc noun*
angel
No es ningún angelito. He's no angel.

angelical *masc & fem adjective*
angelic

las **anginas** *plural fem noun*
throat infection
tener anginas to have a throat infection

el **anglicano** *masc noun*, la **anglicana** *fem*
Anglican

angosto *masc adjective*, **angosta** *fem*
(*Latin America*) **narrow**

la **anguila** *fem noun*
eel

angustiado *masc adjective*, **angustiada** *fem*
worried
Están angustiados porque no saben nada de él. They are really worried because they haven't heard from him.

angustiarse *reflexive verb* **[17]**
to get worried
No hay por qué angustiarse. There's no reason to get worried.

angustioso *masc adjective*, **angustiosa** *fem*
worrying

el **anillo** *masc noun*
ring
el Señor de los Anillos the Lord of the Rings
• el **anillo de boda** wedding ring

♪ **animado** *masc adjective*, **animada** *fem*
1 **lively** (*bar, party, etc*)
2 **in good spirits**
Estaba muy animada. She was in high spirits.

animal *masc & fem adjective*
▷ see **animal** *noun*
stupid
¡Qué animal eres! You're so stupid!

♪ el **animal** *masc noun* ▷ see **animal** *adj*
1 **animal**
2 **brute**
Es un animal. He's a brute.

Spanish-English

el **animal doméstico** *masc noun*
1 **domestic animal**
2 **pet**
¿Tienes algún animal doméstico? Do you have any pets?

animar *verb* [17]
1 **to liven up** (*a party, etc*)
2 **to cheer up** (*a person*)
3 **to cheer on**

animarse *reflexive verb* [17]
to cheer up
¡Anímate! Cheer up!

el **ánimo** *masc noun*
1 **No tengo ánimo para nada.** I don't feel in the mood for anything.
Se la ve con mucho ánimo. She's in high spirits.
2 **¡Ánimo!** Cheer up!

el **aniversario** *masc noun*
anniversary

anoche *adverb*
last night
Anoche no dormí bien. I didn't sleep well last night.
antes de anoche the night before last

anochecer *verb* [35]
▷ see **anochecer** *noun*
to get dark
Está anocheciendo. It's getting dark.

el **anochecer** *masc noun*
▷ see **anochecer** *verb*
nightfall
al anochecer at nightfall

anónimo *masc adjective*, **anónima** *fem*
▷ see **anónimo** *noun*
anonymous

el **anónimo** *masc noun* ▷ see **anónimo** *adj*
anonymous letter

anormal *masc & fem adjective*
abnormal

anotar *verb* [17]
to write down

la **ansiedad** *fem noun*
anxiety

ante *preposition* ▷ see **ante** *noun*
before
ante el juez before the judge

el **ante** *masc noun* ▷ see **ante** *prep*
suede

anteanoche *adverb*
▷ see **antenoche** *adv*
the night before last

anteayer *adverb* ▷ see **antier** *adv*
the day before yesterday

antemano *adverb*
de antemano in advance

la **antena** *fem noun*
1 **aerial**
2 **antenna**
• **la antena parabólica** satellite dish

antenoche *adverb*
▷ see **anteanoche** *adv*
(*Latin America*) **the night before last**

los **anteojos** *plural masc noun*
(*Latin America*) **glasses**

los **antepasados** *plural masc noun*
ancestors

anterior *masc & fem adjective*
previous
la noche anterior the previous night
anterior a algo prior to something

antes *adverb*
1 **before**
la noche antes the night before
Deberías haberlo dicho antes. You should have said it before.
2 **antes de** before
antes del viernes before Friday
Piénsalo antes de comprarlo. Think about it before you buy it.
3 **earlier**
Este año la primavera ha llegado antes. This year spring has come earlier.
A las cinco está bien, no hace falta que vengas antes. Five is fine, you don't need to come any earlier.
4 **first**
Ésta va antes. This goes first.
5 **lo antes posible** as soon as possible

el **antibiótico** *masc noun*
antibiotic

la **anticipación** *fem noun*
con mucha anticipación well in advance
con dos días de anticipación two days in advance

el **anticipo** *masc noun*
advance

la **anticoncepción** *noun*
contraception

el **anticonceptivo** *masc noun*
contraceptive

a b c d e f g h i j k l m n ñ o p q r s t u v w x y z

anticuado *masc adjective*, **anticuada** *fem*
old-fashioned

el **antídoto** *masc noun*
antidote

antier *adverb* ▷ see **anteayer** *adv*
(*Latin America*) **the day before yesterday**

♪ la **antigüedad** *fem noun*
1 **en la antigüedad** in the old days
2 **antique**
una tienda de antigüedades an antique shop
3 **seniority** (*at work*)

♪ **antiguamente** *adverb*
in the old days

♪ **antiguo** *masc adjective*, **antigua** *fem*
1 **old**
una costumbre muy antigua a very old tradition
2 **ancient**
una civilización antigua an ancient civilization
3 **former**
el antiguo presidente the former president

las **Antillas** *plural fem noun*
las Antillas the West Indies

♪ **antipático** *masc adjective*, **antipática** *fem*
unpleasant
Es muy antipático. He's very unpleasant.
¡Qué mujer más antipática! What a horrible woman!

antojarse *reflexive verb* **[17]**
Se le antojó un helado. He fancied an ice-cream.
Se me antojó comprar el jarrón. I felt like buying the vase.

la **antropología** *fem noun*
anthropology

anual *masc & fem adjective*
annual

anualmente *adverb*
yearly

♪ **anunciar** *verb* **[17]**
1 **to announce** (*a piece of news, a decision*)
2 **to advertise** (*a product, a service*)

♪ el **anuncio** *masc noun*
1 **announcement**
2 **advertisement**

el **anzuelo** *masc noun*
hook

añadidura *in phrase*
por añadidura in addition

añadir *verb* **[19]**
to add

♪ el **año** *masc noun*
1 **year**
el año pasado last year
los años cincuenta the fifties
2 (*talking about age*) **¿Cuántos años tienes?** How old are you?
Mi madre tiene cincuenta años. My mother is fifty.
• el **año bisiesto** leap year
• el **Año Nuevo** New Year

♪ **apagado** *masc adjective*, **apagada** *fem*
1 **off**, **turned off**
con la luz apagada with the light off
¿Está apagada la televisión? Is the television off?
2 **out**
El fuego estaba casi apagado. The fire was almost out.

♪ **apagar** *verb* **[28]**
1 **to switch off** (*the television, the light*)
2 **to put out** (*a fire, a cigarette*)

el **apagón** *masc noun*
power cut

el **aparato** *masc noun*
1 **appliance**
2 **los aparatos de laboratorio** laboratory equipment
3 **piece of apparatus** (*in the gym*)
• los **aparatos eléctricos** electrical appliances

♪ el **aparcamiento** *masc noun*
car park

♪ **aparcar** *verb* **[31]**
to park

aparecer *verb* **[35]**
1 **to appear** (*a person or symptom*)
2 **to turn up** (*things that got lost*)

aparente *masc & fem adjective*
apparent

la **apariencia** *fem noun*
appearance
A juzgar por las apariencias. Judging by appearances.
En apariencia no estaba roto. It appeared not to be broken.
Un niño de apariencia delicada. A delicate-looking child.

apartado *masc adjective*, **apartada** *fem*
isolated

el apartamento *masc noun*
(*Latin America*) **flat, apartment**

apartar *verb* **[17]**
1 **to move away**
Aparta la manta del fuego. Move the blanket away from the fire.
2 **to move out of the way**
Aparta la planta para que pueda ver. Move the plant out of the way so that I can see.

apartarse *reflexive verb* **[17]**
to move away
Se apartó de la ventana. She moved away from the window.

aparte *adverb*
1 **aside**
poner algo aparte to put something aside
llamar a alguien aparte to call somebody aside
2 **separately**
Esto lo pago aparte. I'll pay for this separately.
3 **aparte de eso** apart from that

apasionado *masc adjective*, **apasionada** *fem*
passionate

apasionar *verb* **[17]**
El deporte me apasiona. I have a passion for sports.
La ópera no me apasiona. I'm not wild about opera.

apearse de *reflexive verb* **[17]**
1 **to get off** (*a bus, a train*)
2 **to get out of** (*a car*)
3 **to dismount from** (*a horse*)

apellidarse *reflexive verb* **[17]**
Me apellido Alejos. My surname is Alejos.

el apellido *masc noun*
surname
¿Qué apellido tienes? What's your surname?
- el **apellido de soltera** maiden name

apenas *adverb*
1 **hardly**
Apenas hay suficiente. There's hardly enough.
2 **hardly ever**
Ahora apenas nos vemos. We hardly ever see each other now.
3 **scarcely**
Hace apenas tres horas que se fueron. It's scarcely three hours since they left.
Apenas lo veo. I can scarcely see it.
4 **just**
Apenas me había sentado, cuando sonó el teléfono. I had just sat down when the telephone rang.

el apéndice *masc noun*
appendix

la apendicitis *fem noun*
appendicitis

el aperitivo *masc noun*
1 **aperitif** (*before a meal*)
2 **nibbles** (*food*)

apetecer *verb* **[35]**
No me apetece. I don't feel like it.
¿Te apetece ir a cenar fuera? Do you fancy going out for dinner?
Me apetecen las sardinas. I fancy the sardines.
Haz lo que te apetezca. Do whatever you feel like.

WORD TIP Use *apetece, apetecía*, etc if what you feel like, or don't feel like, is singular or an infinitive. Use *apetecen, apetecían*, etc if what you like, or don't like, is plural.

el apetito *masc noun*
appetite
No tengo apetito. I don't feel hungry.
Me ha abierto el apetito. It has given me an appetite.

el apio *masc noun*
celery

aplastar *verb* **[17]**
to squash

aplaudir *verb* **[19]**
to applaud

el aplauso *masc noun*
round of applause
los aplausos del público the applause of the audience

el aplazamiento *masc noun*
postponement

aplazar *verb* **[22]**
to postpone

aplicado *masc adjective*, **aplicada** *fem*
hard-working

aplicar *verb* **[31]**
to apply

el apodo *masc noun*
nickname

apostar *verb* **[24]**
1 **to bet**
Te apuesto cincuenta euros. I bet you fifty euros.

Te apuesto a que no viene. I bet she won't come.
apostar a las carreras to bet on the horses
Apostaron por el favorito. They bet on the favourite.
2 apostar por to back, to go for

el **apóstrofo** *masc noun*
(*Grammar*) **apostrophe**

apoyar *verb* **[17]**
1 **to support** (*a candidate, a plan, etc*)
2 **to lean**
Apoyé la bicicleta en la pared. I leaned the bicycle against the wall.
3 **to rest**
Apoya la cabeza en este cojín. Rest your head on this cushion.

apoyarse *reflexive verb* **[17]**
apoyarse en to lean on
Me apoyé en la puerta. I leaned against the door.

el **apoyo** *masc noun*
support

apreciar *verb* **[17]**
1 **to appreciate**
2 apreciar a alguien to be fond of somebody
La aprecio mucho. I'm very fond of her.

el **aprecio** *masc noun*
sentir aprecio por alguien to be fond of somebody

♪ **aprender** *verb* **[18]**
to learn
aprender español to learn Spanish
aprender a conducir to learn to drive
aprender algo de memoria to learn something by heart
¿Qué has aprendido hoy? What did you learn today?

el **aprendiz** *masc noun*, la **aprendiza** *fem*
apprentice

el **aprendizaje** *masc noun*
apprenticeship

apretado *masc adjective*, **apretada** *fem*
tight

apretar *verb* **[29]**
1 **to press** (*a button*)
2 **to tighten** (*a bolt or knot*)
3 apretar el acelerador to put your foot on the accelerator
4 **to be too tight** (*shoes*)
5 **to squeeze**
Me apretó el brazo. She squeezed my arm.

el **apretón** *masc noun*
un apretón de manos a handshake

el **aprieto** *masc noun*
predicament
meterse en un aprieto to get into a predicament
poner a alguien en un aprieto to put somebody in an awkward situation

aprisa *adverb*
quickly

♪ **aprobar** *verb* **[24]**
1 **to approve** (*a plan, a decision, etc*)
2 **to approve of** (*behaviour, an idea*)
3 **to pass**
aprobar un examen to pass an exam

aprovechado *masc adjective*, **aprovechada** *fem*
Es un aprovechado. He takes advantage of people.

♪ **aprovechar** *verb* **[17]**
1 **to make the most of** (*an opportunity, an offer, a skill*)
Quiero aprovechar esta oportunidad para ... I want to take this opportunity to ...
Aproveché para decírselo. I took the chance to tell him.
2 **to make use of**
Podemos aprovechar esta madera. We can use this wood.
3 (*a person*) **to take advantage of**
4 (*at meals*) ¡Que aproveche! Enjoy your meal!

♪ **aproximadamente** *adverb*
approximately, **roughly**

aproximado *masc adjective*, **aproximada** *fem*
approximate, **rough**

aproximar *verb* **[17]**
to bring nearer

aproximarse *reflexive verb* **[17]**
1 aproximarse a algo **to go up to something**
Se aproximó a la ventana. She went up to the window.
Se aproximó a mí. **He came up to me.**
2 **to approach**
Se aproximaba el momento. The moment was approaching.

apto *masc adjective*, **apta** *fem*
apto para algo suitable for something

la **apuesta** *fem noun*
bet
hacerle una apuesta a alguien to make a bet with somebody ▸▸

Me hicieron una apuesta. They made a bet with me.

apuntar *verb* **[17]**
1 **to write down** (*a telephone number, an address, etc*)
2 **to point out**
Apuntó con el dedo hacia la torre. She pointed out the tower.
3 **to aim**
Me apuntó con la pistola. He aimed the gun at me.

apuntarse *reflexive verb* **[17]**
apuntarse a algo to put your name down for something
Se apuntó a clases de guitarra. She put her name down for guitar classes.
¡Yo me apunto! I'm up for that!

los **apuntes** *plural masc noun*
notes
tomar apuntes to take notes

apurado *masc adjective*, **apurada** *fem*
(*Latin America*) **in a hurry**

apurarse *reflexive verb* **[]**
(*Latin America*) **to hurry**
¡Apúrate! Hurry up!

el **apuro** *masc noun*
estar en un apuro to be in a tight spot
pasar apuros to go through a bad patch

aquel *masc adjective*, **aquella** *fem*
▷ see **aquel** *pron*
1 **that**
en aquel momento at that moment
en aquella habitación in that room
2 **aquellos, aquellas** those
aquellos hombres those men
aquellas mujeres those women

aquel *masc pronoun*, **aquella** *fem*
▷ see **aquel** *adj*
1 **that one**
Quiero aquel. I want that one (*for a masc noun*).
Quiero aquella. I want that one (*for a fem noun*).
2 **aquellos, aquellas** those
Estas no, dame aquellos. Not these, give me those (*for a masc pl noun*).
Estas no, dame aquellas. Not these, give me those (*for a fem pl noun*).

aquél, **aquélla**, **aquéllos**, **aquéllas** *pronoun*

WORD TIP The pronouns *aquel, aquella, aquellos,* and *aquellas* take an accent when it is not clear whether a pronoun or an adjective is being used.
▷ **aquel, aquella**

aquello *pronoun*
that
¿Qué es aquello? What's that?
Aquello que vimos. What we saw.

WORD TIP *aquello* never changes.

aquí *adverb*
here
Lo puse aquí abajo. I put it down here.
Aquí llegan. Here they are.
Debe estar por aquí. It must be around here.
El vino es de aquí. The wine is from here.

árabe *masc & fem adjective* ▷ **see árabe** *noun*
1 **Arab** (*country*)
2 **Arabic** (*letter, number*)

un & una **árabe** *masc & fem noun*
▷ **see árabe** *adj*
1 **Arab** (*person*)
2 **el árabe** Arabic (*the language*)

WORD TIP Adjectives and nouns for nationality, regional origin, and language do not have capital letters in Spanish.

Aragón *masc noun*
Aragon (*a region of North-East Spain*)

aragonés *masc adjective & noun*, **aragonesa** *fem adjective & noun*
1 **Aragonese**
2 **un aragonés, una aragonesa**
Aragonese (*person*)

WORD TIP Adjectives and nouns for nationality and regional origin do not have capital letters in Spanish.

la **araña** *fem noun*
spider

arañar *verb* **[17]**
to scratch

el **arañazo** *masc noun*
scratch

el **árbitro** *masc noun*, la **árbitra** *fem*
1 **referee**
2 **umpire**

el **árbol** *masc noun*
tree
• el **árbol de Navidad** Christmas tree

el **arbusto** *masc noun*
bush

el **arcén** *masc noun*
hard shoulder (*on the motorway*)

el **archivador** *masc noun*
1 **filing cabinet**
2 **ring binder**

archivar *verb* **[17]**
to file

el **archivo** *masc noun*
1 **archive**
2 **file** (*on a computer*)

la **arcilla** *fem noun*
clay

el **arco** *masc noun*
1 **arch**
2 **bow** (*for arrows, for a violin*)
3 (*Latin America*) **goal**
• el **arco iris** rainbow

arder *verb* **[18]**
to burn
El bosque estaba ardiendo. The forest was burning.

ardiente *masc & fem adjective*
burning

la **ardilla** *fem noun*
squirrel

el **área** *fem noun*
area
las áreas más peligrosas the most dangerous areas
• el **área de penalty** penalty area

WORD TIP *área* takes *el* or *un* in the singular even though it is feminine.

la **arena** *fem noun*
sand

Argentina *fem noun*
Argentina
Soy de Argentina. I'm from Argentina.

argentino *masc adjective*, **argentina** *fem* ▷ see **argentino** *noun*
Argentinian

un **argentino** *masc noun*, una **argentina** *fem* ▷ see **argentino** *adj*
Argentinian

WORD TIP Adjectives and nouns for nationality and regional origin do not have capital letters in Spanish.

el **argot** *masc noun*
slang
• el **argot juvenil** youth slang

el **argumento** *masc noun*
1 **argument**
2 **plot** (*of a film, a play, etc*)

aries *masc & fem noun* ▷ see **Aries** *noun*
Aries
Soy aries. I'm Aries.

WORD TIP Use a small letter in Spanish to say *I am Aries*, etc with star signs.

Aries *masc noun* ▷ see **aries** *noun*
Aries

la **aritmética** *fem noun*
arithmetic

el **arma** *fem noun*
weapon
• el **arma blanca** knife (*as a weapon*)
• el **arma de fuego** firearm
• las **armas nucleares** nuclear weapons

WORD TIP *arma* takes *el* or *un* in the singular even though it is feminine.

armado *masc adjective*, **armada** *fem*
armed

armar *verb* **[17]**
1 **to arm**
2 **to assemble** (*a piece of furniture*)
3 **to pitch** (*a tent*)
4 (*informal*) **armar ruido** to make a noise
armar jaleo to make a racket
armar un escándalo to cause a scene

armarse *reflexive verb* **[17]**
1 **armarse un lío** to get confused
Me armé un lío con las fechas. I got confused with the dates.
2 **armarse de paciencia** to be patient

🔑 el **armario** *masc noun*
1 **wardrobe**
2 **cupboard**

la **armonía** *fem noun*
harmony

la **armónica** *fem noun*
harmonica

armonioso *masc adjective*, **armoniosa** *fem*
harmonious

el **aro** *masc noun*
1 **hoop**
2 **hoop earring**

el **aroma** *masc noun*
1 **scent**
2 **aroma**

aromático *masc adjective*, **aromática** *fem*
aromatic

el **arpa** *fem noun*
harp

WORD TIP *arpa* takes *el* or *un* in the singular even though it is feminine.

la **arqueología** *fem noun*
archaeology

el **arqueólogo** *masc noun*, la **arqueóloga** *fem*
archaeologist

el **arquero** *masc noun*, la **arquera** *fem*
(*Latin America*) **goalkeeper**

el **arquitecto** *masc noun*, la **arquitecta** *fem*
architect

la **arquitectura** *fem noun*
architecture

arrancar *verb* [31]
1 **to tear out**
arrancar una hoja del cuaderno to tear out a sheet from the notebook
2 **to tear off**
arrancar una etiqueta to tear off a label
3 **to pull up** (*a plant*)
4 **to pull off** (*a button*)
5 **to snatch**
Me arrancó el libro de las manos. She snatched the book from my hands.
6 **to start** (*cars, engines*)
7 **to boot up** (*computers*)

arrastrar *verb* [17]
to drag (*an object*)

arrastrarse *reflexive verb* [17]
to crawl

arrebatar *verb* [17]
to snatch

arreglado *masc adjective*, **arreglada** *fem*
1 **tidy**
Deja tu habitación arreglada. Leave your room tidy.
2 **well dressed**
Siempre va muy arreglado. He's always very well dressed.

arreglar *verb* [17]
1 **to fix**
2 **to mend**
3 **to tidy** (*a room, a house*)
4 **to sort out** (*a problem*)
No te preocupes, yo lo arreglaré. Don't worry, I'll sort it out.

arreglarse *reflexive verb* [17]
1 **to get ready**
Me arreglo enseguida y salimos. I'll get ready straight away and we can go out.
2 **to dress up**
Mi hermana siempre se arregla mucho. My sister always dresses up a lot.
3 **arreglárselas** to manage
Se las arregla muy bien sola. She manages very well on her own.

arrepentirse *reflexive verb* [14]
arrepentirse de algo to regret something
No me arrepiento. I don't regret it.

arrestar *verb* [17]
to arrest
Queda usted arrestado. You're under arrest.

el **arresto** *masc noun*
arrest

arriba *adverb*
1 **up**
aquí arriba up here
Lo puse más arriba. I put it a bit higher up.
2 **de arriba** above
el cajón de arriba the drawer above
3 **upstairs**
Ha ido arriba. He's gone upstairs.
Viven en el piso de arriba. They live upstairs.
4 **arriba de todo** at the very top
de arriba abajo from top to bottom

arriesgado *masc adjective*, **arriesgada** *fem*
risky

arriesgar *verb* [28]
to risk

arriesgarse *reflexive verb* [28]
to take a risk

la **arroba** *fem noun*
1 **@, at** (*in email addresses*)
juanrobledo@easycom.com
juanrobledo@easycom.com (*said as* **punto, com** *for* **dot, com**)
2 **former measurement of weight**

arrodillarse *reflexive verb* [17]
to kneel down
Estaba arrodillado. He was on his knees.

arrogante *masc & fem adjective*
arrogant

arrojar *verb* [17]
to throw

arropar *verb* [17]
1 **to wrap up** (*a child, a sick person*)
2 **to tuck in** (*in bed*)

arroparse *reflexive verb* [17]
to wrap up
Arrópate bien. Wrap up well.

el **arroyo** *masc noun*
stream

el **arroz** *masc noun*
rice

la **arruga** *fem noun*
wrinkle

arrugar *verb* [28]
1 **to wrinkle**
2 **to crease**
3 **to crumple up**

arruinar *verb* [17]
to ruin

arruinarse *reflexive verb* [17]
to go bankrupt

⚷ el **arte** *masc noun*
art
las artes the arts
• el **arte moderno** modern art
• las **artes gráficas** graphic arts

WORD TIP *arte* is *masc* in the singular, but *fem* in the plural.

la **artesanía** *fem noun*
1 **crafts**
artesanía tradicional traditional crafts
objetos de artesanía handicrafts
2 **craftsmanship**
3 **craftwork**
la artesanía de la zona the local craftwork

el **artesano** *masc noun*, la **artesana** *fem*
1 **craftsman**
2 **craftswoman**

ártico *masc adjective*, **ártica** *fem*
▷ see **Ártico** *noun*
Arctic

WORD TIP Adjectives and nouns for regional origin do not have capital letters in Spanish.

el **Ártico** *masc noun* ▷ see **ártico** *adj*
el Ártico the Arctic

la **articulación** *fem noun*
joint (*in your arm, leg, etc*)

⚷ el **artículo** *masc noun*
article
• el **artículo definido** definite article
• los **artículos de papelería** stationery

artificial *masc & fem adjective*
artificial

⚷ el & la **artista** *masc & fem noun*
artist

artístico *masc adjective*, **artística** *fem*
artistic

la **arveja** *fem noun*
(*Latin America*) **pea**

el **arzobispo** *masc noun*
archbishop

el **asa** *fem noun*
handle
Tómalo por el asa. Take it by the handle.

WORD TIP *asa* takes *el* or *un* in the singular even though it is feminine.

⚷ el **asado** *masc noun*
roast

la **asamblea** *fem noun*
meeting

asar *verb* [17]
1 **to roast** (*meat*)
2 **to bake** (*vegetables*)

ascender *verb* [36]
1 **to be promoted**
Ha ascendido. He's been promoted.
2 **to promote** (*an employee*)
3 **to rise** (*temperature, prices or a balloon*)
ascender a to amount to
La cuenta asciende a quinientos euros. The bill amounts to five hundred euros.

el **ascenso** *masc noun*
promotion

⚷ el **ascensor** *masc noun*
lift

el **asco** *masc noun*
¡Qué asco! How disgusting!
Esta sopa me da asco. This soup is disgusting.
La película es un asco. The film is disgusting.

asegurar *verb* [17]
1 **to assure**
Te aseguro que ... I can assure you that ...
2 **to insure**
3 **to secure**

asegurarse *reflexive verb* [17]
to make sure
Asegúrate de cerrar la llave. Make sure you turn the tap off.

asentir *verb* [14]
asentir con la cabeza to nod (*in agreement*)

⚷ el **aseo** *masc noun*
toilet
• los **aseos de señoras** the Ladies

asesinar *verb* [17]
to murder

el **asesinato** *masc noun*
murder

el **asesino** *masc noun*, la **asesina** *fem*
murderer

Spanish-English

el **asesor** *masc noun*, la **asesora** *fem*
adviser

la **asfixia** *fem noun*
1 **asphyxia**
2 **suffocation**
Tenía una sensación de asfixia. I felt I was suffocating.

asfixiante *masc & fem adjective*
1 **asphyxiating** (*air, fumes*)
2 **suffocating** (*heat*)

asfixiarse *reflexive verb* [17]
1 **to suffocate**
2 **to choke to death**

así *adverb*
1 **like this**
Hazlo así. Do it like this.
2 **like that**
El pueblo se llama Robellón, o algo así. The village is called Robellón, or something like that.
3 **that way**
Me llevaré el coche, así podremos volver pronto. I'll take the car, that way we can come back early.
4 **así que** so
Así que te vas de vacaciones. So you're going on holiday.
5 **así es** that's right
6 **así, así** so, so
'¿Te gusta?'—'Así, así.' 'Do you like it?'—'So, so.'
7 **¡Así me gusta!** That's what I like to see!
¡Así se hace! Well done!

Asia *fem noun*
Asia

asiático *masc adjective & noun*, **asiática** *fem adjective & noun*
1 **Asian**
2 **un asiático, una asiática** Asian (*person*)

WORD TIP Adjectives and nouns for nationality and regional origin do not have capital letters in Spanish.

el **asiento** *masc noun*
seat
• el **asiento delantero** front seat
• el **asiento trasero** back seat

la **asignatura** *fem noun*
subject

el **asilo** *masc noun*
home (*for old people*)
• el **asilo político** political asylum

la **asistenta** *fem noun*
cleaning lady
¿Hay servicio de asistenta? Is there a maid service?

el & la **asistente** *masc & fem noun*
assistant
• el **asistente social** social worker

asistir *verb* [19]
asistir a algo to attend something
Asistió a la reunión. He attended the meeting.
No ha asistido a clases hoy. She has not been to school today.

el **asma** *fem noun*
asthma

WORD TIP *asma* takes *el* or *un* in the singular even though it is feminine.

asmático *masc adjective*, **asmática** *fem*
asthmatic

la **asociación** *fem noun*
association

asociar *verb* [17]
to associate (*ideas, words, etc*)

asociarse *reflexive verb* [17]
to go into partnership (*in business*)

asolar *verb* [17]
to devastate (*a region, coast, etc*)

asomar *verb* [17]
asomar la cabeza to stick your head out
Abrió la ventana y asomó la cabeza. She opened the window and stuck her head out.
'No asomar la cabeza por la ventana' 'Do not lean out of the window'

asomarse *reflexive verb* [17]
Se asomó a la ventana. He had a look out of the window.
'Prohibido asomarse por la ventana' 'Do not lean out of the window'

asombrar *verb* [17]
to amaze
Me asombra su actitud. Her attitude amazes me.

asombrarse *reflexive verb* [17]
to be amazed

el **asombro** *masc noun*
surprise
con cara de asombro with a look of surprise on her face

asombroso *masc adjective*, **asombrosa** *fem*
amazing

el **aspecto** *masc noun*
look
¿Qué aspecto tenían? What did they look like?
Una mujer de aspecto elegante. An elegant-looking woman.
Tienes muy buen aspecto. You look very well.
Tiene aspecto de policía. He looks like an policeman.

áspero *masc adjective*, **áspera** *fem*
rough

el **aspirador** *masc noun* ▷ **aspiradora**

la **aspiradora** *fem noun*
vacuum cleaner
pasar la aspiradora to vacuum
Tengo que pasar la aspiradora en el salón. I must vacuum the living room.

la **aspirina** *fem noun*
aspirin

el **asterisco** *masc noun*
asterisk

la **astilla** *fem noun*
splinter

la **astrología** *fem noun*
astrology

el **astrólogo** *masc noun*, la **astróloga** *fem*
astrologer

el & la **astronauta** *masc & fem noun*
astronaut

la **astronomía** *fem noun*
astronomy

el **astrónomo** *masc noun*, la **astrónoma** *fem*
astronomer

asturiano *masc adjective & noun*, **asturiana** *fem adjective & noun*
1 **Asturian**, **from Asturias** (*a region in north-west Spain*)
2 **un asturiano, una asturiana** Asturian

WORD TIP Adjectives and nouns for nationality and regional origin do not have capital letters in Spanish.

astuto *masc adjective*, **astuta** *fem*
1 **shrewd**
2 **crafty**
Eso fue muy astuto por su parte. That was very crafty of her.

el **asunto** *masc noun*
1 **matter**
asuntos de negocios business matters
un asunto complicado a complicated matter
2 **business**
No quiero saber nada de este asunto. I don't want to know anything about this business.
No es asunto tuyo. It's none of your business.

asustar *verb* [17]
to frighten

asustarse *reflexive verb* [17]
to get frightened
Me asusté al oír un ruido. I got frightened when I heard a noise.

atacar *verb* [31]
to attack

el **atajo** *masc noun*
short cut

el **ataque** *masc noun*
1 **attack**
2 **fit**
un ataque de celos a fit of jealousy
Me dio un ataque de risa. I got a fit of the giggles.
• el **ataque cardíaco** heart attack

atar *verb* [17]
to tie (up)

el **atardecer** *masc noun*
dusk
al atardecer at dusk

atardecer *verb* [35]
to get dark
Estaba atardeciendo. It was getting dark.

atascar *verb* [31]
to block (*a pipe*)

atascarse *reflexive verb* [31]
to get blocked

el **atasco** *masc noun*
1 **traffic jam**
2 **blockage**

el **ataúd** *masc noun*
coffin

✱ la **atención** *fem noun*
attention
prestar atención to pay attention
No pones atención en lo que haces. You don't concentrate on what you are doing.
¡Atención, por favor! Your attention, please!

atender *verb* **[36]**
1 **to pay attention**
Atiende a la profesora. Pay attention to your teacher.
2 **¿La atiende alguien?** Are you being served?

el **atentado** *masc noun*
attack
Un atentado contra el presidente. An assasination attempt on the president.
• el **atentado terrorista** terrorist attack

atentamente *adverb*
1 **attentively**
2 **Le saluda atentamente.** Yours faithfully, Yours sincerely

atento *masc adjective*, **atenta** *fem*
attentive

el **ateo** *masc noun* la **atea** *fem*
atheist

♪ el **aterrizaje** *masc noun*
landing (*of a plane*)

♪ **aterrizar** *verb* **[22]**
to land (*planes*)

aterrorizar *verb* **[22]**
to terrify

el **ático** *masc noun*
1 **top-floor apartment**
2 **loft**

el **atizador** *masc noun*
poker

atlántico *masc adjective*, **atlántica** *fem*
▷ see **Atlántico** *noun*

el **Atlántico** *masc noun*
▷ see **atlántico** *adj*
el Atlántico the Atlantic

el **atlas** *masc noun*
atlas

el & la **atleta** *masc & fem noun*
athlete

atlético *masc adjective*, **atlética** *fem*
1 **athletic** (*person*)
2 **una competición atlética** an athletics competition

el **atletismo** *masc noun*
athletics

atómico *masc adjective*, **atómica** *fem*
atomic

el **átomo** *masc noun*
atom

♪ el **atracador** *masc noun*, la **atracadora** *fem*
1 **robber**
2 **mugger**

♪ **atracar** *verb* **[31]**
1 **to hold up** (*a bank or a shop*)
2 **to mug** (*a person*)

la **atracción** *fem noun*
attraction

♪ el **atraco** *masc noun*
1 **hold-up** (*of a bank or a shop*)
2 **mugging**

atractivo *masc adjective*, **atractiva** *fem*
attractive

atraer *verb* **[42]**
to attract

atragantarse *reflexive verb* **[17]**
atragantarse con algo to choke on something

atrapar *verb* **[17]**
to catch

♪ **atrás** *adverb*
1 **back**
Nos sentamos demasiado atrás. We sat too far back.
hacia atrás backwards
la parte de atrás the back
2 **at the back**
Esto va atrás. This goes at the back.
3 **quedarse atrás** to be left behind

atrasado *masc adjective*, **atrasada** *fem*
1 **slow** (*watch or clock*)
Llevo el reloj atrasado. My watch is slow.
2 **backward** (*country*)
3 **old-fashioned** (*ideas, people*)
4 **behind**
Voy atrasado en los estudios. I'm behind at school.
Van muy atrasados con los ensayos. They're very behind with the rehearsals.

atrasar *verb* **[17]**
1 **to put back** (*a watch or clock*)
Hay que atrasar los relojes una hora. We have to put the clocks back an hour.
2 **to lose time** (*a watch or clock*)
Este reloj atrasa. This watch loses time.
3 **to postpone**

atrasarse *reflexive verb* **[17]**
to lose time (*a watch or clock*)

atravesar *verb* **[29]**
to cross

atrayente *masc & fem adjective*
appealing

atreverse *reflexive verb* **[18]**
to dare
No me atrevo a preguntarle. I don't dare ask him.

atrevido *masc adjective*, **atrevida** *fem*
1 **daring**
2 **cheeky**
¡Qué niño más atrevido! What a cheeky child!

atropellar *verb* **[17]**
to run over, **to knock down**
Lo atropelló un coche. He was run over by a car.

el **atún** *masc noun*
tuna

el **audífono** *masc noun*
hearing aid

✓ el **aula** *fem noun*
1 **classroom**
2 **lecture theatre**

WORD TIP *aula* takes *el* or *un* in the singular even though it is feminine.

el **aullido** *masc noun*
howl

aumentar *verb* **[17]**
1 **to increase**
Aumentó en un cinco por ciento. It increased by five per cent.
2 **to rise** (*temperature, pressure*)

el **aumento** *masc noun*
1 **increase**
2 **rise**

✓ **aun** *adverb* ▷ see **aún** *adv*
even
aun así even so
ni aun con tu ayuda not even with your help

✓ **aún** *adverb* ▷ see **aun** *adv*
1 **still**
Aún estoy esperando. I'm still waiting.
2 **yet**
Aún no se lo he dicho a ellos. I haven't told them yet.
3 **even**
Este es aún mejor. This one is even better.

✓ **aunque** *conjunction*
1 **although**
Aunque estaba cansada, la ayudé. Although I was tired, I helped her.
2 **even if**, **even though**
Aunque parezca mentira, ... Even if it seems untrue, ...
Aunque llegues tarde, llámame. Even if you arrive late, give me a ring.

WORD TIP When *aunque* means *even if*, it is followed by a verb in the subjunctive.

el & la **au pair** *masc & fem noun, pl:* **au pairs**
au pair

el **auricular** *masc noun*
1 **receiver** (*of a phone*)
2 **los auriculares** headphones

✓ **ausente** *masc & fem adjective*
absent
estar ausente to be absent, to be away

Australia *fem noun*
Australia
Soy de Australia. I'm from Australia.

australiano *masc adjective*, **australiana** *fem* ▷ see **australiano** *noun*
Australian

un **australiano** *masc noun*, una **australiana** *fem*
▷ see **australiano** *adj*
Australian

WORD TIP Adjectives and nouns for nationality and regional origin do not have capital letters in Spanish.

Austria *fem noun*
Austria
Soy de Austria. I'm from Austria.

austriaco *masc adjective & noun*, **austriaca** *fem adjective & noun*
1 **Austrian**
2 **un austriaco, una austriaca** Austrian

WORD TIP Adjectives and nouns for nationality and regional origin do not have capital letters in Spanish.

auténtico *masc adjective*, **auténtica** *fem*
authentic

✓ el **auto** *masc noun*
(*Latin America*) **car**

autoadhesivo *masc adjective*, **autoadhesiva** *fem*
self-adhesive

la **autobiografía** *fem noun*
autobiography

✓ el **autobús** *masc noun*
bus
coger el autobús to catch the bus
perder el autobús **to miss the bus**

✓ el **autocar** *masc noun*
coach

Spanish–English
a b c d e f g h i j k l m n ñ o p q r s t u v w x y z

la **autoescuela** *fem noun*
driving school

el **autógrafo** *masc noun*
autograph

automático *masc adjective*, **automática** *fem*
automatic

el **automóvil** *masc noun*
car

el **automovilismo** *masc noun*
1 **motoring**
2 **motor racing**

el & la **automovilista** *masc & fem noun*
motorist

la **autonomía** *fem noun*
1 **autonomy**
2 **autonomous region** (*one of the seventeen self-governing areas into which Spain is divided*)

autonómico *masc adjective*, **autonómica** *fem*
regional (*relating to the seventeen autonomous regions into which Spain is divided*)

la **autopista** *fem noun*
motorway

el **autor** *masc noun*, la **autora** *fem*
author

la **autoridad** *fem noun*
authority

autoritario *masc adjective*, **autoritaria** *fem*
authoritarian

la **autorización** *fem noun*
authorization

autorizar *verb* [22]
to authorize

el **autoservicio** *masc noun*
1 **self-service restaurant**
2 **supermarket**

el **autostop**, **auto-stop** *masc noun*
hitch-hiking
hacer autostop to hitch-hike

el & la **autostopista** *masc & fem noun*
hitch-hiker

la **autovía** *fem noun*
dual carriageway

el & la **auxiliar** *masc & fem noun*
assistant
- el & la **auxiliar de vuelo** flight attendant

el **auxilio** *masc noun*
aid
acudir en auxilio de alguien to go to somebody's aid
primeros auxilios first aid

la **avalancha** *fem noun*
avalanche

avanzar *verb* [22]
1 **to move forward** (*traffic, people*)
2 **to make progress** (*students, researchers*)
3 **to wind on** (*a tape*)

la **avaricia** *fem noun*
greed

avaricioso *masc adjective*, **avariciosa** *fem*
greedy

Avda. *abbreviation*
(=*Avenida*) **Ave.**, **Avenue** (*in addresses*)

el **AVE** *masc noun*
(=*Alta Velocidad Española*) **Spanish high-speed train**

el **ave** *fem noun*
bird
un ave a bird
las aves rapiñas birds of prey

WORD TIP *ave* takes *el* or *un* in the singular even though it is feminine.

la **avellana** *fem noun*
hazelnut

la **avenida** *fem noun*
avenue

la **aventura** *fem noun*
adventure

aventurero *masc adjective*, **aventurera** *fem*
adventurous

avergonzado *masc adjective*, **avergonzada** *fem*
1 **ashamed**
2 **embarrassed**

la **avería** *fem noun*
breakdown (*of a car, etc*)
sufrir una avería to break down

averiado *masc adjective*, **averiada** *fem*
1 **broken down**
2 **out of order**

el **avestruz** *masc noun*
ostrich

el **avión** *masc noun*
aeroplane
- el **avión a reacción** jet (*plane*)

avisar *verb* [17]
1 **avisar a alguien de algo** to let somebody know about something
Le avisé del problema. I let him know about the problem.
Me avisaron que llegarían tarde. They told me they would be late.
2 **to warn**
Les avisé del peligro que corrían. I warned them about the danger they were in.
3 **to call**
avisar al médico to call the doctor

el **aviso** *masc noun*
1 **warning**
El profesor ya le ha dado tres avisos. The teacher has already given him three warnings.
sin previo aviso without prior warning
2 **notice**
hasta nuevo aviso until further notice
3 **Último aviso para los pasajeros del vuelo ...** Last call for passengers on flight ...

la **avispa** *fem noun*
wasp

la **axila** *fem noun*
armpit

⚷ **ayer** *adverb*
yesterday
antes de ayer the day before yesterday

⚷ la **ayuda** *fem noun*
1 **help**
ir en ayuda de alguien to go to somebody's help
2 **aid** (*to a country, etc*)

el & la **ayudante** *masc & fem noun*
helper, **assistant**

⚷ **ayudar** *verb* [17]
to help
¿En qué puedo ayudarle? How can I help you?

⚷ el **ayuntamiento** *masc noun*
1 **town council**
2 **city council**
3 **town hall**

⚷ la **azafata** *fem noun*
1 **flight attendant**
2 **trade fair attendant**

el **azar** *masc noun*
1 **chance**
por azar by chance
2 **al azar** at random

el **azote** *masc noun*
smack

la **azotea** *fem noun*
(flat) roof

⚷ el & la **azúcar** *masc* or *fem noun*
sugar
un terrón de azúcar a sugar lump
- el **azúcar blanco** white sugar
- el **azúcar de caña** cane sugar
- el **azúcar glas, el azúcar glaseado** icing sugar
- el **azúcar moreno** brown sugar

WORD TIP The compounds with *azúcar* can also be feminine.

el **azucarero** *masc noun*
sugar bowl

⚷ **azul** *masc & fem adjective* ▷ **see azul** *noun*
blue
ojos azules blue eyes

⚷ el **azul** *masc noun* ▷ **see azul** *adj*
blue
- el **azul celeste** sky blue
- el **azul claro** light blue
- el **azul marino** navy blue

el **azulejo** *masc noun*
tile

Spanish-English

a b c d e f g h i j k l m n ñ o p q r s t u v w x y z

B b

la **baca** *fem noun*
luggage-rack

el **bacalao** *masc noun*
cod

el **bachillerato** *masc noun*
Bachillerato (*the two-year secondary education course leading to university entrance*)

la **baguette** *fem noun*
baguette, **French stick**

Bahamas *plural fem noun*
las Bahamas the Bahamas
las islas Bahamas the Bahama Islands

bahameño *masc adjective & noun*, **bahameña** *fem adjective & noun*
1 **Bahamian**
2 **un bahameño, una bahameña**
Bahamian (*person*)

WORD TIP Adjectives and nouns for nationality and regional origin do not have capital letters in Spanish.

la **bahía** *fem noun*
bay

bailar *verb* **[17]**
to dance
bailar flamenco to do flamenco dancing

el **bailarín** *masc noun*, la **bailarina** *fem*
dancer

el **baile** *masc noun*
1 **dance**
2 **dancing**
una clase de baile a dancing class

mini-info ***baile***
En España hay muchos bailes tradicionales pero el flamenco, una combinación de guitarra, canto y baile es el más famoso; hoy también la salsa y los ritmos latinos se bailan por todo el mundo.

bajar *verb* **[17]**
1 **to bring down**
¿Puedes bajarme el abrigo? Could you bring down my coat?
2 (*Computers*) **to download** (*a program, a file*)
3 **to take down**
Baja las maletas a recepción. Take the suitcases down to reception.
4 **to go down**
El ascensor está bajando. The lift's going down.
Bajamos por las escaleras. We went down the stairs.
Baje por esta calle hasta llegar a la plaza. Go down this street until you get to the square (*formal use*).
5 **to come down**
¡Ya bajo! I'm coming down!
6 **to fall** (*temperatures, prices*)
7 **to turn down** (*the volume*)
Baja la tele. Turn the television down.
8 **to lower** (*a blind*)
9 **to reduce** (*prices*)

bajarse *reflexive verb* **[17]**
bajarse de un coche to get out of a car
Se bajó de la bicicleta. He got off the bike.

bajo *masc adjective*, **baja** *fem*
▷ see **bajo** *adv, noun, prep*
1 **short**
Soy bastante bajo I'm quite short (*boy speaking*).
Soy bastante baja I'm quite short (*girl speaking*).
2 **low**
Los precios están bajos. Prices are low.
Pon la música baja. Put the music on low.

bajo *adverb* ▷ see **bajo** *adj, noun, prep*
1 **low**
volar bajo to fly low
2 **quietly**
hablar bajo to speak quietly

bajo *preposition* ▷ see **bajo** *adj, adv, noun*
1 **under**
bajo los árboles under the trees
2 **La temperatura está bajo cero.** The temperature's below zero.

el **bajo** *masc noun* ▷ see **bajo** *adj, adv, prep*
ground floor

la **bala** *fem noun*
bullet

el **balancín** *masc noun*
1 **seesaw**
2 **swing seat**
3 **rocking chair**

la **balanza** *fem noun*
scales

balbucear *verb* **[17]**
to stammer

el **balcón** *masc noun*
balcony

la **baldosa** *fem noun*
tile

las **Baleares** *plural fem noun*
las islas Baleares the Balearic Islands

la **ballena** *fem noun*
whale

el **ballet** *masc noun*
ballet

el **balón** *masc noun*
ball
un balón de fútbol a football

♪ el **baloncesto** *masc noun*
basketball

el **balonmano** *masc noun*
handball

el **balonvolea** *masc noun*
volleyball

la **balsa** *fem noun*
1 **raft**
2 **pond**

la **banca** *fem noun*
banking

el **banco** *masc noun*
1 **bench** (*in a park*)
2 **pew** (*in church*)
3 **bank** (*for loans, savings*)
Trabaja en un banco. She works in a bank.

la **banda** *fem noun*
1 **band** (*of musicians*)
2 **gang** (*of criminals*)
• la **banda sonora** soundtrack

la **bandeja** *fem noun*
tray

la **bandera** *fem noun*
flag

la **banderilla** *fem noun*
banderilla (*a decorated dart used in bullfighting*)

el **bandido** *masc noun*, la **bandida** *fem*
bandit

el **banquero** *masc noun*, la **banquera** *fem*
banker

la **banqueta** *fem noun*
stool

el **banquete** *masc noun*
banquet
un banquete de bodas a wedding banquet

♪ el **bañador** *masc noun*
1 **swimming trunks**
2 **swimming costume**

♪ **bañar** *verb* **[17]**
bañar a un bebé to bath a baby

bañarse *reflexive verb* **[17]**
1 **to have a bath**
Voy a bañarme esta noche. I'm going to have a bath tonight.
2 **to have a swim**
¿Te apetece bañarte? Do you fancy going for a swim?

♪ la **bañera** *fem noun*
bath (*bathtub*)

♪ el **baño** *masc noun*
1 **bathroom**
¿Dónde está el baño? Where's the bathroom?
2 **bath**
darse un baño to have a bath
Voy a darme un baño. I'm going to have a bath.
3 **swim**
darse un baño to go for a swim
¿Te apetece darte un baño? Do you fancy going for a swim?

♪ el **bar** *masc noun*
bar

la **baraja** *fem noun*
pack of cards

barajar *verb* **[17]**
to shuffle (*a pack of cards*)

la **barandilla** *fem noun*
rail

la **baratija** *fem noun*
knick-knack

♪ **barato** *masc adjective*, **barata** *fem*
cheap
Es muy barato. It's very cheap.

la **barba** *fem noun*
beard
afeitarse la barba to shave off your beard
dejarse barba to grow a beard
Voy a dejarme barba. I'm going to grow a beard.

la **barbacoa** *fem noun*
barbecue

barbadense *masc & fem adjective & noun*
1 **Barbadian**
2 **un & una barbadense Barbadian** (*person*)

WORD TIP Adjectives and nouns for nationality and regional origin do not have capital letters in Spanish.

Spanish–English

Barbados *masc noun*
Barbados

♂ la **barbaridad** *fem noun*
1 **atrocity**
2 (*saying something is very bad*) **Nos cobraron una barbaridad.** They charged us a fortune.
3 **Eso es una barbaridad.** That's far too much.
4 **Deja de decir barbaridades.** Stop talking nonsense.
5 **¡Qué barbaridad!** That's terrible!

el **barbero** *masc noun*
barber

la **barbilla** *fem noun*
chin

la **barca** *fem noun*
boat
- la **barca de pesca** fishing boat
- la **barca de remos** rowing boat

el **Barça** *masc noun*
(*informal*) **Barcelona Football Club**

Barcelona *fem noun*
Barcelona

♂ el **barco** *masc noun*
1 **boat**
viajar en barco to travel by boat
2 **ship**
- el **barco de guerra** warship
- el **barco de pesca** fishing boat

el **barniz** *masc noun*
varnish
- el **barniz de uñas** nail varnish

el **barómetro** *masc noun*
barometer

♂ la **barra** *fem noun*
1 **rail** (*for clothes*)
2 **bar**
Nos sirvieron en la barra. They served us at the bar.
- la **barra de jabón** bar of soap
- la **barra de labios** lipstick
- la **barra de pan** baguette

barrer *verb* **[18]**
to sweep

la **barrera** *fem noun*
barrier

♂ la **barriga** *fem noun*
stomach, **tummy**
tener dolor de barriga to have stomachache
Tengo dolor de barriga. I have stomachache.

el **barril** *masc noun*
barrel

♂ el **barrio** *masc noun*
area (*of a town*)
- los **barrios bajos** the slums

el **barro** *masc noun*
1 **mud**
lleno de barro covered in mud
2 **clay** (*for making pots*)

los **bártulos** *plural masc noun*
(*informal*) **stuff**, **things**
Llévate todos tus bártulos. Take all your stuff away.

basar *verb* **[17]**
to base
basar algo en algo to base something on something
En eso baso mi opinión. I base my views on that.

basarse *reflexive verb* **[17]**
¿En qué te basas para decir eso? What basis do you have for saying that?

la **base** *fem noun*
1 **base**
2 **a base de** by
Lo aprendió a base de repetirlo. He learnt it by repeating it.
- la **base de datos** database
- la **base de maquillaje** foundation (*make-up*)

básico *masc adjective*, **básica** *fem*
basic

♂ **bastante** *masc & fem adjective*
▷ see **bastante** *adv, pron*
1 **enough**
Tenemos bastante pan. We've got enough bread.
No tenemos bastantes sillas. We don't have enough chairs.
2 **quite a lot of**
bastante gente quite a lot of people
Bebimos bastante café. We drank quite a lot of coffee.
Compramos bastantes regalos. We bought quite a lot of presents.

WORD TIP *bastante* takes *-s* in the plural when it is an adjective.

bastante *adverb, pronoun*
▷ see **bastante** *adj*
1 **enough**
Con esto tenemos bastante. We have enough with this.
Compramos bastante para toda la semana.

a **b** c d e f g h i j k l m n ñ o p q r s t u v w x y z

We bought enough for the whole week.
¿Has comido bastante? Have you eaten enough?
2 **quite**
Estaba bastante contenta. She was quite happy.
Ha mejorado bastante. He's improved quite a lot.

WORD TIP *bastante* does not change when it is an adverb or pronoun.

bastar *verb* **[17]**
1 **to be enough**
Con eso basta. That's enough.
¡Ya basta! That's enough!
2 **Basta con preguntarle.** You just need to ask him.

el **bastón** *masc noun*
walking stick

el **bastoncillo** *masc noun*
cotton bud

♪ la **basura** *fem noun*
1 **rubbish**
Hay que sacar la basura. We must put the rubbish out.
2 **dustbin, bin**
tirar algo a la basura to put something in the dustbin
Tíralo a la basura. Throw it in the dustbin.

el **basurero** *masc noun*
▷ see **basurero** *noun*
rubbish tip

el **basurero** *masc noun*, la **basurera** *fem*
▷ see **basurero** *masc noun*
refuse collector

la **bata** *fem noun*
1 **dressing gown**
2 **una bata de médico** a white doctor's coat

la **batalla** *fem noun*
battle

el **bate** *masc noun*
bat

la **batería** *fem noun* ▷ see **batería** *masc & fem noun*
1 **battery** (*for a car*)
2 **drum kit**
tocar la batería to play the drums

el & la **batería** *masc & fem noun*
▷ see **batería** *fem noun*
drummer

el **batido** *masc noun*
milkshake
un batido de fresa a strawberry milkshake

la **batidora** *fem noun*
food mixer

batir *verb* **[19]**
1 **to beat** (*in recipes*)
batir los huevos beat the eggs
2 **to whip** (*cream*)
3 (*Sports*) **batir un récord** to break a record

el **baúl** *masc noun*
trunk (*for clothes*)

el **bautismo** *masc noun*
baptism

bautizar *verb* **[22]**
to christen

el **bautizo** *masc noun*
christening

la **baya** *fem noun*
berry

la **bayeta** *fem noun*
cloth (*for wiping*)

el **bebé** *masc noun*
baby (***el bebé*** *can be a girl or boy*)

♪ **beber** *verb* **[18]**
to drink
¿Quieres beber algo? Do you want something to drink?

♪ la **bebida** *fem noun*
drink
una bebida refrescante a refreshing drink

la **beca** *fem noun*
1 **grant**
2 **scholarship**

♪ el **béisbol** *masc noun*
baseball

el **belén** *masc noun*
nativity scene, crib

belga *masc & fem adjective & noun*
1 **Belgian**
2 **un & una belga** Belgian (*person*)

WORD TIP Adjectives and nouns for nationality and regional origin do not have capital letters in Spanish.

Bélgica *fem noun*
Belgium

la **belleza** *fem noun*
beauty

bello *masc adjective*, **bella** *fem*
beautiful

bendito *masc adjective*, **bendita** *fem*
1 **blessed**
2 **holy** (*water, bread in church*)

Spanish–English

beneficiar *verb* **[17]**
to benefit

el **beneficio** *masc noun*
1 **benefit**
2 **profit**

benéfico *masc adjective*, **benéfica** *fem*
charity
una organización benéfica a charity

la **berenjena** *fem noun*
aubergine

el **berro** *masc noun*
watercress

la **besamel** *fem noun*
white sauce

besar *verb* **[17]**
to kiss

el **beso** *masc noun*
kiss
darle un beso a alguien to give someone a kiss
Dame un beso. Give me a kiss.
Me dio un beso en la mejilla. He gave me a kiss on the cheek.

bestia *masc & fem adjective* ▷ see **bestia** *noun*
1 (*informal*) **ignorant**
2 **No seas bestia y habla bien.** Don't be so rude, mind your language.

la **bestia** *fem noun* ▷ see **bestia** *adj*
1 **beast** (*animal*)
2 (*informal*) **idiot**
Es una bestia, no sabe nada. He's so thick, he doesn't know a thing.
3 **brute**

el **betún** *masc noun*
shoe polish

la **Biblia** *fem noun*
Bible

la **biblioteca** *fem noun*
library

el **bibliotecario** *masc noun*, la **bibliotecaria** *fem*
librarian

el **bicho** *masc noun*
creepy-crawly

la **bici** *fem noun*
bike
montar en bici to ride a bike
Vine en bici. I came by bike.

la **bicicleta** *fem noun*
bicycle
montar en bicicleta to ride a bicycle
¿Sabes montar en bicicleta? Can you ride a bicycle?

el **bien** *masc noun* ▷ see **bien** *adv, adj*
good
la diferencia entre el bien y el mal the difference between good and evil

bien *adverb, adjective* ▷ see **bien** *noun*
1 **well**
Lo has hecho muy bien. You've done it very well.
No me siento bien. I don't feel well.
'¿Cómo están tus padres?'—'Muy bien, gracias.' 'How are your parents?'—'Very well, thank you!'
Hablas muy bien español. You speak very good Spanish.
2 **all right**
¿Estás bien en esa silla? Are you all right in that chair?
Así está bien. It's all right like this.
3 **nice**
Huele bien. It smells nice.
Sabe bien. It tastes nice.
4 **properly**
No funciona bien. It doesn't work properly.
5 (*in exclamations*) **¡Bien!** That's right!
¡Bien hecho! Well done!
¡Muy bien! All right!, Ok!

el **bienestar** *masc noun*
welfare

la **bienvenida** *fem noun* ▷ see **bienvenido** *adj*
welcome
dar la bienvenida a alguien to welcome somebody
Le dieron una cálida bienvenida. She was given a warm welcome.

bienvenido *masc adjective*, **bienvenida** *fem* ▷ see **bienvenida** *noun*
welcome
¡Bienvenido! Welcome! (*speaking to one person*)
¡Bienvenidos! Welcome! (*speaking to two or more people*)
Aquí siempre sois bienvenidos. You're always welcome here (*familiar form*).

el **bigote** *masc noun*
moustache

el **bikini** *masc noun*
bikini

a b c d e f g h i j k l m n ñ o p q r s t u v w x y z

bilingüe *masc & fem adjective*
bilingual

el **billar** *masc noun*
1 **billiards**
2 **pool**
3 **snooker**

los **billares** *plural masc noun*
amusement arcade

♪ el **billete** *masc noun*
1 **note** (*money*)
un billete de cincuenta euros a fifty-euro note
2 **ticket**
un billete de tren a train ticket
- el **billete de banco** bank note
- el **billete de ida** single ticket
- el **billete de ida y vuelta** return ticket
- el **billete sencillo** single ticket

la **billetera** *fem noun*
wallet

el **billetero** *masc noun*
wallet

la **biografía** *fem noun*
biography

la **biología** *fem noun*
biology

el **biólogo** *masc noun*, la **bióloga** *fem*
biologist

el **biquini** *masc noun*
bikini

el **bisabuelo** *masc noun*, la **bisabuela** *fem*
1 **great-grandfather**
2 **great-grandmother**
3 **mis bisabuelos** my great-grandparents

el **bisnieto** *masc noun*, la **bisnieta** *fem*
1 **great-grandson**
2 **great-granddaughter**
3 **mis bisnietos** my great-grandchildren

♪ el **bistec** *masc noun*
steak

el **bizcocho** *masc noun*
sponge cake

♪ **blanco** *masc adjective*, **blanca** *fem*
▷ see **blanco** *noun*
white
una bandera blanca a white flag

el **blanco** *masc noun* ▷ see **blanco** *adj*
1 (*Colour*) **white**
2 **un blanco** a white man
una blanca a white woman
3 **target**
dar en el blanco to hit the target

blando *masc adjective*, **blanda** *fem*
1 **soft**
un colchón blando a soft mattress
La mantequilla se ha puesto blanda. The butter's gone soft.
2 **tender** (*meat*)
3 **soft** (*person*)

WORD TIP *blando* does not mean *bland* in English; for the meaning of *bland* see ▷ SOSO.

el **bloc** *masc noun*
writing pad

♪ el **bloque** *masc noun*
block
un bloque de pisos a block of flats

bloquear *verb* **[17]**
to block
Un camión bloqueaba la calle. A lorry was blocking the street.

♪ la **blusa** *fem noun*
blouse

♪ **bobo** *masc adjective*, **boba** *fem*
(*informal*) **silly**
Eres bobo. You are silly.

♪ la **boca** *fem noun*
1 **mouth**
No abrió la boca en toda la tarde. He didn't say a word all afternoon.
2 (*in expressions*) **boca abajo** face down (*cards, photographs*)
boca arriba face up (*cards, photographs*)
Pon el vaso boca arriba. Put the glass the right way up.
- la **boca de incendios** fire hydrant
- la **boca de metro** entrance to the underground (railway)
- la **boca de riego** irrigation hydrant

♪ la **bocacalle** *fem noun*
side street
Es la segunda bocacalle a la derecha. It's the second turning on the right.

♪ el **bocadillo** *masc noun*
1 **sandwich** (*made with French bread and no butter*)
un bocadillo de queso a cheese baguette
2 **speech bubble** (*in a cartoon*)

el **bocado** *masc noun*
1 **mouthful (of food)**
2 **bite to eat**

la **bocata** *fem noun*
sandwich

Spanish–English

la **bocatería** *fem noun*
sandwich bar

el **bochorno** *masc noun*
1 **Hoy hace bochorno.** It's really muggy today.
2 **embarrassment**
¡Qué bochorno pasamos! We were so embarrassed!
Fue un bochorno. It was really embarrassing.

la **bocina** *fem noun*
horn (*of a car*)

la **boda** *fem noun*
wedding
- las **bodas de oro** golden wedding
- las **bodas de plata** silver wedding

la **bodega** *fem noun*
1 **cellar**
2 **wine merchant's**
3 **wine bar**

la **bofetada** *fem noun*
slap

el **bofetón** *masc noun*
slap

la **boina** *fem noun*
beret

la **bola** *fem noun*
1 **ball**
2 **scoop** (*of ice cream*)
3 (*informal*) **fib**
contar bolas to tell fibs
- la **bola de billar** billiard ball
- la **bola de nieve** snowball

la **bolera** *fem noun*
bowling alley

el **boletín** *masc noun*
1 **bulletin**
2 **school report**
- el **boletín informativo** news bulletin
- el **boletín meteorológico** weather report

el **boleto** *masc noun*
1 (*Latin America*) **ticket** (*in buses, cinemas, etc*)
2 **ticket** (*for raffles, lotteries, etc*)
3 **coupon** (*for the football pools*)

el **boli** *masc noun*
(*informal*) **ballpoint pen**

el **bolígrafo** *masc noun*
ballpoint pen

Bolivia *fem noun*
Bolivia

boliviano *masc adjective & noun*, **boliviana** *fem adjective & noun*
1 **Bolivian**
2 **un boliviano, una boliviana** Bolivian (*person*)

WORD TIP Adjectives and nouns for nationality and regional origin do not have capital letters in Spanish.

el **bollo** *masc noun*
bun

la **bolsa** *fem noun*
bag
una bolsa de palomitas a bag of popcorn
mi bolsa de la compra my shopping bag
- la **bolsa de la basura** bin liner
- la **bolsa de plástico** plastic bag
- la **bolsa (de valores)** the stock exchange
- la **bolsa de viaje** travel bag

el **bolsillo** *masc noun*
pocket
un libro de bolsillo a paperback book
un diccionario de bolsillo a pocket dictionary

el **bolso** *masc noun*
handbag
Me robaron el bolso. My handbag was stolen.
- el **bolso de mano**, el **bolso de viaje** overnight bag

la **bomba** *fem noun*
1 **bomb**
Pusieron una bomba en un restaurante. They planted a bomb in a restaurant.
lanzar una bomba to drop a bomb
2 (*informal*) **pasarlo bomba** to have a terrific time
Lo pasamos bomba. We had a terrific time.
3 **pump**
- la **bomba atómica** atomic bomb
- la **bomba de agua** water pump
- la **bomba de bicicleta** bicycle pump

el **bombardeo** *masc noun*
bombing
el bombardeo de Guernica the bombing of Guernica

el **bombero** *masc noun*, la **bombera** *fem*
firefighter

la **bombilla** *fem noun*
light bulb
Se ha fundido la bombilla. The bulb's gone.

el **bombón** *masc noun*
chocolate
una caja de bombones a box of chocolates

a b c d e f g h i j k l m n ñ o p q r s t u v w x y z

bonachón *masc adj*, **bonachona** *fem*
(*informal*) **kind**

la **bondad** *fem noun*
kindness

♪ **bonito** *masc adjective*, **bonita** *fem*
pretty
un pueblo muy bonito a very pretty village
una falda muy bonita a nice skirt
Es una chica muy bonita. She's a very pretty girl.

el **bono** *masc noun*
voucher

boquiabierto *masc adjective*, **boquiabierta** *fem*
astonished
Me quedé boquiabierto. I was astonished.

el **bordado** *masc noun*
embroidery

bordar *verb* **[17]**
to embroider

borde *masc & fem adjective*
▷ see **borde** *noun*
(*informal*) **stroppy**
Se puso muy borde conmigo. He got very stroppy with me.

el **borde** *masc noun* ▷ see **borde** *adj*
1 **edge**
Me di con el borde de la mesa. I bumped myself on the edge of the table.
Se acercó al borde del andén. He went up to the edge of the platform.
2 **rim** (*of a glass or cup*)
3 **llenar algo hasta el borde** to fill something to the brim
4 **el borde del río** the river bank
5 **al borde de la guerra** on the brink of war
al borde de las lágrimas on the verge of tears

bordear *verb* **[17]**
to go round (*the edge of something*)
Bordeamos el lago. We went round the lake.

el **bordillo** *masc noun*
kerb

bordo *masc noun*
a bordo on board (*a plane, boat*)
Subimos a bordo. We went on board.

la **borrachera** *fem noun*
cogerse una borrachera to get drunk

borracho *masc adjective*, **borracha** *fem*
▷ see **borracho** *noun*
drunk
Estaban borrachos. They were drunk.

el **borracho** *masc noun*, la **borracha** *fem*
▷ see **borracho** *adj*
drunk

el **borrador** *masc noun*
1 **rough draft**
Hacedlo primero en borrador. Do it in rough first.
Usa papel de borrador. Use rough paper.
2 **board rubber** (*eraser*)

borrar *verb* **[17]**
1 **to rub out** (*a pencil mark or word*)
2 **to erase** (*a track or tape*)
3 **to clean** (*the blackboard*)
4 **to delete** (*in wordprocessing*)

borrarse *reflexive verb* **[17]**
to fade
Se ha borrado el nombre. The name has faded.

la **borrasca** *fem noun*
1 **area of low pressure**
2 **storm**

el **borrón** *masc noun*
blot

borroso *masc adjective*, **borrosa** *fem*
1 **blurred** (*image, photograph*)
2 **vague** (*memory*)

♪ el **bosque** *masc noun*
1 **wood**
2 **forest**
el bosque ecuatorial the tropical rainforest

bostezar *verb* **[22]**
to yawn

♪ la **bota** *fem noun*
boot
- las **botas de agua** wellingtons
- las **botas de esquiar** ski boots

la **botadura** *fem noun*
launch (*of a ship*)

la **botánica** *fem noun* ▷ see **botánico** *adj*
botany

botánico *masc adjective*, **botánica** *fem*
▷ see **botánica** *noun*
botanic

botar *verb* **[17]**
to launch (*a ship*)

la **botavara** *fem noun*
boom (*of boat*)

el **bote** *masc noun*
1 **boat**
2 **jar**
un bote de aceitunas a jar of olives
3 **can**
un bote de barniz a can of varnish
4 **jump**
pegar un bote to jump
Pegué un bote de alegría. I jumped for joy.
- el **bote de pesca** fishing boat
- el **bote de remos** rowing boat
- el **bote salvavidas** lifeboat

la **botella** *fem noun*
bottle

el **botijo** *masc noun*
drinking jug (*with a spout: with practice you can drink the water as it spurts out in an arc*)

el **botiquín** *masc noun*
medicine cabinet
- el **botiquín de primeros auxilios** first aid kit

el **botón** *masc noun*
button (*on clothes, a machine*)
coser un botón to sew on a button
Se me ha caído un botón. I've lost a button.
el botón de grabar the record button
Aprieta este botón. Press this button.

el **boxeador** *masc noun*, la **boxeadora** *fem*
boxer

boxear *verb* **[17]**
to box

el **boxeo** *masc noun*
boxing
un combate de boxeo a boxing match

las **bragas** *plural fem noun*
knickers, panties
un par de bragas a pair of knickers

la **bragueta** *fem noun*
flies (*in trousers*)

Brasil *masc noun*
Brazil

brasileño *masc adjective & noun*, **brasileña** *fem adjective & noun*
1 **Brazilian**
2 **un brasileño, una brasileña**
Brazilian (*person*)

WORD TIP Adjectives and nouns for nationality and regional origin do not have capital letters in Spanish.

bravo *masc adjective*, **brava** *fem*
▷ see **bravo** *excl*
fierce (*animal*)

bravo *exclamation* ▷ see **bravo** *adj*
¡Bravo! Well done!, Bravo!

el **brazo** *masc noun*
arm
cruzar los brazos to cross your arms
Me cogió del brazo. He took me by the arm.
Iban del brazo. They were walking along arm in arm.
Cogió al niño en brazos. He picked the child up in his arms.
Yo llevaba al bebé en brazos. I was carrying the baby in my arms.

el **brecol** *masc noun*
broccoli

breve *masc & fem adjective*
short
una pausa breve a short pause

brevemente *adverb*
briefly

el **brezo** *masc noun*
heather

el **bribón** *masc noun*, la **bribona** *fem*
rascal

el **bricolaje** *masc noun*
DIY

el **brillante** *masc noun* ▷ see **brillante** *adj*
diamond

brillante *masc & fem adjective*
▷ see **brillante** *noun*
1 **shiny**
2 **bright** (*light or colour*)

brillar *verb* **[17]**
1 **to shine**
2 **to sparkle**

brindar *verb* **[17]**
to toast

el **brindis** *masc noun*
toast
hacer un brindis por alguien to drink a toast to somebody
Hicieron un brindis por los novios. They drank a toast to the newly-weds.

la **brisa** *fem noun*
breeze

británico *masc adjective*, **británica** *fem*
▷ see **británico** *noun*
British

♪ un **británico** *masc noun*, una **británica** *fem* ▷ see **británico** *adj*
1 **British man**
2 **British woman**
3 **los británicos** the British

WORD TIP Adjectives and nouns for nationality and regional origin do not have capital letters in Spanish.

la **brocha** *fem noun*
1 **paintbrush**
2 **brocha de afeitar** shaving brush

el **broche** *masc noun*
brooch

♪ la **broma** *fem noun*
joke
bromas aparte joking apart
Lo he dicho en broma. I was joking.
¡Ni en broma! No way!
hacerle una broma a alguien to play a joke on somebody
Siempre le hacen bromas a su hermano. They're always playing jokes on her brother.

bromear *verb* **[17]**
to joke

bromista *masc & fem adjective* ▷ see **bromista** *noun*
Es muy bromista. He's always joking.

el & la **bromista** *masc & fem noun* ▷ see **bromista** *adj*
Es un bromista. He's always joking.

la **bronca** *fem noun*
1 (*informal*) **armar una bronca** to kick up a fuss
Si no me devuelven el dinero, voy a armar una bronca. If they don't give me the money back I'm going to kick up a fuss.
2 **telling-off**
echar una bronca a alguien to tell somebody off
La profe te va a echar una buena bronca. Teacher's going to give you a real telling-off.

bronceado *masc adjective*, **bronceada** *fem*
suntanned

el **bronceador** *masc noun*
suntan lotion

♪ **broncearse** *reflexive verb* **[17]**
to get a suntan

la **bronquitis** *fem noun*
bronchitis

el **brote** *masc noun*
bud

el **brujo** *masc noun*, la **bruja** *fem*
1 **wizard**
2 **witch**

la **brújula** *fem noun*
compass

la **bruma** *fem noun*
mist

bruto *masc adjective*, **bruta** *fem*
1 **ignorant**
2 **rude**
Es muy bruto, ¡dice unas cosas! He's so rude, he says terrible things!
3 **¡Qué bruto! ¡cómo trata a su hijo!** What a brute he is! What a way to treat his child!

el **buceador** *masc noun*, la **buceadora** *fem*
diver

bucear *verb* **[17]**
to dive

el **budismo** *masc noun*
(*Religion*) **Buddhism**

budista *masc & fem adjective & noun*
1 **Buddhist**
2 **un & una budista** Buddhist

WORD TIP Adjectives and nouns for religion do not have capital letters in Spanish.

♪ **buen** *adjective* ▷ **bueno**

♪ **bueno** *adverb* ▷ see **bueno** *adj*
okay, well, right
'¿Quieres venir?'—'Bueno.' 'Do you want to come?'—'Okay.'
Bueno, no importa. Well, it doesn't matter.
Bueno, no estoy segura. Well, I'm not sure.
Bueno, ya basta. Right, that's enough.

♪ **bueno** *masc adjective*, **buena** *fem* ▷ see **bueno** *adv*
1 **good**
de buena calidad good quality
Es muy buena persona. She's a very good person.
Es muy buen amigo mío. He's a very good friend of mine.
ser bueno para algo to be good at something (*a skill*)
Es muy buena para las matemáticas. She's very good at maths.
¡Buen viaje! Have a good journey!
2 **nice**
¡Qué buen tiempo hace! Isn't the weather nice! ▸▸

Spanish–English
a b c d e f g h i j k l m n ñ o p q r s t u v w x y z

El pastel estaba muy bueno. The cake was very nice.
¡Está buenísimo! It's delicious!

WORD TIP *bueno* becomes *buen* before a masculine singular noun.

- **buenos días** good morning
- **buenas noches** good evening, goodnight
- **buenas tardes** good afternoon, good evening

la **bufanda** *fem noun*
scarf

bufar *verb* **[17]**
to snort

el **bufet** *masc noun*
buffet

el **bufón** *masc noun*
clown (*silly person*)

la **buhardilla** *fem noun*
attic

el **búho** *masc noun*
owl

la **bujía** *fem noun*
spark plug

el **bulto** *masc noun*
1 **piece of luggage**
¿Cuántos bultos llevas? How many pieces of luggage do you have?
2 **bag**
¿Te llevo los bultos? Shall I carry your bags?
Iba cargada de bultos. She was carrying lots of bags.
3 **shape**
Vi un bulto en la oscuridad. I saw a shape in the darkness.
4 **bulkiness**
5 **lump** (*in your body*)

el **bungalow** *masc noun*
cabin, chalet (*in holiday resorts*)

el **buñuelo** *masc noun*
fritter

el **buque** *masc noun*
ship
- el **buque de guerra** warship

la **burbuja** *fem noun*
1 **bubble**
2 **una bebida sin burbujas** a still drink
una bebida con burbujas a fizzy drink

burdo *masc adjective*, **burda** *fem*
coarse

burlarse *reflexive verb* **[17]**
burlarse de alguien to make fun of somebody
¡Deja de burlarte de mí! Stop making fun of me!

la **burocracia** *fem noun*
bureaucracy

la **burrada** *fem noun*
(*informal*) **¡Vaya burrada has dicho!** What a stupid thing to say.
¡No hagas esa burrada! Don't do such a stupid thing.
Sólo dijo burradas. He just talked rubbish.

♪ **burro** *masc adjective*, **burra** *fem*
▷ see **burro** *noun*
stupid
¡Qué burra soy! How stupid of me! (*girl speaking*)

♪ el **burro** *masc noun*, la **burra** *fem*
▷ see **burro** *adj*
1 **donkey**
2 (*informal*) **idiot**
Es un burro. He's really stupid.

el **bus** *masc noun*
bus

la **busca** *fem noun*
search
ir en busca de algo to go in search of something
Fueron en busca del niño perdido. They went to search for the child.

el **buscador** *masc noun*
(*Computers*) **search engine**

♪ **buscar** *verb* **[31]**
1 **to look for**
¿Qué buscas? What are you looking for?
Mi hermana está buscando trabajo. My sister's looking for a job.
Estoy buscando un ayudante. I'm looking for an assistant
2 **to look**
Si no lo encuentras aquí, busca en la oficina. If you don't find it here, look in the office.
3 **ir a buscar algo** to go to pick up something
Mañana iré a buscar mis cosas. I'll go and pick up my things tomorrow.
4 **ir a buscar a alguien** to pick somebody up
Yo te iré a buscar al aeropuerto. I'll pick you up at the airport.

5 **ir a buscar a alguien** to go to get someone
Fueron a buscar a un médico. They went to get a doctor.

la **búsqueda** *fem noun*
search

⚷ la **butaca** *fem noun*
1 **armchair**
2 **seat**
una butaca de patio a seat in the stalls (*in a cinema or theatre*)

el **butano** *masc noun*
butane gas
una bombona de butano a bottle of butane gas

el **buzo** *masc noun*
diver

⚷ el **buzón** *masc noun*
1 **letterbox**
2 **postbox**
• el **buzón de voz** voice mail

Spanish-English

a b c d e f g h i j k l m n ñ o p q r s t u v w x y z

C c

la **caballa** *fem noun*
mackerel

el **caballero** *masc noun*
1 **gentleman**
Es un verdadero caballero. He's a real gentleman.
2 **sir**
Caballero, ¿me deja pasar? Could you let me through, sir?
3 **Caballeros** Gents (*toilets*), men's clothing department (*in a store*)

el **caballo** *masc noun*
1 **horse**
montar a caballo to ride a horse
2 **knight** (*in chess*)
3 **horse** (*in Spanish cards: equivalent to the queen*)
- el **caballo de carreras** racehorse

la **cabaña** *fem noun*
cabin

cabecear *verb* **[17]**
to head (*a ball in football*)

la **cabecera** *fem noun*
1 **headboard** (*of a bed*)
2 **head** (*of table*)
Se sentó a la cabecera de la mesa. He sat at the head of the table.

el **cabello** *masc noun*
hair
Tiene el cabello rubio. She has blonde hair.
- el **cabello liso** straight hair
- el **cabello rizado** curly hair

caber *verb* **[33]**
1 **caber en** to fit into
El monitor no cabe en la caja. The monitor doesn't fit into the box.
No cabemos en el coche. We won't fit into the car.
2 **No cabe nada más.** There's no room for anything else.
¿Caben estos libros en la maleta? Is there room for these books in the suitcase?
3 **caber por algo** to fit through something
No cabe por la puerta. It wouldn't fit through the door.

la **cabeza** *fem noun*
1 **head**
Me duele la cabeza. I've got a headache.
lavarse la cabeza to wash your hair
Tengo que lavarme la cabeza. I've got to wash my hair.
2 **de cabeza** head first
tirarse al agua de cabeza to dive into the water head first
3 **cabeza abajo** upside down
El cuadro está cabeza abajo. The picture's upside down.
4 **a la cabeza de** at the head of
Iban a la cabeza de la manifestación. They were at the head of the demonstration.
- la **cabeza de ajo** bulb of garlic
- el & la **cabeza rapada** skinhead

la **cabina** *fem noun*
1 **cab** (*of a lorry*)
2 **cockpit** (*of a plane*)
3 **cabin** (*on a plane, a boat*)
4 **booth** (*in a language lab*)
- la **cabina de teléfonos**, la **cabina telefónica** telephone box

el **cabo** *masc noun*
1 **end**
al cabo de after, at the end of
al cabo de una semana after one week
2 **end** (*of a piece of string*)
3 **cape** (*in geography*)
el Cabo de Hornos Cape Horn
4 **corporal**

la **cabra** *fem noun*
goat

cabré, **cabría**, **etc** *verb* ▷ **caber**

el **cacahuete** *masc noun*
peanut

el **cacao** *masc noun*
1 **cocoa** (*hot drink*)
2 **lipsalve**

la **cacerola** *fem noun*
saucepan, **pan**

el **cachete** *masc noun*
1 **slap**
2 **cheek**

el **cachorro** *masc noun*, la **cachorra** *fem*
puppy

cada *invariable adjective*
1 **each**
un alumno de cada clase a pupil from each class

Hay diez para cada uno. There are ten for each one.
2 **every**
cada día every day
Me llama cada tres días. She phones me every three days.
3 **cada vez más ...** more and more
Viene cada vez más. She comes more and more.
Se ponía cada vez más rojo. He was going redder and redder.
Juega cada vez mejor. She's playing better and better.
Canta cada vez peor. He sings worse and worse.
Se parecen cada vez más. They look more and more alike.
4 **cada vez menos ...** less and less
Nos visita cada vez menos. She visits us less and less.
Es cada vez menos gordo. He's getting less and less fat.
Se parecen cada vez menos. They look less and less alike.

WORD TIP *cada* never changes.

♪ la **cadena** *fem noun*
1 **chain**
una cadena de hierro an iron chain
tirar de la cadena to flush the toilet
2 **channel** (*on the TV*)
Lo ponen en la segunda cadena. They're showing it on Channel Two.
3 **station** (*on the radio*)
4 **cadenas** *plural* snow chains
- la **cadena antirrobo** bicycle chain
- la **cadena de supermercados** supermarket chain
- la **cadena musical** hi-fi system
- la **cadena perpetua** life imprisonment

♪ la **cadera** *fem noun*
hip

caducar *verb* **[31]**
to expire (*credit cards, cheques, etc*)
Caduca a los tres años. It expires in three years.

♪ **caer** *verb* **[34]**
1 **to fall** (*accidentally*)
El jarrón cayó al suelo. The vase fell to the ground.
2 **dejar caer algo** to drop something (*on purpose*)
Dejé caer la pelota. I dropped the ball.
3 **caerle bien a alguien** to like someone
Tu hermano me cae bien. I like your brother.
4 **caerle mal a alguien** to dislike someone
Ana me cae mal. I don't like Ana.

caerse *reflexive verb* **[34]**
1 **to fall**
Me caí por las escaleras. I fell down the stairs.
Se cayó de la bici. He fell off his bike.
Tropecé y me caí. I tripped and fell down.
2 **caérsele algo a alguien** to drop something (*by accident*)
Se me cayó el plato. I dropped the plate.

♪ el **café** *masc noun*
1 **cafe** (*place*)
2 **coffee**
¿Quieres un café? Do you want a cup of coffee?
- el **café con leche** white coffee
- el **café cortado** coffee with a dash of milk
- el **café descafeinado** decaffeinated coffee
- el **café solo** black coffee

♪ la **cafetera** *fem noun*
coffee maker

♪ la **cafetería** *fem noun*
cafe

caído *masc adjective*, **caída** *fem*
fallen

caiga, **caigo**, **etc** *verb* ▷ **caer**

el **caimán** *masc noun*
alligator

♪ la **caja** *fem noun*
1 **box**
2 **crate**
una caja de naranjas a crate of oranges
3 **checkout** (*in a supermarket*)
Pague en caja. Pay at the checkout.
4 **till** (*in a shop*)
- la **caja de ahorros** savings bank
- la **caja de cambios** gearbox
- la **caja de cartón** cardboard box
- la **caja de las herramientas** toolbox
- la **caja fuerte** safe (*in a bank*)

♪ el **cajero** *masc noun*, la **cajera** *fem*
1 **cashier**
2 **checkout operator**
- el **cajero automático** cash dispenser

el **cajón** *masc noun*
drawer

♪ el **calabacín** *masc noun*
courgette

el **calamar** *masc noun*
squid
calamares a la romana squid rings fried in batter

el **calambre** *masc noun*
1 **cramp**
Me dio un calambre. I got cramp.
2 **electric shock**
La lámpara me ha dado calambre. The lamp gave me an electric shock.

la **calamidad** *fem noun*
disaster

la **calavera** *fem noun*
skull

el **calcetín** *masc noun*
sock
unos calcetines a pair of socks

la **calcomanía** *fem noun*
transfer (*sticker*)

la **calculadora** *fem noun*
calculator

calcular *verb* [17]
1 **to calculate**
1 **to work out**

el **caldo** *masc noun*
1 **stock**
2 **broth**
- el **caldo de verdura** vegetable soup

la **calefacción** *fem noun*
heating
- la **calefacción central** central heating
- la **calefacción de gas** gas heating

el **calendario** *masc noun*
calendar

el **calentador** *masc noun*
1 **boiler**
2 **water heater**

calentar *verb* [29]
1 **to heat (up)**
Voy a calentar la sopa. I'm going to heat the soup.
2 **to give off heat**
Esta estufa calienta mucho. This heater gives off a lot of heat.
3 **calentar los músculos** to warm up (*in sports*)

calentarse *reflexive verb* [29]
to heat up

la **calidad** *fem noun*
quality
materiales de calidad high quality materials
productos de mala calidad poor quality products

calienta, **caliento**, **etc** *verb* ▷ **calentar**

caliente *masc & fem adjective*
1 **hot**
un baño caliente a hot bath
Los platos están muy calientes. The plates are very hot.
2 **warm**
En el salón se está más caliente. It's warmer in the living-room.

la **calificación** *fem noun*
mark
Obtuvo buenas calificaciónes. He got good marks.

callado *masc adjective*, **callada** *fem*
quiet
¡Estate callado! Be quiet!

callar *verb* [17]
to be quiet
Calla, no oigo. Be quiet, I can't hear.
¡Calla ya! Shut up!

callarse *reflexive verb* [17]
to go quiet
Al verla todos se callaron. When they saw her everybody went quiet.
¡Cállate! Shut up!

la **calle** *fem noun*
street (*in addresses, the word* **calle** *is shortened to 'C/'*)
una calle cortada a cul-de-sac
Calle Santa Isabel, **C/ Santa Isabel** Santa Isabel Street
- la **calle de sentido doble** two-way street
- la **calle de sentido único** one-way street

el **callejón** *masc noun*
alley
- el **callejón sin salida** dead end

la **calma** *fem noun*
calm
Hazlo con calma. Do it calmly.
mantener la calma to keep calm
La ciudad está en calma. The city is calm.

calmar *verb* [17]
to calm down

calmarse *reflexive verb* [17]
to calm down
Después de un rato me calmé. After a while I calmed down .

ꟾ el **calor** *masc noun*
1 **heat**
el calor de la estufa the heat of the stove
2 **hacer calor** to be hot (*weather, etc*)
Hace mucho calor. It's very hot.
¡Qué calor hace! It's so hot!
3 **tener calor** to be hot (*people, etc*)
Tengo mucho calor. I'm very hot.
▷ **frío**

ꟾ **caluroso** *masc adjective*, **calurosa** *fem*
hot (*day, place*)

ꟾ **calvo** *masc adjective*, **calva** *fem*
bald
quedarse calvo to go bald

ꟾ el **calzado** *masc noun*
footwear

ꟾ **calzar** *verb* **[22]**
¿Qué número calzas? What shoe size do you take?

ꟾ los **calzoncillos** *plural masc noun*
underpants
unos calzoncillos a pair of underpants

ꟾ la **cama** *fem noun*
bed
¡A la cama! Off to bed!
hacer la cama to make the bed
Tienes que hacer la cama. You must make your bed.
- la **cama de matrimonio** double bed
- la **cama elástica** trampoline
- la **cama individual** single bed
- las **camas gemelas** twin beds

la **cámara** *fem noun* ▷ **see cámara** *masc noun*
1 **camera**
2 **camera woman**
- la **cámara de vídeo** video camera
- la **cámara digital** digital camera
- la **cámara fotográfica** camera

el **cámara** *masc noun* ▷ **see cámara** *fem noun*
camera man

ꟾ el **camarero** *masc noun*, la **camarera** *fem*
1 **waiter**
2 **waitress**
- la **camarera de habitación** chambermaid

ꟾ el **camarón** *masc noun*
shrimp

ꟾ **cambiar** *verb* **[17]**
1 **to change**
Tengo que cambiar libras a euros. I must change pounds into euros.
El tiempo está cambiando. The weather is changing.
2 **cambiar de** to change
cambiar de idea to change your mind
cambiar de canal to change channels
Ha cambiado de trabajo. He's changed his job.
3 **to exchange** (*in a shop*)
Quiero cambiar estos zapatos. I want to exchange these shoes.
4 **cambiar de casa** to move house
5 **cambiar algo a alguien** to swap
Te cambio mi pluma por esa cinta. I'll swap my pen for that tape.

cambiarse *reflexive verb* **[17]**
1 **to get changed**
Voy a cambiarme. I'm going to get changed.
2 **cambiarse de algo** to change
Voy a cambiarme de ropa. I'm going to change my clothes.
Han cambiado de idea. They've changed their minds.
Nos cambiamos de casa el año pasado. We moved house last year.

ꟾ el **cambio** *masc noun*
1 **change**
un cambio a mejor a change for the better
Ha habido un cambio de planes. There's been a change of plan.
2 **exchange** (*in a shop*)
No se admiten cambios. Goods will not be exchanged.
3 **change** (*coins*)
¿Tienes cambio? Do you have any change?
Se ha equivocado al darme el cambio. You've given me the wrong change.
'Cambio' 'Bureau de change' (*for buying euros, etc*)
4 **a cambio de** in exchange for
Le di la mochila a cambio de su riñonera. I gave him the rucksack in exchange for the money belt.
- el **cambio de sentido** U-turn (*in driving*)

el **camello** *masc noun*
camel

la **camilla** *fem noun*
stretcher

ꟾ **caminar** *verb* **[17]**
to walk
Me gusta caminar. I like walking.

la **caminata** *fem noun*
long walk, trek

♪ el **camino** *masc noun*
1 **road**
Todos los caminos están cortados. All the roads are closed.
2 **path**
un camino por el bosque a path through the forest
3 **way**
¿Puede indicarme el camino a la estación? Could you tell me the way to the station? (*formal form*)
Yo sé el camino. I know the way.

♪ el **camión** *masc noun*
1 **lorry, truck**
2 (*Mexico*) **bus**
- el **camión cisterna** petrol tanker
- el **camión de la mudanza** removal van

el **camionero** *masc noun*, la **camionera** *fem*
lorry driver, truck driver

♪ la **camioneta** *fem noun*
van

♪ la **camisa** *fem noun*
shirt

♪ la **camiseta** *fem noun*
1 **T-shirt**
2 **vest**

♪ el **camisón** *masc noun*
nightdress

♪ el **campamento** *masc noun*
camp
Se han ido de campamento. They've gone camping.

la **campana** *fem noun*
bell
tocar la campana to ring the bell

la **campaña** *fem noun*
campaign
- la **campaña electoral** election campaign

♪ el **campeón** *masc noun*, la **campeona** *fem*
champion
los campeones mundiales the world champions

♪ el **campeonato** *masc noun*
championship

♪ el **campesino** *masc noun*, la **campesina** *fem*
1 **country person**
2 **peasant**

♪ el **camping** *masc noun*
campsite
ir de camping to go camping

♪ el & la **campista** *masc & fem noun*
camper (*person*)

♪ el **campo** *masc noun*
1 **country** (*not the city*)
una casa en el campo a house in the country
vivir en el campo to live in the country
2 **countryside**
El campo está muy bonito. The countryside is looking very pretty.
3 **field**
un campo de trigo a field of wheat
- el **campo de fútbol** football pitch

la **cana** *fem noun*
white hair
Le están saliendo canas. He's going grey.

Canadá *masc noun*
Canada

canadiense *masc & fem adjective*
▷ see **canadiense** *noun*
Canadian

un & una **canadiense** *masc & fem noun*
▷ see **canadiense** *adj*
Canadian

WORD TIP Adjectives and nouns for nationality and regional origin do not have capital letters in Spanish.

♪ el **canal** *masc noun*
1 **channel** (*on the TV*)
No cambies de canal. Don't change channels.
2 **channel** (*for water*)
3 **canal**
- el **Canal de la Mancha** English Channel
- el **Canal de Panamá** Panama Canal

el **canario** *masc noun*
canary

canario *masc adjective & noun*, **canaria** *fem adjective & noun*
1 **of or from the Canary Islands**
2 **un canario, una canaria** Canary Islander

WORD TIP Adjectives and nouns for nationality and regional origin do not have capital letters in Spanish.

la **canasta** *fem noun*
(*Latin America*) **basket**

el **canasto** *masc noun*
basket (*usually with a lid*)

cancelar *verb* **[17]**
to cancel

♪ el **cáncer** *masc noun*
cancer
Tiene cáncer. He's got cancer.

- el **cáncer de mama** breast cancer
- el **cáncer de piel** skin cancer

cáncer *masc & fem noun* ▷ see **cáncer, Cáncer** *noun*
Cancer (*sign of the zodiac*)
Soy cáncer. I'm Cancer.

WORD TIP Use a small letter in Spanish to say *I am Cancer*, etc with star signs.

Cáncer *masc noun* ▷ see **cáncer** *noun*
Cancer (*sign of the zodiac*)

♪ la **cancha** *fem noun*
1 **court** (*for tennis, basketball, etc*)
2 **ground** (*for football, hockey, etc*)

♪ la **canción** *fem noun*
song
- la **canción de cuna** lullaby

el **candado** *masc noun*
padlock

el **candelabro** *masc noun*
candlestick
un candelabro dorado a brass candlestick

el **candidato** *masc noun*, la **candidata** *fem*
candidate
el candidato a la presidencia the candidate for the presidency

la **canela** *fem noun*
cinnamon
- la **canela en polvo** ground cinnamon
- la **canela en rama** stick cinnamon

♪ el **cangrejo** *masc noun*
1 **crab**
2 **crayfish**

el **canguro** *masc noun* ▷ see **canguro** *masc & fem noun*
kangaroo

el & la **canguro** *masc & fem noun* ▷ see **canguro** *masc noun*
babysitter

la **canica** *fem noun*
marble
jugar a las canicas to play marbles

♪ la **canoa** *fem noun*
canoe

♪ **cansado** *masc adjective*, **cansada** *fem*
1 **tired**
Estoy muy cansado. I'm very tired.
2 **tiring**
Esperar es muy cansado. Waiting is very tiring.

♪ **cansar** *verb* **[17]**
1 **to make tired**
Le cansa andar. Walking makes him tired.
2 **to be tiring**
Es un trabajo que cansa mucho. It's a very tiring job.
3 **to be boring**
Esta música cansa un poco. This music's a bit boring.

cansarse *reflexive verb* **[17]**
1 **to get tired**
Se cansa muy fácilmente. He gets tired very easily.
2 **to get bored**
Me canso de repetir siempre lo mismo. I get bored always repeating the same thing.

el **Cantábrico** *masc noun*
el mar Cantábrico the Bay of Biscay (*on the north coast of Spain*)

♪ el & la **cantante** *masc & fem noun*
singer

♪ **cantar** *verb* **[17]**
to sing

el **canto** *mascnoun*
singing

la **cantera** *fem noun*
quarry

♪ la **cantidad** *fem noun*
1 **amount**
una enorme cantidad de nieve a huge amount of snow
2 **¿Qué cantidad de vasos necesitamos?** How many glasses do we need?
Mira la cantidad de comida que nos queda. See how much food is left over.
3 **tanta cantidad** so much
No pongas tanta cantidad de leche. Don't put so much milk in.
4 **cantidad de, cantidades de** lots of
Había cantidad de gente. There were lots of people.
'¿Hay flores?'—'Cantidades.' 'Are there flowers?'—'Loads.'
5 **sum**
una cantidad importante de dinero a large sum of money

♪ la **cantina** *fem noun*
1 **cafeteria**
2 **canteen**

la **caña** *fem noun*
1 **cane**
- la **caña de azúcar** sugar cane
- la **caña de pescar** fishing rod

a b c d e f g h i j k l m n ñ o p q r s t u v w x y z

ꞩ la **cañería** *fem noun*
1 **pipe**
2 **plumbing**

el **cañón** *noun*
cannon

la **capa** *fem noun*
1 **layer**
2 **cape**
3 **cloak**
• la **capa de ozono** ozone layer

la **capacidad** *fem noun*
capacity

capaz *masc & fem adjective, pl:* **capaces**
capable
ser capaz de hacer algo to be capable of doing something
Es capaz de hacerlo. He's capable of doing it.
No fueron capaces de darme una respuesta. They weren't able to give me an answer.

ꞩ la **capital** *fem noun*
1 **capital**
la capital de España the capital of Spain
2 **Valencia capital** the city of Valencia (*in contrast to the province*)

el **capitán** *masc noun*, la **capitana** *fem*
captain (*of a team, ship, etc*)

el **capítulo** *masc noun*
1 **chapter**
2 **episode** (*of a TV series*)

el **capó** *masc noun*
bonnet (*of a car*)

el **capricho** *masc noun*
whim

la **capucha** *fem noun*
hood (*of an anorak, etc*)

capricornio *masc & fem noun*
▷ see **Capricornio** *masc noun*
Capricorn
Es capricornio. He's Capricorn.

WORD TIP Use a small letter in Spanish to say *I am Capricorn*, etc, with star signs.

Capricornio *masc noun*
▷ see **capricornio** *masc & fem noun*
Capricorn (*sign of the zodiac*)

ꞩ la **cara** *fem noun*
1 **face**
Tiene una cara bonita. She has a pretty face.
Tienes cara de cansada. You look tired.
tener mala cara to look ill
Tu hermana tiene mala cara. Your sister looks ill.
2 **side**
la otra cara del disco the other side of the record
3 **¿Cara o cruz?** Heads or tails?

el **caracol** *masc noun*
1 **snail**
2 **winkle**

ꞩ el **carácter** *masc noun, pl:* los **caracteres**
character
No tiene mucho carácter. He doesn't have much character.
Es una persona de buen carácter. She's a good-natured person.

la **característica** *fem noun*
characteristic

ꞩ **caramba** *exclamation*
1 **Good heavens!**
2 **Damn it!**

ꞩ el **caramelo** *masc noun*
1 **sweet**
un caramelo de menta a mint
2 **caramel**

la **caravana** *fem noun*
1 **tailback**
una caravana de diez kilómetros a ten-kilometre tailback
Hay caravana para entrar en Sevilla. There's a tailback into Seville.
2 **caravan**

el **carbón** *masc noun*
coal
• el **carbón vegetal** charcoal

la **cárcel** *fem noun*
jail
meter a alguien en la cárcel to put somebody in jail
Lo metieron en la cárcel por robo. He was sent to jail for robbery.

el **cardenal** *masc noun*
1 **bruise**
2 (*Religion*) **cardinal**

cardíaco *masc adjective*, **cardíaca** *fem*
heart
un ataque cardíaco a heart attack

la **carga** *fem noun*
1 **load**
2 **cargo**
3 **refill** (*for a pen*)
4 **burden**
Es una carga para la familia. It's a burden on the family.

5 **charge** (*by police, soldiers*)
¡A la carga! Charge!
• la **carga máxima** maximum load

cargado *masc adjective*, **cargada** *fem*
1 **loaded**
La pistola estaba cargada. The gun was loaded.
2 **ir cargado,** *fem* **cargada de algo** to be loaded with something
Iba cargado de paquetes. He was loaded with parcels.
3 **stuffy**
un ambiente cargado a stuffy atmosphere

cargar *verb* [28]
1 **to load** (*a lorry, a weapon*)
2 **to fill**

el **cargo** *masc noun*
1 **position**
un cargo de responsabilidad a position of responsibility
2 **a cargo de** in charge of
Estoy a cargo del departamento. I'm in charge of the department.
Dejó los niños a mi cargo. She left the children in my care.

el **Caribe** *masc noun*
el Caribe the Caribbean
el mar Caribe the Caribbean Sea

caribeño *masc adjective & noun*, **caribeña** *fem adjective & noun*
1 **Caribbean**
2 **un caribeño, una caribeña** Caribbean

WORD TIP Adjectives and nouns for nationality and regional origin do not have capital letters in Spanish.

♪ el **cariño** *masc noun*
1 **affection**
tenerle cariño a to be fond of
Les tengo cariño. I'm fond of them.
tomarle cariño a to become fond of
Les tomó cariño. He became fond of them.
2 **Con cariño, Maya.** Love, Maya (*as a letter ending*)
3 **dear**
Ven, cariño. Come here, dear.

♪ **cariñoso** *masc adjective*, **cariñosa** *fem*
1 **affectionate, loving** (*a person*)
2 **warm**
un cariñoso saludo best wishes (*as a letter ending*)

el **carmín** *masc noun*
lipstick

el **carnaval** *masc noun*
carnival

♪ el **carné**, **carnet** *masc noun*
card
• el **carné de conducir** driving licence
• el **carné de estudiante** student card
• el **carné de identidad** identity card

♪ la **carne** *fem noun*
1 **meat**
2 **flesh**
• la **carne de cerdo** pork
• la **carne de cordero** lamb
• la **carne de ternera** veal
• la **carne de vaca** beef

♪ la **carnicería** *fem noun*
butcher's (shop)

♪ el **carnicero** *masc noun*, la **carnicera** *fem*
butcher

carnívoro *masc adjective*, **carnívora** *fem*
carnivorous

♪ **caro** *masc adjective*, **cara** *fem*
expensive
un restaurante caro an expensive restaurant
Es demasiado caro. It's too expensive.

la **carpa** *fem noun*
(*Latin America*) **tent**

♪ la **carpeta** *fem noun*
folder
• la **carpeta de anillas** ring binder

el **carpintero** *masc noun*, la **carpintera** *fem*
carpenter

la **carrera** *fem noun*
1 **race**
la carrera de los cien metros the one hundred metres race
echar una carrera to have a race (*against somebody*)
Echamos una carrera. Let's have a race.
Eché una carrera y alcancé el autobús. I ran and caught the bus.
2 **degree course**
hacer una carrera to study for a degree
Quiero hacer una carrera. I want to go to university.
hacer la carrera de algo to study for a degree in something
Quiero hacer la carrera de medicina. I want to study medicine.
• la **carrera automovilística** car race
• la **carrera de obstáculos** steeple chase
• la **carrera de relevos** relay race
• las **carreras de caballos** the races (*with horses*)

la **carreta** *fem noun*
cart

la **carretera** *fem noun*
road
la carretera de Málaga the road to Málaga
Vinimos por carretera. We came by road.
- la **carretera comarcal** B-road
- la **carretera de circunvalación** ring road
- la **carretera nacional** A-road

la **carretilla** *fem noun*
wheelbarrow

el **carril** *masc noun*
lane
- el **carril bus** bus lane

el **carrito** *masc noun*
trolley

el **carro** *masc noun*
1 **cart**
2 (*Latin America*) **car**
- el **carro de combate** tank

la **carta** *fem noun*
1 **letter**
mandar una carta to send a letter
echar una carta al correo to post a letter
2 **menu**
¿Nos trae la carta, por favor? Could you bring us the menu, please?
3 **card** (*in a pack*)
jugar a las cartas to play cards
¿Te gusta jugar a las cartas? Do you like playing cards?
- la **carta certificada** registered letter

el **cartel** *masc noun*
1 **poster** (*for advertising*)
2 **sign**
¿Qué dice el cartel? What does the sign say?

la **cartelera** *fem noun*
la cartelera de cine 'what's on' at the cinema
La obra lleva tres años en cartelera. The play has been running for three years.
La película sigue en cartelera. The film is still showing.

la **cartera** *fem noun*
1 **wallet**
2 **briefcase**
3 **school bag**

el & la **carterista** *masc & fem noun*
pickpocket

el **cartero** *masc noun*, la **cartera** *fem*
1 **postman**
2 **postwoman**

el **cartón** *masc noun*
cardboard

la **casa** *fem noun*
1 **house**
Mi casa tiene tres dormitorios. My house has three bedrooms.
2 **home**
No están en casa. They're not at home.
Estoy pasando unos días en casa de Juan. I'm staying at Juan's for a few days.
El Valencia juega en casa Valencia is playing at home.
- la **casa adosada** semi-detached house
- la **casa de huéspedes** guesthouse
- la **casa rural** house in the country (*for holiday rental*)

casado *masc adjective*, **casada** *fem*
married
estar casado to be married
¿Está casada? Is she married?
Están casados desde hace tres meses. They have been married for three months.

casarse *reflexive verb* **[17]**
to get married
casarse con alguien to marry someone
Se casó con mi primo. She married my cousin.

cascar *verb* **[31]**
to crack (*a nut*)

la **cáscara** *fem noun*
1 **peel**
2 **shell**

el **casco** *masc noun*
1 **helmet**
2 **hoof** (*of a horse*)
3 **empty bottle**
4 **cascos** *plural* **headphones**
- el **casco protector** safety helmet, crash helmet
- el **casco urbano** the town centre

el **caserío** *masc noun*
1 **farmhouse**
2 **hamlet**

casero *masc adjective*, **casera** *fem*
▷ see **casero** *noun*
homemade
productos caseros homemade products

el **casero** *masc noun*, la **casera** *fem*
▷ see **casero** *adj*
1 **landlord**
2 **landlady**

la **caseta** *fem noun*
1 **kennel**
2 **hut** (*for a watchman, a guard*)
3 **stand** (*in a fair*)

⚷ el **casete** *masc noun* ▷ see **casete, cassette** *noun*
cassette recorder

⚷ el & la **casete** *masc & fem noun* ▷ see **casete, cassette** *noun*
cassette

⚷ **casi** *adverb*
1 **almost, nearly**
Son casi las cuatro. It's almost four o'clock.
Casi me caigo. I nearly fell over.
Casi todos son turistas. Almost all of them are tourists.
2 **hardly**
Casi no había gente. There was hardly anybody there.
casi nadie hardly anyone
No había casi nadie. There was hardly anyone there.
casi nunca hardly ever
No viene casi nunca. She hardly ever comes.

la **casilla** *fem noun*
1 **square** (*in a crossword*)
2 **box** (*on a form*)
3 (*Latin America*) **post office box**

⚷ el **caso** *masc noun*
1 **case**
en ese caso in that case
en caso de accidente in case of accident
en todo caso, en cualquier caso in any case
en el peor de los casos if the worst comes to the worst
2 **El caso es que ...** The thing is that ...
3 **hacer caso de algo** to pay attention to something
Haz caso de las señales. Pay attention to the signs.
4 **hacerle caso a alguien** to do as one is told
No me hace caso. He doesn't do as I tell him to.

la **caspa** *fem noun*
dandruff

⚷ el & la **cassette** *masc & fem noun*
cassette

la **castaña** *fem noun* ▷ see **castaño** *adj*
chestnut

castaño *masc adjective*, **castaña** *fem* ▷ see **castaña** *fem noun*
chestnut brown

el **castaño** *masc noun* ▷ see **castaño** *adj*
chestnut tree

las **castañuelas** *plural fem noun*
castanets (*the hand-held pair of clackers used in flamenco dancing*)

⚷ **castellano** *masc adjective*, **castellana** *fem* ▷ see **castellano** *noun*
Castilian

⚷ un **castellano** *masc noun*, una **castellana** *fem* ▷ see **castellano** *adj*
1 **Castilian** (*person from Castile*)
2 **el castellano** **Castilian Spanish** (*the Spanish spoken in the central part of Spain*)

WORD TIP Adjectives and nouns for nationality, regional origin and language, do not have capital letters in Spanish.

⚷ **castigar** *verb* **[28]**
1 **to punish**
2 **castigar a alguien por algo** to punish someone for something
Le castigaron por llegar tarde. She was punished for coming in late.
3 **to give a detention to** (*at school*)
La profesora me dejó castigado. The teacher gave me a detention.

el **castigo** *masc noun*
punishment

Castilla *fem noun*
Castile (*name of the central part of Spain*)

⚷ el **castillo** *masc noun*
castle
• el **castillo de arena** sandcastle

la **casualidad** *fem noun*
1 **chance**
por casualidad by chance
Lo vi por casualidad. I saw it by chance.
2 **Da la casualidad de que ...** It so happens that ...
3 **coincidence**
¡Qué casualidad! What a coincidence!

⚷ **catalán** *masc adjective & noun*, **catalana** *fem adjective & noun*
1 **Catalan**
2 **un catalán, una catalana** Catalan (*person from Catalonia*)
el catalán Catalan (*the language spoken in Cataluña*)

WORD TIP Adjectives and nouns for nationality, regional origin, and language do not have capital letters in Spanish.

⚷ **Cataluña, Catalunya** *fem noun*
Catalonia (*a region of north-east Spain*)

la **catarata** *fem noun*
1 **waterfall**
2 **cataract** (*of the eye*)

el catarro *masc noun*
cold
coger un catarro to catch a cold
Vas a coger un catarro! You're going to catch a cold!

catear *verb* [17]
(*informal*) **to fail**
He cateado las mates. I've failed maths.
Me han cateado en inglés. I've been failed in English.

la catedral *fem noun*
cathedral

la categoría *fem noun*
1 **category**
2 **de primera categoría** first class
un hotel de mucha categoría a top-of-the-range hotel
un restaurante de poca categoría a third-rate restaurant

católico *masc adjective & noun*, **católica** *fem adjective & noun*
1 **Catholic**
2 **un católico, una católica** Catholic

WORD TIP Adjectives and nouns for religion do not have capital letters in Spanish.

catorce *number*
1 **fourteen**
Tiene catorce años. He's fourteen (years old).
2 (*in dates*) **fourteenth**
el catorce de mayo the fourteenth of May

el caucho *masc noun*
rubber

la causa *fem noun*
1 **cause**
la causa del accidente the cause of the accident
2 **a causa de** because of
A causa de eso se marcharon pronto. Because of that they left early.

causar *verb* [17]
to cause
Ha causado muchos problemas. He's caused a lot of problems.

el cautiverio *masc noun*
captivity
mantener a alguien en cautiverio to keep someone in captivity

el cautivo *masc noun*, **la cautiva** *fem*
prisoner

el cava *masc noun*
cava (*sparkling wine from Cataluña*)

cavar *verb* [17]
to dig

la caverna *fem noun*
cave

cayendo *verb* ▷ **caer**

la caza *fem noun*
hunting
ir de caza to go hunting

la cazadora *fem noun*
jacket
la cazadora de piel leather jacket

cazar *verb* [22]
to hunt

la cazuela *fem noun*
casserole

el CD *masc noun*
CD

la cebada *fem noun*
barley

la cebolla *fem noun*
onion

la cebolleta *fem noun*
spring onion

el cebollino *masc noun*
chives

ceder *verb* [18]
1 **to give in**
Finalmente cedí. I finally gave in.
2 **ceder algo a alguien** to give up
Le cedí mi asiento a un anciano. I gave up my seat to an elderly man.
3 **ceder el paso** to give way

el cederom *masc noun*
CDROM

la ceguera *fem noun*
blindness

la ceja *fem noun*
eyebrow

la celda *fem noun*
cell (*in a prison*)

la celebración *fem noun*
celebration

celebrar *verb* [17]
1 **to celebrate**
Tenemos que celebrarlo. We must celebrate it.
2 **to hold** (*a meeting*)

celebrarse *reflexive verb* [17]
to be held
La recepción se celebró en el Hotel Victoria. The reception was held in the Victoria Hotel.

célebre *masc & fem adjective*
famous

⚷ el **celo** *masc noun*
Sellotape

los **celos** *plural masc noun*
1 **jealousy**
2 **tener celos de alguien** to be jealous of somebody
Tiene celos de su hermana pequeña. She's jealous of her little sister.
3 **darle celos a alguien** to make somebody feel jealous
Lo hace para darte celos. He does it to make you feel jealous.

celoso *masc adjective*, **celosa** *fem*
jealous

el **celular** *masc noun*
(*Latin America*) **mobile phone**

el **cementerio** *masc noun*
cemetery

el **cemento** *masc noun*
cement

⚷ la **cena** *fem noun*
1 **supper**
¿Qué hay de cena? What's for supper?
2 **dinner** (*in the evening*)

⚷ **cenar** *verb* [17]
to have dinner (*in the evening*)
Normalmente cenamos a las nueve. We normally have dinner at nine.
Cenamos fuera. We went out for dinner.

⚷ el **cenicero** *masc noun*
ashtray

ceñido *masc adjective*, **ceñida** *fem*
tight
una camiseta muy ceñida a very tight T-shirt

la **ceniza** *fem noun*
ash

⚷ el **ceño** *masc noun*
fruncir el ceño to frown

⚷ el **centavo** *masc noun*
1 **one hundredth**
2 **cent** (*in the dollar system*)

el **centenar** *masc noun*
hundred
un centenar de libros (about) a hundred books
centenares de cartas hundreds of letters

⚷ el **centenario** *masc noun*
centenary

⚷ el **centeno** *masc noun*
rye

la **centésima** *fem noun*
▷ see **centésimo** *adj*
hundredth
una centésima de segundo a hundredth of a second

centésimo *masc adjective*, **centésima** *fem*
▷ see **centésima** *noun*
hundredth

centígrado *masc adjective*, **centígrada** *fem*
centigrade

⚷ el **centímetro** *masc noun*
centimetre

⚷ **céntimo** *masc noun*
1 **cent** (*in the euro system*)
El euro se divide en cien céntimos. The euro is divided into a hundred cents.
2 **penny**
No tengo ni un céntimo. I don't have a penny.

⚷ **central** *masc & fem adjective*
▷ see **central** *noun*
central

⚷ la **central** *fem noun* ▷ see **central** *adj*
1 **head office**
2 **power station**
- la **central de correos** general post office
- la **central nuclear** nuclear power
- la **central telefónica** telephone exchange

⚷ **céntrico** *masc adjective*, **céntrica** *fem*
central
un barrio céntrico a central part of town

centrifugar *verb* [28]
to spin-dry

⚷ el **centro** *masc noun*
centre
el centro de la ciudad the town centre, the city centre
Estaba justo en el centro. It was right in the middle.
- el **centro comercial** shopping mall
- el **centro cultural** cultural centre ⏩

- el **centro polideportivo** sports complex

mini-info centro

Madrid está en el centro de España y de la plaza de Puerta del Sol se miden todas las distancias por carretera a otros puntos del país.

cepillar *verb* **[17]**
to brush

cepillarse *reflexive verb* **[17]**
to brush
cepillarse los dientes to brush your teeth
cepillarse el pelo to brush your hair

el **cepillo** *masc noun*
brush
- el **cepillo de dientes** toothbrush
- el **cepillo del pelo** hairbrush

la **cera** *fem noun*
wax

la **cerámica** *fem noun*
pottery

cerca *adverb*
1 **near**, **close**
Viven aquí cerca. They live near here.
Ponlos cerca el uno del otro. Put them close to each other.
2 **nearby**
Mi casa está cerca. My house is nearby.
3 **cerca de** near
Se sentó cerca de mí. He sat near me.
Vivo cerca del colegio. I live near the school.
Vive muy cerca de mí. She lives very near me.
4 **cerca de** almost, about (*with amounts*)
cerca de diez mil personas almost ten thousand people

la **cercanía** *fem noun*
closeness
las cercanías the surrounding area
Barcelona y sus cercanías Barcelona and its surrounding area
en las cercanías del aeropuerto in the area near the airport

cercano *masc adjective*, **cercana** *fem*
nearby, **near**
las casas cercanas the nearby houses
en un futuro cercano in the near future
estar cercano a algo to be near something
los pueblos que están cercanos al aeropuerto the villages near the airport

el **cerdo** *masc noun*, la **cerda** *fem*
1 **pig**
2 el **cerdo** pork
No como cerdo. I don't eat pork.

los **cereales** *plural masc noun*
cereals

la **ceremonia** *fem noun*
ceremony

la **cereza** *fem noun*
cherry

la **cerilla** *fem noun*
match

el **cero** *masc noun*
1 **zero**
tres grados bajo cero three degrees below zero
El prefijo de Birmingham es cero, uno, dos, uno. The Birmingham dialling code is 0121.
2 **love** (*in tennis*)
3 **nil** (*in sport*)
Empatamos cero a cero. We drew nil-nil.

cerrado *masc adjective*, **cerrada** *fem*
1 **closed**
La ventana está cerrada. The window's closed.
2 **El grifo está cerrado.** The tap's turned off.
3 **cerrado con llave** locked
'Cerrado por obras' 'Closed for Repairs'

la **cerradura** *fem noun*
1 **lock**
2 **el ojo de la cerradura** the keyhole

cerrar *verb* **[29]**
1 **to close**
Cierrra la puerta. Close the door.
Cerramos a las ocho. We close at eight.
2 **Han cerrado la fábrica.** The factory has been closed.
3 **cerrar con llave** to lock up
No te olvides de cerrar con llave. Don't forget to lock up.
4 **to turn off** (*a tap*)
cerrar el grifo to turn off the tap
5 **to put the top on** (*a bottle*)
Cierra la botella. Put the top on the bottle.
¿Has cerrado el frasco? Have you put the lid on the jar?

cerrarse *reflexive verb* **[29]**
to close
La puerta se cerró. The door closed.

certificado *masc adjective*, **certificada** *fem* ▷ see **certificado** *noun*
registered (*letters, parcels*)

el **certificado** *masc noun*
▷ see **certificado** *adj*
certificate

certificar *verb* **[31]**
to certify

♪ la **cervecería** *fem noun*
1 **brewery**
2 **bar** (*selling different kinds of beer*)

♪ la **cerveza** *fem noun*
beer
¿Quieres una cerveza? Do you want a beer?
- la **cerveza de barril** draught beer
- la **cerveza negra** stout
- la **cerveza rubia** lager

♪ el **césped** *masc noun*
lawn
'Prohibido pisar el césped' 'Keep off the grass'

la **cesta** *fem noun*
basket
- la **cesta de mimbre** wicker basket
- la **cesta de Navidad** Christmas hamper

el **cesto** *masc noun*
basket

chalado *masc adjective*, **chalada** *fem*
(*informal*) **wacky**

el **chalé**, **chalet** *masc noun*
1 **villa**
2 **detached house** (*on an estate*)
- el **chalé adosado** semi-detached house (*on an estate*)

♪ el **chaleco** *masc noun*
waistcoast
un chaleco de punto a sleeveless sweater
- el **chaleco antibalas** bullet-proof vest
- el **chaleco salvavidas** life jacket

♪ el & la **champán**, el & la **champaña** *masc & fem noun*
champagne

♪ el **champiñón** *masc noun*
mushroom

♪ el **champú** *masc noun*
shampoo

♪ las **chanclas** *plural fem noun*
flip-flops

♪ el **chándal** *masc noun*
tracksuit

chao *exclamation*
(*Latin America*) **bye**, **bye-bye**

la **chapa** *fem noun*
1 **top** (*of a bottle*)
2 **badge**
una chapa de policía a police badge

el **chapapote** *masc noun*
oil (*polluting a beach*)

♪ el **chaparrón** *masc noun*
downpour

♪ la **chaqueta** *fem noun*
jacket
- la **chaqueta de punto** cardigan

la **charca** *fem noun*
pond

el **charco** *masc noun*
puddle
No pises los charcos. Don't walk in the puddles.

♪ la **charcutería** *fem noun*
delicatessen (*specializing in pork products*)

♪ **charlar** *verb* **[17]**
to chat

el **chasco** *masc noun*
disappointment
Me llevé un chasco. I felt really disappointed.

♪ el **chat** *masc noun*
chatroom

♪ el **cheque** *masc noun*
cheque
un cheque a nombre de Alberto López a cheque payable to Alberto López
cobrar un cheque to cash a cheque
- el **cheque de viaje**, el **cheque de viajero** traveller's cheque

♪ el **chequeo** *masc noun*
checkup
hacerse un chequeo to have a checkup

chévere *adjective*
(*Latin America*) **great**, **fantastic**

♪ la **chica** *fem* ▷ see **chico** *noun, adj*
1 **girl**
2 **girlfriend**
▷ **chico** *noun*

el **chichón** *masc noun*
bump
Me di un golpe en la cabeza y me ha salido un chichón. I banged my head and now I've got a bump.

♪ el **chicle** *masc noun*
chewing gum
¿Quieres un chicle? Do you want some chewing gum?
- el **chicle de globos** bubblegum

chico *masc adjective*, **chica** *fem*
▷ see **chico** *noun*
small
Estos zapatos son muy chicos. These shoes are very small.

el **chico** *masc noun*, la **chica** *fem*
▷ see **chico** *adj*
1 **boy**
un chico y dos chicas a boy and two girls
unos chicos some children (*all boys, or boys and girls*)
Había unos chicos jugando en la calle. There were some children playing in the street.
2 **guy**
Sale con un chico. She's going out with a guy.

chico *masc adjective*, **chica** *fem*
▷ see **chico** *noun*
small
Estos zapatos son muy chicos. These shoes are very small.

chiflado *masc adjective*, **chiflada** *fem*
(*informal*) **wacky**

Chile *masc noun* ▷ see **chile** *noun*
Chile

el **chile** *masc noun* ▷ see **Chile** *noun*
chilli (*hot pepper*)

chileno *masc adjective & noun*, **chilena** *fem adjective & noun*
1 **Chilean**
2 **un chileno, una chilena** Chilean (*person*)

WORD TIP Adjectives and nouns for nationality and regional origin do not have capital letters in Spanish.

chillar *verb* **[17]**
1 **to shout**
2 **to scream**

la **chimenea** *fem noun*
1 **chimney**
2 **fireplace**

China *fem noun*
(la) China China

la **chincheta** *fem noun*
drawing pin

chino *masc adjective & noun*, **china** *fem adjective & noun*
1 **Chinese**
2 **un chino, una china** Chinese man, Chinese woman
3 **el chino** Chinese (*the language*)

WORD TIP Adjectives and nouns for nationality, regional origin, and language do not have capital letters in Spanish.

Chipre *fem noun*
Cyprus

chirriar *verb* **[32]**
to squeak (*doors, hinges, etc*)

chis *exclamation*
1 **Shush!**
2 **¡Chis, chis!** Hey! (*calling somebody in the street*)

el **chisme** *masc noun*
1 **piece of gossip**
Siempre está contando chismes. He's always gossiping
2 **thing**
¿Para qué sirve este chisme? What's this thing for?

la **chispa** *fem noun*
1 **spark**
2 **una chispa de algo** (*informal*) a small amount of something
una chispa de ginebra a dash of gin
Ponle una chispa de sal. Add a pinch of salt to it.

chispa *invariable adjective*
(*informal*) **tipsy**
Estaba un poco chispa. She was a bit tipsy.

el **chiste** *masc noun*
joke
contar un chiste to tell a joke
• el **chiste verde** dirty joke

chocar *verb* **[31]**
1 **to crash**
Dos coches chocaron en la autopista. Two cars crashed on the motorway.
2 **chocar con algo** to crash into something
Chocaron con una farola. They crashed into a lamp-post.
Me choqué con ella. I bumped into her.

el **chocolate** *masc noun*
chocolate
una barra de chocolate a bar of chocolate
• el **chocolate con leche** milk chocolate
• el **chocolate negro** dark chocolate

la **chocolatina** *fem noun*
chocolate bar

el **chófer** *masc noun*
driver (*of car, taxi, etc*)

el **chollo** *masc noun* (*informal*)
1 **cushy job**
2 **bargain**

el **choque** *masc noun*
1 **crash**
un choque frontal a head-on collision
2 **clash**
choques entre manifestantes y la policía clashes between demonstrators and police

el **chorizo** *masc noun*
chorizo (*a spicy dark red, salami-shaped sausage*)

> mini-info **chorizo**
>
> El chorizo es una salchicha parecida al salami. Es muy apreciado y en su primer viaje espacial en 1998, el astronauta Pedro Duque se llevó en su equipaje un chorizo de León.

la **chorrada** *fem noun*
(*informal*)
1 **nonsense**
decir chorradas to talk nonsense
Eso es una chorrada. That's nonsense.
2 **tiny thing**
Se enfada por cualquier chorrada. He gets upset over the tiniest thing.

la **choza** *fem noun*
hut

el **chubasco** *masc noun*
(heavy) shower
Habrá chubascos en el noroeste. There will be heavy showers in the north-west.

la **chuchería** *fem noun*
trinket

la **chuleta** *fem noun*
chop
- la **chuleta de cerdo** pork chop

chupar *verb* **[17]**
to suck

chuparse *reflexive verb* **[17]**
to suck
chuparse el dedo to suck your thumb

el **churro** *masc noun*
1 **twists of batter deep-fried in olive oil** (*eaten hot with coffee or drinking chocolate*)
2 (*informal*) **botched job**
3 (*informal*) **piece of luck**

chutar *verb* **[17]**
to shoot (*at goal*)

el **cibercafé** *masc noun*
Internet cafe
¿Dónde hay un cibercafé? Where is there an Internet cafe?

el & la **cibernauta** *masc & fem noun*
surfer (*on the Internet*)

la **cicatriz** *fem noun*
scar

el **ciclismo** *masc noun*
cycling

el & la **ciclista** *masc & fem noun*
cyclist

ciego *masc adjective*, **ciega** *fem*
▷ see **ciego** *noun*
blind
quedarse ciego to go blind

el **ciego** *masc noun*, la **ciega** *fem*
▷ see **ciego** *adj*
blind person
los ciegos the blind

el **cielo** *masc noun*
1 **sky**
2 **heaven**
ir al cielo to go to heaven
¡Cielos! Good heavens!

cien *number*
hundred
cien personas a hundred people
el cien por cien a hundred per cent
cien mil euros a hundred thousand euros ▷ **ciento**

la **ciencia** *fem noun*
1 **science**
2 **ciencias** science (*as a subject at school*)
- la **ciencia ficción** science fiction
- las **Ciencias de la Información** Media Studies
- las **Ciencias Empresariales** Business Studies
- las **ciencias naturales** natural science

el **cieno** *masc noun*
silt

científico *masc adjective*, **científica** *fem*
▷ see **científico** *noun*
scientific

el **científico** *masc noun*, la **científica** *fem*
▷ see **científico** *adj*
scientist

ciento *number* ▷ see **cien** *number*
1 **hundred**
ciento cinco one hundred and five
cientos de cartas hundreds of letters
doscientos diez two hundred and ten ▷ **cien**
2 **por ciento** per cent
Suspendieron el ocho por ciento. Eight per cent failed. ⏩

Aprobaron un noventa por ciento. Ninety per cent passed.

WORD TIP Spanish uses *el* or *un* with percentages.

cierra, cierro, etc *verb* ▷ **cerrar**

cierto *masc adjective*, **cierta** *fem*
1 **true**
Sí, es cierto. Yes, it's true.
2 **certain**
cierta clase de negocios certain types of business
en cierta ocasión on a certain occasion
3 (*in expressions*) **en cierto modo** in a way
En cierto modo, lo entiendo. In a way, I understand.
hasta cierto punto up to a point
por cierto by the way
Por cierto, ¿has llamado a Ana? By the way, have you phoned Ana?

el **ciervo** *masc noun*
1 **deer**
2 **stag**

la **cifra** *fem noun*
figure
una cifra muy alta a very high figure

el **cigarrillo** *masc noun*
cigarrette

la **cigüeña** *fem noun*
stork

el **cilindro** *masc noun*
cylinder

la **cima** *fem noun*
top (*of a mountain*)

cinco *number*
1 **five**
Julia tiene cinco años. Julia's five (years old).
2 (*saying the date*) **fifth**
Hoy es día cinco. Today is the fifth.
3 (*telling the time*) **five**
Son las cinco. It's five o'clock.
a las dos y cinco at five past two

cincuenta *number*
fifty
Mi madre tiene cincuenta años. My mum's fifty (years old).
cincuenta y ocho fifty-eight
los años cincuenta the fifties

el **cine** *masc noun*
cinema
ir al cine to go to the cinema
Vámonos al cine. Let's go to the cinema.
¿Qué ponen en el cine? What's on at the cinema?
- el **cine de barrio** local cinema

el & la **cineasta** *masc & fem noun*
film-maker

la **cinta** *fem noun*
1 **ribbon**
una cinta para el pelo a hair ribbon
2 **tape**
grabar una cinta to record a tape
- la **cinta adhesiva** adhesive tape
- la **cinta de vídeo** video tape
- la **cinta magnetofónica** magnetic tape
- la **cinta métrica** tape measure
- la **cinta virgen** blank tape

la **cintura** *fem noun*
waist
¿Cuánto tienes de cintura? What's your waist measurement?

el **cinturón** *masc noun*
belt
Es cinturón negro de karate. He's a karate black belt.
- el **cinturón de seguridad** seatbelt

el **circo** *masc noun*
circus

la **circulación** *fem noun*
1 **circulation**
2 **traffic**

circular *verb* ▷ see **circular** *adj, noun* **[17]**
1 **to flow** (*liquids, blood, water*)
2 **to drive**
Circulen por la derecha. Drive on the right.
El coche circulaba a mucha velocidad. The car was travelling very fast.

circular *masc & fem adjective*
▷ see **circular** *verb, noun*
circular

la **circular** *fem noun* ▷ see **circular** *verb, adj*
circular (*letter, note*)

el **círculo** *masc noun*
circle

la **circunferencia** *fem noun*
circumference

la **circunstancia** *fem noun*
1 **reason**
Por alguna circunstancia no pudo hacerlo. He couldn't do it for some reason.
2 **circumstances**
bajo ninguna circunstancia under no circumstances

en estas circunstancias in these circumstances
dadas las circunstancias given the circumstances

el **cirio** *masc noun*
candle

♪ la **ciruela** *fem noun*
plum
- la **ciruela pasa** prune

la **cirugía** *fem noun*
surgery
- la **cirugía estética** cosmetic surgery
- la **cirugía láser** laser surgery

el **cirujano** *masc noun*, la **cirujana** *fem*
surgeon

el **cisne** *masc noun*
swan

♪ la **cita** *fem noun*
1 appointment
Tengo cita con el médico. I've got an appointment to see the doctor.
El dentista me ha dado cita para el jueves. The dentist has given me an appointment for Thursday.
darse cita to arrange to meet
Se dieron cita en el bar. They arranged to meet in the bar.
2 date
Esta noche tengo una cita con mi novio. I've got a date with my boyfriend tonight.
3 quotation

citar *verb* [17]
1 to quote (*a writer or book*)
2 to mention
Citó algunos casos. He mentioned a few cases.
3 to give an appointment
El médico me ha citado para esta tarde. The doctor's given me an appointment for this afternoon.

citarse *reflexive verb* [17]
to arrange to meet
Se citaron para las cinco. They arranged to meet at five.

♪ la **ciudad** *fem noun*
1 town
2 city
- la **ciudad dormitorio** dormitory town
- la **ciudad universitaria** university campus

el **ciudadano** *masc noun*, la **ciudadana** *fem*
citizen

civil *masc & fem adjective* ▷ see **civil** *noun*
1 civil
un matrimonio civil a civil marriage
casarse por lo civil to have civil wedding
2 civilian
la población civil the civilian population

el & la **civil** *masc & fem noun* ▷ see **civil** *adj*
civilian

el **clarinete** *masc noun*
clarinet

♪ **claro** *masc adjective*, **clara** *fem*
▷ see **claro** *adv*
1 clear
Está muy claro. It's very clear.
Su explicación fue muy clara. His explanation was very clear.
2 light
un verde claro a light green
un chico de ojos claros a boy with light-coloured eyes
3 bright
un día claro a bright day, sunny day

♪ **claro** *adverb* ▷ see **claro** *adj*
1 clearly
Habla más claro. Speak more clearly.
Lo veo claro. I can see it clearly.
2 ¡Claro! Of course!
¡Claro que sí! Yes, of course!
¡Claro que no! No, of course not!

♪ la **clase** *fem noun*
1 class (*in school, in society*)
la clase de matemáticas the maths class
una familia de clase media a middle-class family
Tenemos clase de español tres veces por semana. We have Spanish classes three times a week.
Toda la clase se va de excursión. The whole class is going on an excursion.
2 dar clase de algo to teach something
Mi padre da clase de física en un colegio. My father teaches physics in a school.
dar clase de algo to have lessons in something
Da clases de música por las tardes. She has music lessons in the evenings.
dar clase a alguien to teach somebody
Me da clases de inglés. He teaches me English.
3 classroom
¿En qué clase están? What classroom are they in?
4 kind, type
de primera clase top-quality ⏩

¿Qué clase de material? What kind of material?
5 **class** (*in travel*)
viajar en segunda clase to travel second class
6 **class** (*elegance*)
Tiene mucha clase. She has a lot of class.
- la **clase ejecutiva**, la **clase preferente** business class
- la **clase social** social class
- la **clase turista** economy class

clásico *masc adjective*, **clásica** *fem*
1 **classic**
la clásica broma the classic joke
2 **classical** (*music, decorations*)
3 **traditional** (*methods*)

la **clasificación** *fem noun*
1 **classification**
2 **qualifying** (*in sports*)
sin posibilidades de clasificación with no chance of qualifying
3 **table** (*in sports*)
La clasificación final es la siguiente ... The final table is as follows ...

clasificar *verb* [31]
to put in order (*papers, cards, etc*)

clasificarse *reflexive verb* [17]
to qualify
clasificarse para algo to qualify for something
Se clasificaron para la final. They qualified for the final.

clavar *verb* [17]
to hammer
Clavó un clavo en la pared. He hammered a nail into the wall.

clave *invariable adjective* ▷ see **clave** *noun*
key
un factor clave a key factor

la **clave** *fem noun* ▷ see **clave** *adj*
1 **key** (*to a mystery, a problem*)
La clave es ... The key to it is ...
2 **code**
un mensaje en clave a coded message
3 (*in music*) **clef**
- la **clave de sol** treble clef

la **clavija** *fem noun*
1 **peg**
2 **plug** (*for electrical appliances*)

el **clavo** *masc noun*
1 **nail**
2 **clove** (*of spice*)

el **claxon** *masc noun*
horn (*of a car*)

♪ el **clic** *masc noun*
click
un doble clic a double click
hacer clic en algo to click on something
Haz clic en el icono. Click on the icon.

♪ el **cliente** *masc noun*, la **clienta** *fem*
1 **customer**
2 **client** (*of a company, a lawyer*)
3 **guest** (*in a hotel*)

♪ el **clima** *masc noun*
climate

climatizado *masc adjective*, **climatizada** *fem*
air-conditioned

la **clínica** *fem noun*
private hospital

el **clip** *masc noun*
paper clip
- el **clip para el pelo** hairgrip

el **club** *masc noun*
club
un club de jóvenes a youth club

la **coartada** *fem noun*
alibi

♪ **cobarde** *masc & fem adjective*
▷ see **cobarde** *noun*
cowardly

♪ el & la **cobarde** *masc & fem noun*
▷ see **cobarde** *adj*
coward

♪ el **cobrador** *masc noun*, la **cobradora** *fem*
conductor

♪ **cobrar** *verb* [17]
1 **to get paid**
Cobro mil cuatrocientos euros al mes. I get paid one thousand four hundred euros a month.
Cobramos a fin de mes. We get paid at the end of the month.
Cobra el paro. He's paid unemployment benefit.
Cobra bastante de pensión. He gets a good pension.
2 **to charge**
Me cobraron sesenta euros por todo. They charged me sixty euros for everything.
cobrar de más to overcharge
cobrar de menos to undercharge

3 **to collect** *(a debt, the rent, dues)*
Han venido a cobrar el alquiler. They've come to collect the rent.
4 **to cash**
cobrar un cheque de viajero to cash a traveller's cheque

♪ el **cobre** *masc noun*
copper

♪ la **cocaína** *fem noun*
cocaine

♪ **cocer** *verb* [41]
1 **to boil** *(eggs, vegetables)*
cocer algo a fuego lento to simmer something over a low heat
2 **to bake**

♪ el **coche** *masc noun*
1 **car**
ir en coche to go by car
2 **carriage** *(of train)*
- el **coche bomba** car bomb
- el **coche de alquiler** hire car
- el **coche de bomberos** fire engine
- el **coche de carreras** racing car
- el **coche restaurante** restaurant car

♪ el **cochecito de bebé** *masc noun*
pram

♪ la **cochera** *fem noun*
bus depot

el **cocido** *masc noun*
stew *(containing meat and chickpeas)*

♪ la **cocina** *fem noun*
1 **kitchen**
¿Dónde está la cocina? Where's the kitchen?
2 **cooker**
3 **cooking**
la cocina española Spanish cooking
un libro de cocina a cookery book
- la **cocina de gas**, la **cocina de butano** gas cooker
- la **cocina eléctrica** electric cooker

♪ **cocinar** *verb* [17]
to cook
Cocina muy bien. He cooks very well.
cocinar algo a fuego lento to cook something on a low heat

♪ el **cocinero** *masc noun*, la **cocinera** *fem*
cook

♪ el **coco** *masc noun*
1 **coconut**
2 *(informal)* **head**
Me duele el coco. I've got a headache

♪ el **cocotero** *masc noun*
coconut tree

♪ el **cocodrilo** *masc noun*
crocodile

♪ el **cóctel** *masc noun*
1 **cocktail**
2 **cocktail party**

el **código** *masc noun*
code
- el **código de barras** bar code
- el **código postal** postcode

♪ el **codo** *masc noun*
elbow

la **codorniz** *fem noun*
quail

♪ **coger** *verb* [3]
1 **to take**
coger el autobús to take the bus
La cogí del brazo. I took her by the arm.
No quería coger el dinero. He didn't want to take the money.
2 **to get**
coger el teléfono to answer the phone
Voy a coger entradas para el concierto. I'm going to get some concert tickets.
Coge por la Calle Díaz. Go down Díaz Street.
3 **to catch**
coger un resfriado to catch a cold
coger una insolación to get sunstroke
No pudo coger la pelota. He couldn't catch the ball.
Cogieron al asesino. They caught the murderer.
Coge el metro en Sol. Catch the metro at Sol (station).
4 **to pick**
coger fresas to pick strawberries
coger algo del suelo to pick something up from the floor

cogerse *reflexive verb* [3]
1 **cogerse de algo** to hold on to something
Cógete de la barra. Hold on to the rail.
2 **Se cogieron de la mano.** They took each other by the hand.

WORD TIP In Spain *coger* is the usual word for *to take, catch* etc, but in parts of Latin America it is the four-letter word. In Latin America always use *tomar* instead.

cogido *masc adjective*, **cogida** *fem*
1 **taken**
Esta silla ya está cogida. This chair is already taken.
2 **ir cogidos de la mano** to walk hand in hand
ir cogidos del brazo to walk arm in arm

cohibido *masc adjective*, **cohibida** *fem*
1 **awkward**
2 **inhibited**

la **coincidencia** *fem noun*
coincidence
¡Qué coincidencia! What a coincidence!

coincidir *verb* **[19]**
1 **to coincide**
2 **coincidir en algo to agree about something**

coja, **cojas**, **etc** *verb* ▷ **coger**

el **cojín** *masc noun*
cushion

cojo *masc adjective*, **coja** *fem*
1 **lame**
Es cojo. He's lame (*ser because it's permanent*).
2 **Está coja.** She has a limp (*estar because it's temporary*).

la **col** *fem noun*
cabbage
• las **coles de Bruselas** Brussels sprouts

la **cola** *fem noun*
1 **tail**
2 **queue**
hacer cola to queue up
saltarse la cola to jump the queue
Me puse a la cola. I joined the queue.
3 **glue**
Lo pegué con cola. I glued it.
• la **cola de carpintero** wood glue

la **colada** *fem noun*
laundry
hacer la colada to do the washing

el **colador** *masc noun*
strainer

colar *verb* **[24]**
to strain (*vegetables*)

colarse *reflexive verb* **[24]**
1 **to jump the queue**
Esa señora se ha colado. That lady has jumped the queue.
2 **colarse en un sitio** to get in somewhere without paying
Se coló en el cine. He got into the cinema without paying.

la **colcha** *fem noun*
bedspread

el **colchón** *masc noun*
mattress
• el **colchón de aire** air bed

la **colección** *fem noun*
collection

coleccionar *verb* **[17]**
to collect

el & la **coleccionista** *masc & fem noun*
collector

el & la **colega** *masc & fem noun*
colleague

el **cole** *masc noun*
(*informal*) **school**

el **colegial** *masc noun*, la **colegiala** *fem*
1 **schoolboy**
2 **schoolgirl**

el **colegio** *masc noun*
school
Mi hermano ya va al colegio. My brother's going to school now.
• el **colegio mayor** hall of residence
• el **colegio privado** private school
• el **colegio público** state school

la **coleta** *fem noun*
ponytail

colgar *verb* **[23]**
1 **to hang**
2 **colgar la ropa** to hang out the washing
3 **colgar un cuadro** to hang up a picture
4 **to hang up** (*when telephoning*)
Cuelga el teléfono. Hang up.
Me ha colgado. She's hung up on me.
No cuelgue. Hold the line (*polite form*).

colgarse *reflexive verb* **[23]**
(*Computers*) **to crash**

la **coliflor** *fem noun*
cauliflower

la **colilla** *fem noun*
cigarette end

la **colina** *fem noun*
hill

la **colisión** *fem noun*
collision

el **collar** *masc noun*
1 **necklace**
un collar de perlas a string of pearls
2 **collar** (*for a dog*)

el **colmo** *masc noun*
¡Esto es el colmo! This is the last straw!
¡Y para colmo ... ! And to cap it all ... !
el colmo de la incompetencia the height of incompetence

la **colocación** *fem noun*
job
Está buscando colocación. He's looking for a job.

♪ **colocar** *verb* **[31]**
1 **to put**
Colócalo ahí. Put it there.
¿Dónde coloco esta silla? Where should I put this chair?
2 **Aún tenemos que colocar los muebles.** We still have to arrange the furniture.
3 **colocar a alguien** to get somebody a job
Su tío lo ha colocado. His uncle's got him a job.

colocarse *reflexive verb* **[31]**
to find a job
Se ha colocado muy bien. She's found a very good job.

Colombia *fem noun*
Colombia

colombiano *masc adjective & noun*, **colombiana** *fem adjective & noun*
1 **Colombian**
2 **un colombiano, una colombiana** Colombian

WORD TIP Adjectives and nouns for nationality and regional origin do not have capital letters in Spanish.

♪ la **colonia** *fem noun*
1 **(eau de) cologne**
2 **colony**
3 **una colonia de vacaciones** a summer camp

coloquial *masc & fem adjective*
colloquial

el **coloquio** *masc noun*
discussion

♪ el **color** *masc noun*
colour
¿De qué color es? What colour is it?
Es de color azul. It's blue.
colores claros light colours
telas de colores coloured fabrics

colorado *masc adjective*, **colorada** *fem*
red
ponerse colorado to go red
¡Te has puesto colorado! You've gone red!

el **colorante** *masc noun*
colouring

♪ **colorear** *verb* **[17]**
to colour
Coloréalo de rojo. Colour it red.

♪ el **colorete** *masc noun*
blusher

♪ la **columna** *fem noun*
1 **column**
2 **spine**
la columna vertebral the spine

columpiar *verb* **[17]**
to push (*on a swing*)

columpiarse *reflexive verb* **[17]**
to play on a swing

el **columpio** *masc noun*
swing (*in a park*)

la **coma** *fem noun* ▷ see **coma** *masc noun*
1 **comma**
2 **decimal point** (*In Spain a comma is used in decimals.*)
dos coma cinco two point five

el **coma** *masc noun* ▷ see **coma** *fem noun*
(*Medicine*) **coma**
entrar en coma to go into a coma

la **comadrona** *fem noun*
midwife

el & la **comandante** *masc & fem noun*
major

la **comba** *fem noun*
skipping rope
saltar a la comba to skip
jugar a la comba to skip

el **combate** *masc noun*
1 **combat** (*between soldiers*)
2 **fight** (*in boxing*)

la **combinación** *fem noun*
1 **combination**
2 **slip** (*girl's clothing*)

combinar *verb* **[17]**
to combine

la **comedia** *fem noun*
comedy
• la **comedia musical** musical

♪ el **comedor** *masc noun*
1 **dining-room**
2 **dining hall**
3 **canteen**

♪ **comentar** *verb* **[17]**
1 **to talk about**
Comentamos la noticia. We talked about the news.
2 **to mention**
Me lo comentó de pasada. He mentioned it to me in passing.
3 **to remark**
Comentó que ... He remarked that ...

♪ el **comentario** *masc noun*
comment
sin comentarios no comment

a b c d e f g h i j k l m n ñ o p q r s t u v w x y z

comenzar *verb* **[25]**
to begin, to start
¿Cuándo comienzan las clases? When do lessons start?
Hemos comenzado los preparativos. We've begun the preparations.
Comenzó explicando que ... He began by explaining that ...
comenzar a hacer algo to begin to do something
Ha comenzado a llover. It's begun to rain.
Comencé a estudiar español hace dos años. I began learning Spanish two years ago.

WORD TIP To say, to begin by, use *comenzar* + *-ando*, *or -iendo*; to say, to begin to, use *comenzar a* + *infinitive*.

comer *verb* **[18]**
1 **to eat**
¿Te gusta comer pescado? Do you like eating fish?
2 (*Spain*) **to have lunch**
En casa comemos a la una. At home we have lunch at one.
¿Qué había de comer? What was for lunch?
3 (*Latin America*) **to have dinner**
4 **to take** (*a piece in chess, draughts*)
Te como el caballo. I take your knight.

comercial *masc & fem adjective*
commercial
un centro comercial a shopping centre
el centro comercial de la ciudad the commercial centre of the town

el & la **comerciante** *masc & fem noun*
shopkeeper

el **comercio** *masc noun*
1 **trade**
el comercio de animales exóticos the trade in exotic animals
2 **shop**
un comercio pequeño a small shop

los **comestibles** *plural masc noun*
food

la **cometa** *fem noun*
1 **kite**
hacer volar una cometa to fly a kite
2 **comet**

cometer *verb* **[18]**
1 **to commit** (*a crime*)
2 **to make** (*a mistake*)
He cometido un error. I've made a mistake.

el **cómic** *masc noun*
comic

cómico *masc adjective*, **cómica** *fem*
▷ see **cómico** *noun*
1 **funny** (*situation, face*)
2 **comic** (*actor*)

el & la **cómico** *masc & fem noun*
▷ see **cómico** *adj*
comedian

la **comida** *fem noun*
1 **food**
Tenemos suficiente comida. We have enough food.
2 **meal**
tres comidas al día three meals a day
Mi comida fuerte es a mediodía. I have my main meal at midday.
3 (*Spain*) **lunch**
a la hora de la comida at lunch time
4 (*Latin America*) **dinner** (*at night*)
• la **comida rápida** fast food

comienza, **comienzo**, **etc** *verb* ▷ **comenzar**

el **comienzo** *masc noun*
beginning
al comienzo in the beginning
el comienzo del año escolar the beginning of the school year

las **comillas** *plural fem noun*
inverted commas
poner algo entre comillas to put something in inverted commas

el **comino** *masc noun*
cumin

la **comisaría** *fem noun*
police station

la **comisión** *fem noun*
commission

como *conjunction* ▷ see **cómo, como** *adv*
1 **as, in the way that**
Lo hice como me dijeron. I did it as I was told to.
Como tú quieras. Just as you like.
Hazlo como quieras. Do it however you want to.
2 **since, because**
Como no llamaste, no te esperé. Since you didn't call, I didn't wait for you.
3 **if**
Como no tengas cuidado te vas a caer. If you're not careful you'll fall.

como *adverb* ▷ see **cómo** *adv*, **como** *conj*
1 **like** (*in comparisons*)
uno como éste one like this one
ser como ... to be like ...
Eres como tu padre. You're like your father.
tan ... como ... as ... as ...
Es tan negro como el carbón It's as black as coal.
como si as if
Es como si fuéramos niños. It's as if we were children.
2 **such as** (*giving examples*)
metales como el oro y la plata metals such as gold and silver
3 **around**
Eran como cincuenta personas. There were around fifty people.
como a las dos y media around half past two
4 **como mucho** at the most
como poco at least
Serán como mucho quince niños. There will be at most fifteen children.

cómo *adverb* ▷ see **como** *adv, conj*
1 (*in questions*) **how**
¿Cómo estás? How are you?
¿Cómo se escribe tu nombre? How do you write your name?
No sé cómo se enteraron. I don't know how they found out.
2 (*in questions*) **what**
¿Cómo es? What's she like?
¿Cómo es tu casa? What's your house like?
3 (*when you don't hear*) **¿Cómo?** Pardon?
4 (*in exclamations*) **¡Cómo quema!** It's so hot!
¡Cómo se parecen! They are so like each other!
¡Cómo no! Of course!, Please do!
¡Cómo! ¿no lo has hecho? What! you haven't done it?

WORD TIP *cómo*, with an accent, is used for questions (¿...?) and exclamations (¡...!).

la **cómoda** *fem noun*
chest of drawers

el **comodín** *masc noun*
joker (*in a pack of cards*)

cómodo *masc adjective*, **cómoda** *fem*
comfortable
¿Estás cómodo? Are you comfortable?
un sillón muy cómodo a very comfortable armchair
ponerse cómodo to make yourself comfortable
Ponte cómoda. Make yourself comfortable (*speaking to a girl*).

el **compact disc**, el **compacto** *masc noun*
1 **CD**
2 **CD player**

el **compañero** *masc noun*, la **compañera** *fem*
1 **colleague**
mis compañeros de trabajo my workmates
2 **un compañero de clase** a school mate
su compañera de piso her flatmate
3 **partner** (*in a relationship*)

la **compañía** *fem noun*
company
el director de la compañía the manager of the company
hacerle compañía a alguien to keep somebody company
Yo le hacía compañía. I kept her company.

la **comparación** *fem noun*
comparison
hacer una comparación entre dos cosas to make a comparison between two thing
Haz una comparación entre los dos dibujos. Make a comparison between the two pictures.
en comparación con in comparison with
Es alto en comparación con su hermano. He's tall in comparison with his brother.

comparar *verb* **[17]**
to compare

compartir *verb* **[19]**
to share
compartir algo con alguien to share something with somebody
Compartieron su comida conmigo. They shared their food with me.

el **compás** *masc noun*
1 **time, rhythm**
llevar el compás to keep time
2 **pair of compasses**

compensar *verb* **[29]**
to compensate

la **competencia** *fem noun*
competition (*in business, etc*)
Nos hacen la competencia. They're in competition with us.

la **competición** *fem noun*
competition (*in sports*)

competir *verb* **[57]**
to compete

compita, compito, etc *verb* ▷ **competir**

completamente *adverb*
completely

completar *verb* **[17]**
to complete

completo *masc adjective*, **completa** *fem*
1 **complete**
2 **full**
El hotel está completo. The hotel is full.
'Completo' 'No vacancies'

complicado *masc adjective*, **complicada** *fem*
complicated

complicar *verb* **[31]**
to complicate

complicarse *reflexive verb* **[31]**
to become complicated
La situación se ha complicado. The situation has become complicated.

componer *verb* **[11]**
1 **to make up**
El equipo está compuesto de once jugadores. The team is made up of eleven players.
2 **to compose** (*music, a poem*)
3 (*Latin America*) **to repair**
Hay que componer el radio.

componerse *reflexive verb* **[11]**
componerse de to be made up of
Su dieta se compone sólo de verduras. His diet is made up only of vegetables.

el **comportamiento** *masc noun*
behaviour
mal comportamiento bad behaviour

comportarse *reflexive verb* **[17]**
to behave
comportarse mal to behave badly

la **composición** *fem noun*
composition

el **compositor** *masc noun*, la **compositora** *fem*
composer

la **compra** *fem noun*
purchase
Fue una buena compra. It was a good buy.
ir de compras to go shopping
Mañana nos vamos de compras. We're going shopping tomorrow.
hacer la compra to do the shopping
Su padre siempre hace la compra. Her father always does the shopping.

el **comprador** *masc noun*, la **compradora** *fem*
buyer

comprar *verb* **[17]**
1 **to buy**
2 **comprarle algo a alguien** to buy something for somebody (*as a present*)
Le compré a Juan un videojuego para su cumpleaños. I bought Juan a videogame for his birthday.
3 **comprarle algo a alguien** to buy something from somebody
Voy a comprarle su bicicleta. I'm going to buy his bike from him.

comprender *verb* **[18]**
to understand
No comprendo la pregunta. I don't understand the question.
No me comprenden. They don't understand me.

la **comprensión** *fem noun*
comprehension
un ejercicio de comprensión a comprehension test

la **compresa** *fem noun*
sanitary towel

el **comprimido** *masc noun*
pill

comprobar *verb* **[24]**
to check
Hay que comprobar la factura. We must check the bill.

el **compromiso** *masc noun*
1 **appointment**, **commitment**
Mañana no puedo, tengo un compromiso. Tomorrow is out, I've got an appointment.
Tiene muchos compromisos. She has a lot of commitments.
2 **commitment**
3 **obligation**
sin compromiso without obligation
4 **poner a alguien en un compromiso** to put somebody in an awkward situation
Ahora me has puesto en un compromiso. Now you've put me in an awkward situation.
• el **compromiso político** political commitment

el **computador** *masc noun*
(*Latin America*) **computer**
▷ **ordenador**

la **computadora** *fem noun*
(*Latin America*) **computer**
▷ **ordenador**

común *masc & fem adjective*
common
en común in common
No tenemos nada en común. We have nothing in common.
trabajar en común to work together

la **comunicación** *fem noun*
1 **communication**
2 **ponerse en comunicación con alguien** to get in touch with someone
Se puso en comunicación conmigo en cuanto llegó. He got in touch with me as soon as he arrived.
3 **cortarse la comunicación** to be cut off (*on the phone*)
Se ha cortado la comunicación. I've been cut off.
4 (*in transport*) **Las comunicaciones son buenas.** The communications are good.
un barrio con buenas comunicaciones an area with good public transport services

comunicar *verb* **[31]**
1 **to be busy** (*when telephoning*)
Está comunicando. The line is busy.
2 **to inform**
Debo comunicarles que ... I must inform you that ...

comunicarse *reflexive verb* **[31]**
1 **to communicate**
comunicarse por carta to communicate by letter
2 **to be in touch**
No puedo comunicarme con él. I can't get in touch with him.

la **comunidad** *fem noun*
community
• la **Comunidad Europea** the European Community

la **comunión** *fem noun*
communion
(*Religion*) **hacer la primera comunión** to take first communion

con *preposition*
1 **with**
Vine con mi primo. I came with my cousin.
Divídelo con un cuchillo. Divide it up with a knife.
2 **to**
hablar con alguien to speak to somebody
estar casado con alguien to be married to somebody
3 **and**
bistec con patatas steak and chips
pan con mantequilla bread and butter
4 **con tal de que** as long as
Te lo dejo, con tal de que lo cuides. I'll lend it to you as long as you look after it.

el **concejal** *masc noun*, la **concejala** *fem*
councillor
Su tía es concejala. Her aunt is a councillor.

la **concentración** *fem noun*
concentration

concentrar *verb* **[17]**
to concentrate

concentrarse *reflexive verb* **[17]**
to concentrate
Me concentré en mi trabajo. I concentrated on my work.

la **concha** *fem noun*
shell

concienzudo *masc adjective*, **concienzuda** *fem*
conscientious

el **concierto** *masc noun*
concert
un concierto de música rock a rock concert

la **conclusión** *fem noun*
conclusion
llegar a una conclusión to reach a conclusion

concurrido *masc adjective*, **concurrida** *fem*
1 **busy** (*bar, street, market*)
2 **well-attended** (*concert, exhibition*)

el **concurso** *masc noun*
competition
un programa concurso a quiz show
• el **concurso hípico** show-jumping competition

el **conde** *masc noun*, la **condesa** *fem noun*
1 **count**
2 **countess**

la **condición** *fem noun*
condition
a condición de que, con la condición de que on condition that
Te lo presto con la condición de que me lo devuelvas mañana. I'll lend it to you on condition that you give it back tomorrow.

el **condón** *masc noun*
condom

conducir *verb* **[60]**
1 **to drive**
Yo conduzco. I'll drive.
2 **to lead**
el camino que conduce al pueblo the road that leads to the village

♪ el **conductor** *masc noun*, la **conductora** *fem*
driver

conduje, **condujo** *verb* ▷ **conducir**

conduzca, **conduzco, etc** *verb* ▷ **conducir**

conectar *verb* **[17]**
to connect
conectar la impresora al ordenador to connect the printer to the computer

el **conejillo de Indias** *masc noun*
guinea pig

el **conejo** *masc noun*, la **coneja** *fem*
rabbit

la **conexión** *fem noun*
connection

♪ la **conferencia** *fem noun*
1 **lecture**
2 **long-distance call**
una conferencia interurbana a long-distance telephone call
• la **conferencia de prensa** press conference

confesar *verb* **[29]**
to confess

la **confianza** *fem noun*
1 **trust**
una persona de confianza a person you can trust
2 **tener confianza en alguien** to have confidence in somebody
Tiene mucha confianza en sí mismo. He's very self-confident.
3 **tener confianza con alguien** to know somebody very well
Tenemos mucha confianza. We know each other very well.

confiar *verb* **[32]**
to trust
Confío en ti. I trust you.

la **confidencia** *fem noun*
confidence
hacerle una confidencia a alguien to tell somebody something in confidence

confirmar *verb* **[17]**
to confirm

♪ la **confitería** *fem noun*
patisserie, **pastry shop**

la **confitura** *fem noun*
fruit preserve

♪ **conforme** *masc & fem adjective*
1 **estar conforme** to agree
No estoy conforme. I don't agree.
¿Conformes? Do you agree? (*speaking to more than one person*)
2 **¡Conforme!** Ok! (*one person replying*)
estar conforme con algo to be happy with something
Estoy conforme con tu decisión. I'm happy with your decision.
No estoy conforme con el precio. I'm not happy witht he price.

confortable *masc & fem adjective*
comfortable

confortar *verb* **[17]**
to comfort

♪ **confundir** *verb* **[19]**
1 **to confuse**
No me confundas. Don't confuse me.
2 **to get mixed up**
He confundido las fechas. I've got the dates mixed up.
3 **confundir a alguien con alguien** to mistake somebody for somebody else
La confundí con Cristina. I mistook her for Cristina.

confundirse *reflexive verb* **[19]**
1 **to make a mistake**
Creo que se ha confundido con la cuenta. I think you've made a mistake with the bill. (*speaking formally*)
2 **Se confundió de número.** He got the wrong number.

♪ la **confusión** *fem noun*
confusion

♪ **confuso** *masc adjective*, **confusa** *fem*
1 **confusing**
Esto es muy confuso. This is very confusing.
2 **confused**
Estaba confusa. She was confused.

♪ **congelado** *masc adjective*, **congelada** *fem*
1 **frozen**
alimentos congelados frozen food
¡Estoy congelada! I'm freezing!
2 **Murió congelado.** He died from exposure.
3 **Tenía un dedo congelado.** He had frostbite in one finger.

♪ el **congelador** *masc noun*
1 **freezer compartment**
2 **deep freezer**

♪ **congelar** *verb* **[17]**
to freeze

congelarse *reflexive verb* **[17]**
to freeze
¡Me estoy congelando! I'm freezing!

♪ **conjugar** *verb* **[28]**
to conjugate

conjunto *masc adjective*, **conjunta** *fem*
▷ see **conjunto** *noun*
joint
un esfuerzo conjunto a joint effort

el **conjunto** *masc noun* ▷ see **conjunto** *adj*
1 **group**
un conjunto de personas a group of people
un conjunto de música pop a pop group
2 **collection**
un conjunto de cosas a collection of things
3 **outfit**
un conjunto de falda y chaleco a matching skirt and waistcoat
4 **en conjunto** as a whole
En conjunto el trabajo está bien. As a whole the work is all right.

♪ **conmigo** *pronoun*
1 **with me**
Ven conmigo. Come with me.
2 **to me**
No habló conmigo. He didn't talk to me.
3 **conmigo mismo** *masc*, **conmigo misma** *fem* with myself
No estoy contento conmigo mismo. I'm not happy with myself.

WORD TIP *con* + *mí* becomes *conmigo*, which does not change.

♪ **conocer** *verb* **[35]**
1 **to know** (*people, places, stories, etc*)
Los conozco de vista. I know them by sight.
¿Conoces España? Do you know Spain?
Conozco la historia. I know the story.
2 **to meet, to get to know**
Conocí a su hermana en Santander. I met her sister in Santander.
3 **to recognize**
Te conocí por la forma de andar. I recognized you by the way you walk.

conocerse *reflexive verb* **[35]**
1 **to know each other**
Se conocen bien. They know each other well.
2 **to get to know each other**
Nos conocimos en Jaca. We got to know each other in Jaca.

WORD TIP For the other Spanish verb for *to know* ▷ **saber**.

conocido *masc adjective*, **conocida** *fem*
▷ see **conocido** *noun*
1 **well-known** (*actor, song*)
una canción conocida a well-known song
2 **familiar**
una cara conocida a familiar face

el **conocido** *masc noun*, la **conocida** *fem*
▷ see **conocido** *adj*
acquaintance

♪ el **conocimiento** *masc noun*
knowledge

conozca, **conozco**, **etc** *verb* ▷ **conocer**

♪ **conque** *conjunction*
so
Conque esta es tu novia. So, this is your girlfriend.

la **consecuencia** *fem noun*
consequence

♪ **conseguir** *verb* **[64]**
1 **to achieve**
Han conseguido su objetivo. They've achieved their objective.
2 **to get**
He conseguido un trabajo. I've got a job.
3 **conseguir hacer algo** to manage to do something
Conseguimos persuadirle que se quedara. We managed to persuade him to stay.

el **consejero** *masc noun*, la **consejera** *fem*
1 **adviser**
2 **board member** (*of a company*)
3 **minister** (*in some autonomous Spanish parliaments*)
• el **consejero delegado** la **consejera delegada** managing director

♪ el **consejo** *masc noun*
1 **piece of advice**
Te doy un consejo. I'll give you a piece of advice.
2 **consejos** advice
No hacen caso de mis consejos. They don't follow my advice.
3 **board** (*of a company, school, etc*)
4 **council** (*in local government*)
• el **consejo de administración** board of directors
• el **Consejo de Europa** the Council of Europe
• el **consejo de ministros** cabinet meeting
• el **consejo escolar** board of governors (*of a school*)

♪ el & la **conserje** *masc & fem noun*
1 **caretaker** (*in a school, a public building*)
2 **receptionist** (*in a hotel*)

conservador *masc adjective*, **conservadora** *fem*
▷ see **concervador** *noun*
conservative

el **conservador** *masc noun*, la **conservadora** *fem*
▷ see **concervador** *adj*
conservative

conservar *verb* **[17]**
1 **to preserve** (*food*)
2 **to keep up** (*traditions*)
3 **to keep**
Conservo todas sus cartas. I keep all her letters.
Intenta conservar la calma. Try to keep calm.

conservarse *reflexive verb* **[17]**
to keep (*foods*)
Las manzanas se conservan bien. Apples keep well.

las **conservas** *plural fem noun*
tinned food

considerable *masc & fem adjective*
considerable
un número considerable de estudiantes a considerable number of students

la **consideración** *fem noun*
consideración
tomar algo en consideración to take something into consideration
Tienes que tomar en consideración el tiempo que tardarás en llegar. You must take into consideration the time it will take you get here.

considerar *verb* **[17]**
to consider

consiga, **consigo**, **consiguiendo**, **etc** *verb* ▷ **conseguir**

la **consigna** *fem noun*
left-luggage office

consigo *pronoun*
1 **with him**, **with her**
Lo trae consigo. He's bringing it with him., She's bringing it with her.
2 **consigo mismo** with himself
consigo misma with herself
No está contento consigo mismo. He is not happy with himself.
Está enfadada consigo misma. She is angry with herself.
3 **with them**
El dinero que tenían consigo. The money they had with them.
4 **with you** (*when talking politely*)
Si usted quiere lo puede traer consigo. If you wish, you can bring it with you.

WORD TIP *con* + *sí* becomes *consigo*, which does not change.

consistir *verb* **[19]**
consistir en algo to consist of something
Consiste en tres sillas y una mesa. It consists of three chairs and a table.
El trabajo consiste en ... The job involves ...

la **consonante** *fem noun*
consonant (*all the letters except* ***a, e, i, o, u***)

constante *masc & fem adjective*
constant

constipado *masc adjective*, **constipada** *fem* ▷ see **constipado** *noun*
estar constipado to have a cold
No fui a la piscina porque estaba constipada. I didn't go to the pool because I had a cold.

WORD TIP *constipado* does not mean *constipated* in English; for the meaning of *constipated* ▷ **estreñido**.

el **constipado** *masc noun*
▷ see **constipado** *adj*
cold
coger un constipado to catch a cold

constiparse *reflexive verb* **[17]**
to catch a cold
Me he constipado. I've caught a cold.

el **constructor** *masc noun*, la **constructora** *fem*
builder

construir *verb* **[54]**
to build

construya, **construyendo**, **construyo**, **etc** *verb* ▷ **construir**

el & la **cónsul** *masc & fem noun*
consul

el **consulado** *masc noun*
consulate

la **consulta** *fem noun*
1 **surgery**
horas de consulta surgery hours
Pasa consulta de cuatro a siete. His surgery hours are from four to seven.
2 **hacer una consulta a aguien** to ask something
¿**Te puedo hacer una consulta? Can I ask you a question?**
un libro de consulta a reference book

consultar *verb* **[17]**
1 **to consult**
consultarle algo a alguien to consult somebody about something
Se lo voy a consultar al médico. I'm going to consult the doctor about it.
2 **to look up**
Tengo que consultarlo en el diccionario. I have to look it up in the dictionary.

el **consultorio** *masc noun*
surgery

la **consumición** *fem noun*
drink (*in a bar, cafe*)
consumición mínima cuatro euros minimum charge four euros

el **consumo** *masc noun*
consumption

el & la **contable** *masc & fem noun*
accountant

el **contacto** *masc noun*
1 **contact**
estar en contacto to be in contact
2 **ignition** (*in a car*)

el **contado** *masc noun*
al contado cash
pagar al contado to pay cash
Lo compré al contado. I paid for it in cash.

el **contador** *masc noun*
meter (*for electricity, water, in a taxi*)

contagiar *verb* **[17]**
to pass on (*an illness*)
No quiero contagiarte el resfriado. I don't want to give you my cold.

contagiarse *reflexive verb* **[17]**
to become infected
Se ha contagiado de su hermana. She's got it from her sister.

la **contaminación** *fem noun*
1 **pollution** (*of the environment*)
2 **contamination** (*by radioactivity*)

contaminar *verb* **[17]**
1 **to pollute** (*the air, water, sea*)
2 **to contaminate** (*with radioactivity*)

contar *verb* **[24]**
1 **to count**
Cuenta el dinero. Count the money.
2 **contar con alguien** to count on somebody
Puedes contar conmigo. You can count on me.
3 **to tell**
Cuéntamelo. Tell me about it.
Le conté el secreto. I told him the secret.
4 **to count**
Eso no cuenta. That doesn't count.
El trabajo cuenta para mi nota final. The essay counts towards my final mark.

el **contenedor** *masc noun*
1 **container**
2 **skip**
3 **un contenedor de vidrio** a bottle bank

contener *verb* **[9]**
1 **to contain**
No contiene conservantes. It does not contain preservatives.
2 **to hold back** (*tears, laughter, breath*)
contener la respiración to hold your breath
No pudo contener la risa. She couldn't stop herself laughing.

el **contenido** *masc noun*
1 **contents**
el contenido de la botella the contents of the bottle
2 **content**
el contenido del libro the content of the book

contento *masc adjective*, **contenta** *fem*
1 **happy**
Mis padres están muy contentos. My parents are very happy.
2 **pleased**
Estoy contento de verte. I'm pleased to see you.

la **contestación** *fem noun*
1 **answer**
No nos dio una contestación. He didn't give us an answer.
2 **reply**
Quedo a la espera de su contestación. Looking forward to your reply.

el **contestador**, el **contestador automático** *masc noun*
answering machine

contestar *verb* **[17]**
1 **to answer**
No contestó. He didn't answer.
contestar el teléfono to answer the phone
2 **contestar a** to reply to (*a letter, a question*)
No ha contestado a mi carta. He hasn't replied to my letter.

el **contexto** *masc noun*
context

contigo *pronoun*
1 **with you**
Yo voy contigo. I'm going with you. ▸▸

2 to you
No hablo contigo. I'm not talking to you.
3 contigo mismo *masc*, **contigo misma** *fem* with yourself
¿Estás contento contigo mismo? Are you pleased with yourself?

WORD TIP *con* + *ti* becomes *contigo*, which does not change.

ʃ el **continente** *masc noun*
continent

la **continuación** *fem noun*
continuation
A continuación ... Next ...

ʃ **continuamente** *adverb*
continuously

ʃ **continuar** *verb* [20]
to continue
Continuaron viviendo allí. They went living there.
Continúe todo recto. Keep going straight on. (*street directions, polite form*)
Continuará. To be continued.

continuo *masc adjective*, **continua** *fem*
constant

ʃ **contra** *preposition*
against
Son dos contra uno. It's two against one.
Lo apoyó contra la pared. He leant it against the wall.
El coche chocó contra el árbol. The car crashed into the tree.
estar en contra de algo to be against something
Estoy en contra de la decisión. I'm against the decision.

el & la **contrabandista** *masc & fem noun*
smuggler

el **contrabando** *masc noun*
1 smuggling
2 smuggled goods

contrario *masc adjective*, **contraria** *fem*
▷ see **contrario** *noun*
1 opposite
la dirección contraria the opposite direction
Soy contrario a las reformas. I'm opposed to the reforms.
pasarse al bando contrario to go over to the opposing side
todo lo contrario quite the opposite
2 de lo contrario otherwise

el **contrario** *masc noun*
▷ see **contrario** *adj*
1 opposite
al contrario on the contrary
Al contrario, me gusta mucho. On the contrary, I like it a lot.
Es al contrario. It's the opposite way round.
2 por el contrario on the other hand

contrarreloj *adjective*
a contrarreloj against the clock
una carrera a contrarreloj a race against the clock

la **contraseña** *fem noun*
password

el **contrato** *masc noun*
contract

la **contribución** *fem noun*
1 contribution
2 tax

ʃ el **control** *masc noun*
1 control
estar bajo control to be under control
2 llevar el control de algo to keep a check on something
Ella lleva el control de los gastos en casa. She keeps a check on the household expenses.
3 checkpoint
• el **control de la natalidad** birth control
• el **control de pasaportes** passport control
• el **control remoto** remote control

controlar *verb* [17]
1 to control
2 to keep a check on
controlar el peso to keep a check on your weight
controlar las entradas y salidas to keep an eye on the comings and goings

controvertido *masc adjective*, **controvertida** *fem*
controversial
una decisión controvertida a controversial decision

convencer *verb* [44]
1 to convince
2 to persuade
Le convencimos para que fuera. We persuaded him to go.
3 No me convence mucho la idea. I'm not sure about the idea.

conveniente *masc & fem adjective*
1 convenient
2 advisable

♪ **convenir** *verb* **[15]**
1 **to be advisable**
Conviene informarse antes. It's advisable to find out in advance.
Te conviene descansar. It would be advisable to rest.
Te conviene preguntar. You should ask.
2 **convenirle a alguien** to suit someone
Me conviene el sábado. Saturday suits me.
Lo hace porque le conviene. He does it because it suits him.
3 **convenir en algo** to agree on something
Convinieron en reunirse en la oficina del director. They agreed to meet in the headmaster's office.
4 **Sueldo a convenir.** Salary negotiable.

el **convento** *masc noun*
convent

convenza, **convenzo**, **etc** *verb* ▷ **convencer**

♪ la **conversación** *fem noun*
conversation

conversar *verb* **[17]**
(*Latin America*) **to chat**

♪ **convertir** *verb* **[14]**
1 **convertir algo en algo** to turn something into something
Convirtió las libras en euros. He converted the pounds into euros.
2 **to convert** (*to a religion*)

convertirse *reflexive verb* **[14]**
1 **convertirse en algo** to turn into something
Se convirtió en una estrella. She turned into a star.
2 **to convert**
Se convirtió al budismo. She converted to Buddhism.

convierta, **convierto**, **etc** *verb* ▷ **convertir**

el **coñac** *masc noun*
brandy

el & la **cooperante** *masc & fem noun*
voluteer aid worker

cooperar *verb* **[17]**
to cooperate

♪ la **copa** *fem noun*
1 **wine glass**
una copa de vino a glass of wine
2 **drink**
tomar una copa to have a drink
Te invito a una copa. I'll buy you a drink.
3 **cup** (*prize in sports, etc*)
la Copa de Europa the European Cup

la **copia** *fem noun*
copy
• la **copia de seguridad** back-up copy

♪ **copiar** *verb* **[17]**
1 **to copy** (*cheat in exams, etc*)
2 **to make a copy of** (*a document*)
3 **to copy down** (*notes, etc*)

el **coraje** *masc noun*
courage

♪ el **corazón** *masc noun*
1 **heart**
una persona de gran corazón a kind-hearted person
Sufre del corazón. He has heart trouble.
2 **sweetheart**
Vamos, corazón. Let's go sweetheart.

♪ la **corbata** *fem noun*
tie

el **corcho** *masc noun*
cork

♪ el **cordero** *masc noun*
lamb
una pierna de cordero a leg of lamb
una chuleta de cordero a lamb chop

la **cordillera** *masc noun*
mountain range

♪ el **cordón** *masc noun*
1 **string**
2 **flex** (*of electrical appliance*)
• el **cordón de zapato** shoelace

♪ el **coro** *masc noun*
choir
a coro in chorus

la **corona** *fem noun*
1 **crown**
2 **wreath**
una corona de flores a wreath of flowers

el & la **coronel** *masc noun*
colonel

el **corral** *masc noun*
farmyard

♪ la **correa** *fem noun*
1 **strap**
2 **lead** (*for a dog*)
• la **correa de reloj** watchstrap

♪ la **corrección** *fem noun*
correction

correctamente *adverb*
1 **politely**
2 **correctly**
¿Has rellenado el formulario correctamente? Have you filled in the form correctly?

Spanish-English

correcto *masc adjective*, **correcta** *fem*
1 **correct**, **right**
la respuesta correcta the right answer
2 **polite**
Siempre es muy correcto. He's always very polite.

el **corrector ortográfico** *masc noun*
spelling checker

el **corredor** *masc noun*, la **corredora** *fem*
runner
- el **corredor de coches** racing driver
- el **corredor de fondo** long-distance runner

corregir *verb* **[48]**
to correct

el **correo** *masc noun*
1 **post**
mandar algo por correo to send something by post
Mándalo por correo aéreo. Send it by air mail.
echar algo al correo to post something
2 **Correos** the post office
Voy a Correos. I'm going to the post office.

WORD TIP *Correos* is spelt with a capita C; it is never used with *el* when it means post office.

- el **correo aéreo** airmail
- el **correo electrónico** electronic mail; email
- el **correo urgente** special delivery

correr *verb* **[18]**
1 **to run**
¡Corre, que vas a perder el bus! Run, you're going to miss the bus!
Salió corriendo de la habitación. She ran out of the room.
echar a correr to start running
En seguida echaron a correr. They started running straight away.
2 **to go fast** (*cars, bikes, drivers*)
Este coche corre mucho. This car goes very fast
3 (*expressing speed*) **Hice la comida corriendo.** I made dinner quickly.
Vino corriendo a verme. She rushed to see me.
4 **to draw**
Por favor, corre las cortinas. Please draw the curtains.

correrse *reflexive verb* **[17]**
to move up
Córrete a un lado. Move up to make room.

correspondiente *masc & fem adjective*
corresponding

el & la **corresponsal** *masc & fem noun*
correspondent (*in journalism*)

la **corrida** *fem noun* ▷ see **corrido** *adj*
bullfight
Corrida de toros en Almería Bullfights in Almería (*title of poster*)

corrido *masc adjective*, **corrida** *fem*
▷ see **corrida** *noun*
embarrassed

corriente *masc & fem adjective*
▷ see **corriente** *noun*
1 **common**
un error muy corriente a very common mistake
una chica normal y corriente an ordinary kind of girl
Lo más corriente es ... The most usual thing is ...
2 **running**
agua corriente en todas las habitaciones running water in all rooms
3 **estar al corriente de algo** to be aware of something
Siempre está al corriente de lo que pasa. She's always up to date with what's going on.

la **corriente** *fem noun* ▷ see **corriente** *adj*
1 **current** (*in the sea*)
La corriente es muy fuerte. The current's very strong.
2 **current** (*electricity*)
No hay corriente. There's no electricity.
3 **draught**
Hace corriente. There's a draught.

corrija, **corrijo**, **etc** *verb* ▷ **corregir**

corrompido *masc adjective*, **corrompida** *fem*
corrupt

corrupto *masc adjective*, **corrupta** *fem*
corrupt

el **cortacésped** *masc noun*
lawnmower

cortado *masc adjective*, **cortada** *fem*
▷ see **cortado** *noun*
1 **closed** (*road, street, mountain pass*)
2 **off**
La leche está cortada. The milk is off.
3 **ser muy cortado** (*informal*) to be very shy
Su novio es un poco cortado. Her boyfriend's a bit shy.
4 **embarrassed**
estar cortado (*informal*) to be embarrassed

a b c d e f g h i j k l m n ñ o p q r s t u v w x y z

el **cortado** *masc noun* ▷ see **cortado** *adj*
small cup of coffee (*with a dash of milk*)

cortar *verb* **[17]**
1 **to cut**
cortar un pastel to cut a cake
cortar algo por la mitad to cut something in two
Corta la tarta por la mitad. Cut the cake in two.
2 **cortar el césped** to mow the lawn
3 **to chop**
cortar leña to chop wood
cortar un árbol to chop down a tree
4 **to cut off**
Nos han cortado la luz. Our electricity has been cut off.

cortarse *reflexive verb* **[17]**
1 **to cut oneself**
Me he cortado la mano. I've cut my hand.
2 **cortarse el pelo** to have your hair cut
Mañana me voy a cortar el pelo. I'm going to have my hair cut tomorrow.
3 **to be cut off**
Se ha cortado el agua. The water's been cut off.
4 **to go off**
Se ha cortado la leche. The milk's gone off.

el **cortaúñas** *masc noun*
nail clippers

el **corte** *masc noun* ▷ see **corte** *noun*
1 **cut**
hacerse un corte to cut yourself
Se hizo un corte en el dedo. He cut his finger.
un corte de pelo a haircut
Ha habido un corte de agua. The water's been cut off.
2 **corte y confección** dressmaking
3 (*informal*) **embarrassment**
¡Qué corte! How embarrassing!

la **corte** *fem noun* ▷ see **corte** *noun*
court
la Corte Suprema the Supreme Court
las Cortes the Spanish Parliament (*in Madrid*)

cortés *masc & fem adjective*
polite

la **corteza** *fem noun*
1 **bark** (*of a tree*)
2 **rind** (*of cheese*)
3 **crust** (*of bread*)
4 **peel** (*of an orange or a lemon*)

la **cortina** *fem noun*
curtain

corto *masc adjective*, **corta** *fem*
short

la **cosa** *fem noun*
1 **thing**
Se llevó todas sus cosas. He took all his things.
Te he comprado una cosa. I've bought something for you.
¿Qué tal van las cosas? How are things?
2 **alguna cosa** something
Por si pasa alguna cosa. In case something happens.
3 **alguna cosa** anything (*in questions*)
¿Buscas alguna cosa en especial? Are you looking for anything in particular?
¿Quiere alguna otra cosa? Do you want anything else?
4 **cualquier cosa** anything
Si necesitas alguna cosa, dímelo. If you need anything, tell me.

la **cosecha** *fem noun*
1 **harvest**
2 **crop**
3 **vintage** (*of wine*)

cosechar *verb* **[17]**
to harvest

coser *verb* **[18]**
to sew

cosmético *masc adjective*, **cosmética** *fem*
▷ see **cosmético** *noun*
cosmetic

el **cosmético** *masc noun*
▷ see **cosmético** *adj*
cosmetic

las **cosquillas** *plural fem noun*
hacerle cosquillas a alguien to tickle somebody
tener cosquillas to be ticklish

la **costa** *fem noun*
coast

el **costado** *masc noun*
side

costar *verb* **[24]**
1 **to cost**
¿Cuánto cuesta? How much does it cost?
Cuesta muy caro. It's very expensive.
La comida cuesta poco. Food is cheap.
Me costó barato. It didn't cost me very much.
2 **to be hard**
Cuesta mucho entenderlo. It's very hard to understand. ⏩

Cuesta un poco acostumbrarse. It takes a bit of getting used to.
Me costó hacerlo. I found it difficult to do.

Costa Rica *fem noun*
Costa Rica

costarricense *masc & fem adjective & noun*
1 Costa Rican
2 *un & una* **costarricense** Costa Rican

WORD TIP Adjectives and nouns for nationality and regional origin do not have capital letters in Spanish.

el **coste** *masc noun*
cost

la **costilla** *fem noun*
rib

costoso *masc adjective*, **costosa** *fem*
expensive

la **costra** *fem noun*
scab

la **costumbre** *fem noun*
1 habit
Viene los martes por costumbre. He comes on Tuesdays out of habit.
Tengo la costumbre de hacerlo así. I'm in the habit of doing it this way.
2 **de costumbre** as usual
el lugar de costumbre the usual place
3 custom

la **costura** *fem noun*
1 needlework
2 seam

cotidiano *masc adjective*, **cotidiana** *fem*
daily

cotilla *masc & fem noun*
gossip
Es muy cotilla. He's such a gossip.

cotillear *verb* [17]
to gossip

el **cráneo** *fem noun*
skull

la **creación** *fem noun*
creation

creador *masc adjective*, **creadora** *fem*
▷ see **creador** *noun*
creative

el **creador** *masc noun*, la **creadora** *fem*
▷ see **creador** *adj*
creator

crear *verb* [17]
to create

crecer *verb* [35]
1 to grow
Su hermana ha crecido mucho. His sister's grown a lot.
2 to grow up
Creció en Escocia. She grew up in Scotalnd.

el **crédito** *masc noun*
1 credit (*in a shop*)
2 loan (*from a bank*)
• el **crédito hipotecario** mortgage

creer *verb* [37]
1 to think
Creo que se llama Nekane. I think she's called Nekane.
¿Crees que me llamará? Do you think he'll phone me?
Creo que sí. I think so.
Creo que no. I don't think so.
2 to believe
No lo creo. I don't believe it.
¿Crees en Dios? Do you believe in God?

creíble *masc & fem adjective*
believable

la **crema** *fem noun*
cream
• la **crema bronceadora** suntan lotion
• la **crema hidratante** moisturizer

la **cremallera** *fem noun*
zip
subirse la cremallera to do up your zip

el **crepúsculo** *masc noun*
twilight

creyendo, **creyó**, **etc** *verb* ▷ **creer**

crezca, **crezco**, **etc** *verb* ▷ **crecer**

el **crío** *masc noun*, la **cría** *fem*
1 child
2 **la cría** baby animal
una cría de leopardo a baby leopard

el **criado** *masc noun*, la **criada** *fem*
servant

criar *verb* [17]
1 to bring up
Lo crió su tía. He was brought up by his aunt.
2 to breed
criar ganado to breed cattle

criarse *reflexive verb* [17]
to grow up
Se crió en un pueblo. He grew up in a village.

♪ el **crimen** *masc noun*
1 **crime**
cometer un crimen to commit a crime
2 **murder**
cometer un crimen to commit murder

el & la **criminal** *masc & fem noun*
criminal

la **crisis** *fem noun*
1 **crisis**
2 (*Medicine*) **attack**

♪ el **cristal** *masc noun*
1 **glass**
Es de cristal. It's made of glass.
2 **window pane**
limpiar los cristales to clean the windows.
La pelota rompió un cristal. The ball broke a window pane.
3 **piece of broken glass**
El suelo estaba lleno de cristales. The floor was covered with broken glass.

el **cristianismo** *masc noun*
Christianity

cristiano *masc adjective & noun*, **cristiana** *fem adjective & noun*
1 **Christian**
2 **un cristiano, una cristiana** Christian

WORD TIP Adjectives and nouns for religion do not have capital letters in Spanish.

Cristo *masc noun*
(*Religion*) **Christ**

el **criterio** *masc noun*
1 **judgement**
2 **guideline**

la **crítica** *fem noun*
1 **criticism**
Recibió duras críticas. He came in for a lot of harsh criticism.
2 **review**
La película ha recibido muy buenas críticas. The film has had very good reviews.

criticar *verb* **[31]**
1 **to criticize** (*a person, a plan*)
2 **to review** (*a film, an album*)

el **cromo** *masc noun*
sticker

♪ el **cruce** *masc noun*
1 **crossroads**
2 **'Cruce peligroso'** 'Dangerous Junction'
3 **crossing**
• el **cruce de peatones** pedestrian crossing

el **crucero** *masc noun*
cruise (*on a ship*)

♪ el **crucigrama** *masc noun*
crossword

crudo *masc adjective*, **cruda** *fem*
1 **raw**
una zanahoria cruda a raw carrot
2 **La carne está cruda.** The meat is raw.
3 **harsh**
la cruda realidad the harsh reality

cruel *masc & fem adjective*
cruel

la **crueldad** *fem noun*
cruelty
Trataron a los prisioneros con gran crueldad. The prisoners were treated with great cruelty.

la **cruz** *fem noun*, **cruces** *plural*
1 **cross**
2 **¿Cara o cruz?** Heads or tails?
• la **Cruz Roja** the Red Cross

♪ **cruzar** *verb* **[22]**
1 **to cross** (*a street, road*)
cruzar la calle to cross the road.
Crucé la calle corriendo. I ran across the road.
2 **to cross** (*your arms, legs*)
cruzar los brazos to cross your arms

cruzarse *reflexive verb* **[22]**
1 **to cross** (*roads, paths, letters*)
2 **to pass each other**
Me crucé con ella en la calle. I met her in the street.
Los dos coches se cruzaron. The two cars passed each other.

♪ el **cuaderno** *masc noun*
1 **exercise book**
2 **notebook**

la **cuadra** *fem noun*
stable

♪ **cuadrado** *masc adjective*, **cuadrada** *fem*
▷ see **cuadrado** *noun*
square
de forma cuadrada square-shaped

♪ el **cuadrado** *masc noun*
▷ see **cuadrado** *adj*
square (*shape*)

♪ el **cuadro** *masc noun*
1 **painting**
2 **picture**
3 (*in designs*) **a cuadros**, **de cuadros** checked
una tela a cuadros a checked cloth

el cual *masc pronoun*, **la cual** *fem pron*, **los cuales** *masc plural*, **las cuales** *fem plural* ▷ see **cuál** *pron*

1 (*talking about people*) **Pregunté a mi hermano, el cual me dio las señas.** I asked my brother, who gave me the address. (*el cual* for *hermano*)
Las chicas a las cuales invité. The girls whom I invited (*las cuales* for *chicas*).

2 (*talking about things*) **La casa en la cual se encontraron drogas.** The house in which drugs were found (*la cual* for *casa*).
Los ingredientes con los cuales se prepara este plato. The ingredients with which this dish is made (*los cuales* for *ingredientes*).

3 (*talking about something mentioned before*) **lo cual** which
No ha llamado, lo cual es extraño. He hasn't rung, which is strange.

4 **por lo cual** therefore

cuál *masc & fem pronoun*, **cuáles** *plural masc & fem* ▷ see **cual** *pron*

1 **what**
¿Cuál es su profesión? What's your profession?
¿Cuáles son tus preferencias? What are your preferences?

2 **which, which one**
¿Cuál te gusta más? Which one do you like best?

WORD TIP *cuál* with an accent is used for questions (¿...?).

cualesquiera *adjective, pronoun* ▷ **cualquiera**

la **cualidad** *fem noun*
quality

cualquier *adjective* ▷ **cualquiera**

cualquiera, **cualesquiera** *adjective* ▷ see **cualquiera** *pron*
any
Traéme cualquier vaso., Traéme un vaso cualquiera. Bring me any glass.
Cualquier alumna sabe eso., Una alumna cualquiera sabe eso. Any schoolgirl knows that.

WORD TIP *cualquiera* becomes *cualquier* before a singular noun.

cualquiera *pronoun* ▷ see **cualquiera** *adj*

1 **anybody, anyone**
Cualquiera lo sabe. Anybody knows that.

2 **any one (of them)**
Cualquiera servirá. Any one of them will do.

3 **either** (*of two people or things*)
'¿Cuál de los dos quieres?'—'Cualquiera.' 'Which of the two do you want?'—'Either of them.'

4 **whichever one** (*of more than two people or things*)
Coge cualquiera que quieras. Pick whichever one you want.
Toma cualesquiera que quieras. Take whichever ones you want.

WORD TIP *cualquiera* is singular; *cualesquiera* is plural.

cuando *conjunction* ▷ see **cuándo** *adv*
when
Cuando estuve en Barcelona. When I was in Barcelona.
Cuando la vea la próxima semana. When I see her next week.

cuándo *adverb* ▷ see **cuando** *conj*
when?
¿Cuándo la conociste? When did you meet her?
¿Desde cuándo? Since when?
No sé cuándo llegará. I don't know when he'll arrive.

WORD TIP *cuándo* with an accent, is used for questions (¿...?).

cuanto *adverb, adjective & pronoun*, **cuanta** *fem* ▷ see **cuánto** *adv, adj, pron*

1 **as much, as much as**
Corta cuanta tela necesites. Cut as much fabric as you need.
Tengo cuanto necesito. I've got as much as I need.
Llama cuanto quieras. Phone as much as you want.

2 **cuantos, cuantas** as many as
Compra cuantos libros necesites. Buy as many books as you need.
Tengo cuantos necesito. I have as many as I need.

3 **unos cuantos, unas cuantas** a few
unos cuantos empleados a few employees
unas cuantas señoras a few ladies

4 **cuanto más ...** the more ...
Cuanto más pides, más te darán. The more you ask, the more you'll be given.

5 **cuanto menos ...** the less ...
Cuanto menos ruido hagas mejor. The less noise you make, the better.

cuánto *adverb, adjective & pronoun*, **cuánta** *adjective & pronoun*

1 **cuánto, cuánta** how much
¿Cuánto café quieres? How much coffee do you want?

¿Cuánto cuesta? How much does it cost?
'Pon agua'—'¿Cuánta?' 'Add some water'—'How much?'
¿Cuanto tiempo has tardado en hacerlo? How long did you take to do it?

2 **cuántos, cuántas** how many
¿Cuántas tazas saco? How many cups should I put out?
Dime cuántos necesitas. Tell me how many you need.

3 (*in exclamations*) **¡Cuántas personas hay!** What a lot of people there are!
¡Cuántas hay! What a lot there are!
¡Cuánta comida has hecho! What a lot of food you've prepared!
¡Cuánto ha quedado! What a lot is left over!
¡Cuánto te quiero! How I love you!

WORD TIP *cuánto*, with an accent, is used for questions (¿...?) and exclamations (¡...!).

ʆ **cuarenta** *number*
forty
cuarenta y siete forty-seven
Mi madre tiene cuarenta años. My mum's forty.

la **cuaresma** *fem noun*
Lent

la **cuarta** *fem noun*
fourth gear
meter la cuarta to change into fourth

cuartel *noun*
barracks
- el **cuartel general** headquarters

ʆ el **cuarto** *masc noun* ▷ see **cuarto** *adj*

1 **quarter** (*when telling the time*)
a las doce menos cuarto at quarter to twelve
Son las dos y cuarto. It's quarter past two.

2 **quarter**
un cuarto de kilo a quarter of a kilo
Corté la tarta en cuatro cuartos. I cut the cake into four quarters.

3 **room**
el cuarto de los niños the children's bedroom
- el **cuarto de baño** bathroom
- el **cuarto de estar** living room
- los **cuartos de final** quarter finals

ʆ **cuarto** *masc adjective*, **cuarta** *fem* ▷ see **cuarto** *noun*
fourth
en el cuarto piso on the fourth floor
llegar en cuarto lugar to finish in fourth position

ʆ **cuatro** *number*

1 **four**
Juan tiene cuatro años. Juan's four (years old).
Son las cuatro. It's four o'clock.

2 **fourth** (*in dates*)
el cuatro de mayo the fourth of May

ʆ **cuatrocientos, cuatrocientas** *number*
four hundred
cuatrocientos quince four hundred and fifteen

Cuba *fem noun*
Cuba

cubano *masc adjective & noun*, **cubana** *fem adjective & noun*

1 **Cuban**

2 **un cubano, una cubana** Cuban

WORD TIP Adjectives and nouns for nationality and regional origin do not have capital letters in Spanish.

ʆ **cubierto** *masc adjective*, **cubierta** *fem* ▷ see **cubierto** *noun*
covered
estar cubierto de algo to be covered with something
El suelo estaba cubierto de papeles. The ground was covered with paper.

el **cubierto** *masc noun* ▷ see **cubierto** *adj*

1 **los cubiertos** the cutlery
Pon los cubiertos en la mesa. Put the knives and forks on the table.

2 **poner otro cubierto en la mesa** to lay another place at the table
- los **cubiertos de plata** silver cutlery

ʆ el **cubo** *masc noun*

1 **cube**

2 **bucket**
un cubo de agua a bucket of water
- el **cubo de la basura** bin

el **cubrecama** *masc noun*
bedspread

ʆ **cubrir** *verb* **[46]**
to cover

cubrirse *reflexive verb* **[46]**

1 **to cover yourself**
Me cubrí las rodillas. I covered my legs.

2 **to cloud over**
El cielo se ha cubierto. The sky has clouded over.

ʆ la **cucaracha** *fem noun*
cockroach

la cuchara *fem noun*
spoon
- la **cuchara de postre** dessert spoon
- la **cuchara sopera** soup spoon

la cucharada *fem noun*
spoonful

la cucharadita *fem noun*
teaspoonful

la cucharilla, la **cucharita** *fem noun*
teaspoon
una cucharilla de café, una cucharita de café a coffee spoon

cuchichear *verb* **[17]**
to whisper

la cuchilla *fem noun*
blade
- la **cuchilla de afeitar** razor blade

el cuchillo *masc noun*
knife

cuelga, **cuelgo**, **etc** *verb* ▷ **colgar**

el cuello *masc noun*
1 **neck**
2 **collar**
el cuello de la camisa the shirt collar
un jersey de cuello alto a polo-neck jumper

el cuenco *masc noun*
bowl

cuenta, **cuento**, **etc** *verb* ▷ **contar**

la cuenta *fem noun* ▷ see **cuento** *noun*
1 **bill**
¿Nos trae la cuenta, por favor? Could you bring us the bill, please?
2 **account** (*in a bank*)
hacer cuentas to do the accounts
Haz las cuentas de lo que te debo. Work out how much I owe you.
trabajar por su cuenta to be self-employed
Mi padre trabaja por su propia cuenta. My father's self-employed.
3 **darse cuenta de algo** to realize something
Me di cuenta de que había perdido la cartera. I realized I'd lost my wallet.
4 **sum**
hacer una cuenta to do a sum
llevar la cuenta de algo to keep count of something
Lleva la cuenta de lo que está gastando. Keep count of what he's spending.
5 **más de la cuenta** too much
Bebió más de la cuenta. He drank too much.
6 **bead** (*of a necklace*)
- la **cuenta atrás** countdown
- la **cuenta corriente** current account
- la **cuenta de ahorros** savings account

el cuento *masc noun*
1 **short story**
2 **tale**
3 **No me vengas con tus cuentos.** Don't come to me with your stories.
- el **cuento de hadas** fairy tale

la cuerda *fem noun*
1 **rope**
2 **saltar a la cuerda** to skip
3 **darle cuerda a algo** to wind something up
darle cuerda a un reloj to wind a clock

el cuerno *masc noun*
1 **horn**
2 **antler**

el cuero *masc noun*
leather
un bolso de cuero a leather bag
- el **cuero cabelludo** scalp

el cuerpo *masc noun*
body

el cuervo *masc noun*
crow

cuesta, **cueste**, **etc** *verb* ▷ **costar**

la cuesta *fem noun*
1 **slope**
subir una cuesta to go up a slope
ir cuesta arriba to go uphill
ir cuesta abajo to go downhill

la cuestión *fem noun*
matter
Hablaremos de esta cuestión más tarde. We'll talk about this later.
La cuestión es ... The thing is ...

la cueva *fem noun*
cave

cueza, **cuezo**, **etc** *verb* ▷ **cocer**

el cuidado *masc noun* ▷ see **cuidado** *excl*
1 **tener cuidado con algo** to be careful with something
Ten cuidado con los vasos. Be careful with the glasses.
¡Cuidado con el escalón! Mind the step!
2 **hacer algo con cuidado** to do something carefully
Lo cogí con cuidado. I picked it up carefully.
3 **care**
el cuidado de la salud health care
- los **cuidados intensivos** intensive care

cuidado *exclamation* ▷ see **cuidado** *noun*
¡Cuidado! Watch out!
¡Cuidado con el perro! Beware of the dog!

cuidadoso *masc adjective*, **cuidadosa** *fem*
careful

⚷ **cuidar** *verb* [17]
1 cuidar a alguien
cuidar de alguien to look after someone
Yo cuido a los niños. I look after the children.
Cuidan de su padre enfermo. They look after their sick father.

cuidarse *reflexive verb*
to take care of yourself
¡Cuídate! Take care!, Take care of yourself!

⚷ la **culebra** *fem noun*
snake

el **culebrón** *masc noun*
soap opera (*TV entertainment*)

⚷ el **culo** *masc noun* (*informal*)
bum

⚷ la **culpa** *fem noun*
1 fault
Es su culpa. It's his fault.
No es mi culpa. It's not my fault.
Luis tiene la culpa. It's Luis's fault.
2 echarle la culpa a alguien to blame someone
Me echan la culpa de lo que pasó. They blame me for what happened.
3 guilt
Ella tiene la culpa. She's the guilty one.

culpable *masc & fem adjective*
▷ see **culpable** *noun*
1 guilty
sentirse culpable de algo to feel guilty about something
2 ser culpable de un crimen to be guilty of a crime

el & la **culpable** *masc & fem noun*
▷ see **culpable** *adj*
guilty one
Él es el culpable. He's the guilty one.

⚷ **culpar** *verb* [17]
to blame
culpar a alguien de algo to blame somebody for something
Le culparon del incendio. He was blamed for the fire.

cultivar *verb* [17]
1 to grow (*fruit, vegetables*)
2 to cultivate (*land*)

el **culto** *masc noun*
1 cult
2 worship
la libertad de culto the freedom of worship

⚷ la **cultura** *fem noun*
1 culture
2 knowledge
preguntas de cultura general general knowledge questions

el **culturismo** *masc noun*
bodybuilding

⚷ el **cumpleaños** *masc noun*
birthday
fiesta de cumpleaños birthday party
¿Cuándo es tu cumpleaños? When's your birthday?
¡Feliz cumpleaños! Happy Birthday!

⚷ **cumplir** *verb* [19]
1 (*talking about age*) ¿Cuándo cumples años? When's your birthday?
Mañana cumplo quince años. I'll be fifteen tomorrow.
¡Que cumplas muchos más! Many happy returns!
2 to keep (*a promise*)
cumplir una promesa to keep a promise
No has cumplido con tus obligaciones. You haven't done your duty.
3 to fulfil (*conditions*)
4 to carry out (*a task, an order*)
5 to serve
cumplir una condena to serve a sentence

la **cuna** *fem noun*
1 cradle
2 cot

el **cuñado** *masc noun*, la **cuñada** *fem*
1 brother-in-law
2 sister-in-law

cupe, **cupiera**, **cupo**, **etc** *verb* ▷ **caber**

⚷ el **cura** *masc noun* ▷ see **cura** *noun*
priest

la **cura** *fem noun* ▷ see **cura** *noun*
cure

curar *verb* [17]
1 to cure (*an illness, a sick person*)
2 to dress (*a wound*)

curarse *reflexive verb* [17]
to get better

curioso *masc adjective*, **curiosa** *fem*
curious
¡Qué curiosa eres! You're so curious!
Lo curioso es que ... The funny thing is ...
Es curioso que ... It's strange that ...

cursar *verb* **[17]**
1 **to study** (*physics, maths, etc*)
2 **to be in** (*a year at school, etc*)
Estoy cursando cuarto de ESO. I'm in year four of ESO.

el **curioso** *masc noun*, la **curiosa** *fem*
busybody

el **cursillo** *masc noun*
(short) course

el **currículum** *masc noun*
CV, curriculum vitae

la **cursiva** *fem noun*
italics
en cursiva in italics

el **curso** *masc noun*
1 **year** (*in school*)
¿En qué curso estás? What year are you in?
Mi hermana está en el primer curso. My sister's in first year.
2 **course** (*programme of study*)
- el **curso escolar** academic year
- el **curso intensivo** intensive course

el **cursor** *masc noun*
cursor

la **curva** *fem noun* ▷ see **curvo** *adj*
bend
una curva peligrosa a sharp bend
tomar una curva to take a bend

curvo *masc adjective*, **curva** *fem*
▷ see **curva** *noun*
curved

cuyo *masc adjective*, **cuya** *fem*
whose
El amigo cuyo ordenador utilicé. The friend whose computer I used.
Las chicas cuya familia llegó ayer. The girls whose family arrived yesterday.

WORD TIP *cuyo, cuya* agrees with the thing owned; *ordenador* and *familia* above.

Spanish-English

a b c d e f g h i j k l m n ñ o p q r s t u v w x y z

D d

el **dado** *masc noun*
dice
tirar los dados to throw the dice

la **dama** *fem noun*
lady
damas y caballeros ladies and gentlemen
• la **dama de honor** bridesmaid

dan *verb* ▷ **dar**

danés *masc adjective & noun*, **danesa** *fem adjective & noun*
1 **Danish**
2 **un danés, una danesa** Dane (*person*)
el danés Danish (*the language*)

WORD TIP Adjectives and nouns for nationality, regional origin, and language do not have capital letters in Spanish.

la **danza** *fem noun*
dance
estudiar danza to study dance

dañar *verb* **[17]**
to damage

dañino *masc adjective*, **dañina** *fem*
harmful

el **daño** *masc noun*
1 **hacerle daño a alguien** to hurt someone
No quiero hacerte daño. I don't want to hurt you.
hacerse daño to hurt yourself
Te vas a hacer daño. You are going to hurt yourself.
¿Se hizo daño al caer? Did she hurt herself when she fell?
Me hice daño en la pierna. I hurt my leg.
2 **damage**
Diez casas sufrieron daños. Ten houses suffered damage.

dar *verb* **[4]**
1 **to give**
Dale esta carta a María. Give this letter to María.
Me dio su número de teléfono. He gave me his telephone number.
Dame un beso. Give me a kiss.
Dale recuerdos. Give him my regards.
¿Me da un kilo de tomates? Can I have a kilo of tomatoes?
Me dieron un premio. I got a prize.
dar las gracias to say thank you
darle de comer a alguien to feed somebody
Les dio de comer a los niños. He fed the children.
2 **to turn on**
dar la luz to turn on the light
darle a un botón to press a button
darle a un interruptor to flick a switch
3 **to strike** (*the hour*)
El reloj dio las doce. The clock struck twelve.
4 **to give** (*a party*)
Va a dar una fiesta mañana. He's having a party tomorrow.
¿Qué dan en el cine? What's on at the cinema?
5 **to say**
dar los buenos días to say good morning
6 **to go for** (*a stroll, a walk, a drive, etc*)
dar un paseo to go for a walk
Vamos a dar una vuelta en el coche. We're going for a drive.
7 (*saying something has an effect*) **Me dio miedo.** It scared me.
Este jersey da mucho calor. This jumper is very warm.
Las patatas fritas le dieron sed. The crisps made him thirsty.
8 (*with rooms, buildings, etc*) **dar a un lugar** to open onto a place
La puerta da al salón. The door opens into the living room.
La habitación da al mar. The room looks onto the sea.

darse *reflexive verb* **[4]**
1 **to have**
darse un baño to have a bath
darse una ducha to have a shower
2 **darse un golpe** to bump yourself
Me di con el pie en el bordillo. I hit my foot on the kerb.
3 (*with skills*) **Se le dan bien las matemáticas.** She's good at maths.
No se me da bien pintar. I'm not good at painting.

el **dardo** *masc noun*
dart
jugar a los dardos to play darts

la **dársena** *fem noun*
1 **bay** (*in a bus station*)
2 **dry dock** (*for ships*)

a b c d e f g h i j k l m n ñ o p q r s t u v w x y z

♪ el **dato** *masc noun*
1 **piece of information**
No tengo todos los datos. I don't have all the information.
2 **los datos** data
- los **datos informativos** information
- los **datos personales** personal details

♪ **dC** *abbreviation*
(= *después de Cristo*) **AD**

d. de J.C. *abbreviation*
(= *después de Jesucristo*) **AD**

♪ **de** *preposition* ▷ see **dé** *verb*
1 **of**
el nombre del libro the name of the book
un vaso de leche a glass of milk
una caja de naranjas a box of oranges
un tercio del total a third of the total
el mes de marzo the month of March
2 (*to show belonging*) **el coche de mis padres** my parents' car
Esto es de Juan. This is Juan's.
Fuimos a casa de Isa. We went to Isa's house.
3 **from**
Soy de Sevilla. I'm from Sevilla.
de Madrid a Bilbao from Madrid to Bilbao
de la cabeza a los pies from head to toe
No hemos tenido noticias de María. We haven't heard from María.
4 **made of**
flores de plástico plastic flowers
una silla de madera a wooden chair
Es de hierro. It's made of iron.
5 (*describing people, things*) **un hombre de veinte años** a twenty-year-old man
una moneda de dos euros a two-euro coin
una clase de español a Spanish lesson
una película de miedo a horror film
una niña de pelo corto a girl with short hair
Es la chica del jersey a rayas. It's the girl with the striped jumper.
6 (*showing use*) **los vasos del vino** the wine glasses
el cubo de la basura the rubbish bin
7 (*to say something is best, biggest, etc*) **el mejor de todos** the best of all
la ciudad más grande del mundo the biggest city in the world
el más inteligente de la clase the cleverest in the class
el más bonito de los tres the prettiest of the three
8 **than** (*in comparisons*)
más de quince more than fifteen
El doble de lo que yo gano. Twice what I earn.
9 (*in names*) **la estación de Victoria** Victoria Station
la ciudad de Barcelona Barcelona
10 (*in time expressions*) **a las dos de la tarde** at two in the afternoon
de día by day
Viajaron de día. They travelled by day.
Trabajan de noche. They work at night.
11 **trabajar de algo** to work as something
Trabajo de enfermera. I work as a nurse.

WORD TIP *de* + *el* becomes *del*.

dé *verb* ▷ **dar**

♪ **debajo** *adverb, preposition*
1 **underneath**
Pon un plato debajo. Put a plate underneath.
2 **El que está debajo.** The one that's underneath.
3 **debajo de** under, underneath
Está debajo del sofá. It's under the sofa.
4 **por debajo de** below, under
a temperaturas por debajo de los cinco grados at temperatures below ten degrees
El agua entró por debajo de la puerta. The water came in under the door.

WORD TIP *debajo* is used by itself; *debajo de* is followed by a noun or pronoun.

♪ el **deber** *masc noun* ▷ see **deber** *verb*
1 **duty**
cumplir con tu deber to do your duty
2 **los deberes** homework
hacer los deberes to do your homework
Aún no he hecho los deberes. I haven't done my homework yet.

♪ **deber** *verb* **[18]** ▷ see **deber** *noun*
1 **to owe**
Te debo veinte euros. I owe you twenty euros.
2 **must**
Debes intentarlo. You must try.
Deberás estudiar mucho. You will have to study hard.
3 **should**
Deberías descansar. You should have a rest.
Deberías haber seguido mis consejos. You should have followed my advice.

debido *masc adjective*, **debida** *fem*
1 **due**
a su debido tiempo in due course
con el debido respeto with due respect
con el debido cuidado with the necessary care
2 **como es debido** properly
Pórtate como es debido. Behave properly.

3 **debido a** due to
No podía trabajar debido al accidente. She was unable to work due to the accident.

♪ **débil** *masc & fem adjective*
weak

♪ la **década** *fem noun*
decade
la década de los sesenta the sixties

♪ la **decena** *fem noun*
una decena de libros about ten books
Divídelos por decenas. Divide them into tens.

decente *masc & fem adjective*
decent

la **decepción** *fem noun*
disappointment

WORD TIP *decepción* does not mean *deception* in English; for the meaning of *deception* ▷ **engaño**.

♪ **decepcionar** *verb* **[17]**
to disappoint
La película nos decepcionó. The film disappointed us.

♪ **decidir** *verb* **[19]**
to decide
Decidí quedarme. I decided to stay.

decidirse *reflexive verb* **[19]**
1 **to make up your mind**
Aún no se ha decidido. She hasn't made up her mind.
2 **decidirse a hacer algo** to decide to do something
Se decidió a ir de vacaciones. She decided to go on holiday.
Se decidió a aprender a conducir. He decided to learn to drive.

♪ **décimo** *masc adjective*, **décima** *fem*
tenth
el décimo piso the tenth floor
una décima parte a tenth

♪ **decir** *verb* **[5]**
1 **to say**
Dice que sí viene. He says he is coming.
¿Qué dijiste? What did you say?
Aquí dice que ... It says here that ...
¡No me digas! You don't say!
2 **to tell**
Me ha dicho que no viene. He's told me he's not coming.
Dime lo que quieres. Tell me what you want.
No digas mentiras. Don't tell lies.
3 (*on the phone*) **¿Diga?**, **¿Dígame?** Hello?
4 (*when someone speaks to you*) **Dime.** Yes?
'¡Alicia!'—'¿Dime?' 'Alicia!'—'Yes?'

♪ la **decisión** *fem noun*
decision
tomar una decisión to make a decision

declarar *verb* **[17]**
1 **to declare**
declarar la guerra to declare war
¿Algo que declarar? Anything to declare? (*at customs*)
2 **to give evidence**
Se ha negado a declarar. He's refused to give evidence.

declararse *reflexive verb* **[17]**
declararse culpable to plead guilty
declararse inocente to plead not guilty

el **decorador** *masc noun*, la **decoradora** *fem*
interior designer

decorar *verb* **[17]**
to decorate

♪ el **dedo** *masc noun*
1 **finger**
hacer dedo to hitch-hike
2 **el dedo del pie** toe
el dedo gordo del pie the big toe
• el **dedo anular** ring finger
• el **dedo corazón** middle finger
• el **dedo índice** index finger
• el **dedo meñique** little finger
• el **dedo pulgar** thumb

♪ el **defecto** *masc noun*
flaw, **defect**

♪ **defectuoso** *masc adjective*, **defectuosa** *fem*
faulty

♪ **defender** *verb* **[36]**
to defend

defenderse *reflexive verb* **[36]**
1 **to defend yourself**
2 **to get by**
Me defiendo en inglés. I get by in English.

♪ la **defensa** *fem noun*
1 **defence**
2 **defender** (*in sport*)
• la **defensa personal** self-defence

el **defensor** *masc noun*, la **defensora** *fem*
defender
• el **defensor del pueblo** ombudsman

♪ **deficiente** *masc & fem adjective*
deficient
una alimentación deficiente en vitaminas a diet deficient in vitamins

la **definición** *fem noun*
definition

definitivo *masc adjective*, **definitiva** *fem*
definitive

dejar *verb* [17]
1 **to leave**
Quiere dejar el colegio. She wants to leave school.
Ha dejado a su novia. He's left his girlfriend.
¡Déjala en paz! Leave her alone!
2 **to let**
¡Déjame entrar! Let me in!
No la dejan salir los domingos. They don't let her go out on Sundays.
3 **to lend**
¿Me dejas un boli? Can you lend me a pen?
Le he dejado mis apuntes. I've lent him my notes.
4 **dejar caer algo** to drop something
Dejó caer los libros en el escritorio. She dropped the books on the desk.
5 **dejar de hacer algo** to stop doing something
¡Deja de molestar! Stop being a nuisance!
dejar de fumar to give up smoking
No dejes de llamarme cuando llegues. Make sure you phone me when you get there.

dejarse *reflexive verb* [17]
1 **to leave**
Me he dejado las gafas en el coche. I left my glasses in the car.
2 **dejarse barba** to grow a beard
dejarse el pelo largo to grow your hair long

del *preposition*
of the
el respaldo del asiento the back of the chair

WORD TIP *de* + *el* becomes *del*. ▷ **de**

el **delantal** *masc noun*
apron

delante *adverb, preposition*
1 **ir delante** to go on ahead
2 **de delante** front
el asiento de delante the front seat
la parte de delante the front part
3 **por delante: Entraron por delante.** They came in through the front.
Lleva un bolsillo por delante. It has a pocket at the front.
4 **delante de** in front of
delante de mí in front of me
Está delante de la iglesia. It's in front of the church.

WORD TIP *delante* is used by itself; *delante de* is followed by a noun or pronoun.

delantero *masc adjective*, **delantera** *fem*
▷ see **delantero** *noun*
front
la rueda delantera the front wheel

el **delantero** *masc noun*, la **delantera** *fem*
▷ see **delantero** *adj*
forward (*in sport*)

deletrear *verb* [17]
to spell
¿Me lo deletreas? Could you spell it for me?

el **delfín** *masc noun*
dolphin

delgado *masc adjective*, **delgada** *fem*
thin

delicado *masc adjective*, **delicada** *fem*
1 **delicate**
una situación delicada a delicate situation
2 **fragile** (*a piece of china, etc*)
3 **sensitive** (*skin*)

delicioso *masc adjective*, **deliciosa** *fem*
delicious

el & la **delincuente** *masc & fem noun*
criminal

el **delito** *masc noun*
crime
cometer un delito to commit a crime

demás *invariable adjective*
▷ see **demás** *pron*
los demás alumnos the rest of the pupils
las demás cartas the rest of the letters

WORD TIP *demás* never changes.

demás *pronoun* ▷ see **demás** *adj*
1 **lo demás** the rest
Lo demás lo traigo mañana. I'll bring the rest tomorrow.
Aquí está todo lo demás. Here's everything else.
2 **los demás, las demás** the rest, the others
los problemas de los demás other people's problems
Los demás se quedan aquí. The rest can stay here.

demasiado *masc adjective & pronoun*, **demasiada** *fem adj & pron*
▷ see **demasiado** *adv*
1 **too much**
Gasta demasiado. He spends too much.

Gasta demasiado dinero. He spends too much money.
Hay demasiada comida. There is too much food.
Preparó demasiados. She got too much ready.
Hacía demasiado calor. It was too hot.
2 too many
demasiadas veces too many times, too often
Eran demasiados. There were too many of them.
Hay demasiadas personas aquí. There are too many people here.

demasiado *adverb*
▷ see **demasiado** *adj, pron*
1 too much
No trabajes demasiado. Don't work too hard.
2 too
Los billetes eran demasiado caros. The tickets were too expensive.

la **democracia** *fem noun*
democracy

demoler *verb* [38]
to demolish

la **demolición** *fem noun*
demolition

el **demonio** *masc noun*
devil

la **demora** *fem noun*
delay
sin demora without delay

demos, **den** *verb* ▷ **dar**

la **densidad** *fem noun*
1 thickness (*of vegetation*)
2 density

dentado *masc adjective*, **dentada** *fem*
jagged

el **dentífrico** *masc noun*
toothpaste

el & la **dentista** *masc & fem noun*
dentist

dentro *adverb, preposition*
1 inside
desde dentro from inside
aquí dentro in here
allí dentro in there
Ponlo aquí dentro. Put it in here.
2 inside, indoors
Está dentro. She's inside.
pasar dentro to go inside, to go indoors
3 dentro de inside, in
dentro del edificio inside the building
dentro de la caja in the box
dentro de dos semanas in two weeks' time
dentro de poco shortly
4 por dentro on the inside
Por dentro es verde. It's green on the inside.
Lo limpié por dentro. I've cleaned the inside.

WORD TIP *dentro* is used by itself; *dentro de* is followed by a noun or pronoun.

la **denuncia** *fem noun*
1 report (*to the police*)
2 statement

denunciar *verb* [17]
to report (*a person, crime*)
Hay que denunciarlo en la comisaría. You must report it at the police station.

el **departamento** *masc noun*
1 department
2 (*Latin America*) apartment, flat

depender *verb* [18]
to depend
depender de algo to depend on something
Depende del resultado. It depends on the result.
'¿Se lo vas a decir?'—'Depende.' 'Are you going to tell him?'—'It depends.'

el **dependiente** *masc noun*, la **dependienta** *fem*
shop assistant

el **deporte** *masc noun*
sport
hacer deporte to play sports
Me gusta hacer deporte. I like playing sports.
- los **deportes acuáticos** water sports
- los **deportes de invierno** winter sports

mini-info **deporte**
La pelota vasca es el deporte más rápido del mundo; la pelota alcanza una velocidad de unas 260 kilómetros por hora.

deportista *masc & fem adjective*
▷ see **deportista** *noun*
sporty
Soy muy deportista. I do a lot of sport.
Jack es muy buen deportista. Jack's very good at games.

el & la **deportista** *masc & fem noun*
▷ see **deportista** *adj*
1 sportsman
2 sportswoman

deportivo *masc adjective*, **deportiva** *fem*
▷ see **deportivo** *noun*
sports
ropa deportiva sports clothes, casual clothes
un club deportivo a sports club

el **deportivo** *masc noun*
▷ see **deportivo** *adj*
sports car

depositar *verb* [17]
1 **to place**
Deposite su solicitud en esta caja. Place your application in this box.
2 **to deposit** (*money in an account*)

el **depósito** *masc noun*
deposit

deprimente *masc & fem adjective*
depressing

deprimido *masc adjective*, **deprimida** *fem*
depressed
Ha estado muy deprimida. She has been very depressed.

deprimirse *reflexive verb* [19]
to get depressed

deprisa *adverb*
fast, **quickly**
No lo hagas tan deprisa. Don't do it so quickly.
Andaba muy deprisa. He was walking very fast.
¡Deprisa, vístete! Hurry up and get dressed!

la **derecha** *fem noun* ▷ see **derecho** *adj*
1 **right** (*when talking of right and left*)
girar a la derecha to turn right
Está a la derecha. It's on the right., It's on the right-hand side.
la segunda calle a la derecha the second street on the right
Se sentaron a mi derecha. They sat on my right.
En Europa se conduce por la derecha. In Europe you drive on the right.
2 **right hand**
Escribo con la derecha. I write with my right hand.
3 (*in politics*) **la derecha** the right
ser de derechas to be right-wing

derecho *masc adjective*, **derecha** *fem*
▷ see **derecha** *noun*, **derecho** *adv, noun*
1 **right** (*talking about left and right*)
la mano derecha your right hand
el guante derecho the right glove
en el cuadro superior derecho in the top right-hand square
2 **straight** (*when talking about pictures*)
No está derecho. It's not straight.
Ponlo derecho. Put it straight.
Siéntate derecho. Sit up straight.

derecho *adverb* ▷ see **derecho** *adj, noun*
straight
Siga todo derecho. Go straight on.
Me fui derecho al director. I went straight to the headmaster.

el **derecho** *masc noun* ▷ see **derecho** *adj, adv*
1 **right**
tener derecho a algo to have the right to something
Tienes derecho a reclamar. You have the right to complaim.
2 **law**
estudiar derecho to study law
• el **derecho penal** criminal law
• los **derechos humanos** human rights

derramar *verb* [17]
to spill
He derramado el café en la alfombra. I've spilt the coffee on the carpet.

derramarse *reflexive verb* [7]
to spill
Se derramó la leche. The milk has spilt.

derribar *verb* [17]
1 **to demolish** (*a building or wall*)
2 **to break down** (*a door*)
3 **to shoot down** (*a plane*)

derrotar *verb* [17]
to defeat

des *verb* ▷ **dar**

desabrochar *verb* [17]
to undo (*a jacket or shirt*)

desabrocharse *reflexive verb* [17]
to undo
Se desabrochó la chaqueta. He undid his jacket.

desafilado *masc adjective*, **desafilada** *fem*
blunt

desafortunadamente *adverb*
unfortunately

desafortunado *masc adjective*, **desafortunada** *fem*
1 **unlucky** (*person*)
2 **unfortunate** (*event*)

desagradable *masc & fem adjective*
unpleasant

♪ **desanimado** *masc adjective*, **desanimada** *fem*
discouraged

♪ **desaparecer** *verb* [35]
1 **to disappear**
La tradición está desapareciendo. The tradition is dying out.
2 **to go missing** (*talking about a person or an object*)

la **desaparición** *fem noun*
disappearance

♪ **desaprovechar** *verb* [17]
to waste (*paper, time, an opportunity*)

♪ el **desarrollo** *masc noun*
development

♪ el **desastre** *masc noun*
disaster

♪ **desatar** *verb* [17]
to untie

desatarse *reflexive verb* [17]
to come undone (*knots, laces*)

desatornillar *verb* [17]
to unscrew

♪ **desayunar** *verb* [17]
1 **to have breakfast**
Desayuné muy temprano. I had breakfast very early.
2 **to have for breakfast**
Desayuno café y tostadas. I have coffee and toast for breakfast.

♪ el **desayuno** *masc noun*
breakfast
tomar el desayuno to have breakfast

desbordar *verb* [17]
to exceed

desbordarse *reflexive verb* [17]
to overflow
El río se desbordó. The river overflowed its banks.

♪ **descafeinado** *masc adjective*, **descafeinada** *fem*
decaffeinated

♪ **descalificar** *verb* [31]
to disqualify

descalzarse *reflexive verb* [22]
to take your shoes off

♪ **descalzo** *masc adjective*, **descalza** *fem*
barefoot

♪ **descansado** *masc adjective*, **descansada** *fem*
rested

♪ **descansar** *verb* [17]
to rest
descansar la vista to rest your eyes
Necesitas descansar. You need to rest.

♪ el **descansillo** *masc noun*
landing (*on stairs*)

♪ el **descanso** *masc noun*
1 **rest**
2 **half-time**

el **descapotable** *masc noun*
convertible (*car*)

descargar *verb* [28]
1 **to unload** (*goods*)
2 **to download** (*data, images*)

♪ **descender** *verb* [36]
1 **to descend** (*a plane*)
2 **to go down** (*a mountaineer*)
3 **to fall** (*prices, temperature*)

el **descenso** *masc noun*
1 **fall** (*in temperature, etc*)
2 **descent**

♪ **descolgar** *verb* [23]
1 **to pick up** (*the phone*)
2 **dejar el teléfono descolgado** to leave the phone off the hook
3 **to take down** (*a picture, curtains*)

descomponerse *reflexive verb* [11]
(*Latin America*) **to break down**

descompuesto *masc adjective*, **descompuesta** *fem*
(*Latin America*) **broken**
El radio está descompuesto. The radio's not working.

♪ **desconectar** *verb* [17]
to disconnect
¿Has desconectado el ordenador? Have you disconnected the computer?

♪ **desconfiar** *verb* [32]
desconfiar de alguien to mistrust someone
Desconfía de toda la gente. He mistrusts everybody., He doesn't trust anybody.

♪ **descongelar** *verb* [17]
to defrost

decongelarse *reflexive verb* [17]
to defrost

Spanish-English
a b c d e f g h i j k l m n ñ o p q r s t u v w x y z

desconocido *masc adjective*, **desconocida** *fem*
▷ see **desconocido** *noun*
unknown

el **desconocido** *masc noun*, la **desconocida** *fem*
▷ see **desconocido** *adj*
stranger

descontento *masc adjective*, **descontenta** *fem*
▷ see **descontento** *noun*
dissatisfied
quedar descontento con algo to be dissatisfied with something

el **descontento** *masc noun*
▷ see **descontento** *adj*
dissatisfaction

describir *verb* [52]
to describe

la **descripción** *fem noun*
description

descrito *verb* ▷ **describir**

descubrir *verb* [53]
1 **to discover**
2 **to unveil** (*a statue*)

el **descuento** *masc noun*
discount

descuidado *masc adjective*, **descuidada** *fem*
1 **careless** (*person*)
2 **neglected**
El jardín está muy descuidado. The garden is very neglected.

desde *preposition*
1 **from**
Se ve desde la ventana. You can see it from the window.
Puedes mandarlo desde Madrid. You can send it from Madrid.
Mídelo desde este extremo hasta el otro. Measure it from this end to the other.
2 (*with exact times*) **from**
desde el primer momento from the start
desde las tres hasta las cinco from three to five o'clock
3 **desde luego** of course
Desde luego les conozco. Of course I know them.
4 (*with an exact time as the start*) **since**
Vivo aquí desde 2002. I have been living here since 2002.
5 (*saying* **how long**) **desde hace** for
No les veo desde hace años. I haven't seen them for years.
Trabajo allí desde hace tres meses. I've been working there for three months.
6 (*asking* **how long?**) **desde cuándo** for
¿Desde cuándo vives en Coventry? How long have you lived in Coventry?
¿Desde cuándo son novios? How long have they been going out?

WORD TIP In phrases with *desde* Spanish uses the present tense when the activity or state is still going on.

desear *verb* [17]
1 **to wish**
Te deseo lo mejor. I wish you all the best.
Te deseo un feliz cumpleaños. Wishing you a happy birthday (*in a card*)
2 **to want**
Deseaba ir a la fiesta. She wanted to go to the party.
¿Qué desea? Can I help you? (*in a shop*)
Estoy deseando verte. I'm looking forward to seeing you.
Están deseando que llegue el verano. They can't wait for the summer to come.

desembarcar *verb* [31]
1 **to unload**
2 **to disembark**

desempleado *masc adjective*, **desempleada** *fem*
▷ see **desempleado** *noun*
unemployed

el **desempleado** *masc noun*, la **desempleada** *fem*
▷ see **desempleado** *adj*
unemployed person

el **desempleo** *masc noun*
unemployment
cobrar subsidio de desempleo to get unemployment benefit

desenchufar *verb* [17]
to unplug

desenroscar *verb* [31]
to unscrew (*a lid, a screw*)

desenvolver *verb* [45]
to unwrap

el **deseo** *masc noun*
1 **wish**
pedir un deseo to make a wish
Se cumplió mi deseo. My wish came true.
con mis mejores deseos best wishes
2 **desire**

desfavorable *masc & fem adjective*
unfavourable

♪ el **desfile** *masc noun*
parade
- el **desfile de modelos** fashion show

♪ la **desgracia** *fem noun*
misfortune
por desgracia unfortunately

WORD TIP *desgracia* does not mean *disgrace* in English; for the meaning of *disgrace* ▷ **vergüenza**.

desgraciadamente *adverb*
unfortunately

♪ **desgraciado** *masc adjective*, **desgraciada** *fem*
1 **unhappy**
Soy muy desgraciado. I'm very unhappy.
2 **ill-fated**
aquel desgraciado día that ill-fated day

♪ **deshacer** *verb* [7]
1 **to undo** (*a knot*)
2 **to unwrap** (*a parcel*)
deshacer las maletas to unpack
3 **to take apart** (*a clock, etc*)
4 **to crumble** (*a biscuit, etc*)

deshacerse *reflexive verb* [7]
1 **to come undone** (*a knot or seam*)
2 **to melt** (*ice*)
3 to come apart
Se deshizo en mis manos. It came apart in my hands.
4 deshacerse de algo to get rid of something
Voy a deshacerme de este sofá. I'm going to get rid of this sofa.

el **deshielo** *masc noun*
thaw

♪ **desierto** *masc adjective*, **desierta** *fem* ▷ see **desierto** *noun*
deserted

♪ el **desierto** *masc noun* ▷ see **desierto** *adj*
desert

♪ **designar** *verb* [17]
to appoint

♪ **desigual** *masc & fem adjective*
1 **uneven** (*a surface or road*)
2 **unequal** (*a fight*)

desmaquillarse *reflexive verb* [17]
to take off your make-up

♪ **desmayarse** *reflexive verb* [17]
to faint

♪ **desmontar** *verb* [17]
1 **to take apart** (*a machine, etc*)
2 **to take down** (*a tent*)

♪ **desnudar** *verb* [17]
to undress

desnudarse *reflexive verb* [17]
to take your clothes off, to get undressed

♪ **desnudo** *masc adjective*, **desnuda** *fem*
1 **naked** (*person, body*)
2 **bare** (*arms, shoulders*)
con los hombros desnudos with bare shoulders

♪ **desobedecer** *verb* [35]
to disobey
Desobedeció el reglamento. She disobeyed the rules.

desobedezca, **desobedezco**, **etc** *verb* ▷ **desobedecer**

♪ **desobediente** *masc & fem adjective*
disobedient
Eres muy desobediente. You are very disobedient.

♪ el **desodorante** *masc noun*
deodorant

♪ el **desorden** *masc noun*
mess

desorganizado *masc adjective*, **desorganizada** *fem*
disorganized

el **despacho** *masc noun*
1 **office**
2 **study** (*at home*)
- el **despacho de billetes** ticket office
- el **despacho de lotería** lottery agency

♪ **despacio** *adverb*
slowly
Hazlo despacio. Do it slowly.
¡Más despacio! Slower!

♪ la **despedida** *fem noun*
farewell
una cena de despedida a farewell dinner

♪ **despedir** *verb* [57]
1 **to say goodbye to**
Fuimos todos a despedirla. We all went to say goodbye to her.
¿Vendrás a despedirme a la estación? Will you come to see me off at the station?
2 **to sack, to fire** (*an employee*)
Lo despidieron. He was sacked.
3 **to lay off** (*the workforce*)
Han despedido a la mitad de la plantilla. They've laid off half the employees.

despedirse *reflexive verb* [57]
to say goodbye
Se fue sin depedirse. He went without saying goodbye.
despedirse de alguien to say goodbye to someone
Nos despedimos del director el último día. We said goodbye to the headmaster on the last day.

despegar *verb* [28]
1 **to take off** (*a plane*)
2 **to peel off** (*a label or a sticker*)

despegarse *reflexive verb* [28]
to come unstuck

el **despegue** *masc noun*
takeoff (*of a plane*)

despejado *masc adjective*, **despejada** *fem*
clear (*sky, day*)

despejar *verb* [17]
to clear (*a room of people*)

desperdiciar *verb* [17]
to waste (*food, paper, an opportunity, etc*)

el **desperdicio** *masc noun*
1 **waste**
Es un desperdicio tirar esta comida. It's a waste to throw this food away.
2 **los desperdicios** scraps

el **despertador** *masc noun*
alarm (clock)
poner el despertador to set the alarm
Puse el despertador para las siete de la mañana. I set the alarm for seven a.m.

despertar *verb* [29]
to wake up
¿Puedes despertarme a las siete? Can you wake me up at seven?

despertarse *reflexive verb* [29]
to wake up
Me desperté a las diez. I woke up at ten.

despida, **despido**, **etc** *verb* ▷ **despedir**

despierta, **despierto**, **etc** *verb*
▷ see **despierto** *adj* ▷ **despertar**

despierto *masc adjective*, **despierta** *fem*
▷ see **despierto** *verb*
awake

despistado *masc adjective*, **despistada** *fem* ▷ see **despistado** *noun*
absent-minded

el **despistado** *masc noun*, la **despistada** *fem* ▷ see **despistado** *adj*
scatterbrain

desplegar *verb* [30]
to unfold

despliega, **despliego**, **etc** *verb* ▷ **desplegar**

después *adverb, preposition*
1 **afterwards**
poco después shortly afterwards
Después me fui. Afterwards I went away .
2 **later**
Lo haré después. I'll do it later.
Se vieron mucho después. They saw each other much later.
3 **después de** after
después de todo after all
después de las clases after school
Después de verte me sentí mejor. After seeing you I felt better.

WORD TIP *después* is used by itself; *después de* is followed by a noun or pronoun.

el **destino** *masc noun*
1 **destination**
¿Qué destino tiene? What's its destination?
el vuelo con destino a Milán the plane to Milan
2 **fate**

el **destornillador** *masc noun*
screwdriver

la **destrucción** *fem noun*
destruction

destruir *verb* [54]
to destroy

el **desván** *masc noun*
attic

la **desventaja** *fem noun*
disadvantage
estar en desventaja to be at a disadvantage

desvestirse *reflexive verb* [57]
to undress, **to get undressed**

desviar *verb* [32]
to divert (*a plane or traffic*)

el **desvío** *masc noun*
diversion
tomar un desvío to make a detour

el **detalle** *masc noun*
detail
Me describió el lugar con todo detalle. He described the place to me in great detail.

el & la **detective** *masc & fem noun*
detective
• el **detective privado** private detective

detener *verb* **[9]**
1 **to stop** (*traffic*)
2 **to arrest**
¡Queda detenido! You're under arrest!

detenerse *reflexive verb* **[9]**
to stop
detenerse a hacer algo to stop to do something
Me detuve a descansar. I stopped to rest.

el **detergente** *masc noun*
1 **washing powder**
2 **washing-up liquid**

el **determinante** *masc noun*
(*Grammar*) **determiner**

detestar *verb* **[17]**
to detest

detrás *adverb*
1 **behind**
Creo que están detrás. I think they're behind.
2 **detrás de** behind
detrás de la estación behind the station
Ponte detrás de mí. Go behind me.
3 **por detrás** at the back
Se abrocha por detrás. It buttons up at the back.
Entraron por detrás. They got in at the back.

WORD TIP *detrás* is used by itself; *detrás de* is followed by a noun or pronoun.

la **deuda** *fem noun*
debt
Tiene muchas deudas. He has a lot of debts.

devolver *verb* **[45]**
1 **to return**, **to give back** (*something that you have borrowed*)
Lo devolví a su dueño. I returned it to its owner.
Te devolveré el libro mañana. I'll give you the book back tomorrow.
2 **to take back** (*something you've bought*)
He devuelto la camisa. I've taken the shirt back.
3 **to refund**
Me devolvieron el coste de las entradas. I was refunded the cost of the tickets.
4 **to be sick** (*vomit*)
Creo que voy a devolver. I think I'm going to be sick.

devuelto, **devuelvo**, **etc** *verb* ▷ **devolver**

di *verb* ▷ **dar**

el **día** *masc noun*
1 **day**
todos los días every day
¿Qué día es hoy? What day is it today?
cada día every day
buenos días good morning
2 (*talking about dates*) **el día tres de mayo** the third of May
3 **hacerse de día** to get light (*at dawn*)
Aún no se ha hecho de día. It's not light yet.
en pleno día in broad daylight
4 **estar al día** to be up to date
poner a alguien al día to bring someone up to date
Me puso al día de todo lo sucedido. He brought me up to date on everything that had happened.
- el **día de fiesta** holiday
- el **día de los enamorados** St Valentine's Day
- el **día de los Inocentes** the 28th of December (*equivalent to April Fool's Day in Spain*)
- el **día del padre** Father's Day
- el **día de Reyes** Twelfth Night (*6 January*)
- el **día festivo** public holiday
- el **día laborable** working day
- el **día libre** day off

diabético *masc adjective & noun*, **diabética** *fem adjective & noun*
1 **diabetic**
2 **un diabético, una diabética** diabetic

el **diablo** *masc noun*
devil

el **diagnóstico** *masc noun*
diagnosis
emitir un diagnóstico to make a diagnosis

diagonal *masc & fem adjective*
▷ see **diagonal** *noun*
diagonal

la **diagonal** *fem noun* ▷ see **diagonal** *adj*
diagonal

el **diagrama** *masc noun*
diagram

el **dial** *masc noun*
dial

el **diálogo** *masc noun*
1 **conversation**
2 **dialogue**

el **diamante** *masc noun*
diamond

el **diámetro** *masc noun*
diameter

la **diapositiva** *fem noun*
slide (*for a projector*)

diario *masc adjective*, **diaria** *fem*
▷ see **diario** *noun*
1 **daily**
la rutina diaria the daily routine
a diario every day
Se escriben a diario. They write to each other every day.
2 **a day**
Ensayan dos horas diarias. They practise two hours a day.
3 **de diario** everyday
ropa de diario everyday clothes

el **diario** *masc noun* ▷ see **diario** *adj*
1 **diary**
llevar un diario to keep a diary
2 **newspaper**

la **diarrea** *fem noun*
diarrhoea

dibujar *verb* **[17]**
to draw

el **dibujo** *masc noun*
drawing
hacer un dibujo to do a drawing
- el **dibujo técnico** technical drawing
- los **dibujos animados** cartoons

el **diccionario** *masc noun*
dictionary

dice, **dicho**, **etc** *verb* ▷ **decir**

diciembre *masc noun*
December
en diciembre in December
el 25 de diciembre on 25 December

WORD TIP Months of the year start with small letters in Spanish.

el **dictado** *masc noun*
dictation

diecinueve *number*
1 **nineteen**
Tiene diecinueve años. She's nineteen (years old).
2 (*saying the date*) **nineteenth**
el diecinueve de agosto the nineteenth of August

dieciocho *number*
1 **eighteen**
Tiene dieciocho años. She's eighteen (years old).
2 (*saying the date*) **eighteenth**
el dieciocho de agosto the eighteenth of August

dieciséis *number*
1 **sixteen**
Tiene dieciséis años. She's sixteen (years old).
2 (*saying the date*) **sixteenth**
el dieciséis de agosto the sixteenth of August

diecisiete *number*
1 **seventeen**
Tiene diecisiete años. She's seventeen (years old).
2 (*saying the date*) **seventeenth**
el diecisiete de agosto the seventeenth of August

el **diente** *masc noun*
tooth
Se le ha caído un diente. She's lost a tooth.
Ya le están saliendo los dientes. He's already teething.
- el **diente de ajo** clove of garlic

diera, **dieras**, **etc** *verb* ▷ **dar**

el **diesel** *masc noun*
diesel

la **dieta** *fem noun*
diet
estar a dieta to be on a diet
ponerse a dieta to go on a diet

diez *number*
1 **ten**
Tiene diez años. She's ten (years old).
2 (*saying the date*) **tenth**
el diez de agosto the tenth of August
3 (*telling the time*) **ten**
Son las diez. It's ten o'clock.
a las diez y cinco at five past ten

la **diferencia** *fem noun*
1 **difference**
Hay poca diferencia de precio. There's not much difference in price.
2 **a diferencia de** unlike
a diferencia de su padre unlike his father

diferente *masc & fem adjective*
different
ser diferente a, ser diferente de to be different from
Es diferente a su hermana. She is different from her sister.
Son diferentes de los demás. They are different from the others.

difícil *masc & fem adjective*
difficult

♪ la **dificultad** *fem noun*
difficulty
con muchas dificultades with great difficulty

diga, **digo**, **etc** *verb* ▷ **decir**

diluir *verb* **[54]**
1 **to dilute**
2 **to thin** *(paint)*

la **dimensión** *fem noun*
dimension

la **dimisión** *fem noun*
resignation
presentar la dimisión to hand in your resignation

dimitir *verb* **[19]**
to resign

dimos *verb* ▷ **dar**

Dinamarca *fem noun*
Denmark

♪ el **dinero** *masc noun*
money
¿Cuánto dinero tienes? How much money have you got?
No tengo dinero. I haven't got any money.
Es gente de dinero. They are wealthy people.
- el **dinero de bolsillo** pocket money
- el **dinero en efectivo** cash
- el **dinero suelto** change

♪ el **dinosaurio** *masc noun*
dinosaur

dio *verb* ▷ **dar**

♪ el **dios** *masc noun*, la **diosa** *fem*
▷ see **Dios** *noun*
1 **god**
2 **goddess**

♪ el **Dios** *masc noun* ▷ see **dios** *noun*
God
gracias a Dios thank heavens
¡Por Dios! For heaven's sake!
¡Dios mío! Oh, my God!
¡Sabe Dios! God knows!

el **diploma** *masc noun*
diploma

diplomático *masc adjective*, **diplomática** *fem*
▷ see **diplomático** *noun*
diplomatic

el **diplomático** *masc noun*, la **diplomática** *fem*
▷ see **diplomático** *adj*
diplomat

el **diputado** *masc noun*, la **diputada** *fem*
member of parliament

dirá, **diré**, **etc** *verb* ▷ **decir**

♪ la **dirección** *fem noun*
1 **address**
Mi dirección es ... My address is ...
2 **direction**
¿En qué dirección se fueron? What direction did they go in?
Venían en dirección contraria. They were coming the other way.
3 *(on signs)*
'Dirección prohibida' 'No entry'
'Dirección obligatoria' 'One way'
4 **management** *(of a company)*

♪ **directo** *masc adjective*, **directa** *fem*
▷ see **directo** *adv*
1 **direct**
¿Hay un vuelo directo a Santiago? Is there a direct flight to Santiago?
2 **un tren directo** a through train
3 *(in television and radio)* **en directo** live
una retransmisión en directo a live broadcast

♪ **directo** *adverb* ▷ see **directo** *adj*
direct
El autobús va directo al aeropuerto. The bus goes direct to the airport.

♪ el **director** *masc noun*, la **directora** *fem*
1 **headmaster**
2 **headmistress**
3 **manager** *(of a company)*
4 **director** *(of a film or play)*
5 **editor** *(of a newspaper)*
- el **director de orquesta** conductor

♪ **dirigir** *verb* **[49]**
1 **to manage** *(a company)*
2 **to direct** *(a film or play)*
3 **to conduct** *(an orchestra)*
4 **dirigir algo a alguien** to address something to somebody *(a message or a letter)*
La carta venía dirigida a mí. The letter was addressed to me.
No me dirigió la palabra en toda la tarde. He didn't say a word to me all afternoon.

dirigirse *reflexive verb* **[49]**
dirigirse a algo, dirigirse hacia algo to head towards something
Se dirigió hacia la puerta. He headed towards the door.

la **discapacidad** *fem noun*
disability
¿Tiene alguna discapacidad? Does she have a disability?

la **disciplina** *fem noun*
discipline

la **disco** *fem noun* ▷ see **disco** *masc*
disco (*for dancing*)

el **disco** *masc noun* ▷ see **disco** *fem*
1 **record**
grabar un disco to make a record
2 **disk** (*for a computer*)
3 **traffic light**
El disco se ha puesto rojo. The lights are red.
- el **disco compacto** compact disc
- el **disco compacto interactivo** interactive compact disc
- el **disco duro** hard disk
- el **disco flexible** floppy disk
- el **disco sencillo** single

la **discoteca** *fem noun*
disco

la **disculpa** *fem noun*
apology
pedir disculpas a alguien por algo to apologize to someone for something
Le pidió disculpas por su comportamiento. He apologized to her for his behaviour.

disculparse *reflexive verb* **[17]**
to apologize
Se disculpó por llegar tarde. She apologized for arriving late.

la **discusión** *fem noun*
1 **argument**
2 **discussion**

discutir *verb* **[19]**
1 **to argue**
Ha discutido con su novio. She's had an argument with her boyfriend
2 **to discuss**

el **diseñador** *masc noun*, la **diseñadora** *fem*
designer
- el **diseñador gráfico**, la **diseñadora gráfica** graphic designer

diseñar *verb* **[17]**
to design

el **diseño** *masc noun*
design

el **disfraz** *masc noun*
1 **disguise**
2 **costume, fancy dress outfit**
un disfraz de pirata a pirate outfit
una fiesta de disfraces a fancy dress party

disfrazarse *reflexive verb* **[22]**
to dress up
disfrazarse de algo to dress up as something
Me disfracé de bruja. I dressed up as a witch.

disfrutar *verb* **[17]**
to enjoy yourself
disfrutar de algo to enjoy something
Disfruté mucho de las vacaciones. I really enjoyed my holiday.

disgustar *verb* **[17]**
to upset

disgustarse *reflexive verb* **[17]**
to get upset

el **disgusto** *masc noun*
1 **argument**
2 **llevarse un disgusto** to get upset

WORD TIP *disgusto* does not mean *disgust* in English; for the meaning of *disgust* ▷ **asco**.

el **diskette** *masc noun*
diskette, floppy disk

la **disminución** *fem noun*
decrease

disminuir *verb* **[54]**
1 **to decrease**
El número de visitantes ha diminuido. The number of visitors has decreased.
2 **to reduce** (*speed, costs*)

el **disolvente** *masc noun*
solvent

disolver *verb* **[45]**
to dissolve

disolverse *reflexive verb* **[45]**
to dissolve

disparar *verb* **[17]**
1 **to fire, to shoot** (*with a gun*)
2 **to shoot** (*in football, etc*)

el **disparo** *masc noun*
shot

disponible *masc & fem adjective*
available

la **disposición** *fem noun*
1 **aptitude**
2 **estar a la disposición de alguien** to be at somebody's disposal

dispuesto *masc adjective*, **dispuesta** *fem*
1 **ready**
Todo está dispuesto. Everything's ready.
2 **estar dispuesto a hacer algo** to be prepared to do something
No estoy dispuesto a esperar. I'm not prepared to wait.

la **disputa** *fem noun*
1 **argument**
2 **dispute**

disputarse *reflexive verb* [17]
1 **to compete for** (*a title, a cup*)
2 **to fight over** (*an inheritance, a bill*)

el **disquete** *masc noun*
diskette, **floppy disk**

la **disquetera** *fem noun*
disk drive

la **distancia** *fem noun*
distance
Está a poca distancia. It's not far.
¿A qué distancia está el colegio de tu casa? How far is the school from your house?
Los dos postes están a una distancia de dos metros. The two posts are two metres apart.

diste *verb* ▷ **dar**

distinguir *verb* [50]
to distinguish

distinguirse *reflexive verb* [50]
1 **distinguirse por algo** to distinguish yourself by something
2 **distinguirse de algo** to differ from something

distintivo *masc adjective*, **distintiva** *fem*
distinctive

& **distinto** *masc adjective*, **distinta** *fem*
different
ser distinto a algo to be different from something
Son muy distintos. They are very different.
Es distinto al resto. It's different from the rest.

WORD TIP *distinto* does not mean *distinct* in English; for the meaning of *distinct* ▷ **claro**.

la **distracción** *fem noun*
1 **entertainment**
Es su distracción favorita. It's his favourite entertainment.
La tele le sirve de distracción. Television is a way of passing the time for him.
2 (*lack of attention*) **Se lo quitaron en un momento de distracción.** They stole it from her when she wasn't paying attention.

& **distraer** *verb* [42]
1 **to distract**
distraer a alguien de algo to distract somebody from something
El ruido la distrajo de la película. The noise distracted her from the film.
2 to keep busy
La costura me distrae. Sewing keeps me busy.

distraerse *reflexive verb* [42]
1 **to let your attention wander**
Se distrajo un momento y se lo robaron. His attention wandered for a moment and he got robbed.
2 to keep busy
Se distrae con la jardinería. Gardening keeps him busy.

el **distribuidor** *masc noun*, la **distribuidora** *fem*
distributor

distribuir *verb* [54]
to distribute

el **distrito** *masc noun*
district
- el **distrito postal** postal area

& la **diversión** *fem noun*
1 **fun**
por diversión for fun
2 (*leisure activity*) **un lugar lleno de diversiones** a place with plenty of things to do

WORD TIP *diversión* does not mean *diversion* in English; for the meaning of *diversion* ▷ **desvío**.

& **divertido** *masc adjective*, **divertida** *fem*
1 **funny**
Es un chico muy divertido. He's really funny.
2 **enjoyable**
La fiesta fue muy divertida. The party was really enjoyable.

& **divertir** *verb* [14]
to amuse

divertirse *reflexive verb* [14]
to enjoy yourself, **to have fun**
¡Que te diviertas! Enjoy yourself!, Have fun!

dividir *verb* [19]
to divide

la **divisa** *fem noun*
currency
- las **divisas extranjeras** foreign currency

Spanish–English

la **división** *fem noun*
division

divorciado *masc adjective*, **divorciada** *fem* ▷ see **divorciado** *noun*
divorced
Mis padres están divorciados. My parents are divorced.

el **divorciado** *masc noun*, la **divorciada** *fem* ▷ see **divorciado** *adj*
divorcee

divorciarse *reflexive verb* **[17]**
to get divorced
Se divorciaron en México. They got divorced in Mexico.

el **divorcio** *masc noun*
divorce

el **DNI** *masc noun*
(*= Documento Nacional de Identidad*) **identity card**

doblar *verb* **[17]**
1 **to fold** (*a piece of paper or clothes*)
2 **to bend** (*a piece of metal or your leg*)
3 **to double** (*an offer or amount*)
4 **doblar la esquina** to turn the corner

doble *masc & fem adjective* ▷ see **doble** *noun*
double

el **doble** *masc noun* ▷ see **doble** *adj*
el doble de: el doble de personas twice as many people
el doble de harina que de azúcar twice as much flour as sugar
el doble de peso twice the weight
el doble de largo twice the length

los **dobles** *plural masc noun* ▷ see **doble** *adj, noun*
doubles (*in tennis*)
la final de los dobles femeninos the final of the women's doubles

doce *number*
1 **twelve**
Tiene doce años. She's twelve (years old).
2 (*saying the date*) **twelfth**
el doce de enero the twelfth of January
3 (*telling the time*) **twelve**
a las doce at twelve o'clock
Son las doce del mediodía. It's twelve noon.
a las doce de la noche at midnight

doceavo *masc adjective*, **doceava** *fem*
twelfth

la **docena** *fem noun*
dozen
una docena de huevos a dozen eggs

el **doctor** *masc noun*, la **doctora** *fem*
doctor

la **documentación** *fem noun*
1 **papers**
No llevaba mi documentación. I didn't have my papers on me.
2 **documents** (*for a car*)

documental *masc & fem adjective* ▷ see **documental** *noun*
un programa documental a documentary

el **documental** *masc noun* ▷ see **documental** *adj*
documentary

el **documento** *masc noun*
document
- el **documento de identidad** identity card

el **dólar** *masc noun*
dollar

doler *verb* **[38]**
to hurt
Me duele el tobillo. My ankle hurts.
No duele nada. It doesn't hurt at all.
¿Te duele mucho? Does it hurt a lot?
Me duele la cabeza. I've got a headache.
Le dolía el estómago. He had stomachache.

el **dolor** *masc noun*
pain
Tengo dolor de garganta. I have a sore throat.
Tengo dolor de muelas. I have toothache.

doméstico *masc adjective*, **doméstica** *fem*
domestic

el **domicilio** *masc noun*
address
en su domicilio particular in his own home

el **domingo** *masc noun*
Sunday
el domingo on Sunday
el domingo pasado last Sunday
los domingos on Sundays
cada domingo every Sunday
Los domingos nos vamos a la piscina. We go to the pool on Sundays.
el domingo por la mañana on Sunday morning
- el **domingo de Resurrección** Easter Sunday

WORD TIP Names of months and days start with small letters in Spanish.

el **dominical** *masc noun*
1 **Sunday newspaper**
2 **Sunday supplement**

el **dominó** *masc noun*
dominoes
jugar al dominó to play dominoes

🔑 **don** *masc noun*
Mr
Don Juan Pozo Mr Juan Pozo (*don is used to show respect. It goes before the person's first name.*)

la **donación** *fem noun*
donation

🔑 **donde** *adverb* ▷ see **dónde** *adv*
where
El sitio donde nací. The place where I was born.
El lugar a donde nos dirigimos. The place we're going to.
Iré a donde quiera. I'll go wherever I want.
Ponlo donde sea. Put it down anywhere.

🔑 **dónde** *adverb* ▷ see **donde** *adv*
where
¿De dónde eres? Where are you from?
¿Dónde está mi abrigo? Where's my coat?
No sé dónde lo guarda. I don't know where he keeps it.
¿Por dónde se va a la oficina de correos? What's the way to the post office?

WORD TIP *dónde*, with an accent, is used for questions (¿...?).

el **donut** *masc noun*
doughnut

🔑 **doña** *fem noun*
Mrs, Ms
Doña María del Valle Mrs María del Valle (*doña is used to show respect. It goes before the person's first name.*)

🔑 **dorado** *masc adjective*, **dorada** *fem*
gold, **golden** (*in colour*)

dormido *masc adjective*, **dormida** *fem*
asleep
estar dormido to be asleep
quedarse dormido to fall asleep

🔑 **dormir** *verb* **[51]**
1 **to sleep**
¿Has dormido bien? Did you sleep well?
¡A dormir! Time for bed!
Ya es hora de irse a dormir. It's time to go to bed.
2 **to get to sleep**
No puedo dormir. I can't get to sleep.
No he dormido nada. I couldn't sleep at all.
3 **estar durmiendo** to be asleep
Juan está todavía durmiendo. Juan is still asleep.
4 **dormir la siesta** to have a nap

dormirse *reflexive verb* **[51]**
1 **to fall asleep**
No puedo dormirme. I can't get to sleep.
2 **to oversleep**
Me dormí y llegué tarde al trabajo. I overslept and was late for work.

🔑 el **dormitorio** *masc noun*
1 **bedroom**
2 **dormitory**

🔑 el **dorso** *masc noun*
back (*of a piece of paper, a hand, an animal*)

dos *number*
1 **two**
Tiene dos años. She's two (years old).
2 (*saying the date*) **second**
el dos de enero the second of January
3 (*telling the time*) **two**
Son las dos. It's two o'clock.
a las dos y media at half past two

doscientos, **doscientas** *number*
two hundred
doscientos veinte two hundred and twenty

doy *verb* ▷ **dar**

el **dragón** *masc noun*
dragon

el **drama** *masc noun*
1 **drama**
2 **play**

dramático *masc adjective*, **dramática** *fem*
dramatic

🔑 la **droga** *fem noun*
drug

el **drogadicto** *masc noun*, la **drogadicta** *fem*
drug addict

la **droguería** *fem noun*
1 **hardware shop** (*specializing in household items*)
2 **chemist's**

🔑 la **ducha** *fem noun*
shower
darse una ducha to have a shower

🔑 **ducharse** *reflexive verb* **[17]**
to have a shower

Spanish-English

la **duda** *fem noun*
1 **doubt**
Sin duda es el mejor. It's undoubtedly the best.
No me queda la menor duda. I have no doubts whatsoever.
2 **query**
¿Tienes alguna duda? Do you have any queries?
Tengo algunas dudas. I have a few queries.

dudar *verb* [17]
to doubt
Lo dudo. I doubt it.
No dudes en preguntar. Don't hesitate to ask.
Dudo que sepa hacerlo. I doubt he knows how to do it.

WORD TIP *dudar que* is followed by a verb in the subjunctive.

duela, **duelo**, **etc** *verb* ▷ **doler**

el **dueño** *masc noun*, la **dueña** *fem*
1 **owner**
Se lo devolví a la dueña. I returned it to its owner.
¿Quién es el dueño de este coche? Who's the owner of this car?
2 **landlord** (*of a pub or a guesthouse*)
3 **landlady** (*of a pub or a guesthouse*)

duerma, **duermo**, **etc** *verb* ▷ **dormir**

dulce *masc & fem adjective* ▷ see **dulce** *noun*
sweet

el **dulce** *masc noun* ▷ see **dulce** *adj*
los dulces sweet things

la **duna** *fem noun*
dune

duodécimo *masc adjective*, **duodécima** *fem*
twelfth

el **duque** *masc noun*, la **duquesa** *fem*
1 **duke**
2 **duchess**

la **duración** *fem noun*
length
la duración de la película the length of the film
un disco de larga duración an LP

durante *preposition*
1 **during**
durante aquel tiempo during that time
Lo haré durante las vacaciones. I'll do it during the holidays.
durante todo el partido throughout the match
2 (*for a specific period of time*) **for**
No se vieron durante tres semanas. They didn't see each other for three weeks.

durar *verb* [17]
to last
¿Cuánto dura? How long is it?
No dura mucho. It's not very long.
La guerra duró tres años. The war lasted three years.

el **durazno** *masc noun*
(*Latin America*) **peach**

la **dureza** *fem noun*
hardness

duro *masc adjective*, **dura** *fem*
▷ see **duro** *adv, noun*
1 **hard**
Al secarse se pone duro. It goes hard when it dries.
Fue un golpe muy duro para todos. It was a hard blow for all of us.
2 **strict** (*teacher*)
un profesor muy duro a very strict teacher
3 **tough** (*meat*)
4 **stale** (*bread*)
5 **ser duro de oído** to be hard of hearing

duro *adverb* ▷ see **duro** *adj, noun*
hard
estudiar duro to study hard

el **duro** *masc noun* ▷ see **duro** *adj, adv*
five-peseta coin (*no longer used*)
No tengo ni un duro. I'm broke.

el **DVD** *masc noun*
DVD (*player, disk*)

a b c d e f g h i j k l m n ñ o p q r s t u v w x y z

E e

e *conjunction*
and
español e inglés Spanish and English
padres e hijos parents and children

WORD TIP And is normally *y* in Spanish, but *e* before words beginning with *i-* or *hi-*.

⚷ **echar** *verb* [17]
1 **to throw, to throw out**
Échale agua al fuego. Throw water on the fire.
Eché la botella a la basura. I threw the bottle out.
Los eché de mi casa. I threw them out of my house.
echar una carta (al correo) to post a letter
echar a alguien del trabajo to sack someone
Lo han echado del trabajo. He's been sacked.
2 **to put**
Échale más leche al café. Put more milk in the coffee.
Tengo que echar gasolina al coche. I must put some petrol in the car.
3 **to show**
Echan una película en la tele. They're showing a film on the television.
¿Qué echan en el cine? What's on at the cinema?
4 **echar de menos a alguien** to miss somebody
Echamos de menos a mi hermana. We miss my sister.
Te hecho mucho de menos. I miss you a lot.

⚷ **echarse** *verb reflexive* [17]
1 **echarse al suelo** to throw yourself on the ground
2 **to move**
echarse para atrás to move backwards
Se echó a la derecha. He moved to the right.
Me eché a un lado. I moved to one side.
3 **echarse una siesta** to have a nap

el **eclipse** *masc noun*
eclipse

el **eco** *masc noun*
echo

ecológico *masc adjective*, **ecológica** *fem*
ecological
un desastre ecológoco an environmental disaster

ecologista *masc & fem adjective*
ecologist

la **economía** *fem noun*
1 **economy**
la economía europea the European economy
2 **economics**
estudiar economía to study economics

económico *masc adjective*, **económica** *fem*
1 **economic**
una crisis económica an economic crisis
2 **financial**
los problemas económicos de la zona the financial problems of the area
3 **cheap**
un vuelo económico a cheap flight
4 **thrifty** (*person*)

⚷ la **ecuación** *fem noun*
equation

el **ecuador** *masc noun* ▷ see **Ecuador** *noun*
the equator (*in geography*)

Ecuador *masc noun* ▷ see **ecuador** *noun*
Ecuador (*the Latin American country on the equator*)

ecuatoriano *masc adjective & noun*, **ecuatoriana** *fem adjective & noun*
1 **Ecuadorian**
2 **un ecuatoriano, una ecuatoriana** Ecuadorian

WORD TIP Adjectives and nouns for nationality and regional origin do not have capital letters in Spanish.

⚷ la **edad** *fem noun*
age
¿Qué edad tienes? How old are you?
Carmen y yo tenemos la misma edad. Carmen and I are the same age.
Una mujer de unos treinta años de edad. A woman of about thirty.
Está en la edad del pavo. She's at the awkward age.
- la **edad de piedra** the Stone Age
- la **edad media** the Middle Ages

la **edición** *fem noun*
1 **edition**
2 **one of a series**
la sexta edición del festival the sixth in the series of festivals
• la **edición de bolsillo** pocket edition

el **edificio** *masc noun*
building

editar *verb* **[17]**
1 **to publish**
2 **to edit** (*a text, in IT*)

la **editorial** *fem noun*
publishing company

el **edredón** *masc noun*
quilt
• el **edredón nórdico** duvet

♂ la **educación** *fem noun*
1 **education**
el ministerio de educación the ministry of education
2 **manners**
¡Qué mala educación! What bad manners!
Eso es de mala educación. That's bad manners.
• la **educación a distancia** distance learning
• la **educación física** physical education
• la **educación secundaria** secondary education

educado *masc adjective*, **educada** *fem*
polite
una persona bien educada a polite person
una persona mal educada a rude person

♂ **educar** *verb* **[31]**
1 **to educate**
Me eduqué en un colegio público. I was educated in a state school.
2 **to bring up**
La educó su tía. Her aunt brought her up.

EE.UU. *abbreviation*
(= *los Estados Unidos*) **USA**

WORD TIP *Estados Unidos* is often used without *los*.

efectivo *masc adjective*, **efectiva** *fem*
▷ see **efectivo** *noun*
effective (*remedy, method*)

el **efectivo** *masc noun* ▷ see **efectivo** *adj*
cash
pagar en efectivo to pay cash
mil euros en efectivo a thousand euros in cash

el **efecto** *masc noun*
1 **effect**
La pastilla no me hizo efecto. The pill didn't have any effect on me.
2 **en efecto that's right**
En efecto llegaron a las diez. That's right, they arrived at ten.
• el **efecto invernadero** greenhouse effect
• los **efectos especiales** special effects
• los **efectos secundarios** side effects

♂ **efectuar** *verb* **[20]**
to carry out
efectuar una búsqueda to carry out a search
El tren efectuará su salida a las nueve y treinta. The train will depart at 9:30.

eficaz *masc & fem adjective, pl:* **eficaces**
effective
un remedio eficaz an effective treatment

egoísta *masc & fem adjective & noun*
1 **selfish**
2 **Eres un egoísta., Eres una egoísta.** You're very selfish.

ejecutar *verb* **[17]**
to execute

ejecutivo *masc adjective*, **ejecutiva** *fem*
▷ see **ejecutivo** *noun*
executive

el **ejecutivo** *masc noun*, la **ejecutiva** *fem*
▷ see **ejecutivo** *adj*
executive

el **ejemplar** *masc noun*
1 **copy** (*of a book*)
2 **issue** (*of a magazine*)
3 **specimen** (*of an animal, a plant*)

el **ejemplo** *masc noun*
example
por ejemplo for example
Ese caso es un mal ejemplo. That case is a bad example.
dar buen ejemplo to set a good example
El capitán de equipo tiene que dar buen ejemplo. The captain of the team has to set a good example.

♂ el **ejercicio** *masc noun*
exercise
hacer ejercicio to take exercise
Hago ejercicio dotos los días. I take exercise every day.

♂ el **ejército** *masc noun*
army
alistarse en el ejército to join the army
• el **ejército de aire** air force
• el **ejército de tierra** army

la **emisora** *fem noun*
radio station

la **emoción** *fem noun*
1 **emotion**
2 **excitement**
una película llena de emoción a really exciting film
¡Qué emoción! How exciting!

emocionado *masc adjective*, **emocionada** *fem*
1 **moved**
2 **excited**

emocional *masc & fem adjective*
emotional

emocionante *masc & fem adjective*
1 **moving**
Hubo emocionantes escenas en el aeropuerto. There were moving scenes at the airport.
2 **exciting**
una película emocionante an exciting film
¡Qué emocionante! How exciting!

el **emoticón** *masc noun*
smiley, **emoticon**

el **empacho** *masc noun*
(*informal*) **tener empacho** to have a stomach-ache (*from over-eating*)
Se cogió un empacho de pasteles. He ate so many cakes he had a stomachache.

el **empalme** *masc noun*
junction (*on a railway*)

la **empanada** *fem noun*
pastie
una empanada de atún a tuna pie

empapado *masc adjective*, **empapada** *fem*
soaking wet
Venían empapados. They were soaking wet.

empaparse *verb* **[17]**
to get soaking wet

empastar *verb* **[17]**
to fill (*a tooth*)

el **empaste** *masc noun*
filling (*for a tooth*)

empatar *verb* **[17]**
to draw
Empataron dos a dos. They drew two all

el **empate** *masc noun*
1 **draw** (*in sport*)
2 **tie** (*in voting, etc*)

empecé *verb* ▷ **empezar**

empeorar *verb* **[17]**
1 **to get worse**
La situación ha empeorado. The situation has got worse.
2 **to make worse**
Va a empeorar las cosas. It's going to make things worse.

el **emperador** *masc noun*
emperor

la **emperatriz** *fem noun*, **emperatrices** *plural*
empress

⚷ **empezar** *verb* **[25]**
to begin, **to start**
El colegio empieza el quince de septiembre. School begins on the fifteenth of September.
Empiezo el colegio en enero. I start school in January.
Empezaré otra vez. I'll start again.
Empezó diciendo que ... He began by saying that ...
empezar a hacer algo to begin to do something
Empezó a llover. It started to rain.

WORD TIP To say, to begin by, use *empezar* + *-ando*, *or -iendo*; to say, to begin to, use *empezar a* + *infinitive*.

empiece, **empieza**, **empiezo**, **etc** *verb* ▷ **empezar**

empinado *masc adjective*, **empinada** *fem*
steep (*slopes, streets*)

el **emplazamiento** *masc noun*
situation, **location**

⚷ el **empleado** *masc noun*, la **empleada** *fem*
employee
los empleados the staff (*in a company*).
Todos los empleados se beneficiarán. All the staff will benefit.

emplear *verb* **[17]**
1 **to employ**
Emplean 300 trabajadores en la fábrica. They employ 300 workers at the factory.
2 **to use**
Emplearon materiales viejos. They used old materials.

⚷ el **empleo** *masc noun*
1 **employment**
2 **job**
buscar empleo to look for a job
3 **estar sin empleo** to be unemployed

empollar *verb* **[17]**
1 (*informal*) **to swot** (*for exams*)
2 **to incubate** (*eggs*)

el **empollón** *masc noun*, la **empollona** *fem*
(*informal*) **swot**

emprendedor *masc adjective*, **emprendedora** *fem*
enterprising

la **empresa** *fem noun*
company

empujar *verb* **[17]**
to push

en *preposition*
1 **in**
en español in Spanish
en invierno in winter
Ponlo en el cajón. Put it in the drawer.
Vivo en Londres. I live in London.
2 **into**
Entró en la casa. He went into the house.
3 **on**
Está en la mesa. It's on the table.
Viven en el segundo piso. They live on the second floor.
4 **at**
Estaré en casa toda la tarde. I'll be at home all afternoon.
Es muy buena en inglés. She's very good at English.
5 **by**
ir en coche to go by car

la **enagua** *fem noun, pl:* las **enaguas**
petticoat

enamorado *masc adjective*, **enamorada** *fem*
in love
estar enamorado de alguien to be in love with someone
Está enamorado de ella. He is in love with her.
Está enamorada de él. She is in love with him.

enamorarse *reflexive verb* **[17]**
to fall in love
Se enamoraron. They fell in love.
enamorase de alguien to fall in love with someone
Se enamoró de ella. He fell in love with her.

el **enano** *masc noun*, la **enana** *fem*
dwarf

encantado *masc adjective*, **encantada** *fem*
1 **¡Encantado de conocerle!** Pleased to meet you! (*boy speaking; formal style*)
¡Encantada de conocerle! Pleased to meet you! (*girl speaking; formal style*)
2 **delighted**
Están encantados con la casa. They're delighted with the house.
3 **enchanted** (*castle, life*)

encantador *masc adjective*, **encantadora** *fem*
▷ see **encantador** *noun*
1 **lovely** (*thing*)
2 **charming** (*person*)

el **encantador** *masc noun*, la **encantadora** *fem*
▷ see **encantador** *adj*
magician
• el **encantador de serpientes** snake-charmer

encantar *verb* **[17]**
Me encanta el regalo. I love the present.
Nos encanta el hotel. We love the hotel.
Le encantan las joyas. She loves the jewels.
Nos encantaría venir a verte. We'd love to come and see you.

WORD TIP Use *encanta, encantó, encantaba, encantaría, etc* if what you love is singular or an infinitive. Use *encantan, encantaron, encantaban, encantarían, etc* if what you love is plural.

encargado *masc adjective*, **encargada** *fem* ▷ see **encargado** *noun*
encargado de algo responsible for something
La persona encargada del reparto. The person responsible for the delivery.

el **encargado** *masc noun*, la **encargada** *fem* ▷ see **encargado** *adj*
manager

el **encendedor** *masc noun*
lighter

encender *verb* **[36]**
1 **to light** (*a cigarette, match*)
2 **to turn on** (*the lights, tv*)

encendido *masc adjective*, **encendida** *fem*
1 **on** (*radio, cooker*)
2 **burning** (*match, hay*)

el **encerado** *masc noun*
blackboard

encerrar *verb* **[36]**
1 **to lock up** (*a person*)
2 **to lock away** (*papers, money*)

enchufar *verb* **[17]**
1 **to plug in** (*to the socket*)
2 **to turn on** (*the tv, the kettle*)

el **enchufe** *masc noun*
plug (*for a socket*)

la **enciclopedia** *fem noun*
encyclopedia

encienda, **enciendo**, **etc** *verb* ▷ **encender**

encima *adverb*
1 **on, on top**
Ponlo ahí encima. Put it on there.
Había un plástico encima. There was a piece of plastic on top.
No llevaba el carnet de identidad encima. He didn't have his identity card on him.
2 **el de encima, la de encima** the top one
el piso de encima the flat above
3 **encima de** on, on top of (*someting*)
encima del armario on top of the wardrobe
Está encima de la cama. It's on the bed.
Llevaba una gabardina encima de la chaqueta. I was wearing a raincoat over my jacket.
4 **por encima de** above, over (*something*)
Las temperaturas están por encima de lo normal. Temperatures are above normal.
5 **encima de** as well, too
Encima de llegar tarde se queja. He arrives late and he complains as well.
¡Y encima no me lo devolvió! And on top of that he didn't give it back to me!

WORD TIP *encima* is used by itself; *encima de* is followed by a noun or pronoun.

encontrar *verb* **[24]**
to find
No encuentro mis gafas en ninguna parte. I can't find my glasses anywhere.
Las encontré en la cocina. I found them in the kitchen.

encontrarse *reflexive verb* **[24]**
1 **encontrarse con** to meet
Me encontré con ella en la calle. I met her in the street.
2 **to feel**
No me encuentro bien. I don't feel well.
3 **to find**
Me encontré un billete de diez euros. I found a ten-euro note.

encuentra, **encuentras**, **encuentro**, **etc** *verb* ▷ **encontrar**

la **encuesta** *fem noun*
survey
- la **encuesta de opinión** opinion poll

el **enemigo** *masc noun*, la **enemiga** *fem*
enemy

la **energía** *fem noun*
energy
- la **energía nuclear** nuclear energy
- la **energía solar** solar energy

enérgico *masc adjective*, **enérgica** *fem*
energetic

enero *masc noun*
January
en enero in January
el 14 de enero on 14 January

WORD TIP Names of months and days start with small letters in Spanish.

enfadado *masc adjective*, **enfadada** *fem*
1 **angry**
2 **annoyed**

enfadar *verb* **[17]**
1 **to make angry**
2 **to annoy**

enfadarse *reflexive verb* **[17]**
1 **to get annoyed**
Se enfadó conmigo. He got annoyed with me.
No te enfades. Don't get annoyed.
2 **to get angry**
Se enfadó muchísimo. He got really angry.
3 **to get cross**
Mamá se va a enfadar. Mum's going to get cross.

el **énfasis** *masc noun*
emphasis

enfermar *verb* **[17]**
to get ill

la **enfermedad** *fem noun*
illness, disease

la **enfermería** *fem noun*
1 **nursing**
2 **infirmary**

el **enfermero** *masc noun*, la **enfermera** *fem*
nurse

enfermo *masc adjective*, **enferma** *fem*
▷ see **enfermo** *noun*
ill
Está gravemente enferma. She's seriously ill.
caer enfermo to fall ill

el **enfermo** *masc noun*, la **enferma** *fem*
▷ see **enfermo** *adj*
1 **sick person**
los enfermos sick people
2 **patient**

Spanish–English
a b c d e f g h i j k l m n ñ o p q r s t u v w x y z

enfrente *adverb*
opposite
La estación está enfrente de la catedral. The station is opposite the cathedral.
de enfrente: la casa de enfrente the house opposite

engañar *verb* [17]
1 **to deceive**
2 **to cheat, to swindle**
3 **to be unfaithful to**

engañarse *reflexive verb* [17]
to fool yourself

el **engaño** *masc noun*
1 **deception**
2 **swindle**

engordar *verb* [17]
1 **to put on weight**
Ha engordado mucho. He's put on a lot of weight.
2 **to be fattening**
La mantequilla engorda. Butter is fattening.

la **enhorabuena** *fem noun*
¡Enhorabuena por ganar el premio! Congratulations on winning the prize!
darle la enhorabuena a alguien to congratulate someone

enjuagar *verb* [28]
to rinse
enjuagar los platos to rinse the plates

enjuagarse *reflexive verb* [28]
enjuagarse el pelo to rinse your hair

enmohecerse *reflexive verb* [35]
to go mouldy

enojado *masc adjective*, **enojada** *fem*
(*Latin America*) **angry**

enojar *verb* [17]
(*Latin America*) **to annoy**

enojarse *reflexive verb* [17]
to get annoyed
Se enojó conmigo. He got annoyed with me.
No te enojes. Don't get annoyed.

enorme *masc & fem adjective*
huge

enormemente *adverb*
extremely, very
Estaba enormemente preocupado. He was extremely worried.

enrollar *verb* [17]
to roll up

enroscar *verb* [31]
1 **to wind**
2 **to screw on**

la **ensaimada** *fem noun*
pastry (*shaped like a spiral and dusted with icing sugar*)

la **ensalada** *fem noun*
salad
- la **ensalada de frutas** fruit salad
- la **ensalada mixta** mixed salad

la **ensaladera** *fem noun*
salad bowl

la **ensaladilla**, la **ensaladilla rusa** *fem noun*
potato salad

el **ensayo** *masc noun*
1 **rehearsal**
2 **essay**
3 **try** (*in rugby*)
- el **ensayo general** dress rehearsal

enseguida *adverb*
right away
Enseguida lo traigo. I'll bring right away.

la **enseñanza** *fem noun*
1 **teaching**
la enseñanza de música the teaching of music
2 **education**
- la **enseñanza primaria** primary education
- la **enseñanza secundaria** secondary education
- la **enseñanza superior** higher education

enseñar *verb* [17]
1 **to teach**
Enseña matemáticas. She teaches maths.
enseñarle a alguien a hacer algo to teach somebody something
Mi padre me enseñó a nadar. My father taught me to swim.
2 **to show**
Enséñame tus fotos. Show me your photos.
Nos enseñó la casa. He showed us the house.

ensuciar *verb* [17]
to make dirty
No ensucies la mesa. Don't make the table dirty.
Ensucié el mantel de aceite de oliva. I got olive oil on the tablecloth.

ensuciarse *reflexive verb* [17]
to get dirty
Te vas a ensuciar las manos. You're going to get your hands dirty.
Me he ensuciado las botas de barro. I've got mud on my boots.

entender *verb* [36]
1 **to understand**
Entiendo lo que dicen. I can understand what they're saying.
¿Entiendes la pregunta? Do you understand the question?
No le entiendo. I can't understand you. (*formal use*)
2 **entender algo mal** to misunderstand something
La entendí mal. I misunderstood her.
3 **entender de algo** to know about something
Entiendo un poco de fontanería. I know a bit about plumbing.
Entiendo un poco de español. I can understand a little bit of Spanish.

entenderse *reflexive verb* [36]
entenderse con alguien to get along with someone
Se entiende muy bien con su hermana. She gets along very well with her sister.
Nos entendemos muy bien. We get along very well.

entendido *masc adjective*, **entendida** *fem*
1 **understood**
Queda bien entendido. It's clearly understood.
¿Entendido? Is that clear?
2 **ser entendido en algo** to know about something
Es muy entendido en informática. He knows a lot about computers.

enterarse *reflexive verb* [17]
1 **enterarse de algo** to find out about something
2 **enterarse de lo que pasa** to realize what is happening

entero *masc adjective*, **entera** *fem*
whole
un día entero a whole day
Estuve esperando tres horas enteras. I was waiting for three whole hours.

enterrar *verb* [29]
to bury

entienda, **entiendes**, **entiendo**, **etc**
verb ▷ **entender**

entonces *adverb*
1 **then**
Entonces llegó Carlos. Then Carlos arrived.
Desde entonces vivimos en Marbella. Since then we've lived in Marbella.
2 **so, ok**
Entonces nos vemos mañana. So we'll see each other tomorrow.

la **entrada** *fem noun*
1 **entrance**, **way in**
¿Dónde está la entrada? Where is the entrance?
2 **ticket** (*for the cinema, a match, bullfight, etc*)
¿Cuánto cuesta la entrada? How much is a ticket?
Tenemos que sacar las entradas. We must buy the tickets.
Los niños pagan media entrada. It's half-price for children.
'Entrada libre' 'Admission free'
3 **entry**
la entrada de nuevos miembros en la Unión Europea the entry of new members into the European Union
4 **tackle** (*in football*)
5 **starter** (*on menus*)
6 **deposit** (*for a purchase*)

entrar *verb* [17]
1 **to enter**, **to get in**
Entraron por una ventana They got in through a window.
2 **to come in**
¡Entra! Come in!
3 **to go in**
Llama antes de entrar. Knock before you go in.
Entraron en la clase corriendo. They ran into the classroom.
4 **entrar en** to go into
Entramos en la sala de espera. We went into the waiting rom.
5 **dejar entrar a alguien** to let someone in
No le dejes entrar. Don't let him in.
6 **hacer entrar a alguien** to show someone in
Le hizo entrar a su oficina. He showed him in.
7 **to fit**
No entra por la puerta. It doesn't fit through the door.
El desayuno no entra en el precio. Breakfast is not included in the price.
8 **to join**
Entraron en la UE. They joined the EU.
9 (*with feelings of cold, hunger, etc*) **Me entró hambre.** I got hungry.
Te va a entrar frío si te sientas fuera. You'll get cold if you sit outside.
10 (*informal*) (*about understanding something*) **No me entra.** I don't get it.
No le entran las matemáticas. He just doesn't get maths.

entre *preposition*
1 **between**
Estaba sentado entre Jaime y Margarita. I was sitting between Jaime and Margarita.
Lo hicimos entre todos. We did it between us.
2 **among**
Lo encontré entre mis papeles. I found it among my papers.
3 **by** (*in maths*)
Nueve dividido entre tres. Nine divided by three.

entreabierto *masc adjective*, **entreabierta** *fem*
half-open

el **entreacto** *masc noun*
interval

la **entrega** *fem noun*
1 **delivery** (*of goods*)
2 **presentation** (*of a prize, award*)
3 **la fecha límite para la entrega de solicitudes** the deadline for handing in applications

entregar *verb* **[28]**
1 **to deliver, to hand in**
Vino a entregar una carta. He came to deliver a letter.
Tenemos que entregar el trabajo el próximo lunes. We have to hand in the essay next Monday.
Me entregó los documentos. He handed me the documents.
2 **to present** (*a prize, an award*)
El alcalde entregó los premios. The mayor presented the prizes.
3 **to surrender** (*a town, weapons*)
4 **to hand over** (*a criminal, a prisoner*)

entregarse *reflexive verb* **[28]**
to give yourself up
Se entregó a la policía. He gave himself up to the police.

el **entremés** *masc noun*, **entremeses** *plural*
starter (*in a meal*)

el **entrenador** *masc noun*, la **entrenadora** *fem*
1 **manager** (*of a professional sports team*)
2 **trainer** (*of a team, horse, dog, etc*)

el **entrenamiento** *masc noun*
training

entrenar *verb* **[17]**
to train
Entrenamos los martes y jueves. We train on Tuesdays and Thursdays.

entrenarse *reflexive verb* **[17]**
to train

entretanto *adverb*
in the meantime

entretenido *masc adjective*, **entretenida** *fem*
entertaining

la **entrevista** *fem noun*
interview
- la **entrevista de trabajo** job interview

entrevistar *verb* **[17]**
to interview

entumecido *masc adjective*, **entumecida** *fem*
numb

entusiasmar *verb* **[17]**
Me entusiasma la idea. I really like the idea.
Le entusiasma el deporte. She's really keen on sports.
A mi padre no le entusiasma viajar. My father's not keen on travel.

entusiasmarse *reflexive verb* **[17]**
entusiasmarse con algo to get keen about something
Se entusiasmaron con la idea. They got keen on the idea.

el **entusiasmo** *masc noun*
enthusiasm

enviar *verb* **[32]**
to send
Te enviaré un mensaje de texto. I'll send you a text message.

la **envidia** *fem noun*
1 **envy**
Se muere de envidia. He's green with envy.
2 **jealousy**
tenerle envidia a alguien to be jealous of someone
Me tienen envidia. They're jealous of me.
Le tiene envidia a su hermana. She's envious of her sister.

envidiar *verb* **[17]**
to be envious of
Me envidia que saqué mejores notas que ella. She's envious that I got better marks than she did.

envidioso *masc adjective*, **envidiosa** *fem*
envious

§ **envolver** *verb* **[45]**
to wrap up
envolver un regalo to wrap up a present

§ **envuelto** *masc adjective*, **envuelta** *fem*
1 **wrapped**
envuelto para regalo gift-wrapped
2 **estar envuelto en algo** to be involved in something
Está envuelto en un asunto de drogas. He's involved in something to do with drugs.

envuelto *verb* ▷ **envolver**

la **epidemia** *fem noun*
epidemic

el **episodio** *masc noun*
episode

la **época** *fem noun*
1 **time**
En aquella época vivíamos en Málaga. At that time we were living in Málaga.
Es de la época de los romanos. It's from the time of the Romans.
2 **season**
en la época de la cosecha at harvest time

el **equilibrio** *masc noun*
balance
estar en equilibrio to be in balance
perder el equilibrio to lose your balance

§ el **equipaje** *masc noun*
luggage
- el **equipaje de mano** hand luggage

§ el **equipo** *masc noun*
1 **team**
el equipo visitante the away team
formar un buen equipo to make a good team
El trabajo en equipo es muy importante. Team work is very important.
2 **equipment**
- el **equipo de alta fidelidad** hi-fi system
- el **equipo de música** sound system

la **equis** *fem noun*
(*the Spanish name for*) **letter X**

la **equitación** *fem noun*
horse riding

equivaler *verb* **[43]**
equivaler a algo to be equivalent to something
Veinte euros equivalen a quice libras. Twenty euros are equivalent to fifteen pounds.

§ **equivocado** *masc adjective*, **equivocada** *fem*
wrong
Estás equivocada. You're wrong. (*talking to a girl*)

§ **equivocarse** *reflexive verb* **[31]**
1 **to make a mistake**
Me he equivocado. I've made a mistake.
equivocarse de algo to make a mistake about something
Me equivoqué de carpeta. I took the wrong folder.
Se equivocó de calle. He took the wrong street.
2 **to be wrong**
Te equivocas si piensas eso. You're wrong if you think like that.

era, **érais**, **eras**, **eres**, **etc** *verb* ▷ **ser**

el **error** *masc noun*
mistake
cometer un error to make a mistake
un error de cálculo a miscalculation
- el **error tipográfico** typing error

eructar *verb* **[17]**
to burp

el **eructo** *masc noun*
burp

es *verb* ▷ **ser**

§ **esa**, **ésa** *fem adjective & pronoun*
that, **that one**
▷ **ese** *adj, pron*

§ **esas**, **ésas** *fem plural adjective & pronoun*
those, **those ones**
▷ **ese** *adj, pron*

la **escala** *fem noun*
1 **stopover**
Hicieron escala en Florida. They stopped over in Florida.
2 **scale** (*of a map, measurements*)
a gran escala on a large scale
3 **scale** (*in music*)

la **escalada** *fem noun*
1 **(rock) climbing**
2 **climb**

el **escalador** *masc noun*, la **escaladora** *fem*
climber

escalar *verb* **[17]**
1 **to climb** (*a mountain*)
2 **to move up** (*a league table*)

la **escalera** *fem noun*
staircase
bajar la escalera to go down the stairs
subir la escalera to go up the stairs
una escalera de mano a ladder
- la **escalera de caracol** spiral staircase
- la **escalera de incendios** fire escape
- la **escalera mecánica** escalator

el **escalofrío** *masc noun*
1 **shiver** (*from cold*)
tener escalofríos to be shivering
2 **shudder** (*with horror*)
darle escalofríos a alguien to make someone shudder

el **escalón** *masc noun*
step

el **escalope** *masc noun*
escalope

el **escándalo** *masc noun*
1 **scandal**
¡Su comportamiento fue un escándalo! His behaviour was really outrageous!
2 **racket**
armar un escándalo to make a racket
¡Qué escándalo están armando! what a racket they are making!
- el **escándalo político** political scandal

escandaloso *masc adjective*, **escandalosa** *fem*
1 **shocking** (*behaviour or clothes*)
2 **noisy** (*people*)

Escandinavia *fem noun*
Scandinavia

escandinavo *masc adjective & noun*, **escandinava** *fem adjective & noun*
1 **Scandinavian**
2 **un escandinavo, una escandinava** Scandinavian

WORD TIP Adjectives and nouns for nationality and regional origin do not have capital letters in Spanish.

el **escáner** *masc noun*
1 **scanner**
2 **scan**

escapar *verb* **[17]**
to escape
escapar de algo to escape from something

escaparse *reflexive verb* **[17]**
1 **to escape**
Se ha escapado de la cárcel. He's escaped from prison.
2 **to run away**
escaparse de casa to run away from home
3 **to leak** (*gas, water, etc*)

el **escaparate** *masc noun*
shop window

el **escarabajo** *masc noun*
beetle

la **escarcha** *fem noun*
frost

la **escasez** *fem noun*, *pl:* las **escaseces**
shortage
Hay escasez de agua. There's a water shortage.

la **escayola** *fem noun*
plaster (*for broken bones*)

la **escena** *fem noun*
scene

el **escenario** *masc noun*
stage

el **esclavo** *masc noun*, la **esclava** *fem*
slave

la **esclusa** *fem noun*
lock (*on a canal*)

la **escoba** *fem noun*
broom

escocés *masc adjective*, **escocesa** *fem*
▷ see **escocés** *noun*
Scottish

un **escocés** *masc noun*, una **escocesa** *fem*
▷ see **escocés** *adj*
Scot
los escoceses the Scots

WORD TIP Adjectives and nouns for nationality and regional origin do not have capital letters in Spanish.

Escocia *fem noun*
Scotland
Soy de Escocia. I'm from Scotland.

escoger *verb* **[3]**
to choose
Escoge el que te guste más. Choose the one you like best. (*familiar form*)
Escoged el que os guste más. Choose the one you like best. (*familiar plural form*)

escoja, escojo, etc *verb* ▷ **escoger**

escolar *masc & fem adjective*
▷ see **escolar** *noun*
school
la vida escolar school life

el & la **escolar** *masc & fem noun*
▷ see **escolar** *adj*
1 **schoolboy**
2 **schoolgirl**

esconder *verb* **[18]**
to hide

esconderse *reflexive verb* **[18]**
to hide
esconderse de alguien to hide from someone
Se escondió del profesor. She hid from the teacher.

escondido *masc adjective*, **escondida** *fem*
hidden

escorpio, **escorpión** *masc & fem noun*
▷ see **escorpión** *noun*
Scorpio (*star sign*)
Soy escorpio. I'm Scorpio.

WORD TIP Use a small letter in Spanish to say *I am Scorpio*, etc with star signs.

el **escorpión** *masc noun*
▷ see **escorpio** *noun*
scorpion

♪ **escribir** *verb* **[52]**
1 **to write**
escribir una novela to write a novel
Le escribí una postal. I wrote him a postcard.
2 **escribir a máquina** to type

escribirse *reflexive verb*
to spell
¿Cómo se escribe tu nombre? How do you spell your name?
Se escribe así. You spell it like this.

escrito *verb* ▷ **escribir**

el **escritor** *masc noun*, la **escritora** *fem*
writer

el **escritorio** *masc noun*
1 **desk**
2 (*Latin America*) **office**

♪ **escuchar** *verb* **[17]**
1 **to listen**
Escuchamos atentamente. We listened carefully.
2 **to listen to**
Escúchame. Listen to me.
Escucha bien lo que digo. Listen carefully to what I say.

♪ la **escuela** *fem noun*
school (*usually primary*)
- la **escuela nocturna** night school
- la **escuela primaria** primary school

el **escultor** *masc noun*, la **escultora** *fem*
sculptor

la **escultura** *fem noun*
sculpture

escupir *verb* **[19]**
1 **to spit**
escupirle a alguien to spit at someone
Le escupió en la cara. She spat in his face.
2 **to spit out**
Escupió la comida. He spat out the food.

el **escúter** *masc noun*
motor scooter

♪ **ese** *masc adjective*, **esa** *fem* ▷ see **ese** *pron*
1 **that**
ese libro that book
esa chica that girl
Ese chico es mi primo. That boy is my cousin.
¿Quién es esa chica? Who is that girl?
2 **esos, esas** those
esos zapatos those shoes
esas camisas those shirts
Esos chicos son de mi clase. Those boys are in my class.
¿Quienes son esos chicos? Who are those boys?

♪ **ese**, **esa**, **ése**, **ésa** *pronoun* ▷ see **ese** *adj*
1 **that one**
Ese es más bonito. That one is nicer (*for a masc noun*).
Me gusta más esa. I like that one better (*for a fem noun*).
¿Quién es esa? Who is that? (*girl*)
¿Quién es ese? Who is that? (*boy*)
2 **esos, esas** those ones
Esos son más bonitos. Those ones are prettier (*for a masc pl noun*).
Me gustan más esas. I like those ones better (*for a fem pl noun*).

el **esfuerzo** *masc noun*
effort
hacer un esfuerzo to make an effort

el **esguince** *masc noun*
sprain

el **eslogan** *masc noun*
slogan

eslovaco *masc adjective & noun*, **eslovaca** *fem adjective & noun*
1 **Slovak**
2 **un eslovaco, una eslovaca** Slovak

WORD TIP Adjectives and nouns for nationality and regional origin do not have capital letters in Spanish.

Eslovaquia *fem noun*
Slovakia

Eslovenia *fem noun*
Slovenia

esloveno *masc adjective & noun*, **eslovena** *fem adjective & noun*
1 **Slovene**
2 un esloveno, una eslovena Slovene

WORD TIP Adjectives and nouns for nationality and regional origin do not have capital letters in Spanish.

eso *pronoun*
1 **that**
Eso no importa. That doesn't matter.
¿Qué es eso? What's that?
Por eso no vinimos. That's why we didn't come.
2 **a eso de ...** about ...
a eso de las ocho about eight o'clock

WORD TIP *eso* never changes.

la **ESO** *fem*
(= *Educación Secundaria Obligatoria*) **secondary education programme** (*for the 12-16 age group in Spain*)

esos *masc plural adjective*, **esas** *fem plural adjective*
those
▷ **ese** *adj, pron*

esos, **ésos**, **esas**, **ésas** *pronoun*
those ones
▷ **ese** *adj, pron*

la **espada** *fem noun*
sword

espabilado *masc adjective*, **espabilada** *fem*
alert, **on-the-ball**

el **espacio** *masc noun*
1 **space**, **room**
dejar un espacio leave a space
No tenemos suficiente espacio. We don't have enough room.
2 **el espacio** space
la exploración del espacio the exploration of space

los **espaguetis** *plural masc noun*
spaghetti

la **espalda** *fem noun*
1 **back**
Me duele la espalda. My back hurts.
nadar a espalda to swim backstroke
¿Sabes nadar a espalda? Can you do the backstoke?

España *fem noun*
Spain

español *masc adjective*, **española** *fem*
▷ see **español** *noun*
Spanish

un **español** *masc noun*, una **española** *fem*
▷ see **español** *adj*
1 **Spaniard**
los españoles the Spaniards, the Spanish
2 **el español** Spanish (*the language*)

WORD TIP Adjectives and nouns for nationality, regional origin, and language do not have capital letters in Spanish.

el **espantapájaros** *masc noun, pl:* los **espantapájaros**
scarecrow

espantoso *masc adjective*, **espantosa** *fem*
1 **horrific** (*crime*)
2 **horrible**
un vestido espantoso a horrible dress
Tiene un gusto espantoso. He has a horrible sense of taste.
3 **Hacía un frío espantoso.** It was terribly cold.
Tengo un sueño espantoso. I'm terribly sleepy.

el **esparadrapo** *masc noun*
sticking plaster

el **esparcimiento** *masc noun*
relaxation

el **espárrago** *masc noun*
asparagus

la **especia** *fem noun*
spice

especial *masc & fem adjective*
special

la **especialidad** *fem noun*
speciality

especializarse *reflexive verb* [22]
to specialize
Voy a epecializarme en ciencias. I'm going to specialize in science.

el **espectáculo** *masc noun*
1 **sight**
Era un espectáculo espantoso. It was a terrible sight.
2 **show**
el mundo del espectáculo show business

el **espectador** *masc noun*, la **espectadora** *fem*
spectator

el **espejo** *masc noun*
mirror
• el **espejo retrovisor** rear-view mirror

♪ la **espera** *fem noun*
wait
una corta espera a short wait
estar a la espera de algo to be waiting for something
Estabamos a la espera de su llamada. We were waiting for her call.

la **esperanza** *fem noun*
hope
Hay pocas esperanzas de encontrarlos. There's little hope of finding them.
darle esperanzas a alguien to raise somebody's hopes
No quiero darle esperanzas de que vendrá. I don't want to raise his hopes that she'll come.

♪ **esperar** *verb* **[17]**
1 **to wait**
Espera aquí. Wait here. (*informal use*)
Espere un momento. Wait a minute. (*formal use*)
2 **to wait for**
Te he estado esperando más de una hora. I've been waiting for you for more than an hour.
3 **to hope**
Espero que vengas. I hope you'll come.
Espero que sí., Eso espero. I hope so.
4 **to expect**
No esperaba esa respuesta. I didn't expect that answer.

♪ **espeso** *masc adjective*, **espesa** *fem*
thick

el **espesor** *masc noun*
thickness

la **espesura** *fem noun*
thickness
Tiene diez centímetros de espesura. It's ten centimetres thick.

el & la **espía** *masc & fem noun*
spy

espiar *verb* **[32]**
to spy on

la **espina** *fem noun*
thorn

las **espinacas** *fem plural noun*
spinach

el **espionaje** *masc noun*
spying, **espionage**

espléndido *masc adjective*, **espléndida** *fem*
1 **splendid** (*occasion, weather, house*)
2 **generous** (*a person*)

el **espliego** *masc noun*
lavender

la **esponja** *fem noun*
sponge

♪ el **esposo** *masc noun*, la **esposa** *fem noun*
1 **husband**
el esposo de mi hermana my sister's husband
2 **wife**
la esposa de Juan Juan's wife
3 **las esposas** handcuffs
Le pusieron esposas. He was handcuffed.

la **espuma** *fem noun*
1 **foam**
2 **lather** (*of soap*)
3 **froth** (*of beer*)
- la **espuma de afeitar** shaving foam
- la **espuma para el pelo** styling mousse

espumoso *masc adjective*, **espumosa** *fem*
1 **foaming**
2 **frothy** (*beer*)
3 **un vino espumoso** a sparkling wine

el **esqueleto** *masc noun*
skeleton

♪ el **esquí** *masc noun*
1 **ski**
2 **skiing**
practicar el esquí to go skiing
- el **esquí acuático** waterskiing
- el **esquí nórdico**, el **esquí de fondo** cross-country skiing

♪ el **esquiador** *masc noun*, la **esquiadora** *fem*
skier

♪ **esquiar** *verb* **[32]**
to ski

esquimal *masc & fem adjective & noun*
1 **Eskimo**
2 **un & una esquimal** Eskimo

WORD TIP Adjectives and nouns for nationality and regional origin do not have capital letters in Spanish.

la **esquina** *fem noun*
corner (*of a street*)
doblar la esquina to turn the corner
Vivo en la esquina de la calle León con la calle Viriato. I live on the corner of León Street and Viriato Street.

♪ **esta** *fem adjective*
this
▷ **este**, **esta** *adjective*

Spanish–English

a b c d e f g h i j k l m n ñ o p q r s t u v w x y z

esta, ésta *fem pronoun*
this one
▷ **este** *pronoun*

está, estás, etc *verb* ▷ **estar**

la **estación** *fem noun*
1 **station** (*for trains, buses*)
2 **season** (*of the year*)
la estación de las lluvias the rainy season
El otoño es mi estación preferida. Autumn is my favourite season.
• la **estación de autobuses** bus station
• la **estación de esquí** ski resort
• la **estación de servicio** petrol station

el **estacionamiento** *masc noun*
(*Latin America*) **car park**

estacionar *verb* **[17]**
to park
estacionar en doble fila to double-park

estacionario *masc adjective*, **estacionaria** *fem*
stationary

el **estadio** *masc noun*
stadium
• el **estadio de fútbol** football stadium

estado *verb* ▷ see **estado** *noun* ▷ **estar**

el **estado** *masc noun* ▷ see **estado** *verb*
1 **state**
2 **en buen estado** in good condition (*a picture, table, etc*)
3 **estar en estado** to be pregnant
• el **estado civil** marital status
• el **estado de bienestar** welfare state
• el **estado de cuenta** bank statement

los **Estados Unidos** *plural masc noun*
United States

WORD TIP *Estados Unidos* is often used without *los*

estadounidense *masc & fem adjective*
American, US

WORD TIP Adjectives and nouns for nationality and regional origin do not have capital letters in Spanis

la **estafa** *fem noun*
swindle
¡Qué estafa! What rip-off!

estáis *verb* ▷ **estar**

la **estampilla** *fem noun*
(*Latin America*) **stamp**

estallar *verb* **[17]**
1 **to explode** (*a bomb*)
2 **to burst** (*a balloon*)
3 **to blow out** (*a tyre*)

la **estancia** *fem noun*
stay
Su estancia en Madrid durará tres días. His stay in Madrid will last three days.

estando *verb* ▷ **estar**

el **estanco** *masc noun*
tobacconist's (*also selling stamps, post cards, stationery, etc*)

el **estanque** *masc noun*
pond

el **estante** *masc noun*
shelf

la **estantería** *fem noun*
1 **shelves**
2 **bookcase**

estar *verb* **[2]**
1 (*saying where someone or something is*) **to be**
¿Dónde está mi abrigo? Where's my coat?
¿Has estado en Buenos Aires? Have you been to Buenos Aires?
Estaré en Leeds un mes. I'll be in Leeds for a month.
2 (*asking, saying how someone is feeling*)
¿Cómo estás? How are you? (*about a boy or girl*)
Estoy muy bien, gracias. I'm very well, thank you (*boy or girl speaking.*)
Estoy mal. I'm not well (*boy or girl speaking*)
¿Cómo está? How is he?, How is she?
Está mal. He's not well., She's not well.
Estoy contento. I'm happy (*boy speaking*).
Estoy contenta. I'm happy (*girl speaking*).
3 (*saying how someone or something is*)
Esta paella está muy buena. This paella is very good.
La sopa está fría. The soup is cold.
Con ese vestido estás muy guapa. You look very nice in that dress.
Todavía no está terminado. It's not finished yet.
Esa falda te está corta. This skirt is too short for you.
Está casada. She's married.
4 (*saying what's happening*) **to be + -ing**
Está nevando. It's snowing.
Están viajando por África. They're travelling around Africa.
Estaban sentados allí. They were sitting over there.
5 **estar de + noun** to be (*doing something*)
Está de viaje. She's away on a trip.
Están de vacaciones. They're on holiday.
6 (*with dates*)
Estamos a tres de julio. It's the third of July.

7 *(asking, saying if something's ready)*
¿Están ya las fotocopias? Are the photocopies ready?
Sí, ya están. Yes, they're ready.
Pulsas el botón y ya está. You press the button and that's it.

WORD TIP For the other Spanish verb for *to be* ▷ **ser**.

estarse *reflexive verb* **[2]**
to stay
Se está horas mirando la tele. He watches TV for hours.
Se estuvo sentado toda la tarde. He was sitting down all afternoon.
¡Estate quieto! Keep still!

está, **estaré**, **etc** *verb* ▷ **estar**

estaría, **estarías**, **etc** *verb* ▷ **estar**

la **estatua** *fem noun*
statue

el **estatus** *masc noun*
status

este *masc adjective*, **esta** *fem*
▷ see **este** *pron, noun*
1 **this**
en este momento at this moment
en esta caja in this box
2 **estos, estas** those
estos chicos these boys
estas chicas these girls

este, **esta**, **éste**, **ésta** *pronoun*
▷ see **este** *adj, noun*
1 **this one**
Quiero este. I want this one *(for a masc noun)*.
Quiero esta. I want that one *(for a fem noun)*.
2 **estos, estas** those
Estas no, dame aquellos. Not these, give me those *(for a **masc pl** noun)*.
Estas no, dame aquellas. Not these, give me those *(for a **fem pl** noun)*.

este *masc noun, invariable adjective*
▷ see **este** *adj, pron*
east
ir hacia el este to go east
la costa este de Escocia the east coast of Scotland
al este de Granada to the east of Granada
en el este de España in the east of Spain

esté, **estén** *verb* ▷ **estar**

la **estera** *fem noun*
1 **rush matting**
2 **rush mat**
3 **beach mat**

el **estéreo** *masc noun*
stereo

estés *verb* ▷ **estar**

el & la **esteticista** *masc & fem noun*
beautician

el **estilo** *masc noun*
1 **style**
2 **ni nada por el estilo** or anything like that
o algo por el estilo or something of the kind

estimado *masc adjective*, **estimada** *fem*
dear *(in formal letters)*
Estimado Señor Pérez Dear Mr Pérez
Estimada Señora Dear Madam

estirar *verb* **[17]**
to stretch

esto *pronoun*
this
¿Qué es esto? What is this?
Esto es lo más importante. This is the most important thing.

WORD TIP *esto* never changes.

el **estofado** *masc noun*
stew

el **estómago** *masc noun*
stomach
Me duele el estómago. I've got stomachache.

Estonia *fem noun*
Estonia

estonio *masc adjective & noun*, **estonia** *fem adjective & noun*
1 **Estonian**
2 **un estonio, una estonia** Estonian

WORD TIP Adjectives and nouns for nationality and regional origin do not have capital letters in Spanish.

estornudar *verb* **[17]**
to sneeze

el **estornudo** *masc noun*
sneeze

estoy *verb* ▷ **estar**

estrecho *masc adjective*, **estrecha** *fem*
1 **narrow**
una calle estrecha a narrow street
2 **tight**
Me queda muy estrecho. It's too tight for me.

la **estrella** *fem noun*
star
- la **estrella de cine** film star
- la **estrella fugaz** shooting star

Spanish-English

estrellarse *reflexive verb* **[17]**
to crash
estrellarse contra algo to crash into something
Se estrelló contra un árbol. He crashed into a tree.

estrenar *verb* **[17]**
to show for the first time out (*films, plays*)
La película se estrena el próximo lunes. The film comes out next Monday.
El domingo estrenaré los zapatos. I'll wear my new shoes on Sunday.
Aún no he estrenado la bici. I haven't used the new bike yet.

el **estreno** *masc noun*
première, first showing (*of a film*)

estreñido *masc adjective*, **estreñida** *fem*
constipated

estresado *masc adjective*, **estresada** *fem*
stressed

estricto *masc adjective*, **estricta** *fem*
strict

estropear *verb* **[17]**
1 **to break**
Vas a estropear la tele si sigues haciendo eso. You'll wreck the TV if you carry on doing that.
2 **to spoil**
El tiempo nos estropeó las vacaciones. The weather spoiled our holidays.
3 **to damage**
Me estropeó el coche. He damaged my car.
4 **to ruin** (*a carpet or dress, for example*)

estropearse *reflexive verb* **[17]**
1 **to break down**
Se ha estropeado el coche otra vez. The car's broken down again.
2 **to go off** (*fruit*)
3 **to go bad** (*milk or fish*)
4 **to get ruined** (*a carpet or dress, for example*)

la **estructura** *fem noun*
structure

el **estuche** *masc noun*
case (*for glasses, pencils, etc*)

el & la **estudiante** *masc & fem noun*
student

estudiar *verb* **[17]**
1 **to study**
estudiar medicina to study medicine
2 **to learn**
Tenemos que estudiar dos temas para mañana. We have to study two topics for tomorrow.

el **estudio** *masc noun*
1 **studio** (*in a house*)
2 **studio flat**
3 **study**
el estudio de la naturaleza the study of nature

los **estudios** *plural masc noun*
studies
- los **estudios de mercado** market research
- los **estudios superiores** higher education

la **estufa** *fem noun*
1 **heater**
2 **fire**

estupendo *masc adjective*, **estupenda** *fem*
great
¿Ganaste? ¡Estupendo! Did you win? Great!

estúpido *masc adjective*, **estúpida** *fem*
▷ see **estúpido** *noun*
stupid

el **estúpido** *masc noun*, la **estúpida** *fem*
▷ see **estúpido** *adj*
stupid person
Es un estúpido. He's really stupid.

estuve, **estuviste**, **etc** *verb* ▷ **estar**

estuviera, **estuvieras**, **etc** *verb* ▷ **estar**

la **etapa** *fem noun*
stage
por etapas in stages

el **etcétera** *masc noun*
etcetera

la **eternidad** *fem noun*
eternity

la **ética** *fem noun*
ethics

la **etiqueta** *masc noun*
1 **label**
2 **price tag**

el **euro** *masc noun*
euro
El euro se divide en cien céntimos. The euro is divided into a hundred cents.

el **eurodiputado** *masc noun*, la **eurodiputada** *fem*
MEP, Member of the European Parliament

Europa *fem noun*
Europe

a b c d e f g h i j k l m n ñ o p q r s t u v w x y z

europeo *masc adjective & noun*, **europea** *fem adjective & noun*
1 **European**
2 **un europeo, una europea** European

WORD TIP Adjectives and nouns for nationality and regional origin do not have capital letters in Spanish.

la **eurozona** *fem noun*
eurozone

Euskadi *fem noun*
the Basque Country (*Euskadi is the Basque language name for the area of Spain bordering South-West France*)

euskera *masc & fem adjective, masc noun*
1 **Basque**
2 **el euskera** Basque (*the language*)

WORD TIP Adjectives and nouns for nationality, regional origin, and language do not have capital letters in Spanish.

la **evaluación** *fem noun*
assessment

evaporarse *reflexive verb* **[17]**
to evaporate

la **evidencia** *fem noun*
evidence

evidente *masc & fem adjective*
obvious

evidentemente *adverb*
obviously

evitar *verb* **[17]**
1 **to avoid**
Evitan tomar la responsabilidad. They avoid taking responsibility.
2 **to prevent**
evitar un accidente to prevent an accident

la **evolución** *fem noun*
evolution

exactamente *adverb*
exactly

exacto *masc adjective*, **exacta** *fem*
1 **exact**
2 **accurate**

exagerar *verb* **[17]**
to exaggerate

♪ el **examen** *masc noun*
exam
hacer un examen to take an exam
presentarse a un examen to sit an exam
aprobar un examen to pass an exam
- el **examen oral** oral exam

examinar *verb* **[17]**
to examine

examinarse *reflexive verb* **[17]**
to take an exam

excelente *masc & fem adjective*
excellent

la **excepción** *fem noun*
exception
hacer una excepción to make an exception
a excepción de with the exception of

excepcional *masc & fem adjective*
exceptional

excepcionalmente *adverb*
exceptionally

♪ **excepto** *preposition*
except for

exclusivo *masc adjective*, **exclusiva** *fem*
exclusive

la **excursión** *fem noun*
trip
irse de excursión to go away on a trip
Nos vamos de excursión al campo. We're going on a trip into the countryside.

la **excusa** *fem noun*
excuse
poner excusas to make excuses

exigente *masc & fem adjective*
demanding

exigir *verb* **[49]**
to demand

exiliado *masc adjective*, **exiliada** *fem*
exiled

existir *verb* **[19]**
1 **to exist**
2 **Existen motivos para pensarlo.** There are reasons to think that.

el **éxito** *masc noun*
success
tener éxito to be successful

WORD TIP *éxito* does not mean *exit* in English; for the meaning of *exit* ▷ **salida**.

♪ la **experiencia** *fem noun*
experience
- la **experiencia laboral** work experience

experimentado *masc adjective*, **experimentada** *fem*
experienced

el **experimento** *masc noun*
experiment

el **experto** *masc noun*, la **experta** *fem*
expert

la **explicación** *fem noun*
explanation

explicar *verb* [31]
to explain

explorar *verb* [17]
to explore

explotar *verb* [17]
to explode

la **exportación** *fem noun*
export
La lana es la exportación más importante. Wool is the most important export.

exportar *verb* [17]
to export
Rusia exporta mucha madera y petróleo. Russia exports a lot of oil and timber.

la **exposición** *fem noun*
exhibition

expresar *verb* [17]
to express

la **expresión** *fem noun*
expression

expreso *masc adjective*, **expresa** *fem*
▷ see **expreso** *noun*
express

el **expreso** *masc noun* ▷ see **expreso** *adj*
1 **express train**
2 **espresso** (*coffee*)

extenderse *reflexive verb* [36]
to stretch out
Se extiende hasta Tierra del Fuego. It stretches as far as Tierra del Fuego.

exterior *masc & fem adjective*
▷ see **exterior** *noun*
1 **outer** (*layer*)
2 **outside** (*temperature*)
3 **la parte exterior de la casa** the outside of the house
4 **foreign**
- la **política exterior** foreign policy

el **exterior** *masc noun* ▷ see **exterior** *adj*
1 **exterior, outside**
el exterior de la casa the outside of the house
2 **outward appearance**
En su exterior estaba tranquilo. His outward appearance was calm.

externo *masc adjective*, **externa** *fem*
external, outward

la **extinción** *fem noun*
extinction
una especie en peligro de extinción an endangered species

extincto *masc adjective*, **extincta** *fem*
extinct

el **extintor** *masc noun*
extinguisher
- el **extintor (de incendios)** fire extinguisher

extraescolar *masc & fem adjective*
out-of-school
las actividades extraescolares out-of-school activities

extrañar *verb* [17]
Le extrañó verla allí. He was surprised to see her there.
Me extraña que no hayan llamado. I'm surprised they haven't phoned.

extranjero *masc adjective*, **extranjera** *fem* ▷ see **extranjero** *noun*
foreign

el **extranjero** *masc noun*, la **extranjera** *fem* ▷ see **extranjero** *adj, noun*
foreigner

extranjeros

Más de 50 millones de extranjeros visitan España cada año de los cuales 14 millones son del Reino Unido. Actualmente casi un millón viven allí permanentemente y otros dos millones tienen una residencia secundaria (casa) en el país.

el **extranjero** *masc noun*
▷ see **extranjero** *adj, noun*
vivir en el extranjero to live abroad
Viaja mucho al extranjero. He travels abroad a lot.

extraño *masc adjective*, **extraña** *fem*
▷ see **extraño** *noun*
strange

🗝 el **extraño** *masc noun*, la **extraña** *fem*
▷ see **extraño** *adj*
stranger

extraordinario *masc adjective*, **extraordinaria** *fem*
extraordinary

el & la **extraterrestre** *masc & fem noun*
alien (*from outer space*)

extremo *masc adjective*, **extrema** *fem*
▷ see **extremo** *noun*
extreme

el **extremo** *masc noun* ▷ see **extremo** *adj, noun*
extreme
con extremo cuidado extremely carefully

el **extremo** *masc noun*, la **extrema** *fem*
▷ see **extremo** *adj, noun*
winger (*in sports*)

extrovertido *masc adjective*, **extrovertida** *fem*
extrovert

Spanish–English

F f

a b c d e f g h i j k l m n ñ o p q r s t u v w x y z

la **fábrica** *fem noun*
factory

fabricar *verb* **[31]**
to manufacture

fácil *masc & fem adjective*
easy
Es un trabajo fácil. It's an easy job.
ser fácil de hacer to be easy to do
Es fácil de entender. It's easy to understand.

la **facilidad** *fem noun*
ease
Lo hice con facilidad. I did it with ease.
tener facilidad de palabra to have a way with words

fácilmente *adverb*
easily

la **factura** *fem noun*
bill, **invoice**
la factura del gas the gas bill

la **facultad** *fem noun*
1 (*part of a university*) **faculty**
la Facultad de Medicina the Faculty of Medicine
un compañero de facultad a fellow student
2 (*ability*) **faculty**
perder facultades to lose your faculties

facultativo *masc adjective*, **facultativa** *fem*
1 **optional**
2 **medical**

la **faena** *fem noun*
chore
• las **faenas de la casa** housework

el **faisán** *masc noun*, los **faisanes** *plural*
pheasant

la **falda** *fem noun*
skirt
• la **falda de tubo** straight skirt

la **falda escocesa** *fem noun*
1 **tartan skirt** (*for a woman*)
2 **kilt** (*for a man*)

la **falla** *fem noun*
flaw

fallar *verb* **[17]**
1 **to fail** (*equipment, brakes*)
Fallaron los frenos. The brakes failed.
2 **to go wrong** (*a plan*)
Algo ha fallado. Something's gone wrong.
Me falló la puntería. I missed. (*the target*)

el **fallo** *masc noun*
1 **fault**
El motor tiene un fallo. There's something wrong with the engine.
2 **failure**
un fallo en el sistema a failure in the system
3 **verdict** (*in a court*)
• el **fallo humano** human error

la **falsificación** *fem noun*
forgery
El cuadro es una falsificación. The picture is a forgery.

falso *masc adjective*, **falsa** *fem*
1 **false** (*document, name*)
2 **fake** (*diamond, picture*)

la **falta** *fem noun*
1 **lack**
una falta de algo a lack of something
la falta de personal staff shortage
por falta de dinero due to lack of money
2 **poner una falta a alguien** to mark someone absent
Ya tiene tres faltas. He's been absent three times already.
3 **foul** (*in sport*)
sacar la falta to take the free kick
4 **infringement**, **fault**
una falta grave a serious infringement
5 **hacer falta hacer algo** to need to do something
Hace falta comprar pan. We need to buy bread.
No hace falta cambiarlo. We don't need to change it.
No hace falta que me esperes. You don't need to wait for me.
6 **hacerle falta algo a alguien** to need something
Me hace falta un bolígrafo. I need a pen.
No me hace falta nada más, gracias. I don't need any more, thank you.

WORD TIP What you need is always the subject of *hacer falta*.

• la **falta de asistencia** absence (*from school*)
• la **falta de educación** bad manners
• la **falta de ortografía** spelling mistake

faltar *verb* **[17]**
1 **to be missing**
¿Quién falta? Who's missing?
2 (*not to turn up*) **faltar a algo** to be absent from something
faltar al colegio to be absent from school
3 (*saying you need, lack something*) **Nos falta práctica.** We need practice.
Le falta interés. He lacks interest.
Nos faltan mil euros para poder comprarlo. We need a thousand euros to buy it.
Nos faltó tiempo. We didn't have enough time.
4 (*in time expressions*) **Sólo faltan tres horas.** There are only three hours to go.
Faltan diez días para mi cumpleaños. It's ten days to my birthday.
Falta poco para el verano. It's not long before it's summer.

WORD TIP What you need, who is missing, etc is always the subject of *faltar*.

la **fama** *fem noun*
1 **fame**
2 **reputation**
tener buena fama to have a good reputation
tener fama de mentiroso to have a reputation for being a liar

la **familia** *fem noun*
family
pasar las fiestas en familia to spend the holiday with the family

familiar *masc & fem adjective*
▷ see **familiar** *noun*
1 **family**
Tiene problemas familiares. She has family problems.
2 **familiar**
Su cara me resulta familiar. Her face is familiar.

el & la **familiar** *masc & fem noun*
▷ see **familiar** *adj*
relative

famoso *masc adjective*, **famosa** *fem*
famous
ser famoso, *fem* **famosa por algo** to be famous for something
Es famosa por su poesía. She is famous for her poetry.

la **fantasía** *fem noun*
1 **fantasy**
un mundo de fantasía a fantasy world
2 **imagination**
tener mucha fantasía to have a lot of imagination

el **fantasma** *masc noun*
ghost

fantástico *masc adjective*, **fantástica** *fem*
fantastic

farmacéutico *masc adjective*, **farmacéutica** *fem*
▷ see **farmacéutico** *noun*
pharmaceutical

el **farmacéutico** *masc noun*, la **farmacéutica** *fem*
▷ see **farmacéutico** *adj*
chemist, pharmacist

la **farmacia** *fem noun*
chemist's, pharmacy
• la **farmacia de guardia** duty chemist

el **faro** *masc noun*
1 **lighthouse**
2 **headlamp**

la **farola** *fem noun*
1 **streetlight**
2 **lamp post**

fascinar *verb* **[17]**
to fascinate

fastidiar *verb* **[17]**
1 **to bother**
¡Deja de fastidiarme! Stop bothering me!
2 **to be annoying**
Sólo lo hacen para fastidiar. They only do it to annoy.
¡Deja de fastidiar! Stop being a pain!

fastidiarse *reflexive verb* **[17]**
(*showing irritation*) **¡Que se fastidie!** He'll have to put up with it!
¡Te fastidias! Tough!

el **fastidio** *masc noun*
annoyance
¡Qué fastidio! How annoying!

fatal *masc & fem adjective* ▷ see **fatal** *adv*
1 (*informal*) **awful**
Me siento fatal. I feel awful.
El tiempo fue fatal. The weather was awful.
2 **fatal** (*accident, illness*)

fatal *adverb* ▷ see **fatal** *adj*
(*informal*) **really badly**
hacer algo fatal to do something really badly
Canto fatal. I am hopeless at singing.

el **favor** *masc noun*
1 **favour**
Me pidió un favor. She asked me a favour.
hacerle un favor a alguien to do someone a favour ▸▸

¿**Me haces un favor?** Can you do me a favour
estar a favor de algo to be in favour of something
Estoy a favor de la propuesta. I'm in favour of the proposal.
2 **por favor** please
Pase, por favor. Please come in. (*formal use*)

favorito *masc adjective*, **favorita** *fem*
favourite

el **fax** *masc noun*
fax

la **fe** *fem noun*
faith

febrero *masc noun*
February
en febrero in February
el 14 de febrero on 14 February

WORD TIP Names of months and days start with small letters in Spanish.

la **fecha** *fem noun*
date
¿**A qué fecha estamos hoy?** What's the date today?
- la **fecha de caducidad** use-by date
- la **fecha de nacimiento** date of birth

la **felicidad** *fem noun*
1 **happiness**
2 (*in general*) **¡Felicidades!** Congratulations!
3 (*for birthdays*) **¡Felicidades!** Happy birthday!

felicitar *verb* **[17]**
1 (*in general*) **felicitar a alguien** to congratulate someone
¡Te felicito! Congratulations!
2 (*for birthdays*) **felicitar a alguien** to wish someone happy birthday
¡Te felicito! Happy birthday!

feliz *masc & fem adjective*, **felices** *plural*
happy
¡Feliz Año Nuevo! Happy New Year!
¡Feliz Navidad! Merry Christmas!
¡Feliz cumpleaños! Happy birthday!
¡Felices Pascuas! Happy Easter!

el **felpudo** *masc noun*
doormat

femenino *masc adjective*, **femenina** *fem*
1 **women's** (*team, fashion*)
el equipo femenino the women's team
2 **feminine** (*style, manners, noun*)
3 **female**
el sexo femenino the female sex

el **femenino** *masc noun*
▷ see **femenino** *adj*
(*Grammar*) **feminine**

fenomenal *masc & fem adjective*
▷ see **fenomenal** *adv*
(*informal*) **great**
una fiesta fenomenal a great party

fenomenal *adverb* ▷ see **fenomenal** *adj*
pasarlo fenomenal to have a great time
¡Lo pasamos fenomenal! We had a great time!

feo *masc adjective*, **fea** *fem*
ugly

la **feria** *fem noun*
fair

feroz *masc & fem adjective*, *pl:* **feroces**
fierce

la **ferretería** *fem noun*
ironmonger's, hardware store

el **ferrocarril** *masc noun*
railway

el **ferry** *masc noun*, *pl:* **ferrys**, **ferries**
ferry

festivo *masc adjective*, **festiva** *fem*
1 **festive** (*atmosphere*)
2 **un día festivo** a public holiday

fiable *masc & fem adjective*
reliable

el **fiambre** *masc noun*
cold cut of meat

fiarse *reflexive verb* **[32]**
1 **fiarse de algo** to believe something
No te fíes de los periódicos. Don't believe what you read in the newspapers.
2 **fiarse de alguien** to trust someone
No te fíes de él. Don't trust him.

la **fibra** *fem noun*
fibre

la **ficción** *fem noun*
fiction

la **ficha** *fem noun*
1 **counter** (*in board games*)
2 **index card**
3 **token** (*for a public telephone in a bar, etc*)
- la **ficha médica** medical card
- la **ficha policial** police record
- la **ficha técnica** (technical) specifications, product description

el **fideo** *masc noun*
noodle

♪ la **fiebre** *fem noun*
1 **temperature**
tener fiebre to have a temperature
Le ha subido la fiebre. His temperature has gone up.
Le ha bajado la fiebre. Her temperature has gone down.
2 **fever**
• la **fiebre del heno** hay fever

♪ **fiel** *masc & fem adjective*
1 **faithful**
No le es fiel a su mujer. He's not faithful to his wife.
2 **loyal** (*friend*)
3 **accurate** (*translation, copy*)

♪ la **fiesta** *fem noun*
1 **party**
Dan una fiesta mañana. They are having a party tomorrow.
2 **public holiday**
Mañana es fiesta. Tomorrow's a holiday.

la **figura** *fem noun*
figure

figurar *verb* **[17]**
to appear (*on a list, document*)
Su nombre no figura en la lista. Your name is not on the list. (*formal use*)

figurarse *reflexive verb* **[17]**
to imagine
Me figuro que sí. I imagine so.

♪ **fijar** *verb* **[17]**
1 **to fix**
fijar una fecha to fix a date
2 **to stick** (*bills, posters*)
No fijar carteles. Stick no bills.

fijarse *reflexive verb* **[17]**
1 **fijarse en algo** to take note of something
Fíjate en el nombre de la calle. Look carefully at the name of the street.
2 **fijarse en algo** to notice something
Se fija en todo. She notices everything.

♪ **fijo** *masc adjective*, **fija** *fem*
1 **fixed**
precios fijos fixed prices
Está fijo a la pared. It's fixed to the wall.
¿Está la escalera bien fija? Is the ladder steady?
2 **permanent** (*jobs*)

♪ la **fila** *fem noun*
1 **line**
en fila india in single file
ponerse en fila to stand in a line
Tuvimos que ponernos en fila. We had to line up.
2 **row** (*of seats in theatre, cinema*)

♪ el **filete** *masc noun*
1 **fillet** (*of meat or fish*)
filetes de lenguado fillets of sole
un filete de cerdo a pork fillet, a pork steak

♪ **filmar** *verb* **[17]**
1 **to shoot** (*a film*)
2 **to film** (*a person, an event*)

♪ la **filosofía** *fem noun*
philosophy

♪ el **fin** *masc noun*
1 **end**
el fin de mes the end of the month
a fines de junio at the end of June
llegar al fin de algo to get to the end of something
2 **por fin, al fin** at last
Por fin llegaste. At last you've arrived.
3 **en fin** well
En fin, ¿qué le vamos a hacer? Well, what's to be done about it?
• el **fin de año** New Year's Eve
• el **fin de semana** weekend

♪ **final** *masc & fem adjective* ▷ see **final** *noun*
final

♪ el **final** *masc noun* ▷ see **final** *adj, noun*
1 **end**
el final del partido the end of the match
al final de la calle at the end of the street
el final de las vacaciones the end of the holidays
2 **ending**
una película con final feliz a film with a happy ending
3 **al final** in the end
Al final lo conseguí. In the end I got it.

♪ la **final** *fem noun* ▷ see **final** *adj, noun*
final (*of a competition*)

♪ la **finca** *fem noun*
1 **plot of land**
2 **farm**

finlandés *masc adjective & noun*, **finlandesa** *fem adjective & noun*
1 **Finnish**
2 (*person*) **un finlandés, una finlandesa** Finn
el finlandés Finnish (*the language*)

WORD TIP Adjectives and nouns for nationality, regional origin, and language do not have capital letters in Spanish.

♪ **Finlandia** *fem noun*
Finland

fino *masc adjective*, **fina** *fem*
▷ see **fino** *noun*
1 **fine** (*hair, sand, line*)
2 **thin** (*layer, slice*)
3 **slender** (*waist or finger*)
4 **subtle** (*sense of humour*)
5 **refined** (*manners, person*)
6 **acute** (*senses*)
tener el oído muy fino to have a very acute sense of hearing
tener el olfato muy fino to have a very acute sense of smell

el **fino** *masc noun* ▷ see **fino** *adj*
dry sherry

la **firma** *fem noun*
1 **signature**
2 **company**

firmar *verb* [17]
to sign

firme *masc & fem adjective*
1 **steady** (*ladders, chairs*)
con pulso firme with a steady hand
2 **firm** (*beliefs, physique, attitude*)
mostrarse firme con alguien to be firm with somebody

la **física** *fem noun* ▷ see **físico** *adj, noun*
physics

físico *masc adjective*, **física** *fem*
▷ see **física, físico** *noun*
physical

el **físico** *masc noun*, la **física** *fem*
▷ see **físico** *adj, noun*
physicist

el **físico** *masc noun* ▷ see **físico** *adj, noun*
1 **physique**
2 **appearance**

la **fisioterapia** *fem noun*
physiotherapy

flaco *masc adjective*, **flaca** *fem*
thin

flamenco *masc adjective*, **flamenca** *fem*
▷ see **flamenco** *noun*
flamenco
el baile flamenco flamenco dancing

el **flamenco** *masc noun*
▷ see **flamenco** *adj*
1 **flamenco dancing**
2 **flamingo** (*bird*)

el **flan** *masc noun*
crème caramel

la **flauta** *fem noun*
flute
• la **flauta dulce** recorder

la **flecha** *fem noun*
arrow

el **flequillo** *masc noun*
fringe

flexible *masc & fem adjective*
flexible

flojo *masc adjective*, **floja** *fem*
1 **loose** (*knot, screw*)
2 **slack** (*rope*)
3 **weak** (*coffee or tea*)
4 **poor** (*a piece of work*)
5 **lazy** (*pupil, student*)

la **flor** *fem noun*
flower
de flores flower-patterned
una falda de flores a flower-patterned skirt
estar en flor to be in flower

el **florero** *masc noun*
vase

el & la **florista** *masc & fem noun*
florist

la **floristería** *fem noun*
florist's

la **flota** *fem noun*
fleet

flotar *verb* [17]
to float

fluido *masc adjective*, **fluida** *fem*
▷ see **fluido** *noun*
1 **fluid** (*substance*)
2 **free-flowing** (*traffic*)
La circulación está fluida. The traffic is flowing freely.

el **fluido** *masc noun* ▷ see **fluido** *adj*
fluid

fluir *verb* [54]
to flow

el **flujo** *masc noun*
flow

la **foca** *fem noun*
seal (*animal*)

el **foco** *masc noun*
1 **focus**
el foco de atención the focus of attention
2 **spotlight**

folclórico *masc adjective*, **folclórica** *fem*
folk
la musica folclórica folk music

el **folleto** *masc noun*
1 **leaflet**
2 **brochure**

el **fondo** *masc noun*
1 **bottom**
el fondo del lago the bottom of the lake
al fondo del baúl at the bottom of the trunk
sin fondo bottomless
llegar al fondo de algo to get to the bottom of something
Llegaron al fondo de la cuestión. They got to the bottom of the matter.
2 **back**
Está al fondo de la sala. It's at the back of the room.
3 **end**
al fondo del pasillo at the end of the corridor
4 **kitty**
Tenemos un fondo común para estas cosas. We have a kitty for these things.
5 **los fondos** funds
recaudar fondos to raise funds
6 **a fondo** in depth
estudiar algo a fondo to study something in depth
prepararse a fondo to prepare thoroughly
7 **de fondo** background
el ruido de fondo background noise
la música de fondo background music

el **fontanero** *masc noun*, la **fontanera** *fem*
plumber

el **footing** *masc noun*
jogging
hacer footing to go jogging

el **forastero** *masc noun*, la **forastera** *fem*
stranger

la **forma** *fem noun*
1 **shape**
en forma de cruz in the shape of a cross
con la forma de una hoja leaf-shaped
Tiene forma cuadrada. It's square.
2 **way**
Es mi forma de ser. It's the way I am.
3 **en forma** fit
mantenerse en forma to keep fit
4 **de todas formas** anyway
De todas formas, estamos en contacto. Anyway, we're in touch.

la **formación** *fem noun*
1 **education**
un chico con una buena formación a well-educated boy
2 **training**
- la **formación profesional** vocational training

formal *masc & fem adjective*
1 **reliable** (*person*)
2 **formal** (*dinner, or invitation*)
3 **firm** (*offer*)

formar *verb* [17]
1 **to form**
formar parejas to get into pairs (*in a class, for games, etc*)
formar un grupo de música to form a band
2 **to make up**
El equipo está formado por doce miembros. The team is made up of twelve members.
3 **to train** (*teachers, engineers, etc*)

formarse *reflexive verb* [17]
to form
Se formó un atasco. A traffic jam formed.
Se está formando hielo en la carretera. Ice is forming on the road.

formidable *masc & fem adjective*
fantastic (*informal*)

la **fórmula** *fem noun*
formula

el **formulario** *masc noun*
form

la **fortuna** *fem noun*
1 **fortune** (*riches*)
ganar una fortuna to earn a fortune
2 **luck** (*good fortune*)
Tuve la buena fortuna de conocerlos. I was lucky enough to meet them.
por fortuna fortunately

forzar *verb* [26]
1 **to force**
Me forzaron a aceptar. They forced me to accept.
2 **forzar la vista** to strain your eyes

forzarse *reflexive verb* [26]
forzarse a hacer algo to force yourself to do something
Me fuerzo a ir al gimnasio tres veces por semana. I force myself to go to the gym three times a week.

la **fosa** *fem noun*
pit
- las **fosas nasales** nostrils

♪ el **fósforo** *masc noun*
match (*to make fire*)

♪ la **foto** *fem noun*
photo
sacar una foto to take a photo
Sacamos muchas fotos durantes las vacaciones. We took many pictures during the holiday.

la **fotocopia** *fem noun*
photocopy

la **fotocopiadora** *fem noun*
photocopier

fotocopiar *verb* **[17]**
to photocopy

♪ la **fotografía** *fem noun*
1 **photography**
2 **photograph**
sacar una fotografía to take a photograph

el **fotógrafo** *masc noun*, la **fotógrafa** *fem*
photographer

fracasar *verb* **[17]**
to fail

el **fracaso** *masc noun*
failure

la **fractura** *fem noun*
fracture

frágil *masc & fem adjective*
fragile

♪ la **frambuesa** *fem noun*
raspberry
la mermelada de frambuesas raspberry jam

francés *masc adjective & noun*, **francesa** *fem adjective & noun*
1 **French**
un coche francés a French car
2 (*person*) **un francés** Frenchman
3 (*person*) **una francesa** Frenchwoman
4 **los franceses** the French (*people*)
5 **el francés** French (*the language*)

WORD TIP Adjectives and nouns for nationality, regional origin, and language do not have capital letters in Spanish.

♪ **Francia** *fem noun*
France

♪ el **frasco** *masc noun*
1 **bottle**
2 **jar**
un frasco de mermelada a jar of jam

♪ la **frase** *fem noun*
1 **sentence**
2 **phrase**
• la **frase hecha** set phrase

el **fraude** *masc noun*
fraud

♪ la **frecuencia** *fem noun*
frequency
con frecuencia often

♪ **frecuente** *masc & fem adjective*
frequent

♪ **frecuentemente** *adverb*
often, frequently

♪ el **fregadero** *masc noun*
sink (*in the kitchen*)

♪ **fregar** *verb* **[30]**
1 **to wash**
fregar los platos to wash the dishes
fregar el suelo to mop the floor
2 **to scrub**

freír *verb* **[53]**
to fry

frenar *verb* **[17]**
1 **to brake** (*when driving*)
2 **to slow down** (*a process*)

el **freno** *masc noun*
brake

♪ el **frente** *masc noun* ▷ see **frente** *fem*
1 **front** (*in a war, in weather reports*)
2 **al frente** forwards
dar un paso al frente to step forwards
3 **al frente de** at the head of
estar al frente del desfile to be at the head of the procession
4 **de frente** head on
Los camiones chocaron de frente. The lorries collided head on.
5 **frente a** opposite
Está frente a la iglesia. It's opposite the church.
6 **hacer frente a algo** to face something (*a problem, an attacker*)

♪ la **frente** *fem noun* ▷ see **frente** *masc*
forehead

♪ la **fresa** *fem noun*
strawberry
la mermelada de fresas strawberry jam

♪ **fresco** *masc adjective*, **fresca** *fem*
▷ see **fresco** *noun*
1 **cool**
una bebida fresca a cool drink
una brisa fresca a cool breeze
2 **Hoy hace fresco.** It's chilly today.

a b c d e f g h i j k l m n ñ o p q r s t u v w x y z

3 **fresh** (*vegetables, fish, milk*)
pescado fresco fresh fish
4 **pintura fresca** wet paint
5 (*informal*) **ser muy fresco** to have a nerve
Es muy fresca. She's got a nerve.
¡Qué fresco! What a nerve!

♪ el **fresco** *masc noun* ▷ see **fresco** *adj*
fresh air
tomar el fresco to get some fresh air
estar al fresco to be out in the fresh air
Hace fresco. It's chilly.

fría, **frío**, **etc** *verb* ▷ **freír**

friega, **friego**, **friegue**, **etc** *verb* ▷ **fregar**

♪ el **frigorífico** *masc noun*
fridge

♪ el **frijol** *masc noun*
bean

♪ **frío** *masc adjective*, **fría** *fem* ▷ see **frío** *noun*
cold
un día frío a cold day

♪ el **frío** *masc noun* ▷ see **frío** *adj*
1 **cold**
2 **hacer frío** to be cold (*weather, etc*)
Hace frío. It's cold.
¡Qué frío hace! It's so cold!
3 **tener frío** to be cold (*people, etc*)
Tengo mucho frío. I'm very cold.
▷ **calor**

♪ **frito** *masc adjective*, **frita** *fem*
fried
huevos fritos fried eggs

♪ la **frontera** *fem noun*
border
Cruzamos la frontera en Irún. We crossed the border at Irún.

♪ el **frontón** *masc noun*
1 (*Sport*) **pelota court**
2 (*Sport*) **the game of pelota** (*a traditional Basque game*)

frotar *verb* [17]
to rub

frotarse *reflexive verb* [17]
to rub

fruncir *verb* [66]
fruncir el ceño to frown

frustrante *masc & fem adjective*
frustrating

frustrar *verb* [17]
1 **to frustrate** (*a person*)
2 **to spoil** (*plans*)

♪ la **fruta** *fem noun*
fruit
fruta de la temporada fruit in season

♪ la **frutería** *fem noun*
fruit shop

el **frutero** *masc noun*
fruit bowl

el **fruto** *masc noun*
fruit
- los **frutos secos** nuts and dried fruits

fue *verb* ▷ **ser, ir**

♪ el **fuego** *masc noun*
1 **fire**
encender el fuego to light the fire
¿Tienes fuego? Have you got a light?
prenderle fuego a algo to set fire to something
Prendió fuego al bosque. She set fire to the woods.
2 (*in cooking*) **cocinar algo a fuego lento** to cook something on a low heat
- los **fuegos artificiales** fireworks

la **fuente** *fem noun*
1 **spring** (*water source*)
2 **fountain**
3 **large dish**
una fuente de servir a serving dish
una fuente de horno an oven-proof dish

fuera, **fuéramos**, **etc** *verb*
▷ see **fuera** *adv* ▷ **ser, ir**

♪ **fuera** *adverb* ▷ see **fuera** *verb*
1 **out**
¡Sal fuera! Go out!
ahí fuera out there
Salimos a cenar fuera. We went out for dinner.
El jefe está fuera. The boss is away.
2 **outside**
Están esperando fuera. They're waiting outside.
Deja las cajas fuera. Leave the boxes outside.
Por fuera es plateado. It's silver on the outside.
la parte de fuera de la maleta the outside of the suitcase
3 **fuera de** out of, outside of
fuera de peligro out of danger
estar fuera de lugar to be out of place
estar fuera de juego to be offside
Están fuera del país. They're abroad.

fueron *verb* ▷ **ser, ir**

♪ **fuerte** *masc & fem adjective* ▷ see **fuerte** *adv*
1 **strong**
ser fuerte to be strong
un olor fuerte a strong smell
una escena fuerte a violent scene
2 **loud**
No pongas la música tan fuerte. Don't play the music so loud.
3 **big**
un beso fuerte a big kiss
Tomamos una comida fuerte al mediodía. We have a big meal at lunchtime.
4 **hard** (*blow, punch*)
5 **severe**
un dolor fuerte a severe pain

♪ **fuerte** *adverb* ▷ see **fuerte** *adj*
1 **hard**
Pégale fuerte. Hit it hard.
2 **tight**
Agárralo fuerte. Hold it tight.
3 **a lot**
Comimos fuerte. We ate a lot.

♪ la **fuerza** *fem noun*
1 **strength**
tener fuerza to be strong
No tuvo fuerza para levantarlo. He wasn't strong enough to lift it.
Empuja con todas tus fuerzas. Push as hard as you can.
2 **force**
por la fuerza by force
Lo obligaron a salir por la fuerza. They forced him to go outside.
3 **a fuerza de** by
Aprobó a fuerza de estudiar mucho. He passed by studying hard.
- la **fuerza aérea** air force
- la **fuerza de voluntad** willpower
- las **fuerzas armadas** armed forces

la **fuga** *fem noun*
1 **leak** (*of gas, water*)
una fuga de gas a gas leak
2 **escape**
un intento de fuga an attempted escape
darse a la fuga to run away

fui, fuimos, fuiste, etc *verb* ▷ **ser, ir**

el **fumador** *masc noun*, la **fumadora** *fem*
smoker
'No fumadores' 'No-smoking section'

♪ **fumar** *verb* **[17]**
to smoke
¿Fumas? Do you smoke?
No fumo. I don't smoke.

la **función** *fem noun*
1 **function**
2 **performance**
- la **función de noche** late-night performance

♪ **funcionar** *verb* **[17]**
1 **to work**
¿Cómo funciona? How does it work?
'No funciona' 'Out of order'
2 **to run**
Funciona con electricidad. It runs on electricity.

el **funcionario** *masc noun*, la **funcionaria** *fem*
civil servant
Mi padre es funcionario. My father's a civil servant.

la **funda** *fem noun*
1 **cover** (*for a cushion, pillow, etc*)
2 **sleeve** (*of a record*)
3 **pillowcase**

fundamental *masc & fem adjective*
fundamental

fundir *verb* **[19]**
to melt

fundirse *reflexive verb* **[19]**
1 **to melt**
2 **to be founded** (*companies*)

el **funeral** *masc noun*
funeral

la **funeraria** *fem noun*
undertaker's

♪ la **furgoneta** *fem noun*
van

la **furia** *fem noun*
fury
estar hecho una furia (*informal*) to be furious

♪ **furioso** *masc adjective*, **furiosa** *fem*
furious
ponerse furioso to get furious

el **fusible** *masc noun*
fuse
Saltaron los fusibles. The fuses blew.

el **fusil** *masc noun*
rifle

fusionar *verb* [17]
to merge

⸙ el **futbito** *masc noun*
five-a-side football

⸙ el **fútbol** *masc noun*
football
jugar al fútbol to play football

mini-info **fútbol**
Uruguay ganó la primera Copa Mundial de fútbol que se celebró en su país en julio de 1930.

⸙ el **futbolín** *masc noun*
1 **table football**
2 **los futbolines** amusement arcade

⸙ el & la **futbolista** *masc & fem noun*
footballer

⸙ el **fútbol sala** *masc noun*
indoor football

⸙ **futuro** *masc adjective*, **futura** *fem*
▷ see **futuro** *noun*
future

⸙ el **futuro** *masc noun* ▷ see **futuro** *adj*
future
en el futuro in future

Spanish-English

a b c d e f g h i j k l m n ñ o p q r s t u v w x y z

G g

las **gafas** *plural fem noun*
glasses
llevar gafas to wear glasses
- las **gafas de sol** sunglasses

el **galápago** *masc noun*
1 **giant turtle**
2 **terrapin**

la **galaxia** *fem noun*
galaxy

la **galería** *fem noun*
gallery
- la **galería comercial** shopping mall
- la **galería de arte** art gallery

galés *masc adjective*, **galesa** *fem*
▷ see **galés** *noun*
Welsh

un **galés** *masc noun*, una **galesa** *fem*
▷ see **galés** *adj*
1 **Welshman**
los galeses the Welsh (*people*)
2 **Welshwoman**
3 **el galés** Welsh (*the language*)

WORD TIP Adjectives and nouns for nationality, regional origin, and language do not have capital letters in Spanish.

Gales *masc noun*
el país de Gales Wales
Soy de Gales. I'm from Wales.

Galicia *fem noun*
Galicia (*the province in North-West Spain*)

gallego *masc adjective & noun*, **gallega** *fem adjective & noun*
1 **Galician**
2 **un gallego, una gallega** Galician
3 **el gallego** Galician (*the language of Galicia*)

WORD TIP Adjectives and nouns for nationality, regional origin, and language do not have capital letters in Spanish.

la **galleta** *fem noun*
biscuit

la **gallina** *fem noun*
hen

el **gallo** *masc noun*
cockerel

galopar *verb* **[17]**
to gallop

la **gama** *fem noun*
range (*of products, etc*)
una amplia gama de colores a wide range of colours

la **gamba** *fem noun*
prawn
gambas a la plancha grilled prawns

el **gamberro** *masc noun*, la **gamberra** *fem*
rowdy, **hooligan**
Es muy gamberro. He's a real rowdy.

la **gana** *fem noun*
1 **darle la gana a alguien** to feel like it
Lo hago, porque me da la gana. I do it just because I feel like it.
No quiero hacerlo, porque no me da la gana. I don't want to do it, because I don't feel like it.
Siempre hace lo que le da la gana. She always does just as she pleases.
2 **tener ganas de hacer algo** to feel like doing something
Tengo ganas de verlos. I want to see them.
No tengo ganas de ir al cine. I don't feel like going to the cinema.
3 (*in expressions*) **hacer algo sin ganas** to do something half-heartedly
hacer algo de buena gana to do something willingly
hacer algo de mala gana to do something reluctantly

el **ganado** *masc noun*
cattle
el ganado lanar sheep
el ganado vacuno cattle (*cows*)

el **ganador** *masc noun*, la **ganadora** *fem*
winner

ganador *masc adjective*, **ganadora** *fem*
winning
el equipo ganador the winning team

la **ganancia** *fem noun*
profit

ganar *verb* **[17]**
1 **to win**
ganar una carrera to win a race
ganar una medalla to win a medal
Ganaron el primer premio. They won first prize.

2 **to earn**
Gano bastante dinero. I earn a lot of money.
3 **ganarle a alguien en algo to beat someone at something**
Le gané. I beat her.
Les ganamos en natación, pero ellos nos ganaron en fútbol. We beat them at swimming, but they beat us at football.

ganarse *reflexive verb* [17]
to earn
Se ganó veinte libras repartiendo folletos. She earned twenty pounds handing out leaflets.
ganarse la vida to earn your living
Se gana la vida pintando. He earns his living by painting.

el **gancho** *masc noun*
hook

♪ la **ganga** *fem noun*
bargain
¡Qué ganga! What a bargain!

el **ganso** *masc noun*, la **gansa** *fem*
1 **goose**
2 (*informal*) **ser un ganso** to be a clown
hacer el ganso to clown around

el **garaje** *masc noun*
garage

la **garantía** *fem noun*
guarantee
estar bajo garantía to be under guarantee

garantizar *verb* [22]
to guarantee

el **garbanzo** *masc noun*
chickpea

la **garganta** *fem noun*
throat
Me duele la garganta. I have a sore throat.

el **gas** *masc noun*
gas
una cocina a gas a gas cooker
- los **gases tóxicos** toxic fumes

la **gaseosa** *fem noun*
lemonade

el **gasoil**, **gasóleo** *masc noun*
1 **diesel**
2 **heating oil**

♪ la **gasolina** *fem noun*
petrol
Voy a echar gasolina al coche. I'm going to put some petrol in the car.
- la **gasolina sin plomo** unleaded petrol

la **gasolinera** *fem noun*
petrol station

♪ **gastar** *verb* [17]
1 **to spend**
Gasta todo lo que gana. He spends everything he earns.
2 **to use**
Me gastó todo el champú. She used up all my shampoo.
Mi coche gasta mucha gasolina. My car uses a lot of petrol.
3 **to take** (*in shoe sizes, etc*)
¿Qué número de pie gastas? What shoe size do you take?
4 **to waste**
Gasta mucho en caramelos. He wastes a lot of money on sweets.

gastarse *reflexive verb* [17]
to run out
Se han gastado las pilas. The batteries have run out.

el **gasto** *masc noun*
expense
Tenemos muchos gastos. We have a lot of expenses.
- los **gastos de envío** postage and packing
- los **gastos de desplazamiento** travel expenses

la **gastronomía** *fem noun*
gastronomy

gatear *verb* [17]
to crawl

♪ el **gato** *masc noun*, la **gata** *fem*
cat

la **gaviota** *fem noun*
seagull

el **gazpacho** *masc noun*
gazpacho (*a cold soup made with tomatoes, cucumber, and other vegetables*)

el **gel** *masc noun*
gel

la **gelatina** *fem noun*
jelly

el **gemelo** *masc noun*, la **gemela** *fem*
twin

los **gemelos** *plural masc noun*
1 **binoculars**
2 **twins**

géminis *masc & fem noun*
▷ see **Géminis** *noun*
Gemini (*person born under Gemini*)
Soy géminis. I'm Gemini.

WORD TIP Use a small letter in Spanish to say *I am Gemini*, etc with star signs.

Géminis *masc noun* ▷ see **géminis** *noun*
Gemini (*the constellation*)

gemir *verb* **[57]**
to groan
gemir de dolor to groan with pain

la **generación** *fem noun*
generation

general *masc & fem adjective*
▷ see **general** *noun*
general
en general in general
por lo general generally
en términos generales in general terms

el & la **general** *masc & fem noun*
▷ see **general** *adj*
general
el general Serrano General Serrano

generalmente *adverb*
generally

generoso *masc adjective*, **generosa** *fem*
generous

la **genética** *fem noun*
genetics

♂**genial** *masc & fem adjective*
1 **brilliant**
una idea genial a brilliant idea
2 (*informal*) **great**, **brilliant**
¡Es genial! It's great!

el **genio** *masc noun*
1 **genius**
Ana es un genio. Ana is a genius.
2 **temper**
tener mal genio to be bad-tempered
¡Vaya genio! What a temper!

♂la **gente** *fem noun*
people
Vino mucha gente. Lots of people came.
La gente dice que ... People say that ...
La gente de por aquí es muy simpática. The people round here are very nice.

WORD TIP *gente* takes a singular verb in Spanish.

la **geografía** *fem noun*
geography

la **geometría** *fem noun*
geometry

el **geranio** *masc noun*
geranium

el & la **gerente** *masc & fem noun*
manager
el gerente de la fábrica the factory manager

la **gestión** *fem noun*
1 **management**
la gestión de la empresa the management of the company
2 **Papá tiene que hacer una gestión en el banco.** Dad has some business to do at the bank.

el **gesto** *masc noun*
gesture
Me hizo un gesto para que me acercara. He gestured to me to come over.
Hice un gesto de asentimiento. I nodded to say yes.

Gibraltar *masc noun*
Gibraltar
el Estrecho de Gibraltar the Straits of Gibraltar

el **gigabyte** *masc noun*
gigabyte
un disco duro de treinta gigabytes a thirty gigabyte hard disk

el **gigante** *masc noun*, la **giganta** *fem*
giant

la **gimnasia** *fem noun*
gymnastics
hacer gimnasia to do PE
Es bueno hacer gimnasia. It's good to do PE.
una clase de gimnasia a PE class
- la **gimnasia de mantenimiento** keep-fit exercises

el **gimnasio** *masc noun*
gym

el **gin tonic** *masc noun*
gin and tonic

la **ginebra** *fem noun*
gin

♂**girar** *verb* **[17]**
1 **to turn**
Gira a la derecha en el semáforo. Turn right at the traffic lights.
girar la cabeza to turn your head
2 **to go round**
La tierra gira alrededor del sol. The earth goes round the sun.
3 **to spin**
4 **girar un cheque** to write out a cheque
5 **girar dinero** to send money

el **girasol** *masc noun*
sunflower

el **gitano** *masc noun*, la **gitana** *fem*
gypsy

el **glaciar** *masc noun*
glacier

el **globo** *masc noun*
balloon

la **gloria** *fem noun*
glory

la **glorieta** *fem noun*
1 **square** (*in a town*)
2 **roundabout** (*on the road*)

glotón *masc adjective*, **glotona** *fem*
greedy

gobernar *verb* **[17]**
1 **to rule**
2 **to govern**

el **gobierno** *masc noun*
government

✓el **gol** *masc noun*
goal
marcar un gol to score a goal
ganar por tres goles a dos to win by three goals to two
perder por un gol a cero to lose by one goal to nil

el **golf** *masc noun*
golf
jugar al golf to play golf

el & la **golfista** *masc & fem noun*
golfer

el **golfo** *masc noun*
1 **gulf** (*in geography*)
2 **scoundrel**
¡Qué golfo eres! What a scoundrel you are!
3 **little rascal** (*to a child*)

la **golondrina** *fem noun*
swallow

la **golosina** *fem noun*
sweet
No comas tantas golosinas. Don't eat so many sweets.

✓el **golpe** *masc noun*
1 **blow**
Fue un duro golpe. It was a hard blow.
2 **knock**
darse un golpe to knock yourself
Se dió un golpe en la cabeza. He knocked his head.
3 **darle un golpe a alguien** to hit someone
Le dio un golpe en la cara. She hit him in the face.
4 **tap**
dar unos golpes en la mesa to tap the table
5 **de golpe** with a bang
La ventana se cerró de golpe. The window slammed shut.
Cerré el baúl de golpe. I slammed the trunk shut.

✓**golpear** *verb* **[17]**
1 **to hit**
Le golpeé la cabeza con la revista. I hit him on the head with the magazine.
2 **to bang**
La ventana golpeaba por el viento. The window was banging in the wind.
3 **to beat**
golpear un tambor to beat a drum

golpearse *reflexive verb* **[17]**
to bang
Se golpeó la pierna con la mesa. She banged her leg on the table.

la **goma** *fem noun*
1 **rubber**
botas de goma rubber boots
2 **una goma elástica** a rubber band
• la **goma de borrar** rubber (*for pencil writing*)
• la **goma espuma** foam rubber

✓**gordo** *masc adjective*, **gorda** *fem*
▷ see **gordo** *noun*
1 **fat**
ponerse gordo to get fat
¡Qué gordo te has puesto! You've got so fat.
2 **thick** (*book, sweater*)
3 **serious** (*problem or mistake*)

el **gordo** *masc noun*, la **gorda** *fem*
▷ see **gordo** *adj*
1 **fat man** (*or boy*)
2 **fat woman** (*or girl*)
3 el gordo **jackpot** (*in the state lottery*)
Le tocó el gordo. He won the jackpot.

el **gorila** *masc noun*
gorilla

la **gorra** *fem noun*
cap

el **gorro** *masc noun*
cap

la **gota** *fem noun*
1 **drop**
2 **una gota de** (*informal*) a drop of
Tomaré una gota de café. I'll have a drop of coffee.

gotear *verb* **[17]**
to drip

gozar *verb* **[22]**
to enjoy
Gozo mucho oyendo música. I enjoy listening to music a lot.
gozar de algo to enjoy something
Todos gozamos del espectáculo. We all enjoyed the show.

la **grabación** *fem noun*
recording

el **grabador** *masc noun*
tape recorder

la **grabadora** *fem noun*
tape recorder
• la **grabadora de DVD** DVD recorder

grabar *verb* **[17]**
to record
grabar música de Internet to record music on the Internet

la **gracia** *fem noun*
1 **joke**
2 **tener gracia** to be funny
Esa broma no tiene gracia. That joke isn't funny.
Tiene mucha gracia contando cosas. She's very good at telling funny stories.
Me hace gracia verlo. Seeing it makes me laugh.
3 **no hacerle gracia alguien**
No me hace ninguna gracia ir. I don't like the idea of going at all.

las **gracias** *plural fem noun*
thank you
muchas gracias thank you very much
'Muchas gracias.'—'A Usted.' 'Thank you very much.'—'Thank you' (*polite form*).
darle las gracias a alguien to thank someone
Antes de irme, les di las gracias. Before leaving, I thanked them.

gracioso *masc adjective*, **graciosa** *fem*
funny

el **grado** *masc noun*
degree
veinte grados centígrados twenty degrees centigrade
cinco grados bajo cero five degrees below zero

gradual *masc & fem adjective*
gradual

graduarse *reflexive verb* **[20]**
to graduate

el **gráfico** *masc noun*
graph
• los **gráficos** graphics (*in computing*)

la **gramática** *fem noun*
grammar

el **gramo** *masc noun*
gram

gran *adjective* ▷ **grande**

Gran Bretaña *fem noun*
Great Britain

grande, **gran** *adjective*
1 **big, large**
una casa grande a big house
La chaqueta me queda muy grande. The jacket's very big for me.
un gran número de personas a large number of people
Deme una más grande. Give me a larger size.
2 **great**
una gran oportunidad a great opportunity
Es una gran actora. She's a great actor.
Soy un gran aficionado del Atlético. I'm a great Atlético fan.
3 **grown-up**
Cuando sea grande ... When I'm grown up ...
Ya eres muy grande para hacer eso. You're too old to do that.

WORD TIP *grande* becomes *gran* before a singular noun. *grande* shows size; *gran* shows greatness.

los **grandes almacenes** *plural masc noun*
department store
Los venden en los grandes almacenes. They're sold in department stores.

el **Gran Hermano** *masc noun*
Big Brother

el **granizado** *masc noun*
crushed ice drink
granizado de limón iced lemon drink

granizar *verb* **[22]**
to hail

el **granizo** *masc noun*
hail

la **granja** *fem noun*
farm

el **granjero** *masc noun*, la **granjera** *fem*
farmer
Es granjero. He's a farmer.

el **grano** *masc noun*
1 **grain**
un grano de arena a grain of sand
2 **(coffee) bean**
3 **spot**, **pimple**
Me ha salido un grano. I've got a spot.

la **grapa** *fem noun*
staple

la **grapadora** *fem noun*
stapler

grapar *verb* [17]
to staple

la **grasa** *fem noun*
1 **fat**
el contenido de grasa the fat content
La comida tiene mucha grasa. The food is very fatty.
2 **grease**
El horno estaba lleno de grasa. The oven was covered in grease.

grasiento *masc adjective*, **grasienta** *fem*
greasy

⚷ **gratis** *adjective, adverb*
free
entrada gratis free entry
Entramos gratis. We got in free.

WORD TIP *gratis* never changes.

gratuito *masc adjective*, **gratuita** *fem*
free
La entrada es gratuita. Entry is free.

la **grava** *fem noun*
gravel

⚷ **grave** *masc & fem adjective*
serious
una enfermedad grave serious illness
Está muy grave. He's seriously ill.

la **gravedad** *fem noun*
1 **gravity** (*in physics*)
2 **seriousness** (*of a problem*)

Grecia *fem noun*
Greece
Ancient Greece la Grecia antigua

griego *masc adjective & noun*, **griega** *fem adjective & noun*
1 **Greek**
2 **un griego, una griega** Greek
3 **el griego** Greek (*the language*)

WORD TIP Adjectives and nouns for nationality, regional origin, and language do not have capital letters in Spanish.

⚷ el **grifo** *masc noun*
tap
abrir el grifo to turn on the tap
cerrar el grifo to turn off the tap

el **grillo** *masc noun*
cricket (*insect*)

la **gripe** *fem noun*
flu
tener gripe to have flu
Hoy no viene, tiene gripe. She's not coming today, she's got flu.
- la **gripe aviar** bird flu

WORD TIP *gripe* does not mean *gripe* in English; for the meaning of *gripe* ▷ **queja**

⚷ **gris** *masc & fem adjective* ▷ **see gris** *noun*
grey
No me gustan los grises. I don't like the grey ones.

⚷ el **gris** *masc noun* ▷ **see gris** *adj*
grey

⚷ **gritar** *verb* [17]
to shout
¡No grites! Don't shout!
gritar de alegría to shout for joy
gritar de dolor to scream with pain

el **grito** *masc noun*
1 **shout**
dar un grito to shout
2 **cry**, **scream**
un grito de protesta a cry of protest
un grito de dolor a cry of pain
un grito de horror a scream of horror

la **grosella** *fem noun*
redcurrant

la **grosería** *fem noun*
rude remark
No digas groserías. Don't be so rude.
¡Qué grosería! How rude!

grosero *masc adjective*, **grosera** *fem*
rude

la **grúa** *fem noun*
1 **crane**
2 **break-down truck**
No aparcar, llamamos grúa. Parked cars will be towed away. (*street sign*)

grueso *masc adjective*, **gruesa** *fem*
1 **thick**
2 **fat**

gruñón *masc adjective*, **gruñona** *fem*
grumpy

el grupo *masc noun*
group
salir en grupo to go out in a group
un grupo musical a group (*playing music*)

la **gruta** *fem noun*
grotto

el **guante** *masc noun*
glove

guapo *masc adjective*, **guapa** *fem*
good-looking
¡Qué guapa es! Isn't she good-looking!
¡Qué guapo es! Isn't he handsome!
¡Qué guapo estás! How smart you're looking!

el & la **guarda** *masc & fem noun*
1 **guard**
2 **keeper** (*in a park, museum*)

el **guardabarros** *masc noun*
mudguard

el & la **guardaespaldas** *masc & fem noun*, *pl:* **guardaespaldas**
bodyguard

guardar *verb* **[17]**
1 **to keep**
Guardo todas sus cartas. I keep all his letters.
2 **to put away**
Guarda tus cosas. Put your things away.
3 (*Computers*) **to save**
Hay que guardar tu trabajo. You must save your work.

el **guardarropa** *masc noun*
cloakroom (*in restaurant, theatre, etc*)

la **guardería infantil** *fem noun*
nursery

el & la **guardia** *masc & fem noun*
1 **policeman**
2 **policewoman**
3 **la Guardia Civil** the Civil Guard (*Spanish national police force with dark green uniforms*)
- el **guardia jurado** security guard
- el **guardia urbano** policeman

el **guardián** *masc noun*, la **guardiana** *fem*
1 **guard**
2 **guardian**

la **guarnición** *fem noun*
1 **side dish**
2 **topping**

guarro *masc adjective*, **guarra** *fem*
▷ see **guarro** *noun*
1 (*informal*) **filthy**
2 **disgusting** (*person*)

el **guarro** *masc noun*, la **guarra** *fem*
▷ see **guarro** *adj*
(*informal*) **filthy pig**

guatemalteco *masc adjective & noun*, **guatemalteca** *fem adjective & noun*
1 **Guatemalan**
2 **un guatemalteco, una guatemalteca** Guatemalan

WORD TIP Adjectives and nouns for nationality and regional origin do not have capital letters in Spanish.

guau *exclamation*
wow!

guay *invariable adjective, adverb*
(*informal*) **fantastic**, **cool**
¡Qué música más guay! What cool music!
Lo pasé guay. I had a cool time.

la **guayaba** *fem noun*
guava

la **guerra** *fem noun*
war
la guerra del Golfo the Gulf War

la **guerrilla** *fem noun*
guerrilla unit

el **guerrillero** *masc noun*, la **guerrillera** *fem*
guerrilla, **guerrilla fighter**

la **guía** *fem noun*
1 **guide** (*a book, map, etc*)
una guía de restaurantes a restaurant guide
2 **map** (*of a city or town*)
una guía urbana de Sevilla a town map of Sevilla
- la **guía del ocio** entertainment guide
- la **guía telefónica** telephone directory

el & la **guía** *masc & fem noun*
guide (*person*)
Es guía turístico. He's a tourist guide.

guiar *verb* **[32]**
to guide

guiarse *reflexive verb* **[32]**
guiarse por un mapa to follow a map

el **guijarro** *masc noun*
pebble

guiñar *verb* **[17]**
to wink

el **guiño** *masc noun*
wink

el **guión** *masc noun*
1 **dash**
2 **hyphen**
una palabra con guión a hyphenated word
3 **script** (*of a film*)

el & la **guionista** *masc & fem noun*
scriptwriter

el **guisante** *masc noun*
pea

guisar *verb* **[17]**
to cook
Guisa muy bien. He's a very good cook.

la **guitarra** *fem noun* ▷ see **guitarra** *masc & fem noun*
guitar
la guitarra española the Spanish guitar

el & la **guitarra** *masc & fem noun*
▷ see **guitarra** *fem*
guitarist

el & la **guitarrista** *masc & fem noun*
guitarist

el **gusano** *masc noun*
worm

♪ **gustar** *verb* **[17]**
1 (*to say what you like, don't like*) **Me gusta el café.** I like coffee. (*__café__ is singular, so __gusta__*)
Me gusta nadar. I like swimming. (*__nadar__ is an infinitive, so __gusta__*)
No me gustan las matemáticas. I don't like maths. (*__matemáticas__ is plural, so __gustan__*)
A mi padre le gustan las fresas. My dad likes strawberries. (*__fresas__ is plural, so __gustan__*)
¿Te gustó la película? Did you like the film? (*__película__ is singular, so __gustó__*)
No me gustaron los amigos de Paco. I didn't like Paco's friends. (*__amigos__ is plural, so __gustaron__*)
Antes no me gustaban las fiestas. I didn't use to like parties. (*__fiestas__ is plural, so __gustaban__*)
¿Te gustaría visitar Bilbao? Would you like to visit Bilbao? (*__visitar__ is an infinitive, so __gustaría__*)
A nosotros nos gustaría ir a Guatemala. We would like to go to Guatemala. (*__ir__ is an infinitive, so __gustaría__*)
2 **me gusta más ... que ...** I prefer ... to ...
Me gusta más jugar al tenis que nadar. I like playing tennis better than swimming. (*__jugar__ is an infinitive, so __gusta__*)
A Belén le gustan más los gatos que los perros. Belén prefers cats to dogs. (*__gatos__ is plural, so __gustan__*)

WORD TIP Use *gusta, gustó, gustaba, gustaría, etc* if what you like, or don't like, is *singular* or an infinitive. Use *gustan, gustaron, gustaban, gustarían, etc* if what you like, or don't like is *plural*.

el **gusto** *masc noun*
1 **taste**
Tiene buen gusto. It tastes nice.
Tengo mal gusto en la boca. I have a nasty taste in my mouth.
tener gusto a algo to taste of something
Tiene gusto a menta. It tastes of mint.
2 **taste** (*likes and dislikes*)
Tiene muy buen gusto. She has very good taste.
3 (*in introductions*) **Mucho gusto.** Pleased to meet you.

Spanish-English

a b c d e f g h i j k l m n ñ o p q r s t u v w x y z

H h

ha *verb* ▷ **haber**

el **haba** *fem noun*
1 **bean**
2 **broad bean**

WORD TIP *haba* takes *el* or *un* in the singular even though it is feminine.

habéis *verb* ▷ **haber**

haber *verb* **[6]**
1 (*forming past tenses using* **have** *and* **had**) **to have**
Ha venido Laura. Laura has come.
He comprado el pan. I have bought the bread.
No habían llegado. They hadn't arrived.
No había comido cuando llegamos. She had not eaten when we arrived.
2 **haber de** to have to, must
He de ir a la oficina. I have to go to the office.
Ha de ser tarde. It must be late.
3 (*with the singular forms:* **hay**, **había**, *etc*) **hay** there is, there are
había there was, there were
habrá there will be
Hay una carta para ti. There's a letter for you.
No hay sopa. There isn't any soup.
Hay muchos errores. There are many mistakes.
Ha habido varios cambios. There have been several changes.
Había un señor en la puerta. There was a man at the door.
Había más de treinta personas. There were more than thirty people.
Hubo un accidente ayer. There was an accident yesterday.
Hubo cinco muertos. There were five dead.
Habrá bocadillos y bebidas. There will be sandwiches and drinks.
'¿Qué van a tomar de postre?'—'¿Hay helado?' 'What would you like for pudding?'—'Have you got ice cream?'
4 (*in expressions*) **'Gracias.'—'No hay de qué.'** 'Thank you.'—'Don't mention it.'
Hola ¿qué hay? Hello, how are things?
5 (*to say* **must** *with the forms:* **hay que**, **había que**, *etc*) **Hay que comprar leche.** We must buy milk.
Habrá que hacerlo. It'll have to be done.
Hay que leer las instrucciones. We must read the instructions.
¿Qué hay que hacer? What needs to be done?

WORD TIP The choice of *I, must, you must, we need, etc* depends on who you are speaking to.

había, **habías**, **etc** *verb* ▷ **haber**

habido, *verb* ▷ **haber**

habiendo, *verb* ▷ **haber**

hábil *masc & fem adjective*
1 **skilful**
un político muy hábil a very clever politician
Es una jugadora hábil. She is a skilful player.
2 **working**
un día hábil a working day

la **habilidad** *fem noun*
skill

la **habitación** *fem noun*
room
- la **habitación doble** double room
- la **habitación individual** single room
- la **habitación sencilla** single room

el & la **habitante** *masc & fem noun*
inhabitant
¿Cuántos habitantes tiene Granada? How many people live in Granada?

el **habla** *fem noun*
1 (*answering the phone*) **al habla** speaking
'¿Está el Señor López?'—'Al habla.' 'Is Sr López there?'—'Speaking.'
2 **speech**
Se quedó sin habla. He was speechless.
3 (*with languages*) **un país de habla hispana** a Spanish-speaking country

WORD TIP *habla* takes *el* or *un* in the singular even though it is feminine.

hablador *masc adjective*, **habladora** *fem*
▷ see **hablador** *noun*
talkative

el **hablador** *masc noun*, la **habladora** *fem*
▷ see **hablador** *adj*
1 **chatterbox**
2 **gossip**

hablar *verb* **[17]**
1 **to speak**
hablar en voz baja to speak in a low voice
Habla con acento inglés. She speaks with an English accent.
Sabe hablar inglés. He speaks English.

¿Hablas algún idioma? Do you speak any foreign languages?
'Se habla inglés' 'English spoken' (*shop notice*)
2 **to speak** (*on the phone*)
¿Quién habla? Who's speaking, please?
Está hablando por teléfono. He's on the phone.
3 **to talk**
No habla mucho. She doesn't talk much.
hablar con alguien to talk to somebody
Está hablando con mi madre. He's talking to my mother.
hablar de algo to talk about something
Habla mucho de ti. She talks about you a lot.
Habló de sus proyectos. He talked about his plans.

habrá, **habría**, **etc** *verb* ▷ **haber**

hacer *verb* **[7]**
1 **to make**
hacer un ruido to make a noise
hacer un pastel to make a cake
hacer la cama to make the bed
2 **to do**
hacer los deberes to do your homework
No sé qué hacer. I don't know what to do.
¿Qué haces? What are you doing?
¿Qué hace tu padre? What does your father do? (*for a living*)
3 **to cook**
hacer la comida to cook lunch
hacer la cena to cook dinner
4 **to build** (*a house, road*)
5 (*for heat, cold, weather conditions*) **Hace frío.** It's cold.
Hace calor. It's hot.
Hacía mucho viento. It was very windy.
Este verano ha hecho muy buen tiempo. The weather's been very good this summer.
6 **hacer a alguien hacer algo** to make someone do something
Le hice repetirlo. I made him do it again.
Eso me hizo pensar. That made me think.
7 (*for time*) **Hace tres días.** Three days ago.
Hace tres días que se fueron. They left three days ago.
Eso pasó hace mucho tiempo. That happened a long time ago.
La vi hace poco. I saw her a little while ago.
¿Cuánto tiempo hace que vives aquí? How long have you been living here?
Hacía dos meses que no iba a verlos. I hadn't been to see them for two months.
Trabaja aquí desde hace tres meses. She's been working here for three months.

WORD TIP In phrases where *desde hace* means *for* in time expressions, Spanish uses the present tense and English the present perfect (have been + ing).

hacerse *reflexive verb* **[7]**
1 **to become**
hacerse famoso to become famous
Se hicieron amigos. They became friends.
Se están haciendo viejos. They're getting old.
2 **hacerse algo** to do something to yourself
Me he hecho un corte en el dedo. I've cut my finger.
3 **hacerse algo** to make something for yourself
Me he hecho un vestido. I've made myself a dress.
Se ha hecho una mesa para la cocina. She's made a table for her kitchen.
4 (*used impersonally*) **¿Cómo se hace?** How do you do it?

el **hacha** *fem noun*
axe

WORD TIP *hacha* takes *el* or *un* in the singular even though it is feminine.

hacia *preposition*
1 **towards**
hacia el norte northwards
Vinieron hacia mí. They came towards me.
Muévelo hacia abajo. Move it down.
2 (*with time*) **about**
Llamaré hacia las dos de la tarde. I'll call at about two o'clock.
Te pagaré hacia final de mes. I'll pay you towards the end of the month.

la **hacienda** *fem noun*
ranch (*especially in Latin America*)

el **hada** *fem noun*
fairy

WORD TIP *hada* takes *el* or *un* in the singular even though it is feminine.

haga, **hago**, **etc** *verb* ▷ **hacer**

Haití *masc noun*
Haiti

haitiano *masc adjective & noun*, **haitiana** *fem adjective & noun*
1 **Haitian** ▸▸

Spanish–English
a b c d e f g h i j k l m n ñ o p q r s t u v w x y z

2 un haitiano, una haitiana Haitian

WORD TIP Adjectives and nouns for nationality, regional origin, and language do not have capital letters in Spanish.

halagar *verb* **[28]**
to flatter

el **halcón** *masc noun*
falcon

hallar *verb* **[17]**
to find
No hallaron una solución. They couldn't find a solution.

hallarse *reflexive verb* **[17]**
(*formal*)
1 **to be**
El pueblo se halla cerca del mar. The village is near the sea.
2 **to feel**
Me hallaba tranquilo. I was feeling calm.

la **hamaca** *fem noun*
hammock

el **hambre** *fem noun*
hunger
tener hambre to be hungry
¿Tienes hambre? Are you hungry?
No, no tengo hambre. No, I'm not hungry.
Sí, me muero de hambre. Yes, I'm starving.
El ejercicio da hambre. Exercise makes you hungry.

WORD TIP *hambre* takes *el* or *un* in the singular even though it is feminine. Use *tener* to say you're feeling hungry, hot, etc

la **hamburguesa** *fem noun*
hamburger

la **hamburguesería** *fem noun*
hamburger bar

el **hámster** *masc noun*
hamster

han *verb* ▷ **haber**

harán, **haré**, **etc** *verb* ▷ **hacer**

la **harina** *fem noun*
flour
- la **harina con levadura** self-raising flour
- la **harina integral** wholemeal flour

hartarse *reflexive verb* **[17]**
to get fed up
hartarse de algo to get fed up with something
Me harté de esperar. I got fed up with waiting.
Me estoy hartando de este estilo. I'm getting fed up with this style.

harto *masc adjective*, **harta** *fem*
estar harto de algo to be fed up with something
Estoy harta de tus excusas. I'm fed up with your excuses.
Están hartos de comer lo mismo. They're fed up with eating the same thing.

has *verb* ▷ **haber**

hasta *preposition*
1 **until**
Me quedo hasta la semana que viene. I'm staying until next week.
hasta que until
Esperamos hasta que paró de llover. We waited until it stopped raining.
No lo mandes hasta que yo lo diga. Don't send it until I tell you.
2 (*in greetings*) **¡Hasta mañana!** See you tomorrow!
¡Hasta luego! See you later!
¡Hasta pronto! See you soon!
¡Hasta el sábado! See you on Saturday!
3 **up to**
Hasta hace tres meses. Up to three months ago.
hasta ahora up to now
Hasta ahora no lo hemos visto. We haven't seen him up to now.
4 **even**
Hasta un niño sabe eso. Even a child knows that.

hay *verb* ▷ **haber**

haya, **hayas**, **etc** *verb* ▷ **haber**

haz *verb* ▷ **hacer**

he *verb* ▷ **haber**

el **hechizo** *masc noun*
1 **spell**
2 **fascination**

hecho *masc adjective*, **hecha** *fem*
▷ see **hecho** *noun*
1 **made**
hecho a mano hand-made
zapatos hechos a mano hand-made shoes
2 **done**
un trabajo bien hecho a job well done
¡Bien hecho! Well done!

el **hecho** *masc noun* ▷ see **hecho** *adj*
1 **fact**
El hecho es que ... The fact is ...
¿Cuáles son los hechos? What are the facts?
de hecho in fact
2 **action**
Tenemos que pasar de las palabras a los hechos. We must stop talking and take action.

a b c d e f g h i j k l m n ñ o p q r s t u v w x y z

la **helada** *fem noun*
frost

♪ la **heladería** *fem noun*
ice cream parlour

♪ el **heladero** *masc noun*, la **heladera** *fem*
ice cream seller

♪ **helado** *masc adjective*, **helada** *fem*
▷ see **helado** *noun*
1 **frozen**
El río estaba helado. The river was frozen.
La pobre chica estaba helada. The poor girl was frozen.
2 **freezing**
Estoy helado. I'm freezing.
La casa está helada. The house is freezing.
Tienes las manos heladas. Your hands are freezing.

♪ el **helado** *masc noun* ▷ see **helado** *adj*
ice cream
un helado de fresa a strawberry ice cream
helados de todos sabores ice creams of all flavours

♪ **helar** *verb* **[29]**
to freeze
Esta noche va a helar. There's going to be a frost tonight.

helarse *reflexive verb* **[29]**
to freeze
El río se ha helado. The river has frozen over.

la **hélice** *fem noun*
propeller

♪ el **helicóptero** *masc noun*
helicopter

♪ **hemos** *verb* ▷ **haber**

el **heno** *masc noun*
hay

♪ **heredar** *verb* **[17]**
to inherit
heredar el trono to succeed to the throne

♪ el **heredero** *masc noun*, la **heredera** *fem*
heir
Es la heredera de una fortuna. She is the heir to a fortune.

♪ la **herida** *fem noun* ▷ see **herido** *adj*
injury

♪ **herido** *masc adjective*, **herida** *fem*
▷ see **herida** *noun*
1 **injured**
estar gravemente herido to be seriously injured
2 **wounded**
Resultó herido en la pelea. He was wounded in the fight.

♪ **herir** *verb* **[14]**
1 **to wound**
Fue herido de muerte. He was fatally wounded.
2 **to hurt**
Hirieron mis sentimientos. They hurt my feelings.

♪ la **hermana** *fem noun*
▷ see **hermano** *noun*
sister
Tengo una hermana. I have one sister.
- la **hermana gemela** twin sister
- la **hermana política** sister-in-law

♪ el **hermanastro** *masc noun*, la **hermanastra** *fem*
1 **stepbrother**
2 **stepsister**
3 **half-brother**
4 **half-sister**

♪ el **hermano** *masc noun*
▷ see **hermana** *noun*
1 **brother**
Tengo dos hermanos. I have two brothers.
2 **hermanos** brothers and sisters
¿Tienes hermanos? Do you have any brothers and sisters?
- el **hermano gemelo** twin brother
- el **hermano político** brother-in-law

♪ **hermoso** *masc adjective*, **hermosa** *fem*
beautiful

♪ el **héroe** *masc noun*
hero

♪ la **heroína** *fem noun*
1 **heroine**
2 **heroin** (*the drug*)

♪ la **herramienta** *fem noun*
tool

♪ **hervir** *verb* **[14]**
to boil
hervir las patatas to boil the potatoes
El agua está hirviendo. The water is boiling.

♪ **hice** *verb* ▷ **hacer**

hidratante *masc & fem adjective*
moisturizing

♪ la **hiedra** *fem noun*
ivy

♪ el **hielo** *masc noun*
ice
un cubito de hielo an ice cube

la **hierba** *fem noun*
1 **grass**
'No pisar la hierba' 'Do not walk on the grass'
2 **herb**
hierbas aromáticas aromatic herbs
3 **una hierba mala** a weed
• las **hierbas de cocina** herbs (*for cooking*)

el **hierro** *masc noun*
iron

el **hígado** *masc noun*
liver

higiénico *masc adjective*, **higiénica** *fem*
hygienic

el **higo** *masc noun*
fig

la **hija** *fem noun* ▷ see **hijo** *noun*
daughter
• la **hija política** daughter-in-law

el **hijo** *masc noun* ▷ see **hija** *noun*
1 **son**
Su hijo se llama Carlos. Their son is called Carlos.
2 **hijos** children
Tienen tres hijos. They have three children.
• el **hijo político** son-in-law

el **hilo** *masc noun*
thread

el **himno** *masc noun*
hymn

el & la **hincha** *masc & fem noun*
supporter
Es hincha del Sevilla. He's a Seville supporter.

hinchado *masc adjective*, **hinchada** *fem*
swollen

hinchar *verb* [17]
1 **to blow up** (*a balloon*)
2 **to pump up** (*a tyre*)

hincharse *reflexive verb* [17]
to swell up
Se me ha hinchado el tobillo. My ankle has swollen up.

la **hinchazón** *fem noun*
swelling

hindú *masc & fem adjective & noun*
1 **Hindu**
2 **un & una Hindu** Hindu
los hindúes the Hindus

WORD TIP Adjectives and nouns for religion do not have capital letters in Spanish.

el **hinduismo** *masc noun*
(*Religion*) **el hinduismo** Hinduism

WORD TIP Religions are spelt with a small letter in Spanish.

el **hipermercado** *masc noun*
hypermarket

hipnotizar *verb* [25]
to hypnotize

el **hipo** *masc noun*
hiccups
tener hipo to have hiccups

la **hipoteca** *fem noun*
mortgage

hispano *masc adjective*, **hispana** *fem*
▷ see **hispano** *noun*
1 **Hispanic** (*to do with Spanish*)
países de habla hispana Spanish-speaking countries
2 **Hispanic, Spanish American** (*in the United States*)

un **hispano** *masc noun*, una **hispana** *fem*
▷ see **hispano** *adj*
Hispanic
En Estados Unidos hay cada vez más hispanos. There are more and more Hispanics in the United States.

WORD TIP Adjectives and nouns for nationality, regional origin, and language do not have capital letters in Spanish.

Hispanoamérica *fem noun*
Latin America

hispanoamericano *masc adjective & noun*, **hispanoamericana** *fem adjective & noun*
1 **Latin American**
2 **un hispanoamericano, una hispanoamericano** Latin American

hispanohablante *masc & fem adjective*
▷ see **hispanohablante** *noun*
Spanish-speaking
una comunidad hispanohablante a Spanish-speaking community

el & la **hispanohablante** *masc & fem noun*
▷ see **hispanohablante** *adj*
Spanish speaker

WORD TIP Adjectives and nouns for nationality and regional origin do not have capital letters in Spanish.

mini-info ***hispanohablantes***
Más de 350 millones de personas hablan español como primera lengua.

♪ la **historia** *fem noun*
1 **history**
la historia de Chile the history of Chile
2 **story**
una apasionante historia de aventuras an exciting adventure story
una historia de miedo a horror story

♪ **histórico** *masc adjective*, **histórica** *fem*
1 **historical**
documentos históricos historical documents
2 **historic**
un acontecimiento histórico a historic event

♪ la **historieta** *fem noun*
cartoon

♪ **hizo** *verb* ▷ **hacer**

♪ el **hogar** *masc noun*
home
una persona sin hogar a homeless person
las labores del hogar the housework
Éste es mi hogar. This is my home.

♪ la **hoguera** *fem noun*
bonfire

♪ la **hoja** *fem noun*
1 **leaf** (*of a tree, plant*)
2 **sheet** (*of paper, metal*)
3 **page** (*of a book*)

♪ **hola** *exclamation*
hello

Holanda *fem noun*
Holland

holandés *masc adjective & noun*, **holandesa** *fem adjective & noun*
1 **Dutch**
2 **un holandés** Dutchman
una holandesa Dutchwoman
3 **el holandés** Dutch (*the language*)

WORD TIP Adjectives and nouns for nationality, regional origin, and language do not have capital letters in Spanish.

holgazán *masc adjective*, **holgazana** *fem*
lazy

♪ el **hombre** *masc noun*
1 **man** (*the human race*)
El hombre moderno es más numeroso. Modern man is more numerous.
2 (*in exclamations*) **¡Hombre, por supuesto!** Of course!
¡Hombre! ¡Tú por aquí! Hey! Look who's here!
• el **hombre del tiempo** weatherman
• el **hombre de negocios** businessman
• el **hombre rana** frogman

♪ el **hombro** *masc noun*
shoulder

el **homenaje** *masc noun*
tribute
rendir homenaje a alguien to pay tribute to someone

♪ **homosexual** *masc & fem adjective*
▷ see **homosexual** *noun*
homosexual

♪ el & la **homosexual** *masc & fem noun*
▷ see **homosexual** *adj*
homosexual

♪ **hondo** *masc adjective*, **honda** *fem*
▷ see **hondo** *adv*
deep
un pozo hondo a deep well
en lo más hondo del lago in the deepest part of the lake

♪ **hondo** *adverb* ▷ see **hondo** *adj*
deeply
respirar hondo to breathe deeply

Honduras *fem noun*
Honduras

hondureño *masc adjective & noun*, **hondureña** *fem adjective & noun*
1 **Honduran**
2 **un hondureño, una hondureña** Honduran

WORD TIP Adjectives and nouns for nationality, regional origin, and language do not have capital letters in Spanish.

♪ **honesto** *masc adjective*, **honesta** *fem*
honest

♪ el **hongo** *masc noun*
1 **fungus**
2 **tener hongos** to have athlete's foot
3 (*Latin America*) **mushroom**

♪ el **honor** *masc noun*
honour
en honor de in honour of
una recepción en honor del equipo visitante a reception in honour of the visiting team

la **honra** *fem noun*
honour

la **honradez** *fem noun*
honesty

honrado *masc adjective*, **honrada** *fem*
honest

♪ la **hora** *fem noun*
1 **hour**
media hora half an hour
hora y media an hour and a half

a las quince horas at three p.m.
La película dura dos horas. The film lasts two hours.
El bus sale cada hora. The bus leaves every hour.
Hablamos horas y horas. We talked for hours.

2 time
¿Qué hora es? What's the time?
¿Tiene hora? Have you got the time?
¿Me puede dar la hora? Could you tell me what time it is?
¿A qué hora empieza? What time does it start?
Ya es hora de entrar. It's time to go in.
a la hora de comer at lunchtime
llegar a la hora to arrive on time

3 (*in expressions*) a todas horas all the time
a última hora at the last minute
a primera hora de la mañana first thing in the morning
una noticia de última hora some news just in

4 (*at the doctor's, dentist's*) pedir hora to make an appointment
He pedido hora con el dentista. I've made an appointment to see the dentist.

- la **hora punta** rush hour
- las **horas de trabajo** working hours
- las **horas de visita** visiting hours
- las **horas extra** overtime

las **horas libres** *plural fem noun*
free time
¿Qué haces en tus horas libres? What do you do in your free time?

el **horario** *masc noun*
1 timetable
- el **horario de clase** school timetable
- el **horario de visitas** visiting hours

la **horchata** *fem noun*
tiger nut milk (*thick, white, cold drink made from tiger nuts*)

la **horchatería** *fem noun*
refreshment stall (*selling horchata*)

horizontal *masc & fem adjective*
horizontal

el **horizonte** *masc noun*
horizon

la **hormiga** *fem noun*
ant

el **hormigón** *masc noun*
concrete

el **horno** *masc noun*
1 oven
verduras al horno oven-cooked vegetables
En verano la ciudad es como un horno. In summer the town is like an oven.
2 kiln
- el **horno microondas** microwave oven

el **horóscopo** *masc noun*
horoscope

la **horquilla** *fem noun*
hairpin

horrible *masc & fem adjective*
horrible

el **horror** *masc noun*
horror
¡Qué horror! (*informal*) How awful!

horrorizar *verb* [22]
to horrify

horroroso *masc adjective*, **horrorosa** *fem*
1 horrific (*crime*)
2 (*informal*) awful (*dress, book, picture*)

la **hortaliza** *fem noun*
vegetable

hospedarse *reflexive verb* [17]
to stay, to put up at
Nos hospedamos en una pensión. We stayed in a guesthouse.

el **hospital** *masc noun*
hospital

la **hospitalidad** *fem noun*
hospitality

el **hostal** *masc noun*
(small, inexpensive) hotel

la **hostelería** *fem noun*
hotel industry

el **hotel** *masc noun*
hotel
un hotel de cuatro estrellas a four-star hotel

el **hotelero** *masc noun*, la **hotelera** *fem*
hotel manager

hoy *adverb*
1 today
Hoy es mi cumpleaños. It's my birthday today.
el periódico de hoy today's paper
¿A qué estamos hoy? What day is it today?
2 hoy día, hoy en día nowadays
Hoy en día el cuarenta por ciento de los alumnos van a la universidad. Nowadays forty per cent of pupils go to university.

el **hoyo** *masc noun*
hole (*in the ground, for golf*)

hube, **hubo**, **etc** *verb* ▷ **haber**

hubiera, **hubieras**, **etc** *verb* ▷ **haber**

la **hucha** *fem noun*
moneybox

hueco *masc adjective*, **hueca** *fem*
▷ see **hueco** *noun*
hollow

el **hueco** *masc noun*
1 **hollow** (*in a surface*)
2 **hole**
3 **gap** (*in your timetable, schedule*)
4 **space**
un hueco para aparcar a parking space
Hazme un hueco. Make some room for me.
- el **hueco de la escalera** stairwell

huela, **huelo**, **etc** *verb* ▷ **oler**

la **huelga** *fem noun*
strike
hacer huelga to strike
estar en huelga to be on strike
- la **huelga de celo** work-to-rule
- la **huelga de hambre** hunger strike

la **huella** *fem noun*
1 **footprint**
2 **track** (*of an animal, a tyre*)
- las **huellas dactilares** fingerprints

el **huérfano** *masc noun*, la **huérfana** *fem*
orphan

la **huerta** *fem noun* ▷ **huerto**

el **huerto** *masc noun*
1 **vegetable garden**
2 **orchard**

el **hueso** *masc noun*
1 **bone**
romperse un hueso to break a bone
2 **stone** (*in fruit*)

el & la **huésped** *masc & fem noun*
guest

huesudo *masc adjective*, **huesuda** *fem*
bony

el **huevo** *masc noun*
egg
- el **huevo de Pascua** Easter egg
- el **huevo duro** hard-boiled egg
- el **huevo escalfado** poached egg
- el **huevo frito** fried egg
- el **huevo pasado por agua** boiled egg
- los **huevos revueltos** scrambled eggs

huir *verb* **[54]**
to flee, **to run away**
huir de la policía to flee from the police

humano *masc adjective*, **humana** *fem*
▷ see **humano** *noun*
1 **human**
la especie humana race
Es humano cometer errores. It's human to make mistakes.
2 **humane**
una política humana hacia los animales a humane policy to animals

el **humano** *masc noun*, la **humana** *fem*
▷ see **humano** *adj*
human being

la **humedad** *fem noun*
1 **dampness**
La casa tiene humedad. The house is damp.
2 **humidity**
3 **moisture**

húmedo *masc adjective*, **húmeda** *fem*
1 **damp** (*house, weather, clothes*)
2 **humid** (*climate*)
3 **moist** (*lips, eyes*)

humillar *verb* **[17]**
to humiliate

el **humo** *masc noun*
smoke

el **humor** *masc noun*
1 **humour**
tener sentido del humor to have a sense of humour
2 **mood**
estar de buen humor to be in a good mood
estar de mal humor to be in a bad mood
No estoy de humor para verlos. I'm not in the mood to see them.

hundir *verb* **[19]**
to sink

hundirse *reflexive verb* **[19]**
1 **to sink** (*ships, coins*)
2 **to collapse** (*buildings, mines*)

húngaro *masc adjective & noun*, **húngara** *fem adjective & noun*
1 **Hungarian**
2 (*person*) un húngaro, una húngara Hungarian
3 el húngaro Hungarian (*the language*)

WORD TIP Adjectives and nouns for nationality, regional origin, and language do not have capital letters in Spanish.

Hungría *fem noun*
Hungary

el **huracán** *masc noun*
hurricane
un huracán de categoría cuatro a category four hurricane

hurra *exclamation*
hurrah!

huyas, **huyo**, **etc** *verb* ▷ **huir**

I i

iba, iban, etc *verb* ▷ **ir**

ibérico *masc adjective*, **ibérica** *fem*
Iberian (*to do with Spain & Portugal*)

el iceberg *masc noun*, **icebergs** *plural*
iceberg

el icono *masc noun*
icon

la ida *fem noun*
departure
un billete de ida a single ticket
un billete de ida y vuelta a return ticket

la idea *fem noun*
idea
Tengo una idea. I've got an idea.
No tienen ni idea de cómo hacerlo. They have no idea how to do it.
'¿A qué hora llegan?'—'No tengo ni idea.' 'What time will they arrive?'—'I have no idea.'

ideal *masc & fem adjective*
ideal

idéntico *masc adjective*, **idéntica** *fem*
identical
Es idéntico a su padre. He's just like his father.

la identidad *fem noun*
identity
un carné de identidad an identity card

la identificación *fem noun*
identification

identificar *verb* **[31]**
to identify

identificarse *reflexive verb* **[31]**
1 **to identify yourself**
2 **identificarse con alguien** to identify with somebody
Me identifico con sus ideales sociales. I identify with her social ideals.

el idioma *masc noun*
language
Hablo tres idiomas. I speak three languages.

idiota *masc & fem adjective*
▷ see **idiota** *noun*
stupid

el & la idiota *masc & fem noun*
▷ see **idiota** *adj*
idiot

ido *verb* ▷ **ir**

la iglesia *fem noun*
church
ir a la iglesia to go to church
casarse por la iglesia to have a church wedding

ignorante *masc & fem adjective*
ignorant

ignorar *verb* **[17]**
1 **to ignore**
No me gusta que me ignoren. I don't like being ignored.
2 **not to know**
Ignoro las razones. I don't know the reasons.

igual *masc & fem adjective* ▷ see **igual** *adv*
1 **same**
uno de igual tamaño one of the same size
Son iguales. They are the same.
Parecen todos iguales. They all look the same.
ser igual a algo to be the same as something
Era igual a éste. It was the same as this one.
ser igual que algo to be the same as something
No es igual que los demás. It's not the same as the others.
2 **equal**
dos equipos iguales two equal teams
ser [1] igual a algo to be equal to something
Cien centímetros son iguales a un metro. A hundred centimetres are equal to one metre.
3 **dar igual a alguien: Todo le da igual.** He doesn't care about anything.
Les da igual lo uno que lo otro. Either way it makes no difference to them.
'¿Quieres salir o quedar en casa?'—'Me da igual.' 'Do you want to go out or stay at home?'—'I don't mind.'

igual *adverb* ▷ see **igual** *adj*
1 **the same**
Suenan igual. They sound the same.
2 **equally**
Los quiero a todos igual. I like them all equally.

Los dos sistemas son igual de buenos. Both systems are equally good.
3 (*in comparisons*) **igual que** just like
Es géminis, igual que yo. She's a Gemini, just like me.
Es igual de alto que su padre. He's as tall as his father.
Es igual de ancho que la mesa. It's as wide as the table.
4 **maybe**
Igual la vemos en la fiesta. Maybe we'll see her at the party.
Igual no viene. He may not even come.
5 **al igual que** just like
6 **anyway**
¿Tú no quieres venir? Yo voy igual. Don't you want to come? Well, I'm going anyway.

♪ la **igualdad** *fem noun*
equality
en igualdad de condiciones on equal terms
• la **igualdad de oportunidades** equal opportunities

♪ **igualmente** *adverb*
1 **equally**
Son todos igualmente buenos. They are all equally good.
2 (*to return good wishes*)
'Que pases un buen fin de semana.'—'Igualmente.' 'Have a good week end.'—'You too.'

♪ **ilegal** *masc & fem adjective*
illegal

♪ **ilegalmente** *adverb*
illegally

♪ **ileso** *masc adjective*, **ilesa** *fem*
unhurt, **uninjured**

ilimitado *masc adjective*, **ilimitada** *fem*
unlimited

♪ la **iluminación** *fem noun*
1 **lighting** (*in a room, hall*)
2 **illumination** (*of a building, statue*)

♪ **iluminar** *verb* [17]
1 **to light** (*a room, hall*)
2 **to illuminate** (*a building, statue*)

♪ la **ilusión** *fem noun*
1 **illusion**
2 **hope**
Su ilusión es ir a América. She hopes to go to America.
3 **hacerle ilusión hacer algo** to really want to do something
Me hace ilusion ir al circo. I really want to go to the circus.

la **ilustración** *fem noun*
illustration

ilustrar *verb* [17]
to illustrate

♪ la **imagen** *fem noun, pl:* las **imágenes**
1 **image**
Es la viva imagen de su madre. She's the image of her mother.
El presidente trata de mejorar su imagen. The president is trying to improve his image.
2 **picture** (*on a TV screen*)
3 **reflection** (*in a mirror*)

♪ la **imaginación** *fem noun*
imagination
No tienes imaginación. You have no imagination.
Son imaginaciones suyas. He's just imagining things.

♪ **imaginar** *verb* [17]
to imagine

imaginarse *reflexive verb* [17]
to imagine
Me imagino que vendrá mañana. I imagine he'll come tomorrow.
Me imagino que sí. I imagine so.
Me imagino que no. I suppose not

♪ el **imán** *masc noun*, **imanes** *plural*
magnet

♪ **imbécil** *masc & fem adjective*
▷ see **imbécil** *noun*
stupid

♪ el & la **imbécil** *masc & fem noun*
▷ see **imbécil** *adj*
idiot

♪ **imitar** *verb* [17]
to imitate

la **impaciencia** *fem noun*
impacience

♪ **impaciente** *masc & fem adjective*
impatient

impactante *masc & fem adjective*
1 **shocking** (*piece of news*)
2 **powerful** (*advertising*)

el **impacto** *masc noun*
impact

♪ **impar** *masc & fem adjective*
odd (*number*)

impecable *masc & fem adjective*
impeccable

impedir *verb* **[57]**
1 **to prevent**
impedirle a alguien hacer algo to prevent someone from doing something
El dolor le impedía caminar. The pain prevented her from walking.
impedirle a alguien que haga algo to prevent someone from doing something
Tienes que impedirle que se vaya. You have to prevent him from going.
2 **impedir el paso a alguien** to block someone's way

el **imperativo** *masc noun*
(*Grammar*) **imperative**

el **imperdible** *masc noun*
safety pin

imperfecto *masc adjective*, **imperfecta** *fem* ▷ see **imperfecto** *noun*
imperfect

el **imperfecto** *masc noun*
▷ see **imperfecto** *adj*
(*Grammar*) **imperfect**

el **impermeable** *masc noun*
raincoat

impersonal *masc & fem adjective*
impersonal

implicar *verb* **[31]**
to involve

imponer *verb* **[11]**
to impose (*a condition, a punishment*)

la **importación** *fem noun*
import
artículos de importación imported goods

la **importancia** *fem noun*
importance
darle importancia a algo to attach importance to something
No le di importancia a lo que dijo. I didn't attach any importance to what he said.

importante *masc & fem adjective*
1 **important**
Lo importante es ... The important thing is ...
2 **significant** (*quantities, sums, amounts*)
una importante suma de dinero a significant sum of money

importar *verb* **[17]**
1 **to import** (*goods*)
2 **to matter**
Importa mucho el color. The colour matters a lot.
No importa. It doesn't matter.
Me importa mucho. It matters a lot to me.
Me importa ayudarles. I want to help them.
¿Y a ti que te importa? What's it to do with you?
3 (*making polite requests*) **¿Le importaría comprobarlo?** Would you mind checking it?
¿Le importa que abra la ventanilla? Do you mind if I open the window?

el **importe** *masc noun*
amount

imposible *masc & fem adjective*
impossible
misión imposible mission impossible

la **impresión** *fem noun*
impression
causar una buena impresión to make a good impression
Me da la impresión de que ... I have the feeling that ...

impresionante *masc & fem adjective*
1 **incredible** (*success, amount*)
2 **shocking** (*scene, pictures*)

impresionar *verb* **[17]**
1 **to impress**
Quiere impresionarte. She wants to impress you.
2 **to shock**
La violencia de la película me impresionó mucho. The film's violence shocked me.
Me impresionó mucho verlos discutir. Seeing them argue really shook me.

impreso *masc adjective*, **impresa** *fem*
▷ see **impreso** *noun*
printed

el **impreso** *masc noun* ▷ see **impreso** *adj*
form
• el **impreso de solicitud** application form

la **impresora** *fem noun*
printer
• la **impresora láser** laser printer

imprevisible *masc & fem adjective*
1 **unpredictable**
2 **unforeseeable**

imprevisto *masc adjective*, **imprevista** *fem* ▷ see **imprevisto** *noun*
unforeseen, unexpected

el **imprevisto** *masc noun*
▷ see **imprevisto** *adj*
unforeseen event

improviso *in phrase*
de improviso unexpectedly, out of the blue

imprudente *masc & fem adjective*
▷ see **imprudente** *noun*
careless
un conductor imprudente a careless driver

el & la **imprudente** *masc & fem noun*
▷ see **imprudente** *adj*
careless person
Es un imprudente conduciendo. He's a careless driver.

el **impuesto** *masc noun*
tax
- el **impuesto sobre la renta** income tax

impulsivo *masc adjective*, **impulsiva** *fem*
impulsive

inaccesible *masc & fem adjective*
1 **inaccessible** (*place*)
2 **unapproachable** (*person*)

inaceptable *masc & fem adjective*
unacceptable

inadecuado *masc adjective*, **inadecuada** *fem*
1 **inappropriate**
2 **inadequate**

inadmisible *masc & fem adjective*
unacceptable

inadvertido *masc adjective*, **inadvertida** *fem*
pasar inadvertido to go unnoticed

inalámbrico *masc adjective*, **inalámbrica** *fem*
1 **wireless** (*technology*)
2 **cordless** (*phone*)

incapaz *masc & fem adjective*, *pl:* **incapaces**
incapable
ser incapaz de hacer algo to be incapable of doing something
Fui incapaz de entenderlo. I was unable to understand it.
Son incapaces de hacerlo. They are incapable of doing it.

el **incendio** *masc noun*
fire
- el **incendio forestal** forest fire
- el **incendio provocado** arson attack

la **incertidumbre** *fem noun*
uncertainty

incierto *masc adjective*, **incierta** *fem*
uncertain

incitar *verb* **[17]**
incitar a alguien a hacer algo to incite someone to do something

incluido *masc adjective*, **incluida** *fem*
included
Dos mil euros, todo incluido. Two thousand euros, everything included.
Seremos diez personas, nosotros incluidos. There will be ten people including us.

incluir *verb* **[54]**
1 **to include**
2 **to enclose** (*something in a letter*)

inclusive *adverb*
inclusive
las páginas veinte a treinta inclusive pages twenty to thirty inclusive

incluso *adverb*
even
Es incluso difícil para los profesores. It's even difficult for the teachers.

incluya, **incluyo**, **etc** *verb* ▷ **incluir**

incoloro *masc adjective*, **incolora** *fem*
colourless

incómodo *masc adjective*, **incómoda** *fem*
uncomfortable

incompetente *masc & fem adjective*
incompetent

incompleto *masc adjective*, **incompleta** *fem*
incomplete

incomprensible *masc & fem adjective*
incomprehensible

incondicional *masc & fem adjective*
unconditional

inconsciente *masc & fem adjective*
unconscious

inconveniente *masc & fem adjective*
▷ see **inconveniente** *noun*
inconvenient

el **inconveniente** *masc noun*
▷ see **inconveniente** *adj*
1 **disadvantage**, **drawback**
El plan tiene varios inconvenientes. The plan has several drawbacks.
2 **objection**
No tenemos ningún inconveniente salir más temprano. We have no objection to leaving earlier.

incorporar *verb* **[17]**
to incorporate

incorporarse *reflexive verb* **[17]**
1 **to sit up**
2 **incorporarse a algo** to join something (*a club, a group*)

incorrecto *masc adjective*, **incorrecta** *fem*
incorrect

increíble *masc & fem adjective*
incredible

indecente *masc & fem adjective*
indecent

indeciso *masc adjective*, **indecisa** *fem*
1 **indecisive**
2 **undecided**
Están indecisos sobre la cantidad. They're undecided about the quantity.

indefenso *masc adjective*, **indefensa** *fem*
defenceless

indefinidamente *adverb*
indefinitely, **for good**

indefinido *masc adjective*, **indefinida** *fem*
1 **indefinite**
2 **vague** (*outline, smell*)

indemnizar *verb* **[22]**
to compensate
Los indemnizaron con veinte mil euros. They received twenty thousand euros in compensation.
indemnizar a alguien por algo to compensate someone for something

la **indemnización** *fem noun*
compensation
Le pagaron una indemnización. They paid her compensation.

la **independencia** *fem noun*
independence

independiente *masc & fem adjective*
independent

la **India** *fem noun*
(la) India India

la **indicación** *fem noun*
1 **indication**
2 **sign**
Hay una indicación en el camino. There's a sign on the road.
Me hizo una indicación para que lo siguiese. He signalled to me to follow him.

indicar *verb* **[31]**
1 **to indicate**
Hay una flecha que indica el camino. There's an arrow indicating the way.
2 **to point out**
Me indicó el lugar en el mapa. He pointed out the place on the map.

el **índice** *masc noun*
index

indiferente *masc & fem adjective*
indifferent
Es indiferente al peligro. He is indifferent to danger.
El precio me es indiferente. The price doesn't matter to me.

indígena *masc & fem adjective*
native

> **mini-info** ***indígenas***
> Mucho antes de llegar Cristóbal Colón a las Américas en 1492 varias poblaciones indígenas, unas bastante avanzadas, vivían allí. En México había los Aztecas; en Guatemala, los Maya y en el Perú, los Incas.

la **indigestión** *fem noun*
indigestion

indigesto *masc adjective*, **indigesta** *fem*
indigestible

la **indignación** *fem noun*
1 **indignation**
2 **outrage**

indignar *verb* **[17]**
1 **indignar a alguien** to make someone angry
2 **to outrage**

indignarse *reflexive verb* **[17]**
to get very angry

indio *masc adjective & noun*, **india** *fem adjective & noun*
1 **Indian**
2 **un indio, una india** Indian

WORD TIP Adjectives and nouns for nationality, regional origin, and language do not have capital letters in Spanish. In Latin America *indio* refers to the native peoples of Latin America, not the Indian subcontinent.

la **indirecta** *fem noun* ▷ see **indirecto** *adj*
hint
soltar una indirecta to drop a hint

indirecto *masc adjective*, **indirecta** *fem*
▷ see **indirecta** *noun*
indirect

indiscreto *masc adjective*, **indiscreta** *fem*
indiscreet

indispensable *masc & fem adjective*
essential

indispuesto *masc adjective*, **indispuesta** *fem*
estar indispuesto to be unwell

individual *masc & fem adjective*
1 **individual**
2 **single**
una cama individual a single bed

los **individuales** *plural masc noun*
singles (*in tennis*)
la final de los individuales masculinos the final of the men's singles

el **individuo** *masc noun*
1 **person**
un individuo con pelo largo a person with long hair
2 (*pejorative*) **character**
un individuo con muy mal aspecto a nasty-looking character

la **industria** *fem noun*
industry

industrial *masc & fem adjective*
industrial

ineficaz *masc & fem adjective*, **ineficaces** *plural*
1 **ineffective** (*remedy, measure*)
2 **inefficient** (*person*)

inepto *masc adjective*, **inepta** *fem*
incompetent

inesperado *masc adjective*, **inesperada** *fem*
unexpected

inevitable *masc & fem adjective*
unavoidable
Era inevitable que pasase. It was bound to happen.

inexperto *masc adjective*, **inexperta** *fem*
inexperienced

la **infancia** *fem noun*
childhood

infantil *masc & fem adjective*
1 **for children**
un programa infantil a children's programme
2 **childish**
Eres muy infantil. You're very childish.
3 **childlike**

el **infarto** *masc noun*
heart attack
Le dio un infarto. He had a heart attack.

la **infección** *fem noun*
infection

infectar *verb* [17]
to infect

infectarse *reflexive verb* [17]
to become infected
La herida se infectó. The wound became infected.

infeliz *masc & fem adjective*, **infelices** *plural*
unhappy
ser infeliz to be unhappy

inferior *masc & fem adjective*
1 **lower** (*shelf, part, etc*)
2 **inferior** (*quality*)

infiel *masc & fem adjective*
unfaithful
serle infiel a alguien to be unfaithful to someone

el **infierno** *masc noun*
hell

el **infinitivo** *masc noun*
infinitive

infinito *masc adjective*, **infinita** *fem*
▷ see **infinito** *noun*
infinite

el **infinito** *masc noun* ▷ see **infinito** *adj*
infinity

inflable *masc & fem adjective*
inflatable

la **inflación** *fem noun*
inflation

inflamable *masc & fem adjective*
inflammable

inflar *verb* [17]
1 **to inflate** (*a tyre*)
2 **to blow up** (*a balloon*)

la **influencia** *fem noun*
influence

influir *verb* [54]
to influence

la **información** *fem noun*
1 **information**
Busco información sobre el servicio de autobuses. I'm looking for information about the bus service.
Es una información muy práctica. It's a very useful piece of information.
2 (*in newspaper or TV news*) **news**
la información internacional the foreign news
3 'Información' 'Information Desk' (*in an airport, station, etc*) ▸▸

Spanish–English

4 (*in telephoning*) **directory enquiries**
llamar a información to call directory enquiries

informal *masc & fem adjective*
1 **informal** (*chat, meal*)
2 **casual** (*clothes*)
3 **unreliable** (*person*)

informar *verb* **[17]**
to inform
Me informaron mal. I was misinformed.
¿Podría informarme sobre ... ? Could you give me information about ... ?

informarse *reflexive verb* **[17]**
to find out information
Me informaré sobre el horario. I'll find out about the timetable.

la **informática** *fem noun*
computing, **information technology**

el **informe** *masc noun*
report

la **infracción** *fem noun*
offence
cometer una infracción to commit an offence
- la **infracción de tráfico** traffic offence

la **infusión** *fem noun*
herbal tea
la infusión de menta peppermint tea

el **ingeniero** *masc noun*, la **ingeniera** *fem*
engineer
- el **ingeniero agrónomo**, la **ingeniera agrónoma** agonomist
- el **ingeniero de caminos**, la **ingeniera de caminos** civil engineer

ingenuo *masc adjective*, **ingenua** *fem*
▷ see **ingenuo** *noun*
naive

el **ingenuo** *masc noun*, la **ingenua** *fem*
▷ see **ingenuo** *adj*
Eres un ingenuo. You're so naive.

Inglaterra *fem noun*
England
Soy de Inglaterra. I'm from England.

inglés *masc adjective*, **inglesa** *fem*
▷ see **inglés** *noun*
English

un **inglés** *masc noun*, una **inglesa** *fem*
▷ see **inglés** *adj*
1 **Englishman**
2 **Englishwoman**
3 **los ingleses** the English, English people
4 **el inglés** English (*the language*)
¿Hablas inglés? Do you speak English.

WORD TIP Adjectives and nouns for nationality, regional origin, and language do not have capital letters in Spanish.

ingrato *masc adjective*, **ingrata** *fem*
ungrateful

el **ingrediente** *masc noun*
ingredient

el **ingreso** *masc noun*
1 **admission** (*to hospital, university*)
2 **deposit** (*in a bank account*)
3 **los ingresos** income

inicial *masc & fem adjective*
▷ see **inicial** *noun*
initial

la **inicial** *fem noun* ▷ see **inicial** *adj*
initial
Estas son mis iniciales. These are my initials.

la **iniciativa** *fem noun*
initiative
por iniciativa propia on her own initiative

injusto *masc adjective*, **injusta** *fem*
unfair

inmaduro *masc adjective*, **inmadura** *fem*
immature

las **inmediaciones** *plural fem noun*
surrounding area
en las inmediaciones de Bilbao in the area surrounding Bilbao

inmediatamente *adverb*
immediately

inmediato *masc adjective*, **inmediata** *fem*
immediate
de inmediato immediately
Volvieron de inmediato. They came back immediately.

inmenso *masc adjective*, **inmensa** *fem*
1 **immense** (*happiness, quantity*)
2 **huge** (*house, room*)

la **inmigración** *fem noun*
immigration

el & la **inmigrante** *masc & fem noun*
immigrant

la **inmobiliaria** *fem noun*
1 **estate agent's**
2 **building company** (*developing housing, tourist resorts, etc*)

inmoral *masc & fem adjective*
immoral

a b c d e f g h i j k l m n ñ o p q r s t u v w x y z

inmunizar *verb* **[22]**
to immunize

innecesario *masc adjective*, **innecesaria** *fem*
unnecessary

la **innovación** *fem noun*
innovation

innumerable *masc & fem adjective*
countless

la **inocentada** *fem noun*
practical joke
gastarle una inocentada a alguien to play a practical joke on someone (*Often one played on 28 December, which is similar to April Fool's Day.*)

inocente *masc & fem adjective*
1 **innocent**
2 **naive**▷ **día**

inofensivo *masc adjective*, **inofensiva** *fem*
harmless

inolvidable *masc & fem adjective*
unforgettable
unas vacaciones inolvidables an unforgetable holiday

inoxidable *masc & fem adjective*
rust-proof
el acero inoxidable stainless steel

inquieto *masc adjective*, **inquieta** *fem*
1 **worried**
2 **restless**

la **inquietud** *fem noun*
1 **worry**
2 **interest**
Es una persona con inquietudes. She's a person with many interests.
3 **restlessness**

el **inquilino** *masc noun*, la **inquilina** *fem*
tenant

inscribir *verb* **[52]**
1 **to register** (*on a course*)
2 **to engrave**

inscribirse *reflexive verb* **[52]**
to register

la **inscripción** *fem noun*
1 **registration** (*on a course*)
La inscripción es el martes. Registration is on Tuesday.
2 **inscription**

el **insecto** *masc noun*
insect

insertar *verb* **[17]**
to insert

insignificante *masc & fem adjective*
insignificant

insistir *verb* **[19]**
to insist
insistir en algo to insist on something
Insiste en que es verdad. She insists that it's true.

la **insolación** *fem noun*
sunstroke
coger una insolación to get sunstroke

insolente *masc & fem adjective*
rude

insólito *masc adjective*, **insólita** *fem*
unheard of
un aconteciemiento insólito an unheard of event

insonorizado *masc adjective*, **insonorizada** *fem*
soundproofed

insoportable *masc & fem adjective*
unbearable

la **inspección** *fem noun*
inspection

inspeccionar *verb* **[17]**
to inspect

el **inspector** *masc noun*, la **inspectora** *fem*
inspector

la **inspiración** *fem noun*
inspiration

inspirar *verb* **[17]**
to inspire

inspirarse *reflexive verb* **[17]**
inspirarse en algo to be inspired by something
Se inspiró en la naturaleza. He was inspired by nature.

la **instalación** *fem noun*
installation

instalar *verb* **[17]**
to install (*a washing machine, a computer*)

instalarse *reflexive verb* **[17]**
to install yourself
Se instaló en el sillón. He installed himself in the armchair.

instantáneo *masc adjective*, **instantánea** *fem*
1 **instant** (*coffee, soup*)
2 **immediate** (*reaction, result*)

el **instante** *masc noun*
moment
Vuelvo en un instante. I'll be back in a moment.
Un instante, por favor. One moment, please.
Hacían preguntas a cada instante. They asked questions constantly.

el **instinto** *masc noun*
instinct
por instinto instinctively
- el **instinto de conservación** survival instinct

el **instituto** *masc noun*
1 **institute**
2 **(secondary) school**

la **instrucción** *fem noun*
1 **education**
2 **las instrucciones** instructions (*for a computer, TV, etc*)

el **instructor** *masc noun*, la **instructora** *fem*
instructor
- el **instructor de autoescuela** driving instructor
- el **instructor de esquí** ski instructor

instruir *verb* [54]
1 **to instruct**
2 **to educate**

el **instrumento** *masc noun*
instrument
tocar un instrumento to play an instrument

insuficiente *masc & fem adjective*
▷ see **insuficiente** *noun*
inadequate

el **insuficiente** *masc noun*
▷ see **insuficiente** *adj*
fail (*in exams*)

insultar *verb* [17]
to insult

el **insulto** *masc noun*
insult

intacto *masc adjective*, **intacta** *fem*
undamaged, **in one piece**
El envío llegó intacto. The consignment arrived undamaged.

integral *masc & fem adjective*
1 **comprehensive** (*plan, education*)
2 **wholemeal** (*flour, bread*)

íntegro *masc adjective*, **íntegra** *fem*
complete (*text*)
la versión íntegra de la película the full-length version of the film

el **integrismo** *masc noun*
(*Religion*) **fundamentalism**

intelectual *masc & fem adjective*
▷ see **intelectual** *noun*
intellectual

el & la **intelectual** *masc & fem noun*
▷ see **intelectual** *adj*
intellectual

la **inteligencia** *fem noun*
intelligence

inteligente *masc & fem adjective*
1 **intelligent**
2 **smart** (*bomb, terminal*)

la **intención** *fem noun*
intention
Esa fue mi intención. That was my intention.
No era mi intención ofenderla. I didn't mean to offend her.
Tiene buenas intenciones. She means well.
Lo hizo con la intención de ayudar. He did it with the intention of helping.

intensivo *masc adjective*, **intensiva** *fem*
intensive

intenso *masc adjective*, **intensa** *fem*
intense

intentar *verb* [17]
to try
¡Inténtalo otra vez! Try again!
intentar hacer algo to try to do something
Intenté cerrarlo. I tried to shut it.
Intenta llegar temprano. Try to arrive early.

el **intento** *masc noun*
attempt
Lo consiguió al tercer intento. She succeeded at the third attempt.

intercambiar *verb* [17]
1 **to exchange** (*ideas*)
2 **to swap** (*stamps, magazines, toys*)

intercambiarse *reflexive verb* [17]
to swap
Se intercambiaron los números de teléfono. They swapped telephone numbers.

el **intercambio** *masc noun*
1 **exchange** (*of ideas*)
2 **swap** (*of stamps, magazines*)

3 **exchange** (*visit*)
Fui a Málaga de intercambio. I went to Málaga on an exchange.

♪ el **interés** *masc noun*
interest
su interés por la historia her interest in history
Es de gran interés para mí. It's of great interest to me.

♪ **interesante** *masc & fem adjective*
interesting
una película interestante an interesting film
Resultó poco interesante. It wasn't very interesting.

♪ **interesar** *verb* [17]
1 **interesarle algo a alguien** to be interested in something
Me interesa el deporte. I'm interested in sport.
¿Te interesa la historia? Are you interested in history?
2 **to have to do with**
Eso no le interesa. That doesn't have anything to do with her.

interesarse *reflexive verb* [17]
interesarse por algo to take an interest in something
Se interesa por todo lo que hago. He takes an interest in everything I do.

♪ el **interfono** *masc noun*
1 **entryphone**
2 **intercom**

♪ **interior** *masc & fem adjective*
▷ see **interior** *noun*
1 **interior**
una escalera interior an interior staircase
un piso interior a flat with windows facing into an inner courtyard
2 **inside**
en la parte interior on the inside

♪ el **interior** *masc noun* ▷ see **interior** *adj*
1 **inside**
el interior de la caja the inside of the box
En mi interior, tenía miedo. Deep down inside, I was afraid.
2 **interior** (*of a country*)

♪ **intermedio** *masc adjective*, **intermedia** *fem* ▷ see **intermedio** *noun*
1 **intermediate** (*level, stage*)
2 **medium**
de tamaño intermedio medium-sized

♪ el **intermedio** *masc noun*
▷ see **intermedio** *adj*
interval

♪ **intermitente** *masc & fem adjective*
flashing (*light*)

♪ **internacional** *masc & fem adjective*
international
un vuelo internacional an international flight

♪ el **internado** *masc noun*
boarding school

♪ el & la **internauta** *masc & fem noun*
surfer (*on the Internet*)

♪ **Internet** *masc noun*
Internet
la era de Internet the age of the Internet
en Internet on the Internet
estar conectado a Internet to be on the Internet

WORD TIP *Internet* in Spanish is normally used without *el*.

♪ **interno** *masc adjective*, **interna** *fem*
▷ see **interno** *noun*
internal

♪ el **interno** *masc noun*, la **interna** *fem*
▷ see **interno** *adj*
boarder (*in a boarding school*)

♪ **interpretar** *verb* [17]
1 **to interpret** (*a comment, a text*)
2 **interpretar un papel** to play a part (*in a play, a film, etc*)
interpretar una canción to sing a song
interpretar una pieza de música to perform a piece of music

♪ el & la **intérprete** *masc & fem noun*
1 **interpreter**
2 **performer** (*of a piece of music*)
3 **singer** (*of a song*)

la **interrogación** *fem noun*
interrogation

♪ el & la **interrogante** *masc & fem noun*
1 **question**
Quedan muchos interrogantes sin responder. There are many questions left unanswered.
2 **question mark**
Pon un interrogante. Write a question mark.

♪ **interrogar** *verb* [28]
1 **to question** (*a suspect*)
2 **to interrogate** (*a prisoner*)

interrumpir *verb* **[19]**
1 **to interrupt**
Perdone que interrumpa. Excuse my interrupting.
¡No me interrumpas! Don't interrupt.
2 **to stop**
Las lluvias interrumpieron las obras. The rain stopped the building works.

la **interrupción** *fem noun*
interruption

el **interruptor** *masc noun*
switch

interurbano *masc adjective*, **interurbana** *fem*
long-distance
una llamada interurbana a long-distance call
un tren interurbano an intercity train

el **intervalo** *masc noun*
interval

la **intervención** *fem noun*
intervention

intervenir *verb* **[15]**
1 **to take part**
intervenir en las discusiones to take part in the discussions
2 **to intervene**
No quiero intervenir. I don't want to intervene.
3 **intervenir a alguien** to operate on somebody

la **interviú** *fem noun*
interview

intimidar *verb* **[17]**
to intimidate

íntimo *masc adjective*, **íntima** *fem*
1 **private**
su vida íntima her private life
una cena íntima a very private dinner
2 **intimate**
un ambiente íntimo an intimate atmosphere
3 **close** (*friend, friendship*)

intolerante *masc & fem adjective*
intolerant

la **intoxicación** *fem noun*
poisoning
- la **intoxicación alimenticia** food poisoning

intransitivo *masc adjective*, **intransitiva** *fem*
intransitive

la **intriga** *fem noun*
intrigue

introducir *verb* **[60]**
1 **to introduce**
introducir cambios to introduce changes
2 **to insert**
Introduzca la moneda en la ranura. Insert the coin in the slot.

introducirse *reflexive verb* **[60]**
to get in
El ladrón se introdujo por la ventana. The burglar got in through the window.
El agua se introducía por las ranuras. The water was coming in through the cracks.

el **intruso** *masc noun*, la **intrusa** *fem*
intruder

intuitivo *masc adjective*, **intuitiva** *fem*
intuitive

la **inundación** *fem noun*
flood
Ha habido inundaciones en Cataluña. There have been floods in Catalonia.

inútil *masc & fem adjective*
useless
Es inútil intentarlo. It's useless trying.

invadir *verb* **[19]**
to invade

el **inválido** *masc noun*, la **inválida** *fem*
disabled person
los inválidos disabled people

la **invasión** *fem noun*
invasion

inventar *verb* **[17]**
1 **to invent**
2 **to make up** (*a story, a game*)

inventarse *reflexive verb* **[17]**
to invent, **to make up**
Se inventó una excusa. He made up an excuse.

el **invento** *masc noun*
invention
el invento del teléfono
the invention of the telephone

el **invernadero** *masc noun*
greenhouse

la **inversión** *fem noun*
investment

inverso *masc adjective*, **inversa** *fem*
reverse (*order*)
hacer algo a la inversa to do something the other way round

♂ la **investigación** *fem noun*
1 **investigation** (*of a crime, an accident*)
2 **research**
• la **investigación de mercado** market research

♂ el **invierno** *masc noun*
winter
en invierno in winter
el invierno pasado last winter

invisible *masc & fem adjective*
invisible

♂ la **invitación** *fem noun*
invitation
una invitación para la boda an invitation to the wedding

♂ el **invitado** *masc noun*, la **invitada** *fem*
guest

♂ **invitar** *verb* [17]
1 **to invite**
invitar a alguien a una fiesta to invite someone to a party
Me han invitado a su casa. They've invited me to their house.
2 (*offering to pay*) **¡Yo invito!** It's on me!
Te invito a cenar. I'll take you out for dinner.
Nos invitó a una copa. He bought us a drink.

involuntario *masc adjective*, **involuntaria** *fem*
involuntary

♂ la **inyección** *fem noun*
injection

♂ **ir** *verb* [8]
1 **to go** (*to a place*)
¿Adónde vas? Where are you going?
Voy a casa de Alicia. I'm going to Alicia's house.
Iremos al museo. We'll go to the museum.
Aún no va al colegio. She doesn't go to school yet.
El camino va a la playa. The road goes to the beach.
¿Cómo se va a la estación? How do you get to the station?
2 **to go** (*belong in a particular place*)
¿Dónde van los platos? Where do the plates go?
3 **to come**
¡Ya voy! I'm coming!
'¡Fernando!'—'¡Voy!' '¡Fernando!'—'Coming!'
4 (*talking about progress*) **¿Cómo van las cosas?** How are things going?
¿Cómo te va? How are you?
¿Cómo va el enfermo? How's the patient doing?
Todo va muy bien. Everything is going well.
Le va muy bien en el trabajo. Things are going well for him at work.
Me fue muy mal en la entrevista. Things went very badly at the interview.
5 (*for how something works*) **La lavadora no va bien.** The washing machine is not working properly.
6 (*for how clothes, etc look*) **El negro te va bien.** Black suits you.
Iba con un abrigo marrón. He was wearing a brown coat.
Iban bien vestidos. They were well dressed.
ir con algo to go with something
Esos zapatos no van con esa falda. Those shoes don't go with that skirt.
7 (*talking about activities*) **ir de vacaciones** to go on holiday
ir de compras to go shopping
ir a la compra to do the shopping
Siempre voy yo a la compra. I'm always the one who does the shopping.
8 (*saying how you go*) **ir a pie** to go on foot
ir de pie to stand (all the way)
ir a caballo to go on horseback
ir en coche to go by car
ir en avión to go by plane
ir en bicicleta to go by bike
Fueron en coche. They drove here.
¿Vamos en taxi? Shall we go by taxi?
Va en bicicleta a todas partes. She goes everywhere by bike.
9 **ir a hacer algo** to be going to do something
Voy a comprar leche. I'm going to buy some milk.
Voy a ser médico. I'm going to be a doctor.
Iré a recogerla. I'll go to pick her up.
¡Te vas a caer! You're going to fall!
Iba a mandártelo hoy. I was going to send it to you today.
Dijo que lo iba a pensar. She said she was going to think it over.
Se lo voy a decir. I'm going to tell him.
10 **ir a por algo** to go to get something, to fetch something
Voy a por pan. I'm going to get some bread.
ir a por alguien to go to get someone, to fetch somebody ▸▸

Ha ido a por su madre. He's gone to get his mother.
Fuimos a por ella. We went to fetch her.

11 **ir a hacer algo** to go to do something
¿Has ido a verla? ¿Have you been to see her?
Fuimos a ver su casa nueva. We went to see their new house.

12 (*talking about a process*) **ir haciendo algo Su salud va mejorando.** Her health is getting better.
Poco a poco va aprendiendo. She's learning little by little.
La situación ha ido empeorando. The situation has been getting worse and worse.
Iban acercándose. They were getting closer.

13 (*in suggestions and orders*) **¡Vamos!** Come on!
¡Vamos, date prisa! Come on, hurry up!
Vamos a trabajar. Let's get to work.
Vamos a discutir el asunto. Let's discuss the matter.

14 (*expressing surprise, annoyance*) **¡Vaya, si es Carlos!** Hey, it's Carlos!
¡Vaya, se ha fundido la luz! Oh dear, the light has gone!
¡Vaya, no lo encuentro! Bother, I can't find it!
¡Vaya hombre, un billete de cincuenta euros! Hey look, a fifty-euro note!

15 (*saying you don't agree*) **'¿Te molesta?'—'¡Qué va!'** 'Do you mind?'—'Not at all!'
'¿Lo ha hecho él solo?'—'¡Qué va!' 'Did he do it on his own?'—'Not likely!'

irse *reflexive verb* [8]
1 **to leave**
Nos fuimos pronto. We left early.
Bueno, me voy. Well, I'm off.
Vámonos, que se hace tarde. Let's go, it's getting late.
2 **to go away**
Se fueron a casa. They went off home.
3 **to go** (*pain*)
¿Se te ha ido el dolor de cabeza? Has your headache gone?

la **ira** *fem noun*
rage
en un arrebato de ira in a fit of rage

Irak *masc noun*
Iraq

Irán *masc noun*
Iran

iraní *masc & fem adjective & noun, pl:* **iraníes**
1 **Iranian**
2 **un & una iraní** Iranian

WORD TIP Adjectives and nouns for nationality, regional origin, and language do not have capital letters in Spanish.

iraquí *masc & fem adjective & noun, pl:* **iraquíes**
1 **Iraqi**
2 **un & una iraquí** Iraqi

WORD TIP Adjectives and nouns for nationality, regional origin, and language do not have capital letters in Spanish.

Irlanda *fem noun*
Ireland
Soy de Irlanda. I'm from Ireland.

irlandés *masc adjective,* **irlandesa** *fem*
▷ see **irlandés** *noun*
Irish

un **irlandés** *masc noun,* una **irlandesa** *fem*
▷ see **irlandés** *adj*
1 **Irishman**
2 **Irishwoman**
3 **los irlandeses** the Irish, Irish people
4 **el irlandés** Irish (*the language*)

WORD TIP Adjectives and nouns for nationality, regional origin, and language do not have capital letters in Spanish.

la **ironía** *fem noun*
irony

irónico *masc adjective,* **irónica** *fem*
ironic

irreal *masc & fem adjective*
unreal

irresponsable *masc & fem adjective*
irresponsible

la **irritación** *fem noun*
irritation

irritar *verb* [17]
1 **to irritate** (*eyes, throat, skin*)
2 **to irritate, to annoy**

irritarse *reflexive verb* [17]
1 **to become irritated** (*eyes, throat, skin*)
2 **to get annoyed, to get irritated**

la **isla** *fem noun*
island

el **islam**, el **Islam** *masc noun*
(*Religion*) **Islam**

WORD TIP *Islam* is always used with *el* and may be written with a capital *I*.

islámico *masc adjective*, **islámica** *fem adjective*
Islamic

WORD TIP Adjectives and nouns for religion do not have capital letters in Spanish.

islandés *masc adjective & noun*, **islandesa** *fem adjective & noun*
1 **Icelander**
2 **un islandés, una islandesa** Icelander

WORD TIP Adjectives and nouns for nationality and regional origin do not have capital letters in Spanish.

Islandia *fem noun*
Iceland

Israel *masc noun*
Israel

israelí *masc & fem adjective & noun*, *pl:* **israelíes**
1 **Israeli**
2 **un & una israelí** Israeli

WORD TIP Adjectives and nouns for nationality and regional origin do not have capital letters in Spanish.

Italia *fem noun*
Italy

italiano *masc adjective & noun*, **italiana** *fem adjective & noun*
1 **Italian**
2 **un italiano, una italiana** Italian
3 **el italiano** Italian (*the language*)

WORD TIP Adjectives and nouns for nationality, regional origin, and language do not have capital letters in Spanish.

el **itinerario** *masc noun*
itinerary, **route**

el **IVA** *masc noun*
(= *Impuesto al Valor Añadido*) **VAT** (*Value Added Tax*)

la **izquierda** *fem noun* ▷ see **izquierdo** *adj*
1 **left** (*when talking of left and right*)
girar a la izquierda to turn left
Está a la izquierda. It's on the left., It's on the left-hand side.
la segunda calle a la izquierda the second street on the left
Se sentaron a mi izquierda. They sat on my left.
En Gran Bretaña se conduce por la izquierda. In Great Britain you drive on the left.
2 **left hand**
Escribo con la izquierda. I write with my left hand.
3 (*in politics*) **la izquierda** the left
ser de izquierdas to be left-wing

izquierdo *masc adjective*, **izquierda** *fem* ▷ see **izquierda** *noun*
left (*when talking of left and right*)
la mano izquierda your left hand
el guante izquierdo the left glove
en el cuadro superior izquierdo in the top left-hand square

Spanish–English

a b c d e f g h i j k l m n ñ o p q r s t u v w x y z

Jj

el **jabalí** *masc noun*, jabalíes *plural*
wild boar

el **jabón** *masc noun*
soap
una pastilla de jabón a bar of soap

la **jabonera** *fem noun*
soapdish

jalar *verb* [ ]
(*Latin America*) **to pull**

el **jalón** *masc noun*
(*Latin America*) **pull**

Jamaica *fem noun*
Jamaica

jamaicano *masc adjective & noun*, **jamaicana** *fem adjective & noun*
1 **Jamaican**
2 **un jamaicano, una jamaicana** Jamaican

WORD TIP Adjectives and nouns for nationality and regional origin do not have capital letters in Spanish.

jamás *adverb*
never
No lo he visto jamás. I've never seen it.
Nunca jamás volveré. I'll never ever go back again.

el **jamón** *masc noun*
ham
- el **jamón de York** cooked ham
- el **jamón serrano** cured raw ham

Japón *masc noun*
(el) Japón Japan

japonés *masc adjective & noun*, **japonesa** *fem adjective & noun*
1 **Japanese**
2 **un japonés, una japonesa** Japanese
3 **el japonés** Japanese (*the language*)

WORD TIP Adjectives and nouns for nationality, regional origin, and language do not have capital letters in Spanish.

el **jaque mate** *masc noun*
(*Chess*) **checkmate**
dar jaque mate a alguien to checkmate somebody

el **jarabe** *masc noun*
syrup
jarabe para la tos cough mixture

el **jardín** *masc noun*
1 **garden**
Nuestra casa tiene un jardín. Our house has a garden.
- el **jardín de infancia** nursery school

el **jardinero** *masc noun*, la **jardinera** *fem*
gardener

la **jarra** *fem noun*
jug

el **jarro** *masc noun*
jug

el **jarrón** *masc noun*
vase

la **jaula** *fem noun*
cage

el **jefe** *masc noun*, la **jefa** *fem*
1 **boss** (*at work*)
2 **manager** (*of a company*)
3 **chief**
el jefe de policía the chief of police
el jefe de bomberos the chief fire officer
4 **leader** (*of a group*)

el **jengibre** *masc noun*
ginger

el **jerez** *masc noun*
sherry

el **jersey** *masc noun*, jerseys *plural*
sweater

Jesucristo *masc noun*
Jesus Christ

el **jinete** *masc noun*
1 **rider**
2 **jockey**

los **JJ.OO.** *plural masc abbreviation*
(= *los Juegos Olímpicos*) **Olympic Games**

la **jornada** *fem noun*
day
una jornada de trabajo a working day
trabajar media jornada to work half days
trabajar jornada completa to work full time

joven *masc & fem adjective*, *pl:* **jóvenes**
▷ see **joven** *noun*
young
la moda joven young fashion
las personas jóvenes young people

♪ el & la **joven** *masc & fem noun, pl:* **jóvenes**
▷ see **joven** *adj*
1 **young man**
2 **young woman**
3 **los jóvenes** young people

el **jovencito** *masc noun,* la **jovencita** *fem*
1 **young man**
2 **young woman**

la **joya** *fem noun*
1 **piece of jewellery**
No me gustan las joyas. I don't like jewellery.
2 **gem** (*stone, person*)
Esa chica es una joya. That girl's a real gem.

la **joyería** *fem noun*
jeweller's shop

la **jubilación** *fem noun*
retirement

jubilado *masc adjective,* **jubilada** *fem*
▷ see **jubilado** *noun*
retired

el **jubilado** *masc noun,* la **jubilada** *fem*
▷ see **jubilado** *adj*
pensioner
los jubilados retired people

jubilarse *reflexive verb* **[17]**
to retire

el **judaísmo** *masc noun*
Judaism

WORD TIP Adjectives and nouns for religion do not have capital letters in Spanish.

♪ la **judía** *fem noun* ▷ see **judío** *adj, noun*
bean
- las **judías blancas** haricot beans
- las **judías pintas** kidney beans
- las **judías verdes** green beans

judío *masc adjective,* **judía** *fem*
▷ see **judío** *noun*
Jewish

el **judío** *masc noun,* la **judía** *fem*
▷ see **judío** *adj*
Jew

WORD TIP Adjectives and nouns for religions and peoples do not have capital letters in Spanish.

el **judo** *masc noun*
judo
hacer judo to do judo

juega, juego, etc *verb* ▷ see **juego** *noun*
▷ **jugar**

♪ el **juego** *masc noun* ▷ see **juega, juego, etc** *verb*
1 **game**
Sólo es un juego. It's only a game.
2 **gambling**
Es aficionado al juego. He likes gambling.
3 **play**
juego limpio fair play
fuera de juego offside
después de diez minutos de juego after ten minutes of play
4 **set**
un juego de llaves a set of keys
5 **hacer juego con algo** to match something
No hace juego con los pantalones. It doesn't match the trousers.
- el **juego de azar** game of chance
- el **juego de manos** conjuring trick
- el **juego de palabras** play on words
- los **juegos de mesa** board games
- los **Juegos Olímpicos** the Olympic Games
- los **Juegos Paralímpicos** the Paralympic Games

juegue, etc *verb* ▷ **jugar**

la **juerga** *fem noun*
(*informal*) **irse de juerga** to go out partying
Nos fuimos de juerga. We went out partying.

el & la **juerguista** *masc & fem noun*
(*informal*) **party animal**

♪ el **jueves** *masc noun*
Thursday
el jueves on Thursday
el jueves pasado last Thursday
los jueves on Thursdays
cada jueves every Thursday
Reparten los jueves. They deliver on Thursdays.

WORD TIP Names of months and days start with small letters in Spanish.

el & la **juez** *masc & fem noun,* la **jueza** *fem,* **jueces, juezas** *plural*
1 **judge**
2 **referee**

WORD TIP *juez* and *jueces* can be men and women judges; *jueza* and *juezas* are for women.

el **jugador** *masc noun,* la **jugadora** *fem*
1 **player**
2 **gambler**

♪ **jugar** *verb* **[27]**
1 **to play**
jugar al fútbol to play football
jugar a la pelota to play ball ▸▸

¿A qué quieres jugar? What do you want to play?
2 **to gamble**
Ahora ya no juega. He doesn't gamble any more.
3 **to move** (*in board games*)
Te toca jugar a ti. It's your turn to move.

el **jugo** *masc noun*
juice
- el **jugo de fruta** fruit juice

jugoso *masc adjective*, **jugosa** *fem*
juicy

el **juguete** *masc noun*
toy
un coche de juguete a toy car

la **juguetería** *fem noun*
toyshop

el **juicio** *masc noun*
1 **trial** (*in court*)
2 **sense**
No tiene ningún juicio. He has no sense.
perder el juicio to lose one's mind

♪ **julio** *masc noun*
July
en julio in July
el 28 de julio on 28 July

WORD TIP Names of months and days start with small letters in Spanish.

la **jungla** *fem noun*
jungle

♪ **junio** *masc noun*
June
en junio in June
el primero de junio on 1 June

WORD TIP Names of months and days start with small letters in Spanish.

júnior *adjective*
junior
los jugadores júniors the junior players

la **junta** *fem noun*
1 **committee**
2 **board** (*of a company*)
3 **meeting**
4 **regional government**
una junta autonómica a regional government (*in Spain's devolved government system*)
la Junta de Andalucía the Andalusian Regional Government

♪ **juntar** *verb* **[17]**
1 **to put together**
Juntad las mesas. Put the tables together.
2 **to join**

juntarse *reflexive verb* **[17]**
1 **to join**
Los cables se juntan así. You join the wires like this.
2 **to get together**
Me junté con unos amigos. I met some friends.
Se han juntado otra vez. They've got together again.
3 **to get closer**
Juntaos más. Get closer together.

♪ **junto** *masc adjective*, **junta** *fem*
1 **together**
Ahora todos juntos. All together now.
No los pongas tan juntos. Don't put them so close together.
2 **junto a** next to
Ponlo junto a la ventana. Put it next to the window.
3 **junto con** together with
Bátelo junto con los huevos. Beat it up together with the eggs.

el **jurado** *masc noun*
jury

jurar *verb* **[17]**
to swear
Es verdad. Te lo juro. It's true. I swear.

jurídico *masc adjective*, **jurídica** *fem*
legal

justamente *adverb*
1 **fairly**
No lo han tratado justamente. He hasn't been fairly treated.
2 **exactly**
¡Justamente! Exactly!
Justamente eso es lo que yo quería decir. That's exactly what I meant.

la **justicia** *fem noun*
justice

justificar *verb* **[31]**
to justify

♪ **justo** *masc adjective*, **justa** *fem*
▷ see **justo** *adv*
1 **fair**
una sociedad justa a fair society
No has sido justo con él. You haven't been fair to him.
2 **exact**
la cantidad justa the exact amount
Son ciento cincuenta euros justos. That's exactly one hundred and fifty euros.
3 **lo justo** just enough
Viven con lo justo. They have just enough to live on.

Tengo lo justo para el autobús. I have just enough for the bus fare.

4 **tight** (*clothes, shoes*)
Te está un poco justo. It's a bit tight on you.
Los zapatos me quedan muy justos. The shoes are too tight on me.

justo *adverb* ▷ see **justo** *adj*
just
justo a tiempo just in time
justo en frente del cine just opposite the cinema
justo en el centro right in the middle

juvenil *masc & fem adjective*
1 **youthful** (*appearance*)
2 **young** (*fashion*)
3 **junior** (*team or competition*)

la **juventud** *fem noun*
youth
la juventud de hoy the youth of today

el **juzgado** *masc noun*
court

juzgar *verb* [28]
1 **to judge**
Te he juzgado mal. I've misjudged you.
2 **to try** (*a case, a person in court*)

K k

kaki *invariable adjective*
khaki

WORD TIP *kaki* never changes.

el **kárate** *masc noun*
karate
hacer kárate to do karate

el **karting** *masc noun*
go-karting
to go go-karting hacer karting

el **ketchup** *masc noun*
ketchup

Kg. *abbreviation*
(= *kilogramo*) **kg**, **kilogram**

el **kilo** *masc noun*
kilo

el **kilogramo** *masc noun*
kilogram

el **kilómetro** *masc noun*
kilometre
Está a cinco kilómetros de la costa. It's five kilometres from the sea.

el **kiosco** *masc noun*
1 **kiosk** (*selling sweets, cigarettes, etc*)
2 **newspaper kiosk**
3 **stand**
un kiosko de helados an ice cream stand
el kiosko de la orquesta the bandstand

el **kiwi** *masc noun*
1 **kiwi fruit**
2 **kiwi** (*New Zealand bird*)

Km. *abbreviation*
(= *Kilómetro*) **km**, **kilometre**

el **koala** *masc noun*
koala bear

L l

la *fem determiner* ▷ see **la** *pron*
1 (*before fem sing nouns*) **the**
la moto the motor bike
la casa grande the big house
2 (*with parts of the body, clothes*) **Se rompió la pierna.** She broke her leg.
Se afeitó la barba. He shaved off his beard.
Me quité la chaqueta. I took my jacket off.
3 (*talking about time*) **a las diez de la mañana** at ten in the morning
Iré la próxima semana. I'll go next week.
4 (*when* **la** *is not translated*)
irse a la cama to go to bed
la maleta de Isabel Isabel's suitcase
la señora Martínez Mrs Martínez
No me gusta la sandía. I don't like watermelon.
5 (*for a fem noun, which is known about, e.g.* **la** *camisa below.*) **Me gustó la verde.** I liked the green one.
La mía es roja. Mine is red.
Esa es la tuya. That one is yours.
Esta es la de Ana. This one is Ana's.

WORD TIP See also *el*, *los* and *las*.

la *fem pronoun* ▷ see **la** *determiner*
1 (*as direct object*) **her** (*person*)
La acompañé a casa. I took her home.
Voy a verla mañana. I am going to see her tomorrow.
2 (*as direct object*) **it** (*thing*)
Compré una camiseta, pero la voy a devolver. I bought a T-shirt, but I'm going to take it back.
¡Dámela ahora! Give it to me now!
3 (*as direct object*) **you** (*polite form*)
A usted la llamaron hace un momento. They called you a moment ago.

el **labio** *masc noun*
lip

laborable *masc & fem adjective*
un día laborable a working day

el **laboratorio** *masc noun*
laboratory

la **laca** *fem noun*
1 **lacquer**
2 **hairspray**
• la **laca de uñas** nail varnish

la **ladera** *fem noun*
slope

el **lado** *masc noun*
1 **side**
el otro lado the other side
al otro lado de la carretera on the other side of the road
hacerse a un lado to move aside
Hazte a un lado. Move aside.
2 **al lado de** next to
al lado de Miguel next to Miguel
Se sentó a mi lado. He sat next to me.
Viven en la casa de al lado. They live next door.
3 **de lado**
Ponlo de lado. Put it on its side.
tumbarse de lado to lie on your side
4 **por todos lados** everywhere
Lo he buscado por todos lados. I've looked for it everywhere.
5 **en ningún lado**, **por ningún lado** nowhere, not anywhere
No está por ningún lado. It's nowhere.
No lo encuentro en ningún lado. I can't find it anywhere.
6 **en algún lado** somewhere
Debe estar en algún lado. It must be somewhere.
7 **por otro lado ...** on the other hand ...
Por otro lado, hay el problema de ... On the other hand, there's the problem of ...

ladrar *verb* **[17]**
to bark

el **ladrillo** *masc noun*
brick

el **ladrón** *masc noun*, la **ladrona** *fem*
1 **thief**
2 **burglar**
3 **robber** (*of banks*)

el **lagarto** *masc noun*
lizard

el **lago** *masc noun*
lake

la **lágrima** *fem noun*
tear

la **laguna** *fem noun*
1 **lake**
2 **lagoon**

lamentar *verb* **[17]**
to regret
Lo lamento mucho. I'm very sorry. ⏩

Lamento no poder ayudarle. I'm sorry I can't help you.
Lamento tener que informarle de ... I regret to have to inform you that ...

lamer *verb* **[18]**
to lick

la **lámpara** *fem noun*
lamp
- la **lámpara de pie** standard lamp

la **lana** *fem noun*
wool
una chaqueta de lana a wool jacket
pura lana virgen pure new wool

la **langosta** *fem noun*
lobster

el **langostino** *masc noun*
king prawn

la **lanza** *fem noun*
spear

el **lanzamiento** *masc noun*
launch (*of rocket, product*)

lanzar *verb* **[22]**
1 **to throw** (*a ball or stone*)
2 **to launch** (*a product or an attack*)

lanzarse *reflexive verb* **[22]**
1 **to throw yourself**
Se lanzó al agua. He threw himself into the water.
lanzarse en paracaídas to parachute
2 **lanzarse sobre alguien** to pounce on someone
Se lanzó sobre el ladrón. He pounced on the burglar.

el **lápiz** *masc noun*, **lápices** *plural*
pencil
- los **lápices de colores** crayons
- el **lápiz de labios** lipstick
- el **lápiz de ojos** eyeliner

largo *masc adjective*, **larga** *fem*
▷ see **largo** *noun*
1 **long**
una falda larga a long skirt
un largo recorrido a long journey
Te está muy largo. It's too long for you.
2 **a lo largo de** along
a lo largo de la costa along the coast
3 **a lo largo de** throughout
a lo largo del día throughout the day

el **largo** *masc noun* ▷ see **largo** *adj*
length
¿Cuánto mide de largo? How long is it?
Mide cinco metros de largo. It is five metres long.

las *plural fem determiner* ▷ see **las** *pron*
1 (*before fem plural nouns*) **the**
Deja las cajas ahí. Leave the boxes there.
2 (*with parts of the body, clothes*) **Se lavó las manos.** She washed her hands.
Me quité las botas. I took my boots off.
3 (*talking about time*) **a las ocho de la mañana** at eight in the morning
Son las siete y cinco. It's five past seven.
4 (*when **las** is not translated*) **las maletas de Isabel** Isabel's suitcases
Me gustan las naranjas. I like oranges.
5 (*for a fem plural noun, which is known about, e.g. **las camisetas** below*) **Las mías son rojas.** Mine are red.
Esas son las tuyas. Those are yours.
Me gustaron las verdes. I liked the green ones.
6 **Éstas son las de Ana.** These ones are Ana's.
las mías y las de usted mine and yours
Me gustan más las de Toni. I like Toni's better.
las que yo compré the ones I bought
las que quieras whichever you want

WORD TIP See also *el*, *la* and *los*.

las *plural fem pronoun* ▷ see **las** *determiner*
1 (*as direct object*) **them** (*people, things*)
Las vi ayer. I saw them yesterday.
Te las puedes llevar. You can take them with you.
Quiero verlas. I want to see them.
¡Dámelas ahora! Give them to me now!
2 (*as direct object*) **you** (*plural polite form*)
¿Las atienden, señoras? Are you being served, ladies?

el **láser** *masc noun*
laser
un rayo láser a laser beam

la **lástima** *fem noun*
¡Qué lástima! What a shame!
Su madre me da lástima. I feel sorry for her mother.
Es una lástima que no puedas venir. How sad that you can't come.

WORD TIP *ser una lástima que* is followed by a verb in the subjunctive.

la **lata** *fem noun*
1 **tin**
una lata de tomates a tin of tomatoes
en lata tinned
unas sardinas en lata tinned sardines
2 (*informal*) **nuisance**
¡Qué lata! What a nuisance!

Es una lata tener que esperar. It's a nuisance having to wait.
dar la lata (*informal*) to be a nuisance
Siempre están dando la lata. They're always such a nuisance.

⚷ el **latín** *masc noun*
Latin

WORD TIP Use a small letter for languages in Spanish.

⚷ **Latinoamérica** *fem noun*
Latin America

latinoamericano *masc adjective & noun*, **latinoamericana** *fem adjective & noun*
1 **Latin American**
2 **un latinoamericano, una latinoamericana** Latin American

WORD TIP Adjectives and nouns for nationality and regional origin do not have capital letters in Spanish.

el **latón** *masc noun*
brass

⚷ el **laurel** *masc noun*
1 **laurel**
2 **bay tree**
una hoja de laurel a bayleaf

⚷ el **lavabo** *masc noun*
1 **washbasin**
2 **toilet**
¿Dónde están los lavabos? Where are the toilets?

⚷ el **lavado** *masc noun*
wash
- el **lavado a mano** handwashing
- el **lavado en seco** dry cleaning

⚷ la **lavadora** *fem noun*
washing machine
- la **lavadora automática** automatic washing machine

la **lavanda** *fem noun*
lavender

⚷ la **lavandería** *fem noun*
1 **laundry**
2 **laundrette**

⚷ el **lavaplatos** *masc noun*, lavaplatos *plural*
dishwasher

⚷ **lavar** *verb* **[17]**
1 **to wash**
lavar los platos to wash the dishes
Lavé la ropa. I washed the clothes.
Lavó el coche. He washed the car.
2 **lavar un abrigo en seco** to dry-clean a coat

lavarse *reflexive verb* **[17]**
to wash
lavarse las manos to wash your hands
lavarse los dientes to clean your teeth
lavarse el pelo to wash your hair
Me lavo la cabeza todos los días. I wash my hair everyday.

⚷ el **lavavajillas** *masc noun*, *pl:* los **lavavajillas**
dishwasher

⚷ el **lazo** *masc noun*
ribbon

⚷ **la** *fem pronoun* ▷ **see la** *determiner*
1 (*as direct object*) **her** (*person*)
La acompañé a casa. I took her home.
Voy a verla mañana. I am going to see her tomorrow.
2 (*as direct object*) **it** (*thing*)
Compré una camiseta, pero la voy a devolver. I bought a T-shirt, but I'm going to take it back.
¡Dámela ahora! Give it to me now!
3 (*as direct object*) **you** (*polite form*)
A usted la llamaron hace un momento. They called you a moment ago.

⚷ **le** *masc & fem pronoun*
1 (*as indirect object*) **him**
Le di las llaves. I gave him the keys.
Le mandé el paquete el lunes. I sent him the parcel on Monday.
¿Qué le quitaron? What did they take from him?
Tengo algo que decirle. I've got something to tell him.
Dale las llaves. Give him the keys.
2 (*as indirect object*) **her**
Le mandé el paquete el lunes. I sent her the parcel on Monday.
Me encontré con Inés y le di las llaves. I met Inés and gave her the keys.
¿Qué le quitaron? What did they take from her?
Tengo algo que decirle. I've got something to tell her.
Dale las llaves. Give her the keys.
3 (*as indirect object*) **you** (*polite form*)
Tengo algo que decirle. I've got something to tell you.
Le mandé el paquete el lunes. I sent you the parcel on Monday.
¿Le llevo las maletas a su habitación? Shall I carry your suitcases to your room?
4 (*as indirect object*) **it**
Le puse la tapa. I put the lid on it.
Le puse otra estantería. I added another shelf to it.

Spanish–English

la lección *fem noun*
lesson

la leche *fem noun*
milk
- la **leche descremada**, la **leche desnatada** skimmed milk
- la **leche en polvo** powdered milk
- la **leche entera** full-cream milk

la lechuga *fem noun*
lettuce

el **lector** *masc noun*, la **lectora** *fem*
reader
- el **lector de DVD** DVD player

la lectura *fem noun*
reading

WORD TIP *lectura* does not mean *lecture* in English; for the meaning of *lecture* ▷ **conferencia**.

leer *verb* **[37]**
to read
Estoy leyendo una novela I'm reading a novel.
¿Has leído a Lorca? Have you read Lorca?

legal *masc & fem adjective*
legal

legendario *masc adjective*, **legendaria** *fem*
legendary

las legumbres *plural fem noun*
1 **pulses** (*beans, lentils, etc*)
2 **vegetables**

lejano *masc adjective*, **lejana** *fem*
distant
Son parientes lejanos. They are distant relatives.

el **Lejano Oriente** *masc noun*
the Far East

la lejía *fem noun*
bleach

lejos *adverb*
1 **far**
No está muy lejos. It's not very far.
¿Está lejos de aquí? Is it far from here?
Está demasiado lejos para ir andando. It's too far to walk.
2 **a long way**
Está muy lejos. It's a long way (away).
Está lejos del centro. It's a long way from the centre.
Viven lejos de aquí. They live a long way from here.
3 **desde lejos** from a long way off
Desde lejos se ve la catedral. You can see the cathedral from a long way off.

la lengua *fem noun*
1 **tongue**
morderse la lengua to bite your tongue
2 **language**
una lengua muy difícil a very difficult language
- la **lengua materna** mother tongue

el lenguado *masc noun*
sole (*the fish*)

el lenguaje *masc noun*
language
- el **lenguaje corporal** body language

lentamente *adverb*
slowly

la lente *fem noun*
lens
- las **lentes de contacto** contact lenses

la lenteja *fem noun*
lentil

los **lentes** *plural masc noun*
(*Latin America*) **glasses**

la **lentilla** *fem noun*
contact lens

lento *masc adjective*, **lenta** *fem*
▷ see **lento** *adv*
slow
Son muy lentos. They're very slow.

lento *adverb* ▷ see **lento** *adj*
slowly
Caminan muy lento. They're walking very slowly.

la leña *fem noun*
firewood

el leño *masc noun*
log

leo *masc & fem noun* ▷ see **Leo** *noun*
Leo
Es leo. She's Leo.

WORD TIP Use a small letter in Spanish to say *I am Leo*, etc with star signs.

el Leo *masc noun* ▷ see **leo** *noun*
Leo (*star sign*)

el león *masc noun*, la **leona** *fem*
1 **lion**
2 **lioness**

el leopardo *masc noun*
leopard

los **leotardos** *plural masc noun*
woollen tights

les *plural masc & fem pronoun*
1 *(as indirect object)* **them**
Les di las llaves. I gave them the keys.
Les mandé el paquete el martes. I sent them the parcel on Tuesday.
Tengo algo que decirles. I've got something to tell them.
Dales las llaves. Give them the keys.
¿Qué les quitaron? What did they take from them?
Les puse la tapa. I put the lids on them.
2 *(as indirect object)* **you** *(plural polite form)*
Les mandé el paquete el martes. I sent you the parcel on Tuesday.
Tengo algo que darles. I've got something to give you.

la **lesión** *fem noun*
injury

letón *masc adjective & noun*, **letona** *fem adjective & noun*
1 **Latvian**
2 **un letón, una letona** Latvian

WORD TIP Adjectives and nouns for nationality and regional origin do not have capital letters in Spanish.

Letonia *fem noun*
Latvia

la **letra** *fem noun*
1 **letter** *(of the alphabet)*
2 **handwriting**
Tiene muy buena letra. Her handwriting is very good.
Casi no se le entiende la letra. You can hardly read his handwriting.
3 **lyrics** *(of a song)*
- la **letra mayúscula** capital letter
- la **letra minúscula** lower-case letter

el **letrero** *masc noun*
notice, **sign**

la **levadura** *fem noun*
yeast

leve *masc & fem adjective*
minor *(injury)*

levantar *verb* **[17]**
1 **to lift**
levantar un peso to lift a weight
Levanta la tapa. Lift the lid.
2 **to raise**
levantar la mano to raise your hand
levantar la voz to raise your voice
3 **to pick up**
Levantamos a la niña del suelo. We picked the girl up from the floor.
4 **levantar la mesa** to clear the table

levantarse *reflexive verb* **[17]**
1 **to get up** *(out of bed)*
Me levanto a las siete. I get up at seven o'clock.
Los domingos nos levantamos tarde. On Sundays we get up late.
2 **to get up**, **to stand up**
Todos se levantaron. Everyone stood up.
levantarse de la mesa to get up from the table

la **ley** *fem noun*
law
violar la ley to break the law

la **leyenda** *fem noun*
1 **legend**
2 **key** *(to a map)*

leyó *verb* ▷ **leer**

libanés *masc adjective & noun*, **libanesa** *fem adjective & noun*
1 **Lebanese**
2 **un libanés, una libanesa** Lebanese

WORD TIP Adjectives and nouns for nationality and regional origin do not have capital letters in Spanish.

Líbano *masc noun*
(el) Líbano Lebanon

liberar *verb* **[17]**
1 **to free**
2 **to liberate**

la **libertad** *fem noun*
freedom
- la **libertad condicional** parole
- la **libertad de expresión** freedom of speech

la **libra** *fem noun* ▷ see **libra, Libra** *noun*
pound
diez libras esterlinas ten pounds sterling

libra *masc & fem noun* ▷ see **libra, Libra** *noun*
Libra
Susana es libra. Susana's Libra.

WORD TIP Use a small letter in Spanish to say *I am Libra*, etc with star signs.

el **Libra** *masc noun* ▷ see **libra** *noun*
Libra *(star sign)*

librar *verb* **[17]**
librar a alguien de algo to save someone from something ⏩

Los libraron de morir ahogados. He saved them from drowning.

librarse *reflexive verb* **[17]**
1 **librarse de algo** to save yourself from something
Se libró de morir ahogado. He saved himself from drowning.
Me libré del castigo. I escaped punishment.
2 **librarse de una obligación** to get out of an obligation
Se libró de lavar los platos. He got out of doing the dishes.

libre *masc & fem adjective*
1 **free**
un país libre a free country
en mis ratos libres in my free time
Tengo el día libre. I'm free all day.
¿Está libre este asiento? Is this seat free?
los quinientos metros libres the five hundred metres freestyle
2 **trabajar por libre** to work freelance
Trabaja por libre como traductora. She works as a freelance translator.

la **librería** *fem noun*
1 **bookshop**
2 **bookcase**

WORD TIP *librería* does not mean *library* in English; for the meaning of *library* ▷ **biblioteca**.

la **libreta** *fem noun*
notebook

el **libro** *masc noun*
book
- el **libro de bolsillo** paperback
- el **libro de reclamaciones** complaints book (*in hotels etc*)
- el **libro de texto** text book

mini-info ***libro de familia***
Cada familia en España recibe un Libro de Familia del gobierno como registro oficial. Hay que presentar este libro cuando los hijos tienen 14 años por ejemplo, para obtener su Documento Nacional de Identidad (DNI).

la **licencia** *fem noun*
licence, permit

el **licenciado** *masc noun*, la **licenciada** *fem*
graduate

la **licenciatura** *fem noun*
university degree

el **licor** *masc noun*
liqueur

la **licuadora** *fem noun*
liquidizer

el & la **líder** *masc & fem noun*
leader (*of a political party, union, etc*)

la **liebre** *fem noun*
hare

la **liga** *fem noun*
league
la liga de fútbol the football league

ligeramente *adverb*
slightly

ligero *masc adjective*, **ligera** *fem*
1 **light** (*not heavy*)
un paquete ligero a light parcel
tener el sueño ligero to be a light sleeper
2 **slight**
un ligero sabor a almendras a slight taste of almonds
Hay un ligero problema. There's a slight problem.
3 **thin** (*fabric*)
4 **fast**
un caballo muy ligero a very fast horse

la **lima** *fem noun*
1 **file** (*tool*)
2 **lime** (*fruit*)
- la **lima de uñas** nail file

limitar *verb* **[17]**
1 **to limit**
Tuvieron que limitar el número de estudiantes. They had to limit the number of students.
2 **limitar con un país** to border on a country
España limita con Francia. Spain borders on France.

limitarse *reflexive verb* **[17]**
limitarse a algo: Me limité a hacer sólo una pregunta. I lmited myself to asking one question.
Me limité a ayudarlos con el ordenador. I just helped them with the computer.

el **límite** *masc noun*
1 **limit**
Hay un tiempo límite. There's a time limit.
2 **la fecha límite** the deadline
3 **border** (*of a country*)
- el **límite de velocidad** speed limit

el **limón** *masc noun*
lemon

la **limonada** *fem noun*
lemonade

el **limonero** *masc noun*
lemon tree

la **limosna** *fem noun*
pedir limosna to beg
Nunca doy limosna. I never give money to beggars.

el **limpiaparabrisas** *masc noun*, *pl:* los **limpiaparabrisas**
windscreen wiper

limpiar *verb* [17]
1 **to clean**
limpiar la casa to clean the house
Limpié los zapatos. I cleaned my shoes.
2 **to clean off**
Limpió la mancha que había en la mesa. She cleaned the dirty mark off the table.
3 **to wipe**
4 **Limpió la mesa con un trapo.** He wiped the table.
5 **limpiar algo en seco** to dry-clean something
Hay que limpiarlo en seco. It must be dry-cleaned.

la **limpieza** *fem noun*
1 **cleanliness**
2 **cleaning**
hacer la limpieza to do the cleaning
la señora de la limpieza the cleaning lady
- la **limpieza de cutis** facial
- la **limpieza en seco** dry-cleaning

la **limpieza general** *fem noun*
spring-clean
Voy a hacer una limpieza general. I'm going to have a spring-clean.

limpio *masc adjective*, **limpia** *fem*
1 **clean**
¿Tienes las manos limpias? Are your hands clean?
2 **clear** (*sky*)
un cielo limpio, sin nubes a clear, cloudless sky
3 **fair** (*game, business deal*)
4 **pasar algo a limpio** to make a fair copy of something
Tuve que pasar a limpio la redacción. I had to make a fair copy of the essay.

el **lince**
lynx (*the animal*)

lindo *masc adjective*, **linda** *fem*
lovely

la **línea** *fem noun*
1 **line** (*mark*)
una línea recta a straight line
2 **line** (*of a poem, letter, etc*)
escribirle unas líneas a alguien to drop someone a line
leer entre líneas to read between the lines
3 **line** (*in telecommunications*)
Se ha cortado la línea. The line has gone dead.
4 **line** (*of products*)
una nueva línea de juegos a new line of games
5 **de primera línea** top-quality
productos de primera línea top-quality products
un jugador de primera línea a top player
6 **line** (*of the railway, metro*)
el final de la línea the end of the line
No hay servicio en la línea 5. There is no service on Line 5.
7 **route** (*of a bus service*)
No hay servicio en la línea 5. There is no service on route number 5.
No hay línea directa. There is no direct service.
8 **figure**
cuidar la línea to watch your figure
- la **línea aérea** airline
- la **línea de llegada** finishing line
- la **línea de meta** goal line
- la **línea regular** airline (*operating scheduled flights*)
- la **línea telefónica** telephone line

el **lino** *masc noun*
linen

la **linterna** *fem noun*
torch

el **lío** *masc noun* (*informal*)
1 **mess**
hacerse un lío to get muddled up
¡Vaya lío! What a mess!
Me hice un lío con las fechas. I got the dates all muddled up.
2 **trouble**
¡No te metas en líos! Keep out of trouble!
armar un lío to kick up a fuss
Armó un lío tremendo. He kicked up a real fuss.

la **liquidación** *fem noun*
1 **sale**
2 **liquidation** (*of a business*)
entrar en liquidación to go into liquidation
3 **settlement** (*of a debt, an account*)
- la **liquidación por cierre** closing-down sale
- la **liquidación total** clearance sale

líquido *masc adjective*, **líquida** *fem*
▷ see **líquido** *noun*
liquid

el **líquido** *masc noun* ▷ see **líquido** *adj*
liquid

liso *masc adjective*, **lisa** *fem*
1 **smooth** (*skin, surface*)
2 **straight** (*hair*)
3 **flat** (*ground*)

la **lista** *fem noun* ▷ see **listo** *adj*
1 **list**
hacer una lista to make a list
No estás en la lista. You're not on the list.
2 **register** (*at school*)
pasar lista to take the register
- la **lista de bodas** wedding list
- la **lista de espera** waiting list
- la **lista de la compra** shopping list
- la **lista de precios** price list
- la **lista de vinos** wine list

el **listín** *masc noun*
telephone directory, **phone book**

listo *masc adjective*, **lista** *adjective*
▷ see **lista** *noun*
1 **clever**
Se cree muy lista. She thinks she's very clever.
2 **ready**
estar listo to be ready
Ya estamos listos para salir. We're ready to go now.

la **litera** *fem noun*
1 **bunk bed** (*piece of furniture*)
2 **berth** (*in a ship*)
3 **couchette** (*on a train*)

la **literatura** *fem noun*
literature

el **litro** *masc noun*
litre

Lituania *fem noun*
Lithuania

lituano *masc adjective & noun*, **lituana** *fem adjective & noun*
1 **Lithuanian**
2 **un lituano, una lituana** Lithuanian

WORD TIP Adjectives and nouns for nationality and regional origin do not have capital letters in Spanish.

la **llama** *fem noun*
1 **flame**
2 **llama**

la **llamada** *fem noun*
call
- la **llamada a cobro revertido** reverse-charge call
- la **llamada interurbana** long-distance call
- la **llamada telefónica** telephone call
- la **llamada urbana** local call

llamar *verb* [17]
1 **to call**
Te llama tu madre. Your mother is calling you.
llamar al médico to call the doctor
Llamamos a un taxi. We called a taxi.
La llamamos Tintina. We call her Tintina.
2 **to phone**
¿Cuándo llamarás? When will you phone?
llamar a alguien por teléfono to phone someone
Lo llamé por teléfono. I phoned him.

llamarse *reflexive verb* [17]
to be called
Se llama Ángeles. She's called Ángeles.
¿Cómo te llamas? What's your name?

llano *masc adjective*, **llana** *fem*
flat, **level** (*ground*)

la **llave** *fem noun*
1 **key**
cerrar algo con llave to lock something
Cerró la puerta con llave. He locked the door.
2 **switch** (*for a light*)
3 (*Latin America*) **tap**
4 **spanner**
- la **llave de contacto** ignition key
- la **llave de judo** judo hold
- la **llave inglesa** adjustable spanner
- la **llave maestra** master key

el **llavero** *masc noun*
keyring

la **llegada** *fem noun*
arrival
A su llegada al hotel ... On his arrival at the hotel ...

llegar *verb* [28]
1 **to arrive**
¿Cuándo llegan tus primos? When are your cousins arriving?
Llegan a las siete. They arrive at seven.
Siempre llega tarde. He's always late.
Llegó justo a tiempo. He was just in time.
llegar a un lugar to arrive somewhere
Llegó a Madrid. He arrived in Madrid
Llegó al aeropuerto a las dos. She arrived at the airport at two o'clock.
Cenaremos cuando lleguemos a casa.

We'll have dinner when we get home.
llegar de un lugar to arrive from somewhere
Acaba de llegar de Caracas. He's just arrived from Caracas.

2 **to come**
Ya llega el invierno. Winter is coming.
Pensé que nunca llegaría este momento. I thought this moment would never come.

3 to reach
Las cortinas llegan hasta el suelo. The curtains go down to the floor.
No llego a la lámpara. I can't reach the lamp.
Esa cuerda no llega al otro lado. That rope won't reach the other side.
Llegué a la conclusión de que mentía. I reached the conclusion that he was lying.
Llegamos a un acuerdo. We reached an agreement.

4 **to be enough**
Con tres litros de leche llega para todos. Three litres of milk will be enough for everybody.
No me llega el dinero. I have'nt got enough money.

5 **llegar a hacer algo** to get to do something
Llegué a conocerlo. I got to meet him.
No llegué a verlo. I didn't get to see it.

6 **llegar a ser** to become
Llegó a ser famoso. He became famous.
Nunca llegó a director. He never became director.

♪ llenar *verb* [17]

1 **to fill**
llenar la bañera to fill the bath
Llene el depósito, por favor. Fill up the tank, please.
llenar algo de algo to fill something up with something
Llené la bañera de agua. I filled the bath up with water.
Le llenaron la cabeza de ideas. They filled his head with ideas.

2 **fill in** (*a form*)
Llenó la solicitud. She filled in the application form.

llenarse *reflexive verb* [17]

to fill up
El tren siempre se llena aquí. The train always fills up here.
llenarse de algo to fill with something
El cubo se llenó de agua. The bucket filled with water.
Se le llenaron los ojos de lágrimas. Her eyes filled with tears.

♪ lleno *masc adjective*, llena *fem*

1 **full**
estar lleno de algo to be full of something
La botella está llena de agua. The bottle is full of water.

2 **covered**
estar lleno de algo to be covered with something
El suelo estaba lleno de papeles. The floor was covered with papers.

3 **full** (*of food*)
No gracias, estoy lleno. No thanks, I'm full.

♪ llevar *verb* [17]

1 **to take** (*from one place to another*)
Te lo puedes llevar. You can take it with you.
Le llevé unas flores. I took her some flowers.
Llevaré una botella de vino a la fiesta. I'll take a bottle of wine to the party.
Te lo llevaré el sábado. I'll bring it on Saturday.
Yo te puedo llevar a la estación. I can take you to the station.
La llevé a comer a un restaurante. I took her for lunch to a restaurant.
La llevé en coche a su casa. I drove her home.

2 **to carry**
Yo llevaba al niño en brazos. I was carrying the baby in my arms.
Los atracadores llevaban pistolas. The robbers carried guns.

3 **to have**
¿Qué llevas en el bolso? What have you got in your bag?
No llevo las llaves encima. I don't have the keys on me.

4 **to wear**
No llevo reloj. I'm not wearing a watch.
Llevaba un vestido verde. She was wearing a green dress.

5 **to take** (*time*)
Lleva tiempo. It takes time.
Me llevó dos semanas terminarlo. It took me two weeks to finish it.

6 **to be** (*talking about time*)
¿Cuánto tiempo llevas trabajando aquí? How long have you been working here?
Llevamos dos semanas en Londres. We've been in London for two weeks.
Lleva media hora hablando por teléfono. He's been on the phone for half an hour.
El tren lleva una hora de retraso. The train's an hour late.

7 (*to be taller than, ahead of, etc*) **Le llevo cuatro años.** I'm four years older than him. ▸▸

♪ indicates key words

Mi hijo te lleva unos centímetros. My son is a few centimetres taller than you.
Nos llevan tres días de ventaja. They have a three-day lead over us.

8 **to lead**
El camino que lleva al río. The road that leads to the river.
¿Adónde lleva este camino? ¿Where does this road go?

9 **to run** (*to be in charge of*)
Su padre lleva la tienda. Her father runs the shop.
Lleva la contabilidad de la empresa. He does the company accounts.

llevarse *reflexive verb* **[17]**

1 **to take (away)**
Se llevó los discos. He took the records.
Ya puedes llevarte esto. You can take this away now.
Nos lo llevamos a la playa. We took him off to the beach.
Los ladrones se llevaron las joyas. The thieves went off with the jewels.

2 **llevarse bien con alguien** to get on with someone
Se llevan bien. They get on well.
Nos llevamos mal. We don't get on.

llorar *verb* **[17]**
to cry
Lo hizo llorar. She made him cry.

llover *verb* **[38]**
to rain
Está lloviendo. It's raining.

la **llovizna** *fem noun*
drizzle

llueva, **llueve**, **etc** *verb* ▷ **llover**

la **lluvia** *fem noun*
rain
un día de lluvia a rainy day
- la **lluvia ácida** acid rain

lluvioso *masc adjective*, **lluviosa** *fem*
rainy

lo *determiner* ▷ **see lo** *pron*

1 (*lo + adjective*) **the ... thing**
Lo mejor es ... The best thing is ...
Lo curioso es ... The funny thing is ...
Prefiero lo salado a lo dulce. I prefer savoury things to sweet things.

2 (*for someone's belongings*) **lo mío** mine
Esto es lo tuyo. That's yours.
Esto es lo de mi madre. This is my mother's.
Lo vuestro está en la habitación. Your things are in the bedroom.
Lo de Marta lo he puesto en la mesa. I've put Marta's things on the table.

3 (*talking about an event*) **¿Sabes lo de Eva?** Have you heard about Eva?
Le conté lo tuyo. I told her about you.
Lo de Pablo es muy raro. It's really strange this thing with Pablo.
Lo del accidente fue horrible. That thing about the accident was horrible.

4 **lo que** what
Eso es lo que yo compré. That's what I bought.
Toma lo que quieras. Take whatever you want.
Dime todo lo que sepas. Tell me everything you know.

lo *masc pronoun* ▷ **see lo** *determiner*

1 (*as direct object*) **him**
Lo vi ayer. I saw him yesterday.
Voy a verlo mañana. I am going to see him tomorrow.

2 (*as direct object*) **it** (*thing*)
Lo metí en tu bolso. I put it in your bag.
Léelo en voz alta. Read it aloud.
Ya lo sé. I know.

3 (*as direct object*) **you** (*polite form*)
A usted no lo llamaron. They didn't call you.

el **lobo** *masc noun*
wolf

local *masc & fem adjective* ▷ **see local** *masc noun*
local

el **local** *masc noun* ▷ **see local** *masc & fem adj*
premises

la **localidad** *fem noun*

1 **town**
una pequeña localidad a small town

2 **seat** (*in a cinema, concert hall, etc*)
'No hay localidades' 'Sold out'

la **loción** *fem noun*
lotion
- la **loción bronceadora** suntan lotion
- la **loción para después del afeitado** aftershave lotion

loco *masc adjective*, **loca** *fem* ▷ **see loco** *noun*
mad
¡Estás loco! You're mad!
estar loco por alguien to be crazy about somebody
Estaba loco por ella. He was crazy about her.
(*informal*) **volver loco a alguien** to drive someone mad

¡Este niño me va a volver loco! That child's going to drive me mad!
Las fresas la vuelven loca. She loves strawberries.

ℰ el **loco** *masc noun*, la **loca** *fem*
▷ see **loco** *adj*
1 **madman**
2 **madwoman**

ℰ la **locomotora** *fem noun*
engine (*of a train*)

ℰ la **locura** *fem noun*
1 **madness**
2 (*mad thing, idea*) **Eso es una locura.** That's crazy.
Es otra de sus locuras. It's another of his crazy ideas.

ℰ el **locutor** *masc noun*, la **locutora** *fem*
1 **announcer**
2 **newsreader**
• el **locutor deportivo** sports commentator

lógico *masc adjective*, **lógica** *fem*
logical

ℰ **lograr** *verb* [17]
1 **to achieve**
lograr la victoria to achieve victory
2 **lograr hacer algo** to manage to do something
Logré terminar el ejercicio. I managed to finish the exercise.
No lograron terminarlo. They didn't manage to finish it.
lograr que alguien haga algo to get someone to do something
Lograron que lo hiciera a tiempo. They got him to finish it in time.

WORD TIP *lograr que* is followed by a verb in the subjunctive.

ℰ la **lombriz** *fem noun*
earthworm

ℰ el **lomo** *masc noun*
1 **back** (*of an animal*)
2 **spine** (*of a book*)
3 (*Latin America*) **steak**
• el **lomo de cerdo** loin of pork

ℰ la **loncha** *fem noun*
slice
una loncha de bacon a rasher of bacon
una loncha de jamón a slice of ham

londinense *masc & fem adjective & noun*
1 **London**
2 **un & una londinense** Londoner

WORD TIP Adjectives and nouns for regional origin do not have capital letters in Spanish.

ℰ **Londres** *masc noun*
London

ℰ la **longaniza** *fem noun*
spicy pork sausage

ℰ la **longitud** *fem noun*
length
Tiene doce metros de longitud. It's twelve metres long.
• la **longitud de onda** wavelength

ℰ el **loro** *masc noun*, la **lora** *fem*
parrot

ℰ **los** *plural masc determiner* ▷ see **los** *pron*
1 (*before masc plural nouns*) **the**
Deja los libros ahí. Leave the books there.
2 (*when **los** is not translated*) **los discos de Isabel** Isabel's records
No me gustan los tomates. I don't like tomatoes.
3 (*for parts of the body, clothes*) **Se frotó los ojos.** She rubbed her eyes.
Me puse los zapatos. I put my shoes on.
4 (*for a masc plural noun, which is known about, e.g. **los pañuelos** below*)
Los míos son rojos. Mine are red.
Ésos son los tuyos. Those are yours.
Me gustaron los verdes. I liked the green ones.
5 **Estos son los de Ana.** These ones are Ana's.
los míos y los de usted mine and yours
Me gustan más los de Toni. I like Toni's better.
los que yo compré the ones I bought
los que quieras whichever ones you want

WORD TIP See also *el*, *la* and *las*.

ℰ **los** *plural masc pronoun* ▷ see **los** *determiner*
1 (*as direct object*) **them**
Los vi ayer. I saw them yesterday.
Te los puedes llevar. You can take them with you.
Quiero verlos. I want to see them.
¡Dámelos ahora! Give them to me now!
2 (*as direct object*) **you** (*plural polite form*)
Los oí, caballeros. I heard you, gentlemen.

el **lote** *masc noun*
batch
un lote de pedidos a batch of orders

ℰ la **lotería** *fem noun*
lottery
Les tocó la lotería. They won the lottery.

las **luces** *masc noun* ▷ **luz**
• las **luces cortas**, **luces de cruce** dipped headlights
• las **luces de freno** brake lights
• las **luces largas** full beam

la lucha *fem noun*
1 **fight, struggle**
la lucha contra el cáncer the fight against cancer
la lucha por la supervivencia the struggle for survival
2 **wrestling**

luchar *verb* **[17]**
1 **to fight** (*in combat*)
Luchó en la guerra del Golfo. He fought in the Gulf War.
2 **to fight, to struggle**
luchar por algo to fight for something
Lucharon por la paz. They fought for peace.
3 **to wrestle** (*in sport*)

luego *adverb*
1 **then**
Luego vino su madre. Then her mother came.
2 **later**
Luego te veo. I'll see you later.
¡Hasta luego! See you later!
3 **afterwards**
Luego te arrepentirás. You'll be sorry afterwards.
Luego podemos cenar. We can have dinner afterwards.
4 **then**
Primero está su casa y luego la mía. First comes her house and then mine.
Primero iré al banco y luego a tu casa. I'll go to the bank first and then to your house.

el lugar *masc noun*
1 **place**
un lugar precioso a beautiful place
en cualquier lugar anywhere
en otro lugar somewhere else
por cualquier otro lugar anywhere else
Tiene que estar en algún lugar. It must be somewhere.
2 **tener lugar** to take place
El concierto tendrá lugar en la plaza. The concert will take place in the square.
3 (*saying the order of things*) **en primer lugar** first of all
En primer lugar, hay que recordar ... First of all, we must remember ...
en segundo lugar ... secondly ...
en último lugar last of all
Llegó en último lugar. He finished last (*in a race*).
4 **room**
No hay lugar para nada más. There's no room for anything else.
5 **en lugar de** instead of
En lugar de ir de compras, fuimos a la piscina. Instead of going shopping, we went to the pool.
- el **lugar de nacimiento** place of birth

lúgubre *masc & fem adjective*
gloomy

el lujo *masc noun*
luxury
un apartamento de lujo a luxury apartment

lujoso *masc adjective*, **lujosa** *fem*
luxurious

luminoso *masc adjective*, **luminosa** *fem*
1 **bright** (*room, idea*)
2 **luminous**

la luna *fem noun*
1 **moon**
Esta noche hay luna. The moon is out tonight.
2 **mirror**
3 **shop window**
- la **luna creciente** waxing moon
- la **luna de miel** honeymoon
- la **luna llena** full moon
- la **luna menguante** waning moon

el lunar *masc noun*
1 **mole** (*on your skin*)
2 **polka dot**
una camisa de lunares a polka-dot shirt

el lunes *masc noun*
Monday
el lunes on Monday
el lunes pasado last Monday
los lunes on Mondays
cada lunes every Monday
La tienda está cerrada los lunes. The shop is closed on Mondays.
Te llamaré el lunes por la tarde. I'll phone you on Monday evening.

WORD TIP Names of months and days start with small letters in Spanish.

la lupa *fem noun*
magnifying glass

el luto *masc noun*
mourning
ir de luto to be in mourning
ponerse de luto to go into mourning

Luxemburgo *masc noun*
Luxembourg

la luz *fem noun, pl:* **las luces**
1 **light**
dar la luz to switch on the light
apagar la luz to switch off the light
2 **electricity**
Se ha ido la luz. The electricity's gone off.
3 **dar a luz** to give birth
Dio a luz a un niño. She gave birth to a boy.
- la **luz del sol** sunlight

M m

los **macarrones** *plural masc noun*
macaroni

la **macedonia** *fem noun*
fruit salad

la **maceta** *fem noun*
flowerpot

machista *masc & fem adjective*
▷ see **machista** *noun*
sexist
un comportamiento machista sexist behaviour

el & la **machista** *masc & fem noun*
▷ see **machista** *adj*
male chauvinist
Mi jefe es un machista asqueroso. My boss is a disgusting male chauvinist.

macho *masc adjective*
male
un ratón macho a male mouse
una ballena macho a bull whale

la **madera** *fem noun*
1 **wood**
Son de madera. They're made of wood.
una silla de madera a wooden chair
2 **timber**
madera canadiense importada imported Canadian timber

la **madrastra** *fem noun*
stepmother
Se lleva muy bien con su madrastra. He gets on very well with his stepmother.

la **madre** *fem noun*
1 **mother**
Es huérfano de madre. He doesn't have a mother.
2 *(exclamation)* **¡Madre mía!** My goodness!
- la **madre soltera** single mother
- la **madre política** mother-in-law

Madrid *fem noun*
Madrid

madrileño *masc adjective*, **madrileña** *fem*
▷ see **madrileño** *noun*
of Madrid, from Madrid
las iglesias madrileñas the churches of Madrid
los inviernos madrileños the Madrid winters

un **madrileño** *masc noun*, una **madrileña** *fem noun* ▷ see **madrileño** *adj*
person from Madrid
Se casó con un madrileño. She married a man from Madrid.

WORD TIP Adjectives and nouns for nationality and regional origin do not have capital letters in Spanish.

la **madrina** *fem noun*
godmother

la **madrugada** *fem noun*
dawn
de madrugada at dawn
Nos levantamos de madrugada. We got up at dawn.
Llegamos de madrugada. We arrived in the early hours of the morning.
a las cuatro de la madrugada at four in the morning

madrugar *verb* **[28]**
to get up early

madurar *verb* **[17]**
1 **to ripen** *(fruit, etc)*
2 **to mature** *(people, ideas)*

maduro *masc adjective*, **madura** *fem*
1 **ripe** *(fruit, etc)*
2 **mature** *(person)*
Es muy poco maduro. He's quite immature.

el **maestro** *masc noun*, la **maestra** *fem noun*
1 **teacher** *(in primary school)*
2 **master** *(of a trade)*
un maestro carpintero a master carpenter
Su mamá es maestra panadera. Her mum's a master baker.

la **magdalena** *fem noun*
fairycake

la **magia** *fem noun*
magic
como por arte de magia as if by magic

mágico *masc adjective*, **mágica** *fem*
magical

magnético *masc adjective*, **magnética** *fem*
magnetic

Spanish-English

♪ el **magnetofón**, **magnetófono** *masc noun*
tape recorder

♪ **magnífico** *masc adjective*, **magnífica** *fem*
1 **wonderful**
2 **magnificent**

♪ el **mago** *masc noun*, la **maga** *fem*
1 **magician**
2 **wizard**

♪ la **mahonesa** *fem noun*
mayonnaise

el **mail** *masc noun*
email (*the message*)

♪ el **maíz** *masc noun*
1 **sweetcorn**
una mazorca de maíz a corn on the cob
2 **maize**
el maíz transgénico genetically modified maize

♪ **mal** *masc & fem adjective* ▷ see **mal** *adv, noun*
1 **bad**
Es un mal amigo. He's a bad friend.
Vinieron en mal momento. They came at a bad time.
No está mal. It's not bad.
2 **wrong**
Está mal criticar. It's wrong to criticize.
La respuesta está mal. The answer's wrong.
3 **ill**
¿Te sientes mal? Do you feel ill?
Su padre está muy mal. His father's very ill.

WORD TIP *mal* is used before a masc singular noun instead of *malo*. In other situations use *malo, mala.* ▷ **malo**

♪ **mal** *adverb* ▷ see **mal** *adj, noun*
1 **badly**
Está muy mal pintado. It's really badly painted.
Lo leyó muy mal. She read it very badly.
El país marcha mal. The country's not doing well.
Le va muy mal en el trabajo. He's doing very badly at work.
2 **wrong**
Lo hizo mal. He did it wrong.
Hace mal en no pedir perdón. He's wrong not to apologize.
3 **contestarle mal a alguien** to answer someone back
Le contestó mal a la profesora. He answered the teacher back.
4 **Te oigo mal.** I can't hear you very well.
5 **Olía muy mal.** There was a nasty smell.
La comida sabe mal. The food tastes horrible.
6 **portarse mal** to misbehave
entender mal algo to misunderstand something
Entendió mal lo que le dije. She misunderstood what I said to her.
7 **¡Menos mal!** Thank goodness!

♪ el **mal** *masc noun* ▷ see **mal** *adj, adv*
evil
el bien y el mal good and evil

los **malabarismos** *plural masc noun*
hacer malabarismos to juggle
Hace malabarismos con plátanos. She juggles bananas.

el & la **malabarista** *masc & fem noun*
juggler

la **malanga** *fem noun*
eddo

♪ **malcriado** *masc adjective*, **malcriada** *fem* ▷ see **malcriado** *noun*
1 **spoilt**
una niña malcriada a spoilt little girl
2 **naughty**

♪ el **malcriado** *masc noun*, la **malcriada** *fem* ▷ see **malcriado** *adj*
Es un malcriado. He's really spoilt.

♪ la **maldición** *fem noun*
1 **curse**
La bruja les echó una maldición. The witch put a curse on them.
2 **soltar una maldición** to swear
3 **¡Maldición!** Damn!

maleducado *masc adjective*, **maleducada** *fem* ▷ see **maleducado** *noun*
rude
¡Qué niños tan maleducados! What rude children!

♪ el **maleducado** *masc noun*, la **maleducada** *fem* ▷ see **maleducado** *adj*
Es una maleducada. She's really rude.

♪ el **malentendido** *masc noun*
misunderstanding
Desgraciadamente, hubo un malentendido. Unfortunately there was a misunderstanding.

♪ la **maleta** *fem noun*
suitcase
hacer la maleta to pack a suitcase

a b c d e f g h i j k l m n ñ o p q r s t u v w x y z

Ya he hecho la maleta. I've already packed my suitcase.

♪ el **maletero** *masc noun*
boot (*of a car*)
No cabe nada más en el maletero. There's no room for anything else in the boot.

♪ el **maletín** *masc noun*
1 **briefcase**
2 **overnight case**
3 **el maletín del médico** the doctor's bag

♪ el **malhumor** *masc noun*
bad temper
estar de malhumor to be in a bad mood

el **mall** *masc noun*
(*Latin America*) **shopping centre**

la **malla** *fem noun*
1 **mesh** (*of net*)
una bolsa de malla a string bag
2 **leotard** (*for gymnastics*)
3 **mallas** leggings
• la **malla de alambre** wire mesh

♪ **Mallorca** *fem noun*
Majorca

mallorquín *masc adjective & noun*, **mallorquina** *fem adjective & noun*
1 **Majorcan**
2 **un mallorquín, una mallorquina** Majorcan

WORD TIP Adjectives and nouns for nationality and regional origin do not have capital letters in Spanish.

♪ **malo** *masc adjective*, **mala** *fem*
1 **bad**
de mala calidad bad quality
una mala costumbre a bad habit
Es malo para la salud. It's bad for your health.
2 **naughty**, **nasty**
¡Qué niño más malo! What a naughty child!
No seas mala y devuélveselo. Don't be nasty, give it back to her.
3 **Ayer hizo malo.** The weather was bad yesterday.
Nos hizo muy malo durante las vacaciones. We had horrible weather during the holidays.
4 **estar malo** to be ill
El pobre está muy malo. The poor thing is in a really bad way.
No puede venir porque está mala. She can't come because she's ill.
5 **estar malo** to be off (*food*)
La leche está mala. The milk's gone off.
6 **estar malo** to taste horrible
La sopa estaba muy mala. The soup was horrible.
7 **ser malo para algo** to be bad at something (*a skill*)
Soy malo para las matemáticas. I'm bad at maths. ▷ **mal**

♪ la **mamá** *fem noun*
(*informal*) **mum**
Dile a tu mamá que la espero abajo. Tell your mum I'll wait for her downstairs.
La maestra quiere hablar con todas las mamás. The teacher wants to talk to all our mums.

♪ el **mamífero** *masc noun*
mammal
¿Los canguros son mamíferos? Are kangaroos mammals?

♪ la **manada** *fem noun*
1 **herd** (*of cattle*)
2 **pack** (*of dogs*)
3 **gang** (*of young people*)

♪ la **mancha** *fem noun*
1 **stain**
una mancha de chocolate a chocolate stain
quitar una mancha to remove a stain
2 **mark**
• la **mancha de petróleo** oil slick

♪ **manchar** *verb* **[17]**
1 **to get (something) dirty**
Me has manchado la camiseta. You've got my tee-shirt all dirty.
Mancharon la alfombra de barro. They got mud all over the carpet.
2 **to stain**
Manché el mantel de café. I got coffee stains on the tablecloth.

mancharse *reflexive verb* **[17]**
to get yourself dirty
Cuidado, no te manches. Careful, don't get yourself dirty.
Se manchó los pantalones de barro. He got mud all over his trousers.

manchego *masc adjective & noun*, **manchega** *fem adjective & noun*
1 **Manchegan**, **from La Mancha** (*a region in central Spain*)
2 **un manchego, una manchega** person from La Mancha

WORD TIP Adjectives and nouns for nationality and regional origin do not have capital letters in Spanish.

el **manchón** *masc noun*
stain

Spanish–English

mandar *verb* [17]
1 **to order**
2 **Le gusta mandar.** She likes to give the orders.
3 **mandar a alguien hacer algo** to tell somebody to do something
Me mandó recoger la habitación. She told me to tidy my bedroom.
Haz lo que te mandan. Do as you're told.
4 **to send**
mandarle una carta a alguien to send somebody a letter
Le mandó una postal a su novia. He sent his girfriend a postcard.
Los mandé a comprar fruta. I sent them to buy some fruit.
5 **mandar llamar a alguien** to send for someone
Mandó llamar al doctor. She sent for the doctor.

la **mandarina** *fem noun*
mandarin, **tangerine**

el **mando** *masc noun*
1 **command**
estar al mando de algo to be in charge of something
Estaba al mando del pelotón. She was in charge of the platoon.
2 **controls** (*of a machine, TV set*)
• el **mando a distancia** remote control

manejar *verb* [17]
1 **to use** (*a computer, dictionary*)
2 **to operate** (*a machine*)
3 **to manage** (*a business*)
4 (*Latin America*) **to drive** (*a vehicle*)
¿Sabes manejar? Can you drive?

la **manera** *fem noun*
1 **way**
Busca la manera más fácil de hacerlo. Find the easiest way to do it.
Lo hice a mi manera. I did it my way.
Es su manera de ser. It's the way he is.
No hubo manera de arreglarlo. There was no way of fixing it.
2 **de alguna manera** somehow
Me las arreglaré de alguna manera. I'll manage it somehow.
3 **de cualquier manera**
any old how
Puedes decorarlo de cualquier manera. You can decorate it any way you want.
4 **de una manera u otra** one way or another
5 **¡De ninguna manera!** No way!
'¿Me dejas el coche?'—'¡De ninguna manera!' 'Can I borrow your car?'—'No way!'
6 **de todas maneras** anyway
De todas maneras no pensaba comprarlo. I wasn't thinking of buying it anyway.
7 **de manera que** so
De manera que al final no la vi. So I didn't see her after all.

la **manga** *fem noun*
1 **sleeve**
una camisa de manga corta a short-sleeved shirt
sin mangas sleeveless
2 **hose** (*for watering*)

el **mango** *masc noun*
1 **handle** (*of a knife, tool*)
2 **mango** (*fruit*)

la **manguera** *fem noun*
hosepipe

la **manía** *fem noun*
1 **Tiene la manía del orden.** He's obsessed with tidiness.
Es maja pero tiene sus manías. She's nice but she has her funny little ways.
2 **tenerle manía a alguien** to have it in for somebody
Tu hermano me tiene manía. Your brother has it in for me.

maniático *masc adjective*, **maniática** *fem*
▷ see **maniático** *noun*
fussy
Es un poco maniática con la comida. She's a bit fussy about her food.

el **maniático** *masc noun*, la **maniática** *fem*
▷ see **maniático** *adj*
Es un maniático de la limpieza. He's obsessed with cleanliness.

la **manifestación** *fem noun*
1 **demonstration**
una manifestación en contra de la guerra a demonstration against the war
2 **sign** (*of emotion, disapproval*)
3 **manifestaciones** statements

manifestar *verb* [29]
1 **to express** (*disapproval, an opinion*)
Quiero manifestar mi agradecimiento. I would like to express my gratitude.
2 **to show** (*emotions*)

manifestarse *reflexive verb* [29]
1 **to demonstrate**
manifestarse en contra de algo to demonstrate against something

a b c d e f g h i j k l m n ñ o p q r s t u v w x y z

2 **manifestarse en contra de algo** to speak out against something
Se manifestó en contra del racismo. She spoke out against racism.
3 **to become evident**

el **manillar** *masc noun*
handlebars
Tengo el manillar flojo. My handlebars are loose.

♪ **manipular** *verb* [17]
1 **to operate** (*a machine*)
2 **to manipulate** (*data, information*)
3 **to handle** (*goods*)
Hay que tener las manos limpias para manipular alimentos. You have to have clean hands to handle food.

el **maniquí** *masc noun*
mannequin

la **manivela** *fem noun*
handle

♪ la **mano** *fem noun* ▷ see **mano** *masc*
1 **hand**
levantar la mano to put your hand up
ir de la mano to go hand in hand
Dame la mano. Hold my hand.
Lo tiene en la mano izquierda. He has it in his left hand.
coger a alguien de la mano to take somebody's hand
Cogió al niño de la mano. She took the child's hand.
Iban cogidos de la mano. They were walking hand in hand.
2 **darle la mano a alguien** to shake somebody's hand
Se dieron la mano. They shook hands.
3 **decir adiós con la mano** to wave goodbye
4 **coat** (*of paint*)
una mano de pintura a coat of paint
5 (*in expressions*) **hecho a mano** handmade
6 **a mano izquierda** on the left
a mano derecha on the right

el **mano** *masc noun*, la **mana** *fem*
▷ see **mano** *fem*
(*Latin America*) **buddy**, **mate**

el **manómetro** *masc noun*
pressure gauge

♪ la **mansión** *fem noun*
mansion
una mansión restaurada de la época victoriana a restored Victorian mansion

manso *masc adjective*, **mansa** *fem*
1 **tame** (*an animal*)
2 **gentle** (*a person*)

♪ la **manta** *fem noun*
blanket
una manta de lana a woollen blanket
• la **manta eléctrica** electric blanket

la **manteca** *fem noun*
lard

♪ el **mantecado** *masc noun*
almond delicacy (*eaten at Christmas*)

♪ el **mantel** *masc noun*
tablecloth

♪ **mantendrá**, **mantendría**, **etc** *verb* ▷ **mantener**

♪ **mantener** *verb* [9]
1 **to keep**
mantener la calma to keep calm
mantener el equilibrio to keep your balance
2 **to support** (*a family*)
Tiene que mantener a sus seis hermanos. He has to support his six brothers and sisters.

mantenerse *reflexive verb* [9]
to keep
mantenerse en equilibrio to keep your balance
mantenerse en contacto con alguien to keep in touch with somebody
Se mantuvo en contacto con sus compañeros de colegio. She kept in touch with her school friends.

♪ **mantengo**, **mantenga**, **etc** *verb* ▷ **mantener**

el **mantenimiento** *masc noun*
1 **maintenance**
2 **Hace ejercicios de mantenimiento.** She does keep-fit exercises.

♪ la **mantequilla** *fem noun*
butter
mantequilla sin sal unsalted butter
pan con mantequilla bread and butter

♪ la **mantilla** *fem noun*
mantilla (*traditional lace headscarf*)

♪ **mantuve**, **mantuvo**, **etc** *verb* ▷ **mantener**

manual *masc & fem adjective*
manual

la **manzana** *fem noun*
1 **apple**
zumo de manzana apple juice
2 **block** (*in a town*)
dar una vuelta a la manzana to go round the block

la **manzanilla** *fem noun*
1 **camomile tea**
Tomé una manzanilla para calmarme los nervios. I had a camomile tea to settle my nerves.
2 **dry sherry**

el **manzano** *masc noun*
apple tree
Los manzanos están en flor. The apple trees are in bloom.

mañana *adverb* ▷ see **mañana** *noun*
tomorrow
pasado mañana the day after tomorrow
¡Hasta mañana! See you tomorrow!
mañana por la tarde tomorrow afternoon

la **mañana** *fem noun* ▷ see **mañana** *adv*
morning
por la mañana in the morning
mañana por la mañana tomorrow morning
a la mañana siguiente the next morning
a las once de la mañana at eleven o'clock in the morning

el **mapa** *masc noun*
map
- el **mapa de carreteras** road map
- el **mapa de sitio** site map (*on website*)

el **maquillaje** *masc noun*
make-up

maquillar *verb* **[17]**
to make up
La vestí y maquillé para la foto. I dressed her and made her up for the photo.

maquillarse *reflexive verb* **[17]**
to put your make-up on
Apenas se maquilla. She hardly wears any make-up.

la **máquina** *fem noun*
machine
escribir a máquina to type
- la **máquina de afeitar** electric shaver
- la **máquina de coser** sewing machine
- la **máquina de escribir** typewriter
- la **máquina expendedora** vending machine
- la **máquina fotográfica** camera
- la **máquina tragamonedas** slot machine

la **maquinaria** *fem noun*
machinery

la **maquinilla** *fem noun*
safety razor
una maquinilla desechable a disposable razor

el **mar** *masc noun*
sea
viajar por mar to travel by sea
- el **mar Cantábrico** Bay of Biscay
- el **mar de Irlanda** Irish Sea
- el **mar del Norte** North Sea
- el **mar Mediterráneo** Mediterranean Sea

el & la **maratón** *masc & fem noun*
marathon
participar en el maratón de Nueva York to take part in the New York marathon

la **maravilla** *fem noun*
wonder
Es una maravilla de casa. It's a wonderful house
Baila de maravilla. He's a fantastic dancer.

maravilloso *masc adjective*, **maravillosa** *fem*
wonderful
Hace un tiempo maravilloso aquí. The weather's fantastic here.

la **marca** *fem noun*
1 **mark**
El cuadro ha dejado una marca en la pared. The picture has left a mark on the wall.
2 **brand**
artículos de marca brand products
ropa de marca designer clothes
3 **record** (*in sports*)
batir una marca to break a record
establecer una nueva marca to establish a new record
- la **marca registrada** registered trademark

el **marcador** *masc noun*
scoreboard
¿Cómo va el marcador? What's the score?

marcar *verb* **[31]**
1 **to mark**
La experiencia me marcó mucho. The experience really marked me.
2 **Mi reloj marca las nueve.** My watch says nine o'clock.
El termómetro marcaba cinco grados. The thermometer was registering five degrees.
3 **marcar un número** to dial a number
Marca 00 44 para Gran Bretaña. Dial 00 44 for Britain.

4 **marcar un gol** to score a goal
5 **marcar el ritmo, marcar el compás** to beat time

♪ la **marcha** *fem noun*
1 **hike**
ir de marcha to go hiking
Fuimos de marcha a la montaña. We went hiking in the mountains.
¡En marcha! Let's go!
2 **march** (*demonstration*)
3 **gear** (*in a car*)
cambiar de marcha to change gear
meter la marcha atrás to go into reverse
un coche de cinco marchas a car with five gears
4 **speed**
disminuir la marcha to reduce speed
5 **estar en marcha** to be running (*engines, machines*)
6 **poner en marcha** to start (*a car, machine*)
7 (*in expressions*) **ir de marcha** to go out partying
una discoteca con mucha marcha a really fun disco
¡Qué marcha tiene ese grupo! This group's really wild!

♪ **marchar** *verb* [17]
1 **to go, to work**
¿Cómo marcha el negocio? How's the business going?
Esto no marcha. This isn't working.
2 **to march**
3 (*in bars, cafes*) **¡Marchando dos cafés!** Two coffees coming up!

marcharse *reflexive verb* [17]
to leave
Nos marchamos mañana. We're leaving tomorrow.

♪ el **marco** *masc noun*
1 **frame** (*of picture, etc*)
el marco de la puerta the doorframe
2 **setting** (*for events*)
3 **goalposts**

♪ la **marea** *fem noun*
tide
Está subiendo la marea. The tide's coming in.
Cuando baje la marea. When the tide goes out.
- la **marea alta** high tide
- la **marea baja** low tide
- la **marea negra** oil slick

♪ **mareado** *masc adjective*, **mareada** *fem*
1 **sick**
Estoy mareado. I feel sick.
2 **dizzy**
Se siente mareada. She feels dizzy.
3 **estar mareado** to be muddled up
Estoy mareada con tantos números. I'm muddled up with all these numbers.

♪ **marear** *verb* [17]
1 **to make you feel sick**
El movimiento del bote la mareaba. The motion of the boat made her feel sick.
2 **to make you dizzy**
¿Te ha mareado el tiovivo? Has the roundabout made you dizzy?
3 **to confuse**
Me marearon a preguntas. They asked me so many questions my head was spinning.

marearse *reflexive verb* [17]
1 **to get dizzy**
2 **to feel faint**
3 **to get tipsy**

♪ el **mareo** *masc noun*
1 **sick feeling**
Me dan mareos si viajo en coche. I get carsick.
2 **seasickness**
tabletas para el mareo seasick tablets
3 **dizziness**

♪ el **marfil** *masc noun*
ivory
Está prohibida la importación de marfil. Importation of ivory is forbidden.

♪ la **margarina** *fem noun*
margarine
una margarina baja en grasas a low-fat margarine

♪ la **margarita** *fem noun*
1 **daisy**
2 **marguerite** (*larger flower*)

♪ el **margen** *masc noun*
margin
escribir algo en el margen to write something in the margin

♪ el **marido** *masc noun*
husband

♪ la **marina** *fem noun*
navy
la marina mercante the merchant navy

Spanish–English

el marinero *masc noun*
sailor
Mi abuelo fue marinero. My grandfather was a sailor.

la **marioneta** *fem noun*
puppet

la mariposa *fem noun*
1 **butterfly**
2 **nadar mariposa** to swim butterfly
¿Sabes nadar mariposa? Can you swim butterfly?
• la **mariposa nocturna** moth

la mariquita *fem noun*
ladybird

el marisco *masc noun*
shellfish, seafood
Pedimos marisco y cerveza. We ordered seafood and beer.

el mármol *masc noun*
marble
una escalera de mármol a marble staircase

marrón *masc & fem adjective*
▷ see **marrón** *noun*
brown
una falda marrón a brown skirt
unos zapatos marrones a pair of brown shoes
unos pantalones marrón claro a pair of light brown trousers

el marrón *masc noun* ▷ see **marrón** *adj*
brown
Prefiero el marrón al verde. I prefer brown to green.

el martes *masc noun*
Tuesday
el martes on Tuesday
el martes pasado last Tuesday
los martes on Tuesdays
cada martes every Tuesday
El bar está cerrado los martes. The bar is closed on Tuesdays.

WORD TIP Names of months and days start with small letters in Spanish.

el martillo *masc noun*
hammer
Esto se arregla pronto con un martillo y unos clavos. This can soon be fixed with a hammer and some nails.
• el **martillo neumático** pneumatic drill

marzo *masc noun*
March
en marzo in March
el 17 de marzo on 17 March

WORD TIP Names of months and days start with small letters in Spanish.

más *adjective, adverb, pronoun*
▷ see **más** *prep*
1 **more**
tres más three more
Pon más azúcar. Add more sugar.
¿Necesitas más? Do you need any more?
No comas más. Don't eat any more.
Éste me gusta más. I like this one more.
2 **Hay que hacerlo más rápido.** We must do it faster.
3 (*to say 'most'*) **el de más peso** the heaviest one
los más altos the tallest ones
los de más prestigio the most prestigious ones
el libro con más páginas the book with the most pages
El que más me gusta. The one I like the most.
4 (*in comparisons*) **más blanco que la nieve** whiter than snow
Es un poco más grande. It's a bit bigger.
Es mucho más grande. It's much bigger.
Ayer vino más gente que hoy. More people came yesterday than today.
Es más interesante que su primer libro. It's more interesting than his first book.
Me gusta más el de piel que el de tela. I like the leather one more than the cloth one.
5 (*in comparisons: with numbers*) **más de ...** more than ...
más de veinte kilos more than twenty kilos
Vinieron más de veinte personas. More than twenty people came.
6 **de más** to spare, to be left over
Hay tres pasteles de más. There are three cakes left over.
Tengo un billete de más. I have a spare ticket.
Hay tres sillas de más. There are three chairs too many.
7 (*in time expressions*) **No me quedo más.** I won't stay any longer.
No lo hagas más. Don't do it again.
No les he visto más. I've never seen them again.
8 **no ... más** only
No tardo más de diez minutos. I'll only take ten minutes.
No es más que un resfriado. It's only a cold.

a b c d e f g h i j k l m n ñ o p q r s t u v w x y z

9 (*in expressions*) **alguien más** anybody else
¿Esperas a alguien más? Are you expecting anybody else?
nadie más nobody else
No quiero nada más. I don't want anything else.
algo más anything else
¿Querías algo más? Did you want anything else?
más que nunca more than ever
más o menos more or less

10 (*in exclamations*) **¡Qué niña más bonita!** What a beautiful little girl!
¡Qué libros más pesados! What heavy books!

🗝 **más** *preposition* ▷ see **más** *adv, adj, pron*
plus
cinco más siete five plus seven

la **masa** *fem noun*
1 **dough**
Espera que suba la masa. Wait for the dough to rise.
2 **pastry**
• la **masa de hojaldre** puff pastry

el **masaje** *masc noun*
massage

la **máscara** *fem noun*
mask

la **mascarilla** *fem noun*
mask

🗝 **masculino** *masc adjective*, **masculina** *fem* ▷ see **masculino** *noun*
1 **men's** (*team, fashion*)
el equipo masculino the men's team
2 **masculine** (*style, manners, noun*)
3 **male**
el sexo masculino the male sex

el **masculino** *masc noun* ▷ see **masculino** *adj*
(*Grammar*) **masculine**

🗝 **masticar** *verb* [31]
to chew

el **mástil** *masc noun*
1 **mast**
2 **flagpole**

🗝 el **matador** *masc noun*
matador (*bullfighter who kills one of the six bulls at a* **corrida de toros**)

la **matanza** *fem noun*
1 **massacre** (*of people*)
2 **slaughter** (*of animals*)

🗝 **matar** *verb* [17]
to kill
¡Han matado al Presidente! The President's been killed!
Lo mató a cuchilladas. She stabbed him to death.
Estas botas me matan. These boots are killing me.

matarse *reflexive verb* [17]
1 **to kill yourself**
Si te vas me mato. If you leave I'll kill myself.
Su primo se mató de un tiro. His cousin shot himself.
2 **to get killed**
Si sigues conduciendo así, te vas a matar. If you carry on driving like that you're going to get killed.

mate *masc & fem adjective* ▷ see **mate** *noun*
matt

el **mate** *masc noun* ▷ see **mate** *adj*
jaque mate checkmate

🗝 las **matemáticas** *plural fem noun*
maths
Soy un negado para las matemáticas. I'm hopeless at maths.

🗝 la **materia** *fem noun*
1 **matter**
materia orgánica organic matter
materia grasa fat
2 **subject** (*of study, of a book*)
• la **materia prima** raw material

material *masc & fem adjective* ▷ see **material** *noun*
material

el **material** *masc noun* ▷ see **material** *adj*
material
materiales para la construcción building materials

maternal *masc & fem adjective*
maternal

🗝 **materno** *masc adjective*, **materna** *fem*
1 **motherly**
2 **Su lengua materna es el bengalí.** Bengali is her mother tongue.
3 **sus abuelos maternos** his maternal grandparents

el **matiz** *masc noun*
shade (*of a colour*)

la **matrícula** *fem noun*

1 **registration**
hacer la matrícula to register
¿Has hecho la matrícula de la clase de ténis? Have you registered for the tennis lessons?

2 **registration number** (*of a car*)
un coche con matrícula de Sevilla a car with a Seville number plate
Tiene un BMW con matrícula personalizada. She has a BMW with a personalized number plate.

- la **matrícula de honor** distinction (*for school work*)

el **matrimonio** *masc noun*

1 **marriage**

2 **married couple**
Son un matrimonio muy unido. They're a very close couple.

- el **matrimonio civil** civil wedding

máximo *masc adjective*, **máxima** *fem*

1 **maximum**
el precio máximo the maximum price

2 **top** (*speed*)

3 **highest**
el punto máximo the highest point

mayo *masc noun*

May
en mayo in May
el dos de mayo the second of May
Nos conocimos el cuatro de mayo. We met on the fourth of May.

WORD TIP Names of months and days start with small letters in Spanish.

la **mayonesa** *fem noun*

mayonnaise
No se puede preparar mayonesa sin aceite de oliva. You can't make mayonnaise without olive oil.

mayor *masc & fem adjective*
▷ see **mayor** *noun*

1 **greater**
una cantidad tres veces mayor a quantity three times greater
la mayor parte de los estudiantes most of the students

2 **greatest**
el mayor desastre the greatest disaster

3 **higher**
un número mayor que cien a number higher than one hundred

4 **highest**
el mayor número de casos the highest number of cases

5 **bigger**
¿Tienes una talla mayor? Do you have a bigger size?

6 **biggest**
el de mayor tamaño the biggest one

7 **older**
su hermano mayor his older brother
Es tres años mayor que su hermana. He's three years older than his sister.

8 **oldest**
mi hermana mayor my oldest sister
Soy el mayor de todos mis hermanos. I'm the oldest of all my brothers and sisters.

9 **adult**, **grown-up**
una persona mayor an adult
ser mayor de edad to be of age (*over 18*)
Cuando seas mayor ... When you're grown up ...

10 **elderly**
una señora mayor an elderly lady
Ya son muy mayores. They're quite old now.

el & la **mayor** *masc & fem noun*
▷ see **mayor** *adj*

1 **adult**

2 **los mayores** grown-ups, adults
Había más niños que mayores en la fiesta. There were more children than grown-ups at the party.
No hables así con tus mayores. Don't speak like that to your elders.

3 **los mayores** the elderly

la **mayoría** *fem noun*

majority
la mayoría de ... most of ...
Se ha vendido la mayoría de los artículos. Most of the items have been sold.

la **mayúscula** *fem noun*

capital letter
Se escribe con mayúscula. It's spelt with a capital letter.

mayúsculo *masc adjective*, **mayúscula** *fem* ▷ see **mayúscula** *noun*

1 **capital** (*letter*)
Cardiff se escribe con c mayúscula. Cardiff is spelled with a capital c.

2 (*informal*) **terrible** (*mistake, fright*)
Cometió un error mayúsculo. He committed a terrible mistake.

el **mazapán** *masc noun*

marzipan

♪ **me** *pronoun*

1 (*as direct object*) **me**
Me invitó a su fiesta. She invited me to her party.
No me han visto. They haven't seen me.

2 (*as indirect object*) **to me**
Me mintió. He lied to me.
Me lo dieron mis primas My cousins gave it to me.
Me lo ha comprado mi madre. My mother bought it for me.
¿Puedes enviármelos? Can you send them to me?
No me dijo nada. She didn't say anything to me.

3 (*in reflexive verbs*) **myself**
Me corté. I cut myself.
Me reí mucho. I laughed a lot.
Voy a bañarme. I'm going for a swim.
Me senté a la mesa. I sat at the table.

4 (*with parts of the body, clothes*) **Me quité el abrigo.** I took my coat off.
Me limpié los pies al entrar. I wiped my feet at the door.

5 (*to have something done*) **El sábado iré a cortarme el pelo.** I'll go and have my hair cut on Saturday.
¿Me abres esto? Will you open this for me?

mecánico *masc adjective*, **mecánica** *fem* ▷ see **mecánico** *noun*
mechanical

♪ el **mecánico** *masc noun*, la **mecánica** *fem* ▷ see **mecánico** *adj*
mechanic
Mi hermana es mecánica. My sister's a mechanic.

♪ la **mecanografía** *fem noun*
typing
Soy una negada para la mecanografía. I'm hopeless at typing.

la **mecedora** *fem noun*
rocking chair

♪ el **mechero** *masc noun*
lighter
un mechero desechable a disposable lighter

la **medalla** *fem noun*
medal
la medalla de oro the gold medal

la **media** *fem noun* ▷ see **media** *fem noun*
average
la media de altura the average height
una media de cien euros diarios an average of a hundred euro per day
la media europea the European average

♪ la **media** *fem noun* ▷ see **media** *noun*

1 **stocking**

2 **unas medias** tights

3 (*Latin America*) **sock**

4 (*telling the time*) **a las dos y media** at half past two
tres horas y media three and a half hours

5 (*in expressions*) **hacer algo a medias** to do things by halves
Siempre hace las cosas a medias He always leaves things half-done.
Lo dejó a medias. He didn't finish it.
pagar a medias to pay half each
Lo hicimos a medias. We did it between the two of us.

♪ **mediados** *plural masc noun*
a mediados de año halfway through the year
hacia mediados de abril around mid-April
Se fue a mediados de semana. He left midweek.

♪ **mediano** *masc adjective*, **mediana** *fem*

1 **medium**
Es de peso mediano. He's of medium weight.
¿Lo tienen en talla mediana? Do you have it in medium size?

2 **average**
un hombre de mediana inteligencia a man of average intelligence
una canción de mediana calidad a mediocre song

♪ la **medianoche** *fem noun*
midnight
a medianoche at midnight

♪ el **medicamento** *masc noun*
medicine
recetar un medicamento to prescribe a medicine

♪ la **medicina** *fem noun*
medicine
estudiar medicina to study medicine
tomarse la medicina to take your medicine

♪ **médico** *masc adjective*, **médica** *fem* ▷ see **médico** *noun*
medical
un reconocimiento médico a medical examination

el **médico** *masc noun*, la **médica** *fem*
▷ see **médico** *adj*
doctor
- el **médico de cabecera** family doctor

la **medida** *fem noun*
1 **tomar medidas a algo** to measure something
2 **measurement**
¿Qué medidas tiene la mesa? What are the measurements of the table?
3 **un traje a medida** a made-to-measure suit
4 **a medida que ...** as ...
A medida que pase el tiempo lo entenderás. As time goes by you'll understand.
5 **en gran medida** to a large extent
en cierta medida to a certain extent
en la medida de lo posible as far as possible

medieval *masc & fem adjective*
medieval

el **medio ambiente** *masc noun*
environment
el Ministerio de Medio Ambiente the Ministry of the Environment

medio *masc adjective*, **media** *fem*
▷ see **medio** *adv, noun*
1 **half**
medio kilo half a kilo
media docena half a dozen
2 **average**
de estatura media of average height
el ciudadano medio the average citizen
3 **half** (*in time expressions*)
- la **media hora** half an hour
- la **media pensión** half board (*in a hotel*)

medio *adverb* ▷ see **medio** *adj, noun*
half
Ya está medio convencido. He's half convinced now.
Estaba medio borracha. She was half drunk.

el **medio** *masc noun* ▷ see **medio** *adj, adv*
1 **middle**
Ponlo en el medio. Put it in the middle.
la casa de en medio the house in the middle
No pudimos conversar en medio de todo aquel jaleo. We couldn't talk amid all that racket.
2 **quitarse de en medio** to get out of the way
3 **way**
Es el mejor medio de hacerlo. It's the best way to do it.
No hubo medio de localizarlo. There was no way of finding him.
Lo intenté por todos los medios. I tried every possible way.
Trata por todos los medios de convencerlo. Try any way you can to persuade him.
4 **means**
por cualquier medio by any means
por medio de un interruptor by means of a switch
Lo conseguí por medio de un amigo. I obtained it through a friend.
- los **medios de comunicación** the media
- los **medios de transporte** means of transport

el **mediodía** *masc noun*
midday
al mediodía at midday

medir *verb* **[57]**
1 **to measure**
Midió la mesa. She measured the table.
2 **to be** (*in width, length, height*)
¿Cuánto mide de ancho? How wide is it?
Mide sesenta centímetros de largo. It's sixty centimetres long.
¿Cuánto mides? How tall are you?
Mido un metro sesenta. I'm one metre sixty.

mediterráneo *masc adjective*, **mediterránea** *fem*
▷ see **Mediterráneo** *noun*
Mediterranean
el clima mediterráneo the Mediterranean climate

WORD TIP Adjectives for regional origin do not have capital letters in Spanish.

el **Mediterráneo** *masc noun*
▷ see **mediterráneo** *adj*
el Mediterráneo the Mediterranean

mejicano *masc adjective & noun*, **mejicana** *fem adjective & noun* ▷ **mexicano, mexicana**

Méjico *masc noun* ▷ **México**

la **mejilla** *fem noun*
cheek
Me arden las mejillas. My cheeks are stinging.

el **mejillón** *masc noun*
mussel

mejor *masc & fem adjective* ▷ see **mejor** *adv, noun*
1 **better**
Éste es de mejor calidad. This one is better quality.
los mejores aguacates the best avocados

cuanto antes mejor the earlier the better
Tu bici es mejor que la mía. Your bike is better than mine.
Es mejor que no vayamos. It's better if we don't go.
2 **best**
el mejor alumno de la clase the best pupil in the class
Lo mejor sería esperar aquí. The best thing would be to wait here.

♪ **mejor** *adverb* ▷ see **mejor** *adj, noun*
1 **better**
Isabel toca la guitarra mejor. Isabel plays the guitar better.
mejor que better than
mejor que el otro better than the other one
Canta mejor que nadie. He sings better than anybody.
cada vez mejor better and better
2 **best**
Es la que mejor dibuja. She's the one that draws the best.
Hazlo lo mejor que puedas. Do your best.
3 a lo mejor maybe
A lo mejor es de Sara. Maybe it's Sara's.
A lo mejor no voy. I might not go.
4 Mejor no preguntes. It's better if you don't ask.
Mejor déjalo así. It's better if you leave it like this.
Mejor venid en tren. You'd be better coming by train.

♪ el & la **mejor** *masc & fem noun*
▷ see **mejor** *adj, noun*
el mejor, la mejor the best one
Escoge el mejor. Pick the best one.
Estas naranjas son las mejores que he visto. These oranges are the best I've seen.

la **mejora** *fem noun*
improvement

♪ **mejorar** *verb* [17]
1 **to improve**
Tiene que mejorar la letra. Hee must improve his handwriting.
2 **to get better**
Ha mejorado del estómago. He's got over his stomach problems.

mejorarse *reflexive verb* [17]
to get better
¡Que te mejores! Get well soon!
¿Se mejoró del resfriado? Is her cold better?

♪ **mellizo** *masc adjective*, **melliza** *fem*
▷ see **mellizo** *noun*
twin
hermanas mellizas twin sisters

♪ el **mellizo** *masc noun*, la **melliza** *fem*
▷ see **mellizo** *adj*
twin

♪ el **melocotón** *masc noun*
peach

la **melodía** *fem noun*
melody

♪ el **melón** *masc noun*
melon

♪ la **memoria** *fem noun*
1 **memory**
aprenderse algo de memoria to learn something by heart
Se ha aprendido el poema de memoria. He's learnt the poem by heart.
2 memorias memoirs

mencionar *verb* [17]
to mention

mendigar *verb* [17]
to beg

el **mendigo** *masc noun*, la **mendiga** *fem*
beggar

la **menestra** *fem noun*
menestra de verduras vegetable stew

♪ el **meñique** *masc noun*
little finger

♪ **menor** *masc & fem adjective*
▷ see **menor** *noun*
1 **younger**
mi hermana menor my younger sister
Soy menor que tú. I'm younger than you.
2 **youngest**
el menor de la familia the youngest of the family
3 **less**
Su importancia es cada vez menor. It gets less and less important all the time.
en menor grado to a lesser extent
4 **least**
con el menor esfuerzo posible with as little effort as possible
5 **minor**
de menor importancia of minor importance
6 **smaller**
un número menor de alumnos a smaller number of pupils ▸▸

Spanish–English
a b c d e f g h i j k l m n ñ o p q r s t u v w x y z

Spanish–English

7 **smallest**
hasta el menor detalle even the smallest detail
8 **No tengo la menor idea.** I haven't got the slightest idea.

♪ el & la **menor** *masc & fem noun* ▷ see **menor** *adj*
minor (*under 18*)
no apto para menores not suitable for under-18s

♪ **menos** *invariable adjective* ▷ see **menos** *adv, pron, prep*
1 **less**
de menos peso of less weight
2 **fewer**
Hay menos gente que ayer. There are fewer people than yesterday.

♪ **menos** *adverb* ▷ see **menos** *adj, pron, prep*
1 **less**
Ahora sale menos. He goes out less now.
Ahora los veo menos. I see less of them.
cada vez menos less and less
2 **least**
el menos alto the shortest one
las menos informadas the least well-informed
Es lo menos que esperaba. It's the least I expected.
Compro siempre los menos caros. I always buy the least expensive ones.
el que corre menos the slowest runner of all
3 (*in comparisons*) **menos que ...** less than ...
Habla menos que yo. He speaks less than I do.
Cuesta menos que el otro. It costs less than the other one.
4 (*in comparisons with numbers*) **menos de ...** less than ...
adultos de menos de treinta años adults aged under thirty
Cuesta menos de cien euros. It costs less than a hundred euros.
Vinieron menos de veinte. Fewer than twenty came.

♪ **menos** *pronoun* ▷ see **menos** *adj, adv, prep*
1 **less**
Ahora compramos menos. We buy less now.
2 (*in expressions*) **al menos**, **por lo menos** at least
de menos under
cobrar de menos cobrar de menos
Hay diez tarjetas de menos. There are ten cards too few.
¡Menos mal! Thank goodness!

♪ **menos** *preposition* ▷ see **menos** *adj, adv, pron*
1 **except**
todos menos su madre everybody except her mother
2 (*telling the time*) **a las dos menos veinte** at twenty minutes to two
Son las ocho menos diez. It's ten to eight.

♪ el **mensaje** *masc noun*
message
Te dejó un mensaje. She left you a message.
¿Hay algún mensaje para mí? Are there any messages for me.
• el **mensaje de texto** text message

♪ el **mensajero** *masc noun*, la **mensajera** *fem*
1 **messenger**
2 **courier**
un servicio de mensajeros a courier service

menso *masc adjective*, **mensa** *fem*
(*Latin America*) **stupid**

♪ **mensual** *masc & fem adjective*
monthly
un boletín mensual a monthly bulletin
dos cientos euros mensuales two hundred euros a month

♪ **mensualmente** *adverb*
monthly
Se cobrará mensualmente. It will be charged monthly.

♪ la **menta** *fem noun*
mint
un caramelo de menta a mint
¿Por qué no tomas un té de menta? Why don't you have a peppermint tea?

♪ **mental** *masc & fem adjective*
mental
Hizo un esfuerzo mental para recordarlo. He made a mental effort to remember it.

♪ la **mente** *fem noun*
mind
Perdón, tenía la mente en otra cosa. Sorry, my mind was on something else.
Se le quedó la mente en blanco. Her mind went blank.

♪ **mentir** *verb* **[14]**
to lie
Nos está mintiendo. He's lying to us.
No me mientas más. Stop lying to me.

la mentira *fem noun*
lie
decir mentiras to tell lies
¡Mentira! No fui yo. That's a lie! It wasn't me.

el mentiroso *masc noun*, **la mentirosa** *fem*
liar

el mentón *masc noun*
chin
Me di en el mentón contra la mesa. I bumped my chin on the table.

el menú *masc noun*
menu
el menú del día the set menu
- el **menú desplegable** (*Computing*) pull-down menu

menudo *masc adjective*, **menuda** *fem*
1 **small**
Es muy menuda. She's quite small.
2 **a menudo** often
Nos vemos a menudo. We see each other often.
3 **¡Menudo problema!** What a problem!
¡Menuda moto! What an incredible motorbike!

el mercado *masc noun*
market
ir al mercado to go to the market
- el **Mercado Común** the Common Market
- el **mercado negro** black market

las mercancías *plural fem noun*
goods
mercancías importadas imported goods
un tren de mercancías a goods train

la mercería *fem noun*
haberdashery (*selling sewing materials, buttons, etc*)

merecer *verb* [35]
1 **to deserve**
Mereces un castigo. You deserve to be punished.
2 **merecer la pena** to be worthwhile
La película merece la pena. The film is worth seeing.
No merece la pena volver. It's not worth going back.

merecerse *reflexive verb* [35]
to deserve
No me merezco que me traten así. I don't deserve to be treated like this.
Se lo tiene bien merecido. It serves him right.

merendar *verb* [29]
to have a teatime snack
Siempre merienda pan y chocolate. He always has bread and chocolate in the afternoon.
¿Quieres merendar algo? Do you want something to eat for tea?
¡A merendar! Teatime!

merezca, merezco, etc *verb* ▷ **merecer**

meridional *masc & fem adjective*
southern

la merienda *fem noun*
▷ see **merienda** *verb*
1 **afternoon snack**
2 **ir de merienda** to go for a picnic
- la **merienda campestre** picnic

merienda, meriendo, etc *verb*
▷ see **merienda** *noun* ▷ **merendar**

el mérito *masc noun*
merit

la merluza *fem noun*
hake

la mermelada *fem noun*
jam
mermelada de fresas strawberry jam
mermelada de naranjas marmalade

WORD TIP *mermelada* does not mean *marmalade* in English, but *jam* in general.

el mes *masc noun*
month
el mes que viene next month
mil euros al mes a thousand euros a month
hace dos meses two months ago
un bebé de siete meses a seven-month-old baby

la mesa *fem noun*
table
poner la mesa to set the table
quitar la mesa, recoger la mesa to clear the table
sentarse a la mesa to sit at the table
¡A la mesa! Food's ready!

el mesero *masc noun*, **la mesera** *fem* (*Latin America*)
1 **waiter**
2 **waitress**

la mesita *fem noun*
una mesita de noche a bedside table

el mesón *masc noun*
1 **restaurant** (*traditional kind*)
2 **inn**

♪ la **meta** *fem noun*
1 **aim**
Tiene como meta ser actriz. Her aim is to become an actress.
2 **finishing line** (*in race*)

♪ el **metal** *masc noun*
metal
metales pesados heavy metals

♪ **metálico** *masc adjective*, **metálica** *fem*
metallic

♪ **meteorológico** *masc adjective*, **meteorológica** *fem*
meteorological
un parte meteorológico a weather forecast

♪ **meter** *verb* **[18]**
1 **to put (something) in**
Metió la mano. He put his hand in.
Mételo en la carpeta. Put it in the folder.
2 **to fit**
¿Puedes meter algo más en la maleta? Can you fit anything else in the suitcase?
3 **meter un gol** to score a goal
4 **meter la primera** to put the car in first gear
meter la marcha atrás to put the car into reverse

meterse *reflexive verb* **[18]**
1 **meterse en** to get in(to)
meterse en la cama to get into bed
2 **meterse en algo** to get involved in something
Se metió en un asunto turbio. He got mixed up in some shady business.
No te metas en mis asuntos. Mind your own business.

el **método** *masc noun*
method

♪ **métrico** *masc adjective*, **métrica** *fem*
metric

♪ el **metro** *masc noun*
1 **underground railway**
el Metro de Londres the London Underground
2 **metre**
los cien metros libres the hundred metres freestyle

♪ **mexicano** *masc adjective & noun*, **mexicana** *fem adjective & noun*
1 **Mexican**
2 **un mexicano, una mexicana** Mexican

WORD TIP Adjectives and nouns for nationality and regional origin do not have capital letters in Spanish.

♪ **México** *masc noun*
Mexico

♪ la **mezcla** *fem noun*
1 **mixture**
Añadí una pizca de sal a la mezcla. I added a pinch of salt to the mixture.
2 **mix**
una mezcla de culturas a mix of cultures

♪ **mezclar** *verb* **[17]**
1 **to mix**
Hay que mezclarlo con agua. It has to be mixed with water.
2 **to mix up**
Has mezclado todos los papeles. You've mixed up all the papers.

mezclarse *reflexive verb* **[17]**
mezclarse en algo to get mixed up in something
Evitó mezclarse en el asunto. She avoided getting mixed up in the matter.

♪ la **mezquita** *fem noun*
mosque

♪ **mi** *masc & fem adjective*
my
mi madre my mother
mis amigos my friends

♪ **mí** *pronoun*
1 (*after prepositions*) **me**
detrás de mí behind me
Se olvidaron de mí. They forgot about me.
¿Es para mí? Is it for me?
Me lo dio a mí. He gave it to me.
2 **A mí me gusta.** I like it.
A mí me parece que ... I think that ...
3 **mí mismo, mí misma** myself
Voy a guardar el último para mí mismo. I'm going to keep the last one for myself.
Sé cuidar de mí misma. I can look after myself.
4 **por mí ...** as far as I'm concerned ...

♪ el **micrófono** *masc noun*
microphone

el **microondas** *masc noun*, *pl:* los **microondas**
microwave oven

♪ el **microscopio** *masc noun*
microscope
Lo miré en el microscopio. I looked at it under the microscope.

mida, **midiendo**, **midió**, **mido**, **etc** *verb*
▷ **medir**

a b c d e f g h i j k l m n ñ o p q r s t u v w x y z

el **miedo** *masc noun*
fear
¡Qué miedo! How frightening!
tener miedo to be scared
Tengo mucho miedo. I'm really scared.
¿Tienes miedo de intentarlo? Are you afraid of trying?
Le tengo miedo a la ocuridad. I'm afraid of the dark.
Le da miedo la altura. She's afraid of heights.
Les da miedo ir solos. They're afraid of going on their own.

miedoso *masc adjective*, **miedosa** *fem*
¡No seas miedoso! Don't be so scared!
Es muy miedoso. He's afraid of everything.

la **miel** *fem noun*
honey

el & la **miembro** *masc & fem noun*
▷ see **miembro** *masc noun*
member
Se hizo miembro del partido. She became a member of the party.

el **miembro** *masc noun*
▷ see **miembro** *masc & fem noun*
limb (*of the body*)

mienta, **miento**, **etc** *verb* ▷ **mentir**

mientras *adverb* ▷ see **mientras** *conj*
meanwhile
mientras tanto in the meantime
Mientras tanto él estaba esperando en la estación. In the meantime he was waiting at the station.

mientras *conjunction* ▷ see **mientras** *adv*
1 **while**
Pon la mesa mientras yo hago la comida. Lay the table while I cook the meal.
2 **as long as**
Mientras yo viva ... As long as I'm alive ...

el **miércoles** *masc noun*
Wednesday
el miércoles on Wednesday
el miércoles pasado last Wednesday
los miércoles on Wednesdays
cada miércoles every Wednesday
Abren los miércoles. They're open on Wednesdays.

WORD TIP Names of months and days start with small letters in Spanish.

la **miga** *fem noun*
crumb

mil *number*
thousand
mil cien one thousand one hundred
mil doscientos cincuenta one thousand two hundred and fifty
cinco mil euros five thousand euros
Acudieron miles de personas. Thousands of people attended.

el **milagro** *masc noun*
miracle

el **milenio** *masc noun*
millennium

milésimo *masc adjective*, **milésima** *fem*
thousandth

la **mili** *fem noun*
(*informal*) **military service**
Hizo la mili en Ceuta. He did his military service in Ceuta.

el **milímetro** *masc noun*
milimetre
Tiene diez milímetros de espesor. It's ten millimetres thick.

militar *masc & fem adjective*
▷ see **militar** *noun*
military

el & la **militar** *masc & fem noun*
▷ see **militar** *adj*
soldier
Su tía es militar. His aunt's a soldier.

millón *number*
million
un millón de euros a million euros
un millón dos cientos mil one million two hundred thousand
tres millones de habitantes three million inhabitants
un millón de gracias thank you ever so much

el **millonario** *masc noun*, la **millonaria** *fem*
millionaire

mimado *masc adjective*, **mimada** *fem*
spoilt (*child*)

la **mina** *fem noun*
mine
una mina de carbón a coalmine

mineral *masc & fem adjective*
▷ see **mineral** *noun*
mineral

el **mineral** *masc noun* ▷ see **mineral** *adj*
mineral

Spanish-English

minero *masc adjective*, **minera** *fem*
▷ see **minero** *noun*
mining
una zona minera a mining area

♪ el **minero** *masc noun*, la **minera** *fem*
▷ see **minero** *adj*
miner

♪ la **mini** *fem noun*
(*informal*) **mini**

♪ la **minifalda** *fem noun*
miniskirt

♪ **mínimo** *masc adjective*, **mínima** *fem*
▷ see **mínimo** *noun*
minimum
la cantidad mínima the minimum quantity
No me importa lo más mínimo. I couldn't care less.

♪ el **mínimo** *masc noun* ▷ see **mínimo** *adj*
minimum
un mínimo de cien euros a minimum of one hundred euros
cinco años como mínimo at least five years

♪ el **ministerio** *masc noun*
ministry
el Ministerio del Interior the Interior Ministry (*the Home Office in the UK*)

♪ el **ministro** *masc noun*, la **ministra** *fem*
minister
la Ministra de Salud Pública the Public Health Minister

♪ la **minoría** *fem noun*
minority

♪ **mintamos**, **mintió**, **etc** *verb* ▷ **mentir**

♪ la **minúscula** *fem noun*
▷ see **minúsculo** *adj*
small letter
¿Se escribe con mayúscula o minúscula? Is it spelt with a capital or a small letter?

minúsculo *masc adjective*, **minúscula** *fem*
▷ see **minúscula** *noun*
tiny

♪ **minusválido** *masc adjective*, **minusválida** *fem*
▷ see **minusválido** *noun*
disabled

♪ el **minusválido** *masc noun*, la **minusválida** *fem*
▷ see **minusválido** *adj*
disabled person
coches para minusválidos cars for the disabled

♪ el **minuto** *masc noun*
minute

♪ **mío** *masc adjective*, **mía** *fem* ▷ see **mío** *pron*
mine
una amiga mía a friend of mine
unos dibujos míos some of my drawings

♪ el **mío** *pronoun*, la **mía** *fem* ▷ see **mío** *adj*
mine
El mío es verde. Mine is green.
¿Dónde están las mías? Where are mine?

miope *masc & fem adjective*
shortsighted

♪ la **mirada** *fem noun*
look
una mirada alegre a happy look
bajar la mirada to look down
dirigirle una mirada a alguien to look at somebody
Me dirigió una mirada. She looked at me.
echarle una mirada a algo to have a look at something
Voy a echarle una mirada al periódico. I'm going to have a look at the newspaper.

♪ **mirar** *verb* **[17]**
1 **to look**
Miré afuera. I looked outside.
Mira en el cajón Look in the drawer.
2 **mirar algo** to look at something
Me miró. He looked at me.
¡No me mires así! Don't look at me like that!
Miró la foto con interés. He looked at the photo with interest.
3 **to watch**
mirar la tele to watch TV
4 **mirar fijamente** to stare at
Miraba fijamente la pantalla. He was staring at the screen.

mirarse *reflexive verb* **[17]**
mirarse en el espejo to look at yourself in the mirror
mirarse las manos to look at your hands

el **mirlo** *masc noun*
blackbird

♪ la **misa** *fem noun*
mass
ir a misa to go to mass

♪ **miserable** *masc & fem adjective*
1 **wretched** (*conditions*)
2 **mean** (*person*)

a b c d e f g h i j k l m n ñ o p q r s t u v w x y z

♪ la **miseria** *fem noun*
1 **misery**
2 **poverty**
Viven en la miseria. They live in poverty.
3 **pittance**
Gana una miseria. He earns a pittance.

♪ el **misil** *masc noun*
missile

♪ **mismo** *masc adjective*, **misma** *fem*
▷ see **mismo** *adv, pron*
1 **same**
al mismo tiempo at the same time
Iba en la misma dirección que yo. She was going in the same direction as me.
Llevan los mismos zapatos. They have the same shoes.
2 **very**
en este mismo lugar in this very spot
en ese mismo momento right at that moment
3 **yo mismo** I myself
Lo vi yo mismo. I saw it myself.
Lo dijo ella misma. She said it herself.
Eso mismo dije yo. That's just what I said.

♪ **mismo** *adverb* ▷ see **mismo** *adj, pron*
right
ahora mismo right now
Está ahí mismo. It's right there.
al lado mismo de casa right next to the house

♪ **mismo** *masc pronoun*, **misma** *fem pronoun*
▷ see **mismo** *adj, adv*
1 **el mismo** the same one
He usado la misma. I've used the same one.
Sara tiene los mismos que tú. Sara has the same ones as you.
2 **lo mismo** the same thing
Siempre dice lo mismo. He always says the same thing.
Tiene lo mismo que yo. She has the same as me.
dar lo mismo to not matter
Da lo mismo el color. The colour doesn't matter.

♪ el **misterio** *masc noun*
mystery

♪ **misterioso** *masc adjective*, **misteriosa** *fem*
mysterious

♪ la **mitad** *fem noun*
1 **half**
la mitad del pastel half the cake
a mitad de precio at half-price
2 **halfway**
llenar algo hasta la mitad to half-fill something
Llenó la botella hasta la mitad. She half-filled the bottle.
A mitad de camino paramos a comer. We stopped halfway to eat.
Lo he leído hasta la mitad. I'm halfway through reading it.
3 **cortar algo por la mitad** to cut something in two
Cortó la manzana por la mitad. He cut the apple in two.

♪ el **mito** *masc noun*
myth
mitos griegos Greek myths

♪ **mixto** *masc adjective*, **mixta** *fem*
mixed

el **mobiliario** *masc noun*
furniture
• el **mobiliario de cocina** kitchen fittings

♪ la **mochila** *fem noun*
1 **backpack**
2 **school bag**

♪ los **mocos** *plural masc noun*
tener mocos to have a runny nose
limpiarse los mocos to wipe your nose

♪ la **moda** *fem noun*
fashion
la moda juvenil young fashion
estar de moda to be in fashion
pasarse de moda to go out of fashion
Están muy de moda. They are very fashionable.
Siempre va a la última moda. He's always wearing the latest fashion.

♪ los **modales** *plural masc noun*
manners
tener buenos modales to have good manners

♪ el **modelo** *masc noun* ▷ see **modelo** *masc & fem noun*
model
el último modelo the latest model
utilizar algo como modelo to use something as a model

♪ el & la **modelo** *masc & fem noun*
▷ see **modelo** *masc noun*
model (*in fashion*)
Sale con una modelo brasileña. He's going out with a Brazilian model.

Spanish–English

moderno *masc adjective*, **moderna** *fem*
1 **modern**
2 **trendy**

modesto *masc adjective*, **modesta** *fem*
1 **modest** (*person, attitude*)
2 **humble** (*status, lifestyle*)

modificar *verb* [31]
to change

el **modisto** *masc noun*, la **modista** *fem*
1 **dressmaker**
2 **(fashion) designer**

el **modo** *masc noun*
1 **way**
Lo haré a mi modo. I'll do it my way.
A mi modo de ver ... To my way of thinking ...
No hubo modo. There was no way (of doing it).
Lo hizo de cualquier modo. He did it any old way.
¡De ningún modo! No way!
De cualquier modo, te llamaré antes. In any case, I'll phone you first.
2 **de modo que ...** so ...
3 **¿De modo que te vas?** So you're off, are you?
4 **de modo que ...** so that ...
Déjalo aquí de modo que la vea cuando vuelva. Leave it here so that he sees it when he comes back.
5 (*in expressions*) **de todos modos** anyway
De todos modos, no iba a comprarlo. Anyway I wasn't going to buy it.
en cierto modo somehow
• el **modo de empleo** instructions for use

mohoso *masc adjective*, **mohosa** *fem*
mouldy

mojado *masc adjective*, **mojada** *fem*
wet
calcetines mojados wet socks

mojar *verb* [17]
to wet
Me has mojado la camisa. You've wet my shirt.

mojarse *reflexive verb* [17]
to get wet
Me mojé volviendo a casa. I got wet coming home.
Se me mojó el pelo. My hair got wet.

moler *verb* [38]
to grind

molestar *verb* [17]
1 **to disturb**
'No molestar' 'Do not disturb'
No molestes a tu madre, que está trabajando. Don't disturb your mother, she's working.
2 **to bother**
¿Te molesta que ponga la tele? Do you mind if I put the TV on?
Perdone que le moleste. Sorry to bother you. (*polite form*)
3 **to annoy**
Me molesta que no me hayan invitado. I'm annoyed that they haven't invited me.

molestarse *reflexive verb* [17]
1 **to get upset**
Se molestó porque fuimos sin ella. She got upset because we went without her.
2 **molestarse en hacer algo** to bother to do something
No se molestó en preguntar. She didn't bother to find out.

la **molestia** *fem noun*
1 **trouble**
No es ninguna molestia. It's no trouble at all.
causar molestias a alguien to be a nuisance to someone
Los niños no me causaron ninguna molestia. The children were no nuisance at all.
2 **tomarse la molestia de hacer algo** to take the trouble to do something
Ni se tomó la molestia de avisarme. He didn't even bother to let me know.
3 **Perdone la molestia.** Sorry to bother you.
4 **Si no es molestia ...** If you don't mind ...
¿Me llevas, si no es molestia? Would you mind giving me a lift?

molesto *masc adjective*, **molesta** *fem*
1 **annoying**
un ruido molesto an annoying noise
2 **uncomfortable**
3 **estar molesto** to be upset
Sé que está molesta conmigo. I know she's upset with me.

el **momento** *masc noun*
moment
dentro de un momento in a moment
de momento at the moment
justo en ese momento right at that moment
¡Un momento! Just a moment!
en cualquier momento any moment
en este momento right now

ℰ la **monarquía** *fem noun*
monarchy

ℰ el **monasterio** *masc noun*
monastery

ℰ la **moneda** *fem noun*
1 **coin**
una moneda de dos euros a two euro coin
2 **currency**
Quería pagar en moneda suiza. He wanted to pay in Swiss currency.

ℰ el **monedero** *masc noun*
purse

ℰ la **monja** *fem noun*
nun

ℰ el **monje** *masc noun*
monk

ℰ **mono** *masc adjective*, **mona** *fem*
▷ see **mono** *noun*
1 **cute** (*baby, puppy*)
2 **pretty** (*person, garment*)

ℰ el **mono** *masc noun*, la **mona** *fem*
▷ see **mono** *adj*
monkey

ℰ el **monopatín** *masc noun*
skateboard

ℰ el **monstruo** *masc noun*
monster

ℰ la **montaña** *fem noun*
mountain
en la montaña in the mountains
• la **montaña rusa** roller coaster

el **montañismo** *masc noun*
mountain climbing

montañoso *masc adjective*, **montañosa** *fem*
mountainous

ℰ **montar** *verb* [17]
1 **to get in**
montar en el coche to get in the car
2 **to get on**
montar en el avión to get on the plane
3 **to ride**
montar a caballo to ride a horse
montar en la moto to get on the motorbike
montar en bicicleta to ride a bike
4 **to get on** (*a horse*)
Montó su caballo y se fue. He got on his horse and left.
5 **to put on** (*a play*)
6 **to set up** (*a business, exhibition*)
7 **to put up** (*a tent*)
8 **montar un escándalo** (*informal*) to cause a scene

montarse *reflexive verb* [17]
1 **to get on**
Se montó en el tren. He got on the train.
2 **to get in**
montarse en un coche to get into a car

ℰ el **monte** *masc noun*
1 **mountain**
2 **woodland**
• el **monte de piedad** pawnbroker's shop

ℰ el **montón** *masc noun*
1 **pile**
Puse todas las revistas en un montón. I put all the magazines in a pile.
2 **un montón de algo, montones de algo** loads of something
Había un montón de niños. There were loads of children.
Tiene montones de dinero. She has loads of money.
Me gusta un montón. (*informal*) I like it a lot.
3 **del montón** (*informal*) run-of-the mill
un cantante del montón an run-of-the mill singer

ℰ el **monumento** *masc noun*
monument
un monumento a los caídos a war memorial

ℰ la **moqueta** *fem noun*
fitted carpet

ℰ la **mora** *fem noun* ▷ see **moro** *adj*
blackberry
recoger moras to pick blackberries

ℰ **morado** *masc adjective*, **morada** *fem*
▷ see **morado** *noun*
purple

ℰ el **morado** *masc noun* ▷ see **morado** *adj*
purple

moral *masc & fem adjective*
▷ see **moral** *noun*
moral
el apoyo moral moral support

ℰ la **moral** *fem noun* ▷ see **moral** *adj*
1 **morals**
No tienen ninguna moral. They have no morals.
2 **morale**
estar bajo de moral to feel low

ℰ la **morcilla** *fem noun*
black pudding

morder *verb* [38]
to bite
No te preocupes, no muerde. Don't worry, he doesn't bite.

el **mordisco** *masc noun*
bite
darle un mordisco a algo to bite (on) something
Le dio un mordisco a la manzana. He took a bite out of the apple.

moreno *masc adjective*, **morena** *fem*
1 **dark** (*hair*)
2 **Es morena.** She's dark-haired.
3 **estar moreno** to be tanned
ponerse moreno to get tanned

morir *verb* [55]
to die
morir ahogado to drown
morir en un accidente to be killed in an accident

morirse *reflexive verb* [55]
1 **to die**
Se murió de un infarto. He died of a heart attack.
Me muero de hambre. I'm starving.
Me muero de ganas de verla. I'm dying to see her.
¡Me muero de frío! I'm freezing!
2 **morirse por hacer algo** to be dying to do something
Se muere por ir a la playa. He's dying to go to the beach.

moro *masc adjective*, **mora** *fem*
▷ see **moro** *noun*
Moorish

un **moro** *masc noun*, una **mora** *fem*
▷ see **moro** *adj*
1 **Moor** (*the Muslim occupiers of parts of Spain between 711 and 1492*)
2 **North African**

WORD TIP Adjectives and nouns for nationality and regional origin do not have capital letters in Spanish.

mortal *masc & fem adjective*
1 **fatal** (*illness, accident*)
2 **lethal** (*blow, dose*)

la **mosca** *fem noun*
fly

el **mosquito** *masc noun*
mosquito

la **mostaza** *fem noun*
mustard

el **mostrador** *masc noun*
1 **counter** (*in a shop*)
2 **bar** (*in a pub*)
3 **check-in desk** (*at an airport*)

mostrar *verb* [24]
to show
Muéstrame cómo se hace. Show me how to do it.

mostrarse *reflexive verb* [24]
mostrarse interesado en algo to show interest in something
mostrarse amable to be kind
mostrarse contento to be happy

el **motivo** *masc noun*
1 **cause**
el motivo del accidente the cause of the accident
2 **reason**
por motivos personales for personal reasons

la **moto** *fem noun*
motorbike
montar en moto to ride a motorbike
montar en la moto to get on the motorbike
• la **moto acuática** jetski

la **motocicleta** *fem noun*
motorbike

el & la **motociclista** *masc & fem noun*
motorcyclist

el **motor** *masc noun*
engine
• el **motor a reacción** jet engine

la **motora** *fem noun*
motorboat

el & la **motorista** *masc & fem noun*
motorcyclist

WORD TIP *motorista* does not mean *motorist* in English; for the meaning of *motorist* ▷ **automovilista**

mover *verb* [38]
to move
Ayúdame a mover estas cajas. Help me to move these boxes.

moverse *reflexive verb* [38]
to move
No me atreví a moverme. I didn't dare move.
No te muevas. Don't move.
Deja de moverte. Stop fidgeting.

el **móvil** *masc noun*
mobile phone
Llámame al móvil. Call me on my mobile.

♪ el **movimiento** *masc noun*
movement
ponerse en movimiento to start moving

♪ el **mozo** *masc noun*, la **moza** *fem*
1 **young boy**
2 **young girl**
• el **mozo de estación** porter

el **MP3** *masc noun*
MP3 player

♪ el **muchacho** *masc noun*, la **muchacha** *fem*
1 **boy**
2 **girl**

♪ la **muchedumbre** *fem noun*
crowd

♪ **mucho** *masc adjective*, **mucha** *fem*
▷ see **mucho** *adv, pron*
1 **a lot of**
mucha lluvia a lot of rain
mucho lodo a lot of mud
Sucedió hace mucho tiempo. It happened a long time ago.
2 **much**
No queda mucho tiempo. There's not much time left.
¿Queda mucha cerveza? Is there much beer left?
3 **many**
¿Había muchos niños? Were there many children?
muchas veces many times
4 (*in expressions*) **Hacía mucho frío.** It was very cold.
Tengo mucho sueño. I'm very sleepy.
5 **Tengo mucha prisa.** I'm in a real hurry.
6 **muchas gracias** thanks a lot
mucho gusto nice to meet you
Lo haré con mucho gusto. I'd be very pleased to do it.

♪ **mucho** *adverb* ▷ see **mucho** *adj, pron*
1 **a lot**
Lo usan mucho. They use it a lot.
Eso es mucho mejor. That's a lot better.
Salen mucho. They go out a lot.
trabajar mucho to work very hard
Voy a estudiar mucho. I'm going to study very hard.
2 **very**
Lo siento mucho. I'm very sorry.
'¿Te interesa?'—'Mucho.' 'Are you interested?'—'Very.'
3 **mucho más** much more
Es mucho más grande. It's much bigger.
4 (*in expressions*) **mucho antes** long before
mucho después long after
5 **como mucho** at the most
quince kilómetros como mucho fifteen kilometres at the most
6 **ni mucho menos** far from it

♪ **mucho** *masc pronoun*, **mucha** *fem*
▷ see **mucho** *adj, adv*
1 **a lot**
Tienes mucho que aprender. You have a lot to learn.
Traté de sacar el agua, pero aún quedaba mucha. I tried to get the water out, but there was still a lot left.
2 **much**
No tengo mucho. I haven't got much.
3 **many**
No quedan muchas. There aren't many left.
Muchos se sorprendieron. Many were surprised.
4 (*in time expressions*) **Tardan mucho.** They are taking a long time.
¿Hace mucho que ha llamado? Is it a long time since she called?
Hace mucho que no sé nada de ella. It's a long time since I last heard from her.
No falta mucho para mi cumpleaños. It's not long to my birthday now.

♪ la **mudanza** *fem noun*
removal
un camión de mudanzas a removal van
estar de mudanza to be in the process of moving

♪ **mudar** *verb* **[17]**
1 **to move** (*from one house to another*)
2 **mudar a un bebé** to change a baby

mudarse *reflexive verb* **[17]**
1 **to change your clothes**
2 **to move**
mudarse de casa to move house

mudo *masc adjective*, **muda** *fem*
dumb

♪ el **mueble** *masc noun*
piece of furniture
muebles de oficina office furniture
muebles de época antique furniture

♪ la **muela** *fem noun*
back tooth
tener dolor de muelas to have toothache
• la **muela del juicio** wisdom tooth

♪ **muera**, **muero**, **etc** *verb* ▷ **morir**

♪ **muerda**, **muerdo**, **etc** *verb* ▷ **morder**

♪ la **muerte** *fem noun*
death
una muerte repentina a sudden death
amenazas de muerte death threats
estar condenado a muerte to be sentenced to death

♪ **muerto** *masc adjective*, **muerta** *fem*
▷ see **muerto** *noun*
dead
Están muertos. They're dead.
muerto de sed dying of thirst
Estoy muerto de frío. I'm freezing to death.
Estamos muertos de hambre. We're starving.
Las niñas estaban muertas de cansancio. The girls were dead tired.

WORD TIP Always use *estar* for 'to be' with *muerto, ta.*

♪ el **muerto** *masc noun*, la **muerta** *fem*
▷ see **muerto** *adj*
dead person
Hubo un muerto en la explosión. One person died in the explosion.
No ha habido muertos. There were no casualties.

♪ **muestra**, **muestro**, **etc** *verb* ▷ **mostrar**

♪ **mueva**, **muevo**, **etc** *verb* ▷ **mover**

♪ la **mujer** *fem noun*
1 **woman**
mujeres diputadas women members of parliament
2 **wife**
mi mujer my wife

♪ la **muleta** *fem noun*
crutch

el **mulo** *masc noun*, la **mula** *fem*
mule

♪ la **multa** *fem noun*
fine
Me pusieron una multa. I was fined.

multicolor *masc & fem adjective*
multicoloured

♪ la **multiplicación** *fem noun*
multiplication

♪ **multiplicar** *verb* **[31]**
to multiply
Multiplica trece por siete. Multiply thirteen by seven.

♪ **mundial** *masc & fem adjective*
▷ see **mundial** *noun*
world
un récord mundial a world record
la economía mundial the world economy
de fama mundial world-famous

♪ el **mundial** *masc noun* ▷ see **mundial** *adj*
el mundial de fútbol the World Cup

♪ el **mundo** *masc noun*
1 **world**
2 **todo el mundo** everybody, everyone

las **municiones** *plural fem noun*
ammunition

♪ **municipal** *masc & fem adjective*
1 **municipal** (*library, elections*)
2 **local** (*taxes*)

♪ la **muñeca** *fem noun*
1 **doll**
jugar a las muñecas to play dolls
2 **wrist**
• la **muñeca de trapo** rag doll

♪ el **muñeco** *masc noun*
1 **dummy**
2 **doll**
• el **muñeco de peluche** soft toy

♪ la **muralla** *fem noun*
wall (*of a city, as defence, etc*)
la Gran Muralla de China the Great Wall of China

♪ el **murciélago** *masc noun*
bat

♪ **muriendo**, **murió**, **etc** *verb* ▷ **morir**

el **murmullo** *masc noun*
1 **whispering**
hablar en un murmullo to whisper
2 **murmur**

♪ **murmurar** *verb* **[17]**
1 **to whisper**
2 **to murmur**
3 **murmurar sobre alguien** to gossip about someone
Se murmura que ... The rumour is that ...

♪ el **muro** *masc noun*
wall

♪ el **músculo** *masc noun*
muscle

♪ el **museo** *masc noun*
1 **museum**
2 **gallery**
un museo de pintura an art gallery

- el **museo de arte moderno** modern art museum
- el **museo de cera** waxworks

ℰ la **música** *fem noun*
music
- la **música clásica** classical music
- la **música en directo**, **música en vivo** live music
- la **música pop** pop music

musical *masc & fem adjective*
musical

ℰ el & la **músico** *masc & fem noun*
1 **musician**
2 **composer**

ℰ el **muslo** *masc noun*
1 **thigh**
2 **leg** (*of chicken*)

musulmán *masc adjective & noun*, **musulmana** *fem adjective & noun*
1 **Muslim**
2 **un musulmán, una musulmana** Muslim

WORD TIP Adjectives and nouns for religion do not have capital letters in Spanish.

mutuo *masc adjective*, **mutua** *fem*
mutual

ℰ **muy** *adverb*
1 **very**
Es muy fácil. It's very easy.
Está muy bien. It's very good.
Muy bien, sigamos. Ok, let's go on.
2 **too**
Era muy pequeño para entenderlo. He was too small to understand it.
3 (*in letters*) **Muy señor mío:** Dear Sir,

N n

el **nabo** *masc noun*
turnip

el **nácar** *masc noun*
mother-of-pearl

nacer *verb* **[35]**
to be born
¿Dónde naciste? Where were you born?
Nací en Nottingham. I was born in Nottingham.

nacido *masc adjective*, **nacida** *fem*
born
nacido en Sevilla born in Seville
un niño recién nacido a new-born baby

el **nacimiento** *masc noun*
1 **birth**
Es madrileño de nacimiento. He was born in Madrid.
2 **crib** (*nativity scene*)

la **nación** *fem noun*
nation

nacional *masc & fem adjective*
national

la **nacionalidad** *fem noun*
nationality
¿De qué nacionalidad eres? What nationality are you?
Es de nacionalidad británica. He's British.

nada *adverb* ▷ see **nada** *pron*
at all
No me gusta nada. I don't like it at all.
No me ayudan nada. They don't help me at all.

nada *pronoun* ▷ see **nada** *adv*
1 **nothing, not ... anything**
No queda nada. There's nothing left.
No hay nada nuevo. There's nothing new.
No me dijeron nada. They didn't say anything to me.
Yo no sé nada de eso. I don't know anything about that.
Es mejor que nada. It's better than nothing.
2 (*in expressions*) **nada de: No tengo nada de dinero.** I have no money at all.
nada más nothing else
No quiero nada más. I don't want anything else.
Sólo quiero hablar con ella, nada más. I only want to speak to her, nothing else.
Nada más, gracias. That's all thank you.
nada más que only
No quiero nada más que un kilo. I only want one kilo.
De nada. You're welcome.
'Gracias.'—'De nada.' 'Thank you.'—'You're welcome.'
3 **love** (*in tennis*)
treinta nada thirty love

nadar *verb* **[17]**
to swim
nadar a braza to swim breaststroke

nadie *pronoun*
nobody, not ... anybody
Nadie llamó., No llamó nadie. Nobody phoned.
Nadie sabrá. No one will know.
No se lo dije a nadie. I didn't tell anybody.

el **nailon** *masc noun*
nylon

el **naipe** *masc noun*
card, playing card
juegos de naipes card games

la **nana** *fem noun*
lullaby

naranja *invariable adjective*
▷ see **naranja** *noun*, **naranjo** *noun*
orange
unos pantalones naranja a pair of orange trousers

WORD TIP *naranja* never changes.

la **naranja** *fem noun* ▷ see **naranja** *adj, noun*, **naranjo** *noun*
orange (*the fruit*)
un zumo de naranja an orange juice

el **naranja** *masc noun* ▷ see **naranja** *adj, noun*, **naranjo** *masc noun*
orange (*the colour*)

la **naranjada** *fem noun*
orangeade

el **naranjo** *masc noun* ▷ see **naranja** *adj, noun*
orange tree

el & la **narcotraficante** *masc & fem noun*
drugs trafficker

el **narcotráfico** *masc noun*
drugs trade

la **nariz** *fem noun*
nose
sonarse la nariz to blow your nose
Me sale sangre de la nariz. I've got a nosebleed.

la **nata** *fem noun*
cream
- la **nata líquida** single cream
- la **nata montada** whipped cream
- la **nata para montar** double cream

la **natación** *fem noun*
swimming

las **natillas** *plural fem noun*
cold custard (*eaten as a pudding*)

natural *masc & fem adjective*
natural (*state, ingredients, ability, etc*)
historia natural natural history
Es natural que lo hagan. It's natural that they should do it.

WORD TIP *ser natural que* is followed by a verb in the subjunctive.

la **naturaleza** *fem noun*
nature
respetar la naturaleza to respect nature
- la **naturaleza humana** human nature
- la **naturaleza muerta** still life

naturalmente *adverb*
naturally

las **náuseas** *plural fem noun*
nausea
tener náuseas to feel sick
El olor me daba náuseas. The smell made me feel sick.

nauseabundo *masc adjective*, **nauseabunda** *fem*
nauseating

la **navaja** *fem noun*
penknife
- la **navaja de afeitar** cut-throat razor

la **nave** *fem noun*
ship
- la **nave espacial** spaceship
- la **nave industrial** industrial premises

navegar *verb* [28]
1 **to navigate**
2 **to sail**
3 (*Computers*) **navegar en Internet** to surf the Internet
navegar por la red to surf the Net

la **Navidad** *fem noun*
1 **Christmas**
el día de Navidad Christmas Day
feliz Navidad Merry Christmas
2 **Navidades** the Christmas season
Pasaré las Navidades con mi familia. I'll spend Christmas with my family.

nazca, **nazco**, **etc** *verb* ▷ **nacer**

la **neblina** *fem noun*
mist
Hay neblina. It's misty.

necesario *masc adjective*, **necesaria** *fem*
necessary
No es necesario hacer todos los ejercicios. It's not necessary to do all the exercises.
No es necesario que lo hagas. There's no need for you to do it.

WORD TIP *ser necesario que* is followed by a verb in the subjunctive.

la **necesidad** *fem noun*
need
No hay necesidad de llamarlos. There's no need to call them.
En caso de necesidad me lo prestará. She'll lend it to me if necessary.

necesitar *verb* [17]
to need
No necesitas llevar el pasaporte. You don't need to take your passport.
'Se necesita camarero con experiencia' 'Experienced waiter required' (*on sign*)

la **nectarina** *fem noun*
nectarine

neerlandés *masc adjective & noun*, **neerlandesa** *fem adjective & noun*
1 **Dutch**
2 **un neerlandés, una neerlandesa** Dutchman, Dutchwoman
3 **el neerlandés** Dutch (*the language*)

WORD TIP Adjectives and nouns for nationality, regional origin, and language do not have capital letters in Spanish.

nefasto *masc adjective*, **nefasta** *fem*
1 **disastrous** (*consequences*)
2 **awful** (*weather, taste in clothes*)

negar *verb* [30]
1 **to deny**
Lo niega todo. He denies everything.
2 **to refuse**
Nos negaron su ayuda. They refused to help us.

Spanish–English

negarse *reflexive verb* **[30]**
to refuse
negarse a hacer algo to refuse to do something
Se niega a ayudarme. He refuses to help me.

negativo *masc adjective*, **negativa** *fem*
negative

la **negociación** *fem noun*
negotiation

negociar *verb* **[17]**
to negotiate

el **negocio** *masc noun*
1 **business** (*firm*)
montar un negocio to set up a business
un viaje de negocios a business trip
2 **los negocios** business (*commercial dealings*)
Se dedica a los negocios. She's in business.
3 **deal**
hacer un buen negocio to make a good deal

negro *masc adjective*, **negra** *fem*
▷ see **negro** *noun*
black
Llevaba un traje negro. He was wearing a black suit.

el **negro** *masc noun* ▷ see **negro** *adj*
1 (*Colour*) **black**
2 **un negro** a black man
una negra a black woman

neozelandés *masc adjective*, **neozelandesa** *fem*
▷ see **neozelandés** *noun*
1 **(of) New Zealand**
el gobierno neocelandés the New Zealand government
2 **from New Zealand**
Es neocelandesa. She is from New Zealand.

un **neozelandés** *masc noun*, una **neozelandesa** *fem*
▷ see **neozelandés** *adj*
New Zealander

WORD TIP Adjectives and nouns for nationality and regional origin do not have capital letters in Spanish.

el **nervio** *masc noun*
nerve
Tengo muchos nervios. I'm very nervous.

nervioso *masc adjective*, **nerviosa** *fem*
nervous
ponerse nervioso to get nervous

el **neumático** *masc noun*
tyre

la **neumonía** *fem noun*
pneumonia

neutro *masc adjective*, **neutra** *fem*
1 **neutral**
2 **neuter** (*in grammar*)

la **nevada** *fem noun*
snowfall

nevar *verb* **[29]**
to snow
Está nevando. It's snowing.

la **nevasca** *fem noun*
snow storm

la **nevera** *fem noun*
fridge

ni *conjunction*
1 **ni ... ni ...** neither ... nor ...
ni uno ni otro neither one nor the other
No es ni grande ni pequeño. It's neither big nor small.
2 **no ... ni ...** neither ... nor ...
No vino él ni su hermana. Neither he nor his sister came.
No es mío ni suyo. It's not mine and it's not hers either.
una casa sin luz ni agua corriente a house with neither electricity nor running water
'Yo no pienso ir.'—'Ni yo tampoco.' 'I don't intend going.'—'Neither do I.'
3 **not one**, **not a single one**
Ni uno de ellos llamó. Not one of them called.
No vendieron ni un libro. They didn't sell a single book.
4 **¡Ni hablar!** No way!
'¿Puedes hacerlo ahora?'—'¡Ni hablar!' 'Can you do it now?'—'No way!'

Nicaragua *fem noun*
Nicaragua

nicaragüense *masc & fem adjective & noun*
1 **Nicaraguan**
2 **un & una nicaragüense** Nicaraguan

WORD TIP Adjectives and nouns for nationality and regional origin do not have capital letters in Spanish.

el **nido** *masc noun*
nest

a b c d e f g h i j k l m n ñ o p q r s t u v w x y z

la niebla *fem noun*
fog
Hay mucha niebla. It's very foggy.

el nieto *masc noun*, **la nieta** *fem*
1 **grandson**
2 **granddaughter**
3 **mis nietos** my grandchildren

nieva, nieve, etc *verb* ▷ **nevar**

la nieve *fem noun*
1 **snow**

ningún *adjective* ▷ **ninguno**

ninguno *masc adjective*, **ninguna** *fem*
▷ **see ninguno** *pron*
not ... any, no
No trajeron ninguna caja. They didn't bring any boxes.
No he comprado ningún libro. I didn't buy any books.
No hay ninguna necesidad. There's no need.

WORD TIP *ninguno* becomes *ningún* before a masc singular noun.

ninguno *pronoun* ▷ **see ninguno** *adj*
1 **neither, not ... either**
Ninguno de los dos vale. Neither of them is suitable.
Ninguno de los dos me gusta. I don't like either of them.
2 **none, not ... any**
ninguno de los que estaban allí none of those who were there.
No compró ninguno. He didn't buy any of them.
3 **nobody**
Ninguno lo vio. Nobody saw him.
Toca mejor que ninguno. He plays better than anybody.

la niña *fem noun*
1 **girl**
2 **child**
La conozco desde niña. I've known her since I was a child.

la niñera *fem noun*
nanny

la niñez *fem noun*
childhood

el niño *masc noun*
1 **boy**
2 **child**
De niño era muy tímido. He was very shy as a child.
Van a tener un niño. They're going to have a baby.
3 **niños** children
ropa de niños children's clothes

mini-info niños refugiados
En abril de 1937, tras el bombardeo de Guernica, unos 4000 niños vascos llegaron a Inglaterra refugiados de la Guerra Civil en España.

el nitrógeno *masc noun*
nitrogen

el nivel *masc noun*
1 **level**
el nivel del agua the level of the water
2 **standard**
- **el nivel de vida** standard of living

no *adverb*
1 (*in replies*) **no**
'¿Es tuyo?'—'No.' 'Is it yours?'—'No.'
No, no quiero. No, I don't want to.
'¿Es nuevo?'—'Creo que no.' 'Is it new?'—'I don't think so.'
Ellos lo saben, pero yo no. They know, but I don't.
2 **not**
no mucho not much
ahí no not there
No es mi amigo. He's not my friend.
No sabe nadar. He can't swim.
No se sabe. It's not known.
3 (*with other negatives*) **No comió nada.** He didn't eat anything.
No vi a nadie. I didn't see anybody.
No voy nunca al cine. I never go to the cinema.
No se parecen en nada. They are not similar at all.
4 (*asking for confirmation*) **Somos siete ¿no?** There are seven of us, aren't there?
Tú hablaste con ella, ¿no? You spoke to her, didn't you?
5 (*before a noun*) **non-**
la no violencia non-violence
los no fumadores non smokers

la noche *fem noun*
1 **night**
a las once de la noche at eleven o'clock at night
esta noche tonight
por la noche at night
el lunes por la noche Monday night
la noche anterior the night before
de noche at night
buenas noches goodnight
hacerse de noche to get dark
2 **evening**
a las ocho de la noche at eight o'clock ▸▸

Spanish–English

in the evening
esta noche this evening
por la noche in the evening
el lunes por la noche Monday evening
la noche anterior the previous evening
de noche in the evening
buenas noches good evening

la **Nochebuena** *fem noun*
Christmas Eve

la **Nochevieja** *fem noun*
New Year's Eve

nocturno *masc adjective*, **nocturna** *fem*
1 **nocturnal**
2 **evening**
clases nocturnas evening classes

nomás *adverb*
(*Latin America*) **Démelo así nomás.** Just give it to me like that.

nombrar *verb* [17]
1 **to mention**
2 **to appoint**

el **nombre** *masc noun*
1 **name**
¿Qué nombre tiene el grupo? What's the name of the group?
¿Qué nombre le van a poner al niño? What are they going to call the baby?
2 (*on forms*) **'Nombre'** 'First name'
'Nombre y apellidos' 'Full name'
3 **noun**
• el **nombre de pila** first name

no obstante *in phrase*
no obstante nevertheless
No obstante nos fuimos y disfrutamos mucho. Nevertheless we went and had a good time.

el **nordeste**, el **noreste** *masc noun*
northeast

la **norma** *fem noun*
rule

normal *masc & fem adjective*
normal
Eso es normal. That's normal.
un jugador normal y corriente a run-of-the-mil player

normalmente *adverb*
normally
Normalmente no salgo de noche. I don't normally go out at night.

el **noroeste** *masc noun*
northwest

norte *masc noun, invariable adjective*
north
ir hacia el norte to go north
la costa norte de España the north coast of Spain
al norte del Sevilla to the north of Seville
en el norte de Francia in the north of France

Norteamérica *fem noun*
North America

norteamericano *masc adjective & noun*, **norteamericana** *fem adjective & noun*
1 **North American**
2 **un norteamericano, una norteamericana** North American

WORD TIP Adjectives and nouns for nationality and regional origin do not have capital letters in Spanish.

Noruega *fem noun*
Norway

noruego *masc adjective & noun*, **noruega** *fem adjective & noun*
1 **Norwegian**
2 **un noruego, una noruega** Norwegian
3 **el noruego** Norwegian (*the language*)

WORD TIP Adjectives and nouns of nationality, regional origin, and language do not have capital letters in Spanish.

nos *pronoun*
1 (*as direct object*) **us**
Nos invitaron a la fiesta. They invited us to the party.
Viene a vernos mañana. He is coming to see us tomorrow.
2 (*as indirect object*) **to us, us**
Nos mintió. He lied to us.
Danos las llaves. Give us the keys.
3 (*with reflexive verbs*) **ourselves**
Nos divertimos. We enjoyed ourselves.
Nos reímos mucho. We laughed a lot.
Vamos a bañarnos. Let's go for a swim.
Nos sentamos a la mesa. We sat down at the table.
(*with parts of the body, clothes*) **Nos quitamos los abrigos.** We took our coats off.
4 (*showing interaction*) **each other**
Siempre nos ayudamos. We always help each other.

nosotros *plural masc pronoun*, **nosotras** *plural fem pronoun*
1 (*as subject*) **we**
Lo hicimos nosotras. We did it.
nosostros mismos we ourselves
2 (*after prepositions*) **us**
Estaban hablando con nosotros. They were talking to us.

Iban detrás de nosotros. They were behind us.
Es de nosotros. It's ours.

WORD TIP *nosotros* is used to refer to two or more males, or males and females.

la **nota** *fem noun*
1 **note**
tomar nota de algo to write something down
Toma nota de eso. Write that down.
tomar notas to take notes
2 **mark** (*in school*)
¿Qué nota has sacado en física? What did you get in physics?
sacar buenas notas to get good marks
- la **nota musical** note

notable *masc & fem adjective*
▷ see **notable** *noun*
distinct
una notable mejora a distinct improvement

el **notable** *masc noun* ▷ see **notable** *adj*
pass mark (*between 70% and 85%*)

notar *verb* [17]
to notice
Notó que la puerta estaba abierta. She noticed that the door was open.
Te noto preocupado. You look worried.
Se nota que ... You can tell that ...

el **notario** *masc noun*, la **notaria** *fem*
notary public (*a kind of lawyer*)

la **noticia** *fem noun*
1 (*noticia: singular*) **una noticia interesante** an interesting piece of news
La noticia me sorprendió. The news surprised me.
Nos dio la buena noticia. He gave us the good news.
2 (*noticias: plural*) **news**
las noticias de las nueve the nine o'clock news
Tengo buenas noticias. I've got good news.

novecientos *masc number*, **novecientas** *fem number*
nine hundred
novecientos veinte nine hundred and twenty

la **novela** *fem noun*
novel

noveno *masc adjective*, **novena** *fem*
ninth
el noveno piso the ninth floor

noventa *number*
ninety
noventa y siete ninety-seven
los años noventa the nineties
Tiene noventa años. She's ninety (years old).

la **novia** *fem noun*
1 **bride**
2 **fiancée**
3 **girlfriend**

noviembre *masc noun*
November
en noviembre in November
el 11 de noviembre on 11 November

WORD TIP Names of months and days start with small letters in Spanish.

la **novillada** *fem noun*
bullfight for young bulls

los **novillos** *plural masc noun*
hacer novillos to play truant

el **novio** *masc noun*
1 **groom** (*at a wedding*)
los novios the bride and groom
2 **fiancé**
3 **boyfriend**
Llevan tres meses de novios. They've been going out for three months.

la **nube** *fem noun*
cloud
un cielo cubierto de nubes a cloudy sky

nublado *masc adjective*, **nublada** *fem*
cloudy
Estaba nublado. It was cloudy.

nublarse *reflexive verb* [17]
to cloud over
Se nubló por la tarde. It clouded over in the afternoon.

la **nubosidad** *fem noun*
cloud cover

nuclear *masc & fem adjective*
▷ see **nuclear** *noun*
nuclear

la **nuclear** *fem noun* ▷ see **nuclear** *adj*
nuclear power station

el **nudillo** *masc noun*
knuckle

el **nudo** *masc noun*
knot
hacer un nudo to tie a knot

Spanish–English

la **nuera** *fem noun*
daughter-in-law

♪ **nuestro** *masc adjective*, **nuestra** *fem*
▷ see **nuestro** *pron*
our
nuestra casa our house
nuestros padres our parents
un familiar nuestro a relative of ours

♪ el **nuestro** *masc pronoun*, la **nuestra** *fem*
ours
La nuestra es verde. Ours is green.
Los nuestros están en el salón. Ours are in the living room.
Aquel es el nuestro. That one is ours.

♪ **nueve** *number*
1 **nine**
Jaime tiene nueve años. Jaime's nine (years old).
2 (*saying the date*) **ninth**
el nueve de marzo the ninth of March
3 (*when telling the time*) **nine**
a las nueve y diez at ten past nine
Son las nueve. It's nine o'clock.

♪ **nuevo** *masc adjective*, **nueva** *fem*
1 **new**
mis zapatos nuevos my new shoes
No dijo nada nuevo. She didn't say anything new.
¿Qué hay de nuevo? What's new?
Ha surgido un nuevo problema. A new problem has cropped up.
2 **de nuevo** again
Tenemos que empezar de nuevo. We have to start again.

♪ la **nuez** *fem noun*
1 **walnut**
2 **Adam's apple**
- la **nuez moscada** nutmeg

♪ el **número** *masc noun*
1 **number**
Dame tu número. Give me your telephone number.
2 **issue** (*of a magazine, newspaper*)
3 **size** (*for shoes, clothes*)
¿Qué número de zapatos calzas? What size shoes do you take?
- el **número de teléfono** telephone number
- el **número primo** prime number
- el **número romano** Roman numeral

♪ **nunca** *adverb*
never
nunca más never again
casi nunca hardly ever
más que nunca more than ever
Nunca he estado en Valencia. I've never been to Valencia.

nutritivo *masc adjective*, **nutritiva** *fem*
nourishing

a b c d e f g h i j k l m n ñ o p q r s t u v w x y z

Ñ ñ

ñoño *masc adjective*, **ñoña** *fem*
pathetic (*feeble*)
No seas ñoño. Don't be so pathetic.

Spanish-English

O o

o *conjunction*

1 **or**
antes o después sooner or later
plata u oro silver or gold
11 ó 12 11 or 12

2 **o ... o ...** either ... or ...
O me acompañas o te quedas aquí. Either you come with me or you stay here.

3 **o sea** so
¿O sea que no te importa? So you don't mind?

4 **o sea ...** in other words ...
las niñas, o sea Juana y Maite the girls, in other words Juana and Maite

WORD TIP *o* is the usual word for English *or*, but it becomes *u* before another word starting with *o*. When *o* is between numbers, it becomes *ó*.

el **oasis** *masc noun, pl:* los **oasis**
oasis

obedecer *verb* [35]
to obey
Se niega a obedecerme. He refuses to obey me.

obedezca, **obedezco**, **etc** *verb* ▷ **obedecer**

la **obediencia** *fem noun*
obedience

obediente *masc & fem adjective*
obedient

el **obispo** *masc noun*
bishop

objetivo *masc adjective*, **objetiva** *fem* ▷ see **objetivo** *noun*
objective

el **objetivo** *masc noun* ▷ see **objetivo** *adj*
objective

el **objeto** *masc noun*
object
- los **objetos de valor** valuables
- **objetos perdidos** lost property office (*no article*)

obligar *verb* [28]
obligar a alguien a hacer algo to make somebody do something
Lo obligaron a salir. They made him leave.
Nos obligó a hacerlo de nuevo. She made us do it again.

obligarse *reflexive verb* [28]
obligarse a hacer algo to make yourself do something
Se obliga a hacer ejercicio todos los días. He makes himself take exercise every day.

obligatorio *masc adjective*, **obligatoria** *fem*
compulsory

la **obra** *fem noun*

1 **deed**
una buena obra a good deed

2 **play**
una obra de Shakespeare a Shakespeare play

3 **obras** building work
estar en obras to be having some building work done
Estamos en obras. We're having some building work done.
'Obras' 'Roadworks'
- la **obra de arte** work of art
- la **obra maestra** masterpiece

el **obrero** *masc noun*, la **obrera** *fem*
worker

obsceno *masc adjective*, **obscena** *fem*
obscene

la **obscuridad** *fem noun* ▷ **oscuridad**

obscuro *masc adjective*, **obscura** *fem* ▷ **oscuro**

la **observación** *fem noun*

1 **observation**
La tienen en observación. She's under observation.

2 **remark**
Hizo varias observaciones al respecto. She made several remarks about it.

observador *adjective masc*, **observadora** *fem* ▷ see **observador** *noun*
observant

el **observador** *masc noun*, la **observadora** *fem* ▷ see **observador** *adj*
observer

a b c d e f g h i j k l m n ñ o p q r s t u v w x y z

⚷ **observar** *verb* **[17]**
1 **to watch**
observar un eclipse to watch an eclipse
2 **to comment**
Observó que todavía quedaba mucho que hacer. He commented that there was still a lot to be done.

⚷ el **observatorio** *masc noun*
observatory

la **obsesión** *fem noun*
obsession
Tiene una obsesión con la limpieza. He has an obsession with cleanliness.
Tiene la obsesión de que la siguen. She's obsessed with the idea that she's being followed.

⚷ el **obstáculo** *masc noun*
obstacle
superar un obstáculo to overcome an obstacle

obstinado *masc adjective*, **obstinada** *fem*
obstinate

obstinarse *reflexive verb* **[17]**
obstinarse en hacer algo to insist on doing something
Se obstinó en abrir la puerta. He insisted on opening the window.

⚷ **obtendré**, **obtendría**, **etc** *verb* ▷ **obtener**

⚷ **obtener** *verb* **[9]**
1 **to obtain, to get**
Obtuvo las mejores notas. She got the best marks.
2 **to win**
obtener el premio to win the prize

⚷ **obtenga**, **obtengo**, **obtuve**, **etc** *verb* ▷ **obtener**

⚷ **obvio** *masc adjective*, **obvia** *fem*
obvious
Es obvio que la quiere. It's obvious that he loves her.

la **oca** *fem noun*
goose

⚷ la **ocasión** *fem noun*
1 **occasion**
2 **opportunity**
Si hay ocasión. If there's an opportunity.
3 (*in advertising*) **precios de ocasión** bargain prices
coches de ocasión second-hand cars

⚷ **ocasionar** *verb* **[17]**
to cause
La tormenta ocasionó muchos daños. The storm caused a lot of damage.

⚷ **occidental** *masc & fem adjective*
western
la costa occidental the western coast

⚷ el **Occidente** *masc noun*
the West (*Europe and America*)

⚷ el **océano** *masc noun*
ocean
el océano Atlántico the Atlantic Ocean
el océano Pacífico the Pacific Ocean

⚷ **ochenta** *number*
eighty
Tiene ochenta años. She's eighty (years old).
ochenta y cinco eighty-five
los años ochenta the eighties

⚷ **ocho** *number*
1 **eight**
Tiene ocho años. She's eight (years old).
2 **eighth** (*in dates*)
Estamos a ocho. It's the eighth today.
3 **eight** (*in clock time*)
Son las ocho. It's eight o'clock.

⚷ **ochocientos**, **ochocientas** *number*
eight hundred
ochocientos siete eight hundred and seven

el **ocio** *masc noun*
spare time
en mis ratos de ocio in my spare time

ocioso *masc adjective*, **ociosa** *fem*
idle

el **ócorro** *masc noun*
okra

octavo *masc adjective*, **octava** *fem*
eighth
el octavo piso the eighth floor

⚷ **octubre** *masc noun*
October
en octubre in October
el 31 de octubre on 31 October

WORD TIP Names of months and days start with small letters in Spanish.

mini-info
12 de octubre

El 12 de octubre es el Día de la Hispanidad, fiesta nacional de España y los 23 países hispanohablantes cuando se celebra el descubrimiento de América por Cristóbal Colón en 1492.

la **ocupación** *fem noun*
occupation

ocupado *masc adjective*, **ocupada** *fem*
1 **busy**
Está muy ocupado. He's very busy.
2 **engaged**, **busy**
La línea está ocupada. The line is engaged.
3 **taken**
¿Está ocupado este asiento? Is this seat taken?

ocupar *verb* [17]
1 **ocupar un asiento** to have a seat
Ocupa el asiento 11b. He's in seat 11b.
¿Quién ocupa esa habitación? Who's in that room?
2 **to occupy** (*land, a building*)
3 **to spend** (*time*)
¿En qué ocupas tu tiempo libre? How do you spend your free time?
Ocupo mi tiempo libre jugando al tenis. I spend my free time playing tennis.

ocuparse *reflexive verb* [17]
ocuparse de algo, de alguien to take care of something, someone
Yo me ocupo de ello. I'll look after that.
¿Quién se ocupa de los niños? Who takes care of the children?

ocurrir *verb* [19]
to happen
¿Qué le ocurre? What's the matter with him?
Me ocurrió una cosa muy graciosa. Something really funny happened to me.

ocurrirse *reflexive verb* [19]
Se me ocurre que podemos ... I think we can ...
¿Se te ocurre alguna idea? Can you think of anything?
No se me ocurre nada. I just can't think of anything.

odiar *verb* [17]
to hate
Odio el invierno. I hate the winter.

el **odio** *masc noun*
hate, **hatred**
Le tiene odio. She hates him.

oeste *masc noun, invariable adjective*
west
ir hacia el oeste to go west
la costa oeste de Irlanda the west coast of Ireland
al oeste de Madrid to the west of Madrid
en el oeste de España in the west of Spain

ofender *verb* [18]
to offend

ofenderse *reflexive verb* [18]
to take offence

la **oferta** *fem noun*
offer
una oferta de trabajo a job offer
estar de oferta to be on offer
Esos zapatos están de oferta. Those shoes are on offer.

oficial *masc & fem adjective*
▷ see **oficial** *noun*
official

el & la **oficial** *masc & fem noun*
▷ see **oficial** *adj*
officer

la **oficina** *fem noun*
office
- la **oficina de cambio** bureau de change
- la **oficina de correos** post office
- la **oficina de (información y) turismo** tourist (information) office
- la **oficina de objetos perdidos** lost property (office)

el & la **oficinista** *masc & fem noun*
office worker
Es oficinista. He's an office worker.

el **oficio** *masc noun*
1 **trade**
2 **service** (*in church*)

ofrecer *verb* [35]
to offer
Ofreció ir a buscarla a la estación. He offered to collect her from the station.

ofrecerse *reflexive verb* [35]
to volunteer
ofrecerse para hacer algo to offer to do something
Se ofreció para llevarnos en el coche. She offered to take us in the car.

ofrezca, **ofrezco**, **etc** *verb* ▷ **ofrecer**

el **oído** *masc noun*
1 **ear**
tener dolor de oídos to have earache
2 **tener buen oído** to have a good ear (*for music*)

oiga, **oigo**, **etc** *verb* ▷ **oír**

oír *verb* [56]
1 **to hear**
No oigo nada. I can't hear anything.

2 **to listen to**
oír las noticias to listen to the news
Me gusta oír música. I like listening to music.
3 (*calling to someone*) **¡Oye! No olvides la carta.** Hey! Don't forget the letter.
¡Oiga! ¿Cuánto le debemos? Excuse me! How much do we owe you? (*to a waiter, barman, etc*)

ʃ **ojalá** *exclamation*
1 (*as a reply*) **I hope so**
'Seguro que te van a invitar.'—'¡Ojalá!' 'Of course you'll be invited.'—'I hope so!'
2 (*with wishes*) **¡Ojalá me llame!** I hope he rings me!
¡Ojalá que venga! I hope she comes!

WORD TIP A verb following *ojalá* goes in the *subjunctive*.

ʃ el **ojo** *masc noun*
1 **eye**
con los ojos cerrados with your eyes closed
Tiene los ojos azules. He has blue eyes.
Tiene los ojos claros. He has pale eyes. (*blue, green, or grey rather than brown*)
2 (*on signs, etc*) **¡Ojo!** Careful!
¡Ojo! Pinta Wet Paint
• el **ojo de la cerradura** keyhole

ʃ la **ola** *fem noun*
wave
• la **ola de calor** heatwave
• la **ola de frío** cold spell

ʃ **ole**, **olé** *exclamation*
olé (*at bullfights, flamenco dancing, etc*)

ʃ **oler** *verb* **[39]**
to smell
oler una flor to smell a flower
oler a algo to smell of something
Huele a ajo. It smells of garlic.

ʃ las **olimpiadas** *plural fem noun*
Olympic Games
las Olimpiadas del 2012 the 2012 Olympic Games

ʃ **olímpico** *masc adjective*, **olímpica** *fem adjective*
Olympic
los Juegos olímpicos the Olympic Games

ʃ la **oliva** *fem noun*
olive
el aceite de oliva olive oil

ʃ el **olivo** *masc noun*
olive tree

ʃ la **olla** *fem noun*
pan
• la **olla a presión** pressure cooker

ʃ el **olor** *masc noun*
smell
Tiene un olor raro. It has a funny smell.
Tiene olor a almendras. It smells of almonds.

ʃ **olvidar** *verb* **[17]**
to forget
¡Olvídalo! Forget it!
Olvidé el paraguas. I forgot my umbrella.

olvidarse *reflexive verb* **[17]**
to forget
Se me olvidó llamarte. I forgot to ring you.
Se me olvidó la cartera. I forgot my wallet.
olvidarse de to forget
Me olvidé de traerlo. I forgot to bring it.

ʃ el **ombligo** *masc noun*
navel

omitir *verb* **[19]**
to omit

ʃ **once** *number*
1 **eleven**
Tiene once años. She's eleven (years old).
2 **eleventh** (*in dates*)
Hoy estamos a once. It's the eleventh today.
3 **eleven** (*in clock time*)
Son las once. It's eleven o'clock.

onceavo *masc adjective*, **onceava** *fem*
eleventh

ʃ la **onda** *fem noun*
wave
estar en la onda (*informal*) to be trendy
¡No estás en la onda! You're not with it!
• la **onda corta** short wave
• la **onda larga** long wave
• la **onda media** medium wave

ondulado *masc adjective*, **ondulada** *fem*
wavy

la **ONG** *fem noun*
(*= Organización No-Gubernamental*) **NGO** (*Non-Governmental Organization*)

la **ONU** *fem noun*
(*= Organización de las Naciones Unidas*) **UN** (*United Nations*)
un país miembro de la ONU a UN member country

opcional *masc & fem adjective*
optional

♪ la **ópera** *fem noun*
opera

♪ la **operación** *fem noun*
operation
Ha sufrido una operación. He's had an operation.
• **operación retorno** the rush to get back to the cities at the end of major holidays
• **operación salida** the rush to get out of the cities when major holidays begin

el **operador** *masc noun*, la **operadora** *fem*
operator

♪ **operar** *verb* **[17]**
1 **to operate on** (*a person*)
¿Tendrán que operarlo? Will they have to operate on him?
La operaron de la pierna. She had an operation on her leg.
2 **to produce** (*a change*)

operarse *reflexive verb* **[17]**
to have an operation
Se va a operar del corazón. She's going to have a heart operation.

♪ **opinar** *verb* **[17]**
1 **to think**
Opino que ... I think that ...
¿Qué opinas del diseño? What do you think of the design?
2 **to express an opinion**
Prefiero no opinar. I prefer not to give an opinion.

♪ la **opinión** *fem noun*
opinion
en mi opinión in my opinion
cambiar de opinión to change your mind
He cambiado de opinión. I've changed my mind.
¿Cuál es tu opinión? What do you think?
• la **opinión pública** public opinion

♪ **oponer** *verb* **[11]**
1 **to raise** (*an objection*)
2 **oponer resistencia** to put up a fight

oponerse *reflexive verb* **[11]**
oponerse a algo to be against something
Me opongo a la idea. I'm against the idea.
Se oponen a los cambios de las reglas. They are against the changes in the rules.

♪ la **oportunidad** *fem noun*
chance, opportunity
aprovechar una oportunidad to make the most of an opportunity
Tuve la oportunidad de visitar el castillo. I had the chance to visit the castle.

♪ **oportuno** *masc adjective*, **oportuna** *fem*
right, good
Es un momento oportuno. It's the right moment.

la **oposición** *fem noun*
1 **opposition**
2 **oposiciones** competitive public exams for a government job

♪ **optativo** *masc adjective*, **optativa** *fem*
optional

el **óptico** *masc noun*, la **óptica** *fem*
optician

el **optimismo** *masc noun*
optimism

optimista *masc & fem adjective*
▷ see **optimista** *noun*
optimistic

el & la **optimista** *masc & fem noun*
▷ see **optimista** *adj*
optimist

♪ **opuesto** *masc adjective*, **opuesta** *fem*
1 **conflicting** (*views, opinions*)
2 **opposite**
Venían en dirección opuesta. They were coming from the opposite direction.

♪ la **oración** *fem noun*
1 (*Gramar*) **sentence**
2 **prayer**

♪ **oral** *masc & fem adjective* ▷ see **oral** *noun*
oral

♪ el **oral** *masc noun* ▷ see **oral** *adj*
oral exam

♪ el **orden** *masc noun* ▷ see **orden** *fem noun*
1 (*arranging*) **order**
en orden alfabético in alphabetical order
en orden de importancia in order of importance
arreglados en orden de tamaño arranged according to size
Ponlos en orden. Put them in order.
2 **mantener el orden** to keep order
poner la habitación en orden to tidy up the room
¡Orden! Order!

♪ la **orden** *fem noun* ▷ see **orden** *fem noun*
1 **order**
dar una orden to give an order
2 **warrant**
una orden de detención an arrest warrant
3 (*Religion*) **order**
una orden religiosa a religious order

ordenado *masc adjective*, **ordenada** *fem*
tidy
Es muy ordenado. He's very tidy.

el ordenador *masc noun*
computer

ordenar *verb* [17]
1 **to tidy up** (*a room, house*)
2 **to put in order**
ordenar algo alfabéticamente to put something in alphabetical order
3 **to order**
Nos ordenó seguir. He ordered us to carry on.

ordinario *masc adjective*, **ordinaria** *fem*
1 **vulgar**
Su novio es muy ordinario. Her boyfriend's very vulgar.
2 **usual**
3 **run-of-the-mill**
un vino ordinario a run-of-the-mill wine

WORD TIP *ordinario* does not mean *ordinary* in English; for the meaning of *ordinary* ▷ **corriente**.

la oreja *fem noun*
ear

orgánico *masc adjective*, **orgánica** *fem adjective*
organic

la organización *fem noun*
organization

organizar *verb* [22]
1 **to organize**
2 **to arrange**
Organicé una visita a las cuevas. I arranged a visit to the caves.

el órgano *masc noun*
organ

el orgullo *masc noun*
pride
Tiene mucho orgullo. He's very proud.

orgulloso *masc adjective*, **orgullosa** *fem*
proud
estar orgulloso de algo to be proud of something
Está muy orgulloso de su bici He's very proud of his bike.

la orientación *fem noun*
1 (*aspect*) **¿Qué orientación tiene la casa?** Which way does the house face?
2 **bearings** (*in navigation*)
3 **orientation** (*tendency*)
- **la orientación profesional** careers guidance

oriental *masc & fem adjective*
eastern
la costa oriental the eastern coast

orientar *verb* [17]
1 **to give directions to**
Me orientó para ir a Correos. She gave me directions to get to the Post Office.
2 **to give guidance to** (*a young person, student*)
3 **to place**
La orienté hacia el este. I placed it facing east.

orientarse *reflexive verb* [17]
to get your bearings

el Oriente *masc noun*
the East (*the countries east of Europe*)
el Lejano Oriente the Far East
el Oriente Medio the Middle East

original *masc & fem adjective*
▷ see **original** *noun*
original

el original *masc noun* ▷ see **original** *adj*
original

la orilla *fem noun*
1 **bank**
sentados a la orilla del río sitting on the river bank
a orillas del Duero on the banks of the Duero
2 **shore**
una casa a orillas del mar a house by the sea

ornamental *masc & fem adjective*
ornamental

el oro *masc noun*
gold
una medalla de oro a gold medal

la orquesta *fem noun*
orchestra
una orquesta de jazz a jazz band

la ortiga *fem noun*
nettle

la ortografía *fem noun*
spelling

la oruga *fem noun*
caterpillar

os *pronoun*
1 **you**
Os vimos desde la ventana. We saw you from the window.
¿Os dieron suficiente información? Did they give you enough information? ▸▸

2 **to you**
Os mintió. He lied to you.
3 **yourselves**
Os tenéis que portar bien. You must behave yourselves.
4 **each other**
¿Os conocéis? Do you know each other?
5 (*with reflexive verbs*) **¿Os divertisteis?** Did you have a good time?
Iros a bañar. Go for a swim.
6 (*with parts of the body, clothes*) **Os podéis quitar los abrigos.** You can take your coats off.
¿Os habéis lavado las manos? Have you washed your hands?
7 (*to have something done*) **Os tenéis que cortar el pelo.** You must get your hair cut.

WORD TIP Use *os* to talk to more than one person who you know them well. See also *tú* and *vosotros*.

osado *masc adjective*, **osada** *fem*
bold

la **oscuridad** *fem noun*
darkness

oscuro *masc adjective*, **oscura** *fem*
dark
a oscuras in the dark

el **osito** *masc noun*
un osito de peluche a teddy bear

el **oso** *masc noun*, la **osa** *fem*
bear
- el **oso polar** polar bear

la **ostra** *fem noun*
1 **oyster**
2 **¡Ostras!** Good grief!

la **OTAN** *fem noun*
(= *Organización del Tratado del Atlántico Norte*) **NATO**
un miembro de la OTAN a member of NATO

el **otoño** *masc noun*
autumn
en otoño in the autumn
el otoño pasado last autumn

otro *masc adjective*, **otra** *fem*
▷ see **otro** *pron*
1 **another**
¿Te has comprado otro CD? Have you bought another CD?
Añade otros dos. Add another two.
2 **other**
en otros colores in other colours
La otra tarde le vi. I saw him the other evening.
¿No tienes ningún otro color? Don't you have any other colours?
3 **otra cosa** something else
¿Quieres alguna otra cosa? Do you want something else?
Me gustaría comprarle otra cosa. I would like to buy her something else.
Eso es otra cosa diferente. That's something different.
No me gusta ninguna otra cosa. I don't like anything else.
4 **otra vez** again
Hazlo otra vez. Do it again.

otro, **otra** *pronoun* ▷ see **otro** *adj*
1 **another one**
Este no, dame otro. Not this one, give me another one.
2 **el otro, la otra** the other one
El otro te queda mejor. The other one suits you better.
Las otras están en el cajón. The other ones are in the drawer.
Los otros vendrán en coche. The others will come by car.
A otros les gustaría. Other people would like it.
3 (*in time expressions*) **un mes sí y otro no** every other month
de un día para otro from one day to the next

la **oveja** *fem noun*
sheep

el **OVNI** *masc noun*
(= *Objeto Volante No Identificado*) **UFO**

oxidado *masc adjective*, **oxidada** *fem*
rusty

el **oxígeno** *masc noun*
oxygen

oye, **oyendo**, **oyó** *verb* ▷ **oír**

el **ozono** *masc noun*
ozone
el agujero en la capa de ozono the hole in the ozone layer

P p

el **pabellón** *masc noun*
1 **block** (*part of a building, etc*)
2 **pavilion** (*in a trade fair, etc*)
3 **summerhouse**
• el **pabellón deportivo** sports hall

♪ la **paciencia** *fem noun*
patience
tener paciencia to be patient
Ten paciencia, ya vendrá. Be patient, she'll soon be here.

paciente *masc & fem adjective*
▷ see **paciente** *noun*
patient

el & la **paciente** *masc & fem noun*
▷ see **paciente** *adj*
patient

el **Pacífico** *masc noun* ▷ see **pacífico** *adj*
el Pacífico the Pacific, the Pacific Ocean

padecer *verb* **[35]**
to suffer
padecer de algo to suffer from something
Padece del corazón. He has heart trouble.

♪ el **padrastro** *masc noun*
stepfather

♪ el **padre** *masc noun*
1 **father**
2 **mis padres** my parents
3 (*Religion*) **el padre Antonio** Father Anthony

♪ el **padrino** *masc noun*
1 **godfather**
2 **mis padrinos** my godparents
• el **padrino de boda** man, giving away the bride (*usually her father, who also acts as best man*)

♪ la **paella** *fem noun*
paella (*rice dish, containing chicken and seafood*)

la **paga** *fem noun*
1 **pocket money**
¡Me ha suspendido la paga! She's stopped my pocket money!
2 **pay**
Recibimos la paga el día treinta. We get our pay on the thirtieth.
• la **paga extra** bonus pay (*a month's salary, usually paid at Christmas and in July*)

♪ **pagar** *verb* **[28]**
1 **to pay**
¿Cuánto pagaste por la bici? How much did you pay for the bike?
2 **to pay for** (*tickets, drinks, etc*)
Tengo que pagar el café. I have to pay for the coffee.
3 **to pay off** (*a debt*)
4 **to repay** (*a favour*)

♪ la **página** *fem noun*
page
en la página ocho on page eight
• la **página web** web page

♪ el **pago** *masc noun*
payment
efectuar un pago to make a payment
• el **pago al contado** cash payment
• el **pago anticipado** payment in advance
• el **pago inicial** down payment

♪ el **país** *masc noun*
country
los países de habla hispana Spanish-speaking countries

♪ el **paisaje** *masc noun*
landscape

los **Países Bajos** *plural masc noun*
los Países Bajos the Netherlands

♪ el **País de Gales** *masc noun*
el País de Gales Wales

♪ el **País Vasco** *masc noun*
el País Vasco the Basque Country (*a region in northern Spain with its own language and culture*)

♪ la **paja** *fem noun*
1 **straw**
un sombrero de paja a straw hat
un tejado de paja a thatched roof
2 **una pajita** a drinking straw

la **pajarita** *fem noun*
bow tie

♪ el **pájaro** *masc noun*
bird

♪ la **pala** *fem noun*
1 **spade**
2 **shovel**
3 **bat** (*for table tennis*)
4 **slice** (*for serving cake, fish, etc*)

la **palabra** *fem noun*
1 **word**
una redacción de quinientas palabras a five hundred word essay
No entendí ni una palabra. I didn't understand a word.
2 **word, promise**
Cumplió con su palabra. He kept his word.
Faltó a su palabra. She broke her word.
3 **speech**
el don de la palabra the gift of speech
4 **pedir la palabra** to ask permission to speak
• la **palabra compuesta** compound word

palabras

Muchas palabras usadas en la vida diaria son de origen árabe. Se identifican porque comienzan con las letras al-, ar-, az-; por ejemplo alfombra, arroz, azúcar. También hay muchos nombres como el río *Guadalquivir* o la *Alhambra*.

la **palabrota** *fem noun*
swearword
decir palabrotas to swear
No digas palabrotas. Don't swear.

el **palacio** *masc noun*
palace
• el **palacio de congresos** conference centre
• el **palacio de deportes** sports centre

la **palanca** *fem noun*
1 **lever**
abrir algo haciendo palanca to lever something open
2 **crowbar**
• la **palanca de cambios** gearstick
• la **palanca de mando** joystick

la **paleta** *fem noun*
1 **palette** (*for paints*)
2 **spatula** (*for cooking*)
3 **trowel** (*for cementing*)
4 **bat** (*for table tennis*)

palidecer *verb* **[35]**
to go pale

pálido *masc adjective*, **pálida** *fem*
pale
Tiene la tez pálida. She has a pale complexion.
Estás muy pálido. You're looking very pale.

el **palillo** *masc noun*
1 **chopstick**
2 (*Music*) **drumstick**
• el **palillo de dientes** toothpick

la **palma** *fem noun*
1 **palm tree**
2 **palm** (*of hand*)
dar palmas to clap your hands

el **palmera** *fem noun*
palm tree

el **palmero** *fem noun*
palm grower

el **palo** *masc noun*
1 **stick**
2 **pole** (*for tents*)
3 **club** (*for golf*)
4 **mast** (*of a ship*)
• el **palo de escoba** broomstick

la **paloma** *fem noun*
1 **pigeon**
2 **dove**
• la **paloma de la paz** dove of peace

las **palomitas** *plural fem noun*
popcorn

la **palta** *fem noun*
(*South America*) **avocado (pear)**

el **pan** *masc noun*
1 **bread**
una rebanada de pan a slice of bread
una barra de pan a French loaf
¿Quieres pan con mantequilla? Do you want bread and butter?
2 **loaf**
Cómprame dos panes. Buy me two loaves.
• el **pan blanco** white bread
• el **pan de molde** tin loaf
• el **pan integral** wholemeal bread
• el **pan rallado** breadcrumbs
• el **pan tostado** toast

WORD TIP *pan* does not mean *pan* in English; for the meaning of *pan* ▷ **cacerola**.

la **pana** *fem noun*
corduroy
unos pantalones de pana a pair of corduroy trousers

la **panadería** *fem noun*
bakery

el **panadero** *masc noun*, la **panadera** *fem*
baker

Panamá *masc noun*
Panama
el Canal de Panamá the Panama Canal

panameño *masc adjective & noun*, **panameña** *fem adjective & noun*
1 **Panamanian**
2 **un panameño, una panameña** Panamanian

WORD TIP Adjectives and nouns for nationality and regional origin do not have capital letters in Spanish.

la **pancarta** *fem noun*
banner

la **panceta** *fem noun*
belly pork

♪ la **pandereta** *fem noun*
tambourine
tocar la pandereta to play the tambourine

♪ el **panecillo** *masc noun*
bread roll

el **pánico** *masc noun*
panic
tenerle pánico a algo to be terrified of something
Les tiene pánico a los perros. He's terrified of dogs.

el **panorama** *masc noun*
1 **view, panorama**
Tiene un bello panorama de la sierra. It has a beautiful view of the mountains.
2 **outlook**
El panorama es deprimente. The outlook is depressing.

♪ la **pantalla** *fem noun*
1 **screen** (*of a TV, computer*)
2 **shade** (*of a lamp*)
- la **pantalla grande** big screen

♪ el **pantalón** *masc noun*
trousers
un pantalón a pair of trousers

♪ los **pantalones** *plural masc noun*
trousers
un par de pantalones, unos pantalones a pair of trousers
- los **pantalones cortos** shorts
- los **pantalones de peto** dungarees
- los **pantalones vaqueros** jeans

el **pantano** *masc noun*
1 **marsh, swamp**
2 **reservoir**

pantanoso *masc adjective*, **pantanosa** *fem*
marshy, swampy

♪ la **pantorrilla** *fem noun*
calf (*of your leg*)

♪ el **panty, panti** *masc noun*
tights
comprar unos pantys to buy a pair of of tights

el **pañal** *masc noun*
nappy
- el **pañal desechable** disposable nappy

el **paño** *masc noun*
cloth
un paño a piece of cloth
- el **paño de cocina** dishcloth

♪ el **pañuelo** *masc noun*
1 **handkerchief**
2 **headscarf**
3 **neckerchief**

la **papa** *fem noun*
(*Latin America*) **potato**
- las **papas fritas**
1 **chips**
2 **crisps**

♪ el **Papa** *masc noun*
(*Religion*) **Pope**

♪ el **papá** *masc noun*
1 **daddy**
2 (*informal*) **mis papás** my mum and dad

el **papagayo** *masc noun*
parrot

la **papaya** *masc noun*
pawpaw

♪ el **papel** *masc noun*
paper
un trozo de papel a piece of paper
Hay un papel en la mesa. There is piece of paper on the table.
- el **papel aluminio** aluminium foil
- el **papel de envolver** wrapping paper
- el **papel de lija** sandpaper
- el **papel higiénico** toilet paper
- el **papel pintado** wallpaper

♪ la **papelera** *fem noun*
1 **wastepaper basket**
2 **litter bin** (*in the street*)

la **papelería** *fem noun*
stationer's

las **paperas** *plural fem noun*
mumps

Spanish-English

el **paquete** *masc noun*
1 **parcel**
mandar un paquete to send a parcel
2 **packet**
un paquete de cigarrillos a packet of cigarettes

Paquistán *masc noun*
Pakistan

paquistaní *masc & fem adjective & noun*
1 **Pakistani**
2 **un & una paquistaní** Pakistani

WORD TIP Adjectives and nouns for nationality and regional origin do not have capital letters in Spanish.

par *masc & fem adjective* ▷ see **par** *noun*
even
un número par an even number

el **par** *masc noun* ▷ see **par** *adj*
1 **pair**
un par de zapatos a pair of shoes
2 **couple**
un par de veces a couple of times
3 **de par en par** wide open
La puerta estaba abierta de par en par. The door was wide open.

para *preposition*
1 **for**
Es para ti. It's for you.
Sirve para limpiar compactos. It's for cleaning CDs.
¿Para qué lo quieres? What do you want it for?
Hay suficiente para todos. There's enough for everybody.
2 (*with times, dates*) **by**
Tiene que estar listo para las tres. It has to be ready by three o'clock.
Estará terminado para el doce. It'll be finished by the twelfth.
Tráeme la falda para mañana. Bring me the skirt by tomorrow.
3 **to**
Se lo dijo para sí. He said it to himself.
Me quedé en casa para ver la película. I stayed at home to watch the film.
Es demasiado largo para recordarlo. It's too long to remember.
4 (*showing direction*) **Vamos para la estación.** We're going to the station.
Me voy para casa. I'm going home.
5 **para que** so that
Déjalo ahí para que lo vea. Leave it there so that he'll see it.

WORD TIP *para que* is followed by a verb in the subjunctive.

el **parabrisas** *masc noun, pl:* los **parabrisas**
windscreen

el **paracaídas** *masc noun, pl:* los **paracaídas**
parachute
lanzarse en paracaídas to parachute
Se lanzaron en paracaídas desde el avión. They parachuted out of the plane.

el **parachoques** *masc noun, pl:* los **parachoques**
bumper

la **parada** *fem noun* ▷ see **parado** *adj, noun*
stop (*for buses, etc*)
- la **parada del autobús** bus stop
- la **parada de taxis** taxi rank

el **paradero** *masc noun*
(*Latin America*) **bus stop**

parado *masc adjective*, **parada** *fem* ▷ see **parada** *noun*, **parado** *noun*
1 **unemployed**
2 (*Latin America*) **estar parado** to stand

el **parado** *masc noun*, la **parada** *fem* ▷ see **parada** *noun*, **parado** *adj*
unemployed person
Hay un millón de parados. There are one million unemployed.

el **parador** *masc noun*
Spanish state-owned hotel (*in a restored historic building, e.g. a castle, monastery, etc*)

el **paraguas** *masc noun, pl:* los **paraguas**
umbrella

el **Paraguay** *masc noun*
Paraguay

paraguayo *masc adjective & noun*, **paraguaya** *fem adjective & noun*
1 **Paraguayan**
2 **un paraguayo, una paraguaya** Paraguayan

WORD TIP Adjectives and nouns for nationality and regional origin do not have capital letters in Spanish.

el **paraíso** *masc noun*
paradise

paralelo *masc adjective*, **paralela** *fem* ▷ see **paralelo** *noun*
parallel
ser paralelo a algo to be parallel to something

el **paralelo** *masc noun* ▷ see **paralelo** *adj*
parallel

el **parapente** *masc noun*
paragliding
practicar parapente to go paragliding

a b c d e f g h i j k l m n ñ o p q r s t u v w x y z

♪ **parar** *verb* **[17]**
1 **to stop**
Para el coche. Stop the car.
Paramos un momento. We stopped for moment.
parar de hacer algo to stop doing something
No paró de hablar durante toda la tarde. He didn't stop talking all afternoon.
Bailamos sin parar. We didn't stop dancing.
2 **to save** (*in football, hockey*)
parar un gol to make a save
3 **ir a parar** to end up
Fueron a parar al hospital. They ended up in hospital.
¡No sé adónde vamos a ir a parar! I don't know what the world is coming to!
4 **Para un momento.** Hang on a minute.

pararse *reflexive verb* **[17]**
1 **to stop**
Se paró a pensar. He stopped to think.
No te pares ahí. Don't stop there.
Mi reloj se ha parado. My watch has stopped.
2 (*Latin America*) **to stand up**

el **pararrayos** *masc noun*, *pl:* los **pararrayos**
lightning conductor

el **parasol** *masc noun*
1 **visor** (*in car*)
2 **parasol**

la **parcela** *fem noun*
plot of land

WORD TIP *parcela* does not mean *parcel* in English; for the meaning of *parcel* ▷ **paquete**.

♪ el **parche** *masc noun*
patch

♪ el **parchís** *masc noun*
ludo
jugar al parchís to play ludo

♪ **parecer** *verb* **[35]**
1 **to seem**, **to look**
El coche parece nuevo. The car seems new.
Parece que no vienen. It seems they're not coming
Parece de madera. It looks as if it's made of wood.
Parece que está roto. It seems to be broken.
Parece que va a llover. It looks like rain.
2 (*when giving your opinion*) **Me parece demasiado complicado.** It seems too complicated to me.
¿Qué te pareció la película? What did you think of the film?
Me parece que llegan hoy. I think they arrive today.
Me parece que no. I don't think so.
Me parece que sí. It looks that way.
Le pareció muy mal que no llamasen. He thought it was really bad of them not to call.
3 **según parece**, **al parecer** apparently
Según parece, hay un retraso de tres horas. Apparently there's a three hour delay.

parecerse *reflexive verb* **[35]**
to look like, **to be like**
Se parece mucho a su padre. She looks very like her father.
Se parece mucho a su hermano. He's very like his brother.
Me parezco mucho a mi padre. I look very like my father.

♪ **parecido** *masc adjective*, **parecida** *fem*
▷ see **parecido** *noun*
1 **similar**
Es muy parecida a su tía. She's very similar to her aunt.
2 **ser bien parecido** to be good-looking

♪ el **parecido** *masc noun* ▷ see **parecido** *adj*
similarity
El parecido es increíble. The similarity is incredible.
Tiene un gran parecido con su prima, She's a lot like her cousin.

♪ la **pared** *fem noun*
wall

♪ la **pareja** *fem noun*
1 **couple**
2 **partner**
mi pareja my partner (*man or woman*)
3 **pair**
trabajar en pareja to work in pairs
4 (*one of a pair*) **He perdido la pareja de este guante.** I've lost my other glove.

♪ el **paréntesis** *masc noun*, *pl:* los **paréntesis**
brackets
entre paréntesis in brackets

♪ **parezca**, **parezco**, **etc** *verb* ▷ **parecer**

♪ el & la **pariente** *masc & fem noun*
relative
una pariente lejana a distant relative

♪ el **parking** *masc noun*
car park

♪ el **parlamento** *masc noun*
parliament

el **paro** *masc noun*
1 **unemployment**
estar en paro to be unemployed
cobrar el paro to get unemployment benefit
2 **strike**
un paro de 24 horas a 24-hour strike
• el **paro cardíaco** heart failure

parpadear *verb* [17]
to blink

el **párpado** *masc noun*
eyelid

el **parque** *masc noun*
park
• el **parque de atracciones** amusement park
• el **parque de bomberos** fire station
• el **parque eólico** wind farm
• el **parque infantil** play park
• el **parque móvil** fleet (*of cars, lorries, etc*)
• el **parque nacional** national park
• el **parque natural** nature reserve
• el **parque temático** theme park
• el **parque zoológico** zoo

mini-info ***parque nacional***
El primer parque nacional se estableció en 1918 en España y hoy hay once, con más de 200 parques regionales.

parquear *verb* []
(*Latin America*) **to park**

el **parqueo** *masc noun*
(*Latin America*) **parking**

el **parquímetro** *masc noun*
parking meter

el **párrafo** *masc noun*
paragraph

la **parrilla** *fem noun*
grill
trucha a la parrilla grilled trout
chuletas a la parrilla barbecued chops

la **parroquia** *fem noun*
1 **parish**
2 **parish church**

la **parte** *fem noun* ▷ see **parte** *masc noun*
1 **part**
la parte antigua de la ciudad the old part of town
Es parte de Asia. It's part of Asia.
Forma parte del programa. It's part of the syllabus.
2 **share**
mi parte del trabajo my share of the work
una tercera parte de la herencia a third of the inheritance
3 **la mayor parte de** most of
la mayor parte de los profesores most of the teachers
4 **en parte** partly
En parte tienen razón. They're partly right.
5 **de parte de** on behalf of
¿De parte de quién? Who's calling? (*on the phone*)
saludos de parte de Juan Juan says hello
Felicítalos de mi parte. Give them my congratulations.
6 (*to give your point of view*) **(yo) por mi parte ...** as far as I'm concerned ...
(ellos) por su parte ... as far as they're concerned ...
7 (*in expressions meaning 'where'*) **en alguna parte**, **por alguna parte** somewhere
en cualquier parte, **por cualquier parte** anywhere
en todas partes, **por todas partes** everywhere
No vamos a ninguna parte. We're not going anywhere.
• la **parte de la oración** part of speech

el **parte** *masc noun* ▷ see **parte** *fem noun*
report
• el **parte meteorológico** weather report

la **partera** *fem noun*
midwife

la **participación** *fem noun*
1 **participation**
2 **share in lottery ticket**

participar *verb* [17]
to participate, **to take part**
participar en algo to take part in something

el **participio** *masc noun*
participle
• el **participio pasado** past participle

particular *masc & fem adjective*
1 **private** (*lessons, teacher, etc*)
un colegio particular a private school
2 **mi teléfono particular** my home telephone number
nuestro domicilio particular our home address
3 **special**
Tiene un olor particular. It has a very special smell.
Y eso ¿qué tiene de particular? What's so

strange about that?
Es muy particular. He's very peculiar.

la **partida** *fem noun*
game
una partida de ajedrez a game of chess

♪ el **partido** *masc noun*
1 **party** (*political*)
un partido de izquierdas a left-wing party
2 **game**, **match**
un partido de rugby a rugby match

♪ **partir** *verb* **[19]**
1 **to cut** (*a loaf, melon, etc*)
partir algo por la mitad to cut something in half
Partió la manzana por la mitad. He cut the apple in half.
2 **to break** (*a branch, twig*)
Lo partió en dos. She broke it in two.
3 **to crack** (*a nut*)
4 **to leave** (*trains, people*)
El tren parte a medianoche. The train leaves at midnight.
5 **a partir de** from
a partir de ese momento from that moment on
a partir de ahora from now on

partirse *reflexive verb* **[19]**
to break
Me partí un diente. I broke a tooth.
La rama se partió. The branch broke.

la **partitura** *fem noun*
score (*in music*)

el **parto** *masc noun*
labour (*in pregnancy*)
estar de parto to be in labour

♪ la **pasa** *fem noun*
raisin

♪ **pasado** *masc adjective*, **pasada** *fem*
▷ see **pasado** *noun*
1 **last** (*with days, months, seasons*)
el verano pasado last summer
el domingo pasado last Sunday
2 **after**
pasado mañana the day after tomorrow
Son las diez pasadas. It's past ten o'clock.
Pasados los exámenes, nos vamos de vacaciones. After the exams, we're going on holiday.
3 **off** (*milk, fruit*)
La leche está pasada. The milk is off.
4 **overcooked** (*meat*)
El filete está muy pasado. The steak is overcooked.

el **pasado** *masc noun* ▷ see **pasado** *adj*
1 **past**
en el pasado in the past.
2 **past tense**

♪ el **pasaje** *masc noun*
ticket
sacar un pasaje para ... to buy a ticket to ...

♪ el **pasajero** *masc noun*, la **pasajera**, *fem*
passenger

el **pasamanos** *masc noun*,
pl: los **pasamanos**
1 **banister**
2 **handrail**

♪ el **pasaporte** *masc noun*
passport
sacar el pasaporte to get a passport
Tengo que renovar el pasaporte. I must renew my passport.

♪ **pasar** *verb* **[17]**
1 **to pass**
¿Me pasas las tijeras? Could you pass me the scissors?
Me pasó el balón. He passed the ball to me.
Nos pasó el resfriado. She gave us her cold.
2 **to go past**
Pasó un bus hace cinco minutos. A bus went past five minutes ago.
3 **to come past**, **to call in**
Pasaron por aquí. They came past this way.
El cartero pasa a las diez. The postman comes at ten.
Pasaré por tu casa. I'll call in at your house.
4 **to get past**
No podíamos pasar. We couldn't get past.
5 **to go in**
Pasaron todos al salón. They all went into the living room.
6 **to come in**
Pase, por favor. Please come in. (*polite form*)
7 **to sift**
Pasó la harina por el cedazo. He sifted the flour.
8 **pasar la aspiradora** to vacuum
Pasé la aspiradora por la habitación. I vacuumed the bedroom.
9 **to happen**
¿Qué pasa? What's happening?
No le ha pasado nada. Nothing has happened to him.
¿Qué te pasa? What's the matter?
No pasa nada. Nohing's the matter.
10 **to spend** (*time*)
Siempre pasamos las vacaciones en Canarias. We always spend our holidays in the Canary Islands.

Pasé la noche en casa de Candela. I spent the night at Candela's house.
11 **pasarlo bien, mal** to have a good, bad time
Lo pasamos muy bien. We had a very good time.
Lo pasé muy mal en las vacaciones. I had a terrible time on my holidays.
12 (*when telephoning*) **Le paso con el Señor Muñoz.** I'll put you through to Mr Muñoz.

pasarse *reflexive verb* **[17]**
1 **to go off** (*milk, fish*)
2 **to go bad** (*vegetables, fruit*)
3 **to spend** (*time*)
Nos pasamos las vacaciones en Murcia. We spent our hoildays in Murcia.
Se pasa todo el tiempo leyendo. She spends all her time reading.
4 **to call by**
Pásate por mi casa a las siete. Call by at my house at seven.
5 **to go past** (*too far*)
Nos pasamos de parada. We missed our stop.

el **pasatiempo** *masc noun*
hobby
Mi pasatiempo favorito es tocar la guitarra. My favourite hobby is playing the guitar.

la **Pascua** *fem noun*
1 **Easter**
¡Felices Pascuas! Happy Easter!
2 **Christmas**
¡Felices Pascuas! Merry Christmas!

pasear *verb* **[17]**
1 **to go for a walk**
Me gusta pasear por la playa. I like walking on the beach.
sacar al perro a pasear to take the dog for a walk
2 **to go out** (*in the car, on bike, etc*)
pasear en coche to go for a drive
Fuimos a pasear en bici. We went for a bike ride.

pasearse *reflexive verb* **[17]**
to go for a walk

el **paseo** *masc noun*
1 **walk**
2 **stroll**
3 **dar un paseo** to go out
Vamos a dar un paseo. Let's go for a walk.
dar un paseo en coche to go for a drive
dar un paseo en bicicleta to go for a bike ride

el **pasillo** *masc noun*
corridor
al fondo del pasillo at the end of the corridor

la **pasión** *fem noun*
passion

pasivo *masc adjective*, **pasiva** *fem*
passive
un fumador pasivo a passive smoker

el **paso** *masc noun*
1 **step**
paso a paso step by step
un paso importante an important step
dar un paso adelante to take a step forward
2 **footsteps**
oír pasos to hear footsteps
3 **passing**
el paso del tiempo the passing of time
4 **float** (*in a procession*)
5 (*on signs*) **'Ceda el paso'** 'Give way'
6 **'Prohibido el paso'** 'No entry'
7 **Te viene de paso., Te pilla de paso.** It's on your way.
- el **paso a nivel** level crossing
- el **paso de cebra** zebra crossing
- el **paso de peatones** pedestrian crossing
- el **paso elevado** flyover
- el **paso subterráneo**

1 **subway** (*for pedestrians*)
2 **underpass** (*for cars*)

la **pasta** *fem noun*
1 **paste**
pasta de tomates tomato paste
2 **biscuit**
3 **pastry**
4 **pasta**
- la **pasta de dientes** toothpaste

el **pastel** *masc noun*
cake
un pastel de chocolate a chocolate cake

la **pastelería** *fem noun*
cake shop

la **pastilla** *fem noun*
tablet, pill
pastillas para dormir sleeping pills
- la **pastilla de jabón** bar of soap

el **pasto** *masc noun*
(*Latin America*) **grass**

el **pastor** *masc noun*, la **pastora** *fem*
1 **shepherd**
2 **shepherdess**
3 **minister** (*of religion*)
- el **pastor alemán** Alsatian, German shepherd

ℰ la **pata** *fem noun* ▷ see **pato** *noun*
1 **leg**
2 **paw**
Se ha lastimado la pata. She's hurt her paw.
3 (*informal*) **meter la pata** to put your foot in it
He metido la pata de nuevo. I've put my foot in it again.

ℰ la **patada** *fem noun*
kick
darle una patada a alguien to kick someone
Le dio una patada al árbitro. He kicked the referee.
darle una patada a algo to kick something
Le dio una patada a la puerta. He kicked the door.

la **patata** *fem noun*
potato
• las **patatas bravas** spicy sautéed potatoes

las **patatas fritas** *plural fem noun*
1 **chips**, **french fried potatoes**
2 **crisps**

paternal *masc & fem adjective*
paternal

la **patera** *fem noun*
small boat (*used by illegal immigrants*)

ℰ el **patín** *masc noun*
1 **roller skate**
2 **ice skate**
3 **skateboard**
4 **pedalo**
• los **patines de hielo** ice skates
• los **patines en línea** Rollerblades®

el **patinador** *masc noun*, la **patinadora** *fem*
skater

ℰ el **patinaje** *masc noun*
1 **roller skating**
2 **ice skating**
• el **patinaje artístico** figure skating
• el **patinaje en línea** rollerblading

ℰ **patinar** *verb* **[1]**
1 **to roller-skate**
2 **to ice-skate**
3 **to rollerblade**
4 **to slip**
Patiné en una mancha de aceite. I slipped on a patch of oil.
5 **to skid** (*cars, bikes*)

ℰ el **patio** *masc noun*
1 **courtyard**
2 **patio**
3 **playground** (*of school*)

ℰ el **pato** *masc noun*, la **pata** *fem noun*
duck

ℰ la **patria** *fem noun*
homeland

patrocinar *verb* **[17]**
to sponsor

ℰ el **patrón** *masc noun*
1 **boss**
2 **skipper** (*of a boat*)
3 **landlord** (*of a guesthouse, a bar*)

la **patrona** *fem noun*
1 **boss**
2 **landlady** (*of a guesthouse, a bar*)

la **patrulla** *fem noun*
patrol
una patrulla de rescate a rescue party

la **patrullera** *fem noun*
patrol boat

el **patrullero** *masc noun*
1 **patrol boat**
2 **patrol plane**
3 **patrol car**

ℰ la **pausa** *fem noun*
pause
hacer una pausa to have a break
Haremos una pausa a mediodía. We'll have a break at midday.

ℰ el **pavo** *masc noun*, la **pava** *fem*
turkey
• el **pavo real** peacock

ℰ el **payaso** *masc noun*, la **payasa** *fem*
clown

ℰ la **paz** *fem noun*, *pl:* las **paces**
1 **peace**
2 **hacer las paces** to make up
Nos peleamos pero al final hicimos las paces. We had a fight, but we made up in the end.
3 **dejar a alguien en paz** to leave somebody alone
¡Deja a tu hermano en paz! Leave your brother alone!
¡Estos niños nunca me dejan en paz! These children never give me a moment's peace!

PD *abbreviation*
P.S. (*at the end of a letter*)

el **peaje** *masc noun*
toll (*on a bridge, motorway*)
una carretera de peaje a toll road

el **peatón** *masc & fem noun*
pedestrian

peatonal *masc & fem adjective*
pedestrian, for pedestrians

la **peca** *fem noun*
freckle

el **pecado** *masc noun*
sin

el **pecho** *masc noun*
1 **chest**
2 **bust** (*woman's*)
3 **breast**
dar el pecho a un bebé to breastfeed a baby

la **pechuga** *fem noun*
breast (*of chicken, turkey, etc*)
una pechuga de pollo a chicken breast

el **pedal** *masc noun*
pedal
- el **pedal de arranque** kickstart

el **pedazo** *masc noun*
piece
un pedazo de queso a piece of cheese
hacer pedazos algo to smash something to pieces
Hizo pedazos el vaso. He smashed the glass to pieces.
El jarrón se cayó y se hizo pedazos. The vase fell and smashed to pieces.

el **pedido** *masc noun*
order (*in buying, selling*)
hacer un pedido to place an order

pedir *verb* **[57]**
1 **to ask for**
pedir ayuda to ask for help
pedir un favor to ask a favour
pedir consejo to ask for advice
Piden medio millón por el cuadro. They're asking half a million for the picture.
Me pidió que le comprara el libro. He asked me to buy him the book.
2 **pedir perdón** to apologize
3 **pedir prestado algo** to ask to borrow something
pedir dinero prestado to ask to borrow some money
Me pidió prestada la moto. He asked to borrow my motorbike.
4 **pedir hora** to make an appointment (*at the doctor's, dentist's*)
5 **to order** (*in a restaurant, cafe*)
¿Qué vas a pedir? What are you going to order?
Pedí pollo, no pescado. I ordered chicken, not fish.

WORD TIP For the other Spanish verb for *to ask* ▷ **preguntar**.

pegajoso *masc adjective*, **pegajosa** *fem*
sticky
Tienes las manos pegajosas. Your hands are sticky.

el **pegamento** *masc noun*
glue

pegar *verb* **[28]**
1 **to stick**
He pegado una foto suya en la pared. I've stuck a picture of him on the wall.
2 **to glue**
Pegué los pedazos del plato. I glued the pieces of the plate together.
copiar y pegar to copy and paste (*in word processing*)
3 **to hit**
Me pegó. He hit me.
(*informal*) **pegarle una patada a alguien** to kick somebody
Le pegó una patada a su hermano. He kicked his brother.
(*informal*) **pegarle una paliza a alguien** to give somebody a beating
(*informal*) **pegarle un susto a alguien** to give somebody a fright
¡Me pegaste un susto tremendo! You gave me a terrible fright!
Le pegaron una buena paliza. They gave him a real beating.
4 (*in expressions*) **pegar un grito** to yell
pegar un salto to jump
pegar saltos de alegría to jump for joy
Me vas a pegar el resfriado. You're going to give me your cold.

pegarse *reflexive verb* **[28]**
1 **to hit each other**
Empezaron a pegarse. They started hitting each other.
2 **to stick**
Este sello no se pega. This stamp won't stick.

la **pegatina** *fem noun*
sticker

el **peinado** *masc noun*
hairstyle
Ese peinado no te sienta. That hairstyle doesn't suit you.

peinar *verb* **[17]**
1 **to comb**
2 **to brush**

peinarse *reflexive verb* **[17]**
1 **to comb your hair**
2 **to brush your hair**

♪ el **peine** *masc noun*
comb

la **pela** *fem noun*
(*informal*) **penny**
No me quedan pelas. I haven't got a penny.

♪ **pelar** *verb* **[17]**
1 **to peel** (*potatoes, apples*)
2 (*informal*) **pelar a alguien** to cut somebody's hair

pelarse *reflexive verb* **[17]**
1 **to peel** (*from sunburn*)
Se me está pelando la nariz. My nose is peeling.
2 (*informal*) **to have your hair cut**
¡Te pelaste! You've had your hair cut!

♪ el **peldaño** *masc noun*
1 **step**
Cuidado con el útimo peldaño. Be careful of the bottom step.
2 **rung**
una escala de diez peldaños a ladder with ten rungs

♪ la **pelea** *fem noun*
1 **fight**
2 **row**
Tuvo una pelea con su novio. She had a row with her boyfriend.

♪ **pelear** *verb* **[17]**
1 **to fight**
2 **to quarrel**
Pelean por cualquier cosa. They fight over anything.

pelearse *reflexive verb* **[17]**
1 **to fight**
Había dos chicos peleándose. There were two boys fighting.
2 **to quarrel**
Se pelearon por dinero. They quarrelled over money.
Siempre se pelea con su novio. She's always quarrelling with her boyfriend.

♪ la **película** *fem noun*
1 **film**
¿Qué película ponen hoy? What film are they showing today?
una película de terror a horror film
una película de risa a comedy film
una película de suspense a thriller
2 **film** (*for a camera*)
un rollo de película a roll of film

♪ el **peligro** *masc noun*
danger
estar en peligro, correr peligro to be in danger
fuera de peligro out of danger
un peligro para la salud a health risk
un peligro de incendio a fire hazard
poner a alguien en peligro to put somebody at risk
Puso en peligro a su familia. She put her family at risk.

> mini-info **peligro**
> El lince ibérico está en peligro de extinción; sólo quedan entre 100 y 120 ejemplares.

♪ **peligroso** *masc adjective*, **peligrosa** *fem*
dangerous
una curva peligrosa a dangerous bend

♪ **pelirrojo** *masc adjective*, **pelirroja** *fem*
1 **red-haired**
2 **pelo pelirrojo** red hair

pellizcar *verb* **[31]**
to pinch
¡No me pellizques! Stop pinching me!

el **pellizco** *masc noun*
pinch
Le di un pellizco en el brazo. I pinched her arm.

♪ el **pelo** *masc noun*
1 **hair**
pelo liso, pelo lacio straight hair
pelo rizado curly hair
Tengo el pelo negro. I've got black hair.
2 **un pelo de la barba** a whisker
3 **fur** (*of an animal*)
4 **tomarle el pelo a alguien** to pull somebody's leg
Te están tomando el pelo. They're pulling your leg.
Creí que era verdad, pero me estaba tomando el pelo. I thought it was true, but she was pulling my leg.

♪ la **pelota** *fem noun*
ball (*for football, tennis etc*)
una pelota de fútbol a football
• la **pelota vasca** pelota (*Basque game played in a walled court*)

la **peluca** *fem noun*
wig

el **peluche** *masc noun*
un juguete de peluche a cuddly toy
un osito de peluche a teddy bear

peludo *masc adjective*, **peluda** *fem*
hairy

la **peluquería** *fem noun*
hairdresser's

el **peluquero** *masc noun*, la **peluquera** *fem*
hairdresser

la **pena** *fem noun*
1 **shame**
¡Qué pena! What a shame!
Es una pena que no puedas venir. It's a shame you can't come.
2 **sadness**
Me da pena verla así. It makes me sad to see her like that.
3 **Sara me da mucha pena.** I'm really sorry for Sara.
4 **sentence**
la pena de muerte the death sentence
5 **valer la pena** to be worth it
No vale la pena. It's not worth it.
Vale la pena ver la película. The film's worth seeing.
6 **penas** problems
Cuéntame tus penas. Tell me all your problems.

el **penalti** *masc noun*
penalty

pendiente *masc & fem adjective*
▷ see **pendiente** *noun*
unresolved
una cuenta pendiente an unpaid bill
un asunto pendiente an unresolved problem

el **pendiente** *masc noun*
▷ see **pendiente** *adj, fem noun*
earring
He perdido la pareja de este pendiente. I've lost my other earring.

la **pendiente** *fem noun*
▷ see **pendiente** *adj, masc noun*
slope
una pendiente muy pronunciada a very steep slope
un camino en pendiente an uphill path

el **pene** *masc noun*
penis

penetrar *verb* **[17]**
to penetrate

la **península** *fem noun*
peninsula
la Península Ibérica the Iberian Peninsula

el **penique** *masc noun*
penny
Vale ochenta peniques. It's only worth eighty pence.

el **pensamiento** *masc noun*
thought
Creo que me adivina el pensamiento. I think she can read my thoughts.

pensar *verb* **[29]**
1 **to think**
Pienso que está bien. I think it's all right.
Piénsalo bien antes de decidir. Think about it carefully before deciding anything.
Pensándolo bien ... On second thoughts ...
2 **pensar en alguien** to think about somebody
Estaba pensando en ti. I was thinking about you.
3 **pensar en algo** to think of something
¿En qué piensas? What are you thinking about?
Pienso en las vacaciones. I'm thinking about the holidays.
4 **pensar de alguien** to think of someone
¿Qué piensas del nuevo entrenador? What do you think of the new coach?
5 **pensar hacer algo** to intend to do something
Pensamos volver mañana. We're intending to come back tomorrow.
¿Piensas llamarlo? Are you thinking of calling him?

la **pensión** *fem noun*
1 **pension**
cobrar la pensión to draw your pension
2 **guesthouse**
3 **media pensión** half board
• la **pensión completa** full board
• la **pensión de viudedad** widow's pension

el & la **pensionista** *masc & fem noun*
pensioner

peor *masc & fem adjective* ▷ see **peor** *adv, noun*
1 **worse**
No hay nada peor. There's nothing worse.
Éstas son peores que las de la otra tienda. These are worse than the ones in the other shop.
mucho peor much worse
2 **worst**
mi peor enemigo my worst enemy
en el peor de los casos in the worst case scenario
3 **peor para ti** it's your loss

peor *adverb* ▷ see **peor** *adj, noun*
worse
cada vez peor worse and worse
de mal en peor from bad to worse
Yo juego peor que tú. I play worse than you do.
Ella canta aún peor. She sings even worse.
Tu hermano juega aún peor que Iñaki. Your brother plays even worse than Iñaki.

♪ el & la **peor** *masc & fem noun*
▷ see **peor** *adjective, adverb*
el peor, la peor the worst one
Es el peor del equipo. He's the worst one in the team.
los peores, las peores the worst ones
Estas uvas son las peores que he probado. These grapes are the worst ones I've tasted.

♪ el **pepinillo** *masc noun*
gherkin

♪ el **pepino** *masc noun*
cucumber
Corta el pepino en rodajas. Slice the cucumber.

♪ **pequeño** *masc adjective*, **pequeña** *fem*
▷ see **pequeño** *noun*
1 **small**
un coche pequeño a small car
Dame otro más pequeño. Give me a smaller one.
La chaqueta me está pequeña. The jacket's too small for me.
2 **little**
un pequeño esfuerzo a little effort
3 **young**
mi hermana pequeña my little sister
Vivimos allí de pequeños. We lived there when we were young.

♪ el **pequeño** *masc noun*, la **pequeña** *fem*
▷ see **pequeño** *adj*
small child
Hay dos pequeños en el jardín. There are two little boys in the garden.
¿Cómo se llama la pequeña? What's the little girl's name?
¿Han comido los pequeños? Have the little ones eaten?

♪ la **pera** *fem noun*
pear
Déme un kilo de peras. Give me a kilo of pears.

el **peral** *masc noun*
pear tree

♪ la **percha** *fem noun*
1 **hanger**
2 **coat hook**

♪ **perder** *verb* **[36]**
1 **to lose**
perder la paciencia to lose patience
perder el conocimiento to lose consciousness
He perdido la cartera. I've lost my wallet.
Perdimos tres partidos seguidos. We lost three games in a row.
2 **to miss**
perder el tren to miss the train
Perdimos el vuelo. We missed the flight.
Has perdido una gran oportunidad. You've missed a great opportunity.
3 **perder el tiempo** to waste time
No pierdas el tiempo. Don't waste your time.
Pierde horas enteras mirando por la ventana. He wastes hours on end staring out of the window.
4 **perder la costumbre** to get out of the habit

perderse *reflexive verb* **[36]**
1 **to get lost**
Me he perdido. I'm lost.
¿Se ha perdido? Are you lost? (*polite form*)
No os perdáis en el bosque. Don't get lost in the woods.
2 **perderse algo** to lose something (*glasses, money, etc*)
Se me ha perdido la llave. I've lost my key.
3 **perderse algo** to miss something (*a programme, a chance*)
No quiero perderme el último episodio. I don't want to miss the final episode.
No te la pierdas esta oportunidad. Don't miss ithis opportunity.

♪ la **pérdida** *fem noun*
1 **loss**
2 **Es una pérdida de tiempo.** It's a waste of time.
3 **Está enfrente del supermercado, no tiene pérdida.** It's opposite the supermarket, you can't miss it.

la **perdiz** *fem noun*
partridge

♪ el **perdón** *masc noun*
▷ see **perdón** *exclamation*
pardon
pedir perdón to apologize, to say sorry
Le pedí perdón por lo que había dicho. I apologized to her for what I'd said.

perdón *exclamation* ▷ see **perdón** *noun*
1 **excuse me**
Perdón, ¿usted es el gerente? Excuse me, are you the manager?
2 **sorry**
Perdón, no te vi. Sorry, I didn't see you.

perdonar *verb* [17]
1 **to forgive**
No la he perdonado. I haven't forgiven her.
2 **to let off** (*without a punishment*)
Te perdono el castigo. I'll let you off.
3 (*when interrupting, apologizing, etc*) **¡Perdona!** Sorry!
¡Perdone! Excuse me! (*polite form*)
Perdone la molestia. Sorry to bother you.

la **peregrinación** *fem noun*
pilgrimage
irse de pereginación to go on a pilgrimage

el **perejil** *masc noun*
parsley
perejil picado chopped parsley

la **pereza** *fem noun*
laziness

perezoso *masc adjective*, **perezosa** *fem*
lazy
No seas tan perezoso. Don't be so lazy.

perfeccionar *verb* [17]
1 **to improve** (*a skill*)
Quiero perfeccionar mi español. I want to improve my Spanish.
2 **to perfect**

perfectamente *adverb*
perfectly
Te entiendo perfectamente. I understand you perfectly.

perfecto *masc adjective*, **perfecta** *fem*
perfect
Tiene un dominio perfecto del inglés. She has a perfect command of English.

el **perfil** *masc noun*
profile
Me parece mejor visto de perfil. It looks better to me from the side.

el **perfume** *masc noun*
perfume
un frasco de perfume a bottle of perfume

la **perfumería** *fem noun*
perfume shop

el **periódico** *masc noun*
newspaper
un periódico semanal a weekly newspaper

el & la **periodista** *masc & fem noun*
journalist

el **período**, **periodo** *masc noun*
period (*of time*)
un período bastante largo quite a long period

el **periquito** *masc noun*
budgie

la **perla** *fem noun*
pearl

permanecer *verb* [35]
1 **to stay** (*in a place*)
Permanecí un año en Sevilla. I stayed for a year in Seville.
2 **to remain**
permanecer callado to remain silent
permanecer a la escucha to stay tuned

permanente *masc & adjective*
▷ see **permanente** *noun*
permanent
'Servicio permanente' '24 hour service'

la **permanente** *fem noun*
▷ see **permanente** *adj*
perm
hacerse la permanente to have your hair permed

permanezca, **permanezco**, **etc** *verb*
▷ **permanecer**

el **permiso** *masc noun*
1 **permission**
darle permiso a alguien para hacer algo to give somebody permission to do something, to allow somebody to do something
Nos dio permiso para copiar las cartas. He gave us permission to copy the letters.
No le dieron permiso para ir a la fiesta. He wasn't allowed to go the party.
2 **con permiso** may I come in? (*when you knock on a door*), excuse me (*to get past someone*)
3 **leave**
estar de permiso to be on leave
un permiso de una semana a week's leave
4 **permit**
- el **permiso de conducir** driving licence
- el **permiso de trabajo** work permit

permitir *verb* [19]
1 **to allow**
Me permitió llevarlo. She allowed me to take it away.
No nos permitieron entrar. They didn't allow us in.
2 **No te permito que me contestes.** I won't have you answering me back.

3 (*asking permission*) **¿Me permite?** May I?
¿Me permite una sugerencia? May I make a suggestion?
4 **to make possible**
Este proceso permite ahorrar más combustible. This process makes it possible to save more fuel.

pero *conjunction*
1 **but**
Es ligero, pero muy fuerte. It's light, but very strong.
2 (*showing surprise, impatience*) **Pero ¿qué haces ahí arriba?** Just what are you doing up there?
¡Pero ya te dije que no viene! How many times do I have to tell you he's not coming!

el **perrito** *masc noun*
puppy
- el **perrito caliente** hot dog

el **perro** *masc noun*, la **perra** *fem*
dog
- el **perro callejero** stray dog
- el **perro guardián** guard dog
- el **perro guía** guide dog

la **persecución** *fem noun*
1 **pursuit**
Salieron en persecución de los ladrones. They set off in pursuit of the thieves.
2 **persecution**

perseguir *verb* **[64]**
to pursue

la **persiana** *fem noun*
blind

persiga, **persigo**, **persiguió**, **etc** *verb* ▷ **perseguir**

persistir *verb* **[19]**
to persist

la **persona** *fem noun*
1 **person**
Él es una persona importante. He is an important person.
Vino en persona para agradecernos. She came in person to thank us.
Nos dio cuatro por persona. He gave us four each.
2 **las personas** people
Había diez personas. There were ten people.

el **personaje** *masc noun*
1 **character** (*in a book, play*)
2 **important figure**, **celebrity**
un personaje del mundo del cine an important figure in the film world

personal *masc & fem adjective*
▷ see **personal** *noun*
personal

el **personal** *masc noun*
▷ see **personal** *adjective*
staff

la **personalidad** *fem noun*
personality

la **perspectiva** *fem noun*
1 **perspective**
2 **prospect**
Las perspectivas son buenas. The prospects are good.

persuadir *verb* **[19]**
to persuade
persuadir a alguien de que haga algo to persuade somebody to do something
Trata de persuadirla de que se quede. Try to persuade her to stay.

pertenecer *verb* **[35]**
to belong
pertenecer a alguien to belong to somebody
Pertenece a mi tía. It belongs to my aunt.
¿A quién pertenece? Who does it belong to?

pertenezca, **pertenezco**, **etc** *verb* ▷ **pertenecer**

Perú, **el Perú** *masc noun*
Peru

peruano *masc adjective & noun*, **peruana** *fem adjective & noun*
1 **Peruvian**
2 **un peruano, una peruana** Peruvian

WORD TIP Adjectives and nouns for nationality and regional origin do not have capital letters in Spanish.

la **pesa** *fem noun*
weight
hacer pesas to do weightlifting

la **pesadilla** *fem noun*
nightmare
Tuve otra pesadilla anoche. I had another nightmare last night.

pesado *masc adjective*, **pesada** *fem*
▷ see **pesado** *noun*
1 **heavy** (*box, suitcase*)
2 **ser muy pesado** to be boring (*a job, book, film*)
3 **ser muy pesado** to be a pain
Tu hermanito es muy pesado. Your little brother's a real pain.

♪ el **pesado** *masc noun*, la **pesada** *fem*
▷ see **pesado** *adj*
(*informal*) **bore**, **pain**
¡Eres un pesado! You're such a pain!

♪ **pesar** *verb* **[17]**
1 **to weigh**
Peso sesenta kilos. I weigh sixty kilos.
Hay que pesar el equipaje. The luggage has to be weighed.
2 **pesar mucho** to be very heavy
Puedo llevarlo, no pesa mucho. I can carry it, it's not very heavy.
¿Te pesan mucho las bolsas? Are the bags too heavy for you?

la **pesca** *fem noun*
fishing
ir de pesca to go fishing

♪ la **pescadería** *fem noun*
fishmonger's

♪ el **pescado** *masc noun*
fish (*as food*)
El pescado alimenta mucho. Fish is very nourishing. ▷ **pez**

el **pescador** *masc noun*, la **pescadora** *fem*
1 **fisherman**
2 **fisherwoman**

pescar *verb* **[31]**
1 **to fish**
ir a pescar to go fishing
Salieron a pescar tiburón. They went out shark-fishing
2 **to catch**
No pescamos nada. We didn't catch anything.

♪ la **peseta** *fem noun*
peseta (*Spanish currency before the euro; 500 pesetas = 3.00 euros*)

pesimista *masc & fem adjective*
▷ see **pesimista** *noun*
pessimistic

el & la **pesimista** *masc & fem noun*
▷ see **pesimista** *adj*
pessimist

♪ el **peso** *masc noun*
weight
perder peso to lose weight
ganar peso to put on weight
vender al peso to sell by weight
• el **peso bruto** gross weight

pesquero *masc adjective*, **pesquera** *fem*
fishing
la industria pesquera the fishing industry

♪ la **pestaña** *fem noun*
eyelash

♪ el **pétalo** *masc noun*
petal

el **petardo** *masc noun*
banger (*firework*)

♪ el **petróleo** *masc noun*
oil
una refinería de petróleo an oil refinery

el **petrolero** *masc noun*
oil tanker (*ship*)

♪ el **pez** *masc noun*, *pl:* los **peces**
fish (*as a living creature*)
Vimos cientos de peces. We saw hundreds of fish. ▷ **pescado**
• el **pez de colores** goldfish
• el **pez espada** swordfish

♪ el **piano** *masc noun*
piano
tocar el piano to play the piano
• el **piano de cola** grand piano

picado *masc adjective*, **picada** *fem*
1 **decayed** (*tooth*)
Tengo una muela picada. I have a cavity in one of my back teeth.
2 **minced** (*meat*)
3 **choppy** (*choppy*)
El mar estaba picado. The sea was choppy.
4 (*informal*) **estar picado** to be miffed
Está picada porque no la llamaste. She's miffed that you didn't call her.

♪ la **picadura** *fem noun*
bite, **sting**
una picadura de mosquito a mosquito bite
Tenía picaduras de abeja por todo el cuerpo. He was covered in bee stings.

picante *masc & fem adjective*
hot (*spicy*)
una salsa picante a hot sauce

el **picaporte** *masc noun*
door handle

♪ **picar** *verb* **[31]**
1 **to sting** (*insects*)
2 **to mince** (*meat*)
3 **to chop** (*vegetables*)
4 **to rot** (*teeth*)
5 **to be hot** (*spicy foods*)
Esta salsa pica mucho. This sauce is very hot.
6 **to itch**
Me pica la nariz. My nose is itching.
7 **Me pican los ojos.** My eyes are stinging.

8 **to nibble** (*bar snacks*)
Nos trajo algo para picar. He brought us something to nibble.

el **pico** *masc noun*
1 **beak**
2 **pick** (*for digging*)
3 **peak** (*of a mountain*)
4 **corner** (*of a table*)
5 **un cuello de pico** a V-neck
6 **... y pico** ... and something
Le costó tres mil y pico. It cost him three thousand and something.
Llegaron a las cinco y pico. They arrived just after five.

pida, **pido**, **pidió**, **etc** *verb* ▷ **pedir**

el **pie** *masc noun*
1 **foot**
ir a pie to walk, to go on foot
Si no viene el taxi iremos a pie. If the taxi doesn't come we'll walk.
Tuvo que volver a pie. He had to walk back.
2 **de pie** standing
estar de pie to be standing.
ponerse de pie to stand up
3 **base** (*of a lamp, glass*)

la **piedra** *fem noun*
1 **stone**
un banco de piedra a stone bench
tener piedras en el riñón to have kidney stones
2 **flint** (*of a lighter*)
- la **piedra filosofal** philosopher's stone
- la **piedra preciosa** precious stone

la **piel** *fem noun*
1 **skin**
tener la piel seca to have dry skin
2 **peel** (*of fruit*)
3 **fur**
un abrigo de pieles a fur coat
4 **leather**
un bolso de piel a leather bag

piensa, **pienso**, **etc** *verb* ▷ **pensar**

la **pierna** *fem noun*
leg
cruzar las piernas to cross your legs

la **pieza** *fem noun*
1 **piece**
2 (*Latin America*) **bedroom**
- la **pieza de recambio**, la **pieza de repuesto** spare part

el **pijama** *masc noun*
pyjamas
un pijama de algodón a pair of cotton pyjamas

la **pila** *fem noun*
1 **pile**
una pila de libros a pile of books
2 **battery**
Funciona con pilas. It runs on batteries.
3 **sink** (*in a kitchen*)
4 **basin** (*in a bathroom*)

la **píldora** *fem noun*
pill

el & la **piloto** *masc & fem noun*
pilot

el **pimentón** *masc noun*
1 **paprika**
2 **cayenne pepper**

la **pimienta** *fem noun*
pepper
- la **pimienta blanca** white pepper
- la **pimienta negra** black pepper

el **pimiento** *masc noun*
pepper
- el **pimiento rojo** red pepper
- el **pimiento verde** green pepper

el **pimpón** *masc noun*
table tennis

el **pincel** *masc noun*
1 **paintbrush**
2 **make-up brush**

el & la **pinchadiscos** *masc & fem noun*, *pl:* **pinchadiscos**
disc jockey, DJ

pinchar *verb* **[17]**
1 **to prick**
Las espinas le pinchaban la cara. The thorns pricked his face.
2 **to be prickly**
3 **to burst** (*a balloon*)
Me ha pinchado el globo. He's burst my balloon.
4 **to have a puncture**
Creo que hemos pinchado. I think we've got a puncture.
5 (*Computers*) **to click on**
6 (*informal*) **to give an injection to**

pincharse *reflexive verb* **[17]**
1 **to burst** (*balloons*)
Se le pincharon todos los globos. All his balloons burst. ▸▸

2 **to puncture**
Se me ha pinchado una rueda. I've got a puncture.

el **pinchazo** *masc noun*
puncture
Tuvimos un pinchazo. We had a puncture.

el **pincho** *masc noun*
1 **bar snack**
2 **prickle** (*on bush*)

el **pingüino** *masc noun*
penguin

el **pino** *masc noun*
pine tree
muebles de pino pine furniture

la **pinta** *fem noun*
1 **Tiene pinta de oficinista.** He looks like an office worker.
¡Qué pinta más rara! That looks really odd!
La comida tiene muy buena pinta. The food looks delicious.
2 **pint** (*of beer, etc*)

las **pintadas** *plural fem noun*
graffiti

pintado *masc adjective*, **pintada** *fem*
painted
pintado a mano hand-painted
La casa estaba pintada de blanco. The house was painted white.

pintar *verb* **[17]**
to paint
Lo pinté de negro. I painted it black.

el **pintor** *masc noun*, la **pintora** *fem*
painter

pintoresco *masc adjective*, **pintoresca** *fem*
picturesque

la **pintura** *fem noun*
1 **paint**
pintura amarilla yellow paint
una mano de pintura a coat of paint
2 **painting**
una pintura abstracta an abstract painting
3 **pinturas** crayons
- la **pintura al óleo** oil painting

la **pinza** *fem noun*
1 **clothes peg**
2 **hairgrip**
3 **pincer**
4 **dart** (*in clothing*)

las **pinzas** *plural fem noun*
tweezers

la **piña** *fem noun*
1 **pineapple**
jugo de piña pineapple juice
2 **pine cone**

la **pipa** *fem noun*
1 **pipe**
fumar en pipa to smoke a pipe
2 **pipas** sunflower seeds

la **piragua** *fem noun*
canoe

el **piragüismo** *masc noun*
canoeing

la **pirámide** *fem noun*
pyramid

los **Pirineos** *plural masc noun*
los Pirineos the Pyrenees

el **piropo** *masc noun*
compliment

el **pirulí** *masc noun*
lollipop

pisar *verb* **[17]**
1 **to step**
pisar a alguien to step on somebody's foot
pisar algo to tread on something
2 **'Prohibido pisar el césped'.** 'Keep off the grass'.

piscina *noun*
swimming pool
una piscina al aire libre an open-air swimming pool
la parte honda de la piscina the deep end of the pool
la parte poco profunda de la piscina the shallow end of the pool

piscis *masc & fem noun* ▷ see **Piscis** *noun*
Pisces
Soy piscis. I'm Pisces.

WORD TIP Use a small letter in Spanish to say *I am Pisces*, etc with star signs.

Piscis *masc noun* ▷ see **piscis** *noun*
Pisces

el **piso** *masc noun*
1 **floor**, **storey**
Vivo en el tercer piso. I live on the third floor.
un edificio de cinco pisos a five-storey building
un autobús de dos pisos a double-decker bus

2 flat
un piso de dos cientos metros cuadrados. a four-hundred square metre flat
3 (*Latin America*) **floor** (*of a room*)

♪ la **pista** *fem noun*
1 track
seguirle la pista a alguien to be on somebody's trail
La policía les está siguiendo la pista. The police are on their trail.
2 racecourse
- la **pista de aterrizaje** runway
- la **pista de atletismo** athletics track
- la **pista de esquí** ski slope
- la **pista de hielo** ice rink
- la **pista de patinaje** skating rink
- la **pista de tenis** tennis court

el **pistacho** *masc noun*
pistachio

♪ la **pistola** *fem noun*
gun

pitar *verb* **[17]**
1 to blow a whistle
2 to toot the horn (*in a car*)

el **pito** *masc noun*
1 whistle
tocar el pito to blow the whistle
2 horn
tocar el pito to toot the horn

♪ la **pizarra** *fem noun*
1 blackboard
2 slate
techos de pizarra slate roofs

la **placa** *fem noun*
1 plate, sheet (*of metal*)
2 badge
- la **placa de matrícula** number plate

el **placer** *masc noun*
pleasure

♪ el **plan** *masc noun*
1 plan
hacer planes to make plans
¿Qué planes tienes para las vacaciones? What are your plans for the holidays?
2 (*informal*) **en plan ...: viajar en plan económico** to travel on the cheap
Lo dije en plan de broma. I was only kidding.
- el **plan de capacitación** training scheme
- el **plan de estudios** syllabus

♪ la **plancha** *fem noun*
1 iron (*for clothes*)
pasarle la plancha a una camisa to iron a shirt
No necesita plancha. It doesn't need ironing.
2 (*in cooking*) **a la plancha** grilled
pescado a la plancha grilled fish
3 sheet
una plancha de plástico a sheet of plastic
- la **plancha de vela** sailboard

♪ **planchar** *verb* **[17]**
to iron
Te planché el pantalón. I ironed your trousers.

planear *verb* **[17]**
1 to plan
2 to glide

♪ el **planeta** *masc noun*
planet
descubrir un planeta nuevo to discover a new planet

♪ **plano** *masc adjective*, **plana** *fem*
▷ see **plano** *noun*
flat (*land, field*)
un terreno plano a flat plot of land

♪ el **plano** *masc noun* ▷ see **plano** *adj*
1 street map
un plano de Madrid a street map of Madrid
2 plan (*of a building*)

♪ la **planta** *fem noun*
1 plant
regar las plantas to water the plants
2 floor
en la sexta planta on the sixth floor
- la **planta baja** ground floor

plantar *verb* **[17]**
to plant

♪ el **plástico** *masc noun*
plastic
bolsas de plástico plastic bags

♪ la **plata** *fem noun*
1 silver
cubiertos de plata silver cutlery
la medalla de plata the silver medal.
2 (*Latin America*) **money**
Perdió un montón de plata. He lost loads of money.

la **plataforma** *fem noun*
platform
- la **plataforma de lanzamiento** launching pad
- la **plataforma petrolera** oil rig

♪ indicates key words

el **plátano** *masc noun*
banana
un rácimo de plátanos a bunch of bananas

la **plática** *fem noun*
(*Latin America*) **talk**

platicar *verb* **[31]**
(*Latin America*) **to talk, to chat**

el **platillo** *masc noun*
saucer
- el **platillo volante** flying saucer

el **plato** *masc noun*
1 **plate**
lavar los platos to wash the dishes
2 **dish**
un plato típico de Cataluña a typical Catalan dish
3 **course**
Tomaré pescado de primer plato. I'll have fish for the first course.
¿Y de segundo plato? And for your second course?
- el **plato combinado** complete meal served on one plate
- el **plato de postre** dessert plate
- el **plato del día** dish of the day
- el **plato fuerte** main course
- el **plato llano** dinner plate

la **playa** *fem noun*
1 **beach**
pasar el día en la playa to spend the day on the beach
2 **seaside**
veranear en la playa to spend your summer holidays at the seaside

la **playera** *fem noun*
canvas shoe

la **plaza** *fem noun*
1 **square** (*in a town, city*)
la Plaza Mayor the Main Square
2 **market**
Los martes hay plaza. Tuesday is market day.
3 **seat** (*on bus, train*)
¿Quedan plazas? Are there any seats left?
4 **position** (*at work*)
Hay plazas vacantes. There are vacancies.
- la **plaza de aparcamiento** parking space
- la **plaza de toros** bullring

el **plazo** *masc noun*
1 **period**
un plazo de dos meses a two-months period
El plazo de entrega acaba el día once. The deadline is on the eleventh.
2 (*in expressions*) **a corto plazo** in the short term
a largo plazo in the long term
planes a largo plazo long-term plans
pagar algo a plazos to pay for something in instalments
- el **plazo de vencimiento** expiry date (*of passport, licence, etc*)

plegar *verb* **[30]**
to fold

pleno *masc adjective*, **plena** *fem*
1 **full**
2 **en pleno verano** in the middle of summer
en pleno centro right in the centre of town

pliega, pliego, pliegue, etc *verb* ▷ **plegar**

el **plomo** *masc noun*
1 **lead**
sin plomo lead-free
2 **fuse**
Se han fundido los plomos. The fuses have blown.
3 **ser un plomo** to be a real drag
¡Esa película es un plomo! That film's a real drag!

la **pluma** *fem noun*
1 **feather**
2 **pen**

el **plumier** *masc noun*
pencil case

plural *masc & fem adjective*
▷ see **plural** *noun*
plural

el **plural** *masc noun*
(*Grammar*) **plural**
en plural in the plural

la **población** *fem noun*
population

pobre *masc & fem adjective*
▷ see **pobre** *noun*
poor
Su familia es muy pobre. His family is very poor.
¡Pobre Jaime! Poor Jaime!
Esta pobre chica está enferma. This poor girl is ill.

el & la **pobre** *masc & fem noun*
▷ see **pobre** *adj*
poor person
los pobres the poor

¡La pobre! Ha perdido el billete. Poor thing! She's lost her ticket.

la **pobreza** *fem noun*
poverty
Vimos tanta pobreza. We saw so much poverty.

la **pocilga** *fem noun*
pigsty
Tu habitación está hecha una pocilga. Your room is a pigsty.

poco *masc adjective*, **poca** *fem*
▷ see **poco** *pron, adv*
1 **little**
con poco esfuerzo with little effort
Hay poco pan. There isn't much bread.
Es poca cosa. It's not much.
2 **few**
pocos días más tarde a few days later
pocas veces not often
Había pocas personas. There were only a few people.
Pocas veces la he tenido que esperar. It's not often I've had to wait for her.
Ha venido pocas veces aquí. She's only been here a few times.
Cuesta unos pocos euros. It costs just a few euros.

poco, **poca** *pronoun* ▷ see **poco** *adj, adv*
1 **little**
Basta con poco. A little is enough.
Queda poco. There's not much left.
poco a poco little by little
2 **few**
Vinieron pocos. Only a few came.
Quedan pocas de las viejas costumbres. Few of the old customs remain.
Pon unos pocos aquí. Put a few here.
3 **un poco** a bit
Espera un poco. Wait a bit.
un poco de sal a bit of salt
Me fastidia un poco. It's a bit irritating.
4 (*in time expressions*) **hace poco** not long ago
Hace poco que me llamó. He called me not long ago.
Aún voy a tardar un poco. I'm going to take a little more time.
Falta poco para las cinco. It's almost five o'clock.
dentro de poco soon
poco antes de comer shortly before eating
poco después de su llegada not long after he arrived

poco *adverb* ▷ see **poco** *adj, pron*
not very much
Habla poco. He doesn't talk very much.
un cantante poco conocido a little-known singer
Soy muy poco paciente. I'm very impatient.
Están poco interesados. They aren't very interested.
Nos vemos muy poco. We hardly ever see each other.

poder *verb* **[10]** ▷ see **poder** *noun*
1 (*expressing ability*) **can**, **to be able to**
Puedo hacerlo para mañana. I can do it by tomorrow.
¿Puedes venir hoy? Can you come today?
No puede levantarlo. He can't lift it.
No pude ir. I couldn't go.
Pueden hacerlo solos. They can do it on their own.
Hazlo lo mejor que puedas. Do it as best you can.
¿Podrás ayudarme? Will you be able to help me?
¿Pudiste encontrarlo? Were you able to find it?
2 (*asking permission politely*) **may**
¿Se puede? May I come in?
¿Puedo abrir la ventana? May I open the window?
¿Podría usar tu ordenador? May I use your computer?
3 (*expressing possibility*) **Podría suceder.** It could happen.
Puede que se haya roto. It may have got broken.
Has podido romperlo. You could have broken it.
Puede que llegue más tarde. He might come later.
'¿Se habrán olvidado?'—'Puede ser.' 'Could they have forgotten?'—'They might have.'
Puede ser que no lo sepa. It might be that she doesn't know.
Puede ser que se haya perdido. He might have got lost.
4 (*making suggestions*) **Podrías preguntar.** You could ask.
Podríamos comer fuera. We could eat out.
5 (*in difficult situations*) **to cope**
¡Ya no puedo más! I can't cope any more!
No puede con tanto trabajo. She can't cope with so much work.
6 (*when telling someone off*) **¡Podrías haberlo dicho!** You might have said so!
7 **Si puede ser.** If possible.

♪ el **poder** *masc noun* ▷ see **poder** *verb*
power
Llegaron al poder en 1997. They came to power in 1997.

poderoso *masc adjective*, **poderosa** *fem*
powerful

♪ **podrá**, **podré**, **podría**, **etc** *verb* ▷ **poder**

podrido *masc adjective*, **podrida** *fem*
rotten

el **poema** *masc noun*
poem

la **poesía** *fem noun*
poetry

el & la **poeta** *masc & fem noun*
poet

el **póker** *masc noun*
poker (*card game*)
¿Sabes jugar al póker? Do you know how to play poker?

polaco *masc adjective & noun*, **polaca** *fem adjective & noun*
1 **Polish**
2 **un polaco, una polaca** Pole
3 **Polish** (*the language*)

WORD TIP Adjectives and nouns for nationality, regional origin and language, do not have capital letters in Spanish.

polémico *masc adjective*, **polémica** *fem*
controversial
una decisión polémica a controversial decision

♪ el & la **policía** *masc & fem noun* ▷ see **policía** *fem noun*
police officer
Mi hermana es policía. My sister's a policewoman.
Pregunta al policía. Ask the policeman.

♪ la **policía** *fem noun* ▷ see **policía** *noun*
police (*the force*)
- la **policía antidisturbios** riot police

policíaco *masc adjective*, **policíaca** *fem*
una novela policíaca a detective novel

♪ el **polideportivo** *masc noun*
sports centre

el **polígono industrial** *masc noun*
industrial estate

la **polilla** *fem noun*
moth

♪ la **política** *fem noun* ▷ see **político** *adj, noun*
1 **politics**
2 **policy** (*of a government, an organization, etc*)
la política exterior foreign policy

♪ **político** *masc adjective*, **política** *fem* ▷ see **política** *noun*, **político** *noun*
political

el **político** *masc noun*, la **política** *fem* ▷ see **política** *fem noun*, **político** *adj*
politician

la **póliza** *fem noun*
policy (*insurance document*)

el **pollito** *masc noun*, la **pollita** *fem*
chick

♪ el **pollo** *masc noun*
chicken
- el **pollo asado** roast chicken

♪ el **polo** *masc noun*
1 **pole** (*in physics, geography*)
los polos positivo y negativo the positive and negative poles
2 **ice-lolly**
3 (*Sports*) **polo**
- el **Polo Norte** North Pole

♪ **Polonia** *fem noun*
Poland

la **polución** *fem noun*
pollution

♪ el **polvo** *masc noun*
1 **dust**
quitar el polvo a los muebles to dust the furniture
2 (*informal*) **estar hecho polvo** to be worn out
Después de la excursión nos quedamos hechos polvo. We were worn out after the trip.
Este sofá está hecho polvo. This sofa's a wreck.
3 **polvos** face powder
- los **polvos de talco** talcum powder

el **polvorón** *masc noun*
pastry (*made with almonds; eaten at Christmas time*)

la **pomada** *fem noun*
ointment

♪ el **pomelo** *masc noun*
grapefruit

♪ **pondría**, **pondrías**, **etc** *verb* ▷ **poner**

poner *verb* **[11]**
1 **to put**
Ponlo en la mesa. Put it on the table.
Lo puse en el armario. I put it in the wardrobe.
Pusimos diez euros cada uno. We put in ten euros each.
Le puso la silla al caballo. She put the saddle on the horse.
2 (*in cafés, etc*) **¿Qué les pongo?** What can I get you?
¿Me pone un café? Can I have a coffee please?
¿Le pongo más sopa? Would you like some more soup?
3 **to turn on** (*the radio, a CD, etc*)
poner la tele to put on the telly
poner música to put on some music
Pon el volumen más alto. Turn the volume up.
4 **to set** (*a clock, timer, etc*)
poner el despertador to set the alarm clock
Puse el despertador a las ocho. I set the alarm clock for eight.
5 **to install** (*heating, an alarm system, etc*)
Van a poner calefacción central. They're going to install central heating.
6 **to fit** (*a carpet*)
7 (*with names*) **¿Qué nombre le vais a poner al niño?** What are you going to call the baby?
Le pusieron el apodo de 'el Rubio'. They nicknamed him 'Blondy'.
8 (*with films, plays, etc*) **poner una película** to show a film
poner una obra de teatro to put on a play
¿Qué ponen en el 'Roxy'? What's on at the 'Roxy'?
9 **to start up**
poner un negocio to start up a business
poner una tienda to open a shop
10 (*on the phone*) **¿Me pone con el señor Muñoz?** Could you put me through to Mr Muñoz?
11 **poner a alguien + adjective** to make somebody + adjective
poner a alguien triste to make somebody sad
No me pongas nerviosa. Don't make me nervous.
poner a alguien de mal humor to put somebody in a bad mood
Me pone siempre de mal humor. He always puts me in a bad mood.
12 **poner la mesa** to lay the table
13 **poner atención** to pay attention
14 **ponerle una inyección a alguien** to give somebody an injection

ponga, pongo, etc *verb* ▷ **poner**

el **poni** *masc noun*
pony

popular *masc & fem adjective*
popular

por *preposition*
1 **for**
por ejemplo for example
por esa razón for that reason
Lo hago por tu bien. I'm doing it for your benefit.
Me ofrecieron dos mil euros por el coche viejo. They offered me two thousand euros for the old car.
2 **through**
No entra por la ventana. It won't go in through the window.
Me enteré por mi hermana. I heard through my sister.
Pasamos por Toledo. We went through Toledo.
3 **by** (*by means of*)
mandar algo por correo to send something by post
viajar por carretera to travel by road
¿Cuánto cuesta enviarlos por avión? How much does it cost to send them by air?
Nos mantenemos en contacto por correo electrónico. We keep in touch by email.
Lo dijeron por la tele. They said so on TV.
4 **by** (*someone*)
diseño por Santiago Calatrava design by Santiago Calatrava
Fue criado por su tía. He was brought up by his aunt.
5 **because of**
Suspendieron el partido por la lluvia. The game was cancelled because of the rain.
Lo expulsaron por mala conducta. He was thrown out for bad behaviour.
Por eso no lo hice. That's why I didn't do it.
6 **¿Por qué?** Why?
'¿Por qué lo hiciste?'—'Porque me dio la gana.' 'Why did you do it?'—'Because I felt like it.' (*See also: porque*)
7 (*in calculations*) **Cinco por tres son quince.** Five times three is fifteen.
Mide tres metros por cuatro. It measures three metres by four.
8 (*in time expressions*) **por la mañana** in the morning
9 **por la noche** at night
10 (*saying where*) **por todos lados** everywhere
andar por la calle to walk along the road
Lo dejé por aquí. I left it around here somewhere. ⏩

Viven por la Avenida de Sitges. They live somewhere around Sitges Avenue.
¿Por dónde queda la estación? Whereabouts is the station?

11 (*saying the rate*) **per**, **each**
treinta euros por persona thirty euros per person
a cien kilómetros por hora at a hundred kilometres an hour
por ciento per cent
un descuento del diez por ciento a ten per cent discount
un diez por ciento de los estudiantes ten per cent of the students

WORD TIP Spanish always has *el* or *un* before percentages.

12 (*in expressions*) **por adelantado** in advance
por escrito in writing
por fin at last
Me levanto por lo general a las ocho. I usually get up at eight.
por lo tanto therefore
por supuesto of course

el **porcentaje** *masc noun*
percentage

el **porche** *masc noun*
porch

la **porción** *fem noun*
1 **portion**
una porción de tarta a slice of cake
2 **share**

porque *conjunction*
because
Está enfadado porque no le saludaste. He's annoyed because you didn't say hello.
'¿Por qué hiciste eso?'—'Porque sí.' 'Why did you do that?'—'Just because I felt like it.'
'¿Por qué no viniste ayer?'—'Porque no.' 'Why didn't you come yeserday?'—'I didn't feel like it.'

WORD TIP *¿por qué?*, two words and accented, is *why?*; *porque*, one word, is *because*.

el **porrón** *masc noun*
wine bottle (*from which you drink, holding it away from your mouth*)

la **portada** *fem noun*
1 **title page** (*of a book*)
2 **cover** (*of a magazine*)
3 **front page** (*of a newspaper*)

el **portaequipajes** *masc noun*, *pl:* los **portaequipajes**
1 **roof rack**
2 **luggage rack** (*on a train*)

portarse *reflexive verb* **[17]**
to behave
portarse mal to behave badly
¡Pórtate bien! Behave yourself!

portátil *masc & fem adjective*
▷ see **portátil** *noun*
portable

el **portátil** *masc noun* ▷ see **portátil** *adj*
laptop (computer)

el **portazo** *masc noun*
dar un portazo to slam the door
Oí un portazo. I heard a door slamming.

la **portería** *fem noun*
goal

el **portero** *masc noun*, la **portera** *fem*
1 **goalkeeper**
2 **caretaker**
3 **porter**
• el **portero automático** entry-phone

portorriqueño *masc adjective & noun*, **portorriqueña** *fem adjective & noun*
1 **Puerto Rican**
2 **un portorriqueño, una portorriqueña** Puerto Rican

WORD TIP Adjectives and nouns for nationality and regional origin do not have capital letters in Spanish.

Portugal *masc noun*
Portugal

portugués *masc adjective & noun*, **portuguesa** *fem adjective & noun*
1 **Portuguese**
2 **un portugués, una portuguesa** Portuguese man, Portuguese woman
3 **Portuguese** (*the language*)

WORD TIP Adjectives and nouns for nationality, regional origin, and language do not have capital letters in Spanish.

el **porvenir** *masc noun*
future

posar *verb* **[17]**
1 **to pose**
2 **to put down**

posarse *reflexive verb* **[17]**
to land (*birds*)

poseer *verb* **[37]**
1 **to own**
2 **to hold** (*a title, record*)

la **posibilidad** *fem noun*
1 **possibility**
Es una posibilidad. It's a possibility.

2 **tener posibilidades de hacer algo** to have a good chance of doing something
Tienen muchas posibilidades de ganar. They have a good chance of winning.
¿Qué posibilidades tienen? What are their chances?

posible *masc & fem adjective*
▷ see **posible** *adv*
possible
a ser posible if possible
No fue posible impedirlo. It was impossible to avoid it.
Es posible que venga hoy. She may come today.
Hice todo lo posible para ayudarla. I did all I could to help her.

posible *adverb* ▷ see **posible** *adj*
lo más tarde posible as late as possible
Hazlo lo mejor posible. Do the best you can.

la **posición** *fem noun*
position
en quinta posición in fifth place
mantener algo en posición vertical to keep something upright
• la **posición social** social status

positivo *masc adjective*, **positiva** *fem*
positive

postal *masc & fem adjective*
▷ see **postal** *noun*
postal

la **postal** *fem noun* ▷ see **postal** *adj*
postcard

el **poste** *masc noun*
1 **post**
2 **pole**

el **póster** *masc noun*
poster

posterior *masc & fem adjective*
1 **back**
el asiento posterior the back seat
la parte posterior de la casa the back of the house
2 **subsequent**, **later**
en años posteriores in later years

la **postilla** *fem noun*
scab

postizo *masc adjective*, **postiza** *fem*
false
una dentadura postiza a set of false teeth

el **postre** *masc noun*
pudding, **dessert**
¿Qué hay de postre? What's for pudding?
De postre tenemos ... For dessert, we have ...

potable *masc & fem adjective*
agua potable drinking water

potencial *masc & fem adjective*
potential

la **práctica** *fem noun*
1 **practice**
He perdido la práctica. I'm out of practice.
Lo aprenderás con la práctica. You'll learn with practice.
2 **prácticas** *plural* practical work (*in school subjects*), teaching practice (*for trainee teachers*)

practicar *verb* **[31]**
1 **to practise**
practicar el violín to practise the violin
2 **practicar deportes** to do sports

práctico *masc adjective*, **práctica** *fem*
practical
una solución muy práctica a very practical solution
Tiene gran sentido práctico. He's a very practical person.

la **pradera** *fem noun*
grassland, **prairie**

el **prado** *masc noun*
meadow

la **precaución** *fem noun*
1 **precaution**
tomar precauciones to take precautions
2 **caution**
actuar con precaución to act with caution

precedente *masc & fem adjective*
previous

el **precio** *masc noun*
price
precios de saldo bargain prices
¿Qué precio tiene? How much is it?
Los precios han subido mucho. Prices have gone up a lot.
• el **precio al por mayor** wholesale price
• el **precio al por menor** retail price
• el **precio fijo** fixed price

precioso *masc adjective*, **preciosa** *fem*
1 **beautiful**
¡Qué vestido más precioso! What a beautiful dress! ▸▸

Spanish–English

2 **precious**
piedras preciosas precious stones

el **precipicio** *masc noun*
precipice

la **precipitación** *fem noun*
1 **rush**
hacer algo con mucha precipitación to do something in a rush
Salió con mucha precipitación. He rushed out.
2 **precipitaciones** (*plural*) rainfall
Habrá precipitaciones moderadas. There will be moderate rainfall.

precipitarse *reflexive verb* **[17]**
to rush
No te precipites. Don't rush into anything.
precipitarse hacia algo to rush towards something
Todos se precipitaron hacia la salida de emergencia. Everyone rushed for the emergency exit.

precisamente *adverb*
precisely

la **precisión** *fem noun*
precision

preciso *masc adjective*, **precisa** *fem*
1 **precise**
Necesito datos más precisos. I need more precise information.
Llegaron en el momento preciso. They arrived just in time.
En este preciso momento no puedo. Right now I can't.
2 **ser preciso** to be necessary
si es preciso if necessary
No es preciso pagar por adelantado. It's not necessary to pay in advance.
Es preciso que vayas hoy. You must go today.

predilecto *masc adjective*, **predilecta** *fem*
favourite

preescolar *masc & fem adjective*
preschool
un programa de educación preescolar a preschool educational programme

la **preferencia** *fem noun*
1 **preference**
tener preferencia por algo to have a preference for something
2 **right of way**
Yo tenía preferencia. I had right of way.
3 **priority**
tener preferencia to have priority
Tendremos preferencia sobre los que llegan después. We'll have priority over those who arrive after us.

preferible *masc & fem adjective*
preferable
ser preferible a algo to be preferable to something
Es preferible que no venga. It's better if he doesn't come.

preferido *masc adjective*, **preferida** *fem*
favourite
Mi comida preferida es la china. My favourite food is Chinese.

preferir *verb* **[14]**
to prefer
¿Cuál prefieres? Which do you prefer?
preferir algo a algo to prefer something to something
Prefiero el campo a la playa. I prefer the country to the seaside.
Preferiría no tener que ir. I'd rather not have to go.

prefiera, **prefiero**, **etc** *verb* ▷ **preferir**

el **prefijo** *masc noun*
1 **prefix**
2 **dialling code**
el prefijo de España the dialling code for Spain

la **pregunta** *fem noun*
question
hacer una pregunta to ask a question

preguntar *verb* **[17]**
to ask
Pregúntale si quiere venir. Ask him if he wants to come.
Le pregunté sobre los vuelos. I asked her about the flights.
preguntar por alguien to ask about someone
Me preguntó por tus padres. He asked me about your parents.

preguntarse *reflexive verb* **[17]**
to wonder
Me pregunto si dice la verdad. I wonder if he's telling the truth.

WORD TIP For the other Spanish verb for *to ask* ▷ **pedir**.

el **prejuicio** *masc noun*
prejudice
tener prejuicios contra algo to be prejudiced against something

a b c d e f g h i j k l m n ñ o p q r s t u v w x y z

prematuro *masc adjective*, **prematura** *fem*
premature

premiar *verb* **[17]**
premiar a alguien to give somebody a prize

♪ el **premio** *masc noun*
prize
el premio al mejor ensayo the prize for the best essay
ganar un premio to win a prize
¿Qué dan de premio? What's the prize?
Me tocó el premio gordo. I won the jackpot.
darle un premio a alguien to give someone a prize
- el **premio gordo** jackpot (*in the lottery*)

prender *verb* **[18]**
1 **to catch** (*a criminal*)
2 **to light** (*cigarette, match*)
La leña no prende. The wood won't light.
3 **prenderle fuego a algo** to set fire to something
Le prendió fuego a la casa. She set fire to the house.
4 (*Latin America*) **to turn on** (*the radio, the lights*)

♪ la **prensa** *fem noun*
la prensa the press
leer la prensa to read the newspapers

♪ **preocupado** *masc adjective*, **preocupada** *fem*
worried
estar preocupado por algo to be worried about something
Estoy preocupada por Carmen. I'm worried about Carmen.

♪ **preocupar** *verb* **[17]**
to worry
Me preocupan los exámenes. I'm worried about the exams.
¿Qué te preocupa? What's worrying you?

preocuparse *reflexive verb* **[17]**
to get worried
Se preocupó porque no la llamé. She got worried because I didn't phone her.
No se preocupe. Don't worry about it. (*polite form*)
No te preocupes. Don't worry about it. (*informal form*)

la **preparación** *fem noun*
1 **preparation**
2 **training** (*in sport*)
3 **un trabajador con muy buena preparación** a highly trained worker

♪ **preparar** *verb* **[17]**
1 **to prepare**
preparar la cena to prepare dinner
preparar un examen to prepare for an exam
2 **to train** (*a player, athlete*)
3 **to coach** (*a student*)
4 **preparar la cuenta** to draw up the bill

prepararse *reflexive verb* **[17]**
to get ready
Es hora de prepararnos para salir. It's time we got ready to go.

los **preparativos** *plural masc noun*
preparations

la **preposición** *fem noun*
preposition

la **presa** *fem noun*
1 **dam**
2 **reservoir**
3 **prey**
4 **ser presa del terror** to be seized with panic

la **presencia** *fem noun*
presence
en presencia de sus padres in front of his parents

la **presentación** *fem noun*
1 **introduction**
hacer las presentaciones to do the introductions
2 **presentation**

el **presentador** *masc noun*, la **presentadora** *fem*
presenter

♪ **presentar** *verb* **[17]**
1 **to introduce**
Te presento a mi novio. This is my boyfriend.
Nos presentó a su jefe. He introduced us to his boss.
2 **to present** (*a programme*)
3 **to submit** (*an application*)
4 **to launch** (*a product*)
5 **to show** (*a permit, passport*)

presentarse *reflexive verb* **[17]**
1 **to introduce yourself**
2 **to arrive**
Se presentaron sin avisar a nadie. They arrived without letting anybody know.
3 **presentarse voluntario** to volunteer
4 **presentarse a un examen** to sit an exam
5 **presentarse a un concurso** to enter a competition ▸▸

6 **presentarse para un cargo** to apply for a post
7 **presentarse a la presidencia** to run for the presidency

presente *masc & fem adjective*
▷ see **presente** *noun*
present, here (*when calling the register*)

el **presente** *masc noun* ▷ see **presente** *adj*
present

el **preservativo** *masc noun*
condom

la **presidencia** *fem noun*
presidency

el **presidente** *masc noun*, la **presidenta** *fem*
president
el presidente del gobierno the prime minister

la **presión** *fem noun*
1 **pressure**
2 **la presión atmosférica** atmospheric pressure

♪ **preso** *masc adjective*, **presa** *fem*
▷ see **preso** *noun*
estar preso to be in prison
meter preso a alguien to send somebody to prison
Metieron presos a los delincuentes. The criminals were sent to prison.

♪ el **preso** *masc noun*, la **presa** *fem*
▷ see **preso** *adj*
prisoner
• el **preso político** political prisoner

el **préstamo** *masc noun*
loan
• el **préstamo hipotecario** mortgage

♪ **prestar** *verb* **[17]**
1 **to lend**
Le presté dinero para el coche. I lent him money for the car.
¿Me prestas tu abrigo? Could you lend me your coat?
2 **prestar atención** to pay attention

el **prestidigitador** *masc noun*, la **prestidigitadora** *fem*
conjurer

presumido *masc adjective*, **presumida** *fem* ▷ see **presumido** *noun*
conceited

el **presumido** *masc noun*, la **presumida** *fem* ▷ see **presumido** *adj*
Es un presumido. He's so conceited.

presumir *verb* **[19]**
to show off
Presumen de casa grande. They like to boast about how big their house is.
Presume de guapa. She thinks she's so good-looking.

el **presupuesto** *masc noun*
1 **budget** (*in business, government*)
2 **estimate** (*for repairs, etc*)

pretender *verb* **[18]**
1 **to try**
¿Qué pretende conseguir? What is he trying to achieve?
¿Qué pretendes decir con eso? What are you getting at?
Pretendía que pagase yo. She was trying to get me to pay for it.
2 **pretender que alguien haga algo** to expect somebody to do something
Pretende que yo le ayude. He expects me to help him.

WORD TIP *pretender* in Spanish, does not mean *to pretend*; for the meaning of *pretend* ▷ **fingir**

el **pretexto** *masc noun*
pretext, excuse
Siempre tiene algún pretexto para no hacerlo. He always has some excuse or other for not doing it.

prevenir *verb* **[15]**
1 **to prevent**
Previene la malaria. It prevents malaria.
2 **to warn**
Hay que prevenirles de las inundaciones. We must warn them about the floods.

prever *verb* **[16]**
to foresee

previsto *masc adjective*, **prevista** *fem*
a la hora prevista at the scheduled time
Está previsto que vengan mañana. They're due to come tomorrow.

♪ la **primavera** *fem noun*
spring
en primavera in spring
la primavera pasada last spring

♪ **primer** *adjective*
first

a b c d e f g h i j k l m n ñ o p q r s t u v w x y z

▷ **primero, primera** *adjective*
el primer ministro the prime minister
en el primer piso on the first floor

WORD TIP *primer* is used instead of *primero* before a masc singular noun.

ʆ **primero** *masc adjective, pronoun,* **primera** *fem* ▷ see **primero** *adv*
first
primera clase first class
Sólo leí las veinte primeras páginas. I only read the first twenty pages.
el primero de mayo the first of May
Soy el primero. I'm first.
Llegó en primer lugar. He finished in first position.

ʆ **primero** *adverb* ▷ see **primero** *adj, pron*
first
Yo estaba primero. I was here first.
Primero vamos a informarnos. First of all, let's find out.

la **primicia** *fem noun*
1 **scoop** (*news story*)
2 **first showing** (*of film*)

ʆ el **primo** *masc noun,* la **prima** *fem*
cousin
Hoy vienen mis primos Julio y Sara My cousins Julio and Sara are coming today.

ʆ la **princesa** *fem noun*
princess

ʆ **principal** *masc & fem adjective*
main
la calle principal del pueblo the village's main street

ʆ el **príncipe** *masc noun*
prince
un príncipe ruso a Russian prince
los Príncipes de Asturias the Prince and Princess of Asturias (*Príncipe de Asturias is the title of Spain's crown prince*)

el **principiante** *masc noun,* la **principianta** *fem*
beginner

ʆ el **principio** *masc noun*
1 **beginning**
a principios de mes at the beginning of the month
a principios de siglo at the turn of the century
al principio de la temporada at the beginning of the season
un buen principio a good start
2 **principle**
Se niega por principio a hacerlo. He refuses to do it on principle.

ʆ la **prisa** *fem noun*
1 **hurry**
tener prisa to be in a hurry
Tengo mucha prisa. I'm in a real hurry.
darse prisa to hurry up
Date prisa, que llegamos tarde. Hurry up or we'll be late.
2 **de prisa** fast
hacer algo de prisa to do something fast
Hizo los deberes de prisa. He rushed through his homework.
a toda prisa in a hurry
3 **correr prisa** to be urgent
Este trabajo corre prisa. This job is urgent.

la **prisión** *fem noun*
prison

el **prisionero** *masc noun,* la **prisionera** *fem*
prisoner

los **prismáticos** *plural masc noun*
binoculars

privado *masc adjective,* **privada** *fem*
private
la vida privada private life
en privado in private

privar *verb* **[17]**
privar a alguien de algo to deprive somebody of something
Lo privaron de su libertad. He was deprived of his freedom.

privarse *reflexive verb* **[17]**
privarse de algo to deprive yourself of something
Se priva de todo lujo. She deprives herself of all luxuries.

privilegiado *masc adjective,* **privilegiada** *fem*
privileged

el **privilegio** *masc noun*
privilege

probable *masc & fem adjective*
probable
Es probable que lo traiga hoy. He'll probably bring it today.

el **probador** *masc noun*
changing room

probar *verb* **[24]**
1 **to try**
Prueba a abrirlo con esta llave. Try opening it with this key.
Es la primera vez que lo pruebo. It's the first time I've tried it.
Probar no cuesta nada. There's no harm in trying.
2 **to taste**
Pruébalo. Taste it.
¿Has probado la sopa? Have you tasted the soup?
3 **to test** (*the brakes*)
4 **to prove**
Esta carta prueba que mintió. This letter proves she lied.
No pudo probar su inocencia. He could not prove his innocence.

probarse *reflexive verb* **[24]**
to try on
Quisiera probarme este vestido. I'd like to try on this dress.
¿Quiere probárselo? Would you like to try it on?

la **probeta** *fem noun*
test tube
un niño probeta a test-tube baby

el **problema** *masc noun*
problem
un problema muy importante a major problem
resolver un problema to solve a problem

procedente *masc & fem adjective*
from
el vuelo procedente de Londres the flight from London

proceder *verb* **[18]**
1 **proceder de algo** to come from something
Su familia procede de Italia. His family comes from Italy.
2 **to proceed**
Hay que proceder con cautela. We must proceed with caution.

el **procesador** *masc noun*
un procesador de textos a word processor

la **procesión** *fem noun*
procession

el **proceso** *masc noun*
1 **process**
un proceso químico a chemical process
2 **processing**
• el **proceso de datos** data processing

procurar *verb* **[17]**
procurar hacer algo to try to do something
Procura terminarlo para el viernes. Try to finish it by Friday.

la **producción** *fem noun*
production

producir *verb* **[60]**
1 **to produce**
producir coches to produce cars
2 **to cause**
La tormenta produjo daños importantes. The storm caused extensive damage.

el **producto** *masc noun*
product
un producto químico a chemical product
productos alimenticios foodstuffs
• el **producto lácteo** dairy product

productor *masc adjective*, **productora** *fem* ▷ see **productor** *noun*
producing
países productores de petróleo oil-producing countries

el **productor** *masc noun*, la **productora** *fem* ▷ see **productor** *adj*
producer

produje, **produzca**, **etc** *verb* ▷ **producir**

el & la **profe** *masc & fem noun*
teacher (*informal*)

la **profesión** *fem noun*
profession, **trade**
Es arquitecta de profesión. She's an architect by profession.
Era fontanero de profesión. He was a plumber by trade.
Profesión: guardia jurado Occupation: Security guard

profesional *masc & fem adjective*
professional
Es fotógrafa profesional. She's a professional photographer.

el **profesor** *masc noun*, la **profesora** *fem*
1 **teacher** (*in a secondary school*)
Soy profesor de francés. I'm a teacher of French.
2 **lecturer** (*in a university*)

la **profundidad** *fem noun*
depth

profundo *masc adjective*, **profunda** *fem*
deep
un río muy profundo a very deep river
una laguna poco profunda a shallow lake

𝄞 el **programa** *masc noun*
1 **programme** (*on TV, radio*)
un programa sobre la pobreza a programme about poverty
2 (*Computers*) **program**
Puedes bajar el programa gratis. You can download the program free.
• el **programa informático** computer program

el **programador** *masc noun*, la **programadora** *fem*
programmer

programar *verb* [17]
to program (*a computer*)

progresar *verb* [17]
to progress

el **progreso** *masc noun*
progress
hacer progresos to make progress

𝄞 **prohibido** *masc adjective*, **prohibida** *fem*
forbidden
Está terminantemente prohibido. It's strictly forbidden.
'Prohibido fumar' 'No smoking'
'Prohibido el paso', **'Prohibida la entrada'** 'No entry'
'Prohibido pisar el césped' 'Keep off the grass'

𝄞 **prohibir** *verb* [58]
to prohibit
Se prohíbe la entrada a menores de dieciséis años. No admission to persons under 16.
Nos han prohibido escribirnos. They've forbidden us to write to each other.

prolongar *verb* [28]
to prolong

prolongarse *reflexive verb* [28]
to go on (*matches, parties*)

el **promedio** *masc noun*
average
un promedio de quince libras por semana an average of fifteen pounds a week
una vez a la semana como promedio once a week on average

la **promesa** *fem noun*
promise
cumplir con una promesa to keep a promise
faltar a una promesa to break a promise

𝄞 **prometer** *verb* [18]
to promise
Prometió llamarme. She promised to call me.
Vendrá pronto, te lo prometo. He'll come soon, I promise.

el **prometido** *masc noun*, la **prometida** *fem*
1 **fiancé** (*man*)
2 **fiancée** (*woman*)

la **promoción** *fem noun*
promotion

𝄞 el **pronombre** *masc noun*
pronoun

𝄞 el **pronóstico** *masc noun*
1 **forecast** (*for weather, events*)
2 **prognosis** (*for illness*)
• el **pronóstico del tiempo** weather forecast

𝄞 **pronto** *masc adjective*, **pronta** *fem*
▷ see **pronto** *adv*
prompt
una pronta respuesta a prompt reply
Le deseo una pronta mejoría. I wish her a speedy recovery.

𝄞 **pronto** *adverb* ▷ see **pronto** *adj*
1 **soon**
Vengan tan pronto como sea posible. Come as soon as possible.
¡Hasta pronto! See you soon!
2 **quickly**
Respondieron muy pronto. They answered very quickly.
3 **early**
Se marcharon pronto. They left early.
4 **de pronto** all of a sudden

la **pronunciación** *fem noun*
pronunciation

pronunciar *verb* [17]
to pronounce
¿Cómo se pronuncia este nombre? How do you pronounce this name?

la **propaganda** *fem noun*
1 **advertising**
hacer propaganda de un producto to advertise a product
2 **propaganda** (*in politics*)

la **propiedad** *fem noun*
property
ser propiedad de alguien to belong to somebody
Es propiedad del estado. It's state property.
• la **propiedad privada** private property

el **propietario** *masc noun*, la **propietaria** *fem*
owner
El propietario vive en el sótano. The owner lives in the basement.
Es propietaria de cinco hoteles. She owns five hotels.

la **propina** *fem noun*
tip
Le dejé dos euros de propina. I left him a two euro tip.

propio *masc adjective*, **propia** *fem*
1 **own**
mi propio hermano my own brother
Tiene coche propio. She has her own car.
2 (*for emphasis*) **La propia Elena lo admitió.** Elena herself admitted it.
El propio director se equivocó. The headmaster himself made a mistake.

proponer *verb* **[11]**
1 **to suggest**
Nos propuso ir a cenar fuera. He suggested we went out for dinner.
Propongo que vayas en tren. I suggest you go by train.
2 **to propose**
proponer una idea to propose an idea
proponer un trato to make a proposition
3 **to put forward** (*a candidate*)

proponerse *reflexive verb* **[11]**
1 **to set yourself a goal**
Me propuse encontrar un trabajo. I set myself the goal of finding a job.
Siempre consigue lo que se propone. He always achieves what he sets out to do.
¿Qué se proponen? What have they got in mind?
2 **to decide**
Se propuso ir a verlos. He decided to go and see them.

la **proporción** *fem noun*
proportion
en proporción in proportion
las proporciones del edificio the dimensions of the building

la **proposición** *fem noun*
proposal

el **propósito** *masc noun*
intention

la **prórroga** *fem noun*
1 **extension** (*of time limit*)
2 **extra time** (*in sports*)

el **prospecto** *masc noun*
1 **patient information leaflet** (*supplied with medicine*)
2 **advertising leaflet**

próspero *masc adjective*, **próspera** *fem*
1 **prosperous**
2 **¡Próspero Año Nuevo!** A prosperous New Year to you!

la **prostituta** *fem noun*
prostitute

el & la **protagonista** *masc & fem noun*
1 **leading player** (*in a play*)
2 **main character** (*in a film, a story*)
3 **leading figure**
los protagonistas de la guerra civil the leading figures in the civil war

la **protección** *fem noun*
protection

protector *masc adjective*, **protectora** *fem*
▷ see **protector** *noun*
1 **protective**
2 **Sociedad Protectora de Animales** Society for the Prevention of Cruelty to Animals

el **protector** *masc noun*, la **protectora** *fem*
▷ see **protector** *adj*
protector

proteger *verb* **[3]**
to protect
Te protegerá del frío. It will protect you from the cold.

protegerse *reflexive verb* **[3]**
to protect yourself

protegido *masc adjective*, **protegida** *fem*
protected

la **protesta** *fem noun*
protest
en señal de protesta in protest

protestante *masc & fem adjective & noun*
1 **Protestant**
2 **un & una protestante** Protestant

WORD TIP Adjectives and nouns for religion do not have capital letters in Spanish.

protestar *verb* **[17]**
to protest

el **provecho** *masc noun*
1 **benefit**
Siempre piensa en su propio provecho. He always thinks of his own interests.
sacar provecho de algo to benefit from something

Sacó mucho provecho de su viaje a Paris. He greatly benefited from his trip to Paris.
2 ¡Buen provecho! Enjoy your meal!

proveniente *masc & fem adjective*
personas provenientes de otros países people from other countries

el **proverbio** *masc noun*
proverb

♂ la **provincia** *fem noun*
province
una ciudad de provincias a provincial town

provisional *masc & fem adjective*
provisional

provocador *masc adjective*, **provocadora** *fem*
▷ see **provocador** *noun*
provocative

el **provocador** *masc noun*, la **provocadora** *fem*
▷ see **provocador** *adj*
political agitator

♂ **provocar** *verb* [31]
1 to provoke (*a person*)
2 to cause (*an explosion, fire*)
Provocaron el incendio forestal. They caused the forest fire.

la **proximidad** *fem noun*
proximity

♂ **próximo** *masc adjective*, **próxima** *fem*
1 next
la próxima semana next week
la próxima parada the next stop
2 (*in time*) en fecha próxima in the near future
Ya está próximo su aniversario. It will soon be their anniversary.

♂ el **proyecto** *masc noun*
1 project
2 plan
¿Qué proyectos tienes para el verano? What are your plans for the summer?
3 Tengo varios trabajos en proyecto. I've got several jobs lined up.

el **proyector** *masc noun*
projector

prudente *masc & fem adjective*
sensible
Sé prudente conduciendo. Drive carefully.

♂ la **prueba** *fem noun* ▷ see **prueba** *verb*
1 proof
No tienen pruebas. They have no proof.
2 test
3 hacer la prueba to try
Hice la prueba y funcionó. I tried and it worked.
Haz la prueba de limpiarlo con lejía. Try cleaning it with bleach.
4 a prueba on trial
unos trabajadores a prueba workers on probation
5 a prueba de ... ...-proof
a prueba de balas bullet-proof
a prueba de agua waterproof

♂ , **prueba**, **etc** *verb* ▷ see **prueba** *noun* ▷ **probar**

♂ el **psicólogo** *masc noun*, la **psicóloga** *fem*
psychologist

♂ el & la **psiquiatra** *masc & fem noun*
psychiatrist

publicar *verb* [31]
to publish

la **publicidad** *fem noun*
1 publicity
2 advertising

♂ **público** *masc adjective*, **pública** *fem*
▷ see **público** *noun*
public
el transporte público public transport

♂ el **público** *masc noun* ▷ see **público** *adj*
1 public
Prefiere no cantar en público. She prefers not to sing in public.
2 audience

♂ **pude**, **pudo**, **etc** *verb* ▷ **poder**

pudrir *verb* [59]
to rot

pudrirse *reflexive verb* [59]
to rot

♂ el **pueblo** *masc noun*
1 village
2 small town
3 people
el pueblo español the Spanish people

♂ el **puente** *masc noun*
1 bridge
2 hacer puente to take a long weekend
- el **puente aéreo** shuttle service
- el **puente colgante** suspension bridge
- el **puente levadizo** drawbridge
- el **puente peatonal** footbridge

♂ la **puerca** *fem noun*
pig, sow

el **puerco** *masc noun*
pig, boar

el **puerro** *masc noun*
leek

la **puerta** *fem noun*
1 **door**
Llaman a la puerta. Someone's knocking at the door.
Quedamos en la puerta del cine. We arranged to meet outside the cinema.
2 **gate**
la puerta del jardín the garden gate
- la **puerta de embarque** gate (*in an airport*)
- la **puerta giratoria** revolving door
- la **puerta principal** main door
- la **puerta trasera** back door

el **puerto** *masc noun*
1 **port**
2 **harbour**
- el **puerto de montaña** mountain pass
- el **puerto deportivo** marina
- el **puerto marítimo** seaport
- el **puerto pesquero** fishing port

Puerto Rico *masc noun*
Puerto Rico

puertorriqueño *masc adjective & noun*, **puertorriqueña** *fem adjective & noun*
1 **Puerto Rican**
2 **un puertorriqueño, una puertorriqueña** Puerto Rican

WORD TIP Adjectives and nouns for nationality and regional origin do not have capital letters in Spanish.

pues *conjunction*
1 **well**
Pues bien, como te iba diciendo ... Well, as I was telling you ...
Pues no estoy seguro. Well, I'm really sure.
Pues mira, ahora no me acuerdo. Well, look, I can't remember now.
2 (*for emphasis*) **¡Pues no vayas!** Well, don't go then!
Pues si no te gusta el libro, no lo leas. If you don't like the book, don't read it then.
¡Pues claro! Of course!
¡Pues claro que no! Of course not!
'¿Lo querías tú?'—'¡Pues sí!' 'Did you want it?'—'Yes, of course I did!'

puesto *masc adjective*, **puesta** *fem*
▷ see **puesto** *noun, conj*
1 **set** (*tables, cutlery*)
La mesa estaba puesta. The table was laid.
2 **on** (*clothes*)
Llevaba el abrigo puesto. I had my coat on.

el **puesto** *masc noun* ▷ see **puesto** *adj, conj*
1 **position**
llegar en primer puesto to finish in first position
Sacó el primer puesto en el examen. She came top in the exam.
2 **job**
un puesto fijo a permanent job
puestos vacantes vacancies
Perdió su puesto de trabajo. He lost his job.
3 **stall** (*in a market*)
- el **puesto de socorro** first-aid post
- el **puesto de trabajo** job

puesto *conjunction* ▷ see **puesto** *adj, noun*
puesto que ... since ...
Puesto que no ha venido, me voy. Since he hasn't come, I'm leaving.

la **pulga** *fem noun*
flea

la **pulgada** *fem noun*
inch
una pantalla de diecisiete pulgadas a seventeen inch screen

el **pulgar** *masc noun*
thumb

pulir *verb* **[19]**
to polish

el **pulmón** *masc noun*
lung
Padece de los pulmones. He has lung problems.

el **pulpo** *masc noun*
octopus

pulsar *verb* **[17]**
1 **to press** (*a key, a button*)
2 **to pluck** (*a string*)

la **pulsera** *fem noun*
1 **bracelet**
2 **watchstrap**

el **pulso** *masc noun*
1 **pulse**
Le tomó el pulso. He took her pulse.
2 **tener buen pulso** to have a steady hand
Me temblaba el pulso. My hand was shaking.
3 **a pulso**
dibujar algo a pulso to draw something freehand
Lo levantó a pulso. He lifted it with his hands.
4 **echar un pulso** to arm-wrestle

la **punta** *fem noun*
1 **point** (*of a knife, a needle*)
Acaba en punta. It's pointed.
2 **tip** (*of pencil, tongue, finger, etc*)
3 **end**
a la otra punta del pasillo at the other end of the corridor
4 **las puntas** ends (*of hair*)
cortarse las puntas to have your hair trimmed
tener las puntas abiertas to have split ends
5 **sacar punta a un lápiz** to sharpen a pencil

la **puntada** *fem noun*
stitch

el **puntapié** *masc noun*
kick
darle un puntapié a alguien to kick someone

la **puntería** *fem noun*
aim (*in shooting*)
Tiene buena puntería. He's a good shot.

la **puntilla** *fem noun*
1 **ponerse de puntillas** to stand on tiptoe
andar de puntillas to walk on tiptoe
2 **lace edging**

♪ el **punto** *masc noun*
1 **point**
punto por punto point by point
hasta cierto punto up to a point
Llevan tres puntos de ventaja. They're three points ahead.
Es mi punto débil. It's my weak point.
2 **estar a punto de hacer algo** to be about to do something
Estaba a punto de salir cuando me llamó. I was about to leave when he called me.
3 **dot**
el punto sobre la 'i' the dot on the 'i'
rosa.ramirez@easycom.com (*said as rosa* **punto** *ramirez* **arroba** *easycom* **punto** *com*)
4 (*in time expressions*) **en punto** on the dot
a las dos en punto at two on the dot
llegar en punto to arrive exactly on time
5 **stitch**
de punto knitted
una falda de punto a knitted skirt
hacer punto to knit
6 (*talking about food*) **estar algo en su punto** to be just right
La carne está en su punto. The meat is just right.
- el **punto de vista** point of view
- el **punto final** full stop (*in punctuation*)
- el **punto muerto** neutral (*gear*)
- el **punto y coma** semicolon

♪ la **puntocom** *fem noun*
una puntocom a dot-com company

el **punto negro** *masc noun*
1 **black spot** (*for accidents*)
2 **blackhead** (*on skin*)

♪ la **puntuación** *fem noun*
1 **punctuation**
2 **score** (*in sports*)
Nuestro equipo obtuvo la máxima puntuación. Our team got the highest score.
3 **marks** (*in an exam*)

puntual *masc & fem adjective*
punctual
ser puntual to be always on time
Llegaron puntuales. They arrived on time.

♪ el **puñetazo** *masc noun*
punch
Me dio un puñetazo. He punched me.
Di un puñetazo en la mesa. I thumped on the table with my fist.

♪ el **puño** *masc noun*
1 **fist**
Cerró el puño. He clenched his fist.
2 **cuff** (*of a shirt*)
3 **handle** (*of a tool*)

♪ la **pupila** *fem noun*
pupil (*of your eye*)

♪ el **pupitre** *masc noun*
desk (*in school*)

el **puré** *masc noun*
purée
- el **puré de guisantes** pea soup
- el **puré de patatas** mashed potatoes

♪ **puro** *masc adjective*, **pura** *fem*
▷ see **puro** *noun*
pure
el aire puro del campo the pure country air
Es de pura lana. It's made of pure wool.
la pura verdad the simple truth
de puro aburrimiento out of sheer boredom

♪ el **puro** *masc noun* ▷ see **puro** *adj*
cigar

♪ **púrpura** *masc & fem adjective*
purple

♪ **puse**, **puso**, **etc** *verb* ▷ **poner**

♪ el **puzzle** *masc noun*
jigsaw puzzle

Spanish–English

a b c d e f g h i j k l m n ñ o p q r s t u v w x y z

Q q

que *pronoun* ▷ see **que** *conj*
1 **who**
el hombre que me lo dijo the man who told me
los que están interesados those who are interested
2 **which, that**
el libro que recomendé the book which I recommended
la marca que me gusta the brand (that) I like
3 **el que prefiero** the one (that) I prefer
las que vimos ayer the ones (that) we saw yesterday

que *conjunction* ▷ see **que** *pron*
1 **that**
Sé que le gusta. I know (that) he likes it.
Confirmó que viene. She confirmed that she's coming.
Dijo que no lo necesitaba. She said (that) she didn't need it.
Nos pidió que le ayudásemos. He asked us to help him.
2 (*in comparisons*) **than**
Es más alto que yo. He's taller than me.
3 (*in wishes*) **Que te mejores pronto.** Get well soon.
Que pases unas buenas vacaciones. Have a nice holiday.
4 (*in orders*) **Que pasen.** Show them in.
¡Que te calles! Shut up!
5 (*for emphasis*) **¡Que es mío!** I'm telling you it's mine!
'¿Te importa?'—'¡Que no!' 'Do you mind?'—'I've already told you that I don't!'
¡Que te he dicho que sí me gusta! I've already told you I like it!
6 (*expressing surprise*) **¿Que tiene veinte años?** She's twenty?
7 **yo que tú ...** if I were you ...

qué *adjective* ▷ see **qué** *adv, pron*
1 **which**
¿Qué abrigo es el tuyo? Which coat is yours?
¿Qué países visitaste? What countries did you visit?
2 **what** (*in exclamations*)
¡Qué casa tan bonita! What a pretty house!
¡Qué ojos tan grandes tienes! What big eyes you have!

qué *adverb* ▷ see **qué** *adj, pron*
¡Qué bonito! How nice!
¡Qué bien! Great!
¡Qué bien toca! Doesn't he play well!
¡Qué egoísta eres! You're so selfish!

qué *pronoun* ▷ see **qué** *adj, adv*
1 **what**
¿Qué es eso? What's that?
¿A qué te refieres? What are you referring to?
2 **¿Qué?** What?
3 **¿Qué tal?** How are you doing?
¿Qué tal va? How's it going?
¿Qué hay? How are things?
¿Qué hay de nuevo? What's new?
4 **¡Qué va!** No way!

WORD TIP *qué*, with an accent, is used in questions and for emphasis.

el **quebradero** *masc noun*
worry

el **quebrado** *masc noun*
fraction

quebrar *verb* **[29]**
to break
Me ha quebrado el lápiz. He's broken my pencil.
¡No lo quiebres! Don't break it!

quedar *verb* **[17]**
1 **to be left**
Quedan tres paquetes. There are three packets left.
¿Te queda dinero? Do you have any money left?
No queda leche. There's no milk left.
Quedaban quince kilómetros. There were still fiteen kilometres to go.
2 (*in time expressions*) **Aún queda tiempo.** There's still time.
Aún quedan dos días. There are still two days to go.
¿Cuánto tiempo me queda? How much time do I have left?
Quedaban quince minutos para el final de la clase. It was still fifteen minutes till the end of the class.
3 (*saying what happened*) **Quedó viudo.** He was widowed.
Quedaron solos. They were left alone.
Quedó ciego tras el accidente. He was left

a b c d e f g h i j k l m n ñ o p q r s t u v w x y z

blind after the accident.
quedar en último lugar to end up last

4 (*about how something looks*) **Así queda mejor.** It's better like this.
Queda muy feo con esa tela. It's horrible with that material.

5 (*arranging to meet*) **Quedamos en la plaza.** We arranged to meet in the square.
¿Te apetece quedar? Would you like to meet?
¿Quedamos para el sábado? Shall we meet on Saturday?

6 (*about clothes, hairstyles, etc*) **Me queda apretado.** It's too tight on me.
¿Te queda bien? Does it fit you?
Ese color te queda muy bien. That colour really suits you.
Esos vaqueros te quedan fenomenal. Those jeans look great on you.

7 (*impressions*) **Quiere quedar bien con mi familia.** She wants to make a good impression on my family.

8 **Va a quedar mal si no lo hacemos.** It will look bad if we don't do it.
Quedamos muy mal con sus padres. We made a bad impression on her parents.

9 **quedar en algo** to agree on something
Quedamos en vernos hoy. We agreed to see each other today.

10 **to be** (*talking about where something is*)
Queda bastante lejos. It's quite a long way away.
Queda cerca de mi casa. It's near my house.
¿Dónde queda la estación? Where is the station?

quedarse *reflexive verb* **[17]**

1 **to stay**
Se quedó en la cama. He stayed in bed.
Prefiero quedarme en casa. I'd rather stay at home.
quedarse con algo to keep something
Se quedó con mi revista. He kept my magazine.
Quédese con la vuelta. Keep the change.

2 (*saying what happened*) **quedarse ciego** to go blind
quedarse calvo to lose your hair
quedarse asombrado to be amazed
Se quedó dormido. He fell asleep.
quedarse callado to remain silent
quedarse sin trabajo to lose your job

WORD TIP If the person is female, the adjective is *ciega*, *calva*, *asombrada*, etc.

♪ la **queja** *fem noun*
complaint, **gripe**
presentar una queja to make a complaint
Presentó una queja al gerente por el mal servicio. She made a complaint to the manager about the bad service.
Estamos hartos de sus quejas. We're sick of his complaining.

los **quehaceres** *plural masc noun*
chores

♪ **quejarse** *reflexive verb* **[17]**
to complain
Se quejan de la comida. They complain about the food.
Se quejó de que tardé mucho. She complained about how long I took.

quemado *masc adjective*, **quemada** *fem*
burnt

la **quemadura** *fem noun*
burn

♪ **quemar** *verb* **[17]**

1 **to burn**

2 **to scald**
El vapor me ha quemado la mano. The steam has scalded my hand.

3 **to be very hot**
La sopa quema mucho. The soup's really hot.

4 **quemar un motor** to burn out an engine

5 **quemar calorías** to burn up calories

6 **¡Cómo quema el sol!** The sun's really scorching!

quemarse *reflexive verb* **[17]**

1 **to burn yourself**
Me quemé la mano. I burnt my hand.

2 **to scald yourself**

3 **to get burnt**
¡Cómo te has quemado! You've really got burnt! (*in the sun*)
El mantel se quemó un poco. The tablecloth got a bit burnt.

4 **to burn down**
La casa se quemó toda. The house burned down.

quepo, **quepa**, **quepamos**, **etc** *verb* ▷ **caber**

♪ **querer** *verb* **[12]**

1 **to want**
Queremos volver a casa. We want to go home.
No quiero ir al cine. I don't want to go to the cinema.
¿Qué quieres para tu cumpleaños? What do you want for your birthday?
¿Quieres apagar la tele, por favor? Would you mind switching off the television, please? ▸▸

Spanish-English

querer que alguien haga algo to want somebody to do something
Quiero que me lo compres. I want you to buy it for me.

WORD TIP *querer que* is followed by a verb in the subjunctive.

2 **to love**
Te quiero. I love you.
3 (*making offers*) **¿Quieres beber algo?** Would you like something to drink?
Si quieres voy más tarde. If you like I'll go later.
4 (*in shops, cafés, etc*) **Yo quiero un café.** I'll have a coffee.
Quisiera ver vestidos largos. I would like to see some long dresses.
Quisiera reservar una mesa para cuatro. I'd like to book a table for four.
5 **querer decir algo** to mean something
¿Qué quieres decir? What do you mean?
¿Qué quiere decir esto? What does this mean?

quererse *reflexive verb* **[17]**
to love each other
Si os queréis tanto ¿por qué no os casáis? If you love each other so much, why don't you get married?

querido *masc adjective*, **querida** *fem*
dear
Querido Pablo: Dear Pablo, (*starting a letter*)

querrá, **querré**, **querría**, **etc** *verb* ▷ **querer**

el **queso** *masc noun*
cheese
- el **queso para untar** cheese spread
- el **queso rallado** grated cheese

la **quiebra** *fem noun*
bankruptcy

quien *pronoun* ▷ see **quién** *pron*
1 **who**
Creo que fue Iñaki quien lo sugirió. I think it was Iñaki who suggested it.
No fui yo quien lo dijo. It wasn't me who said it.
Ellos son quienes no quisieron ir. They're the ones who didn't want to go.
(*when* **quien** *may not be translated*) **la chica con quien bailé anoche** the girl I danced with last night
las personas con quienes habló the people he spoke to
2 **whom**, **who**
Isabel, a quien vi ayer ... Isabel, whom I saw yesterday ...

quién *pronoun* ▷ see **quien** *pron*
1 **who**
¿Quién es? Who is it?
¿Quiénes son esos chavales? Who are those lads?
¡Quién lo hubiese dicho! Who would have said!
2 **which**
¿Quién de vosotros es Carlos? Which of you is Carlos?
3 **¿De quién?** Whose?
¿De quién es esta cartera? Whose is this wallet?
¿De quiénes son estas motos? Who do these motorbikes belong to?

WORD TIP *quién* with an accent is used for questions (¿...?).

quienquiera *pronoun*
whoever

quiera, **quiere**, **etc** *verb* ▷ **querer**

quieto *masc adjective*, **quieta** *fem*
still
¡Estate quieto! Keep still!

WORD TIP *quieto* does not mean *quiet* in English; for the meaning of *quiet* ▷ **silencioso**.

la **química** *fem noun* ▷ see **químico** *adj*, **químico** *noun*
chemistry
Estudié química y física. I studied chemistry and physics.

químico *masc adjective*, **química** *fem* ▷ see **química** *noun*, **químico** *noun*
chemical

el **químico** *masc noun*, la **química** *fem* ▷ see **química** *noun*, **químico** *adj*
chemist

quince *number*
1 **fifteen**
Tiene quince años. He's fifteen (years old).
2 **fifteenth** (*in dates*)
Hoy estamos a quince. It's the fifteenth today.
Llegará el día quince. She'll arrive on the fifteenth.
3 **quince días** a fortnight

el **quinceañero** *masc noun*, la **quinceañera** *fem*
teenager

la **quincena** *fem noun*
una quincena a fortnight
la primera quincena de mayo the first two weeks in May

a b c d e f g h i j k l m n ñ o p q r s t u v w x y z

la **quiniela** *fem noun*
pools coupon
rellenar una quiniela to fill in a pools coupon
jugar a las quinielas to do the pools

♪ **quinientos**, **quinientas** *number*
five hundred
quinientos cinco five hundred and five

quinto *masc adjective*, **quinta** *fem*
fifth
el quinto piso the fifth floor
llegar en quinto lugar to finish in fifth position

♪ el **quiosco** *masc noun*
1 **news-stand**
2 **el quiosco de los helados** the ice cream stand
Está frente al quiosco de bebidas. It's opposite the drinks stand.
3 **kiosk**

♪ el **quiosquero** *masc noun*, la **quiosquera** *fem*
1 **newspaper vendor**
2 **kiosk attendant**

quirúrgico *masc adjective*, **quirúrgica** *fem*
surgical
una intervención quirúrgica a surgical operation

♪ **quise**, **quisiera**, **quiso**, **etc** *verb* ▷ **querer**

el **quitaesmalte** *masc noun*
nail varnish remover

el **quitanieves** *masc noun*, *pl:* los **quitanieves**
snowplough

♪ **quitar** *verb* **[17]**
1 **to take off**
Quita los pies de la mesa. Take your feet off the table.
No puedo quitar la tapa. I can't get the lid off.
2 **Le quité los zapatos al niño.** I took the child's shoes off.
3 **quitarle algo a alguien** to take something from someone
Le quitaron la cartera. They took his wallet.
4 **to take away**
Quita esa silla de ahí. Take that chair away from there.
Le han quitado el carnet de conducir. They've taken his driving licence away.
5 **to remove**
quitar la suciedad to remove the dirtiness
quitar el polvo to dust

quitarse *reflexive verb* **[17]**
1 **to come out** (*a stain, mark*)
2 **to go away** (*a pain*)
3 **quitarse algo** to take something off
Se quitó el abrigo. He took his coat off.

♪ **quizá**, **quizás** *adverb*
perhaps

Spanish–English

R r

el **rábano** *masc noun*
radish

la **rabia** *fem noun*
1 **dar rabia a alguien** to annoy somebody
Eso me da mucha rabia. That makes me very annoyed.
Le dio mucha rabia que no se lo dijeran. It really annoyed him that they didn't tell him.
2 **tenerle rabia a alguien** to hate somebody
Le tengo rabia. I hate him.
3 **rabies**

el **rabo** *masc noun*
tail

la **racha** *fem noun*
1 **gust** (*of wind*)
2 **una racha de mala suerte** a spell of bad luck
pasar una mala racha to go through a bad patch
tener una buena racha to be on a winning streak

el **racimo** *masc noun*
bunch
un racimo de uvas a bunch of grapes

la **ración** *fem noun*
portion
una ración de gambas a portion of prawns (*in a tapas bar*)

racionar *verb* **[17]**
to ration

el **racismo** *masc noun*
racism

racista *masc & fem adjective & noun*
1 **racist**
2 **el & la racista** racist

el **radar** *masc noun*
1 **radar**
2 **speed camera**

la **radiación** *fem noun*
radiation

radiactivo *masc adjective*, **radiactiva** *fem*
radioactive

el **radiador** *masc noun*
radiator

la **radio** *fem noun* ▷ see **radio** *masc noun*
radio
escuchar la radio to listen to the radio
oír algo por la radio to hear something on the radio
poner la radio to switch on the radio

el **radio** *masc noun* ▷ see **radio** *fem noun*
1 **radius**
2 (*Latin America*) **radio**

el **radiocassette** *masc noun*
radio cassette player

la **radiografía** *fem noun*
X-ray
hacerse una radiografía to have an X-ray taken

la **ráfaga** *fem noun*
1 **gust**
una ráfaga de viento a gust of wind
2 **burst** (*of gunfire*)
una ráfaga de ametralladora a burst of machine-gun fire

la **raíz** *fem noun*, *pl:* las **raíces**
root
echar raíces to take root
a raíz de as a result of
• **la raíz cuadrada** square root

rallado *masc adjective*, **rallada** *fem*
1 **grated**
2 **pan rallado** breadcrumbs

el **rallador** *masc noun*
grater

rallar *verb* **[17]**
to grate

la **rama** *fem noun*
branch

el **ramo** *masc noun*
1 **bunch** (*of flowers*)
2 **bouquet**

la **rampa** *fem noun*
ramp
• **la rampa de lanzamiento** launch pad

la **rana** *fem noun*
frog

a b c d e f g h i j k l m n ñ o p q r s t u v w x y z

ℰ la **ranura** *fem noun*
coin slot
introducir la moneda en la ranura to put the coin in the slot

el **rape** *masc noun*
1 **monkfish**
2 **llevar el pelo cortado al rape** to have your hair closely cropped

ℰ **rápidamente** *adverb*
quickly

ℰ **rápido** *masc adjective*, **rápida** *fem*
▷ see **rápido** *adverb, noun*
1 **quick**, **fast**
la comida rápida fast food
2 **rapid**

ℰ **rápido** *adverb* ▷ see **rápido** *adjective & noun*
fast, **quickly**
Lo más rápido que podía. As fast as I could.

ℰ el **rápido** *masc noun* ▷ see **rápido** *adjective, adverb*
express train

la **raqueta** *fem noun*
1 **racket**
2 **snowshoe**

raramente *adverb*
rarely

ℰ **raro** *masc adjective*, **rara** *fem*
1 **strange**
¡Qué raro que no venga! How strange that he hasn't come!
2 **rare**
Es raro que vengan turistas a esta zona. It's rare for tourists to come to this area.

el **rascacielos** *invarable masc noun*
skyscraper

rascar *verb* **[31]**
to scratch

rascarse *reflexive verb* **[31]**
to scratch yourself
Se rascó la nariz. He scratched his nose.

rasgar *verb* **[28]**
to tear

el **rasguño** *masc noun*
scratch

el **rastrillo** *masc noun*
rake

el **rastro** *masc noun*
1 **trail**
sin dejar rastro without a trace
2 **flea market**

la **rata** *fem noun*
rat

ℰ el **ratero** *masc noun*, la **ratera** *fem*
1 **pickpocket**
2 **petty thief**

ℰ el **rato** *masc noun*
1 **while**
dentro de un rato in a while
después de un rato after a while
al poco rato soon afterwards
al rato after a while
Tardaré un rato en hacerlo. It will take me a while to do it.
Ya hace rato que se han ido. They went a while ago.
2 **time**
pasar el rato to kill time
Pasamos unos buenos ratos allí. We had good times there.
¿Qué haces en tus ratos libres? What do you do in your spare time?

ℰ el **ratón** *masc noun*
mouse

la **raya** *fem noun*
1 **line**
2 **dash** (*in punctuation*)
3 **parting** (*in your hair*)
hacerse la raya to part your hair
4 **a rayas** striped (*dress, cloth*)
una falda a rayas a striped skirt
5 **skate** (*kind of fish*)

rayar *verb* **[17]**
1 **to scratch**
2 **rayar en** to border on
Raya en lo ridículo. It's bordering on the ridiculous.

el **rayo** *masc noun*
1 **ray**
un rayo de luz a ray of light
2 **bolt of lightning**
- el **rayo láser** laser beam
- los **rayos X** X-rays

la **raza** *fem noun*
1 **race**
2 **breed**
un perro de raza a pedigree dog

Spanish–English

♪ la **razón** *fem noun*
1 **reason**
por alguna razón for some reason
con razón with good reason
por razones de salud for health reasons
¿Por qué razón se marchó? Why did he go away?
2 **tener razón** to be right
Tienes razón. You're right.
No tienes razón en eso. You're wrong about that.
darle la razón a alguien to agree that somebody is right
Nos dieron la razón. They agreed with us.
3 **reason, sanity**
perder la razón to lose your mind
4 (*on notices*) **Razón: 279452** Call 279452 for information.

razonable *masc & fem adjective*
reasonable

la **reacción** *fem noun*
reaction

reacio *masc adjective*, **reacia** *fem*
reluctant

el **reactor** *masc noun*
1 **reactor**
2 **jet**

real *masc & fem adjective*
1 **real**
2 **true**
una historia real a true story
3 **royal**
el palacio real the royal palace

la **realidad** *fem noun*
reality
hacerse realidad to become true
en realidad in fact

realista *masc & fem adjective*
1 **realistic**
Es muy realista. He's very realistic.
2 **royalist**

el **realizador** *masc noun*, la **realizadora** *fem*
producer

realizar *verb* **[22]**
1 **to carry out** (*a task*)
2 **to make** (*a visit, a trip*)
3 **to fulfil** (*a dream*)

realizarse *reflexive verb* **[22]**
1 **to come true** (*dreams*)
2 **to fulfil yourself**

♪ la **rebaja** *fem noun*
1 **reduction**
Lo rebajó a cuarenta euros. He reduced it to forty euros.
hacer una rebaja to give a reduction
Me hizo una rebaja de diez euros. He gave me a ten euro reduction.
2 **las rebajas** the sales
Esa tienda está de rebajas. This shop has a sale on.

rebajar *verb* **[17]**
1 **to bring down** (*prices*)
2 **to reduce the price of** (*an item*)
Todas las faldas están rebajadas. All the skirts are reduced.

la **rebanada** *fem noun*
slice

el **rebaño** *masc noun*
1 **flock** (*of sheep*)
2 **herd** (*of goats*)

la **rebeca** *fem noun*
cardigan

rebelarse *reflexive verb* **[17]**
to rebel

rebelde *masc & fem adjective*
▷ see **rebelde** *noun*
1 **rebel**
2 **unruly** (*child*)
3 **una tos rebelde** a persistent cough

el & la **rebelde** *masc & fem noun*
▷ see **rebelde** *adjective*
rebel

la **rebelión** *fem noun*
rebellion

rebobinar *verb* **[17]**
to rewind (*tapes*)

rebotar *verb* **[17]**
1 **to bounce**
La pelota rebotó en el poste. The ball bounced off the post.
2 **to ricochet**

rebuznar *verb* **[17]**
to bray (*donkeys*)

el **recado** *masc noun*
1 **message**
Me han dejado un recado. They left a message for me.
2 **errand**
hacer un recado to go on an errand

a b c d e f g h i j k l m n ñ o p q r s t u v w x y z

recalentar *verb* **[29]**
1 **to reheat** (*food*)
2 **to overheat** (*engines*)

el **recambio** *masc noun*
1 **spare part**
2 **refill** (*for a pen*)

recargar *verb* **[28]**
1 **to recharge** (*batteries, etc*)
2 **to top up** (*mobile phones*)

la **recepción** *fem noun*
reception

el & la **recepcionista** *masc & fem noun*
receptionist

la **receta** *fem noun*
1 **recipe**
2 **prescription**

rechazar *verb* **[22]**
to turn down, **to reject**

recetar *verb* **[17]**
to prescribe

el **recibidor** *masc noun*
entrance hall

♪ **recibir** *verb* **[19]**
1 **to receive**
He recibido un menaje de texto de Lola. I've received a text from Lola.
2 **to get**
Recibí una llamada de Maricarmen. I got a phone call from Maricarmen.
3 **Lo recibieron con los brazos abiertos.** He was welcomed with open arms.
4 **ir a recibir a alguien** to go to meet somebody
Fuimos a recibirlos a la estación. We went to meet them at the station.
5 (*letter endings*) **Recibe un fuerte abrazo.** Best wishes
Reciba un cordial saludo. Yours sincerely

♪ el **recibo** *masc noun*
1 **receipt**
2 **bill** (*for water, electricity*)

el **reciclaje** *masc noun*
recycling (*of waste*)

reciclar *verb* **[17]**
to recycle

♪ **recién** *adverb*
1 **Pasteles recién hechos.** Freshly baked cakes.
'Recién pintado' 'Wet paint'
2 (*Latin America*) **just**, **only just**
• los **recién casados** newly-weds
• los **recién llegados** newcomers
• el **recién nacido** newborn baby

♪ **reciente** *masc & fem adjective*
recent

♪ **recientemente** *adverb*
recently

el **recipiente** *masc noun*
container

recitar *verb* **[17]**
to recite

la **reclamación** *fem noun*
1 **complaint**
hacer una reclamación to make a complaint
2 **claim**
hacer una reclamación al seguro to make a claim on insurance

♪ **reclamar** *verb* **[17]**
1 **to complain**
2 **to demand** (*rights, money, better conditions*)

♪ **recoger** *verb* **[3]**
1 **to pick up**
Recoge ese papel del suelo. Pick up that piece of paper off the floor.
Fui a recogerlos a la estación. I went to pick them up from the station.
2 **to tidy up**
Tienes que recoger tu habitación. You must tidy up your room.
recoger la mesa to clear the table
3 **to collect** (*money, signatures*)
4 **to pick** (*fruit, flowers*)

recogerse *reflexive verb* **[3]**
recogerse el pelo to tie your hair back

la **recogida** *fem noun*
collection (*of rubbish, mail*)

la **recomendación** *fem noun*
1 **recommendation**
2 **reference** (*for a job*)

♪ **recomendar** *verb* **[29]**
to recommend

la **recompensa** *fem noun*
reward

recompensar *verb* **[17]**
to reward

reconciliarse *reflexive verb* **[17]**
reconciliarse con alguien to make it up with somebody
Se ha reconciliado con su novia. He's made it up with his girlfriend.

reconocer *verb* **[35]**
1 **to recognize**
No la reconocí. I didn't recognize her.
2 **to admit** (*a mistake*)
3 **to examine** (*a patient*)

el **reconocimiento** *masc noun*
1 **recognition** (*of a voice, facts*)
2 **examination** (*of a patient*)
• el **reconocimiento médico** medical examination

reconozca, **reconozcas**, **etc** *verb* ▷ **reconocer**

el **récord** *masc noun*, *pl*: los **récords**
record

recordar *verb* **[24]**
1 **to remember**
Lo recuerdo muy bien. I remember it very well.
Recuerdo que terminamos pronto. I remember that we finished early.
2 **to remind**
Me recuerda a su madre. He reminds me of his mother.
3 **recordarle a alguien que haga algo** to remind somebody to do something
Recuérdale que compre pan. Remind him to buy bread.

recorrer *verb* **[18]**
1 **to cover** (*a distance*)
2 **to travel around** (*a country*)
3 **to go round** (*an exhibition, museum, etc*)

el **recorrido** *masc noun*
1 **distance**
2 **journey**
3 **route**

el **recreo** *masc noun*
break (*at school*)

la **recta** *fem noun*
straight line

el **rectángulo** *masc noun*
rectangle

recto *masc adjective*, **recta** *fem*
▷ see **recto** *adv*
1 **straight** (*lines*)
2 **honest**

recto *adverb* ▷ see **recto** *adj*
seguir todo recto to carry straight on
Siga todo recto hasta el semáforo. Carry straight on until the traffic lights.

recuerda, **recuerdo**, **etc** *verb* ▷ **recordar**

el **recuerdo** *masc noun*
1 **memory**
Tengo buenos recuerdos de Valencia. I've got happy memories of Valencia.
2 **souvenir**
'Recuerdo de España' 'Souvenir from Spain'
3 **recuerdos** *plural* regards, greetings
Dale recuerdos a tu hermana de mi parte. Say hello to your sister from me.

recuperar *verb* **[17]**
1 **to get back** (*money, strength*)
2 **recuperar tiempo** to make up for lost time

recuperarse *reflexive verb* **[17]**
recuperarse de una enfermedad to get well after an illness

la **red** *fem noun*
1 **net**
2 **network**
3 **la Red** the Net (*Internet*)

la **redacción** *fem noun*
1 **essay**
2 **editorial team** (*in a newspaper*)

el **redactor** *masc noun*, la **redactora** *fem*
editor

redondo *masc adjective*, **redonda** *fem*
round
en números redondos in round figures

la **reducción** *fem noun*
reduction

reducido *masc adjective*, **reducida** *fem*
1 **small** (*amount, size*)
2 **reduced** (*prices*)

reducir *verb* **[60]**
to reduce

reduje, **reduzca**, **reduzco**, **etc** *verb* ▷ **reducir**

reembolsar *verb* **[17]**
to refund

el **reembolso** *masc noun*
refund

reemplazar *verb* **[22]**
to replace
reemplazar a alguien to stand in for somebody
Me reemplazó durante las vacaciones. She stood in for me over the holidays.

el **reemplazo** *masc noun*
replacement

la **referencia** *fem noun*
reference
referencias references (*for a job*)
hacer referencia a to refer to
No hizo referencia al tema. He didn't refer to the subject.

referirse *reflexive verb* **[14]**
referirise a to refer to
Se refiere a ti. She's referring to you.
¿A qué te refieres? What are you referring to?

la **refinería** *fem noun*
refinery

reflejar *verb* **[17]**
to reflect

reflejarse *reflexive verb* **[17]**
to be reflected

el **reflejo** *masc noun*
1 **reflection**
2 **reflex**
3 **los reflejos** highlights (*in hair*)

la **reflexión** *fem noun*
reflection

reflexionar *verb* **[17]**
to think it over
Hay que reflexionar antes de tomar una decisión. We must think it over before we take a decision.

la **reforestación** *fem noun*
reforestation

la **reforma** *fem noun*
1 **reform** (*of laws, system, etc*)
2 **alteration** (*to a house, etc*)
'cerrado por reformas' 'closed for repairs'

reformar *verb* **[1]**
1 **to reform** (*a law, system, etc*)
2 **to alter** (*a house, etc*)
reformar la casa to do up the house

el **refrán** *masc noun*
saying

refrescante *masc & fem adjective*
refreshing

refrescar *verb* **[31]**
1 **to get cooler** (*weather*)
2 **to air** (*room*)
3 **to refresh** (*your memory*)

♪ el **refresco** *masc noun*
soft drink
tomar un referesco to have a soft drink

el **refrigerio** *masc noun*
light refreshments

el **refugiado** *masc noun*, la **refugiada** *fem*
refugee
un refugiado económico an economic refugee

refugiarse *reflexive verb* **[17]**
to take shelter
refugiarse de algo to take shelter from something
Nos refugiamos de la lluvia. We took shelter from the rain.

el **refugio** *masc noun*
shelter
dar refugio a alguien to give somebody shelter
un refugio de montaña a mountain refuge

la **regadera** *fem noun*
watering can

♪ **regalar** *verb* **[17]**
1 **to give** (*as a present*)
Mi tío me ha regalado un reloj. My uncle has given me a watch.
¿Qué vas a regalarle por Navidad? What are you going to give her for Christmas?
2 **to give away**
Están regalando bolígrafos. They're giving away ball-point pens.
¿Te gusta? Te lo regalo. Do you like it? You can have it.

♪ el **regalo** *masc noun*
1 **present**
un regalo de cumpleaños a birthday present
2 (*in promotions*) **de regalo: Compre dos y llévese uno de regalo.** Buy two and get one free.

regañar *verb* **[17]**
1 **to tell off**
Mi madre me regañó por llegar tarde. My mother told me off because I got home late.
2 **regañar con alguien** to quarrel with somebody
Ha regañado con su hermano. He's had an argument with his brother.

regar *verb* **[30]**
to water

♪ el **régimen** *masc noun*
diet
ponerse a régimen to go on a diet
Tengo que ponerme a régimen. I must go on a diet.

la **región** *fem noun*
region

regional *masc & fem adjective*
regional

registrar *verb* **[17]**
1 **to search**
Nos registraron. We were searched.
La policía registró la casa. The police searched the house.
2 **to go through**
Me registraron todos los papeles. They went through all my papers.
3 **to register** (*a birth, car*)
4 **to record** (*temperature*)

registrarse *reflexive verb* **[17]**
1 **to register**
2 **to check in** (*at a hotel*)
Se registró a las cinco. She checked in at five o'clock.

el **registro** *masc noun*
1 **search** (*by police, etc*)
2 **register**
• el **registro civil** registry office

la **regla** *fem noun*
1 **ruler** (*for measuring*)
2 **rule**
por regla general as a general rule
3 **estar con la regla** to have your period

el **reglamento** *masc noun*
regulations

regresar *verb* **[17]**
to return, **to come back**
Siempre regresan tarde. They always come back late.

el **regreso** *masc noun*
return

regular *adverb, masc & fem adjective*
1 **regular**
de tamaño regular regular-sized
'¿Qué tal está tu padre?'—'Regular.' 'How's your father?'—'So-so.'
2 **poor** (*mark*)
3 **por lo regular** as a general rule

la **regularidad** *fem noun*
regularity
con regularidad regularly

rehacer *verb* **[7]**
1 **rehacer algo** to do something again
2 **Rehizo su vida.** She rebuilt her life.

el & la **rehén** *masc & fem noun, pl:* **rehenes**
hostage

la **reina** *fem noun*
queen
la reina Sofía Queen Sofía
la reina de España the queen of Spain

el **reinado** *masc noun*
reign
durante el reinado del rey Juan Carlos in the reign of King Juan Carlos

reinar *verb* **[17]**
to reign

el **reino** *masc noun*
kingdom
el Reino Unido the United Kingdom

reír *verb* **[61]**
to laugh
echarse a reír to start laughing

reírse *reflexive verb* **[61]**
reírse de algo to laugh about something
Se están riendo de ti. They're laughing at you.
reírse a carcajadas to roar with laughter

la **reja** *fem noun*
1 **railing**
2 **grille**
estar entre rejas to be behind bars

la **relación** *fem noun*
1 **relationship**
Se ha roto su relación. Their relationshp has broken down.
2 **connection**
con relación a, **en relación con** compared to
con relación al año pasado compared to last year
• las **relaciones públicas** public relations

relacionado *masc adjective*, **relacionada** *fem*
related

relacionar *verb* **[17]**
to relate
relacionar algo con algo to relate something to something

relacionarse *reflexive verb* **[17]**
1 **to be related** (*facts, figures*)
2 **relacionarse con alguien** to get to know someone
Se relacionó con muchos deportistas. He got to know many sports people.

relajar *verb* **[17]**
to relax

relajarse *reflexive verb* **[17]**
to relax

el **relámpago** *masc noun*
flash of lightning

♂ la **religión** *fem noun*
religion

religioso *masc adjective*, **religiosa** *fem*
religious

♂ **rellenar** *verb* **[17]**
1 **rellenar un impreso** to fill in a form
2 **to stuff** (*a chicken, peppers*)
3 **to fill again**

relleno *masc adjective*, **rellena** *fem*
▷ see **relleno** *noun*
relleno de algo filled with something
stuffed (*chicken, peppers*)

el **relleno** *masc noun* ▷ see **relleno** *adjective*
1 **filling** (*for a pie*)
2 **stuffing** (*for a chicken*)

♂ el **reloj** *masc noun*
1 **clock**
2 **watch**
Mi reloj va atrasado. My watch is slow.
- el **reloj de pulsera** wristwatch
- el **reloj despertador** alarm clock
- el **reloj digital** digital clock

la **relojería** *fem noun*
shop selling watches and clocks

remar *verb* **[17]**
to row

el **remate** *masc noun*
1 **shot** (*in football*)
un remate de cabeza a header
2 **smash** (*in tennis*)

remediar *verb* **[17]**
1 **to help doing something**
No lo puede remediar. He can't help it.
2 **to put something right**
No pudimos remediarlo. We couldn't put it right.

el **remedio** *masc noun*
1 **remedy**
remedios naturales natural remedies
No hay más remedio. There's no other alternative.
2 (*Latin America*) **medicine**

remendar *verb* **[29]**
to mend (*clothes, etc*)

el **remite** *masc noun*
name and address (*of sender, for returning a letter*)

♂ el & la **remitente** *masc & fem noun*
sender (*of a letter*)

el **remo** *masc noun*
oar

remojar *verb* **[17]**
to soak

el **remojo** *masc noun*
poner algo en remojo to soak something
poner los garbanzos en remojo to put the chickpeas to soak

la **remolacha** *fem noun*
beetroot

remolcar *verb* **[31]**
to tow

el **remolino** *masc noun*
1 **whirlpool**
2 **whirlwind**

el **remolque** *masc noun*
1 **trailer**
2 **llevar algo a remolque** to tow something

el **remordimiento** *masc noun*
feeling of guilt
tener remordimientos de conciencia to feel guilty

remoto *masc adjective*, **remota** *fem*
remote

remover *verb* **[38]**
1 **to stir** (*a sauce, the soup*)
2 **to toss** (*a salad*)
3 **to turn over** (*soil*)

remueva, **remuevo**, **etc** *verb* ▷ **remover**

el **renacuajo** *masc noun*
tadpole

el **rencor** *masc noun*
guardarle rencor a alguien to bear someone a grudge

la **rendición** *fem noun*
surrender

rendir *verb* **[57]**
1 **to tire out**
2 **to be profitable** (*businesses*)
3 **to be productive** (*worker*)

rendirse *reflexive verb* **[57]**
to surrender
¿Te rindes? Do you give up?

♂ la **RENFE** *fem noun*
(*= Red Nacional de Ferrocarriles Españoles*) **the Spanish national rail network**

el **renglón** *masc noun*
line (*of print, text*)

la **renta** *fem noun*
1 **rent**
2 **income**

rentable *masc & fem adjective*
profitable

renovar *verb* **[1]**
1 **to renew** (*a passport, licence*)
2 **to renovate** (*a house, a room*)
3 **to update** (*your clothes*)

renunciar *verb* **[17]**
renunciar a to give up (*a right, an idea*)
renunciar a un puesto to resign from a job

la **reparación** *fem noun*
repair
un taller de reparaciones a repair shop

reparar *verb* **[17]**
1 **to repair**
2 **to mend** (*clothes*)
3 **reparar en algo** to notice something

repartir *verb* **[19]**
1 **to deliver**
Repartimos a domicilio. We make home deliveries.
2 **to hand out** (*leaflets, exam papers*)
3 **to share**
Lo repartiremos entre todos nosotros. We'll share it between us.

el **reparto** *masc noun*
1 **delivery**
2 **share-out**
hacer el reparto del dinero to share out the money
- el **reparto a domicilio** home delivery service

repasar *verb* **[17]**
1 **to revise**
repasar los apuntes to revise your notes
2 **to check** (*figures*)
3 **to clean** (*a room*)

el **repaso** *masc noun*
1 **revision**
darles un repaso a los apuntes to revise your notes
2 **check** (*for mistakes*)
3 **clean-up** (*of a room*)

repente *in phrase*
de repente all of a sudden

repentino *masc adjective*, **repentina** *fem*
sudden

la **repetición** *fem noun*
repetition
- la **repetición de la jugada** action replay

repetir *verb* **[57]**
1 **to repeat**
¿Puede repetirlo? Would you say that again?
2 **to have a second helping**
¿Quieres repetir? Would you like a second helping?

la **repisa** *fem noun*
1 **shelf**
2 **ledge** (*of a window*)
3 **mantlepiece** (*of chimney*)

repita, **repitió**, **repito**, **etc** *verb* ▷ **repetir**

repleto *masc adjective*, **repleta** *fem*
full up
estar repleto de algo to be packed with something
una sala repleta de gente a room packed with people

el **repollo** *masc noun*
cabbage

reponer *verb* **[11]**
1 **to replace** (*stores, stocks*)
2 **to repeat** (*a series, programme*)

reponerse *reflexive verb* **[11]**
to recover
reponerse de una enfermedad to recover from an illness

el **reportaje** *masc noun*
1 **article** (*in a newspaper*)
2 **report** (*on TV*)

el **reportero** *masc noun*, la **reportera** *fem*
reporter

reposar *verb* **[17]**
1 **to rest**
2 **dejar reposar** to leave to stand

el **reposo** *masc noun*
rest

la **repostería** *fem noun*
confectionery

el & la **representante** *masc & fem noun*
representative

representar *verb* **[17]**
1 **to represent** (*your school, a person*)
Representa el concepto de libertad. It represents the idea of liberty.
2 **to put on** (*a play*)
representar una obra to perform a play
3 **to play** (*a part*)

la **reproducción** *fem noun*
reproduction

el **reproductor** *masc noun*
player
- el **reproductor de discos compactos** CD player
- el **reproductor de MP3** MP3 player

reproducir *verb* **[60]**
to reproduce

reproducirse *reflexive verb* **[60]**
to reproduce

el **reptil** *masc noun*
reptile

la **república** *fem noun*
republic

♂ la **República Dominicana** *fem noun*
the Dominican Republic

repugnante *masc & fem adjective*
disgusting

repuesto *masc noun*
spare part
de repuesto, una rueda de repuesto a spare wheel

la **reputación** *fem noun*
reputation

el **requesón** *masc noun*
cottage cheese

el **requisito** *masc noun*
requirement

la **resaca** *fem noun*
hangover

resbaladizo *masc adjective*, **resbaladiza** *fem*
slippery

resaltar *verb* **[17]**
1 **to stand out** (*colours*)
2 **to stress** (*the strong points*)

resbalar *verb* **[17]**
to slip

resbalarse *reflexive verb* **[17]**
to slip
resbalarse con una piel de plátano to slip on a banana skin

rescatar *verb* **[17]**
to rescue

el **rescate** *masc noun*
rescue
una operación de rescate a rescue operation

la **reserva** *fem noun*
1 **reservation** (*in a hotel, etc*)
hacer una reserva to make a reservation
2 **reserve**
los jugadores de reserva the reserve players
3 **supply** (*of fuel*)
4 **reservation**, **doubt**
Tengo mis reservas. I have my doubts.
- la **reserva natural** nature reserve

la **reservación** *fem noun*
(*Latin America*) **reservation**

reservado *masc adjective*, **reservada** *fem*
reserved

♂ **reservar** *verb* **[17]**
1 **to put by** (*savings, food*)
2 **to book** (*a room, a table*)

♂ el **resfriado** *masc noun*
cold
tener un resfriado to have a cold

resfriarse *reflexive verb* **[32]**
to catch a cold
Me he resfriado. I've caught a cold.

♂ la **residencia** *fem noun*
1 **residence**
un permiso de residencia a residence permit
2 **hall of residence** (*for students*)
- la **residencia de ancianos** old people's home

residir *verb* **[19]**
residir en to live in
Reside en Londres. She lives in London.

♂ los **residuos** *plural masc noun*
waste
- los **residuos nucleares** nuclear waste
- los **residuos tóxicos** toxic waste

la **resistencia** *fem noun*
1 **resistance**
2 **stamina**
tener mucha resistencia to have a lot of stamina

resistir *verb* **[19]**
1 **to resist**
2 **to stand** (*pain, cold, heat*)
¡No lo resisto! I can't stand it!

resistirse *reflexive verb* **[19]**
to resist

resolver *verb* **[45]**
1 **to solve** (*a crime, a mystery*)
2 **to sort out** (*problems*)
3 **to decide** (*a match, etc*)

el **resorte** *masc noun*
spring (*in a mechanism*)

el **respaldo** *masc noun*
1 **back** (*of a chair*)
2 **support** (*for a person*)

el **respecto** *masc noun*
1 **al respecto: No hay más información al respecto.** There is no more informaton about it.
2 **con respecto a: Con respecto a lo que me contaste, ...** Regarding what you told me, ...

respetable *masc & fem adjective*
respectable

respetar *verb* [17]
1 **to respect** (*a person*)
2 **to obey** (*rules, the law, etc*)

el **respeto** *masc noun*
respect
tenerle mucho respeto a alguien to have a lot of respect for someone

la **respiración** *fem noun*
breathing
contener la respiración to hold your breath

respirar *verb* [17]
to breathe

responder *verb* [18]
1 **to answer**
responder a un mail to answer an email
No me respondió. He didn't answer me.
2 **to respond** (*to treatment*)
3 **responder por algo, alguien** to be reponsible for something, someone

la **responsabilidad** *fem noun*
responsibility

responsable *masc & fem adjective*
▷ see **responsable** *noun*
responsible

el & la **responsable** *masc & fem noun*
▷ see **responsable** *adjective*
1 **person responsible**
2 **person in charge**
¿Quién es el responsable? Who's the person in charge?

la **respuesta** *fem noun*
1 **answer**, **reply** (*to a message, enquiry etc*)
2 **response** (*from the public*)

restante *masc & fem adjective*
remaining
lo restante the remainder

restar *verb* [17]
to take away (*in maths*)

el **restaurante** *masc noun*
restaurant

restaurar *verb* [17]
to restore

el **resto** *masc noun*
1 **rest**
el resto de la clase the rest of the clase
2 **los restos** leftovers (*from a meal*)
3 **los restos** remains (*of a body*)

la **restricción** *fem noun*
restriction

restringir *verb* [49]
to restrict

restringirse *reflexive verb* [49]
to restrict yourself

el **resultado** *masc noun*
result
un resultado muy positivo a very positive result
unos resultados inesperados some unexpected results

resultar *verb* [17]
1 **to come of**
¿Qué resultará de esto? What's going to come of this?
2 **to be**
Así resulta más fácil. It's easier this way.
Varios manifestantes reultaron heridos. Several demonstrators were injured.

el **resumen** *masc noun*
summary

resumir *verb* [19]
1 **to summarize**
2 **to sum up**
Resumiendo, ... To cut a long story short, ...

retener *verb* [9]
1 **to keep** (*a person from doing something, etc*)
2 **to remember**

retirar *verb* [17]
1 **to take away** (*a passport, a licence*)
2 **to move back**
Retira esa silla. Move that chair back.

retirarse *reflexive verb* [17]
1 **to move back**
2 **to retire**

Spanish–English
a b c d e f g h i j k l m n ñ o p q r s t u v w x y z

retrasado *masc adjective*, **retrasada** *fem*
▷ see **retrasado** *noun*
1 **mentally handicapped**
2 **behind** (*in schedule, etc*)
Vamos muy retrasados con el trabajo. We're very late with the job.
3 **Mi reloj va retrasado.** My watch is slow.

el **retrasado** *masc noun*, la **retrasada** *fem*
▷ see **retrasado** *adj*
mentally handicapped person
los retrasados mentales the menatlly handicapped

retrasar *verb* [17]
1 **to delay** (*a trip*)
2 **to put back** (*a watch*)

retrasarse *reflexive verb* [17]
1 **to be late**
Me retrasé unos minutos. I was a few minutes late.
2 **to fall behind** (*in studies*)

♪ el **retraso** *masc noun*
1 **delay**
una media hora de retraso a half-hour delay
Llevan retraso. They're late.
2 **con retraso** late
Llegaron con retraso. They arrived late.

el **retrato** *masc noun*
portrait

♪ el **retrete** *masc noun*
toilet

el **retrovisor** *masc noun*
1 **rear-view mirror**
2 **wing mirror**

el **reuma** *masc noun*
rheumatism

♪ la **reunión** *fem noun*
1 **meeting**
asistir a una reunión to attend a meeting
2 **reunion**
una reunión de antiguos alumnos a reunion of former pupils

reunir *verb* [62]
1 **to gather** (*information*)
2 **to call together** (*members, students, etc*)
3 **to have**
Reúne los elementos que busco. It has everything I'm looking for.
4 **reunir dinero** to raise money

reunirse *reflexive verb* [62]
to meet, **to get together**

la **revancha** *fem noun*
1 **revenge**
tomarse la revancha to get your own back
2 **return game**
jugar la revancha to play a rematch

revelar *verb* [17]
1 **to reveal**
2 **to develop** (*a film*)

la **reverencia** *fem noun*
bow, **curtsey**
hacer una reverencia to bow, to curtsey

reventar *verb* [17]
1 **to burst** (*balloons, tyres, etc*)
2 **to explode**

el **reverso** *masc noun*
back

el **revés** *masc noun*
1 **al revés** inside out
Tu jersey está al revés. Your jumper is inside out.
2 **al revés** upside down
Ese cuadro está al revés. That picture's upside down.
3 **inside**
el revés del abrigo the inside of the coat
4 **backhander** (*in tennis*)
el revés de la página the back of the page

revisar *verb* [17]
1 **to check** (*a bill, a machine, writing*)
2 **to revise**
3 **to service** (*a car*)

la **revisión** *fem noun*
1 **revision**
2 **(medical) checkup**
3 **service** (*for a car, etc*)

♪ el **revisor** *masc noun*, la **revisora** *fem*
ticket inspector

♪ la **revista** *fem noun*
magazine

la **revolución** *fem noun*
revolution

revolver *verb* [45]
1 **to stir** (*soup, sauce*)
2 **to turn upside down**
Me revolvieron todos los cajones. They went through all my drawers.
Le habían revuelto todos sus papeles. They'd left all his papers in a mess.

el **revólver** *masc noun*
pistol

Spanish–English

revuelto *masc adjective*, **revuelta** *fem*
1 **in a mess**
Los papeles estaban todos revueltos. All the papers were in a mess.
2 **rough** (*sea*)
3 **unsettled** (*weather*)

el **rey** *masc noun*
1 **king**
2 **los reyes de España** the King and Queen of Spain

mini-info **rey**

España tiene una familia real. El actual rey se llama Don Juan Carlos de Borbón y Borbón y la reina Doña Sofía. Felipe, Príncipe de Asturias, es el heredero al trono español.

rezar *verb* **[22]**
to pray

ría, **rían**, **etc** *verb* ▷ **reír**

la **riada** *fem noun*
flood

la **ribera** *fem noun*
riverbank
la ribera del Tajo the bank of the Tagus

rico *masc adjective*, **rica** *fem* ▷ **see rico** *noun*
1 **rich** (*people*)
2 **good** (*food*)
La sopa está muy rica. The soup is very good.

el **rico** *masc noun*, la **rica** *fem* ▷ **see rico** *adj*
rich person
los ricos the rich

ridículo *masc adjective*, **ridícula** *fem* ▷ **see ridículo** *noun*
ridiculous

el **ridículo** *masc noun* ▷ **see ridículo** *adjective*
hacer el ridículo to make a fool of yourself
dejar a alguien en ridículo to make a fool of somebody
Lo dejó en ridículo. She made afool of him.

ríe, **ríen**, **etc** *verb* ▷ **reír**

riega, **riego**, **riegue**, **etc** *verb* ▷ **regar**

la **rienda** *fem noun*
rein

el **riesgo** *masc noun*
risk
un riesgo para la salud a health hazard
correr un riesgo to run a risk
Corres el riesgo de que te suspendan. You're running the risk of being failed.

la **rifa** *fem noun*
raffle

el **rímel** *masc noun*
mascara

el **rincón** *masc noun*
1 **corner** (*of a room*)
2 **en el rincón de mi habitación** in the corner of my bedroom
Lo buscamos en todos los rincones. We looked everywhere for it.

el **rinoceronte** *masc noun*
rhinoceros

la **riña** *fem noun*
1 **fight**
una riña callejera a street fight
2 **quarrel**
Tuvo una riña con su novia. He had a quarrel with his girlfriend.

el **riñón** *masc noun*
1 **kidney**
2 **los riñones** lower back
tener dolor de riñones to have backache

el **río** ▷ **see río** *verb masc noun*
river
ir río abajo to go downstream
ir río arriba to go upstream

rió ▷ **see río** *noun verb* ▷ **reir**

la **riqueza** *fem noun*
wealth

la **risa** *fem noun*
1 **laugh**
una risa histérica an hysterical laugh
¡Qué risa! What a laugh!
(*informal*) **morirse de risa** to die of laughter
Nos moríamos de risa. We were dying of laughter.
2 **risas** *plural* laughter
Se oían risas. You could hear laughter.

el **ritmo** *masc noun*
rhythm
llevar el ritmo to keep time
marcar el ritmo to beat time

el & la **rival** *masc & fem noun*
rival

rizado *masc adjective*, **rizada** *fem*
curly

el **rizo** *masc noun*
curl

robar *verb* **[17]**
1 **to steal**
robarle algo a alguien to steal something from somebody

a b c d e f g h i j k l m n ñ o p q r s t u v w x y z

Les robó dinero a sus padres. He stole money from his parents.
2 to rob
robar un banco to rob a bank
robar en una casa to rob a house
3 to rip (somebody) off
¡Me han robado! I've been ripped off!

el **roble** *masc noun*
oak

el **robo** *masc noun*
1 robbery
¡Esto es un robo! This is a rip-off!
2 burglary
3 break-in

la **roca** *fem noun*
rock

el **rocío** *masc noun*
dew

la **rodaja** *fem noun*
slice (*of chorizo, fruit, etc*)
cortar en rodajas to slice

rodar *verb* [24]
1 to roll (*stones, logs, etc*)
2 to turn (*a wheel*)
3 to shoot (*a film*)

rodeado *masc adjective*, **rodeada** *fem*
surrounded
rodeado de espectadores surrounded by on-lookers

rodear *verb* [17]
to surround

la **rodilla** *fem noun*
knee
ponerse de rodillas to kneel down

♪ **rogar** *verb* [24]
to beg
Te ruego que me perdones. I beg you to forgive me.
Le rogué que volviera. I begged her to come back.
'Se ruega no fumar' 'No smoking'

♪ **rojo** *masc adjective*, **roja** *fem*
▷ see **rojo** *noun*
red
ponerse rojo to go red

♪ el **rojo** *masc noun* ▷ see **rojo** *adj*
red

el **rollo** *masc noun*
1 roll (*of paper, film*)
un rollo de tela a roll of fabric
un rollo de papel higiénico a toilet roll
2 coil (*of rope, wire*)
3 (*informal*) bore
¡Vaya rollo de película! What a boring film!
4 (*informal*) business
Es mal rollo. It's a bad business.

romántico *masc adjective*, **romántica** *fem*
romantic

el **rompecabezas** *masc noun*, *pl:* los **rompecabezas**
puzzle

♪ **romper** *verb* [40]
1 to break
Vas a romper la silla. You're going to break the chair.
romper algo en mil pedazos to smash something to pieces
2 to tear
Rompió la carta en pedazos. He tore up the letter.
3 to break down
Los bomberos rompieron la puerta. The firemen broke down the door.

romperse *reflexive verb* [40]
1 to break (*by itself*)
La lámpara se ha roto. The lamp has broken.
2 to break (*a leg, arm, rib, etc*)
Se rompió el brazo. She broke her leg.

el **rompiente** *masc noun*
breaker (*wave*)

el **ron** *masc noun*
rum

roncar *verb* [31]
to snore

ronco *masc adjective*, **ronca** *fem*
hoarse
quedarse ronco to go hoarse

la **ronda** *fem noun*
1 round
Esta ronda la pago yo. It's my round.
2 patrol
hacer la ronda to be on patrol

ronronear *verb* [31]
to purr

♪ la **ropa** *fem noun*
clothes
la ropa sucia dirty clothes ▸▸

cambiarse de ropa to change your clothes
quitarse la ropa to take your clothes off
- la **ropa interior** underwear

el **ropero** *masc noun*
wardrobe

rosa *invariable adjective* ▷ see **rosa** *noun*
pink

WORD TIP *rosa, adjective*, never changes.

la **rosa** *fem noun* ▷ see **rosa** *adj*
rose (*flower and plant*)

rosado *masc adjective*, **rosada** *fem* ▷ see **rosado** *noun*
pink

el **rosado** *masc noun* ▷ see **rosado** *adj*
1 **pink** (*colour*)
2 **rosé** (*wine*)

el **rosario** *masc noun*
(*Religion*) **rosary**

el **rosbif** *masc noun*
roast beef

el **rostro** *masc noun*
1 **face**
2 (*informal*) **¡Qué rostro!** What a nerve!

roto *masc adjective*, **rota** *fem*
1 **broken**
2 **torn**
3 **worn out** (*shoes*)

la **rotonda** *fem noun*
roundabout

el **rotulador** *masc noun*
felt-tip pen

rubio *masc adjective*, **rubia** *fem*
blond, **blonde**
un chico rubio a blond boy
una actriz rubia a blonde actress
una cerveza rubia a lager
Soy rubia, pero mi novio es moreno. I'm blonde, but my boyfriend has dark hair.

ruborizarse *reflexive verb* [22]
to blush

la **rueda** *fem noun*
1 **wheel**
2 **tyre**
- la **rueda delantera** front wheel
- la **rueda de prensa** press conference
- la **rueda de repuesto** spare wheel

rugir *verb* [49]
to roar (*lions, wind, waves*)

el **ruido** *masc noun*
noise
hacer ruido to make a noise
Estaban haciendo much ruido. They were making a lot of noise.

ruidoso *masc adjective*, **ruidosa** *fem*
noisy

la **ruina** *fem noun*
1 **ruin**
La empresa está en la ruina. The company is in a terrible state.
La casa está en ruinas. The house is in ruins.
2 **las ruinas** ruins
unas ruinas romanas some roman ruins
las ruinas del castillo the ruins of the castle

el **ruiseñor** *masc noun*
nightingale

el **rulo** *masc noun*
roller (*curler*)

la **rulot** *fem noun*
caravan

Rumania, **Rumanía** *fem noun*
Romania

rumano *masc adjective & noun*, **rumana** *fem adjective & noun*
1 **Romanian**
2 **un rumano, una rumana** Romanian
el rumano Romanian (*the language*)

WORD TIP Adjectives and nouns for nationality, regional origin, and language do not have capital letters in Spanish.

el **rumbo** *masc noun*
course
el rumbo que han tomado los acontecimientos the course which events have taken
Colón salió con rumbo al Nuevo Mundo. Columbus set sail for the New World.
La nave espacial va rumbo a Marte. The spaceship is on course to Mars.

el **rumor** *masc noun*
1 **rumour**
2 **murmur**

Rusia *fem noun*
Russia

ruso *masc adjective & noun*, **rusa** *fem adjective & noun*

1 **Russian**

2 **un ruso, una rusa** Russian
el ruso Russian (*the language*)

WORD TIP Adjectives and nouns for nationality, regional origin, and language do not have capital letters in Spanish.

la **ruta** *fem noun*
route

la **rutina** *fem noun*
routine
por rutina out of habit

S s

♪ el **sábado** *masc noun*
Saturday
el sábado on Saturday
el sábado pasado last Saturday
los sábados on Saturdays
cada sábado every Saturday
Jugamos los sábados. We play on Saturdays.

WORD TIP Names of months and days start with small letters in Spanish.

♪ la **sábana** *fem noun*
sheet (*for a bed*)

el **saber** *masc noun* ▷ see **saber** *verb*
knowledge

♪ **saber** *verb* **[13]** ▷ see **saber** *noun*
1 **to know** (*facts*)
Ya lo sé. I know.
No lo sabe. He doesn't know.
Sabe mucho del tema. He knows a lot about it.
Sabía que no le gustaría hacerlo. I knew he wouldn't want to do it.
saber algo de memoria to know something by heart
2 (*know how to do something*) **can**
¿Sabes hablar francés? Can you speak French?
Sabe montar en bicicleta. She can ride a bike.
No sé tocar la guitarra. I can't play the guitar.
3 **to find out**
Lo supe por su hermana. I found out through her sister.
4 **to taste**
¡Qué bien sabe! It tastes really good!
La comida sabe muy rica. The food tastes very nice.
saber a algo to taste of something
Sabe a fresa. It tastes of strawberry.

WORD TIP For the other Spanish verb for *to know* ▷ **conocer**.

la **sabiduría** *fem noun*
wisdom

sabio *masc adjective*, **sabia** *fem*
wise

♪ el **sabor** *masc noun*
taste
Tiene un sabor a fresa. It tastes like strawberry.

♪ **sabrá**, **sabré**, **sabría**, **etc** *verb* ▷ **saber**

sabroso *masc adjective*, **sabrosa** *fem*
tasty

el **sacacorchos** *masc noun*, *pl:* los **sacacorchos**
corkscrew

♪ el **sacapuntas** *masc noun*, *pl:* los **sacapuntas**
pencil sharpener

♪ **sacar** *verb* **[31]**
1 **to take out**
sacar al perro a pasear to take the dog for a walk
sacar la basura to take the rubbish out
Saqué diez libras de la caja. I took ten pounds from the till.
Sacó su monedero del bolso. She took her purse out of her bag.
sacar a alguien a bailar to ask somebody to dance
Lo sacó a bailar. She asked him to dance.
2 **to bring out** (*a books, a DVD*)
sacar un libro to publish a book
sacar un disco to release a record
3 **to get, to buy**
sacar entradas to buy tickets
Todavía no he sacado los billetes. I haven't bought the tickets yet.
4 **to pull out** (*a pistol, a knife*)
Sacó su pistola He pulled out his gun.
5 **to get** (*marks*)
sacar buenas notas to get good marks
sacar malas notas to get bad marks
He sacado un siete en matemáticas. I got seven (out of ten) in maths.
6 **to take** (*a picture*)
sacar una foto to take a photo
sacar una fotocopia to make a photocopy
7 **to serve** (*in tennis*)
Te toca a ti sacar. It's your service.
8 **to kick off** (*in football*)
Va a sacar Gómez. Gómez is going to kick off.

sacarse *reflexive verb* **[31]**
1 **sacarse una muela** to have a tooth out
2 **sacarse una foto** to have one's photograph taken
Me saqué una foto frente al palacio. I had my photograph taken in front of the palace.

el **sacerdote** *masc noun*
priest

♪ el **saco** *masc noun*
1 **sack**
2 (*Latin America*) **coat**
• el **saco de dormir** sleeping bag

sacrificar *verb* **[31]**
1 **to sacrifice**
2 **to put down** (*an animal*)

el **sacrificio** *masc noun*
sacrifice

la **sacudida** *fem noun*
1 **shake**
Le di una sacudida. I gave it a shake.
2 **El coche iba dando sacudidas.** The car went shaking and jerking along.

sacudir *verb* **[19]**
1 **to shake** (*a bottle, cloth*)
2 **to shake off**
Sacudió las migas del mantel. She shook the crumbs off the tablecloth.

sacudirse *reflexive verb* **[19]**
to shake off
Se sacudió el polvo de la chaqueta. He shook the dust off his jacket.

sagaz *masc & fem adjective*
shrewd

sagitario *masc & fem noun*
▷ see **Sagitario** *noun*
Sagittarius
Es sagitario. She's Sagittarius.

WORD TIP Use a small letter in Spanish to say *I am Sagittarius*, etc with star signs.

Sagitario *masc noun* ▷ see **sagitario** *noun*
Sagittarius

sagrado *masc adjective*, **sagrada** *fem*
1 **sacred**
2 **holy**

♪ la **sal** *fem noun*
salt
• las **sales de baño** bath salts

♪ la **sala** *fem noun*
1 **room**
2 **hall**
3 **ward** (*in a hospital*)
• la **sala de espera** waiting room
• la **sala de estar** living room
• la **sala de exposiciones** exhibition hall
• la **sala de fiestas** night club
• la **sala de juegos** games room
• la **sala de profesores** staff room

salado *masc adjective*, **salada** *fem*
salty
agua salada salt water
Está muy salado. It's very salty.

♪ el **salario** *masc noun*
1 **wages** (*weekly*)
2 **salary** (*monthly*)

♪ la **salchicha** *fem noun*
sausage

el **salchichón** *masc noun*
salami sausage

saldar *verb* **[17]**
1 **to settle** (*a debt*)
2 **to sell off**

el **saldo** *masc noun*
1 **balance** (*of an account*)
2 **settlement**
3 **los saldos** the sales (*in shopping*)
precios de saldo sale prices
• el **saldo negativo** debit balance
• el **saldo positivo** credit balance

♪ **saldrá**, **saldré**, **saldría**, **salga**, **salgo**, **etc** *verb* ▷ **salir**

el **salero** *masc noun*
salt cellar

♪ la **salida** *fem noun*
1 **exit**
2 **departure** (*of flight, etc*)

♪ **salir** *verb* **[63]**
1 **to go out**
Salen mucho por la noche. They go out a lot in the evenings.
Está saliendo con Ana. He's going out with Ana.
2 **to come out**
Salieron uno a uno. They came out one by one.
Salimos del cole a las tres y media. We come out of school at half past three.
La noticia salió en el periódico. The news came out in the paper.
3 **to get out**
No pude salir. I couldn't get out.
4 **to leave**
El vuelo sale a las cinco. The flight leaves at five. ▸▸

salir de un sitio to leave a place
Salgo de casa a las ocho. I leave home at eight.
Salió de la casa corriendo. He ran out of the house.
5 salir en la televisión to appear on television
6 to turn out
Las cosas salieron bien. Things turned out well.
Todo salió como esperábamos. Everything turned out as we expected.
7 Las vacaciones nos salieron muy caras. Our holidays cost us a lot.
Si compras tres, sale más barato. It works out cheaper if you buy three.
El retrato te ha salido perfecto. Your picture has turned out just right.
El examen me salió fatal. The exam was really bad.
8 (*about spots, hair*) Me ha salido un grano. I've got a spot.
Le están saliendo canas. His hair's starting to go grey.
Le salía sangre de la nariz. His nose was bleeding.

salirse *reflexive verb* [63]
1 **to leave**
salirse del colegio to leave school
Jaime se ha salido del grupo. Jaime has left the group.
El coche se salió de la carretera. The car left the road.
2 (*with liquids*) El agua se salió del fregadero. The sink overflowed.
Se ha salido la leche. The milk has boiled over.

la **saliva** *fem noun*
saliva

salmón *invariable adjective*
▷ see **salmón** *noun*
salmon-pink

el **salmón** *masc noun*
▷ see **salmón** *adjective*
salmon
- el **salmón ahumado** smoked salmon

el **salón** *masc noun*
1 **living room**
2 **function room**
- el **salón de actos** assembly hall
- el **salón de belleza** beauty salon
- el **salón de fiestas** reception room

salpicar *verb* [31]
to splash

la **salsa** *fem noun*
1 **sauce**
2 **gravy**
3 **salsa** (*music*)
- la **salsa besamel** white sauce

el **saltamontes** *masc noun*, *pl:* los **saltamontes**
grasshopper

saltar *verb* [17]
to jump
saltar al suelo to jump to the ground
saltar de la cama to jump out of bed
saltar un muro to jump over a wall
saltar por encima de la verja to jump over the fence

saltarse *reflexive verb* [17]
1 **to skip** (*a page, a meeting*)
2 (*in driving*) Nos saltamos un semáforo en rojo. We jumped a red light.

el **salto** *masc noun*
jump
dar un salto to jump
- el **salto con pértiga** pole vault
- el **salto de altura** high jump
- el **salto de longitud** long jump

la **salud** *fem noun* ▷ see **salud** *exclamation*
health
estar bien de salud to be in good health

salud *exclamation* ▷ see **salud** *noun*
1 **Cheers!**
¡A tu salud! Cheers!
2 (*Latin America*) **Bless you!**

saludable *masc & fem adjective*
healthy

saludar *verb* [17]
1 **to say hello**
Nos saludó con la mano. She waved hello to us.
2 (*formal letter endings*) Le saluda atentamente, Jaime Rodríguez Yours sincerely, Jaime Rodríguez, Yours faithfully, Jaime Rodríguez

el **saludo** *masc noun*
1 **greeting**
Te envían sus saludos. They send their regards.
Dale saludos de mi parte. Give him my regards.
2 (*informal letter endings*) Un afectuoso saludo, Bea Best wishes, Bea

salvadoreño *masc adjective & noun*, **salvadoreña** *fem adjective & noun*
1 **Salvadorean**
2 **un salvadoreño, una salvadoreña** Salvadorean

WORD TIP Adjectives and nouns for nationality and regional origin do not have capital letters in Spanish.

salvaje *masc & fem adjective*
▷ see **salvaje** *noun*
1 **savage**
2 **wild**

el & la **salvaje** *masc & fem noun*
▷ see **salvaje** *adj*
savage

el **salvamanteles** *masc noun*, *pl:* los **salvamanteles**
table mat

el **salvamento** *masc noun*
rescue
una operación de salvamento a rescue operation

salvar *verb* [17]
to save (*lives*)

salvarse *reflexive verb* [17]
to survive

el **salvavidas** *masc noun*, *pl:* los **salvavidas**
life jacket

salvo *preposition, conjunction*
except
salvo que unless

San *masc adjective*
Saint (*San is used for most male saints*)
San Andrés Saint Andrew ▷ **santo**

San Salvador *masc noun*
San Salvador (*the country in Central America*)

sanar *verb* [17]
1 **to recover** (*patients*)
2 **to heal** (*injuries*)

la **sandalia** *fem noun*
sandal

la **sandía** *fem noun*
watermelon

el **sándwich** *masc noun*
(toasted) sandwich

sangrar *verb* [17]
to bleed

la **sangre** *fem noun*
blood

la **sangría** *fem noun*
sangria (*a cold punch made with red wine and lemonade*)

sano *masc adjective*, **sana** *fem*
healthy

la **sanidad** *fem noun*
1 **health**
2 **public health**
la sanidad pública the health service

WORD TIP *sanidad* does not mean *sanity* in English; for the meaning of *sanity* ▷ **razón**.

sanitario *masc adjective*, **sanitaria** *fem*
1 **health**
un control sanitario a health inspection
2 **sanitary**
las condiciones sanitarias the sanitary conditions

santo *masc adjective*, **santa** *fem*
▷ see **santo** *noun*
holy

el **santo** *masc noun*, la **santa** *fem noun*
▷ see **santo** *adjective & noun*
1 **saint**
Santo Tomás Saint Thomas
Santa María Saint Mary
2 **name day** (*The day of the saint many people are named after.*)

mini-info **santo**

Cada día del año tiene el nombre de un santo y los españoles y latinoamericanos con ese nombre, celebran ese día igual que su cumpleaños.

el **santuario** *noun*
shrine

el **sapo** *masc noun*
toad

el **saque** *masc noun*
1 **serve** (*in tennis*)
2 **kick-off** (*in football*)
- el **saque de banda** throw in
- el **saque de esquina** corner kick

el **sarampión** *masc noun*
measles

el **sarcasmo** *masc noun*
sarcasm

la **sardina** *fem noun*
sardine

el & la **sargento** *masc & fem noun*
sergeant

Spanish-English
a b c d e f g h i j k l m n ñ o p q r s t u v w x y z

el **sarpullido** *masc noun*
rash
Me ha salido un sarpullido. I've come out in a rash.

la **sartén** *fem noun*
frying pan

el & la **sastre** *masc & fem noun*
tailor

el **satélite** *masc noun*
satellite

el **satén** *masc noun*
satin

la **satisfacción** *fem noun*
satisfaction

satisfacer *verb* **[7]**
to satisfy
Sólo para satisfacer mi curiosidad. Just to satisfy my curiosity.
Satisface todos nuestros requisitos. It satisfies all our requirements.

satisfacerse *reflexive verb* **[7]**
to be satisfied

satisfecho *masc adjective*, **satisfecha** *fem*
satisfied
Estamos muy satisfechos con los resultados. We are very happy with the results.

el **sauce** *masc noun*
willow

el **saxofón** *masc noun*
saxophone

sazonado *masc adjective*, **sazonada** *fem*
seasoned

sazonar *verb* **[17]**
to season

se *pronoun*
1 (*with reflexive verbs*) **himself, herself**
Se cortó. He cut himself., She cut herself.
2 **itself**
Se desconecta solo. It disconnects itself.
3 **themselves**
¿Se han portado bien? Did they behave themselves?
4 **yourself** (*polite form*)
Espero que no se haya hecho daño. I hope you haven't hurt yourself.
5 **yourselves** (*polite form*)
¿Se han divertido ustedes? Did you enjoy yourselves?
6 (*showing interaction*) **each other**
Se quieren. They love each other.
Se miraron. They looked at each other.
Se lavó las manos. He washed his hands., She washed her hands.
Se pusieron la ropa. They put their clothes on.
7 **him, to him, her, to her, etc**
Se lo pregunté. I asked him., I asked her.
Se lo mandaré. I'll send it to him., I'll send it to her.
Cuando les vea se lo preguntaré. I'll ask them when I see them.
Cuando les vea se la daré. I'll give it to them when I see them.
Se lo dije a usted ayer. I told you yesterday (*polite form*).

WORD TIP To avoid *le* + *lo*, *les* + *los*, etc *se* is used instead of *le*, *les*.

8 (*in impersonal phrases*) **Se hace así.** It's done like this.
'Se vende piso' 'Flat for sale'
'Se habla inglés' 'English spoken'
9 (*with certain verbs*) **reírse: Me reí mucho.** I laughed a lot.
caerse: Se cayó. He fell down., She fell down.
pelearse: Se han peleado. They've had a fight.
levantarse: Se levantaron. They got up.

WORD TIP Many verbs in Spanish are used with the pronoun *-se* but are not translated with *himself*, *herself*, etc in English.

sé *verb* ▷ **ser**, **saber**

sea, **seas** *verb* ▷ **ser**

la **secadora** *fem noun*
dryer

el **secador de pelo** *masc noun*
hairdryer

secar *verb* **[31]**
to dry

secarse *reflexive verb* **[31]**
1 **to dry, to dry up**
¿Cuánto tarda en secarse la pintura? How long does the paint take to dry?
El río se seca completamente en el verano. The river dries up completely in summer.
2 **to dry yourself**
secarse el pelo to dry your hair
Sécate las manos con este trapo. Dry your hands with this cloth.

la **sección** *fem noun*
1 **section**
2 **department**

seco *masc adjective*, **seca** *fem*
dry
limpieza en seco dry-cleaning

la **secretaría** *fem noun*
secretary's office

⚷ el **secretario** *masc noun*, la **secretaria** *fem noun*
secretary

secreto *masc adjective*, **secreta** *fem*
▷ see **secreto** *noun*
secret

el **secreto** *masc noun*
▷ see **secreto** *adjective*
secret

el **secuestrador** *masc noun*, la **secuestradora** *fem noun*
1 **hijacker**
2 **kidnapper**

secuestrar *verb* [17]
1 **to kidnap**
2 **to hijack**

el **secuestro** *masc noun*
1 **kidnapping**
2 **hijacking**

secundario *masc adjective*, **secundaria** *fem*
secondary

⚷ la **sed** *fem noun* ▷ see **sed** *verb*
thirst
tener sed to be thirsty
¿Tienes sed? Are you thirsty?
Sí, tengo sed. Yes, I'm thirsty.

WORD TIP Use *tener* to say you're thirsty, hot, etc.

⚷ **sed** *verb* ▷ see **sed** *noun* ▷ **ser**

la **seda** *fem noun*
silk

el **sedal** *masc noun*
fishing line

la **sede** *fem noun*
la sede de las Olimpiadas the venue for the Olympics
la sede de la empresa the company's head office
la sede del gobierno the seat of government

⚷ **seguida** *in phrase* ▷ see **seguido** *adjective, adverb*
en seguida right away
Voy en seguida. I'll be there right away.

seguido *masc adjective*, **seguida** *fem*
▷ see **seguida** *in phrase*, **seguido** *adverb*
1 **tres días seguidos** three days in a row
Dan las dos películas seguidas. Two films are shown one after the other.
Los tres autobuses vinieron seguidos. The three buses came one after the other.
2 **seguido de alguien** followed by somebody
Entró seguido de su ayudante. He came in followed by his assistant.

seguido *adverb* ▷ see **seguida** *in phrase*, **seguido** *adjective*
todo seguido straight on
Vaya todo seguido. Go straight on.

⚷ **seguir** *verb* [64]
1 **to follow**
seguir a alguien to follow somebody
seguir una pista to follow up a clue
seguir un consejo to follow a piece of advice
2 **to go on, to continue**
Sigamos. Let's go on.
El camino sigue hasta el pueblo. The road goes on to the village.
3 **seguir haciendo algo** to carry on doing something
Seguí leyendo. I carried on reading.
Siguen viviendo en Sevilla. They're still living in Seville.
4 **to go on** (*in a car, walking*)
Siga todo recto. Go straight on. (*polite form, singular*)
Sigan por esta calle. Carry on down this street. (*polite form, plural*)

⚷ **según** *preposition, conjunction*
▷ see **según** *adverb*
1 **according to**
según las normas according to the rules
Según dijo él. From what he said.
2 **as**
Según los vayas acabando. As you finish them.

según *adverb* ▷ see **según** *preposition, conjunction*
'¿Te interesa apuntarte?'—'Según.' 'Would you be interested in enrolling?'—'It depends.'

la **segunda** *fem noun*
▷ see **segundo** *adjective & noun*
la segunda second gear

⚷ **segundo** *masc adjective*, **segunda** *fem*
▷ see **segunda** *noun*, **segundo** *noun*
second
llegar en segundo lugar to finish in second place
Viven en el segundo piso. They live on the second floor.
Viajan en segunda clase. They travel second class.

el **segundo** *masc noun*
▷ see **segunda** *noun*, **segundo** *adjective*
1 **second**
Espera un segundo. Wait a moment.
2 **el segundo** the main course
De segundo, tenemos ... For the main course, we have ...

la **seguridad** *fem noun*
1 **security**
2 **safety**
por razones de seguridad for safety reasons
3 **certainty**
Lo sé con seguridad. I know for certain.
• la **seguridad nacional** national security
• la **seguridad social** social security

seguramente *adverb*
probably
Seguramente irán. They'll probably go.
Seguramente no están. I expect they're not there.

seguro *masc adjective*, **segura** *fem*
▷ see **seguro** *adv, noun*
1 **safe**
Aquí me siento seguro. I feel safe here.
La escalera no es muy segura. The ladder isn't very safe.
2 **seguro de sí mismo, segura de sí misma** self-confident
Es muy segura de sí misma. She's very self-confident.
3 **sure**
Estoy completamente seguro. I'm absolutely certain.
¿Estás seguro de que se pone así? Are you sure this is the way to put it on?
4 **definite**
No es seguro todavía. It's not definite yet.
5 **reliable**
Es un método muy seguro. It's a very reliable method.

seguro *adverb* ▷ see **seguro** *adj, noun*
definitely
Irán seguro. They'll definitely go.
Seguro que no están. I bet they're not there.

el **seguro** *masc noun* ▷ see **seguro** *adj, adv*
1 **insurance**
hacerse un seguro to take out insurance
¿Tienes seguro médico? Have you got medical insurance?
2 **clasp** (*of a bracelet*)
3 **safety catch** (*on a gun*)
4 **el Seguro** Social Security
• el **seguro a todo riesgo** comprehensive insurance
• el **seguro contra incendios** fire insurance

seis *number*
1 **six**
Tiene seis años. He's six (years old).
2 **sixth** (*in dates*)
el seis de junio the sixth of June
3 **six** (*in telling the time*)
Son las seis. It's six o'clock.

seiscientos, **seiscientas** *number*
six hundred
seiscientos dos six hundred and two

la **selección** *fem noun*
1 **selection**
2 **team**
la selección española the Spanish team

seleccionar *verb* **[17]**
to select

la **selectividad** *fem noun*
university entrance exam

el **self-service** *masc noun*
self-service restaurant

el **sello** *masc noun*
stamp
un sello para Gran Bretaña a stamp for Britain
un sello de setenta céntimos a seventy cent stamp
• el **sello discográfico** record label

la **selva** *fem noun*
forest
• la **selva amazónica** Amazon rainforest
• la **selva tropical** tropical rainforest

el **semáforo** *masc noun*
traffic lights
saltarse un semáforo en rojo to go through a red light
Cuando llegue al semáforo, gire a la derecha. When you get to the traffic lights, turn right.

la **semana** *fem noun*
week
la próxima semana next week
entre semana during the week
Hace una semana. It's a week now.
• la **Semana Santa** Holy Week
en Semana Santa during Holy Week (*a time of great religious celebrations in many Spanish-speaking countries*)

semanal *masc & fem adjective*
weekly

semanalmente *adverb*
weekly

sembrar *verb* **[29]**
1 **to sow**
2 **to plant**

semejante *masc & fem adjective*
similar
Es muy semejante al antiguo. It's very similar to the old one.

la **semifinal** *fem noun*
semifinal

la **semilla** *fem noun*
seed

la **sémola** *fem noun*
semolina

sencillo *masc adjective*, **sencilla** *fem*
▷ see **sencillo** *masc*
1 **simple**
2 **modest**
3 **straightforward** (*person*)

♪ el **sencillo** *masc noun* ▷ see **sencillo** *adj*
1 **single** (*record*)
2 **single** (*ticket*)
3 (*Latin America*) **change**

la **senda** *fem noun*
path

el **senderismo** *masc noun*
hiking
hacer senderismo to go hiking

el & la **senderista** *masc & fem noun*
hiker

el **sendero** *masc noun*
path

el **seno** *masc noun*
1 **breast**
2 **bosom**

la **sensación** *fem noun*
1 **feeling**
una sensación de tristeza a feeling of sadness
Tengo la sensación de que ... I have the feeling that ...
2 **sense**
una sensación de pérdida a sense of loss
3 **sensation, stir**
causar sensación to cause a sensation
Su llegada causó sensación. Her arrival caused a sensation.

sensacional *masc & fem adjective*
sensational
una noticia sensacional a sensational piece of news

la **sensatez** *fem noun*
sense
tener sensatez to be sensible
actuar con sensatez to act sensibly

sensato *masc adjective*, **sensata** *fem*
sensible
un chico muy sensato a very sensible boy

la **sensibilidad** *fem noun*
sensitivity

sensible *masc & fem adjective*
1 **sensitive**
2 **noticeable**
un cambio sensible a noticeable change

WORD TIP *sensible* does not mean *sensible* in English; for the meaning of *sensible* ▷ **sensato**.

sensiblemente *adverb*
considerably

♪ **sentado** *masc adjective*, **sentada** *fem*
estar sentado to be sitting
Están sentados en la terraza. They are sitting on the terrace.
Estabámos sentados a la mesa. We were sitting at the table.
Permanezcan sentados, por favor. Please remain seated.

♪ **sentar** *verb* **[29]**
1 **to sit**
Sienta al niño en su silla. Sit the baby in his chair.
2 **to suit**
El rojo me sienta fatal. Red doesn't suit me at all.
Ese vestido te sienta muy bien. That dress really suits you.
3 **sentarle bien a alguien** to agree with somebody (*food*)
sentarle mal a alguien to not agree with somebody (*food*)
Los pimientos me sientan mal. Peppers don't agree with me.

sentarse *reflexive verb* **[29]**
to sit down
Siéntate. Sit down.
Siéntese. Do sit down (*polite form*).

el **sentido** *masc noun*
1 **meaning**
el sentido de la palabra the meaning of the word
No tiene sentido. It doesn't make sense.
2 **consciousness**
perder el sentido to lose consciousness
3 **direction**
Venían en sentido contrario. They were

coming from the opposite direction.
una calle de sentido único a one-way street
en sentido de las agujas del reloj clockwise
en el sentido contrario al de las agujas del reloj anticlockwise
- el **sentido común** common sense
- el **sentido del humor** sense of humour

sentimental *masc & fem adjective*
sentimental
¿Qué tal tu vida sentimental? How's your love life?

el **sentimiento** *masc noun*
1 **feeling**
2 **Te acompaño en el sentimiento.** My condolences.

sentir *verb* **[14]**
1 **to feel**
sentir dolor to feel pain
sentir sed to feel thirsty
sentir alegría to feel happy
2 **to hear**
sentir pasos to hear footsteps
3 (*saying you're sorry*) **Lo siento mucho.** I'm very sorry.
Siento llegar tarde. Sorry I'm late.
Sentimos tener que comunicarle que ... We regret to inform you that ...

WORD TIP If you only say you are sorry, use *lo siento, lo sentimos*, etc. If you mention the reason, use *sentir* + the reason, without *lo*.

sentirse *reflexive verb* **[14]**
to feel
¿Cómo te sientes? How do you feel?
Me siento cansado. I feel tired.
No se sentía bien y se fue a casa. He wasn't feeling well and he went home.

la **seña** *fem noun*
1 **sign**
hacer una seña to make a sign
Me hizo señas para que entrase. He made signs to me to come in.
2 **señas** address
¿Quieres darme tus señas? Would you like to give me your address?

la **señal** *fem noun*
1 **sign**
las señales de carretera the road signs
Es una buena señal. It's a good sign.
hacer una señal to make a sign
Nos está haciendo señales. She's signalling to us.
2 **tone** (*in an answering machine message*)
Deje su mensaje después de la señal. Leave your message after the tone.
3 **deposit** (*when you buy something*)
- la **señal de marcar** dial tone
- la **señal de tráfico** traffic sign

señalar *verb* **[17]**
1 **to point**
Señaló hacia la casa. He pointed to the house.
2 **to point out**
Señaló que ... She pointed out that ...
3 **to fix** (*a date, time*)

señalarse *reflexive verb* **[17]**
Se señaló la pierna. He pointed at his leg.

el **señor** *masc noun*
1 **Mr**
el señor Muñoz Mr Muñoz
los señores López Mr and Mrs López
2 (*referring to a man politely*) **gentleman**, **man**
Hay un señor esperando. There's a gentleman waiting.
Perdone señor, ¿me deja pasar? Excuse me, sir, could I get past?
3 (*in letters*) **Muy señor mío: ...** Dear Sir, ...
4 (*for emphasis*) **No señor, eso no se hace.** You just don't do that.
Si señor, es verdad. Yes, that's quite right.

la **señora** *fem noun*
1 **Mrs**, **Ms**
la señora Gómez Mrs Gómez, Ms Gómez (*Spanish women keep their surnames after marrying.*)
2 (*referring to a woman politely*) **lady**
Una señora nos ayudó. A lady helped us.
Perdone señora, ¿me deja pasar? Excuse me, madam, could I get past?
señoras y señores ladies and gentlemen
3 **wife**
Le llamó su señora. Your wife rang you.
4 (*for emphasis*) **No señora, no fui yo.** It definitely wasn't me.
Sí señora, es mío. It certainly is mine.

la **señorita** *fem noun*
1 **Miss**, **Ms**
la señorita García Miss García, Ms García
Aquí están mis deberes, señorita. Here's my homework, Miss. (*speaking to your teacher*)
2 **young lady**
Le llama una señorita. A young lady is on the line for you.
3 (*for emphasis*) **No señorita, no se lo dejo.** I am certainly not lending it to you.

sepa, **sepan**, **etc** *verb* ▷ **saber**

la **separación** *fem noun*
1 **gap**
2 **separation**

separado *masc adjective*, **separada** *fem*
1 **separated**
2 **por separado** separately

separar *verb* [17]
1 **to separate**
2 **to move (something) away**
Separa la silla de la chimenea. Move the chair away from the fire.

separarse *reflexive verb* [17]
1 **to separate** (*couples*)
2 **Se separaron hace dos años.** They separated two years ago.

♪ **septiembre** *masc noun*
September
en septiembre in September
el 11 de septiembre on 11 September

WORD TIP Names of months and days start with small letters in Spanish.

séptimo *masc adjective*, **séptima** *fem*
seventh
el séptimo piso the seventh floor

♪ la **sequía** *fem noun*
drought

♪ **ser** *verb* [1] ▷ see **ser** *noun*
1 (*describing people, things*) **to be**
Es alta y morena. She's tall and dark.
Es muy simpática. She's very nice.
Es muy bonito. It's very pretty.
Estas naranjas son buenísimas. These oranges are really nice
2 (*asking and saying who's there*) **¿Quién es?** Who is it? (*when someone's at the door*)
Hola, soy yo. Hello, it's me (*on the phone*).
3 (*when paying*) **¿Cuánto es?** How much is that?
Son veinte euros. That's twenty euros.
4 (*in dates, times*) **Hoy es once.** Today's the eleventh.
Eran las seis y media. It was half past six.
5 (*saying what you do*) **Soy estudiante.** I'm a student.
Mi madre es abogada. My mother's a lawyer.
6 (*saying where, when things happen*) **Eso fue el año pasado.** That was last year.
La fiesta es en el gimnasio. The party's in the gym.
7 (*saying where you come from*) **ser de** to be from
Soy de Chester. I'm from Chester.
Es irlandés. He's Irish.
Ella es de Argentina. She's from Argentina.
8 (*showing ownership*) **Era de mi hermana.** It was my sister's.
El coche es de Juan. The car belongs to Juan.
9 (*saying how many you are*) **Somos cuatro.** There are four of us.
Eran tres. There were three of them.
10 (*saying what something is made of*) **ser de** to be made of
Es de madera. It's made of wood.
La silla es de metal. The chair's made of metal.
11 (*saying if someone is married, single*) **Es soltero.** He's single.
Es casada. She's married.
12 (*To form the passive with* **-ado** *and* **-ido** *forms of verbs*) **to be + -ed**
El puente fue derribado el año pasado. The bridge was demolished last year.
La casa fue construida en 1998. The house was built in 1998.
13 (*in expressions*)
ya sea ... o ... either ... or ...
ya sea por carta o por teléfono either by post or by telephone
14 **o sea, ...** so ..., that is ...
O sea, que no lo has terminado. So, you haven't finished.
Dentro de una semana, o sea el próximo jueves. In a week, that is next Thursday.
a no ser que + *subjunctive* unless
A no ser que le interese. Unless he's interested.

WORD TIP For the other Spanish verb for *to be* ▷ **estar**.

el **ser** *masc noun* ▷ see **ser** *verb*
being
• **un ser humano** human being
• **un ser vivo** living being

♪ **será**, **seré**, **sería**, **etc** *verb* ▷ **ser**

la **serie** *fem noun*
1 **series**
fabricación en serie mass production
2 **fuera de serie** exceptional

♪ **serio** *masc adjective*, **seria** *fem*
1 **serious**
ponerse serio to have a serious expression
un problema serio a serious problem
2 **reliable** (*person*)
3 **reputable** (*company*)
4 **Lo digo en serio.** I mean it.

Spanish–English
a b c d e f g h i j k l m n ñ o p q r s t u v w x y z

la **serpiente** *fem noun*
snake

serrano *masc adjective*, **serrana** *fem*
mountain, from the mountains
un pueblo serrano a mountain village

el **servicio** *masc noun*
1 **service**
servicio incluido service included
servicio a domicilio home delivery service
estar fuera de servicio to be out of service
2 **estar de servicio** to be on duty
3 **'Servicios'** 'Toilets'
- el **servicio de atención al cliente** customer services
- el **servicio militar** military service
- los **servicios públicos** public services

la **servilleta** *fem noun*
serviette

servir *verb* [57]
1 **to serve**
servir la sopa to serve the soup
¿Te sirvo más vino? Would you like some more wine?
2 **to be of use**
Estas herramientas ya no sirven. These tools are no use any more.
No sirve para nada. It's useless.
Yo no sirvo para camarera. I'm no good as a waitress.
3 **servir para algo** to be used for something
¿Para qué sirve este interruptor? What's this switch for?
Esto no nos sirve para abrirlo. This is no use for opening it.

servirse *reflexive verb* [57]
to help yourself to
Sírvete más. Help yourself to some more.
Se sirvió ensalada. She helped herself to some salad.

sesenta *number*
sixty
Tiene sesenta años. He's sixty (years old).
sesenta y dos sixty-two
los años sesenta the sixties

la **sesión** *fem noun*
1 **session**
2 **performance**
la sesión de noche the evening performance
- la **sesión continua** continuous performance

la **seta** *fem noun*
mushroom
- la **seta venenosa** toadstool

setecientos, **setecientas** *number*
seven hundred
setecientos ochenta seven hundred and eighty

setenta *number*
seventy
Tiene setenta años. He's seventy (years old).
setenta y dos seventy-two
los años setenta the seventies

el **seto** *masc noun*
hedge

severo *masc adjective*, **severa** *fem*
1 **severe** (*person, punishment*)
2 **harsh** (*climate*)

el **sexo** *masc noun*
sex

sexto *masc adjective*, **sexta** *fem*
sixth
el sexto piso the sixth floor

sexual *masc & fem adjective*
sexual
tener relaciones sexuales con alguien to have sex with someone

si *conjunction* ▷ see **sí** *adv, pron*
if
Si nos invitan, iremos. If they invite us, we'll go.
No sé si podré. I don't know if I'll be able to.
Si lo hubiese sabido ... If I'd known ...
Si tuviese dinero, lo compraría. If I had the money I'd buy it.

sí *adverb* ▷ see **si** *conj*, **sí** *pron*
yes
Sí, es cierto. Yes, it's true.
'¿Lo vas a comprar?'—'Sí.' 'Are you going to buy it?'—'Yes I am.'
'¿Es suyo?'—'Creo que sí.' 'Is it hers?'—'I think so.'
Ellos no lo saben, pero yo sí. They don't know, but I do.

sí *pronoun* ▷ see **sí** *adv*, **si** *conj*
1 **himself, herself**
Lo dijo para sí. He said it to himself., She said it to herself.
2 (*polite form*) **yourself, yourselves**
Lo pensaron para sí. You thought of it yourselves.

3 **itself**
Este problema es, en sí mismo ... This problem is, in itself ...
4 **themselves**
Los dos hermanos lo quieren todo para sí. Both brothers want everything for themselves.
5 (*emphasizing a particular person*) **sí mismo, sí misma** himself, herself
Se ríe de sí misma. She laughs at herself.
Lo hizo por sí mismo. He did it by himself.
Quiere hacerlo por sí misma. She wants to do it by herself.
Lo dividieron entre sí. They divided it between themselves

♪ el **sida** *masc noun*
(*= Síndrome de inmunodeficiencia adquirida*) **Aids** (*= Aquired Immune Deficiency Syndrome*)

♪ **sido** *verb* ▷ **ser**

♪ la **sidra** *fem noun*
cider

♪ **siempre** *adverb*
1 **always**
casi siempre almost always
Siempre van al mismo club. They always go to the same club.
2 **para siempre** for ever
Se quedaron allí para siempre. They stayed there for ever after.
3 **como siempre** as usual
la historia de siempre the usual story
4 **siempre que** whenever
Siempre que puedo. Whenever I can.

♪ **siendo** *verb* ▷ **ser**

♪ **sienta**, **siento**, **etc** *verb* ▷ **sentar, sentir**

♪ la **sierra** *fem noun*
1 **saw**
2 **mountain range**
Veranean en la sierra. They spend their summer holidays in the mountains.

♪ la **siesta** *fem noun*
afternoon nap
echarse una siesta to have a nap
Está durmiendo la siesta. He's having a nap.

siete *number*
1 **seven**
Tiene siete años. She's seven (years old).
2 **seventh** (*in dates*)
Hoy es siete de abril. It's the seventh of April today.
3 **seven** (*in clock time*)
Son las siete. It's seven o'clock.

♪ **siga**, **sigan**, **etc** *verb* ▷ **seguir**

♪ la **sigla** *fem noun*
abbreviation
S.A. son las siglas de sociedad anónima. S.A. is the abbreviation for 'sociedad anónima.'

♪ el **siglo** *masc noun*
century
el siglo XX the 20th century (*Use roman numbers for centuries in Spanish*)
Hace un siglo que no nos vemos. (*informal*) We haven't seen each other for ages.

el **significado** *masc noun*
meaning

♪ **significar** *verb* [31]
to mean
¿Qué significa esto? What does this mean?
Eso no significa nada para él. That doesn't mean anything to him.

el **signo** *masc noun*
1 **sign**
¿De qué signo eres? What sign are you?
2 **mark**
- el **signo de exclamación** exclamation mark
- el **signo de interrogación** question mark
- el **signo del zodiaco** star sign

♪ **sigo**, **sigue**, **etc** *verb* ▷ **seguir**

♪ **siguiente** *masc & fem adjective*
▷ see **siguiente** *noun*
next, **following**
al día siguiente ... the next day ...

♪ el & la **siguiente** *masc & fem noun*
▷ see **siguiente** *adjective*
El siguiente, por favor. Next, please.

♪ **siguió** *verb* ▷ **seguir**

la **sílaba** *fem noun*
syllable

♪ **silbar** *verb* [17]
to whistle

el **silbato** *masc noun*
whistle (*the instrument*)

el **silbido** *masc noun*
whistle (*the noise*)

♪ el **silencio** *masc noun*
silence

♪ **silenciosamente** *adverb*
quietly

silencioso *masc adjective*, **silenciosa** *fem*
quiet

Spanish–English

la **silla** *fem noun*
chair
- la **silla eléctrica** electric chair
- la **silla de ruedas** wheelchair

el **sillín** *masc noun*
saddle (*on a bicycle*)

el **sillón** *masc noun*
armchair

el **símbolo** *masc noun*
symbol

similar *masc & fem adjective*
similar
similar a algo similar to something

la **similitud** *fem noun*
similarity

el **simio** *masc noun*
ape

simpático *masc adjective*, **simpática** *fem*
nice
Es muy simpático. He's very nice.

WORD TIP *simpático* does not mean *sympathetic* in Spanish; for the meaning of *sympathetic* ▷ **comprensivo**.

simple *masc & fem adjective*
1 **simple**
2 **mere**
una simple formalidad a mere formality

simplemente *adverb*
simply

simplificar *verb* **[31]**
to simplify

simular *verb* **[17]**
1 **to pretend**
2 **to fake**

simultáneo *masc adjective*, **simultánea** *fem*
simultaneous

sin *preposition*
1 **without**
sin esfuerzo without effort
sin duda without a doubt
Lo hice sin pensar. I did it without thinking.
un agua mineral sin gas a still mineral water
una cerveza sin alcohol a non-alcoholic beer
Estamos sin azúcar. We're out of sugar.
Nos quedamos sin dinero. We ran out of money.
2 (*in expressions*) **sin querer** unintentionally
sin hogar homeless
sin sentido senseless
sin embargo nevertheless
Sin embargo nos quedamos. Nevertheless we stayed.

la **sinagoga** *fem noun*
synagogue

sinceramente *adverb*
1 **sincerely**
2 **quite honestly**

la **sinceridad** *fem noun*
sincerity

sincero *masc adjective*, **sincera** *fem*
sincere

el & la **sindicalista** *masc & fem noun*
trade unionist

el **sindicato** *masc noun*
trade union

el **singular** *masc noun*
(*Grammar*) **singular**
en singular in the singular

siniestro *masc adjective*, **siniestra** *fem*
▷ see **siniestro** *noun*
sinister

el **siniestro** *masc noun*
▷ see **siniestro** *adjective*
1 **accident**
2 **disaster**

sino *conjunction*
but
No es verde, sino amarillo. It's not green but yellow.

WORD TIP *sino* is used after *no* to correct what has just been said.

sinónimo *masc adjective*, **sinónima** *fem*
▷ see **sinónimo** *noun*
synonymous

el **sinónimo** *masc noun*
▷ see **sinónimo** *adjective*
synonym (*word meaning the same as another*)
'Empezar' y 'comenzar' son sinónimos. 'Empezar' and 'comenzar' are synonyms.

sintético *masc adjective*, **sintética** *fem*
synthetic

sintieron, **sintió**, **etc** *verb* ▷ **sentir**

el **síntoma** *masc noun*
symptom

sintonizar *verb* **[22]**
to tune in

a b c d e f g h i j k l m n ñ o p q r s t u v w x y z

♪ el & la **sinvergüenza** *masc & fem noun*
1 **swine**
2 **crook**
3 **rascal**

♪ **siquiera** *adverb*
1 **at least**
Dales siquiera un poco de dinero. Give them at least a bit of money.
2 **ni siquiera** not even
Ni siquiera me reconoció. She didn't even recognise me.

la **sirena** *fem noun*
1 **mermaid**
2 **siren** (*in a factory*)

el **sistema** *masc noun*
system

♪ el **sitio** *masc noun*
1 **place**
Ponlo otra vez en su sitio. Put it back in its place.
2 **room**
hacer sitio to make room
No tengo sitio en la maleta. I haven't got any room in my suitcase.
Hay sitio para uno más. There's room for one more.
3 **seat**
Hay un sitio al lado de la ventana. There's a seat by the window.
4 (*in expressions*) **en algún sitio** somewhere
en cualquier sitio anywhere
en ningún sitio nowhere
en otro sitio somewhere else
5 **siege**
• el **sitio web** web site

la **situación** *fem noun*
1 **situation**
2 **position**
La situación de la casa es buena. The house is in a good position.

♪ **situado** *masc adjective*, **situada** *fem*
situated

situar *verb* **[20]**
1 **to site** (*a building*)
2 **to set** (*a plot in a novel*)

situarse *reflexive verb* **[20]**
1 **to be situated**
2 **situarse en primer puesto** to be in first position
3 **situarse bien en la vida** to do very well for yourself in life

el **smoking** *masc noun*
dinner jacket

WORD TIP *smoking* does not mean *smoking* in English; for the meaning of *smoking* ▷ **fumar**.

el **SMS** *masc noun*
text message
enviar un SMS to send a text message

el **sobaco** *masc noun*
armpit

♪ **sobra** *fem noun*
1 **de sobra** to spare
Tenemos pan de sobra. We have bread to spare.
Hay una silla de sobra. There's a spare chair.
Como estaba de sobra me fui. I wasn't needed, so I left.
2 **las sobras** leftovers (*of food*)

♪ **sobrar** *verb* **[17]**
1 (*saying something is left over*) **Va a sobrar dinero.** There will be money left over.
Nos ha sobrado vino. We have wine left over.
2 (*saying there is too much*) **Sobran tres sillas.** There are three chairs too many.
Nos sobra tiempo. We have plenty of time.
Le sobraba una entrada. He had a spare ticket.

♪ **sobre** *preposition* ▷ see **sobre** *noun*
1 **on**
Está sobre la cama. It's on the bed.
2 **above**
la lámpara que está sobre el sofá the lamp above the sofa
sobre el nivel del mar above sea level
3 **over**
el puente sobre el río the bridge over the river
4 **about**
un artículo sobre el cambio climatológico an article about climate change
5 **sobre todo** especially

♪ el **sobre** *masc noun* ▷ see **sobre** *preposition*
envelope

la **sobredosis** *fem noun, pl:* las **sobredosis**
overdose

sobrenatural *masc & fem adjective*
supernatural

sobrepasar *verb* **[17]**
to exceed

sobresaliente *masc & fem adjective*
▷ see **sobresaliente** *noun*
outstanding, excellent

el sobresaliente *masc noun*
▷ see **sobresaliente** *adj*
mark between 8.5 and 10 (out of 10)

sobresalir *verb* [63]
1 **sobresalir en algo** to do very well in something
Sobresale en los idiomas. She does very well in languages.
2 **to overhang**

el sobresalto *masc noun*
fright
llevarse un sobresalto to get a fright

el & la sobreviviente *masc & fem noun*
survivor

sobrevivir *verb* [19]
to survive
sobrevivir a algo to survive something
No sobrevivió a la operación. He didn't survive the operation.

el sobrino *masc noun*, **la sobrina** *fem*
1 **nephew**
2 **niece**
mis sobrinos my nephews and nieces, my nephews

sociable *masc & fem adjective*
sociable

social *masc & fem adjective*
social

socialista *masc & fem adjective & noun*
1 **socialist**
2 **el & la socialista** socialist

la sociedad *fem noun*
society
• **la sociedad anónima** public limited company
• **la sociedad de consumo** consumer society

el socio *masc noun*, **la socia** *fem noun*
member
hacerse socio de algo to join something
Se hizo socia del club de tenis. She joined the tennis club

socorrer *verb* [18]
to help

el & la socorrista *masc & fem noun*
lifeguard
¿Hay un socorrista en la playa? Is there a lifeguard at the beach?

el socorro *masc noun*
1 **help**
pedir socorro to ask for help
2 **¡Socorro!** Help!

el sofá *masc noun*
sofa

sofocar *verb* [31]
to put out (*a fire*)

sofocarse *reflexive verb* [31]
to get worked up

sois *verb* ▷ **ser**

la soja *fem noun*
soya

el sol *masc noun*
sun
un día de sol a sunny day
sentarse al sol to lie in the sun
al ponerse el sol at sunset
Hacía sol. It was sunny.
El sol estaba saliendo. The sun was rising.

solamente *adverb*
only

el & la soldado *masc & fem noun*
soldier

soleado *masc adjective*, **soleada** *fem*
sunny
un piso soleado a sunny flat

la soledad *fem noun*
loneliness

soler *verb* [38]
1 **soler hacer algo** to usually do something
Suelen verse. They usually see each other.
Suele salir por las noches. He usually goes out in the evenings.
2 **used to**
Solía venir los lunes. She used to come on Mondays.

solicitar *verb* [17]
1 to ask for (*permission, an interview*)
2 **to apply for** (*a job*)

la solicitud *masc noun*
application

sólido *masc adjective*, **sólida** *fem*
1 **solid**
2 **sound**

solitario *masc adjective*, **solitaria** *fem*
lonely

solo *masc adjective*, **sola** *fem* ▷ see **sólo** *adv*
1 **alone**
Vive solo. He lives alone.
Cuando me quedé solo. When I was left alone.
2 **lonely**
sentirse solo to feel lonely
Está muy sola. She's very lonely.
3 **on your own**
Desde que murió su madre está sola. Since her mother died, she's been on her own.
4 **by yourself**
Lo hice sola. I did it by myself.
5 (*by itself*) **un café solo** a black coffee
un coñac solo a neat brandy
6 (*just one*) **con una sola mano** with one hand
sin una sola queja without a single complaint

sólo *adverb* ▷ see **solo** *adj*
only

el **solomillo** *masc noun*
fillet steak

soltar *verb* **[24]**
1 **to let go of**
¡Suéltame! Let go of me!
Le solté la mano. I let go of his hand.
2 **to release** (*a prisoner*)
3 **to untie**
soltar un nudo to untie a knot
4 **soltar al perro** to let the dog off the lead
5 (*with shouts, laughs*) **soltar un grito** to let out a cry
soltar una carcajada to let out a laugh
soltar una palabrota to come out with a swearword

soltarse *reflexive verb* **[24]**
1 **to come undone** (*a knot, bow*)
2 **soltarse de algo** to let go of something
Se soltó de mi mano. He let go of my hand.
No te sueltes de la barandilla. Don't let go of the banister.
3 **soltarse el pelo** to let your hair down

soltero *masc adjective*, **soltera** *fem* ▷ see **soltero** *noun*
single

el **soltero** *masc noun*, la **soltera** *fem noun* ▷ see **soltero** *adjective*
1 **bachelor** (*male*)
2 **single woman**

la **soltura** *fem noun*
con soltura with ease, without difficulty
hablar español con soltura to speak Spanish fluently

soluble *masc & fem adjective*
soluble

la **solución** *fem noun*
solution

solucionar *verb* **[17]**
1 **to solve**
2 **to settle** (*a conflict*)

la **sombra** *fem noun*
1 **shadow**
2 **shade**
dar sombra to give shade
sentarse en la sombra to sit in the shade
• la **sombra de ojos** eye shadow

el **sombrero** *masc noun*
hat

la **sombrilla** *fem noun*
1 **sunshade**
2 **parasol**

sombrío *masc adjective*, **sombría** *fem*
1 **dark** (*street, room*)
2 **gloomy** (*face, look*)

somos, **son** *verb* ▷ **ser**

sonar *verb* **[24]**
1 **to ring** (*a doorbell, telephone*)
Está sonando el teléfono. The telephone's ringing.
2 **to sound**
Suena raro. It sounds strange.
Suena a hueco. It sounds hollow.
3 **to be familiar**
Me suena mucho su cara. Her face is very familiar to me.
¿Carlos Ramírez? No me suena. Carlos Ramírez? The name doesn't ring a bell.

sonarse *reflexive verb* **[24]**
sonarse la nariz to blow one's nose

soñar *verb* **[24]**
to dream
Anoche soñé contigo. I dreamt about you last night.

el **sondeo** *masc noun*
survey

el **sonido** *masc noun*
sound

sonreír *verb* **[61]**
to smile
Me sonrió. He smiled at me.

sonreírse *reflexive verb* **[61]**
to smile

sonría, sonríe, sonrío, etc *verb* ▷ **sonreír**

la **sonrisa** *fem noun*
smile

sonrojarse *verb* [17]
to blush

la **sopa** *fem noun*
soup
sopa de pescado fish soup

soplar *verb* [17]
1 **to blow**
soplar el polvo de la mesa to blow the dust off the table
El viento sopla del oeste. The wind blows from the west.
2 **to blow out**
soplar las velas to blow out the candles
3 (*with secrets, answers*) **soplarle la respuesta a alguien** to pass on the answer to someone (*in an exam*)

soportar *verb* [17]
1 **to stand** (*a person, situation*)
No soporto a Rafael. I can't stand Rafael.
2 **to bear** (*pain*)
3 **to withstand** (*heat*)

el **soporte** *masc noun*
support

el **sorbete** *masc noun*
sorbet

el **sorbo** *masc noun*
1 **sip**
beber a sorbos to sip
2 **gulp**
beberse algo de un sorbo to drink something in one gulp
Se lo bebió de un sorbo. He drank it in one gulp.

sordo *masc adjective*, **sorda** *fem* ▷ see **sordo** *noun*
deaf

el **sordo** *masc noun*, la **sorda** *fem noun* ▷ see **sordo** *adj*
deaf person

sordomudo *masc adjective*, **sordomuda** *fem* ▷ see **sordomudo** *noun*
deaf and dumb

el **sordomudo** *masc noun*, la **sordomuda** *fem noun* ▷ see **sordomudo** *adj*
deaf mute

sorprendente *masc & fem adjective*
surprising

sorprender *verb* [18]
to surprise
Me sorprende que se retrase. I'm surprised he's late.

sorprenderse *reflexive verb* [18]
to be surprised

sorprendido *masc adjective*, **sorprendida** *fem*
surprised

la **sorpresa** *fem noun*
surprise

la **sortija** *fem noun*
ring

soso *masc adjective*, **sosa** *fem*
1 **dull**
2 **bland**

el **soso** *masc noun*, la **sosa** *fem noun* ▷ see **soso** *adj*
bore

la **sospecha** *fem noun*
suspicion
Tengo la sospecha de que ... I have a suspicion that ...

sospechar *verb* [17]
to suspect

sospechoso *masc adjective*, **sospechosa** *fem*
suspicious
Me parece sospechoso. I find it suspicious.

el **sostén** *masc noun*
1 **support**
2 **bra**

sostener *verb* [9]
1 **to support** (*an arch, ceiling, family*)
2 **to bear** (*a weight, load*)

el **sótano** *masc noun*
1 **basement**
2 **cellar**

soy *verb* ▷ **ser**

Sr. *abbreviation*
(*short for: Señor*) **Mr**

Sra. *abbreviation*
(*short for: Señora*) **Mrs**, **Ms**

Sres. *abbreviation*
(*short for: Señores*) **Mr & Mrs**

Srta. *abbreviation*
(*short for: Señorita*) **Miss**, **Ms**

su *masc & fem adjective*
1 **his**, **her**
su casa her house, his house
Ahí está con sus padres. There she is with her parents., There he is with his parents.
2 **its**
El perro duerme en su caseta. The dog sleeps in its kennel.
3 **their**
Es su coche. It's their car.
4 **your** (*polite form, singular & plural*)
Aquí tiene su sombrero. Here's your hat.
¿Son éstos sus zapatos? Are these your shoes?

suave *masc & fem adjective*
1 **soft**
2 **smooth**
3 **gentle** (*voice, climate*)
4 **mild** (*weather*)

el **suavizante** *masc noun*
1 **fabric softener**
2 **hair conditioner**

subdesarrollado *masc adjective*, **subdesarrollada** *fem*
underdeveloped (*country*)

subestimar *verb* **[17]**
underestimate

la **subida** *fem noun*
1 **rise** (*in temperature, prices*)
2 **climb** (*up a hill, mountain*)

subir *verb* **[19]**
1 **to go up**
subir al tercer piso to go up to the third floor
El ascensor está subiendo. The lift is going up.
La temperatura ha subido tres grados. The temperature has gone up three degrees.
2 **to come up**
¡Sube! Come up!
3 **to bring up**
Súbeme un vaso de agua. Bring me up a glass of water.
Suba el equipaje, por favor. Bring the luggage up, please. (*polite form*)
4 **to take up**
¿Le subo las maletas a su habitación? Shall I take the luggage up to your room?
5 **to put up**
Han subido el precio de la gasolina. They've put up the price of petrol again.
6 (*with vehicles*) **subir al tren** to get on the train
subir a un coche to get into a car
subir a bordo to go on board
7 **to turn up** (*the volume*)
Subió un poco la música. He turned up the music a bit.
8 **to raise**
subir una persiana to raise a blind
9 **to rise** (*water, rivers*)
El agua está subiendo. The water is rising.
10 **to come in** (*tides*)

subirse *reflexive verb* **[19]**
1 **subirse al tren** to get on the train
subirse a un coche to get into a car
2 **subirse a un árbol** to climb up a tree
3 **to pull up** (*trousers, socks*)
subirse los calcetines to pull up your socks

súbitamente *adverb*
suddenly

súbito *masc adjective*, **súbita** *fem*
sudden

el **subjuntivo** *masc noun*
subjunctive

el **submarinismo** *masc noun*
scuba diving

el & la **submarinista** *masc & fem noun*
1 **scuba diver**
2 **submariner**

el **submarino** *masc noun*
submarine

subrayar *verb* **[17]**
to underline

el **subsidio** *masc noun*
subsidy
- el **subsidio de desempleo** unemployment benefit
- el **subsidio de invalidez** disability allowance

subterráneo *masc adjective*, **subterránea** *fem*
▷ see **subterráneo** *noun*
underground

el **subterráneo** *masc noun*
▷ see **subterráneo** *adjective*
subway, **underpass**

los **subtítulos** *plural masc noun*
subtitles (*in films*)

el **suburbio** *masc noun*
1 **slum area** (*on the outskirts of a town*)
2 **suburb**

la **subvención** *fem noun*
subsidy

subvencionar *verb* **[17]**
to subsidize

♪ **suceder** *verb* **[18]**
1 **to happen**
¿Qué sucede? What's happening?
Le ha sucedido algo. Something's happened to him.
Lo que sucede es que ... The thing is that ...
2 **to succeed** (*to the throne*)

el **suceso** *masc noun*
1 **event**
2 **incident**
la página de sucesos accidents and crimes report (*in a newspaper*)

la **suciedad** *fem noun*
1 **grime**
2 **dirtiness**

♪ **sucio** *masc adjective*, **sucia** *fem*
1 **dirty**
Tienes la camisa sucia. Your shirt is dirty.
2 **en sucio** in rough
El trabajo sólo está en sucio. The essay is only in rough.

la **sucursal** *fem noun*
1 **branch** (*of a bank, a business*)
2 **office** (*of a company*)

♪ la **sudadera** *fem noun*
sweatshirt

♪ **Sudamérica** *fem noun*
South America

sudamericano *masc adjective & noun*, **sudamericana** *fem adjective & noun*
1 **South American**
2 **un sudamericano, una sudamericana** South American

WORD TIP Adjectives and nouns for nationality and regional origin do not have capital letters in Spanish.

sudar *verb* **[17]**
to sweat

el **sudeste** *masc noun*
southeast

el **sudoeste** *masc noun*
southwest

el **sudor** *masc noun*
sweat

Suecia *fem noun*
Sweden

sueco *masc adjective & noun*, **sueca** *fem adjective & noun*
1 **Swedish**
2 **un sueco, una sueca** Swede
el sueco Swedish (*the language*)

WORD TIP Adjectives and nouns for nationality, regional origin, and language do not have capital letters in Spanish.

el **suegro** *masc noun*, la **suegra** *fem*
1 **father-in-law**
2 **mother-in-law**
3 **mis suegros** my parents in law

la **suela** *fem noun* ▷ see **suela** *verb*
sole

suela, **suelas**, **etc** *verb* ▷ see **suela** *noun* ▷ **soler**

el **sueldo** *masc noun*
1 **salary**
2 **pay**
un aumento de sueldo a pay rise

♪ el **suelo** *masc noun* ▷ see **suelo** *verb*
1 **floor**
2 **ground**
tirarse al suelo to throw yourself to the ground

♪ **suelo** *verb* ▷ see **suelo** *noun* ▷ **soler**

suelta, **suelte**, **suelto**, **etc** *verb* ▷ **soltar**

suelto *masc adjective*, **suelta** *fem* ▷ see **suelto** *noun*
1 **loose**
El perro está suelto. The dog is loose.
2 **separately**
Los venden sueltos. They are sold separately.

el **suelto** *masc noun* ▷ see **suelto** *adjective*
change (*coins*)
¿Tienes suelto? Have you got any change?

♪ **suena**, **suene**, **sueno**, **etc** *verb* ▷ **sonar**

♪ **sueña**, **sueñe**, **sueño**, **etc** *verb* ▷ **soñar**

♪ el **sueño** *masc noun*
1 **dream**
Mi sueño es vivir en Los Ángeles. My dream is to live in Los Angeles.
2 **tener sueño** to be sleepy

♪ la **suerte** *fem noun*
luck
tener suerte to be lucky
traer mala suerte to bring bad luck
¡Qué mala suerte! What bad luck!
¡Suerte! Good luck!

♪ el **suéter** *masc noun*
sweater

suficiente *masc & fem adjective & pronoun* ▷ see **suficiente** *noun*
enough
Tenemos suficiente dinero. We have enough money.
No traigas más, tenemos suficientes. Don't bring any more, we've got enough.

el **suficiente** *masc noun* ▷ see **suficiente** *adj, pron*
(*in school*) **pass** (*equivalent to 50%*)

sufrir *verb* **[19]**
1 **to suffer**
Sufre mucho. He's suffering a lot.
2 **to have**
sufrir un accidente to have an accident
Sufre una grave enfermedad. He has a serious illness.

la **sugerencia** *fem noun*
suggestion

sugerir *verb* **[14]**
to suggest

sugiera, **sugiero**, **sugirieron**, **etc** *verb* ▷ **sugerir**

suicidarse *reflexive verb* **[17]**
to commit suicide

el **suicidio** *masc noun*
suicide

Suiza *fem noun*
Switzerland

suizo *masc adjective & noun*, **suiza** *fem adjective & noun*
1 **Swiss**
2 **un suizo, una suiza** Swiss

WORD TIP Adjectives and nouns for nationality and regional origin do not have capital letters in Spanish.

⚷ el **sujetador** *masc noun*
bra

sujeto *masc adjective*, **sujeta** *fem* ▷ see **sujeto** *noun*
1 **secure**
Está bien sujeto. It's really secure.
2 **estar sujeto a algo** to be liable to something
Está sujeto a modificaciones. It's liable to change.

⚷ el **sujeto** *masc noun* ▷ see **sujeto** *adj*
subject

la **suma** *fem noun*
1 **addition**
2 **en suma** in short

sumar *verb* **[17]**
to add

⚷ **supe**, **supiste**, **etc** *verb* ▷ **saber**

⚷ **super**, **súper** *invariable adjective, adverb*
(*informal*) **super**
Cantan super bien. They sing really well.
Me lo pasé super bien. I had a great time.

WORD TIP *super, súper* never changes.

superar *verb* **[17]**
1 **to overcome** (*fear, problems*)
2 **to get over** (*a shock*)
3 **to exceed** (*expectations, temperatures*)

la **superficie** *fem noun*
surface

superior *masc & fem adjective*
1 **superior**
Es superior a los demás.. It's superior to the rest.
2 **upper** (*lip, floor, storey*)
3 **higher** (*number, level, class*)

⚷ el **supermercado** *masc noun*
supermarket

la **superstición** *fem noun*
superstition

supersticioso *masc adjective*, **supersticiosa** *fem*
superstitious

supervisar *verb* **[17]**
supervise

el **supervisor** *masc noun*, la **supervisora** *fem noun*
supervisor

el & la **superviviente** *masc & fem noun*
survivor

suplementario *masc adjective*, **suplementaria** *fem*
additional

⚷ el **suplemento** *masc noun*
supplement
Hay que pagar un suplemento. You have to pay an additional charge.

supondrá, **supondré**, **supondría**, **etc** *verb* ▷ **suponer**

suponer *verb* **[11]**
1 **to suppose**
Supongo que sí. I suppose so.
2 **to involve**
Supone volver a hacerlo. It involves doing it again.

Spanish–English

suponga, **supongo**, **etc** *verb* ▷ **suponer**

el **supositorio** *masc noun*
suppository

suprimir *verb* **[19]**
1 **to suppress** (*news*)
2 **to abolish**
3 **to delete**

supuesto *in phrase*
por supuesto of course
Por supuesto que te acompañamos. Of course we'll go with you.

supuse, **supuso** *verb* ▷ **suponer**

sur *masc noun, invariable adjective*
south
ir hacia el sur to go south
la costa sur de Inglaterra the south coast of England
al sur de Murcia south of Murcia
en el sur de España in the south of Spain

Suramérica *fem noun*
South America

suramericano *masc adjective & noun*, **suramericana** *fem adjective & noun*
1 **South American**
2 **un suramericano, una suramericana** South American

WORD TIP Adjectives and nouns for nationality and regional origin do not have capital letters in Spanish.

el **sureste** *masc noun*
southest

el **surf** *masc noun*
surfing
practicar el surf to go surfing

el & la **surfista** *masc & fem noun*
surfer (*in the sea*)

el **suroeste** *masc noun*
southwest

surtido *masc adjective*, **surtida** *fem*
▷ see **surtido** *noun*
1 **assorted**
2 **una tienda bien surtida** a well-stocked shop

el **surtido** *masc noun* ▷ see **surtido** *adj*
1 **assortment**
2 **selection**

el **surtidor** *masc noun*
petrol pump

suspender *verb* **[18]**
1 **to fail** (*in exams*)
Hemos suspendido. We've failed.
He suspendido la física. I've failed physics.
2 **to suspend** (*a payment, service*)
3 **to cancel**
suspender un partido to cancel a match

el **suspense** *masc noun*
suspense
una película de suspense a thriller (*film*)

el **suspenso** *masc noun*
1 **fail** (*in an exam*)
2 **estar en suspenso** to be in suspense

suspirar *verb* **[17]**
to sigh

el **suspiro** *masc noun*
sigh

la **sustancia** *fem noun*
substance

el **sustantivo** *masc noun*
noun

sustituir *verb* **[54]**
1 **to replace**
sustituir algo por algo to replace something with something
Sustituimos el azucar por la miel. We replaced the honey with sugar.
2 **sustituir a alguien** to stand in for someone (*at work*), to substitute for someone (*in sports*)
Lo sustituyó en su ausencia. She stood in for him in his absence.
Zamorano sustituyó a Salas en el minuto 20. Zamorano came on for Salas in the twentieth minute.

el **sustituto** *masc noun*, la **sustituta** *fem noun*
1 **replacement**
2 **substitute**
3 **locum**

el **susto** *masc noun*
fright
darle un susto a alguien to give someone a fright
¡Qué susto me has dado! What a fright you gave me!
¡Qué susto me llevé! I got such a fright!

sustraer *verb* **[42]**
to subtract

a b c d e f g h i j k l m n ñ o p q r **s** t u v w x y z

susurrar *verb* **[17]**
to whisper

sutil *masc & fem adjective*
subtle

suyo *masc adjective*, **suya** *fem*
▷ see **suyo** *pron*

1 **his, hers**
Esto es suyo. This is his., This is hers.
un conocido suyo a friend of his, a friend of hers
una vecina suya a neighbour of his, a neighbour of hers

2 **theirs**
Estos son suyos. These are theirs.
Venían con un amigo suyo. They came with a friend of theirs.
Venían con unos amigos suyos. They came with some friends of theirs.

3 **yours** (*polite* ***usted*** *form*)
un colega suyo a colleague of yours

WORD TIP *suyo, suya* agrees with the thing you have or own: *conocido, vecina*, etc above. *suyo, suya* goes after the noun.

suyo *pronoun* ▷ see **suyo** *adj*

1 **his, hers**
El suyo es gris. His is grey., Hers is grey.
Las suyas son mejores. His are better., Hers are better.

2 **yours** (*polite 'usted' form*)
Aquí tiene el suyo. Here is yours.

3 **theirs**
Este es mi coche. El suyo es más grande. This is my car. Theirs is bigger.
Estos son los nuestros. Los suyos son más grandes. These are ours. Theirs are bigger.

WORD TIP *el suyo, la suya* agrees with the thing you have or own.

Spanish–English

T t

a b c d e f g h i j k l m n ñ o p q r s t u v w x y z

*el **tabaco** *masc noun*
1 **tobacco**
2 **cigarettes**
Tengo que comprar tabaco. I must buy some cigarettes.

*el **tabaquismo** *masc noun*
tobacco addiction

*la **taberna** *fem noun*
bar (*selling wine*)

*la **tabla** *fem noun*
1 **plank**
2 **board**
3 **pleat**
4 **table** (*of figures*)
- la **tabla de gimnasia** circuit training
- la **tabla de multiplicar** multiplication table
- la **tabla de planchar** ironing board
- la **tabla de vela** sailboard

el **tablao** *masc noun*
- el **tablao flamenco** flamenco dance bar

el **tablero** *masc noun*
1 **board** (*for chess, draughts*)
2 **noticeboard**
- el **tablero chino** Chinese checkers
- el **tablero de damas** draughtboard

el **tablón** *masc noun*
plank
- el **tablón de anuncios** noticeboard

*el **taburete** *masc noun*
stool

tacaño *masc adjective*, **tacaña** *fem*
▷ see **tacaño** *noun*
stingy

el **tacaño** *masc noun*, la **tacaña** *fem noun*
▷ see **tacaño** *adj*
miser

tachar *verb* **[17]**
to cross out

el **taco** *masc noun*
1 **cue** (*in billiards*)
2 **stud** (*on a sports boot*)
3 (*informal*) **swearword**
decir tacos to swear

*el **tacón** *masc noun*
heel
zapatos de tacón alto high-heeled shoes
- el **tacón de aguja** stiletto heel

la **táctica** *fem noun*
1 **tactic**
2 **tactics**

el **tacto** *masc noun*
1 **sense of touch**
2 **feel**
3 **tact**
Fue una falta de tacto. It was very tactless.

***TAF** *abbreviation* (= *Transferencia Automática de Fondos*) **automatic funds transfer**

la **tajada** *fem noun*
slice (*of melon, etc*)

***tal** *masc & fem adjective* ▷ **see tal** *adv*
1 **such**
Tal cosa es imposible. Such a thing is impossible.
Lo hizo de tal manera que ... She did it in such a way that ...
Tales eran sus problemas que ... Such were his problems that ...
2 (*for emphasis*) **Nunca había visto tal cantidad de lluvia.** I had never seen such a lot of rain.
3 (*when you don't know someone*) **Una tal Señora González pregunta por ti.** Someone called Mrs González is asking for you.

***tal** *adverb* ▷ **see tal** *adj*
1 (*informal*) (*asking questions*) **¿Qué tal?** How are things?
¿Qué tal estás? How are you doing?
¿Qué tal es su novia? What's his girlfriend like?
¿Qué tal estuvo la película? How was the film?
2 **tal vez** maybe
Tal vez iré el viernes. Maybe I'll go on Friday.
3 **tal cual** just the way it was
Lo dejaron tal cual. They left it just as it was.

el **talco** *masc noun*
talc
polvos de talco talcum powder

el **talento** *masc noun*
talent

♂ el **TALGO** *masc noun*
(= *Tren Articulado Ligero Goicoechea Oriol*) **express train** (*in Spain*)

♂ la **talla** *fem noun*
size (*for clothes, hats*)
unos pantalones de la talla 40 a pair of size 40 trousers
¿Qué talla de pantalones usa? What size of trousers do you take? (*polite form*)

♂ el **taller** *masc noun*
1 **workshop**
2 **garage**
llevar el coche al taller to take the car to the garage

♂ el **talón** *masc noun*
heel

el **talonario** *masc noun*
chequebook

♂ el **tamaño** *masc noun*
size
un tamaño más grande a larger size
de tamaño familiar family-sized
¿De qué tamaño es? What size is it?
¿Tiene un tamaño más pequeño? Do you have a smaller size?

♂ **también** *adverb*
too, as well
Ella también vive allí. She lives there too.
'Tengo quince años.'—'Yo también.' 'I'm fifteen.'—'Me too.'
'Yo quiero tarta.'—'Nosotros también.' 'I want some cake.'—'We do too.'
También estudia griego. He also studies Greek.

el **tambor** *masc noun*
drum

♂ **tampoco** *adverb*
1 **not ... either**
Él tampoco irá. He won't go either.
Ella no irá tampoco. She won't go either.
Ellos tampoco quieren jugar. They don't want to play either.
Ellas no pueden jugar tampoco. They can't play either.

WORD TIP *Tampoco* can be used with or without *no*, but its position in the sentence changes accordingly.

2 (*in short replies*) **neither do I** (*you, he, she, etc*)
'A mí no me gusta.'—'A mí tampoco.' 'I don't like it.'—'Neither do I.'
'A mí no me apetece ir.'—'A nosotros tampoco.' 'I don't feel like going.'—'Neither do we.'

el **tampón** *masc noun*
tampon

♂ **tan** *adverb*
1 **so** (*+ adverb or adjective*)
No es tan fácil. It's not so easy.
No corras tan rápido. Don't run so fast.
¡Qué casa tan grande! What a big house!
2 **such a** (*+ noun*)
Es una persona tan egoísta. He's such a selfish person.
Es una chica tan guapa. She's such a good-looking girl.
3 (*in comparisons*) **tan ... como ...** as ... as ...
Es tan alta como su padre. She's as tall as her father.
No era tan caro como el otro. It wasn't as expensive as the other one.
4 (*saying the result*) **tan ... que ...** so ... that ...
Era tan grande que no cabía por la puerta. It was so big that it would not fit through the door.

el **tanque** *masc noun*
tank

♂ **tanto** *masc adjective*, **tanta** *fem*
▷ **see tanto** *adv, noun, pron*
1 **so much**
tanto dinero so much money
tanta sal so much salt
Puso tanto azúcar al café, que no se podía beber. He put so much sugar in the coffee that it was undrinkable.
2 **so many**
tantos libros so many books
tantas cajas so many boxes
Había tanta gente que no cabíamos. There were so many people that there wasn't room for us.
3 **tanto ... como ..., tanta ... como ...** as much ... as ...
No gasta tanta gasolina como el coche viejo. It doesn't use as much petrol as the old car.
4 **tantos ... como ..., tantas ... como ...** as many ... as ...
Hay tantos alumnos como el año pasado. There are as many students as last year.
No hay tantas golondrinas como antes. There aren't as many swallows as before.

♂ **tanto** *adverb* ▷ **see tanto** *adj, pron, noun*
1 **so**
No corras tanto. Don't go so fast.
Se enfadó tanto. He got so upset. ▸▸

a b c d e f g h i j k l m n ñ o p q r s t u v w x y z

2 so much
No deberías gastar tanto. You shouldn't spend so much.
3 so often
Yo no los visito tanto. I don't visit them all that often.
4 so long
Lleva tanto hacerlo. It takes so long to do.
5 Pesa tanto como éste. It's as heavy as this one.
6 (*with* **mejor** *and* **peor**) **tanto mejor** so much the better
Si le gusta, tanto mejor. If she likes it, so much the better.
tanto peor so much the worse
Si no le gusta, tanto peor. If she doesn't like it, so much the worse.

el **tanto** *masc noun* ▷ **see tanto** *adj, adv, pron*
1 point, goal
marcar un tanto to score a point, to score a goal
2 an amount
Gana un tanto de cada venta. She gets an amount on each sale.
• el **tanto por ciento** percentage

tanto *masc pronoun*, **tanta** *fem* ▷ **see tanto** *adj, adv, noun*
1 tanto so much (*for a masc noun*)
tanta so much (*for a fem noun*)
No hace falta tanto., No hace falta tanta. We don't need so much.
2 tantos so many (*for a masc plural noun*)
tantas so many (*for a fem plural noun*)
Vinieron tantos que no había sillas libres. So many came that there weren't any chairs left.
Vendieron tantas que no quedan más. They sold so many that there are none left.
3 (*talking about time*) **tanto** so long
No tardes tanto como ayer. Don't take as long as yesterday.
'Me llevará dos días hacerlo.'—'¿Tanto?.' 'It'll take me two days to do it.'—'As long as that?.'
4 (*in expressions*) **por lo tanto** therefore
mientras tanto in the meantime
entre tanto in the meantime

la **tapa** *fem noun*
1 lid
2 top
tapa de rosca screw top
3 cover (*of a book*)
4 tapa (*snack eaten in a 'tapas' bar*)
un bar de tapas a tapas bar
comer de tapas to eat tapas for lunch (*or supper, etc*)

> mini-info **tapas**
> Comenzaron como un pedazo de pan para cubrir el vaso para protegerlo de las moscas. Hoy en día se trata de una variedad enorme de pinchos o raciones para acompañar una bebida.

tapar *verb* **[17]**
1 to cover
2 to put the top on
3 to fill in
tapar un agujero to fill in a hole
4 to block up (*a window, a door*)
5 to blot out (*sunlight, the view*)

el **tapón** *masc noun*
1 cork
2 top (*of a bottle*)
3 plug (*of a basin, bath, sink*)

la **taquigrafía**
shorthand

la **taquilla** *fem noun*
1 box office
un éxito de taquilla a box office hit
2 ticket office

tardar *verb* **[17]**
1 to take (*time*)
¿Cuánto se tarda de Sevilla a Córdoba? How long does it take from Seville to Cordoba?
Tarda un par de horas. It takes a couple of hours.
2 to take a long time
Tardó mucho en contestarme. She took a long time to answer.
¡No tardes! Don't be long!
No tardes en volver. Come back soon.
3 a más tardar at the latest
a las cuatro a más tardar at four o'clock at the latest

tarde *adverb* ▷ **see tarde** *noun*
late
llegar tarde to be late
Se acuesta tarde. He goes to bed late.
Más vale tarde que nunca. better late than never.

la **tarde** *fem noun* ▷ **see tarde** *adv*
afternoon, evening
a las tres de la tarde at three in the afternoon
por la tarde in the afternoon, in the evening
Buenas tardes. Good afternoon., Good evening.

♪ la **tarea** *fem noun*
1 **task**
2 **las tareas de la casa** the housework
3 **homework**

♪ la **tarifa** *fem noun*
1 **price list**
2 **fare** (*for buses, taxis*)
3 **charge** (*for electricity, gas, postage*)

♪ la **tarjeta** *fem noun*
card
sacarle a alguien la tarjeta amarilla to show somebody the yellow card
sacarle a alguien la tarjeta roja to show somebody the red card
- la **tarjeta de crédito** credit card
- la **tarjeta de cumpleaños** birthday card
- la **tarjeta de embarque** boarding card
- la **tarjeta de fidelidad** loyalty card
- la **tarjeta de Navidad** Christmas card
- la **tarjeta postal** postcard
- la **tarjeta de prepago** top-up card
- la **tarjeta SIM** SIM card

la **tarrina** *fem noun*
tub (*for food*)

♪ el **tarro** *masc noun*
jar

♪ la **tarta** *fem noun*
1 **cake**
2 **tart**
- la **tarta de cumpleaños** birthday cake
- la **tarta helada** ice-cream cake

la **tartera** *fem noun*
sandwich box

♪ la **tasa** *fem noun*
1 **rate**
2 **valuation**
3 **tax**
- la **tasa de desempleo** rate of unemployment
- la **tasa de interés** interest rate

♪ el **tatuaje** *masc noun*
tatoo

♪ **tauro** *masc & fem noun*
Taurus
Es tauro. He's Taurus.

WORD TIP Use a small letter in Spanish to say *I am Taurus*, etc with star signs.

♪ **Tauro** *masc noun*
Taurus

♪ el **taxi** *masc noun*
taxi

♪ el & la **taxista** *masc & fem noun*
taxi driver

♪ la **taza** *fem noun*
1 **cup**
una taza de café a cup of coffee
2 **(toilet) bowl**

♪ el **tazón** *masc noun*
bowl

♪ **te** *pronoun*
1 **you**
Te quiero. I love you.
Te vi ayer. I saw you yesterday.
2 **to you**
Te lo mandaré por correo. I'll post it to you.
3 (*with parts of the body, personal belongings*) **¿Te has cortado el dedo?** Have you cut your finger?
¿Quieres quitarte los zapatos? Do you want to take your shoes off?
4 (*about having things done*) **¿Te has cortado el pelo?** Have you had your hair cut?
5 **yourself**
Cuídate mucho. Look after yourself.
6 **Siéntate.** Sit down.

WORD TIP *te* is used to refer to a person you know well. ▷ **usted, vosotros**

♪ el **té** *masc noun*
tea
a la hora del té at tea time
Queremos té para dos. We'd like tea for two.

♪ el **teatro** *masc noun*
theatre

♪ el **tebeo** *masc noun*
comic (*for children*)

♪ el **techo** *masc noun*
1 **ceiling**
2 (*Latin America*) **roof**
3 **los sin techo** the homeless

♪ la **tecla** *fem noun*
key

♪ el **teclado** *masc noun*
keyboard

la **técnica** *fem noun* ▷ see **técnico** *adj, noun*
technique

técnico *masc adjective*, **técnica** *fem*
▷ see **técnica** *noun*, **técnico** *noun*
technical

el **técnico** *masc noun*, la **técnica** *fem noun*
▷ see **técnica** *noun*, **técnico** *adj*
technician

a b c d e f g h i j k l m n ñ o p q r s t u v w x y z

la **tecnología** *fem noun*
technology

la **teja** *fem noun*
tile

el **tejado** *masc noun*
roof

los **tejanos** *plural masc noun*
jeans

tejer *verb* **[18]**
1 **to weave**
2 **to knit**

la **tela** *fem noun*
1 **fabric**
una tela de algodón a cotton fabric
2 **canvas** (*for painting*)

la **telaraña** *fem noun*
1 **spider's web**
2 **cobweb**
3 **spider diagram**

la **tele** *fem noun*
(*informal*) **telly**, **TV**
ver la tele to watch telly
ver algo en la tele to see something on TV
poner la tele to switch on the telly

el **telediario** *masc noun*
television news

el **teleférico** *masc noun*
cablecar

telefonear *verb* **[17]**
to telephone

telefónico *masc adjective*, **telefónica** *fem*
telephone
una conversación telefónica a telephone conversation
el listín telefónico telephone book

el **teléfono** *masc noun*
telephone
contestar el teléfono to answer the phone
colgar el teléfono to hang up
No tenemos teléfono. We don't have a phone.
llamar por teléfono a alguien to phone somebody
Al llegar, me llamó por teléfono. When she arrived, she phoned me.
- el **teléfono celular** (*Latin America*) mobile phone
- el **teléfono inalámbrico** cordless phone
- el **teléfono móvil** mobile phone

el **telegrama** *masc noun*
telegram

la **telenovela** *fem noun*
TV serial

el **telescopio** *masc noun*
telescope

la **televisión** *fem noun*
television
ver la televisión to watch television
poner la televisión to switch on the television
El rey habló por televisión. The king spoke on television.
Hoy ponen una película en la televisión. There's a film on the television today.

el **televisor** *masc noun*
television set
- el **televisor de pantalla grande** wide-screen television

el **tema** *masc noun*
1 **subject**
2 **issue**
un tema polémico a contentious issue

temblar *verb* **[29]**
1 **to shiver**
2 **to shake**
Le temblaban las manos. His hands were shaking.

temer *verb* **[18]**
to fear (*danger, punishment*)
Tememos lo peor. We fear the worst.
temer a alguien to be afraid of somebody
Sus alumnos le temen. His pupils are afraid of him.

temerse *reflexive verb* **[18]**
1 **to fear**
2 **Me temo que no podré venir.** I'm afraid I won't be able to come.

la **temperatura** *fem noun*
temperature
Hace una temperatura de quince grados. The temperature is fifteen degrees.
Ha subido la temperatura. The temperature has risen.

la **tempestad** *fem noun*
storm

templado *masc adjective*, **templada** *fem*
1 **mild** (*climate*)
2 **warm**
3 **lukewarm**

♪ la **temporada** *fem noun*
season
fuera de temporada out of season
la temporada alta the high season
la temporada baja the low season

♪ **temprano** *masc adjective*, **temprana** *fem* ▷ see **temprano** *adv*
early

♪ **temprano** *adverb* ▷ see **temprano** *adj*
early
tarde o temprano sooner or later
llegar temprano to arrive early

la **tendencia** *fem noun*
tendency

tender *verb* [36]
1 **tender a** to tend to
Tienden a visitarnos más en invierno. They tend to visit us more often in winter.
2 **tender la ropa** to hang out the washing

tenderse *reflexive verb* [36]
to lie down
tenderse al sol to lie down in the sun

el **tendero** *masc noun*, la **tendera** *fem noun*
shopkeeper

♪ **tendrá**, **tendré**, **tendría**, **etc** *verb* ▷ **tener**

♪ el **tenedor** *masc noun*
fork

♪ **tener** *verb* [9]
1 **to have**
Tengo un hermano. I have a brother.
Tiene los ojos marrones. He has brown eyes.
tener dolor de cabeza to have a headache
No tengo tiempo. I haven't got the time.
¿Tienes hora? Have you got the time?
Ha tenido un niño. She has had a baby.
2 (*saying your age*) **to be**
¿Cuántos años tienes? How old are you?
Tengo catorce años. I'm fourteen (years old).
Ella tiene quince años. She's fifteen (years old).
3 **to be** (*hot, cold, hungry, thirsty, etc*)
tener calor to be hot
tener frío to be cold
tener hambre to be hungry
tener sed to be thirsty
Tengo calor. I'm hot.
4 **to be** (*careful, afraid, right, in a hurry, etc*)
tener cuidado to be careful
tener miedo to be afraid
tener razón to be right
tener prisa to be in a hurry
tener sueño to feel sleepy
No tengo miedo del perro. I'm not afraid of the dog.
Tenemos prisa. We're in a hurry.
5 **tener que hacer algo** to have to do something, must
Tengo que estudiar. I have to study.
Tengo que ir al dentista. I must go to the dentist's.
Tendría que ir al banco. I should go to the bank.
Tienes que hacer lo que diga el médico. You must do as the doctor says.
6 **tener que ver con alguien** to have to do with someone
No tiene nada que ver contigo. It has nothing to do with you.
7 (*saying something is done*) **tener + -ado, -ido form of the verb**
Lo tienen controlado. They've got it under control.
Lo tengo hecho. I've done it.
8 **tenerle envidia de alguien** to be jealous of somebody
Le tiene envidia. He's jealous of her.

♪ **tenga**, **tengo**, **etc** *verb* ▷ **tener**

el & la **teniente** *masc & fem noun*
lieutenant

♪ el **tenis** *masc noun*
tennis
• el **tenis de mesa** table tennis

♪ el & la **tenista** *masc & fem noun*
tennis player

la **tensión** *fem noun*
1 **tension**
2 **stress**
3 **blood pressure**
tomarse la tensión to have your blood pressure taken

la **tentación** *fem noun*
temptation

tentar *verb* [29]
to tempt

teñir *verb* [65]
to dye

teñirse *reflexive verb* [65]
to dye
teñirse el pelo to have your hair dyed

tercer *masc adjective*
third *adjective*
el tercer piso the third floor

WORD TIP *tercer* is used instead of *tercero* before a masc singular noun. ▷ **tercero**

tercero *masc adjective*, **tercera** *fem*
third
el tercer piso the third floor
la tercera puerta a la derecha the third door on the right
llegar en tercer lugar to finish in third position
- **el Tercer Mundo** the Third World

WORD TIP *tercero* becomes *tercer* before a masculine singular noun.

el **terciopelo** *masc noun*
velvet

terminado *masc adjective*, **terminada** *fem*
finished

terminal *masc & fem adjective* ▷ see **terminal** *noun*
terminal

la **terminal** *fem noun* ▷ see **terminal** *adj*
1 **terminal**
2 **bus station**

terminar *verb* [17]
1 **to finish**
Ya he terminado. I've finished now.
¿Cuándo termina el trimestre? When does term end?
Terminó la novela en tres horas. He finished the novel in three hours.
terminar de + infinitive to finish +ing
He terminado de revisarlo. I've finished checking it.
2 **terminar con algo** to finish with something
¿Has terminado con el libro? Have you finished with the book?
terminar con alguien to finish with someone
Ha terminado con su novio. She's broken up with her boyfriend.
3 **to end up**
Terminamos en una discoteca. We ended up in a disco.
Terminó harta. In the end she got fed up.
Terminaron por pelearse. They ended up having a fight.
4 **to end in**
terminar en algo to end in something
Su nombre termina en 't'. Her name ends in 't'.
Termina en punta. It's pointed.

terminarse *reflexive verb* [17]
1 **to be over**
La clase se termina a las doce. The lesson will be over at twelve.
2 **Se ha terminado la leche.** We've run out of milk.
Se me terminó la tinta del boli. My pen ran out (of ink).

el **termo**® *masc noun*
Thermos®

el **termómetro** *masc noun*
thermometer

la **ternera** *fem noun* ▷ see **ternero** *masc noun*
1 **veal**
2 **beef**

el **ternero** *masc noun*, la **ternera** *fem* ▷ see **ternera** *noun*
calf

la **terraza** *fem noun*
1 **balcony**
2 **terrace** (*of a cafe, bar*)
Desayunamos en la terraza. We had breakfast on the terrace.

el **terremoto** *masc noun*
earthquake

el **terreno** *masc noun*
1 **plot of land**
2 **field**
3 **land**
La casa tiene mucho terreno. The house has a lot of land.
4 **el terreno de juego** football pitch

terrible *masc & fem adjective*
terrible

el **territorio** *masc noun*
territory

el **terrón** *masc noun*
lump (*of sugar, earth*)

el **terror** *masc noun*
terror

el **terrorismo** *masc noun*
terrorism

terrorista *masc & fem adjective & noun*
1 **terrorist**
2 **un & una terrorista** terrorist

el **tesoro** *masc noun*
treasure

ʆ el **test** *masc noun*
1 **test**
2 **un examen tipo test** a multiple-choice exam

el **testamento** *masc noun*
will
hacer testamento to make your will

el & la **testigo** *masc & fem noun*
witness

el **tétano** *masc noun*
tetanus

ʆ la **tetera** *fem noun*
1 **teapot**
2 **kettle**

ʆ el **texto** *masc noun*
text

ʆ **ti** *pronoun*
1 **you**
detrás de ti behind you
Se olvidaron de ti. They forgot about you.
A mí no me dijo nada. ¿Y a ti? He hasn't told me anything. - Has he told you?
2 **to you**
Te lo dio a ti. He gave it to you.
3 **¿A ti te gusta?** Do you like it?
¿A ti qué te parece? What do you think?
4 **ti mismo, ti misma** yourself
Sabes cuidar de ti misma. You can look after yourself.

WORD TIP *ti is never written with an accent.*

ʆ la **tía** *fem noun*
aunt

tibio *masc adjective*, **tibia** *fem*
lukewarm

ʆ el **tiburón** *masc noun*
shark

tiembla, **tiemblo**, **etc** *verb* ▷ **temblar**

ʆ el **tiempo** *masc noun*
1 **time**
al mismo tiempo at the same time
por un tiempo for a time
la mayor parte del tiempo most of the time
Tenemos bastante tiempo. We've got plenty of time.
Ha pasado mucho tiempo desde entonces. It's been a long time since then.
Hace mucho tiempo que no la veo. I haven't seen her for a long time.
¿Cuánto tiempo hace que se fueron? How long ago did they go?
2 (*in expressions*) **a tiempo** on time
llegar a tiempo to be on time
¿Cada cuánto tiempo? How often?
cada cierto tiempo every so often
a su debido tiempo in due course
en aquellos tiempos in those days
trabajar a tiempo completo to work full time
trabajar a tiempo parcial to work part time
3 **weather**
el pronóstico del tiempo the weather forecast
Nos hizo buen tiempo. We had nice weather.
El tiempo fue espantoso. The weather was dreadful.
4 **half** (*in matches*)
el primer tiempo the first half
el segundo tiempo the second half
5 (*Grammar*) **tense**
• el **tiempo libre** spare time

ʆ la **tienda** *fem noun*
1 **shop**
una tienda de discos a record shop
una tienda de recuerdos a souvenir shop
• la **tienda de comestibles** grocer's
• la **tienda de campaña** tent

tiendo, **tiendes**, **etc** *verb* ▷ **tender**

tierno *masc adjective*, **tierna** *fem*
1 **tender**
2 **affectionate**

ʆ la **tierra** *fem noun*
1 **land**
viajar por tierra to travel overland
tomar tierra to land (*aeroplanes*)
2 **earth**, **soil**
3 **ground**
4 **la Tierra** the Earth (*the planet*)
volver a la Tierra to return to Earth
5 **homeland**
volver a su tierra to go back to your homeland
• la **tierra adentro** inland
• la **tierra firme** solid ground

el **tiesto** *masc noun*
flowerpot

ʆ el **tigre** *masc noun*
tiger

ʆ las **tijeras** *plural fem noun*
scissors
un par de tijeras, unas tijeras a pair of scissors

♪ el **timbre** *masc noun*
bell, doorbell
tocar el timbre to ring the bell

♪ **tímido** *masc adjective*, **tímida** *fem*
1 **shy**
2 **timid**

la **tina** *fem noun*
(*Latin America*) **bathtub**

la **tinta** *fem noun*
ink

♪ **tinto** *masc adjective & masc noun*
un vino tinto a red wine
Es un tinto de la Rioja. It's a red wine from the Rioja.

la **tintorería** *fem noun*
dry cleaner's

tiña, tiñeron, tiño, tiñó, etc *verb* ▷ **teñir**

♪ el **tío** *masc noun*
1 **uncle**
2 **mis tíos** my uncles, my aunt and uncle
3 (*informal*) **guy, bloke**
¡Qué tío más pesado! What a bore that guy is!

♪ el **tiovivo** *masc noun*
merry-go-round

típico *masc adjective*, **típica** *fem*
1 **typical**
2 **traditional**
un plato típico de la región a traditional regional dish

♪ el **tipo** *masc noun*
1 **type**
coches de todo tipo cars of all types
Me gusta este tipo de trabajo. I like this type of work.
2 **figure, physique**
Tiene buen tipo. She's got a good figure.
3 (*informal*) **guy, bloke**
- el **tipo de cambio** exchange rate
- el **tipo de interés** interest rate

los **tirantes** *plural masc noun*
braces

♪ **tirar** *verb* **[17]**
1 **to throw**
tirar algo al suelo to throw something on the floor
2 **tirarle algo a alguien** to throw something to somebody, to throw something at somebody
Tírame ese boli. Throw me that pen.
Me tiró una piedra. He threw a stone at me.
3 **to throw away, to throw out** (*as rubbish*)
tirar algo a la basura to through something out
Hay que tirar esos papeles. We need to throw those papers away.
4 **to pull**
'Tirar' 'Pull' (*on a door*)
Tira un poco más. Pull a bit harder.
5 **tirar de algo** to pull something
Tira de la cuerda cuando yo te diga. Pull the rope when I tell you.
6 **to shoot**
tirar a puerta to shoot at goal
tirar una flecha to shoot an arrow
tirar una bomba to drop a bomb
7 **to knock over**
Tiré la taza sin querer. I knocked the cup over by accident.
8 **tirar abajo** to knock down
tirar la puerta abajo. to knock the door down.
Tiraron el cine abajo. They knocked the cinema.
9 **to get by**
Vamos tirando. We're getting by.

tirarse *reflexive verb* **[17]**
tirarse al suelo to throw yourself to the ground
tirarse al río to jump into the river
tirarse al agua del trampolín to dive into the water from the diving board
tirarse en paracaídas to parachute, to bale out

♪ la **tirita** *fem noun*
sticking plaster

tiritar *verb* **[17]**
to shiver
tiritar de frío to shiver with cold

el **tiro** *masc noun*
1 **shot**
disparar un tiro to fire a shot
Se oyeron tiros. Shots were heard.
Lo mataron de un tiro. They shot him dead.
2 **shot** (*in sport*)
- el **tiro al blanco** target shooting
- el **tiro a portería** shot at goal
- el **tiro libre** free kick

el **tirón** *masc noun*
1 **pull**
darle un tirón a algo to pull something
Le dio un tirón de pelo. She pulled her hair.
2 (*informal*) **de un tirón** in one go
Se leyó el libro de un tirón. She read the book in one go.

el **títere** *masc noun*
1 **puppet**
2 **títeres** puppet show

el **titular** *masc noun*
1 **headline** (*in newspaper*)
2 **account holder** (*in bank, etc*)

⚷ el **título** *masc noun*
1 **title** (*of a book*)
2 **heading** (*of a document*)
• el **título universitario** university degree

⚷ la **tiza** *fem noun*
chalk
una tiza a piece of chalk

⚷ la **toalla** *fem noun*
towel

⚷ el **tobillo** *masc noun*
ankle

el **tobogán** *masc noun*
1 **slide** (*in a park*)
2 **emergency chute** (*from a plane*)
3 **toboggan**

⚷ el **tocadiscos** *masc noun*, *pl:* los **tocadiscos**
record player

⚷ el **tocador** *masc noun*
dressing table

⚷ **tocar** *verb* **[31]**
1 **to touch**
'No tocar' 'Do not touch' (*in a shop*)
Me tocó el hombro. He touched me on the shoulder.
2 **to play** (*an instrument*)
tocar el piano to play the piano
3 **to ring**
Tienes que tocar el timbre. You must ring the bell.
4 **tocarle a alguien hacer algo** to be somebody's turn to do something
Te toca jugar. It's your turn to play.
5 **tocarle a alguien algo** to win something
Les ha tocado la lotería. They've won the lottery.
Me ha tocado el primer premio. I've won the first prize.

tocarse *reflexive verb* **[31]**
to touch
Se tocó la cabeza. He touched his head.
Los dos cables se están tocando. The two cables are touching.

⚷ el **tocino** *masc noun*
bacon

⚷ **todavía** *adverb*
1 **still**
Todavía queda suficiente pan. There's still enough bread.
Todavía nos vemos. We still see each other.
2 **yet**
Todavía no han llegado. They haven't arrived yet.
No salgas todavía. Don't go out yet.
3 **even**
todavía más temprano even earlier
Quieren todavía más. They want even more.

⚷ **todo** *masc adjective*, **toda** *fem*
▷ **see todo** *noun, pron*
1 **all**
todos mis amigos all my friends
todas las canciones all the songs
viajar por todo el mundo to travel all over the world
2 **whole**
toda la mañana the whole morning
toda la semana the whole week
Se comió toda la tarta. She ate the whole cake.
3 **every**
Vienen todos los días. They come every day.
Revisamos todos las cajones. We checked all the drawers.
4 (*for emphasis*) **Estaba toda nerviosa.** She was all nervous.
Está todo roto. It's completely broken.
Siga todo recto. Carry straight on.
5 (*in expressions*) **a toda velocidad** at top speed
Fue toda una aventura. It was quite an adventure.

el **todo** *masc noun* ▷ **see todo** *adj, pron*
el todo the whole

⚷ **todo**, **toda** *pronoun* ▷ **see todo** *adj, noun*
1 **everything**
a pesar de todo despite everything
Se lo conté todo. I told him everything.
2 **all**
todo o nada all or nothing
3 **todos, todas** everybody
Vinieron todos. Everybody came.
Todos estábamos de acuerdo. We were all in agreement.
4 (*in expressions*) **ante todo**, **la seguridad ante todo** security above all else
de todo, **Tienen de todo.** They've got all sorts of things.
sobre todo, **Sobre todo no te olvides de los billetes.** Above all, don't forget the tickets.

tomar *verb* **[17]**
1 **to take**
tomar el autobús to take the bus
Tomamos la primera calle a la izquierda. We took the first street on the left.
Toma, tu billete. Here, here's your ticket.
La tomó de la mano. She took her hand.
Hay que tomar las pastillas después de comer. You must take the tablets after eating.
tomar algo en serio to take something seriously
No toma nada en serio. He doesn't anything seriously.
2 **to have** (*something to drink, to eat*)
tomar el desayuno to have breakfast
Voy a tomar postre. I'm going to have a dessert.
¿Te apetece tomar algo? Would you like something to drink?
¿Quieres tomar un café? Would you like a coffee?
3 **tomar el sol** to sunbathe
4 **tomar el aire** to get some fresh air

tomarse *reflexive verb* **[17]**
to take
tomarse unos días libres to take some days off
Nos tomamos un día para visitar Granada. We took a day out to visit Granada.
Se tomó la medicina. She took the medicine.

el **tomate** *masc noun*
tomato
una salsa de tomate a tomato sauce

la **tonelada** *fem noun*
ton

la **tónica** *fem noun*
tonic water

el **tono** *masc noun*
1 **tone**
en tono serio in a serious tone
2 **shade**
telas de tonos suaves materials in soft shades
- el **tono de llamada** ring tone
- el **tono de marcar** dial tone
- el **tono de ocupado** engaged tone

la **tontería** *fem noun*
decir tonterías to talk nonsense
¡Qué tonterías dices! What nonsense you talk!
Se pelearon por una tontería. They fell out over something very silly.

tonto *masc adjective*, **tonta** *fem*
▷ see **tonto** *noun*
silly
una pregunta tonta a silly question

el **tonto** *masc noun*, la **tonta** *fem*
▷ see **tonto** *adj*
idiot

el **topo** *masc noun*
mole (*the animal*)

el **torbellino** *masc noun*
whirlwind

torcer *verb* **[41]**
1 **to turn**
torcer la cabeza to turn your head
torcer la esquina to turn the corner
Tuerce a la derecha al final de la calle. Turn right at the end of the road.
2 **to wring out** (*clothes*)

torcerse *reflexive verb* **[41]**
to twist
torcerse el tobillo to twist your ankle

torcido *masc adjective*, **torcida** *fem*
1 **crooked**
una línea torcida a crooked line
El cuadro está torcido. The picture's crooked.
2 **twisted**
3 **bent**

el **torero** *masc noun*, la **torera** *fem noun*
bullfighter

la **tormenta** *fem noun*
storm
- la **tormenta de nieve** snowstorm

el **tornado** *masc noun*
tornado

el **torneo** *masc noun*
tournament

el **tornillo** *masc noun*
screw

el **toro** *masc noun*
1 **bull**
2 **los toros** bullfighting
ir a los toros to go to a bullfight
¿Te gustan los toros? Do you like bullfighting?

la **toronja** *fem noun*
(*Latin America*) **grapefruit**

torpe *masc & fem adjective*
1 **clumsy**
2 **awkward**

ʃ la **torre** *fem noun*
1 **tower**
2 **rook**, **castle** (*in chess*)
- la **torre de alta tensión** pylon
- la **torre de control** control tower

ʃ la **torta** *fem noun*
1 **cake**
2 (*informal*) **slap**
Le dio una torta. She slapped him.

ʃ la **tortilla** *fem noun*
1 **omelette**
2 (*Mexico*) **tortilla** (*made of corn flour*)
- la **tortilla española** Spanish omelette (*with potatoes*)
- la **tortilla francesa** French omelette (*with eggs only*)

la **tortuga** *fem noun*
1 **tortoise**
2 **turtle**

torturar *verb* [17]
to torture

la **tos** *fem noun*
cough
Tengo tos. I've got a cough.

toser *verb* [18]
to cough

ʃ la **tostada** *fem noun*
una tostada a piece of toast
Tomo tostadas para desayunar. I have toast for breakfast.

el **tostador** *masc noun*
toaster

la **tostadora** *fem noun*
toaster

ʃ **tostar** *verb* [24]
1 **to toast** (*bread*)
2 **to roast** (*coffee*)

tostarse *reflexive verb* [24]
to tan, **to go brown**

ʃ **total** *masc & fem adjective* ▷ see **total** *noun*
1 **total**
el precio total the total price
2 (*when summing up*) **so**
Total, no lo sabemos aún. So, we still don't know.

el **total** *masc noun* ▷ see **total** *adj*
total
¿Cuánto es el total? What's the total?
Son mil quinientas en total. It's one thousand five hundred in total.

la **totalidad** *fem noun*
la totalidad del colegio the whole school
la totalidad de los alumnos all the pupils

tóxico *masc adjective*, **tóxica** *fem*
toxic
residuos tóxicos toxic waste

el **toxicómano** *masc noun*, la **toxicómana** *fem*
drug addict

ʃ **trabajador** *masc adjective*, **trabajadora** *fem* ▷ see **trabajador** *noun*
hard-working
Son muy trabajadores. They are very hard-working.

ʃ el **trabajador** *masc noun*, la **trabajadora** *fem* ▷ see **trabajador** *adj*
worker

ʃ **trabajar** *verb* [17]
to work
trabajar a tiempo completo to work full time
trabajar a tiempo parcial to work part time
Mi padre trabaja en un banco. My father works in a bank.
Elena trabaja de camarera. Elena works as a waitress.
Trabaja para una empresa americana. She works for an American company.

ʃ el **trabajo** *masc noun*
1 **work**
estar sin trabajo to be out of work
vivir cerca del trabajo to live close to where you work
Costó mucho trabajo encontrarlo. It was hard work finding it.
2 **job**
buscar trabajo to look for a job
quedarse sin trabajo to lose your job
3 **essay**
un trabajo sobre el cambio climatológico an essay on climate change
- el **trabajo a tiempo completo** full-time work
- el **trabajo a tiempo parcial** part-time work
- el **trabajo fijo** steady job
- los **trabajos manuales** handicrafts

el **trabalenguas** *masc noun*, *pl:* los **trabalenguas**
tongue twister

el **tractor** *masc noun*
tractor

la **tradición** *fem noun*
tradition

tradicional *masc & fem adjective*
traditional

la **traducción** *fem noun*
translation

traducir *verb* **[60]**
to translate
Tradúzcalo al inglés. Translate it into English.

el **traductor** *masc noun*, la **traductora** *fem*
translator

traduje, **traduzca**, **traduzco**, **etc** *verb* ▷ **traducir**

traer *verb* **[42]**
1 **to bring**
Trae a Enrique. You bring Enrique.
He traído la comida. I've brought the food.
La trajo a la estación. He brought her to the station.
Me trae un café con leche, por favor. I'd like a white coffee, please.
2 **to have**
El periódico trae un artículo sobre Ávila. The newspaper has an article on Ávila in it.

el & la **traficante** *masc & fem noun*
dealer
- el **traficante de armas** arms dealer
- el **traficante de drogas** drugs dealer

el **tráfico** *masc noun*
1 **traffic**
2 **trade**
- el **tráfico de armas** arms trade
- el **tráfico de drogas** drug dealing

el & la **tragaperras** *masc & fem noun, pl:* **tragaperras**
(*informal*) **slot machine**

tragar *verb* **[28]**
to swallow

tragarse *reflexive verb* **[28]**
to swallow
Se tragó el chicle. He swallowed his chewing gum.

la **tragedia** *fem noun*
tragedy

trágico *masc adjective*, **trágica** *fem*
tragic

la **traición** *fem noun*
1 **betrayal**
2 **una traición** an act of treachery

el **traidor** *masc noun*, la **traidora** *fem*
traitor

traiga, **traigo**, **trajo**, **etc** *verb* ▷ **traer**

el **traje** *masc noun* ▷ **see traer** *verb*
1 **suit**
2 **costume** (*national, regional*)
- el **traje de baño** swimsuit, swimming trunks
- el **traje de luces** bullfighter's costume
- el **traje típico** traditional dress

la **trampa** *fem noun*
trap
caer en la trampa to fall into the trap

el **tramposo** *masc noun*, la **tramposa** *fem*
cheat

el **trampolín** *masc noun*
1 **springboard**, **diving board**
2 **trampoline**
3 **ski jump**

el **tranquillo** *masc noun*
knack
cogerle el tranquillo a algo to get the knack of something
Pronto le cogeras el tranquillo. You'll soon get the knack of it.

tranquilo *masc adjective*, **tranquila** *fem*
1 **quiet**
un barrio tranquilo a quiet neighbourhood
2 **calm**
un ambiente tranquilo a calm environment
Es muy tranquilo. He's very calm.
Está bastante tranquila ante el examen. She's quite calm about the exam.
¡Tranquilo! Keep calm!

el **transbordador** *masc noun*
ferry
- el **transbordador espacial** space shuttle

transbordar *verb* **[17]**
1 **to transfer** (*luggage, goods*)
2 **to change** (*trains*)

el **transbordo** *masc noun*
change
hacer transbordo to change (*trains, buses*)
Haz transbordo en Sol. Change at Sol.

el & la **transeúnte** *masc & fem noun*
passer-by

el **tránsito** *masc noun*
traffic
Hay mucho tránsito a esa hora. There's a lot of traffic at that time.

la **transferencia** *fem noun*
transfer
- la **transferencia bancaria** bank transfer

transformar *verb* **[17]**
1 **to transform**
2 **to turn into**
Transformaron el garaje en una oficina. They turned the garage into an office.

transformarse *reflexive verb* **[17]**
to be turned into

la **transfusión** *fem noun*
transfusion

la **transmisión** *fem noun*
broadcast
- la **transmisión en diferido** pre-recorded broadcast
- la **transmisión en directo** live broadcast

la **transparencia** *fem noun*
1 **transparency**
2 **slide** (*in photography, for OHP*)

transparente *masc & fem adjective*
transparent

transportar *verb* **[17]**
to transport, **to carry** (*people, goods*)

⚷ el **transporte** *masc noun*
transport

⚷ el **tranvía** *masc noun*
tram

el **trapo** *masc noun*
cloth
- el **trapo de cocina** tea towel
- el **trapo del polvo** duster

⚷ **tras** *preposition*
1 **after**
uno tras otra one after another
hora tras hora hour after hour
Tras despedirme, subí al autocar. After saying goodbye, I got into the coach.
2 **behind**
La puerta se cerró tras ella. The door closed behind her.

⚷ **trasero** *masc adjective*, **trasera** *fem*
1 **back**
la puerta trasera the back door
2 **rear**
la rueda trasera the rear wheel

el **traslado** *masc noun*
transfer (*of an employee*)

trasnochar *verb* **[17]**
to stay up late

el **trasplante** *masc noun*
transplant
un trasplante de hígado a liver transplant

el **tratado** *masc noun*
treaty

el **tratamiento** *masc noun*
1 **treatment**
2 **processing**

⚷ **tratar** *verb* **[17]**
1 **to treat**
Me tratan muy bien. They treat me very well.
Trátalo con cuidado. Treat it carefully.
Hay que tratar el agua. The water must be treated.
2 (*speaking to somebody*) **tratar a alguien de usted** to speak to somebody using the 'usted' form
tratar a alguien de tú to speak to somebody using the 'tú' form
3 **tratar de hacer algo** to try to do something
Tratamos de ayudarla. We tried to help her.
Trata de llamarme antes de las cinco. Try to call me before five.
4 **tratar de algo** to be about something
¿De qué trata la película? What's the film about?

tratarse *reflexive verb* **[17]**
tratarse de algo to be about something
Se trata de Javier. It's about Javier.
Se trata de la vida en Hollywod. It's about life in Hollywood.

⚷ **través** *in phrases*
a través de algo through something, across something
a través del cristal through the window
a través de los campos across the fields
Lo encontré a través de Internet. I found it on the Internet.

travieso *masc adjective*, **traviesa** *fem*
naughty

el **trayecto** *masc noun*
journey, **route**
final de trayecto end of the journey (*on public transport*)
Hace el trayecto Málaga-Granada. It does the Málaga-Granada route.

trazar *verb* **[22]**
1 **to trace**
2 **to draw** (*a map*)
3 **to draw up** (*a plan*)

trece *number*
1 **thirteen**
Tiene trece años. She's thirteen (years old).
2 **thirteenth** (*in dates*)
el trece de mayo the thirteenth of May

treinta *number*
1 **thirty**
Tiene treinta años. She's thirty (years old).
treinta y siete thirty-seven
2 **thirtieth** (*in dates*)
el treinta de mayo the thirtieth of May

tremendo *masc adjective*, **tremenda** *fem*
1 **tremendous**
una tremenda victoria a tremendous victory
una tremenda derrota a tremendous defeat
2 **naughty**
un niño tremendo a naughty boy

el **tren** *masc noun*
train
el tren a Barcelona the train to Barcelona
coger el tren to catch the train
viajar en tren to travel by train
- el **tren de aterrizaje** landing gear
- el **tren de alta velocidad** high-speed train
- el **tren de cercanías** local train
- el **tren directo** through train
- el **tren de largo recorrido** long-distance train
- el **tren de montaje** assembly line

mini-info **tren**
El AVE (tren de alta velocidad) viaja a 350 kilómetros por hora y si llega con más de 5 minutos de retraso se le devuelve el importe del billete al viajero.

trepar *verb* **[17]**
to climb
trepar a un árbol to climb a tree

tres *number*
1 **three**
Tiene tres años. She's three (years old).
2 **third** (*in dates*)
el tres de mayo the third of May
3 **three** (*in clock time*)
Son las tres. It's three o'clock.

trescientos, **trescientas** *number*
three hundred
trescientos veinte three hundred and twenty

el **triángulo** *masc noun*
triangle

la **tribu** *fem noun*
tribe

el **tribunal** *masc noun*
1 **court**
2 **the judges** (*in a competition*)

el **trigo** *masc noun*
wheat

los **trillizos** *plural masc noun*, las **trillizas** *plural fem noun*
triplets

el **trimestre** *masc noun*
1 **term** (*in school*)
2 **quarter** (*three months*)

el **trineo** *masc noun*
sledge

Trinidad *fem noun*
Trinidad

trinitense *masc & fem adjective & noun*
1 **Trinidadian**
2 **un & una trinitense** Trinidadian

WORD TIP Adjectives and nouns for nationality and regional origin do not have capital letters in Spanish.

triniteño *masc adjective & noun*, **triniteña** *fem adjective & noun*
1 **Trinidadian**
2 **un triniteño, una triniteña** Trinidadian

WORD TIP Adjectives and nouns for nationality and regional origin do not have capital letters in Spanish.

la **tripa** *fem noun*
1 (*informal*) **tummy**
2 (*informal*) **belly**
3 **tripas** guts

triple *masc & fem adjective* ▷ **see triple** *noun*
triple

el **triple** *masc noun* ▷ **see triple** *adj*
el triple del precio original three times the original price
Es el triple de ancho. It's three times as wide.

triplicarse *reflexive verb* **[31]**
to triple
El precio se ha triplicado. The price has tripled.

la **tripulación** *fem noun*
crew

el & la **tripulante** *masc & fem noun*
crew member

triste *masc & fem adjective*
1 **sad**
2 **gloomy**

la tristeza *fem noun*
sadness

triunfar *verb* [17]
to triumph

el triunfo *masc noun*
1 **victory**
2 **triumph**

trivial *masc & fem adjective*
trivial

el trofeo *masc noun*
trophy

el trombón *masc noun*
trombone

la trompeta *fem noun*
trumpet

tronar *verb* [24]
to thunder

el tronco *masc noun*
1 **trunk**
2 **log**

el trono *masc noun*
throne

tropezar *verb* [25]
to trip
tropezar con algo to trip over something
Tropezó con una piedra. He tripped over a stone.

tropezarse *reflexive verb* [25]
tropezarse con alguien to bump into someone
Nos tropezamos con Paco en la calle. We bumped into Paco in the street.

el trópico *masc noun*
tropic

tropiece, tropiezo, etc *verb* ▷ **tropezar**

trotar *verb* [17]
to trot

el trozo *masc noun*
piece
un trozo de tela a piece of cloth
un trozo de queso a piece of cheese

la trucha *fem noun*
trout

el truco *masc noun*
trick
un truco de cartas a card trick

el trueno *masc noun*
thunder clap
Hubo truenos. There was thunder.

tu *adjective*
your
tu casa your house
tus amigos your friends

tú *pronoun* ▷ see **tu** *adj*
1 **you**
Tú sí lo sabes. You do know it.
2 **tú mismo, tú misma** yourself
Hazlo tú mismo. Do it yourself.
3 **tratar a alguien de tú** to speak to somebody using the 'tú' form

WORD TIP *tú* is used to refer to a person you know well. ▷ **usted, vosotros**

el tubo *masc noun*
tube
- **el tubo de escape** exhaust pipe

la tuerca *fem noun*
nut

tuerza, tuerzo, etc *verb* ▷ **torcer**

tuesta, tueste, tuesto, etc *verb* ▷ **tostar**

el tulipán *masc noun*
tulip

la tumba *fem noun*
1 **grave**
2 **tomb**

tumbar *verb* [17]
1 **to knock down**
tumbar a alguien de un puñetazo to floor somebody (*with a punch*)
2 **to lay down**

tumbarse *reflexive verb* [17]
to lie down
Se tumbó en el sofá. He lay down on the sofa.

la tumbona *fem noun*
deckchair

tunecino *masc adjective & noun*, **tunecina** *fem adjective & noun*
1 **Tunisian**
2 **un tunecino, una tunecina** Tunisian

WORD TIP Adjectives and nouns for nationality and regional origin do not have capital letters in Spanish.

el túnel *masc noun*
tunnel

Túnez *masc noun*
Tunisia

el **turbante** *masc noun*
turban

turco *masc adjective & noun*, **turca** *fem adjective & noun*
1 **Turkish**
2 **un turco, una turca** Turk
el turco Turkish (*the language*)

WORD TIP Adjectives and nouns for nationality, regional origin, and language do not have capital letters in Spanish.

el **turismo** *masc noun*
1 **tourism**
la oficina de turismo the tourist office
hacer turismo to go sightseeing
2 **saloon car**

turístico *masc adjective*, **turística** *fem*
tourist
una ruta turística a tourist route

el & la **turista** *masc & fem noun*
tourist

turnarse *reflexive verb* **[17]**
to take turns

el **turno** *masc noun*
1 **turn**
tocarle el turno a alguien to be somebody's turn
Te toca el turno a ti. It's your turn.
2 **shift**
hacer turnos de siete horas to work seven-hour shifts
- el **turno de noche** night shift

Turquía *fem noun*
Turkey

el **turrón** *masc noun*
nougat (*traditionally eaten at Christmas*)

tutear *verb* **[17]**
tutear a alguien to speak to somebody using the 'tú' form

tutearse *reflexive verb* **[17]**
to use the 'tú' form to each other

el **tutor** *masc noun*, la **tutora** *fem*
1 **class teacher**
2 **guardian**

tuvo, **tuvieron**, **tuviste**, **etc** *verb* ▷ **tener**

tuyo *masc adjective*, **tuya** *fem*
▷ **see tuyo** *pron*
yours
Esto es tuyo. This is yours.
Estos son tuyos. These are yours.
un amigo tuyo a friend of yours
unos amigos tuyos some friends of yours
una vecina tuya a neighbour of yours
unos vecinos tuyos some neighbours of yours

WORD TIP *tuyo, tuya* agrees with the thing you have or own: *amigos*, *vecina*, etc above. *tuyo, tuya* goes after the noun.

tuyo, **tuya** *pronoun* ▷ **see tuyo** *adj*
yours
El tuyo es verde., La tuya es verde. Yours is green.
Los tuyos son mejores., Las tuyas son mejores. Yours are better.

WORD TIP *el tuyo, la tuya* agrees with the thing you have or own.

U u

u *conjunction*
or
plata u oro silver or the gold

WORD TIP The usual word for *or*, *o*, becomes *u* before words beginning with *o-* or *ho-*.

ubicado *masc adjective*, **ubicada** *fem*
situated

Ucrania *fem noun*
Ukraine

ucraniano *masc adjective, noun*, **ucraniana** *fem adjective, noun*
1 **Ukrainian**
2 **un ucraniano, una ucraniana** Ukrainian
el ucraniano Ukrainian (*the language*)

WORD TIP Adjectives and nouns for nationality, regional origin, and language do not have capital letters in Spanish.

Ud. *abbreviation*
you

WORD TIP singular polite form; short for *usted*

Uds. *abbreviation*
you

WORD TIP plural polite form; short for *ustedes*

la **UE** *fem noun*
(= *Unión Europea*) **EU** (*European Union*)

la **úlcera** *fem noun*
ulcer

últimamente *adverb*
lately

⚷ **último** *masc adjective*, **última** *fem*
▷ see **último** *noun*
1 **last**
Llegó último. He came in last.
El último día fuimos a la playa. On the last day we went to the beach.
2 **latest**
su última película her latest film
lo último en equipo audio the latest in audio equipment
3 **bottom**
el último alumno de la clase the bottom student in the class

WORD TIP *úlitimo, última* goes before the noun.

⚷ el **último** *masc noun*, la **última** *fem*
▷ see **último** *adj*
el último the last one
el último de la serie the last inthe series
Ésta es la última que queda. This is the last one left.

el **ultramarinos** *masc noun*, *pl:* los **ultramarinos**
grocer's shop

⚷ **un** *masc determiner*, **una** *fem determiner*
a, an
un hombre a man
una manzana an apple
Tiene un gato. She has a cat.
un ala a wing
un hacha an axe

WORD TIP *un* is used instead of *una*, with fem nouns starting with stressed *a* or *ha*. ▷ **unos**

⚷ **un** *number* ▷ **see un** *determiner*
one, a, an
un año one year, a year
Lleva un año abierto. It's been open for one year.

WORD TIP *un* means *one* before masc singular nouns. ▷ **uno** *number*

⚷ **único** *masc adjective*, **única** *fem*
▷ see **único** *noun*
1 **unique**
una oportunidad única a unique oportunity
2 **only**
su único hijo her only child
Es hija única. She's an only child.
3 **talla única** one size

⚷ el **único** *masc noun*, la **única** *fem*
▷ see **único** *adjective*
el único, la única the only one
El único que funciona. The only one that works.

la **unidad** *fem noun*
1 **unit**
2 **unity**
• la **unidad de cuidados intensivos**, la **unidad de vigilancia intensiva** intensive care unit

unido *masc adjective*, **unida** *fem*
1 **united**
2 **close** (*family, community*)
Las dos familias están muy unidas. The two families are very close.

⚷ indicates key words

uniforme *masc & fem adjective*
▷ see **uniforme** *noun*
1 **uniform** (*size, speed*)
2 **even** (*surface*)

el **uniforme** *masc noun*
▷ see **uniforme** *adj*
uniform

la **Unión Europea** *fem noun*
European Union

unir *verb* **[19]**
1 **to unite** (*groups of people*)
2 **to join** (*buildings*)
3 **to combine** (*qualities*)
El diseño une la elegancia con la eficacia. The design combines elegance and efficiency.

unirse *reflexive verb* **[19]**
1 **to unite** (*workers, employees*)
2 **to merge** (*organizations*)

la **universidad** *fem noun*
university
ir a la universidad to go to university
estar en la universidad to be at university
- la **universidad a distancia** open university
- la **universidad laboral** technical college

universitario *masc adjective*, **universitaria** *fem*
▷ see **universitario** *noun*
university
profesores universitarios university teachers

el **universitario** *masc noun*, la **universitaria** *fem*
▷ see **universitario** *adj*
university student

el **universo** *masc noun*
universe

uno, **una** *number* ▷ see **uno** *pronoun*
1 **one**
un hombre one man
una chica one girl
Compré sólo uno. I bought only one.
Hay una razón. There is one reason.
2 **first** (*in dates*)
el uno de enero the first of January
3 **la una** one o'clock
Es la una. It's one o'clock.
Llegaron a la una. They arrived at one o'clock.

WORD TIP *uno* becomes *un* before a masculine singular noun. ▷ **un**

uno, **una** *pronoun* ▷ see **uno** *number*
one
una para ti one for you
de uno en uno one by one

unos, **unas** *adjective*
unos, unas some, a few
Unos lo saben y otros no. Some know and some don't.
Compré unos sobres. I bought some envelopes.
Se quedarán unas horas. They will stay for a few hours. ▷ **un, una, uno, una**

la **uña** *fem noun*
nail (*of fingers, toes*)
una uña del dedo del pie a toe nail

la **urbanización** *fem noun*
housing estate

urbano *masc adjective*, **urbana** *fem*
urban

la **urgencia** *fem noun*
1 **urgency**
2 (*in hospitals*) **la sala de urgencias** the accident and emergency ward
'Urgencias' 'Accident and Emergency'

urgente *masc & fem adjective*
1 **urgent**
2 **express** (*letters*)

urgentemente *adverb*
urgently
Quiere verte urgentemente. She wants to see you urgently.

Uruguay *masc noun*
Uruguay

uruguayo *masc adjective & noun*, **uruguaya** *fem adjective & noun*
1 **Uruguayan**
2 **un uruguayo, una uruguaya** Uruguayan

WORD TIP Adjectives and nouns for nationality and regional origin do not have capital letters in Spanish.

usado *masc adjective*, **usada** *fem*
1 **used**
2 **second-hand**
ropa usada second-hand clothes

usar *verb* **[17]**
1 **to use**
Hay que usar aceite. You have to use oil.
2 **to wear** (*clothes, perfume*)
¿Qué perfume usas? What perfume do you use?

el **uso** *masc noun*
use
instrucciones de uso instructions for use

⚷ **usted** *pronoun*
1 **you**
Usted sí lo sabe. You do know it.
2 **usted mismo, usted misma** yourselves
Hágalo usted mismo., Hágalo usted misma. Do it yourself.
3 **tratar a alguien de usted** to speak to somebody using the 'usted' form

WORD TIP *usted, ustedes* are the polite forms for *you.* ▷ **tú, vosotros**

⚷ **ustedes** *pronoun*
you (*polite form: to more than one person*)
ustedes mismos, ustedes mismas yourselves

usual *masc & fem adjective*
usual

el **usuario** *masc noun*, la **usuaria** *fem*
user

el **utensilio** *masc noun*
1 **tool**
2 **utensil**

⚷ **útil** *masc & fem adjective*
useful

⚷ **utilizar** *verb* **[22]**
to use
Lo utilizan para mantenerse en contacto They use it to keep in touch.
Se utiliza para limpiar ... It's used for cleaning ...

⚷ la **uva** *fem noun*
grape
las uvas de la suerte the twelve grapes (*one for each month of the year*) eaten traditionally in Spain at midnight on New Year's Eve
tomar las uvas to eat grapes (*at midnight on New Year's Eve*)

V v

ℰ la **vaca** *fem noun*
cow

ℰ las **vacaciones** *plural fem noun*
holiday, holidays
irse de vacaciones to go on holiday
tomarse unas vacaciones to take a holiday
estar de vacaciones to be on holiday
las vacaciones de Navidad the Christmas holidays
Pasamos las vacaciones en la Costa Brava. We spent the holidays on the Costa Brava.

> mini-info **vacaciones**
>
> En España cada trabajador tiene derecho a 20 días laborales pagados. Además hay 14 días festivos anuales. Hay 7 nacionales, 5 que se celebran a nivel regional y 2 días para las fiestas locales.

vaciar *verb* **[32]**
to empty

vacilar *verb* **[17]**
1 **to hesitate**
Lo hizo sin vacilar. He did it without hesitating.
Vacilaba entre quedarse o no. She was hesitating whether to stay or not.
2 (*informal*) **to fool around**
¡Deja de vacilar! Stop fooling about!
3 (*Latin America*) **to enjoy yourself**

ℰ **vacío** *masc adjective*, **vacía** *fem*
▷ see **vacío** *noun*
empty
una botella vacía an empty bottle
las calles vacías the empty streets

el **vacío** *masc noun* ▷ see **vacío** *adj*
vacuum

la **vacuna** *fem noun*
vaccine

vacunar *verb* **[17]**
to vaccinate

ℰ el **vado** *masc noun*
1 **dropped kerb**
2 **'Vado Permanente'** 'Keep clear'

vagabundo *masc adjective*, **vagabunda** *fem* ▷ see **vagabundo** *noun*
un perro vagabundo a stray dog

el **vagabundo** *masc noun*, la **vagabunda** *fem* ▷ see **vagabundo** *adj*
vagrant

vago *masc adjective*, **vaga** *fem*
▷ see **vago** *noun*
1 **vague**
2 **lazy**

el **vago** *masc noun*, la **vaga** *fem*
▷ see **vago** *adj*
layabout

el **vagón** *masc noun*
1 **carriage** (*of train*)
2 **wagon**

la **vainilla** *fem noun*
vanilla

ℰ **valdrá**, **valdré**, **valdría**, **etc** *verb* ▷ **valer**

el **vale** *masc noun* ▷ see **valer** *verb*, **vale** *excl*
1 **voucher**
2 **credit slip**

ℰ **vale** *exclamation* ▷ see **vale** *noun*, **valer** *verb*
okay
'Tú te encargas de las bebidas.'—'¡Vale!.' 'You look after the drinks.'—'Okay!'

valenciano *masc adjective & noun*, **valenciana** *fem adjective & noun*
1 **Valencian**
2 **un valenciano, una valenciana** Valencian (*person from Valencia*)
el valenciano Valencian (*the language spoken in Valencia*)

> **WORD TIP** Adjectives and nouns for nationality, regional origin, and language do not have capital letters in Spanish.

ℰ **valer** *verb* **[43]**
1 **to cost**
¿Cuánto vale? How much is it?
Vale cincuenta euros. It's fifty euros.
2 **to be worth**
Vale bastante dinero. It's worth quite a lot of money.
3 **valer la pena** to be worth the trouble
Vale la pena el esfuerzo. It's worth the effort.
No vale la pena. It's not worth the trouble.
4 **to be valid** (*tickets, coupons, etc*)
5 **to be allowed**
No vale preguntar. You're not allowed to ask.
Eso no vale. That's not fair.

ʃ **valga**, **valgo**, **etc** *verb* ▷ **valer**

válido *masc adjective*, **válida** *fem*
valid

valiente *masc & fem adjective*
brave

valioso *masc adjective*, **valiosa** *fem*
valuable

ʃ el **valle** *masc noun*
valley

el **valor** *masc noun*
1 **value**
2 **courage**

valorar *verb* **[17]**
1 **to value** (*goods, advice, etc*)
2 **to assess** (*a situation*)

el **vals** *masc noun*
waltz

vamos *exclamation*
1 **¡Vamos!** Come on!!
2 **Vamos, ...** Well, ...
▷ **ir**

el **vandalismo** *masc noun*
vandalism

vanidoso *masc adjective*, **vanidosa** *fem*
vain

vano *masc adjective*, **vana** *fem*
1 **futile**
Todo fue en vano. It was futile.
2 **vain** (*person*)

el **vapor** *masc noun*
steam
verduras al vapor steamed vegetables

ʃ el **vaquero** *masc noun*
1 **cowboy**
2 **unos vaqueros** a pair of jeans

variado *masc adjective*, **variada** *fem*
varied

variar *verb* **[32]**
to vary (*prices, temperatures*)

la **varicela** *fem noun*
chicken pox

la **variedad** *fem noun*
variety

ʃ **varios** *plural masc adjective & pronoun*, **varias** *plural fem adjective & pronoun*
several
La vimos varias veces. We saw her several times.
Hay varios similares. There are several similar ones.

varón *masc adjective & noun*
male
un hijo varón a male child

varonil *masc & fem adjective*
manly

vasco *masc adjective & noun*, **vasca** *fem adjective & noun*
1 **Basque**
2 **un vasco, una vasca** Basque
el vasco Basque (*the language*)

WORD TIP Adjectives and nouns for nationality, regional origin, and language do not have capital letters in Spanish.

la **vasija** *fem noun*
vessel

ʃ el **vaso** *masc noun*
glass
un vaso de agua a glass of water
un vaso de papel a paper cup

ʃ **vaya** *exclamation*
¡Vaya moto que se ha comprado! Hey, look a that motorbike he's bought himself!

Vd. *abbreviation*
you

WORD TIP singular polite form; short for *usted*

Vds. *abbreviation*
you

WORD TIP plural polite form; short for *ustedes*

la **vecindad** *fem noun*
neighbourhood

ʃ **vecino** *masc adjective*, **vecina** *fem*
▷ see **vecino** *noun*
neighbouring
los países vecinos the neighbouring countries

ʃ el **vecino** *masc noun*, la **vecina** *fem*
▷ see **vecino** *adj*
1 **neighbour**
2 **local resident**

ʃ **vegetariano** *masc adjective*, **vegetariana** *fem adj*
▷ see **vegetariano** *noun*
vegetarian

ʃ el **vegetariano** *masc noun*, la **vegetariana** *fem*
▷ see **vegetariano** *adj*
vegetarian

el **vehículo** *masc noun*
vehicle
- el **vehículo espacial** spacecraft

veía, **veían**, **etc** *verb* ▷ **ver**

veinte *number*
1 **twenty**
Tiene veinte años. She's twenty (years old).
los años veinte the twenties (*1920-1929*)
2 **twentieth** (*in dates*)
el veinte de diciembre the twentieth of December
3 (*in the 24-hour time system*) **a las veinte horas** at twenty hundred hours (*8 p.m.*)

la **vejez** *fem noun*
old age

la **vela** *fem noun*
1 **candle**
2 **sail**
3 **sailing**
4 **pasar la noche en vela** to be awake all night
He pasado toda la noche en vela. I've been awake all night.

el **velero** *masc noun*
1 **sailing ship**
2 **sailing boat**

la **velocidad** *fem noun*
1 **speed**
a toda velocidad at top speed
la velocidad máxima the maximum speed
disminuir la velocidad to slow down
2 **gear** (*in a car, bicycle*)
una bici de cinco velocidades a bike with five gears

la **vena** *fem noun*
vein

vencedor *masc noun*, **vencedora** *fem noun*
winner

vencer *verb* **[44]**
1 **vencer a alguien** to defeat somebody
Vencieron al equipo visitante. They defeated the visiting team.
2 **to win**
Venció dos a uno. He won two to one.
3 **to expire** (*passports, contracts*)

vencido *masc adjective*, **vencida** *fem*
defeated

la **venda** *fem noun*
bandage

vendar *verb* **[17]**
1 **to bandage** (*a wound*)
2 **vendarle los ojos a alguien** to blindfold somebody

el **vendaval** *masc noun*
gale

el **vendedor** *masc noun*, la **vendedora** *fem*
1 **seller**
2 **salesman**, **saleswoman**
3 **shop assistant**
- el **vendedor ambulante** street seller

vender *verb* **[18]**
to sell
Venden de todo. They sell everything.
Los venden a cinco euros el kilo. They're selling them for five euros a kilo.
Le he vendido la bicicleta. I've sold him the bicycle.
'Se vende' 'For sale'
Se venden muy bien. They sell very well.

la **vendimia** *fem noun*
wine harvest

vendrá, **vendré**, **vendría**, **etc** *verb* ▷ **venir**

el **veneno** *masc noun*
poison

venenoso *masc adjective*, **venenosa** *fem*
poisonous

venezolano *masc adjective & noun*, **venezolana** *fem adjective & noun*
1 **Venezuelan**
2 **un venezolano, una venezolana** Venezuelan

WORD TIP Adjectives and nouns for nationality and regional origin do not have capital letters in Spanish.

Venezuela *fem noun*
Venezuela

venga *exclamation* ▷ see **venga** *verb*
¡Venga! Come on!

venga, **vengo**, **etc** *verb* ▷ see **venga** *excl* ▷ **venir**

la **venganza** *fem noun*
revenge

vengarse *reflexive verb* **[28]**
vengarse de alguien to get one's revenge on someone
Se vengó de él. She got her revenge on him.

ƒ venir *verb* **[15]**

1 **to come**
Ven a las siete. Come at seven.
Ya vienen. They're coming now..
Vino a verte. He came to see you.
Viene de Italia. It comes from Italy.

2 **venir a por algo** to come to fetch something
Vengo a por el paquete. I've come to fetch the parcel.
venir por alguien to come to collect somebody
Vengo por ti a las cinco. I'll come for you at five.

3 **to be**
La noticia viene en la primera página. The news is on the front page.

4 **venirle bien a alguien** to suit someone
Mañana me viene bien. Tomorrow suits me.
Esa camisa te viene bien. That shirt suits you.
¿Te viene bien quedar en la entrada? Is it okay for you if we meet at the entrance?
Esta parada de metro me viene muy bien. This tube station's very convenient for me.

5 (*in time expressions*) **La semana que viene.** Next week.
El domingo que viene. Next Sunday.

ƒ la **venta** *fem noun*
sale
estar en venta to be for sale
Salió a la venta. It went on sale.

la **ventaja** *fem noun*
advantage
las ventajas y desventajas the advantages and disadvantages

ƒ la **ventana** *fem noun*
window (*of a house*)

ƒ la **ventanilla** *fem noun*
1 **window** (*in a train, car*)
2 **till** (*in a bank*)
3 **ticket counter** (*for train tickets, cinema tickets*)

la **ventilación** *fem noun*
ventilation

el **ventilador** *masc noun*
fan

la **ventisca** *fem noun*
blizzard

ƒ ver *verb* **[16]**

1 **to see**
Los vi ayer. I saw them yesterday.
No lo veo. I can't see it.
No veo nada desde aquí. I can't see anything from here.
No veo bien de lejos. I'm shortsighted.
Ya veo cuál es el problema. I can see the problem now.
Ya veremos lo que hacemos. We'll see what we do.

2 **to watch**
ver la tele to watch TV
Anoche vimos una película muy buena. We watched a very good film last night.

3 **to think**
Lo que ha hecho no lo veo bien. I don't think what he's done is right.

4 **tener que ver con algo** to have something to do with something
Eso no tiene nada que ver. That has nothing to do with it.

5 (*in exclamations*) **'Mira lo que me compré.' —'¿A ver?'** 'Look what I've bought.'— 'Let's see?'
A ver. ¿Qué te pasa? Right, what's the matter with you?

verse *reflexive verb* **[16]**

1 **to see yourself**
verse en el espejo to see yourself in the mirror

2 **to see each other**
Nos vemos todos los días. We see each other every day.

3 **to meet**
Nos vimos ayer. We met yesterday.

el & la **veraneante** *masc & fem noun*
holidaymaker

veranear *verb* **[17]**
veranear en to spend your summer holidays in
Veranean en la montaña. They spend their summer holidays in the mountains.

ƒ el **verano** *masc noun*
summer
en verano in summer
el verano pasado last summer
Pasamos las vacaciones de verano en Mallorca. We spend the summer holidays in Mallorca.

veras *in phrase*
de veras
Lo siento de veras. I really am sorry.
¡De veras! Really!

la **verbena** *fem noun*
1 **open-air dance**
2 **festival** (*for a town or village's patron saint*)

el **verbo** *masc noun*
(*Grammar*) **verb**

la **verdad** *fem noun*
1 **truth**
la pura verdad the absolute truth
Dime la verdad. Tell me the truth.
La verdad es que ... The truth is that ...
La verdad, no me acuerdo. I don't remember, honestly.
2 **ser verdad** to be true
Eso es verdad. That's true.
3 (*in questions*) **¿No te gusta, verdad?** You don't like it, do you?
¿Sabes hacerlo, verdad? You know how to do it, don't you?
Sí vienen, ¿verdad? They are coming, aren't they?
4 (*in expressions*) **de verdad**
un amigo de verdad a real friend
De verdad que no lo quiero. Really, I don't want it.

verdadero *masc adjective*, **verdadera** *fem*
1 **true**
una historia verdadera a true story
su verdadero nombre his true name
2 (*for emphasis*) **Es un verdadero idiota.** He's a real idiot.

verde *masc & fem adjective* ▷ see **verde** *noun*
1 **green**
una blusa verde oscuro a dark green blouse
Tiene los ojos verdes. She has green eyes.
2 **dirty** (*story, etc*)
un chiste verde a dirty joke

el **verde** *masc noun* ▷ see **verde** *adj*
1 **green**
2 **los Verdes** the Greens (*in politics*)
- el **verde botella** bottle-green

la **verdulería** *fem noun*
greengrocer's

la **verdura** *fem noun*
vegetable
un puesto de verduras a vegetable stall
Las verduras son muy saludables. Vegetables are very healthy.

vergonzoso *masc adjective*, **vergonzosa** *fem*
1 **timid** (*person*)
2 **shameful** (*act, behaviour*)

la **vergüenza** *fem noun*
1 **shame**
Me da vergüenza pensarlo. I'm ashamed to think about it.
¡Qué poca vergüenza tienes! Have you no shame at all?
2 **embarrassment**
No quiero, me da vergüenza. I don't want to, I'm too embarrassed.
Me da vergüenza hablar en público. I feel embarrassed when I have to speak in public.
¡Qué vergüenza! How embarrassing!
3 **disgrace**
Es una vergüenza. It's a disgrace.
¡Qué vergüenza! That's terrible.

la **verruga** *fem noun*
1 **wart**
2 **verruca**

la **versión** *fem noun*
version
una película en versión original a film which has not been dubbed (*a subtitled foreign film*)

el **vertedero** *masc noun*
rubbish tip

vertical *masc & fem adjective*
vertical
en posición vertical in a vertical position

el **vertido** *masc noun*
1 **spillage** (*of pollutants, etc*)
2 **los vertidos** effluent

el **vértigo** *masc noun*
vertigo
Me da vértigo mirar abajo. Looking down makes me dizzy.

el **vestíbulo** *masc noun*
1 **hall**
2 **foyer**

vestido *masc adjective*, **vestida** *fem* ▷ see **vestido** *noun*
dressed
ir bien, mal vestido to be well, badly dressed
Iba vestida de azul. She dressed in blue.
Tenemos que ir vestidos de uniforme. We have to wear uniform.

el **vestido** *masc noun* ▷ see **vestido** *adj*
dress
- el **vestido de noche** evening dress
- el **vestido de novia** wedding dress

vestir *verb* [57]
to dress
vestir bien, mal to dress well, badly

vestirse *reflexive verb* [57]
1 **to get dressed**
Ya es hora de vestirnos. It's time to get dressed.
2 **to dress**
Se viste a la última moda. She wears the latest fashions.
Me gusta vestirme de azul. I like wearing blue.

el **vestuario** *masc noun*
1 **wardrobe**
2 **changing room**

el **veterinario** *masc noun*, la **veterinaria** *fem*
veterinary surgeon

vez *fem noun, pl:* las **veces**
1 **time**
una vez once
dos veces twice
tres veces al año three times a year
La primera vez que fui al extranjero. The first time I went to abroad.
¿Has estado alguna vez en Italia? Have you ever been to Italy?
2 (*in expressions*) **a la vez** at the same time, at once
algunas veces sometimes
a veces sometimes
cada vez each time
de vez en cuando from time to time
De vez en cuando nos manda una carta. Occasionally he sends us a letter.
en vez de instead of
otra vez again
por última vez for the last time
rara vez seldom
tal vez perhaps, maybe
3 **cada vez más** more and more
Hay cada vez más turistas. There are more and more tourists.
4 **cada vez menos** less and less, fewer and fewer
Hay cada vez menos peces en el río. There are fewer and fewer fish in the river.
5 (*telling stories*) **Érase una vez ...** Once upon a time ...

la **vía** *fem noun*
1 **way, path**
2 **en vías de, un país en vías de desarrollo** a developing country
3 (*in sending things*) **por vía aérea** by air
por vía marítima by sea
- la **vía de acceso** slip road
- la **vía férrea** railway track
- la **Vía Láctea** Milky Way

viajar *verb* [17]
to travel
viajar en avión to travel by plane
viajar a México to travel to Mexico

el **viaje** *masc noun*
journey, trip
un viaje de quince días a two-week trip
estar de viaje to be away
hacer un viaje to go on a journey, to go on a trip
salir de viaje to go on a journey, to go on a trip
¡Buen viaje! Have a good journey!
- el **viaje de negocios** business trip
- el **viaje de novios** honeymoon
- el **viaje organizado** package tour

el **viajero** *masc noun*, la **viajera** *fem*
1 **traveller**
2 **passenger**

la **víbora** *fem noun*
viper

vibrar *verb* [17]
to vibrate

el **vicio** *masc noun*
1 **vice**
2 **bad habit**
Tengo el vicio de morderme las uñas. I have the bad habit of biting my nails.

la **víctima** *fem noun*
victim
El número de víctimas mortales asciende a 25. The death toll has risen to 25.

la **victoria** *fem noun*
victory

la **vid** *fem noun*
vine (*grapes*)

la **vida** *fem noun*
life
estar con vida to be alive
llevar una vida muy activa to lead a very busy life
Se gana la vida como mecánico. He earns his living as amechanic.
La vida está muy cara. The cost of living is very high.

el **vídeo** *masc noun*
video
en vídeo on video

la **videocámara** *fem noun*
video camera

el **videoclub** *masc noun*
video shop

el **videojuego** *masc noun*
video game

el **vidrio** *masc noun*
glass

viejo *masc adjective*, **vieja** *fem*
▷ see **viejo** *noun*
old (*car, house, custom*)

el **viejo** *masc noun*, la **vieja** *fem*
▷ see **viejo** *adj*
1 **old man**
2 **old woman**

el **viento** *masc noun*
1 **wind**
Hace viento. It's windy.
El viento sopla del este. The wind is blowing from the east.
2 **guy rope** (*of tent*)

el **vientre** *masc noun*
1 **belly**
2 **womb**

el **viernes** *masc noun*
Friday
el viernes on Friday
el viernes pasado last Friday
los viernes on Fridays
cada viernes every Friday
Hay mercado los viernes. There's a market on Fridays.

WORD TIP Names of months and days start with small letters in Spanish.

vigésimo *masc adjective*, **vigésima** *fem*
twentieth

el **villancico** *masc noun*
Christmas carol

el **vinagre** *masc noun*
vinegar

vine, **viniste**, **vino**, **etc** *verb* ▷ **venir**

el **vino** *masc noun*
wine
- el **vino blanco** white wine
- el **vino de mesa** table wine
- el **vino tinto** red wine

el **viñedo** *masc noun*
vineyard

violar *verb* **[17]**
1 **to break** (*rules, regulations*)
2 **to rape** (*a person*)

la **violencia** *fem noun*
violence

violento *masc adjective*, **violenta** *fem*
1 **violent**
2 **embarrassing** (*situation*)

violeta *invariable adjective & fem noun*
1 **violet** (*colour*)
2 **la violeta** violet (*the flower*)

el **violín** *masc noun*
violin
tocar el violín to play the violin

el **violoncelo**, **violonchelo** *masc noun*
cello

virar *verb* **[17]**
to swerve
El coche viró para esquivar al perro. The car swerved to avoid the dog.

la **virgen** *fem noun*
virgin
la Virgen María the Virgin Mary

virgo *masc & fem noun* ▷ see **Virgo** *noun*
Virgo
Es virgo. He's Virgo.

WORD TIP Use a small letter in Spanish to say *I am Virgo*, etc with star signs.

Virgo *masc noun* ▷ see **virgo** *noun*
Virgo

la **virtud** *fem noun*
virtue

el **virus** *masc noun*, *pl:* los **virus**
(*Computers, Medicine*) **virus**
un software anti virus a piece of anti-virus software

el **visado** *masc noun*
visa

la **visibilidad** *fem noun*
visibility

visible *masc & fem adjective*
visible

la **visión** *fem noun*
1 **vision**
2 **sight**
perder la visión to lose your sight

la **visita** *fem noun*
1 **visit**
una visita a la feria a visit to the fair
horario de visita visiting times
hacerle una visita a alguien to visit somebody
Les hizo una visita. She visited them.

2 **visitor**
Tienes una visita. You have a visitor.
Tienen visita. They have visitors.
3 **hit** (*on a web site*)

♪ **visitar** *verb* **[17]**
to visit
visitar el casco urbano to visit the old part of town
visitar a mis abuelos to visit my grandparents

la **víspera** *fem noun*
la víspera the day before
la víspera del partido the day before the match

♪ la **vista** *fem noun*
1 **view**
una vista preciosa a beautifu view
El hotel tiene vistas al mar. The hotel has views over the sea.
2 **eyesight**
tener buena, mala vista to have good, bad eyesight
perder la vista to lose your sight
El sol me hace daño a la vista. The sun's hurting my eyes.
La conocemos de vista. We know her by sight.
3 (*the direction you look*) **bajar la vista** to look down
levantar la vista to look up
4 **estar a la vista** to be within sight
no estar a la vista to be out of sight
5 **¡Hasta la vista!** See you!

♪ **vistieron**, **vistió**, **etc** *verb* ▷ **vestir**

♪ **visto** *verb* ▷ **see visto** *adj* ▷ **ver**

visto *masc adjective*, **vista** *fem*
▷ **see ver** *verb*
1 **clear**
Está visto que ... It's clear that ...
2 **por lo visto** apparently
Por lo visto se perdieron.. Apparently hey got lost.
3 **estar bien, mal visto** to be acceptable, unacceptable
Está muy mal visto. It's just not acceptable.

la **vitamina** *fem noun*
vitamin

la **vitrina** *fem noun*
shop window

el **viudo** *masc noun*, la **viuda** *fem*
1 **widower**
2 **widow**

viva *exclamation*
¡Viva! Hurray!
¡Viva la novia! Three cheers for the bride!

la **vivienda** *fem noun*
1 **housing**
el problema de la vivienda the housing problem
2 **dweling** (*could be a flat, huse etc*)
un bloque de viviendas a block of flats

♪ **vivir** *verb* **[19]**
1 **to live**
Vivo en la calle Altamira. I live in Altamira Street.
Vive en casa de su hermana. She lives with her sister.
Vivimos un año en Alicante. We lived inAlicante for a year.
2 **to live through, to have**
Vivimos unos momentos muy felices. We lived through some happy times.

vivo *masc adjective*, **viva** *fem*
alive
en vivo live (*broadcast, concert, etc*)
Todavía están vivos. They're still alive.

WORD TIP Always use *estar* for 'to be' with *vivo*.

el **vocabulario** *masc noun*
vocabulary

la **vocal** *fem noun*
vowel (*the letters* **a, e, i, o, u**)

volante *masc & fem adjective*
▷ **see volante** *noun*
flying

el **volante** *masc noun* ▷ **see volante** *adj*
steering wheel

♪ **volar** *verb* **[24]**
1 **to fly** (*planes, birds, people*)
Fue la primera vez que volé. It was the first time I flew.
2 **to blow up**
volar un edificio to blow up a building

el **volcán** *masc noun*
volcano

volcar *verb* **[24]**
1 **to knock over**
2 **to turn over**
El camión volcó. The lorry turned over.
3 **to empty** (*a box, a drawer*)

volcarse *reflexive verb* **[24]**
1 **to turn over** (*vehicles*)
2 **volcarse en algo** to do all you can for something ⏩

Se vuelca en su familia. She does all she can for her family.

el **vóleibol**, **voleibol** *masc noun*
volleyball
jugar al vóleibol to play volleyball

la **voltereta** *fem noun*
somersault

el **volumen** *masc noun*
volume
subir el volumen to turn up the volume
¡Baja el volumen! Turn the volume down!

la **voluntad** *fem noun*
1 **will**
Lo hicieron de buena voluntad. They did it willingly.
Lo hice por mi propia voluntad. I did it of my own free will.
2 **wish**
la voluntad de los padres the parents' wishes

voluntario *masc adjective*, **voluntaria** *fem* ▷ see **voluntario** *noun*
voluntary

el **voluntario** *masc noun*, la **voluntaria** *fem* ▷ see **voluntario** *adj*
volunteer

♪ **volver** *verb* **[45]**
1 **to come back**
Ya ha vuelto. He's already come back.
¿Cuándo volverás? When will you come back?
Volveré a eso de las siete. I'll be back by about seven.
¿Cuándo volviste de tu viaje? When did you get back from your trip?
2 **to go back**
volver al colegio to go back to school
¿Quieres que volvamos a casa? Do you want us to go back home?
Ha vuelto con su novia. He's gone back to his girlfriend.
No había vuelto a Sevilla desde el verano pasado. I hadn't been back to Seville since last summer.
3 **to turn**
volver la página to turn the page
Volvió la cabeza. She turned her head.
Al volver la esquina ... When I turned the corner ...
4 **volver a hacer algo** to do something again
Volví a revisarlo. I checked it again.
¡No lo vuelvas a hacer! Don't do it again!
Tenemos que volver a empezar. We have to start again.
5 **volver loco a alguien** to drive someone mad
Me vuelve loca con tantas preguntas. She's driving me mad with all her questions.
6 **volver en sí** to come round (*after fainting*)

volverse *reflexive verb* **[45]**
1 **to turn around**
Me volví para ver mejor. I turned around to see better.
2 **volverse de espaldas** to turn your back
¡No te vuelvas de espaldas cuando te estoy hablando! Don't turn your back on me when I'm talking to you!
3 **to come back**
volverse a casa to come back home
Se volvieron a las doce. They came back at twelve o'clock.
4 **to become**
volverse loco to go crazy
Se ha vuelto muy vanidosa. She's become very vain.
La situación se ha vuelto grave. The situation has become serious.

vomitar *verb* **[17]**
to be sick
tener ganas de vomitar to feel sick

vosotros, **vosotras** *pronoun*
you
¿Vosotras queréis ir? Do you want to go?
vosotros mismos *masc*, **vosotras mismas** *fem* yourselves

WORD TIP *vosotros* is used to refer to two or more males, or males and females, who you know well.

votar *verb* **[17]**
1 **to vote on** (*a measure*)
2 **to vote for** (*a party, a candidate*)
¿Por quién votaste? Who did you vote for?
Siempre vota a los verdes. She always votes for the Greens.

el **voto** *masc noun*
1 **vote**
un voto a favor a vote for
un voto en contra a vote against
un voto secreto a secret ballot
2 **vow**
- el **voto de censura** vote of no confidence
- el **voto en blanco** blank ballot paper

♪ **voy** *verb* ▷ **ir**

♪ la **voz** *fem noun*, *pl:* las **voces**
voice
oír voces to hear voices
tener la voz tomada to be hoarse
hablar en voz baja quietly
hablar en voz alta to speak loudly
leer algo en voz alta to read something out loud

♪ el **vuelo** *masc noun*
flight
el vuelo 453 con destino Cardiff flight 453 to Cardiff
• el **vuelo regular** scheduled flight

♪ la **vuelta** *fem noun*
1 **change** (*coins*)
2 **turn**
una vuelta a la derecha a turn to the right
3 **return**
la vuelta al colegio the return to school (*after the summer holidays*)
A la vuelta iremos al cine. We'll go to the cinema when we come back.
4 **stage** (*in a competition*)
5 **round** (*in elections*)
6 **dar una vuelta** to go out (*for a walk, a drive, etc*)
dar una vuelta en coche to go for a drive
¿Quieres dar una vuelta? Do you want to go out for a walk?
7 **dar la vuelta a algo**
dar la vuelta a la página to turn over the page
dar la vuelta a la esquina to turn the corner
dar una vuelta a la manzana to go round the block
dar la vuelta al mundo to go round the world
Dale la vuelta al cuadro. Turn the picture round the other way.
dar la vuelta a un disco to turn a record over
8 **dar una vuelta alrededor de algo** to go out for a tour around something
Dieron una vuelta alrededor de la ciudad. They went out for a tour round the city.

el **vuelto** *masc noun*
(*Latin America*) **change** (*coins*)

♪ **vuelva**, **vuelvo**, **etc** *verb* ▷ **volver**

vuestro *masc adjective*, **vuestra** *fem*
▷ see **vuestro** *pron*
your (*talking to more than one person*)
vuestra casa your house
un familiar vuestro a relative of yours

vuestro, **vuestra** *pronoun*
▷ see **vuestro** *adj*
yours
La vuestra es verde. Yours is green.
Los vuestros están en el salón. Yours are in the living room.
Aquel es el vuestro. That one is yours.

vulgar *masc & fem adjective*
1 **vulgar**
2 **common**

W w

el **walkman**® *masc noun*
personal stereo

ꟹ el **wáter** *masc noun*
toilet

el **whisky** *masc noun*
whisky

ꟹ el **windsurf** *masc noun*
windsurfing
hacer windsurf to go windsurfing

X x

el **xilófono** *masc noun*
xylophone

Y y

y *conjunction*
1 **and**
Amanda y yo Amanda and I
2 (*with numbers*) **treinta y siete** thirty-seven
3 (*in clock time*) **la una y media** half past one
a las diez y veinte at twenty past ten
4 (*for emphasis*) **¿Y a mí qué?** So, what's it to me?

WORD TIP *y* becomes *e* before words beginning with *i-* or *hi-*.

ya *adverb*
1 **already**
Ya está hecho. It's already done.
¿Has comido ya? Have you already eaten?
2 **yet**
¿Han llegado ya? Have they arrived yet?
3 **any more**
Ya no importa. It doesn't matter any more.
4 **now**
Tenemos que decidirnos ya. We must decide now.
Ya es hora de irnos. We must go now.
5 (*in the future*) **Ya veremos.** We'll see about that.
Ya te contaré. I'll tell you about it.
6 (*for emphasis*) **Ya lo sé.** I know.
Ya entiendo. I understand.
Ya era hora. About time too.
¡Ya está! That's it!
¡Ya voy! I'm just coming!
¡Ya lo creo! You bet!
7 (*in expressions*) **'Esto es de Juan'—'Ya.'** 'This is Juan's'—'I know.'
Preparados, listos, ¡Ya! Ready, steady, go!
'Yo no he sido'—'Ya, ya.' 'It wasn't me'—'Yeah, yeah!'
8 **ya que** since
Ya que vas a estar aquí. Since you're going to be here.

el **yate** *masc noun*
yacht

la **yedra** *fem noun*
ivy

la **yegua** *fem noun*
mare

la **yema** *fem noun*
1 **yolk**
2 **la yema del dedo** the fingertip

el **yerno** *masc noun*
son-in-law

yo *pronoun*
1 **I**
Yo no lo sé. I don't know.
2 **me**
Soy yo. It's me.
3 **yo mismo, yo misma** myself
Lo haré yo mismo. I'll do it myself.

el **yoga** *masc noun*
yoga

el **yogur** *masc noun*
yoghurt

el **yudo** *masc noun*
judo

Z z

⚷ la **zanahoria** *fem noun*
carrot

el **zancudo** *masc noun*
(*Latin America*) **mosquito**

la **zapatería** *fem noun*
shoe shop

el **zapatero** *masc noun*, la **zapatera** *fem*
1 **shoemaker**
2 **shoe repairer's**

la **zapatilla** *fem noun*
1 **slipper**
2 **canvas shoe**
- la **zapatilla de ballet** ballet shoe
- la **zapatilla de deporte** trainer
- la **zapatilla de esparto** espadrille

⚷ el **zapato** *masc noun*
shoe
- el **zapato bajo** flat shoe
- el **zapato de tacón** high heeled shoe

mini-info ***Zara***

España tiene muchos diseñadores de moda famosos pero es la marca de ropa Zara la que se conoce por todo el mundo. Se fundó en 1963 y hoy tiene más de 15.000 sucursales en 44 países.

la **zarzamora** *fem noun*
blackberry

la **zarzuela** *fem noun*
Spanish light opera

el **zodíaco**, **zodiaco** *masc noun*
zodiac

⚷ la **zona** *fem noun*
area
Viven en la zona. **They live locally.**
- la **zona (azul)** short-term parking area (*requiring a parking disk*)
- la **zona comercial** commercial district
- la **zona peatonal** pedestrian precinct

zonzo *masc adjective*, **zonza** *fem*
(*Latin America: informal*) **silly**, **daft**

el **zoo** *masc noun*
zoo

el **zoológico** *masc noun*
zoo

el **zorro** *masc noun*, la **zorra** *fem*
1 **fox**
2 **vixen**

el **zueco** *masc noun*
clog

zumbar *verb* **[17]**
to buzz

⚷ el **zumo** *masc noun*
juice
- el **zumo de fruta** fruit juice
- el **zumo de naranja** orange juice

zurdo *masc adjective*, **zurda** *fem*
left-handed

Writing a letter

Text messaging and email

Family and friends

Home and local area

Healthy living and the human body

Food and eating out

Sports and leisure activities

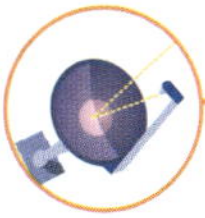

Media and communication

Travel and transport

Holidays and tourism

School life

Careers and future plans

Jobs and work experience

Time

Numbers

Writing a letter

A formal letter

San Pedro, 22 de noviembre de 2009

Sra María Navarro
Marqués del Duero, 25
29670 San Pedro de Alcántara

Hotel Paraíso
Calle Elche
03110 Alicante

Muy Señor mío

Recibí el folleto de su hotel; muchas gracias.

Quisiera reservar una habitacíon con baño y wc, para dos personas con pensión completa del 27 de abril al 12 de mayo. Adjunto encontrará un cheque de 100 euros.

Dándole las gracias por anticipado.
Le saluda atentamente

María de Navarro

- The name of the town and the date the letter is being written go at the top right.
- The sender's name and address go on the left.
- The name and the address the letter is being sent to go on the right.

- Muy Señor mío/Estimado Señor Ramírez (*to a man*)
- Muy Señora mía/Estimada Señora Gómez (*to a woman*)

- Le saluda atentamente/cordialmente.
- Atentamente.

A letter to a friend

Chester, 23 de abril de 2009

Querida Catalina

Gracias por tu carta. Bueno pues, vas a venir a Chester en junio, ¡fantástico! Vas a visitar mi colegio. Será muy interesante. Es un colegio bastante grande con buenas instalaciones. Podrás ayudarme con mi español. Voy bien en español y el profe es muy simpático. También podremos visitar el pueblo un poco. Chester es muy bonito.
El fin de semana pasado, fui a Londres con mi amiga. Cogimos el tren (el viaje dura dos horas en tren). Fuimos de compras y después al cine. Siempre hay mucho que hacer y ver allí. Vámonos en junio si quieres.

Espero recibir noticias tuyas pronto ... contesta ¡rápido!

Un abrazo
Susan

- The name of the town and the date the lett is being written go at the top right.

- Querido (*to a boy*)
- Querida (*to a girl*)

To a whole family or group:

- Hola/saludos a todos
- Queridos todos
- Queridos amigos

- Gracias por tun carta/tu invitacíon/tu regalito.
- Acabo de recibir su invitacíon/su carta que me agradó mucho (*formal*).
- Espero recibir noticias tuyas pronto.
- Saluda a tus padres/tu hermano, etc.

- Hasta pronto
- Besos
- Un (fuerte) abrazo

Text messaging and email

Text messaging

- Certain words or syllables can be represented by letters or numbers that sound the same but take up less space, e.g. mñn, mñna = mañana.
- Accents are often left out. The syllables '*-pe*, *-te*' and '*-ca*' can be replaced by the letters P, T and K etc.
- Another way of shortening words is to leave out certain letters, especially vowels. For example, 'adiós' becomes 'a2' and 'cuando' becomes 'q&d'.
- 'Emoticons' are very popular, e.g. :-) = *sonrisa*, :-(= *cara feliz*, :-D = *sonrisa de oreja a oreja*

hl cm tva? vi a t hna ayr. s m simpatik
Hola, ¿cómo te va ? Vi a tu hermana ayer. Es muy simpática
bbtt. stas bn ? vams al cin o 1kf mñn ?
Buenas tardes. ¿Estás bien? ¿Vamos al cine o a un café mañana?

Abbreviation	Full Word	Abbreviation	Full Word	Abbreviation	Full Word
sn	sin	fsta	fiesta	msj	mensaje
simpatik	simpática	hna	hermana	pbrlm	problema
cin	cine	gf	jefe	xq	porque
fin d smn	fin de semana	ayr	ayer	x	por
atamñn	hasta mañana	j+	jamás	q&d	cuando
d+sia2	demasiados	dbres	deberes	na-	nada menos
taptec1kf?	te apetece un café ?	t&q	te quiero	resp s t gsta	responde si te gusta
lgo	luego	q	que	hno	hermano
bdias	buenos días	kf	café	hl cm tva?	¿hola cómo te va ?
bbtt	buenas tardes	qn	quién	s3ad	estresado
s	es	qay d nvo?	¿qué hay de nuevo	xfa	por favor
s dcir	es decir	l100to	lo siento	sp	siempre
dacurd	de acuerdo	eia	ella	stas bn?	estás bien?
npn	no pasa nada	mñn, mñna	mañana	stas ocu ?	¿estás ocupado ?
trist	triste	mdr	muerto de risa	vstrs	vosotros

Email

un correo electrónico, un email = an email
una dirección de correo electrónico = an email address
enviar un correo electrónico, un email = to send an email
recibir un correo electrónico, un email = to receive an email
un archivo = a file
un archivo adjunto = an attachment
una arroba = an @ sign
borrar un mensaje = to delete a message
un sitio web = a website
hacer click (en) = to click (on)
responder = reply
reenviar = forward
asunto = subject
copiar y pegar = to cut and paste
correo basura = spam

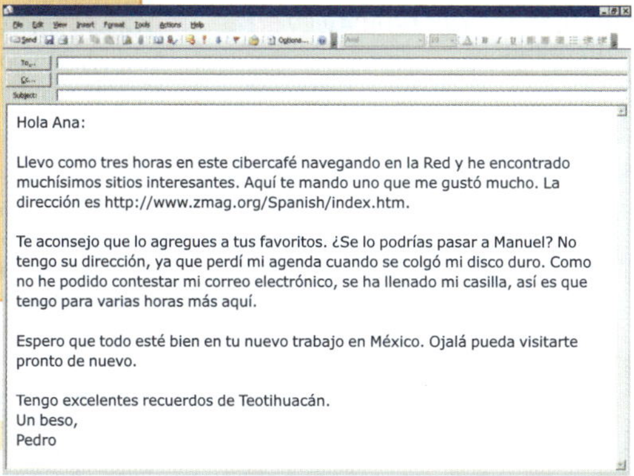

Hola Ana:

Llevo como tres horas en este cibercafé navegando en la Red y he encontrado muchísimos sitios interesantes. Aquí te mando uno que me gustó mucho. La dirección es http://www.zmag.org/Spanish/index.htm.

Te aconsejo que lo agregues a tus favoritos. ¿Se lo podrías pasar a Manuel? No tengo su dirección, ya que perdí mi agenda cuando se colgó mi disco duro. Como no he podido contestar mi correo electrónico, se ha llenado mi casilla, así es que tengo para varias horas más aquí.

Espero que todo esté bien en tu nuevo trabajo en México. Ojalá pueda visitarte pronto de nuevo.

Tengo excelentes recuerdos de Teotihuacán.
Un beso,
Pedro

Family and friends

Relationships

En mi familia, somos cinco.
There are five of us in my family.
Hay mis padres.
There are my parents.
mi padre/mi madre
my father/my mother
mi padrastro/mi madrastra
my stepfather/my stepmother
Tiene hijos.
He has children/She has children.
un hijo/una hija
a son/a daughter
Tengo un hermano/una hermana.
I have a brother/a sister.
un hermanastro/una hermanastra
a half-brother/a half-sister
un mellizo/una melliza
a twin brother/a twin sister
Soy hijo único.
I'm an only child (*boy speaking*).
Soy hija única.
I'm an only child (*girl speaking*).
Me llevo bien/No me llevo bien con ...
I get on well/I don't get on well with ...
- **mis abuelos.**
- my grandparents.
- **mi abuela/mi abuelo.**
- my grandmother/my grandfather.
- **mi tío/mi tía.**
- my uncle/my aunt.
- **mi primo** (*boy*)/**mi prima** (*girl*).
- my cousin.

Status

Es ... She/He is ...
- **soltero / soltera.** single.
- **casado** (*man*) / **casada** (*woman*). married.
- **viudo** (*man*) / **viuda** (*woman*). widower / widow.

Está ... She/He is ...
- **muerto** (*man*) / **muerta** (*woman*). dead.
- **prometido / prometida.** engaged.
- **separado** (*man*) / **separada** (*woman*). separated.
- **divorciado** (*man*) / **divorciada** (*woman*). divorced

estar contento/ contenta
to be happy

estar triste
to be sad

estar enfada enfadada
to be angry

tener sueño
to be tired

estar enamorado/ enamorada
to be in love

tener mi
to be afra

tener calor
to be hot

tener frío
to be cold

tener hambr
to be hungry

Descriptions

Mi mejor amiga (girl) **se llama ...**
Mi mejor amigo (boy) **se llama ...**
My best friend is called ...
Es ... He/She is ...
alto/alta. tall.
bajo/baja. short.
rubio/rubia. blond.
moreno/morena. dark-haired.
simpático/simpática. really nice.
pesado/pesada. a pain.
Tengo un amigo/una amiga que tiene quince años
I have a friend who is fifteen years old ...
... a quien le encanta el deporte.
... and who loves sport.
... a quien le encantan los juegos vídeo.
... and who loves video games.

ay ...
nere is ...

una cocina.
a kitchen.

una sala de estar.
a living room.

un comedor.
a dining room.

un WC.
a toilet.

un dormitorio.
a bedroom.

un cuarto de baño.
a bathroom.

un estudio.
an office/a study.

un garaje.
a garage.

un jardín.
a garden.

¿Vives ... Do you live...
- **en el centro?** in the city centre?
- **en las afueras?** in the suburbs?
- **en el campo?** in the country?
- **a orillas del mar?** at the seaside?
- **en la montaña?** in the mountains?

Vivo en el norte/sur/este/oeste/centro de ...
I live in the north/south/east/west/centre of ...
Es una ciudad industrial/moderna/animada.
It's an industrial/modern/lively town.
Es un pueblo agrícola/tranquilo/turístico.
It's a farming/quiet/touristy village.

En mi ciudad, hay ...
In my town there is/are ...

- **unas tiendas.** shops.
- **unos restaurantes.** restaurants.
- **unas cafeterías.** cafes.
- **unos hoteles.** hotels.
- **un museo.** a museum.
- **una iglesia.** a church.
- **una piscina.** a swimming pool.
- **un cine.** a cinema.
- **un teatro.** a theatre.
- **un centro de reciclaje.** a recycling centre.
- **un polideportivo.** a sports stadium.
- **un ayuntamiento.** a town hall.
- **una farmacia.** a chemist's/ pharmacy.

en la planta baja
on the ground floor
en la primera planta
on the first floor

Vivo en ...
I live in ...
- **una casa.** a house.
- **un apartamento en el segundo piso.** a flat on the second floor.

Mi casa es pequeña/grande/moderna/vieja.
My home is small/big/modern/old.

Healthy living and the human body

Me gusta ... I like ...
Me gustan ... I like ... (+ *plural*)
No me gusta ... I don't like ...
No me gustan ... I don't like ... (+ *plurc*

- **la gaseosa.** fizzy drinks.
- **el alcohol.** alcohol.
- **el agua.** water.
- **el zumo de fruta.** fruit juice.
- **la leche.** milk.
- **el café.** coffee.
- **la fruta.** fruit.
- **los dulces/caramelos.** sweets.
- **la verdura.** vegetables.
- **la carne.** meat.

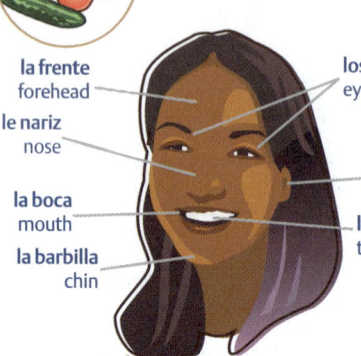

Hay que evitar beber ...
You must avoid drinking ...
No debes fumar.
You mustn't smoke.

Es saludable/sano.
It's healthy.
No es saludable/san
It's unhealthy.

Para mantenerse en forma, hay que ...
To keep healthy, you have to ...

- **levantarse temprano.** get up early.
- **acostarse temprano.** go to bed early.
- **hacer deporte.** take exercise.
- **ir a pie/caminar.** walk.

todos los días
every day
una vez a la/por semana
once a week
de vez en cuando
now and then
nunca
never
siempre
always

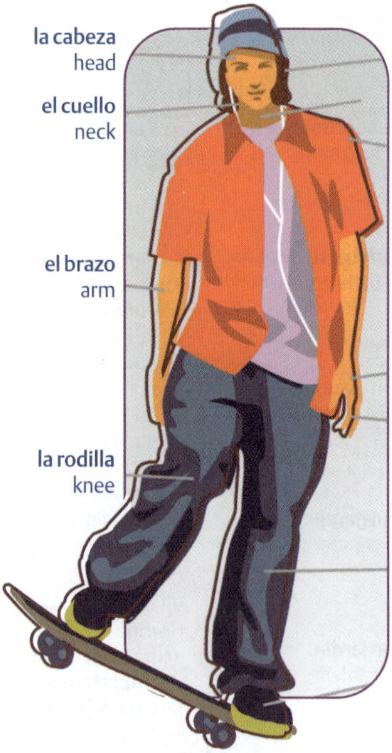

el desayuno breakfast
el almuerzo/la comida lunch
la cena dinner
Como fruta una vez al día.
I eat fruit once a day.
Tengo hambre. I'm hungry.
Tengo sed. I'm thirsty.
Tengo ganas de dormir. I'm sleepy.
Me duele la cabeza. I have a headache.
Tengo alergia. I have an allergy.

hacer las compras ...
to go shopping (for food) ...

en la pastelería
at the cake shop

en la tienda de comestibles
at the grocer's

en la panadería
at the baker's

At a restaurant/cafe

Quisiera reservar... I'd like to reserve ...
una mesa para cuatro personas.
a table for four people.
¿Qué desea? What would you like?
Me gustaría tomar ... I'd like ...
- **un café.** a coffee.
- **una taza de té.** a cup of tea.
- **un zumo de naranja.** an orange juice.

¿Tiene usted helado de vainilla?
Have you got vanilla ice cream?
Para comenzar/como entrada deme ...
For a starter, I'll have ...
- **una sopa de cebolla.** onion soup.
- **una ensalada de tomate.** tomato salad.

en la carnicería
at the butcher's

en la charcutería
at the delicatessen

en el mercado
at the market

en el supermercado
at the supermarket

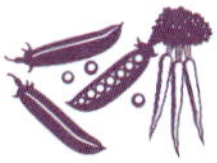

en Internet
on the Internet

Como plato fuerte/principal ...
For my main course ...
- **el pollo asado** roast chicken
- **el filete de ternera** fillet steak

con ... with ...
- **guisantes.** peas.
- **patatas fritas.** chips.

De postre, me gustaría ...
For dessert, I'd like ...
- **la tarta de pera.** pear tart.
- **el mousse de chocolate.** chocolate mousse.

Para beber ...
To drink, I'll have ...
- **agua mineral.** mineral water.
- **un vino (blanco/tinto).** (white/red) wine.

La cuenta, por favor. The bill, please.
¿Cuánto es? How much is it?

Sports and leisure activities

Mi pasatiempo preferido es ...
My favourite pastime is ...
- **salir con amigos.** going out with friends.
- **ir al centro (de la ciudad).** going into town.
- **ir de compras.** going shopping.
- **ir a un concierto.** going to concerts.
- **la lectura.** reading.
- **escuchar la música.** listening to music.
- **ver la tele.** watching TV.
- **jugar a la consola.** playing on a games console.
- **ir de fiestas/ir de discotecas.** going to parties/discos.
- **ir a montar en bici.** going cycling.

¿Vamos al parque?
Shall we go to the park?
Nos encontramos en el gimnasio.
We'll meet up at the gym.
Prefiero ir al estadio.
I'd rather go to the stadium.
¡Nos vemos ...
See you ...
- **en el cine!** at the cinema!
- **en el partido!** at the match!
- **¡en el centro recreativo!** at the leisure centre!
- **en la disco!** at the disco!

hacer el esquí.
going skiing.

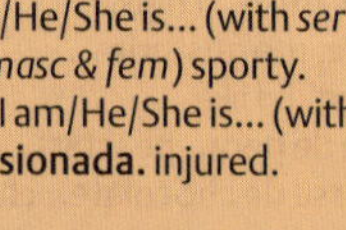

Soy/Es*... I am/He/She is... (with *ser*)
- **deportisa.** (*masc & fem*) sporty.

Estoy/Está*... I am/He/She is... (with *estar*)
- **lesionado/lesionada.** injured.
- **bien.** well.

Me gusta mantenerme en forma. I like to keep fit.
Me siento mal. I feel ill.
Me duele. It hurts.
*Spanish avoids specifying I, *yo*; he, *él*; she *ella* etc. unless emphasis is needed.

Mi pasatiempo preferido es ...
My favourite pastime is ...

la natación.
going swimming.

hacer vela.
going sailing.

montar a caballo.
going horse-riding.

Me gusta/No me gusta el deporte.
I like/I don't like playing sport .
Mi deporte favorito es... My favourite sport is...
- **jugar al fútbol.** playing football.
- **jugar al tenis.** playing tennis.
- **jugar al vóleibol.** playing volleyball.
- **el atletismo.** athletics.
- **el ciclismo de montaña.** mountain biking.
- **el montañismo.** mountaineering.
- **el submarinismo.** scuba diving.
- **el windsurf.** windsurfing.
- **el monopatinaje.** skateboarding.
- **el patinaje/el patinaje sobre hielo/el patinaje sobre ruedas.** skating/ice skating/roller skating

hacer el senderismo.
going hiking.

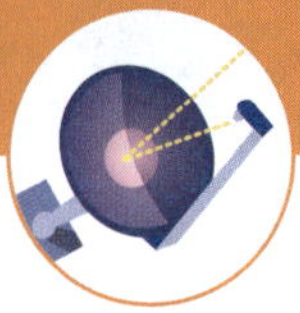

Media and communication

Television and cinema

ver la tele to watch TV
¿Qué programas hay en la tele?
What's on the telly?
Hay ... There's ...
- **un programa de deporte.** a sports programme.
- **un documental.** a documentary.
- **un culebrón.** a soap.
- **un concurso.** a game show.
- **las noticias/el noticiero.** the news.

¿En qué cadena está?
What channel is it on?
Mi serie preferida es ...
My favourite series is ...
ir al cine. to go to the cinema.
Ponen ... They're showing ...
- **una película policíaca.** a detective film.
- **dibujos animados.** cartoons.
- **una comedia.** a comedy.
- **una película de terror.** a horror film.

Vi Star Wars hace poco.
I saw Star Wars recently.

Top 10 media gadgets

un televisor (pantalla grande)
a (wide screen) TV
una antena parabólica a satellite dish
un MP3 an MP3 player
un DVD a DVD player
una consola de juegos a games console
un ordenador portátil laptop computer
una cámara digital a digital camera
una cámara vídeo a video camera
una cadena hifi a music system
un (teléfono) móvil a mobile phone

On the telephone

¡Diga! Hallo!
¿Puedo hablar con ... ?
Can I speak to ... ?
¿Quién llama? Who's calling?
No cuelgues. Hold on.
¿Puedo dejar un mensaje?
Can I leave a message?
Volveré a llamar más tarde.
I'll call back later.

Radio, newspapers, and magazines

escuchar la radio to listen to the radio
Leo el periódico todos los días.
I read the newspaper every day.
Mi revista favorita/mi periódico preferido es ...
My favourite magazine/newspaper is ...

On the computer

Con el ordenador... On my computer, I...
- **nevego en Internet.** surf the web.
- **mando mails a mis amigos.** email friends.
- **descargo música.** download music.
- **veo DVDs.** watch dvds.
- **hago los deberes.** do homework.
- **busco algo en Internet.** look something up on the Internet.

- **el ordenador** computer
- **el sitio web, el web** website
- **Internet** *masc* (normally used without *el*) Internet
- **el blog, la bitácora** blog
- **la webcam, la cámara** web, webcam

Travel and transport

Voy ...
I'm going...

en avión.
by plane.

en tren.
by train.

en coche.
by car.

en autobús.
by bus.

en barco.
by ship.

en bici.
by bike.

en autocar.
by coach.

en taxi.
by taxi.

en moto.
on a motorbike.

salir/la salida to leave/departure
llegar/la llegada to arrive/arrival
viajar/un viaje to travel/a journey
el equipaje luggage

¿Nos encontramos ... ? Shall we meet ... ?
- **en el aeropuerto** at the airport
- **en el puerto** at the port
- **en la estación** at the station
- **en la estación de buses** at the bus station

Quisiera ...
I'd like ...
- **comprar un billete de ida solo/de ida y vuelta a Madrid.**
- a single/a return to Madrid.
- **comprar un billete.**
- to buy a ticket.
- **reservar un asiento.**
- to reserve a seat.
- **consultar el horario.**
- to check the timetable.

¿De qué vía/andén sale el tren?
What platform does the train leave from?

¿A qué hora sale el tren?
What time does the train leave?

¿Dónde está la parada de autobuses?
Where is the bus stop?

La estación de metro está aquí cerca.
The underground station is close by.

El año pasado fui a Francia.
Last year, I went to France.

¿Cuánto tiempo dura el vuelo?
How long is the flight?

Fuimos en coche.
We travelled by car.

No he ido nunca al extranjero.
I have never been abroad.

urante las vacaciones, me alojaré ...
uring the holidays, I am going to stay ...
en un hotel. in a hotel.
en un albergue juvenil.
in a youth hostel.
en una casa de campo.
in a holiday home in the country.
en un camping. at a campsite.
en la costa. by the sea.
en las montañas. in the mountains.
en el campo. in the country.
en la playa. at the beach.

Me gusta/No me gusta...
I like/I don't like...

- **el tiempo.** the weather.
- **el clima.** the climate.
- **la gente.** the people.
- **el idioma, la lengua.** the language.
- **el paisaje.** the scenery.
- **la comida.** the food.
- **la música.** the music.
- **la cultura.** the culture.
- **la arquitectura.** the architecture.

- **hacer turismo.** to go sight-seeing.
- **sacar fotos.** to take photos.
- **visitar los museos.** to visit museums.
- **tomar el sol.** to sunbathe.
- **relajarme.** to relax.
- **ir a las fiestas locales.** to go to local festivals.

medio ambiente the environment
:ológico, ecológica environmentally
endly
ecoturismo ecotourism
protección del medio ambiente
nservation
lvar el planeta saving the planet
s emisiones de carbono carbon
nissions
huella de carbono carbon footprint
dióxido de carbono carbon dioxide
cambio climático climate change
calentamiento global global warming
i colegio se vuelve ecológico. My
hool is going green.

El verano pasado, fui a España.
Last summer, I went to Spain.
Este año, voy a quedarme en casa.
This year, I'll stay at home.
Cada verano, voy a Marruecos.
Every summer, I go to Morocco.
El próximo verano, voy a ir a Bilbao.
Next summer, I'll be going to Bilbao.

Estoy de acuerdo/No estoy de acuerdo.
I agree/I disagree.
Estoy a favor de/Estoy en contra de...
I am for/against...
en me opinión in my opinion
una ventaja an advantage
una desventaja a disadvantage

School life

Voy al colegio a pie. I walk to school.
Mi colegio se llama ... My school is called ...
Estoy en el tercero de ESO. I'm in Year 10.
Hay 25 alumnos en mi curso.
There are 25 pupils in my class.
Los cursos comienzan a las ocho y media.
Lessons start at half past eight.
Una clase dura 45 minutos.
A lesson lasts 45 minutes.
Los lunes, a las nueve, tengo matemáticas.
On Mondays at nine o'clock I have maths.
Hago inglés y español.
I do English and Spanish.
Soy fuerte en/voy bien en ... (*boy or girl*)
I'm good at ...
Soy débil en ...
I'm not very good at ...
Estoy estudiando para el examen de ...
I'm studying for the ... exam.
Tenemos muchos deberes.
We have a lot of homework.
Al mediodía, como en la cantina.
At midday, I have lunch in the canteen.

Mi asignatura preferida es ...
My favourite subject is ...

el francés. French.

la química. chemistry.

el diseño. art.

el inglés. English.

las ciencias. science.

la música. music.

el alemán. German.

la física. physics.

la educaci física PE.

el español. Spanish.

la biología. biology.

la informá computing

la tecnología. technology.

la geografía. geography.

las mates. maths.

la historia. history.

Classroom instructions

¡Pasa! Come in! (*to one pupil*)
¡Entrad! Come in! (*to two or more pupils*)
Sacad vuestros cuadernos.
Take out your exercise books.
Abrid vuestros libros a la página 23.
Open your books at page 23.
En silencio, por favor.
Quietly, please.
Escuchad bien. Listen carefully.
Escuchad y repetid. Listen and repeat.
Trabaja con una pareja. Work with a partner. (*to one pupil*)
Leed el primer párrafo.
Read the first paragraph.
Escribid una descripción de ...
Write a description of ...
Buscad las palabras en un diccionario.
Look up the words in a dictionary.

Classroom objects

un libro de texto a textbook
un cuaderno an exercise book
un lápiz a pencil
un bolígrafo a ballpoint pen
un rotulador a felt-tip pen
una regla a ruler
una goma a rubber
un sacapuntas a pencil sharpener
unas tijeras scissors
una calculadora a calculator

Mi ambición es ...
My ambition is to...

estudiar.
study.

viajar al extranjero.
go abroad.

trabajar con niños.
work with children.

trabajar al aire libre.
work outdoors.

ser médico/médica.
be a doctor.

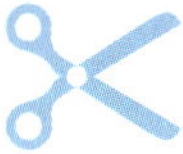
ser peluquero/ peluquera.
be a hairdresser.

ser secretaria.
be a secretary.

ser contable.
be an accountant.

ser mecánico/ mecánica.
be a car mechanic.

abc
ser profesor/ profesora.
be a teacher.

Este año estoy cursando el GCSE.
This year, I'm studying for my GCSEs.
El año que viene, voy a hacer 8 exámenes.
Next year, I'll sit 8 exams.
Depués, me gustaría ...
Then, I'd like to ...
Más tarde, quisiera ...
Later on, I'd like to ...
Tengo la intencíon de ... I plan to ...
Quiero ... I want to ...

Mi ambición es ...
My ambition is to ...
- **estudiar.** study.
- **ir a la universidad.** go to university.
- **hacer un diploma.** do a diploma.
- **hacer un aprendizaje.** do an apprenticeship.
- **hacer la práctica laboral.** go on a work placement.
- **encontrar un empleo.** find a job.
- **viajar al extranjero.** go abroad.

Me gustaría ser ...
I'd like to be ...
- **profesor/profesora.** a teacher.
- **médico/médica.** a doctor.

Me gustaría trabajar ...
I'd like to work ...
- **con niños.** with children.
- **al aire libre.** outdoors.
- **en turismo.** in tourism.

Para mí, un empleo es ideal si ...
For me, a job is ideal if ...
- **es interesante.** it's interesting.
- **paga bien.** it's well paid.
- **me gusta.** I like it.

Cuando tenga treinta años ...
When I'm thirty ...
estaré casado/casada. I'll be married.
Tendré una familia. I'll have a family.
Iré de vacaciones. I'll go on holiday.

Jobs and work experience

Sally Roberts

Dirección
27 Park Road
London N8 6PJ
tél: 0208 340 6549

sallyroberts@hotmail.com

Fecha de nacimiento: el dos de mayo 1993
Lugar de nacimiento: Londres
Nacionalidad: británica

Datos académicos
Preparacíon de los A levels (equivalente al bachillerato)
Asignaturas: inglés, español, música

Desde 2009	Alexandra Park Sixth Form Centre (instituto)
2009	8 GCSE's (equivalente al Certificado: Graduada en Educacíon Secundaria) Optativas: matemáticas, ciencias, inglés, español, geografía, arte y diseño, música, tecnología
2004–2009	Park View Secondary School (colegio)

Experiencia profesional

2009	mes de agosto trabajando en una oficina local vendedora en una zapatería local
2008	seis meses los sábados,
2007	de canguro para una familia vecina

Otro
Lenguas extranjeras: español (nivel avanzado oral y escrito), francés/alemán (nivel básico)

Informática: formacíon a nivel medio en Microsoft Word

Cualidades personales: organizada, responsable, extrovertida

Aficiones: Deporte, natacíon y surf, cine, lectura
Miembro del grupo local de arte dramático y de la orquesta de colegio

Writing a CV

- Remember the order of the information:
  - personal details
  - education
  - work experience
  - language skills (whether spoken or written), computer skills, interests and membership of any clubs or voluntary organizations.
- Check your spelling and grammar – if possible, get a Spanish speaker to help you with this.
- In Spain and Latin America, it is quite usual to include a passport-sized photo with your job application.
- Always handwrite a covering letter.

Spanish companies often use a graphologist (handwriting expert)

Tengo ...
I have ...
- **un empleo para el verano.** a summer job.
- **un empleo a tiempo completo.** a full-time job.
- **un empleo a tiempo parcial.** a part-time job.

El año pasado, hice las prácticas laborales.
Last year I did work experience.
Fue interesante.
It was interesting.

un empleado an employee (*man*)
una empleada an employee (*woman*)
un empleador an employer
el salario the salary/wages
los horas the hours
los títulos the qualifications
una carta de solicitud
letter of application/supporting statement
el currículo CV

Me gustaría ...
I'd like to ...
- **trabajar en una tienda.**
  work in a shop.
- **hacer de canguro.**
  do babysitting.
- **hacer jardinería.**
  do gardening.
- **lavar coches.**
  wash cars.

Ya he trabajado en ...
I've already worked in ...
- **una oficina.** an office.
- **una fábrica.** a factory.
- **una gasolinera.** a petrol station.
- **un supermercado.** a supermarket.

Tengo experiencia. I have experience.
No he trabajado nunca. I've never worke
He repartido periódicos.
I did a paper round.
durante un mes/un año for a month/a ye

Encontré el empleo ... I found the job ...
- **fascinante.** fascinating.
- **pesado.** boring.
- **bien remunerado.** well paid.
- **mal pagado.** badly paid.

Gané ... I earned ...
- **7 euros la hora.** 7 euros an hour.
- **150 euros al mes.** 150 euros a month.

Days of the week

lunes Monday
martes Tuesday
miércoles Wednesday
jueves Thursday
viernes Friday
sábado Saturday
domingo Sunday

The seasons

la primavera spring
el verano summer
el otoño autumn
el invierno winter

Ionths

nero January
:brero February
ıarzo March
bril April
ıayo May
ınio June
ılio July
gosto August
eptiembre September
ctubre October
oviembre November
iciembre December

Ii cumpleaños es en febrero.
Iy birthday is in February.
e fue en marzo.
he left in March.
legamos el 11 de noviembre.
Ve're arriving on 11th November.
icardo nació el 2 de agosto.
ichard was born on 2nd August.
n el año 2006 (dos mil seis) in 2006
n el año 1999 in 1999

The time

¿Qué hora es? What time is it?
Es la una. It's one o'clock.
Son las cuatro y media.
It's half past four.
Son las seis y cuarto.
It's quarter past six.
Son las seis menos cuarto.
It's quarter to six.
Son las nueve y diez.
It's ten past nine.
Son las nueve menos diez.
It's ten to nine.
Es el mediodía. It's midday.
Es la media noche. It's midnight.
Son las diecinueve horas. It's 7pm (19.00).
Son las trece horas y quince minutos.
It's 1.15pm (13.15).

la una
one o' clock

las cuatro y media
half past four

las seis y cuarto
quarter past six

las seis menos cuarto
quarter to six

las nueve y diez
ten past nine

las nueve menos diez
ten to nine

las 19 horas
7pm (19.00)

las trece horas y quince minutos
1.15pm (13.15)

el mediodía
midday

la media noche
midnight

Numbers

One is *uno* in Spanish, but it is *un* before a masculine noun and *una* before a feminine noun, so *un lápiz* but *una mesa*, *veintiún hombres*, *veintiuna mesas*, etc.

0	cero			
1	uno, un; *fem* una	1st	1°	primero, primer; *fem* primera
2	dos	2nd	2°	segundo, *fem* segunda
3	tres	3rd	3°	tercero, tercer; *fem* tercera
4	cuatro	4th	4°	cuarto, *fem* cuarta
5	cinco	5th	5°	quinto, *fem* quinto
6	seis	6th	6°	sexto, *fem* sexta
7	siete	7th	7°	séptimo, *fem* séptima
8	ocho	8th	8°	octavo, *fem* octava
9	nueve	9th	9°	noveno, *fem* novena
10	diez	10th	10°	décimo, *fem* décima
11	once	11th	11°	undécimo, *fem* decimoprimera
12	doce	12th	12°	duodécimo, *fem* decimosegunda
13	trece	13th	13°	decimotercero, *fem* decimotercera
14	catorce	14th	14°	decimocuarto, *fem* decimocuarta
15	quince	15th	15°	decimoquinto, *fem* decimoquinta
16	dieciséis	16th	16°	decimosexto, *fem* decimosexta
17	diecisiete	17th	17°	decimoséptimo, *fem* decimoséptima
18	dieciocho	18th	18°	decimoctavo, *fem* decimoctava
19	diecinueve	19th	19°	decimonoveno, *fem* decimonovena
20	veinte	20th	20°	vigésimo, *fem* vigésima
21	veintiuno	21st	21°	vigesimoprimero, *fem* -a
22	veintidós	22nd	22°	veintidós or vigesimosegundo, *fem* -a
23	veintitrés	23rd	23°	veintitrés or vigesimotercero, *fem* -a
24	veinticuatro	24th	24°	veinticuatro or vigesimocuarto, *fem* -a
25	veinticinco	25th	25°	veinticinco or vigesimoquinto, *fem* -a
26	veintiséis	26th	26°	veintiséis or vigésimosexto, *fem* -a
27	veintisiete	27th	27°	veintisiete or vigesimoséptimo, *fem* -a
28	veintiocho	28th	28°	veintiocho or vigesimoctavo, *fem* -a
29	veintinueve	29th	29°	veintinueve or vigesimonoveno, *fem* -a
30	treinta	30th	30°	treinta or trigésimo, *fem* -a
31	treinta y uno	31st	31°	treinta y uno, *fem* treinta y una
32	treinta y dos	32nd	32°	treinta y dos
40	cuarenta	40th	40°	cuarenta or cuadragésimo, *fem* -a
50	cincuenta	50th	50°	cincuenta or quincuagésimo, *fem* -a
60	sesenta	60th	60°	sesenta or sexagésimo, *fem* -a
70	setenta	70th	70°	setenta or septuagésimo, *fem* -a
80	ochenta	80th	80°	ochenta or octogésimo, *fem* -a
90	noventa	90th	90°	noventa or nonagésimo, *fem* -a
100	cien	100th	100°	centésimo, *fem* centésima
101	ciento uno	101st	101°	ciento uno, *fem* ciento una
200	doscientos	200th	200°	doscientos, *fem* doscientas
201	doscientos uno	201st	201°	doscientos uno, *fem* doscientas una
500	quinientos	500th	500°	quinientos, *fem* quinientas
700	setecientos	700th	700°	setecientos, *fem* setecientas
900	novecientos	900th	900°	novecientos, *fem* novecientas

When writing longer numbers Spanish uses a space or a full stop instead of a comma – for example, 1 000 or 1.000 rather than 1,000. Ordinals take a raised º or ª after the number.

1.000	mil	1000th	1.000°	milésimo, *fem* -a
1.001	mil uno	1001st	1.001°	mil uno
2.000	dos mil	2000th	2.000°	dos mil
2.007	dos mil siete	2007th	2.007°	dos mil siete
1.000.000	un millón	1000000th	1.000.000°	millonésimo, *fem* -a

Spanish verb tables

The following verb tables show you how Spanish verbs are formed. They fall in to three categories – main irregular verbs, the three regular verb patterns using *hablar*, *comer* and *vivir* as models, and other irregular verbs.

Main Spanish irregular verbs (pages 352–367)

The following Spanish verbs are unlike any others – they are irregular. The way that they are formed is given in the following section. When you look up a verb in this dictionary, you will see that it has a number in square brackets ([1], [2] etc.) This number tells you which verb to look up in this section.

[1]	**ser**	to be	[9]	**tener**	to have
[2]	**estar**	to be	[10]	**poder**	to be able
[3]	**coger**	to take	[11]	**poner**	to put
[4]	**dar**	to give	[12]	**querer**	to want, to love
[5]	**decir**	to say, to tell	[13]	**saber**	to know (facts)
[6]	**haber**	to have	[14]	**sentirse**	to feel
[7]	**hacer**	to make, to do	[15]	**venir**	to come
[8]	**ir**	to go	[16]	**ver**	to see

Regular Spanish verbs (pages 368–370)

All other Spanish verbs belong to verb families. These are the **-ar**, **-er** and **-ir** verbs. The ones with regular patterns follow the ones given in full here. In this dictionary, the numbers in square brackets ([17] , [18] or [19]) tell you which verb pattern to follow.

-ar verbs	[17]	habl**ar**	to speak, to talk
-er verbs	[18]	com**er**	to eat
-ir verbs	[19]	viv**ir**	to live

Other irregular verbs (pages 371–381)

However, some of the verbs in the **-ar**, **-er** and **-ir** regular verb families have differences from the regular patterns. These verbs are also numbered in the dictionary to tell you where to find them in this centre section. These verbs follow the regular verb patterns, apart from the forms that are given on pages 371-381.

Reflexive verbs

Many Spanish verbs may also be used reflexively with the appropriate pronouns (*me/te/se/nos/os/se*) for each person. Remember that when a verb is used reflexively its meaning may change, so check carefully in the dictionary. A typical example is **[14] sentirse** on page 365.

Irregular verbs

[1] ser

Present

soy	I am
eres	
es	
somos	
sois	
son	

Preterite

fui	I was
fuiste	
fue	
fuimos	
fuisteis	
fueron	

Future

seré	I will be
serás	
será	
seremos	
seréis	
serán	

Imperfect

era	I was, used to be
eras	
era	
éramos	
erais	
eran	

Gerund

siendo	being

Conditional

sería	I would be
serías	
sería	
seríamos	
seríais	
serían	

Present subjunctive*

sea	I am
seas	
sea	
seamos	
seáis	
sean	

*after hoping, wanting, it's a shame, etc

Imperfect subjunctive*

fuera	I was, were
fueras	
fuera	
fuéramos	
fuerais	
fueran	

*after hoping, wanting, etc

si fuera él, lo vendería
if it were him, he'd sell it

Imperative (command form)

sé (*tú*)	be (*singular*)
sea (*usted*)	be (*singular formal*)
seamos (*nosotros*)	let us be
sed (*vosotros*)	be (*plural*)
sean (*ustedes*)	be (*plural formal*)

Past participle*

sido	been

ha sido terrible
it's been terrible

*used to form the tenses with **haber**

[2] estar

Present

estoy I am
estás
está
estamos
estáis
están

Preterite

estuve I was
estuviste
estuvo
estuvimos
estuvisteis
estuvieron

Future

estaré I will be
estarás
estará
estaremos
estaréis
estarán

Imperfect

estaba I was, used to be
estabas
estaba
estábamos
estabais
estaban

Gerund

estando being

Conditional

estaría I would be
estarías
estaría
estaríamos
estaríais
estarían

Present subjunctive*

esté I am
estés
esté
estemos
estéis
estén

*after hoping, wanting, it's a shame, etc

Imperfect subjunctive*

estuviera I was, I were
estuvieras
estuviera
estuviéramos
estuvierais
estuvieran

*after hoping, wanting, etc

si estuviera aquí, todo saldría bien
if she/he were here, everything would turn out well

Imperative (command form)

está (*tú*) be (*singular*)
esté (*usted*) be (*singular formal*)
estemos (*nosotros*) let us be, let's be
estad (*vosotros*) be (*plural*)
estén (*ustedes*) be (*plural formal*)

Past participle*

estado been
han estado aquí
they've been here

*used to form the tenses with **haber**

[3] coger

Present

cojo	I take, am taking
coges	
coge	
cogemos	
cogéis	
cogen	

Preterite

cogí	I took
cogiste	
cogió	
cogimos	
cogisteis	
cogieron	

Future

cogeré	I will take
cogerás	
cogerá	
cogeremos	
cogeréis	
cogerán	

Imperfect

cogía	I was taking, used to take
cogías	
cogía	
cogíamos	
cogíais	
cogían	

Gerund

cogiendo	taking

Conditional

cogería	I would take
cogerías	
cogería	
cogeríamos	
cogeríais	
cogerían	

Present subjunctive*

coja	I take
cojas	
coja	
cojamos	
cojáis	
cojan	

* after hoping, wanting, it's a shame, etc

Present continuous **estar + cogiendo**

estoy cogiendo	I am taking
estás cogiendo	
está cogiendo	
estamos cogiendo	
estáis cogiendo	
están cogiendo	

Imperative (command form)

coge (*tú*)	take (*singular*)
coja (*usted*)	take (*singular formal*)
cojamos (*nosotros*)	let us take, let's take
coged (*vosotros*)	take (*plural*)
cojan (*ustedes*)	take (*plural formal*)

Past participle*

cogido taken

han cogido las botellas

they've taken the bottles

* used to form the tenses with **haber**

[4] dar

Present
doy I give
das
da
damos
dais
dan

Preterite
di I gave
diste
dio
dimos
disteis
dieron

Future
daré I will give
darás
dará
daremos
daréis
darán

Imperfect
daba I gave, used to give
dabas
daba
dábamos
dabais
daban

Gerund
dando giving

Conditional
daría I would give
darías
daría
daríamos
daríais
darían

Present subjunctive*
dé I give
des
dé
demos
deis
den

*after hoping, wanting, it's a shame, etc

Present continuous **estar + dando**
estoy dando I am giving
estás dando
está dando
estamos dando
estáis dando
están dando

Imperative (command form)
da (*tú*) give (*singular*)
dé (*usted*) give (*singular formal*)
demos (*nosotros*) let us give, let's give
dad (*vosotros*) give (*plural*)
den (*ustedes*) give (*plural formal*)

Past participle*
dado given
me han dado la noticia
they've given me the news
*used to form the tenses with **haber**

[5] decir

Present
digo I say, am saying
dices
dice
decimos
decís
dicen

Preterite
dije I said
dijiste
dijo
dijimos
dijisteis
dijeron

Future
diré I will say
dirás
dirá
diremos
diréis
dirán

Imperfect
decía I was saying, used to say
decías
decía
decíamos
decíais
decían

Gerund
diciendo saying

Conditional
diría I would say
dirías
diría
diríamos
diríais
dirían

Present subjunctive*
diga I say
digas
diga
digamos
digáis
digan

* after hoping, wanting, it's a shame, etc

Present continuous **estar+diciendo**
estoy diciendo I am saying
estás diciendo
está diciendo
estamos diciendo
estáis diciendo
están diciendo

Imperative (command form)
di (*tú*) say (*singular*)
diga (*usted*) say (*singular formal*)
digamos (*nosotros*) let us say, let's say
decid (*vosotros*) say (*plural*)
digan (*ustedes*) say (*plural formal*)

Past participle*
dicho said
¿qué ha dicho?
what has she/he said?

* used to form the tenses with **haber**

[6] haber

Present

he I have
has
ha
hemos
habéis
han

Preterite

hube I had
hubiste
hubo
hubimos
hubisteis
hubieron

Future

habré I will have
habrás
habrá
habremos
habréis
habrán

Imperfect

había I was having, used to have
habías
había
habíamos
habíais
habían

Gerund

habiendo having

Conditional

habría I would have
habrías
habría
habríamos
habríais
habrían

Present subjunctive*

haya I have
hayas
haya
hayamos
hayáis
hayan

* after hoping, wanting, it's a shame, etc

Imperfect subjunctive*

hubiera I had, were to have
hubieras
hubiera
hubiéramos
hubierais
hubieran
si hubieran venido, nos habríamos ido
if they had come, we would have gone

* after if, hoping, wanting, etc

Imperative (command form)

he (*tú*) have (*singular*)
haya (*usted*) have (*singular formal*)
hayamos (*nosotros*) let us have, let's have
habed (*vosotros*) have (*plural*)
hayan (*ustedes*) have (*plural formal*)

Past participle*

habido been
ha habido un desastre
there's been a disaster

* used to form the tenses with **haber**

hay = there is/there are
había = there used to be
hubo = there was/there were

Irregular verbs

[7] hacer

Present

hago	I make, am making/I do, am doing
haces	
hace	
hacemos	
hacéis	
hacen	

Preterite

hice	I made/I did
hiciste	
hizo	
hicimos	
hicisteis	
hicieron	

Future

haré	I will make/I will do
harás	
hará	
haremos	
haréis	
harán	

Imperfect

hacía	I was making, used to make/was doing, used to do
hacías	
hacía	
hacíamos	
hacíais	
hacían	

Gerund

haciendo	making/doing

Conditional

haría	I would make/ I would do
harías	
haría	
haríamos	
haríais	
harían	

Present subjunctive*

haga	I make/I do
hagas	
haga	
hagamos	
hagáis	
hagan	

*after hoping, wanting, it's a shame, etc

Present continuous **estar+haciendo**

estoy haciendo	I am making/I am doing
estás haciendo	
está haciendo	
estamos haciendo	
estáis haciendo	
están haciendo	

Imperative (command form)

haz (*tú*)	make/do (*singular*)
haga (*usted*)	make/do (*sing formal*)
hagamos (*nosotros*)	let us make, let's make/let us do, let's do
haced (*vosotros*)	make/do (*plural*)
hagan (*ustedes*)	make/do (*plural formal*)

Past participle*

hecho	made/done

¿qué han hecho?
what have they done?
what have they made?

*used to form the tenses with **haber**

[8] ir

Present

voy	I go, am going
vas	
va	
vamos	
vais	
van	

Preterite

fui	I went
fuiste	
fue	
fuimos	
fuisteis	
fueron	

Future

iré	I will go
irás	
irá	
iremos	
iréis	
irán	

Imperfect

iba	I was going, used to go
ibas	
iba	
íbamos	
ibais	
iban	

Gerund

yendo	going

Conditional

iría	I would go
irías	
iría	
iríamos	
iríais	
irían	

Present subjunctive*

vaya	I go
vayas	
vaya	
vayamos	
vayáis	
vayan	

* after hoping, wanting, it's a shame, etc

Present continuous **estar+yendo**

estoy yendo	I am going
estás yendo	
está yendo	
estamos yendo	
estáis yendo	
están yendo	

Imperative (command form)

ve (*tú*)	go (*singular*)
vaya (*usted*)	go (*singular formal*)
vayamos (*nosotros*)	let us go, let's go
id (*vosotros*)	go (*plural*)
vayan (*ustedes*)	go (*plural formal*)

Past participle*

ido	gone

han ido al partido
they've gone to the match

* used to form the tenses with **haber**

[9] tener

Present
tengo I have, am having
tienes
tiene
tenemos
tenéis
tienen

Preterite
tuve I had
tuviste
tuvo
tuvimos
tuvisteis
tuvieron

Future
tendré I will have
tendrás
tendrá
tendremos
tendréis
tendrán

Imperfect
tenía I was having, used to have
tenías
tenía
teníamos
teníais
tenían

Gerund
teniendo having

Conditional
tendría I would have
tendrías
tendría
tendríamos
tendríais
tendrían

Present subjunctive*
tenga I have
tengas
tenga
tengamos
tengáis
tengan
*after hoping, wanting, it's a shame, etc

Present continuous **estar+teniendo**
estoy teniendo I am having
estás teniendo
está teniendo
estamos teniendo
estáis teniendo
están teniendo

Imperative (command form)
ten (*tú*) have (*singular*)
tenga (*usted*) have (*singular formal*)
tengamos (*nosotros*) let us have, let's have
tened (*vosotros*) have (*plural*)
tengan (*ustedes*) have (*plural formal*)

Past participle*
tenido had
ha tenido un accidente
he's had an accident
*used to form the tenses with **haber**

[10] poder

Present
puedo I am able to, can
puedes
puede
podemos
podéis
pueden

Preterite
pude I was able to, could
pudiste
pudo
pudimos
pudisteis
pudieron

Future
podré I will be able to
podrás
podrá
podremos
podréis
podrán

Imperfect
podía I was able to, used to be able to
podías
podía
podíamos
podíais
podían

Gerund
pudiendo being able to

Conditional
podría I would be able to
podrías
podría
podríamos
podríais
podrían

Present subjunctive*
pueda I am able to, can
puedas
pueda
podamos
podáis
puedan

*after hoping, wanting, it's a shame, etc

Imperfect subjunctive*
pudiera I was able to, were able to
pudieras
pudiera
pudiéramos
pudierais
pudieran
si pudiera, lo compraría
if he could, he'd buy it

*after if, hoping, wanting, etc

Imperative (command form)
The imperative is not used with **poder**.

Past participle*
podido been able to
ha podido hacerlo
she's/he's been able to do it

*used to form the tenses with **haber**

[11] poner

Present

pongo	I put, am putting
pones	
pone	
ponemos	
ponéis	
ponen	

Preterite

puse	I put
pusiste	
puso	
pusimos	
pusisteis	
pusieron	

Future

pondré	I will put
pondrás	
pondrá	
pondremos	
pondréis	
pondrán	

Imperfect

ponía	I was putting, used to put
ponías	
ponía	
poníamos	
poníais	
ponían	

Gerund

poniendo	putting

Conditional

pondría	I would put
pondrías	
pondría	
pondríamos	
pondríais	
pondrían	

Present subjunctive*

ponga	I put
pongas	
ponga	
pongamos	
pongáis	
pongan	

*after hoping, wanting, it's a shame, etc

Present continuous **estar+poniendo**

estoy poniendo	I am putting
estás poniendo	
está poniendo	
estamos poniendo	
estáis poniendo	
están poniendo	

Imperative (command form)

pon (*tú*)	put (*singular*)
ponga (*usted*)	put (*singular formal*)
pongamos (*nosotros*)	let us put, let's put
poned (*vosotros*)	put (*plural*)
pongan (*ustedes*)	put (*plural formal*)

Past participle*

puesto	put

lo ha puesto aquí
she's/he's put it here

*used to form the tenses with **haber**

[12] querer

Present

quiero	I want to/I love
quieres	
quiere	
queremos	
queréis	
quieren	

Preterite

quise	I wanted to/I loved
quisiste	
quiso	
quisimos	
quisisteis	
quisieron	

Future

querré	I will want to/I will love
querrás	
querrá	
querremos	
querréis	
querrán	

Imperfect

quería	I wanted to, used to want to/I loved, used to love
querías	
quería	
queríamos	
queríais	
querían	

Gerund

queriendo	wanting to/loving

Conditional

querría	I would like to/ I would love
querrías	
querría	
querríamos	
querríais	
querrían	

Present subjunctive*

quiera	I want to/I love
quieras	
quiera	
queramos	
queráis	
quieran	

*after hoping, wanting, it's a shame, etc

Imperfect subjunctive*

quisiera	I would like to
quisieras	
quisiera	
quisiéramos	
quisierais	
quisieran	

quisiera hacer una reserva
I'd like to make a booking

*to express wishes, after if, etc

Imperative (command form)

quiere (*tú*)	want (*singular*)
quiera (*usted*)	want (*sing formal*)
queramos (*nosotros*)	let us want to let's want
quered (*vosotros*)	want (*plural*)
quieran (*ustedes*)	want (*plural formal*)

Past participle*

querido	wanted/loved

no ha querido hacerlo
she/he didn't want to do it
nunca lo ha querido
she's never loved him

*used to form the tenses with **haber**

Irregular verbs

[13] saber

Present

sé	I know
sabes	
sabe	
sabemos	
sabéis	
saben	

Preterite

supe	I knew
supiste	
supo	
supimos	
supisteis	
supieron	

Future

sabré	I will know
sabrás	
sabrá	
sabremos	
sabréis	
sabrán	

Imperfect

sabía	I knew, used to know
sabías	
sabía	
sabíamos	
sabíais	
sabían	

Gerund

sabiendo	knowing

Conditional

sabría	I would know
sabrías	
sabría	
sabríamos	
sabríais	
sabrían	

Present subjunctive*

sepa	I know
sepas	
sepa	
sepamos	
sepáis	
sepan	

*after hoping, wanting, it's a shame, etc

Imperfect subjunctive*

supiera	I knew
supieras	
supiera	
supiéramos	
supierais	
supieran	

si lo supiera la dejaría
if he knew, he'd leave her

*after if, etc

Imperative (command form)

sabe (*tú*)	know (*singular*)
sepa (*usted*)	know (*sing formal*)
sepamos (*nosotros*)	let us know let's know
sabed (*vosotros*)	know (*plural*)
sepan (*ustedes*)	know (*plural formal*)

Past participle*

sabido	known

lo ha sabido desde hace mucho
she's/he's known it for a long time

*used to form the tenses with **haber**

[14] sentirse

Present
me siento I feel
te sientes
se siente
nos sentimos
os sentís
se sienten

Preterite
me sentí I felt
te sentiste
se sintió
nos sentimos
os sentisteis
se sintieron

Future
me sentiré I will feel
te sentirás
se sentirá
nos sentiremos
os sentiréis
se sentirán

Imperfect
me sentía I felt, used to feel
te sentías
se sentía
nos sentíamos
os sentíais
se sentían

Gerund
sintiendo feeling

Conditional
me sentiría I would feel
te sentirías
se sentiría
nos sentiríamos
os sentiríais
se sentirían

Present subjunctive*
me sienta I feel
te sientas
se sienta
nos sintamos
os sintáis
se sientan

* after hoping, wanting, it's a shame, etc

Present continuous **estar+sintiendo**
me estoy sintiendo I am feeling
te estás sintiendo
se está sintiendo
nos estamos sintiendo
os estáis sintiendo
se están sintiendo

Past participle*
sentido felt
se ha sentido mejor desde ayer
she's/he's felt better since yesterday

* used to form the tenses with **haber**

[15] venir

Present

vengo	I come, am coming
vienes	
viene	
venimos	
venís	
vienen	

Preterite

vine	I came
viniste	
vino	
vinimos	
vinisteis	
vinieron	

Future

vendré	I will come
vendrás	
vendrá	
vendremos	
vendréis	
vendrán	

Imperfect

venía	I was coming, used to come
venías	
venía	
veníamos	
veníais	
venían	

Gerund

viniendo	coming

Conditional

vendría	I would come
vendrías	
vendría	
vendríamos	
vendríais	
vendrían	

Present subjunctive*

venga	I come
vengas	
venga	
vengamos	
vengáis	
vengan	

*after hoping, wanting, it's a shame, etc

Present continuous **estar+viniendo**

estoy viniendo	I am coming
estás viniendo	
está viniendo	
estamos viniendo	
estáis viniendo	
están viniendo	

Imperative (command form)

ven (*tú*)	come (*singular*)
venga (*usted*)	come (*sing formal*)
vengamos (*nosotros*)	let us come let's come
venid (*vosotros*)	come (*plural*)
vengan (*ustedes*)	come (*plural formal*)

Past participle*

venido	come

ya han venido
they've already come

*used to form the tenses with **haber**

[16] ver

Present

veo	I see, am seeing
ves	
ve	
vemos	
veis	
ven	

Preterite

vi	I saw
viste	
vio	
vimos	
visteis	
vieron	

Future

veré	I will see
verás	
verá	
veremos	
veréis	
verán	

Imperfect

veía	I saw, used to see
veías	
veía	
veíamos	
veíais	
veían	

Gerund

viendo	seeing

Conditional

vería	I would see
verías	
vería	
veríamos	
veríais	
verían	

Present subjunctive*

vea	I see
veas	
vea	
veamos	
veáis	
vean	

* after hoping, wanting, it's a shame, etc

Present continuous **estar+viendo**

estoy viendo	I am seeing
estás viendo	
está viendo	
estamos viendo	
estáis viendo	
están viendo	

Imperative (command form)

ve (*tú*)	see (*singular*)
vea (*usted*)	see (*singular formal*)
veamos (*nosotros*)	let us see, let's see
ved (*vosotros*)	see (*plural*)
vean (*ustedes*)	see (*plural formal*)

Past participle*

visto	seen

ya lo hemos visto
we've already seen it

* used to form the tenses with **haber**

[17] hablar

Present

habl**o**	I speak, am speaking
habl**as**	
habl**a**	
habl**amos**	
habl**áis**	
habl**an**	

Preterite

habl**é**	I spoke
habl**aste**	
habl**ó**	
habl**amos**	
habl**asteis**	
habl**aron**	

Future

habl**aré**	I will speak
habl**arás**	
habl**ará**	
habl**aremos**	
habl**aréis**	
habl**arán**	

Imperfect

habl**aba**	I was speaking, used to speak
habl**abas**	
habl**aba**	
habl**ábamos**	
habl**abais**	
habl**aban**	

Gerund

habl**ando**	speaking

Conditional

habl**aría**	I would speak
habl**arías**	
habl**aría**	
habl**aríamos**	
habl**aríais**	
habl**arían**	

Present subjunctive*

habl**e**	I speak
habl**es**	
habl**e**	
habl**emos**	
habl**éis**	
habl**en**	

*after hoping, wanting, it's a shame, etc

Present continuous **estar+hablando**

estoy hablando	I am speaking
estás hablando	
está hablando	
estamos hablando	
estáis hablando	
están hablando	

Imperative (command form)

habl**a** (*tú*)	speak (*singular*)
habl**e** (*usted*)	speak (*sing formal*)
habl**emos** (*nosotros*)	let us speak let's speak
habl**ad** (*vosotros*)	speak (*plural*)
habl**en** (*ustedes*)	speak (*plural formal*)

Past participle*

habl**ado**	spoken

han hablado ya
they've already spoken

*used to form the tenses with **haber**

[18] comer

Present

com**o**	I eat, am eating
com**es**	
com**e**	
com**emos**	
com**éis**	
com**en**	

Preterite

com**í**	I ate
com**iste**	
com**ió**	
com**imos**	
com**isteis**	
com**ieron**	

Future

com**eré**	I will eat
com**erás**	
com**erá**	
com**eremos**	
com**eréis**	
com**erán**	

Imperfect

com**ía**	I was eating, used to eat
com**ías**	
com**ía**	
com**íamos**	
com**íais**	
com**ían**	

Gerund

com**iendo** eating

Conditional

com**ería**	I would eat
com**erías**	
com**ería**	
com**eríamos**	
com**eríais**	
com**erían**	

Present subjunctive*

com**a**	I eat
com**as**	
com**a**	
com**amos**	
com**áis**	
com**an**	

*after hoping, wanting, it's a shame, etc

Present continuous **estar+comiendo**

estoy comiendo	I am eating
estás comiendo	
está comiendo	
estamos comiendo	
estáis comiendo	
están comiendo	

Imperative (command form)

com**e** (*tú*)	eat (*singular*)
com**a** (*usted*)	eat (*singular formal*)
com**amos** (*nosotros*)	let us eat, let's eat
com**ed** (*vosotros*)	eat (*plural*)
com**an** (*ustedes*)	eat (*plural formal*)

Past participle*

com**ido** eaten

han comido ya

they've already eaten

*used to form the tenses with **haber**

[19] vivir

Present

viv**o**	I live, am living
viv**es**	
viv**e**	
viv**imos**	
viv**ís**	
viv**en**	

Preterite

viv**í**	I lived
viv**iste**	
viv**ió**	
viv**imos**	
viv**isteis**	
viv**ieron**	

Future

viv**iré**	I will live
viv**irás**	
viv**irá**	
viv**iremos**	
viv**iréis**	
viv**irán**	

Imperfect

viv**ía**	I was living, used to live
viv**ías**	
viv**ía**	
viv**íamos**	
viv**íais**	
viv**ían**	

Gerund

viv**iendo**	living

Conditional

viv**iría**	I would live
viv**irías**	
viv**iría**	
viv**iríamos**	
viv**iríais**	
viv**irían**	

Present subjunctive*

viv**a**	I live
viv**as**	
viv**a**	
viv**amos**	
viv**áis**	
viv**an**	

*after hoping, wanting, it's a shame, etc

Present continuous **estar+viviendo**

estoy viviendo	I am living
estás viviendo	
está viviendo	
estamos viviendo	
estáis viviendo	
están viviendo	

Imperative (command form)

viv**e** (*tú*)	live (*singular*)
viv**a** (*usted*)	live (*singular formal*)
viv**amos** (*nosotros*)	let us live, let's live
viv**id** (*vosotros*)	live (*plural*)
viv**an** (*ustedes*)	live (*plural formal*)

Past participle*

viv**ido**	lived

han vivido en Alicante
they've lived in Alicante

*used to form the tenses with **haber**

Irregular -ar verbs

[20] actuar to act
like [17] **hablar** except:

Present	Present subjunctive
actúo	actúe
actúas	actúes
actúa	actúe
actuamos	actuemos
actuáis	actuéis
actúan	actúen

Imperative (command form)
actúa (*tú*)
actúe (*usted*)
actuemos (*nosotros*)
actuad (*vosotros*)
actúen (*ustedes*)

[21] andar to walk
like [17] **hablar** except:

Preterite	Imperfect subjunctive
anduve	anduviera
anduviste	anduvieras
anduvo	anduviera
anduvimos	anduviéramos
anduvisteis	anduvierais
anduvieron	anduvieran

[22] cazar to hunt
like [17] **hablar** except:

Preterite	Present subjunctive
cacé	cace
cazaste	caces
cazó	cace
cazamos	cacemos
cazasteis	cacéis
cazaron	cacen

Imperative (command form)
caza (*tú*)
cace (*usted*)
cacemos (*nosotros*)
cazad (*vosotros*)
cacen (*ustedes*)

[23] colgar to hang
like [17] **hablar** except:

Present	Present subjunctive
cuelgo	**cue**lgue
cuelgas	**cue**lgues
cuelga	**cue**lgue
colgamos	colguemos
colgáis	colguéis
cuelgan	**cue**lguen

Preterite	Imperative (command form)
colgué	**cue**lga (*tú*)
colgaste	**cue**lgue (*usted*)
colgó	colguemos (*nosotros*)
colgamos	colgad (*vosotros*)
colgasteis	**cue**lguen (*ustedes*)
colgaron	

[24] contar to count
like [17] **hablar** except:

Present	Present subjunctive
cuento	**cue**nte
cuentas	**cue**ntes
cuenta	**cue**nte
contamos	contemos
contáis	contéis
cuentan	**cue**nten

Imperative (command form)
cuenta (*tú*)
cuente (*usted*)
contemos (*nosotros*)
contad (*vosotros*)
cuenten (*ustedes*)

Irregular -ar verbs

[25] empezar to begin

like [17] **hablar** except:

Present	Present subjunctive
emp**ie**zo	emp**ie**ce
emp**ie**zas	emp**ie**ces
emp**ie**za	emp**ie**ce
empezamos	empecemos
empezáis	empecéis
emp**ie**zan	emp**ie**cen

Preterite	Imperative (command form)
empecé	emp**ie**za (*tú*)
empezaste	emp**ie**ce (*usted*)
empezó	empecemos (*nosotros*)
empezamos	empezad (*vosotros*)
empezasteis	emp**ie**cen (*ustedes*)
empezaron	

[26] forzar to force

like [17] **hablar** except:

Present	Present subjunctive
f**ue**rzo	f**ue**rce
f**ue**rzas	f**ue**rces
f**ue**rza	f**ue**rce
forzamos	forcemos
forzáis	forcéis
f**ue**rzan	f**ue**rcen

Preterite	Imperative (command form)
forcé	f**ue**rza (*tú*)
forzaste	f**ue**rce (*usted*)
forzó	forcemos (*nosotros*)
forzamos	forzad (*vosotros*)
forzasteis	f**ue**rcen (*ustedes*)
forzaron	

[27] jugar to play

like [17] **hablar** except:

Present	Present subjunctive
j**ue**go	j**ue**gue
j**ue**gas	j**ue**gues
j**ue**ga	j**ue**gue
jugamos	juguemos
jugáis	juguéis
j**ue**gan	j**ue**guen

Preterite	Imperative (command form)
jugué	j**ue**ga (*tú*)
jugaste	j**ue**gue (*usted*)
jugó	juguemos (*nosotros*)
jugamos	jugad (*vosotros*)
jugasteis	j**ue**guen (*ustedes*)
jugaron	

[28] pagar to pay

like [17] **hablar** except:

Preterite	Present subjunctive
pagué	pague
pagaste	pagues
pagó	pague
pagamos	paguemos
pagasteis	paguéis
pagaron	paguen

Imperative (command form)

paga (*tú*)
pague (*usted*)
paguemos (*nosotros*)
pagad (*vosotros*)
paguen (*ustedes*)

Irregular -ar verbs

[29] pensar to think

like [17] **hablar** except:

Present	Present subjunctive
p**ie**nso	p**ie**nse
p**ie**nsas	p**ie**nses
p**ie**nsa	p**ie**nse
pensamos	pensemos
pensáis	penséis
p**ie**nsan	p**ie**nsen

Imperative (command form)
p**ie**nsa (*tú*)
p**ie**nse (*usted*)
pensemos (*nosotros*)
pensad (*vosotros*)
p**ie**nsen (*ustedes*)

[30] regar to water

like [17] **hablar** except:

Present	Present subjunctive
r**ie**go	r**ie**gue
r**ie**gas	r**ie**gues
r**ie**ga	r**ie**gue
regamos	reguemos
regáis	reguéis
r**ie**gan	r**ie**guen

Preterite	Imperative (command form)
regué	r**ie**ga (*tú*)
regaste	r**ie**gue (*usted*)
regó	reguemos (*nosotros*)
regamos	regad (*vosotros*)
regasteis	r**ie**guen (*ustedes*)
regaron	

[31] sacar to take out

like [17] **hablar** except:

Preterite	Present subjunctive
saqué	saque
sacaste	saques
sacó	saque
sacamos	saquemos
sacasteis	saquéis
sacaron	saquen

Imperative (command form)
saca (*tú*)
saque (*usted*)
saquemos (*nosotros*)
sacad (*vosotros*)
saquen (*ustedes*)

[32] vaciar to empty

like [17] **hablar** except:

Present	Present subjunctive
vacío	vacíe
vacías	vacíes
vacía	vacíe
vaciamos	vaciemos
vaciáis	vaciéis
vacían	vacíen

Imperative (command form)
vacía (*tú*)
vacíe (*usted*)
vaciemos (*nosotros*)
vaciad (*vosotros*)
vacíen (*ustedes*)

Irregular -er verbs

[33] caber to fit

like [18] **comer** except:

Present
q**ue**po
cabes
cabe
cabemos
cabéis
caben

Conditional
cabría
cabrías
cabría
cabríamos
cabríais
cabrían

Preterite
c**u**pe
c**u**piste
c**u**po
c**u**pimos
c**u**pisteis
c**u**pieron

Present subjunctive
q**ue**pa
q**ue**pas
q**ue**pa
q**ue**pamos
q**ue**páis
q**ue**pan

Future
cabré
cabrás
cabrá
cabremos
cabréis
cabrán

Imperfect subjunctive
c**u**piera
c**u**pieras
c**u**piera
c**u**piéramos
c**u**pierais
c**u**pieran

Imperative (command form)
cabe (*tú*)
q**ue**pa (*usted*)
q**ue**pamos (*nosotros*)
cabed (*vosotros*)
q**ue**pan (*ustedes*)

[34] caer to fall

like [18] **comer** except:

Present
ca**i**go
caes
cae
caemos
caéis
caen

Imperfect subjunctive
cayera
cayeras
cayera
cayéramos
cayerais
cayeran

Preterite
caí
caíste
cayó
caímos
caísteis
cayeron

Imperative (command form)
cae (*tú*)
ca**i**ga (*usted*)
ca**i**gamos (*nosotros*)
caed (*vosotros*)
ca**i**gan (*ustedes*)

Present subjunctive
ca**i**ga
ca**i**gas
ca**i**ga
ca**i**gamos
ca**i**gáis
ca**i**gan

Gerund
cayendo

Past participle
ca**í**do

[35] conocer to know (person/plac

like [18] **comer** except:

Present
conozco
conoces
conoce
conocemos
conocéis
conocen

Present subjunctive
conozca
conozcas
conozca
conozcamos
conozcáis
conozcan

Imperative (command form)
conoce (*tú*)
conozca (*usted*)
conozcamos (*nosotros*)
conoced (*vosotros*)
conozcan (*ustedes*)

Irregular -er verbs

[36] entender to understand

like [18] **comer** except:

Present	Present subjunctive
ent**ie**ndo	ent**ie**nda
ent**ie**ndes	ent**ie**ndas
ent**ie**nde	ent**ie**nda
entendemos	entendamos
entendéis	entendáis
ent**ie**nden	ent**ie**ndan

Imperative (command form)
ent**ie**nde (*tú*)
ent**ie**nda (*usted*)
entendamos (*nosotros*)
entended (*vosotros*)
ent**ie**ndan (*ustedes*)

[37] leer to read

like [18] **comer** except:

Preterite	Imperfect subjunctive
leí	leyera
leíste	leyeras
leyó	leyera
leímos	leyéramos
leísteis	leyerais
leyeron	leyeran

Gerund	Past participle
leyendo	leído

[38] mover to move

like [18] **comer** except:

Present	Present subjunctive
m**ue**vo	m**ue**va
m**ue**ves	m**ue**vas
m**ue**ve	m**ue**va
movemos	movamos
movéis	mováis
m**ue**ven	m**ue**van

Imperative (command form)
m**ue**ve (*tú*)
m**ue**va (*usted*)
movamos (*nosotros*)
moved (*vosotros*)
m**ue**van (*ustedes*)

[39] oler to smell

like [18] **comer** except:

Present	Present subjunctive
h**ue**lo	h**ue**la
h**ue**les	h**ue**las
h**ue**le	h**ue**la
olemos	olamos
oléis	oláis
h**ue**len	h**ue**lan

Imperative (command form)
h**ue**le (*tú*)
h**ue**la (*usted*)
olamos (*nosotros*)
oled (*vosotros*)
h**ue**lan (*ustedes*)

[40] romper to break

like [18] **comer** except:

Past participle
roto

[41] torcer to turn

like [18] **comer** except:

Present	Present subjunctive
t**ue**rzo	t**ue**rza
t**ue**rces	t**ue**rzas
t**ue**rce	t**ue**rza
torcemos	torzamos
torcéis	torzáis
t**ue**rcen	t**ue**rzan

Imperative (command form)
t**ue**rce (*tú*)
t**ue**rza (*usted*)
torzamos (*nosotros*)
torced (*vosotros*)
t**ue**rzan (*ustedes*)

Irregular -er verbs

[42] traer to bring

like [18] **comer** except:

Present	Preterite
tr**ai**go	traje
traes	trajiste
trae	trajo
traemos	trajimos
traéis	trajisteis
traen	trajeron

Present subjunctive	Imperative (command form)
tr**ai**ga	trae (*tú*)
tr**ai**gas	tr**ai**ga (*usted*)
tr**ai**ga	tr**ai**gamos (*nosotros*)
tr**ai**gamos	traed (*vosotros*)
tr**ai**gáis	tr**ai**gan (*ustedes*)
tr**ai**gan	

Imperfect subjunctive	Gerund
trajera	trayendo
trajeras	
trajera	**Past participle**
trajéramos	traído
trajerais	
trajeran	

[43] valer to cost

like [18] **comer** except:

Present	Present subjunctive
valgo	valga
vales	valgas
vale	valga
valemos	valgamos
valéis	valgáis
valen	valgan

Future	Imperfect subjunctive
valdré	valiera
valdrás	valieras
valdrá	valiera
valdremos	valiéramos
valdréis	valierais
valdrán	valieran

Conditional	Imperative (command form)
valdría	vale (*tú*)
valdrías	valga (*usted*)
valdría	valgamos (*nosotros*)
valdríamos	valed (*vosotros*)
valdríais	valgan (*ustedes*)
valdrían	

[44] vencer to defeat

like [18] **comer** except:

Present	Present subjunctive
venzo	venza
vences	venzas
vence	venza
vencemos	venzamos
vencéis	venzáis
vencen	venzan

Imperative (command form)

vence (*tú*)
venza (*usted*)
venzamos (*nosotros*)
venced (*vosotros*)
venzan (*ustedes*)

[45] volver to come back

like [18] **comer** except:

Present	Imperative (command form)
v**ue**lvo	v**ue**lve (*tú*)
v**ue**lves	v**ue**lva (*usted*)
v**ue**lve	volvamos (*nosotros*)
volvemos	volved (*vosotros*)
volvéis	v**ue**lvan (*ustedes*)
v**ue**lven	

Present subjunctive	Past participle
v**ue**lva	v**ue**lto
v**ue**lvas	
v**ue**lva	
volvamos	
volváis	
v**ue**lvan	

Irregular -ir verbs

[46] abrir to open

like [19] **vivir** except:

Past participle
ab**ie**rto

[47] adquirir to acquire

like [19] **vivir** except:

Present
adqu**ie**ro
adqu**ie**res
adqu**ie**re
adquirimos
adquirís
adqu**ie**ren

Present subjunctive
adqu**ie**ra
adqu**ie**ras
adqu**ie**ra
adquiramos
adquiráis
adqu**ie**ran

Imperative (command form)
adqu**ie**re (*tú*)
adqu**ie**ra (*usted*)
adquiramos (*nosotros*)
adquirid (*vosotros*)
adqu**ie**ran (*ustedes*)

[48] corregir to correct

like [19] **vivir** except:

Present
corr**i**jo
corr**i**ges
corr**i**ge
corregimos
corregís
corr**i**gen

Preterite
corregí
corregiste
corr**i**gió
corregimos
corregisteis
corr**i**gieron

Present subjunctive
corr**i**ja
corr**i**jas
corr**i**ja
corr**i**jamos
corr**i**jáis
corr**i**jan

Imperative (command form)
corr**i**ge (*tú*)
corr**i**ja (*usted*)
corr**i**jamos (*nosotros*)
corregid (*vosotros*)
corr**i**jan (*ustedes*)

[49] dirigir to direct

like [19] **vivir** except:

Present
dirijo
diriges
dirige
dirigimos
dirigís
dirigen

Present subjunctive
dirija
dirijas
dirija
dirijamos
dirijáis
dirijan

Imperative (command form)
dirige (*tú*)
dirija (*usted*)
dirijamos (*nosotros*)
dirigid (*vosotros*)
dirijan (*ustedes*)

[50] distinguir to distinguish

like [19] **vivir** except:

Present
distingo
distingues
distingue
distinguimos
distinguís
distinguen

Present subjunctive
distinga
distingas
distinga
distingamos
distingáis
distingan

Imperative (command form)
distingue (*tú*)
distinga (*usted*)
distingamos (*nosotros*)
distinguid (*vosotros*)
distingan (*ustedes*)

[51] dormir to sleep

like [19] **vivir** except:

Present
d**ue**rmo
d**ue**rmes
d**ue**rme
dormimos
dormís
d**ue**rmen

Preterite
dormí
dormiste
d**u**rmió
dormimos
dormisteis
d**u**rmieron

Present subjunctive
d**ue**rma
d**ue**rmas
d**ue**rma
d**u**rmamos
d**u**rmáis
d**ue**rman

Imperfect subjunctive
d**u**rmiera
d**u**rmieras
d**u**rmiera
d**u**rmiéramos
d**u**rmierais
d**u**rmieran

Imperative (command form)
d**ue**rme (*tú*)
d**ue**rma (*usted*)
d**u**rmamos (*nosotros*)
dormid (*vosotros*)
d**ue**rman (*ustedes*)

Gerund
d**u**rmiendo

Past participle
dormido

Irregular -ir verbs

[52] escribir to write

like [19] **vivir** except:

Past participle
escrito

[53] freír to fry

like [19] **vivir** except:

Present	Imperfect subjunctive
fr**í**o	fr**i**era
fr**í**es	fr**i**eras
fr**í**e	fr**i**era
freímos	fr**i**éramos
freís	fr**i**erais
fr**í**en	fr**i**eran

Preterite	Imperative (command form)
freí	fr**í**e (*tú*)
freíste	fr**í**a (*usted*)
fr**i**ó	fr**i**amos (*nosotros*)
freímos	freíd (*vosotros*)
freísteis	fr**í**an (*ustedes*)
fr**i**eron	

Present subjunctive	Gerund
fr**í**a	fr**i**endo
fr**í**as	
fr**í**a	**Past participle**
fr**i**amos	fr**i**to
fr**i**áis	
fr**í**an	

[54] huir to flee

like [19] **vivir** except:

Present	Imperfect subjunctive
huyo	huyera
huyes	huyeras
huye	huyera
huimos	huyéramos
huís	huyerais
huyen	huyeran

Preterite	Imperative (command form)
huí	huye (*tú*)
huiste	huya (*usted*)
huyó	huyamos (*nosotros*)
huimos	huid (*vosotros*)
huisteis	huyan (*ustedes*)
huyeron	

Present subjunctive	Gerund
huya	huyendo
huyas	
huya	**Past participle**
huyamos	huido
huyáis	
huyan	

[55] morir to die

like [19] **vivir** except:

Present	Present subjunctive
m**ue**ro	m**ue**ra
m**ue**res	m**ue**ras
m**ue**re	m**ue**ra
morimos	m**u**ramos
morís	m**u**ráis
m**ue**ren	m**ue**ran

Preterite	Imperfect subjunctive
morí	m**u**riera
moriste	m**u**rieras
m**u**rió	m**u**riera
morimos	m**u**riéramos
moristeis	m**u**rierais
m**u**rieron	m**u**rieran

Gerund	Past participle
m**u**riendo	m**ue**rto

Irregular -ir verbs

[56] oír to hear

like [19] **vivir** except:

Present	Present subjunctive
oigo	**oi**ga
oyes	**oi**gas
oye	**oi**ga
oímos	**oi**gamos
oís	**oi**gáis
oyen	**oi**gan

Preterite	Imperfect subjunctive
oí	oyera
oíste	oyeras
oyó	oyera
oímos	oyéramos
oísteis	oyerais
oyeron	oyeran

Future	Imperative (command form)
oiré	**oy**e (*tú*)
oirás	**oi**ga (*usted*)
oirá	**oi**gamos (*nosotros*)
oiremos	oíd (*vosotros*)
oiréis	**oi**gan (*ustedes*)
oirán	

Conditional	Gerund
oiría	oyendo
oirías	
oiría	**Past participle**
oiríamos	oído
oiríais	
oirían	

Imperfect
oía
oías
oía
oíamos
oíais
oían

[57] pedir to ask

like [19] **vivir** except:

Present	Present subjunctive
p**i**do	p**i**da
p**i**des	p**i**das
p**i**de	p**i**da
pedimos	p**i**damos
pedís	p**i**dáis
p**i**den	p**i**dan

Preterite	Imperfect subjunctive
pedí	p**i**diera
pediste	p**i**dieras
p**i**dió	p**i**diera
pedimos	p**i**diéramos
pedisteis	p**i**dierais
p**i**dieron	p**i**dieran

Imperative (command form)
p**i**de (*tú*)
p**i**da (*usted*)
p**i**damos (*nosotros*)
pedid (*vosotros*)
p**i**dan (*ustedes*)

[58] prohibir to prohibit

like [19] **vivir** except:

Present	Present subjunctive
prohíbo	prohíba
prohíbes	prohíbas
prohíbe	prohíba
prohibimos	prohibamos
prohibís	prohibáis
prohíben	prohíban

Imperative (command form)
prohíbe (*tú*)
prohíba (*usted*)
prohibamos (*nosotros*)
prohibid (*vosotros*)
prohíban (*ustedes*)

Irregular -ir verbs

[59] pudrir to rot

like [19] **vivir** except:

Past participle
p**o**drido

[60] reducir to reduce

like [19] **vivir** except:

Present	Present subjunctive
reduzco	reduzca
reduces	reduzcas
reduce	reduzca
reducimos	reduzcamos
reducís	reduzcáis
reducen	reduzcan

Preterite	Imperfect subjunctive
reduje	redujera
redujiste	redujeras
redujo	redujera
redujimos	redujéramos
redujisteis	redujerais
redujeron	redujeran

Imperative (command form)
reduce (*tú*)
reduzca (*usted*)
reduzcamos (*nosotros*)
reducid (*vosotros*)
reduzcan (*ustedes*)

[61] reír to laugh

like [19] **vivir** except:

Present	Conditional
río	reiría
ríes	reirías
ríe	reiría
reímos	reiríamos
reís	reiríais
ríen	reirían

Imperfect	Present subjunctive
reía	**r**ía
reías	**r**ías
reía	**r**ía
reíamos	**r**iamos
reíais	**r**iáis
reían	**r**ían

Preterite	Imperfect subjunctive
reí	**r**iera
reíste	**r**ieras
rió	**r**iera
reímos	**r**iéramos
reísteis	**r**ierais
rieron	**r**ieran

Future	Imperative (command form)
reiré	**r**íe (*tú*)
reirás	**r**ía (*usted*)
reirá	**r**iamos (*nosotros*)
reiremos	reíd (*vosotros*)
reiréis	**r**ían (*ustedes*)
reirán	

[62] reunir to gather

like [19] **vivir** except:

Present	Present subjunctive
reúno	reúna
reúnes	reúnas
reúne	reúna
reunimos	reunamos
reunís	reunáis
reúnen	reúnan

Imperative (command form)
reúne (*tú*)
reúna (*usted*)
reunamos (*nosotros*)
reunid (*vosotros*)
reúnan (*ustedes*)

Irregular -ir verbs

[63] salir to go out

like [19] **vivir** except:

Present	Present subjunctive
salgo	salga
sales	salgas
sale	salga
salimos	salgamos
salís	salgáis
salen	salgan

Future	Imperfect subjunctive
saldré	saliera
saldrás	salieras
saldrá	saliera
saldremos	saliéramos
saldréis	salierais
saldrán	salieran

Conditional	Imperative (command form)
saldría	sal (*tú*)
saldrías	salga (*usted*)
saldría	salgamos (*nosotros*)
saldríamos	salid (*vosotros*)
saldríais	salgan (*ustedes*)
saldrían	

[64] seguir to follow

like [19] **vivir** except:

Present	Present subjunctive
sigo	siga
sigues	sigas
sigue	siga
seguimos	sigamos
seguís	sigáis
siguen	sigan

Preterite	Imperfect subjunctive
seguí	siguiera
seguiste	siguieras
siguió	siguiera
seguimos	siguiéramos
seguisteis	siguierais
siguieron	siguieran

Imperative (command form)
sigue (*tú*)
siga (*usted*)
sigamos (*nosotros*)
seguid (*vosotros*)
sigan (*ustedes*)

[65] teñir to dye

like [19] **vivir** except:

Present	Present subjunctive
tiño	tiña
tiñes	tiñas
tiñe	tiña
teñimos	tiñamos
teñís	tiñáis
tiñen	tiñan

Preterite	Imperfect subjunctive
teñí	tiñera
teñiste	tiñeras
tiñó	tiñera
teñimos	tiñéramos
teñisteis	tiñerais
tiñeron	tiñeran

Imperative (command form)
tiñe (*tú*)
tiña (*usted*)
tiñamos (*nosotros*)
teñid (*vosotros*)
tiñan (*ustedes*)

A a

a *determiner*
1 (*before a masc noun*) **un**
a tree un árbol
a boy un chico
2 (*before a fem noun*) **una**
a table una mesa
a girl una chica
3 (*saying how much, how fast, etc*) **five euros a kilo** cinco euros el kilo
fifty kilometres an hour cincuenta kilómetros por hora
three times a day tres veces al día
4 (*saying what you do*) **She's a doctor.** Es médica.
I'm a student. Soy estudiante.

WORD TIP *a* is not translated into Spanish when you say your profession.

to **abandon** *verb*
abandonar [17]

abbey *noun*
la **abadía** *fem*
Westminster Abbey la abadía de Westminster

abbreviation *noun*
la **abreviatura** *fem*

to **abide** *verb*
I can't abide ... No soporto ...

ability *noun*
la **capacidad** *fem*
the ability to do something la capacidad de hacer algo
Do it to the best of your ability. Hazlo lo mejor que puedas.
I did it to the best of my ability. Lo hice lo mejor que pude.

able *adjective*
to be able to do something poder [10] hacer algo
Will you be able to come? ¿Podrás venir?
She wasn't able to come. No pudo venir.

abnormal *adjective*
anormal *masc & fem*

to **abolish** *verb*
abolir [19]

abortion *noun*
el **aborto** *masc*

⚷ **about** *adverb* ▷ see **about** *prep*
1 (*to give an idea of something*) **There are about sixty people.** Hay unas sesenta personas.
at about three o'clock a eso de las tres, como a las tres
about a month ago hace aproximadamente un mes
2 (*almost ready*) **to be about to do something** estar [2] a punto de hacer algo
I'm about to leave the house. Estoy a punto de salir de la casa.

⚷ **about** *preposition* ▷ see **about** *adv*
1 (*on the subject of*) **sobre**
a film about Picasso una película sobre Picasso
What's it about? ¿De qué trata?
2 (*to talk, think on the subject of*) **acerca de**
He wants to talk to you about your exam. Quiere hablarte acerca de tu examen.
to talk about something hablar [17] de algo
What is she talking about? ¿De qué está hablando?
to think about somebody, something pensar [29] en alguien, algo
I'm thinking about you. Estoy pensando en ti.
She's thinking about her holidays. Está pensando en las vacaciones.

⚷ **above** *adverb* ▷ see **above** *prep*
arriba
See above. Ver arriba.
the flat above el piso de arriba

⚷ **above** *preposition* ▷ see **above** *adv*
1 (*about where something is*) **encima de**
above the sink encima del fregadero
the flat above ours el piso que está encima del nuestro
2 (*about numbers*) **por encima de**
temperatures above 20 degrees temperaturas por encima de los veinte grados
3 (*about age*) **mayor**
pupils above 15 years old alumnos mayores de 15 años

⚷ **abroad** *adverb*
to go abroad irse [8] al extranjero
to live abroad vivir [19] en el extranjero
My family lived abroad for three years. Mi familia vivió en el extranjero durante tres años.

abscess *noun*
el **flemón** *masc*

abseiling *noun*
el **rappel** *masc*

absent *adjective*
ausente *masc & fem*
He's absent from school today. Está ausente hoy.
to be absent from faltar [17] a
He was absent from the lesson. Faltó a clase.
She's often absent from school. Falta a menudo al colegio.
• **absent-minded** distraído *masc*, distraída *fem*

absolute *adjective*
absoluto *masc*, **absoluta** *fem*
an absolute disaster un desastre absoluto

absolutely *adverb*
1 (*completely*) **totalmente**
I'm absolutely certain. Estoy totalmente segura.
It's absolutely dreadful. Es realmente terrible.
You're absolutely right. Tienes toda la razón.
2 (*saying you agree*) **Absolutely!** ¡Por supuesto!

to **absorb** *verb*
absorber [18]

abuse *noun* ▷ see **abuse** *verb*
1 (*violence to a child, a woman*) los **malos tratos** *masc plural*
2 (*insults*) los **insultos** *masc plural*
3 (*of alcohol, drugs*) **alcohol abuse** el alcoholismo *masc*
drug abuse la drogadicción *fem*

to **abuse** *verb* ▷ see **abuse** *noun*
to abuse somebody maltratar [17] a alguien

academic *adjective*
académico *masc*, **académica** *fem*
• **academic year** el año académico

to **accelerate** *verb*
acelerar [17]

accelerator *noun*
el **acelerador** *masc*

accent *noun*
el **acento** *masc*
She has a Spanish accent. Tiene acento español.

to **accept** *verb*
aceptar [17]

acceptable *adjective*
aceptable *masc & fem*

access *noun* ▷ see **access** *verb*
el **acceso** *masc*

to **access** *verb* ▷ see **access** *noun*
to access something obtener [9] acceso a algo

accessory *noun*
el **accesorio** *masc*

accident *noun*
1 (*when something goes wrong*) el **accidente** *masc*
a road accident un accidente de carretera
a car accident un accidente de coche
to have an accident tener [9] un accidente
2 (*chance*) la **casualidad** *fem*
It's no accident. No es casualidad.
3 (*by chance*) **by accident** por casualidad
She broke it by accident. Lo rompió sin querer.
4 (*without meaning to*) **by accident** sin querer
I found it by accident. Lo encontré por casualidad.

accidental *adjective*
fortuito *masc*, **fortuita** *fem*
an accidental discovery un descubrimiento fortuito

accident & emergency *noun*
las **urgencias** *fem pl*

accidentally *adverb*
1 (*without meaning to*) **sin querer**
I accidentally knocked over his glass. Le tiré el vaso sin querer.
2 (*by chance*) **por casualidad**
I accidentally discovered that ... Descubrí por casualidad que ...

accommodation *noun*
el **alojamiento** *masc*
I'm looking for accommodation. Busco alojamiento.
What's the hotel accommodation like? ¿Cómo es el alojamiento en hotel?

to **accompany** *verb*
to accompany somebody acompañar [17] a alguien
Two teachers accompanied our party. Dos profesores acompañaron nuestro grupo.

according *in phrase*
according to según
according to Sophie según Sophie
according to the guide book según la guía

accordion *noun*
el **acordeón** *masc*

account *noun*
1 (*in a bank, shop, post office*) la **cuenta** *fem*
a bank account una cuenta bancaria
to open an account abrir [46] una cuenta
I have fifty pounds in my account. Tengo cincuenta libras en mi cuenta.
2 (*description of what happened*) el **relato** *masc*
3 (*in expressions*) **on account of** debido a
The station is closed on account of the strike. La estación está cerrada debido a la huelga.
to take something into account tener [9] algo en cuenta
We will take his illness into account. Tendremos en cuenta su enfermedad.

accountant *noun*
el & la **contable** *masc & fem*
She's an accountant. Es contable.

accuracy *noun*
la **precisión** *fem*

accurate *adjective*
preciso *masc*, **precisa** *fem*

accurately *adverb*
con precisión

to **accuse** *verb*
acusar [17]
to accuse somebody of something acusar a alguien de algo
He was accused of murder. Le acusaron de asesinato.
to accuse somebody of doing something acusar a alguien de hacer algo
She accused me of stealing her pen. Me acusó de haber robado su pluma.

accustomed to *adjective*
to be accustomed to something estar [2] acostumbrado, acostumbrada a algo
She's accustomed to having lots of homework. Está acostumbrada a tener muchos deberes.

ace *adjective* ▷ see **ace** *noun*
(*informal*) **de primera**
He's an ace drummer. Es un baterista de primera.

ace *noun* ▷ see **ace** *adj*
el **as** *masc*
the ace of hearts el as de corazones

to **ache** *verb*
doler [38]
My arm aches. Me duele el brazo.
My muscles ache. Me duelen los músculos.

to **achieve** *verb*
1 **conseguir** [64]
She's achieved a great deal. Consiguió mucho.
to achieve an ambition hacer [7] realidad una ambición
to achieve an aim lograr [17] un objetivo
to achieve success tener [9] éxito

achievement *noun*
el **logro** *masc*
It's been a great achievement. Ha sido todo un logro.

acid *noun*
el **ácido** *masc*
• **acid rain** la lluvia ácida

acne *noun*
el **acné** *masc*

acorn *noun*
la **bellota** *fem*

acrobat *noun*
el & la **acróbata** *masc & fem*

across *preposition*
1 (*from one side to the other*) **a través de**
a barrier across the street una barrera a través de la calle
We walked across the park. Caminamos a través del parque.
They ran across the road. Cruzaron la carretera corriendo.
2 (*on the other side of*) **al otro lado de**
It's across the lake. Está al otro lado del lago.
She lives in the house across the street. Vive en la casa de enfrente.
She was sitting across from me. Estaba sentada en frente de mí.

acrylic *adjective*
acrílico *masc*, **acrílica** *fem*

act *noun* ▷ see **act** *verb*
el **acto** *masc*

to **act** *verb* ▷ see **act** *noun*
actuar [20]

acting *noun*
la **actuación** *fem*
She wants to go into acting. Quiere ser actriz.

action *noun*
la **acción** *fem*
• **action replay** la repetición de la jugada

active *adjective*
activo *masc*, **activa** *fem*

activity *noun*
actividad *fem*
• **activity holiday** las vacaciones con actividades programadas

actor *noun*
el **actor** *masc*
Who's your favourite actor? ¿Quién es tu actor favorito?

actress *noun*
la **actriz** *fem, fem pl:* las **actrices**
Who's your favourite actress? ¿Quién es tu actriz favorita?

actual *adjective*
real *masc & fem*
actual cases casos reales
his actual words sus palabras textuales
in actual fact de hecho
In actual fact, he didn't pay. De hecho, no pagó.

actually *adverb*
(*in fact, as it happens*) **la verdad es que ...**
Actually, I've changed my mind. La verdad es que he cambiado de idea.
He's not actually here at the moment. La verdad es que no está aquí en este momento.
Did she actually say that? ¿Dijo eso de verdad?

acupuncture *noun*
la **acupuntura** *fem*

acute *adjective*
agudo *masc*, **aguda** *fem*
the acute accent as in café: é el acento agudo como en café: é

ad *noun*
el **anuncio** *masc*
to put an ad in the paper poner [11] un anuncio en el periódico
the small ads los anuncios por palabras

AD *abbreviation of Anno Domini*
d. de C. (*después de Cristo*)
in 400 AD en el año 400 d. de C.

to **adapt** *verb*
to adapt something adaptar [17] algo
to adapt to something adaptarse [17] a algo
She's adapted to her new school. Se ha adaptado a su nuevo colegio.

adaptor *noun*
el **adaptador** *masc*

to **add** *verb*
añadir [19]
Add three eggs. Añade tres huevos.
• **to add something up** **sumar** [17] **algo**

addict *noun*
1 (*to drugs*) el **drogadicto** *masc*, la **drogadicta** *fem*
2 (*of television, chocolate*) el **adicto** *masc*, la **adicta** *fem*
She's a telly addict. Es una adicta a la televisión.
He's a football addict. Es un fanático del fútbol.

addicted *adjective*
1 (*to drugs, television, computer games*) **adicto** *masc*, **adicta** *fem*
She's addicted to heroin. Es adicta a la heroína.
He's addicted to the Net. Es un adicto a Internet.
2 (*to food*) **I'm addicted to chocolate.** El chocolate es mi vicio (*informal*) .

addition *noun*
1 (*adding up*) la **suma** *fem*
2 **in addition** además
in addition to además de

additional *adjective*
adicional *masc & fem*
the additional costs los costes adicionales

additive *noun*
el **aditivo** *masc*

address *noun*
1 (*where you live*) la **dirección** *fem*
What's your address? ¿Cuál es tu dirección?
to change your address cambiar [17] de domicilio
2 (*on a form*) el **domicilio** *masc*
• **address book** la libreta de direcciones

adequate *adjective*
suficiente *masc & fem*

adhesive *adjective* ▷ see **adhesive** *noun*
adhesivo *masc*, **adhesiva** *fem*

adhesive *noun* ▷ see **adhesive** *adj*
el **pegamento** *masc*
• **adhesive tape** la cinta adhesiva

adjective *noun*
el **adjetivo** *masc*

to **adjust** *verb*
1 (*the volume, the temperature*) **regular** [17]
2 (*the height, the width*) **ajustar** [17]
3 **to adjust to something** adaptarse [17] a algo
She has adjusted to the changes. Se ha adaptado a los cambios.

adjustable *adjective*
regulable *masc & fem*

administration *noun*
la **administración** *fem*

admiral *noun*
el **almirante** *masc*

admiration *noun*
la **admiración** *fem*

to **admire** *verb*
admirar [17]

admission *noun*
la **entrada** *fem*
'No admission' 'Prohibida la entrada'
'Admission free' 'Entrada gratuita'

to **admit** *verb*
1 (*to confess*) **reconocer** [35]
I must admit that ... debo reconocer que ...
She admits she lied. Admite que mintió.
2 (*to allow in*) **dejar** [1] **entrar**
3 (*a patient*) **ingresar** [1]
She was admitted to hospital. La ingresaron en el hospital.

adolescence *noun*
la **adolescencia** *fem*

adolescent *noun*
el & la **adolescente** *masc & fem*

to **adopt** *verb*
adoptar [17]

adopted *adjective*
adoptado *masc*, **adoptada** *fem*

adoption *noun*
la **adopción** *fem*

to **adore** *verb*
adorar [17]

Adriatic Sea *noun*
the Adriatic Sea el mar Adriático

adult *adjective* ▷ see **adult** *noun*
adulto *masc*, **adulta** *fem*
the adult population la población adulta

adult *noun* ▷ see **adult** *adj*
el **adulto** *masc*, la **adulta** *fem*
• **adult education** la educación para adultos

advance *noun* ▷ see **advance** *verb*
el **avance** *masc*
scientific advances los avances científicos

to **advance** *verb* ▷ see **advance** *noun*
avanzar [22]

advanced *adjective*
avanzado *masc*, **avanzada** *fem*

advantage *noun*
la **ventaja** *fem*
there are several advantages hay varias ventajas
to take advantage of something aprovechar [17] algo
I took advantage of the sales to buy myself some shoes. Aproveché las rebajas para comprarme unos zapatos.
to take advantage of somebody aprovecharse [17] de alguien
They take advantage of the tourists. Se aprovechan de los turistas.

adventure *noun*
la **aventura** *fem*

adventurous *adjective*
1 (*person*) **aventurero** *masc*, **aventurera** *fem*
2 (*design, designer, composer*) **innovador** *masc*, **innovadora** *fem*

adverb *noun*
el **adverbio** *masc*

advertisement, advert *noun*
1 (*on television, radio, in a newspaper*) el **anuncio** *masc*
2 (*small ad in a newspaper*) el **anuncio por palabras**

to **advertise** *verb*
to advertise a product anunciar [17] un producto
to advertise something in the newspaper anunciar [17] algo en el periódico
I saw it advertised on telly. Lo vi anunciado en la tele.
I saw a bike advertised in the paper. Vi un anuncio de una bicicleta en el periódico.

advertising *noun*
la **publicidad** *fem*
I'd like to work in advertising. Me gustaría trabajar en publicidad.

advice *noun* ▷ see **advise** *verb*
los **consejos** *masc plural*
a piece of advice un consejo
His advice is good. Sus consejos son buenos.
to give somebody advice aconsejar [17] a alguien
They gave me good advice. Me aconsejaron bien.
to ask for advice about something pedir [57] consejo sobre algo
Ask for advice about the exam. Pide consejo sobre el examen.

to **advise** *verb* ▷ see **advice** *noun*
aconsejar [17]
to advise somebody to ... aconsejar a alguien que ...
I advised him to study more. Le aconsejé que estudiara más.
I advised her not to wait. Le aconsejé que no esperara.

WORD TIP The verb following *aconsejar* is in the subjunctive.

adviser *noun*
el **asesor** *masc*, la **asesora** *fem*

aerial *noun*
la **antena** *fem*

aerobics *noun*
el **aerobic** *masc*
to do aerobics hacer [7] aerobic

aeroplane *noun*
el **avión** *masc*
We came by aeroplane. Vinimos en avión.

aerosol *noun*
el **aerosol** *masc*, el **spray** *masc*

affair *noun*
1 (*event*) el **asunto** *masc*
international affairs asuntos internacionales
2 (*between lovers*) la **aventura** *fem*
a love affair una aventura amorosa

to **affect** *verb*
afectar [17]

affectionate *adjective*
cariñoso *masc*, **cariñosa** *fem*

to **afford** *verb*
to afford something poder [10] permitirse algo
I can't afford a new DVD. No puedo permitirme un nuevo DVD.
She can afford to fly in first class. Puede permitirse el lujo de viajar en primera.

afraid *adjective*
1 (*frightened*) **to be afraid of something** tener [9] miedo de algo
I'm afraid. Tengo miedo.
I'm afraid of dogs. Tengo miedo de los perros.
2 (*when giving bad news*) **temerse**
I'm afraid so. Me temo que sí.
I'm afraid not. Me temo que no.
I'm afraid there are not tickets left. Me temo que no quedan entradas.

Africa *noun*
África *fem*

African *adjective & noun*
1 **africano** *masc*, **africana** *fem*
2 (*person*) un **africano** *masc*, una **africana** *fem*
the Africans los africanos *masc pl*

WORD TIP Adjectives and nouns for nationality and regional origin do not have capital letters in Spanish.

after *adverb, conjunction, preposition*
(*later in time*) **después, después de**
soon after poco después
after 10 o'clock después de las diez en punto
after lunch después de comer
after school después del colegio
the day after tomorrow pasado mañana
after I've finished my homework después de terminar mis deberes
after all después de todo
After all, she's only six. Después de todo, sólo tiene seis años.

afternoon *noun*
la **tarde** *fem*
this afternoon esta tarde
tomorrow afternoon mañana por la tarde
yesterday afternoon ayer por la tarde
on Saturday afternoon el sábado por la tarde
on Saturday afternoons los sábados por la tarde
at four o'clock in the afternoon a las cuatro de la tarde
every afternoon todas las tardes
Good afternoon! ¡Buenas tardes!

afters *noun*
el **postre** *masc*

aftershave *noun*
la **loción para después del afeitado**

afterwards *adverb*
después
shortly afterwards poco después

again *adverb*
1 (*one more time*) **otra vez, de nuevo**
Try again. Inténtalo otra vez.
I've forgotten it again. Se me ha olvidado otra vez.
You should ask again. Deberías preguntar de nuevo.
I want to see her again. Quiero volver a verla.
Don't do it again. No lo vuelvas a hacer.

WORD TIP Using *volver a* + infinitive is a very common way of expressing *again* in Spanish.

2 (*in expressions*) **again and again** una y otra vez
Never again! ¡Nunca más!

against *preposition*
contra
against the wall contra la pared
to fight against terrorism luchar [17] contra el terrorismo
I'm against the idea. Estoy en contra de la idea.
They are playing against Scotland. Juegan contra Escocia.

age *noun*
1 (*saying how old someone is*) la **edad** *fem*
at the age of fifteen a la edad de quince años
What age is she? ¿Cuántos años tiene?
She's the same age as me. Tiene mi misma edad.
to be under age ser [1] menor de edad
2 (*a long time*) **for ages**
I haven't seen Johnny for ages. Hace siglos que no he visto a Johnny.
I haven't been to London for ages. Hace un montón de tiempo que no voy a Londres.

aged *adjective*
a girl aged fourteen una chica de catorce años
a man aged fifty un hombre de cincuenta años

agenda *noun*
la **agenda** *fem*

agent *noun*
el & la **agente** *masc & fem*

aggressive *adjective*
agresivo *masc*, **agresiva** *fem*

ago *adverb*
an hour ago hace una hora
three days ago hace tres días
five years ago hace cinco años
a long time ago hace mucho tiempo
not long ago no hace mucho tiempo
How long ago was it? ¿Cuánto tiempo hace de eso?

WORD TIP Spanish uses *hace* and the amount of time to say *ago*.

to **agree** *verb*
1 **to agree with somebody** estar [2] de acuerdo con alguien
I agree with Laura. Estoy de acuerdo con Laura.
I don't agree. No estoy de acuerdo.
I agree that ... estoy de acuerdo en que ...
I agree that it's too late now. Estoy de acuerdo en que ya es demasiado tarde.
2 **to agree to do something** aceptar [18] hacer algo
Steve has agreed to help me. Steve ha aceptado ayudarme.
3 (*food, drink*) **Coffee doesn't agree with me.** El café no me sienta bien.

agreement *noun*
el **acuerdo** *masc*

agricultural *adjective*
agrícola *masc & fem*
productos agrícolas farm products

agriculture *noun*
la **agricultura** *fem*

ahead *adverb*
1 (*in directions*) **straight ahead** todo recto
Go straight ahead until you get to the crossroads. Siga todo recto hasta que llegues al cruce (*polite form of* **seguir**).
2 (*saying 'yes'*) **Go ahead!** ¡Adelante!
3 (*in competitions*) **to be ahead** llevar [17] la ventaja
Our team was ten points ahead. Nuestro equipo llevaba diez puntos de ventaja.

aid *noun*
la **ayuda** *fem*
aid to developing countries la ayuda a los países en vías de desarrollo
in aid of en beneficio de
a collection in aid of the homeless una colecta en beneficio de la gente sin hogar

Aids, **AIDS** *noun*
(*= Aquired Immune Deficiency Syndrome*) el **sida** *masc* (*= Síndrome de inmunodeficiencia adquirida*)
to have Aids tener [9] sida

aim *noun* ▷ see **aim** *verb*
el **objetivo** *masc*
We want to achieve all our aims. Queremos conseguir todos nuestros objetivos.
Their aim is to control pollution. Su objetivo es controlar la contaminación.

to **aim** *verb* ▷ see **aim** *noun*
1 (*a weapon*) **to aim a pistol at somebody** apuntar [17] una pistola a alguien
2 (*to intend*) **a campaign aimed at young people** una campaña dirigida a los jóvenes
to aim to do something proponerse [11] hacer algo
We're aiming to finish it today. Nos proponemos terminarlo hoy.

air *noun*
1 (*that you breathe*) el **aire** *masc*
in the open air al aire libre
to go out for a breath of air salir [63] a tomar el aire ▸▸

English–Spanish
a b c d e f g h i j k l m n o p q r s t u v w x y z

2 (*about travel by plane*) **We came by air.** Vinimos en avión.
- **airbag** el airbag
- **air-conditioned** con aire acondicionado
- **air conditioning** el aire acondicionado
- **air force** la fuerza aérea
- **air hostess** la azafata
- **airline** la línea aérea
- **airmail** el correo aéreo
  by airmail por correo aéreo
- **airport** el aeropuerto

aisle *noun*
el **pasillo** *masc*

alarm *noun*
la **alarma** *fem*
a burglar alarm una alarma antirrobo
The alarm has gone off. Ha sonado la alarma.
- **alarm clock** el despertador

album *noun*
el **álbum** *masc*

alcohol *noun*
el **alcohol** *masc*

alcoholic *adjective* ▷ see **alcoholic** *noun*
alcohólico *masc*, **alcohólica** *fem*
alcoholic drinks bebidas alcohólicas

alcoholic *noun* ▷ see **alcoholic** *adj*
el **alcohólico** *masc*, la **alcohólica** *fem*
She's an alcoholic. Es alcohólica.

alert *adjective* ▷ see **alert** *noun*
espabilado *masc*, **espabilada** *fem*

alert *noun* ▷ see **alert** *adj*
la **alerta** *fem*
to be on the alert estar **[2]** alerta

A levels *noun*
la **selectividad** (*Students take 'la selectividad' at the same age as A levels are taken in Britain.) You can explain A levels as follows: Son exámenes que se realizan a dos niveles, AS y A2. Los exámenes AS se hacen después de un año de preparación, generalmente en cuatro o cinco asignaturas; los A2 abarcan un número menor de asignaturas que ya se hayan estudiado para el nivel AS. Ambos exámenes se califican desde A (nota máxima), a N (sin calificar). La calificación de los A levels se toma en cuenta para ingresar a la universidad*)
▷ **selectividad**

alibi *noun*
la **coartada** *fem*

alien *noun*
1 (*foreigner*) el **extranjero** *masc*, la **extranjera** *fem*
2 (*from outer space*) el & la **extraterrestre** *masc & fem*

alike *adjective*
parecido *masc*, **parecida** *fem*
They're all alike. Son todos parecidos.
to look alike parecerse **[35]**
The two brothers look alike. Los dos hermanos se parecen.

alive *adjective*
vivo *masc*, **viva** *fem*
to be alive estar **[2]** vivo

♪ **all** *adjective, adverb* ▷ see **all** *pron*
1 (*with objects, periods of time*) **todo** *masc*, **toda** *fem*
all the knives todos los cuchillos
all the cups todas las tazas
all the time todo el tiempo
all day todo el día
all along desde el primer momento
I knew it all along. Lo supe desde el primer momento.
2 (*entirely*) **completamente**
all alone completamente solo
She's all alone. Está completamente sola.
3 (*in scores*) **three all** tres iguales

♪ **all** *pronoun* ▷ see **all** *adj, adv*
1 (*every one, the whole*) **todo** *masc pronoun*, **toda** *fem pronoun*
It's all I have. Es todo lo que tengo.
They're all there. Están todos allí.
They've eaten it all. Se lo han comido todo.
2 (*in expressions*) **first of all** en primer lugar
after all después de todo
not at all de nada (*the answer to* ***gracias*** *or 'thank you'*)

allergic *adjective*
alérgico *masc*, **alérgica** *fem*
to be allergic to something ser **[1]** alérgico a algo
I'm allergic to cats. Soy alérgica a los gatos.

allergy *noun*
la **alergia** *fem*

alligator *noun*
el **caimán** *masc*

♪ to **allow** *verb*
1 **to allow somebody to do something** dejar **[17]** a alguien hacer algo
We are allowed to go out in the evenings. Nos dejan salir por las noches.
I'm not allowed to go out during the week. No me dejan salir durante la semana.
The teacher allowed them to go out. El maestro les dejó salir.

all right *adverb*
1 (*when you agree*) **de acuerdo**, **vale** (*informal*)
'Come round to my house around six.' - 'All right.' 'Ven a mi casa a eso de las seis.' - 'De acuerdo.'
It's all right by me. Vale.
2 (*the way you want things*) **Is everything all right?** ¿Va todo bien?
Is it all right to leave the door open? ¿Está bien dejar la puerta abierta?
3 (*to talk about how you are*) **bien**
Are you all right? ¿Estás bien?
She's all right now. Ya está bien.
4 (*not bad*) **The meal was all right.** La comida no estuvo mal.

ally *noun*
el **aliado** *masc*, la **aliada** *fem*

almond *noun*
la **almendra** *fem*

almost *adverb*
casi
almost every day casi cada día
almost everybody casi todo el mundo
She's almost five. Tiene casi cinco años.

alone *adjective*
solo *masc*, **sola** *fem*
He lives alone. Vive solo.
Leave me alone! ¡Déjame en paz!
Leave that alone! ¡Deja eso!

along *preposition*
1 **por**
We go for walks along the beach. Nos paseamos por la playa.
2 **a lo largo de**
There are trees all along our road. Hay árboles a lo largo de la calle donde vivimos.
3 (*further away*) **a bit further along** un poco más adelante
She lives along the street from me. Vive más abajo en la misma calle.

aloud *adverb*
en voz alta
to read something aloud leer [37] algo en voz alta

alphabet *noun*
el **alfabeto** *masc*

alphabetical *adjective*
alfabético *masc*, **alfabética** *fem*
in alphabetical order por orden alfabético

Alps *plural noun*
the Alps los Alpes

already *adverb*
ya
They've already left. Ya se han ido.
It's six o'clock already! ¡Ya son las seis!

Alsatian *noun*
el **pastor alemán**

also *adverb*
también
I've also invited Karen. He invitado también a Karen.

to **alter** *verb*
cambiar [17]

alternate *adjective*
on alternate days un día sí y otro no

alternative *adjective*
▷ see **alternative** *noun*
otro *masc*, **otra** *fem*
to look for an alternative solution buscar [31] otra solución

alternative *noun* ▷ see **alternative** *adj*
la **alternativa** *fem*
We have no alternative. No tenemos alternativa.

alternatively *adverb*
o bien
Alternatively, we could go on Saturday. O bien podríamos ir el sábado.

alternative medicine *noun*
la **medicina alternativa**

although *conjunction*
aunque
Although she's ill, she wants to come. Aunque está enferma, quiere venir.

altitude *noun*
la **altitud** *fem*

altogether *adverb*
1 (*all in all*) **en total**
I've spent thirty pounds altogether. He gastado treinta libras en total.
2 (*completely*) **totalmente**
I'm not altogether convinced. No estoy totalmente convencido.

aluminium *noun*
el **aluminio** *masc*

always *adverb*
siempre
I always leave at five. Siempre salgo a las cinco.
I have always lived in Milton. Siempre he vivido en Milton.

am *verb* ▷ **be**

a.m. *abbreviation*
de la mañana
at 8 a.m. a las ocho de la mañana

amateur *noun*
el & la **amateur** *masc & fem*, **amateurs** *masc & fem pl*
- **amateur dramatics** el teatro de amateurs

to **amaze** *verb*
asombrar [17]
What amazes me is ... Lo que me asombra es ...

amazed *adjective*
asombrado *masc*, **asombrada** *fem*
I was amazed to see her. Me quedé asombrado al verla.
She'll be amazed to find out. Se quedará asombrada al enterarse.

amazement *noun*
el **asombro** *masc*
To my amazement she agreed. Para mi gran sorpresa aceptó.

amazing *adjective*
increíble *masc & fem*
They've got an amazing house. Tienen una casa increíble.
She has an amazing number of friends. Tiene un número increíble de amigos.

ambassador *noun*
el **embajador** *masc*, la **embajadora** *fem*

ambition *noun*
la **ambición** *fem*

ambitious *adjective*
ambicioso *masc*, **ambiciosa** *fem*

ambulance *noun*
la **ambulancia** *fem*
- **ambulance driver** el conductor de ambulancia, la conductora de ambulancia

amenities *plural noun*
los **servicios públicos**

America *noun*
América *fem*
in America en América, en Estados Unidos
(*In Spanish,* ***América*** *often means the Latin American countries.*)

American *adjective* ▷ see **American** *noun*
americano *masc*, **americana** *fem*

American *noun* ▷ see **American** *adj*
(*person*) un **americano** *masc*, una **americana** *fem*
the Americans los americanos *masc pl*

> **WORD TIP** Adjectives and nouns for nationality and regional origin do not have capital letters in Spanish.

ammunition *noun*
las **municiones** *fem pl*

among, **amongst** *preposition*
entre
I found it among my books. Lo encontré entre mis libros.
You can decide amongst yourselves. Podéis decidirlo entre vosotros.

amount *noun*
la **cantidad** *fem*
an enormous amount of bread una enorme cantidad de pan
a huge amount of work una enorme cantidad de trabajo
a large amount of money una gran cantidad de dinero
- to **amount to something**
ascender [36] **a**
The bill amounts to five hundred euros. La cuenta asciende a quinientos euros.

amp *noun*
1 (*in electricity*) el **amperio** *masc*
2 (*amplifier*) el **amplificador** *masc*

amplifier *noun*
el **amplificador** *masc*

to **amuse** *verb*
divertir [14]

amusement arcade *noun*
el **salón de juegos recreativos**

amusement park *noun*
el **parque de atracciones**

amusing *adjective*
divertido *masc*, **divertida** *fem*

an *determiner*
1 **un** (*masculine*)
2 **una** (*feminine*)
▷ **a**

anaesthetic *noun*
la **anestesia** *fem*

to **analyse** *verb*
analizar [22]

analysis *noun*
el **análisis** *masc*

ancestor *noun*
el **antepasado** *masc*, la **antepasada** *fem*

anchor *noun*
el **ancla** *fem*

WORD TIP *ancla* takes *el* or *un* in the singular even though it is fem.

anchovy *noun*
el **anchoa** *fem*

WORD TIP *anchoa* takes *el* or *un* in the singular even though it is fem.

ancient *adjective*
1 (*historic*) **antiguo** *masc*, **antigua** *fem*
an ancient castle un castillo antiguo
2 (*very old*) **viejísimo** *masc*, **viejísima** *fem*
an ancient pair of jeans unos vaqueros viejísimos

♪ **and** *conjunction*
1 **y**
Sean and Anna Sean y Anna
boys and girls chicos y chicas
2 (*before words beginning with* ***i*** *or* ***hi***) **e**
Spain and Italy España e Italia
father and son padre e hijo
3 (*in English numbers above 100*) **a hundred and one** ciento uno
two hundred and thirty-one doscientos treinta y uno
4 (*in expressions with -er and -er*) **cada vez más ...**
bigger and bigger cada vez más grande
better and better cada vez mejor

Andalusia *noun*
Andalucía *fem* (*the region in southern Spain*)

Andalusian *adjective & noun*
1 **andaluz** *masc*, **andaluza** *fem*
2 (*person*) un **andaluz** *masc*, una **andaluza** *fem*
the Andalusians los andaluces

WORD TIP Adjectives and nouns for nationality and regional origin do not have capital letters in Spanish.

angel *noun*
el **ángel** *masc*

anger *noun*
la **ira** *fem*

angle *noun*
el **ángulo** *masc*

angrily *adverb*
con enfado

♪ **angry** *adjective*
to be angry estar [2] enfadado, *fem* enfadada
She was angry with me. Estaba enfadada conmigo.
to get angry (about something) enfadarse [17] (por algo)
She got angry with us for being late. Se enfadó con nosotros por llegar tarde.

♪ **animal** *noun*
el **animal** *masc*

ankle *noun*
el **tobillo** *masc*
to break your ankle romperse [40] el tobillo

♪ **anniversary** *noun*
el **aniversario** *masc*
a wedding anniversary un aniversario de boda
the fortieth anniversary of ... el cuarenta aniversario de ...

to **announce** *verb*
anunciar [17]

announcement *noun*
el **anuncio** *masc*

to **annoy** *verb*
1 (*to pester*) **fastidiar** [17]
Don't annoy me! ¡No fastidies!
2 (*to become angry*) **to be annoyed** estar [2] enfadado, *fem* enfadada
to get annoyed (about something) enfadarse [17] (por algo)
He got annoyed about the radio. Se enfadó por la radio.

♪ **annoying** *adjective*
1 (*person*) **pesado** *masc*, **pesada** *fem*
2 (*noise, habit*) **irritante** *masc & fem*
3 (*situation*) **How annoying!** ¡Qué fastidio!
The whole thing's really annoying. Todo es un verdadero fastidio.

annual *adjective*
anual *masc & fem*

anorak *noun*
el **anorak** *masc*, *pl:* los **anoraks**

anorexia *noun*
la **anorexia** *fem*

♪ **another** *adjective, pron*
otro *masc*, **otra** *fem*
Would you like another Coke®? ¿Quieres otra Coca Cola®?
Yes, I'll have another. Sí, me bebo otra. (***otra*** *refers to Coca Cola®*)
We need another three chairs. Necesitamos otras tres sillas.
another two years otros dos años
I'll come another time. Vendré en otro momento.
another one otro, otra
I want to buy another one. Quiero comprar otro.

answer *noun* ▷ see **answer** *verb*
1 (*to a question*) la **respuesta** *fem*
the right answer la respuesta correcta
the wrong answer la respuesta equivocada
2 (*to a problem*) **the answer to a problem** la solución a un problema

to **answer** *verb* ▷ see **answer** *noun*
1 (*a person, the phone*) **contestar [17]**
to answer your mobile contestar el móvil
He has answered my text message. Ha contestado mi mensaje de texto.
Nobody's answering. Nadie contesta.
2 (*the door*) **abrir [46] la puerta**

answering machine *noun*
el **contestador automático**, el **contestador** *masc*
to leave a message on the answering machine dejar [17] un mensaje en el contestador

ant *noun*
la **hormiga** *fem*

Antarctic *noun*
the Antarctic la Antártida

anthem *noun*
el **himno** *masc*
the national anthem el himno nacional

antibiotic *noun*
el **antibiótico** *masc*

anticlockwise *adverb*
en el sentido contrario al de las agujas del reloj
It turns anticlockwise. Gira en el sentido contrario al de las agujas del reloj.

antique *adjective* ▷ see **antique** *noun*
antiguo *masc*, **antigua** *fem*
an antique table una mesa antigua

antique *noun* ▷ see **antique** *adj*
antiques las antigüedades
• **antique shop** la tienda de antigüedades

antiseptic *noun*
el **antiséptico** *masc*

anxious *adjective*
preocupado *masc*, **preocupada** *fem*

anxiously *adverb*
con preocupación

any *adjective* ▷ see **any** *adv, pron*
1 (*asking questions, saying no*) Is there any butter? ¿Hay mantequilla?
There isn't any flour. No hay harina.
Have you got any glasses? ¿Tienes vasos?
I haven't got any glasses. No tengo vasos.
She's gone without any money. Ha ido sin dinero.

WORD TIP *any* is not translated in these examples.

2 (*stating facts*) **cualquier** (+ *noun*)
Any pupil knows that. Cualquier alumno lo sabe.
She could come any day. Podría venir cualquier día.
3 any one cualquiera
Any one will tell you. Cualquiera se lo dirá.
4 to be any more quedar [17] más
Is there any more? ¿Queda más?
Are there any more? ¿Quedan más?
There isn't any more butter. No queda más mantequilla.
There's hardly any more left. No queda casi nada.

any *adverb* ▷ see **any** *adj, pron*
1 (*with -er adjectives*) Are you any better? ¿Te sientes mejor?
2 any more ya no
We don't go there any more. Ya no vamos allí.

any *pronoun* ▷ see **any** *adj, adv*
1 (*in negative statements*) **ninguno** *masc pronoun*, **ninguna** *fem pronoun*
I don't want any. No quiero ninguno, *fem* ninguna.
2 (*in questions*) alguno *masc pronoun*, alguna *fem pronoun*
Do you want any? ¿Quieres alguno, *fem* alguna?

anybody, **anyone** *pronoun*
1 (*in questions and after 'if'*) **alguien**
Does anybody need water? ¿Alguien necesita agua?
Is anybody at home? ¿Hay alguien en casa?
If anybody calls, tell them ... Si alguien llama, dile que ...
2 (*in negative statements*) **not ... anybody** no ... nadie
There isn't anybody at home. No hay nadie en casa.
I don't know anybody there. No conozco a nadie allí.
3 (*anybody at all*) **cualquiera**
Anybody can go. Puede ir cualquiera.
Any one will tell you. Cualquiera se lo dirá.

anyhow *adverb* ▷ **anyway**

anyone *pronoun* ▷ **anybody**

anything *pronoun*
1 (*in questions*) **algo** (*invariable*)
Do you need anything? ¿Necesitas algo?

2 (*in negative statements*) **not ... anything** no ... nada
There isn't anything to eat. No hay nada para comer.
3 (*anything at all*) **cualquier cosa**
Anything could happen. Podría pasar cualquier cosa.

anyway, **anyhow** *adverb*
de todos modos
Anyway, I'll ring you before I leave. De todos modos te llamaré antes de salir.

⚷ **anywhere** *adverb*
1 (*in questions*) **Have you seen my keys anywhere?** ¿Has visto mis llaves en algún sitio?
Are you going anywhere tomorrow? ¿Vas a algún sitio mañana?
2 (*in negative statements*) **not ... anywhere** en ningún sitio
I can't find my keys anywhere. No encuentro mis llaves en ningún sitio.
I'm not going anywhere tonight. Esta noche no voy a ningún sitio.
3 (*to any place*) **a cualquier sitio**
You can take it anywhere. Puedes llevarlo a cualquier sitio.
4 (*in any place*) **en cualquier sitio**
Put your cases down anywhere. Pon las maletas en cualquier sitio.

apart *adjective, adverb*
1 (*separated*) **separado** *masc*, **separada** *fem*
They're too far apart. Están demasiado separados.
His parents live apart. Sus padres viven separados.
2 (*in measurements*) **to be two metres apart** estar [2] a dos metros de distancia
3 (*except*) **apart from** aparte de
Everybody came apart from Judy . Todo el mundo vino aparte de Judy.

apartment *noun*
el **apartamento** *masc*

ape *noun*
el **simio** *masc*

⚷ to **apologize** *verb*
1 **disculparse** [17]
to apologize for something disculparse por algo
He apologized for his behaviour. Se disculpó por su comportamiento
2 **to apologize to somebody** pedirle [57] perdón a alguien
He apologized to Tanya. Le pidió perdón a Tanya.

apology *noun*
la **disculpa** *fem*

apostrophe *noun*
el **apóstrofe** *masc*

apparent *adjective*
aparente *masc & fem*

apparently *adverb*
al parecer, **por lo visto**

appeal *noun* ▷ see **appeal** *verb*
(*call*) **an appeal for calm** un llamamiento a la calma
an appeal for help una solicitud de ayuda

to **appeal** *verb* ▷ see **appeal** *noun*
to appeal to somebody atraer [42] a alguien
Horror films don't appeal to me. Las películas de miedo no me atraen.

to **appear** *verb*
1 (*to come into view*) **aparecer** [35]
Mick appeared at the door. Mick apareció en la puerta.
2 (*on TV*) **to appear on television** salir [63] en televisión
3 (*to seem*) **parecer** [35]
It appears that somebody has taken the key. Parece que alguien se ha llevado la llave.

appendicitis *noun*
la **apendicitis** *fem*

appendix *noun*
el **apéndice** *masc*

appetite *noun*
el **apetito** *masc*

⚷ **appetizing** *adjective*
apetitoso *masc*, **apetitosa** *fem*

to **applaud** *verb*
aplaudir [19]

applause *noun*
los **aplausos** *masc plural*

⚷ **apple** *noun*
la **manzana** *fem*
• **apple tree** el manzano

applicant *noun*
candidato *masc*, **candidata** *fem*

application *noun*
la **solicitud** *fem*
a job application una solicitud de trabajo
• **application form** el impreso de solicitud

to **apply** *verb*

1 (*for a job, a place, etc*) **to apply for something** solicitar [17] algo
I'm going to apply for the job. Voy a solicitar el trabajo.
I've applied for the course. He solicitado que me admitan en el curso.

2 (*to be relevant to*) **to apply to somebody** aplicarse [31] a alguien
It applies to everyone. Se aplica a todos.

appointment *noun*
la **cita** *fem*
to make an appointment at the dentist's pedir [57] cita en el dentista
I've got a hair appointment at 4 o'clock. Tengo cita en la peluquería para las cuatro.

to **appreciate** *verb*
agradecer [35]
I appreciate your help. Te agradezco tu ayuda.

apprentice *noun*
el **aprendiz** *masc*, la **aprendiza** *fem*

apprenticeship *noun*
el **aprendizaje** *masc*

to **approach** *verb*
acercarse [31] a
We are approaching Madrid. Nos acercamos a Madrid.

appropriate *adjective*
apropiado *masc*, **apropiada** *fem*

approval *noun*
la **aprobación** *fem*

to **approve** *verb*
I don't approve of her friends. No me gustan sus amigos.
I don't approve of his methods. No estoy de acuerdo con sus métodos.
Does he approve of the idea? ¿Le parece bien la idea?

approximate *adjective*
aproximado *masc*, **aproximada** *fem*

approximately *adverb*
aproximadamente
approximately fifty people aproximadamente cincuenta personas

apricot *noun*
el **albaricoque** *masc*
- **apricot tree** el albaricoquero *masc*

April *noun*
abril *masc*
in April en abril

WORD TIP Names of months and days start with small letters in Spanish.

- **April Fool** el & la inocente
- **April Fool's Day** el día de los Santos Inocentes (*similar to April Fool's Day, but on the 28 December*)

apron *noun*
el **delantal** *masc*

aquarium *noun*
el **acuario** *masc*

Aquarius *noun*
1 (*the star sign*) el **Acuario** *masc*
2 (*person*) un & una **acuario** *masc & fem*
Sharon's Aquarius. Sharon es acuario.

WORD TIP Use a small letter in Spanish to say *I am ...* etc with star signs. Star signs in Spanish are used without *el, un, la, una*.

Arab *adjective & noun*
1 **árabe** *masc & fem*
the Arab countries los países árabes
2 (*person*) un & una **árabe** *masc & fem*
the Arabs los árabes *masc pl*

WORD TIP Adjectives and nouns for nationality and regional origin do not have capital letters in Spanish.

arch *noun*
el **arco** *masc*

archaelogist *noun*
el **arqueólogo** *masc*, la **arqueóloga** *fem*
She's an archaeologist. Es arqueóloga.

archaeology *noun*
la **arqueología** *fem*

archbishop *noun*
el **arzobispo** *masc*

architect *noun*
el **arquitecto** *masc*, la **arquitecta** *fem*
He's an architect. Es arquitecto.

architecture *noun*
la **arquitectura** *fem*

Arctic *noun*
the Arctic el Ártico

are *verb* ▷ **be**

area *noun*
1 (*region*) la **zona** *fem*
a poor area una zona pobre
in the Leeds area en la zona de Leeds
2 (*of a square, a circle*) el **área** *fem*

WORD TIP *área* takes *el* or *un* in the singular even though it is fem.

aren't *short for* **are not** (*See:* **to be**)

Argentina *noun*
Argentina *fem*

Argentinian *adjective*
▷ see **Argentinian** *noun*
argentino *masc*, **argentina** *fem*

Argentinian *noun*
▷ see **Argentinian** *adj*
(*person*) un **argentino** *masc*, una **argentina** *fem*
the Argentinians los argentinos *masc pl*

WORD TIP Adjectives and nouns for nationality and regional origin do not have capital letters in Spanish.

♪ to **argue** *verb*
discutir [19]
Jack and Jane are always arguing. Jack y Jane siempre están discutiendo.
to argue about something discutir sobre algo
They're arguing about the result. Están discutiendo sobre el resultado.

argument *noun*
la **discusión** *fem*
to have an argument discutir [19]

Aries *noun*
1 (*the star sign*) el **Aries** *masc*
2 (*person*) un & una **aries** *masc & fem*
Davina's Aries. Davina es aries.

WORD TIP Use a small letter in Spanish to say *I am ...* etc with star signs. Star signs in Spanish are used without *el, un, la, una.*

arithmetic *noun*
la **aritmética** *fem*

♪ **arm** *noun*
el **brazo** *masc*
to go arm in arm ir [8] del brazo
to break your arm romperse [40] el brazo
She's broken her arm. Se ha roto el brazo.
• **armchair** el sillón

armed *adjective*
armado *masc*, **armada** *fem*
armed terrorists terroristas armados

armpit *noun*
la **axila** *fem*

arms *plural noun*
las **armas** *fem pl*

army *noun*
el **ejército** *masc*
to join the army alistarse [17] en el ejército

♪ **around** *adverb, preposition*
1 (*with places, times*) **alrededor de**
the countryside around Edinburgh el campo de alrededor de Edinburgo
We'll be there around ten. Estaremos allí alrededor de las diez.
We sat around the table. Nos sentamos alrededor de la mesa.
She has a scarf around her neck. Tiene una bufanda alrededor del cuello.
to travel around the world viajar [17] por el mundo
2 (*with amounts, ages*) **We need around six kilos.** Necesitamos unos seis quilos.
She's around fifteen. Tiene unos quince años.
3 (*nearby*) **Is Phil around?** ¿Está Phil por aquí?
Is there a post office around here? ¿Hay una oficina de correos por aquí?
It's around the corner. Está a la vuelta de la esquina.

♪ to **arrange** *verb*
to arrange to do something quedar [17] en hacer algo
We've arranged to go to the beach on Saturday. Quedamos en ir a la playa el domingo.

arrangement *noun*
1 (*agreement*) el **acuerdo** *masc*
2 (*of things*) la **disposición** *fem*

arrest *noun* ▷ see **arrest** *verb*
He's under arrest. Está detenido.
You're under arrest. Queda detenido.

to **arrest** *verb* ▷ see **arrest** *noun*
arrestar [17]

arrival *noun*
la **llegada** *fem*
Arrivals Llegadas

♪ to **arrive** *verb*
llegar [17]
They arrived at three. Llegaron a las tres.
We arrive in Barcelona at one. Llegamos a Barcelona a la una.

arrow *noun*
la **flecha** *fem*

art *noun*
1 (*painting, sculpture, design*) el **arte** *masc*, las **artes** *fem pl*
modern art el arte moderno
the arts las artes
2 (*school subject*) el **dibujo** *masc*
the art class la clase de dibujo

WORD TIP *arte* singular is masc, but *artes* plural is fem.

English–Spanish
a b c d e f g h i j k l m n o p q r s t u v w x y z

artery *noun*
la **arteria** *fem*

art gallery *noun*
el **museo de arte**

article *noun*
1 (*in a newspaper, magazine*) el **artículo** *masc*
a magazine article un artículo de revista
2 (*Grammar*) el **artículo** *masc*
the definite article el artículo definido (*in Spanish: el, la, los*)
the indefinite article el artículo indefinido (*in Spanish: un, una*)

artichoke *noun*
la **alcachofa** *fem*

artificial *adjective*
artificial *masc & fem*

artist *noun*
el & la **artista** *masc & fem*
He's an artist. Es artista.

artistic *adjective*
artístico *masc*, **artística** *fem*

art school *noun*
la **escuela de Bellas Artes**

as *adverb, preposition* ▷ see **as** *conj*
1 (*in comparisons*) **as ... as ...** tan ... como ...
He's as tall as his brother. Es tan alto como su hermano.
You must be as tired as I am. Debes estar tan cansado como yo.
Do it as quickly as you can. Hazlo tan rápido como puedas.
as much ... as ... tanto *masc*, tanta *fem* como
You have as much time as I do. Tienes tanto tiempo como yo.
as many ... as ... tantos *masc pl*, tantas *fem pl* como
We have as many points as they do. Tenemos tantos puntos como ellos.
She has as many apples as I do. Tiene tantas manzanas como yo.
2 (*saying what you do*) **to work as** trabajar **[17]** de
He works as a taxi driver. Trabaja de taxista.

as *conjunction* ▷ see **as** *adv, prep*
1 (*like*) **como**
as you know como sabes
as usual como siempre
as I told you como te dije
2 (*giving a reason*) **como**
As there were no trains, we took the bus. Como no había trenes, tomamos el autobús.
3 (*in expressions*) **as soon as possible** lo más pronto posible
as long as siempre que
Buy it, as long as it's good quality. Cómpralo, siempre que sea de buena calidad.

WORD TIP *siempre que* is followed by a verb in the subjunctive.

asbestos *noun*
el **asbestos** *masc*

ash *noun*
la **ceniza** *fem*

ashamed *adjective*
to be ashamed estar **[2]** avergonzado, *fem* avergonzada
I was very ashamed of myself. Estaba muy avergonzado.
You should be ashamed of yourself! ¡Debería darte vergüenza!

ashtray *noun*
el **cenicero** *masc*

Asia *noun*
Asia *fem*

Asian *adjective* ▷ see **Asian** *noun*
1 (*from the continent of Asia*) **asiático** *masc*, **asiática** *fem*
2 (*from India*) **indio** *masc*, **india** *fem*
3 (*from Pakistan*) **paquistaní** *masc & fem*

Asian *noun* ▷ see **Asian** *adjective*
1 (*from Asia*) un **asiático** *masc*, una **asiática** *fem*
2 (*from India*) un **indio** *masc*, una **india** *fem*
3 (*from Pakistan*) un & una **paquistaní** *masc & fem*

WORD TIP Adjectives and nouns for nationality and regional origin do not have capital letters in Spanish.

to ask *verb*
1 (*to find out*) **preguntar [17]**
You can ask at reception. Puede preguntar en recepción. (*formal form*)
to ask somebody something preguntarle algo a alguien
I asked him where he lived. Le pregunté dónde vivía.
2 **to ask for something** pedir **[57]** algo
Ask for three coffees. Pide tres cafés.
to ask somebody to do something pedirle **[57]** a alguien que haga algo
Ask Danny to go with you. Pídele a Danny que vaya contigo.
3 **to ask somebody a question** hacerle **[7]** una pregunta a alguien

I asked you a question! ¡Te he hecho una pregunta!

4 (*to invite*) **invitar** [17]
They've asked us to a party at their house. Nos han invitado a una fiesta en su casa.
Paul's asked Janie out on Friday. Paul ha invitado a Janie a salir el viernes.

asleep *adjective*
dormido *masc*, **dormida** *fem*
to be asleep estar [2] dormido
Jason's asleep. Jason está dormido.
to fall asleep quedarse [17] dormido

asparagus *noun*
el **espárrago** *masc*

♪ **aspirin** *noun*
la **aspirina** *fem*

assignment *noun*
la **tarea** *fem*
to hand in an assignment entregar [28] una tarea

to **assist** *verb*
ayudar [17]

assistance *noun*
la **ayuda** *fem*

assistant *noun*
el & la **ayudante** *masc & fem*

association *noun*
la **asociación** *fem*

assorted *adjective*
variado *masc*, **variada** *fem*

assortment *noun*
el **surtido** *masc*
an assortment of sweets un surtido de caramelos

to **assume** *verb*
suponer [11]

to **assure** *verb*
asegurar [17]
You'll like it, I assure you. Te gustará, te lo aseguro.

asterisk *noun*
el **asterisco** *masc*

asthma *noun*
el **asma** *fem*
I have asthma. Sufro de asma.

WORD TIP *asma* takes *el* or *un* in the singular even though it is fem.

♪ **astonishing** *adjective*
asombroso *masc*, **asombrosa** *fem*
Her Spanish is astonishing. Su español es asombroso.

astrologer *noun*
el **astrólogo** *masc*, la **astróloga** *fem*

astrology *noun*
la **astrología** *fem*

astronaut *noun*
el & la **astronauta** *masc & fem*

astronomer *noun*
el **astrónomo** *masc*, la **astrónoma** *fem*

astronomy *noun*
la **astronomía** *fem*

♪ **at** *preposition*

1 (*talking about places*) **en**
at home en casa
at school en el colegio
There's someone at the door. Hay alguien en la puerta.
Dad's at work all day. Papá está en el trabajo todo el día.

2 (*talking about where people live, work*) **en**
at Emma's house en casa de Emma
at the hairdresser's en la peluquería
She's at her brother's this evening. Esta noche está en casa de su hermano.

3 (*talking about the time, periods of time*) **a**
at eight o'clock a las ocho
at night por la noche
We go there at weekends. Nos vamos allí los fines de semana.
at last por fin
He's found a job at last. Por fin ha encontrado un trabajo.

4 (*in email addresses*) la **arroba** *fem*
jason.foster@easylink.com jason-punto-foster-arroba-easylink-punto-com

athlete *noun*
el & la **atleta** *masc & fem*

athletic *adjective* ▷ see **athletics** *noun*
atlético *masc*, **atlética** *fem*

♪ **athletics** *noun* ▷ see **athletic** *adj*
el **atletismo** *masc*

Atlantic *noun*
the Atlantic el Atlántico

atlas *noun*
el **atlas** *masc*

atmosphere *noun*
la **atmósfera** *fem*

atom *noun*
el **átomo** *masc*

atomic *adjective*
atómico *masc*, **atómica** *fem*

♪ to **attach** *verb*
1 (*to fasten*) **sujetar** [17]
2 (*to tie*) **atar** [17]

attachment *noun*
1 (*in an email*) el **adjunto** *masc*
2 (*in a letter*) el **documento adjunto**

attack *noun* ▷ see **attack** *verb*
el **ataque** *masc*

to **attack** *verb* ▷ see **attack** *noun*
atacar [31]

attacker *noun*
el **agresor** *masc*, la **agresora** *fem*

attempt *noun* ▷ see **attempt** *verb*
el **intento** *masc*
at the second attempt al segundo intento

to **attempt** *verb* ▷ see **attempt** *noun*
to attempt to do something intentar [17] hacer algo
I attempted to contact them. Intenté ponerme en contacto con ellos.

to **attend** *verb*
asistir [19] **a**
to attend a class asistir a clase

♪ **attention** *noun*
la **atención** *fem*
to pay attention to somebody prestar [17] atención a alguien
I wasn't paying atttention to the teacher. No estaba prestando atención al profesor.

attic *noun*
el **desván** *masc*, la **buhardilla** *fem*

attitude *noun*
la **actitud** *fem*

to **attract** *verb*
atraer [42]

attraction *noun*
la **atracción** *fem*

attractive *adjective*
atractivo *masc*, **atractiva** *fem*

aubergine *noun*
la **berenjena** *fem*

auction *noun*
la **subasta** *fem*

♪ **audience** *noun*
el **público** *masc*
a member of the audience un espectador

♪ **August** *noun*
agosto *masc*
in August en agosto

WORD TIP Names of months and days start with small letters in Spanish.

♪ **aunt**, **auntie** *noun*
la **tía** *fem*

au pair *noun*
el & la **au pair** *masc & fem*
I'm looking for a job as an au pair. Busco un trabajo de au pair.

Australia *noun*
Australia *fem*

Australian *adjective & noun*
1 **australiano** *masc*, **australiana** *fem*
2 (*person*) un **australiano** *masc*, una **australiana** *fem*
the Australians los australianos *masc pl*

WORD TIP Adjectives and nouns for nationality and regional origin do not have capital letters in Spanish.

Austria *noun*
Austria *fem*

Austrian *adjective & noun*
1 **austriaco** *masc*, **austriaca** *fem*
2 (*person*) un **austriaco** *masc*, una **austriaca** *fem*
the Austrians los austriacos *masc pl*

WORD TIP Adjectives and nouns for nationality and regional origin do not have capital letters in Spanish.

♪ **author** *noun*
el **autor** *masc*, la **autora** *fem*

autobiography *noun*
la **autobiografía** *fem*

autograph *noun*
el **autógrafo** *masc*

automatic *adjective*
automático *masc*, **automática** *fem*

automatically *adverb*
automáticamente

autumn *noun*
el **otoño** *masc*
in the autumn en otoño

availability *noun*
la **disponibilidad** *fem*

available *adjective*
disponible *masc & fem*

avalanche *noun*
la **avalancha** *fem*

avenue *noun*
la **avenida** *fem*

average *adjective* ▷ see **average** *noun*
1 (*talking about age, height, weight*) **medio** *masc*, **media** *fem*
his average speed su velocidad media
The average height of the pupils is ... La estatura media de los alumnos es ...
2 (*neither good nor bad*) **regular** *masc & fem*
The food is average. La comida es regular.

average *noun* ▷ see **average** *adj*
la **media** *fem*
above average por encima de la media
below average por debajo de la media
on average como promedio
My marks are above average. Mis notas están por encima de la media.

avocado *noun*
el **aguacate** *masc*

to **avoid** *verb*
evitar [17]
She avoided me. Me evitó.
to avoid doing something evitar hacer algo
I avoid speaking to him. Evito hablar con él.

awake *adjective*
to be awake estar [2] despierto, *fem* despierta
Is Lola awake? ¿Está despierta Lola?

award *noun*
el **premio** *masc*
the award for the best CD el premio al mejor CD
to win an award ganar [17] un premio

aware *adjective*
to be aware of something ser [1] consciente de algo
I am aware of the problem. Soy consciente del problema.
We are more aware of environmental problems than before. Somos más conscientes de los problemas ecológicos que antes.

away *adverb*
1 (*with distances*) **a long way away** muy lejos
not far away no muy lejos
Go away! ¡vete!
The thieves ran away. Los ladrones se escaparon.
How far away is it? ¿A qué distancia está?
It's two kilometres away. Está a dos kilómetros.
2 (*not at home*) **to be away** estar [2] fuera
I'll be away next week. Estaré fuera la próxima semana.
Laura's gone away for a week. Laura se ha ido por una semana.
We're playing away today. Hoy jugamos fuera de casa.

WORD TIP For expressions like *to give away, to put away*, etc, see *to give, to put*.

• **away match** el partido fuera de casa

awful *adjective*
1 (*very bad*) **espantoso** *masc*, **espantosa** *fem*, **fatal** *masc & fem*
The film was awful! La película era espantosa.
How awful! ¡Qué horror!
I think he's awful. Me cae fatal.
There's an awful lot to do. Hay muchísimo que hacer.
2 (*ill*) **fatal**
I feel awful. Me siento fatal.
3 (*guilty*) **I feel awful about it.** Me siento muy culpable.

awkward *adjective*
1 (*person, question*) **difícil** *masc & fem*
an awkward child un niño difícil
an awkward question una pregunta difícil
2 (*situation, silence*) **incómodo** *masc*, **incómoda** *fem*
It's an awkward situation. Es una situación incómoda .
It's a bit awkward. Es un poco delicado.

axe *noun*
hacha *fem*

WORD TIP *hacha* takes *el* or *un* in the singular even though it is fem.

English-Spanish

B b

baby *noun*
el **bebé** *masc*

to **babysit** *verb*
hacer [7] de canguro

babysitter *noun*
el & la **canguro** *masc & fem*

babysitting *noun*
to go babysitting hacer [7] de canguro

bachelor *noun*
el **soltero** *masc*

back *adjective* ▷ see **back** *adv, noun, verb*
1 (*wheel, seat*) **trasero** *masc*, **trasera** *fem*
the back seat of the car el asiento trasero del coche
2 **the back garden** el jardín de atrás
the back gate la verja de atrás

back *adverb* ▷ see **back** *adj, noun, verb*
1 **to go back** volver [45]
to go back to school volver al colegio
Lisa's gone back to London. Lisa ha vuelto a Londres.
2 **to come back** volver [45]
They've come back from Chile. Han vuelto de Chile.
She's back at work. Ha vuelto al trabajo.
Sue's not back yet. Sue no ha vuelto aún.
She went by bus and walked back. Fue en autobús y volvió andando.
3 **to phone back** volver [45] a llamar
I'll ring back later. Te volveré a llamar más tarde.
4 **to give something back to somebody** devolverle [45] algo a alguien
I gave him back his cassettes. Le devolví sus cintas.
Give it back! ¡Devuélvemelo!

back *noun* ▷ see **back** *adj, adv, verb*
1 (*of a person, a coat, etc*) la **espalda** *fem*
to do something behind somebody's back hacer [7] algo a espaldas de alguien
2 (*of an animal*) el **lomo** *masc*
3 (*of a piece of paper, your hand*) el **dorso** *masc*
on the back of the envelope en el dorso del sobre
4 (*of a car, plane, hall*) el **fondo** *masc*
We have seats at the back. Tenemos asientos al fondo.
The children are at the back of the room. Los niños están al fondo de la habitación.
5 (*of a building*) **la parte de atrás**
a garden at the back of the house un jardín en la parte de atrás de la casa
6 (*of a chair, sofa*) el **respaldo** *masc*
7 (*in football, hockey, etc*) el & la **defensa** *masc & fem*

to **back** *verb* ▷ see **back** *adj, adv, noun*
1 (*a candidate*) **apoyar [17]**
2 (*a horse*) **apostar [24] por**
• **to back up a file**
(*on a computer*) **hacer [7] una copia de seguridad de un archivo**
• **to back somebody up**
apoyar [17] a alguien

backache *noun*
el **dolor de espalda**

backbone *noun*
la **columna vertebral**

back door *noun*
1 (*of a building*) la **puerta de atrás**
2 (*of a car*) la **puerta trasera**

to **backfire** *verb*
(*to turn out badly*) **salir [63] mal**

background *noun*
1 (*of a person*) el **origen** *masc*
2 (*of events, a situation*) el **contexto** *masc*
3 (*in a picture, view*) el **fondo** *masc*
the trees in the background los árboles del fondo
• **background music** la música de fondo
• **background noise** el ruido de fondo

backhand *noun*
el **revés** *masc*

backing *noun*
(*moral support*) el **apoyo** *masc*

backpack *noun* ▷ see **backpack** *verb*
la **mochila** *fem*

to **backpack** *verb* ▷ see **backpack** *noun*
to go backpacking viajar [17] con mochila

back seat *noun*
el **asiento trasero**

backside *noun*
el **trasero** *masc*

backstroke *noun*
el **estilo espalda**
to swim backstroke nadar [17] a espalda

a b c d e f g h i j k l m n o p q r s t u v w x y z

back to front *adverb*
al revés
Your jumper's on back to front. Te has puesto el jersey al revés.

backup *noun*
(*support*) el **apoyo** *masc*
- **backup disk** (*Computers*) el disco de seguridad

backwards *adverb*
(*to lean, to fall*) **hacia atrás**

bacon *noun*
el **bacon** *masc*
bacon and eggs huevos con bacon

♪ **bad** *adjective*
1 (*not good*) **malo** *masc*, **mala** *fem*
a bad moment un mal momento
a bad experience una experiencia mala
It's bad for your health. Es malo para la salud.
2 (*accident, mistake*) **grave** *masc & fem*
a bad accident un accidente grave
3 (*headache, cold*) **fuerte** *masc & fem*
a bad cold un resfriado fuerte
4 (*food*) **podrido** *masc*, **podrida** *fem*
a bad apple una manzana podrida
to go bad estropearse [17]
5 (*rude*) **bad language** lenguaje grosero
6 (*naughty*) **malo** *masc*, **mala** *fem*
Bad dog! ¡(Perro) malo!
7 **to be bad at something** dársele [4] algo mal a alguien
I'm bad at physics. Se me da mal la física.
8 **It's not bad.** No está mal.
His new film's not bad. Su nueva película no está mal.

WORD TIP *malo* becomes *mal* before a masc singular noun.

badge *noun*
1 (*pin-on*) la **chapa** *fem*
2 (*policeman's*) **a police badge** una placa de policía

♪ **badly** *adverb*
1 **mal**
He writes badly. Escribe mal.
I slept badly. Dormí mal.
My exam went badly. El examen me fue mal.
2 **badly hurt** gravemente herido
3 **The car was badly damaged.** El coche quedó muy estropeado.

bad-mannered *adjective*
maleducado *masc*, **maleducada** *fem*

badminton *noun*
el **bádminton** *masc*
to play badminton jugar [27] al bádminton

bad-tempered *adjective*
(*answer, look*) **malhumorado** *masc*, **malhumorada** *fem*
to be bad-tempered (*for a while*) estar [2] de mal humor, (*always*) tener [9] mal genio

♪ **bag** *noun*
1 (*made of plastic, paper*) la **bolsa** *fem*
2 (*handbag*) el **bolso** *masc*

baggage *noun*
el **equipaje** *masc*
- **baggage allowance** la franquicia de equipaje
- **baggage reclaim** la recogida de equipaje

bagpipes *plural noun*
la **gaita** *fem*
to play the bagpipes tocar [31] la gaita

bags *plural noun*
las **maletas** *fem pl*
to pack your bags hacer [7] las maletas

Bahamas *plural noun*
the Bahamas las Bahamas

Bahamian *adjective & noun*
1 **bahameño** *masc*, **bahameña** *fem*
2 (*person*) un **bahameño** *masc*, una **bahameña** *fem*
the Bahamians los bahameños *masc pl*

WORD TIP Adjectives and nouns for nationality and regional origin do not have capital letters in Spanish.

to **bake** *verb*
to bake a cake hornear [17] un pastel
to bake potatoes asar [17] patatas

baked *adjective*
1 (*fruit, vegetables*) **asado** *masc*, **asada** *fem*
baked apples manzanas asadas
a baked potato una patata asada
2 (*fish*) **al horno**
- **baked beans** las judías en salsa de tomate

♪ **baker** *noun*
el **panadero** *masc*, la **panadera** *fem*
to go to the baker's ir [8] a la panadería

bakery *noun*
la **panadería** *fem*

balance *noun*
1 (*steadiness*) el **equilibrio** *masc*
to lose your balance perder [36] el equilibrio
2 (*of your bank account*) el **saldo** *masc*

balanced *adjective*
equilibrado *masc*, **equilibrada** *fem*

ℰ **balcony** *noun*
el **balcón** *masc*

bald *adjective*
calvo *masc*, **calva** *fem*

Balearic Islands *plural noun*
the Balearic Islands las Islas Baleares

ℰ **ball** *noun*
1 (*for tennis, golf*) la **pelota** *fem*
2 (*for football, volleyball*) el **balón** *masc*
3 (*of string, wool*) el **ovillo** *masc*

ballet *noun*
el **ballet** *masc*
• **ballet dancer** el bailarín de ballet, la bailarina de ballet

ℰ **balloon** *noun*
el **globo** *masc*

ballot *noun*
la **votación** *fem*

ballpoint pen *noun*
el **boli** *masc*, el **bolígrafo** *masc*

ban *noun* ▷ see **ban** *verb*
la **prohibición** *fem*
to put a ban on smoking prohibir [58] fumar

to **ban** *verb* ▷ see **ban** *noun*
prohibir [58]

ℰ **banana** *noun*
el **plátano** *masc*
a banana yoghurt **un yogur de plátano**

band *noun*
1 (*playing music*) el **grupo** *masc*
a rock band un grupo de rock
a jazz band (*big*) una orquesta de jazz, (*small*) un conjunto de jazz
a brass band una banda de música
2 **a rubber band** una goma elástica

bandage *noun* ▷ see **bandage** *verb*
la **venda** *fem*

to **bandage** *verb* ▷ see **bandage** *noun*
vendar [17]

bang *exclamation* ▷ see **bang** *noun, verb*
(*like a gun*) **¡pum!**

bang *noun* ▷ see **bang** *excl, verb*
1 (*noise*) el **estallido** *masc*
2 (*of a window*) el **golpe** *masc*
3 (*of a door*) el **portazo** *masc*

to **bang** *verb* ▷ see **bang** *excl, noun*
1 (*a table, a drum*) **golpear** [17]
He banged his fist on the table. Golpeó la mesa con el puño.
2 (*to knock*) **dar** [4] **golpes a**
to bang on the door dar golpes a la puerta
I banged my head on the door. Me di un golpe en la cabeza con la puerta.
I banged into the table. Me choqué con la mesa.
3 **to bang the door** aporrear [17] la puerta

bangle *noun*
la **pulsera** *fem*

banister *noun*, **banisters** *plural noun*
la **barandilla** *noun*

ℰ **bank** *noun*
(*for money*) el **banco** *masc*
I'm going to the bank. Voy al banco.
• **bank account** la cuenta bancaria
• **bank balance** el saldo
• **bank card** la tarjeta bancaria
• **bank holiday** el día festivo
• **banknote** el billete de banco
• **bank statement** el extracto de cuenta

to **baptize** *verb*
bautizar [22]

ℰ **bar** *noun* ▷ see **bar** *verb*
1 (*where you have drinks*) el **bar** *masc*
Janet works in a bar. Janet trabaja en un bar.
2 (*the counter in a bar*) la **barra** *fem*
3 **a bar of chocolate** una tableta de chocolate
4 **a bar of soap** una pastilla de jabón
5 (*of wood, metal*) la **barra** *fem*
a metal bar una barra de metal
6 (*Music*) el **compás** *masc*

ℰ to **bar** *verb* ▷ see **bar** *noun*
(*to block physically*) **bloquear** [17]
to bar someone's way bloquear el paso a alguien

Barbadian *adjective & noun*
1 **barbadense** *masc & fem*
2 (*person*) un & una **barbadense**
the Barbadians los barbadenses

WORD TIP Adjectives and nouns for nationality and regional origin do not have capital letters in Spanish.

barbecue *noun* ▷ see **barbecue** *verb*
la **barbacoa** *fem*
There's a barbecue tonight. Hay una barbacoa esta noche.

to **barbecue** *verb* ▷ see **barbecue** *noun*
to barbecue a chicken asar **[17]** un pollo a la parrilla
barbecued chicken el pollo a la parrilla

barbed wire *noun*
el **alambre de púas**

bare *adjective*
desnudo *masc*, **desnuda** *fem*

barely *adverb*
a penas
She's barely twelve. A penas tiene doce años.

barefoot *adjective*
descalzo *masc*, **descalza** *fem*
to be barefoot estar **[2]** descalzo, *fem* descalza

bargain *noun*
la **ganga** *fem*
I got a bargain. Conseguí una ganga
It's a bargain! ¡Es una ganga!

barge *noun*
la **barcaza** *fem*

bark *noun* ▷ see **bark** *verb*
1 (*of a tree*) la **corteza** *fem*
2 (*of a dog*) el **ladrido** *masc*

to **bark** *verb* ▷ see **bark** *noun*
ladrar [17]

barley *noun*
la **cebada** *fem*

barmaid *noun*
la **camarera** *fem*

barman *noun*
el **camarero** *masc*

barn *noun*
el **granero** *masc*

barometer *noun*
el **barómetro** *masc*

barrel *noun*
el **tonel** *masc*

barrier *noun*
la **barrera** *fem*

base *noun*
la **base** *fem*

baseball *noun*
el **béisbol** *masc*
to play baseball jugar **[27]** al béisbol

based *adjective*
1 **to be based on something** basarse **[17]** en algo
The film is based on a true story. La película se basa en una historia real.
2 **to be based in** (*companies*) tener **[9]** su base en
3 **to be based in** (*people*) vivir **[19]** en
He's based in Bristol. Vive en Bristol.

♪ **basement** *noun*
el **sótano** *masc*
in the basement en el sótano

bash *noun*
1 el **golpe** *masc*
It's got a bash on the bumper. Tiene un golpe en el guardabarros.
2 (*informal*) **I'll have a bash.** Voy a probar.

basic *adjective*
1 (*elementary*) **básico** *masc*, **básica** *fem*
basic knowledge conocimientos básicos
2 **the basic facts** los hechos fundamentales
the basic salary el sueldo base
3 (*without frills*) **sencillo** *masc*, **sencilla** *fem*
The flat's a bit basic. El piso es bastante sencillo.

basically *adverb*
básicamente

basics *noun*
los **rudimentos** *masc plural*

basin *noun*
(*washbasin*) el **lavabo** *masc*

basis *noun*
1 la **base** *fem*
on the basis of something en base a algo
2 **on a regular basis** regularmente

♪ **basket** *noun*
1 la **cesta** *fem*
a shopping basket una cesta de la compra
a linen basket una cesta de ropa sucia
2 **a waste-paper basket** una papelera

basketball *noun*
el **baloncesto** *masc*
to play basketball jugar **[27]** al baloncesto

Basque *adjective & noun*
1 **vasco** *masc*, **vasca** *fem*
the Basque Country el País vasco, Euskadi (*the region's Basque name*)
2 (*person*) un **vasco** *masc*, una **vasca** *fem*
the Basques los vascos
3 (*the language*) el **vasco** *masc*, el **euskera** *masc* (*the language's Basque name*)

WORD TIP Adjectives and nouns for nationality, regional origin, and language do not have capital letters in Spanish.

English–Spanish
a b c d e f g h i j k l m n o p q r s t u v w x y z

bass *noun*
1 el **bajo** *masc*
to play bass tocar [31] el bajo
2 **a double bass** un contrabajo
- **bass drum** el bombo
- **bass guitar** el bajo

bassoon *noun*
el **fagot** *masc*
to play the bassoon tocar [31] el fagot

bat *noun*
1 (*for cricket, baseball*) el **bate** *masc*
2 (*for table tennis*) la **paleta** *fem*
3 (*the animal*) el **murciélago** *masc*

batch *noun*
el **lote** *masc*
a batch of letters un lote de cartas

bath *noun*
1 el **baño** *masc*
I was in the bath. Estaba en el baño.
to have a bath bañarse [17]
2 (*bathtub*) la **bañera** *fem*
The bath's pink. La bañera es rosa.

to **bathe** *verb*
1 (*a wound*) **lavar** [17]
2 (*to go swimming*) **bañarse** [17]

bathroom *noun*
el **cuarto de baño**

bath towel *noun*
la **toalla de baño**

batter *noun*
1 (*for frying*) el **rebozado** *masc*
fish in batter pescado rebozado
2 (*for pancakes*) la **masa** *fem*

battery *noun*
1 (*for a torch, a radio*) la **pila** *fem*
2 (*for a car*) la **batería** *fem*

battle *noun*
la **batalla** *fem*

bay *noun*
1 (*on a coast*) la **bahía** *fem*
the Bay of Biscay el Golfo de Vizcaya
2 (*in a bus station*) la **dársena** *fem*

B.C. *abbreviation*
(*= before Christ*) **a. de C.** (*antes de Cristo*)

to **be** *verb*
(*Spanish has two verbs for* ***to be***, ***ser*** *and* ***estar***)
1 (*saying how someone or something* ***always*** *is*) **ser** [1]
She's blond. Es rubia.
He's tall. Es alto.
It's beautiful. Es precioso.
Honey is sweet. La miel es dulce.
2 (*saying* ***alive*** *or* ***dead***) **estar** [1]
She's dead. Está muerta.
He's still alive. Todavía está vivo.
3 (*saying how someone or something is* ***now***) **estar** [2]
She's angry. Está enfadada.
I'm tired. Estoy cansado (*boy speaking*)., Estoy cansada (*girl speaking*).
The soup is cold. La sopa está fría.
These strawberries are delicious. Estas fresas están deliciosas.
4 (*saying where someone or something is*) **estar** [2]
Dad's in the garden. Papá está en el jardín.
Where's the butter? ¿Dónde está la mantequilla?
It's on the table. Está en la mesa.
When we were in Granada. Cuando estábamos en Granada.
5 **there is, there are** hay
There is one mistake. Hay un error.
There are two children outside. Hay dos niños fuera.
There's more. Hay más.
Is there a problem? ¿Hay algún problema?

WORD TIP *hay* is the same for the singular and plural.

6 (*saying what people do*) **ser** [1]
She's a teacher. Es profesora.
He's a footballer. Es futbolista.

WORD TIP *a* is not translated.

7 (*with married*) **estar** [2]
She's married to Carl. Está casada con Carl.
He's married to my sister. Está casado con mi hermana.
8 (*telling the time*) **ser** [1]
It's exactly one o'clock. Es la una en punto. (***es*** *for one o'clock*)
It's half past five. Son las cinco y media. (***son*** *for the times after one o'clock*)
9 (*with days of the week, dates*) **ser** [1]
What day is it today? ¿Qué día es hoy?
Today's Tuesday. Hoy es martes.
It's the twentieth of May., It's May the twentieth. Es veinte de mayo.
10 (*saying your age*) **tener** [9]
to be x years old tener x años
He's fifteen years old. Tiene quince años.
She's fourteen. Tiene catorce años.
How old are you? ¿Cuántos años tienes?
Sam's two. Sam tiene dos años.
11 (*saying you're hot, cold, hungry, thirsty*) **tener** [9]
I'm hot. Tengo calor.
I'm cold. Tengo frío.
We're hungry. Tenemos hambre.
Are you thirsty? ¿Tienes sed?
12 (*talking about the weather*) **hacer** [7]
It's cold today. Hoy hace frío.

It's hot! ¡Qué calor hace!
It's a nice day. Hace buen día.
13 (*saying where you've been*) **estar** [2]
I've been to Alicante twice. He estado en Alicante dos veces.
Have you been to Spain before? ¿Has estado en España alguna vez?
14 (*for passive verb forms:* ***to be -ed****. Spanish often uses the third person plural in these cases*)
to be loved ser [1] amado
She is liked by everyone. Es apreciada por todos., Todos la aprecian (*third person pl form*).
The house was built in 2003. Construyeron la casa en 2003 (*third person pl form*).
He has been killed. Lo han matado (*third person pl form*).

beach *noun*
la **playa** *fem*
on the beach en la playa
Let's go to the beach. Vamos a la playa.

bead *noun*
la **cuenta** *fem*

beak *noun*
el **pico** *masc*

beam *noun*
1 (*of light*) el **rayo** *masc*
2 (*for a roof*) la **viga** *fem*

bean *noun*
la **alubia** *fem*, la **judía** *fem*
baked beans alubias en salsa de tomate
green beans judías verdes

bear *noun* ▷ see **bear** *verb*
el **oso** *masc*

to **bear** *verb* ▷ see **bear** *noun*
1 **soportar** [17]
I can't bear him. No lo soporto.
I can't bear the idea. No soporto la idea.
2 to bear something in mind tener [9] algo en cuenta
I'll bear it in mind. Lo tendré en cuenta.

beard *noun*
la **barba** *fem*

bearded *adjective*
barbudo *masc*, **barbuda** *fem*

bearings *plural noun*
to get your bearings orientarse [17]

beast *noun*
(*animal*) la **bestia** *fem*
You beast! ¡Bruto!

beat *noun* ▷ see **beat** *verb*
el **ritmo** *masc*

to **beat** *verb* ▷ see **beat** *noun*
1 (*to defeat*) **ganarle a** [17]
We beat them! ¡Les hemos ganado!
He beat me at chess. Me ganó al ajedrez.
You can't beat a good meal. No hay nada mejor que una buena comida.
2 (*to hit repeatedly*) **golpear** [17]
3 (*eggs, a cake mixture*) **batir** [19]
• **to beat somebody up**
darle [4] **una paliza a alguien** (*informal*)

beautician *noun*
el & la **esteticista** *masc & fem*

beautiful *adjective*
precioso *masc*, **preciosa** *fem*
a beautiful day un día precioso
How beautiful! ¡Qué precioso!

beautifully *adverb*
maravillosamente

beauty *noun*
la **belleza** *fem*
• **beauty spot** (*for tourists*) el lugar pintoresco

because *conjunction*
porque
Because it's you. Porque eres tú.
Because it's cold. Porque hace frío.
because of a causa de
because of the accident a causa del accidente

to **become** *verb*
1 **hacerse** [7]
I want to become a lawyer. Quiero hacerme abogado.
She became famous. Se hizo famosa.
We became friends. Nos hicimos amigos.
2 (*become + adjective*) to become bored aburrirse [19]
to become tired cansarse [17]

WORD TIP *become* with an adjective is often translated by a reflexive verb, with *se*, in Spanish.

bed *noun*
1 (*for sleeping in*) la **cama** *fem*
a double bed una cama de matrimonio
a single bed una cama individual
in bed en la cama
to go to bed ir [8] a la cama
She went to bed at nine o'clock. Se fue a la cama a las nueve., Se acostó a las nueve.
2 (*flower bed*) el **macizo** *masc*
• **bedclothes** la ropa de cama

bedding *noun*
la **ropa de cama**

bedroom *noun*
la **habitación** *fem*
my bedroom window la ventana de mi habitación

bedside table *noun*
la **mesilla de noche**

bedsit *noun*
la **habitación amueblada de aquiler**

bedspread *noun*
la **colcha** *fem*

bedtime *noun*
It's bedtime. Es hora de acostarse.

bee *noun*
la **abeja** *fem*

beech *noun*
el **haya** *fem*

WORD TIP *haya* takes *el* or *un* in the singular even though it is fem.

beef *noun*
la **carne de vaca**

beefburger *noun*
la **hamburguesa** *fem*

beer *noun*
la **cerveza** *fem*
Two beers please. Dos cervezas, por favor.
• **beer can** la lata de cerveza

beetle *noun*
el **escarabajo** *masc*

beetroot *noun*
la **remolacha** *fem*

before *adverb, preposition*
▷ see **before** *conj*
1 (*ahead of*) **antes de**
before Monday antes del lunes
before somebody antes que alguien
He left before me. Se fue antes que yo.
the day before el día anterior
the day before the wedding el día anterior a la boda
the day before yesterday anteayer
the week before la semana anterior
2 (*already*) **ya**
I've seen him before somewhere. Ya le he visto en algún sitio.
I had seen the film before. Ya había visto la película.
She'd never tried before. Nunca lo había intentado antes.

before *conjunction* ▷ see **before** *adv, prep*
1 **antes de**
before doing something antes de hacer algo
I closed the windows before leaving. Cerré las ventanas antes de salir.
Phone before you leave. Llámame antes de salir.
2 **antes de que**
Phone me before they leave. Llámame antes de que salgan.
Oh, before I forget ... Ah, antes de que se me olvide ...

WORD TIP *antes de que* is followed by a verb in the subjunctive.

beforehand *adverb*
antes
Phone beforehand. Llama antes.

to **beg** *verb*
1 (*to ask for money*) **mendigar** [28]
2 (*to ask someone to do something*) **suplicarle a** [31]
She begged me not to leave. Me suplicó que no me marchase.

to **begin** *verb*
1 **empezar** [25]
the words beginning with P las palabras que empiezan con P
The meeting begins at ten. La reunión empieza a las diez.
2 **to begin to do something** empezar a hacer algo
I'm beginning to understand. Empiezo a comprender.

beginner *noun*
el & la **principiante** *masc & fem*

beginning *noun*
1 (*start*) el **principio** *masc*
at the beginning al principio
at the beginning of the holidays al principio de las vacaciones
2 (*with a 'day', 'week', 'month', 'year'*) **at the beginning of** a principios de
at the beginning of the month a principios de mes

behalf *noun*
on behalf of en nombre de

to **behave** *verb*
portarse [17]
He behaved badly. Se portó mal.
to behave yourself portarse bien
Behave yourselves! ¡Portaos bien!

behaviour *noun*
el **comportamiento** *masc*

behind *adverb* ▷ see **behind** *noun, prep*
1 (*to the back*) **detrás**
the car behind el coche de detrás
You go behind. Tú vas detrás.
2 (*where you were*) **to leave something behind** olvidarse [17] algo
I've left my keys behind. Me he olvidado las llaves.
to stay behind quedarse [17]
3 (*not making progress*) **He's behind in class.** Va retrasado en clase.

behind *noun* ▷ see **behind** *adv, prep*
el **trasero** *masc*

behind *preposition* ▷ see **behind** *adv, noun*
detrás de
behind the sofa detrás del sofá
behind them detrás de ellos

beige *adjective*
beige *invariable adj*
beige socks calcetines beige

Belgian *adjective & noun*
1 **belga** *masc & fem*
2 (*person*) **un & una belga** *masc & fem*
the Belgians los belgas

WORD TIP Adjectives and nouns for nationality and regional origin do not have capital letters in Spanish.

Belgium *noun*
Bélgica *fem*

belief *noun*
la **creencia** *fem*
his political beliefs sus creencias políticas

to **believe** *verb*
1 **creer** [37]
I believe you. Te creo.
They believed what I said. Se creyeron lo que dije.
I don't believe you! ¡No te creo!
2 **to believe in something** creer en algo
Do you believe in ghosts. ¿Crees en fantasmas?
I believe in God. Creo en Dios.

bell *noun*
1 (*in a church*) la **campana** *fem*
2 (*on a door*) el **timbre** *masc*
Ring the bell! ¡Toca el timbre!
3 (*for a cat, a toy*) el **cascabel** *masc*

to **belong** *verb*
1 (*showing ownership*) **to belong to someone** ser [1] de alguien
That belongs to Lucy. Eso es de Lucy.
2 **to belong to a club** pertenecer [35] a un club
3 (*in a particular place*) **ir** [8]
That chair belongs in the study. Esa silla va en el estudio.
Where does this vase belong? ¿Adónde va este jarrón?

belongings *plural noun*
las **pertenencias** *fem pl*
All my belongings are in London. Todas mis pertenencias están en Londres.

below *adverb* ▷ see **below** *prep*
abajo
the flat below el piso de abajo
Shouts came from below. Se oyeron gritos abajo.

below *preposition* ▷ see **below** *adv*
debajo de
below the window debajo de la ventana
the flat below yours el piso de debajo del tuyo

belt *noun*
el **cinturón** *masc*

bench *noun*
el **banco** *masc*

bend *noun* ▷ see **bend** *verb*
(*in a road, river*) la **curva** *fem*

to **bend** *verb* ▷ see **bend** *noun*
1 (*your arm, your leg, a wire*) **doblar** [17]
2 (*roads, paths, rivers*) **torcer** [41]
The road bends to the right. La carretera tuerce a la derecha.
3 (*people*) **to bend down** agacharse [17]
She bent down to look. Se agachó para mirar.

beneath *preposition*
bajo

benefit *noun*
el **beneficio** *masc*
unemployment benefit el subsidio de desempleo

bent *adjective*
doblado *masc*, **doblada** *fem*

beret *noun*
la **boina** *fem*

berry *noun*
la **baya** *fem*

berth *noun*
la **litera** *fem*

beside *preposition*
(*next to*) **al lado de**
It's beside the table. Está al lado de la mesa.
She was sitting beside me. Estaba sentada a mi lado.

besides *adverb*
además
Besides, it's too late. Además, es demasiado tarde.
four dogs, and six cats besides cuatro perros y además seis gatos

best *adjective* ▷ see **best** *adv*
mejor *masc & fem*
the best song on the album la mejor canción del álbum
It's the best. Es el mejor.
That's the best car. Ese coche es el mejor.
She's my best friend. Es mi mejor amiga.
She's the best at tennis. Es la mejor jugando al tenis.
He's the best at English. Es el mejor en inglés.
The best thing to do is to phone them. Lo mejor es llamarlos por teléfono.
It's the best I can do. Es lo más que puedo hacer.
I did my best to help her. Hice todo lo posible para ayudarla.
- **best man** el padrino de boda

best *adverb* ▷ see **best** *adj*
mejor
best of all lo mejor de todo
He plays best. Es el que mejor juega.
I like Barcelona best. Barcelona es la ciudad que más me gusta.

bet *noun* ▷ see **bet** *verb*
la **apuesta** *fem*

to **bet** *verb* ▷ see **bet** *noun*
apostar [24]
to bet on a horse apostar por un caballo
I bet you he'll forget! ¡Te apuesto algo a que se le olvida!

better *adjective* ▷ see **better** *adv*
1 (*in comparisons*) **mejor** *masc & fem*
She's found a better flat. Ha encontrado un piso mejor.
This road's better than the other one. Esta calle es mejor que la otra.
This pen writes better. Esta pluma escribe mejor.
even better todavía mejor
better still todavía mejor, aún mejor
It's even better than before. Es todavía mejor que antes.
2 (*less bad*) **to get better** mejorar **[17]**
My Spanish is getting better. Mi español está mejorando.
so much the better mucho mejor
the sooner the better cuanto antes mejor
3 (*less ill*) **to be better** estar **[2]** mejor
to feel better sentirse **[14]** mejor
I feel better today. Hoy me siento mejor.
I hope you get better soon. Espero que te mejores pronto.

better *adverb* ▷ see **better** *adj*
I, you, she, etc had better más vale que + *subjunctive*
You'd better phone at once. Más vale que llames ahora mismo.
He'd better not go. Más vale que no vaya.
I'd better go now. Más vale que me vaya ahora.

better off *adjective*
1 (*richer*) **They're better off than us.** Tienen más dinero que nosotros.
2 (*more comfortable*) **mejor** *masc & fem*
You'd be better off in bed. Estarás mejor en la cama.

between *preposition*
entre
between London and Dover entre Londres y Dover
between you and me entre tú y yo
I'll go sometime between Monday and Friday. Iré entre el lunes y el viernes.
It's closed between 2 and 5. Está cerrado de dos a cinco.

to **beware** *verb*
Beware of the dog! ¡Cuidado con el perro!

beyond *preposition*
1 (*in space and time*) **beyond the border** más allá de la frontera
2 (*too complicated for*) **It's beyond me!** ¡No lo entiendo!

Bible *noun*
(*Religion*) **the Bible** la Biblia

bicycle *noun*,
la **bicicleta** *fem*
by bicycle en bicicleta
- **bicycle lane** el carril de bicicletas
- **bicycle pump** la bomba de bicicleta

big *adjective*
1 (*large*) **grande** *masc & fem*
a big house una casa grande
big cities ciudades grandes
It's too big for me. Es demasiado grande para mí.
a big disappointment una gran desilusión

2 (*older*) **mayor** *masc & fem*
my big sister mi hermana mayor
Big Brother el Gran Hermano

WORD TIP *grande* becomes *gran* when it comes before a singular noun.

bigheaded *adjective*
creído *masc*, **creída** *fem*
to be bigheaded ser [1] un creído, *fem* una creída

big screen *noun*
la **pantalla grande**

big toe *noun*
el **dedo gordo del pie**

bike *noun*
1 (*with pedals*) la **bici** *fem*
I go to school by bike. Voy en bici al colegio.
We went for a bike ride. Fuimos a dar una vuelta en bici.
2 (*with a motor*) la **moto** *fem*
We went to the cinema by bike. Fuimos al cine en moto.
She took me into town on her bike. Me llevó al centro en su moto.

bikini *noun*
el **bikini** *masc*

bilingual *adjective*
bilingüe *masc & fem*

bill *noun*
1 (*in a restaurant*) la **cuenta** *fem*
Can I have the bill, please? ¿Me trae la cuenta por favor?
2 (*for gas, electricity, in a hotel*) la **factura** *fem*

billiards *noun*
el **billar** *masc*
to play billiards jugar [27] al billar

billion *noun*
los **mil millones** *masc plural*

bin *noun*
1 (*dustbin*) el **cubo de la basura**
2 (*wastepaper bin*) la **papelera** *fem*

binoculars *plural noun*
los **prismáticos** *masc plural*

biochemistry *noun*
la **bioquímica** *fem*

biography *noun*
la **biografía** *fem*

biologist *noun*
el **biólogo** *masc*, la **bióloga** *fem*

biology *noun*
la **biología** *fem*

bird *noun*
1 (*small*) el **pájaro** *masc*
2 (*large*) el **ave** *fem*

WORD TIP *ave* takes *el* and *un* in the singular even though it is fem.

- **bird flu** la gripe aviar

birdwatching *noun*
to go birdwatching ir [8] a observar pájaros

Biro® *noun*
el **boli** *masc*

birth *noun*
el **nacimiento** *masc*
- **birth certificate** el certificado de nacimiento
- **birth control** el control de la natalidad

birthday *noun*
el **cumpleaños** *masc, pl:* los **cumpleaños**
a birthday present un regalo de cumpleaños
Happy birthday! ¡Feliz cumpleaños!

WORD TIP *cumpleaños* does not change in the plural.

- **birthday cake** la tarta de cumpleaños
- **birthday card** la tarjeta de cumpleaños
- **birthday party** la fiesta de cumpleaños

biscuit *noun*
la **galleta** *fem*

bishop *noun*
el **obispo** *masc*

bit *noun*
1 (*small piece*) el **trozo** *masc*
a bit of string un trozo de cordón
a bit of chocolate un trozo de chocolate
a bit of news una noticia
a bit of advice un consejo
to fall to bits hacerse [7] pedazos
2 (*in a book, film*) la **parte** *fem*
This bit's brilliant! ¡Esta parte es genial!
3 (*small quantity*) **a bit** un poco
a bit of something un poco de algo
a bit of sugar un poco de azúcar
with a bit of luck con un poco de suerte
Wait a bit! ¡Espera un poco!
bit by bit poco a poco
4 (*rather*) **a bit hot** un poco caliente
a bit early un poco pronto
5 (*for a horse*) el **bocado** *masc*

bite *noun* ▷ see **bite** *verb*
1 (*snack*) el **bocado** *masc*
I'll just have a bite before I go. Voy a tomar un bocado antes de irme. ▸▸

English–Spanish
a b c d e f g h i j k l m n o p q r s t u v w x y z

English-Spanish
a b c d e f g h i j k l m n o p q r s t u v w x y z

2 (*insect's*) la **picadura** *fem*
a mosquito bite una picadura de mosquito
3 (*dog's*) el **mordisco** *masc*
It gave me a bite. Me dio un mordisco.

to **bite** *verb* ▷ see **bite** *noun*
1 (*people, dogs*) **morder** [38]
to bite your nails morderse las uñas
2 (*insects*) **picar** [31]

bitter *adjective*
(*taste*) **amargo** *masc*, **amarga** *fem*

black *adjective*
1 (*in colour*) **negro** *masc*, **negra** *fem*
my black jacket mi chaqueta negra
a black coffee un café solo
to turn black volverse [45] negro
2 (*person*) a Black man un negro
a Black woman una negra
- **blackberry** la mora *fem*
- **blackbird** el mirlo *masc*
- **blackboard** la pizarra *fem*
- **blackcurrant** la grosella negra
- **black eye** el ojo morado

blackmail *noun* ▷ see **blackmail** *verb*
el **chantaje** *masc*

to **blackmail** *verb* ▷ see **blackmail** *noun*
chantajear [1]

black pudding *noun*
la **morcilla** *fem*

blade *noun*
la **hoja** *fem*

blame *noun* ▷ see **blame** *verb*
la **culpa** *fem*
to put the blame on somebody echarle [17] la culpa a alguien
to take the blame for something asumir [19] la responsabilidad de algo

to **blame** *verb* ▷ see **blame** *noun*
culpar [17]
to blame somebody for something culpar a alguien de algo
They blamed him for the accident. Lo culparon por el accidente.
She is to blame for it. Ella tiene la culpa.
I blame the parents! ¡Yo culpo a los padres!
I don't blame you! ¡No me extraña!

blank *noun* ▷ see **blank** *adj*
(*on forms*) el **espacio en blanco**

blank *adjective* ▷ see **blank** *noun*
1 (*page, cheque, screen*) **en blanco**
2 (*tape, disk*) **virgen**
3 My mind went blank. Me quedé en blanco.

blanket *noun*
la **manta** *fem*

blast *noun*
1 (*explosion*) la **explosión** *fem*
2 (*of air*) la **ráfaga** *fem*
3 at full blast: to play music at full blast poner [11] la música a todo volumen

blaze *noun* ▷ see **blaze** *verb*
el **incendio** *masc*

to **blaze** *verb* ▷ see **blaze** *noun*
arder [18]

blazer *noun*
el **blázer** *masc*

bleach *noun*
la **lejía** *fem*

to **bleed** *verb*
sangrar [17]
My nose is bleeding. Me está sangrando la nariz.

blend *noun* ▷ see **blend** *verb*
la **mezcla** *fem*

to **blend** *verb* ▷ see **blend** *noun*
mezclar [17]

blender *noun*
la **licuadora** *fem*

to **bless** *verb*
bendecir [5]
(*after a sneeze*) Bless you! ¡Jesús!

blind *adjective* ▷ see **blind** *noun*
ciego *masc*, **ciega** *fem*
to go blind quedarse [17] ciego (*of a boy*), quedarse [17] ciega (*of a girl*)

blind *noun* ▷ see **blind** *adj*
(*in a window*) la **persiana** *fem*

blindness *noun*
la **ceguera** *fem*

to **blink** *verb*
pestañear [17]

blister *noun*
la **ampolla** *fem*

blizzard *noun*
la **tormenta de nieve**

block *noun* ▷ see **block** *verb*
1 (*of flats, offices*) el **bloque** *masc*
a block of flats un bloque de pisos
an office block un bloque de oficinas
2 (*group of buildings*) la **manzana** *fem*
to take a walk round the block dar [4] la vuelta a la manzana

to **block** *verb* ▷ see **block** *noun*
1 (*an exit, a road*) **bloquear [17]**
2 (*a drain, a hole*) **atascar [31]**
The sink's blocked. El fregadero está atascado.

♪ **blond** *adjective*
rubio *masc*, **rubia** *fem*

♪ **blood** *noun*
la **sangre** *fem*
• **blood test** el análisis de sangre

blossom *noun*
la **flor** *fem*
to be in blossom estar [2] en flor

blot *noun*
el **borrón** *masc*

♪ **blouse** *noun*
la **blusa** *fem*

blow *noun* ▷ see **blow** *verb*
el **golpe** *masc*

♪ to **blow** *verb* ▷ see **blow** *noun*
1 (*winds, people*) **soplar [17]**
2 **to blow off** salir [63] volando
My hat blew off. Mi sombrero salió volando.
to blow away salir [63] volando
The tickets blew away. Los billetes salieron volando.
3 (*in explosions*) **The bomb blew a hole in the wall.** La bomba hizo un agujero en la pared.
4 **to blow your nose** sonarse [24] la nariz
• **to blow something out**
(*a candle, flames*) **apagar [28] algo**
• **to blow up**
(*to explode*) **explotar [17]**
• **to blow something up**
1 (*a balloon, a tyre*) **inflar [17] algo**
2 (*a building, a car*) **hacer [7] volar algo**
They blew up the president's residence. Hicieron volar la residencia del presidente.

blow-dry *noun*
el **brushing** *masc*
to have a blow-dry hacerse [7] el brushing

♪ **blue** *adjective* ▷ see **blue** *noun*
azul *masc & fem*
blue eyes ojos azules

blue *noun* ▷ see **blue** *adj*
el **azul**
• **bluebell** el jacinto silvestre

blunder *noun*
la **metedura de pata**

blunt *adjective*
1 (*knife, scissors*) **desafilado** *masc*, **desafilada** *fem*
2 (*pencil*) **sin punta**
3 (*person*) **directo** *masc*, **directa** *fem*

blurred *adjective*
1 (*vision, image*) **borroso** *masc*, **borrosa** *fem*
2 (*photo*) **movido** *masc*, **movida** *fem*

to **blush** *verb*
ponerse [11] colorado, *fem* **colorada**

board *noun* ▷ see **board** *verb*
1 (*plank*) la **tabla** *fem*
2 (*blackboard*) la **pizarra** *fem*
3 (*notice board*) el **tablón de anuncios**
4 (*for a board game*) el **tablero** *masc*
a chess board un tablero de ajedrez
5 (*accommodation*) **full board** pensión completa
half board media pensión
board and lodging comida y alojamiento
6 (*on a boat, ship, plane*) **on board** a bordo
on board the ferry a bordo del ferry

to **board** *verb* ▷ see **board** *noun*
embarcarse [31]

boarder *noun*
(*at a school*) el **interno** *masc*, la **interna** *fem*

board game *noun*
el **juego de mesa**

boarding card *noun*
la **tarjeta de embarque**

boarding school *noun*
el **internado** *masc*

to **boast** *verb*
presumir [19]
He was boasting about his new bike. Estaba presumiendo de su nueva bici.

♪ **boat** *noun*
1 (*in general*) el **barco** *masc*
2 (*rowing boat*) la **barca** *fem*

♪ **body** *noun*
1 (*of a living person*) el **cuerpo** *masc*
2 (*of a dead person*) el **cadáver** *masc*
• **bodybuilding** el culturismo *masc*
• **bodyguard** el & la guardaespaldas *masc & fem*

boil *noun* ▷ see **boil** *verb*
(*swelling*) el **furúnculo** *masc*

to **boil** *verb* ▷ see **boil** *noun*
1 (*liquids*) **hervir [14]**
The water's boiling. El agua está hirviendo.
I'm going to boil some water. Voy a hervir un poco de agua.
2 (*vegetables, pasta, an egg*) **to boil the vegetables** cocer **[41]** las verduras
to boil an egg cocer un huevo
• **to boil over**
salirse [63]

boiled egg *noun*
el **huevo pasado por agua**

boiler *noun*
1 (*for central heating*) el **calentador** *masc*
2 (*industrial*) la **caldera** *fem*

boiling *adjective*
1 (*water*) **que hierve**
2 (*weather*) **It's boiling hot today!** ¡Hoy hace un calor espantoso!

Bolivia *noun*
Bolivia *fem*

Bolivian *adjective* ▷ see **Bolivian** *noun*
boliviano *masc*, **boliviana** *fem*

Bolivian *noun* ▷ see **Bolivian** *adj*
(*person*) un **boliviano** *masc*, una **boliviana** *fem*
the Bolivians los bolivianos

WORD TIP Adjectives and nouns for nationality and regional origin do not have capital letters in Spanish.

bolt *noun* ▷ see **bolt** *verb*
1 (*large*) el **cerrojo** *masc*
2 (*small*) el **pestillo** *masc*

to **bolt** *verb* ▷ see **bolt** *noun*
(*a door*) **cerrar [29] con cerrojo**

bomb *noun* ▷ see **bomb** *verb*
la **bomba** *fem*

to **bomb** *verb* ▷ see **bomb** *noun*
1 (*from the air*) **bombardear [17]**
2 (*in a terrorist attack*) **lanzar [31] una bomba a**

bombing *noun*
1 (*in a war*) el **bombardeo** *masc*
2 (*a terrorist attack*) el **atentado terrorista**

bone *noun*
1 (*of a person, an animal*) el **hueso** *masc*
2 (*of a fish*) la **espina** *fem*

bonfire *noun*
la **hoguera** *fem*

bonnet *noun*
(*of a car*) el **capó** *masc*

bony *adjective*
1 (*fish*) **lleno de espinas** *masc*, **llena de espinas** *fem*
2 (*body*) **huesudo** *masc*, **huesuda** *fem*

to **boo** *verb*
abuchear [17]
The crowd booed the referee. El público abucheó al árbitro.

♪ **book** *noun* ▷ see **book** *verb*
1 (*that you read*) el **libro** *masc*
a book about dinosaurs un libro sobre los dinosaurios
a biology book un libro de biología
2 (*that you write in*) **an exercise book** un cuaderno
3 (*of tickets, stamps, etc*) **a book of tickets** un taco de billetes
a book of stamps un librito de sellos
• **bookcase** la estantería *fem*

♪ to **book** *verb* ▷ see **book** *noun*
reservar [17]
I booked a table for 8 o'clock. Reservé una mesa para las ocho.

♪ **booking** *noun*
la **reserva** *fem*
• **booking office** la taquilla

♪ **booklet** *noun*
el **folleto** *masc*

bookshelf *noun*
el **estante** *masc*

♪ **bookshop** *noun*
la **librería** *fem*

♪ **boot** *noun*
1 (*item of clothing*) la **bota** *fem*
walking boots botas de montaña
wellington boots botas de agua
2 (*short fashion boot*) el **botín** *masc*
3 (*of a car*) el **maletero** *masc*

border *noun*
(*between countries*) la **frontera** *fem*
We crossed the border at Irún. Cruzamos la frontera en Irún.

bore *noun*
1 (*informal: boring person*) el **pesado** *masc*, la **pesada** *fem*
2 (*informal: nuisance*) **What a bore!** ¡Qué rollo!

bored *adjective*
aburrido *masc*, **aburrida** *fem*
to be bored estar **[2]** aburrido
I'm bored. Estoy aburrido (*boy speaking*)., Estoy aburrida (*girl speaking*).
to get bored aburrirse **[19]**

boring *adjective*
aburrido *masc*, **aburrida** *fem*

to **born** *verb*
to be born nacer [35]
She was born on 1 June. Nació el primero de junio.
I was born in Manchester. Nací en Manchester.

to **borrow** *verb*
Can I borrow your bike? ¿Me prestas tu bici?
to borrow something from someone pedirle [57] algo prestado a alguien
I'll borrow some money from Dad. Le pediré dinero prestado a papá.

boss *noun*
el **jefe** *masc*, la **jefa** *fem*

bossy *adjective*
(*informal*) **mandón** *masc*, **mandona** *fem*

both *pronoun, adjective* ▷ see **both** *conj*
los dos *masc*, **las dos** *fem*
both my feet mis dos pies
They both came. Vinieron los dos.
They've both been sold. Los dos están vendidos.
Both sisters were there. Las dos hermanas estaban allí.

both *conjunction* ▷ see **both** *adj, pron*
both ... and tanto ... como
both at home and at school tanto en casa como en colegio
both in summer and in winter tanto en verano como en el invierno

bother *noun* ▷ see **bother** *verb*
los **problemas** *masc plural*
without any bother sin ningún problema
I've had a lot of bother with the car. He tenido muchos problemas con el coche.
It's no bother. No es ningún problema.
It's too much bother. No merece la pena molestarse.

to **bother** *verb* ▷ see **bother** *noun*
1 (*to disturb*) **molestar** [17]
I'm sorry to bother you. Siento molestarte.
2 (*to worry*) **preocuparse** [17]
That doesn't bother me at all. No me preocupa en absoluto.
Don't bother about dinner. No te preocupes de la cena.
3 (*to take the trouble*) **to bother to do something** molestarse [17]
She didn't even bother to come. Ni siquiera se molestó en venir.
Don't bother! ¡No te molestes!

bottle *noun*
la **botella** *fem*
- **bottle bank** el contenedor de botellas

bottle opener *noun*
el **abrebotellas**, *pl:* los **abrebotellas**

bottom *adjective* ▷ see **bottom** *noun*
1 (*lowest*) **de abajo**
the bottom shelf el estante de abajo
the bottom flat el piso bajo
the bottom sheet la sábana bajera
2 (*team, place*) **último** *masc*, **última** *fem*

bottom *noun* ▷ see **bottom** *adj*
1 (*of a page, a hill, a wall, steps*) el **pie** *masc*
at the bottom of the ladder al pie de la escalera
at the bottom of the page al pie de la página
2 (*of a bag, a hole, a street, etc*) el **fondo** *masc*
at the bottom of the lake en el fondo del lago
3 (*of a list*) el **final** *masc*
4 (*of a bottle*) el **culo** *masc*
5 (*buttocks*) el **trasero** *masc*

to **bounce** *verb*
rebotar [17]

bouncer *noun*
el **gorila** *masc* (*informal*)

bound *adjective*
He's bound to be late. Seguro que llega tarde.
That was bound to happen. Eso tenía que pasar.

boundary *noun*
la **línea divisoria**

bow *noun*
1 (*in a shoelace, ribbon*) el **lazo** *masc*
2 (*for playing the violin, shooting arrows*) el **arco** *masc*

bowl *noun* ▷ see **bowl** *verb*
1 (*for cereal*) el **bol** *masc*
2 (*for mixing food in*) el **cuenco** *masc*
3 (*for washing up*) el **barreño** *masc*
4 (*for salad, fruit*) **a salad bowl** una ensaladera
a fruit bowl un frutero

to **bowl** *verb* ▷ see **bowl** *noun*
(*a ball*) **lanzar** [22]

bowling *noun*
(*tenpins*) los **bolos** *masc plural*
to go bowling ir [8] a jugar a los bolos

bow tie *noun*
la **pajarita** *fem*, el **corbatín** *masc*

box *noun*
1 (*container*) la **caja** *fem*
a box of chocolates una caja de bombones
a cardboard box una caja de cartón
2 (*of matches*) la **cajetilla** *fem*
3 (*on a form*) el **recuadro** *masc*

boxer *noun*
1 (*fighter*) el **boxeador** *masc*
2 (*dog*) el **bóxer** *masc*
• **boxer shorts** los calzoncillos *masc plural*

boxing *noun*
el **boxeo** *masc*
a boxing match un combate de boxeo

Boxing Day *noun*
la **fiesta del 26 de diciembre**

box office *noun*
la **taquilla** *fem*

boy *noun*
el **niño** *masc*
a little boy un niño pequeño
• **boyfriend** el novio *masc*

bra *noun*
el **sujetador** *masc*

brace *noun*
el **aparato de los dientes**

bracelet *noun*
la **pulsera** *fem*

braces *plural noun*
los **tirantes** *masc plural*

bracket *noun*
in brackets entre paréntesis

brain *noun*
el **cerebro** *masc*
• **brainwave** la idea genial

brake *noun* ▷ see **brake** *verb*
el **freno** *masc*

to **brake** *verb* ▷ see **brake** *noun*
frenar [17]

bramble *noun*
la **zarzamora** *fem*

branch *noun*
1 (*of a tree*) la **rama** *fem*
2 (*of a shop, a company, a bank*) la **sucursal** *fem*
our Glasgow branch nuestra sucursal de Glasgow

brand *noun*
la **marca** *fem*

brand-new *adjective*
nuevo *masc*, **nueva** *fem*

brandy *noun*
el **coñac** *masc*

brass *noun*
1 (*the metal*) el **latón** *masc*
a brass candlestick un candelabro dorado
2 (*in an orchestra*) **the brass** los metales
• **brass band** la banda de música

Brazil *noun*
Brasil *masc*

Brazilian *adjective & noun*
1 **brasileño** *masc*, **brasileña** *fem*
2 (*person*) un **brasileño** *masc*, una **brasileña** *fem*
the Brazilians los brasileños *masc pl*

WORD TIP Adjectives and nouns for nationality and regional origin do not have capital letters in Spanish.

brave *adjective*
valiente *masc & fem*

bread *noun*
el **pan** *masc*
a slice of bread una rebanada de pan

break *noun* ▷ see **break** *verb*
1 (*short rest*) el **descanso** *masc*
a fifteen-minute break un descanso de quince minutos
to take a break descansar [17] un rato
the Christmas break las vacaciones de Navidad
2 (*in school*) el **recreo** *masc*

to **break** *verb* ▷ see **break** *noun*
romper [40]
He broke a glass. Rompió un vaso.
to break your leg romperse una pierna
I broke my arm. Me rompí un brazo.
to break your promise romper una promesa
to break the rules infringir [49] las reglas
You mustn't break the rules. No debes infringir las reglas.
to break a record batir [19] un récord
to break the news dar [4] la noticia
• to **break down** **averiarse** [17]
The car broke down. El coche se estropeó
• to **break in** The thief broke in through the window. El ladrón entró a robar por la ventana.
The house was broken into. Entraron ladrones en la casa.
• to **break out**
1 (*fires*) **declararse** [17]
2 (*wars, storms*) **estallar** [17]
3 (*prisoners*) **escaparse** [17]
• to **break up**
1 (*family*) **separarse** [17]

2 (*couples*) **romper** [40]
3 (*crowds, clouds*) **dispersarse** [17]
4 (*for the holidays*) **We break up on Thursday.** Empezamos las vacaciones el jueves.

breakdown *noun*
1 (*of a vehicle*) la **avería** *fem*
We had a breakdown on the motorway. Tuvimos una avería en la autopista.
2 (*in talks, negotiations*) la **ruptura** *fem*
3 (*nervous collapse*) la **crisis nerviosa**
to have a (nervous) breakdown sufrir [19] una crisis nerviosa
• **breakdown truck** la grúa

breakfast *noun*
el **desayuno** *masc*
to have breakfast desayunar [17]
We have breakfast at eight. Desayunamos a las ocho.

break-in *noun*
el **robo** *masc*

breast *noun*
1 (*a woman's*) el **pecho** *masc*
2 (*of chicken, of turkey*) la **pechuga** *fem*

breaststroke *noun*
la **braza** *fem*

breath *noun*
el **aliento** *masc*
out of breath sin aliento
to get one's breath recobrar [17] el aliento
to take a deep breath respirar [17] hondo

to **breathe** *verb*
respirar [17]

breathing *noun*
la **respiración** *fem*

breed *noun* ▷ see **breed** *verb*
la **raza** *fem*

to **breed** *verb* ▷ see **breed** *noun*
1 (*animals*) **criar** [32]
2 (*to have babies*) **reproducirse** [60]
Rabbits breed fast. Los conejos se reproducen mucho.

breeze *noun*
la **brisa** *fem*

brewery *noun*
la **cervezería** *fem*

bribe *noun* ▷ see **bribe** *verb*
el **soborno** *masc*

to **bribe** *verb* ▷ see **bribe** *noun*
sobornar [17]

brick *noun*
el **ladrillo** *masc*
a brick wall una pared de ladrillo

bride *noun*
la **novia** *fem*
the bride and groom los novios, el novio y la novia

bridegroom *noun*
el **novio** *masc*

bridesmaid *noun*
la **dama de honor**

bridge *noun*
1 (*over a river*) el **puente** *masc*
a bridge over the Thames un puente sobre el Támesis
2 (*card game*) el **bridge** *masc*
to play bridge jugar [27] al bridge

bridle *noun*
la **brida** *fem*

brief *adjective*
breve *masc & fem*

briefcase *noun*
el **maletín** *masc*

briefly *adverb*
brevemente

briefs *plural noun*
los **calzoncillos** *masc plural*

bright *adjective*
1 (*star, light*) **brillante** *masc & fem*
bright sunshine un sol radiante
2 (*colour*) **vivo** *masc*, **viva** *fem*
bright green socks calcetines de un verde vivo
3 (*clever*) **inteligente** *masc & fem*
She's not very bright. No es muy inteligente.

to **brighten up** *verb*
The weather's brightening up. El tiempo está aclarando.

brilliant *adjective*
1 (*very clever*) **brillante** *masc & fem*
a brilliant surgeon un brillante cirujano
He's brilliant at maths. Es genial para las matemáticas.
2 (*wonderful*) **fenomenal** *masc & fem*
The party was brilliant! ¡La fiesta estuvo fenomenal!

♪ to **bring** *verb*
traer [42]
They brought a present. Trajeron un regalo.
Bring your camera. Trae tu cámara.
It brings good luck. Trae buena suerte.
She's bringing all the children. Trae a todos los niños.
I'll bring the shopping in. Voy a entrar las compras.
- to **bring something back**
devolver [45] **algo**
- to **bring up**
(*children*) **criar** [32]
He was brought up by his aunt. Lo crió su tía.

bristle *noun*
la **cerda** *fem*

Britain *noun*
Gran Bretaña *fem*

♪ **British** *adjective* ▷ see **British** *plural noun*
británico *masc*, **británica** *fem*
the British Isles las islas británicas

♪ **British** *plural noun* ▷ see **British** *adj*
(*the people*) **the British** los británicos *masc plural*

WORD TIP Adjectives and nouns for nationality and regional origin do not have capital letters in Spanish.

broad *adjective*
(*wide*) **ancho** *masc*, **ancha** *fem*
- **broad bean** el haba *fem*

WORD TIP *haba* takes *el* or *un* in the singular even though it is fem.

♪ **broadcast** *noun* ▷ see **broadcast** *verb*
la **emisión** *fem*

♪ to **broadcast** *verb* ▷ see **broadcast** *noun*
(*a programme*) **emitir** [19]

broccoli *noun*
el **brécol** *masc*

♪ **brochure** *noun*
el **folleto** *masc*

broke *adjective*
to be broke no tener [9] un duro (*informal*)

broken *adjective*
roto *masc*, **rota** *fem*
to have a broken leg tener [9] una pierna rota
The window's broken. La ventana está rota.

bronchitis *noun*
la **bronquitis** *fem*

bronze *adjective* ▷ see **bronze** *noun*
de bronce

bronze *noun* ▷ see **bronze** *adj*
el **bronce** *masc*

brooch *noun*
el **broche** *masc*

broom *noun*
(*for sweeping*) la **escoba** *fem*

♪ **brother** *noun*
el **hermano** *masc*
my little brother mi hermanito
My brother's fifteen. Mi hermano tiene quince año.
- **brother-in-law** el cuñado *masc*

♪ **brown** *adjective*
1 (*in colour*) **marrón** *masc & fem*
brown shoes zapatos marrón
2 (*hair, eyes*) **castaño** *masc*, **castaña** *fem*
3 (*tanned in the sun*) **moreno** *masc*, **morena** *fem*
to go brown ponerse [11] moreno, *fem* morena
- **brown bread** el pan integral
- **brown sugar** el azúcar moreno

browser *noun*
el **navegador** *masc*

bruise *noun*
1 (*on a person*) el **moretón** *masc*
2 (*on fruit*) la **magulladura** *fem*

♪ **brush** *noun* ▷ see **brush** *verb*
1 (*for hair, clothes, nails, shoes*) el **cepillo** *masc*
my hair brush mi cepillo del pelo
2 (*for sweeping*) la **escoba** *fem*
3 (*paintbrush*) la **brocha** *fem*

♪ to **brush** *verb* ▷ see **brush** *noun*
1 (*your hair, shoes*) **cepillar** [17]
to brush your hair cepillarse el pelo
She brushed her hair. Se cepilló el pelo.
2 (*your teeth*) **to brush your teeth** limpiarse [17] los dientes
I'm going to brush my teeth. Voy a limpiarme los dientes.

Brussels *noun*
Bruselas *fem*
- **Brussels sprouts** las coles de Bruselas

bubble *noun*
la **burbuja** *fem*
- **bubble bath** el gel de baño
- **bubblegum** el chicle (de globos)

bucket *noun*
el **cubo** *masc*

buckle *noun*
la **hebilla** *fem*

bud *noun*
el **brote** *masc*

Buddhism *noun*
el **budismo** *masc*

Buddhist *noun*
un & una **budista** *masc & fem*

WORD TIP Adjectives and nouns for religion do not have capital letters in Spanish.

budget *noun*
el **presupuesto** *masc*

budgie *noun*
el **periquito** *masc*

buffet *noun*
1 (*on a train*) el **bar** *masc*
2 (*meal*) el **buffet** *masc*
- **buffet car** el coche restaurante

bug *noun*
1 (*informal: insect*) el **bicho** *masc*
2 (*virus*) el **virus** *masc*
a stomach bug un virus en el estómago

to **build** *verb*
construir [54]

builder *noun*
el & la **albañil** *masc & fem*

building *noun*
el **edificio** *masc*
- **building site** el solar
- **building society** la sociedad de crédito hipotecario

built-in *adjective*
empotrado *masc*, **empotrada** *fem*

built-up *adjective*
urbanizado *masc*, **urbanizada** *fem*
a built-up area una zona urbanizada

bulb *noun*
1 (*for a light*) la **bombilla** *fem*
2 (*in gardening*) el **bulbo** *masc*

bulky *adjective*
voluminoso *masc*, **voluminosa** *fem*

bull *noun*
el **toro** *masc*
- **bulldozer** el bulldozer *masc*

bullet *noun*
la **bala** *fem*

bulletin *noun*
el **boletín** *masc*
a news bulletin un boletín de noticias

bullfight *noun*
la **corrida de toros**

mini-info **bullfights**

This Spanish custom, also popular in some Latin American countries, typically takes place on a Sunday afternoon at 5 o'clock. The season lasts from March to October. A recent law makes it illegal for children under 14 to attend a bullfight.

bullfighter *noun*
el **torero** *masc*, la **torera** *fem*

bullfighting *noun*
los toros
Do you like bullfighting? ¿Te gustan los toros?

bullring *noun*
la **plaza de toros**

bully *noun* ▷ see **bully** *verb*
el **bravucón** *masc*, la **bravucona** *fem*
He's a bully. Es un bravucón.

to **bully** *verb* ▷ see **bully** *noun*
intimidar [17]

bum *noun*
el **trasero** *masc* (*informal*)

bump *noun* ▷ see **bump** *verb*
1 (*on the head*) el **chichón** *masc*
2 (*in the road*) el **bache** *masc*
3 (*jolt*) la **sacudida** *fem*
4 (*noise*) el **golpe** *masc*

to **bump** *verb* ▷ see **bump** *noun*
1 (*to bang*) **darse [4] un golpe**
I bumped my head. Me di un golpe en la cabeza.
2 **to bump into something** chocarse **[31]** con algo
I bumped into the table. Me choqué con la mesa.
3 **to bump into somebody** encontrarse **[24]** con alguien
I bumped into Tom. Me encontré con Tom.

bumper *noun*
el **parachoques** *masc*, *pl:* los **parachoques**

bumpy *adjective*
1 (*road*) **lleno de baches** *masc*, **llena de baches** *fem*
2 (*ride, plane landing*) **con muchas sacudidas**

bun *noun*
1 (*small cake*) el **bollo** *masc*
2 (*for a burger*) el **panecillo** *masc*

bunch *noun*
1 (*of flowers*) el **ramo** *masc*
2 (*of carrots, radishes, keys*) el **manojo** *masc*
3 (*of grapes*) **a bunch of grapes** un racimo de uvas

bundle *noun*
1 (*of clothes*) el **fardo** *masc*
2 (*of papers, letters*) el **paquete** *masc*

bungalow *noun*
la **casa de una planta**

bunk *noun*
la **litera** *fem*
• **bunk beds** las literas

bureau de change *noun*
la **casa de cambio**

burger *noun*
la **hamburguesa** *fem*

burglar *noun*
el **ladrón** *masc*, la **ladrona** *fem*
• **burglar alarm** la alarma antirrobo

burglary *noun*
el **robo** *masc*

burn *noun* ▷ see **burn** *verb*
la **quemadura** *fem*

to **burn** *verb* ▷ see **burn** *noun*
1 **quemar** [17]
I've burned the letters. He quemado las cartas.
She burnt herself on the grill. Se quemó en la parrilla.
You'll burn your finger! ¡Te vas a quemar el dedo!
Mum's burnt her cake. A mamá se le ha quemado el pastel.
2 (*woodland, scrub*) **arder** [18]
The forest has been burning for two days. El bosque arde desde hace dos días.
3 (*in the sun*) **quemarse**
I burn easily. Me quemo fácilmente.

burnt *adjective*
quemado *masc*, **quemada** *fem*

to **burst** *verb*
1 (*balloons*) **estallar** [17]
2 (*tyres, pipes*) **reventar** [29]
The tyre burst. Reventó el neumático.
3 **to burst out laughing** echarse [17] a reír
to burst into tears echarse [17] a llorar
to burst into flames empezar [25] a arder

to **bury** *verb*
enterrar [29]

bus *noun*
1 (*in town*) el **autobús** *masc*, el **bus** *masc*
by bus en el autobús
on the bus en el autobús
a bus ticket un billete de autobús
to take the bus tomar [17] el autobús
I go to school by bus. Voy al colegio en el autobús.
We missed the bus. Perdimos el autobús.
2 (*for long distances*) el **autocar** *masc*
to go to London by bus ir [8] a Londres en autocar
• **bus driver** el conductor de autobús, la conductora de autobús

bush *noun*
el **arbusto** *masc*

business *noun*
1 (*commercial dealings*) los **negocios** *masc plural*
a business letter una carta de negocios
He's in Leeds on business. Está en Leeds de viaje de negocios.
2 (*firm, company*) la **empresa** *fem*
small businesses las pequeñas empresas
3 (*concern*) **Mind your own business!** ¡No te metas en lo que no te importa!
That's my business! ¡Eso es asunto mío!
• **business class** la clase preferente
• **businessman** el hombre de negocios
• **business trip** el viaje de negocios
• **businesswoman** la mujer de negocios

bus lane *noun*
el **carril bus**

bus pass *noun*
el **abono de autobús**

bus route *noun*
la **línea de autobús**

bus shelter *noun*
la **marquesina** *fem*

bus station *noun*
la **estación de autobuses**

bus stop *noun*
la **parada de autobús**

bust *noun*
el **busto** *masc*

busy *adjective*
1 (*person*) **ocupado** *masc*, **ocupada** *fem*
Don't disturb him, he's busy. No lo molestes, está ocupado.
to be busy doing something estar [2] ocupado, *fem* ocupada haciendo algo
She's busy painting the kitchen. Está ocupada pintando la cocina.

2 (*day, week*) **ajetreado** *masc*, **ajetreada** *fem*
a very busy day un día muy ajetreado
3 (*station, airport, market, shop*) **muy concurrido** *masc*, **muy concurrida** *fem*
The shops were busy. Las tiendas estaban muy concurridas.
4 (*phones*) **The line's busy.** Está comunicando.

but *conjunction, preposition*
1 (*however*) **pero**
small but strong pequeño pero fuerte
I'll try, but it's difficult. Lo intentaré, pero es difícil.
2 (*to show contradiction*) **not ... but ...** no ... sino ...
not Thursday but Friday no el jueves sino el viernes
3 (*except*) **menos**
anything but that cualquier cosa menos eso
everyone but Leah todos menos Leah
the last but one el penúltimo

butcher *noun*
el **carnicero** *masc*, la **carnicera** *fem*
the butcher's la carnicería

butter *noun* ▷ see **butter** *verb*
la **mantequilla** *fem*
- **buttercup** el botón de oro
- **butterfly** la mariposa

to **butter** *verb* ▷ see **butter** *noun*
untar [17] con mantequilla

button *noun*
el **botón** *masc*
the record button el botón de grabar
- **buttonhole** el ojal

buy *noun* ▷ see **buy** *verb*
a good buy una buena compra
a bad buy una mala compra

to **buy** *verb* ▷ see **buy** *noun*
comprar [17]
I bought the cinema tickets. Compré las entradas para el cine.
to buy something for somebody comprarle algo a alguien
Sarah bought him a sweater. Sarah le compró un jersey.
to buy something from someone comprarle algo a alguien
He bought his bike from Tim. Le compró su bici a Tom .

buyer *noun*
el **comprador** *masc*, la **compradora** *fem*

to **buzz** *verb*
zumbar [17]

buzzer *noun*
el **timbre** *masc*

by *preposition*
1 (*saying how something happens*) **por**
by telephone por teléfono
eaten by a dog comido por un perro
by mistake por equivocación
He got in by the window. Entró por la ventana.
2 (*saying how you do something*) **by bike** en bicicleta
to come by bus venir **[15]** en autobús
to leave by train salir **[63]** en tren
to pay by the hour pagar **[28]** por horas
3 (*saying where something is*) **al lado de**
by the fire al lado del fuego
by the sea al lado del mar
close by cerca
4 (*with time limits*) **para**
It'll be ready by Monday. Estará listo para el lunes.
Kevin was back by four. Kevin estaba de vuelta para las cuatro.
They should have finished by now. Ya deberían haber terminado.
5 (*saying who did something*) **por**
written by Neruda escrito por Neruda
She did it by herself. Lo hizo sola.
6 (*in expressions*)
by the way por cierto
by myself: I was by myself in the house. Estaba solo en la casa. (*boy speaking*)
to take somebody by the hand coger **[3]** a alguien de la mano
to measure two metres by four medir **[57]** dos metros por cuatro

bye *exclamation*
adiós
Bye for now! ¡Hasta luego!

bypass *noun*
la **carretera de circunvalación**

C c

cab *noun*
1 el **taxi** *masc*
to call a cab llamar **[17]** un taxi
2 (*on a lorry*) la **cabina** *fem*

cabbage *noun*
el **repollo** *masc*

cabin *noun*
1 (*on a lorry, plane*) la **cabina** *fem*
2 (*on a ship*) el **camarote** *masc*

cable *noun*
el **cable** *masc*
- **cable car** el teleférico
- **cable television** la televisión por cable

cactus *noun*
el **cactus** *masc*

cafe *noun*
la **cafetería** *fem*

cafetière *noun*
la **cafetera de émbolo**

cage *noun*
la **jaula** *fem*

cagoule *noun*
el **canguro** *masc*

cake *noun*
el **pastel** *masc*
Would you like a piece of cake? ¿Quieres un trozo de pastel?
- **cake shop** la pastelería

to **calculate** *verb*
calcular [17]

calculation *noun*
el **cálculo** *masc*

calculator *noun*
la **calculadora** *fem*

calendar *noun*
el **calendario** *masc*

calf *noun*
1 (*animal*) el **ternero** *masc*, la **ternera** *fem*
2 (*of your leg*) la **pantorrilla** *fem*

to **call** *verb* ▷ see **call** *noun*
1 (*to telephone*) **llamar [17]**
to call a taxi llamar un taxi
to call the doctor llamar al médico
Call this number. Llama a este número.
Thank you for calling. Gracias por su llamada.
I'll call you back later. Te llamo más tarde.
2 (*to name*) **llamar**
They call him Billy. Le llaman Billy.
They've called the baby Julie. Le han puesto Julie al bebé.
to be called llamarse **[17]**
What's he called? ¿Cómo se llama?
Her brother is called Dan. Tiene un hermano que se llama Dan.
- to **call in**
pasar [17]
I'll call in on my way back. Pasaré por tu casa cuando vuelva.

call *noun* ▷ see **call** *verb*
(*on the telephone*) la **llamada** *fem*
a phone call una llamada telefónica
to give somebody a call llamar **[17]** a alguien
Thank you for your call. Gracias por su llamada.
I had several calls this morning. Tuve varias llamadas esta mañana.
- **call box** la cabina telefónica

calm *adjective* ▷ see **calm** *noun, verb*
tranquilo *masc*, **tranquila** *fem*
Try to stay calm. Trata de estar tranquilo.

calm *noun* ▷ see **calm** *adj, verb*
la **calma** *fem*

to **calm** *verb* ▷ see **calm** *adj, noun*
calmar [17]
- to **calm down**
calmarse
He's calmed down a bit. Se ha calmado un poco.
- to **calm somebody down**
calmar a alguien
I tried to calm her down. Intenté calmarla.

calmly *adverb*
con calma

calorie *noun*
la **caloría** *fem*

camcorder *noun*
la **videocámara** *fem*

camel *noun*
el **camello** *masc*

camera *noun*
1 (*for photos*) la **cámara de fotos**
2 (*for films, TV*) la **cámara** *fem*
- **cameraman** el & la cámara *masc & fem*

camp *noun* ▷ see **camp** *verb*
el **campamento** *masc*

to **camp** *verb* ▷ see **camp** *noun*
acampar [17]

campaign *noun*
la **campaña** *fem*

camper *noun*
el & la **campista** *masc & fem*
- **camper van** la caravana

camping *noun*
el **camping** *masc*
to go camping ir [8] de camping
We're going camping in Asturias this summer. Nos vamos de camping a Asturias este verano.

campsite *noun*
el **camping** *masc*

can *noun* ▷ see **can** *verb*
1 (*for food*) la **lata** *fem*
a can of tomatoes una lata de tomates
2 (*for petrol, oil*) el **bidón** *masc*

can *verb* ▷ see **can** *noun*
1 (*saying you are able to*) **poder** [10]
I can lend you £20. Puedo prestarte veinte libras.
I can't be there before ten. No puedo estar allí antes de las diez.
He cannot come. No puede venir.
They couldn't come. No pudieron venir.
2 (*with polite questions, polite orders, etc*) **You can leave your bag here.** Puedes dejar tu bolsa aquí.
Can you open the door, please? ¿Me abres la puerta por favor?
Can I help you? ¿Qué desea? (*in a shop*)
You could go tomorrow. Podrías ir mañana.
You could have told me. Me lo podrías haber dicho.
3 (*saying you know how to*) **saber** [13]
She can't drive. No sabe conducir.
Can you play the piano? ¿Sabes tocar el piano?
4 (*with words like: see, hear, feel, remember, etc*) **I can see her well.** La veo bien.
Can you hear me? ¿Me oyes?
I can remember that ... Me acuerdo de que ...
I can't see you. No te veo.
I can't find my keys. No encuentro mis llaves.

WORD TIP When you use *can* with *see*, *hear*, *feel*, *remember*, etc, it is not translated into Spanish.
▷ **could**

Canada *noun*
Canadá *masc*

Canadian *adjective* ▷ see **Canadian** *noun*
canadiense *masc & fem*

Canadian *noun* ▷ see **Canadian** *adj*
un & una **canadiense** *masc & fem*

WORD TIP Adjectives and nouns for nationality and regional origin do not have capital letters in Spanish.

canal *noun*
el **canal** *masc*

canary *noun*
el **canario** *masc*

Canary Islands *plural noun*
the Canary Islands las Islas Canarias

to **cancel** *verb*
cancelar [17]
The concert's been cancelled. Han cancelado el concierto.

cancer *noun* ▷ see **Cancer** *noun*
el **cáncer** *masc*
to have lung cancer tener cáncer de pulmón

Cancer *noun*
1 (*the star sign*) el **Cáncer** *masc*
2 (*person*) **un & una cáncer** *masc & fem*
I'm Cancer. Soy cáncer.

WORD TIP Use a small letter in Spanish to say *I am ...* etc with star signs. Star signs in Spanish are used without *el, un, la, una*.

candidate *noun*
el **candidato** *masc*, la **candidata** *fem*

candle *noun*
la **vela** *fem*
- **candlestick** el candelabro

candyfloss *noun*
el **algodón de azúcar**

canned *adjective*
en lata
canned tomatoes tomates en lata

cannon *noun*
el **cañón** *masc*

cannot *verb* ▷ **can** *verb*
He cannot come. No puede venir.

canoe *noun*
la **piragua** *fem*

canoeing *noun*
el **piragüismo** *masc*
to go canoeing hacer [7] piragüismo
I like canoeing. Me gusta hacer piragüismo.

English–Spanish
a b c d e f g h i j k l m n o p q r s t u v w x y z

can-opener *noun*
el **abrelatas** *masc, pl:* los **abrelatas**

can't *short for* **cannot** (*See:* **can**)

canteen *noun*
la **cantina** *fem*

canvas *noun*
1 (*fabric*) la **lona** *fem*
2 (*painting*) el **lienzo** *masc*

cap *noun*
1 (*hat*) el **gorro** *masc*
a baseball cap un gorro de béisbol
2 (*on a bottle, tube*) el **tapón** *masc*

capable *adjective*
capaz *masc & fem*
to be capable of doing something ser [1] capaz de hacer algo
They are capable of winning the cup. Son capaces de ganar la copa.

capacity *noun*
la **capacidad** *fem*

capital *adjective* ▷ see **capital** *noun*
1 (*city*) **capital** *masc & fem*
2 (*letter*) **mayúsculo** *masc*, **mayúscula** *fem*
It is written with a capital C. Se escribe con C mayúscula.

capital *noun* ▷ see **capital** *adj*
1 (*city*) la **capital** *fem*
Madrid is the capital of Spain. Madrid es la capital de España.
2 (*letter*) la **mayúscula** *fem*
in capitals en mayúsculas

capitalism *noun*
el **capitalismo** *masc*

capitalist *noun*
el & la **capitalista** *masc & fem*

Capricorn *noun*
1 (*the star sign*) el **Capricornio** *masc*
2 (*person*) un & una **capricornio** *masc & fem*
Linda's Capricorn. Linda es capricornio.

WORD TIP Use a small letter in Spanish to say *I am ...* etc with star signs. Star signs in Spanish are used without *el, un, la, una.*

captain *noun*
1 (*of a ship, team*) el **capitán** *masc*, la **capitana** *fem*
2 (*of a plane*) el & la **comandante** *masc & fem*

captivity *noun*
el **cautiverio** *masc*
to keep someone in captivity mantener [9] a alguien en cautiverio

to **capture** *verb*
capturar [17]

car *noun*
el **coche** *masc*, (*Latin America*) el **carro** *masc*
a car crash un accidente de coche
He parked the car. Aparcó el coche.
We're going by car. Vamos en coche.

carafe *noun*
la **garrafa** *fem*

caramel *noun*
el **caramelo** *masc*

caravan *noun*
la **caravana** *fem*

card *noun*
1 (*for a card game*) la **carta** *fem*
a card game un juego de cartas
to have a game of cards jugar [27] a las cartas
2 (*for phoning, for a cash machine, for Christmas, etc*) la **tarjeta** *fem*
a birthday card una tarjeta de cumpleaños

cardboard *noun*
el **cartón** *masc*

cardigan *noun*
la **chaqueta (de punto)** *fem*

cardphone *noun*
el **teléfono de tarjeta**

care *noun* ▷ see **care** *verb*
1 el **cuidado** *masc*
He took care opening it. Tuvo cuidado al abrirlo.
to take care of somebody cuidar [17] a alguien
He takes care of his mother. Cuida a su madre.
2 (*in expressions: be careful*) **Take care!** ¡Cuidado!, (*when saying goodbye*) ¡Cuídate!

to **care** *verb* ▷ see **care** *noun*
to care about something importarle [17] algo a alguien
She doesn't care if I come in late. A ella no le importa si vuelvo tarde.
I couldn't care less! ¡No me importa en absoluto!
He doesn't care about me. No se preocupa por mí.

career *noun*
la **carrera** *fem*

careful *adjective*
cuidadoso *masc*, **cuidadosa** *fem*
Try to be more careful. Procura ser más cuidadoso.
He's a careful driver. Es un conductor prudente.
Be careful! ¡Ten cuidado!

carefully *adverb*
1 (*with attention*) **atentamente**
Read the instructions carefully. Lea las instrucciones atentamente.
Listen carefully. Escuchad atentamente.
2 (*to handle*) **con cuidado**
She put the vase down carefully. Colocó el jarrón con cuidado.
3 **Drive carefully!** ¡Conduce con precaución!

careless *adjective*
(*person*) **descuidado** *masc*, **decuidada** *fem*
He's very careless. Es muy descuidado.
a careless mistake un error por descuido
This is careless work. Este trabajo está hecho sin cuidado.
careless driving la conducción negligente

caretaker *noun*
1 (*in a school*) **el & la conserje** *masc & fem*
2 (*in a block of flats*) **el portero** *masc*, **la portera** *fem*

car ferry *noun*
el **ferry** *masc*

cargo *noun*
la **carga** *fem*

car hire *noun*
el **alquiler de coches**

Caribbean *adjective*
▷ see **Caribbean** *noun*
caribeño *masc*, **caribeña** *fem*

WORD TIP Adjectives and nouns for nationality and regional origin do not have capital letters in Spanish.

Caribbean *noun* ▷ see **Caribbean** *adj*
the Caribbean el Caribe
the Caribbean Sea el mar Caribe

caricature *noun*
la **caricatura** *fem*

carnation *noun*
el **clavel** *masc*

carnival *noun*
el **carnaval** *masc*

♪ **car park** *noun*
el **aparcamiento** *masc*

♪ **carpenter** *noun*
el **carpintero** *masc*, la **carpintera** *fem*

carpentry *noun*
la **carpintería** *fem*

carpet *noun*
1 (*fitted*) la **moqueta** *fem*
2 (*rug*) la **alfombra** *fem*

car phone *noun*
el **teléfono de coche**

car radio *noun*
la **radio de coche**

carriage *noun*
el **vagón** *masc*

carrier bag *noun*
la **bolsa** *fem*

♪ **carrot** *noun*
la **zanahoria** *fem*

♪ to **carry** *verb*
1 (*a parcel, a school bag, etc*) **llevar** [17]
Can you carry the bag? ¿Puedes llevar la bolsa?
2 (*heavy loads*) **transportar** [17]
The coach was carrying schoolchildren. El autobús transportaba colegiales.
• to **carry on**
seguir [64]
Carry on until the post office. Siga hasta llegar a Correos. (*polite form*)
They carried on talking. Siguieron hablando.
• **carrycot** la cuna portátil

carsick *adjective*
to be carsick marearse [17] al viajar en coche

cart *noun*
el **carro** *masc*

carton *noun*
el **envase** *masc*

♪ **cartoon** *noun*
1 (*film*) los **dibujos animados**
2 (*comic strip*) la **tira cómica**
3 (*in a newspaper*) la **viñeta** *fem*

cartridge *noun*
1 (*for a pen*) el **recambio** *masc*
2 (*for a gun*) el **cartucho** *masc*

to **carve** *verb*
1 (*wood, stone*) **trinchar** [17]
2 (*meat*) **trinchar** [17]

case *noun*
1 (*suitcase*) la **maleta** *fem*
to pack your case hacer [7] la maleta
2 (*for wine bottles*) la **caja** *fem*
3 (*for glasses*) el **estuche** *masc*
4 (*example*) el **caso** *masc*
a case of flu un caso de gripe
in that case en ese caso ▸▸

That's not the case. No se trata de eso.
in case en caso
in case he's late en caso de que llegue tarde
Check first, just in case. Asegúrate, por si acaso.
in any case de todas formas
In any case, it's too late. De todas formas, es demasiado tarde.

cash *noun*
1 (*money*) el **dinero** *masc*
I've got cash. Yo tengo dinero.
2 (*notes and coins*) el **dinero en efectivo**
to pay in cash pagar [28] en efectivo
£50 in cash cincuenta libras en efectivo
- **cash card** la tarjeta de cajero automático
- **cash desk** la caja
- **cash dispenser** el cajero automático

cashew *noun*
el **anacardo** *masc*

cashier *noun*
el **cajero** *masc*, la **cajera** *fem*

cash point *noun*
el **cajero automático**

cash register *noun*
la **caja registradora**

cassette *noun*
la **cinta de cassette**
- **cassette recorder** el cassette

cast *noun*
el **reparto** *masc*
a star-studded cast un reparto estelar

castle *noun*
1 (*building*) el **castillo** *masc*
Windsor Castle el castillo de Windsor
2 (*in chess*) la **torre** *fem*

casual *adjective*
informal *masc & fem*

casualty *noun*
1 (*in an accident*) la **víctima** *fem*
2 (*hospital department*) **urgencias** *plural fem*
He's in casualty. Está en urgencias.

WORD TIP *urgencias* does not take an article.

cat *noun*
el **gato** *masc*, la **gata** *fem*

Catalan *adjective & noun*
1 **catalán** *masc*, **catalana** *fem*
2 (*person*) un **catalán** *masc*, una **catalana** *fem*
the Catalans los catalanes
3 (*the language*) el **catalán** *masc*

WORD TIP Adjectives and nouns for nationality, regional origin and language do not have capital letters in Spanish.

Catalonia *noun*
Cataluña *fem*

catalogue *noun*
el **catálogo** *masc*

catastrophe *noun*
la **catástrofe** *fem*

catch *noun* ▷ see **catch** *verb*
1 (*on a door*) el **pestillo** *masc*
2 (*drawback*) la **trampa** *fem*
What's the catch? ¿Dónde está la trampa?

to **catch** *verb* ▷ see **catch** *noun*
1 (*a ball, a person*) **coger** [3]
Tom caught the ball. Tom cogió la pelota.
You can't catch me! ¡No me coges!
to catch somebody doing something coger [3] a alguien haciendo algo
He was caught stealing money. Lo cogieron robando dinero.
2 (*in fishing, hunting*) **to catch a fish** pescar [31] un pez
to catch a mouse cazar [22] un ratón
3 (*a bus, a plane*) **coger** [3], **tomar** [17]
Did Jason catch his bus? ¿Cogió Jason el autobús?
4 (*a show, a film*) **I want to catch that film.** No quiero perderme esa película.
5 (*an illness*) **coger** [3]
I'm catching a cold. Me estoy resfriando.
He's caught chickenpox. Ha cogido la varicela.
6 (*what somebody says*) **entender** [36]
I didn't catch your name. No entendí bien su nombre. (*polite form*)
- **to catch up with somebody**
alcanzar [22] **a alguien**

category *noun*
la **categoría** *fem*

catering *noun*
el **catering** *masc*

caterpillar *noun*
la **oruga** *fem*

cathedral *noun*
la **catedral** *fem*
Seville cathedral la catedral de Sevilla

Catholic *adjective* ▷ see **Catholic** *noun*
católico *masc*, **católica** *fem*

Catholic *noun* ▷ see **Catholic** *adj*
un **católico** *masc*, una **católica** *fem*
I'm a Catholic. Soy católico.

WORD TIP Adjectives and nouns for religion do not have capital letters in Spanish.

mini-info **Catholic**
Spain is no longer officially a Catholic country but about 43% of the people still go to church regularly. Religious festivals are very popular and most towns and villages have a patron saint.

cattle *plural noun*
el **ganado** *singular masc*

♪ **cauliflower** *noun*
la **coliflor** *fem*
• **cauliflower cheese**
la **coliflor con besamel**

cause *noun* ▷ see **cause** *verb*
la **causa** *fem*
the cause of the accident la causa del accidente
It's for a good cause. Es por una buena causa.

to **cause** *verb* ▷ see **cause** *noun*
causar [17]
to cause problems causar problemas

caution *noun*
la **cautela** *fem*

cautious *adjective*
cauteloso *masc*, **cautelosa** *fem*

cave *noun*
la **cueva** *fem*

caving *noun*
la **espeleología** *fem*
to go caving hacer [7] espeleología

CD *noun*
el **disco compacto**, el **CD** *masc*
• **CD player** el reproductor de discos compactos

♪ **CD-ROM** *noun*
el **CD-ROM** *masc*

♪ **ceiling** *noun*
el **techo** *masc*
on the ceiling en el techo

to **celebrate** *verb*
celebrar [17]
I'm celebrating my birthday today. Hoy celebro mi cumpleaños.

celebrity *noun*
el **famoso** *masc*, la **famosa** *fem*
media celebrities famosos mediáticos

celery *noun*
el **apio** *masc*

cell *noun*
la **célula** *fem*
• **cell phone** el teléfono celular

♪ **cellar** *noun*
el **sótano** *masc*

cello *noun*
el **violonchelo** *masc*
to play the cello tocar [31] el violonchelo

cement *noun*
el **cemento** *masc*

cemetery *noun*
el **cementerio** *masc*

♪ **cent** *noun*
1 *(in the euro system)* el **céntimo** *masc*
2 *(in the dollar system)* el **centavo** *masc*

centenary *noun*
el **centenario** *masc*

centigrade *noun*
el **centígrado** *masc*
ten degrees centigrade diez grados centígrados

♪ **centimetre** *noun*
el **centímetro** *masc*

central *adjective*
central *masc & fem*
central London el centro de Londres
The office is very central. La oficina es muy céntrica.

Central America *noun*
América Central *fem*

♪ **central heating** *noun*
la **calefacción central**

♪ **centre** *noun*
el **centro** *masc*
in the centre of en el centro de
in the town centre en el centro de la ciudad
a shopping centre un centro comercial

♪ **century** *noun*
el **siglo** *masc*
the sixth century el siglo seis
the twentieth century el siglo veinte
in the twenty-first century el siglo veintiuno

cereal *noun*
los **cereales** *masc plural*
to have cereal for breakfast desayunar [17] cereales

ceremony *noun*
la **ceremonia** *fem*

English–Spanish

certain *adjective*
1 (*sure*) **seguro** *masc*, **segura** *fem*
Are you certain of the address? ¿Estás seguro de las señas?
I'm certain of it. Estoy seguro.
to be certain that ... estar **[2]** seguro de que ...
Nicky's certain (that) you're wrong. Nicky está segura de que estás equivocado.
Nobody knows for certain. Nadie lo sabe con seguridad.
2 (*particular*) **cierto** *masc*, **cierta** *fem*
It's only open on certain days. Está abierto solamente ciertos días.

certainly *adverb*
Certainly! ¡Por supuesto!
Certainly not! ¡Claro que no!

certificate *noun*
el **certificado** *masc*

chain *noun*
la **cadena** *fem*

chair *noun*
1 (*in general*) la **silla** *fem*
a kitchen chair una silla de cocina
2 (*with arms*) la **butaca** *fem*
• **chair lift** la telesilla

chalet *noun*
1 (*in the mountains*) el **chalet** *masc*
2 (*in a holiday camp*) el **bungalow** *masc*

chalk *noun*
la **tiza** *fem*

challenge *noun*
el **reto** *masc*
The exam was a real challenge. El examen fue un verdadero reto.

champion *noun*
el **campeón** *masc*, la **campeona** *fem*
the world champion el campeón mundial
the world football champions los campeones mundiales de fútbol

chance *noun*
1 (*opportunity*) la **oportunidad** *fem*
to have the chance to do something tener **[9]** ocasión de hacer algo
I had the chance to go to New York. Tuve la oportunidad de ir a Nueva York.
I haven't had the chance to text him. No he tenido la oportunidad de mandarle un mensaje de texto.
2 (*possibility*) la **posibilidad** *fem*
There's a chance that she'll pass. Existe la posibilidad de que apruebe.
There's little chance of winning. Hay pocas posibilidades de ganar.
by chance por casualidad
Do you have her address, by any chance? ¿Tienes sus señas por casualidad?

change *noun* ▷ see **change** *verb*
1 (*alteration*) el **cambio** *masc*
a change of plan un cambio de planes
They've made some changes to the house. Han hecho algunos cambios en la casa.
It makes a change from hamburgers. Por lo menos, es algo distinto a las hamburguesas.
for a change para variar
Let's eat out for a change. Vamos a comer fuera, para variar.
2 (*of clothes*) **a change of clothes** una muda de ropa
3 (*coins*) el **cambio** *masc*
I haven't any change. No tengo cambio.
Keep the change. Quédese con el cambio.

to **change** *verb* ▷ see **change** *noun*
1 (*to make completely different*) **cambiar [17]**
It changed my life. Cambió mi vida.
Liz never changes. Liz no cambia.
2 (*to switch from one thing to another*) **cambiar [17] de**
We changed trains at Crewe. Cambiamos de tren en Crewe.
She's changed her address. Ha cambiado de dirección.
to change your mind cambiar de opinión
to change the subject cambiar de tema
to change colour cambiar de color
They changed places. Se cambiaron de sitio.
3 (*to swap one for another*) **cambiar [17]**
Have you changed the towels? ¿Has cambiado las toallas?
Can I change it for the larger size? ¿Puedo cambiarlo por una talla más grande?
4 (*to change into different clothes*) **cambiarse [17]**
Mike's gone to change. Mike ha ido a cambiarse.
to change your clothes cambiarse de ropa
I must change my shirt. Tengo que cambiarme de camisa.

changing room *noun*
1 (*for sports, swimming*) el **vestuario** *masc*
2 (*in a shop*) el **probador** *masc*

channel *noun*
1 (*on TV*) el **canal** *masc*
to change channels cambiar **[17]** de canal
2 (*water course*) el **canal** *masc*
the (English) Channel el Canal de la Mancha
to cross the Channel cruzar **[22]** el Canal de la Mancha

Channel Tunnel *noun*
the Channel Tunnel **el Eurotúnel**

chaos *noun*
el **caos** *masc*
It was chaos! ¡Fue un caos!

chapel *noun*
la **capilla** *fem*

chapter *noun*
el **capítulo** *masc*
in Chapter Two en el capítulo número dos

character *noun*
1 (*personality*) el **carácter** *masc*
a house with a lot of character una casa con mucho carácter
2 (*in a book, play, film*) el **personaje** *masc*
the main character el personaje principal

characteristic *noun*
la **característica** *fem*

charcoal *noun*
1 (*for burning*) el **carbón vegetal**
2 (*for drawing*) el **carboncillo** *masc*

ʆ **charge** *noun* ▷ see **charge** *verb*
1 (*what you pay*) el **precio** *masc*
an extra charge un suplemento
The admission charge is £5. El precio de admisión es cinco libras.
There's no charge. Es gratis.
2 (*responsible position*) to be in charge ser [1] el responsable (*a boy*), ser la responsable (*a girl*)
Who's in charge? ¿Quién es el responsable?
Lucy is in charge. Lucy es la responsable.
to be in charge of something or somebody estar [2] a cargo de algo o alguien
Who's in charge of these children? ¿Quién está a cargo de estos niños?
3 (*for a crime*) la **acusación** *fem*
to be on a charge of theft estar [2] acusado de robo

ʆ to **charge** *verb* ▷ see **charge** *noun*
1 (*to get payment*) **cobrar** [17]
They charge ten pounds an hour. Cobran diez libras la hora.
How much do you charge for one day? ¿Cuánto cobran por un día?
We don't charge, it's free. No cobramos, es gratis.
They didn't charge me for the drinks. No me cobraron las bebidas.
2 (*to accuse*) to charge somebody with something acusar [17] a alguien de algo

charity *noun*
la **organización benéfica**

charm *noun*
el **encanto** *masc*

ʆ **charming** *adjective*
encantador *masc*, **encantadora** *fem*

chart *noun*
1 (*table*) la **tabla** *fem*
2 the weather chart el mapa del tiempo
3 the charts las listas de éxitos
number one in the charts número uno en las listas de éxitos

charter flight *noun*
el **vuelo chárter**

chase *noun* ▷ see **chase** *verb*
la **persecución** *fem*
a car chase una persecución en coche

to **chase** *verb* ▷ see **chase** *noun*
perseguir [64]

ʆ **chat** *noun*
la **charla** *fem*
to have a chat with somebody charlar [17] con alguien
• **chatroom** el chat
• **chat show** el programa de entrevistas

to **chatter** *verb*
1 (*to talk*) **cotorrear** [17] (*informal*)
2 (*teeth*) My teeth are chattering. Me castañetean los dientes.

ʆ **chauffeur** *noun*
el & la **chófer** *masc & fem*

ʆ **cheap** *adjective*
barato *masc*, **barata** *fem*
cheap shoes zapatos baratos
That's very cheap! ¡Eso es muy barato!

cheaply *adverb*
to buy cheaply comprar [17] barato
to sell cheaply vender [18] barato
to eat cheaply comer [18] con poco dinero
to dress cheaply vestir [57] con poco dinero

cheap-rate *adjective*
de tarifa reducida
a cheap-rate phone call una llamada de teléfono de tarifa reducida

cheat *noun* ▷ see **cheat** *verb*
el **tramposo** *masc*, la **tramposa** *fem*

to **cheat** *verb* ▷ see **cheat** *noun*
engañar [17]

to check *verb* ▷ see **check** *noun*
(to make sure) **comprobar [24]**
He checked the time. Comprobó la hora.
Check they're all back. Comprueba que ya han llegado todos.
Check with your father. Pregunta a tu padre.
- **to check in**
1 *(for a flight)* **facturar [17] el equipaje**
2 *(at a hotel)* **registrarse [17]**
She checked in at five o'clock. Se registró a las cinco.
- **to check out**
(from a hotel) **irse [17]**

check *noun* ▷ see **check** *verb*
1 *(in a factory, at border controls)* el **control** *masc*
2 *(by a doctor)* el **examen médico**
3 *(in chess)* **Check!** ¡Jaque!
- **check-in** la facturación de equipajes
- **checkout** la caja
at the checkout en caja
- **checkup** el chequeo

cheek *noun*
1 *(of your face)* la **mejilla** *fem*
2 *(nerve)* **What a cheek!** ¡Qué cara! *(informal)*

cheeky *adjective*
1 *(mischievous)* **descarado** *masc*, **descarada** *fem*
2 *(rude)* **impertinente** *masc & fem*

cheer *noun* ▷ see **cheer** *verb*
1 *(applause)* **Three cheers for Tom!** ¡Tres hurras por Tom!
2 *(when you have a drink)* **Cheers!** ¡Salud!

to cheer *verb* ▷ see **cheer** *noun*
(to shout hurray) **vitorear [17]**
- **to cheer on**
animar [17]
- **to cheer somebody up**
animar [17] a alguien
Cheer up! ¡Ánimo!

cheerful *adjective*
alegre *masc & fem*

cheese *noun*
el **queso** *masc*
blue cheese queso azul
a cheese sandwich un sándwich de queso
- **cheesecake** la tarta de queso

chef *noun*
el & la **chef** *masc & fem*

chemical *noun*
el **producto químico**

chemist *noun*
1 *(pharmacist)* el **farmacéutico** *masc*, la **farmacéutica** *fem*
at the chemist's en la farmacia
2 *(scientist)* el **químico** *masc*, la **química** *fem*

chemistry *noun*
la **química** *fem*

cheque *noun*
el **cheque** *masc*
to pay by cheque pagar **[28]** con cheque
to write a cheque extender **[18]** un cheque
- **chequebook** el talonario de cheques
- **cheque guarantee card** la tarjeta bancaria

cherry *noun*
la **cereza** *fem*

chess *noun*
el **ajedrez** *masc*
to play chess jugar **[27]** al ajedrez
- **chessboard** el tablero de ajedrez

chest *noun*
1 *(part of the body)* el **pecho** *masc*
2 *(box)* el **arcón** *masc*

chestnut *noun*
la **castaña** *fem*
- **chestnut tree** el castaño

chest of drawers *noun*
la **cómoda** *fem*

to **chew** *verb*
masticar [31]

chewing gum *noun*
el **chicle** *masc*

chick *noun*
1 *(young hen)* el **pollito** *masc*, la **pollita** *fem*
2 *(young bird)* el **polluelo** *masc*, la **polluela** *fem*

chicken *noun*
el **pollo** *masc*
roast chicken pollo asado
- **chickenpox** la varicela

chicory *noun*
la **endivia** *fem*

chickpea *noun*
el **garbanzo** *masc*

chief *noun*
el **jefe** *masc*, la **jefa** *fem*
- **chief of police** el jefe de policía, la jefa de policía

child *noun*
(boy) el **niño** *masc*, *(girl)* la **niña** *fem*
Jenny's children los niños de Jenny

childish *adjective*
infantil *masc & fem*

childminder *noun*
el **niñero** *masc*, la **niñera** *fem*

Chile *noun*
Chile *masc*

Chilean *adjective* ▷ see **Chilean** *noun*
chileno *masc*, **chilena** *fem*

Chilean *noun* ▷ see **Chilean** *adj*
un **chileno** *masc*, una **chilena** *fem*

WORD TIP Adjectives and nouns for nationality and regional origin do not have capital letters in Spanish.

chilli *noun*
el **chile** *masc*

chilly *adjective*
(*room, weather*) **frío** *masc*, **fría** *fem*
It's chilly today. Hoy hace fresco.

chimney *noun*
la **chimenea** *fem*

chimpanzee *noun*
el & la **chimpancé** *masc & fem*

♪ **chin** *noun*
la **barbilla** *fem*

china *noun*
la **porcelana** *fem*
a china plate un plato de porcelana

China *noun*
China *fem*

Chinese *adjective* ▷ see **Chinese** *noun*
chino *masc*, **china** *fem*
a Chinese man un chino
a Chinese woman una china
a Chinese meal una comida china

Chinese *noun* ▷ see **Chinese** *adj*
1 (*person*) un **chino** *masc*, una **china** *fem*
2 (*the language*) el **chino** *masc*
the Chinese los chinos

WORD TIP Adjectives and nouns for nationality, regional origin and language do not have capital letters in Spanish.

♪ **chip** *noun*
1 (*fried potato*) la **patata frita**
I'd like some chips. Quiero unas patatas fritas.
2 (*microchip*) el **chip** *masc*
3 (*in glass, china*) la **desportilladura** *fem*

chipped *adjective*
desportillado *masc*, **desportillada** *fem*

chives *noun*
las **cebolletas** *plural fem*

♪ **chocolate** *noun*
1 (*the food*) el **chocolate** *masc*
a chocolate ice cream un helado de chocolate
hot chocolate chocolate caliente
milk chocolate chocolate con leche
dark chocolate chocolate sin leche
2 (*item*) **a chocolate** un bombón
a box of chocolates una caja de bombones

♪ **choice** *noun*
la **elección** *fem*
freedom of choice libertad de elección
I had no choice. No tuve más remedio.
It was a good choice. Fue una buena elección.
You have a choice of two flights. Puede elegir entre dos vuelos.

choir *noun*
el **coro** *masc*

choke *noun* ▷ see **choke** *verb*
el **estárter** *masc*

to **choke** *verb* ▷ see **choke** *noun*
atragantarse [17]
She choked on a bone. Se atragantó con un hueso.

♪ to **choose** *verb*
elegir [48]
You chose well. Elegiste bien.
Cathy chose the red one. Cathy eligió el rojo.
It's hard to choose from all these colours. Es difícil elegir entre todos estos colores.

to **chop** *verb* ▷ see **chop** *noun*
1 (*wood*) **cortar** [17]
2 (*vegetables, meat*) **cortar** [17] **en trozos pequeños**
3 (*an onion*) **picar** [31]

chop *noun* ▷ see **chop** *verb*
la **chuleta** *fem*
a lamb chop una chuleta de cordero
• **chopstick** el palillo

chord *noun*
el **acorde** *masc*

chorus *noun*
1 (*of a song*) el **estribillo** *masc*
2 (*a group of singers*) el **coro** *masc*

Christ *noun*
Cristo

christening *noun*
el **bautizo** *masc*

Christian *adjective* ▷ see **Christian** *noun*
cristiano *masc*, **cristiana** *fem*

Christian *noun* ▷ see **Christian** *adj*
un **cristiano** *masc*, una **cristiana** *fem*

Christianity *noun*
(*Religion*) el **cristianismo** *masc*

WORD TIP Adjectives and nouns for religion do not have capital letters in Spanish.

Christian name *noun*
el **nombre de pila**

Christmas *noun*
la **Navidad** *fem*
at Christmas en Navidad
Happy Christmas! ¡Feliz Navidad!
- **Christmas card** la tarjeta de Navidad
- **Christmas carol** el villancico
- **Christmas Day** el día de Navidad
- **Christmas dinner** la cena de Navidad
- **Christmas Eve** la Nochebuena
  on Christmas Eve en Nochebuena
- **Christmas present** el regalo de Navidad
- **Christmas tree** el árbol de Navidad

chunk *noun*
el **trozo** *masc*

church *noun*
la **iglesia** *fem*
to go to church ir [8] a la iglesia
- **churchyard** el cementerio

cider *noun*
la **sidra** *fem*

cigar *noun*
el **puro** *masc*

cigarette *noun*
el **cigarrillo** *masc*

cinema *noun*
el **cine** *masc*
to go to the cinema ir [8] al cine

circle *noun*
el **círculo** *masc*
to sit in a circle sentarse [17] en círculo
to go round in circles dar [4] vueltas

circuit *noun*
1 (*lap*) la **vuelta** *fem*
2 (*racing track*) la **pista** *fem*

circular *adjective*
circular *masc & fem*

circumference *noun*
la **circunferencia** *fem*

circumstances *plural noun*
under the circumstances en estas circunstancias

circus *noun*
el **circo** *masc*

citizen *noun*
el **ciudadano** *masc*, la **ciudadana** *fem*

city *noun*
la **ciudad** *fem*
the city of Seville la ciudad de Sevilla
- **city centre** el centro de la ciudad
  in the city centre en el centro de la ciudad

civilian *noun*
el & la **civil** *masc & fem*

civilization *noun*
la **civilización** *fem*

civil servant *noun*
el **funcionario** *masc*, la **funcionaria** *fem*
She's a civil servant. Es funcionaria.

civil service *noun*
la **administración pública**

civil war *noun*
la **guerra civil**

claim *noun* ▷ see **claim** *verb*
1 (*statement*) la **afirmación** *fem*
2 (*on insurance*) la **reclamación** *fem*

to **claim** *verb* ▷ see **claim** *noun*
asegurar [17]
He claimed he knew nothing about it. Aseguró no saber nada de ello.

to **clap** *verb*
1 **aplaudir** [19]
Everyone clapped. Todo el mundo aplaudió.
2 **to clap your hands** dar [4] palmadas

clapping *noun*
los **aplausos** *masc plural*

clarinet *noun*
el **clarinete** *masc*
to play the clarinet tocar [31] el clarinete

clash *noun* ▷ see **clash** *verb*
el **choque** *masc*

to **clash** *verb* ▷ see **clash** *noun*
1 (*rival groups*) **chocar** [31]
2 (*colours*) **desentonar** [17]
The curtains clash with the wallpaper. Las cortinas desentonan con el papel pintado.

class *noun*
1 (*at school*) la **clase** *fem*
an art class una clase de arte
She's in the same class as me. Está en la misma clase que yo.
2 (*social group*) la **clase** *fem*
the middle class la clase media

classic *adjective*
clásico *masc*, **clásica** *fem*

classical *adjective*
clásico *masc*, **clásica** *fem*
• **classical music** la música clásica

classmate *noun*
el **compañero de clase**, la **compañera de clase**

✎ **classroom** *noun*
la **clase** *fem*

claw *noun*
1 (*of a cat, dog*) la **zarpa** *fem*
2 (*of a crab*) la **pinza** *fem*

clay *noun*
(*for modelling*) la **arcilla** *fem*

✎ **clean** *adjective* ▷ see **clean** *verb*
1 (*not dirty*) **limpio** *masc*, **limpia** *fem*
a clean shirt una camisa limpia
My hands are clean. Tengo las manos limpias.
2 (*air, water*) **puro** *masc*, **pura** *fem*

✎ to **clean** *verb* ▷ see **clean** *adj*
limpiar [17]
I cleaned the whole house. Limpié toda la casa.
to clean your teeth lavarse [17] los dientes
I'm going to clean my teeth. Voy a lavarme los dientes.

cleaner *noun*
1 (*in a public place*) el **limpiador** *masc*, la **limpiadora** *fem*
2 (*cleaning lady*) la **señora de la limpieza**
3 (*cleaning product*) el **producto de limpieza**

✎ **cleaning** *noun*
to do the cleaning hacer [7] la limpieza

cleanser *noun*
1 (*for the house*) el **producto de limpieza**
2 (*for your face*) la **crema limpiadora**

✎ **clear** *adjective* ▷ see **clear** *verb*
1 (*that you can see through*) **transparente** *masc & fem*
clear glass cristal transparente
2 (*cloudless*) **despejado** *masc*, **despejada** *fem*
3 (*easy to understand*) **claro** *masc*, **clara** *fem*
clear instructions instrucciones claras
It's clear that ... Está claro que ...
Is that clear? ¿Está claro?

✎ to **clear** *verb* ▷ see **clear** *adj*
1 (*your papers, rubbish, clothes*) **sacar** [31]
Have you cleared your stuff out of your room? ¿Has sacado todas tus cosas de tu habitación?
2 (*the table*) **recoger** [3]
Can I clear the table? ¿Puedo recoger la mesa?
3 (*a road, a path*) **despejar** [17]
4 (*your throat*) **to clear your throat** aclararse [17] la voz
5 (*fog, smoke*) **disiparse** [17]
The fog cleared. La niebla se disipó.
• **to clear something up**
recoger [3] **algo**
I'll just clear up my books. Voy a recoger mis libros.

clearly *adverb*
1 (*to think, to speak, to hear*) **con claridad**
2 (*obviously*) **claramente**
She was clearly worried. Estaba claramente preocupada.

clementine *noun*
la **clementina** *fem*

✎ **clever** *adjective*
1 (*intelligent*) **inteligente** *masc & fem*
Their children are all very clever. Todos sus hijos son muy inteligentes.
2 (*ingenious*) **ingenioso** *masc*, **ingeniosa** *fem*
a clever idea una idea ingeniosa

click *noun* ▷ see **click** *verb*
el **clic** *masc*
a double click un doble clic

to **click** *verb* ▷ see **click** *noun*
hacer [7] **clic en**
Click on the icon. Haz clic en el icono.

✎ **client** *noun*
el & la **cliente** *masc & fem*

cliff *noun*
el **acantilado** *masc*

✎ **climate** *noun*
el **clima** *masc*

to **climb** *verb*
1 (*the stairs*) **subir** [19]
2 (*a hill, a tree*) **escalar** [17]
We climbed Mont Blanc. Escalamos el Mont Blanc.

climber *noun*
el & la **alpinista** *masc & fem*

✎ **climbing** *noun*
el **alpinismo** *masc*
They go climbing in Italy. Practican el alpinismo en Italia.

clinic *noun*
1 (*in a hospital*) el **consultorio** *masc*
2 (*a private hospital*) la **clínica** *fem*

clip *noun* ▷ see **clip** *verb*
1 (*from a film*) el **clip** *masc*
2 (*for your hair*) la **horquilla** *fem*

English–Spanish

to clip *verb* ▷ see **clip** *noun*
1 **cortar** [17]
2 **to clip together** sujetar [17] con un clip

cloakroom *noun*
1 (*for coats*) el **guardarropa** *masc*
2 (*toilet*) el **lavabo**

clock *noun*
el **reloj** *masc*
to put the clocks forward an hour adelantar [17] los relojes una hora
to put the clocks back atrasar [17] los relojes
- **clock radio** el radiodespertador
- **clockwise** en el sentido de las agujas del reloj

clog *noun*
el **zueco** *masc*

close *adjective* ▷ see **close** *adv, verb*
1 (*result*) **reñido** *masc*, **reñida** *fem*
2 (*relation*) **cercano** *masc*, **cercana** *fem*
(*friend, relationship*) **She's a close friend of mine.** Es muy amiga mía.
3 (*near*) **cerca** *masc & fem*
not very close no muy cerca

close *adverb* ▷ see **close** *adj, verb*
1 (*relationship*) **They are very close.** Son muy unidos.
2 (*near*) **cerca**
close to the cinema cerca del cine
The station's very close. La estación está muy cerca.
She lives close by. Vive cerca.

to close *verb* ▷ see **close** *adj, adv*
cerrar [29]
Close your eyes! ¡Cierra los ojos!
She closed the door. Cerró la puerta.
The post office closes at six. La oficina de correos cierra a las seis.
- **to close down**
(*shops, factories*) **cerrar** [29]

closed *adjective*
cerrado *masc*, **cerrada** *fem*
'Closed on Mondays' 'Cerrado los lunes'

closely *adverb*
de cerca
to examine something closely examinar [17] algo de cerca

closing date *noun*
la **fecha límite**
the closing date for entries la fecha límite para inscribirse

closing-down sale *noun*
la **liquidación por cierre de negocio**

closing time *noun*
la **hora de cierre**

cloth *noun*
1 (*for the floor, for wiping surfaces*) la **bayeta** *fem*
2 (*for polishing*) el **trapo del polvo**
3 (*for drying up*) el **paño de cocina**
4 (*fabric by the metre*) la **tela** *fem*

clothes *plural noun*
la **ropa** *singular fem*
to change your clothes cambiarse [17] de ropa
- **clothes hanger** la percha
- **clothes line** la cuerda de tender
- **clothes peg** la pinza para tender

cloud *noun*
la **nube** *fem*
- **to cloud over**
nublarse [17]
It clouded over in the afternoon. Se nubló por la tarde.

cloudy *adjective*
nublado *masc*, **nublada** *fem*

clove *noun*
el **clavo** *masc*
- **clove of garlic** el diente de ajo

clown *noun*
el **payaso** *masc*, la **payasa** *fem*

club *noun*
1 (*association*) el **club** *masc*
He's in the football club. Está en el club de fútbol.
2 (*in cards*) el **trébol** *masc*
the four of clubs el cuatro de tréboles
3 (*golfing iron*) el **palo de golf**

clue *noun*
1 (*for solving something*) la **pista** *fem*
They have a few clues. Tienen unas cuantas pistas.
I haven't a clue. No tengo ni idea.
2 (*in a crossword*) la **clave** *fem*

clumsy *adjective*
torpe *masc & fem*

clutch *noun* ▷ see **clutch** *verb*
(*in a car*) el **embrague** *masc*

to clutch *verb* ▷ see **clutch** *noun*
to clutch something tener [9] algo firmemente agarrado

coach *noun*
1 (*bus*) el **autobús** *masc*
on the coach en el autobús
by coach en autobús
to travel by coach viajar [17] en autobús

2 (*in sports*) el **entrenador** *masc*, la **entrenadora** *fem*
3 (*railway carriage*) el **vagón** *masc*
• **coach station** la estación de autobuses
• **coach trip** la excursión en autobús

coal *noun*
el **carbón** *masc*
• **coal mine** la mina de carbón
• **coal miner** el minero, la minera

coarse *adjective*
basto *masc*, **basta** *fem*

coast *noun*
la **costa** *fem*
on the east coast en la costa este

⚷ **coat** *noun*
1 (*that you wear*) el **abrigo** *masc*
2 (*layer*) **a coat of paint** una capa de pintura
• **coat hanger** la percha

cobweb *noun*
la **telaraña** *fem*

⚷ **Coca-Cola®** *noun*
la **Coca-Cola®** *fem*

cocaine *noun*
la **cocaína** *fem*

cockerel *noun*
el **gallo** *masc*

cocoa *noun*
1 (*drink*) el **chocolate** *masc*
2 (*powder*) el **cacao** *masc*

coconut *noun*
el **coco** *masc*

cod *noun*
el **bacalao** *masc*

code *noun*
el **código** *masc*
the highway code el código de la circulación
the dialling code for Barcelona el prefijo de Barcelona

⚷ **coeducational** *adjective*
mixto *masc*, **mixta** *fem*

coffee *noun*
el **café** *masc*
a cup of coffee un café
a white coffee un café con leche
A black coffee, please. Un café solo, por favor.
• **coffee break** la pausa para el café
• **coffee cup** la taza de café

coffee machine *noun*
1 (*vending machine*) la **máquina de café**
2 (*electric*) la **cafetera eléctrica**

coffee pot *noun*
la **cafetera** *fem*

coffee table *noun*
la **mesa de centro** *fem*

coffin *noun*
el **ataúd** *masc*

⚷ **coin** *noun*
la **moneda** *fem*
a pound coin una moneda de una libra

coincidence *noun*
la **coincidencia** *fem*

Coke® *noun*
la **Coca-Cola®** *fem*
Two Cokes, please. Dos Coca-Colas, por favor.

colander *noun*
el **colador** *masc*

⚷ **cold** *adjective* ▷ see **cold** *noun*
1 (*thing, substance*) **frío** *masc*, **fría** *fem*
cold milk leche fría
Your hands are cold. Tienes las manos frías.
2 (*weather, temperature*) **It's cold today.** Hoy hace frío.
It's cold in the kitchen. Hace frío en la cocina.
3 (*feeling*) **I'm cold.** Tengo frío.
He was feeling very cold. Tenía mucho frío.

⚷ **cold** *noun* ▷ see **cold** *adj*
1 (*cold weather*) el **frío** *masc*
I don't want to go out in this cold. No quiero salir con este frío.
Come in out of the cold. Entra, que hace frío.
She was shivering with cold. Estaba temblando de frío.
2 (*illness*) el **resfriado** *masc*
a bad cold un fuerte resfriado
to have a cold estar [2] resfriado (*about a boy*), estar resfriada (*about a girl*)
Carol's got a cold. Carol está resfriada.
• **cold sore** la calentura

to **collapse** *verb*
1 (*roofs, walls, houses*) **derrumbarse** [17]
2 (*people*) **He collapsed in his office.** Sufrió un desmayo en su oficina.

collar *noun*
1 (*on a shirt, etc*) el **cuello** *masc*
2 (*for a dog*) el **collar** *masc*
• **collarbone** la clavícula

colleague *noun*
el **compañero** *masc*, la **compañera** *fem*

English–Spanish

to collect *verb*
1 *(as a hobby)* **coleccionar [17]**
I collect stamps. Colecciono sellos.
2 *(a person, a thing)* **recoger [3]**
She collects the children from school. Ella recoge a los niños del colegio.
3 *(a fare, money)* **cobrar [17]**
4 *(data, information)* **reunir [62]**
• **to collect in**
recoger [3]
Collect in the exercise books, Laura. Recoge los cuadernos, Laura.

collection *noun*
1 *(of stamps, CDs, etc)* la **colección** *fem*
2 *(of money)* la **colecta** *fem*
to hold a collection hacer [7] una colecta

collector *noun*
el & la **coleccionista** *masc & fem*

college *noun*
1 *(for higher education)* el **colegio universitario**
to go to college ir [8] a la universidad
2 *(for vocational training)* la **escuela de formación profesional**
3 *(school)* el **instituto** *masc*

collie *noun*
el & la **collie** *masc & fem*

collision *noun*
el **choque** *masc*

Colombia *noun*
Colombia *fem*

Colombian *adjective & noun*
1 **colombiano** *masc*, **colombiana** *fem*
2 un **colombiano** *masc*, una **colombiana** *fem*
the Colombians los colombianos

WORD TIP Adjectives and nouns for nationality and regional origin do not have capital letters in Spanish.

colonel *noun*
el **coronel** *masc*

♪ **to colour** *verb* ▷ see **colour** *noun*
colorear [17]
to colour something red colorear [17] algo de rojo

♪ **colour** *noun* ▷ see **colour** *verb*
el **color** *masc*
What colour is your car? ¿De qué color es tu coche?
What colour is it? ¿De qué color es?
Do you have it in a different colour? ¿Lo tiene en otros colores?
• **colour blind** daltónico *masc*, daltónica *fem*
• **colour film** *(for a camera)* el carrete de color

colourful *adjective*
de colores

colouring book *noun*
el **libro para colorear**

colour supplement *noun*
el **suplemento a color**

column *noun*
la **columna** *fem*

♪ **comb** *noun* ▷ see **comb** *verb*
el **peine** *masc*

♪ **to comb** *verb* ▷ see **comb** *noun*
to comb your hair peinarse [17]
I'll just comb my hair. Voy a peinarme.

to combine *verb*
combinar [17]
They don't combine well. No combinan bien.

combination *noun*
la **combinación** *fem*

♪ **to come** *verb*
venir [15]
The bus is coming. Ya viene el autobús.
Nick came by bike. Nick vino en bici.
Did Jess come to school yesterday? ¿Vino Jess ayer a clase?
Can you come over for a coffee? ¿Puedes venir a tomar un café?
Come quick! ¡Ven rápido!
Come on! ¡Venga!
Come and see! ¡Ven a ver!
Coming! ¡Ya voy!
• **to come apart**
deshacerse [7]
It came apart in my hands. Se deshizo en mis manos.
• **to come back**
volver [45]
She's coming back to collect us. Volverá para recogernos.
• **to come down**
bajar [17]
She came down for breakfast. Bajó a desayunar.
I came down the stairs. Bajé la escalera.
• **to come for**
(a person) **venir [15] a por**
My father's coming for me. Mi padre va a venir a por mí.
• **to come from**
ser [1] de
Ian comes from Scotland. Ian es de Escocia.
The wine comes from Spain. El vino es español.

a b c d e f g h i j k l m n o p q r s t u v w x y z

- to **come in**
  entrar [17]
  Come in! ¡Adelante!
  She came into the kitchen. Entró en la cocina.
- to **come off**
  1 (*buttons*) **desprenderse** [18], (*handles*) **soltarse** [24]
  2 (*lids*) **I can't get the lid to come off.** No puedo quitar la tapa.
- to **come out**
  salir [63]
  They came out when I called. Salieron cuando los llamé.
  The CD's coming out soon. El compacto va a salir pronto.
  The sun hasn't come out yet. El sol no ha salido aún.
- to **come to**
  1 (*to get to*) **llegar** [28] **a**
  When you come to the church turn right. Gira a la derecha cuando llegues a la iglesia.
  2 (*to add up to*) **It comes to 150 euros.** Suma ciento cincuenta euros.
- to **come up**
  subir [19]
  Can you come up a moment? ¿Puedes subir un momento?
- to **come up to somebody**
  acercarse [31] **a alguien**

comedian *noun*
el **cómico** *masc*, la **cómica** *fem*

comedy *noun*
la **comedia** *fem*

♪ **comfortable** *adjective*
1 **cómodo** *masc*, **cómoda** *fem*
This chair's really comfortable. Esta silla es muy cómoda.
2 **to feel comfortable** estar [2] cómodo
Are you comfortable there? ¿Estás cómoda ahí?

comfortably *adverb*
cómodamente

♪ **comic** *noun*
(*magazine*) el **cómic** *masc*
- **comic strip** la tira cómica

comma *noun*
la **coma** *fem*

command *noun*
la **orden** *fem*

comment *noun*
(*in a conversation*) el **comentario** *masc*
He made some rude comments about my friends. Hizo unos comentarios groseros sobre mis amigos.

commentary *noun*
la **crónica** *fem*
the commentary on the match la crónica del partido

commentator *noun*
el & la **comentarista** *masc & fem*
a sports commentator un comentarista deportivo

commercial *adjective*
▷ see **commercial** *noun*
comercial *masc & fem*

commercial *noun*
▷ see **commercial** *adj*
el **anuncio de televisión**

to **commit** *verb*
1 (*a crime*) **cometer** [18]
2 **to commit yourself to doing something** comprometerse [18] a hacer algo

committee *noun*
el **comité** *masc*

common *adjective*
1 **corriente** *masc & fem*
It's a common problem. Es un problema corriente.
2 **in common** en común
They have nothing in common. No tienen nada en común.
- **common sense** el sentido común

to **communicate** *verb*
comunicar [31]

communication *noun*
1 (*message, letter, etc*) la **comunicación** *fem*
2 (*in transport*) **Communications are good.** Las comunicaciones son buenas.

communion *noun*
la **comunión** *fem*

communism *noun*
el **comunismo** *masc*

communist *noun*
un & una **comunista** *masc & fem*

community *noun*
la **comunidad** *fem*
the European Community la comunidad europea

to **commute** *verb*
to commute between Reading and London viajar [17] todos los días de Reading a Londres para ir a trabajar

English–Spanish

a b c d e f g h i j k l m n o p q r s t u v w x y z

commuter *noun*
trains full of commuters trenes llenos de personas que van a trabajar cada día

compact disc *noun*
el **disco compacto**
• **compact disc player** el compacto

company *noun*
1 (*business*) la **compañía** *fem*
an insurance company una compañía de seguros
a theatre company una compañía de teatro
She's set up a company. Ha montado una compañía.
2 (*companionship*) **to keep somebody company** hacer [7] compañía a alguien
The dogs keep me company. Los perros me hacen compañía.

comparatively *adverb*
relativamente

to **compare** *verb*
comparar [17]
if you compare the Spanish with the English... si comparas el español con el inglés...
Our house is small compared with yours. Nuestra casa es pequeña comparada con la tuya.

comparison *noun*
la **comparación** *fem*
in comparison with something en comparación con algo

compartment *noun*
el **compartimento** *masc*

compass *noun*
la **brújula** *fem*

compatible *adjective*
compatible *masc & fem*

compensation *noun*
la **indemnización** *fem*

to **compete** *verb*
to compete in something participar [17] en algo

competent *adjective*
competente *masc & fem*

competition *noun*
1 (*in a magazine, at school*) el **concurso** *masc*
a poetry competition un concurso de poesía
2 (*in sports*) la **competición** *fem*
a fishing competition una competición de pesca
3 (*rivalry*) la **competencia** *fem*

competitor *noun*
(*in sports, business*) el **competidor** *masc*, la **competidora** *fem*

to **complain** *verb*
quejarse [17]
We complained about the hotel. Nos quejamos del hotel.

complaint *noun*
la **queja** *fem*
to make a complaint presentar [17] una queja
She made a complaint to the manager. Presentó una queja al gerente.

complete *adjective* ▷ see **complete** *verb*
completo *masc*, **completa** *fem*
the complete collection la colección completa

to **complete** *verb* ▷ see **complete** *adj*
1 (*your education, a piece of work*) **terminar** [17]
2 (*a form*) **rellenar** [17]

completely *adverb*
completamente

complexion *noun*
el **cutis** *masc*

complicated *adjective*
complicado *masc*, **complicada** *fem*

complication *noun*
la **complicación** *fem*
There were complications. Hubo complicaciones.

compliment *noun*
el **cumplido** *masc*
to pay somebody a compliment hacer [7] un cumplido a alguien

to **compose** *verb*
componer [11]
composed of something compuesto de algo

composer *noun*
el **compositor** *masc*, la **compositora** *fem*

comprehension *noun*
la **comprensión** *fem*
a comprehension test un ejercicio de comprensión

compulsory *adjective*
obligatorio *masc*, **obligatoria** *fem*

computer *noun*
el **ordenador** *masc*, (*Latin America*) la **computadora**

to work on a computer trabajar [17] en ordenador
- **computer engineer** el técnico en informática, la técnica en informática
- **computer game** el juego de ordenador
- **computer program** el programa informático
- **computer programmer** el programador, la programadora
- **computer science** la informática

computing *noun*
la **informática** *fem*

conceited *adjective*
engreído *masc*, **engreída** *fem*

to **concentrate** *verb*
concentrarse [17]
I can't concentrate. No puedo concentrarme.
I was concentrating on the film. Me estaba concentrando en la película.

concentration *noun*
la **concentración** *fem*

concern *noun* ▷ see **concern** *verb*
1 (*business*) **That's no concern of yours.** Eso no es asunto tuyo.
2 (*worry*) la **preocupación** *fem*
There is no cause for concern. No hay razón para preocuparse.

to **concern** *verb* ▷ see **concern** *noun*
(*to affect*) **concernir** [14]
as far as I'm concerned por mi parte
This doesn't concern you. Esto no te concierne.

concert *noun*
el **concierto** *masc*
a concert ticket una entrada para un concierto
to go to a rock concert ir [8] a un concierto de rock

conclusion *noun*
la **conclusión** *fem*

concrete *noun*
el **cemento** *masc*
a concrete floor un suelo de cemento

to **condemn** *verb*
condenar [17]

condition *noun*
la **condición** *fem*
in good condition en buenas condiciones
in bad condition en malas condiciones
weather conditions condiciones meteorológicas
the conditions of sale las condiciones de venta
on one condition con una condición
on condition that you let me pay a condición de que me dejes pagar

conditional *noun*
el **condicional** *masc*

conditioner *noun*
el **suavizante** *masc*

condom *noun*
el **condón** *masc*

conduct *noun* ▷ see **conduct** *verb*
la **conducta** *fem*

to **conduct** *verb* ▷ see **conduct** *noun*
(*an orchestra, a piece of music*) **dirigir** [49]

conductor *noun*
1 (*of an orchestra*) el **director de orquesta**, la **directora de orquesta**
2 (*on a bus*) el **cobrador** *masc*, la **cobradora** *fem*

cone *noun*
1 (*for ice cream*) el **cucurucho** *masc*
2 (*for traffic*) el **cono** *masc*

confectionery *noun*
los **dulces** *masc plural*
She works in a confectionery shop. Trabaja en una confitería.

conference *noun*
la **conferencia** *fem*

to **confess** *verb*
confesar [29]

confession *noun*
la **confesión** *fem*

confidence *noun*
1 (*faith in somebody*) la **confianza** *fem*
to have confidence in somebody tener [9] confianza en alguien
2 (*in yourself*) la **seguridad en sí mismo**
He has a lot of confidence. Tiene mucha seguridad en sí mismo.
You're lacking in confidence. Te falta seguridad en ti mismo.

confident *adjective*
1 (*sure of yourself*) **seguro de sí mismo** *masc*, **segura de sí misma** *fem*
You look very confident. Pareces muy seguro de ti mismo.
She's a confident young woman. Es una joven segura de sí misma.
2 (*sure that something will happen*) **to be confident that** estar [2] seguro de que
I'm confident that it will work out all right. Estoy segura de que saldrá bien.

to **confirm** *verb*
confirmar [17]
We'll confirm the date. Confirmaremos la fecha.

to **confuse** *verb*
confundir [19]
I confuse him with his brother. Lo confundo con su hermano.

confused *adjective*
1 (*facts, account*) **confuso** *masc*, **confusa** *fem*
He gave us a confused story. Contó una historia muy confusa.
2 (*person*) **confundido** *masc*, **confundida** *fem*
Now I'm completely confused. Ahora estoy completamente confundida.
I'm confused about the holiday dates. No estoy seguro de las fechas de las vacaciones.
to get confused confundirse [19]
She got confused. Se confundió.

confusing *adjective*
poco claro *masc*, **poco clara** *fem*
The instructions are confusing. Las instrucciones son poco claras.

confusion *noun*
la **confusión** *fem*

to **congratulate** *verb*
felicitar [17]
I congratulated Tim on his success. Felicité a Tim por su éxito.
We congratulate you on winning. Te felicitamos por haber ganado.

♪ **congratulations** *plural noun*
la **enhorabuena** *singular fem*
Congratulations on the baby! ¡Enhorabuena por el bebé!

conjurer *noun*
el **mago** *masc*, la **maga** *fem*

to **connect** *verb*
conectar [17]

connection *noun*
la **conexión** *fem*
a faulty connection una conexión defectuosa
Sally missed her connection. Sally perdió su conexión.
There's no connection between his letter and my decision. No hay relación entre su carta y mi decisión.

conscience *noun*
la **conciencia** *fem*
to have a guilty conscience no tener [9] la conciencia tranquila

conscious *adjective*
consciente *masc & fem*

consequence *noun*
la **consecuencia** *fem*

consequently *adverb*
por consiguiente

conservation *noun*
la **protección del medio ambiente**

conservative *adjective*
▷ see **conservative** *noun*
conservador *masc*, **conservadora** *fem*

conservative *noun*
▷ see **conservative** *adj*
un **conservador** *masc*, una **conservadora** *fem*

conservatory *noun*
el **jardín de invierno**

to **consider** *verb*
1 (*a suggestion, an idea*) **considerar** [17]
all things considered bien considerado
2 (*to think you might do*) **plantearse** [17]
We're considering buying a flat. Estamos planteándonos comprar un piso.

considerable *adjective*
considerable *masc & fem*
a considerable number of students un número considerable de estudiantes

considerate *adjective*
considerado *masc*, **considerada** *fem*

consideration *noun*
la **consideración** *fem*

considering *preposition*
teniendo en cuenta
considering her age teniendo en cuenta su edad
considering he did it all himself teniendo en cuenta que lo hizo todo él solo

to **consist** *verb*
to consist of consistir [19] en

consistent *adjective*
constante *masc & fem*

console *noun*
(*Computers*) la **consola** *fem*

consonant *noun*
(*Grammar*) la **consonante** *fem*

constant *adjective*
constante *masc & fem*

constantly *adverb*
constantemente

constipated *adjective*
estreñido *masc*, **estreñida** *fem*

to **construct** *verb*
construir [54]

construction *noun*
la **construcción** *fem*

consulate *noun*
el **consulado** *masc*

to **consult** *verb*
consultar [17]

consumer *noun*
el **consumidor** *masc*, la **consumidora** *fem*

consumption *noun*
el **consumo** *masc*

to **contact** *verb* ▷ see **contact** *noun*
ponerse [11] **en contacto con**
I'll contact you tomorrow. Me pondré en contacto contigo mañana.

contact *noun* ▷ see **contact** *verb*
el **contacto** *masc*
We've lost contact. Hemos perdido contacto.
Rob has contacts in the music business. Rob tiene contactos en el mundo de la música.
to be in contact with somebody estar [2] en contacto con alguien
• **contact lens** la lentilla

to **contain** *verb*
contener [9]

container *noun*
el **recipiente** *masc*

to **contaminate** *verb*
contaminar [17]

contemporary *adjective*
contemporáneo *masc*, **contemporánea** *fem*

contents *plural noun*
el **contenido** *singular masc*
the contents of my suitcase el contenido de mi maleta

contest *noun*
1 (*competition*) el **concurso** *masc*
2 (*in sport*) la **competición** *fem*

contestant *noun*
el & la **concursante** *masc & fem*

context *noun*
el **contexto** *masc*

continent *noun*
el **continente** *masc*
on the Continent en Europa continental

continental *adjective*
a continental holiday unas vacaciones en Europa continental

♪ to **continue** *verb*
1 **continuar** [20]
We continued our journey. Continuamos con nuestro viaje.
'To be continued' 'Continuará'
2 **to continue doing something** seguir [64] haciendo algo
Jill continued talking. Jill siguió hablando.

continuous *adjective*
continuo *masc*, **continua** *fem*
• **continuous assessment** la evaluación continua

contraception *noun*
la **anticoncepción** *fem*

contraceptive *noun*
el **anticonceptivo** *masc*

contract *noun*
el **contrato** *masc*

to **contradict** *verb*
contradecir [5]

contradiction *noun*
la **contradicción** *fem*

contrary *noun*
the contrary lo contrario
on the contrary al contrario

contrast *noun*
el **contraste** *masc*

to **contribute** *verb*
(*money*) **contribuir** [54]

contribution *noun*
(*to charity, an appeal*) la **contribución** *fem*

control *noun* ▷ see **control** *verb*
(*of a crowd, animals*) el **control** *masc*
The police have lost control. La policía ha perdido el control.
Everything's under control. Todo está bajo control.

to **control** *verb* ▷ see **control** *noun*
controlar [17]
to control oneself controlarse [17]

controversial *adjective*
controvertido *masc*, **controvertida** *fem*
a controversial decision una decisión controvertida

convenient *adjective*
1 (*simple*) **práctico** *masc*, **práctica** *fem*
Frozen vegetables are very convenient. Las verduras congeladas son muy prácticas.
2 (*suitable*) **to be convenient for somebody** venirle **[15]** bien a alguien o algo
If that's convenient for you. Si te viene bien.
3 (*handy*) **The house is convenient for shops and schools.** La casa está bien situada respecto a tiendas y colegios.

convent *noun*
el **convento** *masc*

conventional *adjective*
1 (*practice*) **convencional** *masc & fem*
2 (*person*) **tradicional** *masc & fem*

conversation *noun*
la **conversación** *fem*

to **convert** *verb*
convertir [14]
We're going to convert the garage into a workshop. Vamos a convertir el garaje en un taller.

to **convince** *verb*
convencer [44]
I'm convinced you're wrong. Estoy convencido de que estás equivocado.

convincing *adjective*
convincente *masc & fem*

cook *noun* ▷ see **cook** *verb*
el **cocinero** *masc*, la **cocinera** *fem*

to **cook** *verb* ▷ see **cook** *noun*
1 (*to make food*) **cocinar [17]**
Who's cooking tonight? ¿Quién cocina esta noche?
I like cooking. Me gusta cocinar.
2 (*the vegetables, the pasta, etc*) **cocer [41]**
Cook the carrots for five minutes. Cuece las zanahorias durante cinco minutos.
3 (*to make a meal*) **hacer [7]**
Fran's busy cooking supper. Fran está haciendo la cena.
4 (*food*) **hacerse [7]**
The sausages are cooking. Las salchichas se están haciendo.
Is the chicken cooked? ¿Está hecho el pollo?

cooker *noun*
la **cocina** *fem*
an electric cooker una cocina eléctrica
a gas cooker una cocina de gas

cookery *noun*
la **cocina** *fem*
- **cookery book** el libro de cocina

cooking *noun*
la **cocina** *fem*
Italian cooking la cocina italiana
home cooking la comida casera
to do the cooking cocinar **[27]**

cool *adjective* ▷ see **cool** *noun, verb*
1 (*cold*) **fresco** *masc*, **fresca** *fem*
a cool drink una bebida fresca
It's cool inside. Dentro hace fresco.
2 (*laid-back*) **tranquilo** *masc*, **tranquila** *fem*
3 (*informal: person*) **to be cool** estar **[2]** en la onda
He's so cool. Está muy en la onda.
4 (*informal: car, jacket*) **molón** *masc*, **molona** *fem*

cool *noun* ▷ see **cool** *adj, verb*
1 (*coldness*) el **fresco** *masc*
Stay in the cool. Quedarse **[17]** al fresco.
2 (*calm*) la **calma** *fem*
to lose one's cool perder **[36]** la calma
He kept his cool. Mantuvo la calma.

to **cool** *verb* ▷ see **cool** *adj, noun*
to cool enfriarse **[32]**
- to **cool down**
enfriarse [32]

to **cooperate** *verb*
cooperar [17]

cop *noun*
el & la **poli** *masc & fem* (*informal*)

to **cope** *verb*
(*to manage*) **defenderse [36]**
She copes well. Se defiende bien.
He can't cope any more. Ya no puede más.
- to **cope with something**
1 (*children, work*) **ocuparse [17] de**
I'll cope with the dishes. Yo me ocupo de los platos.
2 (*a problem*) **hacer [7] frente a**
She's had a lot to cope with. Ha tenido que hacer frente a muchos problemas.

copper *noun*
el **cobre** *masc*

copy *noun* ▷ see **copy** *verb*
1 (*of a document, picture*) la **copia** *fem*
Make ten copies of this letter. Haz diez copias de esta carta.
2 (*of a book*) el **ejemplar** *masc*

to **copy** *verb* ▷ see **copy** *noun*
copiar [17]
I copied (down) the address. Copié las señas.

cord *noun*
1 *(string)* la **cuerda** *fem*
2 *(for a blind, etc)* el **cordón** *masc*

ℰ **cordial** *noun*
el **refresco concentrado**

cordless telephone *noun*
el **teléfono inalámbrico**

core *noun*
(of an apple, pear) el **corazón** *masc*

cork *noun*
1 *(in a bottle)* el **tapón** *masc*
2 *(the material)* el **corcho** *masc*
• **corkscrew** el sacacorchos

corn *noun*
1 *(wheat)* el **trigo** *masc*
2 *(sweetcorn)* el **maíz** *masc*

ℰ **corner** *noun*
1 *(of a street, page)* la **esquina** *fem*
in the bottom right-hand corner of the page en la esquina inferior derecha de la página
on the corner of the street en la esquina de la calle
It's just round the corner. Está a la vuelta de la esquina.
2 *(of a room, cupboard)* el **rincón** *masc*
in a corner of the kitchen en un rincón de la cocina
3 *(of your eye)* **out of the corner of your eye** por el rabillo del ojo
4 *(in football)* el **córner** *masc*

cornflakes *noun*
los **copos de maíz**

Cornwall *noun*
Cornualles *masc*

corpse *noun*
el **cadáver** *masc*

correct *adjective* ▷ see **correct** *verb*
correcto *masc*, **correcta** *fem*
the correct sum la cantidad total correcta
the correct answer la respuesta correcta
the correct choice la elección adecuada
Yes, that's correct. Sí, así es.

to **correct** *verb* ▷ see **correct** *adj*
corregir [48]

correction *noun*
la **corrección** *fem*

correctly *adverb*
correctamente
Have you filled in the form correctly? ¿Has rellenado el formulario correctamente?

to **correspond** *verb*
corresponder [18]

ℰ **correspondence** *noun*
la **correspondencia** *fem*

corridor *noun*
el **pasillo** *masc*

cosmetics *plural noun*
los **cosméticos** *masc plural*

ℰ **cost** *noun* ▷ see **cost** *verb*
el **coste** *masc*
the cost of a new computer el coste de un nuevo ordenador
the cost of living el coste de la vida

ℰ to **cost** *verb* ▷ see **cost** *noun*
costar [24]
How much does it cost? ¿Cuánto cuesta?
The tickets cost ten pounds. Las entradas cuestan diez libras.
It costs too much. Cuesta demasiado.

Costa Rica *noun*
Costa Rica *fem*

Costa Rican *adjective & noun*
1 **costarricense** *masc & fem*
2 un & una **costarricense** *masc & fem*
the Costa Ricans los costarricenses

WORD TIP Adjectives and nouns for nationality and regional origin do not have capital letters in Spanish.

ℰ **costume** *noun*
1 *(fancy dress)* el **disfraz** *masc*
2 *(for an actor)* el **traje** *masc*

cosy *adjective*
(room) **acogedor** *masc*, **acogedora** *fem*
It's cosy by the fire. Se está muy bien al lado del fuego.

cot *noun*
la **cuna** *fem*

cottage *noun*
la **casita en el campo**

ℰ **cotton** *noun*
1 *(fabric)* el **algodón** *masc*
a cotton shirt una camisa de algodón
2 *(thread)* el **hilo** *masc*
• **cotton wool** el algodón en rama

couch *noun*
el **sofá** *masc*

cough *noun* ▷ see **cough** *verb*
la **tos** *fem*
a nasty cough una tos mala
to have a cough tener **[9]** tos

to cough *verb* ▷ see **cough** *noun*
toser [18]

could *verb*

1 (*saying you are able to*) **poder [10]**
I couldn't open it. No podía abrirlo.
They couldn't smoke there. No podían fumar allí.
She did all she could. Hizo todo lo que pudo.

2 (*saying you know how to*) **saber [13]**
He couldn't drive. No sabía conducir.
I couldn't swim then. Entonces no sabía nadar.

3 (*asking permission, suggesting*) **poder [10]**
Could I speak to David? ¿Podría hablar con David?
You could try telephoning. Podrías intentar llamar por teléfono.

4 (*with words like: see, hear, feel, remember, etc*)
I could see her well. La veía bien.
She couldn't hear a thing. No oía nada.
I couldn't find my keys. No encontraba mis llaves.

WORD TIP When you use *could* with *see, hear, feel, remember*, etc, it is not translated into Spanish. ▷ **can**

5 (*for possibilities*) **poder [10]**
They could be home by now. Puede que ya estén en casa.
You could be right. Puede que tengas razón.
I would buy it if I could afford it. Lo compraría si pudiese.
I could have gone if I'd wanted. Habría podido ir si hubiese querido.

WORD TIP The verb in Spanish, telling you what the possibility is, is in the subjunctive.

couldn't *short for* **could not** (*See:* **could**)

council *noun*
el **consejo** *masc*
the town council el ayuntamiento
- **council flat** el piso de protección oficial
- **council house** la casa de protección oficial

councillor *noun*
el **concejal** *masc*, la **concejala** *fem*
Her uncle is a councillor. Su tío es concejal.

to count *verb*

1 (*to reckon up*) **contar [24]**
I counted my money. Conté mi dinero.
Thirty-five not counting the children. Treinta y cinco sin contar a los niños.

2 (*to be allowed*) **That doesn't count.** Eso no vale.

- **to count as**
considerarse [17] como
Children over twelve count as adults. Los niños mayores de doce años se consideran como adultos.

counter *noun*

1 (*in a shop*) el **mostrador** *masc*
2 (*in a cafe*) la **barra** *fem*
3 (*in a post office, bank*) la **ventanilla** *fem*
4 (*for board games*) la **ficha** *fem*

country *noun*

1 (*Spain, Britain, etc*) el **país** *masc*
a foreign country un país extranjero
from another country de otro país

2 (*not the town*) el **campo** *masc*
to live in the country vivir **[19]** en el campo
- **country dancing** el baile folklórico
- **country road** el camino rural
- **countryside** el campo
- **country walk** el paseo por el campo

county *noun*
el **condado** *masc*

couple *noun*

1 (*a pair*) la **pareja** *fem*
a married couple una pareja de casados

2 (*one or two*) **a couple of** un par de
a couple of times un par de veces
I've got a couple of things to do. Tengo que hacer un par de cosas.

courage *noun*
el **valor** *masc*

courgette *noun*
el **calabacín** *masc*

courier *noun*

1 (*delivery service*) la **mensajería** *fem*
by courier por mensajería

2 (*on a package holiday*) el & la **guía** *masc & fem*

course *noun*

1 (*lessons*) el **curso** *masc*
a beginners' course un curso para principiantes
a computer course un curso de informática
to go on a course asistir **[19]** a un curso

2 (*part of a meal*) el **plato** *masc*
the main course el plato principal

3 (*for sport*) **a golf course** un campo de golf

4 (*to show certainty*) **of course** claro
Yes, of course! ¡Sí, claro!
He's forgotten, of course. Se ha olvidado, claro.

court *noun*

1 (*for tennis, squash, basketball*) la **cancha** *fem*
2 (*of law*) el **tribunal** *masc*
- **courtyard** el patio

∫ **cousin** *noun*
el **primo** *masc*, la **prima** *fem*
my cousin Sonia mi prima Sonia

∫ **cover** *noun* ▷ see **cover** *verb*
1 (*for a book*) la **tapa** *fem*
2 (*for a duvet, cushion*) la **funda** *fem*
a duvet cover una funda de edredón

∫ to **cover** *verb* ▷ see **cover** *noun*
1 (*to hide*) **cubrir** [46]
to cover the wound cubrir la herida
The ground was covered with snow. El suelo estaba cubierto de nieve.
He was covered in mud. Estaba cubierto de barro.
2 (*your face, eyes*) **cubrirse** [46]
She covered her face. Se cubrió la cara.

∫ **cow** *noun*
la **vaca** *fem*
mad cow disease la enfermedad de las vacas locas

coward *noun*
el & la **cobarde** *masc & fem*

cowboy *noun*
el **vaquero** *masc*

crab *noun*
el **cangrejo** *masc*

crack *noun* ▷ see **crack** *verb*
1 (*in a wall*) la **grieta** *fem*
2 (*in a cup, plate*) la **raja** *fem*
3 (*a cracking noise*) el **crujido** *masc*

to **crack** *verb* ▷ see **crack** *noun*
1 (*a cup, window, etc*) **hacer** [7] **una raja en**
2 (*a bone*) **fracturar** [17]
3 (*a nut, an egg*) **cascar** [31]
4 (*ice*) **rajarse** [17]
5 (*sticks, etc*) **crujir** [19]

cracker *noun*
(*biscuit*) la **galleta salada**

to **crackle** *verb*
crujir [19]

craft *noun*
(*at school*) los **trabajos manuales**

crafty *adjective*
astuto *masc*, **astuta** *fem*
That was very crafty of her. Eso fue muy astuto por su parte.

cramp *noun*
el **calambre** *masc*
I've got cramp in my leg. Tengo un calambre en la pierna.

crane *noun*
la **grúa** *fem*

to **crash** *verb* ▷ see **crash** *noun*
1 (*cars, planes*) **estrellarse** [17]
The plane crashed. El avión se estrelló.
to crash into something chocar [31] con algo
The car crashed into a tree. El coche chocó con un árbol.
2 (*Computers*) **colgarse** [23]

crash *noun* ▷ see **crash** *verb*
1 (*accident*) el **accidente** *masc*
a car crash un accidente de coche
2 (*smashing noise*) el **estrépito** *masc*
a crash of broken glass un estrépito de cristales rotos
• **crash course** el curso intensivo
• **crash helmet** el casco

∫ **crate** *noun*
1 (*for china*) el **cajón para embalar**
2 (*for bottles, fruit*) la **caja** *fem*

crawl *noun* ▷ see **crawl** *verb*
(*in swimming*) el **crol** *masc*

to **crawl** *verb* ▷ see **crawl** *noun*
1 (*people, babies*) **ir** [8] **a gatas**
2 (*cars in a jam*) **ir** [8] **muy despacio**
We were crawling along. Íbamos muy despacio.

crayon *noun*
1 (*wax*) la **pintura de cera**
2 (*coloured pencil*) el **lápiz de color**

craze *noun*
la **fiebre** *fem*
the craze for computer games la fiebre de los juegos de ordenador

∫ **crazy** *adjective*
loco *masc*, **loca** *fem*
to go crazy volverse [45] loco
to be crazy about someone, something estar [2] loco por alguien, algo
He's crazy about football. A él le encanta el fútbol.
She's crazy about tennis. A ella le encanta el tenis.

to **creak** *verb*
(*a hinge*) **chirriar** [32], (*a floorboard*) **crujir** [19]

∫ **cream** *noun*
1 (*on milk*) la **nata** *fem*
strawberries and cream fresas con nata
2 (*for hands, face, etc*) la **crema** *fem*
• **cream cheese** el queso para untar

crease *noun*
la **arruga** *fem*

creased *adjective*
arrugado *masc*, **arrugada** *fem*

to **create** *verb*
crear [17]

creative *adjective*
creativo *masc*, **creativa** *fem*

creature *noun*
la **criatura** *fem*

creche *noun*
la **guardería** *fem*

credit *noun*
el **crédito** *masc*
to buy something on credit comprar [17] algo a crédito
- **credit card** la tarjeta de crédito

crew *noun*
1 (*on a ship, plane*) la **tripulación** *fem*
2 (*in rowing, for filming*) el **equipo** *masc*
- **crew cut** el corte de pelo al rape

cricket *noun*
1 (*the game*) el **críquet** *masc*
to play cricket jugar [27] al críquet
2 (*the insect*) el **grillo** *masc*
- **cricket bat** el bate de críquet

crime *noun*
1 (*minor offence*) el **delito** *masc*
Theft is a crime. El robo es un delito.
2 (*murder*) el **crimen** *masc*
3 (*within society*) el **crimen** *masc*
the fight against crime la lucha contra el crimen

criminal *adjective* ▷ see **criminal** *noun*
criminal *masc & fem*

criminal *noun* ▷ see **criminal** *adj*
el & la **criminal** *masc & fem*

crisis *noun*
la **crisis** *fem*

crisp *adjective* ▷ see **crisp** *noun*
crujiente *masc & fem*

crisp *noun* ▷ see **crisp** *adj*
la **patata frita**
a packet of (potato) crisps un paquete de patatas fritas

critical *adjective*
1 (*remark, somebody's condition*) **crítico** *masc*, **crítica** *fem*
2 (*moment*) **decisivo** *masc*, **decisiva** *fem*

criticism *noun*
la **crítica** *fem*

to **criticize** *verb*
criticar [31]

Croatia *noun*
Croacia *fem*

crockery *noun*
la **vajilla** *fem*

crocodile *noun*
el **cocodrilo** *masc*

crook *noun*
(*criminal*) el & la **granuja** *masc & fem*

crooked *adjective*
torcido *masc*, **torcida** *fem*
a crooked line una línea torcida

crop *noun*
la **cosecha** *fem*

cross *adjective* ▷ see **cross** *noun, verb*
enfadado *masc*, **enfadada** *fem*
She's very cross. Está muy enfadada.
I'm cross with you. Estoy enfadado contigo.
to get cross enfadarse [17]

cross *noun* ▷ see **cross** *adj, verb*
la **cruz** *fem*

to **cross** *verb* ▷ see **cross** *adj, noun*
1 (*to cross over*) **cruzar** [22]
to cross the road cruzar la calle
to cross your legs cruzar las piernas
2 (*to cross each other*) **cruzarse** [22]
The two roads cross here. Las dos carreteras se cruzan aquí.
- to **cross out**
(*a word, sentence*) **tachar** [17]

cross-Channel *adjective*
a cross-Channel ferry un ferry que cruza el Canal de la Mancha

cross-country *noun*
el **cross** *masc*
cross-country skiing esquí de fondo

crossing *noun*
la **travesía** *fem*
a Channel crossing una travesía por el Canal de la Mancha

cross-legged *adjective*
to sit cross-legged sentarse [29] con las piernas cruzadas

crossroads *noun*
el **cruce** *masc*
at the crossroads en el cruce

crossword *noun*
el **crucigrama** *masc*
I'm doing the crossword. Estoy haciendo el crucigrama.

to **crouch** *verb*
ponerse [11] en cuclillas

crow *noun* ▷ see **crow** *verb*
el **cuervo** *masc*

to **crow** *verb* ▷ see **crow** *noun*
(*cockrels*) **cacarear [17]**

crowd *noun*
la **multitud** *fem*
in the crowd en la multitud
a crowd of 5,000 una multitud de cinco mil personas

crowded *adjective*
lleno de gente *masc*, **llena de gente** *fem*

crown *noun*
la **corona** *fem*

crude *adjective*
1 (*rough and ready*) **rudimentario** *masc*, **rudimentaria** *fem*
2 (*vulgar*) **grosero** *masc*, **grosera** *fem*

cruel *adjective*
cruel *masc & fem*

cruelty *noun*
la **crueldad** *fem*
They were treated with great cruelty. Los trataron con gran crueldad.

cruise *noun*
el **crucero** *masc*
to go on a cruise ir **[8]** de crucero

crumb *noun*
la **miga** *fem*

to **crumple** *verb*
arrugar [28]

crunchy *adjective*
crujiente *masc & fem*

to **crush** *verb*
aplastar [17]

crust *noun*
la **corteza** *fem*

crutch *noun*
la **muleta** *fem*
to be on crutches andar **[21]** con muletas

♪ **cry** *noun* ▷ see **cry** *verb*
el **grito** *masc*

♪ to **cry** *verb* ▷ see **cry** *noun*
1 (*to weep*) **llorar [17]**
2 (*to call out*) **gritar [17]**

crystal *noun*
el **cristal** *masc*

cub *noun*
1 (*animal*) el **cachorro** *masc*
2 (*scout*) el **lobato** *masc*

Cuba *noun*
Cuba *fem*

Cuban *adjective & noun*
1 **cubano** *masc*, **cubana** *fem*
2 un **cubano** *masc*, una **cubana** *fem*
the Cubans los cubanos

WORD TIP Adjectives and nouns for nationality and regional origin do not have capital letters in Spanish.

cube *noun*
el **cubo** *masc*
an ice cube un cubito de hielo

cubic *adjective*
(*for measurements*) **cúbico** *masc*, **cúbica** *fem*
three cubic metres tres metros cúbicos

cubicle *noun*
1 (*in a changing room*) el **vestuario** *masc*
2 (*in a public lavatory*) el **cubículo** *masc*

cuckoo *noun*
el **cuco** *masc*

cucumber *noun*
el **pepino** *masc*

cuddle *noun* ▷ see **cuddle** *verb*
to give somebody a cuddle dar **[4]** un abrazo a alguien

to **cuddle** *verb* ▷ see **cuddle** *noun*
abrazar [22]

cue *noun*
(*used in billiards, pool, snooker*) el **taco** *masc*

cuff *noun*
(*on a shirt*) el **puño** *masc*

cul-de-sac *noun*
el **callejón sin salida**

culture *noun*
la **cultura** *fem*

cunning *adjective*
astuto *masc*, **astuta** *fem*

♪ **cup** *noun*
1 (*for drinking*) la **taza** *fem*
a cup of tea una taza de té
2 (*trophy*) la **copa** *fem*

♪ **cupboard** *noun*
el **armario** *masc*
in the kitchen cupboard en el armario de la cocina

cup tie *noun*
el **partido de copa**

cure *noun* ▷ see **cure** *verb*
la **cura** *fem*

to **cure** *verb* ▷ see **cure** *noun*
curar [17]

curiosity *noun*
la **curiosidad** *fem*

curious *adjective*
curioso *masc*, **curiosa** *fem*

curl *noun* ▷ see **curl** *verb*
el **rizo** *masc*

to **curl** *verb* ▷ see **curl** *noun*
(*hair*) **rizar** [22]

curly *adjective*
rizado *masc*, **rizada** *fem*

currant *noun*
la **pasa de Corinto**

currency *noun*
la **moneda** *fem*
foreign currency moneda extranjera

current *adjective* ▷ see **current** *noun*
actual *masc & fem*
• **current affairs** los sucesos de actualidad

current *noun* ▷ see **current** *adj*
(*of electricity, water*) la **corriente** *fem*

curriculum *noun*
1 (*national*) el **plan de estudios**
2 (*for a single course*) el **programa de estudios**

curry *noun*
el **curry** *masc*
a chicken curry un curry de pollo

cursor *noun*
el **cursor** *masc*

curtain *noun*
la **cortina** *fem*

cushion *noun*
el **cojín** *masc*

custard *noun*
1 (*runny*) las **natillas** *plural fem*
2 (*baked*) el **flan** *masc*

custom *noun*
la **costumbre** *fem*

customer *noun*
el **cliente** *masc*, la **clienta** *fem*
• **customer services** la atención al cliente

customs *plural noun*
la **aduana** *singular fem*
to go through customs pasar [17] por la aduana
• **customs hall** la aduana
• **customs officer** el & la agente de aduana

cut *noun* ▷ see **cut** *verb*
(*injury, haircut*) el **corte** *masc*

to **cut** *verb* ▷ see **cut** *noun*
1 (*with scissors, a knife, a mower, etc*) **cortar** [17]
to cut the grass cortar la hierba
I've cut the bread. He cortado el pan.
You'll cut yourself! ¡Te vas a cortar!
Kevin's cut his finger. Kevin se ha cortado el dedo.
Alicia's had her hair cut. Alicia se ha cortado el pelo.
2 (*prices*) **recortar** [17]
• to **cut something down**
(*a tree*) **cortar** [17] **algo**
• to **cut down on something**
to cut down on fats consumir [19], menos grasas
• to **cut something out**
1 (*a newspaper article*) **recortar** [17] **algo**
2 (*sugar, fatty food, etc*) **suprimir** [19] **algo**
• to **cut something up**
(*food*) **cortar** [17] **algo en trocitos**

cute *adjective*
mono *masc*, **mona** *fem*

cutlery *noun*
la **cubertería** *fem*

CV *noun*
el **currículum**

to **cycle** *verb* ▷ see **cycle** *noun*
montar [17] **en bicicleta**
Do you like cycling? ¿Te gusta montar en bicicleta?
We cycle to school. Vamos al colegio en bicicleta.

cycle *noun* ▷ see **cycle** *verb*
(*bike*) la **bicicleta** *fem*
• **cycle lane** el carril de bicicletas
• **cycle race** la carrera de ciclismo

cycling *noun*
el **ciclismo** *masc*
• **cycling holiday** las vacaciones en bicicleta

cyclist *noun*
el & la **ciclista** *masc & fem*

cylinder *noun*
el **cilindro** *masc*
a gas cylinder una bombona

D d

♪ **dad** *noun*
1 (*father*) el **padre** *masc*
Anna's dad el padre de Ana
My dad works in a bank. Mi padre trabaja en un banco.
2 (*daddy*) el **papá** *masc*
Dad's not home yet. Papá no ha llegado a casa aún.

♪ **daddy** *noun*
el **papá** *masc*

daffodil *noun*
el **narciso** *masc*

daily *adjective* ▷ see **daily** *adv*
diario *masc*, **diaria** *fem*
his daily visit su visita diaria

daily *adverb* ▷ see **daily** *adj*
a diario
She visits him daily. Le visita a diario.

dairy products *plural noun*
los **productos lácteos**

daisy *noun*
la **margarita** *fem*

dam *noun*
la **presa** *fem*

♪ **damage** *noun* ▷ see **damage** *verb*
daño *masc*
The damage is done. El daño ya está hecho.
There's no damage. No ha habido daños.

to **damage** *verb* ▷ see **damage** *noun*
dañar [17]

damn *noun* ▷ see **damn** *excl*
(*informal*) **He doesn't give a damn.** Le importa un comino.

damn *exclamation* ▷ see **damn** *noun*
(*informal*) **Damn!** ¡Maldita sea!

damp *adjective* ▷ see **damp** *noun*
húmedo *masc*, **húmeda** *fem*

damp *noun* ▷ see **damp** *adj*
la **humedad** *fem*
because of the damp a causa de la humedad

♪ **dance** *noun* ▷ see **dance** *verb*
el **baile** *masc*
a folk dance un baile folklórico

♪ to **dance** *verb* ▷ see **dance** *noun*
bailar [17]
I like dancing. Me gusta bailar.

dancer *noun*
el **bailarín** *masc*, la **bailarina** *fem*

dancing *noun*
el **baile** *masc*
I love dancing. Me encanta bailar.

dancing class *noun*
la **clase de baile**
to go to dancing classes ir [8] a clase de baile

dandruff *noun*
la **caspa** *fem*

Dane *noun*
un **danés** *masc*, una **danesa** *fem*
the Danes los daneses

WORD TIP Adjectives and nouns for nationality and regional origin do not have capital letters in Spanish.

danger *noun*
el **peligro** *masc*
to be in danger estar [2] en peligro
to be out of danger estar [2] fuera de peligro

♪ **dangerous** *adjective*
peligroso *masc*, **peligrosa** *fem*
It's dangerous to drive so fast. Es peligroso conducir tan rápido.

Danish *adjective & noun*
1 **danés** *masc*, **danesa** *fem*
2 (*the language*) el **danés** *masc*

WORD TIP Adjectives and nouns for nationality, regional origin and language do not have capital letters in Spanish.

to **dare** *verb*
1 (*to be brave enough*) **atreverse** [18]
How dare you! ¡Cómo te atreves!
to dare to do something atreverse a hacer algo
I didn't dare to suggest it. No me atreví a sugerirlo.
Don't you dare tell her I'm here! ¡No se te ocurra decirle que estoy aquí!
2 (*to challenge someone*) **I dare you!** ¡A que no te atreves! (*informal*)
I dare you to tell him! ¡A que no te atreves a decírselo! (*informal*)

daring *adjective*
osado *masc*, **osada** *fem*
That was a bit daring! ¡Eso fue un poco osado!

dark *adjective* ▷ see **dark** *noun*
1 (*colour, room*) **oscuro** *masc*, **oscura** *fem*
a dark blue suit un traje azul oscuro
She has dark brown hair. Tiene el pelo castaño oscuro.
The kitchen's a bit dark. La cocina es un poco oscura.
It's dark in here. Está oscuro aquí.
2 (*night-time*) **to get dark** oscurecer [35]
It gets dark around five. Oscurece a eso de las cinco.
It's dark already. Ya es de noche.

dark *noun* ▷ see **dark** *adj*
in the dark en la oscuridad
after dark de noche
to be afraid of the dark tener [9] miedo de la oscuridad

darkness *noun*
la **oscuridad** *fem*

darling *noun*
el **querido** *masc*, la **querida** *fem*
See you later, darling! ¡Te veo luego querido!

dart *noun*
el **dardo** *masc*
to play darts jugar [27] a los dardos

data *plural noun*
los **datos** *masc plural*
• **database** la base de datos

⚷ **date** *noun*
1 (*on the calendar*) la **fecha** *fem*
the date of the meeting la fecha de la reunión
What's the date today? ¿Qué día es hoy?
to fix a date for something fijar [17] una fecha para algo
2 (*with a boyfriend, girlfriend*) **I have a date with Jerry on Sunday.** He quedado para salir con Jerry el domingo.
3 (*the fruit*) el **dátil** *masc*
• **date of birth** la fecha de nacimiento

⚷ **daughter** *noun*
la **hija** *fem*
Tina's daughter la hija de Tina
• **daughter-in-law** la nuera

dawn *noun*
el **amanecer** *masc*

⚷ **day** *noun*
el **día** *masc*
three days later tres días más tarde
It rained all day. Llovió todo el día.
It's going to be a nice day tomorrow. Mañana va a hacer buen día.
the day after al día siguiente
the day after tomorrow pasado mañana
the day before el día anterior
the day before yesterday anteayer
every day todos los días
• **day off** el día libre

⚷ **dead** *adjective* ▷ see **dead** *adv*
muerto *masc*, **muerta** *fem*
He's dead. Está muerto.

⚷ **dead** *adverb* ▷ see **dead** *adj*
(*informal: really*) **super**
He's dead nice. Es super majo.
It's dead easy. Es super fácil.
It was dead good. Fue genial.
You're dead right. Tienes toda la razón.
She arrived dead on time. Llegó justo a la hora.
• **dead end** el callejón sin salida
• **deadline** la fecha límite

⚷ **deaf** *adjective*
sordo *masc*, **sorda** *fem*
to go deaf quedarse [17] sordo

deafening *adjective*
ensordecedor *masc*, **ensordecedora** *fem*

deal *noun* ▷ see **deal** *verb*
1 (*involving money*) el **negocio** *masc*
It's a good deal. Es un buen negocio.
2 (*pact*) el **trato** *masc*
I'll make a deal with you. Voy a hacer un trato contigo.
It's a deal! ¡Trato hecho!
3 (*to describe quantity*) **a great deal of energy** mucha energía
I don't have a great deal of time. No tengo mucho tiempo.
a great deal mucho
it has improved a great deal ha mejorado mucho

to **deal** *verb* ▷ see **deal** *noun*
(*in cards*) **repartir** [19]
• **to deal with something**
ocuparse [17] **de algo**
Linda deals with the accounts. Linda se ocupa de las cuentas.
I'll deal with it as soon as possible. Me ocuparé de ello tan pronto como sea posible.

𝆑 **dear** *adjective*
1 (*term of affection*) **querido** *masc*, **querida** *fem*
Dear Jo Querida Jo
2 (*expensive*) **caro** *masc*, **cara** *fem*

death *noun*
la **muerte** *fem*
after his father's death después de la muerte de su padre
• **death penalty** la pena de muerte

debate *noun* ▷ see **debate** *verb*
el **debate** *masc*

to **debate** *verb* ▷ see **debate** *noun*
debatir [19]

𝆑 **debit card** *noun*
la **tarjeta de cobro automático**

debt *noun*
la **deuda** *fem*
to get into debt endeudarse [17]

decade *noun*
década *fem*

decaffeinated *adjective*
descafeinado *masc*, **descafeinada** *fem*

to **deceive** *verb*
engañar [17]

𝆑 **December** *noun*
diciembre *masc*

WORD TIP Names of months and days start with small letters in Spanish.

decent *adjective*
decente *masc & fem*
a decent salary un sueldo decente
a decent meal una comida decente
He seems a decent enough guy. Parece un tipo decente.

𝆑 to **decide** *verb*
decidir [19]
to decide to do something decidir hacer algo
She's decided to buy a car. Ha decidido comprarse un coche.
They've decided not to go on holiday. Han decidido no irse de vacaciones.

decimal *adjective*
decimal *masc & fem*
• **decimal point** el punto decimal, la coma (*Most Spanish-speaking countries use a comma in maths for a decimal point.*)

decision *noun*
la **decisión** *fem*
the right decision la decisión acertada
the wrong decision la decisión errónea
to make a decision tomar [17] una decisión

deck *noun*
(*on a ship*) la **cubierta** *fem*
• **deckchair** la tumbona

to **declare** *verb*
declarar [17]

to **decorate** *verb*
1 (*to put decorations on*) **adornar** [17]
to decorate the Christmas tree adornar el árbol de Navidad
2 (*with paint*) **pintar** [17]
3 (*with wallpaper*) **empapelar** [17]

decoration *noun*
1 (*the act of adornment*) la **decoración** *fem*
2 (*an ornament*) el **adorno** *masc*

decorator *noun*
el **pintor** *masc*, la **pintora** *fem*

decrease *noun* ▷ see **decrease** *verb*
la **disminución** *fem*
a decrease in the number of something una disminución en el número de algo

to **decrease** *verb* ▷ see **decrease** *noun*
disminuir [54]

to **deduct** *verb*
deducir [60]

deep *adjective*
profundo *masc*, **profunda** *fem*
a deep feeling of gratitude un profundo sentimiento de gratitud
a hole two metres deep un agujero de dos metros de profundidad
The river is very deep here. Aquí el río es muy profundo.
How deep is the swimming pool? ¿Qué profundidad tiene la piscina?
• **deep end** (*of a swimming pool*) la parte honda
• **deep freeze** el congelador

deeply *adverb*
profundamente

deer *noun*
el **ciervo** *masc*

defeat *noun* ▷ see **defeat** *verb*
la **derrota** *fem*

to **defeat** *verb* ▷ see **defeat** *noun*
derrotar [17]

defect *noun*
el **defecto** *masc*

defence *noun*
la **defensa** *fem*

to **defend** *verb*
defender [36]

defender *noun*
1 (*supporter of a cause*) el **defensor** *masc*, la **defensora** *fem*
2 (*in football, etc*) el & la **defensa** *masc & fem*

to **define** *verb*
definir [19]

definite *adjective*
1 (*clear*) **claro** *masc*, **clara** *fem*
a definite improvement una clara mejora
a definite advantage una clara ventaja
It's a definite possibility. Es claramente una posibilidad.
2 (*certain*) **seguro** *masc*, **segura** *fem*
It's not definite yet. Aún no es seguro.
3 (*exact*) **preciso** *masc*, **precisa** *fem*
a definite answer una respuesta precisa
I don't have a definite idea of what I want. No tengo una idea precisa de lo que quiero.
• **definite article** el artículo definido

definitely *adverb*
1 (*showing your opinion*) **sin ninguna duda**
The blue one is definitely the biggest. El azul es sin ninguna duda el más grande.
Your French is definitely better than mine. Hablas francés mejor que yo sin ninguna duda.
'Are you sure you like this one better?'— 'Definitely.' ¿Estás seguro de que te gusta más éste?'—'Segurísimo.'
2 (*for certain*) **She's definitely going to be there.** Seguro que va a estar aquí.
Definitely not! ¡En absoluto!
She definitely said she would do it. Dijo que seguro que lo haría.

definition *noun*
la **definición** *fem*

degree *noun*
1 (*amount, measurement*) el **grado** *masc*
thirty degrees treinta grados
2 (*qualification*) **a university degree** un título universitario

delay *noun* ▷ see **delay** *verb*
el **retraso** *masc*
a two-hour delay un retraso de dos horas

to **delay** *verb* ▷ see **delay** *noun*
retrasar [17]
The flight was delayed by bad weather. El mal tiempo retrasó el vuelo.
The decision has been delayed until Thursday. Retrasaron la decisión hasta el jueves.

deliberate *adjective*
deliberado *masc*, **deliberada** *fem*

deliberately *adverb*
a propósito
You did it deliberately. Lo hiciste a propósito.
He left it there deliberately. Lo dejó allí a propósito.

delicate *adjective*
delicado *masc*, **delicada** *fem*

delicatessen *noun*
la **charcutería** *fem*

delicious *adjective*
delicioso *masc*, **deliciosa** *fem*

delighted *adjective*
encantado *masc*, **encantada** *fem*
They're delighted with their new flat. Están encantados con su nuevo piso.
I'm delighted to hear you can come. Estoy encantado de saber que puedes venir.

to **deliver** *verb*
1 (*goods*) **entregar [28]**
the person who delivered the parcel la persona que entregó el paquete
2 (*mail*) **repartir [19]**

delivery *noun*
la **entrega** *fem*

demand *noun* ▷ see **demand** *verb*
la **petición** *fem*

to **demand** *verb* ▷ see **demand** *noun*
exigir [49]

democracy *noun*
la **democracia** *fem*

democratic *adjective*
democrático *masc*, **democrática** *fem*

to **demolish** *verb*
destruir [54]

to **demonstrate** *verb*
1 (*a theory, a skill*) **demostrar [24]**
2 (*a machine, a product, a technique*) **hacer [7] una demostración de**
3 (*to protest*) **manifestarse [29]**
to demonstrate against something manifestarse en contra de algo

demonstration *noun*
1 (*of a machine, product, technique*) la **demostración** *fem*
2 (*protest*) la **manifestación** *fem*

demonstrator *noun*
(*in protest*) el & la **manifestante** *masc & fem*

denim *noun*
la **tela vaquera**
a denim jacket una chaqueta vaquera

Denmark *noun*
Dinamarca *fem*

dense *adjective*
denso *masc*, **densa** *fem*

dent *noun* ▷ see **dent** *verb*
la **abolladura** *fem*

to **dent** *verb* ▷ see **dent** *noun*
abollar [17]

dental *adjective*
dental *masc & fem*
- **dental appointment** la cita con el dentista
- **dental floss** el hilo dental
- **dental hygiene** la higiene dental
- **dental surgeon** el cirujano dentista, la cirujana dentista

♪ **dentist** *noun*
el & la **dentista** *masc & fem*
My mum's a dentist. Mi madre es dentista.

to **deny** *verb*
negar [30]

deodorant *noun*
el **desodorante** *masc*

to **depart** *verb*
salir [63]

♪ **department** *noun*
1 (*in school, university*) el **departamento** *masc*
the language department el departamento de idiomas
2 (*in a shop*) la **sección** *fem*
the men's department la sección de caballeros
- **department store** los grandes almacenes

♪ **departure** *noun*
la **salida** *fem*
- **departure gate** la puerta de embarque
- **departure lounge** la sala de embarque

to **depend** *verb*
to depend on something depender [18] de algo
It depends. Depende.
It depends on the price. Depende del precio.
It depends on what you want. Depende de lo que tú quieras

WORD TIP *depende de lo que* is followed by a verb in the subjunctive.

deposit *noun*
1 (*for renting, making bookings, etc*) el **depósito** *masc*
to pay a deposit pagar [28] un depósito
2 (*for buying something*) la **entrada** *fem*

depressed *adjective*
deprimido *masc*, **deprimida** *fem*

depressing *adjective*
deprimente *masc & fem*

depth *noun*
la **profundidad** *fem*

deputy *noun*
el **segundo** *masc*, la **segunda** *fem*
- **deputy head** el subdirector, la subdirectora

to **descend** *verb*
descender [36]

♪ to **describe** *verb*
describir [52]

♪ **description** *noun*
la **descripción** *fem*

desert *noun*
el **desierto** *masc*
- **desert island** la isla desierta

mini-info **desert**

The Atacama desert in northern Chile is the driest place in the world, suffering almost 400 years of drought until 1971.

to **deserve** *verb*
merecer [35]

design *noun* ▷ see **design** *verb*
el **diseño** *masc*
the design of the plane el diseño del avión
a floral design un diseño de flores
fashion design diseño de moda

to **design** *verb* ▷ see **design** *noun*
diseñar [17]

designer *noun*
el **diseñador** *masc*, la **diseñadora** *fem*

desire *noun* ▷ see **desire** *verb*
el **deseo** *masc*

to **desire** *verb* ▷ see **desire** *noun*
desear [17]

♪ **desk** *noun*
1 (*in an office, at home*) el **escritorio** *masc*
the reception desk la recepción
the information desk Información
2 (*at school*) el **pupitre** *masc*

despair *noun*
la **desesperación** *fem*

desperate *adjective*
1 (*despairing*) **desesperado** *masc*, **desesperada** *fem*
a desperate attempt un intento desesperado ⏩

2 (*impatient*) **to be desperate to do something** estar [2] deseando hacer algo
I'm desperate to see you. Estoy deseando verte.

to **despise** *verb*
despreciar [17]

dessert *noun*
el **postre** *masc*
What's for dessert? ¿Qué hay de postre?

destination *noun*
el **destino** *masc*

to **destroy** *verb*
destruir [54]

destruction *noun*
la **destrucción** *fem*

detached house *noun*
la **casa no adosada**

detail *noun*
el **detalle** *masc*

detailed *adjective*
detallado *masc*, **detallada** *fem*

detective *noun*
1 (*police officer*) el & la **agente** *masc & fem*
2 (*for private investigations*) **a private detective** un detective privado, una detective privada
- **detective novel** la novela policiaca
- **detective story** la novela policiaca

detention *noun*
(*in school*) **to be in detention** estar [2] castigado (*for a boy*), estar castigada (*for a girl*)

detergent *noun*
el **detergente** *masc*

determined *adjective*
decidido *masc*, **decidida** *fem*
to be determined to do something estar [2] determinado a hacer algo
She's determined to leave. Está decidida a irse.

detour *noun*
el **rodeo** *masc*

to **develop** *verb*
1 (*a film*) **revelar** [17]
to get a film developed revelar un carrete de fotos
2 (*people*) **desarrollarse** [17]
how children develop cómo se desarrollan los niños

developing country *noun*
el **país en vías de desarrollo**

development *noun*
el **desarrollo** *masc*

devil *noun*
el **diablo** *masc*

dew *noun*
el **rocío** *masc*

diabetes *noun*
la **diabetes** *fem*

diabetic *adjective* ▷ see **diabetic** *noun*
diabético *masc*, **diabética** *fem*
to be diabetic ser [1] diabético

diabetic *noun* ▷ see **diabetic** *adj*
el **diabético** *masc*, la **diabética** *fem*

diagonal *adjective*
diagonal *masc & fem*

diagnosis *noun*
el **diagnóstico** *masc*

diagram *noun*
el **diagrama** *masc*

to **dial** *verb*
marcar [31]
Dial 00 34 for Spain. Marca 00 34 para España.

dialling tone *noun*
el **tono de marcar**

dialogue *noun*
el **diálogo** *masc*

diameter *noun*
el **diámetro** *masc*

diamond *noun*
1 (*jewel*) el **diamante** *masc*
2 (*in cards*) **diamonds** diamantes
the jack of diamonds la jota de diamantes
3 (*shape*) el **rombo** *masc*

diarrhoea *noun*
la **diarrea** *fem*
to have diarrhoea tener [9] diarrea

diary *noun*
1 (*for dates*) la **agenda** *fem*
I've noted the date of the meeting in my diary. He anotado la fecha de la reunión en mi agenda.
2 (*personal journal*) el **diario íntimo**
to keep a diary tener [9] un diario íntimo

dice *noun*
el **dado** *masc*
to throw the dice tirar [17] los dados

dictation *noun*
el **dictado** *masc*

dictionary *noun*
el **diccionario** *masc*
to look up a word in the dictionary buscar [31] una palabra en el diccionario

did *verb* ▷ **do**

didn't *short for* **did not** (*See:* **to do**)

to **die** *verb*
1 **morir** [55]
My grandmother died in January. Mi abuela murió en enero.
2 **to be dying to do something** estar [2] deseando hacer algo
I'm dying to see them! ¡Estoy deseando verlos!
• to **die out**
desaparecer [35]
The tradition is dying out. La tradición está desapareciendo.

diesel *noun*
el **diesel** *masc*
• **diesel car** el diesel
• **diesel engine** el motor diesel

♪ **diet** *noun*
1 (*what you eat*) la **dieta** *fem*
to have a healthy diet llevar [17] una dieta saludable
2 (*to slim, special requirements*) el **régimen** *masc*
a salt-free diet un régimen sin sal
to be on a diet estar [2] a régimen
to go on a diet ponerse [11] a régimen

♪ **difference** *noun*
1 (*distinction*) la **diferencia** *fem*
I can't see any difference between the two. No puedo ver ninguna diferencia entre los dos.
What's the difference between ...? ¿Qué diferencia hay entre ...?
2 (*alteration*) **It makes a difference.** Eso cambia las cosas.
It makes no difference. Da lo mismo.
It makes no difference what I say. Da lo mismo lo que yo diga.

♪ **different** *adjective*
distinto *masc*, **distinta** *fem*
The two sisters are very different. Las dos hermanas son muy distintas.
She's very different from her sister. Es muy distinta a su hermana.

♪ **difficult** *adjective*
difícil *masc & fem*
It's really difficult. Es muy difícil.
It's difficult to decide. Es difícil decidir.

difficulty *noun*
la **dificultad** *fem*
I had difficulty finding your house. Me resultó difícil encontrar tu casa.

to **dig** *verb*
cavar [17]
to dig a hole cavar un agujero

digestion *noun*
la **digestión** *fem*

digital *adjective*
digital *masc & fem*
a digital camera una cámara digital
a digital radio una radio digital

dignity *noun*
la **dignidad** *fem*

dim *adjective*
1 (*weak*) **tenue** *masc & fem*
a dim light una luz tenue
2 (*informal: unintelligent*) **tonto** *masc*, **tonta** *fem*
She's a bit dim. Es un poco tonta.

dimension *noun*
la **dimensión** *fem*

din *noun*
el **ruido** *masc*
They were making a dreadful din. Estaban haciendo un ruido enorme.
Stop making such a din! ¡Deja de hacer tanto ruido!

dinghy *noun*
a sailing dinghy un bote
a rubber dinghy un bote neumático

♪ **dining room** *noun*
el **comedor** *masc*

♪ **dinner** *noun*
1 (*evening meal*) la **cena** *fem*
to have dinner cenar [17]
to invite somebody to dinner invitar [17] a alguien a cenar
2 (*midday meal*) la **comida** *fem*
to have dinner comer [18]
to have school dinners comer [18] en el colegio

dinner time *noun*
1 (*in the evening*) la **hora de cenar**
2 (*at midday*) la **hora de comer**

dinosaur *noun*
el **dinosaurio** *masc*

♪ **diploma** *noun*
el **diploma** *masc*

direct *adjective* ▷ see **direct** *adv, verb*
directo *masc*, **directa** *fem*
a direct flight un vuelo directo

direct *adverb* ▷ see **direct** *adj, verb*
directo
The bus goes direct to the airport. El autobús va directo al aeropuerto.

to **direct** *verb* ▷ see **direct** *adj, adv*
1 *(a programme, a film, a play, the traffic)* **dirigir [49]**
2 *(give directions to)* **to direct someone somewhere** indicarle **[31]** a alguien el camino a un lugar
I directed them to the station. Les indiqué el camino a la estación.

direction *noun*
1 *(the way to somewhere)* la **dirección** *fem*
in the other direction en la otra dirección
in the direction of the church en dirección a la iglesia
in all directions en todas direcciones
to ask somebody for directions pedir **[57]** a alguien que te indique el camino
2 *(instruction)* **directions for use** instrucciones de uso

directly *adverb*
1 *(to go, fly, deal, ask)* **directamente**
2 *(at once)* **inmediatamente**
directly afterwards inmediatamente después

director *noun*
el **director** *masc*, la **directora** *fem*

directory *noun*
la **guía telefónica**
• **directory enquiries** el servicio de información telefónica

dirt *noun*
la **suciedad** *fem*

dirty *adjective*
sucio *masc*, **sucia** *fem*
My hands are dirty. Tengo las manos sucias.
to get dirty ensuciarse **[17]**
The curtains get dirty quickly. Las cortinas se ensucian rápido.
to get something dirty ensuciar **[17]** algo
I got the floor dirty. Ensucié el suelo.
You'll get your dress dirty. Te vas a ensuciar el vestido.

disability *noun*
la **discapacidad** *fem*
Does he have a disability? ¿Tiene alguna discapacidad?

disabled *adjective*
discapacitado *masc*, **discapacitada** *fem*
disabled people los discapacitados

disadvantage *noun*
1 la **desventaja** *fem*
2 **to be at a disadvantage** estar **[2]** en desventaja

to **disagree** *verb*
no estar [2] de acuerdo
I disagree. No estoy de acuerdo.
I disagree with James. No estoy de acuerdo con James.

to **disappear** *verb*
desaparecer [35]

disappearance *noun*
la **desaparición** *fem*

disappointed *adjective*
decepcionado *masc*, **decepcionada** *fem*
I was disappointed with my marks. Mis notas me decepcionaron.

disappointment *noun*
la **decepción** *fem*

disaster *noun*
el **desastre** *masc*
It was a complete disaster. Fue un completo desastre.

disastrous *adjective*
desastroso *masc*, **desastrosa** *fem*

disc *noun*
el **disco** *masc*
a slipped disc una hernia de disco
a compact disc un disco compacto

discipline *noun*
la **disciplina** *fem*

disc jockey *noun*
el & la **disc-jockey** *masc & fem*

disco *noun*
1 *(dance)* el **baile** *masc*
They're having a disco. Tienen un baile.
2 *(club)* la **disco** *fem*, la **discoteca**

to **disconnect** *verb*
desconectar [17]
Have you disconnected the electricity? ¿Has desconectado la electricidad?

discount *noun*
el **descuento** *masc*

to **discourage** *verb*
1 *(to depress)* **desanimar [17]**
2 *(to persuade not to)* **to discourage somebody from doing something** convencer **[44]** a alguien de que no haga algo

I discouraged her from buying it. La convencí de que no lo comprara.

WORD TIP *convencer a alguien de que no* is followed by a verb in the subjunctive.

to **discover** *verb*
descubrir [46]

discovery *noun*
el **descubrimiento** *masc*

discreet *adjective*
discreto *masc*, **discreta** *fem*

discrimination *noun*
la **discriminación** *fem*
racial discrimination discriminación racial

⚷ to **discuss** *verb*
1 (*a subject, a topic*) **hablar** [17] **de**
to discuss politics hablar de política
2 (*a problem, a plan*) **discutir** [19]
I'm going to discuss it with Phil. Voy a hablarlo con Phil.

discussion *noun*
la **discusión** *fem*

disease *noun*
la **enfermedad** *fem*

disgraceful *adjective*
vergonzoso *masc*, **vergonzosa** *fem*

disguise *noun* ▷ see **disguise** *verb*
el **disfraz** *masc*
to be in disguise ir [8] disfrazado (*talking about a man*), ir disfrazada (*talking about a woman*)

to **disguise** *verb* ▷ see **disguise** *noun*
disfrazar [22]
to disguise oneself as something disfrazarse de algo
He was disguised as a woman. Iba disfrazado de mujer.

disgust *noun*
1 (*indignation*) la **indignación** *fem*
2 (*physical revulsion*) el **asco** *masc*

disgusted *adjective*
1 (*indignant*) **indignado** *masc*, **indignada** *fem*
2 (*physically sick*) **asqueado** *masc*, **asqueada** *fem*

⚷ **disgusting** *adjective*
asqueroso *masc*, **asquerosa** *fem*

⚷ **dish** *noun*
1 (*plate, item on menu*) el **plato** *masc*
to wash the dishes lavar [17] los platos
The dish of the day is paella. El plato del día es paella.
2 (*serving dish*) la **fuente** *fem*
a large white dish una fuente grande blanca
• **dishcloth** el paño de cocina

dishonest *adjective*
deshonesto *masc*, **deshonesta** *fem*

dishonesty *noun*
la **falta de honradez**

⚷ **dishwasher** *noun*
el **lavaplatos** *masc*

WORD TIP *lavaplatos* does not change in the plural.

to **disinfect** *verb*
desinfectar [17]

disinfectant *noun*
el **desinfectante** *masc*

⚷ **disk** *noun*
el **disco** *masc*
a floppy disk un disquete
the hard disk el disco duro
• **disk drive** la disquetera

⚷ **diskette** *noun*
el **disquete** *masc*

to **dislike** *verb*
I dislike sport. No me gusta el deporte.
He dislikes my friends. No le gustan mis amigos.

WORD TIP Use *gusta, gustó, gustaba, gustaría*, etc if what you dislike is singular or an infinitive. Use *gustan, gustaron, gustaban, gustarían*, etc if what you dislike is plural.

dismay *noun*
la **consternación** *fem*

to **dismiss** *verb*
(*an employee*) **despedir** [57]

disobedient *adjective*
desobediente *masc & fem*

to **disobey** *verb*
desobedecer [35]
She disobeyed the rules. Desobedeció el reglamento.

display *noun* ▷ see **display** *verb*
la **exposición** *fem*
a handicrafts display una exposición de artesanía
a window display un escaparate
a firework display fuegos artificiales
to be on display estar [2] expuesto

to **display** *verb* ▷ see **display** *noun*
exponer [11]

disposable *adjective*
desechable *masc & fem*

dispute *noun*
1 (*quarrel*) la **disputa** *fem*
2 (*argument*) la **polémica** *fem*

to **disqualify** *verb*
descalificar [31]

to **dissolve** *verb*
disolver [45]

distance *noun*
la **distancia** *fem*
from a distance de lejos
in the distance a lo lejos
It's within walking distance. Se puede ir andando.

distant *adjective*
distante *masc & fem*

distinct *adjective*
claro *masc*, **clara** *fem*

distinctly *adverb*
1 (*to hear, see*) **claramente**
2 (*very*) It's distinctly odd. Es realmente raro.

to **distract** *verb*
distraer [42]

to **distribute** *verb*
distribuir [54]

distribution *noun*
la **distribución** *fem*

district *noun*
1 (*in a town*) el **barrio** *masc*
a poor district of Barcelona un barrio pobre de Barcelona
2 (*in the country*) la **región** *fem*

to **disturb** *verb*
molestar [17]
Sorry to disturb you. Perdona que te moleste.
'Do not disturb' 'Se ruega no molestar'

ditch *noun*
la **zanja** *fem*

dive *noun* ▷ see **dive** *verb*
la **zambullida** *fem*

to **dive** *verb* ▷ see **dive** *noun*
tirarse [17]
to dive into the water tirarse al agua

diver *noun*
(*deep-sea*) el & la **submarinista** *masc & fem*

diversion *noun*
(*for traffic*) el **desvío** *masc*

to **divide** *verb*
dividir [19]

diving *noun*
1 (*from a board*) los **saltos de trampolín**
2 (*from the surface of the water*) el **submarinismo** *masc*
• **diving board** el trampolín

division *noun*
la **división** *fem*

divorce *noun* ▷ see **divorce** *verb*
el **divorcio** *masc*

to **divorce** *verb* ▷ see **divorce** *noun*
divorciarse [17]
They divorced in Mexico. Se divorciaron en México.
to get divorced divorciarse

divorced *adjective*
divorciado *masc*, **divorciada** *fem*
My parents are divorced. Mis padres están divorciados.

DIY *noun*
el **bricolaje** *masc*
to do DIY hacer [7] bricolaje
a DIY shop una tienda de bricolaje

dizzy *adjective*
to feel dizzy estar [2] mareado
I feel dizzy. Estoy mareada.

DJ *noun*
el & la **disc-jockey** *masc & fem*

to **do** *verb*
1 (*to carry out*) **hacer** [7]
What are you doing? ¿Qué estás haciendo?
I'm doing my homework. Estoy haciendo mis deberes.
What have you done with the hammer? ¿Qué has hecho con el martillo?
2 (*in questions: **do** is not translated*) Did Maria go to the party? ¿Fue María a la fiesta?
Do you want some strawberries? ¿Quieres fresas?
When does it start? ¿Cuándo empieza?
How did you open the door? ¿Cómo has abierto la puerta?
3 (*in negative sentences*) I don't like this kind of music. No me gusta este tipo de música.
Rosie doesn't like spinach. A Rosie no le gustan las espinacas.
You didn't shut the door. No cerraste la puerta.
It doesn't matter. No importa.

4 (*referring to another verb;* **do** *is not translated*) **'Do you live here?' - 'Yes, I do.'** ¿Vives aquí?' - 'Sí.'
She has more money than I do. Tiene más dinero que yo.
'I live in Charlton.' - 'So do I.' 'Vivo en Charlton.' - 'Yo también.'
'I didn't phone Gemma.' - 'Neither did I.' 'No llamé a Gemma.' - 'Yo tampoco.'
5 (*in questions*) **don't you?, doesn't he?, etc** ¿no?
You know Helen, don't you? Conoces a Helen, ¿no?
She left on Thursday, didn't she? Se marchó el jueves , ¿no?
6 (*to be enough*) **That'll do.** Así basta.
It'll do like that. Así vale.
• to **do something up**
1 (*laces, shoes*) **atar** [17]
I did my shoes up. Me até los zapatos.
2 (*a cardigan, a jacket*) **abrochar** [17]
Do your jacket up. Abróchate la chaqueta.
3 (*a house*) **arreglar** [17]
• to **do with**
1 (*to concern*) **tener** [9] **que ver con**
It has nothing to do with him. No tiene nada que ver con él.
2 (*to find useful*) **I could do with a rest.** Me vendría bien un descanso.
• to **do without something**
arreglarse [17] **sin algo**
We can do without mustard. Nos arreglaremos sin mostaza.

♪ **doctor** *noun*
médico *masc & fem*
Her mother's a doctor. Su madre es médico.

document *noun*
el **documento** *masc*

documentary *noun*
el **documental** *masc*

dodgems *plural noun*
the dodgems los cochecitos de choque

doesn't *short for* **does not** (*See:* **to do**)

dog *noun*
el **perro** *masc*, la **perra** *fem*

♪ **do-it-yourself** *noun*
el **bricolage** *masc*

dole *noun*
el **paro** *masc*
to be on the dole estar [2] en el paro

♪ **doll** *noun*
la **muñeca** *fem*

dollar *noun*
el **dólar** *masc*

dolphin *noun*
el **delfín** *masc*

to **dominate** *verb*
dominar [17]

Dominican *adjective & noun*
1 **dominicano** *masc*, **dominicana** *fem*
2 (*person*) un **dominicano** *masc*, una **dominicana** *fem*

WORD TIP Adjectives and nouns for nationality and regional origin do not have capital letters in Spanish.

Dominican Republic *noun*
the Dominican Republic la República Dominicana

domino *noun*
la **ficha de dominó**
to play dominoes jugar [27] al dominó

donation *noun*
la **donación** *fem*

donkey *noun*
el **burro** *masc*

don't *short for* **do not** (*See:* **to do**)

♪ **door** *noun*
la **puerta** *fem*
to open the door abrir [46] la puerta
to shut the door cerrar [29] la puerta
to knock on the door llamar [17] a la puerta

doorbell *noun*
el **timbre** *masc*
to ring the doorbell tocar [31] el timbre
There's the doorbell. Llaman a la puerta.

doorstep *noun*
el **umbral de la puerta**

♪ **dormitory** *noun*
el **dormitorio** *masc*

dot *noun*
1 (*written*) el **punto** *masc*
2 (*on fabric*) el **lunar** *masc*
3 **at ten on the dot** a las diez en punto

♪ **double** *adjective* ▷ see **double** *adv, verb*
doble *masc & fem*
a double helping una ración doble
a double whisky un whisky doble

♪ **double** *adverb* ▷ see **double** *adj, verb*
el doble
double the time el doble de tiempo
double the price el doble del precio

to double *verb* ▷ see **double** *adj, adv*
doblar **[17]**
Double the first number. Dobla el primer número.
Sales have doubled this month. Las ventas se han doblado este mes.

double bass *noun*
el **contrabajo** *masc*
to play the double bass tocar **[31]** el contrabajo

double bed *noun*
la **cama de matrimonio**

double-breasted *adjective*
a double-breasted jacket una chaqueta cruzada

to **double-click** *verb*
to double-click on something **hacer** **[7]** **doble clic en algo**

double-decker bus *noun*
el **autobús de dos pisos**

double glazing *noun*
la **doble ventana** *fem*

double room *noun*
la **habitación doble**

doubles *noun*
(*in tennis, etc*) los **dobles** *masc plural*
to play a game of doubles jugar **[27]** un partido de dobles

doubt *noun* ▷ see **doubt** *verb*
la **duda** *fem*
There's no doubt about it. No hay ninguna duda al respecto.
I have my doubts. Tengo mis dudas.

to **doubt** *verb* ▷ see **doubt** *noun*
to doubt something dudar **[17]** algo
I doubt it. Lo dudo.
I doubt that ... dudo que ...
I doubt (that) they'll do it. Dudo que lo hagan.

WORD TIP *dudar que* is followed by a verb in the subjunctive.

doubtful *adjective*
It's doubtful that ... No es seguro que ...
It's doubtful that she'll want to. No es seguro que quiera.

WORD TIP *no es seguro que* is followed by a verb in the subjunctive.

dough *noun*
la **masa** *fem*

doughnut *noun*
el **donut** *masc*

down *adverb* ▷ see **down** *prep*
abajo
He's down in the cellar. Está abajo, en el sótano.
to come down bajar **[17]**
She came down from the bedroom. Bajó de la habitación.
to go down bajar **[17]**
I went down to the kitchen. Bajé a la cocina.
to sit down **sentarse** **[29]**
She sat down on the sofa. Se sentó en el sofá.

down *preposition* ▷ see **down** *adv*
(*nearby*) **down the road** un poco más allá
There's a chemist's just down the road. Hay una farmacia un poco más allá.
to walk down the street bajar **[17]** la calle
to run down the stairs bajar **[17]** corriendo la escalera

downstairs *adverb*
1 (*on the ground floor*) **abajo**
She's downstairs in the sitting-room. Está abajo en el salón.
The dog sleeps downstairs. El perro duerme abajo.
2 (*after a noun*) **de abajo**
the flat downstairs el piso de abajo
the people downstairs la gente de abajo

to **download** *verb*
(*Computers*) **descargar** **[28]**

to **doze** *verb*
dormitar **[17]**

dozen *noun*
la **docena** *fem*
a dozen eggs una docena de huevos

drag *noun* ▷ see **drag** *verb*
(*informal*) **What a drag!** ¡Qué rollo!
(*informal*) **She's a bit of a drag.** Es un poco pesada.

to **drag** *verb* ▷ see **drag** *noun*
arrastrar **[17]**

dragon *noun*
el **dragón** *masc*

drain *noun* ▷ see **drain** *verb*
1 (*plughole*) el **desagüe** *masc*
2 (*in a street*) la **alcantarilla** *fem*

to **drain** *verb* ▷ see **drain** *noun*
(*the vegetables*) **escurrir** **[19]**

drama *noun*
1 (*subject*) el **arte dramático**
2 (*informal: fuss*) **He made a big drama about it.** Montó una escena por eso.

dramatic *adjective*
dramático *masc*, **dramática** *fem*

draught *noun*
la **corriente de aire**

draughts *noun*
las **damas** *plural fem*
to play draughts jugar [27] a las damas

✓ to **draw** *verb* ▷ see **draw** *noun*
1 (*with a pencil, pen, etc*) **dibujar** [17]
I can't draw horses. No sé dibujar caballos.
She can draw really well. Dibuja muy bien.
to draw a picture hacer [7] un dibujo
2 (*to close*) **to draw the curtains** correr [18] las cortinas
3 (*to attract*) **to draw a crowd** atraer [42] a una multitud
4 (*in a match*) **empatar** [17]
We drew three all. Empatamos a tres.
5 (*when choosing*) **to draw lots for something** echar [17] algo a suertes

✓ **draw** *noun* ▷ see **draw** *verb*
1 (*in a match*) el **empate** *masc*
It was a draw. Fue un empate.
2 (*lottery*) el **sorteo** *masc*
• **drawback** el inconveniente

drawer *noun*
el **cajón** *masc*

✓ **drawing** *noun*
el **dibujo** *masc*
• **drawing pin** la chincheta

dreadful *adjective*
terrible *masc & fem*

dreadfully *adverb*
1 (*to sing, act*) **espantosamente**
2 (*very*) **I'm dreadfully late.** Llego tardísimo.
I'm dreadfully sorry. Lo siento muchísimo.

dream *noun* ▷ see **dream** *verb*
el **sueño** *masc*
to have a dream tener [9] un sueño
I had a horrible dream last night. Tuve un sueño horrible anoche.

to **dream** *verb* ▷ see **dream** *noun*
soñar [24]
to dream about something soñar con algo

drenched *adjective*
empapado *masc*, **empapada** *fem*
to get drenched empaparse [17]
I got drenched on the way home. Me empapé yendo a casa.

✓ **dress** *noun* ▷ see **dress** *verb*
el **vestido** *masc*

✓ to **dress** *verb* ▷ see **dress** *noun*
vestir [57]
to dress a child vestir a un niño
• to **dress up**
disfrazarse [22]
She dressed up as a vampire. Se disfrazó de vampiro.

✓ **dressed** *adjective*
vestido *masc*, **vestida** *fem*
Is Tom dressed? ¿Está Tom vestido?
She was dressed in black trousers and a yellow shirt. Iba vestida con unos pantalones negros y una blusa amarilla.
to get dressed vestirse [57]

dresser *noun*
(*for dishes*) el **aparador** *masc*

dressing gown *noun*
la **bata** *fem*

✓ **dressing table** *noun*
el **tocador** *masc*

✓ **dried** *adjective*
seco *masc*, **seca** *fem*
dried apricots albaricoques secos

dryer *noun* ▷ **drier**

to **drift** *verb*
1 (*boat*) **ir** [8] **a la deriva**
2 (*snow*) **amontonarse** [17]

drill *noun* ▷ see **drill** *verb*
(*tool*) la **taladradora** *fem*

to **drill** *verb* ▷ see **drill** *noun*
(*a hole*) **hacer** [7] **un agujero en**
He drilled a hole in the wall. Hizo un agujero en la pared.

✓ **drink** *noun* ▷ see **drink** *verb*
1 (*any liquid*) la **bebida** *fem*
a hot drink una bebida caliente
a cold drink un refresco
2 (*alcoholic*) **Would you like a drink?** ¿Te apetece beber algo?
to go out for a drink salir [63] a tomar una copa

✓ to **drink** *verb* ▷ see **drink** *noun*
beber [18]
He drank a glass of water. Bebió un vaso de agua.

✓ **drive** *noun* ▷ see **drive** *verb*
1 (*outing in a car*) **to go for a drive** ir [8] a dar una vuelta en coche
2 (*path leading to a house*) la **entrada para coches**

♪ to **drive** *verb* ▷ see **drive** *noun*
1 (*a car, a taxi, a bus, etc*) **conducir [60]**
to drive a car conducir un coche
She drives very fast. Conduce muy rápido.
I'd like to learn to drive. Me gustaría aprender a conducir.
Can you drive? ¿Sabes conducir?
2 (*to go somewhere in a car, taxi, bus, etc*) **ir [8] en coche**
We drove to Seville. Fuimos en coche a Sevilla.
3 **to drive somebody (to a place)** llevar **[17]** en coche a alguien (a un sitio)
Mum drove me to the station. Mamá me llevó en coche a la estación.
to drive somebody home llevar **[17]** a alguien a casa en coche

♪ **driver** *noun*
1 (*of a car, taxi or bus*) el **conductor** *masc*, la **conductora** *fem*
2 (*of a racing car*) el & la **piloto** *masc & fem*

driving instructor *noun*
el **instructor de autoescuela**, la **instructora de autoescuela**

driving lesson *noun*
la **clase de conducir**

♪ **driving licence** *noun*
el **permiso de conducir**

driving school *noun*
la **autoescuela** *fem*

driving test *noun*
el **examen de conducir**
to take your driving test presentarse **[17]** al examen de conducir
Jenny's passed her driving test. Jenny ha aprobado el examen de conducir.
He's failed his driving test. Ha suspendido el examen de conducir.

♪ **drizzle** *noun*
la **llovizna** *fem*

♪ **drop** *noun* ▷ see **drop** *verb*
la **gota** *fem*

♪ to **drop** *verb* ▷ see **drop** *noun*
1 (*an object*) **I dropped my glasses.** Se me cayeron las gafas.
Careful, don't drop it! ¡Cuidado, que no se te caiga!
2 (*a course, a subject, a topic*) **dejar [17]**
I'm going to drop history next year. Voy a dejar la historia el próximo año.
3 (*a person*) **dejar [17]**
Could you drop me at the station? ¿Me podrías dejar en la estación?
4 (*as a warning*) **Drop it!** ¡Déjalo ya!

♪ **drought** *noun*
la **sequía** *fem*

♪ to **drown** *verb*
ahogarse [28]
She drowned in the lake. Se ahogó en el lago.

♪ **drug** *noun*
1 (*medicine*) la **medicina** *fem*
2 (*illegal*) **drugs** las drogas
to be on drugs drogarse **[28]**
- **drug abuse** el consumo de drogas
- **drug addict** el drogadicto, la drogadicta
- **drug addiction** la drogadicción

drum *noun*
el **tambor** *masc*
(*in a band*) **drums** la batería *fem*
to play (the) drums tocar **[31]** la batería
- **drum kit** la batería

drummer *noun*
el & la **batería** *masc & fem*

drunk *adjective* ▷ see **drunk** *noun*
borracho *masc*, **borracha** *fem*

drunk *noun* ▷ see **drunk** *adj*
el **borracho** *masc*, la **borracha** *fem*

♪ **dry** *adjective* ▷ see **dry** *verb*
seco *masc*, **seca** *fem*

♪ to **dry** *verb* ▷ see **dry** *adj*
1 (*the plates, the dishes*) **secar [31]**
to dry the dishes secar los platos
to dry your hair secarse el pelo
to dry oneself secarse
I'm going to dry my hair. Me voy a secar el pelo.
It took ages to dry. Tardó muchísimo en secarse.
2 (*washing, paint*) **to let something dry** dejar **[17]** que algo se seque
- **dry cleaner's** la tintorería

dryer *noun*
1 (*for hair*) el **secador de pelo** *masc*
2 (*for clothing*) la **secadora** *fem*

dual carriageway *noun*
la **autovía** *fem*

dubbed *adjective*
a dubbed film una película doblada

♪ **duck** *noun*
el **pato** *masc*, la **pata** *fem*

due *adjective*
1 (*expected*) **Paul's due back soon.** Paul tiene que volver pronto.
What time is the train due? ¿Cuándo llega el próximo tren?

to be due to do something tener [9] que hacer algo
We're due to leave on Thursday. Tenemos que salir el jueves.
2 (*because of*) **due to** debido a
The match has been cancelled due to bad weather. El partido ha sido cancelado debido al mal tiempo.

duke *noun*
el **duque** *masc*

dull *adjective*
1 (*boring*) **aburrido** *masc*, **aburrida** *fem*
2 (*not sunny*) **dull weather** tiempo gris
It's a dull day today. Hoy hace un día muy gris.

dumb *adjective*
1 (*unable to talk*) **mudo** *masc*, **muda** *fem*
to be deaf and dumb ser [1] sordomudo
2 (*stupid*) **tonto** *masc*, **tonta** *fem* (*informal*)
He asked some dumb questions. Hizo unas preguntas muy tontas.

dummy *noun*
(*for a baby*) el **chupete** *masc*

to **dump** *verb*
1 (*rubbish*) **tirar** [17]
2 (*informal: a person*) **plantar** [17]
She's dumped her boyfriend. Ha plantado a su novio.

dune *noun*
la **duna** *fem*

dungarees *plural noun*
el **pantalón de peto**

dungeon *noun*
la **mazmorra** *fem*

♪ **during** *preposition*
durante
during the night durante la noche
I saw her during the holidays. La vi durante las vacaciones.

dusk *noun*
el **anochecer** *masc*
at dusk al anochecer

dust *noun* ▷ see **dust** *verb*
el **polvo** *masc*

to **dust** *verb* ▷ see **dust** *noun*
quitar [17] **el polvo a**
to dust the table quitarle el polvo a la mesa

dustbin *noun*
el **cubo** *masc* **de la basura**
to put something in the dustbin tirar [17] algo al cubo de la basura

dustman *noun*
el **basurero** *masc*

dusty *adjective*
cubierto de polvo *masc*, **cubierta de polvo** *fem*
The table was very dusty. La mesa estaba toda cubierta de polvo.

Dutch *adjective & noun*
1 **holandés** *masc*, **holandesa** *fem*
2 (*the people*) **the Dutch** los holandeses
3 (*the language*) el **holandés** *masc*

WORD TIP Adjectives and nouns for nationality and regional origin do not have capital letters in Spanish.

duty *noun*
1 el **deber** *masc*
to have a duty to do something tener [9] el deber de hacer algo
You have a duty to inform us. Tienes el deber de informarnos.
2 (*nurses, doctors, chemists*) **to be on duty** estar [2] de guardia
3 (*police*) **to be on duty** estar [2] de servicio
4 **to be on night duty** tener [9] el turno de noche

duty-free *adjective*
libre de impuestos *masc & fem*
the duty-free shops las tiendas libres de impuestos
duty-free purchases artículos libres de impuestos

duvet *noun*
el **edredón** *masc*
• **duvet cover** la funda de edredón

DVD *noun*
el **DVD** *masc*
• **DVD player** el lector de DVD
• **DVD recorder** el grabador de DVD

dwarf *noun*
el **enano** *masc*, la **enana** *fem*

dye *noun* ▷ see **dye** *verb*
el **tinte** *masc*

to **dye** *verb* ▷ see **dye** *noun*
teñir [65]
to dye your hair teñirse el pelo
I'm going to dye my hair pink. Me voy a teñir el pelo de rosa.

dynamic *adjective*
dinámico *masc*, **dinámica** *fem*

dyslexia *noun*
la **dislexia** *fem*

dyslexic *adjective*
disléxico *masc*, **disléxica** *fem*

English–Spanish

E e

each *adjective, pronoun*
1 (*with a noun*) **cada** *masc & fem*
each time cada vez
each boy cada chico
2 (*standing for a noun*) **cada uno** *masc*, **cada una** *fem*
They each have a computer. Cada uno tiene un ordenador.
She gave us an apple each. Nos dio una manzana a cada uno.
each of you cada uno de vosotros
Each of us brought two pounds. Cada uno de nosotros trajo dos libras.
The tickets cost ten pounds each. Las entradas cuestan diez libras cada una.
3 **each other**
We know each other. Nos conocemos.
Do you see each other often? ¿Os veis a menudo?
They love each other. Se quieren.

WORD TIP *each other* is usually translated into Spanish using a reflexive verb with: *nos, os, se*.

eagle *noun*
el **águila** *fem*

WORD TIP *águila* takes *el* or *un* in the singular even though it is feminine.

ear *noun*
1 (*outer ear*) la **oreja** *fem*
2 (*inner ear*) el **oído** *masc*

earache *noun*
to have earache tener [9] dolor de oídos

early *adjective, adverb*
1 (*before the usual time*) **temprano**
Come early. Ven temprano.
We should have started earlier. Deberíamos haber empezado más temprano.
to have an early night acostarse [24] temprano
We're making an early start. Vamos a salir temprano.
2 (*before a set time*) **pronto**
Alice likes to arrive early. A Alice le gusta llegar pronto.
We're early, the train doesn't leave until ten. Hemos llegado pronto, el tren no sale hasta las diez.
3 (*at the beginning of a period*) **primero** *masc*, **primera** *fem*
in the early months of 2006 en los primeros meses del 2006
in the early afternoon a primera hora de la tarde
in the early hours of the morning de madrugada
4 (*in the morning*) **temprano**
I get up early. Me levanto temprano.
It's too early. Es demasiado temprano.
5 (*a while ago*) **earlier** hace un rato
Your brother phoned earlier. Tu hermano llamó hace un rato.

to **earn** *verb*
(*money*) **ganar** [17]
Richard earns ten pounds an hour. Richard gana diez libras por hora.

earnings *plural noun*
los **ingresos** *plural masc*

earphones *plural noun*
los **auriculares** *plural masc*

earring *noun*
el **pendiente** *masc*, (*Latin America*) el **arete** *masc*

earth *noun*
la **tierra** *fem*
life on earth la vida en la tierra
- **earthquake** el terremoto

easily *adverb*
1 (*with no difficulty*) **con facilidad**
2 (*by far*) **con mucho**
He's easily the best. Es con mucho el mejor.

east *adjective, adverb* ▷ see **east** *noun*
este *invariable masc & fem*
the east side el lado este
the east winds los vientos del este
east of Seville al este de Sevilla
to travel east viajar [17] hacia el este

WORD TIP *este* never changes.

east *noun* ▷ see **east** *adj, adv*
el **este** *masc*
in the east en el este

Easter *noun*
1 (*day*) **Pascua** *fem*
2 (*holiday time*) **Semana Santa** *noun*
They're coming at Easter. Vienen en Semana Santa.
- **Easter Day** el Domingo de Pascua
- **Easter egg** el huevo de Pascua

a b c d e f g h i j k l m n o p q r s t u v w x y z

eastern *adjective*
este *invariable masc & fem*
Eastern Europe Europa del Este

easy *adjective*
fácil *masc & fem*
It's easy! ¡Es fácil!
It was easy to decide. Fue fácil decidir.

to **eat** *verb*
1 (*a fruit, vegetables, bread*) **comer** [18]
He was eating a banana. Estaba comiendo un plátano.
We're going to have something to eat. Vamos a comer algo.
2 (*a meal*) **tomar** [17]
We were eating breakfast. Estábamos tomando el desayuno.
3 **to eat out** comer [18] fuera

echo *noun* ▷ see **echo** *verb*
el **eco** *masc*

to **echo** *verb* ▷ see **echo** *noun*
hacer [7] **eco**

eclipse *noun*
el **eclipse** *masc*

ecological *adjective*
ecológico *masc*, **ecológica** *fem*

ecologist *noun*
el & la **ecologista** *masc & fem*

ecology *noun*
la **ecología** *fem*

economic *adjective*
1 (*relating to economics*) **económico** *masc*, **económica** *fem*
2 (*profitable*) **rentable** *masc & fem*

economical *adjective*
económico *masc*, **económica** *fem*
It's more economical to buy a big one. Sale más económico comprar uno grande.

economics *noun*
la **economía** *fem*

to **economize** *verb*
economizar [22]
to economize on something economizar algo
We economized on food. Economizamos la comida.

economy *noun*
la **economía** *fem*

Ecuador *noun*
Ecuador *masc*

Ecuadorian *adjective & noun*
1 **ecuatoriano** *masc*, **ecuatoriana** *fem*
2 un **ecuatoriano** *masc*, una **ecuatoriana** *fem*
the Ecuadorians los ecuatorianos

WORD TIP Adjectives and nouns for nationality and regional origin do not have capital letters in Spanish.

eczema *noun*
el **eczema** *masc*

edge *noun*
1 (*of a table, a plate, a cliff*) el **borde** *masc*
the edge of the table el borde de la mesa
2 (*of a river, a lake*) la **orilla** *fem*
at the edge of the lake en la orilla del lago
3 (*showing nervousness*) **to be on edge** estar [2] nervioso

edible *adjective*
comestible *masc & fem*

Edinburgh *noun*
Edimburgo *masc*

to **edit** *verb*
editar [17]

editor *noun*
1 (*of books*) el **editor** *masc*, la **editora** *noun*
2 (*of a newspaper*) el **director** *masc*, la **directora** *noun*
3 (*Computers*) el **editor** *masc*

to **educate** *verb*
educar [31]

educated *adjective*
culto *masc*, **culta** *fem*

education *noun*
la **educación** *fem*

educational *adjective*
educativo *masc*, **educativa** *fem*

effect *noun*
el **efecto** *masc*
the effect of the accident el efecto del accidente
The special effects were great. Los efectos especiales eran fenomenales.
to have an effect on something afectar [17] a algo
It had a good effect on the whole family. Afectó positivamente a toda la familia.

effective *adjective*
eficaz *masc & fem*

efficient *adjective*
eficiente *masc & fem*

effort *noun*
el esfuerzo *masc*
to make an effort hacer [7] un esfuerzo
Jess made an effort to help us. Jess hizo un esfuerzo para ayudarnos.
He didn't even make the effort to apologize. Ni siquiera se molestó en disculparse.
It's not worth the effort. No merece la pena.

e.g. *abbreviation*
p.ej., **por ejemplo**

egg *noun*
el huevo *masc*
a dozen eggs una docena de huevos
two boiled eggs dos huevos pasados por agua
- **eggcup** la huevera
- **eggshell** la cáscara de huevo
- **egg white** la clara de huevo
- **egg yolk** la yema de huevo

eight *number*
ocho *invariable number*
Rosie's eight. Rosie tiene ocho años.
It's eight o'clock. Son las ocho.

eighteen *number*
dieciocho *invariable number*
Kate's eighteen. Kate tiene dieciocho años.

eighth *adjective* ▷ see **eighth** *noun*
octavo *masc*, **octava** *fem*
on the eighth floor en la octava planta

eighth *noun* ▷ see **eighth** *adj*
1 (*fraction*) **an eighth** una octava parte
2 (*when saying dates*) **the eighth of July** el ocho de julio

eighties *plural noun*
the eighties los años ochenta
in the eighties en los años ochenta

eighty *number*
ochenta *invariable number*
eighty-five ochenta y cinco
She's eighty. Tiene ochenta años.

Eire *noun*
Eire *masc*, **la República de Irlanda**

either *conjunction* ▷ see **either** *pron*
1 (*to give alternatives*) **either ... or** o ... o
You either pay or return it. O pagas o lo devuelves.
I'll phone either Thursday or Friday. Llamaré o el jueves o el viernes.
either one or the other o uno u otro
2 (*when in English you say* **not ... either**) **He doesn't want to go either.** Él tampoco quiere ir.
I don't know them either. Yo tampoco los conozco.

either *pronoun* ▷ see **either** *conj*
1 (*giving alternatives*) **Choose either (of them).** Elige cualquiera (de los dos).
2 (*both*) **Either is possible.** Las dos cosas son posibles.
I don't like either (of them). No me gusta ninguno (de los dos).

elastic *adjective* ▷ see **elastic** *noun*
elástico *masc*, **elástica** *fem*

elastic *noun* ▷ see **elastic** *adj*
el elástico *masc*
- **elastic band** la goma elástica

elbow *noun*
el codo *masc*

elder *adjective*
mayor *masc & fem*
her elder brother su hermano mayor

elderly *adjective* ▷ see **elderly** *noun*
an elderly man un anciano
an elderly woman una anciana
an elderly couple una pareja de ancianos

elderly *plural noun* ▷ see **elderly** *adj*
the elderly los ancianos

eldest *adjective*
mayor *masc & fem*
her eldest brother su hermano mayor

to **elect** *verb*
elegir [48]
She has been elected. Ha sido elegida.

election *noun*
las elecciones *plural fem*
in the election en las elecciones
to call a general election convocar [31] elecciones generales

electric *adjective*
eléctrico *masc*, **eléctrica** *fem*

electrical *adjective*
eléctrico *masc*, **eléctrica** *fem*

electrician *noun*
el & la electricista *masc & fem*

electricity *noun*
la electricidad *fem*
to turn off the electricity desconectar [17] la corriente

electronic *adjective*
electrónico *masc*, **electrónica** *fem*
• **electronic mail** el correo electrónico

electronics *noun*
la **electrónica** *fem*

♪ **elegant** *adjective*
elegante *masc & fem*

element *noun*
el **elemento** *masc*

elephant *noun*
el **elefante** *masc*

♪ **eleven** *number*
once *invariable number*
Josh is eleven. Josh tiene once años.
It's eleven o'clock. Son las once.

♪ **eleventh** *adjective* ▷ see **eleventh** *noun*
onceavo *masc*, **onceava** *fem*
on the eleventh floor en la onceava planta

♪ **eleventh** *noun* ▷ see **eleventh** *adj*
the eleventh of May el once de mayo

to **eliminate** *verb*
eliminar [17]

else *adverb*
1 (*to ask questions and say no*) **más**
Who else? ¿Quién más?
What else? ¿Qué más?
Would you like something else? ¿Quieres otra cosa?
nothing else nada más
I don't want anything else. No quiero nada más.
2 (*in expressions*) **somebody else** otra persona
Somebody else must have done it. Lo ha debido hacer otra persona.
something else otra cosa
everybody else todos los demás
everything else todo lo demás
somewhere else en otra parte
or else si no
Hurry up, or else we'll be late. Date prisa, que si no vamos a llegar tarde.

♪ **email** *noun* ▷ see **email** *verb*
1 (*system*) el **correo electrónico**
to be on email tener [9] una dirección de correo electrónico
2 (*message*) el **email**, el **mail**, el **correo electrónico**
to send somebody an email mandarle [17] un email a alguien

♪ to **email** *verb* ▷ see **email** *noun*
1 (*a message*) **enviar** [32] **por correo electrónico**
2 (*a person*) **to email somebody** mandarle [17] un mail a alguien
• **email address** la dirección de correo electrónico

embarrassed *adjective*
I was terribly embarrassed. Me daba mucha vergüenza.
She feels a bit embarrassed. Le da un poco de vergüenza.

embarrassing *adjective*
(*situation, silence*) **violento** *masc*, **violenta** *fem*
How embarrassing! ¡Qué vergüenza!

embarrassment *noun*
la **vergüenza** *fem*

embassy *noun*
la **embajada** *fem*
the Spanish Embassy la embajada española

to **embroider** *verb*
bordar [17]

embroidery *noun*
el **bordado** *masc*

♪ **emergency** *noun*
1 (*dangerous situation*) la **emergencia** *fem*
In an emergency, break the glass. En caso de emergencia, rompa el cristal.
It's an emergency! ¡Es una emergencia!
2 (*medical*) la **urgencia** *fem*
an emergency operation una operación de urgencia
• **emergency exit** la salida de emergencia
• **emergency landing** el aterrizaje forzoso

emotion *noun*
la **emoción** *fem*

emotional *adjective*
1 (*person*) **to be emotional** estar [2] emocionado
to get emotional emocionarse [17]
She got quite emotional. Se emocionó mucho.
2 (*speech, occasion*) **emotivo** *masc*, **emotiva** *fem*

emperor *noun*
el **emperador** *masc*

emphasis *noun*
el **énfasis** *masc*

to **emphasize** *verb*
recalcar [31]
He emphasized that it wasn't compulsory. Recalcó que no era obligatorio.

English–Spanish
a b c d e f g h i j k l m n o p q r s t u v w x y z

English–Spanish

empire *noun*
el **imperio** *masc*
the Roman Empire el imperio romano

to **employ** *verb*
emplear **[17]**

employee *noun*
el **empleado** *masc*, la **empleada** *fem*

employer *noun*
el **patrón** *masc*, la **patrona** *fem*

employment *noun*
el **empleo** *masc*

empress *noun*
la **emperatriz** *fem*

empty *adjective* ▷ see **empty** *verb*
vacío *masc*, **vacía** *fem*
an empty bottle una botella vacía
The room was empty. La habitación estaba vacía.

to **empty** *verb* ▷ see **empty** *adj*
vaciar **[32]**
I emptied the jug into the sink. Vacié la jarra en el fregadero.

enchanting *adjective*
encantador *masc*, **encantadora** *fem*

to **enclose** *verb*
(with a letter) **adjuntar** **[17]**
Please find enclosed a cheque. Se adjunta un cheque.

encore *noun*
el **bis** *masc*
Encore! ¡Otra!

to **encourage** *verb*
animar **[17]**
to encourage somebody to do something animar a alguien a hacer algo
Mum encouraged me to try again. Mamá me animó a intentarlo otra vez.

encouragement *noun*
el **ánimo** *masc*

encouraging *adjective*
alentador *masc*, **alentadora** *fem*

encyclopedia *noun*
la **enciclopedia** *fem*

end *noun* ▷ see **end** *verb*
1 *(the last part)* el **final** *masc*
at the end of the film al final de la película
by the end of the day al final del día
In the end I went home. Al final me fui a casa.
at the end of the year a finales de año
Sally's coming at the end of June. Sally viene a finales de junio.
2 *(in a book, film)* **'The End'** 'Fin'
3 *(of a table, garden, stick)* el **extremo** *masc*
Hold the other end. Sujeta el otro extremo.
4 *(of a street, road)* el **final** *masc*
at the end of the street al final de la calle
5 *(of a football pitch)* el **lado** *masc*
to change ends cambiar **[17]** de lado

to **end** *verb* ▷ see **end** *noun*
1 *(to make something finish)* **poner** **[11]** **fin a**
They've ended the strike. Han puesto fin a la huelga.
2 *(to finish)* **terminar** **[17]**
The day ended with a dinner. El día terminó con una cena.
• **to end up**
terminar **[17]**
We ended up taking a taxi. Terminamos cogiendo un taxi.
Ross ended up in Buenos Aires. Ross terminó en Buenos Aires.

endangered *adjective*
en peligro
an endangered species una especie en vías de extinción

ending *noun*
el **final** *masc*

endless *adjective*
interminable *masc & fem*

enemy *noun*
el **enemigo** *masc*, la **enemiga** *fem*
to make enemies hacer **[7]** enemigos

energetic *adjective*
energético *masc*, **energética** *fem*

energy *noun*
la **energía** *fem*

engaged *adjective*
1 *(to be married)* **prometido** *masc*, **prometida** *fem*
They're engaged. Están prometidos.
Luisa's engaged. Luisa está prometida.
to get engaged prometerse **[18]**
2 *(on the telephone)* **to be engaged** estar **[2]** comunicando
It's engaged, I'll ring later. Está comunicando, llamaré más tarde.
3 *(toilet)* **ocupado** *masc*, **ocupada** *fem*

engagement *noun*
el **compromiso** *masc*
• **engagement ring** el anillo de compromiso

engine *noun*
1 *(in a car)* el **motor** *masc*
2 *(of a train)* la **locomotora** *fem*

a b c d e f g h i j k l m n o p q r s t u v w x y z

engineer *noun*
1 (*repair person*) el & la **técnico** *masc & fem*
2 (*graduate*) el **ingeniero** *masc*, la **ingeniera** *fem*

England *noun*
Inglaterra *fem*
I'm from England. Soy inglés (*boy speaking*)., Soy inglesa (*girl speaking.*)

English *adjective* ▷ see **English** *noun*
inglés *masc*, **inglesa** *fem*
the English team el equipo inglés

English *noun* ▷ see **English** *adj*
1 (*the language*) el **inglés** *masc*
Do you speak English? ¿Hablas inglés?
He answered in English. Contestó en inglés.
my English class mi clase de inglés
our English teacher nuestro profesor de inglés
2 (*the people*) **the English** los ingleses

WORD TIP Adjectives and nouns for nationality, regional origin, and language do not have capital letters in Spanish.

English Channel *noun*
the English Channel el Canal de la Mancha

Englishman *noun*
un **inglés** *masc*

Englishwoman *noun*
una **inglesa** *fem*

to **enjoy** *verb*
1 **disfrutar [17] de**
Did you enjoy the party? ¿Disfrutaste de la fiesta?
We really enjoyed the concert. Disfrutamos mucho del concierto.
I enjoy swimming. Me gusta nadar.
Do you enjoy living in York? ¿Te gusta vivir en York?
2 **to enjoy yourself** divertirse **[14]**
We really enjoyed ourselves. Nos divertimos muchísimo.
Did you enjoy yourself? ¿Te divertiste? (*informal*)
Did you enjoy yourselves? ¿Os divertisteis? (*informal*)

enjoyable *adjective*
agradable *masc & fem*

to **enlarge** *verb*
ampliar [32]

enlargement *noun*
(*of a photo*) la **ampliación** *fem*

enormous *adjective*
enorme *masc & fem*

enough *adjective, adverb, pronoun*
1 (*food, money, etc*) **suficiente** *masc & fem*
There's enough for everyone. Hay suficiente para todos.
Is there enough bread? ¿Hay suficiente pan?
There aren't enough ice-creams. No hay suficientes helados.
They don't pay me enough. No me pagan lo suficiente.
2 (*with an adjective, adverb*) **lo suficientemente**
big enough lo suficientemente grande
slowly enough lo suficientemente despacio
3 (*in exclamations*) **That's enough!** ¡Basta!
I've had enough! ¡Ya estoy harto!

to **enquire** *verb*
informarse [17]
I'm going to enquire about the trains. Voy a informarme sobre los trenes.

enquiry *noun*
to make enquiries about something pedir **[57]** información sobre algo

to **enrol** *verb*
matricularse [17]
I want to enrol on the course. Quiero matricularme en el curso.

to **enter** *verb*
1 (*a room, a building*) **entrar [17] en**
We all entered the church. Todos entramos en la iglesia.
2 **to enter for an exam** presentarse **[17]** a un examen
I'm entering for seven GCSEs. Me voy a presentar a siete asignaturas de GCSE.

to **entertain** *verb*
1 (*to keep amused*) **entretener [9]**
something to entertain the children algo para entretener a los niños
2 (*to have people round*) **invitar [17] a gente**
They don't entertain much. No invitan a mucha gente.

entertaining *adjective*
entretenido *masc*, **entretenida** *fem*

entertainment *noun*
(*fun*) el **entretenimiento** *masc*
There wasn't much entertainment in the evenings. Por las noches no había mucho entretenimiento.
There's plenty of entertainment in Tossa. Hay muchas atracciones en Tossa.
• **entertainment guide** la guía del ocio

enthusiasm *noun*
el **entusiasmo** *masc*

enthusiast *noun*
el **apasionado** *masc*, la **apasionada** *fem*
to be a rugby enthusiast ser [1] un apasionado del rugby

enthusiastic *adjective*
entusiasta *masc & fem*

entire *adjective*
entero *masc*, **entera** *fem*
the entire class la clase entera

entirely *adverb*
completamente

entrance *noun*
la **entrada** *fem*

entry *noun*
la **entrada** *fem*
'No entry' 'Prohibida la entrada'
- **entry phone** el portero automático

envelope *noun*
el **sobre** *masc*

envious *adjective*
envidioso *masc*, **envidiosa** *fem*
to be envious of something tener [9] envidia de algo
He's envious of my exam results. Tiene envidia de las notas de mis exámenes.

environment *noun*
el **medio ambiente**

environmental *adjective*
medioambiental *masc & fem*

environment-friendly *adjective*
ecológico *masc*, **ecológica** *fem*

envy *noun*
la **envidia** *fem*

epidemic *noun*
la **epidemia** *fem*

epilepsy *noun*
la **epilepsia** *fem*
to have epilepsy tener [9] epilepsia

episode *noun*
el **episodio** *masc*

equal *adjective* ▷ see **equal** *verb*
igual *masc & fem*
in equal quantities en cantidades iguales
equal opportunities la igualdad de oportunidades

to **equal** *verb* ▷ see **equal** *adj*
ser [1] igual a

equality *noun*
la **igualdad** *fem*

to **equalize** *verb*
empatar [17]
They equalized in the last minute. Empataron en el último minuto.

equally *adverb*
(*to share*) **en partes iguales**
We divided it equally. Lo dividimos en partes iguales.

equator *noun*
el **ecuador** *masc*

to **equip** *verb*
equipar [17]
well equipped for the walk bien equipado para la marcha

equipment *noun*
1 (*for sport*) los **artículos deportivos**
2 (*in an office, a lab*) el **material** *masc*

equivalent *adjective*
to be equivalent to something ser [1] equivalente a algo

error *noun*
1 (*in spelling, typing*) la **falta** *fem*
a spelling error una falta de ortografía
2 (*in maths, on a computer*) el **error** *masc*

escalator *noun*
la **escalera mecánica**

escape *noun* ▷ see **escape** *verb*
(*from prison*) la **fuga** *fem*

to **escape** *verb* ▷ see **escape** *noun*
1 (*prisoners*) **fugarse** [28]
2 (*dogs, horses*) **escaparse** [17]

escort *noun*
la **escolta** *fem*
a police escort una escolta policial

especially *adverb*
especialmente

essay *noun*
la **redacción** *fem*
an essay on pollution una redacción sobre la contaminación

essential *adjective*
esencial *masc & fem*
It's essential to reply quickly. Es esencial responder rápidamente.

estate *noun*
1 (*houses*) la **urbanización** *fem*
2 (*of a landowner*) la **propiedad** *fem*
- **estate agent's** la agencia inmobiliaria
- **estate car** la ranchera

estimate *noun* ▷ see **estimate** *verb*
1 (*quote for work*) el **presupuesto** *masc*
2 (*rough guess*) el **cálculo aproximado**

to **estimate** *verb* ▷ see **estimate** *noun*
1 **calcular** [17]
2 **the estimated time of arrival** la hora prevista de llegada

etc. *abbreviation*
etcétera, etc

ethnic *adjective*
étnico *masc*, **étnica** *fem*
an ethnic minority una minoría étnica

EU *noun*
(= *European Union*) la **EU** *fem*, la **Unión Europea**

euro *noun*
el **euro** *masc*
The euro is divided into a hundred cents. El euro se divide en cien céntimos.

Europe *noun*
Europa *fem*

European *adjective & noun*
1 **europeo** *masc*, **europea** *fem*
2 (*person*) un **europeo** *masc*, una **europea** *fem*

WORD TIP Adjectives and nouns for nationality and regional origin do not have capital letters in Spanish.

• **European Union** la Unión Europea

eurozone *noun*
la **eurozona** *fem*

to **evaporate** *verb*
evaporarse [17]

eve *noun*
la **víspera**
Christmas Eve la Nochebuena
New Year's Eve la Nochevieja

even *adjective* ▷ see **even** *adv*
1 (*surface, layer*) **plano** *masc*, **plana** *fem*
2 (*number*) **par** *masc & fem*
Six is an even number. Seis es un número par.
3 (*having the same score*) **igualado** *masc*, **igualada** *fem*
Lee and Tony are even. Lee y Tony están igualados.

even *adverb* ▷ see **even** *adj*
1 (*to show something surprising*) **incluso**
Even I could do it. Incluso yo podría hacerlo.
even if incluso si
even if they arrive incluso si llegan
even so aun así
Even so, we had a good time. Aun así lo pasamos bien.
even though aunque
Even though I had a headache, I enjoyed myself. Aunque tenía un dolor de cabeza, me divertí.
2 (*in comparisons*) **aún**
even more difficult aún más difícil
even faster aún más rápido
even more than aún más que
I liked the song even more than their last one. La canción me gustó aún más que la anterior.
3 (*in negative sentences, after* **without**) **ni siquiera**
Even Lisa didn't like it. Ni siquiera a Lisa le gustó.
without even asking sin ni siquiera preguntar
not even ni siquiera
I don't like animals, not even dogs. No me gustan los animales, ni siquiera los perros.

evening *noun*
1 (*before dark*) la **tarde** *fem*
this evening esta tarde
at six o'clock in the evening a las seis de la tarde
tomorrow evening mañana por la tarde
on Thursday evening el jueves por la tarde
the evening before la tarde anterior
every evening cada tarde
Good evening! ¡Buenas tardes!
the evening meal la cena
2 (*after dark*) la **noche** *fem*
this evening esta noche
at ten in the evening a las diez de la noche
tomorrow evening mañana por la noche
on Thursday evening el jueves por la noche
the evening before la noche anterior
every evening cada noche
Good evening! ¡Buenas noches!
I work in the evening(s). Trabajo por las noches.
3 (*event*) la **velada** *fem*
an evening with Madonna una velada con Madonna
• **evening class** la clase nocturna

event *noun*
1 (*something that happened*) el **acontecimiento** *masc*
2 (*in athletics*) la **prueba** *fem*
the track events las pruebas de atletismo

eventful *adjective*
lleno de incidentes *masc*, **llena de incidentes** *fem*

eventually *adverb*
finalmente

ever *adverb*
1 (*to ask a question*) **alguna vez**
Have you ever been to Spain? ¿Has estado alguna vez en España?
Have you ever noticed that? ¿Lo notaste alguna vez?
2 (*in negative statements*) **nunca**
hardly ever casi nunca
No one ever came. Nunca vino nadie.
3 (*always*) **siempre**
as cheerful as ever tan contento como siempre
the same as ever como siempre
more slowly than ever más despacio que nunca
ever since desde entonces
And it's been raining ever since. Y ha estado lloviendo desde entonces.

every *adjective*
1 (*each*) **todos los** *masc*, **todas las** *fem*
every day todos los días
every Monday todos los lunes
Every house has a garden. Todas las casas tienen jardín.
I've seen every one of his films. He visto todas sus películas.
2 (*showing repetition*) **cada** *masc & fem*
every ten kilometres cada diez kilómetros
every time cada vez
every now and then de vez en cuando
every other day un día sí y otro no

everybody *pronoun*
todo el mundo
everybody knows that ... todo el mundo sabe que ...
everybody else todos los demás

everyone *pronoun* ▷ **everybody**

everything *pronoun*
todo
everything you said todo lo que dijiste
everything else todo lo demás
Everything's ready. Todo está listo.
Everything's fine. Está todo bien.

everywhere *adverb*
por todas partes
There was mud everywhere. Había barro por todas partes.
everywhere she went a todos los sitios a los que fue
Everywhere else is closed. Todos los demás sitios están cerrados.

evidently *adverb*
obviamente

evil *adjective* ▷ see **evil** *noun*
malvado *masc*, **malvada** *fem*

evil *noun* ▷ see **evil** *adj*
el **mal** *masc*

exact *adjective*
exacto *masc*, **exacta** *fem*
the exact amount la cantidad exacta
It's the exact opposite. Es exactamente lo contrario.

exactly *adverb*
exactamente
They're exactly the same age. Tienen exactamente la misma edad.
Yes, exactly Exacto.

to **exaggerate** *verb*
exagerar [17]

exaggeration *noun*
la **exageración** *fem*

exam *noun*
el **examen** *masc*
a history exam un examen de historia
to take an exam presentarse [17] a un examen
I'm taking five exams. Me presento a cinco exámenes.
to pass an exam aprobar [24] un examen
I passed all my exams. Aprobé todos mis exámenes.
to fail an exam suspender [18] un examen
I failed the chemistry exam. Suspendí el examen de química.

mini-info ***exams***

Pupils are assessed and graded regularly by their teachers. They are expected to pass all subjects. If they fail they have to retake (revalidar). At 16 all students receive a certificate stating the number of years studied and their grades.

examination *noun*
el **examen** *masc*

to **examine** *verb*
examinar [17]

examiner *noun*
el **examinador** *masc*, la **examinadora** *fem*

example *noun*
el **ejemplo** *masc*
for example por ejemplo
to set a good example dar [4] buen ejemplo

excellent *adjective*
excelente *masc & fem*

except *preposition*
excepto
except in March excepto en marzo
except Tuesdays excepto los martes
except when it rains excepto cuando llueve

exception *noun*
la **excepción** *fem*
without exception sin excepción
with the exception of con la excepción de

exceptional *masc & fem adjective*
excepcional

to exchange *verb* ▷ see **exchange** *noun*
cambiar [17]
Can I exchange this shirt for a smaller one? ¿Puedo cambiar esta camisa por una más pequeña?

exchange *noun* ▷ see **exchange** *verb*
1 (*of information, students*) el **intercambio** *masc*
an exchange visit un viaje de intercambio
2 (*return*) **in exchange for his help** a cambio de su ayuda
• **exchange rate** el tipo de cambio

excited *adjective*
1 (*happy*) **entusiasmado** *masc*, **entusiasmada** *fem*
to be excited about something estar [2] entusiasmado con algo
She's really excited about the idea. Está entusiasmada con la idea.
to get excited entusiasmarse [17]
2 (*noisy, boisterous*) **alborotado** *masc*, **alborotada** *fem*
The children were too excited. Los niños estaban demasiado alborotados.
to get excited alborotarse [17]
The dogs get excited when they hear the car. Los perros se alborotan cuando oyen el coche.

excitement *noun*
la **emoción** *fem*

exciting *adjective*
emocionante *masc & fem*
a really exciting film una película realmente emocionante

exclamation mark *noun*
el **signo de admiración**

to exclude *verb*
(*from school*) **to be excluded** ser [1] expulsado

excursion *noun*
la **excursión** *fem*

excuse *noun* ▷ see **excuse** *verb*
la **excusa** *fem*
to make excuses poner [11] excusas
Gary has a good excuse. Gary tiene una buena excusa.
That's no excuse. Eso no es excusa.

to excuse *verb* ▷ see **excuse** *noun*
(*in apologies*) **Excuse me!** ¡Perdón!

ex-directory *adjective*
to be ex-directory no estar [2] en la guía telefónica

exercise *noun*
el **ejercicio** *masc*
a maths exercise un ejercicio de matemáticas
physical exercise ejercicio físico

exercise book *noun*
el **cuaderno** *masc*
my Spanish exercise book mi cuaderno de español

exhausted *adjective*
agotado *masc*, **agotada** *fem*

exhaust fumes *noun*
los **gases del tubo de escape**

exhaust pipe *noun*
el **tubo de escape**

exhibition *noun*
la **exposición** *fem*
an art exhibition una exposición de obras de arte

to exist *verb*
existir [19]

exit *noun*
la **salida** *fem*

to expect *verb*
1 (*guests, a baby*) **esperar [17]**
We're expecting about thirty people. Esperamos unas treinta personas.
2 (*an event*) **esperarse [17]**
I didn't expect that. No me esperaba eso.
I didn't expect it at all. No me lo esperaba en absoluto.
Rain is expected tomorrow. Dicen que va a llover mañana.
3 (*to suppose*) **suponer [11]**
I expect you're tired. Supongo que estarás cansado.
I expect she'll bring her boyfriend. Supongo que traerá a su novio.
I expect so. Supongo que sí.

expedition *noun*
la **expedición** *fem*

to **expel** *verb*
to be expelled ser **[1]** expulsado

expenses *noun*
los **gastos** *plural masc*

expensive *adjective*
caro *masc*, **cara** *fem*
the most expensive hotels los hoteles más caros
Those shoes are too expensive for me. Esos zapatos son demasiado caros para mí.

experience *noun*
la **experiencia** *fem*
No previous experience required. No se requiere experiencia previa.

experienced *adjective*
con experiencia
You're not experienced enough for this job. No tienes suficiente experiencia para este trabajo.
'Experienced waiter or waitress required' 'Se precisa camarero o camarera con experiencia'

experiment *noun*
el **experimento** *masc*
to do an experiment hacer **[7]** un experimento

expert *noun*
el **experto** *masc*, la **experta** *fem*
He's a computer expert. Es un experto en informática.

to **expire** *verb*
caducar [31]

expiry date *noun*
la **fecha de caducidad**

to **explain** *verb*
explicar [31]

explanation *noun*
la **explicación** *fem*

to **explode** *verb*
explotar [17]

to **explore** *verb*
explorar [17]

explosion *noun*
la **explosión** *fem*

export *noun* ▷ see **export** *verb*
1 (*item*) el **artículo de exportación**
Cotton is the most important export. El artículo de exportación más importante es el algodón.
2 (*trade*) la **exportación** *fem*

to **export** *verb* ▷ see **export** *noun*
exportar [17]
Spain exports a lot of wine and olive oil. España exporta mucho vino y aceite de oliva.

exposure *noun*
(*of a film*) la **exposición** *fem*
a twenty-four-exposure film un carrete de veinticuatro fotos

express *noun* ▷ see **express** *verb*
express train el rápido *masc*

to **express** *verb* ▷ see **express** *noun*
expresar [17]
to express yourself expresarse **[17]**

expression *noun*
la **expresión** *fem*

to **extend** *verb*
(*a building*) **ampliar [32]**

extension *noun*
1 (*extra room for a house*) la **ampliación** *fem*
2 (*telephone*) la **extensión** *fem*
Can I have extension 2347 please? ¿Me puede poner con la extensión veintitrés cuarenta y siete, por favor? (*In Spanish, telephone numbers are usually said in pairs.*)
- **extension lead** el alargador
- **extension number** el número de extensión

extinct *adjective*
1 (*animal, insect*) **extincto** *masc*, **extincta** *fem*
to become extinct extinguirse **[50]**
2 (*volcano*) **apagado** *masc*, **apagada** *fem*

to **extinguish** *verb*
apagar [28]

extra *adjective, adverb*
They gave us some extra homework. Nos dieron más deberes.
at no extra charge sin coste suplementario
You have to pay extra. Tiene que pagar un suplemento.
Wine is extra. El vino se cobra aparte.
to charge extra for something cobrar **[17]** un suplemento por algo
extra hot super picante
extra large super grande

⚷ extraordinary *adjective*
extraordinario *masc*, **extraordinaria** *fem*

extra-special *adjective*
super especial *masc & fem*

extra time *noun*
(in football, etc) la **prórroga** *fem*

extravagant *adjective*
(person) **derrochador** *masc*, **derrochadora** *fem*

extreme *adjective* ▷ see **extreme** *noun*
extremo *masc*, **extrema** *fem*

extreme *noun* ▷ see **extreme** *adj*
el **extremo** *masc*
to go to extremes llevar **[17]** las cosas al extremo

⚷ extremely *adverb*
extremely difficult dificilísimo
extremely fast rapidísimo

WORD TIP In Spanish, the ending *-ísimo, -ísima* is often used with adjectives to say *very* or *extremely*.

⚷ eye *noun*
el **ojo** *masc*
A girl with blue eyes. Una niña con ojos azules.
Shut your eyes! ¡Cierra los ojos!

- **eyebrow** la ceja
- **eyelash** la pestaña
- **eyelid** el párpado
- **eyeliner** el delineador de ojos
- **eye make-up** el maquillaje de ojos
- **eye shadow** la sombra de ojos
- **eyesight** la vista

F f

fabric *noun*
la **tela** *fem*

fabulous *adjective*
fabuloso *masc*, **fabulosa** *fem*

to **face** *verb* ▷ see **face** *noun*
1 (*to deal with*) **enfrentarse [17] a**
I face that problem every day. Todos los días me enfrento a un problema así.
2 (*to look in the direction of*) **dar [4] a**
It faces south. Da al sur.
The hotel faces the sea. El hotel tiene vista al mar.
3 (*to bear the thought of*) **to be able to face something** soportar algo
I can't face the idea of going back. No soporto la idea de volver.

face *noun* ▷ see **face** *verb*
1 (*of a person*) la **cara** *fem*
a smiling face una cara risueña
He had a sad face. Tenía una cara triste.
to pull a face hacer **[7]** muecas
2 (*of a clock, watch*) la **esfera** *fem*
• **facecloth** la toalla de cara

facilities *plural noun*
sports facilities las instalaciones deportivas
The flat has cooking facilities. El piso tiene cocina.

fact *noun*
el **hecho** *masc*
in fact de hecho
The fact that ... El hecho de que ...
Is that a fact? ¿Es eso cierto?

factory *noun*
la **fábrica** *fem*

to **fail** *verb* ▷ see **fail** *noun*
1 (*a test, an exam*) **suspender [18]**
I failed my physics exam. He suspendido el examen de física.
Three students failed. Tres estudiantes suspendieron.
2 (*to not succeed*) **fracasar [1]**
He failed in his attempt to beat the record. Fracasó en su intento de batir el récord.
3 **to fail to do something** no hacer **[7]** algo
He failed to contact us. No se puso en contacto con nosotros.

fail *noun* ▷ see **fail** *verb*
1 (*in a test, exam*) el **suspenso** *masc*
2 (*neglect*) **without fail** sin falta
He failed to contact us. No se puso en contacto con nosotros.

failure *noun*
1 (*lack of success, unsuccessful thing, person*) el **fracaso** *masc*
It was a terrible failure. Fue un fracaso espantoso.
2 (*technical fault*) **a power failure** un apagón

faint *adjective* ▷ see **faint** *verb*
1 (*dizzy*) **to feel faint** sentirse **[14]** mareado
Chloë is feeling faint. Chloë se siente mareada.
2 (*slight*) **ligero** *masc*, **ligera** *fem*
a faint smell of gas un ligero olor a gas
I haven't the faintest idea. No tengo ni la más remota idea.
3 (*voice, sound*) **débil** *masc & fem*

to **faint** *verb* ▷ see **faint** *adj*
desmayarse [17]
Lisa fainted. Lisa se desmayó.

fair *adjective* ▷ see **fair** *noun*
1 (*just, reasonable*) **justo** *masc*, **justa** *fem*
It's not fair! ¡No es justo!
2 (*hair*) **rubio** *masc*, **rubia** *fem*
She has fair hair. Tiene el pelo rubio.
3 (*skin, complexion*) **blanco** *masc*, **blanca** *fem*
4 (*reasonably good*) **bastante bueno** *masc*, **bastante buena** *fem*
His work is fair. Su trabajo es bastante bueno.

fair *noun* ▷ see **fair** *adj*
la **feria** *fem*
• **fairground** el parque de atracciones

fair-haired *adjective*
to be fair-haired tener **[9]** el pelo rubio

fairly *adverb*
bastante
She's fairly happy. Es bastante feliz.

fairy *noun*
el **hada** *fem*

WORD TIP *hada* takes *el* or *un* in the singular even though it is feminine.

• **fairy tale** el cuento de hadas

faith *noun*
1 (*trust*) la **confianza** *fem*
to have faith in somebody tener **[9]** confianza en alguien
2 (*in God*) la **fe** *fem*

faithful *adjective*
fiel *masc & fem*

faithfully *adverb*
Yours faithfully ... Le saluda atentamente ...

fake *noun*
1 (*thing*) la **falsificación** *fem*
2 (*person*) **impostor** *masc*, **impostora** *fem*

fall *noun* ▷ see **fall** *verb*
la **caída** *fem*
to have a fall caerse [34]

♪ to **fall** *verb* ▷ see **fall** *noun*
1 (*to tumble*) **caerse** [34]
Mind, you'll fall. Cuidado, te vas a caer.
Tony fell off his bike. Tony se cayó de la bici.
She fell downstairs. Se cayó por las escaleras.
My jacket fell on the floor. Mi chaqueta se cayó al suelo.
2 (*temperatures, prices*) **bajar** [17]
It fell to minus five last night. La temperatura bajó a cinco grados bajo cero anoche.

♪ **false** *adjective*
falso *masc*, **falsa** *fem*
a false passport un pasaporte falso
- **false alarm** la falsa alarma
- **false teeth** la dentadura postiza

fame *noun*
la **fama** *fem*

familiar *adjective*
familiar *masc & fem*
Your face is familiar. Tu cara me es familiar.

♪ **family** *noun*
la **familia** *fem*
a family of six una familia de seis personas
the Hughes family la familia Hughes
Ben's one of the family. Ben es uno de la familia.
- **family name** el apellido

famine *noun*
la **hambruna** *fem*

♪ **famous** *adjective*
famoso *masc*, **famosa** *fem*
to be famous for something ser [1] famoso por algo
Spain is famous for bullfighting. España es famosa por los toros.

fan *noun*
1 (*of a pop group*) el & la **fan** *masc & fem* (*informal*)
Sarah's an Oasis fan. Sarah es fan de Oasis.
2 (*of a team*) el & la **hincha** *masc & fem*
Martin's a Chelsea fan. Martin es hincha del Chelsea.
3 (*blowing cool air*) el **ventilador** *masc*
4 (*hand-held*) el **abanico** *masc*

fanatic *noun*
el **fanático** *masc*, la **fanática** *fem*

to **fancy** *verb* ▷ see **fancy** *adj*
1 (*feel like*) **Do you fancy a coffee?** ¿Te apetece un café?
I fancy the cakes. Me apetecen los pasteles.
I don't fancy going out. No me apetece salir.
2 **I really fancy him.** Me gusta mucho.
3 (*showing surprise*) **(Just) fancy that!** ¡Imagínate!
Fancy you being here! ¡Qué casualidad que estés aquí!

WORD TIP Use *apetece, etc* or *gusta, etc* if what you fancy, or don't fancy, is singular or an infinitive in Spanish. Use *apetecen, etc* or *gustan, etc* if what you fancy, or don't fancy, is plural.

fancy *adjective* ▷ see **fancy** *verb*
1 (*equipment*) **sofisticado** *masc*, **sofisticada** *fem*
2 (*hotel*) **de lujo**

fancy dress *noun*
el **disfraz** *masc*
in fancy dress disfrazado *masc*, disfrazada *fem*
a fancy-dress party una fiesta de disfraces

♪ **fantastic** *adjective*
estupendo (*informal*) *masc*, **estupenda** *fem*
a fantastic holiday unas vacaciones estupendas
Really? That's fantastic! ¿De verdad?¡ Eso es estupendo!

♪ **far** *adverb* ▷ see *adj*
1 (*a long way away*) **lejos**
It's not far. No está lejos.
Is it far to Cordoba? ¿Está muy lejos Córdoba?
How far is it to Granada? ¿A qué distancia está Granada?
He took us as far as Bilbao. Nos llevó hasta Bilbao.
2 (*much*) **mucho**
far better mucho mejor
far faster mucho más rápido
There is far too much noise. Hay demasiado ruido.
There are far too many people. Hay demasiada gente.
3 (*to show the extent of something*) **as far as I know** que yo sepa
by far con mucho
She is the prettiest by far. Es con mucho la más bonita. ▸▸

so far hasta ahora
So far everything's going well. Hasta ahora todo va bien.

far *adjective* ▷ see **far** *adv*
(*distant*)
in the far distance a lo lejos
at the far end of the room en el otro extremo de la habitación

fare *noun*
el **precio del billete**
half fare el medio billete
full fare el billete entero
the return fare to Barcelona el billete de ida y vuelta a Barcelona

Far East *noun*
the Far East el Lejano Oriente

farm *noun*
la **granja** *fem*

farmer *noun*
el **agricultor** *masc*, la **agricultora** *fem*

farmhouse *noun*
la **casa de labranza**

farming *noun*
la **agricultura** *fem*

fascinating *adjective*
fascinante *masc & fem*

fashion *noun*
la **moda** *fem*
in fashion de moda
out of fashion pasado de moda

fashionable *adjective*
de moda

fashion model *noun*
el & la **modelo** *masc & fem*

fashion show *noun*
el **desfile de modas**

fast *adverb* ▷ see **fast** *adj*
1 (*quickly*) **rápido**
She swims very fast. Nada muy rápido.
2 (*soundly*) **to be fast asleep** estar [2] profundamente dormido

fast *adjective* ▷ see **fast** *adv*
1 (*quick*) **rápido** *masc*, **rápida** *fem*
a fast car un coche rápido
2 (*when you talk about time*) **My watch is fast.** Mi reloj adelanta.
You're ten minutes fast. Vas diez minutos adelantado.
- **fast food** la comida rápida

to **fasten** *verb*
abrochar
Fasten your seatbelts. Abróchense los cinturones.

fat *adjective* ▷ see **fat** *noun*
gordo *masc*, **gorda** *fem*
a fat man un hombre gordo
to get fat engordar [17]

fat *noun* ▷ see **fat** *adj*
la **grasa** *fem*

fatal *adjective*
fatal *masc & fem*

father *noun*
el **padre** *masc*
my father's office la oficina de mi padre
- **Father Christmas** el Papá Noel
- **father-in-law** el suegro
- **Father's Day** el día del padre

fatty *adjective*
(*food*) **graso** *masc*, **grasa** *fem*

fault *noun*
1 (*responsibility*) la **culpa** *fem*
It's Steve's fault. Es culpa de Steve.
It's not my fault. No es culpa mía.
2 (*in tennis*) la **falta** *fem*

favour *noun*
1 (*kindness*) el **favor** *masc*
to do somebody a favour hacerle [7] un favor a alguien
Can you do me a favour? ¿Me haces un favor?
to ask a favour of somebody pedirle [57] un favor a alguien
2 **to be in favour of something** estar [2] a favor de algo
Estoy a favor de la monarquía. I am in favour of the monarchy.

favourite *adjective*
favorito *masc*, **favorita** *fem*
my favourite band mi grupo favorito

to **fax** *verb* ▷ see **fax** *noun*
1 (*a message*) **enviar [32] por fax**
2 (*a person*) **to fax somebody** mandarle [17] un fax a alguien

fax *noun* ▷ see **fax** *verb*
el **fax** *masc*
- **fax machine** el fax

fear *noun* ▷ see **fear** *verb*
el **miedo** *masc*

to fear *verb* ▷ see **fear** *noun*
temer [18]

feather *noun*
la **pluma** *fem*

feature *noun*
1 (*of your face*) el **rasgo** *masc*
to have delicate features tener [9] rasgos delicados
2 (*of a machine, product*) la **característica** *fem*

February *noun*
febrero *masc*
in February en febrero

WORD TIP Names of months and days start with small letters in Spanish.

fed up *adjective*
(*informal*) **to be fed up with something** estar [2] harto de algo (*boy speaking*), estar harta [2] de algo (*girl speaking*)
I'm fed up with working every day. Estoy harto de trabajar todos los días (*boy speaking*)., Estoy harta de trabajar todos los días (*girl speaking*).

to feed *verb*
dar [4] **de comer a**
Have you fed the dog? ¿Has dado de comer al perro?

to feel *verb*
1 (*tired, ill, etc*) **sentirse** [14]
I feel tired. Estoy cansada.
I don't feel well. No me siento bien.
2 (*cold, hot, thirsty, etc*) **to feel cold** tener [9] frío
to feel thirsty tener [9] sed
to feel afraid tener [9] miedo
3 (*a sting, a touch, etc*) **sentir** [14]
I didn't feel a thing. No sentí nada.
4 **to feel like doing something** tener [9] ganas de hacer algo
I feel like going to the cinema. Tengo ganas de ir al cine.
I feel like some chocolate. Me apetece un poco de chocolate.
Do you feel like a walk? ¿Te apetece dar un paseo?
I don't feel like it. No me apetece.
5 (*to touch*) **tocar** [3]
Feel my forehead. Tócame la frente.

feeling *noun*
1 (*in your mind*) el **sentimiento** *masc*
a feeling of embarrassment un sentimiento de vergüenza
to show your feelings demostrar [24] los sentimientos
to hurt somebody's feelings herir [14] los sentimientos de alguien
2 (*in your body*) la **sensación** *fem*
a dizzy feeling una sensación de mareo
3 (*impression*) la **impresión** *fem*
I have the feeling James doesn't like me. Tengo la impresión de que no le caigo bien a James.

felt-tip (pen) *noun*
el **rotulador** *masc*

female *adjective* ▷ see **female** *noun*
1 (*person, population*) **femenino** *masc*, **femenina** *fem*
2 (*animal, insect*) **hembra** *masc & fem*

female *noun* ▷ see **female** *adj*
(*animal*) la **hembra** *fem*

feminine *adjective*
femenino *masc*, **femenina** *fem*

feminist *noun*
el & la **feminista** *masc & fem*

fence *noun*
la **valla** *fem*

fern *noun*
el **helecho** *masc*

ferry *noun*
el **ferry** *masc, pl:* los **ferries**, **ferrys**

to fetch *verb*
ir [8] **a por**
Tom's fetching the children. Tom ha ido a por los niños.
Fetch me the other knife! ¡Vete a por el otro cuchillo!

fever *noun*
la **fiebre** *fem*

few *adjective, pronoun*
1 (*not many*) **pocos** *masc*, **pocas** *fem*
Few people think that ... Pocas personas piensan que ...
Few believe that ... Pocos creen que ...
2 (*some, several*) **a few** algunos *masc*, algunas *fem*
a few weeks earlier algunas semanas antes
in a few minutes dentro de unos minutos
a few more books unos libros más
Have we any tomatoes? We want a few for the salad. ¿Tenemos tomates? Queremos algunos para la ensalada.
quite a few bastantes *plural masc & fem*
There were quite a few questions. Hubo bastantes preguntas.
Yes, there were quite a few. Sí, hubo bastantes.

fewer *adjective*
menos *masc & fem*
fewer than six menos de seis
I have fewer lessons than she does. Tengo menos clases que ella.
There are fewer tourists this year. Hay menos turistas este año.

WORD TIP Use *menos de* with numbers.

fiancé *noun*
el **prometido** *masc*

fiancée *noun*
la **prometida** *fem*

fiction *noun*
la **ficción** *fem*

field *noun*
el **campo** *masc*
a field of wheat un campo de trigo
a football field un campo de fútbol

fifteen *number*
quince *invariable number*
Lara's fifteen. Lara tiene quince años.

fifth *adjective* ▷ **see fifth** *noun*
quinto *masc*, **quinta** *fem*
on the fifth floor en la quinta planta

fifth *noun* ▷ **see fifth** *adj*
1 (*fraction*) **a fifth** una quinta parte
2 (*in dates*) **the fifth of January** el cinco de enero

fifties *plural noun*
the fifties los años cincuenta
in the fifties en los años cincuenta

fifty *number*
cincuenta *invariable number*
She's fifty. Tiene cincuenta años.
fifty-five cincuenta y cinco

fig *noun*
el **higo** *masc*

fight *noun* ▷ **see fight** *verb*
1 (*a scuffle, in boxing*) la **pelea** *fem*
2 (*in war, against illness, poverty*) la **lucha** *fem*

to **fight** *verb* ▷ **see fight** *noun*
1 (*in war, against poverty, a disease*) **luchar** [17]
2 (*to quarrel*) **pelear** [17]
They're always fighting. Siempre se están peleando.

figure *noun*
1 (*number*) la **cifra** *fem*
a four-figure number un número de cuatro cifras
2 (*body shape*) la **figura** *fem*
She's got a very good figure. Tiene una figura estupenda.
3 (*person*) el **personaje** *masc*
a public figure un personaje público

file *noun* ▷ **see file** *verb*
1 (*container for records of a person, case*) el **archivo** *masc*
2 (*Computers*) el **fichero** *masc*
3 (*folder for documents*) la **carpeta** *fem*

to **file** *verb* ▷ **see file** *noun*
1 (*documents, records*) **archivar** [17]
2 (*nails*) **to file your nails** limarse [17] las uñas

to **fill** *verb*
llenar [17]
She filled my glass. Me llenó el vaso.
- **to fill in**
(*a form*) **rellenar** [17]
- **to fill up**
1 (*rooms, buildings*) **llenarse** [17]
The church filled up with people. La iglesia se llenó de gente.
2 (*a car tank*) **llenar**
Fill her up, please! ¡Lleno, por favor!

filling *noun*
1 (*in cooking*) el **relleno** *masc*
2 (*in a tooth*) el **empaste** *masc*

film *noun*
1 (*in a cinema*) la **película** *fem*
Shall we go and see a film? ¿Vamos a ver una película?
2 (*for a camera*) el **carrete de fotos**
a 24-exposure colour film un carrete de color de veinticuatro fotos
- **film star** la estrella de cine

filthy *adjective*
sucísimo *masc*, **sucísima** *fem*

final *adjective* ▷ **see final** *noun*
1 (*definite*) **final** *masc & fem*
the final result el resultado final
2 (*last*) **último** *masc*, **última** *fem*
the final instalment el último plazo

final *noun* ▷ **see final** *adj*
(*Sport*) la **final** *fem*
the final of the European Cup la final de la Copa de Europa

finally *adverb*
finalmente

to **find** *verb*
encontrar [24]
Did you find your passport? ¿Has encontrado tu pasaporte?

I can't find my keys. No puedo encontrar mis llaves.

- **to find out**

1 (*to enquire*) **informarse [17]**
I don't know, I'll find out. No lo sé, me informaré.

2 (*to discover*) **to find something out** descubrir **[46]** algo
Lucy found out the truth. Lucy descubrió la verdad.

fine *adjective* ▷ see **fine** *noun*

1 (*to talk about your health*) **bien** *masc & fem*
'How are you?'— 'Fine, thanks.' '¿Cómo estás?'— 'Bien, gracias.'

2 (*to say that something is all right*) **bien** *masc & fem adjective*
'Ten o'clock?'— 'Yes, that's fine.' '¿A las diez?'— 'Sí, está bien.'
Friday will be fine. El viernes está bien.

3 (*very good*) **muy bueno** *masc*, **muy buena** *fem*
She's a fine athlete. Es muy buena atleta.

4 (*weather, day*) **bueno** *masc*, **buena** *fem*
If it's fine. Si hace buen tiempo.

5 (*not coarse, not thick*) **fino** *masc*, **fina** *fem*
fine wool lana fina

fine *noun* ▷ see **fine** *adj*
la **multa** *fem*

♪ **finger** *noun*
el **dedo** *masc*

- **fingernail** la uña

♪ **finish** *noun* ▷ see **finish** *verb*

1 (*end*) el **final** *masc*
from start to finish del principio al final

2 (*in a race*) la **llegada** *fem*

♪ **to finish** *verb* ▷ see **finish** *noun*
terminar [17]
Wait, I haven't finished. Espera, no he terminado.
When does school finish? ¿Cuándo termina el colegio?
Have you finished the book? ¿Has terminado el libro?
to finish doing something terminar **[17]** de hacer algo
Have you finished telephoning? ¿Has terminado de llamar por teléfono?

- **to finish with**

terminar [17] con
Have you finished with the computer? ¿Has terminado con el ordenador?

Finland *noun*
Finlandia *fem*

Finn *noun*
un **finlandés** *masc*, una **finlandesa** *fem*

WORD TIP Adjectives and nouns for nationality and regional origin do not have capital letters in Spanish.

Finnish *adjective & noun*

1 **finlandés** *masc*, **finlandesa** *fem*

2 (*the language*) el **finlandés** *masc*

WORD TIP Adjectives and nouns for nationality, regional origin, and language do not have capital letters in Spanish.

♪ **to fire** *verb* ▷ see **fire** *noun*
(*to shoot*) **disparar [17]**
to fire at somebody dispararle a alguien
The police fired at the demonstrators. La policía les disparó a los manifestantes.

♪ **fire** *noun* ▷ see **fire** *verb*

1 (*in general, in a grate*) el **fuego** *masc*
to catch fire prenderse **[18]** fuego
to be on fire estar **[2]** ardiendo
to light the fire encender **[36]** el fuego

2 (*accidental*) el **incendio** *masc*
There was a fire at the school. Hubo un incendio en la escuela.

- **fire alarm** la alarma contra incendios
- **fire brigade** el cuerpo de bomberos
- **fire engine** el coche de bomberos
- **fire escape** la escalera de incendios
- **fire extinguisher** el extintor
- **firefighter** el & la bombero
- **fireplace** la chimenea
- **fire station** la estación de bomberos
- **fireworks** los fuegos artificiales

firm *adjective* ▷ see **firm** *noun*
firme *masc & fem*

firm *noun* ▷ see **firm** *adj*
la **empresa** *fem*

♪ **first** *noun* ▷ see **first** *adj, adv, pron*
(*in dates*) **the first of May** el primero de mayo

mini-info first

The first submarine was designed and built by Isaac Peral between 1884-1887 and the autogiro, a prototype for the helicopter, was invented by Juan de la Cierva in the early 1920s.

♪ **first** *adjective, adverb, pronoun*
▷ see **first** *noun*

1 (*before the others*) **primero** *masc*, **primera** *fem*
for the first time por primera vez
Susan's the first. Susan es la primera.
Christy got here first. Christy llegó aquí primero. ▸▸

Ben came first in the 200 metres. Ben llegó el primero en los doscientos metros.
2 (*to begin with*) **primero**
First, I'm going to make some tea. Primero voy a hacer té.
first of all en primer lugar
at first al principio
At first he didn't want to. Al principio no quería.

WORD TIP *primer* is used instead of *primero* before a masc singular noun.

- **first aid** los primeros auxilios
- **first aid kit** el botiquín de primeros auxilios

first-class *adjective, adverb*
(*ticket, carriage, hotel*) **de primera**
a first-class compartment un compartimento de primera
He always travels first-class. Siempre viaja en primera.

first floor *noun*
la **primera planta** *fem*
on the first floor en la primera planta

firstly *adverb*
en primer lugar

first name *noun*
el **nombre de pila**

fir tree *noun*
el **abeto** *masc*

to **fish** *verb* ▷ see **fish** *noun*
pescar [31]
Dad was fishing for trout. Papá estaba pescando truchas.

fish *noun* ▷ see **fish** *verb*
1 (*as a meal*) el **pescado** *masc*
Do you like fish? ¿Te gusta el pescado?
2 (*in the sea, river*) el **pez** *masc, pl:* los **peces**
- **fish and chips** el pescado con patatas fritas

fisherman *noun*
el **pescador** *masc*

fishing *noun*
la **pesca** *fem*
to go fishing ir [8] a pescar
I love fishing. Me encanta pescar.
Fishing is my favourite sport. La pesca es mi deporte favorito.
- **fishing rod** la caña de pescar
- **fishing tackle** los aparejos de pesca

fist *noun*
el **puño** *masc*

fit *adjective* ▷ see **fit** *noun, verb*
en forma
to keep fit mantenerse [9] en forma
I feel really fit. Me siento muy en forma.

fit *noun* ▷ see **fit** *adj, verb*
el **ataque** *masc noun*
I had a fit. Me dio un ataque.
Your dad'll have a fit when he sees you! ¡A tu padre le va a dar un ataque cuando te vea!

to **fit** *verb* ▷ see **fit** *adj, noun*
1 (*garments, shoes*) **to fit somebody estarle [2] bien a alguien**
This skirt doesn't fit me. Esta falda no me queda bien.
Does it fit you okay? ¿Te está bien?
2 (*to go into*) **entrar [17] en**
Will my cases all fit in the car? ¿Entrarán todas mis maletas en el coche?
3 (*a shelf, a lock, a handle*) **poner [11]**
He fitted a lock on the door. Puso una cerradura en la puerta.

fitness *noun*
el **estado físico**
- **fitness training** el entrenamiento

fitted carpet *noun*
la **moqueta** *fem*

five *number*
cinco *invariable number*
Oskar's five. Oskar tiene cinco años.
It's five o'clock. Son las cinco.

to **fix** *verb*
1 (*to repair*) **arreglar [17]**
Mum's fixed the computer. Mamá ha arreglado el ordenador.
2 (*to decide on*) **fijar [17]**
to fix a date fijar una fecha

fizzy *adjective*
con gas
fizzy water agua con gas

flag *noun*
la **bandera** *fem*

flame *noun*
la **llama** *fem*

flan *noun*
1 (*savoury*) el **quiche** *masc*
an onion flan un quiche de cebolla
2 (*sweet*) la **tarta** *fem*

to **flap** *verb*
1 (*birds: their wings*) **batir [19]**
2 (*flags, sails*) **agitarse [17]**

flash *noun* ▷ see **flash** *verb*
1 (*of light*) el **destello** *masc*
a flash of lightning un relámpago
to do something in a flash hacer [7] algo como un relámpago
2 (*on a camera*) el **flash** *masc*

to **flash** *verb* ▷ see **flash** *noun*
1 (*lights*) **destellar** [17]
to flash past pasar [17] como un rayo
2 (*a light*) to flash your headlights hacer [7] señas con los faros del coche

flask *noun*
1 (*insulated bottle*) el **termo** *masc*
2 (*container*) el **frasco** *masc*

flat *adjective* ▷ see **flat** *noun*
1 (*surface*) **plano** *masc*, **plana** *fem*
2 (*countryside, landscape*) **llano** *masc*, **llana** *fem*
3 (*shoes*) **de tacón bajo**
4 (*deflated*) a flat tyre una rueda pinchada

flat *noun* ▷ see **flat** *adj*
el **piso** *masc*
a third-floor flat un piso en la tercera planta
• **flatmate** el compañero de piso, la compañera de piso

flavour *noun* ▷ see **flavour** *verb*
el **sabor** *masc*
The sauce had no flavour. La salsa no tenía sabor.
What flavour of ice cream would you like? ¿De qué sabor quieres el helado?

to **flavour** *verb* ▷ see **flavour** *noun*
sazonar [17]
vanilla-flavoured con sabor a vainilla

flea *noun*
la **pulga** *fem*

fleet *noun*
1 (*of ships*) la **flota** *fem*
2 (*of vehicles*) el **parque móvil**

flight *noun*
1 (*of a plane, bird*) el **vuelo** *masc*
The flight from Moscow is delayed. El vuelo procedente de Moscú lleva retraso.
2 (*of stairs*) a flight of stairs un tramo de escalera
• **flight attendant** el & la auxiliar de vuelo

to **fling** *verb*
lanzar [22]

flipper *noun*
(*for a swimmer*) la **aleta** *fem*

to **flirt** *verb*
flirtear [17]

to **float** *verb*
flotar [17]

to **flood** *verb* ▷ see **flood** *noun*
inundar [17]

flood *noun* ▷ see **flood** *verb*
1 (*of water*) la **inundación** *fem*
the floods in the south las inundaciones del sur
to be in floods of tears estar [2] llorando a mares
2 (*of letters, complaints*) la **avalancha** *fem*
• **floodlight** el foco

floor *noun*
1 (*of a room, vehicle*) el **suelo** *masc*
on the floor en el suelo
2 (*storey*) la **planta** *fem*
the first floor la primera planta
on the second floor en la segunda planta

flop *noun*
el **fracaso** *masc*

floppy disk *noun*
el **disquete** *masc*

florist *noun*
el & la **florista** *masc & fem*

florist's *noun*
la **floristería** *fem*

flour *noun*
la **harina** *fem*

flower *noun* ▷ see **flower** *verb*
la **flor** *fem*

to **flower** *verb* ▷ see **flower** *noun*
florecer [35]

flu *noun*
la **gripe** *fem*
to have flu tener [9] gripe

fluent *adjective*
to be fluent in a language hablar [17] un idioma con fluidez
She speaks fluent Italian. Habla italiano con fluidez.

fluently *adverb*
con fluidez

fluid *noun*
el **fluido** *masc*

to **flush** *verb*
1 (*to go red*) **enrojecer** [35]
2 (*the lavatory*) to flush the lavatory tirar [17] de la cadena

flute *noun*
la **flauta** *fem*
to play the flute tocar [31] la flauta

fly *noun* ▷ see **fly** *verb*
la **mosca** *fem*

to fly *verb* ▷ see **fly** *noun*
1 (*birds, insects, planes*) **volar [24]**
2 (*time*) **pasar [17] volando**
3 (*to travel in a plane*) **ir [8] en avión**
We flew to Edinburgh. Fuimos en avión a Edimburgo.
We flew from Gatwick. Salimos desde Gatwick.
4 (*a kite*) **hacer [7] volar**

foam *noun*
la **espuma** *fem*
• **foam rubber** la goma espuma

focus *noun* ▷ see **focus** *verb*
to be in focus estar **[2]** enfocado
to be out of focus estar **[2]** desenfocado

to focus *verb* ▷ see **focus** *noun*
(*a camera*) **enfocar [31]**

fog *noun*
la **niebla** *fem*

foggy *adjective*
a foggy day un día de niebla
It was foggy. Había niebla.

foil *noun*
el **papel de aluminio**

fold *noun* ▷ see **fold** *verb*
el **pliegue** *masc*

to fold *verb* ▷ see **fold** *noun*
doblar [17]
• **to fold up**
1 **doblar [17]**
to fold up the sheet doblar la sábana
2 (*by itself*) **doblarse**
The table folds up very easily. La mesa se dobla muy fácilmente.

folder *noun*
la **carpeta** *fem*

to follow *verb*
seguir [64]
followed by a dinner seguido de una cena
Follow me! ¡Sígueme!
Do you follow me? ¿Me sigues?

following *adjective*
siguiente *masc & fem*
the following year el año siguiente

fond *adjective*
to be fond of somebody tenerle **[9]** cariño a alguien
I'm very fond of him. Le tengo mucho cariño.
I'm fond of dogs. Me gustan los perros.

food *noun*
la **comida** *fem*
I like Italian food. Me gusta la comida italiana.
• **food poisoning** la intoxicación alimenticia

fool *noun*
el & la **idiota** *masc & fem*

foot *noun*
1 (*of a person*) el **pie** *masc*
He stepped on my foot. Me pisó el pie.
Lucy came on foot. Lucy vino a pie.
2 (*of an animal*) la **pata** *fem*
3 (*the bottom of something*) el **pie** *masc*
at the foot of the stairs al pie de las escaleras
at the foot of the bed a los pies de la cama
4 (*measurement*) el **pie** *masc*
He is six feet tall. Mide seis pies.

football *noun*
1 (*the game*) el **fútbol** *masc*
to play football jugar **[27]** al fútbol
2 (*a ball*) el **balón de fútbol**

footballer *noun*
el & la **futbolista** *masc & fem*

footpath *noun*
el **sendero** *masc*

for *preposition*
1 (*saying where something goes, or what it does*) **para**
a present for my mother un regalo para mi madre
petrol for the car gasolina para el coche
sausages for lunch salchichas para comer
It's for cleaning. Es para limpiar.
What's it for? ¿Para qué es?
2 (*giving the reason for something*) **por**
for that reason por esa razón
3 (*giving costs*) **por**
I sold my bike for fifty pounds. Vendí mi bicicleta por cincuenta libras.
4 (*giving a destination*) **para**
the bus for Barcelona el autobús para Barcelona
5 (*asking for a translation*) **What's the Spanish for 'bee'?** ¿Cómo se dice 'bee' en español?
6 (*in time expressions*) **I studied Spanish for four years.** Estudié español cuatro años.
I'll be away for four days. Estaré fuera cuatro días.
I've been waiting here for an hour. Llevo esperando aquí una hora.
My brother's been living in London for

three years. Mi hermano lleva tres años viviendo en Londres.

WORD TIP In time expressions in the past or future, *for* is not usually translated

to **forbid** *verb*
prohibir [58]
to forbid somebody to do something prohibir [58] a alguien hacer algo
I forbid you to go out. Te prohíbo salir.

♪ **forbidden** *adjective*
prohibido *masc*, **prohibida** *fem*

force *noun* ▷ see **force** *verb*
la **fuerza** *fem*

to **force** *verb* ▷ see **force** *noun*
forzar [26]
to force somebody to do something forzar a alguien a hacer algo

forecast *noun*
(*for the weather*) el **pronóstico** *masc*

forehead *noun*
la **frente** *fem*

foreign *adjective*
extranjero *masc*, **extranjera** *fem*
in a foreign country en un país extranjero

♪ **foreigner** *noun*
el **extranjero** *masc*, la **extranjera** *fem*

♪ **forest** *noun*
el **bosque** *masc*

forever *adverb*
1 (*for all time*) **para siempre**
I'd like to stay here forever. Me gustaría quedarme aquí para siempre.
2 (*non-stop*) **siempre**
He's forever asking questions. Siempre está preguntando.

forgery *noun*
la **falsificación** *fem*

♪ to **forget** *verb*
olvidarse [17]
I forget his name. Se me ha olvidado su nombre.
We've forgotten the bread! ¡Se nos ha olvidado el pan!
to forget to do something olvidarse [17] de hacer algo
I forgot to phone. Se me olvidó llamar por teléfono.
to forget about something olvidarse [17] de algo
I forgot about the outing. Me olvidé de la excursión.

forgetful *adjective*
olvidadizo *masc*, **olvidadiza** *fem*

to **forgive** *verb*
perdonar [17]
I forgave him. Lo perdoné.
to forgive somebody for doing something perdonar a alguien por algo
I forgave her for losing my ring. La perdoné por perderme el anillo.

♪ **fork** *noun*
el **tenedor** *masc*

♪ **form** *noun* ▷ see **form** *verb*
1 (*document*) el **formulario** *masc*
to fill in a form rellenar [17] un formulario
2 (*shape, kind*) la **forma** *fem*
in the form of something en forma de algo
3 (*fitness*) **to be on form** estar [2] en forma
4 (*school class*) la **clase** *fem*
5 (*school year*) el **curso** *masc*

♪ to **form** *verb* ▷ see **form** *noun*
formar [17]

formal *adjective*
(*invitation, event, complaint*) **formal** *masc & fem*

♪ **former** *adjective*
antiguo *masc*, **antigua** *fem*
a former pupil un antiguo alumno

WORD TIP *antiguo, antigua* meaning *former*, go before the noun.

formula *noun*
la **fórmula** *fem*

fortnight *noun*
quince días *plural masc*
We're going to Spain for a fortnight. Vamos quince días a España.

fortune *noun*
la **fortuna** *fem*
to make a fortune hacer [7] una fortuna

fortunate *adjective*
afortunado *masc*, **afortunada** *fem*

fortunately *adverb*
afortunadamente

♪ **forty** *number*
cuarenta *invariable number*
He's forty. Tiene cuarenta años.
forty-five cuarenta y cinco

forward *adverb* ▷ see **forward** *noun*
hacia adelante
to move forward ir [8] hacia adelante
a seat further forward un asiento de más adelante

English–Spanish

forward *noun* ▷ see **forward** *adv*
el & la **delantero** *masc & fem*

foster child *noun*
el **hijo acogido**, la **hija acogida**

foster family *noun*
la **familia de acogida**

foul *adjective* ▷ see **foul** *noun*
espantoso *masc*, **espantosa** *fem*
The weather's foul. El tiempo está horroroso.

foul *noun* ▷ see **foul** *adj*
(*Sport*) la **falta** *fem*

fountain *noun*
la **fuente** *fem*
• **fountain pen** la pluma

four *number*
cuatro *invariable number*
Simon's four. Simon tiene cuatro años.
It's four o'clock. Son las cuatro.

fourteen *number*
catorce *invariable number*
Susie's fourteen. Susie tiene catorce años.

fourth *adjective* ▷ see **fourth** *noun*
cuarto *masc*, **cuarta** *fem*
on the fourth floor en la cuarta planta

fourth *noun* ▷ see **fourth** *adj*
1 (*fraction*) **a fourth** un cuarto
2 (*in dates*) **the fourth of July** el cuatro de julio

fox *noun*
el **zorro** *masc*

fracture *noun*
la **fractura** *fem*

fragile *adjective*
frágil *masc & fem*

frame *noun*
(*of a picture, photograph*) el **marco** *masc*

France *noun*
Francia *fem*

frantic *adjective*
(*effort, search*) **desesperado** *masc*, **desesperada** *fem*
Mum was frantic with worry. Mamá estaba muerta de preocupación.

freckle *noun*
la **peca** *fem*

to **free** *verb* ▷ see **free** *adj*
1 (*a person*) **poner [11] en libertad**
2 (*an animal*) **soltar [24]**

free *adjective* ▷ see **free** *verb*
1 (*when you don't pay*) **gratis** *masc & fem*
a free ticket un billete gratis
The bus is free. El autobús es gratis.
2 (*at liberty*) **libre** *masc & fem*
to be free to do something ser [1] libre de hacer algo
You're free to do what you think best. Eres libre de hacer lo que te parezca.
to set somebody free poner [11] a alguien en libertad
3 (*not occupied*) **libre** *masc & fem*
Are you free on Thursday? ¿Estás libre el jueves?
4 (*not containing*) **sugar-free** sin azúcar
lead-free sin plomo

freedom *noun*
la **libertad** *fem*

free gift *noun*
el **regalo** *masc*

free kick *noun*
el **tiro libre**

to **freeze** *verb*
1 (*in a freezer*) **congelar [17]**
frozen peas guisantes congelados
2 (*in cold weather*) **helarse [29]**

freezer *noun*
el **congelador** *masc*

freezing *adjective*
1 (*temperatures*) **bajo cero** *invariable masc & fem*
It's freezing outside! ¡Fuera hace un frío que pela! (*informal*)
2 (*hands, feet*) **helado** *masc*, **helada** *fem*
I'm freezing! ¡Estoy helado!

French *adjective & noun*
1 **francés** *masc*, **francesa** *fem*
2 (*the people*) **the French** los franceses
3 (*the language*) el **francés** *masc*
our French teacher nuestro profesor de francés

WORD TIP Adjectives and nouns for nationality, regional origin, and language do not have capital letters in Spanish.

• **French bean** la judía verde
• **French fries** las patatas fritas, (*Latin America*) las papas fritas

Frenchman *noun*
un **francés** *masc*

French stick *noun*
la **barra de pan**

French window *noun*
la **cristalera** *fem*

Frenchwoman *noun*
una **francesa** *fem*

frequently *adverb*
frecuentemente, **a menudo**

♪ **fresh** *adjective*
fresco *masc*, **fresca** *fem*
fresh eggs huevos frescos
I'm going out for some fresh air. Voy fuera a tomar un poco el aire.

♪ **Friday** *noun*
el **viernes** *masc*
every Friday cada viernes
last Friday el viernes pasado
on Friday el viernes
on Fridays los viernes
The shop is closed on Fridays. La tienda está cerrada los viernes.
I'll phone you on Friday evening. Te llamaré el viernes por la tarde.

WORD TIP Names of months and days start with small letters in Spanish.

♪ **fridge** *noun*
la **nevera** *fem*
Put it in the fridge. Ponlo en la nevera.

fried egg *noun*
el **huevo frito**

♪ **friend** *noun*
el **amigo** *masc*, la **amiga** *fem*
a friend of mine un amigo mío (*a boy*), una amiga mía (*a girl*)
to make friends with somebody hacerse [7] amigo de alguien
He made friends with Danny. Se hizo amigo de Danny.

friendly *adjective*
1 (*person*) **simpático** *masc*, **simpática** *fem*
2 (*letter, gesture*) **amable** *masc & fem*

friendship *noun*
la **amistad** *fem*

fries *plural noun*
las **patatas fritas**

fright *noun*
el **susto** *masc*
to get a fright asustarse [17]
to give somebody a fright asustar [17] a alguien
You gave me a fright! ¡Me asustaste!

to **frighten** *verb*
asustar [17]

♪ **frightened** *adjective*
to be frightened of something tenerle [9] miedo a algo
He was frightened of the dark. Le tenía miedo a la oscuridad.
He was frightened of his father. Le tenía miedo a su padre.
I was frightened to tell him. Tenía miedo de decírselo.
Don't be frightened. No tengas miedo., No te asustes.

frightening *adjective*
espantoso *masc*, **espantosa** *fem*

fringe *noun*
(*of hair*) el **flequillo** *masc*

frog *noun*
la **rana** *fem*

♪ **from** *preposition*
1 (*coming from*) **de**
a letter from Tom una carta de Tom
He comes from Dublin. Es de Dublín.
2 (*in distances*) **de**
100 metres from the cinema a cien metros del cine
from seven o'clock onwards de las siete en adelante
3 (*starting from*) **desde**
tickets from ten pounds entradas desde diez libras
from today desde hoy
two years from now dentro de dos años
from then on a partir de entonces
from ... to ... de ... a ...
from Monday to Friday de lunes a viernes
the train from London to Liverpool el tren de Londres a Liverpool
from here to the wall de aquí a la pared
4 (*as a result of*) **de**
She suffers from depression. Sufre de depresión.

♪ **front** *adjective* ▷ see **front** *noun*
delantero *masc*, **delantera** *fem*
the front seat el asiento delantero (*of a car*)
in the front row en la fila de delante

♪ **front** *noun* ▷ see **front** *adj*
1 (*of an envelope, a car, train, queue*) la **parte de delante**
sitting in the front sentado en la parte de delante
from the front por delante
the front of the class el frente de la clase
The address is on the front. Las señas están en la parte de delante.
2 (*of a building*) la **fachada** *fem*
3 (*of a garment*) la **delantera** *fem*
4 **in front of** delante de
in front of the TV delante de la televisión
in front of me delante de mí
• **front door** la puerta de la calle

English–Spanish

frontier *noun*
la **frontera** *fem*

frost *noun*
la **helada** *fem*

frosty *adjective*
1 (*weather, air*) **helado** *masc*, **helada** *fem*
It was frosty this morning. Había helada esta mañana.
2 (*windscreen, grass*) **cubierto de escarcha** *masc*, **cubierta de escarcha** *fem*

to **frown** *verb*
fruncir [66] el ceño

frozen *adjective*
congelado *masc*, **congelada** *fem*
a frozen pizza una pizza congelada

fruit *noun*
la **fruta** *fem*
- **fruit juice** el zumo de fruta
- **fruit machine** la máquina tragaperras
- **fruit salad** la macedonia de frutas

frustrating *adjective*
frustrante *masc & fem*

to **fry** *verb*
freír [53]
We fried the fish. Freímos el pescado.

frying pan *noun*
la **sartén** *fem*

fuel *noun*
el **combustible** *masc*

full *adjective*
1 (*container*) **lleno** *masc*, **llena** *fem*
This glass is full. Este vaso está lleno.
The train was full of tourists. El tren estaba lleno de turistas.
I'm full. Estoy lleno.
2 (*hotel, flight*) **completo** *masc*, **completa** *fem*
3 (*top*) **at full speed** a toda velocidad
at full volume a todo volumen
4 (*complete*) **todo** *masc*, **toda** *fem*
the full story toda la historia
to write your name out in full escribir **[52]** su nombre completo
- **full stop** el punto

full time *noun* ▷ see **full-time** *adj, adv*
el **final de partido**

full-time *adjective, adverb* ▷ see **full time** *noun*
a tiempo completo
a full-time job un trabajo a tiempo completo
to work full-time trabajar **[17]** a tiempo completo

fully *adverb*
completamente

fun *noun*
to have fun divertirse **[14]**
Have fun! ¡Que te diviertas!
We had fun catching the ponies. Nos divertimos atrapando a los poneys.
Skiing is fun. Esquiar es divertido.
I do it for fun. Lo hago para divertirme.
to make fun of somebody reírse **[61]** de alguien
- **funfair** el parque de atracciones

funds *noun*
los **fondos** *plural masc*

funeral *noun*
el **funeral** *masc*, los **funerales** *masc pl*

funny *adjective*
1 (*amusing*) **gracioso** *masc*, **graciosa** *fem*
a funny story una historia graciosa
How funny you are! ¡Qué gracioso eres!
2 (*strange*) **raro** *masc*, **rara** *fem*
a funny noise un ruido raro
That's funny, I'm sure I paid. Qué raro, estoy seguro de que pagué.

fur *noun*
1 (*on an animal*) el **pelaje** *masc*
2 (*for a coat*) la **piel** *fem*
a fur coat un abrigo de piel

furious *adjective*
furioso *masc*, **furiosa** *fem*
She was furious with Steve. Estaba furiosa con Steve.

furnished *adjective*
amueblado *masc*, **amueblada** *fem*
a furnished flat un piso amueblado

furniture *noun*
los **muebles** *plural masc*
a piece of furniture un mueble
to buy some furniture comprar **[17]** muebles

further *adverb*
(*at a greater distance*) **más lejos**
They live even further away. Viven aún más lejos.
further forward más adelante
further back más atrás
further in más adentro
further than the station más allá de la estación
ten kilometres further on diez kilómetros más adelante

fuse *noun*
el **fusible** *masc*

a b c d e f g h i j k l m n o p q r s t u v w x y z

fuss *noun*
el **escándalo** *masc*
to make a fuss montar [17] un escándalo
He made a fuss about the bill. Montó un escándalo a causa de la factura.

fussy *adjective*
1 (*about how things are done*) **quisquilloso** *masc*, **quisquillosa** *fem*
to be fussy about something ser [1] muy quisquilloso para algo
2 (*about food*) **maniático** *masc*, **maniática** *fem*
to be fussy about food ser [1] muy maniático para la comida

future *noun*
el **futuro** *masc*
in future en el futuro
a verb in the future un verbo en el futuro
In future, ask me first. En el futuro, pregúntame antes.

English-Spanish

G g

gadget *noun*
el **aparato** *masc*

to **gain** *verb*
adquirir [47]
to gain weight aumentar **[17]** de peso

galaxy *noun*
la **galaxia** *fem*

gale *noun*
el **vendaval** *masc*

Galicia *noun*
Galicia *fem*

Galician *adjective & noun*
1 **gallego** *masc*, **gallega** *fem*
2 (*person*) un **gallego** *masc*, una **gallega** *fem*
the Galicians los gallegos
3 (*the language*) el **gallego** *masc*

WORD TIP Adjectives and nouns for nationality, regional origin, and language do not have capital letters in Spanish.

gallery *noun*
1 (*public art museum*) el **museo de pintura**
2 (*private art shop*) la **galería de arte**

gambling *noun*
el **juego** *masc*

game *noun*
1 (*with rules*) el **juego** *masc*
a board game un juego de mesa
2 (*of cards, etc*) la **partida** *fem*
a game of cards una partida de cartas
3 (*match*) el **partido** *masc*
a game of football un partido de fútbol
4 (*school sports*) **games** los deportes
Jack's very good at games. Jack es muy buen deportista.
• **games console** la consola de juegos

gang *noun*
1 (*one's friends*) la **panda** *fem*
All the gang were there. Toda la panda estaba allí.
2 (*of criminals*) la **banda** *fem*

gangster *noun*
el & la **gángster** *masc & fem*

gap *noun*
1 (*hole*) el **hueco** *masc*
2 (*interval in time*) el **intervalo** *masc*
a two-year gap un intervalo de dos años
an age gap una diferencia de edad
• **gap year** el año libre antes de entrar a la universidad

garage *noun*
1 (*for parking*) el **garaje** *masc*
2 (*for fuel*) la **estación de servicio**
3 (*for repairs*) el **taller mecánico**

garden *noun*
el **jardín** *masc*

gardener *noun*
1 (*as a job*) el **jardinero** *masc*, la **jardinera** *fem*
2 (*as a hobby*) **She is a keen gardener.** Es una apasionada de la jardinería.

gardening *noun*
la **jardinería** *fem*

garlic *noun*
el **ajo** *masc*

garment *noun*
la **prenda** *fem*

gas *noun*
el **gas** *masc*
• **gas cooker** la cocina de gas
• **gas fire** la estufa de gas
• **gas meter** el contador de gas

gate *noun*
1 (*of a garden*) la **verja** *fem*
2 (*of a field*) el **portillo** *masc*
3 (*at an airport*) la **puerta (de embarque)**

to **gather** *verb*
1 (*crowds*) **juntarse [17]**
A crowd gathered. Se juntó una multitud.
2 (*fruit, vegetables, flowers*) **recoger [3]**
3 (*to make out*) **as far as I can gather ...** según tengo entendido ...

gay *adjective*
(*homosexual*) **gay** *masc & fem*

GCSEs *noun plural*
(*Son exámenes que se realizan alrededor de los 16 años y abarcan hasta 12 asignaturas. Se califican desde A-star (nota máxima), a N (sin calificar). Muchos alumnos estudian para los A levels después de hacer los GCSEs.*)
▷ **A levels**

gear *noun*
1 (*in a car*) la **marcha** *fem*
to change gear cambiar **[17]** de marcha
in third gear en tercera

2 (*equipment*) el **equipo** *masc*
camping gear el equipo de acampada
fishing gear los aparejos de pesca
3 (*things*) las **cosas** *plural fem*
I've left all my gear at Gary's. He dejado todas mis cosas en casa de Gary.
• **gear lever** la palanca de cambio

gel *noun*
el **gel** *masc*
hair gel gel para el pelo

Gemini *noun*
1 (*the star sign*) el **Géminis** *masc*
2 (*a person*) un & una **géminis** *masc & fem*
Steph's Gemini. Steph es géminis.

WORD TIP Use a small letter in Spanish to say *I am ...* etc with star signs. Star signs in Spanish are used without *el, un, la, una.*

gender *noun*
(*of a word*) el **género** *masc*
What is the gender of 'casa'? ¿De qué género es 'casa'?

general *noun* ▷ see **general** *adj*
el **general** *masc*
General O'Donnell el general O'Donnell

general *adjective* ▷ see **general** *noun*
general *masc & fem*
in general en general
• **general election** las elecciones generales
• **general knowledge** la cultura general

generally *adverb*
generalmente

generation *noun*
la **generación** *fem*

generous *adjective*
generoso *masc*, **generosa** *fem*

genetics *noun*
la **genética** *fem*

genius *noun*
el **genio** *masc*
Lisa, you're a genius! Lisa, ¡eres un genio!

gentle *adjective*
1 (*person, voice, nature*) **dulce** *masc & fem*
2 (*breeze, murmur, heat*) **suave** *masc & fem*

gentleman *noun*
el **caballero** *masc*
ladies and gentlemen señoras y caballeros ▷ **gents**

gently *adverb*
1 (*talk*) **dulcemente**
2 (*touch*) **suavemente**
3 (*handle*) **con cuidado**

gents *noun*
1 (*men's toilets*) los **servicios de caballeros**
Where's the gents? ¿Dónde están los servicios de caballeros?
2 (*sign for men's toilets*) **Caballeros**

genuine *adjective*
1 (*real*) **auténtico** *masc*, **auténtica** *fem*
a genuine diamond un diamante auténtico
2 (*sincere*) **sincero** *masc*, **sincera** *fem*
She's very genuine. Es muy sincera.

geography *noun*
la **geografía** *fem*

geology *noun*
la **geología** *fem*

geometry *noun*
la **geometría** *fem*

germ *noun*
el **germen** *masc, pl:* los **gérmenes**

German *adjective & noun*
1 **alemán** *masc*, **alemana** *fem*
my German class mi clase de alemán
our German teacher nuestro profesor de alemán
2 (*person*) un **alemán** *masc*, una **alemana** *fem*
the Germans los alemanes
3 (*the language*) el **alemán** *masc*

WORD TIP Adjectives and nouns for nationality, regional origin, and language do not have capital letters in Spanish.

Germany *noun*
Alemania *fem*

to get *verb*
1 (*to obtain*) **conseguir [64]**
Fred's got a job. Fred ha conseguido un trabajo.
I got fifteen for my exam. Saqué un quince en el examen.
Where did you get that jacket? ¿De dónde has sacado esa chaqueta?
2 (*to receive*) **recibir [19]**
I got your letter yesterday. Recibí tu carta ayer.
I got a bike for my birthday. Me regalaron una bicicleta por mi cumpleaños.
3 (*to fetch*) **ir [8] a buscar**
Go and get some bread. Vete a buscar pan.
I'll get your bag for you. Voy a buscar tu bolso.
4 (*to buy*) **comprar [17]**
I got a nice shirt in the sales. Compré una camisa muy bonita en las rebajas.
5 (*to catch*) **coger [3]**
She got a cold. Cogió un resfriado.
I got the train. Cogí el tren. ▸▸

6 (*informal*) (*to understand*) **entender [36]**
Get it? ¿Entiendes?
7 (*to arrive*) **to get to a place** llegar **[28]** a un lugar
When we got to London it was raining. Cuando llegamos a Londres estaba lloviendo.
How do I get to the cathedral? ¿Cómo llego a la catedral?
We got here this morning. Llegamos esta mañana.
What time did they get there? ¿A qué hora llegaron?
8 (*to become*) **to get tired** cansarse **[17]**
She was getting worried. Se estaba preocupando.
It's getting late. Se está haciendo tarde.
I'm getting hungry. Me está entrando hambre.
9 (*to talk about doing a job*) **to get something done**
I must get some work done. Tengo que trabajar un poco.
He's going to get that shelf put up. Va a colocar ese estante.
10 (*to talk about getting a job done by someone else*) **to get something done**
to get your hair cut cortarse **[17]** el pelo
My father got the house painted. Mi padre hizo pintar la casa.

- to **get back**
volver [45]
Mum gets back at six. Mamá vuelve a las seis.
- to **get something back**
(*to have something returned to you*) **We got the money back.** Nos devolvieron el dinero.
Did you get your books back? ¿Te devolvieron los libros?
- to **get down**
bajar [17]
He got down from the tree. Bajó del árbol.
- to **get into something**
to get into a vehicle entrar **[17]** en un vehículo
He got into the car. Entró en el coche.
- to **get off something**
to get off a vehicle bajarse **[17]** de un vehículo
I got off the train at Banbury. Me bajé del tren en Banbury.
- to **get on**
(*to cope*) **How's Amanda getting on?** ¿Cómo le va a Amanda?
- to **get on something**
to get on a vehicle subir **[19]** a un vehículo
She got on the train at Reading. Subió al tren en Reading.
- to **get on with**
to get on with somebody llevarse **[17]** bien con alguien
She doesn't get on with her brother. No se lleva bien con su hermano.
Thomas and Ben get on well. Thomas y Ben se llevan bien.
- to **get out**
(*to leave*) **to get out of a place** salir **[63]** de un lugar
I've got to get out of here. Tengo que salir de aquí.
Laura got out of the car. Laura salió del coche.
- to **get something out**
sacar [31] algo
Robert got his guitar out. Robert sacó la guitarra.
- to **get together**
verse [16]
We must get together soon. Tenemos que vernos pronto.
- to **get up**
levantarse [17]
I get up at seven. Me levanto a las siete.

ghost *noun*
el **fantasma** *masc*

giant
el **gigante** *masc*

giddy *adjective*
mareado *masc*, **mareada** *fem*
I'm feeling giddy. Me siento mareado.

♪ **gift** *noun*
1 (*present*) el **regalo** *masc*
a Christmas gift un regalo de Navidad
2 (*talent*) **to have a gift for something** estar **[2]** dotado, *fem* dotada para algo
Jo has a real gift for languages. Jo está realmente dotada para los idiomas.

gig *noun*
el **concierto** *masc*

gigabyte *noun*
el **gigabyte** *masc*
a fifty gigabyte hard disk un disco duro de cincuenta gigabytes

ginger *noun*
el **jengibre** *masc*
- **ginger-haired** *adj* pelirrojo *masc*, pelirroja *fem*

Gipsy *noun*
el **gitano** *masc*, la **gitana** *fem*

giraffe *noun*
la **jirafa** *fem*

⚷ **girl** *noun*
1 (*child*) la **niña** *fem*
three boys and four girls tres niños y cuatro niñas
a little girl una niña pequeña
when I was a little girl ... cuando yo era pequeña ...
2 (*teenager, young woman*) la **chica** *fem*
an eighteen-year-old girl una chica de dieciocho años

⚷ **girlfriend** *noun*
1 (*partner in a relationship*) la **novia** *fem*
Darren's girlfriend la novia de Darren
2 (*female friend*) la **amiga** *fem*
Lizzie and her girlfriends have gone to the cinema. Lizzie y sus amigas han ido al cine.

⚷ to **give** *verb*
dar [4]
to give something to somebody darle [4] algo a alguien
I gave Sandy the books. Le di los libros a Sandy.
I'll give you my address. Te daré mis señas.
Give me the key. Dame la llave.
Yasmin's dad gave her the money. El padre de Yasmin le dio el dinero.
- to **give something away**
regalar [17] **algo**
She's given away all her books. Ha regalado todos sus libros.
- to **give something back to somebody**
devolverle [45] **algo a alguien**
I gave her back the keys. Le devolví las llaves.
- to **give in**
ceder [18]
She gave in in the end. Al final cedió.
- to **give up**
rendirse [57]
I give up! ¡Me rindo!
- to **give up doing something**
dejar [17] **de hacer algo**
She's given up smoking. Ha dejado de fumar.

glacier *noun*
el **glaciar** *masc*

⚷ **glad** *adjective*
to be glad to do something alegrarse [17] de hacer algo
I'm glad to hear he's better. Me alegra saber que está mejor.
I'm glad to be back. Me alegro de haber vuelto.

glamorous *adjective*
1 (*life, job*) **con mucho glamour**
2 (*film star*) **elegante** *masc & fem*

⚷ **glass** *noun*
1 (*for a drink*) el **vaso** *masc*
a glass of water un vaso de agua
2 (*for windows, etc*) el **cristal** *masc*
a glass table una mesa de cristal

⚷ **glasses** *plural noun*
las **gafas** *plural fem*, (*Latin America*) los **anteojos** *masc pl*
to wear glasses llevar [17] gafas

global *adjective*
global *masc & fem*
- **global warming** el calentamiento global

globe *noun*
(*model*) el **globo terráqueo**

gloomy *adjective*
1 (*expression*) **lúgubre** *masc & fem*
2 (*weather*) **gris** *masc & fem*

glory *noun*
la **gloria** *fem*

glove *noun*
el **guante** *masc*
a pair of gloves un par de guantes

glue *noun*
el **pegamento** *masc*

⚷ **go** *noun* ▷ see **go** *verb*
1 (*turn in a game*) **Whose go is it?** ¿A quién le toca?
It's my go. Me toca a mí.
2 (*attempt*) **to have a go at doing something** intentar [17] hacer algo
I'll have a go at mending it for you. Intentaré arreglártelo.

⚷ to **go** *verb* ▷ see **go** *noun*
1 (*to travel*) **ir** [8]
to go to a concert ir [8] a un concierto
Mark's gone to the dentist's. Mark ha ido al dentista.
We're going to London tomorrow. Mañana vamos a Londres.
I have never been abroad. No he estado nunca en el extranjero.
Have you been to Spain? ¿Has estado en España? ▸▸

⚷ indicates key words

English–Spanish
a b c d e f g h i j k l m n o p q r s t u v w x y z

2 (*to talk about something that you are about to do*) **to be going to do something** ir **[8]** a hacer algo
I'm going to make some tea. Voy a hacer té.
He was going to phone me. Iba a llamarme.
3 (*person, people*) **irse [8]**
Pauline's already gone. Pauline ya se ha ido.
We're going on holiday tomorrow. Nos vamos de vacaciones mañana.
4 (*trains, planes*) **salir [63]**
The train goes at seven. El tren sale a las siete.
5 (*time*) **pasar [17]**
The time goes quickly. El tiempo pasa rápido.
6 (*to turn out*) **ir [8]**
to go well ir **[8]** bien
Did the party go well? ¿Qué tal fue la fiesta?
to go badly ir **[8]** mal
The party went badly. La fiesta no fue buena.
7 (*pain*) **pasarse [17]**
My headache's gone. Se me ha pasado el dolor de cabeza.
8 (*to be used up*) **The money has all gone.** Se ha acabado el dinero.
9 (*to become*) **to go deaf** quedarse **[17]** sordo
to go pale ponerse **[11]** pálido
Her face went red. Se puso colorada.

• to **go away**
irse [8]
Go away! ¡Vete!

• to **go back**
volver [45]
I'm going back to Madrid in March. Vuelvo a Madrid en marzo.
I'm not going back there again! ¡No voy a volver nunca!
I went back home. Volví a casa.

• to **go down**
1 (*to descend*) **bajar [17]**
to go down the stairs bajar las escaleras
She's gone down to the kitchen. Ha bajado a la cocina.
2 (*to decrease*) **bajar [17]**
Prices have gone down. Los precios han bajado.
3 (*tyres, balloons, airbeds*) **desinflarse [17]**

• to **go in**
entrar [17]
He went in and shut the door. Entró y cerró la puerta.

• to **go into something**
entrar [17] en algo
Fran went into the kitchen. Fran entró en la cocina.
This file won't go into my bag. Esta carpeta no entra en mi bolsa.

• to **go off**
1 (*bombs*) **estallar [17]**
The bomb went off in the street. La bomba estalló en la calle.
2 (*alarm clocks*) **sonar [24]**
My alarm clock went off at six. Mi despertador sonó a las seis.
3 (*fire alarms, burglar alarms*) **dispararse [17]**
The fire alarm went off. La alarma contra incendios se disparó.
4 (*milk, fish, meat*) **echarse [17] a perder**
The meat has gone off. La carne se ha echado a perder.

• to **go off something or someone**
I've gone off coffee. Ya no me gusta el café.
I've gone off him. Ya no me gusta.

• to **go on**
1 (*to happen*) **pasar [17]**
What's going on? ¿Qué pasa?
2 (*to continue*) **to go on doing something** seguir **[64]** haciendo algo
She went on talking. Siguió hablando.
3 (*to talk constantly*) **to go on about something** hablar **[17]** de algo
He's always going on about his dog. Siempre está hablando de su perro.

• to **go out**
1 (*to make an exit*) **salir [63]**
She went out of the kitchen. Salió de la cocina.
I'm going out tonight. Voy a salir esta noche.
2 (*to have a relationship*) **to be going out with somebody** salir **[63]** con alguien
She's going out with my brother. Está saliendo con mi hermano.
3 (*lights, fires*) **apagarse [28]**
The light went out. La luz se apagó.

• to **go past something**
pasar [17] por algo
We went past your house. Pasamos por tu casa.

• to **go round** **to go round to somebody's house** ir **[8]** a casa de alguien
I went round to Fred's last night. Anoche fui a casa de Fred.

• to **go round something**
1 (*a building, a park, a garden*) **recorrer [18] algo**
2 (*a museum, a monument*) **visitar [17] algo**

- to **go through something**
  pasar [17] por algo
  The train went through York. El tren pasó por York.
  You can go through my office. Puedes pasar por mi oficina.
- to **go up**

1 (*to ascend*) **subir [19]**
She's gone up to her room. Ha subido a su habitación.
to go up the stairs subir las escaleras
2 (*to increase*) **subir [19]**
The price of petrol has gone up. El precio de la gasolina ha subido.

goal *noun*
el **gol** *masc*
to score a goal marcar **[31]** un gol
to win by three goals to two ganar **[17]** por tres goles a dos
- **goalkeeper** el portero, la portera

goat *noun*
la **cabra** *fem*

god *noun* ▷ see **God** *noun*
el **dios** *masc*

God *noun* ▷ see **god** *noun*
Dios *masc*
to believe in God creer **[37]** en Dios

godchild *noun*
el **ahijado** *masc*, la **ahijada** *fem*

goddaughter *noun*
la **ahijada** *fem*

goddess *noun*
la **diosa** *fem*

godfather *noun*
el **padrino** *masc*

godmother *noun*
la **madrina** *fem*

godparent *noun*
el **padrino** *masc*, la **madrina** *fem*
my godparents mis padrinos

godson *noun*
el **ahijado** *masc*

goggles *plural noun*
swimming goggles las gafas de natación
skiing goggles las gafas de esquí

go-karting *noun*
el **karting** *masc*
to go go-karting hacer **[7]** karting

gold *noun*
el **oro** *masc*
a gold bracelet una pulsera de oro

goldfish *noun*
el **pez de colores** *pl:* los **peces de colores**

golf *noun*
el **golf** *masc*
to play golf jugar **[27]** al golf

golf club *noun*
1 (*place*) el **club de golf**
2 (*stick used to hit a golf ball*) el **palo de golf**

golf course *noun*
el **campo de golf**

golfer *noun*
el & la **golfista** *masc & fem*

♪ **good** *adjective* ▷ see **good** *noun*
1 (*of high quality*) **bueno** *masc*, **buena** *fem*
a good meal una buena comida
She's a good teacher. Es una buena profesora.
His Spanish is very good. Habla español muy bien.
to feel good sentirse **[14]** bien
2 (*well-behaved*) **bueno** *masc*, **buena** *fem*
Be good! ¡Sé bueno!
3 (*healthy, wholesome*) **to be good for you** ser **[1]** bueno para la salud
Tomatoes are good for you. Los tomates son muy buenos para la salud.
4 (*well*) **to feel good** sentirse **[14]** bien
I'm not feeling too good. No me siento muy bien.
5 (*skilled*) **to be good at something** tener **[9]** facilidad para algo
She's good at languages. Tiene facilidad para las lenguas.
I'm good at cooking. Cocino bien.
6 (*kind*) **amable** *masc & fem*
She's been very good to me. Ha sido muy amable conmigo.
7 (*appealing*) **bien** *masc & fem*
It smelled good. Olía bien.
It tastes good. Sabe bien.
It looks good. Tiene buen aspecto.
8 (*well done*) **Good!** ¡Muy bien!

WORD TIP *bueno* becomes *buen* before a masculine singular noun.

♪ **good** *noun* ▷ see **good** *adj*
1 (*benefit*) el **bien** *masc*
to do good hacer **[7]** bien
to do somebody good hacerle **[8]** bien a alguien
It will do you good. Te hará bien.
2 (*for all time*) **for good** para siempre
I've stopped smoking for good. He dejado de fumar para siempre.

goodbye *exclamation*
▷ see **goodbye** *noun*
adiós

goodbye *noun* ▷ see **goodbye** *excl*
to say goodbye despedirse [57]
We said goodbye at the airport. Nos despedimos en el aeropuerto.
to say goodbye to somebody despedirse de alguien
I must say goodbye to Sam. Tengo que despedirme de Sam.

Good Friday *noun*
el **Viernes Santo**

good-looking *adjective*
guapo *masc*, **guapa** *fem*
Maya's boyfriend's really good-looking. El novio de Maya es muy guapo.

goodness *exclamation*
¡Dios mío!
For goodness' sake! ¡Por Dios!

goods *plural noun*
los **artículos** *plural masc*
• **goods train** el tren de mercancías

goose *noun*
el **ganso** *masc*
• **goose pimples** la carne de gallina

gorgeous *adjective*
precioso *masc*, **preciosa** *fem*
a gorgeous dress un vestido precioso
It's a gorgeous day. Es un día precioso.

gorilla *noun*
el **gorila** *masc*

gosh *exclamation*
¡Dios mío!

gossip *noun* ▷ see **gossip** *verb*
1 (*person*) el & la **cotilla** *masc & fem*
2 (*news*) el **cotilleo** *masc*
What's the latest gossip? ¿Qué hay de nuevo?

to **gossip** *verb* ▷ see **gossip** *noun*
cotillear [17]

government *noun*
el **gobierno** *masc*

mini-info **government**

Spain is a parliamentary democracy and has a written constitution. The central government is responsible for running the country which is divided into 17 autonomous regions (Comunidades Autónomas: CCAA), which control many aspects of regional life.

to **grab** *verb*
1 (*to seize*) **agarrar** [17]
She grabbed my arm. Me agarró el brazo.
2 (*to snatch*) **to grab something from somebody** arrebatarle [17] algo a alguien
He grabbed the book from me. Me arrebató el libro.

graceful *adjective*
elegante *masc & fem*

grade *noun*
(*mark*) la **nota** *fem*
to get good grades sacar [31] buenas notas

gradual *adjective*
gradual *masc & fem*

gradually *adverb*
poco a poco
The weather got gradually better. El tiempo mejoró poco a poco.

graduate *noun*
el **licenciado** *masc*, la **licenciada** *fem*

graffiti *plural noun*
los **grafitti** *plural masc*

grain *noun*
el **grano** *masc*

gram *noun*
el **gramo** *masc*

grammar *noun*
la **gramática** *fem*

grammatical *adjective*
gramatical *masc & fem*
a grammatical error un error gramatical

gran *noun*
la **abuelita** *fem*

grandchildren *plural noun*
los **nietos** *plural masc*

granddad *noun*
(*informal*) el **abuelito** *masc*

granddaughter *noun*
la **nieta** *fem*

grandfather *noun*
el **abuelo** *masc*

grandma *noun*
(*informal*) la **abuelita** *fem*

grandmother *noun*
la **abuela** *fem*

grandpa *noun*
(*informal*) el **abuelito** *masc*

grandparents *plural noun*
los **abuelos** *plural masc*

grandson *noun*
el **nieto** *masc*

granny *noun*
(*informal*) la **abuelita** *fem*

grape *noun*
la **uva** *fem*
a bunch of grapes un racimo de uvas
to buy some grapes comprar **[17]** uvas

grapefruit *noun*
el **pomelo** *masc*

graph *noun*
el **gráfico** *masc*

graphics *noun*
los **gráficos** *plural masc*

grass *noun*
1 (*plant*) la **hierba** *fem*
He was sitting on the grass. Estaba sentado en la hierba.
2 (*lawn*) el **césped** *masc*
to cut the grass cortar **[17]** el césped

grasshopper *noun*
el **saltamontes** *masc, pl:* los **saltamontes**

to **grate** *verb*
rallar [17]
grated cheese queso rallado

grateful *adjective*
agradecido *masc*, **agradecida** *fem*

grater *noun*
el **rallador** *masc*

grave *noun*
la **tumba** *fem*

gravel *noun*
la **grava** *fem*

graveyard *noun*
el **cementerio** *masc*

gravity *noun*
la **gravedad** *fem*

gravy *noun*
la **salsa del asado**

grease *noun*
la **grasa** *fem*

greasy *adjective*
1 (*hands, surface*) **grasiento** *masc*, **grasienta** *fem*
2 (*hair, skin, food*) **graso** *masc*, **grasa** *fem*
to have greasy skin tener **[9]** la piel grasa
I hate greasy food. No soporto la comida grasa.

great *adjective*
1 (*major, important*) **gran** *masc & fem*
a great poet un gran poeta
a great opportunity una gran oportunidad
great expectations grandes esperanzas
2 (*terrific*) **estupendo** *masc*, **estupenda** *fem*
It was a great party! ¡Fue una fiesta estupenda!
Great! ¡Estupendo!
3 **a great deal of something** muchísimo *masc*, muchísima *fem*
I've got a great deal of work. Tengo muchísimo trabajo.
a great many muchos *plural masc*, muchas *plural fem*
There are a great many things still to be done. Aún quedan muchas cosas por hacer.

Great Britain *noun*
Gran Bretaña *fem*

Greece *noun*
Grecia *fem*

greedy *adjective*
glotón *masc*, **glotona** *fem*

Greek *adjective & noun*
1 **griego** *masc*, **griega** *fem*
2 (*person*) un **griego** *masc*, una **griega** *fem*
the Greeks los griegos *plural masc*
3 (*the language*) el **griego** *masc*

WORD TIP Adjectives and nouns for nationality, regional origin, and language do not have capital letters in Spanish.

green *adjective*
1 (*colour*) **verde** *masc & fem*
a green door una puerta verde
2 (*good for the environment*) **verde** *masc & fem*
the Green Party el Partido Verde

green *noun*
1 (*colour*) el **verde** *masc*
a pale green un verde pálido
2 (*vegetables*) **greens** las verduras
3 (*ecologists*) **the Greens** los verdes

greengrocer *noun*
el **verdulero** *masc*, la **verdulera** *fem*
the greengrocer's la verdulería

greenhouse *noun*
el **invernadero** *masc*
- **greenhouse effect** el efecto invernadero

green light *noun*
la **luz verde**

greetings *plural noun*
Season's Greetings! ¡Feliz Navidad!
- **greetings card** la tarjeta de felicitación

grey *adjective*
1 (*colour*) **gris** *masc & fem*
a grey skirt una falda gris
2 (*hair*) **canoso** *masc*, **canosa** *fem*
to have grey hair tener [9] el pelo canoso
• **greyhound** el galgo

grid *noun*
1 (*grating*) la **parrilla** *fem*
2 (*network*) la **red** *fem*

grief *noun*
el **dolor** *masc*

grill *noun* ▷ see **grill** *verb*
la **parilla** *masc*

to **grill** *verb* ▷ see **grill** *noun*
to grill something hacer [7] algo a la parilla
I grilled the sausages. Hice las salchichas a la parilla.
grilled sardines las sardinas a la parilla

grin *noun* ▷ see **grin** *verb*
la **sonrisa** *fem*

to **grin** *verb* ▷ see **grin** *noun*
sonreír [61]

to **grip** *verb*
agarrar [17]

grit *noun*
la **arenilla** *fem*

groan *noun* ▷ see **groan** *verb*
1 (*of pain*) el **gemido** *masc*
2 (*of disgust, boredom*) el **gruñido** *masc*

to **groan** *verb* ▷ see **groan** *noun*
1 (*in pain*) **gemir** [57]
2 (*in disgust, boredom*) **refunfuñar** [17]

grocer *noun*
el **tendero** *masc*, la **tendera** *fem*
My dad's a grocer. Mi padre es tendero.
the grocer's la tienda de comestibles

groceries *plural noun*
las **cosas de comer**
to buy some groceries comprar [17] cosas de comer

groom *noun*
el **novio** *masc*

ground *adjective* ▷ see **ground** *noun*
molido *masc*, **molida** *fem*
• **ground coffee** el café molido

ground *noun* ▷ see **ground** *adj*
1 (*earth, floor*) el **suelo** *masc*
to sit on the ground sentarse [29] en el suelo
to throw something on the ground tirar [17] algo al suelo
2 (*for sport*) el **campo** *masc*
a football ground un campo de fútbol

ground floor *noun*
la **planta baja**
We live on the ground floor. Vivimos en la planta baja.

group *noun*
el **grupo** *masc*

to **grow** *verb*
1 (*plants, hair, people*) **crecer** [35]
Your hair's grown. Te ha crecido el pelo.
My little sister's grown a lot this year. Mi hermana pequeña ha crecido mucho este año.
2 (*fruit, vegetables*) **cultivar** [17]
Our neighbour grows strawberries. Nuestro vecino cultiva fresas.
3 **to grow a beard** dejarse [17] barba
4 (*to become*) **to grow old** envejecer [35]
to grow tired cansarse [17]
to grow smaller hacerse [7] más pequeño
• to **grow up**
crecer [35]
The children are growing up. Los niños están creciendo.
She grew up in Scotland. Creció en Escocia.

to **growl** *verb*
gruñir [65]

grown-up *noun*
el **adulto** *masc*, la **adulta** *fem*

growth *noun*
el **crecimiento** *masc*

grudge *noun*
to bear a grudge against somebody guardarle [17] rencor a alguien
She bears me a grudge. Me guarda rencor.

gruesome *adjective*
horrible *masc & fem*

to **grumble** *verb*
refunfuñar [17]
She's always grumbling. Siempre está refunfuñando.
to grumble about something refunfuñar por algo

guarantee *noun* ▷ see **guarantee** *verb*
la **garantía** *fem*
a one-year guarantee una garantía de un año

to **guarantee** *verb* ▷ see **guarantee** *noun*
garantizar [22]

to **guard** *verb* ▷ see **guard** *noun*
vigilar [17]

guard *noun* ▷ see **guard** *verb*
1 (*soldier*) el & la **guardia** *masc & fem*
a prison guard un guardia de prisiones
2 (*on a train*) el **jefe de tren**, la **jefa de tren**
• **guard dog** el perro guardián

guardian *noun*
el **tutor** *masc*, la **tutora** *fem*

Guatemala *noun*
Guatemala *fem*

Guatemalan *adjective & noun*
1 **guatemalteco** *masc*, **guatemalteca** *fem*
2 un **guatemalteco** *masc*, una **guatemalteca** *fem*
the Guatemalans los guatemaltecos

WORD TIP Adjectives and nouns for nationality and regional origin do not have capital letters in Spanish.

guess *noun* ▷ see **guess** *verb*
la **adivinanza** *fem*
Have a guess! ¡Adivina!
It's a good guess. Lo has adivinado.

to **guess** *verb* ▷ see **guess** *noun*
1 (*to work out*) **adivinar** [17]
Guess who I saw last night! ¡Adivina a quién vi anoche!
You'll never guess! ¡No lo vas a adivinar nunca!
Guess what? ¿Sabes qué?
2 (*to suppose*) **suponer** [11]
I guess so. Supongo que sí.
I guess not. Supongo que no.

guest *noun*
1 (*person coming to your home*) el **invitado** *masc*, la **invitada** *fem*
We've got guests coming tonight. Tenemos invitados esta noche.
2 (*person staying at a hotel*) el & la **cliente** *masc & fem*

♪ **guide** *noun*
1 (*person who helps tourists*) , el & la **guía** *masc & fem*
2 (*guidebook*) la **guía** *fem*
3 (*female member of the scouting movement*) Guide la guía *fem*
• **guidebook** la guía
• **guide dog** el perro lazarillo
• **guideline** la pauta

guilty *adjective*
culpable *masc & fem*
to feel guilty sentirse [14] culpable

guinea pig *noun*
1 (*pet*) la **cobaya** *fem*
2 (*subject of an experiment*) el **conejillo de indias**

guitar *noun*
la **guitarra** *fem*
to play the guitar tocar [31] la guitarra
on the guitar a la guitarra

guitarist *noun*
el & la **guitarrista** *masc & fem*

gum *noun*
1 (*part of your mouth*) la **encía** *fem*
2 (*chewing gum*) el **chicle** *masc*

gun *noun*
1 (*pistol*) la **pistola** *fem*
2 (*rifle*) el **fusil** *masc*

guy *noun*
(*informal*) el **tipo** *masc*
a guy from Newcastle un tipo de Newcastle
He's a nice guy. Es un tipo muy majo.
• **guy rope** el viento (de una tienda de campaña)

♪ **gym** *noun*
1 (*gymnasium*) el **gimnasio** *masc*
to go to the gym ir [8] al gimnasio
2 (*gymnastics*) la **gimnasia** *fem*

♪ **gymnasium** *noun*
el **gimnasio** *masc*

gymnast *noun*
el & la **gimnasta** *masc & fem*

gymnastics *noun*
la **gimnasia** *fem*
to do gymnastics hacer [7] gimnasia

H h

habit *noun*
la **costumbre** *fem*
to have a habit of doing something tener [9] la costumbre de hacer algo
It's a bad habit. Es una mala costumbre.

hacker *noun*
el **pirata informático**, la **pirata informática**

hadn't *short for* **had not** (*See:* **to have**)

to **hail** *verb* ▷ see **hail** *noun*
granizar [22]

hail *noun* ▷ see **hail** *verb*
el **granizo** *masc*
• **hailstone** el granizo
• **hailstorm** la granizada

hair *noun*
1 (*on your head*) el **pelo** *masc*
a hair un pelo
to have short hair tener [9] el pelo corto
to brush your hair cepillarse [17] el pelo
to wash your hair lavarse [17] el pelo
to have your hair cut cortarse [17] el pelo
She's had her hair cut. Se ha cortado el pelo.
2 (*on your body*) el **vello** *masc*
3 (*on an animal, plant*) el **pelo** *masc*
• **hairbrush** el cepillo del pelo

haircut *noun*
el **corte de pelo**
I like your new haircut. Me gusta tu nuevo corte de pelo.
to have a haircut cortarse [17] el pelo

hairdresser *noun*
el **peluquero** *masc*, la **peluquera** *fem*
at the hairdresser's en la peluquería
She's a hairdresser. Es peluquera.

hairdryer *noun*
el **secador de pelo**

hairspray *noun*
la **laca del pelo**

hairstyle *noun*
el **peinado** *masc*

hairy *adjective*
peludo *masc*, **peluda** *fem*

Haiti *noun*
Haití *masc*

Haitian *adjective & noun*
1 **haitiano** *masc*, **haitiana** *fem*
2 un **haitiano** *masc*, una **haitiana** *fem*
the Haitians los haitianos

WORD TIP Adjectives and nouns for nationality and regional origin do not have capital letters in Spanish.

half *adjective, adverb* ▷ see **half** *noun, pron*
1 (*divided by two*) **medio** *masc*, **media** *fem*
one and a half hours una hora y media
It's half price. Está a medio precio.
2 (*asleep, drunk, etc*) **medio**
She was half asleep. Estaba medio dormida.
3 **half a** medio *masc*, media *fem*
half a litre medio litro
half an hour media hora
half an apple media manzana
4 **half the** la mitad de
half the people la mitad de la gente
Half the time he's not here. La mitad del tiempo no está aquí.

half *noun, pronoun* ▷ see **half** *adj, adv*
1 (*one of two equal parts*) la **mitad** *fem*
half of something la mitad de algo
I gave him half of the money. Le di la mitad del dinero.
I only want half. Sólo quiero la mitad.
to cut something in half cortar [17] algo por la mitad
2 (*the fraction*) el **medio** *masc*
three and a half tres y medio
She's five and a half. Tiene seis años y medio.
3 (*in time expressions*) **an hour and a half** una hora y media
It's half past three. Son las tres y media.
4 (*Sport*) el **tiempo** *masc*
the first half el primer tiempo
• **half board** la media pensión

half hour *noun*
la **media hora**
every half hour cada media hora

half price *adjective, adverb*
a mitad de precio
half-price CDs compactos a mitad de precio
I bought it half price. Lo compré a mitad de precio.

half time *noun*
(*Sport*) el **descanso** *masc*
at half time en el descanso

half term *noun*
las **vacaciones de mitad de trimestre**
What are you doing at half term? ¿Qué vas a hacer durante las vacaciones de mitad de trimestre?

halfway *adverb*
1 (*in distance*) **a mitad de camino**
halfway between Málaga and Granada a mitad de camino entre Málaga y Granada
2 **to be halfway through something** ir **[8]** por la mitad de
I'm halfway through my homework. Voy por la mitad de los deberes.

hall *noun*
1 (*in a house*) la **entrada** *fem*
2 (*public building*) el **salón** *masc*
the village hall el salón de actos del pueblo
a concert hall una sala de conciertos

hallo *exclamation* ▷ **hello**

ham *noun*
1 (*cooked*) el **jamón de York**
2 (*cured*) el **jamón serrano**

hamburger *noun*
la **hamburguesa** *fem*

hammer *noun*
el **martillo** *masc*

hammock *noun*
la **hamaca** *fem*

hamster *noun*
el **hámster** *masc, pl:* los **hámsters**

hand *noun* ▷ see **hand** *verb*
1 (*part of your body*) la **mano** *fem*
to have something in your hand tener **[9]** algo en la mano
to be holding hands (*two people*) ir **[8]** cogidos de la mano
They were holding hands. Iban cogidos de la mano.
2 (*of a watch, clock*) la **manecilla** *fem*
the hour hand la manecilla de las horas
3 (*help*) **to give somebody a hand** echar **[17]** una mano a alguien
Can you give me a hand to move the table? ¿Puedes echarme una mano para mover la mesa?
Do you need a hand? ¿Necesitas que te echen una mano?
4 (*to talk about possible options*) **on the one hand ...** por un lado ...
on the other hand ... por otro lado ...

to hand *verb* ▷ see **hand** *noun*
to hand something to somebody pasarle **[17]** algo a alguien
I handed him the keys. Le pasé las llaves.
• **to hand something in** **entregar [17] algo**
It must be handed in on Tuesday. Hay que entregarlo el martes.
• **handbag** el bolso
• **handbrake** el freno de mano
• **handcuffs** las esposas

handful *noun*
el **puñado** *masc*
a handful of something un puñado de algo

handicapped *adjective*
disminuido *masc*, **disminuida** *fem*

handicrafts *plural noun*
las **artesanías** *plural fem*
an exhibition of local handicrafts una exposición de artesanías locales

handkerchief *noun*
el **pañuelo** *masc*
a paper handkerchief un pañuelo de papel

to handle *verb* ▷ see **handle** *noun*
1 (*to touch*) **tocar [31]**
Please do not handle the goods. Se ruega no tocar la mercancía.
2 (*to be in charge of*) **encargarse [28] de**
Gina handles the accounts. Gina se encarga de la contabilidad.
3 (*people*) **tratar [17] a**
She's good at handling people. Es buena para tratar con la gente.
4 (*a situation*) **manejar [17]**
How did they handle the emergency? ¿Cómo manejaron la emergencia?

handle *noun* ▷ see **handle** *verb*
1 (*of a door*) el **picaporte** *masc*
2 (*of a drawer*) el **tirador** *masc*
3 (*of a knife, tool, pan*) el **mango** *masc*
4 (*on a cup, basket*) el **asa** *fem*

WORD TIP *asa* takes *el* or *un* in the singular even though it is feminine.

• **handlebars** el manillar

hand luggage *noun*
el **equipaje de mano**

handsome *adjective*
guapo *masc*
He's a very handsome guy. Es un tipo muy guapo.

handwriting *noun*
la **letra** *fem*

English–Spanish

handy *adjective*

1 (*useful, practical*) **práctico** *masc*, **práctica** *fem*
This knife is very handy. Este cuchillo es muy práctico.

2 (*nearby*) **a mano**
I always keep a notebook handy. Siempre tengo un cuaderno a mano.

to **hang** *verb*

colgar [23]
We hung the mirror on the wall. Colgamos el espejo en la pared.
There was a mirror hanging on the wall. Había un espejo colgado en la pared.

- to **hang on**
  esperar [17]
  Hang on a second! ¡Espera un poco!
- to **hang up**
  (*on the phone*) **colgar** [23]
  She hung up on me. Me colgó.
  Don't hang up. No cuelgues. (*informal*)
- to **hang something up**
  colgar [23] **algo**
  You can hang your coat up in the hall. Puedes colgar el abrigo en la entrada.

hangover *noun*

la **resaca** *fem*
to have a hangover tener [9] resaca

to **happen** *verb*

pasar [17]
What's happening? ¿Qué pasa?
What happened to him? ¿Qué le pasó?
It happened in June. Pasó en junio.
What's happened to the can-opener? ¿Dónde se ha metido el abridor?

happily *adverb*

1 (*cheerfully*) **alegremente**
She smiled happily. Sonrió alegremente.

2 (*willingly*) **con mucho gusto**
I'll happily do it for you. Lo haré por ti con mucho gusto.

happiness *noun*

la **felicidad** *fem*

happy *adjective*

1 (*joyful*) **feliz** *masc & fem, pl:* **felices**
the happy event el feliz acontecimiento
He's a happy person. Es una persona muy feliz.
to make somebody happy hacer [7] feliz a alguien
Happy birthday! ¡Feliz cumpleaños!

2 (*pleased*) **to be happy** alegrarse [17]
I'm so happy for you. Me alegro mucho por ti.
She'd be happy to help. Ayudaría con mucho gusto.

3 (*satisfied*) **contento** *masc*, **contenta** *fem*
to be happy with something estar [2] contento con algo
She's very happy with her present. Está muy contenta con su regalo.
She's not happy with her work. No está contenta con su trabajo.

harbour *noun*

el **puerto** *masc*

hard *adverb* ▷ see **hard** *adj*

1 (*with force*) **con fuerza**
I pushed it hard. Lo empujé con fuerza.
I hit her hard. Le pegué fuerte.

2 (*a great deal*) **mucho**
to study hard estudiar [17] mucho
to try hard esforzarse [26] mucho
to work hard trabajar [17] duro

hard *adjective* ▷ see **hard** *adv*

1 (*substance*) **duro** *masc*, **dura** *fem*
hard stones piedras duras
The carrots are hard. Las zanahorias están duras.

2 (*question, piece of work*) **difícil** *masc & fem*
a hard question una pregunta difícil
It's hard to know what to do. Es difícil saber qué hacer.

- **hard-boiled egg** el huevo duro
- **hard disk** el disco duro

hardly *adverb*

apenas
I can hardly hear him. Apenas lo oigo.
hardly any casi nada
There's hardly any milk. Casi no hay nada de leche.
hardly ever casi nunca
I hardly ever see them. Casi nunca los veo.

hard up *adjective*

(*informal*) **to be hard up** estar [2] mal de dinero

harm *noun* ▷ see **harm** *verb*

el **daño** *masc*
It won't do you any harm. No te va a hacer daño.

to **harm** *verb* ▷ see **harm** *noun*

to harm somebody hacerle [7] daño a alguien
A cup of coffee won't harm you. Una taza de café no te va a hacer daño.

harvest *noun*

la **cosecha** *fem*
to get the harvest in hacer [7] la cosecha

hasn't *short for* **has not** (*See:* **to have**)

a b c d e f g h i j k l m n o p q r s t u v w x y z

hat *noun*
el **sombrero** *masc*

to **hate** *verb*
odiar [17]
I hate geography. Odio la geografía.
I hate ironing. Odio planchar.

hatred *noun*
el **odio** *masc*

haunted *adjective*
embrujado *masc*, **embrujada** *fem*

to **have** *verb*
1 (*to own*) **tener** [9]
We have a dog and a cat. Tenemos un perro y un gato.
to have got something tener [9] algo
What have you got in your hand? ¿Qué tienes en la mano?
Anna has three brothers. Anna tiene tres hermanos.
How many sisters have you got? ¿Cuántas hermanas tienes?
She has a lot of patience. Tiene mucha paciencia.
2 (*to form past tenses, with have, had + -ed words*) **haber** [6]
I've finished. He terminado.
Have you fixed it? ¿Lo has arreglado?
Rosie hasn't arrived yet. Rosie aún no ha llegado.
He had lied. Había mentido.
I have just seen her. Acabo de verla.
Have you been waiting long? ¿Hace mucho que esperas?
3 (*in short questions*) **She's done this before, hasn't she?** Ha hecho esto antes, ¿no?
They have arrived, haven't they? Han llegado ¿no?

WORD TIP In short questions like *hasn't she, haven't you?, has, have* are not translated.

4 **to have to do something** tener [9] que hacer algo
I have to phone my mum. Tengo que llamar a mi madre.
Have you got to go? ¿Tienes que ir?
You don't have to come if you don't want to. No tienes que venir si no quieres.
5 (*to receive*) **tener** [9]
We had a letter from him last week. Tuvimos carta de él la semana pasada.
Have you had any news? ¿Has tenido noticias?
6 (*food, drink*) **tomar** [17]
We had a coffee. Tomamos un café.
What will you have? ¿Qué vais a tomar?
I'll have an omelette. Voy a tomar una tortilla.
to have lunch comer [18]
to have dinner (*in the evening*) cenar [17], (*at midday*) comer [18]
7 (*to experience, to undergo*) **tener** [9]
They had an accident. Tuvieron un accidente.
We had a week in Madrid. Estuvimos una semana en Madrid.
to have a shower ducharse [17]
to have a bath bañarse [17]
8 (*to organize*) **to have a party** dar [4] una fiesta
9 (*to suffer from*) **tener** [9]
He has cancer. Tiene cáncer.
I had flu. Tuve la gripe.
You've got a cold. Estás resfriado.
She has stomachache. Le duele el estómago.
I have a terrible headache. Me duele mucho la cabeza.
10 (*to give birth to*) **tener** [9]
She had twins. Tuvo gemelos.
11 (*to talk about getting a job done by someone else*) **I'm going to have my hair cut.** Voy a cortarme el pelo.
She's had her TV repaired. Ha arreglado la tele.
12 **to have just done something** acabar [17] de hacer algo
Ellie has just arrived. Ellie acaba de llegar
They've just come in. Acaban de entrar.
• to **have something on** **llevar** [17] **algo**
What did she have on? ¿Qué llevaba puesto?

haven't *short for* **have not** (*See:* **to have**)

hawk *noun*
el **halcón** *masc*

hay *noun*
el **heno** *masc*
• **hay fever** la fiebre del heno

hazelnut *noun*
la **avellana** *fem*

he *pronoun*
1 (*'he' is usually part of the verb in Spanish*) **He lives in Newcastle.** Vive en Newcastle.
He's a student. Es estudiante.
He's a very good teacher. Es muy buen profesor.
Here he is! ¡Aquí está!
2 (*to make clear or emphasize who did something*) **él**
She went to the theatre, he went to ▸▸

the cinema. Ella fue al teatro y él fue al cine.
He did it. Lo hizo él.

WORD TIP *he*, like other subject pronouns *I*, *you*, *she*, etc, is generally not translated in Spanish; the form of the verb tells you whether the subject of the verb is *I*, *we*, *they*, etc, so *he* is translated only for emphasis or for clarity.

head *noun*
1 (*part of the body*) la **cabeza** *fem*
at the head of the queue a la cabeza de la cola
He had a cap on his head. Tenía un sombrero en la cabeza.
2 (*of a school*) el **director** *masc*, la **directora** *fem*
3 (*when tossing a coin*) **'Heads or tails?'— 'Heads.'** '¿Cara o cruz?'— 'Cara.'
• to **head for something**
dirigirse [49] a algo
Liz headed for the door. Liz se dirigió a la puerta.

headache *noun*
el **dolor de cabeza**
I've got a headache. Me duele la cabeza.

headlight *noun*
el **faro** *masc*

headline *noun*
el **titular** *masc*
to hit the headlines aparecer [35] en los titulares

headmaster *noun*
el **director** *masc*

headmistress *noun*
la **directora** *fem*

head office *noun*
la **sede** *fem*

headphones *plural noun*
los **auriculares** *plural masc*

headquarters *plural noun*
1 (*of an organization*) la **sede** *fem*
2 (*military*) el **cuartel general**

headteacher *noun*
el **director** *masc*, la **directora** *fem*

health *noun*
la **salud** *fem*
It's bad for your health. Es malo para la salud.
• **health centre** el centro médico

healthy *adjective*
1 (*in good health*) **sano** *masc*, **sana** *fem*
to be healthy estar [2] sano
2 (*good for your health*) **sano** *masc*, **sana** *fem*
a healthy diet una dieta sana

heap *noun*
el **montón** *masc*
I've got heaps of things to do. Tengo montones de cosas que hacer.

to **hear** *verb*
oír [56]
I can't hear you. No te oigo.
I can't hear anything. No oigo nada.
I hear you've bought a dog. He oído que te has comprado un perro.
• to **hear about something**
enterarse [17] de algo
Have you heard about the concert? ¿Te has enterado de lo del concierto?
• to **hear from somebody**
Have you heard from Amanda? ¿Sabes algo de Amanda?
I haven't heard from them. No sé nada de ellos.

hearing aid *noun*
el **audífono** *masc*

heart *noun*
1 (*part of the body*) el **corazón** *masc*
2 (*in cards*) **hearts** los corazones *masc pl*
the jack of hearts la jota de corazones
• **heart attack** el ataque al corazón

heat *noun* ▷ see **heat** *verb*
el **calor** *masc*

to **heat** *verb* ▷ see **heat** *noun*
1 (*to become hot*) **calentarse [29]**
The soup's heating. La sopa se está calentando.
2 (*to make hot*) **to heat something** calentar [29] algo
I'll go and heat the soup. Voy a calentar la sopa.

heater *noun*
la **estufa** *fem*

heating *noun*
la **calefacción** *fem*

heaven *noun*
el **cielo** *masc*

heavy *adjective*
1 (*weighing a lot*) **pesado** *masc*, **pesada** *fem*
a heavy bag una bolsa pesada
to be heavy pesar [17] mucho
My rucksack's really heavy. Mi mochila pesa mucho.
How heavy is it? ¿Cuánto pesa?
2 (*busy*) **ocupado** *masc*, **ocupada** *fem*
I've got a heavy day tomorrow. Mañana tengo un día muy ocupado.
3 (*intense*) **heavy rain** lluvia fuerte
to be a heavy drinker beber [18] mucho

hectic *adjective*
ajetreado *masc*, **ajetreada** *fem*
a hectic day un día muy ajetreado

hedge *noun*
el **seto** *masc*

hedgehog *noun*
el **erizo** *masc*

heel *noun*
1 (*of your foot*) el **talón** *masc*
2 (*of a shoe*) el **tacón** *masc*
high heels los tacones altos

height *noun*
1 (*of a person*) la **estatura** *fem*
He was of average height. Era de estatura mediana.
2 (*of a building*) la **altura** *fem*
3 (*of a mountain*) la **altitud** *fem*

heir *noun*
el **heredero** *masc*, la **heredera** *fem*
the heir to the throne el príncipe heredero, la princesa heredera

helicopter *noun*
el **helicóptero** *masc*

hell *noun*
el **infierno** *masc*

hello *exclamation*
1 (*greeting*) **hola**
2 (*on the telephone*) **¿Dígame?**

helmet *noun*
el **casco** *masc*

help *noun* ▷ see **help** *verb*
la **ayuda** *fem*
to call for help pedir [57] ayuda
Thanks for your help. Gracias por ayudarme.
Do you need any help? ¿Necesitas ayuda?
Help! ¡Socorro!

to **help** *verb* ▷ see **help** *noun*
1 (*to assist*) **ayudar** [17]
to help somebody to do something ayudar [17] a alguien a hacer algo
Can you help me move the table? ¿Me ayudas a mover la mesa?
Can I help you? ¿Qué desea?
2 (*to serve*) **to help yourself to something** servirse [57] algo
Help yourself! ¡Sírvete!
Help yourselves to vegetables. Serviros verdura.
3 (*to avoid*) **I can't help it.** No lo puedo remediar.
I couldn't help thinking that she was right. No podía menos que pensar que ella tenía razón.

helping *noun*
la **porción** *fem*
Would you like a second helping? ¿Quieres repetir?

hem *noun*
el **dobladillo** *masc*

hen *noun*
la **gallina** *fem*

her *adjective* ▷ see **her** *pron*
1 (*before most nouns*) **su** *masc & fem*
her brother su hermano
her house su casa
her children sus niños
2 (*with parts of the body, clothes*) **ella**, **los**, **las**
She cut her finger. Se cortó el dedo.
She's washing her hands. Se está lavando las manos.
She took off her coat. Se quitó el abrigo.

WORD TIP Spanish uses *el, la, los, las* for *her* with parts of the body and clothes.

her *pronoun* ▷ see **her** *adj*
1 (*as a direct object*) **la**
I know her. La conozco.
I saw her last week. La vi la semana pasada.
Are you going to see her? ¿Vas a verla?
Listen to her! ¡Escúchala!
Don't push her! ¡No la empujes!
2 (*as an indirect object*) **le**
I gave her my address. Le di mis señas.
I lent it to her. Se lo dejó.
3 (*after a preposition, in comparisons, after the verb to be*) **ella**
with her con ella
without her sin ella
He's older than her. Él es mayor que ella.
It was her. Era ella.

WORD TIP With an infinitive, or when telling someone to do something, *la* joins onto the verb. *le* becomes *se* before the pronouns *lo* or *la*.

herb *noun*
la **hierba** *fem*

herd *noun*
1 (*of cattle*) la **manada** *fem*
2 (*of goats*) el **rebaño** *masc*

here *adverb*
1 (*in this place*) **aquí**
They live not far from here. Viven no lejos de aquí.
Here they are! ¡Aquí están!
Tom isn't here at the moment. Tom no está aquí en este momento. ▸▸

English–Spanish

2 (*for emphasis*) **Here it is.** Toma.
Here's my address. Toma mis señas.
Here you are. Toma.

hero *noun*
el **héroe** *masc*

heroin *noun* ▷ see **heroine** *noun*
(*the drug*) la **heroína** *fem*

heroine *noun* ▷ see **heroin** *noun*
(*of a story*) la **heroína** *fem*

hers *pronoun*
el suyo *masc*, **la suya** *fem*
I took my hat and she took hers. Yo cogí mi sombrero y ella cogió el suyo.
I phoned my mum and Donna phoned hers. Llamé a mi madre y Donna llamó a la suya.
I've invited my parents and Karen's invited hers. Yo he invitado a mis padres y Karen a los suyos.
I showed her my photos and she showed me hers. Yo le enseñé mis fotos y ella me enseñó las suyas.

WORD TIP The form of *suyo* to choose depends the gender and number of the thing owned.

herself *pronoun*
1 (*reflexive*) **se**
She's hurt herself. Se ha hecho daño.
She washed herself. Se lavó.
2 (*for emphasis*) **ella misma**
She said it herself. Lo dijo ella misma.
3 (*on her own*) **by herself** ella sola
She did it by herself. Lo hizo ella sola.

to **hesitate** *verb*
dudar **[17]**
to hesitate to do something dudar en hacer algo

heterosexual *adjective*
heterosexual *masc & fem*

hi *exclamation*
hola

hiccups *plural noun*
el **hipo** *masc*
to have hiccups tener **[9]** hipo

hidden *adjective*
escondido *masc*, **escondida** *fem*

to **hide** *verb*
1 (*person*) **esconderse** **[18]**
She hid behind the door. Se escondió detrás de la puerta.
2 (*an object*) **to hide something** esconder **[18]** algo
Who's hidden the chocolate? ¿Quién ha escondido el chocolate?

hide-and-seek *noun*
to play hide-and-seek jugar **[27]** al escondite

hi-fi *noun*
el **equipo de alta fidelidad**

high *adjective*
1 (*building, wall, mountain*) **alto** *masc*, **alta** *fem*
on a high shelf en una estantería alta
The wall is very high. La pared es muy alta.
How high is the wall? ¿Qué altura tiene la pared?
The wall is two metres high. La pared tiene dos metros de altura.
2 (*number, price, temperature, speed*) **alto** *masc*, **alta** *fem*
Food prices are very high. El precio de la comida es muy alto.
at high speed a alta velocidad
high winds vientos fuertes

mini-info high
With five mountain ranges and a high plateau, Spain is the highest country in Europe after Switzerland at an average height of 650 metres above sea level.

Highers *plural noun*
(*Son exámenes que se hacen en Escocia, en hasta cinco asignaturas, en el penúltimo año de la educación secundaria.*)

high-heeled *adjective*
de tacón alto
high-heeled shoes los zapatos de tacón alto

high jump *noun*
el **salto de altura**

high-speed train *noun*
el **tren de alta velocidad**

Highway Code *noun*
el **Código de la Circulación**

to **hijack** *verb*
secuestrar **[17]**

hijacking *noun*
el **secuestro** *masc*

hiking *noun*
el **senderismo** *masc*

hilarious *adjective*
divertidísimo *masc*, **divertidísima** *fem*

hill *noun*
1 (*low*) la **colina** *fem*
2 (*higher*) la **montaña** *fem*
3 (*sloping street, road*) la **cuesta** *fem*

a b c d e f g h i j k l m n o p q r s t u v w x y z

him *pronoun*
1 (*as a direct object*) **lo**
I know him. Lo conozco.
I saw him last week. Lo vi la semana pasada.
Are you going to see him? ¿Vas a verlo?
Listen to him! ¡Escúchalo!
Don't push him! ¡No lo empujes!
2 (*as an indirect object*) **le**
I gave him my address. Le di mis señas.
I lent it to him. Se lo dejé.
3 (*after a preposition, in comparisons, after the verb to be*) **él**
with him con él
without him sin él
She's older than him. Ella es mayor que él.
It was him. Era él.

WORD TIP With an infinitive, or when telling someone to do something, *lo* joins onto the verb.*le* becomes *se* before the pronouns *lo* or *la*.

himself *pronoun*
1 (*reflexive*) **se**
He's hurt himself. Se ha hecho daño.
He washed himself. Se lavó.
2 (*for emphasis*) **él mismo**
He said it himself. Lo dijo él mismo.
3 (*on his own*) **by himself** él solo
He did it by himself. Lo hizo él solo.

Hindu *adjective & noun*
hindú *masc & fem*
the Hindus los hindúes

WORD TIP Adjectives and nouns for religion do not have capital letters in Spanish.

Hinduism *noun*
(*Religion*) el hinduismo *masc*

WORD TIP Adjectives and nouns for religion do not have capital letters in Spanish.

hip *noun*
la **cadera** *fem*

hire *noun* ▷ see **hire** *verb*
el **alquiler** *masc*
car hire el alquiler de coches
for hire se alquila

to **hire** *verb* ▷ see **hire** *noun*
alquilar [17]
We're going to hire a car. Vamos a alquilar un coche.

his *adjective* ▷ see **his** *pron*
1 (*before most nouns*) **su** *masc & fem*
his brother su hermano
his house su casa
his children sus niños
2 (*with parts of the body, clothes*) **ella, los, las**
He cut his finger. Se cortó el dedo.
He's washing his hands. Se está lavando las manos.
He took off his gloves. Se quitó los guantes.

WORD TIP Spanish uses *el, la, los, las* for *his* with parts of the body and clothes.

his *pronoun* ▷ see **his** *adj*
el suyo *masc*, **la suya** *fem*
I took my hat and he took his. Yo cogí mi sombrero y él cogió el suyo.
I phoned my mum and Danny phoned his. Llamé a mi madre y Danny llamó a la suya.
I've invited my parents and Steve's invited his. Yo he invitado a mis padres y Steve a los suyos.
I showed him my photos and he showed me his. Yo le enseñé mis fotos y él me enseñó las suyas.

WORD TIP The form of *suyo* to choose depends the gender and number of the thing owned.

historic *adjective*
histórico *masc*, **histórica** *fem*
a historic building un edificio histórico

history *noun*
la **historia** *fem*

hit *noun* ▷ see **hit** *verb*
(*success*) el **éxito** *masc*
their latest hit su último éxito
The film is a huge hit. La película es un gran éxito.

to **hit** *verb* ▷ see **hit** *noun*
1 (*a ball, a door, a table*) **golpear** [17]
He hit the ball. Golpeó la pelota.
2 (*a person*) **to hit somebody** pegarle [28] a alguien
She hit him with her handbag. Le pegó con el bolso.
3 (*to bang*) **to hit your head on something** darse [4] un golpe en la cabeza con algo
He hit his head on the table. Se dio un golpe en la cabeza con la mesa.
4 (*to collide with*) **chocar** [31] **con**
The car hit a tree. El coche chocó con un árbol.
5 (*to knock over*) **She was hit by a car.** La atropelló un coche.

hitch *noun* ▷ see **hitch** *verb*
el **problemita** *masc*
There's been a slight hitch. Ha habido un problemita.

to **hitch** *verb* ▷ see **hitch** *noun*
(*informal*) **to hitch a lift** hacer [7] dedo

to **hitchhike** *verb*
hacer [7] **autostop**
We hitchhiked to Valencia. Hicimos autostop hasta Valencia.

hitchhiker *noun*
el & la **autostopista** *masc & fem*

hitchhiking *noun*
el **autostop** *masc*

HIV-negative *adjective*
seronegativo *masc*, **seronegativa** *fem*

HIV-positive *adjective*
seropositivo *masc*, **seropositiva** *fem*

hobby *noun*
el **pasatiempo** *masc*

hockey *noun*
el **hockey** *masc*
to play hockey jugar [27] al hockey
• **hockey stick** el palo de hockey

to **hold** *verb*
1 (*to have in your hands*) **sostener** [9]
to hold something in your hand sostener algo en la mano
Can you hold the torch? ¿Puedes sostener la linterna?
2 (*to contain*) **contener** [9]
This jug holds a litre. Esta jarra contiene un litro.
3 (*a meeting, a wedding, elections*) **celebrar** [17]
to hold a meeting celebrar una reunión
• to **hold on**
1 (*to wait*) **esperar** [17]
2 (*on the phone*) **Hold on!** ¡Un momento!, ¡No cuelgue!
• to **hold on to something**
agarrarse [17] **a algo**
• to **hold somebody up**
(*to delay*) **entretener** [9] **a alguien**
I don't want to hold you up. No quiero entretenerte.
I was held up at the dentist's. Me entretuve en el dentista.
• to **hold something up**
(*to raise*) **levantar** [17]
He held up his glass. Levantó su vaso.

hold-up *noun*
1 (*delay*) el **retraso** *masc*
2 (*traffic jam*) el **atasco** *masc*
3 (*robbery*) el **atraco** *masc*

hole *noun*
el **agujero** *masc*

holiday *noun*
1 (*time away from school, work*) las **vacaciones** *plural fem*
Where are you going for your holiday? ¿Dónde vas de vacaciones?
Have a good holiday! ¡Que pases unas buenas vacaciones!
to be away on holiday estar [2] de vacaciones
to go on holiday irse [8] de vacaciones
the school holidays las vacaciones escolares
2 (*single day*) **a public holiday** un día de fiesta
Monday's a holiday. El lunes es fiesta.

Holland *noun*
Holanda *fem*

hollow *adjective*
hueco *masc*, **hueca** *fem*

holly *noun*
el **acebo** *masc*

holy *adjective*
santo *masc*, **santa** *fem*

home *adverb* ▷ see **home** *noun*
a casa
Susie's gone home. Susie se ha ido a casa.
I'll call in and see you on my way home. Te iré a visitar de camino a mi casa.
to get home llegar [28] a casa
We got home at midnight. Llegamos a casa a media noche.

home *noun* ▷ see **home** *adv*
1 (*the place where you live*) la **casa** *fem*
to stay at home quedarse [17] en casa
I was at home. Estaba en casa.
to leave home irse [8] de casa
2 (*in sport*) **to play at home** jugar [27] en casa
3 (*place for group living, institution*) la **residencia** *fem*
an old people's home una residencia de ancianos

homeless *adjective*
sin hogar
a homeless person una persona sin hogar

home-made *adjective*
casero *masc*, **casera** *fem*
home-made cakes pasteles caseros

homeopathy *noun*
la **homeopatía** *fem*

homesick *adjective*
1 (*when you miss your family*) **He is homesick.** Echa de menos a su familia.
2 (*when you miss your country*) **He is homesick.** Echa de menos a su país.

homework *noun*
los **deberes** *plural masc*
my Spanish homework mis deberes de español
I did my homework. Hice mis deberes.

homosexual *adjective*
homosexual *masc & fem*

Honduran *adjective & noun*
1 **hondureño** *masc*, **hondureña** *fem*
2 un **hondureño** *masc*, una **hondureña** *fem*
the Hondurans los hondureños

WORD TIP Adjectives and nouns for nationality and regional origin do not have capital letters in Spanish.

Honduras *noun*
Honduras *fem*

♪ **honest** *adjective*
1 (*trustworthy*) **honrado** *masc*, **honrada** *fem*
She seems honest. Parece honrada.
2 (*frank*) **sincero** *masc*, **sincera** *fem*
to be honest ... para serte sincero ...
To be honest, I don't like him. Para serte sincero, no me gusta.

honestly *adverb*
sinceramente

honesty *noun*
la **honradez** *fem*

honey *noun*
la **miel** *fem*

honeymoon *noun*
la **luna de miel**

honour *noun*
el **honor** *masc*

hood *noun*
la **capucha** *fem*

hook *noun*
1 (*for doing up clothes*) el **corchete** *masc*
2 (*for fishing*) el **anzuelo** *masc*
3 (*for hanging pictures, clothes*) el **gancho** *masc*
4 (*on the phone*) **to take the phone off the hook** descolgar [23] el teléfono

hooligan *noun*
el **gamberro** *masc*, la **gamberra** *fem*

hooray *exclamation*
¡hurra!

Hoover® *noun* ▷ see **hoover** *verb*
la **aspiradora** *fem*, el **aspirador** *masc*

to **hoover** *verb* ▷ see **Hoover** *noun*
pasar [17] **la aspiradora por**
I hoovered my bedroom. Pasé la aspiradora por mi habitación.

♪ **hope** *noun* ▷ see **hope** *verb*
la **esperanza** *fem*
to give up hope perder [36] la esperanza

♪ to **hope** *verb* ▷ see **hope** *noun*
esperar [17]
Hoping to see you on Friday. Esperando verte el domingo.
I hope so. Espero que sí.
I hope not. Espero que no.
We hope you'll be able to come. Esperamos que puedas venir.

WORD TIP *esperar que* is followed by a verb in the subjunctive.

hopeless *adjective*
to be hopeless at something ser [1] un negado para algo
She's hopeless at geography. Es una negada para la geografía.

horizon *noun*
el **horizonte** *masc*

horn *noun*
1 (*of an animal*) el **cuerno** *masc*
2 (*of a car*) la **bocina** *fem*
to sound your horn tocar [31] la bocina
3 (*musical instrument*) la **trompa** *fem*
to play the horn tocar [31] trompa

horoscope *noun*
el **horóscopo** *masc*

♪ **horrible** *adjective*
horrible *masc & fem*
The weather was horrible. El tiempo era horrible.
She's really horrible! ¡Es realmente horrible!
He was really horrible to me. Me trató muy mal.

horrific *adjective*
horroroso *masc*, **horrorosa** *fem*
a horrific accident un accidente horroroso

horror *noun*
el **horror** *masc*
• **horror film** la película de terror

♪ **horse** *noun*
el **caballo** *masc*
• **horse racing** las carreras de caballos

hose *noun*
la **manguera** *fem*

♪ **hospital** *noun*
el **hospital** *masc*
to be in hospital estar [2] en el hospital
She's in hospital with appendicitis. Está en el hospital con apendicitis.
He's going to go into hospital. Lo van a ingresar en el hospital.

hospitality *noun*
la **hospitalidad** *fem*

host *noun*
el **anfitrión** *masc*, la **anfitriona** *fem*
My host family is very nice. La familia que me hospeda es muy amable.

hostage *noun*
el **rehén** *masc*, *pl:* los **rehenes**

hostess *noun*
la **anfitriona** *fem*

hot *adjective*
1 (*drink, meal, object*) **caliente** *masc & fem*
a hot drink una bebida caliente
Be careful, the plates are hot! ¡Cuidado! los platos están calientes.
2 (*person*) **to be hot** tener [9] calor
I'm hot. Tengo calor.
I'm very hot. Tengo mucho calor.
I'm too hot. Tengo demasiado calor.
3 (*weather, temperature in a room*) **to be hot** hacer [7] calor
It's hot. Hace calor.
It's hot today. Hace calor hoy.
It's very hot in the kitchen. Hace mucho calor en la cocina.
a hot day un día caluroso
a hot climate un clima cálido
4 (*spicy*) **picante** *masc & fem*
This curry's too hot for me. Este curry es demasiado picante para mí.
• **hot dog** el perrito caliente

hotel *noun*
el **hotel** *masc*

hour *noun*
la **hora** *fem*
two hours later dos horas más tarde
two hours ago hace dos horas
every hour cada hora
We waited for two hours. Esperamos dos horas.
We've been waiting for hours. Llevamos horas esperando.
to be paid by the hour cobrar [17] por hora
I earn six pounds an hour. Gano seis libras por hora.

hourly *adjective* ▷ see **hourly** *adv*
por hora
There is an hourly bus service. Hay un autobús por hora.
He's paid hourly. Le pagan por hora.

hourly *adverb* ▷ see **hourly** *adj*
cada hora
The trains leave hourly. Los trenes salen cada hora.

house *noun*
la **casa** *fem*
Judy's at my house. Judy está en mi casa.
I'm at Judy's house. Estoy en casa de Judy.
I'm going to Judy's house tonight. Voy a casa de Judy esta noche.
I phoned from Judy's house. Llamé desde casa de Judy.

housework *noun*
las **tareas de la casa**
to do the housework hacer [7] las tareas de la casa

housing *noun*
las **viviendas** *plural fem*
the housing shortage la escasez de viviendas

how *adverb*
1 (*to ask in what way something is done*) **cómo**
How did you do it? ¿Cómo lo hiciste?
I know how to do it. Sé cómo hacerlo.
2 (*to ask about somebody's health*) **cómo**
How are you? ¿Cómo estás?
3 (*to ask what something or someone is like*) **How was the party?** ¿Qué tal fue la fiesta?
How do I look? ¿Cómo or qué tal estoy?
4 (*to talk about quantities and measurements*) **How much is it?** ¿Cuánto cuesta?
How far is it? ¿A qué distancia está?
How long will it take? ¿Cuánto tardará?
5 (*in exclamations*) **qué**
How nice! ¡Qué bonito!

however *adverb*
sin embargo

hug *noun*
el **abrazo** *masc*
to give somebody a hug darle [4] un abrazo a alguien
She gave me a hug. Me dio un abrazo.

huge *adjective*
enorme *masc & fem*

to **hum** *verb*
tararear [17]

human *adjective*
humano *masc*, **humana** *fem*
• **human being** el ser humano

humour *noun*
el **humor** *masc*
to have a sense of humour tener [9] sentido del humor

hundred *number*
cien *invariable*
a hundred cien

about a hundred unos cien
about a hundred people unas cien personas
hundreds of people cientos de personas
one hundred and six ciento seis
two hundred and ten doscientos diez
two hundred horses doscientos caballos
three hundred boxes trescientas cajas
six hundred seiscientos *masc*, seiscientas *fem*

WORD TIP *cien* never changes and translates *hundred* in English. When *hundred* is used in the plural or with other numbers, use *ciento, -cientos, -cientas* as above.

Hungarian *adjective & noun*
1 **húngaro** *masc*, **húngara** *fem*
2 *(person)* un **húngaro** *masc*, una **húngara** *fem*
the Hungarians los húngaros *plural masc*
3 *(the language)* el **húngaro** *masc*

WORD TIP Adjectives and nouns for nationality, regional origin, and language do not have capital letters in Spanish.

Hungary *noun*
Hungría *fem*

hunger *noun*
el **hambre** *fem*

WORD TIP *hambre* takes *el* or *un* in the singular even though it is feminine.

♪ **hungry** *adjective*
to be hungry tener [9] hambre
I'm hungry. Tengo hambre.

to **hunt** *verb*
(animals) **cazar** [22]
• to **hunt for**
1 *(to search for)* **buscar**
2 *(animals)* **ir** [8] **a la caza de**

hurricane *noun*
el **huracán** *masc, pl:* los **huracanes**
a category four hurricane un huracán de categoría cuatro

♪ **hurry** *noun* ▷ see **hurry** *verb*
to be in a hurry tener [9] prisa
I'm in a hurry. Tengo prisa.
What's the hurry? ¿Qué prisa hay?

♪ to **hurry** *verb* ▷ see **hurry** *noun*
darse [4] **prisa**
I must hurry. Debo darme prisa.
We hurried home. Nos dimos prisa para llegar a casa.
Hurry up! ¡Date prisa!

♪ to **hurt** *verb*
1 *(to injure)* to hurt somebody hacer [7] daño a alguien
You're hurting me! ¡Me estás haciendo daño!
to hurt yourself hacerse [7] daño
Did you hurt yourself? ¿Te hiciste daño?
to hurt your hand hacerse [7] daño en la mano
I hurt my arm. Me hice daño en el brazo.
2 *(to give pain)* **doler** [38]
My back hurts. Me duele la espalda.
My feet hurt. Me duelen los pies.
That hurts! ¡Eso hace daño!

♪ **husband** *noun*
el **marido** *masc*

♪ **hut** *noun*
la **cabaña** *fem*

hymn *noun*
el **himno** *masc*

♪ **hypermarket** *noun*
el **hipermercado** *masc*

hyphen *noun*
el **guión** *masc*

to **hypnotize** *verb*
hipnotizar [25]

I i

I *pronoun*
1 **yo** (*see Word tip*)
I am Scottish. Soy escocés.
I have two sisters. Tengo dos hermanas.
2 (*for emphasis*) **yo**
I did it. Lo hice yo.
Tony and I Tony y yo
I went but Robert didn't. Yo fui pero Robert no.

WORD TIP *I*, like *he*, *she*, *they* etc, is generally not translated into Spanish; the ending of the verb tells you if the subject of the verb is *yo*, *él*, *ella*, etc, so *I* is translated only for emphasis or for clarity.

Iberia *noun*
Iberia *fem* (*the name for Spain and Portugal together*)

Iberian *adjective*
ibérico *masc*, **ibérica** *fem*
the Iberian Peninsula la Península ibérica

WORD TIP Adjectives and nouns for nationality and regional origin do not have capital letters in Spanish.

ice *noun*
el **hielo** *masc*
• **iceberg** el iceberg, *pl:* los **icebergs**

ice cream *noun*
el **helado** *masc*
a chocolate ice cream un helado de chocolate

ice cube *noun*
el **cubito de hielo**

ice hockey *noun*
el **hockey sobre hielo**
to play ice hockey jugar [27] al hockey sobre hielo

ice rink *noun*
la **pista de hielo**

ice skating *noun*
el **patinaje sobre hielo**
to go ice skating ir [8] a patinar sobre hielo

icing *noun*
el **azúcar glaseado**

icon *noun*
(*Computers*) el **icono** *masc*

ICT *noun*
(= *Information and Communications Technology*) la **informática** *fem*

icy *adjective*
1 (*road*) **cubierto de hielo** *masc*, **cubierta de hielo** *fem*
2 (*very cold*) **helado** *masc*, **helada** *fem*
an icy wind un viento helado

ID card *noun* ▷ **identity card**

idea *noun*
la **idea** *fem*
What a good idea! ¡Qué buena idea!
I've no idea. No tengo ni idea.

ideal *adjective*
ideal *masc & fem*

identical *adjective*
idéntico *masc*, **idéntica** *fem*

identical twins *plural noun*
los **gemelos** *plural masc*, las **gemelas** *plural fem*

identification *noun*
la **identificación** *fem*
Have you got any other identification? ¿Tiene algún otro documento que acredite su identidad?

identity card *noun*
el **carné de identidad**

idiot *noun*
el & la **idiota** *masc & fem*

idiotic *adjective*
idiota *masc & fem*

i.e. *abbreviation*
1 (*in writing*) **i.e.**
2 (*in speech*) **esto es**

if *conjunction*
1 (*in conditionals*) **si**
if Sue's there ... si Sue está allí ...
If it rains we'll go to the cinema. Si llueve iremos al cine.
If I won the lottery ... Si ganase la lotería ...
If I had it, I would give it to you. Si lo tuviera, te lo daría.
if only ... ojalá ...
If only you'd told me. Ojalá me lo hubieses dicho.
even if incluso si
We'll go even if it snows Iremos incluso si nieva.
if I were you ... yo que tú ...
If I were you, I'd forget it. Yo que tú me olvidaría del asunto.

2 (*whether*) **si**
They asked if he had left. Preguntaron si se había ido.

WORD TIP When talking about something that might, or might not, happen, *si* is followed by the subjunctive.

to **ignore** *verb*
1 (*a person*) **ignorar** [17]
She's been ignoring me all evening. Me ha estado ignorando toda la noche.
2 (*what somebody says*) **no hacer** [7] **caso de**
Just ignore it. No le hagas caso.

♪ **ill** *adjective*
enfermo *masc*, **enferma** *fem*
to fall ill enfermar [17]
to be taken ill enfermar [17]
to feel ill sentirse [14] mal

illegal *adjective*
ilegal *masc & fem*

illness *noun*
la **enfermedad** *fem*

illustrated *adjective*
ilustrado *masc*, **ilustrada** *fem*

illustration *noun*
la **ilustración** *fem*

♪ **image** *noun*
la **imagen** *fem*, *fem pl:* las **imágenes**

imagination *noun*
la **imaginación** *fem*

imaginative *adjective*
imaginativo *masc*, **imaginativa** *fem*

to **imagine** *verb*
imaginarse [17]
You can't imagine how hard it was! ¡No puedes imaginarte lo difícil que fue!
Imagine that you're very rich. Imagina que eres muy rico.

to **imitate** *verb*
imitar [17]

imitation *noun*
la **imitación** *fem*

immediate *adjective*
inmediato *masc*, **inmediata** *fem*

♪ **immediately** *adverb*
inmediatamente
I rang them immediately. Los llamé inmediatamente.
immediately before justo antes
immediately after justo después

immigrant *noun*
el & la **inmigrante** *masc & fem*

immigration *noun*
la **inmigración** *fem*

impact *noun*
el **impacto** *masc*

impatience *noun*
la **impaciencia** *fem*

impatient *adjective*
impaciente *masc & fem*
to get impatient with somebody impacientarse [17] con alguien

impatiently *adverb*
con impaciencia

imperfect *noun*
(*Grammar*) el **imperfecto** *masc*

import *noun* ▷ see **import** *verb*
1 (*item*) el **artículo de importación**
Coal is the most important import. El artículo de importación más importante es el carbón.
2 (*trade*) la **importación** *fem*

to **import** *verb* ▷ see **import** *noun*
importar [17]

importance *noun*
la **importancia** *fem*

♪ **important** *adjective*
importante *masc & fem*

♪ **impossible** *adjective*
imposible *masc & fem*
It's impossible to find a telephone. Es imposible encontrar un teléfono.

impressed *adjective*
impresionado *masc*, **impresionada** *fem*

impression *noun*
la **impresión** *fem*
to make a good impression on somebody causar [17] una buena impresión a alguien
I got the impression he was hiding something. Me dio la impresión de que estaba ocultando algo.

♪ to **improve** *verb*
mejorar [17]
to improve something mejorar [17] algo
The weather is improving. El tiempo está mejorando.

improvement *noun*
1 (*change for the better*) la **mejora** *fem*
2 (*gradual progress*) el **progreso** *masc*

English–Spanish

♪ **in** *adverb* ▷ see **in** *prep*

1 (*at home, around*) **to be in** estar [2]
Mick's not in at the moment. Mick no está en este momento.
There was nobody in. No había nadie.

2 (*used as part of a verb*) **to come in** entrar [17]
to go in entrar [17]
to run in entrar [17] corriendo

♪ **in** *preposition* ▷ see **in** *adv*

1 (*to talk about where something or someone is*) **en**
in Spain en España
in town en la ciudad
in my pocket en mi bolsillo
in the newspaper en el periódico
to lie in the sun tumbarse [17] al sol
They live in Barcelona. Viven en Barcelona.
Paul is in my class. Paul está en mi clase.
You can't go out in this weather. No puedes salir con este tiempo.

2 (*to talk about how something is done*) **en**
in Spanish en español
in twos de dos en dos
They sat in a circle. Se sentaron en un círculo.
He wrote it in pencil. Lo escribió a lápiz.

3 (*wearing*) **de**
the girl in the pink skirt la chica de la falda rosa
He was in a suit. Llevaba un traje.
She was dressed in white. Iba vestida de blanco.

4 (*during a month, season, year, period of time*) **en**
in May en mayo
in 2003 en dos mil tres
in winter en invierno
in time con el tiempo
It will improve with time. Va a mejorar con el tiempo.

5 (*during a part of the day*) **por**
in the morning por la mañana
in the night por la noche
at eight in the morning a las ocho de la mañana

6 (*at the end of a period of time*) **dentro de**
I'll phone you in ten minutes. Te llamaré dentro de diez minutos.

7 (*to talk about how long it takes to do something*) **en**
She did it in five minutes. Lo hizo en cinco minutos.

8 (*after a superlative*) **de**
the tallest boy in the class el chico más alto de la clase
the biggest city in the world la ciudad más grande del mundo

♪ **inch** *noun*
la **pulgada** *masc*

♪ to **include** *verb* ▷ see **including** *prep*
incluir [54]
Dinner is included in the price. La cena está incluida en el precio.
Service included. Servicio incluido.

♪ **including** *preposition* ▷ see **include** *verb*
incluido *masc*, **incluida** *fem*
60 pounds including VAT. Sesenta libras IVA incluido.
everyone, including children todo el mundo incluidos los niños
including Sundays incluidos los domingos
not including Sundays sin incluir los domingos

income *noun*
los **ingresos** *plural masc*
• **income tax** el impuesto sobre la renta

inconvenient *adjective*
1 (*place, arrangement*) **poco conveniente** *masc & fem*
2 (*time*) **inoportuno** *masc*, **inoportuna** *fem*

♪ **increase** *noun* ▷ see **increase** *verb*
el **aumento** *masc*

♪ to **increase** *verb* ▷ see **increase** *noun*
aumentar [17]
The price has increased by ten pounds. El precio ha aumentado diez libras.

incredible *adjective*
increíble *masc & fem*

incredibly *adverb*
(*very*) **increíblemente**
The film's incredibly boring. La película es increíblemente aburrida.

indeed *adverb*
1 (*used to emphasize something*) **She's very pleased indeed.** Está contentísima.
I'm very hungry indeed. Tengo muchísima hambre.
Thank you very much indeed. Muchísimas gracias.
2 (*certainly*) **'Can you hear his radio?'— 'Indeed I can!'** '¿Oyes su radio?'— 'Ya lo creo.'
'Do you like it?'— 'I do indeed!' '¿Te gusta?'— 'Sí, muchísimo.'

indefinite article *noun*
(*Grammar*) el **artículo indefinido**

independence *noun*
la **independencia** *fem*

a b c d e f g h i j k l m n o p q r s t u v w x y z

independent *adjective*
independiente *masc & fem*
• **independent school** la escuela privada

index *noun*
el **índice** *masc*
• **index finger** el dedo índice

India *noun*
la **India** *fem*

Indian *adjective & noun*
1 **indio** *masc*, **india** *fem*
2 un **indio** *masc*, una **india** *fem*
the Indians los indios

WORD TIP Adjectives and nouns for nationality and regional origin do not have capital letters in Spanish.

indigestion *noun*
la **indigestión** *fem*
to have indigestion tener [9] indigestión

indirect *adjective*
indirecto *masc*, **indirecta** *fem*

individual *adjective*
▷ see **individual** *noun*
(*for one person: serving, contribution*) **individual** *masc & fem*
individual tuition las clases particulares

individual *noun* ▷ see **individual** *adj*
el **individuo** *masc*

indoor *adjective*
1 (*plant*) **de interior**
2 (*swimming pool*) **cubierto** *masc*, **cubierta** *fem*

indoors *adverb*
dentro
to stay indoors quedarse [17] dentro
to go indoors entrar [17]
It's cooler indoors. Hace más fresco dentro.

industrial *adjective*
industrial *masc & fem*
• **industrial estate** la zona industrial

♪ **industry** *noun*
la **industria** *fem*
the advertising industry la industria de la publicidad

inevitable *adjective*
inevitable *masc & fem*

inevitably *adverb*
inevitablemente

inexperienced *adjective*
inexperto *masc*, **inexperta** *fem*

infected *adjective*
infectado *masc*, **infectada** *fem*

infection *noun*
la **infección** *fem*
an eye infection una infección de ojos
I've got a throat infection. Tengo anginas.

infectious *adjective*
infeccioso *masc*, **infecciosa** *fem*

infinitive *noun*
el **infinitivo** *masc*
in the infinitive en infinitivo

inflation *noun*
la **inflación** *fem*

influence *noun*
la **influencia** *fem*
to be a good influence on somebody ser [1] una buena influencia para alguien

to **inform** *verb*
informar [17]
to inform somebody that ... informar a alguien de que ...
They informed us that there was a problem. Nos informaron de que había un problema.
to inform somebody of something informar a alguien de algo
to keep somebody informed mantener [9] a alguien informado

informal *adjective*
1 (*meal, event*) **informal** *masc & fem*
2 (*language*) **familiar** *masc & fem*
an informal expression una expresión familiar

♪ **information** *noun*
la **información** *fem*
a piece of information un dato
I need some information about flights to Madrid. Necesito información sobre vuelos a Madrid.
• **information desk** el mostrador de información
• **information office** la oficina de información
• **information technology** la informática

infuriating *adjective*
exasperante *masc & fem*

ingredient *noun*
el **ingrediente** *masc*

initials *plural noun*
las **iniciales** *plural fem*
Put your initials here. Pon tus iniciales aquí.

injection *noun*
la **inyección** *fem*
to give somebody an injection ponerle **[11]** una inyección a alguien

to **injure** *verb* ▷ see **injured** *adj*
herir [14]
She injured herself playing tennis. Se hirió jugando al tenis.
He was slightly injured in the accident. Resultó levemente herido en el accidente.

injured *adjective* ▷ see **injure** *verb*
herido *masc*, **herida** *fem*

injury *noun*
la **herida** *fem*

ink *noun*
la **tinta** *fem*

in-laws *plural noun*
los **suegros** *plural masc*

innocent *adjective*
inocente *masc & fem*

> mini-info **innocents**
>
> The 28 December, *el día de los Inocentes* is Spain's April Fool's Day when students play tricks on each other chanting Mariposa Inocente. It is the day the Church remembers the massacre of innocent children decreed by King Herod in an attempt to kill the baby Jesus.

insane *adjective*
loco *masc*, **loca** *fem*

insect *noun*
el **insecto** *masc*
an insect bite una picadura de insecto

to **insert** *verb*
insertar [17]

inside *adverb* ▷ see **inside** *noun, prep*
dentro
to go inside entrar **[17]**
She's inside, I think. Creo que está dentro.

inside *noun* ▷ see **inside** *adv, prep*
el **interior** *masc*
the inside of the oven el interior del horno

inside *preposition* ▷ see **inside** *adv, noun*
dentro de
inside the cinema dentro del cine

inside out *adjective, adverb*
del revés
Your jumper's inside out. Llevas el jersey del revés.

to **insist** *verb*
insistir [19]
if you insist si insistes
to insist on doing something insistir en hacer algo
He insisted on paying. Insistió en pagar.
to insist that insistir en que
Ruth insisted that I was wrong. Ruth insistió en que yo estaba equivocada.

inspection *noun*
la **inspección** *fem*

inspector *noun*
el **inspector** *masc*, la **inspectora** *fem*

inspiration *noun*
la **inspiración** *fem*

to **install** *verb*
instalar [17]

instalment *noun*
1 (*of a TV, radio serial*) el **episodio** *masc*
2 (*payment*) el **plazo** *masc*
to pay by instalments pagar **[28]** a plazos

instance *noun*
1 (*example*) el **ejemplo** *masc*
for instance por ejemplo
2 (*case*) el **caso** *masc*
in this instance en este caso

instant *adjective* ▷ see **instant** *noun*
1 (*coffee, soup*) **instantáneo** *masc*, **instantánea** *fem*
2 (*effect, success*) **inmediato** *masc*, **inmediata** *fem*

instant *noun* ▷ see **instant** *adj*
el **instante** *masc*
Come here this instant! ¡Ven aquí ahora mismo!

instead *adverb*
1 (*as an alternative*) **Ted couldn't go, so I went instead.** Ted no pudo ir, así que fui yo en su lugar.
We didn't go to the concert, we went to Lucy's instead. No fuimos al concierto, fuimos a casa de Lucy.
2 **instead of** en vez de
Instead of pudding I had cheese. En vez de dulce tomé queso.
Instead of playing tennis we went swimming. En vez de jugar al tenis nos fuimos a nadar.

instinct *noun*
el **instinto** *masc*

to **instruct** *verb*
to instruct somebody to do something ordenar **[17]** a alguien que haga algo
The teacher instructed us to stay together.

La profesora nos ordenó que nos quedásemos juntos.

WORD TIP *ordenar que* is followed by the subjunctive.

instructions *plural noun*
las **instrucciones** *plural fem*
Follow the instructions on the packet. Siga las instrucciones del paquete.
'Instructions for use' 'Modo de empleo'

instructor *noun*
el **profesor** *masc*, la **profesora** *fem*
my driving instructor mi profesor de conducir
a skiing instructor un monitor de esquí

instrument *noun*
el **instrumento** *masc*
to play an instrument tocar [31] un instrumento

insulin *noun*
la **insulina** *fem*

insult *noun* ▷ see **insult** *verb*
el **insulto** *masc*

to **insult** *verb* ▷ see **insult** *noun*
insultar [17]

insurance *noun*
el **seguro** *masc*
travel insurance seguro de viaje
fire insurance seguro contra incendios
Have you got medical insurance? ¿Tienes seguro médico?

intelligence *noun*
la **inteligencia** *fem*

intelligent *adjective*
inteligente *masc & fem*

to **intend** *verb*
1 (*to wish*) **querer** [12]
He did it as I intended. Lo hizo como yo quería.
2 (*to plan*) **to intend to do something** tener [9] pensado hacer algo
We intend to spend the night in Rome. Tenemos pensado pasar la noche en Roma.

intensive *adjective*
intensivo *masc*, **intensiva** *fem*
an intensive course un curso intensivo
to be in intensive care estar [2] en cuidados intensivos

intention *noun*
la **intención** *fem*
I have no intention of paying. No tengo ninguna intención de pagar.

interest *noun* ▷ see **interest** *verb*
1 (*hobby*) la **afición** *fem*
What are your interests? ¿Qué aficiones tienes?
2 (*enthusiasm*) el **interés** *masc*
She showed interest. Mostró interés.
to take (an) interest in something interesarse [17] por algo

to **interest** *verb* ▷ see **interest** *noun*
interesar [17]
That doesn't interest me. Eso no me interesa.

interested *adjective*
interesado *masc*, **interesada** *fem*
They seem very interested. Parecen estar muy interesados.
Sean's very interested in cooking. A Sean le interesa mucho la cocina.

interesting *adjective*
interesante *masc & fem*

to **interfere** *verb*
to interfere in something entrometerse [18] en algo
She always interferes in my affairs. Siempre se entromete en mis asuntos.

interior *adjective* ▷ see **interior** *noun*
interior *masc & fem*

interior *noun* ▷ see **interior** *adj*
el **interior** *masc*
• **interior designer** el & la interiorista

international *adjective*
internacional *masc & fem*

Internet *noun*
Internet *masc or fem*
to be on the Internet estar [2] conectado a Internet
Look for it on the Internet. Búscalo en Internet.

WORD TIP Spanish does not use *el* or *la* with *Internet*.

• **Internet cafe** el cibercafé

interpreter *noun*
el & la **intérprete** *masc & fem*

to **interrupt** *verb*
interrumpir [19]

interruption *noun*
la **interrupción** *fem*

interval *noun*
el **intermedio** *masc*

interview *noun* ▷ see **interview** *verb*
la **entrevista** *fem*
a job interview una entrevista de trabajo
a TV interview una entrevista en la tele

to **interview** *verb* ▷ see **interview** *noun*
(*on TV, radio*) **entrevistar** [17]

interviewer *noun*
el **entrevistador** *masc*, la **entrevistadora** *fem*

into *preposition*
1 (*showing movement*) **to get into bed** meterse [18] en la cama
to go into town ir [8] a la ciudad
He's gone into the bank. Ha entrado al banco.
I put the cat into his basket. Puse al gato dentro de su cesta.
We got into the car. Entramos en el coche.
He dived into the pool. Se tiró a la piscina.
She walked into a tree. Se dio contra un árbol.
2 (*showing change, etc*) **to translate something into Spanish** traducir [60] algo al español
to change pounds into euros cambiar [17] libras a euros
The sorcerer changed her into a stone. El mago la convirtió en una piedra.
3 (*used in division in maths*) **Three into fifteen goes five times.** Quince dividido por tres es cinco.

to **introduce** *verb*
presentar [17]
She introduced me to her brother. Me presentó a su hermano.
Can I introduce you to my mother? ¿Te puedo presentar a mi madre?

introduction *noun*
1 (*to a person*) la **presentación** *fem*
I'll make the introductions. Yo haré las presentaciones.
2 (*in a book*) la **introducción** *fem*

to **invade** *verb*
invadir [19]

invalid *noun*
el **inválido** *masc*, la **inválida** *fem*

invasion *noun*
la **invasión** *fem*

to **invent** *verb*
inventar [17]

invention *noun*
el **invento** *masc*

inverted commas *plural noun*
las **comillas** *plural fem*
in inverted commas entre comillas

investigation *noun*
la **investigación** *fem*
an investigation into the fire una investigación sobre el fuego

invisible *adjective*
invisible *masc & fem*

invitation *noun*
la **invitación** *fem*
an invitation to dinner una invitación a cenar

to **invite** *verb*
invitar [17]
Kirsty invited me to lunch. Kirsty me invitó a comer.
He's invited me out on Tuesday. Me ha invitado a salir el martes.

invoice *noun*
la **factura** *fem*

to **involve** *verb*
1 (*to entail*) **suponer** [11]
It involves a lot of work. Supone mucho trabajo.
2 (*to consist of*) **What does the job involve?** ¿En qué consiste el trabajo?
3 (*to participate*) **to be involved in something** tomar [17] parte en algo
I am involved in the new project. Estoy tomando parte en el nuevo proyecto.

Iran *noun*
Irán *masc*

Iranian *adjective & noun*
1 **iraní** *masc & fem* (*pl:* **iraníes**)
2 un & una **iraní** *masc & fem*
the Iranians los iraníes

WORD TIP Adjectives and nouns for nationality and regional origin do not have capital letters in Spanish.

Iraq *noun*
Irak *masc*

Iraqi *adjective & noun*
1 **iraquí** *masc & fem* (*pl:* **iraquíes**)
2 un & una **iraquí** *masc & fem*
the Iraqis los iraquíes

WORD TIP Adjectives and nouns for nationality and regional origin do not have capital letters in Spanish.

Ireland *noun*
Irlanda *fem*
the Republic of Ireland la República Irlandesa
I'm from Ireland. Soy irlandés (*boy speaking*)., Soy irlandesa (*girl speaking*).

iris *noun*
el **lirio** *masc*

Irish *adjective* ▷ see **Irish** *noun*
irlandés *masc*, **irlandesa** *fem*

Irish *noun* ▷ see **Irish** *adj*
1 (*the people*) **the Irish** los irlandeses
2 (*the language*) el **irlandés** *masc*

WORD TIP Adjectives and nouns for nationality, regional origin, and language do not have capital letters in Spanish.

Irishman *noun*
un **irlandés masc**

Irish Republic *noun*
the Irish Republic la República de Irlanda

Irish Sea *noun*
the Irish Sea el mar de Irlanda

Irishwoman *noun* ▷ see **Irish** *noun*
una **irlandesa** *fem*

iron *noun* ▷ see **iron** *verb*
1 (*for clothes*) la **plancha** *fem*
2 (*the metal*) el **hierro** *masc*

to **iron** *verb* ▷ see **iron** *noun*
planchar [17]

ironing *noun*
to do the ironing planchar [17]
• **ironing board** la tabla de planchar

irregular *adjective*
irregular *masc & fem*

irresponsible *adjective*
irresponsable *masc & fem*

irritating *adjective*
irritante *masc & fem*

Islam *noun*
el **Islam** *masc*

Islamic *adjective*
islámico *masc*, **islámica** *fem*

WORD TIP Adjectives and nouns for religion do not have capital letters in Spanish.

island *noun*
la **isla** *fem*

isn't *short for*
1 **is not** (*See:* **to be**)
2 (*in questions*) **It's beautiful, isn't it?** ¿Es hermoso, verdad?

isolated *adjective*
aislado *masc*, **aislada** *fem*

Israel *noun*
Israel *masc*

Israeli *adjective & noun*
1 **israelí** *masc & fem* (*pl:* **israelíes**)
2 un & una **israelí** *masc & fem*
the Israelis los israelíes

WORD TIP Adjectives and nouns for nationality and regional origin do not have capital letters in Spanish.

issue *noun* ▷ see **issue** *verb*
1 (*something you discuss*) el **tema** *masc*
a political issue un tema político
2 (*edition of a magazine*) el **número** *masc*

to **issue** *verb* ▷ see **issue** *noun*
distribuir [54]

it *pronoun*
1 (*as the subject*) **él** *masc*, **ella** *fem* (*see Word Tip*)
'Where's my bag?'— 'It's in the kitchen.' '¿Dónde está mi bolso?'— 'Está en la cocina.'
You should see that film, it's great. Deberías ver esa película, es genial.
'How old is your car?'— 'It's five years old.' '¿Cuántos años tiene tu coche?'— 'Cinco.'
2 (*in impersonal statements*) **Yes, it's true.** Sí, es verdad.
It doesn't matter. No importa.
It's a nice day. Hace buen día.
It's hot. Hace calor.
It's one o'clock. Es la una.
It's two o'clock. Son las dos (*Use* **son** *for two to twelve o'clock*).
3 (*as the direct object*) **lo** *masc*, **la** *fem*
My book? I've lost it. ¿Mi libro? Lo he perdido.
Give me the suitcase, I'll carry it. Dame la maleta, yo la llevo.
Put it there. Ponlo ahí.
Don't leave it there. No lo dejes ahí.
4 (*as the indirect object*) **le**
I gave it another coat of paint. Le di otra mano de pintura.
5 (*saying who you are, what something is*) **It was Bill.** Fue Bill.
It's me. Soy yo.
Who is it? ¿Quién es?
What is it? ¿Qué es?
It was a dress, not a blouse, she bought. Fue un vestido, no una blusa, lo que compró.
6 (*after prepositions*) **ello**
I want to talk about it. Quiero hablar de ello.
Go for it! ¡A por ello!

WORD TIP *it*, like *I*, *she*, *he* etc, is generally not translated into Spanish; the ending of the verb tells you if the subject of the verb is *yo*, *él*, *ella*, etc, so *it* is translated only for emphasis or for clarity.

English–Spanish

IT *noun*
(= *Information Technology*) la **informática** *fem*

Italian *adjective & noun*
1 **italiano** *masc*, **italiana** *fem*
2 (*person*) un **italiano** *masc*, una **italiana** *fem*
the Italians los italianos
3 (*the language*) el **italiano** *masc*
my Italian class mi clase de italiano
our Italian teacher nuestro profesor de italiano

WORD TIP Adjectives and nouns for nationality, regional origin, and language do not have capital letters in Spanish.

italics *noun*
la **cursiva** *fem*
in italics en cursiva

Italy *noun*
Italia *fem*

to **itch** *verb*
1 (*clothes*) **picar** [31]
This sweater itches. Este jersey pica.
2 (*part of the body*) **My back is itching.** Me pica la espalda.
I'm itching all over. Me pica todo el cuerpo.

item *noun*
el **artículo** *masc*

its *adjective*
1 (*before most nouns*) **su** *masc & fem*
The dog was playing with its toy. El perro jugaba con su juguete.
It has its problems. Tiene sus problemas.
2 (*with parts of the body*) **el**, **la**, **los**, **las**
The cat was washing its ears. El gato se lavaba las orejas.

itself *pronoun*
1 (*reflexive*) **se**
The cat is washing itself. El gato se está lavando.
2 (*on its own*) **by itself** solo *masc*, sola *fem*
He left the dog by itself. Dejó al perro solo.

ivory *noun*
el **marfil** *masc*

ivy *noun*
la **hiedra** *fem*

J j

jack *noun*
1 (*in cards*) la **jota** *fem*
the jack of clubs la jota de tréboles
2 (*for a car*) el **gato** *masc*

♪ **jacket** *noun*
la **chaqueta** *fem*
• **jacket potato** la patata asada con la piel

jackpot *noun*
el **premio gordo**
to win the jackpot sacarse [31] el premio gordo

jagged *adjective*
dentado *masc*, **dentada** *fem*

jail *noun* ▷ see **jail** *verb*
la **cárcel** *fem*

to **jail** *verb* ▷ see **jail** *noun*
encarcelar [17]

♪ **jam** *noun*
1 (*for eating*) la **mermelada** *fem*
raspberry jam la mermelada de frambuesas
2 (*in traffic*) el **embotellamiento** *masc*
There was a huge traffic jam. Había un enorme embotellamiento.

Jamaica *noun*
Jamaica *fem*

Jamaican *adjective & noun*
1 **jamaicano** *masc*, **jamaicana** *fem*
2 (*person*) un **jamaicano** *masc*, una **jamaicana** *fem*
the Jamaicans los jamaicanos

WORD TIP Adjectives and nouns for nationality and regional origin do not have capital letters in Spanish..

♪ **January** *noun*
enero *masc*
in January en enero

WORD TIP Names of months and days start with small letters in Spanish.

jammed *adjective*
atascado *masc*, **atascada** *fem*

Japan *noun*
Japón *masc*
in Japan en Japón

Japanese *adjective & noun*
1 **japonés** *masc*, **japonesa** *fem*
2 (*person*) un **japonés** *masc*, una **japonesa** *fem*
the Japanese los japoneses
3 (*the language*) el **japonés** *masc*

WORD TIP Adjectives and nouns for nationality, regional origin, and language do not have capital letters in Spanish.

jar *noun*
el **tarro** *masc*
a jar of jam un tarro de mermelada

javelin *noun*
la **jabalina** *fem*

jaw *noun*
la **mandíbula** *fem*

jazz *noun*
el **jazz** *masc*

jealous *adjective*
celoso *masc*, **celosa** *fem*

jealousy *noun*
los **celos** *plural masc*

jeans *noun*
los **vaqueros** *plural masc*
a pair of jeans unos vaqueros
Look at my new jeans. Mira mis vaqueros nuevos.

jelly *noun*
la **gelatina** *fem*

jellyfish *noun*
la **medusa** *fem*

jersey *noun* ▷ see **Jersey** *noun*
1 (*pullover*) el **jersey** *masc*
2 (*for sport*) la **camiseta** *fem*

Jersey *noun* ▷ see **jersey** *noun*
la **isla de Jersey** (*one of the Channel Islands*)

Jesus *noun*
Jesús *masc*
Jesus Christ Jesucristo

jet *noun*
el **avión a reacción**
• **jet lag** el jet
• **jet-ski** la moto acuática

jetty *noun*
el **embarcadero** *masc*

Jew *noun*
el **judío** *masc*, la **judía** *fem*

WORD TIP Adjectives and nouns for religion do not have capital letters in Spanish.

jewel *noun*
la **joya** *fem*

English–Spanish

jeweller *noun*
el **joyero** *masc*, la **joyera** *fem*
- **jeweller's shop** la joyería

jewellery *noun*
las **joyas** *plural fem*

Jewish *adjective*
judío *masc*, **judía** *fem*
He's Jewish. Es judío.

WORD TIP Adjectives and nouns for religion do not have capital letters in Spanish.

jigsaw *noun*
el **rompecabezas** *invariable masc*

job *noun*
1 (*paid work*) el **trabajo** *masc*
a part-time job un trabajo a tiempo parcial
a job as a secretary un trabajo como secretaria
What's your job? ¿En qué trabajas?
He's got a job at a supermarket. Trabaja en un supermercado.
I'm out of a job right now. Estoy sin trabajo en este momento.
2 (*task*) el **trabajo** *masc*
It's not an easy job. No es un trabajo fácil.
She's made a good job of it. Lo ha hecho muy bien.

jobless *adjective*
sin trabajo, **en paro**

jockey *noun*
el & la **jockey** *masc & fem*

to **jog** *verb*
to go jogging hacer [7] footing
She goes jogging every day. Hace footing todos los días.

to **join** *verb*
1 (*to become a member of*) **hacerse [7] socio de**
He joined the judo club. Se ha hecho socio del club de judo.
2 (*to meet up with*)
I'll join you later. Iré más tarde.
- **to join in**
1 (*people*) **participar [17]**
Ruth never joins in. Ruth nunca participa.
2 (*a discussion, a game*) **to join in something** participar [17] en algo
Will you join in the game? ¿Quieres participar en el juego?

joiner *noun*
el **carpintero** *masc*, la **carpintera** *fem*

joint *noun*
1 (*in body*) la **articulación** *fem*
2 (*of hash*) el **porro** *masc*
3 (*bar, etc*) el **antro** *masc*

joke *noun* ▷ see **joke** *verb*
1 (*funny story*) el **chiste** *masc*
to tell a joke contar [24] un chiste
He's always telling jokes. Siempre está contando chistes.
2 (*trick*) la **broma** *fem*
to play a joke on someone gastarle [17] una broma a alguien
She played a joke on him. Le gastó una broma.

to **joke** *verb* ▷ see **joke** *noun*
bromear [17]
She's only joking. Sólo está bromeando.
You're joking! ¡Qué va!

joker *noun*
1 (*in cards*) el **comodín**
2 (*in class*) el & la **bromista** *masc & fem*

Jordan *noun*
Jordania *fem*

journalism *noun*
el **periodismo** *masc*

journalist *noun*
el & la **periodista** *masc & fem*
Sean's dad is a journalist. El padre de Sean es periodista.

journey *noun*
el **viaje** *masc*
our journey to Seville nuestro viaje a Sevilla
a bus journey un viaje en autobús
My journey to school takes half an hour. Me tardo una hora en ir a la escuela en el autobús.

joy *noun*
la **alegría** *fem*

joy-riding *noun*
el delito de robar un coche para dar una vuelta con él a toda velocidad

joystick *noun*
(*Computers*) el **joystick** *masc*

Judaism *noun*
(*Religion*) el **judaísmo** *masc*

WORD TIP Adjectives and nouns for religion do not have capital letters in Spanish.

judge *noun* ▷ see **judge** *verb*
el **juez** *masc*, la **jueza** *fem*

to **judge** *verb* ▷ see **judge** *noun*
(*a time, distance*) **calcular [17]**

judgement *noun*
1 (*sense*) el **juicio** *fem*
in my judgement a mi juicio
2 (*in a court*) la **sentencia** *fem*

a b c d e f g h i j k l m n o p q r s t u v w x y z

judo *noun*
el **judo** *masc*
She does judo. Hace judo.

jug *noun*
la **jarra** *fem*

to **juggle** *verb*
hacer [7] malabarismos

juggler *noun*
el & la **malabarista** *masc & fem*

juice *noun*
el **zumo** *masc*
Two orange juices, please! ¡Dos zumos de naranja, por favor!

juicy *adjective*
jugoso *masc*, **jugosa** *fem*

July *noun*
julio *masc*
in July en julio

WORD TIP Names of months and days start with small letters in Spanish.

jumble sale *noun*
el **mercadillo de beneficencia**

to **jump** *verb* ▷ see **jump** *noun*
saltar [17]

jump *noun* ▷ see **jump** *verb*
el **salto** *masc*
a parachute jump un salto en paracaídas

jumper *noun*
el **jersey** *masc*

junction *noun*
1 (*of roads, motorways*) el **cruce** *masc*
2 (*on a railway*) el **empalme** *masc*

June *noun*
junio *masc*
in June en junio

WORD TIP Names of months and days start with small letters in Spanish.

junior *adjective*
de primaria
a junior school una escuela de primaria
the juniors los alumnos de primaria

jungle *noun*
la **selva** *fem*

junk *noun*
la **basura** *masc*
- **junk food** la comida basura
  Junk food is bad for you. La comida basura es mala para la salud.
- **junk shop** la tienda de cosas usadas

jury *noun*
el **jurado** *masc*

just *adverb*
1 (*shortly*) **justo**
just before midday justo antes del mediodía
just after the church justo después de la iglesia
2 (*only*) **sólo**
just for fun sólo por diversión
It's just for you. Es para ti.
There's just me and Justine. Sólo somos yo y Justine.
3 **to be just doing something** estar **[2]** haciendo algo
I'm just finishing my homework. Estoy terminando mis deberes.
I'm just coming! ¡Ya voy!
4 **to have just done something** acabar **[17]** de hacer algo
Tom has just arrived. Tom acaba de llegar.
Helen had just called. Helen acababa de llamar.

WORD TIP *have just done something* is translated by *acabo de, etc*, i.e. the present tense in Spanish. *had just done something* is translated by *acababa de, etc*, i.e. the imperfect tense in Spanish.

justice *noun*
la **justicia** *fem*

to **justify** *verb*
justificar [31]

English-Spanish

a b c d e f g h i j k l m n o p q r s t u v w x y z

K k

kangaroo *noun*
el **canguro** *masc*

karate *noun*
el **kárate** *masc*

kebab *noun*
la **brocheta** *fem*

keen *adjective*
You don't look too keen. No pareces muy entusiasmado.
He's a keen photographer. Le gusta mucho la fotografía.
He's not keen on jazz. No le gusta el jazz.
They are keen on the idea. Están interesados en la idea.

♪ to **keep** *verb*
1 (*to store*) **guardar [17]**
I keep my bike in the garage. Guardo mi bici en el garaje.
Where do you keep the CDs? ¿Dónde guardas los CDs?
to keep something for someone guardarle algo a alguien
Will you keep my seat? ¿Me guardas el sitio?
to keep somebody waiting hacer [7] esperar a alguien
He kept us waiting for an hour. Nos hizo esperar una hora.
2 (*for ever*) **quedarse [17] con**
I kept the letter. Me quedé con la carta.
Keep the change! ¡Quédese con el cambio! (*formal use*)
3 (*secrets, etc*) **to keep a secret** guardar [17] un secreto
to keep a promise mantener [9] una promesa
4 (*to stay*) **Keep calm!** ¡Tranquilo! (*boy*), ¡Tranquila! (*girl*)
Keep still! ¡Estate quieto!
Keep out of the sun. No te pongas al sol.
5 **to keep on doing something** seguir [64] haciendo algo
She kept on talking. Siguió hablando.
Keep straight on. Siga todo recto. (*formal use*)
6 (*time after time*) **to keep on doing something** no parar [17] de hacer algo
He keeps on phoning me. No para de llamarme.

kerb *noun*
el **bordillo de la acera**

ketchup *noun*
el **ketchup** *masc*

kettle *noun*
el **hervidor** *masc*
to put the kettle on poner [11] el agua a hervir

♪ **key** *noun*
1 (*for a lock*) la **llave** *fem*
a bunch of keys un manojo de llaves
2 (*on a keyboard*) la **tecla** *fem*
• **keyboard** el teclado *masc*
• **keyhole** el ojo de la cerradura
• **keyring** el llavero

♪ **kick** *noun* ▷ see **kick** *verb*
1 (*with the foot*) la **patada** *fem*
to give somebody a kick darle [4] una patada a alguien
2 (*buzz*) **She gets a kick out of driving fast.** Le encanta conducir rápido.

to **kick** *verb* ▷ see **kick** *noun*
to kick somebody darle [4] una patada a alguien
He kicked the referee. Le dio una patada al árbitro.
to kick the ball darle [4] una patada al balón
• to **kick off**
empezar [25]

kick-off *noun*
el **saque inicial**
The kick-off is at three. El partido empieza a las tres.

♪ **kid** *noun*
1 (*child*) el **niño** *masc*, la **niña** *fem*
Dad's looking after the kids. Papá está cuidando a los niños.
2 (*young goat*) el **cabrito** *masc*, la **cabrita** *fem*

to **kidnap** *verb*
secuestrar [17]

kidnapper *noun*
el **secuestrador** *masc*, la **secuestradora** *fem*

kidney *noun*
el **riñón** *masc*

♪ to **kill** *verb*
matar [17]
The cat killed the bird. El gato mató al pájaro.

The disease kills many people. La enfermedad mata a muchas personas.
She was killed in an accident., She got killed in an accident. Murió en un accidente.

killer *noun*
(*murderer*) el **asesino** *masc*, la **asesina** *fem*
The disease is a killer. La enfermedad es una de las que causa más muertes.

kilo *noun*
el **kilo** *masc*
a kilo of tomatoes un kilo de tomates
half a kilo of sugar medio kilo de azúcar
five euros a kilo cinco euros el kilo

kilogramme *noun*
el **kilogramo** *masc*

kilometre *noun*
el **kilómetro** *masc*

kilt *noun*
la **falda escocesa**

kind *adjective* ▷ see **kind** *noun*
amable *masc & fem*, **bueno** *masc*, **buena** *fem*
Marion was very kind to me. Marion fue muy amable conmigo.
She's very kind. Es muy buena.

kind *noun* ▷ see **kind** *adj*
el **tipo** *masc*, la **clase** *fem*
all kinds of people toda clase de gente
It's a kind of fruit. Es un tipo de fruta.
They sell souvenirs and that kind of thing. Venden recuerdos y cosas por el estilo.

kindness *noun*
la **amabilidad** *fem*

king *noun*
el **rey** *masc*
King Juan Carlos el rey Juan Carlos
the King and Queen of Spain los reyes de España
the king of hearts el rey de corazones

kingdom *noun*
el **reino** *masc*
the United Kingdom el Reino Unido

kiosk *noun*
1 (*for newspapers, snacks*) el **quiosco** *masc*
2 (*phonebox*) la **cabina** *fem*

kiss *noun* ▷ see **kiss** *verb*
el **beso** *masc*
to give somebody a kiss darle [4] un beso a alguien
She gave him a kiss., He gave her a kiss. Le dio un beso

to **kiss** *verb* ▷ see **kiss** *noun*
besar [17]
Kiss me! ¡Bésame!
We kissed each other. Nos besamos.
They kiss each other every time they meet. Se dan un beso cada vez que se encuentran.
to kiss somebody goodbye darle [4] un beso de despedida a alguien

kit *noun*
1 (*set*) a tool kit una caja de herramientas
a first-aid kit un botiquín
2 (*clothes, equipment*) el **equipo** *masc*
Where's my gym kit? ¿Dónde está mi equipo de gimnasia?
3 (*for models, furniture*) el **kit** *masc*

kitchen *noun*
la **cocina** *fem*
the kitchen table la mesa de la cocina
• **kitchen roll** el papel de cocina

kite *noun*
(*toy*) la **cometa** *fem*
to fly a kite hacer [7] volar una cometa
We fly our kites in the park. Hacemos volar las cometas en el parque.

kitten *noun*
el **gatito** *masc*, la **gatita** *fem*

kiwi fruit *noun*
el **kiwi** *masc*

knack *noun*
el **tranquillo** *masc*
I've got the knack of it now. Ya le he cogido el tranquillo.

knee *noun*
la **rodilla** *fem*
to be on your knees estar [2] de rodillas

to **kneel** *verb*
1 (*to be kneeling*) **estar** [2] **de rodillas**
2 (*to kneel down*) **arrodillarse** [17]

knickers *plural noun*
las **bragas** *plural fem*

knife *noun*
1 (*fixed blade*) el **cuchillo** *masc*
2 (*penknife*) la **navaja** *fem*

knight *noun*
(*in chess*) el **caballo** *masc*

to **knit** *verb*
1 (*a scarf, a sweater*) **tejer** [18]
2 (*as an activity*) **hacer** [7] **punto**

knitting *noun*
el **punto** *masc*

knob *noun*
1 *(on a drawer)* el **tirador** *masc*
2 *(on a door)* el **pomo** *masc*
3 *(of butter)* el **pedacito** *masc*

knock *noun* ▷ see **knock** *verb*
el **golpe** *masc*
a knock on the head un golpe en la cabeza
a knock at the door un golpe en la puerta

to **knock** *verb* ▷ see **knock** *noun*
1 **darse [4] un golpe**
I knocked my head. Me di un golpe en la cabeza.
2 *(at the door)* **to knock at the door** llamar **[17]** a la puerta
Someone's knocking at the door. Están llamando a la puerta.
• to **knock down**
1 *(a pedestrian, cyclist)* **atropellar [17]**
She was knocked down by a bus. La atropelló un autobús.
2 *(a building)* **derribar [17]**
• to **knock out**
1 *(in competitions)* **eliminar [17]**
United was knocked out in the first round. El United quedó eliminado en la primera vuelta.
2 *(unconscious)* **dejar [17] sin sentido**

knocker *noun*
la **aldaba** *fem*

knot *noun*
el **nudo** *masc*
to tie a knot in a string hacer **[7]** un nudo a la cuerda

♪ to **know** *verb*
1 *(facts, a language)* **saber [13]**
I know where she is. Sé donde está.
Do you know where their house is? ¿Sabes dónde queda su casa?
I know Spanish and French. Sé español y francés.
He knows it by heart. Se lo sabe de memoria.
Yes, I know. Sí, ya lo sé.
You never know! ¡Nunca se sabe!
2 *(a person, a song, a place)* **conocer [35]**
I know Sharon. Conozco a Sharon.
I don't know her father. No conozco a su padre.
All the people I know. Toda la gente que conozco.
Do you know that song? ¿Conoces esa canción?
Do you know Santiago? ¿Conoces Santiago?
3 **to know how to do something** saber **[13]** hacer algo
Steve knows how to make paella. Steve sabe hacer paella.
4 *(a subject, machines)* **to know all about someting** saber **[13]** de algo
Lindy knows all about computers. Lindy sabe de ordenadores.

knowledge *noun*
los **conocimientos** *plural masc*
scientific knowledge conocimientos científicos
She did it without the knowledge of her parents. Lo hizo sin que supieran sus padres.

knuckle *noun*
el **nudillo** *masc*

koala *noun*
el **koala** *masc*

Koran *noun*
(Religion) el **Corán** *masc*

kosher *adjective*
kosher *invariable adjective*

a b c d e f g h i j k l m n o p q r s t u v w x y z

L l

lab *noun*
el **laboratorio** *masc*

label *noun*
la **etiqueta** *fem*

laboratory *noun*
el **laboratorio** *masc*

Labour *noun*
los laboristas *plural masc*
to vote Labour votar [17] por los laboristas
the Labour Party el partido laborista

lace *noun*
1 (*for a shoe*) el **cordón** *masc*
to do up your laces atarse [17] los cordones
2 (*fabric*) el **encaje** *masc*

to **lack** *verb*
to lack something hacerle [7] falta algo a alguien
He lacks confidence. Le hace falta confianza.
We lack funds. Nos hace falta fondos.

lad *noun*
el **chaval** *masc* (*informal*)

ladder *noun*
1 (*for climbing*) la **escalera** *fem*
2 (*in your tights*) la **carrera** *fem*

ladies *noun* ▷ see **lady** *noun*
1 (*women's toilets*) los **servicios de señoras**
Where's the ladies? ¿Dónde están los servicios de señoras?
2 (*sign for women's toilets*) **Señoras**

♪ **lady** *noun* ▷ see **ladies** *noun*
la **señora** *fem*
ladies and gentlemen señoras y señores

lager *noun*
la **cerveza rubia**

laid-back *adjective*
relajado *masc*, **relajada** *fem*

♪ **lake** *noun*
el **lago** *masc*

♪ **lamb** *noun*
1 (*young sheep*) el **cordero** *masc*
2 (*meat*) el **cordero** *masc*
a lamb chop una chuleta de cordero

lame *adjective*
cojo *masc*, **coja** *fem*

♪ **lamp** *noun*
la **lámpara** *fem*
• **lamppost** la farola
• **lampshade** la pantalla

♪ **land** *noun* ▷ see **land** *verb*
1 (*not the sea*) la **tierra** *fem*
on dry land en tierra firme
2 (*property*) **a piece of land** un terreno
He has land. Tiene tierras.
3 (*country*) el **país** *masc*
a faraway land un país lejano

♪ to **land** *verb* ▷ see **land** *noun*
1 (*planes, passengers*) **aterrizar** [22]
2 (*to leave a ship*) **desembarcar** [31]

landing *noun*
1 (*on the stairs*) el **descansillo** *masc*
2 (*of a plane*) el **aterrizaje** *masc*
3 (*from a boat*) el **desembarco** *masc*

landlady *noun*
1 (*of a rented house*) la **casera** *fem*
2 (*of a pub*) la **dueña** *fem*

landlord *noun*
1 (*of a rented house*) el **casero** *masc*
2 (*of a pub*) el **dueño** *masc*

lane *noun*
1 (*in the country*) el **camino** *masc*
2 (*of a motorway, road*) el **carril** *masc*
a bus lane un carril de autobuses

♪ **language** *noun*
1 (*Spanish, Italian, etc*) el **idioma** *masc*
a foreign language un idioma extranjero
2 (*way of speaking*) el **lenguaje** *masc*
scientific language lenguaje científico
3 **bad language** palabrotas *plural fem*
to use bad language decir [5] palabrotas
• **language lab** el laboratorio de idiomas
• **language school** la academia de idiomas

lap *noun*
1 (*your knees*) las **rodillas** *plural fem*
He sat on his father's lap. Se sentó en las rodillas de su padre.
2 (*in a race*) la **vuelta** *fem*

laptop *noun*
el **portátil** *masc*

♪ **large** *adjective*
grande *masc & fem*
a large house una casa grande
large cities las ciudades grandes
a large number of people un gran número de gente
a large quantity of letters una gran cantidad de cartas

WORD TIP *grande* becomes *gran* when it comes before a singular noun.

laser *noun*
el **láser** *masc*
- **laser beam** el rayo láser
- **laser printer** la impresora láser

♪ **last** *adjective* ▷ see **last** *adv, verb*
1 (*final in a series*) **último** *masc*, **última** *fem*
the last time la última vez
It was the last thing I did. Fue lo último que hice.
to be the last one to do something ser [1] el último en hacer algo
I was the last one to leave. Fui el último en salir.
2 (*previous*) **last week** la semana pasada
last night anoche
my last letter mi última carta

♪ **last** *adverb* ▷ see **last** *adj, verb*
1 (*after all the others*) **Rob arrived last.** Rob llegó el último.
I came last in the race. Llegué en último lugar en la carrera.
2 (*most recently*) **I last saw him in May.** La última vez que lo vi fue en mayo.
3 (*in expressions*) **and last ...** y por último ...
At last! ¡Por fin!
You're here at last! ¡Por fin has llegado!

♪ to **last** *verb* ▷ see **last** *adj, adv*
durar [17]
The film lasted two hours. La película duró dos horas.

♪ **late** *adjective, adverb*
1 (*after the usual time: people*) **tarde**
to be late llegar [28] tarde
We're late. Llegamos tarde.
They arrived late. Llegaron tarde.
to be late for something llegar [28] tarde a algo
We were late for the film. Llegamos tarde a la película.
2 (*after the stated time: buses, trains*) **to be late** llegar con retraso
The train was an hour late. El tren llegó con una hora de retraso.
3 (*late in the day*) **tarde**
We got up late. Nos levantamos tarde.
It's getting late. Se está haciendo tarde.
late last night ayer por la noche ya tarde
Too late! ¡Demasiado tarde!

later *adverb*
más tarde
later that same day ese mismo día más tarde
no later than Thursday no más tarde del jueves
I'll explain it to you later. Te lo explicaré más tarde.
See you later! ¡Hasta luego!

latest *adjective* ▷ see **latest** *noun*
último *masc*, **última** *fem*
the latest news las últimas noticias

latest *noun* ▷ see **latest** *adj*
at the latest a más tardar
the latest in audio equipment lo último en equipo de audio

Latin *noun*
el **latín** *masc*

WORD TIP Adjectives and nouns for languages do not have capital letters in Spanish.

Latin America *noun*
América Latina *fem*

Latin American *adjective & noun*
1 **latinoamericano** *masc*, **latinoamericana** *fem*
2 un **latinoamericano** *masc*, una **latinoamericana** *fem*
the Latin Americans los latinoamericanos

WORD TIP Adjectives and nouns for nationality and regional origin do not have capital letters in Spanish.

Latvia *noun*
Letonia *fem*

Latvian *adjective & noun*
1 **letón** *masc*, **letona** *fem*
2 un **letón** *masc*, una **letona** *fem*
the Latvians los letones

WORD TIP Adjectives and nouns for nationality and regional origin do not have capital letters in Spanish.

♪ **laugh** *noun* ▷ see **laugh** *verb*
la **risa** *fem*
She gave a nervous laugh. Soltó una risa nerviosa.
to do something for a laugh hacer [7] algo por divertirse

to laugh *verb* ▷ see **laugh** *noun*
1 **reírse [61]**
Everybody laughed. Todo el mundo se rió.
2 **to laugh at someone** reírse [61] de alguien
They laughed at me. Se rieron de mí.

laughter *noun*
las **risas** *plural fem*

launch *noun* ▷ see **launch** *verb*
1 (*of a product, a spacecraft*) el **lanzamiento** *masc*
2 (*of a ship*) la **botadura** *fem*

to launch *verb* ▷ see **launch** *noun*
1 (*a product, spacecraft*) **lanzar [22]**
2 (*a ship*) **botar [17]**

launderette *noun*
la **lavandería** *fem*

laundry *noun*
la **lavandería** *fem*

lavatory *noun*
el **servicio** *masc*, el **aseo** *masc*

lavender *noun*
la **lavanda** *fem*

law *noun*
1 (*set of rules*) la **ley** *fem*
the law la ley
to pass a law aprobar [24] una ley
to break the law violar [17] la ley
It's against the law. Es ilegal.
2 (*subject of study*) el **derecho** *masc*

lawn *noun*
el **césped** *masc*
• **lawnmower** el cortacésped

lawyer *noun*
el **abogado** *masc*, la **abogada** *fem*
My mother is a lawyer. Mi madre es abogada.

to lay *verb*
1 (*to put*) **poner [11]**
She laid the money on the table. Puso el dinero en la mesa.
2 **to lay the table** poner [11] la mesa
3 (*an egg*) **poner [11]**

lay-by *noun*
el **área** *fem* **de reposo**
a lay-by un área de reposo

WORD TIP *área* takes *el* or *un* in the singular even though it is feminine.

layer *noun*
la **capa** *fem*

laziness *noun*
la **pereza** *fem*

lazy *adjective*
perezoso *masc*, **perezosa** *fem*

to lead *verb* ▷ see **lead** *adj, noun*
1 (*to a place*) **llevar [17]**
He led us to the beach. Nos llevó a la playa.
The path leads to the sea. El sendero lleva al mar.
2 (*in a match, a race, a competition*) ir [8] ganando
They are leading by three goals. Van ganando por tres goles.
3 (*to a result*) **to lead to something** llevar [17] a algo
One thing leads to another. Una cosa lleva a otra.
It led to an accident. Causó un accidente.
This will lead to problems. Esto traerá problemas.
4 (*one's life*) **llevar [17]**
I lead a quiet life. Llevo una vida tranquila.

lead *adjective* ▷ see **lead** *verb, noun*
(*role, singer*) **principal**

lead *noun* ▷ see **lead** *adj, verb*
1 (*in races, competitions*) **to be in the lead** llevar [17] la delantera
Sam's in the lead. Sam lleva la delantera.
We have a lead of three points. Llevamos una ventaja de tres puntos.
2 (*for electricity*) el **cable** *masc*
3 (*for a dog*) la **correa** *fem*
Put the dog on a lead. Ponle una correa al perro.
4 (*the metal*) el **plomo** *masc*
5 (*for a pencil*) la **mina** *fem*

leader *noun*
1 (*of a gang*) el & la **cabecilla** *masc & fem*
2 (*of a political party*) el & la **líder** *masc & fem*
3 (*in a competition*) el **primero** *masc*, la **primera** *fem*

lead-free petrol *noun*
la **gasolina sin plomo**

lead singer *noun*
el & la **cantante principal**

leaf *noun*
la **hoja** *fem*

leaflet *noun*
el **folleto** *masc*

league *noun*
(*in sport*) la **liga** *fem*

lean *adjective* ▷ see **lean** *verb*
(*meat*) **magro** *masc*, **magra** *fem*

to **lean** *verb* ▷ see **lean** *adj*
1 (*to bend*) **echarse** [17]
Lean forward a bit. Échate para delante un poco.
She leaned out of the window. Se asomó por la ventana.
2 (*to support yourself*) **to lean on something** apoyarse [17] en algo
3 (*to prop*) **to lean something on something** apoyar [17] algo en algo
Lean the ladder against the tree. Apoya la escalera en el árbol.

leap year *noun*
el **año bisiesto**

to **learn** *verb*
aprender [18]
to learn Russian aprender ruso
to learn to drive aprender a conducir

learner driver *noun*
She's a learner driver. Está aprendiendo a conducir.

least *adverb, adjective, pronoun*
1 (*in superlatives*) **menos**
the least expensive hotel el hotel menos caro
the least expensive glasses las gafas menos caras
Tony has the least money. Tony es el que menos dinero tiene.
I like the blue shirt least. La camisa azul es la que menos me gusta.
It's the least I can do. Es lo menos que puedo hacer.
2 (*slightest*) **más mínimo** *masc*, **más mínima** *fem*
I haven't the least idea. No tengo ni la más mínima idea.
He didn't show the least interest. No mostró el más mínimo interés.
3 (*at a minimum*) **at least** por lo menos
There must be at least twenty people. Debe haber por lo menos veinte personas.
4 (*at any rate*) **at least** al menos
At least, that's what I think. Al menos eso creo.

leather *noun*
el **cuero** *masc*
a leather jacket una chaqueta de cuero

to **leave** *verb*
1 (*to go away*) **irse** [8]
They're leaving tomorrow. Se van mañana.
We left at six. Nos fuimos a las seis.
2 (*work, a building, etc*) **salir** [63] **de**
I leave school at four. Salgo del colegio a las cuatro.
She left the cinema at ten. Salió del cine a las diez.
3 (*in a place*) **dejar** [17]
He left his wife at the airport. Dejó a su mujer en el aeropuerto.
You can leave your coats in the hall. Podéis dejar los abrigos en la entrada.
4 (*to abandon*) **dejar** [17] **a**
He left his wife. Dejó a su mujer.
5 (*to forget*) **dejarse** [17]
He left his umbrella on the train. Se dejó el paraguas en el tren.
6 **to leave school** dejar [17] los estudios
Guy left school at sixteen. Guy dejó los estudios a los dieciséis años.
7 **to be left** quedar [17]
There are two cakes left. Quedan dos pasteles.
We have ten minutes left. Nos quedan diez minutos.
I've got no money left. No me queda dinero.
• **to leave out**
1 (*to omit*) **omitir** [19]
I left out the most important part. Omití lo más importante.
2 (*to exclude*) **excluir** [54]
She feels left out. Se siente excluida.

lecture *noun*
1 (*at university*) la **clase** *fem*
2 (*public*) la **conferencia** *fem*

lecturer *noun*
el **profesor** *masc*, la **profesora** *fem*

ledge *noun*
1 (*of a window*) la **repisa** *fem*
2 (*on a cliff*) el **saliente** *masc*

leek *noun*
el **puerro** *masc*

left *adjective* ▷ see **left** *adv, noun*
izquierdo *masc*, **izquierda** *fem*
his left foot el pie izquierdo
on the left hand side a mano izquierda

left *adverb* ▷ see **left** *adj, noun*
(*to turn, look*) **a la izquierda**
Turn left at the church. Gira a la izquierda en la iglesia.

left *noun* ▷ see **left** *adj, adv*
1 (*direction*) la **izquierda** *fem*
the second street on the left la segunda calle a la izquierda
on my left a mi izquierda
It's on the left. Está a la izquierda.
to drive on the left conducir [60] por la izquierda
2 (*in politics*) **the left** la izquierda

left-click *noun* ▷ see **left-click** *verb*
el **clic con el botón izquierdo**

to **left-click** *verb* ▷ see **left-click** *noun*
hacer [7] clic con el botón izquierdo
Left-click the icon. Haz clic en el icono con el botón izquierdo.

left-hand *noun*
the left-hand side la parte izquierda

left-handed *adjective*
zurdo *masc*, **zurda** *fem*

⚷ **left-luggage locker** *noun*
la **consigna automática**

⚷ **left-luggage office** *noun*
la **consigna** *fem*

leftovers *plural noun*
las **sobras** *plural fem*

⚷ **leg** *noun*
1 (*person's*) la **pierna** *fem*
my left leg mi pierna izquierda
to break your leg romperse **[40]** una pierna
to pull somebody's leg tomarle **[17]** el pelo a alguien
They're pulling your leg. Te están tomando el pelo.
2 (*of a table, chair, animal*) la **pata** *fem*
3 (*in cooking*) **a leg of chicken** un muslo de pollo
a leg of lamb una pierna de cordero

legal *adjective*
legal *masc & fem*

legend *noun*
la **leyenda** *fem*

leggings *plural noun*
los **leggings** *plural masc*

⚷ **leisure** *noun*
el **tiempo libre**
in my leisure time en mi tiempo libre
• **leisure centre** el polideportivo

⚷ **lemon** *noun*
el **limón** *masc*
a lemon yoghurt un yogur de limón

⚷ **lemonade** *noun*
1 (*made with real lemons*) la **limonada** *fem*
2 (*fizzy drink*) la **gaseosa** *fem*

lemon juice *noun*
el **zumo de limón**

⚷ to **lend** *verb*
dejar [17]
to lend something to somebody dejarle algo a alguien
I lent Judy my bike. Le dejé mi bici a Judy.
Will you lend it to me? ¿Me lo dejas?

length *noun*
1 (*of fabric, board, etc*) el **largo** *masc*
2 (*of a film, play*) la **duración** *fem*
3 (*of a book, list*) la **extensión** *fem*

⚷ **lens** *noun*
1 (*in a camera*) la **lente** *fem*
2 (*in glasses*) el **cristal** *masc*
3 (*contact lens*) la **lentilla** *fem*

Lent *noun*
la **Cuaresma** *fem*

lentil *noun*
la **lenteja** *fem*

Leo *noun*
1 (*the star sign*) el **Leo** *masc*
2 (*a person*) **un & una leo** *masc & fem*
Mary's Leo. Mary es leo.

WORD TIP Use a small letter in Spanish to say *I am ...* etc with star signs. Star signs in Spanish are used without *el, un, la, una.*

leotard *noun*
la **malla** *fem*

lesbian *noun*
la **lesbiana** *fem*

⚷ **less** *pronoun, adjective, adverb*
1 (*not so much*) **menos**
Richard eats less. Richard come menos.
less time menos tiempo
It's less interesting. Es menos interesante.
less quickly than us menos rápido que nosotros
2 (*with amounts, numbers*) **less than** menos de
less than a kilo menos de un kilo
less than three hours menos de tres horas
3 (*in comparisons*) **less than** menos que
You spend less than me. Gastas menos que yo.

lesson *noun*
la **clase** *fem*
the history lesson la clase de historia
a driving lesson una clase de conducir
to take tennis lessons tomar **[17]** clases de tenis

to **let** *verb*
1 (*to allow*) **dejar [17]**
Let her speak. Déjala hablar.
Will you let me go alone? ¿Me dejas ir sola?
The police let us through. La policía nos dejó pasar.
She lets me use her bike. Me deja usar su bici.
Let me help you. Déjame que te ayude. ▸▸

English–Spanish
a b c d e f g h i j k l m n o p q r s t u v w x y z

2 **to let go of something** soltar **[24]** algo
Let go of my hand. Suéltame la mano.
Let go of me! ¡Suéltame!
3 (*in suggestions, orders*) **Let's go!** ¡Vámonos!
Let's not talk about it. No hablemos de ello.
Let's see if Tuesday is ok. Vamos a ver si el martes conviene.
Let's eat out. Vamos a comer fuera.
4 (*to rent out*) **alquilar [17]**
'Flat to let' 'Se alquila apartamento'
• **to let in**
(*to allow to enter*) **dejar [17] entrar**
Don't let the cat in! ¡No dejes entrar al gato!
• **to let off**
1 (*fireworks*) **tirar [17]**
2 (*a bomb*) **hacer [7] estallar**
3 (*to excuse from*) **perdonar [17]**
She let me off returning the money. Me perdonó que devolviera el dinero.
• **to let out**
(*to allow to leave*) **dejar [17] salir**
Let me out of here! ¡Déjame salir de aquí!

lethal *adjective*
mortal *masc & fem*

letter *noun*
1 (*written message*) la **carta** *fem*
a letter for you from Delia una carta de Delia para ti
2 (*of the alphabet*) la **letra** *fem*
M is the letter after L. M es la letra que viene depués de L.
• **letterbox** el buzón

lettuce *noun*
la **lechuga** *fem*

leukaemia *noun*
la **leucemia** *fem*

level *adjective* ▷ see **level** *noun*
1 (*street, floor*) **plano** *masc*, **plana** *fem*
2 (*ground*) **llano** *masc*, **llana** *fem*

level *noun* ▷ see **level** *adj*
el **nivel** *masc*
at street level a nivel de la calle
• **level crossing** el paso a nivel

lever *noun*
la **palanca** *fem*

liar *noun*
el **mentiroso** *masc*, la **mentirosa** *fem*

liberal *adjective*
liberal *masc & fem*
the Liberal Democrats los demócratas liberales

liberty *noun*
la **libertad** *fem*

Libra *noun*
1 (*the star sign*) el **Libra** *masc*
2 (*a person*) **un & una libra** *masc & fem*
John's Libra. John es libra.

WORD TIP Use a small letter in Spanish to say *I am* ... etc with star signs. Star signs in Spanish are used without *el, un, la, una*.

librarian *noun*
el **bibliotecario** *masc*, la **bibliotecaria** *fem*
Mark's a librarian. Mark es bibliotecario.

library *noun*
la **biblioteca** *fem*
a public library una biblioteca pública

licence *noun*
1 (*for driving, fishing*) el **permiso** *masc*
a driving licence un permiso de conducir
2 (*for a TV*) la **licencia** *fem*

to **lick** *verb*
lamer [18]

lid *noun*
la **tapa** *fem*
She took the lid off. Quitó la tapa.

lie *noun* ▷ see **lie** *verb*
la **mentira** *fem*
to tell lies decir **[5]** mentiras

to **lie** *verb* ▷ see **lie** *noun*
1 (*to be stretched out*) **estar [2] tumbado** (*boy*), **estar [2] tumbada** (*girl*)
Jimmy was lying on the bed. Jimmy estaba tumbado en la cama.
2 (*for a little while*) **to lie down** tumbarse **[17]**
Come and lie down in the sun. Ven a echarte al sol
3 (*object*) **estar [2]**
Her coat lay on the bed. Su abrigo estaba sobre la cama.
4 (*not to tell the truth*) **mentir [14]**
He's lying. Está mintiendo.

lieutenant *noun*
el & la **teniente** *masc & fem*

life *noun*
la **vida** *fem*
all my life toda mi vida
She's full of life Está llena de vida.
That's life! ¡Así es la vida!

lifebelt *noun*
el **salvavidas** *masc, pl:* los **salvavidas**

lifeboat *noun*
el **bote salvavidas**

lifeguard *noun*
el & la **socorrista** *masc & fem*

life jacket *noun*
el **chaleco salvavidas**

lifestyle *noun*
el **estilo de vida**

to lift *verb* ▷ see **lift** *noun*
levantar [17]

lift *noun* ▷ see **lift** *verb*
1 (*in a building*) el **ascensor** *masc*
Let's take the lift. Vamos a coger el ascensor.
2 (*a ride*) **to give somebody a lift somewhere** llevar **[17]** a alguien a un lugar
Tom gave me a lift to the station. Tom me llevó a la estación.
Can you give me a lift? ¿Me puedes llevar?

to light *verb* ▷ see **light** *adj, noun*
1 **encender [36]**
We lit a fire. Encendimos un fuego.

light *adjective* ▷ see **light** *verb, noun*
1 (*not heavy*) **ligero** *masc*, **ligera** *fem*
a light meal una comida ligera
light clothes ropa ligera
2 (*not dark*) **a light room** una habitación con mucha luz
It gets light at six. Se hace de día a las seis.
3 (*in colours*) **claro** *masc*, **clara** *fem*
light green verde claro
He has light blue eyes. Tiene ojos azul claro.

light *noun* ▷ see **light** *verb, adj*
1 (*as opposed to darkness*) la **luz** *fem*
a ray of light un rayo de luz
Bring it into the light. Tráelo a la luz.
2 (*electric*) la **luz** *fem, fem pl:* las **luces**
to turn the light on encender **[36]** la luz
to turn off the light apagar **[28]** la luz
Are your lights on? ¿Tienes las luces encendidas?
3 (*streetlight*) la **farola** *fem*
4 (*for traffic*) **the lights** el semáforo
The lights were green. El semáforo estaba en verde.
5 (*for a cigarette*) **Have you got a light?** ¿Tienes fuego?
• **light bulb** la bombilla

lighter *noun*
el **encendedor** *masc*

lightning *noun*
el **relámpago** *masc*
a flash of lightning un relámpago
The tree was struck by lightning. Cayó un rayo en el árbol.

light switch *noun*
el **interruptor de la luz**

like *preposition, conjunction*
1 (*similar to*) **como**
like this como esto
someone like me alguien como yo
sports like badminton deportes como el badminton
He talks like an old man. Habla como un viejo.
I want a hat like this one. Quiero un sombrero como este.
What's it like? ¿Cómo es?
What was the weather like? ¿Qué tiempo hizo?
2 **to look like someone** parecerse **[35]** a alguien
Cindy looks like her father. Cindy se parece a su padre.
3 (*to indicate how something should be done*) **like this** así
You do it like this. Se hace así.
like that así
Don't talk to me like that! ¡No me hables así!
4 (*as*) **como**
like I said como dije (yo)
5 (*as if*) **It sounds like they've already arrived.** Por lo que se ve, parece que ya han llegado.

to like *verb*
1 (*see Word Tip*) **I like fish.** Me gusta el pescado (***pescado** is singular, so **gusta***).
I like it. Me gusta.
I don't like spicy food. No me gusta la comida picante.
Did you like the film? ¿Te gustó la película?
She likes my brother. Le gusta mi hermano.
I like dogs. Me gustan los perros (***perros** is plural, so **gustan***).
I don't like cats. No me gustan los gatos.
She likes bike riding. Le gusta montar a bici (***montar** is an infinitive, so **gusta***).
Dad likes going fishing. A papá le gusta ir a pescar (*Use **a** when a person is mentioned.*).
2 (*to say which you like most or least*)
I like pistachio best. El que más me gusta es el pistacho.
I like vanilla least. La que menos me gusta es la vainilla.
I like those the best. Los que más me gustan son aquellos.
3 (*to ask or say what you, or someone else, wants*)
I'd like to buy it. Quiero comprarlo.
Would you like a coffee? ¿Quieres un café?
What would you like to eat? ¿Qué quieres comer?
Would you like to go to the beach? ¿Quieres ir a la playa? ▸▸

I would like to use the phone. Quisiera hacer una llamada.

4 *(to say what you wish you could do)*
Me gustaría ser astronauta. I'd like to be an astronaut.
Le gustaría ir a la India. She'd like to go to India.

WORD TIP Use *gusta, gustó, gustaba, gustaría, etc* if what you like, or don't like, is singular or an infinitive in Spanish. Use *gustan, gustaron, gustaban, gustarían, etc* if what you like, or don't like, is plural.

likely *adjective*
probable *masc & fem*
It's not very likely. No es muy probable.
She's likely to phone. Es probable que llame.

WORD TIP *ser probable que* is followed by the subjunctive.

lime *noun*
(the fruit) la **lima** *fem*

limit *noun*
el **límite** *masc*
the speed limit el límite de velocidad

line *noun*
1 *(on paper)* la **línea** *fem*
a straight line una línea recta
to draw a line trazar [22] una línea
2 *(queue)* la **cola** *fem*
to stand in line hacer [7] cola
The children were standing in line. Los niños hacían cola.
3 *(for a phone)* la **línea** *fem*
The line's bad. No se oye bien.
Hold the line, please. No cuelgue, por favor. *(formal use)*

linen *noun*
el **lino** *masc*

to **link** *verb* ▷ see **link** *noun*
(two places) **conectar** [17]
The terminals are linked by a shuttle service. Las terminales están conectadas por un servicio de enlace.

link *noun* ▷ see **link** *verb*
la **conexión** *fem*
What's the link between the two? ¿Qué conexión hay entre los dos?

lion *noun*
el **león** *masc*

lip *noun*
el **labio** *masc*
- **lip-read** leer [37] los labios
- **lipstick** el lápiz de labios

liquid *adjective* ▷ see **liquid** *noun*
líquido *masc*, **líquida** *fem*

liquid *noun* ▷ see **liquid** *adj*
el **líquido** *masc*

liquidizer *noun*
la **licuadora** *fem*

list *noun*
la **lista** *fem*

to **listen** *verb*
escuchar [17]
I wasn't listening. No estaba escuchando.
to listen to something escuchar [17] algo
Listen to the music. Escucha la música.
You're not listening to me. No me estás escuchando.

literature *noun*
la **literatura** *fem*

Lithuania *noun*
Lituania *fem*

Lithuanian *adjective & noun*
1 **lituano** *masc*, **lituana** *fem*
2 un **lituano** *masc*, una **lituana** *fem*
the Lithuanians los lituanos

WORD TIP Adjectives and nouns for nationality, regional origin, and language do not have capital letters in Spanish.

litre *noun*
el **litro** *masc*
a litre of milk un litro de leche

litter *noun*
(rubbish) la **basura** *fem*
- **litter bin** papelera *fem*

little *adjective, pronoun*
1 *(small)* **pequeño** *masc*, **pequeña** *fem*
a little boy un niño pequeño
a little break una pequeña pausa
2 *(not much)* **poco** *masc*, **poca** *fem*
We have very little time. Tenemos muy poco tiempo.
3 **a little** un poco
We have a little money. Tenemos un poco de dinero.
Just a little, please. Sólo un poco, por favor.
It's a little late. Es un poco tarde.
a little more un poco más
a little less un poco menos
4 **little by little** poco a poco

to **live** *verb* ▷ see **live** *adj*
1 *(to be alive)* **vivir** [19]
(for) as long as I live mientras viva
2 *(to reside)* **vivir** [19]
Susan lives in York. Susan vive en York.
They live at number 57. Viven en el número cincuenta y siete.
They live together. Viven juntos.

♪ **live** *adjective* ▷ see **live** *verb*
1 *(broadcast)* **en directo** *masc & fem*
a live concert un concierto en directo
2 *(alive)* **vivo** *masc*, **viva** *fem*

liver *noun*
el **hígado** *masc*

♪ **living** *noun*
to earn a living ganarse [17] la vida
• **living room** el salón

to **load** *verb* ▷ see **load** *noun*
cargar [28]
He loaded the crates onto the van. Cargó las cajas en la camioneta.
to load a program (into a computer) cargar [28] un programa (en un ordenador)

load *noun* ▷ see **load** *verb*
1 *(on a lorry)* el **cargamento** *masc*
2 **a bus-load of tourists** un autobús lleno de turistas
3 *(informal: lots of)* **loads of** un montón de
loads of people un montón de gente
They've got loads of money. Tienen un montón de dinero.

loaf *noun*
a loaf of bread un pan
a loaf of wholemeal bread un pan integral

to **loan** *verb* ▷ see **loan** *noun*
prestar [17]

loan *noun* ▷ see **loan** *verb*
el **préstamo** *masc*

♪ **lobby** *noun*
el **vestíbulo** *masc*

lobster *noun*
la **langosta** *fem*

local *adjective*
the local library la biblioteca del barrio
the local newspaper el periódico local

local *noun*
1 *(pub)* **our local** el bar de nuestro barrio
2 *(people)* **the locals** la gente del lugar

locally *adverb*
en la zona

to **lock** *verb* ▷ see **lock** *noun*
to lock the door cerrar [29] la puerta con llave
The door was locked. La puerta estaba cerrada con llave.

lock *noun* ▷ see **lock** *verb*
1 *(with a key)* la **cerradura** *fem*
2 *(on a canal)* la **esclusa** *fem*

locker *noun*
el **armario** *masc*
• **locker room** el vestuario

lodger *noun*
el **inquilino** *masc*, la **inquilina** *fem*

loft *noun*
el **desván** *masc*

log *noun* ▷ see **log** *verb*
1 *(of tree)* el **tronco** *masc*
2 *(record)* el **diario** *masc*

to **log** *verb* ▷ see **log** *noun*
registrar [17]
• **to log on entrar** [17] **al sistema**
• **to log out salir** [63] **del sistema**

logical *adjective*
lógico *masc*, **lógica** *fem*

lollipop *noun*
la **piruleta** *fem*

London *noun*
Londres *masc*
We went to London. Fuimos a Londres.
the London streets las calles de Londres

Londoner *noun*
el & la **londinense** *masc & fem*

WORD TIP Adjectives and nouns for regional origin do not have capital letters in Spanish.

loneliness *noun*
la **soledad** *fem*

♪ **lonely** *adjective*
solitario *masc*, **solitaria** *fem*
She has a lonely life. Tiene una vida solitaria.
to feel lonely sentirse [14] solo (*a boy*), sentirse [14] sola (*a girl*)

♪ **long** *adjective, adverb* ▷ see **long** *verb*
1 *(to talk about distance, extent)* **largo** *masc*, **larga** *fem*
a long journey un viaje largo
a very long book un libro muy largo
She's got long hair. Tiene el pelo largo.
It's five metres long. Mide cinco metros de largo.
How long is the corridor? ¿Cuánto mide el pasillo de largo?
a long way muy lejos
We're a long way from the cinema. Estamos muy lejos del cine.
2 *(to talk about time)* **largo** *masc*, **larga** *fem*
a long film una película larga ▸▸

a long illness una enfermedad larga
It's been a long day. Ha sido un día muy largo.
How long is the film? ¿Cuánto dura la película?
It's an hour long. Dura una hora.
a long time mucho tiempo
a long time ago hace mucho tiempo
I've been here for a long time. He pasado mucho tiempo aquí.
He stayed for a long time. Se quedó mucho tiempo.
not long afterwards no mucho después
Have you been waiting long? ¿Llevas mucho rato esperando?
This won't take long. Esto no llevará mucho tiempo.
I won't be long. No tardo mucho.

3 (*to talk about how long it takes to do something*) **how long?** ¿cuánto tiempo?
How long have you been here? ¿Cuánto tiempo llevas aquí?
How long did it take you to get there? ¿Cuánto tardaste en llegar?

4 (*for the period of time*) **as long as** mientras
as long as she was alive mientras vivió ella
I'll remember it as long as I live. Lo recordaré mientras viva.

5 (*on condition that*) **as long as** siempre que
You can go as long as you're back by 12 Puedes ir siempre que vuelvas antes de las 12.

WORD TIP *siempre que* is followed by a verb in the subjunctive.

to **long** *verb* ▷ see **long** *adj, adv*
to long to do something tener **[9]** muchas ganas de hacer algo
I'm longing to see you. Tengo muchas ganas de verte.

longer *adverb*
no longer ya no
He doesn't work here any longer. Ya no trabaja aquí.
I no longer know. Ya no lo sé.
They no longer live here. Ya no viven aquí.

long jump *noun*
el **salto de longitud**

long-life milk *noun*
la **leche uperizada**

loo *noun*
el **váter** *masc* (*informal*)

♪ to **look** *verb* ▷ see **look** *noun*

1 (*to see, glance*) **mirar [17]**
I wasn't looking. No estaba mirando.
Look! A squirrel! ¡Mira! ¡Una ardilla!
He looked away. Miró hacia un lado.
He walked away without looking back. Se alejó sin mirar atrás.
She looked down the street. Miró calle abajo.
I looked out of the window. Miré por la ventana
Look where you're going! ¡Mira por dónde vas!
He looked me straight in the eye. Me miró a los ojos.

2 (*to search*) **mirar [17]**
Look under the bed. Mira debajo de la cama.

3 (*to seem*) **parecer [35]**
Melanie looked pleased. Melanie parecía contenta.
You look well. Tienes buen aspecto.
He looks ill. Tiene mal aspecto.
The salad looks delicious. La ensalada tiene un aspecto delicioso.

4 **to look like someone** parecerse **[35]** a alguien
Sally looks like her aunt. Sally se parece a su tía.
They look like each other. Se parecen.
It looks like rain. Parece que va a llover.
What does the house look like? ¿Cómo es la casa?

• **to look after cuidar [17]**
Dad's looking after the baby. Papá está cuidando al niño.
I'll look after your luggage. Yo te cuido el equipaje.

• **to look at mirar [17]**
Andy was looking at the photos. Andy estaba mirando las fotos.

• **to look for buscar [31]**
I'm looking for the keys. Estoy buscando las llaves.
I've been looking for you everywhere. Te he estado buscando por todas partes

• **to look forward to something: I'm looking forward to the holidays.** Estoy deseando que lleguen las vacaciones.
She's looking forward to the trip. Está deseando ir de viaje.

• **to look out** (*to be careful*) **tener [9] cuidado**
Look out, it's hot! ¡Cuidado, quema!

• **to look something up buscar [17] algo**
You can look it up in the dictionary. Puedes buscarlo en el diccionario.

♪ **look** *noun* ▷ see **look** *verb*

1 (*glance*) la **mirada** *fem*
to have a look at something mirar **[17]** algo

to have a look round the town visitar [17] la ciudad
to have a look round the shops ver [16] tiendas
2 (*search*) **to have a look for something** buscar [31] algo

loose *adjective*
1 (*screw, knot*) **flojo** *masc*, **floja** *fem*
2 (*garment*) **amplio** *masc*, **amplia** *fem*
• **loose change** el cambio

lorry *noun*
el **camión** *masc*
• **lorry driver** el camionero, la camionera

to **lose** *verb*
perder [36]
We lost. Perdimos.
We lost the match. Perdimos el partido.
Sam's lost his watch. Sam ha perdido su reloj.

loss *noun*
la **pérdida** *fem*

lost *adjective*
perdido *masc*, **perdida** *fem*
I'm lost. Estoy perdido (*boy speaking*)., Estoy perdida (*girl speaking*).
Are you lost? ¿Te has perdido? (*informal use*), ¿Se ha perdido? (*formal use*)
to get lost perderse [36]
We got lost in the woods. Nos perdimos en el bosque.
• **lost property** los objetos perdidos
• **lost property office** la oficina de objetos perdidos

lot *noun*
1 **a lot** mucho
Jason eats a lot. Jason come mucho.
I spent a lot. Gasté mucho.
I've got a lot to do. Tengo mucho que hacer.
I like her a lot. Me gusta mucho.
Your house is a lot bigger than ours. Tu casa es mucho más grande que la nuestra.
'What are you doing tonight?'— 'Not a lot.' '¿Qué haces esta noche?'— 'No mucho.'
2 **a lot of** mucho *masc*, mucha *fem*
a lot of coffee mucho café
a lot of people mucha gente
a lot of books muchos libros
What a lot of books you've got! ¡Cuántos libros tienes!
3 **lots** mucho *masc*, mucha *fem*
I've got lots to do. Tengo mucho que hacer
'How many seats are there left?'— 'Lots.' '¿Cuántos asientos quedan?'— 'Muchos.'
4 **the lot** todos *plural masc*, todas *plural fem*
'How many did she eat?'— 'The lot.' '¿Cuántos comió?'— 'Todos.'
I bought him some chips and he ate the lot. Le compré unas patatas fritas y se las comió todas.

lottery *noun*
la **lotería** *fem*
to win the lottery tocarle [31] la lotería a alguien
She won the lottery. Le tocó la lotería.

mini-info **lotteries**
The Spanish *Lotería Nacional* is one of the biggest in the world. Each year at Christmas *El Gordo* (The Fat One) is drawn. This marks the start of the Christmas celebrations.

loud *adverb* ▷ see **loud** *adj*
(*when speaking*) **alto**
to say something out loud decir [5] algo en voz alta

loud *adjective* ▷ see **loud** *adv*
(*noise, scream, applause*) **fuerte** *masc & fem*
a loud banging unos golpes fuertes
a loud shout un grito fuerte
The radio is very loud. La radio está muy fuerte.
to speak in a loud voice hablar [17] en voz alta
• **loudspeaker** el altavoz *masc*, *pl*: los altavoces

lounge *noun*
(*in a house, hotel*) el **salón** *masc*

to **love** *verb* ▷ see **love** *noun*
1 (*a person*) **querer** [12]
I love you. Te quiero.
They love each other. Se quieren.
2 (*a thing, a place, an activity*) **She loves London.** Le encanta Londres.
I'd love to come. Me encantaría venir.
I love dancing. Me encanta bailar.
Wayne loves burgers. A Wayne le encantan las hamburguesas.

WORD TIP The subject of *encantar* is what you love, so if what you love is singular, use *encanta* etc, if it is plural, use *encantan* etc.

love *noun* ▷ see **love** *verb*
1 (*in general*) el **amor** *masc*
his love for his country su amor a su patria
her love of animals su amor a los animales
to be in love with somebody estar [2] enamorado, enamorada de alguien
She's in love with Jake. Está enamorada de Jake.
He's in love with Kylie. Está enamorado de Kylie. ▸▸

English–Spanish

2 (*in messages, letters*) **Gina sends her love.** Gina manda recuerdos.
With love from Charlie con cariño de Charlie
Lots of love, Ann. Con mucho cariño, Ann
3 (*in tennis, etc*) **nada** *fem*
15-love 15-nada

lovely *adjective*
1 (*beautiful to look at*) **precioso** *masc*, **preciosa** *fem*
a lovely house una casa preciosa
2 **It's a lovely day.** Hace un día muy bueno.
We had lovely weather. Tuvimos un tiempo muy bueno.
3 (*enjoyable*) **I had a lovely time at their house.** Lo pasé muy bien en su casa.
It's lovely to see you! ¡Qué alegría verte!
4 (*food, meal*) **riquísimo** *masc*, **riquísima** *fem*

lover *noun*
1 (*romantic partner*) **el & la amante** *masc & fem*
2 (*fan*) **a music lover** un amante de la música (*boy*), una amante de la música (*girl*)

low *adjective*
bajo *masc*, **baja** *fem*
a low table una mesa baja
at a low price a un precio bajo
in a low voice en voz baja

lower *adjective*
(*lip, jaw, status*) **inferior** *masc & fem*

loyal *adjective*
leal *masc & fem*

loyalty *noun*
la **lealtad** *fem*
• **loyalty card** la tarjeta de fidelidad

luck *noun*
la **suerte** *fem*
Good luck! ¡Buena suerte!, ¡Suerte!
Bad luck! ¡Qué mala suerte!
with a bit of luck con un poco de suerte

> ***luck***
>
> Black cats and Tuesday the 13th bring bad luck in Spain and Latin America.

luckily *adverb*
afortunadamente
luckily for them afortunadamente para ellos

lucky *adjective*
1 (*to have good luck*) **to be lucky** tener [9] suerte
We were lucky. Tuvimos suerte.
2 (*to bring good luck*) **to be lucky** traer [42] suerte
It's supposed to be lucky. Se supone que trae suerte.
• **lucky number** el número de la suerte

luggage *noun*
el **equipaje** *masc*

lump *noun*
1 (*on the body*) el **bulto** *masc*
2 (*of sugar*) el **terrón** *masc*
3 (*of cheese*) **trozo** *masc*

lung *noun*
el **pulmón** *masc*

Luxembourg *noun*
Luxemburgo *masc*

luxurious *adjective*
lujoso *masc*, **lujosa** *fem*

luxury *noun*
el **lujo** *masc*
a luxury hotel un hotel de lujo

lyrics *plural noun*
la **letra** *fem*

a b c d e f g h i j k l m n o p q r s t u v w x y z

M m

mac *noun*
el **impermeable** *masc*

macaroni *noun*
los **macarrones** *plural masc*

machine *noun*
la **máquina** *fem*

machinery *noun*
la **maquinaria** *fem*

ᶘ **mad** *adjective*
1 (*crazy*) **loco** *masc*, **loca** *fem*
She's completely mad! ¡Está completamente loca!
2 (*angry*) **enfadado** *masc*, **enfadada** *fem*
to be mad with somebody estar [2] enfadado con alguien
My mum will be mad! ¡Mamá se pondrá hecha una furia! (*informal*)
3 (*enthusiastic*) **She's mad about horses.** Le encantan los caballos.
to be mad about somebody estar [2] loco por alguien

ᶘ **madam** *noun*
la **señora** *fem*
Yes, madam. Sí, señora.

madness *noun*
la **locura** *fem*

ᶘ **magazine** *noun*
la **revista** *fem*
a music magazine una revista de música

> **mini-info** ***magazine***
> *Hola* magazine was started in 1944 by the Sánchez Junco family. They launched *Hello*, the English edition, in 1988.

maggot *noun*
el **gusano** *masc*

magic *adjective* ▷ see **magic** *noun*
1 (*casting spells*) **mágico** *masc*, **mágica** *fem*
a magic wand una varita mágica
2 (*great*) **fantástico** *masc*, **fantástica** *fem*

magic *noun* ▷ see **magic** *adj*
la **magia** *fem*

magician *noun*
el **mago** *masc*, la **maga** *fem*

magnet *noun*
el **imán** *masc*

magnifying glass *noun*
la **lupa** *fem*

maid *noun*
la **criada** *fem*

maiden name *noun*
el **apellido de soltera**

ᶘ **mail** *noun*
el **correo** *masc*
to send something by mail mandar [17] algo por correo
I put it in the mail. Lo eché al correo.

mail order *noun*
la **venta por correo**
a mail order catalogue un catálogo de venta por correo
to buy something by mail order comprar [17] algo por correo

ᶘ **main** *adjective*
principal *masc & fem*
the main entrance la entrada principal
• **main course** el plato principal, el plato fuerte

mainly *adverb*
principalmente

main road *noun*
la **carretera principal**

majesty *noun*
1 (*of a view, etc*) la **majestuosidad** *fem*
2 (*king, queen*) la **majestad** *fem*
su majestad your majesty

major *adjective* ▷ see **major** *noun*
muy importante *masc & fem*
a major problem un problema muy importante

major *noun* ▷ see **major** *adj*
el & la **comandante** *masc & fem*

Majorca *noun*
Mallorca *fem*

majority *noun*
la **mayoría** *fem*

ᶘ **make** *noun* ▷ see **make** *verb*
la **marca** *fem*
What make is your bike? ¿De qué marca es tu bici?

♪ to **make** *verb* ▷ see **make** *noun*

1 (*a sandwich, dress, noise*) **hacer [7]**
I made an omelette. Hice una tortilla.
to make a meal preparar **[17]** una comida
She made her bed. Hizo su cama.
Don't make a noise. No hagas ruido.

2 (*to manufacture*) **fabricar [31]**
They make computers. Fabrican ordenadores.
'Made in Spain' 'Fabricado en España'
It's made of plastic. Es de plástico.

3 (*money*) **ganar [17]**
He makes eighty pounds a day. Gana ochenta libras al día.

4 (*payments, changes, phone calls*) **hacer [7]**
They have made a lot of changes. Han hecho muchos cambios.
I have to make a phone call. Tengo que hacer una llamada de teléfono.

5 (*a comment, joke*) **hacer [7]**
May I make a suggestion? ¿Puedo hacer una sugerencia?

6 (*sad, happy, hungry, rich, etc*) **to make somebody sad** poner **[11]** triste a alguien
It made me sad. Me puso triste.
They make me very happy. Me hacen muy feliz.
I'll make you rich. Te haré rico.
It made him really annoyed. Le dio mucha rabia.
It makes me so angry. Me da tanta rabia.
That makes me hungry. Eso me da hambre.
It made me sleepy. Me dio sueño.

7 (*to force*) **to make somebody do something** obligar **[28]** a alguien a hacer algo
She made him give the money back. Le obligó a devolver el dinero.
You can't make me go. No puedes obligarme a ir.

8 (*to cause*) **to make somebody do something** hacer **[7]** a alguien hacer algo
He made me wait. Me hizo esperar.
She makes me laugh. Me hace reír.
Look what you've made me do! ¡Mira lo que me has hecho hacer!

9 (*to add up to*) **sumar [17]**
Two and three make five. Dos y tres suman cinco.

10 (*to turn up*) **I can't make it tonight.** No puedo venir esta noche.

11 (*to cope*) **to make do** arreglárselas **[17]**
to make do with something arreglárselas con algo
We'll have to make do with that. Tendremos que arreglárnoslas con eso.

• **to make up**

1 (*to invent*) **inventarse [17]**
She made up an excuse. Se inventó una excusa.

2 (*after a quarrel*) hacer **[7]** las paces
They've made up now. Han hecho las paces ahora.
to make up with someone hacer **[7]** las paces con alguien

♪ **make-up** *noun*

el **maquillaje** *masc*
I don't wear make-up. Yo no uso maquillaje.
to put on your make-up ponerse **[11]** el maquillaje
Jo's putting on her make-up. Jo se está poniendo el maquillaje.

male *adjective*

1 (*person, population*) **masculino** *masc*, **masculina** *fem*
a male voice una voz masculina

2 (*animal, insect*) **macho** *masc & fem*
a male rat una rata macho

3 (*sex: on a form*) **varón** *masc & fem*

mall *noun*

el **centro comercial**

mammal *noun*

el **mamífero** *masc*

♪ **man** *noun*

1 (*person*) el **hombre** *masc*
four men and five women cuatro hombres y cinco mujeres

2 (*mankind*) el **hombre** *masc*
Modern man is taller than his ancestors. El hombre moderno es más alto que sus antepasados.

to **manage** *verb*

1 (*a business, team*) **dirigir [49]**
She manages a travel agency. Ella dirige una agencia de viajes.

2 (*to cope*) **arreglárselas [17]**
I can manage. Puedo arreglármelas.

3 (*to achieve*) **to manage to do something** conseguir **[64]** hacer algo
I didn't manage to get in touch with her. No conseguí ponerme en contacto con ella.

management *noun*

1 (*running, administration*) la **dirección** *fem*
the management of the company la dirección de la empresa

2 (*management staff*) los **directivos** *plural masc*

manager *noun*
1 (*of a company, bank*) el **director** *masc*, la **directora** *fem*
2 (*of a shop, restaurant*) el **encargado** *masc*, la **encargada** *fem*
3 (*in sport, entertainment*) el & la **manager** *masc & fem*

manageress *noun*
la **encargada** *fem*

managing director *noun*
el **consejero delegado**, la **consejera delegada**

mango *noun*
el **mango** *masc*

maniac *noun*
el **loco** *masc*, la **loca** *fem*
She drives like a maniac. Conduce como una loca.

mankind *noun*
la **humanidad** *fem*

manner *noun*
1 (*way, fashion*) la **forma** *fem*
He was behaving in a ridiculous manner. Se estaba comportando de forma ridícula.
in a manner of speaking por así decirlo
2 (*politeness*) **manners** modales *plural masc*
Have you forgotten your manners? ¿Dónde están tus modales?
to have good manners tener [9] buena educación
It's bad manners to talk like that. No es de buena educación hablar así.

mansion *noun*
la **mansión** *fem*

mantelpiece *noun*
la **repisa de la chimenea**

manual *noun*
el **manual** *masc*

to **manufacture** *verb*
fabricar [31]

manufacturer *noun*
el & la **fabricante** *masc & fem*

many *adjective, pronoun*
1 (*a lot*) **muchos** *masc*, **muchas** *fem*
many people mucha gente
She has got many friends. Tiene muchos amigos.
There aren't many onions left. No quedan muchas cebollas.
Many of them came. Muchos de ellos vinieron.
very many muchos *masc*, muchas *fem*
There aren't very many glasses. No hay muchos vasos.
2 **not many** no muchos *masc*, no muchas *fem*
'Have we got any potatoes?'— 'Not many?' '¿Tenemos patatas?'— 'No muchas.'
3 **so many** tantos *masc*, tantas *fem*
I have so many things to do! ¡Tengo tantas cosas que hacer!
We've never scored so many goals. Nunca hemos marcado tantos goles.
4 **too many** demasiados *masc*, demasiadas *fem*
That's too many! ¡Esos son demasiados!
I've got too many things to do. Tengo demasiadas cosas que hacer.
There were too many people. Había demasiada gente.
5 **How many?** ¿cuántos? *masc*, ¿cuántas? *fem*
How many are there? ¿Cuántos hay?
How many sisters have you got? ¿Cuántas hermanas tienes?
I don't know how many there are. No sé cuántos hay.
6 (*in comparisons*) **as many as** tantos como *masc pl*, tantas como *fem pl*
She has as many as I have. Tiene tantos como yo.
There aren't as many sheep as before. No hay tantas ovejas como antes.
7 (*to say all that*) **as many as** todos los que *plural masc*, todas las que *plural fem*
Take as many as you like. Lleva todos los que quieras.

map *noun*
1 (*of a country, region*) el **mapa** *masc*
a road map un mapa de carreteras
2 (*of a town*) el **plano** *masc*

marathon *noun*
el or la **maratón** *masc or fem*

marble *noun*
1 (*the stone*) el **mármol** *masc*
a marble fireplace una chimenea de mármol
2 (*toy*) la **canica** *fem*
to play marbles jugar [27] a las canicas

march *noun* ▷ see **march** *verb*
la **marcha** *fem*

to **march** *verb* ▷ see **march** *noun*
marchar [17]

March *noun*
el **marzo** *masc*
in March en marzo

WORD TIP Names of months and days start with small letters in Spanish.

mare *noun*
la **yegua** *fem*

margarine *noun*
la **margarina** *fem*

margin *noun*
el **margen** *masc, pl:* los **márgenes**

marijuana *noun*
la **marihuana** *fem*

♪ **mark** *noun* ▷ see **mark** *verb*
1 (*at school*) la **nota** *fem*
I got a good mark for my Spanish homework. Saqué una buena nota en los deberes de español.
What mark did you get for Spanish? ¿Qué nota sacaste en español?
2 (*sign, symbol*) la **marca** *fem*
He made a mark on the wall. Hizo una marca en la pared.
3 (*stain*) la **mancha** *fem*
a dirty mark una mancha de suciedad

♪ to **mark** *verb* ▷ see **mark** *noun*
1 (*to correct*) **corregir** [48]
He marked the exams. Corrigió los exámenes.
2 (*to write*) **marcar** [31]
I've marked the price on the lid. He marcado el precio en la tapa.
3 (*to stain*) **manchar** [17]
The coffee marked the carpet. El café manchó la alfombra.

♪ **market** *noun*
el **mercado** *masc*

marketing *noun*
el **marketing** *masc*

marmalade *noun*
la **mermelada de naranja**

♪ **marriage** *noun*
1 (*relationship*) el **matrimonio** *masc*
2 (*ceremony*) el **casamiento** *masc*

♪ **married** *adjective*
casado *masc*, **casada** *fem*
to be married estar [2] casado
She's married. Está casada.
They've been married for twenty years. Llevan casados veinte años.
a married couple un matrimonio

to **marry** *verb*
to marry somebody casarse [17] con alguien
She married a Spaniard. Se casó con un español.
to get married casarse [17]
They got married in July. Se casaron en julio.

♪ **marvellous** *adjective*
maravilloso *masc*, **maravillosa** *fem*
The weather's marvellous. El tiempo es maravilloso.
How marvellous! ¡Qué maravilla!

marzipan *noun*
el **mazapán** *masc*

mascara *noun*
el **rímel** *masc*

masculine *adjective*
▷ see **masculine** *noun*
masculino *masc*, **masculina** *fem*

masculine *noun* ▷ see **masculine** *adj*
(*in Spanish and other grammars*) el **masculino** *masc*
in the masculine en masculino

to **mash** *verb*
(*potatoes, vegetables*) **triturar** [17]

mashed potatoes *plural noun*
el **puré de patatas**

mask *noun*
la **máscara** *fem*

mass *noun*
1 (*large amount*) **masses of something** un montón de algo
They've got masses of money. Tienen un montón de dinero.
There's masses left over. Queda un montón.
2 (*Religion*) la **misa** *fem*
to go to mass ir [8] a misa

massacre *noun*
la **matanza** *fem*

massage *noun*
el **masaje** *masc*

massive *adjective*
enorme *masc & fem*

mat *noun*
1 (*doormat*) el **felpudo** *masc*
2 (*bathmat*) la **alfombrilla** *fem*
3 (*for a hot dish*) el **salvamanteles** *masc, pl:* los **salvamanteles**

♪ **match** *noun* ▷ see **match** *verb*
1 (*for lighting a fire*) la **cerilla** *fem*
a box of matches una caja de cerillas
2 (*in sports*) el **partido** *masc*
a football match un partido de fútbol
We watched the match. Vimos el partido.
Who won the match? ¿Quién ganó el partido?
They lost the match. Perdieron el partido.

to match *verb* ▷ see **match** *noun*
hacer [7] juego con
The jacket matches the skirt. La chaqueta hace juego con la falda.

mate *noun*
el **amigo** *masc*, la **amiga** *fem*
I'm going out with my mates tonight. Voy a salir esta noche con mis amigos.

material *noun*
1 (*fabric*) la **tela** *fem*
2 (*information*) el **material** *masc*
teaching materials material educativo
3 (*substance*) la **materia** *fem*
raw materials materias primas

mathematics *noun*
las **matemáticas** *plural fem*

maths *noun*
las **matemáticas** *plural fem*
I like maths. Me gustan las matemáticas.
Anna's good at maths. A Anna se le dan bien las matemáticas.

matter *noun* ▷ see **matter** *verb*
1 (*question, issue*) el **asunto** *masc*
Let's say no more about the matter No digamos más sobre el asunto.
2 (*problem*) **What's the matter?** ¿Qué pasa?
What's the matter with Lucy? ¿Qué le pasa a Lucy?
There's something the matter with her. Algo le pasa.
3 (*in expressions*) **As a matter of fact, I've never been to Spain.** La verdad es que nunca he estado en España.
no matter how cheap it is ... por barato que sea ...
No matter how hard I try, you're never happy. Por mucho que me esfuerce, nunca estás contento.

to matter *verb* ▷ see **matter** *noun*
(*to be important*) **importar [17]**
the things that matter lo que importa
It matters a lot to me. Me importa mucho.
It doesn't matter. No importa.
It doesn't matter if it rains. No importa que llueva.
You can write it in Spanish or French, it doesn't matter. Puedes escribirlo en español o en francés, da lo mismo.

mattress *noun*
el **colchón** *masc*

maximum *adjective*
▷ see **maximum** *noun*
máximo *masc*, **máxima** *fem*

maximum *noun* ▷ see **maximum** *adj*
el **máximo** *masc*

may *verb*
1 (*to ask permission*) **May I close the door?** ¿Puedo cerrar la puerta?
2 (*to talk about a possibility*) **She may be ill.** Puede que esté enferma.
We may go to Spain. Puede que vayamos a España.

WORD TIP *puede que* is followed by a verb in the subjunctive.

May *noun*
el **mayo** *masc*
in May en mayo

WORD TIP Names of months and days start with small letters in Spanish.

maybe *adverb*
quizás
maybe not quizás no
Maybe he's forgotten. Quizás se ha olvidado.
Maybe they've got lost. Quizás se han perdido.

mayonnaise *noun*
la **mayonesa** *fem*

mayor *noun* ▷ see **mayoress** *noun*
el **alcalde** *masc*, la **alcaldesa** *fem*

mayoress *noun* ▷ see **mayor** *noun*
la **alcaldesa** *fem*

me *pronoun*
1 (*as a direct or indirect object*) **me**
She knows me. Me conoce.
She gave me the documents. Me dio los documentos.
Can you help me, please? ¿Puedes ayudarme por favor?
Listen to me! ¡Escúchame!
Wait for me! ¡Espérame!
Don't push me! ¡No me empujes!

WORD TIP With an infinitive, or when telling someone to do something, *me* joins onto the verb.

2 (*after prepositions*) **mí**
behind me detrás de mí
They left without me. Se fueron sin mí.
with me conmigo
I took her with me. La traje conmigo.
3 (*in comparisons and with 'to be'*) **yo**
She's older than me. Es mayor que yo.
It's me. Soy yo.
Me too! ¡Yo también!

meadow *noun*
el **prado** *masc*

meal *noun*
la **comida** *fem*
They have three meals a day. Hacen tres comidas al día.
Enjoy your meal! ¡Que aproveche!

mean *adjective* ▷ see **mean** *verb*
1 (*with money*) **tacaño** *masc*, **tacaña** *fem*
2 (*nasty*) **She's really mean to her brother.** Trata muy mal a su hermano.
What a mean thing to do! ¡Qué maldad!

to **mean** *verb* ▷ see **mean** *adj*
1 (*to signify*) **querer** [12] **decir**
What do you mean? ¿Qué quieres decir?
What does that mean? ¿Qué quiere decir eso?
That's not what I meant. Eso no es lo que quería decir.
2 (*to imply*) **suponer** [11]
That means that I'll have to do it again. Eso supone que voy a tener que hacerlo otra vez.
3 (*to intend*) **to mean to do something** tener [9] la intención de algo
I meant to phone my mother. Tenía la intención de llamar a mi madre.
4 (*to be supposed to*) **She was meant to be here at six.** Se supone que ella tenía que estar aquí a las seis.
This is meant to be easy. Se supone que esto es fácil.

meaning *noun*
el **significado** *masc*

means *noun*
el **medio** *masc*
a means of transport un medio de transporte
by means of something por medio de algo
a means of doing something una forma de hacer algo
We have no means of contacting him. No tenemos forma de contactar con él.
by all means por supuesto

meantime *adverb*
for the meantime por ahora
in the meantime mientras tanto

meanwhile *adverb*
mientras tanto
Meanwhile she was waiting at the station. Mientras tanto ella estaba esperando en la estación.

measles *noun*
el **sarampión** *masc*

to **measure** *verb*
medir [57]

measurements *plural noun*
1 (*of a room, an object*) las **medidas** *plural fem*
the measurements of the room las medidas de la habitación
2 (*of a person*) la **medida** *fem*
to take somebody's measurements tomarle [17] las medidas a alguien
my waist measurement mi medida de cintura

meat *noun*
la **carne** *fem*

Mecca *noun*
La Meca *fem*
Fueron a la Meca. They went to Mecca.

mechanic *noun*
el **mecánico** *masc*, la **mecánica** *fem*
He's a mechanic. Es mecánico.

medal *noun*
la **medalla** *fem*
the gold medal la medalla de oro

media *plural noun*
the media los medios de comunicación

medical *adjective* ▷ see **medical** *noun*
médico *masc*, **médica** *fem*

medical *noun* ▷ see **medical** *adj*
la **revisión médica**
to have a medical someterse [18] a una revisión médica

medicine *noun*
1 (*drug*) el **medicamento** *masc*
¿Te has tomado el medicamento? Have you taken your medicine?
2 (*science*) la **medicina** *fem*
alternative medicine medicina alternativa
She's studying medicine. Está estudiando medicina.

medieval *adjective*
medieval *masc & fem*

Mediterranean *noun*
the Mediterranean el Mediterráneo

medium *adjective*
mediano *masc*, **mediana** *fem*
Small, medium or large? ¿Pequeño, mediano o grande?

medium-sized *adjective*
de tamaño mediano *masc & fem*
a medium-sized house una casa de tamaño medio

⚷ to **meet** *verb*
1 *(by chance)* **encontrarse [24] con**
I met Rosie outside the baker's. Me encontré con Rosie en la puerta de la panadería.
2 *(by appointment)* **haber [6] quedado (con)**
We're meeting at six. Hemos quedado a las seis.
I'm meeting him at the museum. He quedado con él en el museo.
Shall we meet after work? ¿Quedamos después del trabajo?
3 *(to get to know)* **conocer [35] a**
I met a Spanish girl last week. Conocí a una chica española la semana pasada.
Have you met Oskar? ¿Conoces a Oskar?
4 *(in introductions)* **Tom, meet Ann.** Tom, te presento a Ann.
Pleased to meet you! ¡Encantado! *(man speaking)*, ¡Encantada! *(woman speaking)*
5 *(off a train, bus, plane)* **recoger [3]**
My dad's meeting me at the station. Mi padre va a ir a recogerme a la estación.

⚷ **meeting** *noun*
la **reunión** *fem*
There's a meeting at ten o'clock. Hay una reunión a las diez.
She's in a meeting. Está en una reunión.

megabyte *noun*
el **megabyte** *masc*

⚷ **melon** *noun*
el **melón** *masc*

to **melt** *verb*
1 *(snow, butter, ice cream)* **derretirse [57]**
It melts in your mouth. Se derrite en la boca.
2 **to melt something** derretir [57] algo
Melt the butter in a saucepan. Derretir la mantequilla en una sartén.

member *noun*
1 *(of a party, committee)* el & la **miembro** *masc & fem*
She's a member of the Labour Party. Es miembro del partido laborista.
2 *(of a club)* el **socio** *masc*, la **socia** *fem*

Member of Parliament *noun*
el **diputado** *masc*, la **diputada** *fem*

memorial *noun*
el **monumento** *masc*
a war memorial un monumento a los caídos

to **memorize** *verb*
to memorize something aprender [18] algo de memoria

memory *noun*
1 *(of a person, computer)* la **memoria** *fem*
You have a good memory! ¡Tienes buena memoria!
I have a bad memory. Tengo mala memoria.
2 *(of the past)* el **recuerdo** *masc*
I have good memories of my stay in Spain. Tengo buenos recuerdos de mi estancia en España.

to **mend** *verb*
1 *(a watch)* **arreglar [17]**
2 *(a road)* **reparar [17]**
3 *(clothes)* **coser [18]**

mental *adjective*
mental *masc & fem*
• **mental arithmetic** los cálculos mentales

to **mention** *verb*
mencionar [17]
Your name was mentioned. Se mencionó tu nombre.
'Thank you.'— 'Don't mention it.' 'Gracias.'— 'De nada.'

⚷ **menu** *noun*
1 *(in a restaurant)* la **carta** *fem*, el **menú** *masc*
What's on on the menu? ¿Qué hay en la carta?
Have you got a set menu? ¿Tienen un menú del día?
I'll take the €20 menu. Tomaré el menú de 20€.
2 *(Computers)* el **menú** *masc*

WORD TIP *el menú* is usually a set menu with limited choice.

MEP *noun*
(= *Member of the European Parliament*) el **eurodiputado** *masc*, la **eurodiputada** *fem*
She's an MEP. Es eurodiputada.

to **merge** *verb*
1 *(documents, companies)* **fusionar [17]**
2 *(roads)* **confluir [54]**

meringue *noun*
el **merengue** *masc*

merit *noun*
el **mérito** *masc*

merry *adjective*
1 *(happy)* **alegre** *masc & fem*
Merry Christmas! ¡Feliz Navidad!
2 *(informal: mildly drunk)* **achispado** *masc*, **achispada** *fem*

merry-go-round *noun*
el **tiovivo** *masc*

English-Spanish

mess *noun*
el **desorden** *masc*
What a mess! ¡Qué desorden!
My papers are in a mess. Mis papeles están desordenados.
Don't make a mess! ¡No desordenes nada!
• **to mess about**
hacer [7] **el tonto**
Stop messing about! ¡Deja de hacer el tonto!
• **to mess about with something**
jugar [27] **con algo**
It's dangerous to mess about with matches. Es peligroso jugar con cerillas.
• **to mess something up**
desordenar [17] **algo**
You've messed up all my papers. ¡Me has desordenado todos mis papeles!

message *noun*
el **mensaje** *masc*
a telephone message un recado

messenger *noun*
el **mensajero** *masc*, la **mensajera** *fem*

messy *adjective*
1 (*dirty*) **It's a messy job.** Es un trabajo sucio.
2 (*untidy*) **He's a messy eater.** Se ensucia mucho comiendo.
Her writing's really messy. Escribe sin poner cuidado.

metal *noun*
el **metal** *masc*

meter *noun*
1 (*electricity, gas, taxi*) el **contador** *masc*
to read the meter leer [37] el contador
2 (*for parking*) **a parking meter** un parquímetro

method *noun*
el **método** *masc*

Methodist *noun*
el & la **metodista** *masc & fem*
I'm a Methodist. Soy metodista.

WORD TIP Adjectives and nouns for religion do not have capital letters in Spanish.

metre *noun*
el **metro** *masc*
It's five metres long. Mide cinco metros de largo.

metric *adjective*
métrico *masc*, **métrica** *fem*

Mexican *adjective* ▷ see **Mexican** *noun*
mexicano *masc*, **mexicana** *fem*

Mexican *noun* ▷ see **Mexican** *adj*
un **mexicano** *masc*, una **mexicana** *fem*

WORD TIP Adjectives and nouns for nationality and regional origin do not have capital letters in Spanish.

Mexico *noun*
México *masc*

microchip *noun*
el **microchip** *masc*, *pl:* los **microchips**

microcomputer *noun*
el **microordenador** *masc*, (*Latin America*) la **microcomputadora** *fem*

microphone *noun*
el **micrófono** *masc*

microscope *noun*
el **microscopio** *masc*

microwave oven *noun*
el **microondas** *masc*, *pl:* los **microondas**

midday *noun*
el **mediodía** *masc*
at midday al mediodía

middle *noun*
1 (*of a place*) el **medio** *masc*
in the middle of the room en medio de la habitación
2 (*of a period of time*) **in the middle of the night** en mitad de la noche
in the middle of the day alrededor del mediodía
in the middle of the year a mediados de año
3 (*of an activity*) **to be in the middle of doing something** estar [2] haciendo algo
When she phoned I was in the middle of washing my hair. Cuando llamó estaba lavándome el pelo.

middle-aged *adjective*
de mediana edad *masc & fem*
a middle-aged woman una mujer de mediana edad
some middle-aged couples unas parejas de mediana edad

middle-class *adjective*
de clase media *masc & fem*
a middle-class family una familia de clase media
some middle-class students unos estudiantes de clase media

Middle East *noun*
the Middle East el Oriente Medio

middle finger *noun*
el **dedo corazón**

midge *noun*
el **mosquito pequeño**

⚷ **midnight** *noun*
la **medianoche** *fem*
at midnight a medianoche

Midsummer's Day *noun*
la **noche de San Juan**

midwife *noun*
la **comadrona** *fem*

might *verb*
I might invite Jo. Puede que invite a Jo.
Amanda might know. Puede que Amanda lo sepa.
He might have forgotten. Puede que se haya olvidado.
'Are you going to phone him?'— 'I might.' '¿Vas a llamarlo?'— 'Quizás.'

migraine *noun*
la **jaqueca** *fem*

mike *noun*
(*informal*) el **micro** *masc*

mild *adjective*
1 (*soap, cheese*) **suave** *masc & fem*
2 (*climate*) **templado** *masc*, **templada** *fem*
It's quite mild today. Hoy no hace frío.

mile *noun*
la **milla** *fem* (*in Spain distances are measured in kilometres; to convert miles roughly to kilometres, multiply by 8 and divide by 5*)
The village is ten miles from Chester. El pueblo está a dieciseis kilómetros de Chester.
It's miles better! ¡Es mil veces mejor!

mileage *noun*
la **distancia en millas**
What's the mileage on your car? ¿Cuántas millas ha hecho tu coche?

⚷ **to milk** *verb* ▷ see **milk** *noun*
ordeñar [17]

⚷ **milk** *noun* ▷ see **milk** *verb*
la **leche** *fem*
full-cream milk leche entera
skimmed milk leche desnatada
semi-skimmed milk leche semidesnatada
- **milk chocolate** el chocolate con leche
- **milkman** el lechero
- **milkshake** el batido

millennium *noun*
el **milenio** *masc*

millimetre *noun*
el **milímetro** *masc*

million *noun*
el **millón** *masc*
a million people un millón de personas
two million people dos millones de personas

millionaire *noun*
el **millonario** *masc*, la **millonaria** *fem*

mince *noun*
la **carne picada**

⚷ **to mind** *verb* ▷ see **mind** *noun*
1 (*to look after*) **cuidar [17]**
Can you mind my bag for me? ¿Me cuidas el bolso?
Could you mind the baby for ten minutes? ¿Puedes cuidar del niño diez minutos?
2 (*to be bothered*) **do you mind if ...?** ¿te importa que ...?
Do you mind if I close the door? ¿Te importa que cierre la puerta?
I don't mind the heat. No me molesta el calor.
I don't mind. No me importa.
Never mind! ¡No importa!
3 (*to be careful*) **Mind the step!** ¡Cuidado con el escalón!

⚷ **mind** *noun* ▷ see **mind** *verb*
1 (*brain*) la **mente** *fem*
a logical mind una mente lógica
It crossed my mind that ... Se me pasó por la cabeza que ...
2 (*opinion*) **to change your mind** cambiar **[17]** de opinión
I've changed my mind. He cambiado de opinión.
to make up your mind decidirse **[19]**
I can't make up my mind. No puedo decidirme.

⚷ **mine** *noun* ▷ see **mine** *pron*
la **mina** *fem*
a coal mine una mina de carbón

⚷ **mine** *pronoun* ▷ see **mine** *noun*
el mío *masc*, **la mía** *fem*
She took her hat and I took mine. Ella cogió su sombrero y yo cogí el mío.
Tessa phoned her mum and I phoned mine. Tessa llamó a su madre y yo llamé a la mía.
Karen's invited her parents and I've invited mine. Karen ha invitado a sus padres y yo a los míos.
She showed me her photos and I showed her mine. Ella me enseñó sus fotos y yo le enseñé las mías.

miner *noun*
el **minero** *masc*, la **minera** *fem*
Her father was a miner. Su padre era minero.

mineral water *noun*
el **agua mineral**

WORD TIP *agua* takes *el* or *un* in the singular even though it is *fem*.

minibus *noun*
el **microbús** *masc*

minimum *adjective*
▷ see **minimum** *noun*
mínimo *masc*, **mínima** *fem*
the minimum age la edad mínima

minimum *noun* ▷ see **minimum** *adj*
el **mínimo** *masc*

miniskirt *noun*
la **minifalda** *fem*

minister *noun*
1 (*in government*) el **ministro** *masc*, la **ministra** *fem*
2 (*of a church*) el **pastor** *masc*, la **pastora** *fem*

minor *adjective*
menor *masc & fem*
a minor problem

minority *noun*
la **minoría** *fem*

mint *noun*
1 (*herb*) la **menta** *fem*
2 (*sweet*) el **caramelo de menta**

minus *preposition*
1 (*in sums*) **menos**
Seven minus three is four. Siete menos tres es cuatro.
2 (*to talk about temperature*) **It was minus ten this morning.** Esta mañana hacía diez grados bajo cero.

minute *noun*
el **minuto** *masc*
It's five minutes' walk from here. Está a cinco minutos andando de aquí.
I'll be ready in two minutes. En dos minutos estoy lista.
Just a minute! ¡Un momento!

miracle *noun*
el **milagro** *masc*

mirror *noun*
1 (*looking-glass*) el **espejo** *masc*
I looked at myself in the mirror. Me miré al espejo.
2 (*rear-view mirror in a car*) el **retrovisor** *masc*

to **misbehave** *verb*
portarse [17] mal

mischief *noun*
to get up to mischief hacer [7] travesuras

mischievous *adjective*
travieso *masc*, **traviesa** *fem*

miser *noun*
el **avaro** *masc*, la **avara** *fem*

miserable *adjective*
1 (*person*) **triste** *masc & fem*
He was miserable without her. Estaba triste sin ella.
I feel really miserable today. Hoy tengo el ánimo por los suelos.
2 (*weather*) **It's miserable weather.** Un tiempo deprimente.

misery *noun*
la **miseria** *fem*
He was in misery. Estaba muy triste.

to **miss** *verb*
1 (*to fail to catch, see, etc*) **perder [36]**
She missed her train. Perdió el tren.
I missed the film. Me perdí la película.
to miss an opportunity perder una oportunidad
2 (*a target, goal*) **The ball missed the goal.** La pelota no entró en la portería.
You missed! ¡Fallaste!
3 (*to be absent from*) **faltar [17] a**
He's missed several classes. Ha faltado a varias clases.
4 (*to long to see*) **I miss you.** Te echo de menos.
She's missing her sister. Echa de menos a su hermana.
I miss Madrid. Echo de menos Madrid.

Miss *noun*
la **señorita** *fem* (*usually abbreviated to* **Srta.**)
Miss Jones la Srta. Jones
Good afternoon, Miss Jones. Buenas tardes, señorita Jones.

missile *noun*
el **misil** *masc*

missing *adjective*
the missing piece la pieza que falta
the missing documents los documentos que faltan
the missing link el eslabón perdido
There's a plate missing. Falta un plato.
There are three forks missing. Faltan tres tenedores.
Is there anybody missing? ¿Falta alguien?
to go missing desaparecer [35]
Several things have gone missing lately.

Han desaparecido varias cosas últimamente.
Three people have gone missing. Han desaparecido tres personas.

mist *noun*
la **neblina** *fem*

to **mistake** *verb* ▷ see **mistake** *noun*
confundir [19]
I mistook you for your brother. Te confundí con tu hermano.

♪ **mistake** *noun* ▷ see **mistake** *verb*
el **error** *masc*
by mistake por error
a spelling mistake una falta de ortografía
to make a mistake cometer [18] un error
Sorry, I made a mistake. Perdona, cometí un error.
It was my mistake. Fue un error mío.

mistaken *adjective*
to be mistaken estar [2] equivocado
She's mistaken. Está equivocada.

mistletoe *noun*
el **muérdago** *masc*

to **misunderstand** *verb*
entender [36] **mal**
I misunderstood. Lo entendí mal.

misunderstanding *noun*
el **malentendido** *masc*
There's been a misunderstanding. Ha habido un malentendido.

to **mix** *verb* ▷ see **mix** *noun*
1 (*to combine*) **mezclar** [17]
Mix all the ingredients together. Mezclar todos los ingredientes.
2 (*to socialize*) **to mix with** tratarse [17] con
She mixes with lots of interesting people. Se trata con mucha gente interesante.
• **to mix up**
1 (*to mess up*) desordenar [17]
You've mixed up all my papers. Has desordenado todos mis papeles.
2 (*to confuse*) **confundir** [19]
I get him mixed up with his brother. Lo confundo con su hermano.
You've got it all mixed up! ¡Te has confundido!

mix *noun* ▷ see **mix** *verb*
1 (*mixture*) la **mezcla** *fem*
a good mix of people una buena mezcla de gente
2 (*set of ingredients*) **cake mix** preparado para hacer un pastel

♪ **mixed** *adjective*
variado *masc*, **variada** *fem*
a mixed programme un programa variado
• **mixed salad** la ensalada mixta

mixer *noun*
la **batidora** *fem*

mixture *noun*
la **mezcla** *fem*
a mixture of jazz and rock una mezcla de jazz y rock

to **moan** *verb*
1 (*in pain*) **gemir** [57]
2 (*to complain*) **quejarse** [17]
Stop moaning! ¡Deja de quejarte!

mobile home *noun*
la **caravana fija**

mobile phone *noun*
el **móvil** *masc noun*, el **teléfono móvil**
to call somebody on their mobile llamar [17] a alguien al móvil

mock *noun* ▷ see **mock** *verb*
(*mock exam*) el **examen de práctica**

to **mock** *verb* ▷ see **mock** *noun*
burlarse [17] **de**
Stop mocking me! ¡Deja de burlarte de mí!

model *noun*
1 (*type*) el **modelo** *masc*
the latest model el último modelo
2 (*fashion model*) el & la **modelo** *masc & fem*
She's a model. Es modelo.
3 (*of a plane, car, etc*) la **maqueta** *fem*
a model of Westminster Abbey una maqueta de la abadía de Westminster
He makes models. Construye maquetas.
• **model aeroplane** el aeromodelo
• **model railway** el ferrocarril de juguete

♪ **modem** *noun*
el **módem** *masc, pl:* los **módems**

moderate *adjective*
moderado *masc*, **moderada** *fem*

modern *adjective*
moderno *masc*, **moderna** *fem*
• **modern languages** las lenguas modernas

to **modernize** *verb*
modernizar [22]

moisturizer *noun*
1 (*lotion*) la **loción hidratante**
2 (*cream*) la **crema hidratante**

mole *noun*
1 (*the animal*) el **topo** *masc*
2 (*mark on skin*) el **lunar** *masc*

moment *noun*
el **momento** *masc*
at the moment en este momento
at the right moment en el momento preciso
at any moment en cualquier momento
for the moment de momento
He'll be here in a moment. Llegará en cualquier momento.

monarchy *noun*
la **monarquía** *fem*

Monday *noun*
el **lunes** *masc*
every Monday cada lunes
last Monday el lunes pasado
on Monday el lunes
on Mondays los lunes
The museum is closed on Mondays. El museo cierra los lunes.
I'll phone you on Monday evening Te llamaré el lunes por la tarde.

WORD TIP Months of the year and days of the week start with small letters in Spanish.

money *noun*
el **dinero** *masc*
I haven't got enough money. No tengo suficiente dinero.
to make money hacer [7] dinero
They gave me my money back (*in a shop.*) Me devolvieron el dinero.
• **money box** la hucha

mongrel *noun*
el **chucho** *masc* (*informal*)

monitor *noun*
(*Computers*) el **monitor** *masc*

monkey *noun*
1 (*animal*) el **mono** *masc*
2 (*informal: child*) **You little monkey!** ¡Diablillo!

monster *noun*
el **monstruo** *masc*

month *noun*
el **mes** *masc*
in the month of May en el mes de mayo
this month este mes
next month el próximo mes
We're leaving next month. Nos vamos el próximo mes.
last month el mes pasado
every month todos los meses
in two months' time dentro de dos meses
at the end of the month a final de mes

monthly *adjective*
mensual *masc & fem*
a monthly payment una mensualidad

monument *noun*
el **monumento** *masc*
a monument to the king un monumento al rey

mood *noun*
el **humor** *masc*
to be in a good mood estar [2] de buen humor
to be in a bad mood estar [2] de mal humor
'Do you want to go out?'— 'I'm not in the mood.' '¿Quieres salir?'— 'No me apetece.'

moody *adjective*
temperamental *masc & fem*

moon *noun*
la **luna** *fem*
by the light of the moon a la luz de la luna

moonlight *noun*
la **luz de la luna**
by moonlight a la luz de la luna

moor *noun*
el **páramo**

moped *noun*
el **ciclomotor** *masc*

moral *adjective* ▷ see **moral** *noun*
moral *masc & fem*

moral *noun* ▷ see **moral** *adj*
la **moraleja** *fem*
the moral of the story la moraleja de la historia

morals *plural noun*
la **moralidad** *fem*

more *adverb, adjective, pronoun*
1 (*extra*) **más**
Julie eats more. Julie come más.
more cake más pastel
a few more glasses unos cuantos vasos más
We need three more. Necesitamos tres más.
more easily más fácilmente
This one is more interesting. Este es más interesante.
2 (*with numbers, amounts*) **more than** más de
more than a kilo más de un kilo
more than two hours más de dos horas
3 (*in comparisons*) **more than** más que
The book's more interesting than the film. El libro es más interesante que la película.
He eats more than me. Come más que yo.

4 (*in expressions*) **more and more** cada vez más
Books are getting more and more expensive. Los libros están cada vez más caros.
more or less más o menos
It's more or less finished. Está más o menos terminado.
any more más
I don't want any more. No quiero más.
I don't like it any more. Ya no me gusta.

⚷ **morning** *noun*
la **mañana** *fem*
this morning esta mañana
tomorrow morning mañana por la mañana
yesterday morning ayer por la mañana
in the morning por la mañana
She doesn't work in the morning. No trabaja por las mañanas.
on Friday morning el viernes por la mañana
on Friday mornings los viernes por la mañana
at six o'clock in the morning a las seis de la mañana
every morning todas las mañanas
Good morning! ¡Buenos días!

Morocco *noun*
Marruecos *masc*

mortgage *noun*
la **hipoteca** *fem*

Moscow *noun*
Moscú *masc*

mosque *noun*
la **mezquita** *fem*

mosquito *noun*
el **mosquito** *masc*, (*Latin America*) el **zancudo** *masc*
a mosquito bite una picadura de mosquito

⚷ **most** *adjective, adverb, pronoun*
1 (*in superlatives*) **más**
the most interesting film la película más interesante
the most exciting story la historia más emocionante
the most boring books los libros más aburridos
I've got the most time. Soy el que más tiempo tiene.
What I hate most is the noise. Lo que más odio es el ruido.
She ate the most. Fue la que más comió.
2 (*nearly all: with a plural noun*) **la mayoría de**
most of my friends la mayoría de mis amigos
Most children like chocolate. A la mayoría de los niños les gusta el chocolate.
3 (*nearly all: with a singular noun*) **most of** la mayor parte de
most of the time la mayor parte del tiempo
Most of it is clear. La mayor parte está claro.
They've eaten most of the chocolate. Se han comido casi todo el chocolate.
4 (*in expressions*) **at most** como máximo
two days, at most como máximo dos días

⚷ **mother** *noun*
la **madre** *fem*
my mother mi madre
Kate's mother la madre de Kate
• **mother-in-law** la suegra
• **Mother's Day** el día de la Madre (*in Spain, the first Sunday in May*)

motivated *adjective*
motivado *masc*, **motivada** *fem*

motivation *noun*
el **motivo** *masc*

motor *noun*
el **motor** *masc*

⚷ **motorbike** *noun*
la **motocicleta** *fem*

motorboat *noun*
la **motora** *fem*

motorcycle *noun*
la **motocicleta** *fem*

motorcyclist *noun*
el & la **motociclista** *masc & fem*

motorist *noun*
el & la **automovilista** *masc & fem*

motor racing *noun*
las **carreras de coches**

⚷ **motorway** *noun*
la **autopista** *fem*

mouldy *adjective*
mohoso *masc*, **mohosa** *fem*

⚷ **mountain** *noun*
la **montaña** *fem*
in the mountains en las montañas
• **mountain bike** la bicicleta de montaña

mountaineer *noun*
el **montañero** *masc*, la **montañera** *fem*

mountaineering *noun*
el **montañismo** *masc*
to go mountaineering hacer [7] montañismo

mountainous *adjective*
montañoso *masc*, **montañosa** *fem*

mouse *noun* ▷ see **mousse** *noun*
(*animal, on a computer*) el **ratón** *masc*

mousse *noun* ▷ see **mouse** *noun*
(*pudding, hair product*) la **mousse** *fem*
chocolate mousse mousse de chocolate

moustache *noun*
el **bigote** *masc*

mouth *noun*
la **boca** *fem*
Open your mouth wide. Abra bien la boca.
Shut your mouth! ¡Cállate la boca!

mouthful *noun*
1 (*of food*) el **bocado** *masc*
2 (*of drink*) el **trago** *masc*

mouth organ *noun*
la **armónica** *fem*
to play the mouth organ tocar [31] la armónica

move *noun* ▷ see **move** *verb*
1 (*to a different house*) la **mudanza** *fem*
2 (*in a game*) **Your move!** ¡Tu turno!

to **move** *verb* ▷ see **move** *noun*
1 (*to change your position, place*) **moverse** [38]
She didn't move. No se movió.
Move up a bit. Córrete un poco.
We moved to another table. Nos cambiamos de mesa.
She moved to a new school. Cambió de colegio.
2 (*to change the position of an object*) **cambiar** [17] **de sitio**
You've moved the picture. Has cambiado el cuadro de sitio.
Can you move your bag, please? ¿Puedes correr tu bolsa, por favor?
3 (*an object, a part of the body*) **mover** [38]
She moved her hand. Movió la mano.
4 (*car, traffic*) **avanzar** [22]
The traffic was moving slowly. El tráfico avanzaba lentamente.
5 **to move forward** avanzar [22]
He moved forward a step. Avanzó un paso.
6 (*to move house*) **mudarse** [17]
We're moving on Tuesday. Nos mudamos el martes.
They've moved house. Se han mudado de casa.
They've moved to Spain. Se han ido a vivir en España.
7 (*emotionally*) **conmover** [38]
It really moved me. Me conmovió de verdad.
to be moved estar [2] conmovido, *fem* conmovida

• **to move in**
mudarse [17]
When are you moving in? ¿Cuándo se mudan?

• **to move out**
mudarse [17]
I'm moving out at the end of the month. Me mudo a finales del mes.

movie *noun*
la **película** *fem*
to go to the movies ir [8] al cine

moving *adjective*
1 (*in motion*) **en marcha** *masc & fem*
a moving vehicle un vehículo en marcha
2 (*emotionally*) **conmovedor** *masc*, **conmovedora** *fem*
It's a very moving film. Es una película muy conmovedora.

MP *noun*
(*= Member of Parliament*) el **diputado** *masc*, la **diputada** *fem*
She's an MP. Es diputada.

MP3 *noun*
el **MP3** *masc*
• **MP3 player** el reproductor de MP3

Mr *noun*
el **señor** *masc* (*usually abbreviated to* **Sr.**)
Mr Angus Brown el Sr. Angus Brown
Good afternoon, Mr Brown. Buenas tardes, señor Brown.

Mrs *noun*
la **señora** *fem* (*usually abbreviated to* **Sra.**)
Mrs Mary Hendry la Sra. Mary Hendry
Good afternoon, Mrs Hendry. Buenas tardes, señora Hendry.

Ms *noun*
la **señora** *fem* (*usually abbreviated to 'Sra.'*)
Ms Jane Brown la Sra. Jane Brown
Good afternoon, Ms Brown. Buenas tardes, señora Brown.

WORD TIP There is no direct equivalent to *Ms* in Spanish, but *señora* may be used whether a woman is married or not.

much *adverb, pronoun, adjective*
1 (*with a verb*) **mucho**
not much no mucho
Do you go out much? ¿Sales mucho?
We don't go out much. No salimos mucho.
She doesn't eat much. No come mucho.
very much mucho
I don't watch television very much. No veo mucho la tele.
2 (*with a comparative*) **mucho**
much more mucho más

much bigger mucho más grande
Your house is much older than mine. Tu casa es mucho más vieja que la mía
He won't stay much longer. No se va a quedar mucho más.
3 (*with a noun*) **mucho** *masc*, **mucha** *fem*
We don't have much time. No tenemos mucho tiempo.
There isn't much butter left. No queda mucha mantequilla.
very much mucho *masc*, mucha *fem*
There isn't very much milk. No queda mucha leche.
4 **not much** no mucho *masc*, no mucha *fem*
'Did you add salt?'— 'Not much.' '¿Has puesto sal?'— 'No mucha.'
5 **so much** tanto *masc*, tanto *fem*
You shouldn't have given me so much coffee. No deberías haberme dado tanto café.
I have so much to do! ¡Tengo tanto que hacer!
We liked it so much! ¡Nos gustó tanto!
6 **too much** demasiado *masc*, demasiada *fem*
too much ink demasiada tinta
I drank too much wine. Bebí demasiado vino.
That's far too much! ¡Eso es demasiado!
7 **how much?** ¿cuánto? *masc*, ¿cuánta? *fem*
How much is it? ¿Cuánto cuesta?
How much do you want? ¿Cuánto quieres?
How much milk do you want? ¿Cuánta leche quieres?
8 **as much as** tanto como *masc*, tanta como *fem*
She drank as much milk as I did. Bebió tanta leche como yo.
There isn't as much as before. No hay tanto como antes.
9 **as much as** tanto como
You can take as much as you like. Puedes coger tanto como quieras.

mud *noun*
el **barro** *masc*

muddle *noun*
el **desorden** *masc*
to be in a muddle estar [2] todo desordenado

muddy *adjective*
lleno de barro *masc*, **llena de barro** *fem*
a muddy road una carretera llena de barro
Your boots are all muddy. Tus botas están llenas de barro.

♪ **muffled** *adjective*
sordo *masc*, **sorda** *fem*
a muffled shout un grito sordo

mug *noun* ▷ see **mug** *verb*
la **taza alta**
a mug of coffee una taza alta de café

to **mug** *verb* ▷ see **mug** *noun*
to mug somebody atracar [31] a alguien
My brother was mugged in the park. Atracaron a mi hermano en el parque.

mugging *noun*
el **atraco** *masc*

multiplication *noun*
la **multiplicación** *fem*

to **multiply** *verb*
multiplicar [31]
to multiply six by four multiplicar seis por cuatro

♪ **mum** *noun*
1 (*mother*) la **madre** *fem*
Tom's mum la madre de Tom
I'll ask my mum. Preguntaré a mi madre.
2 (*within the family*) **mamá** *fem*
Mum's not back yet. Mamá no ha vuelto todavía.

♪ **mummy** *noun*
1 (*mother*) la **mamá** *fem*
Susan's mummy is a teacher. La mamá de Susan es profesora.
2 (*within the family*) **mamá** *fem*
Mummy's not back yet. Mamá no ha vuelto todavía.
3 (*preserved body*) la **momia** *fem*

mumps *noun*
las **paperas** *plural fem*

murder *noun* ▷ see **murder** *verb*
el **asesinato** *masc*

to **murder** *verb* ▷ see **murder** *noun*
asesinar [17]

murderer *noun*
el **asesino** *masc*, la **asesina** *fem*

muscle *noun*
el **músculo** *masc*

♪ **museum** *noun*
el **museo** *masc*
to go to the museum ir [8] al museo

♪ **mushroom** *noun*
el **champiñón** *masc*

♪ **music** *noun*
la **música** *fem*
pop music música pop
classical music música clásica

musical *adjective* ▷ see **musical** *noun*
1 (*instrument, evening, ability*) **musical** *masc & fem*
a musical instrument un instrumento musical
2 (*musically gifted*) **They're a very musical family.** Toda la familia tiene dotes para la música.

musical *noun* ▷ see **musical** *adj*
el **musical** *masc*

musician *noun*
el **músico** *masc*, la **música** *fem*
He is a musician. Es músico.

Muslim *adjective* ▷ see **Muslim** *noun*
musulmán *masc*, **musulmana** *fem*

Muslim *noun* ▷ see **Muslim** *adj*
el **musulmán** *masc*, la **musulmana** *fem*

WORD TIP Adjectives and nouns for religion do not have capital letters in Spanish.

mini-info **Muslim Spain**

The Moors (an Islamic people from North Africa) invaded Spain in 711 AD and stayed until 1492. They left behind many common words, place names, surnames, and buildings.

mussel *noun*
la **mejillón** *masc*

must *verb*
1 (*to say you have to*) **tener [9] que**, **deber [18]**
You must be there at eight. Tienes que estar allí a las ocho., Debes estar allí a las ocho (*speaking to one person*).
You must bring sun block. Debéis llevar filtro solar., Tenéis que llevar filtro solar (*speaking to more than one person*).
I must lock the door. Tengo que cerrar la puerta con llave.
2 (*to say something is probable*) **deber**, **deber de**
You must be tired. Debes estar cansado (*to a boy*)., Debes estar cansada (*to a girl*).
It must be five o'clock. Deben ser las cinco.
He must have forgotten. Debe haberse olvidado.

WORD TIP You can also use *debes de*, *deben de*, *debe de* in these examples.

mustard *noun*
la **mostaza** *fem*

mustn't *short for* **must not** (*See:* **must**)

mutton *noun*
la **carne de ovino** *fem*

my *adjective*
1 (*before most nouns*) **mi** *masc & fem*
my book mi libro
my sister mi hermana
my children mis hijos
2 (*with parts of the body, clothes*) **el**, **la**, **los**, **las**
I cut my finger. Me corté el dedo.
I'm washing my hands. Me estoy lavando las manos.
My feet hurt. Me duelen los pies.
I took off my hat. Me quité el sombrero.

WORD TIP Spanish uses *el*, *la*, *los*, *las* for *my* with parts of the body and clothes.

myself *pronoun*
1 (*reflexive*) **me**
I've hurt myself. Me he hecho daño.
I washed myself. Me lavé.
2 (*for emphasis*) **yo mismo** *masc*, **yo misma** *fem*
I said it myself. Lo dije yo mismo.
3 (*on your own*) **by myself** yo solo *masc*, yo sola *fem*
I did it by myself. Lo hice yo solo (*boy speaking*)., Lo hice yo sola (*girl speaking*).

mysterious *adjective*
misterioso *masc*, **misteriosa** *fem*

mystery *noun*
1 (*enigma*) el **misterio** *masc*
2 (*book*) la **novela de misterio**

N n

Ñ, ñ

ñ is a separate letter in the Spanish alphabet, which has 27 letters. Very few Spanish words start with *k*, *w* and *ñ*.

nail *noun*
1 (*on a finger, toe*) la **uña** *fem*
to bite your nails morderse [38] las uñas
2 (*used for hanging, joining things*) el **clavo** *masc*
- **nailbrush** el cepillo de uñas
- **nail file** la lima de uñas
- **nail scissors** las tijeras de uñas
- **nail varnish** el esmalte de uñas
- **nail varnish remover** el quitaesmalte

name *noun*
1 (*of a person*) el **nombre** *masc*
I've forgotten her name. Se me ha olvidado su nombre.
What's your name? ¿Cómo te llamas?
My name is Lily. Me llamo Lily.
2 (*of a book, film*) el **título** *masc*

names

Traditionally Spaniards have two surnames, using one from their father's side and one from their mother's side. They also use many nicknames, e.g. Francisco, Paco; José, Pepe; Juana, Pacha; María Teresa, Maité.

nanny *noun*
la **niñera** *fem*

napkin *noun*
la **servilleta** *fem*

nappy *noun*
el **pañal** *masc*

narrow *adjective*
estrecho *masc*, **estrecha** *fem*
a narrow street una calle estrecha

nasty *adjective*
1 (*spiteful*) **malo** *masc*, **mala** *fem*
They are really nasty to her. Son realmente malos con ella.
That was a nasty thing to do. Eso fue una crueldad.
to have a nasty temper tener [9] mal carácter
2 (*unpleasant: job, habit*) **desagradable** *masc & fem*
That's a nasty job. Ese es un trabajo desagradable.
3 (*taste, smell*) **repugnante** *masc & fem*
It smells nasty. Tiene un olor repugnante.
4 (*situation*) **feo** *masc*, **fea** *fem*
The situation turned nasty. La cosa se puso fea.

WORD TIP *malo* becomes *mal* before a masc singular noun.

nation *noun*
la **nación** *fem*

national *adjective*
nacional *masc & fem*
- **national anthem** el himno nacional

nationality *noun*
la **nacionalidad** *fem*

national park *noun*
el **parque nacional**

Nativity scene *noun*
el **belén** *masc*

natural *adjective*
1 (*found in nature, not manufactured*) **natural** *masc & fem*
natural resources recursos naturales
I'm a natural blonde. Soy rubia natural.
2 (*born*) **nato** *masc*, **nata** *fem*
He is a natural leader. Es un líder nato.
3 (*normal, expected*) **natural** *masc & fem*
It's natural that he should do that. Es natural que haga eso.

WORD TIP *ser natural que* is followed by a verb in the subjunctive.

naturally *adverb*
naturalmente

nature *noun*
1 (*the natural world*) la **naturaleza** *fem*
the laws of nature las leyes de la naturaleza
2 (*temperament*) la **naturaleza** *fem*
by nature por naturaleza
- **nature reserve** la reserva natural

naughty *adjective*
travieso *masc*, **traviesa** *fem*
Don't be so naughty. No seas tan travieso.
You naughty girl! ¡Mala!

nausea *noun*
las **náuseas** *plural fem*

navel *noun*
el **ombligo** *masc*

English–Spanish
a b c d e f g h i j k l m n o p q r s t u v w x y z

to **navigate** *verb*
navegar [28]

navy *noun*
la **marina** *fem*
My uncle's in the navy. Mi tío está en la marina.

navy-blue *adjective*
azul marino *invariable adj*
navy-blue gloves guantes azul marino

near *adjective* ▷ see **near** *adv, prep*
cercano *masc*, **cercana** *fem*
the nearest shop la tienda más cercana

near *adverb, preposition* ▷ see **near** *adj*
1 (*nearby*) **cerca**
They live quite near. Viven bastante cerca.
to go near to something acercarse **[31]** a algo
Don't go any nearer to the edge. No te acerques más al borde.
2 (*close to*) **cerca de**
I live near the station. Vivo cerca de la estación.
Don't go too near the fire. No te acerques demasiado al fuego.
3 (*in time*) **Your birthday's getting nearer.** Se acerca tu cumpleaños.

nearby *adverb* ▷ see **nearby** *adj*
cerca
There's a park nearby. Hay un parque cerca.

nearby *adjective* ▷ see **nearby** *adv*
cercano *masc*, **cercana** *fem*
a nearby park un parque cercano

nearly *adverb*
casi
nearly empty casi vacío
We're nearly there. Ya casi hemos llegado.

neat *adjective*
1 (*well-organized*) **ordenado** *masc*, **ordenada** *fem*
a neat desk un pupitre ordenado
2 (*your clothes, the way you look*) **arreglado** *masc*, **arreglada** *fem*
She always looks very neat. Siempre va muy arreglada.
3 (*garden*) **muy cuidado** *masc*, **muy cuidada** *fem*

necessarily *adverb*
not necessarily no necesariamente

necessary *adjective*
necesario *masc*, **necesaria** *fem*
if necessary si es necesario

neck *noun*
(*of a person, garment, bottle*) el **cuello** *masc*

necklace *noun*
el **collar** *masc*

nectarine *noun*
la **nectarina** *fem*

need *noun* ▷ see **need** *verb*
la **necesidad** *fem*
There's no need, I've done it already. No hay necesidad, ya lo he hecho.
There's no need to wait. No hay necesidad de esperar.

to **need** *verb* ▷ see **need** *noun*
1 (*to require*) **necesitar [17]**
We need bread. Necesitamos pan.
They need help. Necesitan ayuda.
Do you need the hammer? ¿Necesitas el martillo?
Everything you need. Todo lo que necesites.
2 (*to have to*) **to need to do something** tener **[9]** que hacer algo
I need to drop in at the bank. Tengo que pasarme por el banco.
She'll need to check. Tendrá que comprobarlo.
3 (*to be obliged to*) **You needn't decide today.** No hace falta que decidas hoy.
You needn't wait. No hace falta que esperes.

needle *noun*
la **aguja** *fem*

negative *noun*
(*of a photo*) el **negativo** *masc*

neglected *adjective*
descuidado *masc*, **descuidada** *fem*

neighbour *noun*
el **vecino** *masc*, la **vecina** *fem*
We're going round to the neighbours'. Vamos a casa de los vecinos.

neighbourhood *noun*
el **barrio** *masc*
a nice neighbourhood un barrio agradable

neither *conjunction*
1 (*used in sentences with* **nor**)
neither... nor ni ... ni
I have neither the time nor the money. No tengo ni tiempo ni dinero.
2 (*nor*) **tampoco**
Neither do I. Yo tampoco.
'I didn't go.'— 'Neither did I.' 'No fui.'— 'Yo tampoco.'

3 (*with gustar*) **'I don't like fish.'— 'Neither do I.'** 'No me gusta el pescado.'— 'Ni a mí tampoco.'
'I didn't like the film.'— 'Neither did Kirsty.' 'No me gustó la película.'— 'Ni a Kirsty tampoco.'
'Which do you like?'— 'Neither.' '¿Cuál te gusta?'— 'Ninguno.'

♪ **nephew** *noun*
el **sobrino** *masc*

nerve *noun*
1 (*in the body*) el **nervio** *masc*
2 (*courage*) el **valor** *masc*
to lose one's nerve perder [36] el valor
3 (*cheek*) la **cara** *fem*
You've got a nerve! ¡Vaya cara que tienes! (*informal*)

nervous *adjective*
nervioso *masc*, **nerviosa** *fem*
to feel nervous estar [2] nervioso
• **nervous breakdown** la crisis nerviosa

nest *noun*
el **nido** *masc*

net *noun*
la **red** *fem*
(*Computers*) **the Net** la Red

Netherlands *noun*
the Netherlands los Países Bajos

nettle *noun*
la **ortiga** *fem*

network *noun*
la **red** *fem*

neutral *adjective* ▷ see **neutral** *noun*
1 (*not taking sides*) **neutral** *masc & fem*
2 (*colour*) **neutro** *masc & fem*

neutral *noun* ▷ see **neutral** *adj*
(*in a gearbox*) el **punto muerto**
to be in neutral estar [2] en punto muerto

♪ **never** *adverb*
nunca
He never helps. Nunca ayuda.
Ben never smokes. Ben no fuma nunca.
I've never seen the film. No he visto nunca la película.
'Have you ever been to Spain?'— 'No, never.' '¿Has estado alguna vez en España?'— 'No, nunca.'
Never again! ¡Nunca más!

nevertheless *adverb*
sin embargo

♪ **new** *adjective*
1 (*unused, recently acquired*) **nuevo** *masc*, **nueva** *fem*
a new car un coche nuevo
Have you seen their new house? ¿Has visto su casa nueva?
2 (*different*) **nuevo** *masc*, **nueva** *fem*
to start a new job empezar [25] una nueva vida
Debbie's new boyfriend el nuevo novio de Debbie

♪ **news** *plural noun*
1 (*everyday gossip*) la **noticia** *fem*
a piece of good news una buena noticia
Have you heard the news? ¿Te has enterado de la noticia?
Any news? ¿Hay alguna noticia?
2 (*on TV, radio*) las **noticias** *plural fem*
the midday news las noticias del mediodía

newsagent *noun*
el **vendedor de periódicos**, la **vendedora de periódicos**
at the newsagent's en la tienda de periódicos

♪ **newspaper** *noun*
el **periódico** *masc*

newsreader *noun*
el **presentador** *masc*, la **presentadora** *fem*

♪ **New Year** *noun*
el **Año Nuevo**
Happy New Year! ¡Feliz Año Nuevo!

New Year's Day *noun*
el **día de Año Nuevo**

New Year's Eve *noun*
la **Nochevieja** *fem*

New Zealand *noun*
Nueva Zelanda *fem*

New Zealander *noun*
el **neozelandés** *masc*, la **neozelandesa** *fem*

WORD TIP Adjectives and nouns for nationality and regional origin do not have capital letters in Spanish.

♪ **next** *adjective* ▷ see **next** *adv*
1 (*to talk about the future*) **próximo** *masc*, **próxima** *fem*
next week la próxima semana
next Thursday el próximo jueves
next year el próximo año
the next time I see you la próxima vez que te vea
The next train is at ten. El próximo tren sale a las diez. ▸▸

I'll see you next Thursday. Te veré el próximo jueves.
the week after next la semana que viene no, la otra
2 (*to talk about the past*) **siguiente** *masc & fem*
the next day al día siguiente
The next day we went to Valencia. Al día siguiente fuimos a Valencia.
3 (*following*) **siguiente** *masc & fem*
I'm getting off at the next stop. Me bajo en la siguiente parada.
4 (*neighbouring*) **in the next room** en la habitación de al lado

♂ **next** *adverb* ▷ see **next** *adj*
1 (*afterwards*) **luego**
What did he say next? ¿Qué dijo luego?
2 (*now*) **ahora**
What shall we do next? ¿Qué hacemos ahora?
3 (*beside*) **next to someone, something** al lado de alguien, algo
the girl next to Pat la chica que está al lado de Pat
It's next to the baker's. Está al lado de la panadería.
4 (*virtually*) **It's next to impossible.** Es casi imposible.
I bought it for next to nothing. Lo compré por poquísimo dinero.

next door *adverb* ▷ see **next-door** *adj*
al lado
the girl next door la chica de al lado
They live next door. Viven al lado.

next-door *adjective* ▷ see **next door** *adv*
de al lado *masc & fem*
our next-door neighbours nuestros vecinos de al lado

NGO *noun*
(*= Non-Governmental Organization*) **ONG** *fem* (*Organización No-Gubernamental*)

Nicaragua *noun*
Nicaragua *fem*

Nicaraguan *adjective & noun*
1 **nicaragüense** *masc & fem*
2 un & una **nicaragüense** *masc & fem*
the Nicaraguans los nicaragüenses

WORD TIP Adjectives and nouns for nationality and regional origin do not have capital letters in Spanish.

♂ **nice** *adjective*
1 (*pleasant, enjoyable*) **agradable** *masc & fem*
We had a very nice evening. Pasamos una tarde muy agradable.
Brighton's a very nice town. Brighton es una ciudad muy agradable.
Have a nice time! ¡Que lo pases bien!
2 (*attractive: object, place*) **bonito** *masc*, **bonita** *fem*
That's a nice dress. Ese vestido es bonito.
3 (*attractive: person*) **guapo** *masc*, **guapa** *fem*
You look nice in that dress. Estás muy guapa con ese vestido.
4 (*kind, friendly*) **bueno** *masc*, **buena** *fem*
to be nice to somebody ser [1] bueno con alguien
She's been very nice to me. Ha sido muy buena conmigo.
He's a really nice person. Es muy buena persona.
5 (*food*) **rico** *masc*, **rica** *fem*
The food was really nice. La comida estaba muy rica.
6 (*weather*) **bueno** *masc*, **buena** *masc*
It's a nice day. Hace buen día.
We had nice weather. Tuvimos buen tiempo.

WORD TIP *bueno* becomes *buen* before a masc singular noun.

to **nick** *verb*
(*to steal*) **mangar** [28] (*informal*)

nickname *noun*
el **apodo** *masc*

♂ **niece** *noun*
la **sobrina** *fem*

♂ **night** *noun*
la **noche** *fem*
tomorrow night mañana por la noche
last night anoche
I saw Greg last night. Anoche vi a Greg.
at night por la noche
It's cold at night. Hace frío por la noche.
on Friday night el viernes por la noche
on Friday nights los viernes por la noche
all night long toda la noche
every night todas las noches
to stay the night with somebody pasar [17] la noche con alguien
Good night! ¡Buenas noches!
• **night club** el club nocturno

nightdress *noun*
el **camisón** *masc*

nightie *noun*
el **camisón** *masc*

nightmare *noun*
la **pesadilla** *fem*
to have a nightmare tener [9] una pesadilla

night time *noun*
la **noche** *fem*

nil *noun*
cero *masc*
They won four-nil. Ganaron cuatro a cero.

nine *number*
nueve *invariable number*
Jake's nine. Jake tiene nueve años.
It's nine o'clock. Son las nueve.

nineteen *number*
diecinueve *invariable number*
Jonny's nineteen. Jonny tiene diecinueve años.

nineties *plural noun* ▷ see **ninety** *number*
the nineties los años noventa
in the nineties en los años noventa

ninety *number* ▷ see **nineties** *plural noun*
noventa *invariable number*
He's ninety. Tiene noventa años.
ninety-five noventa y cinco

ninth *adjective* ▷ see **ninth** *noun*
noveno *masc*, **novena** *fem*
on the ninth floor en la novena planta

ninth *noun* ▷ see **ninth** *adj*
1 (*fraction*) **a ninth** una novena parte
2 (*when saying dates*) **the ninth of June** el nueve de junio

nitrogen *noun*
el **nitrógeno** *masc*

no *adjective* ▷ see **no** *adv*
1 (*not any*) **We've got no bread.** No tenemos pan.
No problem! ¡Sin problema!
They've got no children. No tienen hijos.
The room has no windows. La habitación no tiene ninguna ventana.
2 (*on a notice*) **'No smoking'** 'Prohibido fumar'
'No parking' 'Prohibido aparcar'

no *adverb* ▷ see **no** *adj*
no
I said no. He dicho que no.
No thank you. No, gracias.
'Have you seen John?'— 'No, I haven't.' 'Has visto a John?'— 'No.'

nobody *pronoun*
nadie
'Who's there?'— 'Nobody.' '¿Quién está ahí?'— 'Nadie.'
There's nobody there. No hay nadie.
Nobody knows me. Nadie me conoce.
Nobody answered. No contestó nadie.

to **nod** *verb*
(*to say yes*) **asentir [14] con la cabeza**
He nodded. Asintió con la cabeza.

noise *noun*
el **ruido** *masc*
to make a noise hacer **[7]** ruido

noisy *adjective*
ruidoso *masc*, **ruidosa** *fem*

none *pronoun*
ninguno *masc*, **ninguna** *fem*
'How many students failed the exam?'— 'None.' '¿Cuántos estudiantes suspendieron?'— 'Ninguno.'
None of the girls knows him. Ninguna de las chicas lo conoce.
There's none left. No queda nada.
There are none left. No queda ninguno.

nonsense *noun*
las **tonterías** *plural fem*
to talk nonsense decir **[5]** tonterías
Nonsense! She's at least thirty. ¡Tonterías! Tiene por lo menos treinta años.

non-smoker *noun*
el **no fumador** *masc*, la **no fumadora** *fem*

non-stop *adjective* ▷ see **non-stop** *adv*
(*train, flight*) **directo** *masc*, **directa** *fem*

non-stop *adverb* ▷ see **non-stop** *adj*
sin parar
She talks non-stop. Habla sin parar.

noodles *plural noun*
los **fideos** *plural masc*

noon *noun*
el **mediodía** *masc*
at (twelve) noon a mediodía

no one *pronoun*
nadie
'Who's there?'— 'No one.' '¿Quién está ahí?'— 'Nadie.'
There's no one there. No hay nadie.
No one knows me. Nadie me conoce.
No one answered. Nadie contestó.

nor *conjunction*
1 (*used in sentences with neither*) **neither ... nor** ni ... ni
I have neither the time nor the money. No tengo ni tiempo ni dinero.
2 (*neither*) **tampoco**
Nor do I. Yo tampoco.
'I didn't go.'— 'Nor did I.' 'No fui.'— 'Yo tampoco.'
3 (*with* **gustar**) **'I don't like fish.'— 'Nor do I.'** 'No me gusta el pescado.'— 'Ni a mí tampoco.'
'I didn't like the film.'— 'Nor did Kirsty.' 'No me gustó la película.'— 'Ni a Kirsty tampoco.'

English–Spanish
a b c d e f g h i j k l m n o p q r s t u v w x y z

normal *adjective*
normal *masc & fem* **That's absolutely normal.** Eso es absolutamente normal.
to get back to normal volver **[45]** a la normalidad

normally *adverb*
normalmente

north *adjective, adverb* ▷ see **north** *noun*
norte *masc & fem*
the north side la parte norte
a north wind un viento del norte
north of Madrid al norte de Madrid
to travel north viajar **[17]** hacia el norte

WORD TIP *norte* never changes.

north *noun* ▷ see **north** *adj, adv*
el **norte** *masc*
in the north of England en el norte de Inglaterra

North America *noun*
Norteamérica *fem*

North American *adjective & noun*
1 **norteamericano** *masc*, **norteamericana** *fem*
2 (*person*) un **norteamericano** *masc*, una **norteamericana** *fem*
the North Americans los norteamericanos

WORD TIP Adjectives and nouns for nationality and regional origin do not have capital letters in Spanish.

northeast *adjective & adverb*
▷ see **northeast** *noun*
noreste *masc & fem*
in northeast England en el noreste de Inglaterra

WORD TIP *noreste* never changes.

northeast *noun* ▷ see **northeast** *adj, adv*
el **noreste** *masc*

Northern Ireland *noun*
Irlanda del Norte

Northern Irish *adjective*
de Irlanda del norte
He's Northern Irish. Es de Irlanda del norte.

North Pole *noun*
the North Pole el Polo Norte

North Sea *noun*
the North Sea el mar del Norte

northwest *adjective & adverb*
▷ see **northwest** *noun*
noroeste *masc & fem*
in northwest Scotland en el noroeste de Escocia

WORD TIP *noroeste* never changes.

northwest *noun* ▷ see **northwest** *adj, adv*
el **noroeste** *masc*

Norway *noun*
Noruega *fem*

Norwegian *adjective & noun*
1 **noruego** *masc*, **noruega** *fem*
2 (*person*) un **noruego** *masc*, una **noruega** *fem*
the Norwegians los noruegos
3 (*the language*) el **noruego** *masc*

WORD TIP Adjectives and nouns for nationality, regional origin and language do not have capital letters in Spanish.

nose *noun*
la **nariz** *fem*
to blow your nose sonarse **[24]** la nariz

nosebleed *noun*
la **hemorragia nasal**
to have a nosebleed tener **[9]** una hemorragia nasal

nostril *noun*
la **fosa nasal**

not *adverb*
1 (*with adjectives and adverbs*) **no**
not on Saturdays los sábados no
Not all alone! ¡Completamente solo no!
It's not bad. No está mal.
2 (*with verbs*) **no**
It's not my car. No es mi coche.
I don't know. No sé.
Sam didn't phone. Sam no llamó.
We decided not to wait. Decidimos no esperar.
She told me not to cry. Me dijo que no llorara.
3 (*in no way*) **not at all** en absoluto
I'm not at all worried No estoy preocupada en absoluto.
4 (*when somebody says **thank you***) **not at all** de nada
'Thanks very much.'— 'Not at all.' 'Muchas gracias.'— 'De nada.'

note *noun*
1 (*short letter*) la **nota** *fem*
She left me a note. Me dejó una nota.
2 (*reminder*) el **apunte** *masc*
to take notes tomar **[17]** apuntes

3 (*banknote*) el **billete** *masc*
a ten-pound note un billete de diez libras
4 (*in music*) la **nota** *fem*
• **notebook** el cuaderno *masc*
• **notepad** el bloc *masc*

♪ nothing *pronoun*
1 (*in general*) **nada**
nothing new nada nuevo
nothing special nada especial
'What did you say?'— 'Nothing.' '¿Qué dijiste?'— 'Nada.'
2 (*with verbs*) **no ... nada**
She knows nothing. No sabe nada.
There was nothing there. No había nada allí.
I saw nothing. No vi nada.
There's nothing happening. No está pasando nada.
There's nothing new. No hay nada nuevo.
They do nothing but fight. No hacen más que pelearse.

♪ to notice *verb* ▷ see **notice** *noun*
notar [17]
I didn't notice anything. No noté nada.

♪ notice *noun* ▷ see **notice** *verb*
1 (*sign*) el **letrero** *masc*
2 (*to pay attention*) **to take notice of somebody** hacerle [7] caso a alguien
Don't take any notice of her! ¡No le hagas caso!
3 (*advance warning*) **to do something at short notice** hacer [7] algo con poca antelación
They cancelled the match at short notice. Cancelaron el partido con poca antelación.
• **notice board** el tablón de anuncios

♪ nought *noun*
el **cero** *masc*

♪ noun *noun*
el **nombre** *masc*

♪ novel *noun*
la **novela** *fem*

novelist *noun*
el & la **novelista** *masc & fem*

♪ November *noun*
el **noviembre** *masc*
in November en noviembre

WORD TIP Names of months and days start with small letters in Spanish.

♪ now *adverb*
1 (*at the present time*) **ahora**
Where is he now? ¿Dónde está ahora?
They live in the country now. Ahora viven en el campo.
Now's your chance Esta es tu oportunidad.
2 **He's busy just now.** Está ocupado en este momento.
I saw her just now in the corridor. Acabo de verla en el pasillo.
3 (*to talk about the past*) **ya**
They've all gone home now. Ya se han ido todos a casa.
It was too late to change now. Ya era demasiado tarde para cambiar.
4 (*nowadays*) **hoy en día**
Divorce is easier now. Hoy en día es más fácil divorciarse.
5 (*to emphasize a statement, question*)
Now, look here! ¡Espera un momento!
Now, who's next? ¿Bueno ¿ahora a quién le toca?
6 (*in expressions*) **Now, now.** ¡Vamos, vamos!
Now, now, don't cry. Vamos, vamos, no llores.
now and then de vez en cuando
We see each other now and then. Nos vemos de vez en cuando.
now then vamos a ver
Now then, what's going on here? Vamos a ver ¿qué es lo que pasa aquí?
from now on de ahora en adelante
She will work hard from now on. Trabajará duro de ahora en adelante.
just now en este momento
He's busy just now. Está ocupado en este momento.
I saw her just now in the corridor. Acabo de verla en el pasillo.
right now ahora mismo
Do it right now! ¡Hazlo ahora mismo!

♪ nowadays *adverb*
hoy en día
Nowadays they are quite common. Hoy en día son bastante comunes.

♪ nowhere *adverb, pronoun*
1 (*no place*) **ninguna parte**
There's nowhere to park. No hay sitio donde aparcar.
Nowhere was open yet. Todavía no había nada abierto.
The car just appeared out of nowhere. El coche apareció de la nada.
2 (*in no place*) **en ninguna parte**
nowhere in Spain en ninguna parte de España
She was nowhere to be found. No se la encontraba por ningún lado. ▸▸

3 (*to no place*) **a ninguna parte**
'Where did she go after work?'— 'Nowhere.' '¿Dónde fue después del trabajo?'— 'A ninguna parte.'
4 (*nowhere near*) **Warsaw is nowhere near Moscow.** Varsovia está lejísimos de Moscú.
His answer was nowhere near right. Se equivocó por mucho.

nuclear *adjective*
nuclear *masc & fem*
a nuclear power station una central nuclear

nude *noun*
el **desnudo** *masc*
in the nude desnudo *masc*, desnuda *fem*

nuisance *noun*
1 (*person*) el **pesado** *masc*, la **pesada** *fem*
He's a real nuisance. Es un verdadero pesado.
2 **It's a nuisance.** Es un fastidio.

numb *adjective*
entumecido *masc*, **entumecida** *fem*
My fingers are numb with cold. Tengo los dedos entumecidos del frío.

number *noun*
el **número** *masc*
my new phone number mi nuevo número de teléfono
a large number of visitors un gran número de visitantes
I live at number thirty-one. Vivo en el número treinta y uno.
The third number is a 7. El tercer número es un siete.
- **number plate** la matrícula

nun *noun*
la **monja** *fem*

nurse *noun*
el **enfermero** *masc*, la **enfermera** *fem*
Janet's a nurse. Janet es enfermera.

nursery *noun*
1 (*for children*) la **guardería** *fem*
2 (*for plants*) el **vivero** *masc*
- **nursery school** el jardín de infancia

nursing *noun*
la **enfermería** *fem*

nut *noun*
1 (*walnut*) la **nuez** *fem*
2 (*almond*) la **almendra** *fem*
3 (*peanut*) el **cacahuete** *masc*
4 (*hazelnut*) la **avellana** *masc*
5 (*for a bolt*) la **tuerca** *fem*

nylon *noun*
el **nylon** *masc*

O o

oak *noun*
el **roble** *masc*

oar *noun*
el **remo** *masc*

oasis *noun*
el **oasis** *masc, pl:* los **oasis**

obedient *adjective*
obediente *masc & fem*

to **obey** *verb*
(*a person*) **obedecer** [35]
to obey the rules respetar [17] las reglas

object *noun* ▷ see **object** *verb*
el **objeto** *masc*

to **object** *verb* ▷ see **object** *noun*
oponerse [11]
If you don't object ... Si no te opones ...
She objected to my suggestion. Se opuso a mi sugerencia.

objection *noun*
la **objeción** *fem*, el **inconveniente** *masc*

oboe *noun*
el **oboe** *masc*
to play the oboe tocar [31] el oboe

obsessed *adjective*
obsesionado *masc*, **obsesionada** *fem*
She's obsessed with her diet. Está obsesionada con su dieta.

obsession *noun*
la **obsesión** *fem*
He has an obsession with cleanliness. Tiene obsesión con la limpieza.

obvious *adjective*
obvio *masc*, **obvia** *fem*

obviously *adverb*
evidentemente
The house is obviously empty. Evidentemente la casa está vacía.
'Do you want to come too?'— 'Obviously, but it's a bit difficult.' '¿Tú quieres venir también?'— 'Evidentemente, pero es un poco difícil.'

occasion *noun*
la **ocasión** *fem*
a special occasion una ocasión especial
on various occasions en varias ocasiones

occasional *adjective*
He sends us the occasional letter. De vez en cuando nos manda una carta.

occasionally *adverb*
de vez en cuando

occupation *noun*
la **ocupación** *fem*

occupied *adjective*
ocupado *masc*, **ocupada** *fem*

to **occur** *verb*
1 **ocurrir** [19]
The accident occurred on Monday. El accidente ocurrió el lunes.
2 **ocurrir**
It occurred to me that we might lose them. Se me ocurrió que podríamos perderlos.
It had never occurred to her. Nunca se le había ocurrido.

ocean *noun*
el **océano** *masc*
the Atlantic Ocean el océano Atlántico
the Pacific Ocean el océano Pacífico

o'clock *adverb*
at ten o'clock a las diez
exactly five o'clock las cinco en punto
It's one o'clock. Es la una.
It's three o'clock. Son las tres.

🔑 **October** *noun*
el **octubre** *masc*
in October en octubre

WORD TIP Names of months and days start with small letters in Spanish.

🔑 **odd** *adjective*
1 (*strange*) **raro** *masc*, **rara** *fem*
That's odd, I'm sure I heard the phone. Qué raro, estoy seguro de que oí el teléfono.
2 (*number*) **impar** *masc & fem*
Three is an odd number. El tres es un número impar.
3 (*sock, shoe*) **desparejado** *masc*, **desparejada** *fem*
an odd sock un calcetín desparejado

odds and ends *plural noun*
los **cachivaches** *plural masc*

🔑 indicates key words

English–Spanish

of *preposition*

1 (*belonging to*) **de**
the name of the flower el nombre de la flor
the end of my work el final de mi trabajo
the beginning of the concert el principio del concierto
the sixth of June el seis de junio

WORD TIP *de + el* becomes *del*.

2 (*with quantities*) **a kilo of tomatoes** un kilo de tomates
some of them algunos *masc*, algunas *fem*
a lot of them muchos *masc*, muchas *fem*
We ate a lot of it. Comimos mucho.
Ray has two bikes but he's selling one of them. Ray tiene dos bicicletas, pero va a vender una.

3 (*about people*) **a friend of mine** un amigo mío, una amiga mía
two of us dos de nosotros
There are two of us. Somos dos.

4 (*saying what something is made of*) **de**
a bracelet made of silver una pulsera de plata
a cup of tea una taza de té

5 (*with tastes, smells*) **a taste of lemons** un sabor a limones
a strong smell of fish un fuerte olor a pescado

off *adjective, adverb, preposition*

1 (*electricity, lights*) **apagado** *masc*, **apagada** *fem*
Is the telly off? ¿Está apagada la tele?
to turn off the lights apagar **[28]** la luz
Switch the engine off. Apaga el motor.

2 (*tap, water, gas*) **cerrado,** *masc*, **cerrada** *fem*
to turn off the tap cerrar **[29]** el grifo

3 (*not at work, school*) **a day off** un día libre
Caro took three days off work. Caro se tomó tres días libres en el trabajo.
Maya's off school today. Maya no ha venido al colegio hoy.
He's off sick. No ha venido al trabajo porque está enfermo.

4 (*to show movement*) **I'm off.** Me voy.
to take something off (*to remove*) quitar **[17]** algo
Take your books off the table. Quita los libros de la mesa.
He took his shirt off. Se quitó la camisa.

5 (*down from*) **It fell off the chair.** Se cayó de la silla.
He got off the train. Bajó del tren.
Don't jump off the wall! ¡No saltes del muro!

6 (*cancelled*) **suspendido,** *fem* **suspendida**
The match is off. El partido se ha suspendido.

7 (*food, drink*) **to be off** estar malo, *fem* mala
The milk's off. La leche está cortada.

offence *noun*

1 (*crime*) el **delito** *masc*

2 (*hurt feelings*) **to take offence** ofenderse **[18]**
He takes offence easily. Se ofende fácilmente.

offer *noun* ▷ see **offer** *verb*

1 (*of help, a job*) la **oferta** *fem*
a job offer una oferta de trabajo

2 (*in a shop*) **'On special offer'** 'De oferta especial'

to **offer** *verb* ▷ see **offer** *noun*

1 (*a present, reward, job*) **ofrecer [35]**
He offered her a coffee. Le ofreció una café.

2 **to offer to do something** ofrecerse **[35]** a hacer algo
Mike offered to drive me to the station. Mike se ofreció a llevarme a la estación.

office *noun*

la **oficina** *fem*
He's still in the office. Todavía está en la oficina.
He works in an office. Trabaja de oficinista.

- **office block** el bloque de oficinas
- **office worker** el & la oficinista

officer *noun*

el & la **oficial** *masc & fem*

official *adjective*

oficial *masc & fem*
the official version la versión oficial

off-licence *noun*

la **tienda de vinos y licores**

offside *adverb*

fuera de juego

often *adverb*

a menudo
He's often late. A menudo llega tarde.
I'd like to see Eric more often. Me gustaría ver a Eric más a menudo.
Do you go often? ¿Vas a menudo?
How often? ¿Con qué frecuencia?
How often do you see Rosie? ¿Con qué frecuencia ves a Rosie?

oil *noun*

el **aceite** *masc*
olive oil aceite de oliva
suntan oil aceite bronceador
Check the oil before starting the engine.

Revisa el aceite antes de encender el motor.

- **oil painting** el óleo

ointment *noun*
la **pomada** *fem*

OK, okay *adjective, adverb*
1 (*showing agreement*) **vale**
OK, tomorrow at ten. Vale, mañana a las diez.
2 (*to ask or give permission*) **Is it OK to use the phone?** ¿Puedo usar el teléfono?
Is it OK with you if I come on Friday? ¿Te va bien si vengo el viernes?
It's OK if you don't want to do it. No pasa nada si no quieres hacerlo.
3 (*person*) **majo** (*informal*) *masc*, **maja** *fem*
Daisy's OK. Daisy es maja.
4 (*nothing special*) **The film was OK.** La película no estuvo mal.
5 (*not ill*) **Are you OK?** ¿Estás bien?
I'm OK now. Ahora estoy bien.

old *adjective*
1 (*not young, not new*) **viejo** *masc*, **vieja** *fem*
an old man un hombre viejo
an old lady una señora vieja
an old friend of mine un viejo amigo mío
old people los ancianos
Bring some old clothes. Trae ropa vieja.
the oldest restaurant in town el restaurante más antiguo de la ciudad
2 (*previous*) **antiguo** *masc*, **antigua** *fem*
my old school mi antiguo colegio
their old address su antigua dirección
Her old car was a Fiat. Su antiguo coche era un Fiat.
in the old days antiguamente
3 (*to talk about age*) **How old are you?** ¿Cuántos años tienes?
James is ten years old. James tiene diez años.
a three-year-old child un niño de tres años
my older sister mi hermana mayor
She's older than me. Es mayor que yo.
He's a year older than me. Es un año mayor que yo.

- **old age** la vejez
- **old-age pensioner** el & la pensionista

old-fashioned *adjective*
1 (*clothes, music, style*) **pasado de moda** *masc*, **pasada de moda** *fem*
2 (*person*) **anticuado** *masc*, **anticuada** *fem*
My parents are so old-fashioned. Mis padres son tan anticuados.

olive *noun*
la **aceituna** *fem*

- **olive oil** el aceite de oliva
- **olive tree** el olivo

mini-info: olives
Spain is the world's leading olive producer and the average Spaniard consumes 10 litres of olive oil a year.

Olympic Games, Olympics *plural noun*
los **Juegos Olímpicos**

ombudsman *noun*
the ombudsman el defensor del pueblo *masc*, la defensora del pueblo *fem*

omelette *noun*
la **tortilla** *fem*
a cheese omelette una tortilla de queso

to **omit** *verb*
omitir [19]

on *adjective* ▷ see **on** *prep*
1 (*TV, light, oven, radio*) **to be on** estar **[2]** encendido, *fem* encendida
All the lights were on. Todas las luces estaban encendidas.
Is the radio on? ¿Está encendida la radio?
I've put the microwave on. He encendido el microondas.
You left the tap on! ¡Dejaste abierto el grifo!
2 (*machine*) **estar en marcha**
The dishwasher's on. El lavaplatos está en marcha.
3 (*clothes*) **I put my best jeans on.** Me puse los mejores vaqueros.
What did she have on? ¿Qué llevaba puesto?
He had nothing on. Estaba desnudo.
4 (*happening*) **What's on TV?** ¿Qué ponen en la tele?
What's on this week at the cinema? ¿Qué ponen en el cine esta semana?
Is the party still on? ¿No se ha suspendido la fiesta?
5 (*continuing*) **Is the programme still on?** ¿Sigue en pie el programa?
He keeps on about his accident. No para de hablar de su accidente.

on *preposition* ▷ see **on** *adj*
1 (*showing position*) **en**
on the desk en la mesa
on the road en la carretera
on the beach en la playa
on the left (hand side) a la izquierda
the first turn on the right la primera calle a la derecha ▸▸

2 (*in expressions of time*) **on March 21st** el 21 de marzo
on rainy days los días de lluvia
He's arriving on Tuesday. Llega el martes.
It's shut on Saturdays. Cierra los sábados.
on Monday morning el lunes por la mañana
on Thursday afternoons los jueves por la tarde
on her birthday el día de su cumpleaños
3 (*for buses, trains, etc*) **She arrived on the bus.** Llegó en autobús.
I met Jackie on the train. Me encontré con Jackie en el tren.
I slept on the plane. Dormí en el avión.
Let's go on our bikes! ¡Vayamos en las bicis!
4 (*happening*) **on TV** en la tele
on the radio en la radio
It's come out on DVD. Ha salido en DVD.
5 (*showing an activity*) **to be on holiday** estar de vacacciones
to be on strike estar [2] de huelga
I'm on the phone. Estoy hablando por teléfono.
Are you on the computer? ¿Estás usando el ordenador?

once *adverb*
1 (*one time*) **una vez**
once a day una vez al día
more than once más de una vez
once upon a time érase una vez
Try once more. Inténtalo una vez más.
I've tried once already. Ya lo he intentado una vez.
We've seen her once or twice. La hemos visto un par de veces.
2 (*in expressions: immediately*) **at once** inmediatamente, enseguida
The doctor came at once. El médico vino inmediatamente.
(*: at the same time*) **at once** a la vez
I can't do two things at once. No puedo hacer dos cosas a la vez.

one *number* ▷ see **one** *pron*
1 (*the number*) **uno** *masc*, **una** *fem*
one apple una manzana
one son un hijo
It's one o'clock. Es la una.
2 (*only*) **único** *masc*, **única** *fem*
Sunday is my one free day. El domingo es mi único día libre.

WORD TIP *uno* becomes *un* before a masc singular noun.

one *pronoun* ▷ see **one** *number*
1 **uno** *masc*, **una** *fem*
one of us uno de nosotros, una de nosotras
one of my friends uno de mis amigos, una de mis amigas
One never knows. Uno nunca sabe., Una nunca sabe.
If you want a pen I've got one. Si quieres un boli yo tengo uno.
2 **this one** este *masc*, esta *fem*
I like that jumper, but this one's cheaper. Me gusta ese jersey, pero este es más barato.
Do you want this shirt or this one? ¿Quieres esta camisa o esta otra?
3 **that one** ese *masc*, esa *fem*
'Which video?'— 'That one.' '¿Qué vídeo?'— 'Ese.'
4 **that one (there)** aquel *masc*, **aquella** *fem*
'Which CD?'— 'That one.' '¿Qué CD?'— 'Aquel.'
5 **which one?** ¿cuál?
'My foot's hurting.'— 'Which one?' 'Me duele el pie.'— '¿Cuál?'
'I was talking to those boys.'— 'Which ones?' 'Estaba hablando con esos chicos.'— '¿Cuáles?'
6 **another one** otro *masc*, otra *fem*
I've already had a coffee, but I'll have another one. Ya he tomado un café pero voy a tomar otro.
I liked the tee-shirt so much that I bought another one. Me gustó tanto la camiseta que compré otra.

one's *adjective*
to wash one's hands lavarse [17] las manos
One must pay one's debts. Uno debe pagar sus deudas.

oneself *pronoun*
1 (*reflexive*) **se**
to wash oneself lavarse [17]
to hurt oneself hacerse [7] daño
2 (*for emphasis*) **uno mismo,** *fem* **una misma**
One has to do everything oneself. Hay que hacerlo todo uno mismo., Hay que hacerlo todo una misma.

one-way street *noun*
la **calle de sentido único**

onion *noun*
la **cebolla** *fem*

online, on-line *adjective, adverb*
en línea
You have to be online to download it. Tienes que estar en línea para bajarlo.
What do I have to do to go online? ¿Qué debo hacer para conectarme con Internet?

only *adjective* ▷ see **only** *adv, conj*
único *masc*, **única** *fem*
the only free seat el único asiento libre
the only thing to do lo único que se puede hacer
I am an only child. Soy hijo único.

only *adverb, conjunction* ▷ see **only** *adj*
1 (*with a verb*) **sólo**
They've only got two bedrooms. Sólo tienen dos habitaciones.
Anne's only free on Fridays. Anne sólo tiene libres los viernes.
There are only three left. Sólo quedan tres.
'How long did they stay?'— 'Only two days.' '¿Cuánto tiempo se quedaron?'— 'Sólo dos días.'
2 (*but*) **pero**
I'd walk, only it's raining. Iría andando, pero está lloviendo.
3 (*for emphasis*) **only just: I've only just seen it.** Acabo de verlo.

onto *preposition*
sobre
It fell onto the tablecloth. Cayó sobre el mantel.
She climbed onto the wall. Se subió al muro.
The band came out onto the stage. El grupo salió al escenario.

open *adjective* ▷ see **open** *noun, verb*
abierto *masc*, **abierta** *fem*
The door's open. La puerta está abierta.
The baker's is open. La panadería está abierta.

open *noun* ▷ see **open** *adj, verb*
in the open al aire libre

to open *verb* ▷ see **open** *adj, noun*
1 (*a door, etc*) **abrir** [46]
Can you open the door for me? ¿Me puedes abrir la puerta?
Sam opened his eyes. Sam abrió los ojos.
The banks open at nine. Los bancos abren a las nueve.
2 (*by itself*) **abrirse** [46]
The door opened. La puerta se abrió.

open-air *adjective*
al aire libre
an open-air swimming pool una piscina al aire libre

opener *noun*
el **abridor** *masc*

opening *noun*
1 (*space*) la **abertura** *fem*
2 (*opportunity*) la **oportunidad** *fem*

opera *noun*
la **ópera** *fem*

to **operate** *verb*
1 (*a machine*) **manejar** [17]
Can you operate a crane? ¿Sabes manejar una grúa?
This button operates the wipers. Este botón hace funcionar los limpiabrisas.
2 (*on a patient*) **operar** [17]
Will they have to operate on him? ¿Tendrán que operarlo?

operation *noun*
la **operación** *fem*
She's had an operation. La han operado.

opinion *noun*
la **opinión** *fem*
in my opinion en mi opinión
• **opinion poll** la encuesta de opinión

opponent *noun*
el & la **oponente** *masc & fem*

opportunity *noun*
la **oportunidad** *fem*
to have the opportunity of doing something tener [9] la oportunidad de hacer algo
I took the opportunity to see her. Aproveché la oportunidad para verla.

opposed *adjective*
to be opposed to something oponerse [11] a algo
They are opposed to any change in the rules. Se oponen a cualquier cambio de las reglas.

opposite *adjective* ▷ see **opposite** *adv, noun, prep*
1 (*direction, side, view*) **opuesto** *masc*, **opuesta** *fem*
She went off in the opposite direction. Se fue en la dirección opuesta.
2 (*facing*) **de enfrente**
in the house opposite en la casa de enfrente

opposite *adverb* ▷ see **opposite** *adj, noun, prep*
enfrente
They live opposite. Viven enfrente.

opposite *noun* ▷ see **opposite** *adj, adv, prep*
the opposite lo contrario
The opposite of narrow is wide. Lo contrario de estrecho es ancho.
No, quite the opposite. No, todo lo contrario.

opposite *preposition* ▷ see **opposite** *adj, adv, noun*
enfrente de
opposite the station enfrente de la estación

opposition *noun*
la **oposición** *fem*

optician *noun*
el & la **oculista** *masc & fem*
I have to go the optician's. Tengo que ir a la óptica.

optimist *noun*
el & la **optmista** *masc & fem*
I'm an optimist. Soy optimista.

optimistic *adjective*
optimista *masc & fem*

or *conjunction*
1 (*to show alternatives*) **o, u**
English or Spanish? ¿Inglés o español?
silver or gold plata u oro
Yesterday or today? ¿Ayer u hoy?

WORD TIP *o* is the usual translation for *or*, but *u* must be used before a word starting with *o-* or *ho-*.

2 (*when in English you say* **not ... or ...**) **ni ... ni ...**
not in June or July ni en junio ni en julio
I don't have a cat or a dog. No tengo ni un gato ni un perro.
3 (*otherwise*) **si no**
Phone Mum, or she'll worry. Llama a mamá, si no se va a preocupar.

oral *noun*
(*exam*) el **oral** *masc*
the Spanish oral el oral de español

orange *adjective* ▷ see **orange** *noun*
naranja
my orange socks mis calcetines naranja

WORD TIP *naranja* does not change in the plural.

orange *noun* ▷ see **orange** *adj*
1 (*the fruit*) la **naranja** *fem*
an orange juice un zumo de naranja
an orange tree un naranjo
2 (*the colour*) el **naranja** *masc*
Orange suits you. El naranja te queda bien.

orchard *noun*
el **huerto** *fem*

orchestra *noun*
la **orquesta** *fem*
a symphony orchestra una orquesta sinfónica

order *noun* ▷ see **order** *verb*
1 (*arrangement*) el **orden** *masc*
in the right order ordenado, *fem* ordenada
The books are in the right order. Los libros están ordenados.
Put them in order. Ponlos en orden.
in the wrong order desordenado, *fem* desordenada
in alphabetical order en orden alfabético
2 (*command*) la **orden** *fem*
That's an order. Es una orden.
3 (*in a restaurant, cafe*) **Can I take your orders?** ¿Les tomo la nota?
4 (*not functioning*) **'Out of order'** 'No funciona'
5 (*to show purpose*) **in order to do something** para hacer algo
We hurried in order to be on time. Nos dimos prisa para llegar a tiempo.

to **order** *verb* ▷ see **order** *noun*
1 (*in a restaurant*) **pedir** [57]
We ordered steaks. Pedimos filetes.
2 (*in a shop*) **encargar** [23]
I ordered her new album. Encargué su nuevo álbum.
3 (*a taxi*) **llamar** [17] **a**
4 (*to command*) **ordenar** [17]
I order you to get out. Os ordeno que salgáis.

ordinary *adjective*
normal *masc & fem*
an ordinary day un día normal
I wore my ordinary clothes. Me puse la ropa de todos los días.

organ *noun*
1 (*Music*) el **órgano** *masc*
to play the organ tocar [31] el órgano
2 (*of the body*) el **órgano** *masc*
an organ transplant un trasplante de órgano

organic *adjective*
1 (*food*) **biológico** *masc*, **biológica** *fem*
2 (*farming*) **ecológico** *masc*, **ecológica** *fem*

organization *noun*
la **organización** *fem*

to **organize** *verb*
organizar [22]

original *adjective*
original *masc & fem*
The original version was better. La versión original era mejor.
It's a really original novel. Es una novela realmente original.

originally *adverb*
al principio
Originally we wanted to take the car. Al principio queríamos llevar el coche.
He's from Ireland originally. Es de origen irlandés.

Orkneys *plural noun*
the Orkneys las Órcadas *plural fem*

ornament *noun*
el **adorno** *masc*

orphan *noun*
el **huérfano** *masc*, la **huérfana** *fem*

other *adjective, pronoun*
1 (*with a singular noun*) **otro** *masc*, **otra** *fem*
the other day el otro día
We took the other road. Cogimos la otra carretera.
the other one el otro, *fem* la otra
I don't like this book, give me the other one. No me gusta este libro, dame el otro.
As well as this book he bought one other. Además de este libro compró otro más.
2 (*with a plural noun*) **otros** *masc*, **otras** *fem*
the other two cars los otros dos coches
He has two other brothers. Tiene otros dos hermanos.
He has two other sisters. Tiene otras dos hermanas.
3 (*the remainder*) **the others** los otros, *fem* las otras, los demás, *fem* las demás
Where are the others? ¿Dónde están los otros?
All the others have left. Todos los demás se han ido.
4 (*in expressions*) **somebody or other** alguien
something or other algo
somewhere or other en algún sitio
every other week una semana sí y otra no

otherwise *adverb* ▷ see **otherwise** *conj*
(*in other ways*) **aparte de eso**
The flat's a bit small but otherwise it's lovely. El piso es pequeño, pero aparte de eso es precioso.

otherwise *conjunction* ▷ see **otherwise** *adv*
(*or else*) **si no**
I'll phone home, otherwise they'll worry. Voy a llamar a casa, si no van a preocuparse.

ought *verb*
deber [18]
I ought to go now. Debería irme ahora.
They ought to know the address. Deberían saber las señas.
You oughtn't to have any problems. No deberías tener ningún problema.

WORD TIP *ought* is translated by the conditional tense of *deber*: *debería, deberías*, etc.

our *adjective*
1 **nuestro** *masc*, **nuestra** *fem*
our brother nuestro hermano
our house nuestra casa
our friends nuestros amigos
our houses nuestras casas
2 (*with parts of the body, clothes*) **el**, **la**, **los**, **las**
We changed our clothes before going out. Nos cambiamos de ropa antes de salir.
We got our shoes dirty. Nos ensuciamos los zapatos.
We should wash our hands. Deberíamos lavarnos las manos.

WORD TIP Spanish uses *el, la, los, las* for *our* with parts of the body and clothes.

ours *pronoun*
1 (*for a singular noun*) **el nuestro** *masc*, **la nuestra** *fem*
Their team's stronger than ours. Su equipo es más fuerte que el nuestro.
The class next door is noisier than ours. La clase de al lado es más ruidosa que la nuestra.
2 (*for a plural noun*) **los nuestros** *masc*, **las nuestras** *fem*
They brought their parents, so we had to bring ours. Trajeron a sus padres, así que tuvimos que traer a los nuestros.
She showed us her photos and we showed her ours. Ella nos enseñó sus fotos y nosotros le enseñamos las nuestras.

ourselves *pronoun*
1 (*reflexive*) **nos**
We introduced ourselves. Nos presentamos.
We wore ourselves out playing tennis. Nos agotamos jugando al tenis.
2 (*for emphasis*) **nosotros solos** *masc*, **nosotras solas** *fem*
In the end we did it ourselves. Al final lo hicimos nosotros solos.

out *adverb*
1 (*outside*) **fuera**
out in the rain bajo la lluvia
It's cold out there. Hace frío ahí fuera.
They're out in the garden. Están en el jardín.
2 (*of a room, for the evening or day, as a couple*) **to go out** salir [63]
He went out of the room. Salió de la habitación. ⏩

English–Spanish
a b c d e f g h i j k l m n o p q r s t u v w x y z

Are you going out this evening? ¿Vas a salir esta noche?
Alison's going out with Danny at the moment. Alison está saliendo ahora con Danny.
He's asked me out. Me ha pedido que salga con él.
3 (*absent*) **to be out** no estar [2]
when they were out cuando ellos no estaban
My mum's out. Mi madre no está.
4 (*light, fire*) **apagado,** *fem* **apagada**
Are all the lights out? ¿Están apagadas todas las luces?
The fire was out. El fuego estaba apagado.
5 (*to show movement*) **to drink out of a glass** beber [18] de un vaso
He threw it out of the window. Lo tiró por la ventana.
She took the photo out of her bag. Sacó la foto del bolso.
He got out of the car. Bajó del coche.
6 (*in statistics*) **out of: Four out of ten people have tried it.** Cuatro de cada diez personas lo han probado.

outing *noun*
la **excursión** *fem*
to go on an outing ir [8] de excursión

outline *noun*
(*of an object*) el **contorno** *masc*

out-of-date *adjective*
1 (*no longer valid*) **caducado** *masc*, **caducada** *fem*
My passport's out of date. Mi pasaporte está caducado.
2 (*old-fashioned*) **pasado de moda** *masc*, **pasada de moda** *fem*
He always wears such out-of-date clothes. Siempre lleva ropa tan pasada de moda.

outside *adjective* ▷ see **outside** *adv, noun, prep*
exterior *masc & fem*

outside *adverb* ▷ see **outside** *adj, noun, prep*
fuera
It's cold outside. Hace frío fuera.

outside *noun* ▷ see **outside** *adj, adv, prep*
la **parte de fuera**
It's blue on the outside. La parte de fuera es azul.

outside *preposition* ▷ see **outside** *adj, adv, noun*
fuera de
I'll meet you outside the cinema. Te veo fuera del cine.

outskirts *plural noun*
las **afueras** *plural fem*
on the outskirts of York en las afueras de York

outstanding *adjective*
excepcional *masc & fem*

oven *noun*
el **horno** *masc*
I've put it in the oven. Lo he puesto en el horno.

over *adverb, preposition*
1 (*above*) **encima de**
There's a mirror over the sideboard. Hay un espejo encima del aparador.
2 (*to show movement*) **por encima de**
She jumped over the fence. Saltó por encima de la valla.
He threw the ball over the wall. Tiró la pelota por encima del muro.
3 (*more than*) **más de**
It will cost over a hundred pounds. Costará más de cien libras.
He's over sixty. Tiene más de sesenta años.
4 (*during*) **durante**
over the weekend durante el fin de semana
over Christmas durante las Navidades
5 (*finished*) **when the meeting's over** cuando la reunión haya acabado
It's all over now. Ahora todo ha acabado.
6 (*in expressions*) **over here** aquí
The drinks are over here. Las bebidas están aquí.
over there allí
She's over there talking to Julian. Está allí, hablando con Julián.
over the phone por teléfono
to ask someone over invitar [17] a alguien
Can you come over on Saturday? ¿Puedes venir el sábado?
all over the place por todas partes
all over the house por toda la casa

overcast *adjective*
nublado *masc*, **nublada** *fem*

overcrowded *adjective*
abarrotado *masc*, **abarrotada** *fem*

overdose *noun*
la **sobredosis** *fem*

overdraft *noun*
el **descubierto** *masc*

to **overflow** *verb*
1 (*water*) **derramarse** [17]
2 (*river*) **desbordarse** [17]

overseas *adverb*
en el extranjero
Dave works overseas. Dave trabaja en el extranjero.

⚷ to **overtake** *verb*
(*another car*) **adelantar** [17]

⚷ **overtime** *noun*
las **horas extras**
to work overtime trabajar [17] horas extras

⚷ to **owe** *verb*
deber [18]
I owe Rick ten pounds. Le debo diez libras a Rick.

owing *adjective*
1 (*still to pay*) **a pagar**
There's five pounds owing. Quedan cinco libras a pagar.
2 **owing to** (*because of*) debido a
owing to the snow debido a la nieve

⚷ **owl** *noun*
el **búho** *masc*

⚷ **own** *adjective* ▷ see **own** *verb*
1 (*to show possession*) **propio** *masc*, **propia** *fem*
my own computer mi propio ordenador
I've got my own room. Tengo mi propia habitación.
2 (*by yourself*) **on your own** solo, *fem* sola
Annie did it on her own. Annie lo hizo sola.

WORD TIP *propio* and *propia* go before the noun.

⚷ to **own** *verb* ▷ see **own** *adj*
tener [9]

owner *noun*
el **dueño** *masc*, la **dueña** *fem*

oxygen *noun*
el **oxígeno** *masc*

oyster *noun*
la **ostra** *fem*

ozone layer *noun*
la **capa de ozono**

P p

Pacific *noun*
the Pacific Ocean el océano Pacífico

pack *noun* ▷ see **pack** *verb*
1 (*packet*) el **paquete** *masc*
2 (*of cards*) **a pack of cards** una baraja

to **pack** *verb* ▷ see **pack** *noun*
1 (*before a journey*) **hacer [7] las maletas**
He's already packed. Ya ha hecho la maleta.
I'll pack my case tonight. Voy a hacer la maleta esta noche.
2 (*breakables*) **embalar [1]**
These plates must be packed carefully. Hay que embalar estos platos con cuidado.

package *noun*
el **paquete** *masc*
• **package holiday** el viaje organizado
• **package tour** el viaje organizado

packed lunch *noun*
la **comida preparada desde casa**

packet *noun*
1 (*pack*) el **paquete** *masc*
a packet of biscuits un paquete de galletas
2 (*bag*) la **bolsa** *fem*
a packet of crisps una bolsa de patatas fritas

packing *noun*
to do your packing hacer [7] las maletas

pad *noun*
(*of paper*) el **bloc** *masc*

paddle *noun* ▷ see **paddle** *verb*
1 (*for a canoe*) **pala** *fem*
2 (*in the sea, etc*) **chapoteo** *masc*

to **paddle** *verb* ▷ see **paddle** *noun*
1 (*a canoe*) **remar [17]**
2 (*in the sea, etc*) **chapotear [17]**

padlock *noun*
el **candado** *masc*

page *noun*
la **página** *fem*
on page seven en la página siete

pain *noun*
el **dolor** *masc*
to have a pain dolerle [38] a alguien
I've got a pain in my leg. Me duele la pierna.
Where's the pain? ¿Dónde te duele?
to be a pain in the neck ser [1] un pesado (*boy*), ser [1] una pesada (*girl*)
Kirsty's a real pain in the neck. Kirsty es una verdadera pesada.
• **painkiller** el analgésico

paint *noun* ▷ see **paint** *verb*
la **pintura** *fem*
'Wet paint' 'Recién pintado'

to **paint** *verb* ▷ see **paint** *noun*
pintar [17]
to paint something pink pintar algo de rosa

paintbrush *noun*
1 (*artist's*) el **pincel** *masc*
2 (*for decorating*) la **brocha** *fem*

painter *noun*
el **pintor** *masc*, la **pintora** *fem*

painting *noun*
1 (*picture*) el **cuadro** *masc*
a painting by Monet un cuadro de Monet
2 (*activity*) la **pintura** *fem*
I prefer painting to drawing. Prefiero la pintura al dibujo.

pair *noun*
1 (*of items, clothes*) el **par** *masc*
a pair of socks un par de calcetines
a pair of shoes un par de zapatos
a pair of jeans unos vaqueros
a pair of trousers unos pantalones
a pair of knickers unas bragas
a pair of scissors unas tijeras
2 (*of people*) la **pareja** *fem*
to work in pairs trabajar [17] en parejas

Pakistan *noun*
Paquistán *masc*

Pakistani *adjective & noun*
1 **paquistaní** *masc & fem*
My grandparents are Pakistani. Mis abuelos son paquistaníes.
2 (*person*) el & la **paquistaní** *masc & fem*
the Pakistanis los paquistaníes
My brother's married to a Pakistani. Mi hermano está casado con una paquistaní.

WORD TIP Adjectives and nouns for nationality and regional origin do not have capital letters in Spanish.

palace *noun*
el **palacio** *masc*

pale *adjective*
1 (*complexion*) **pálido** *masc*, **pálida** *fem*
to turn pale palidecer [35]
You look pale! ¡Estás pálida!
2 (*with colours*) **pale green** verde pálido
pale green curtains cortinas verde pálido

WORD TIP *verde pálido* and other combinations do not change in the plural.

palm *noun*
1 (*of your hand*) la **palma** *fem*
2 (*the tree*) la **palmera** *fem*

pamphlet *noun*
el **folleto** *masc*

pan *noun*
1 (*saucepan*) la **cacerola** *fem*
a pan of water una cacerola de agua
2 (*frying-pan*) la **sartén** *fem*

pancake *noun*
el **crepe** *masc*

panel *noun*
1 (*for a discussion*) el **panel** *masc*, (*for a quiz show*) el **equipo** *masc*
2 (*for a wall, bath*) el **panel** *masc*
• **panel game** el concurso por equipos

panic *noun* ▷ see **panic** *verb*
el **pánico** *masc*

to **panic** *verb* ▷ see **panic** *noun*
dejarse [17] llevar por el pánico
Don't panic! ¡No pierdas la calma!

panties *plural noun*
las **bragas** *plural fem*

pantomime *noun*
la **pantomima** *fem*

pants *plural noun*
los **calzoncillos** *plural masc*

paper *noun*
1 (*for writing, drawing, wrapping*) el **papel** *masc*
a sheet of paper una hoja de papel
a paper hanky un pañuelo de papel
2 (*newspaper*) el **periódico** *masc*
It was in the paper. Salió en el periódico.
to do a paper round repartir [19] los periódicos
• **paperback** el libro de bolsillo
• **paper boy** el repartidor de periódicos
• **paperclip** el clip
• **paper girl** la repartidora de periódicos
• **paper towel** la toalla de papel

parachute *noun*
el **paracaídas** *masc, pl:* los **paracaídas**

parade *noun*
el **desfile** *masc*

paradise *noun*
el **paraíso** *masc*

paragraph *noun*
el **párrafo** *masc*
New paragraph Punto y aparte

Paraguayan *adjective & noun*
1 **paraguayo** *masc*, **paraguaya** *fem*
2 (*person*) el **paraguayo** *masc*, la **paraguaya** *fem*
the Paraguayans los paraguayos

WORD TIP Adjectives and nouns for nationality and regional origin do not have capital letters in Spanish.

parallel *adjective*
paralelo *masc*, **paralela** *fem*
Our road is parallel to the High Street. Nuestra calle es paralela a la Calle Mayor.

Paralympics, **Paralympic Games** *plural noun*
los **Juegos Paralímpicos**

paralysed *adjective*
paralizado *masc*, **paralizada** *fem*

parcel *noun*
el **paquete** *masc*
He's left his parcel of books behind. Se ha dejado el paquete de libros.

pardon *noun*
I beg your pardon. Perdón (*familiar form*)., Perdone (*polite form*).
Pardon? ¿Cómo dices? (*familiar form*), ¿Cómo dice? (*polite form*)

parents *plural noun*
my parents mis padres
a parents' evening una reunión de padres

park *noun* ▷ see **park** *verb*
el **parque** *masc*

to **park** *verb* ▷ see **park** *noun*
1 (*person*) **aparcar [31]**
You can park outside the house. Puedes aparcar fuera de la casa.
2 (*a car*) **to park a car** aparcar [31] un coche
Where did you park the car? ¿Dónde has aparcado el coche?

parking *noun*
el **aparcamiento** *masc*
'No parking' 'No aparcar'
• **parking meter** el parquímetro
• **parking space** el sitio para aparcar
• **parking ticket** la multa

parliament *noun*
el **parlamento** *masc*
the Spanish parliament las Cortes

English-Spanish

parrot *noun*
el **loro** *masc*

parsley *noun*
el **perejil** *masc*

part *noun*
1 la **parte** *fem*
a part of the garden una parte del jardín
the last part of the concert la última parte del concierto
That's part of your job. Eso es parte de tu trabajo.
2 **to take part in something** participar [17] en algo
3 (*in a play*) el **papel** *masc*
4 (*for a car, machine*) la **pieza** *fem*
spare parts piezas de repuesto

particular *adjective*
particular *masc & fem*
nothing in particular nada en particular

particularly *adverb*
especialmente
not particularly interesting no especialmente interesante

partly *adverb*
en parte

partner *noun*
1 (*in a game*) la **pareja** (*man or woman*)
2 (*the person you live with*) el **compañero**, la **compañera**
3 (*in business*) el **socio**, la **socia**

partridge *noun*
la **perdiz** *fem*

part-time *adjective, adverb*
a tiempo parcial
part-time work trabajo a tiempo parcial
to work part-time trabajar [17] a tiempo parcial

party *noun*
1 (*celebration*) la **fiesta** *fem*
a Christmas party una fiesta de Navidad
to have a birthday party celebrar [17] una fiesta de cumpleaños
We've been invited to a party at the Smiths' house. Estamos invitados a una fiesta en casa de los Smith.
2 (*group*) el **grupo** *masc*
a party of schoolchildren un grupo de colegiales
a rescue party un equipo de rescate
3 (*in politics*) el **partido** *masc*
the Labour Party el Partido laborista

pass *noun* ▷ see **pass** *verb*
1 (*to let you in*) el **pase** *masc*
2 (*for bus, train travel*) el **abono** *masc*
3 (*in mountains*) el **puerto de montaña**
4 (*in an exam*) el **aprobado** *masc*
to get a pass in history sacar [31] un aprobado en historia

to pass *verb* ▷ see **pass** *noun*
1 (*a place, building*) **pasar** [17] **por**
We passed your house. Pasamos por tu casa.
2 (*to overtake*) **adelantar** [17] **a**
We passed a bus. Adelantamos a un autobús.
3 (*to give*) **pasar** [17]
Could you pass me the salt please? ¿Me pasas la sal, por favor?
4 (*time*) **pasar** [17]
The time passed slowly. El tiempo pasaba lentamente.
5 (*in an exam*) **aprobar** [24]
Did you pass? ¿Aprobaste?
to pass an exam aprobar un examen

passenger *noun*
el **pasajero** *masc*, la **pasajera** *fem*

passion *noun*
la **pasión** *fem*

passionate *adjective*
apasionado *masc*, **apasionada** *fem*

passive *adjective* ▷ see **passive** *noun*
pasivo *masc*, **pasiva** *fem*

passive *noun* ▷ see **passive** *adj*
(*Grammar*) la **voz pasiva**

Passover *noun*
la **Pascua judía**

passport *noun*
el **pasaporte** *masc*
an EU passport un pasaporte de la Unión Europea
I have to get a passport. Tengo que sacar el pasaporte.

password *noun*
la **contraseña** *fem*

past *adjective* ▷ see **past** *adv, noun, prep*
1 (*recent*) **último** *masc*, **última** *fem*
in the past few weeks en las últimas semanas
2 (*over*) **Winter is past.** Ya ha pasado el invierno.

WORD TIP *último* always goes before the noun.

past *noun* ▷ see **past** *adj, adv, prep*
(*Grammar*) el **pasado** *masc*
in the past en el pasado

a b c d e f g h i j k l m n o p q r s t u v w x y z

past *adverb, preposition* ▷ see **past** *adj, noun*
1 (*alongside*) **to go past something** pasar [17] por delante de algo
We went past the school. Pasamos por delante del colegio.
Go past the station and turn left. Pasa la estación y gira a la izquierda.
Ahmed went past in his new car. Ahmed pasó en su coche nuevo.
2 (*the other side of*) **más allá de**
It's just past the post office. Está un poquito más allá de la oficina de correos.
3 (*to talk about the time*) **ten past six** las seis y diez
half past four las cuatro y media
It's a quarter past two. Son las dos y cuarto.

pasta *noun*
la **pasta** *fem*
I like pasta. Me gusta la pasta.

pasteurized *adjective*
pasteurizado *masc*, **pasteurizada** *fem*

pastry *noun*
la **masa** *fem*

patch *noun*
1 (*of colour*) la **mancha** *fem*
2 (*for repairs*) el **parche** *masc*

path *noun*
(*track*) el **camino** *masc*, (*very narrow*) el **sendero** *masc*

patience *noun*
1 (*calm*) la **paciencia** *fem*
2 (*card game*) el **solitario** *masc*
to play patience hacer [7] solitarios

patient *adjective* ▷ see **patient** *noun*
paciente *masc & fem*
to be patient tener [9] paciencia

patient *noun* ▷ see **patient** *adj*
el & la **paciente** *masc & fem*
heart patients los enfermos del corazón

patiently *adverb*
pacientemente

patio *noun*
el **patio** *masc*

patrol *noun*
la **patrulla** *fem*
• **patrol car** el coche patrulla

pattern *noun*
1 (*on wallpaper, fabric*) el **diseño** *masc*
2 (*for dressmaking*) el **patrón** *masc*
3 (*for knittting*) el **modelo** *masc*

pavement *noun*
la **acera** *fem*
on the pavement en la acera
a pavement cafe un café con terraza

paw *noun*
la **pata** *fem*

pawn *noun*
el **peón** *masc*

pay *noun* ▷ see **pay** *verb*
el **sueldo** *masc*

to **pay** *verb* ▷ see **pay** *noun*
1 **pagar** [28]
to pay cash pagar al contado
to pay by cheque pagar con cheque
to pay by credit card pagar con tarjeta de crédito
I'm paying. Pago yo.
2 **to pay for something** pagar [28] algo
Tony paid for the drinks. Tony pagó las bebidas.
It's all paid for. Todo está pagado.
3 **to pay somebody back** (*money*) devolverle [45] dinero a alguien
4 (*attention*) **to pay attention** prestar [17] atención
5 **to pay a visit to somebody** hacer [7] una visita a alguien

payment *noun*
el **pago** *masc*

pay phone *noun*
el **teléfono público**

PC *noun*
(*Computers*) el **PC** *masc*

pea *noun*
el **guisante** *masc*
pea soup crema de guisantes

peace *noun*
la **paz** *fem*
We went into the garden for some peace and quiet. Salimos al jardín para poder estar tranquilos.
Just leave her in peace. Déjala tranquila.

peaceful *adjective*
tranquilo *masc*, **tranquila** *fem*

peach *noun*
el **melocotón** *masc*
a peach tree un melocotonero

peacock *noun*
el **pavo real**

peak *noun*
(*of a mountain*) el **pico** *masc*
- **peak period** la temporada alta
- **peak rate** la tarifa máxima
- **peak time** la hora punta

peanut *noun*
el **cacahuete** *masc*
- **peanut butter** la mantequilla de cacahuete

pear *noun*
la **pera** *fem*
a pear tree un peral

pearl *noun*
la **perla** *fem*

peasant *noun*
el **campesino** *masc*, la **campesina** *fem*

pebble *noun*
el **guijarro** *masc*

pedal *noun* ▷ see **pedal** *verb*
el **pedal** *masc*

to **pedal** *verb* ▷ see **pedal** *noun*
pedalear [17]

pedestrian *noun*
el **peatón** *masc*, la **peatona** *fem*
- **pedestrian crossing** el paso peatonal
- **pedestrian precinct** la zona peatonal

pee *noun*
to have a pee hacer [7] pis (*informal*)

peel *noun* ▷ see **peel** *verb*
1 (*of an apple*) la **piel** *fem*
2 (*of an orange*) la **cáscara** *fem*

to **peel** *verb* ▷ see **peel** *noun*
(*fruit, vegetables*) **pelar [17]**

peg *noun*
(*hook*) el **gancho** *masc*
a clothes peg una pinza de la ropa
a tent peg una piqueta

pen *noun*
1 (*ballpoint*) el **bolígrafo** *masc*, el **boli** *masc* (*informal*)
2 (*fountain pen*) la **pluma** *fem*

penalty *noun*
1 (*fine*) la **multa** *fem*
2 (*in football, rugby*) el **penalty** *masc*
- **penalty area** el área de castigo

WORD TIP *área* takes *el* and *un* in the singular even though it is fem.

pence *plural noun*
los **peniques** *plural masc*

pencil *noun*
el **lápiz** *masc*
to write in pencil escribir [52] a lápiz
You have to write in pencil. Hay que escribir a lápiz.
- **pencil case** el estuche para lápices
- **pencil sharpener** el sacapuntas

WORD TIP *sacapuntas* does not change in the plural.

pendant *noun*
el **colgante** *masc*

penfriend *noun*
el **amigo por correspondencia**, la **amiga por correspondencia**
My Spanish penfriend is called Cristina. Mi amiga por correspondencia española se llama Cristina.

penis *noun*
el **pene** *masc*

penknife *noun*
la **navaja** *fem*

penny *noun*
el **penique** *masc*

pension *noun*
la **pensión** *fem*
a retirement pension una pensión de jubilación

pensioner *noun*
el & la **pensionista** *masc & fem*

people *plural noun*
1 (*when you count them*) la **persona** *fem*
ten people diez personas
several people varias personas
How many people are coming? ¿Cuántas personas van a venir?
2 (*giving a general idea*) la **gente** *fem*
The people round here are very nice. La gente de por aquí es muy simpática.
There are some bad people in the village. Hay gente mala en el pueblo.
People say he's very rich. La gente dice que es muy rico.

WORD TIP *gente* takes a singular verb.

pepper *noun*
1 (*the spice*) la **pimienta** *fem*
2 (*the vegetable*) el **pimiento** *masc*
a green pepper un pimiento verde
- **peppermill** el molinillo de pimienta
- **pepperpot** el pimentero

peppermint *noun*
la **menta** *fem*
a peppermint tea una infusión de menta

per *preposition*
por
ten pounds per person diez libras por persona

per cent *adverb*
por ciento
sixty per cent of the students un sesenta por ciento de los estudiantes
a hundred per cent of the applicants el cien por cien de los solicitantes

WORD TIP Spanish always has *el* or *un* before percentages.

percentage *noun*
el **porcentaje** *masc*

percussion *noun*
la **percusión** *fem*
to play percussion tocar [31] la percusión

perfect *adjective*
1 (*faultless*) **perfecto** *masc*, **perfecta** *fem*
She speaks perfect English. Habla un inglés perfecto.
2 (*ideal*) **ideal** *masc & fem*
the perfect place for a picnic el sitio ideal para un picnic
• **perfect tense** (*Grammar*) el perfecto, el pretérito perfecto

perfectly *adverb*
perfectamente

to **perform** *verb*
1 (*a piece of music, role*) **interpretar** [17]
2 (*a play*) **representar** [17]
3 (*a song*) **cantar** [17]

performance *noun*
1 (*playing, acting*) la **interpretación** *fem*
a wonderful performance of Macbeth una maravillosa interpretación de Macbeth
2 (*a show*) el **espectáculo** *masc*
The performance starts at eight. El espectáculo empieza a las ocho.
3 (*how well someone does*) la **actuación** *fem*

performer *noun*
el & la **artista** *masc & fem*

♪ **perfume** *noun*
el **perfume** *masc*
a bottle of perfume un frasco de perfume

♪ **perhaps** *adverb*
quizás
Perhaps he's missed the train. Quizás ha perdido el tren.
Perhaps it's in the drawer? ¿A lo mejor está en el cajón?

period *noun*
1 (*of time*) el **periodo** *masc*
a two-year period un periodo de dos años
2 (*in school*) la **clase** *fem*
a forty-five-minute period una clase de cuarenta y cinco minutos
3 (*menstruation*) la **regla** *fem*, el **periodo** *masc*
to have your period tener [9] la regla

perm *noun*
la **permanente** *fem*

permanent *adjective*
permanente *masc & fem*

permanently *adverb*
permanentemente

permission *noun*
el **permiso** *masc*
to get permission to do something conseguir [64] permiso para hacer algo

permit *noun* ▷ see **permit** *verb*
el **permiso** *masc*

to **permit** *verb* ▷ see **permit** *noun*
permitir [19]
to permit somebody to do something permitir a alguien hacer algo
Smoking is not permitted. Está prohibido fumar.
weather permitting ... si el tiempo lo permite ...

♪ **person** *noun*
la **persona** *fem*
He's a very unpleasant person. Es una persona muy antipática.
There's room for one more person. Hay sitio para una persona más.
She's appearing in person. Aparecerá en persona.

WORD TIP *persona* is fem, but it is used for males or females.

personal *adjective*
personal *masc & fem*

personality *noun*
la **personalidad** *fem*

personally *adverb*
personalmente
Personally, I'm against it. Personalmente, estoy en contra.

personal stereo *noun*
el **walkman**® *masc*

perspiration *noun*
el **sudor** *masc*

to **persuade** *verb*
convencer [44]
to persuade somebody to do something convencer a alguien para que haga algo
Try to persuade her to come with us. Trata de convencerla para que nos acompañe.
We persuaded Tim to wait a bit. Convencimos a Tim para que esperara un poco.

WORD TIP *para que* is followed by a verb in the subjunctive.

peseta *noun*
la **peseta** *fem* (*Former Spanish currency replaced by the euro; 500 pesetas = 3.00 euros.*)

pessimistic *adjective*
pesimista *masc & fem*

pest *noun*
1 (*insect, rodent, etc*) la **plaga** *fem*
2 (*annoying person*) el **pesado** *masc*, la **pesada** *fem*

to **pester** *verb*
fastidiar [17]

pet *noun*
1 (*animal*) la **mascota**, el **animal doméstico**
a pet dog un perro de compañía
Do you have a pet? ¿Tienes mascota?
2 (*favourite person*) el **favorito** *masc*, la **favorita** *fem*
Julie is teacher's pet. Julie es la favorita de la maestra.

petal *noun*
el **pétalo** *masc*

pet name *noun*
el **apodo cariñoso**

petrol *noun*
la **gasolina** *fem*
lead-free petrol gasolina sin plomo
to fill up with petrol llenar [17] el depósito de gasolina
to run out of petrol quedarse [17] sin gasolina
- **petrol pump** el surtidor
- **petrol station** la gasolinera
- **petrol tank** el depósito de gasolina

petticoat *noun*
la **enagua** *fem*

pharmacist *noun*
el **farmacéutico** *masc*, la **farmacéutica** *fem*

pharmacy *noun*
la **farmacia** *fem*

pheasant *noun*
el **faisán** *masc*

philosophy *noun*
la **filosofía** *fem*

to **phone** *verb* ▷ see **phone** *noun*
1 (*person*) **llamar** [17] **por teléfono**
He arrived while I was phoning. Llegó mientras llamaba por teléfono.
2 (*a person*) **to phone somebody** llamar [17] a alguien
I'll phone you tonight. Te llamaré esta noche.

phone *noun* ▷ see **phone** *verb*
el **teléfono** *masc*
She's on the phone. Está hablando por teléfono.
I was on the phone to Sophie. Estaba hablando por teléfono con Sophie.
You can book by phone. Puedes reservar por teléfono.
- **phone book** la guía telefónica
- **phone box** la cabina telefónica

phone call *noun*
la **llamada telefónica**
Phone calls are free. Las llamadas telefónicas son gratis.
to make a phone call hacer [7] una llamada (telefónica)

phone card *noun*
la **tarjeta telefónica**

phone number *noun*
el **número de teléfono**

photo *noun*
la **foto** *fem*
to take a photo hacer [7] una foto
I took a photo of their house. Hice una foto de su casa.
to take a photo of somebody hacerle [7] una foto a alguien
He took three photos of me. Me hizo tres fotos.

photocopier *noun*
la **fotocopiadora** *fem*

photocopy *noun* ▷ see **photocopy** *verb*
la **fotocopia** *fem*

to **photocopy** *verb*
▷ see **photocopy** *noun*
fotocopiar [17]

photograph *noun*
▷ see **photograph** *verb*
la **fotografía** *fem*
to take a photograph hacer [7] una fotografía
to take a photograph of somebody hacerle una fotografía a alguien

I took a photograph of her. Le hice una fotografía.

to **photograph** *verb*
▷ see **photograph** *noun*
fotografiar [32]

photographer *noun*
el **fotógrafo** *masc*, la **fotógrafa** *fem*

photography *noun*
la **fotografía** *fem*

phrase *noun*
la **frase** *fem*
• **phrase-book** el manual de conversación

physical *adjective*
físico *masc*, **física** *fem*

physicist *noun*
el **físico** *masc*, la **física** *fem*

⚷ **physics** *noun*
la **física** *fem*
nuclear physics la física nuclear

physiotherapist *noun*
el & la **fisioterapeuta** *masc & fem*

physiotherapy *noun*
la **fisioterapia** *fem*

pianist *noun*
el & la **pianista** *masc & fem*

piano *noun*
el **piano** *masc*
a piano lesson una clase de piano
to play the piano tocar [31] el piano
Steve played it on the piano. Steve lo tocó al piano.

⚷ **pick** *noun* ▷ see **pick** *verb*
Take your pick! ¡Escoge!

⚷ to **pick** *verb* ▷ see **pick** *noun*
1 (*to choose*) **escoger** [3]
Pick a card. Escoge una carta.
2 (*for a team*) **seleccionar** [17]
I've been picked for Saturday. Me han seleccionado para el sábado.
3 (*fruit*) **recoger** [3]
4 (*flowers*) **coger** [3]
• **to pick up**
1 (*to lift*) **coger** [3]
to pick up the phone coger el teléfono
He picked up the papers and went out. Cogió los papeles y salió.
2 (*from the floor*) **recoger** [3]
Pick up that piece of paper. Recoge ese papel.
3 (*to collect together*) **recoger** [3]
I'll pick up the toys. Voy a recoger los juguetes.
4 (*a person, an item*) **recoger** [3]
I'll pick you up at six. Te recogeré a las seis.
He picked her up from the airport. Fue a buscarla al aeropuerto.
I'll pick up the keys tomorrow. Recogeré las llaves mañana.
5 (*to learn*) **aprender** [18]
You'll soon pick it up. Lo aprenderás pronto.

picnic *noun*
el **picnic** *masc*
to have a picnic hacer [7] un picnic

pickpocket *noun*
el & la **carterista** *masc & fem*

⚷ **picture** *noun*
1 (*painting*) el **cuadro** *masc*
a picture by Picasso un cuadro de Picasso
He painted a picture of a horse. Pintó un caballo.
2 (*drawing*) el **dibujo** *masc*
Draw me a picture of your house. Hazme un dibujo de tu casa.
3 (*in a book*) la **ilustración** *fem*
a book with lots of pictures un libro con muchas ilustraciones
4 (*cinema*) **the pictures** el cine
to go to the pictures ir [8] al cine

pie *noun*
1 (*sweet*) el **pastel** *masc*
an apple pie un pastel de manzana
2 (*savoury*) la **empanada** *fem*
a meat pie una empanada de carne

⚷ **piece** *noun*
1 (*bit*) el **trozo** *masc*
a big piece of cheese un trozo grande de queso
a piece of furniture un mueble
four pieces of luggage cuatro maletas
a piece of information un dato
That's a piece of luck! ¡Qué suerte!
2 (*that you fit together*) la **pieza** *fem*
the pieces of a jigsaw las piezas de un rompecabezas
to take something to pieces desmontar [17] algo
3 (*coin*) la **moneda** *fem*
a 50p piece una moneda de cincuenta peniques

pierced *adjective*
to have pierced ears tener [9] agujeros en las orejas

⚷ **pig** *noun*
el **cerdo** *masc*, la **cerda** *fem*

pigeon *noun*
la **paloma** *fem*

piggy bank *noun*
la **hucha** *fem*

pigsty *noun*
la **pocilga** *fem*
Your room is a pigsty. Tu habitación está hecha una pocilga.

pigtail *noun*
la **trenza** *fem*

pile *noun*
1 (*neat stack*) la **pila** *fem*
a pile of plates una pila de platos
2 (*heap*) el **montón** *masc*
a pile of dirty shirts un montón de camisas sucias
• **to pile something up**
1 (*neatly*) **apilar [17] algo**
2 (*in a heap*) **amontonar [17] algo**

pilgrimage *noun*
la **peregrinación** *fem*
to go on a pilgrimage irse [8] de peregrinación

⚷ **pill** *noun*
la **pastilla** *fem*
the pill (*contraceptive*) la píldora
to be on the pill tomar [17] la píldora

pillow *noun*
la **almohada** *fem*
• **pillow case** el almohadón

pilot *noun*
el & la **piloto** *masc & fem*

pimple *noun*
el **grano** *masc*

pin *noun*
1 (*for sewing*) el **alfiler** *masc*
2 (*on a plug*) **a three-pin plug** un enchufe de tres clavijas
• **to pin up**
1 (*a hem*) **prender [18] con alfileres**
2 (*a notice*) **poner [11]**

PIN *noun*
(= *Personal Identification Number*) el **PIN** *masc*

pinball *noun*
el **flipper** *masc*
a pinball machine un flipper
to play pinball jugar [27] al flipper

pinch *noun* ▷ see **pinch** *verb*
el **pellizco** *masc*

to **pinch** *verb* ▷ see **pinch** *noun*
1 (*with your fingers*) **to pinch somebody** pellizcar [31] a alguien
2 (*to steal*) **mangar [28]** (*informal*)
Somebody's pinched my bike. Alguien me ha robado la bici.

pine *noun*
el **pino** *masc*
a pine table una mesa de pino
pine trees pinos

⚷ **pineapple** *noun*
la **piña** *fem*

pine cone *noun*
la **piña** *fem*

ping-pong *noun*
el **ping-pong** *masc*
to play ping-pong jugar [27] al ping-pong

⚷ **pink** *adjective*
rosa
my pink dress mi vestido rosa
pink socks calcetines rosa

WORD TIP *rosa adj* does not change in the plural.

pint *noun*
la **pinta** *fem*

pip *noun*
la **pepita** *fem*

pipe *noun*
1 (*for gas, water*) la **tubería** *fem*
2 (*for smoking*) la **pipa** *fem*
He smokes a pipe. Fuma en pipa.

Pisces *noun*
1 (*the star sign*) el **Piscis** *masc*
2 (*person*) un & una **piscis** *masc & fem*
Kirsty's Pisces. Kirsty es pisces.

WORD TIP Use a small letter in Spanish to say *I am ...* etc with star signs. Star signs in Spanish are used without *el, un, la, una*.

pistachio *noun*
el **pistacho** *masc*

pit *noun*
el **foso** *masc*

⚷ **pitch** *noun* ▷ see **pitch** *verb*
el **campo** *masc*
a football pitch un campo de fútbol

⚷ to **pitch** *verb* ▷ see **pitch** *noun*
to pitch a tent montar [17] una tienda

⚷ **pity** *noun* ▷ see **pity** *verb*
1 (*shame*) la **lástima** *fem*
What a pity! ¡Qué lástima!
It would be a pity to miss the beginning. Sería una lástima perderse el principio.

2 (*for a person*) la **piedad** *fem*
to have pity on somebody tener **[9]** piedad de alguien
Have pity on us! ¡Ten piedad de nosotros!

♪ to **pity** *verb* ▷ see **pity** *noun*
to pity somebody compadecer **[35]** a alguien

♪ **pizza** *noun*
la **pizza** *fem*

♪ **place** *noun* ▷ see **place** *verb*
1 (*spot, seat, destination*) el **sitio** *masc*
in a warm place en un sitio caliente
all over the place por todos sitios
a place for the car un sitio para el coche
to change places cambiarse **[17]** de sitio
Will you keep my place? ¿Me guardas el sitio?
Rome is a wonderful place. Roma es un lugar maravilloso.
2 (*in a race*) el **lugar** *masc*
in first place en primer lugar
3 (*home*) **at your place** en tu casa
We'll go round to Zafir's place. Iremos a casa de Zafir.
4 (*event*) **to take place** tener **[9]** lugar
The competition will take place at four. La competición tendrá lugar a las cuatro.
5 (*position*) **If I was in your place ...** Si yo estuviese en tu lugar ...
• **place mat** el individual
• **place setting** el cubierto

♪ to **place** *verb* ▷ see **place** *noun*
poner [11]
He placed his cup on the table. Puso su taza en la mesa.

♪ **plain** *adjective*
1 (*simple*) **sencillo** *masc*, **sencilla** *fem*
plain cooking la cocina sencilla
2 (*unflavoured*) **natural** *masc & fem*
a plain yoghurt un yogur natural
3 (*chocolate*) **plain chocolate** chocolate sin leche
4 (*not patterned*) **liso** *masc*, **lisa** *fem*
plain curtains cortinas lisas
5 (*unattractive*) **poco atractivo** *masc*, **poco atractiva** *fem*

plait *noun*
la **trenza** *fem*

♪ **plan** *noun* ▷ see **plan** *verb*
1 (*arrangement in advance*) el **plan** *masc*
What are your plans for this summer? ¿Qué planes tienes para este verano?
to go according to plan salir **[63]** según el plan
Everything went according to plan. Todo salió según el plan.
2 (*map*) el **plano** *masc*

♪ to **plan** *verb* ▷ see **plan** *noun*
1 (*to intend*) **planear [17]**
Ricky's planning a trip to Italy. Ricky está planeando un viaje a Italia.
to plan to do something planear **[17]** hacer algo
We're planning to leave at eight. Planeamos salir a las ocho.
2 (*to organize*) **organizar [22]**
I'm planning my day. Estoy organizándome el día.
3 (*a house, garden*) **diseñar [17]**
a well-planned kitchen una cocina bien diseñada

plane *noun*
el **avión** *masc*
We went by plane. Fuimos en avión.

planet *noun*
el **planeta** *masc*

♪ **plant** *noun* ▷ see **plant** *verb*
la **planta** *fem*
a house plant una planta de interior
I have to water the plants. Tengo que regar las plantas.

♪ to **plant** *verb* ▷ see **plant** *noun*
plantar [17]
I've planted daffodils in these pots. He plantado narcisos en estas macetas.
They planted the fields with wheat. Plantaron los campos de trigo.

♪ **plaster** *noun*
1 (*sticking plaster*) la **tirita** *fem*
2 (*for walls*) el **yeso** *masc*
3 (*for a broken limb*) **to have your leg in plaster** tener **[9]** una pierna escayolada

plastic *noun*
el **plástico** *masc*
a plastic bag una bolsa de plástico

♪ **plate** *noun*
el **plato** *masc*
a plate of chips un plato de patatas fritas

♪ **platform** *noun*
1 (*in a station*) el **andén** *masc*, la **vía**
the train arriving at platform six el tren que llega al andén número seis
2 (*for lecturing, performing*) el **estrado** *masc*

play *noun* ▷ see **play** *verb*
1 (*drama*) la **obra** *fem*
a play by Shakespeare una obra de Shakespeare
Our school is putting on a play. Nuestro colegio está preparando una obra.
2 (*in sports*) el **juego** *masc*
out of play fuera de juego
Play was interrupted three times. Se interrumpió el juego tres veces.

to **play** *verb* ▷ see **play** *noun*
1 (*a game, sport*) **jugar** [27]
to play tennis jugar al tenis
The children were playing with a ball. Los niños estaban jugando con una pelota.
Wales play Scotland tomorrow. Gales juega mañana contra Escocia.
They were playing cards. Estaban jugando a las cartas.
2 (*music, an instrument*) **tocar** [31]
Omar plays the drums. Omar toca la batería.
They play all kinds of music. Tocan todo tipo de música.
3 (*a tape, a CD, a record*) **poner** [11]
Play me your new CD. Ponme tu nuevo compacto.
4 (*a role*) **Who's playing Hamlet?** ¿Quién hace el papel de Hamlet?
I'm playing the baddy. Yo represento el malo.

player *noun*
1 (*in sport*) el **jugador** *masc*, la **jugadora** *fem*
a football player un jugador de fútbol
2 (*musician*) el **músico** *masc*, la **música** *fem*
a guitar player un guitarrista
She's a trumpet player. Es trompetista.

playground *noun*
el **patio de recreo**

playing card *noun*
el **naipe** *masc*

playing field *noun*
el **campo de juego**

playroom *noun*
el **cuarto de los juguetes**

pleasant *adjective*
agradable *masc & fem*
a very pleasant smell un olor muy agradable
She's not very pleasant. Es poco agradable.
Have a pleasant time! ¡Que lo pasen bien!

please *adverb*
por favor
Two coffees, please. Dos cafés, por favor.
Could you turn the TV off, please? ¿Puedes apagar la tele, por favor?
Please may I have a clean fork? ¿Me trae un tenedor limpio, por favor?

pleased *adjective*
contento *masc*, **contenta** *fem*
I'm very pleased. Estoy muy contento.
I was really pleased! ¡Me puse muy contento!
She was pleased with her present. Se puso muy contenta con su regalo.
Pleased to meet you! ¡Encantado de conocerte! (*boy speaking*), Encantada de conocerte! (*girl speaking*)

pleasure *noun*
1 (*pleasant thing*) el **placer** *masc*
It's a pleasure to hear him play. Es un placer oírlo tocar.
2 (*as a polite reply*) **with pleasure** con mucho gusto
'Thank you very much.'— 'It's a pleasure.' 'Muchas gracias.'— 'De nada.'

plenty *pronoun*
1 (*lots*) **bastante**
He's got plenty of experience. Tiene bastante experiencia.
There's plenty of bread. Hay bastante pan.
There are plenty of cases. Hay bastantes casos.
She's got plenty of ideas. Tiene bastantes ideas.
There were plenty of them. Había bastantes.
2 (*quite enough*) **de sobra**
We've got plenty of time for a coffee. Tenemos tiempo de sobra para tomar un café.
Thank you, that's plenty! Gracias, eso es suficiente.

pliers *plural noun*
los **alicates** *plural masc*

plug *noun*
1 (*electrical*) el **enchufe** *masc*
2 (*in a bath, sink*) el **tapón** *masc*
to pull out the plug quitar [17] el tapón
• **to plug something in**
enchufar [17] **algo**

plum *noun*
(*la*) **ciruela** *fem*
a plum tart una tarta de ciruelas
a plum tree un ciruelo

plumber *noun*
el **fontanero** *masc*, la **fontanera** *fem*
He's a plumber. Es fontanero.

plump *adjective*
regordete *masc*, **regordeta** *fem*

plural *noun*
(*Grammar*) el **plural** *masc*
in the plural en plural

plus *preposition*
más
three children plus the baby tres niños más el bebé
Two plus three equals five. Dos más tres es igual a cinco.

p.m. *adverb*
at two p.m. a las dos de la tarde
at nine p.m. a las nueve de la noche

WORD TIP Use *de la tarde* for times up to 8 p.m., and *de la noche* for times after that.

poached egg *noun*
el **huevo escalfado**

♪ **pocket** *noun*
el **bolsillo** *masc*
She had her hands in her pockets. Tenía las manos en los bolsillos.

♪ **pocket money** *noun*
1 (*for children*) la **paga** *fem*
2 (*for minor purchases*) el **dinero para gastos personales**

poem *noun*
el **poema** *masc*

poet *noun*
el & la **poeta** *masc & fem*

poetry *noun*
la **poesía** *fem*

♪ **point** *noun* ▷ see **point** *verb*
1 (*in time*) el **momento** *masc*
at this point in time en este momento
At that point the police arrived. En ese momento llegó la policía.
to be on the point of doing something estar [2] a punto de hacer algo
He was on the point of leaving. Estaba a punto de marcharse.
2 (*in space*) el **punto** *masc*
the highest point on the island el punto más alto de la isla
3 (*tip*) la **punta** *fem*
the point of a nail la punta de un clavo
4 (*in games, contests, exams*) el **punto** *masc*
fifteen points to eleven quince puntos a once
5 (*subject*) el **punto** *masc*
We discussed various points. Tratamos diversos puntos.
6 (*meaning, main issue*) **I don't see the point of that.** No lo entiendo.
That's not the point. No se trata de eso.
7 (*purpose*) el **sentido** *masc*
What's the point of waiting? ¿Qué sentido tiene esperar?
There's no point in phoning, he's out. No tiene sentido llamar, ha salido.
8 (*argument*) **That's a good point!** ¡Es verdad!
She made the point that ... Observó que ...
9 (*feature*) **her strong point** su punto fuerte
She doesn't see his bad points. No le ve los defectos.
10 (*in decimal numbers*) **6 point 4** seis coma cuatro (*Use a comma for the decimal point, so 6.4 = 6,4*)

♪ to **point** *verb* ▷ see **point** *noun*
señalar [17]
a notice pointing to the station un cartel señalando hacia la estación
It's rude to point. Es de mala educación señalar con el dedo.
to point at somebody señalar [17] a alguien
He pointed at one of the children. Señaló a uno de los niños.
He pointed his finger at me. Me señaló con el dedo.
• **to point out**
señalar [17]
I'll point her out to you. Te la señalaré.
James pointed out the cathedral. James señaló la catedral.
He pointed out to them that he was ill. Les señaló que estaba enfermo.

♪ **pointless** *adjective*
(*attempt*) **vano** *masc*, **vana** *fem*
It's pointless arguing with him. No tiene sentido discutir con él.

♪ **point of view** *noun*
el **punto de vista**
from my point of view desde mi punto de vista

poison *noun* ▷ see **poison** *verb*
el **veneno** *masc*

to **poison** *verb* ▷ see **poison** *noun*
envenenar [17]

poisonous *adjective*
venenoso *masc*, **venenosa** *fem*

poker *noun*
1 (*for a fire*) el **atizador** *masc*
2 (*the card game*) el **póker** *masc*

Poland *noun*
Polonia *fem*

polar bear *noun*
el **oso polar**

pole *noun*
1 (*for a tent*) el **mástil** *masc*
2 (*point of the globe*) el **polo** *masc*
the North Pole el Polo Norte

Pole *noun*
(*person*) un **polaco** *masc*, una **polaca** *fem*

WORD TIP Adjectives and nouns for nationality and regional origin do not have capital letters in Spanish.

police *plural noun*
the police la policía
The police are coming. Ya viene la policía.

WORD TIP *policía* takes a singular verb.

- **police car** el coche de policía
- **policeman** el policía
- **police officer** el & la agente
- **police station** la comisaría
- **policewoman** la mujer policía

mini-info *police*
Spain has three police forces; a local force for towns over 5000 inhabitants; the national force for towns over 20 000 inhabitants. The Civil Guard controls rural areas, roads, coasts and airports.

policy *noun*
1 (*plan*) la **política** *fem*
2 (*document*) la **póliza** *fem*

polish *noun* ▷ see **polish** *verb*
1 (*for furniture*) la **cera** *fem*
2 (*for shoes*) el **betún** *masc*

to **polish** *verb* ▷ see **polish** *noun*
(*shoes, furniture*) **sacar [31] brillo a**

Polish *adjective & noun*
1 **polaco** *masc*, **polaca** *fem*
2 (*the people*) **the Polish** los polacos
3 (*the language*) el **polaco** *masc*

WORD TIP Adjectives and nouns for nationality, regional origin and language do not have capital letters in Spanish.

polite *adjective*
educado *masc*, **educada** *fem*
to be polite to somebody ser [1] educado, *fem* educada con alguien
You should be more polite to your teacher. Deberías ser más educado con tu profesora.

political *adjective*
político *masc*, **política** *fem*

politician *noun*
el **político** *masc*, la **política** *fem*

politics *plural noun*
la **política** *fem*

polluted *adjective*
contaminado *masc*, **contaminada** *fem*
The river is very polluted. El río está muy contaminado.

pollution *noun*
la **contaminación** *fem*

polo-necked *adjective*
de cuello alto
a polo-necked sweater un jersey de cuello alto

polythene bag *noun*
la **bolsa de plástico**

pond *noun*
1 (*natural*) la **laguna** *fem*
2 (*man-made*) el **estanque** *masc*

pony *noun*
el **poni** *masc*
- **ponytail** la cola de caballo

poodle *noun*
el **caniche** *masc*

pool *noun*
1 (*swimming pool*) la **piscina** *fem*
2 (*of water, blood*) el **charco** *masc*
3 (*the game*) el **billar americano**
to have a game of pool jugar [27] al billar americano
4 (*competition*) **the football pools** las quinielas
to do the pools hacer [7] las quinielas

poor *adjective*
1 (*having little money*) **pobre** *masc & fem*
a poor area una zona pobre
a poor family una familia pobre
2 (*unfortunate*) **pobre** *masc & fem*
Poor Tanya failed her exam. La pobre Tanya suspendió el examen.
3 (*bad*) **malo** *masc*, **mala** *fem*
This is poor quality. Esto es de mala calidad.
The weather was pretty poor. El tiempo fue bastante malo.

pop *noun*
el **pop** *masc*
a pop concert un concierto de pop
a pop star una estrella del pop
a pop song una canción de pop
- **to pop into**
entrar [17] un momento
I'll just pop into the bank. Voy a entrar un momento en el banco.

popcorn *noun*
las **palomitas de maíz**

pope *noun*
(*Religion*) el **papa** *masc*

poppy *noun*
la **amapola** *fem*

popular *adjective*
popular *masc & fem*

population *noun*
la **población** *fem*

mini-info population

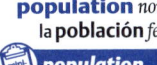

Mexico City with more than 20 million inhabitants, and growing, is the largest city in the world; its population is larger than the entire population of Australia.

porch *noun*
el **porche** *masc*

⚷ **pork** *noun*
el **cerdo** *masc*
a pork chop una chuleta de cerdo

porridge *noun*
las **gachas** *plural fem*

⚷ **port** *noun*
1 (*for ships*) el **puerto** *masc*
2 (*the drink*) el **oporto** *masc*

portable *adjective*
portátil *masc & fem*
a portable computer un portátil

porter *noun*
1 (*at a station, airport*) el **mozo de las maletas**
2 (*in a hotel*) el **portero** *masc*

portion *noun*
(*of food*) la **ración** *fem*

portrait *noun*
el **retrato** *masc*

Portugal *noun*
Portugal *masc*

Portuguese *adjective & noun*
1 **portugués** *masc*, **portuguesa** *fem*
2 (*person*) el **portugués** *masc*, la **portuguesa** *fem*
the Portuguese los portugueses
3 (*the language*) el **portugués** *masc*

WORD TIP Adjectives and nouns for nationality, regional origin and language do not have capital letters in Spanish.

posh *adjective*
elegante *masc & fem*
a posh house una casa elegante

position *noun*
la **posición** *fem*

positive *adjective*
1 (*sure*) **seguro** *masc*, **segura** *fem*
I'm positive he's left. Estoy seguro de que se ha ido.
2 (*enthusiastic*) **positivo** *masc*, **positiva** *fem*
a positive reaction una reacción muy positiva
Try to be more positive. Intenta tener una actitud más positiva.

⚷ **possession** *noun*
1 (*ownership*) la **posesión** *fem*
She took possession of the house. Tomó posesión de la casa.
2 **possessions** (*belongings*) las pertenencias
All my possessions are in the flat. Todas mis pertenencias están en el piso.

possibility *noun*
la **posibilidad** *fem*

⚷ **possible** *adjective*
posible *masc & fem*
if possible si es posible
It's possible. Es posible.
as quickly as possible tan rápidamente como sea posible

possibly *adverb*
1 (*maybe*) **posiblemente**
'Will you be at home at midday?'—'Possibly.' '¿Estarás en casa a mediodía?'—'Posiblemente.'
2 (*for emphasis*) **How can you possibly believe that?** Pero, ¿cómo puedes creerte eso?
I can't possibly arrive before Thursday. No puedo llegar antes del jueves de ninguna manera.

⚷ to **post** *verb* ▷ see **post** *noun*
to post a letter echar **[17]** una carta al correo
to post something to somebody mandarle **[17]** algo a alguien
I'll post the books to you. Te mandaré los libros por correo.

⚷ **post** *noun* ▷ see **post** *verb*
1 (*postal system*) el **correo** *masc*
to send something by post mandar **[17]** algo por correo
2 (*letters*) **Is there any post for me?** ¿Hay alguna carta para mí?
3 (*pole*) el **poste** *masc*
4 (*job*) el **puesto** *masc*
the post advertised in the paper el puesto anunciado en el periódico
- **postbox** el buzón
- **postcard** la postal
- **postcode** el código postal

poster *noun*
1 (*for decoration*) el **póster** *masc, pl:* los **pósters**
I've bought a Coldplay poster. He comprado un póster de Coldplay.
2 (*for advertising*) el **cartel** *masc*
I saw the poster for the concert. Vi el cartel del concierto.

postman *noun*
el **cartero** *masc*
Pat is a postman. Pat es cartero.
Has the postman been? ¿Ha pasado el cartero?

post office *noun*
la **oficina de correos**
He went to the post office. Fue a la oficina de correos.

to **postpone** *verb*
posponer [11]

postwoman *noun*
la **cartera** *fem*
My mother is a postwoman. Mi madre es cartera.

pot *noun*
1 (*jar*) el **tarro** *masc*
a pot of honey un tarro de miel
2 (*teapot*) la **tetera** *fem*
I'll make a pot of tea. Voy a hacer té.
3 (*for a plant*) la **maceta** *fem*
4 (*for cooking*) **the pots and pans** los cacharros

potato *noun*
la **patata** *fem*, (*Latin America*) la **papa**
fried potatoes patatas fritas
• **potato crisps** las patatas fritas de bolsa

pottery *noun*
la **cerámica** *fem*

pound *noun*
(*money, weight*) la **libra** *fem*
fourteen pounds catorce libras
a pound of apples una libra de manzanas
How much is that in pounds? ¿Cuánto es eso en libras?

to **pour** *verb*
1 (*a liquid*) **echar** [17]
He poured the milk into the pan. Echó la leche en la cacerola.
2 (*a drink*) **servir** [57]
to pour the tea servir el té
I poured him a drink. Le serví una bebida.
3 (*to rain heavily*) **llover** [38] **a cántaros**
It's pouring with rain. Está lloviendo a cántaros.

poverty *noun*
la **pobreza** *fem*

powder *noun*
el **polvo** *masc*

power *noun*
1 (*electricity*) la **corriente eléctrica**
2 (*energy*) la **energía** *fem*
nuclear power energía nuclear
3 (*over people*) el **poder** *masc*
to be in power estar [2] en el poder
• **power cut** el apagón

powerful *adjective*
poderoso *masc*, **poderosa** *fem*

power point *noun*
el **enchufe** *masc*

power station *noun*
la **central eléctrica**

practical *adjective*
práctico *masc*, **práctica** *fem*
• **practical joke** la broma pesada

practice *noun*
1 (*in general*) la **práctica** *fem*
in practice en la práctica
theory and practice la teoría y la práctica
2 (*training: for sport*) el **entrenamiento** *masc*
hockey practice el entrenamiento de hockey
to be out of practice estar [2] desentrenado
3 (*training: for an instrument*) **to do your piano practice** hacer [7] los ejercicios de piano
Musicians must keep in practice. Los músicos tienen que practicar continuamente.
He's out of practice. Le falta práctica.

to **practise** *verb*
1 (*in general*) **practicar** [31]
I went to Granada to practise my Spanish. Fui a Granada para practicar mi español.
2 (*for sport*) **entrenar** [17]
The team practises on Wednesdays. El equipo entrena los miércoles.

to **praise** *verb*
elogiar [17]
to praise somebody for something elogiar [17] a alguien por algo
We praised them for their efforts. Los elogiamos por sus esfuerzos.

pram *noun*
el **cochecito de bebé**

prawn *noun*
la **gamba** *fem*

to **pray** *verb*
rezar [22]

a b c d e f g h i j k l m n o p q r s t u v w x y z

prayer *noun*
la **oración** *fem*

precious *adjective*
precioso *masc*, **preciosa** *fem*

precise *adjective*
preciso *masc*, **precisa** *fem*

to **predict** *verb*
predecir [5]

♪ to **prefer** *verb*
preferir [14]
I prefer coffee to tea. Prefiero el café al té.
I'd prefer to go to Paris. Preferiría ir a París.

pregnant *adjective*
embarazada *fem*

pregnancy *noun*
el **embarazo** *masc*

prejudice *noun*
el **prejuicio** *masc*
a prejudice un prejuicio
racial prejudice los prejuicios raciales

prejudiced *adjective*
to be prejudiced tener [9] prejuicios

premiere *noun*
el **estreno** *masc*

preparation *noun*
1 (*act of preparing*) la **preparación** *fem*
2 (*arrangements in advance*) los **preparativos**
the Christmas preparations los preparativos para Navidad

♪ to **prepare** *verb*
1 (*to make ready*) **preparar** [17]
to prepare somebody for something preparar [17] a alguien para algo
Our teacher is preparing us for the exam. La profesora nos está preparando para el examen.
Prepare yourself for a shock! ¡Prepárate!
2 (*food*) **preparar** [17]
She prepared a paella. Preparó una paella.
3 **to prepare for something** prepararse para algo
I've got to prepare for the exam. Tengo que prepararme para el examen.

prepared *adjective*
1 (*ready*) **preparado** *masc*, **preparado** *fem*
to be prepared for something estar [2] preparado para algo
I wasn't prepared for the news. No estaba preparada para la noticia.
2 (*willing*) **dispuesto** *masc*, **dispuesta** *fem*
I'm prepared to pay half. Estoy dispuesta a pagar la mitad.

preposition *noun*
(*Grammar*) la **preposición** *fem*

♪ **pre-recorded** *adjective*
pregrabado *masc*, **pregrabada** *fem*

to **prescribe** *verb*
recetar [17]

prescription *noun*
la **receta** *fem*
on prescription con receta

♪ **present** *adjective* ▷ see **present** *verb, noun*
1 (*attending*) **presente** *masc & fem*
Is Tracy present? ¿Está presente Tracy?
to be present at something asistir [19] a algo
Fifty people were present at the funeral. Cincuenta personas asistieron al funeral.
2 (*current*) **actual** *masc & fem*
the present situation la situación actual
at the present time en este momento

♪ **present** *noun* ▷ see **present** *adj, verb*
1 (*gift*) el **regalo** *masc*
to give somebody a present hacerle [17] un regalo a alguien
He gave Laura a present. A Laura le hizo un regalo.
2 (*the current time*) el **presente** *masc*
That's all for the present. Eso es todo por ahora.
3 (*Grammar*) el **presente** *masc*
in the present (tense) en presente

♪ to **present** *verb* ▷ see **present** *adj, noun*
1 (*to hand over*) **entregar** [28]
to present something to somebody entregarle algo a alguien
The headteacher will present the prize to her. El director le entregará el premio.
2 (*a TV programme*) **presentar** [17]

presenter *noun*
(*on TV*) el **presentador** *masc*, la **presentadora** *fem*

♪ **president** *noun*
el **presidente** *masc*, la **presidenta** *fem*

to **press** *verb* ▷ see **press** *noun*
1 (*a button, doorbell*) **pulsar** [1]
She pressed the button. Pulsó el botón.
2 (*to push*) **empujar** [17]
Press here to open. Para abrir, empuje aquí.

press *noun* ▷ see **press** *verb*
the press la prensa
- **press conference** la rueda de prensa

English–Spanish

pressure *noun*
la **presión** *fem*
- **pressure gauge** el manómetro
- **pressure group** el grupo de presión

to **pretend** *verb*
fingir [49]
to pretend to do something fingir hacer algo
He's pretending not to hear. Está fingiendo no oír.

♪ **pretty** *adjective* ▷ see **pretty** *adv*
bonito *masc*, **bonita** *fem*
a pretty dress un vestido bonito

♪ **pretty** *adverb* ▷ see **pretty** *adj*
bastante *masc & fem*
It was pretty embarrassing. Fue bastante vergonzoso.

to **prevent** *verb*
1 (*a crime, an accident*) **prevenir [15]**
2 (*a war, disaster*) **evitar [17]**
3 **to prevent somebody from doing something** impedir **[57]** a alguien hacer algo
There's nothing to prevent you from leaving. No hay nada que te impida irte.

previous *adjective*
anterior *masc & fem*
the previous day el día anterior

previously *adverb*
antes

♪ **price** *noun*
el **precio** *masc*
the price per kilo el precio por kilo
CDs have gone up in price. Los compactos han subido de precio.
- **price list** la lista de precios
- **price ticket** la etiqueta del precio

pride *noun*
el **orgullo** *masc*

priest, *noun*
el **sacerdote** *masc*

♪ **primary school** *noun*
la **escuela primaria**
- **primary school teacher** el maestro, la maestra

♪ **prime minister** *noun*
el **primer ministro** *masc*, la **primera ministra** *fem*

prince *noun*
el **príncipe** *masc*
Prince Charles el príncipe Carlos

princess *noun*
la **princesa** *fem*
Princess Anne la Princesa Ana

♪ **principal** *adjective* ▷ see **principal** *noun*
principal *masc & fem*

♪ **principal** *noun* ▷ see **principal** *adj*
el **director** *masc*, la **directora** *fem*

print *noun*
1 (*on a page*) la **letra** *fem*
in small print en letra pequeña
2 (*photo*) la **copia** *fem*
a colour print una copia a color

♪ **printer** *noun*
(*machine*) la **impresora** *fem*

print-out *noun*
la **copia en papel**

prison *noun*
la **cárcel** *fem*
in prison en la cárcel

prisoner *noun*
el **preso** *masc*, la **presa** *fem*

♪ **private** *adjective*
1 (*not public*) **privado** *masc*, **privada** *fem*
in private en privado
a private school una escuela privada
'Private property' 'Propiedad privada'
2 (*lesson*) **particular** *masc & fem*
to have private lessons tener **[9]** clases particulares

privilege *noun*
el **privilegio** *masc*

♪ **prize** *noun*
el **premio** *masc*
the prize for the best athlete el premio al mejor atleta
to win a prize ganar **[17]** un premio
- **prize-giving** la entrega de premios
- **prizewinner** el ganador, la ganadora

♪ **probable** *adjective*
probable *masc & fem*
the most probable explanation la explicación más probable
It's probable that it will rain. Es probable que llueva.

probably *adverb*
probablemente

♪ **problem** *noun*
el **problema** *masc*
It's a serious problem. Es un problema grave.
She has a weight problem. Tiene problemas con el peso.
No problem! ¡No hay problema!

a b c d e f g h i j k l m n o p q r s t u v w x y z

procession *noun*
1 (*parade*) el **desfile** *masc*
2 (*at a religious festival*) la **procesión** *fem*

produce *noun* ▷ see **produce** *verb*
los **productos** *plural masc*

to **produce** *verb* ▷ see **produce** *noun*
1 (*to give out*) **producir** [60]
It produces a lot of heat. Produce mucho calor.
2 (*to show*) **presentar** [17]
I produced my passport. Presenté mi pasaporte.

producer *noun*
el **productor** *masc*, la **productora** *fem*

♪ **product** *noun*
el **producto** *masc*
dairy products productos lácteos

production *noun*
1 (*of a film*) la **producción** *fem*
2 (*of a play, an opera*) la **puesta en escena**
a new production of Hamlet una nueva puesta en escena de Hamlet
3 (*by a factory*) la **producción** *fem*

profession *noun*
la **profesión** *fem*

professional *adjective*
▷ see **professional** *noun*
profesional *masc & fem*
She's a professional singer. Es cantante profesional.

professional *noun*
▷ see **professional** *adj*
el & la **profesional** *masc & fem*
He's a professional. Es un profesional.

professor *noun*
el **catedrático** *masc*, la **catedrática** *fem*

profit *noun*
los **beneficios** *plural masc*

profitable *adjective*
rentable *masc & fem*

♪ **program** *noun* ▷ see **programme** *noun*
(*Computers*) el **programa**
a computer program un programa de ordenador
You can download the program from the website. Puedes bajar el programa del sitio web.

♪ **programme** *noun* ▷ see **program** *noun*
el **programa** *masc*
What's your programme for tomorrow? ¿Qué programa tienes para mañana?

programmer *noun*
el **programador** *masc*, la **programadora** *fem*

progress *noun*
1 el **progreso** *masc*
to make progress (*in your work*) hacer [7] progresos
2 **to be in progress** estar [2] en curso

project *noun*
1 (*at school*) el **trabajo** *masc*
2 (*plan*) el **proyecto** *masc*
a project to build a bridge un proyecto para construir un puente

projector *noun*
el **proyector** *masc*

promise *noun* ▷ see **promise** *verb*
la **promesa** *fem*
to make a promise hacer [7] una promesa
to break a promise no cumplir [19] con una promesa
It's a promise! ¡Lo prometo!

to **promise** *verb* ▷ see **promise** *noun*
to promise to do something prometer [18] hacer algo
I've promised to be home by ten. He prometido estar en casa a las diez.

to **promote** *verb*
ascender [36]
She's been promoted. La han ascendido.

♪ **promotion** *noun*
1 (*at work*) el **ascenso** *masc*
2 (*special offer*) la **promoción** *fem*

prompt *adjective*
pronto *masc*, **pronta** *fem*
a prompt reply una pronta respuesta

pronoun *noun*
(*Grammar*) el **pronombre** *masc*

♪ to **pronounce** *verb*
pronunciar [17]
It's hard to pronounce. Es difícil de pronunciar.
How do you pronounce it? ¿Cómo se pronuncia?

pronunciation *noun*
la **pronunciación** *fem*

proof *noun*
las **pruebas** *plural fem*
They've got proof. Tienen pruebas.
There's no proof. No hay pruebas.

English–Spanish

propaganda *noun*
la **propaganda** *fem*

propeller *noun*
la **hélice** *fem*

proper *adjective*
1 (*real, genuine*) **de verdad**
a proper doctor un médico titulado
I need a proper meal. Necesito una comida de verdad.
2 (*correct*) **adecuado** *masc*, **adecuada** *fem*
the proper tool la herramienta adecuada
Leave it in its proper place. Déjalo en su sitio.

properly *adverb*
bien
Hold it properly. Sujétalo bien.
Is it properly wrapped? ¿Está bien envuelto?

property *noun*
la **propiedad** *fem*
'Private property' 'Propiedad privada'

to **propose** *verb*
1 (*to suggest*) **proponer** [11]
2 (*in engagements*) **He proposed to her.** Le pidió que se casara con él.

prostitute *noun*
la **prostituta** *fem*

to **protect** *verb*
proteger [3]

protection *noun*
la **protección** *fem*

protein *noun*
la **proteína** *fem*

protest *noun* ▷ see **protest** *verb*
la **protesta** *fem*
in spite of their protests a pesar de sus protestas

to **protest** *verb* ▷ see **protest** *noun*
1 (*to grumble*) **protestar** [17]
He protested about the noise. Protestó por el ruido.
2 (*to demonstrate*) **manifestarse** [29]

Protestant *adjective & noun*
1 **protestante** *masc & fem*
2 el & la **protestante** *masc & fem*

WORD TIP Adjectives and nouns for religion do not have capital letters in Spanish.

protester *noun*
el & la **manifestante** *masc & fem*

protest march *noun*
la **manifestación** *fem*

proud *adjective*
orgulloso *masc*, **orgullosa** *fem*
I'm very proud of you. Estoy muy orgullosa de vosotros.

to **prove** *verb*
probar [24]

proverb *noun*
el **refrán** *masc*

to **provide** *verb*
proveer [37]
They've provided us with food. Nos han provisto de comida.

provided *conjunction*
siempre que
provided you do it siempre que tú lo hagas

WORD TIP *siempre que* is followed by a verb in the subjunctive.

province *noun*
la **provincia** *fem*

⚷ **prune** *noun*
la **ciruela pasa**

PS *abbreviation*
(*at the end of a letter*) **PD**

psychiatrist *noun*
el & la **psiquiatra** *masc & fem*
He's a psychiatrist. Es psiquiatra.

psychological *adjective*
psicológico *masc*, **psicológica** *fem*

psychologist *noun*
el **psicólogo** *masc*, la **psicóloga** *fem*
She's a psychologist. Es psicóloga.

psychology *noun*
la **psicología** *fem*

PTO *abbreviation*
(*= Please Turn Over*) **sigue al dorso**

pub *noun*
el **bar** *masc*

⚷ **public** *adjective* ▷ see **public** *noun*
público *masc*, **pública** *fem*
the public library la biblioteca pública
• **public address system** el sistema de megafonía

a b c d e f g h i j k l m n o p q r s t u v w x y z

English–Spanish

public *noun* ▷ see **public** *adj*
the public el público
in public en público
It's open to the public at weekends. Está abierto al público los fines de semana.

public holiday *noun*
el **día de fiesta**
The first of January is a public holiday. El uno de enero es fiesta.

publicity *noun*
la **publicidad** *fem*

public school *noun*
el **colegio privado**

public transport *noun*
el **transporte público**

to **publish** *verb*
publicar [31]

publisher *noun*
1 (*person*) el **editor** *masc*, la **editora** *fem*
2 (*company*) la **editorial** *fem*

pudding *noun*
(*dessert*) el **postre** *masc*
For pudding we've got strawberries. De postre tenemos fresas.

puddle *noun*
el **charco** *masc*

Puerto Rican *adjective & noun*
1 **puertorriqueño** *masc*, **puertorriqueña** *fem*
2 (*person*) el **puertorriqueño** *masc*, la **puertorriqueña** *fem*
the Puerto Ricans los puertorriqueños

WORD TIP Adjectives, and nouns for nationality and regional origin do not have capital letters in Spanish.

puff pastry *noun*
el **hojaldre** *masc*

to **pull** *verb*
tirar [17]
to pull a rope tirar de una cuerda
Pull hard! ¡Tira fuerte!
• **to pull down**
(*a blind*) **bajar** [17]
• **to pull in**
(*at the roadside*) **parar** [17]
• **to pull something out**
sacar [31] **algo**
He pulled a letter out of his pocket. Sacó una carta del bolsillo.

pullover *noun*
el **jersey** *masc*
a wool pullover un jersey de lana

pulse *noun*
el **pulso** *masc*
The doctor took my pulse. El médico me tomó el pulso.

pump *noun* ▷ see **pump** *verb*
la **bomba** *fem*
a bicycle pump una bomba de bicicleta

to **pump** *verb* ▷ see **pump** *noun*
(*oil, water*) **bombear** [17]
They were pumping the water out of the cellar. Estaban bombeando el agua del sótano.
• **to pump up**
(*a tyre*) **inflar** [17]

punch *noun* ▷ see **punch** *verb*
1 (*in boxing*) el **puñetazo** *masc*
2 (*the drink*) el **ponche** *masc*

to **punch** *verb* ▷ see **punch** *noun*
1 (*a person*) to punch somebody darle [4] un puñetazo a alguien
He punched me. Me dio un puñetazo.
2 (*a ticket*) **picar** [31]

punctual *adjective*
puntual *masc & fem*

punctuation *noun*
la **puntuación** *fem*
• **punctuation mark** el signo de puntuación

puncture *noun*
el **pinchazo** *masc*
We had a puncture. Tuvimos un pinchazo.

to **punish** *verb*
castigar [28]

punishment *noun*
el **castigo** *masc*

pupil *noun*
1 (*in a school*) el **alumno** *masc*, la **alumna** *fem*
2 (*of your eye*) la **pupila** *fem*

puppet *noun*
el **títere** *masc*

puppy *noun*
el **cachorro** *masc*, la **cachorra** *fem*
a labrador puppy un cachorro de labrador

to **purchase** *verb*
comprar [17]
to purchase something from somebody comprarle algo a alguien

a b c d e f g h i j k l m n o p q r s t u v w x y z

English–Spanish

pure *adjective*
puro *masc*, **pura** *fem*

purple *adjective*
morado *masc*, **morada** *fem*
a purple tee-shirt una camiseta morada

purpose *noun*
1 (*reason*) el **propósito** *masc*
What was the purpose of her call? ¿Qué propósito tenía su llamada?
2 **on purpose** a propósito
She did it on purpose. Lo hizo a propósito.

to **purr** *verb*
ronronear [17]

purse *noun*
el **monedero** *masc*
I'm always forgetting my purse. Siempre me olvido del monedero.

push *noun* ▷ see **push** *verb*
el **empujón** *masc*
to give something a push dar [4] un empujón a algo
• **pushchair** la sillita de niño

to **push** *verb* ▷ see **push** *noun*
1 (*to shove*) **empujar** [17]
He pushed me. Me empujó.
Stop pushing! ¡Deja de empujar!
2 (*a bell, button*) **apretar** [29]
• **to push something away**
apartar [17] **algo**
She pushed her plate away. Apartó su plato.

to **put** *verb*
1 (*to place*) **poner** [11]
You can put it in the fridge. Puedes ponerlo en la nevera.
Where did you put my bag? ¿Dónde has puesto mi bolso?
Put your suitcase here. Pon tu maleta aquí.
Put your address here. Pon tus señas aquí.
2 (*to put inside*) **meter** [18]
I put it in the drawer. Lo metí en el cajón.
• **to put away**
guardar [17]
I'll put the shopping away. Voy a guardar la compra.
• **to put back**
volver [45] **a poner**
He put it back in the wardrobe. Lo volvió a poner en el armario.
• **to put down**
poner [11]
She put the vase down on the table. Puso el jarrón en la mesa.
• **to put off**
1 (*to postpone*) **aplazar** [22]
He put off my lesson till Thursday. Aplazó mi clase hasta el jueves.
2 (*to turn you against*) **It put me off Chinese food!** ¡Hizo que se me quitaran las ganas de tomar comida china!
Don't be put off! ¡No te desanimes!
• **to put on**
1 (*clothing, make-up*) **ponerse** [11]
I'll just put my shoes on. Voy a ponerme los zapatos.
2 (*lights, heating*) **encender** [36]
Could you put the lamp on? ¿Puedes encender la lámpara?
3 (*the TV, radio*) **poner** [11]
Shall we put on the telly? ¿Ponemos la tele?
Don't put on Oasis again. No vuelvas a poner a Oasis.
4 (*a play*) **montar** [17]
We're putting on a Spanish play. Estamos montando una obra española.
• **to put out**
1 (*to put outside*) **sacar** [31]
Put the rubbish out. Saca la basura.
2 (*a light, a fire, a cigarette*) **apagar** [28]
She put the lights out. Apagó las luces.
3 (*part of your body*) **to put out your hand** extender [36] la mano
• **to put through**
pasar [17] **con**
I'll put you through to the manager. Le paso con el gerente.
• **to put up**
1 (*your hand*) **levantar** [17]
He put up his hand. Levantó la mano.
2 (*a picture*) **poner** [11]
I've put up some photos in my room. He puesto algunas fotos en mi habitacion.
3 (*a notice*) **colgar** [23]
4 (*the price*) **subir** [19]
They've put up the price of the tickets. Han subido el precio de las entradas.
5 (*for the night*) **Can you put me up on Friday?** ¿Puedo quedarme a dormir en tu casa el viernes?
• **to put up with something**
aguantar [17] **algo**
I don't know how she puts up with it. No sé cómo lo aguanta.

a b c d e f g h i j k l m n o p q r s t u v w x y z

puzzle *noun*
el **rompecabezas** *masc*, el **puzzle** *masc*

WORD TIP *rompecabezas* does not change in the plural.

puzzled *adjective*
confuso *masc*, **confusa** *fem*

♪ **pyjamas** *plural noun*
el **pijama** *masc*
a pair of pyjamas un pijama
Where are my pyjamas? ¿Dónde está mi pijama?

pylon *noun*
la **torre de alta tensión**

pyramid *noun*
la **pirámide**

Pyrenees *noun*
the Pyrenees los Pirineos (*The mountains between Spain and France.*)

English–Spanish

a b c d e f g h i j k l m n o p q r s t u v w x y z

Q q

quail *noun*
la **codorniz** *fem*

qualification *noun*
1 (*certificate, degree, etc*) el **título** *masc*
2 **qualifications** la titulación *fem*
vocational qualifications la titulación profesional

qualified *adjective*
1 (*as a teacher*) **cualificado** *masc*, **cualificada** *fem*
She's a qualified ski instructor. Es una monitora de esquí cualificada.
2 (*having a degree, diploma*) **titulado** *masc*, **titulada** *fem*
a qualified architect un arquitecto titulado

to **qualify** *verb*
1 (*in sport*) **clasificarse** [31]
They've qualified for the quarter finals. Se han clasificado para los cuartos de final.
2 **to qualify for a benefit** tener [9] derecho a un beneficio
We qualify for a reduction. Tenemos derecho a una reducción.

quality *noun*
la **calidad** *fem*
good quality jeans vaqueros de buena calidad
a poor quality recording una grabación de calidad inferior

quantity *noun*
la **cantidad** *fem*

quarantine *noun*
la **cuarentena** *fem*

quarrel *noun* ▷ see **quarrel** *verb*
la **pelea** *fem*
to have a quarrel tener [9] una pelea

to **quarrel** *verb* ▷ see **quarrel** *noun*
pelearse [17]
They're always quarrelling. Siempre se están peleando.

quarry *noun*
la **cantera** *fem*

⚷ **quarter** *noun*
1 (*fraction*) la **cuarta parte** *fem*
a quarter of the class una cuarta parte de la clase
three quarters of the class las tres cuartas partes de la clase
2 (*when telling the time*) el **cuarto** *masc*
a quarter past ten las diez y cuarto
a quarter to ten las diez menos cuarto
at a quarter to one a la una menos cuarto
a quarter of an hour un cuarto de hora
three quarters of an hour tres cuartos de hora
an hour and a quarter una hora y cuarto
3 (*with weights, measures*) **a quarter of a kilo** un cuarto de kilo
three quarters of a litre tres cuartos de litro
• **quarter finals** los cuartos de final

quartet *noun*
el **cuarteto** *masc*
a jazz quartet un cuarteto de jazz

quay *noun*
el **muelle** *masc*

⚷ **queen** *noun*
la **reina** *fem*
Queen Elizabeth la reina Isabel
the Queen of Spain la reina de España

query *noun*
la **pregunta** *fem*
Do you have any queries? ¿Hay alguna duda?

⚷ to **question** *verb* ▷ see **question** *noun*
interrogar [28]
She was questioned about her business interests. La interrogaron acerca de sus negocios.

⚷ **question** *noun* ▷ see **question** *verb*
1 (*when you ask*) la **pregunta** *fem*
to ask a question hacer [7] una pregunta
I asked her a question. Le hice una pregunta.
He didn't answer my question. No contestó a mi pregunta.
2 (*problem*) la **cuestión** *fem*
the question of his frequent absences la cuestión de sus frecuentes faltas de asistencia
It's a question of time. Es cuestión de tiempo.
It's out of the question! ¡Bajo ningún concepto!
• **question mark** el signo de interrogación

questionnaire *noun*
el **cuestionario** *masc*
to fill in a questionnaire rellenar [17] un cuestionario

queue *noun* ▷ see **queue** *verb*
1 (*of people*) la **cola** *fem*
to stand in a queue estar [2] en la cola
2 (*of cars*) la **fila** *fem*

to **queue** *verb* ▷ see **queue** *noun*
hacer [7] cola
We were queueing for hours. Estábamos haciendo cola durante horas.

♪ **quick** *adjective*
rápido *masc*, **rápida** *fem*
a quick lunch una comida rápida
It's quicker by motorway. Es más rápido por la autopista.
to have a quick look at something echarle [17] un vistazo rápido a algo
Quick! there's the bus! ¡De prisa, que viene el autobús!
Be quick! ¡Date prisa!

quickly *adverb*
rápidamente
I'll just quickly phone my mother. Voy a llamar rápidamente a mi madre.

♪ **quiet** *adjective*
1 (*person, machine*) **silencioso** *masc*, **silenciosa** *fem*
a quiet engine un motor silencioso
The children are very quiet. Los niños están muy silenciosos.
to keep quiet no hablar [17]
Please keep quiet. Por favor, no hablen.
2 (*music, voice*) **suave**
some quiet music una música suave
in a quiet voice en voz baja
3 (*neighbourhood*) **tranquilo** *masc*, **tranquila** *fem*
a quiet street una calle tranquila
We had a quiet day at home. Pasamos un día tranquilo en casa.

quietly *adverb*
1 (*to move*) **sin hacer ruido**
He got up quietly. Se levantó sin hacer ruido.
2 (*to speak*) **en voz baja**
3 (*to read, play*) **en silencio**

quilt *noun*
el **edredón** *masc*
a continental quilt un edredón nórdico

♪ **quite** *adverb*
1 **bastante**
quite often bastante a menudo
It's quite cold outside. Hace bastante frío fuera.
That's quite a good idea. Es una idea bastante buena.
He sings quite well. Canta bastante bien.
2 **not quite** no ... todavía
The meat's not quite cooked. La carne no está hecha todavía.
'Was it like this?'—'Not quite.' '¿Era así?'—'No exactamente.'
3 **quite a ...** bastante
quite a lot of money bastante dinero
quite a few people bastante gente
I have quite a lot of friends here. Tengo bastantes amigos aquí.

quiz *noun*
el **concurso** *masc*

quotation *noun*
la **cita** *fem*

quotation marks *plural noun*
(*Grammar*) las **comillas** *plural fem*
in quotation marks entre comillas

quote *noun* ▷ see **quote** *verb*
1 (*from a book, speech*) la **cita** *fem*
2 (*for work*) el **presupuesto** *masc*
We asked the builder for a quote. Le pedimos un presupuesto al contratista.
3 (*in text*) **in quotes** entre comillas

to **quote** *verb* ▷ see **quote** *noun*
citar [17]

English-Spanish

a b c d e f g h i j k l m n o p q r s t u v w x y z

English–Spanish

R r

rabbi *noun*
el **rabino** *masc*, la **rabina** *fem*

rabbit *noun*
el **conejo** *masc*

race *noun*
1 (*sports event*) la **carrera** *fem*
a cycle race una carrera de bicicletas
to have a race echar [17] una carrera
2 (*ethnic group*) la **raza** *fem*

racer *noun*
(*bike*) la **bicicleta de carreras**

racetrack *noun*
1 (*for horses*) la **pista de carreras**
2 (*for cars*) el **circuito** *masc*
3 (*for cycles*) el **velódromo** *masc*

racing *noun*
las **carreras** *plural fem*
- **racing car** el coche de carreras
- **racing driver** el & la piloto de carreras

racial *adjective*
racial *masc & fem*
racial discrimination discriminación racial

racism *noun*
el **racismo** *masc*

racist *adjective* ▷ see **racist** *noun*
racista *masc & fem*

racist *noun* ▷ see **racist** *adj*
el & la **racista** *masc & fem*

racket *noun*
1 (*for tennis*) la **raqueta** *fem*
2 (*noise*) el **jaleo** *masc*
What a racket! ¡Qué jaleo!

radar *noun*
el **radar** *masc*

radiator *noun*
el **radiador** *masc*

radio *noun*
la **radio** *fem*
to listen to the radio escuchar [17] la radio
to hear something on the radio oír [56] algo en la radio
- **radio station** la emisora de radio

radish *noun*
el **rabanito** *masc*

radius *noun*
el **radio** *masc*

raffle *noun*
la **rifa** *fem*

raft *noun*
la **balsa** *fem*

rag *noun*
el **trapo** *masc*

rage *noun*
la **furia** *fem*
He went red with rage. Se puso rojo de furia.
She's in a rage. Está furiosa.

rail *noun*
1 (*railway*) **to go by rail** ir [8] en tren
2 (*on a balcony, bridge*) la **baranda** *fem*
3 (*on stairs*) el **pasamanos** *masc, pl:* los **pasamanos**
4 (*for a train*) el **raíl** *masc*

railings *plural noun*
la **verja** *fem*

railway *noun*
1 (*transport system*) el **ferrocarril** *masc*
the railways los ferrocarriles
2 (*track*) la **vía férrea**
They were playing on the railway. Estaban jugando en la vía férrea.
- **railway carriage** el vagón de tren

railway line *noun*
1 (*track*) la **vía férrea**
2 (*route*) la **línea de ferrocarril**

railway station *noun*
la **estación de trenes**
opposite the railway station enfrente de la estación de trenes

rain *noun* ▷ see **rain** *verb*
la **lluvia** *fem*
I went out in the rain. Salí cuando llovía.
We were caught in the rain Nos cogió la lluvia.
It looks like rain. Parece que va a llover.

to **rain** *verb* ▷ see **rain** *noun*
llover [38]
It's raining. Está lloviendo.
It's going to rain. Va a llover.
- **rainbow** el arco iris
- **raincoat** el impermeable
- **rainfall** las precipitaciones

rainy *adjective*
lluvioso *masc*, **lluviosa** *fem*

a b c d e f g h i j k l m n o p q r s t u v w x y z

to **raise** *verb*
1 *(to lift up)* **levantar [17]**
She raised her head. Levantó la cabeza.
2 *(prices, salaries)* **subir [19]**
3 *(some money)* **recaudar [17]**
to raise money for something recaudar dinero para algo
4 *(the standards)* **mejorar [17]**
5 *(a child, family)* **criar [17]**

raisin *noun*
la **pasa** *fem*

rally *noun*
1 *(meeting)* la **concentración** *fem*
2 *(sports event)* el **rally** *masc, pl:* los **rallys**
3 *(in tennis)* el **peloteo** *masc*

rambler *noun*
el & la **excursionista** *masc & fem*

rambling *noun*
to go rambling ir **[8]** de excursión

ramp *noun*
(for a wheelchair) la **rampa** *fem*

range *noun*
1 *(choice)* la **gama** *fem*
a wide range of colours una amplia gama de colores
2 *(of mountains)* la **cordillera** *fem*

rap *noun*
1 *(knock on a door)* el **golpe** *masc*
2 *(music)* el **rap** *masc*

rape *noun* ▷ see **rape** *verb*
la **violación** *fem*

to **rape** *verb* ▷ see **rape** *noun*
violar [17]

♪ **rare** *adjective*
1 *(not common)* **poco común** *masc & fem*
a rare bird un pájaro poco común
2 *(steak)* **poco hecho** *masc*, **poco hecha** *fem*
a rare steak un filete poco hecho

♪ **raspberry** *noun*
la **frambuesa** *fem*
raspberry jam mermelada de frambuesa
a raspberry tart una tarta de frambuesas

rat *noun*
la **rata** *fem*

♪ **rate** *noun*
1 *(speed)* el **ritmo** *masc*
I read at a rate of 100 pages a day. Leo a un ritmo de cien páginas por día.
at this rate a este paso
at any rate en todo caso
2 *(level)* el **índice** *masc*
the birth rate el índice de natalidad
rate of interest tipo de interés
3 *(charge)* la **tarifa** *fem*
reduced rates tarifas reducidas
What are the rates for children? ¿Cuáles son las tarifas para niños?

rather *adverb*
1 *(somewhat)* **bastante**
I'm rather busy. Estoy bastante ocupado.
rather a lot of bastante
I've got rather a lot of work. Tengo bastante trabajo.
There are rather a lot of mistakes. Hay bastantes errores.
2 *(showing a preference)* **I'd rather wait.** Preferiría esperar.
I'd rather walk than go by bus. Prefiero andar a ir en autobús.
I'd rather not think about that. Prefiero no pensar en eso.
3 *(in expressions)* **rather than** en vez de
We went to Spain rather than France. Fuimos a España en vez de Francia.
in summer rather than winter en verano más que en invierno

raw *adjective*
crudo *masc*, **cruda** *fem*

ray *noun*
el **rayo** *masc*

razor *noun*
(safety razor) la **máquina de afeitar**
• **razor blade** la cuchilla

RE *noun*
(= Religious Education) la **religión** *fem*

reach *noun* ▷ see **reach** *verb*
el **alcance** *masc*
to be out of somebody's reach estar **[2]** fuera del alcance de alguien
The book was out of my reach. El libro estaba fuera de mi alcance.
to be within somebody's reach estar **[2]** al alcance de alguien
The cup was within my reach. La taza estaba a mi alcance.
The hotel is within easy reach of the sea. El hotel está muy cerca del mar.

to **reach** *verb* ▷ see **reach** *noun*
1 *(your destination)* **llegar [28] a**
We reached the church. Llegamos a la iglesia.
The team reached the final. El equipo llegó a la final. ⏩

2 (*to stretch far enough*) **alcanzar [22]**
I stood on a box to reach it. Me subí a una caja para alcanzarlo.
I can't reach! ¡No alcanzo!

to **read** *verb* ▷ see **reading** *noun*
leer [37]
What are you reading at the moment? ¿Qué estás leyendo en este momento?
I'm reading a detective novel. Estoy leyendo una novela policiaca.
I read about it in the paper. Lo leí en el periódico.
He read out the list. Leyó la lista.

reading *noun* ▷ see **read** *verb*
la **lectura** *fem*
I don't like reading. No me gusta la lectura.
Some easy reading for the beach. Lectura fácil para la playa.

> mini-info ***reading***
> One of the first novels ever written was the *Don Quijote* by Miguel de Cervantes; part one came out in 1605 and part two in 1615. The novel has continued to be very influential ever since.

ready *adjective*
1 (*food*) **preparado** *masc*, **preparada** *fem*
Supper's not ready yet. La cena aún no está preparada.
to get something ready (*a meal, things*) preparar **[17]** algo
He got the meal ready. Preparó la comida.
I'll get your room ready. Voy a preparar tu habitación.
2 (*person*) **listo** *masc*, **lista** *fem*
Are you ready to leave? ¿Estás listo para salir?
to get ready prepararse **[17]**
I'm getting ready to go out. Me estoy preparando para salir.
I was getting ready for bed. Estaba preparándome para irme a la cama.

ready-cooked meal *noun*
la **comida precocinada**

real *adjective*
verdadero *masc*, **verdadera** *fem*
Is that his real name? ¿Es ése su verdadero nombre?
Her real father is dead. Su verdadero padre está muerto.
He's a real bore. Es un verdadero pesado.
It's a real diamond. Es un diamante de verdad.

to **realize** *verb*
darse [4] cuenta
I hadn't realized. No me había dado cuenta.
to realize (that) ... darse cuenta de que ...
I didn't realize (that) he was French. No me di cuenta de que era francés.
Do you realize what time it is? ¿Te das cuenta de la hora que es?

really *adverb*
1 (*in fact*) **The tomato is really a fruit.** El tomate en realidad es una fruta.
Is it really midnight? ¿De verdad son las doce de la noche?
'Do you like it?" "Not really.' '¿Te gusta?'— 'No mucho.'
2 (*for emphasis*) **The film was really good.** La película fue buenísima.
It was really hot. Hacía mucho calor.
I really don't know. Realmente no lo sé.
really and truly de verdad
3 (*to show surprise*) **Really?** ¿De verdad?
'She is very famous.'— 'Really?' 'Es muy famosa.'— '¿De verdad?'

reason *noun*
la **razón** *fem*
the reason for something la razón de algo
the reason for the delay la razón del retraso
the reason why I phoned la razón por la que llamé

reasonable *adjective*
razonable *masc & fem*

rebel *noun*
el & la **rebelde** *masc & fem*

rebellion *noun*
la **rebelión** *fem*

receipt *noun*
el **recibo** *masc*
Could I have a receipt please? ¿Me podría dar un recibo, por favor?

to **receive** *verb*
recibir [19]
I received your letter. Recibí tu carta.
She received a blow to the head. Recibió un golpe en la cabeza.
to receive treatment ser **[1]** tratado
He received an honorary doctorate. Le confirieron un doctorado honoris causa.

receiver *noun*
el **auricular** *masc*
to pick up the receiver descolgar **[23]** el auricular
to put down the receiver colgar **[23]** el auricular

recent *adjective*
reciente *masc & fem*
a recent change un cambio reciente

recently *adverb*
recientemente

reception *noun*
1 (*in a hotel, office, etc*) la **recepción** *fem*
He's waiting at reception. Está esperando en recepción.
2 (*social event*) la **recepción** *fem*
a big wedding reception un gran banquete de bodas
3 (*on TV, radio*) la **recepción** *fem*
4 (*response, reaction*) la **acogida** *fem*
to get a good reception tener [9] buena acogida

receptionist *noun*
el & la **recepcionista** *masc & fem*
My sister works as a receptionist. Mi hermana trabaja como recepcionista.

recipe *noun*
la **receta** *fem*
Can I have the recipe for your salad? ¿Me puedes dar tu receta de la ensalada?

to **reckon** *verb*
creer [37]
I reckon it's a good idea. Creo que es una buena idea.

to **recognize** *verb*
reconocer [35]

to **recommend** *verb*
recomendar [29]
Can you recommend a dentist? ¿Puedes recomendarme un dentista?
I recommend the fish soup. Recomiendo la sopa de pescado.

recommendation *noun*
la **recomendación** *fem*

to **record** *verb* ▷ see **record** *noun*
(*onto a tape, CD*) **grabar** [17]
They're recording a new album. Están grabando un nuevo álbum.

record *noun* ▷ see **record** *verb*
1 (*in sport, etc*) el **récord** *masc, pl:* los **récords**
to hold the world record tener [9] el récord mundial.
It's a world record. Es un récord mundial.
record sales récord de ventas
2 (*document*) el **documento** *masc*
official records documentos oficiales
3 (*of events*) **to keep a record of something** llevar [17] un registro de algo
the hottest summer on record el verano más caluroso del que se tienen datos
4 (*personal details*) **medical records** historial médico
to have a (criminal) record tener [9] antecedentes penales
I'll just check your records. Voy a mirar tu ficha.
5 (*of attendance*) el **registro** *masc*
He keeps a record of attendance at meetings. Lleva un registro de asistencia a las reuniones.
6 (*of music*) el **disco** *masc*
a Robbie Williams record un disco de Robbie Williams

recorder *noun*
1 (*musical instrument*) la **flauta dulce**
to play the recorder tocar [31] la flauta dulce
2 (*electrical device*) **a cassette recorder** un cassette
a video recorder una cámara de vídeo

recording *noun*
la **grabación** *fem*

record player *noun*
el **tocadiscos** *masc, pl:* los **tocadiscos**

to **recover** *verb*
(*from an illness*) **recuperarse** [17]
She's recovered now. Ya se ha recuperado.

recovery *noun*
(*from an illness*) la **recuperación** *fem*
• **recovery vehicle** la grúa

rectangle *noun*
el **rectángulo** *masc*

rectangular *adjective*
rectangular *masc & fem*

to **recycle** *verb*
reciclar [17]

recycling *noun*
el **reciclaje** *masc*

red *adjective*
1 (*in general*) **rojo** *masc*, **roja** *fem*
a red shirt una camisa roja
a bright red car un coche rojo vivo
2 (*in the face*) **to go red** ponerse [11] colorado (*boy*), ponerse [11] colorada (*girl*)
3 (*hair*) **to have red hair** ser [1] pelirrojo
4 (*wine*) **tinto** *masc*, **tinta** *fem*

Red Cross *noun*
the Red Cross la Cruz Roja

redcurrant *noun*
la **grosella** *fem*
redcurrant jelly jalea de grosellas

red-haired *adjective*
pelirrojo *masc*, **pelirroja** *fem*

red light *noun*
la **luz roja**

to **reduce** *verb*
reducir [60]
They've reduced the price. Han reducido el precio.

reduced *adjective*
(*price, weight, numbers*) **reducido** *masc*, **reducida** *fem*
reduced-price tickets entradas a precios reducidos

reduction *noun*
1 (*in numbers, size, spending*) la **reducción** *fem*
a reduction in costs una reducción de gastos
2 (*in price*) la **rebaja** *fem*
a 5% reduction una rebaja del cinco por ciento

redundant *adjective*
(*from a job*) **He was made redundant.** Lo despidieron por reducción de plantilla.

to **refer to** *verb*
referirse [14] **a**
She's referring to you. Se refiere a ti.

referee *noun*
(*in sport*) **el & la árbitro** *masc & fem*

reference *noun*
1 (*allusion*) la **referencia** *fem*
to make reference to something hacer [7] referencia a algo
2 (*for a job*) la **referencia** *fem*
She gave me a good reference. Me dio una buena referencia.

referendum *noun*
el **referendum** *masc, pl:* los **referendums**

refill *noun*
1 (*for a pen*) el **recambio** *masc*
2 (*for a lighter*) la **carga** *fem*

to **reflect** *verb*
reflejar [17]

reflection *noun*
1 (*in a mirror*) el **reflejo** *masc*
2 (*thought*) la **reflexión** *fem*
on reflection pensándolo bien

reflexive *adjective*
reflexivo *masc*, **reflexiva** *fem*
a reflexive verb un verbo reflexivo

refreshing *adjective*
refrescante *masc & fem*

refreshment *noun*
el **refresco** *masc*

refrigerator *noun*
la **nevera** *fem*

refuge *noun*
el **refugio** *masc*
a mountain refuge un refugio (de montaña)
to take refuge refugiarse [17]
He took refuge in the ruins. Se refugió en las ruinas.

refugee *noun*
el **refugiado** *masc*, la **refugiada** *fem*

refund *noun* ▷ see **refund** *verb*
el **reembolso** *masc*

to **refund** *verb* ▷ see **refund** *noun*
reembolsar [17]

refuse *noun* ▷ see **refuse** *verb*
(*rubbish*) los **desperdicios** *plural masc*

to **refuse** *verb* ▷ see **refuse** *noun*
negarse [30]
I refused. Me negué.
to refuse to do something negarse a hacer algo
He refuses to help. Se niega a ayudar.

regards *plural noun*
los **recuerdos** *plural masc*
Regards to your parents. Recuerdos a tus padres.
Nat sends his regards. Nat manda recuerdos.

reggae *noun*
el **reggae** *masc*

region *noun*
la **región** *fem*
an industrial region una región industrial

regional *adjective*
regional *masc & fem*

register *noun* ▷ see **register** *verb*
(*in a school*) la **lista** *fem*

to **register** *verb* ▷ see **register** *noun*
inscribirse [52]
He registered for a German course. Se inscribió en un curso de alemán.

registered letter *noun*
la **carta certificada**

registration number *noun*
(*of a vehicle*) el **número de matrícula**

to **regret** *verb*
to regret something arrepentirse **[14]** de algo

regular *adjective*
1 (*shape, pulse, verb*) **regular** *masc & fem*
2 (*frequent*) **regular visits** visitas frecuentes
3 (*customer*) **habitual** *masc & fem*

regularly *adverb*
regularmente

♪ **regulation** *noun*
la **norma** *fem*
safety regulations normas de seguridad
It's against the regulations. Va contra el reglamento.

rehearsal *noun*
el **ensayo** *masc*

to **rehearse** *verb*
ensayar [17]

reign *noun* ▷ see **reign** *verb*
el **reinado** *masc*

to **reign** *verb* ▷ see **reign** *noun*
reinar [17]

rein *noun*
la **rienda** *fem*

to **reject** *verb*
rechazar [22]

related *adjective*
1 (*subject, ideas*) **relacionado** *masc*, **relacionada** *fem*
2 (*people*) **We're not related.** No somos parientes.

relation *noun*
el & la **pariente** *masc & fem*
my relations mis parientes

relationship *noun*
la **relación** *fem*
We have a good relationship. Tenemos una buena relación.

relative *noun*
el & la **pariente** *masc & fem*
all my relatives todos mis parientes

to **relax** *verb*
relajarse [17]
I'm going to relax and watch telly tonight. Esta noche voy a relajarme y ver la tele.

relaxation *noun*
el **esparcimiento** *masc*
Tennis is her relaxation. El tenis es su esparcimiento.

relaxed *adjective*
relajado *masc*, **relajada** *fem*

relaxing *adjective*
relajante *masc & fem*

relay race *noun*
la **carrera de relevos**

release *noun* ▷ see **release** *verb*
1 (*of a film*) el **estreno** *masc*
this week's new releases los estrenos de esta semana
2 (*of a prisoner, hostage*) la **puesta en libertad**

to **release** *verb* ▷ see **release** *noun*
1 (*a film*) **estrenar [17]**
2 (*a record, video*) **sacar [31]**
3 (*a person*) **poner [11] en libertad**

reliable *adjective*
1 (*person*) **responsable** *masc & fem*
2 (*information*) **fidedigno** *masc*, **fidedigna** *fem*

relief *noun*
el **alivio** *masc*
What a relief! ¡Qué alivio!

relieved *adjective*
aliviado *masc*, **aliviada** *fem*
I was relieved to hear you'd arrived. Fue un alivio oír que habías llegado.

religion *noun*
la **religión** *fem*

religious *adjective*
religioso *masc*, **religiosa** *fem*
Jane's not religious. Jane no es religiosa.

reluctant *adjective*
reacio *masc*, **reacia** *fem*
He's reluctant to go. Se muestra reacio a ir.

to **rely** *verb*
to rely on somebody contar **[24]** con alguien
I'm relying on you for Saturday. Cuento contigo para el sábado.

♪ to **remain** *verb*
1 (*to stay*) **quedarse [17]**
The best thing is to remain silent. Lo mejor es quedarse callado.
How long do you intend to remain in the country? ¿Cuánto tiempo piensa quedarse en el país?
2 (*to be left*) **quedar [17]**
This is all that remains of the city. Esto es todo lo que queda de la ciudad.
There are less than five minutes remaining. Quedan menos de cinco minutos.

English–Spanish
a b c d e f g h i j k l m n o p q r s t u v w x y z

English–Spanish

remark *noun*
el **comentario** *masc*
to make remarks about something hacer [7] comentarios sobre algo

ᶴ to **remember** *verb*
acordarse [24]
I don't remember. No me acuerdo.
to remember something acordarse de algo
I can't remember the number. No me acuerdo del número.
to remember to do something acordarse de hacer algo
Remember to shut the door! ¡Acuérdate de cerrar la puerta!
I remembered to bring the CDs. Me acordé de traer los compactos.

ᶴ to **remind** *verb*
recordar [24]
to remind somebody of something recordarle a alguien a algo
It reminds me of Paris. Me recuerda París.
to remind somebody of somebody recordarle a alguien a alguien
He reminds me of Frank. Me recuerda a Frank.
to remind somebody to do something recordarle a alguien que haga algo
Remind your mother to pick me up. Recuérdale a tu madre que me recoja.
Oh, that reminds me ... ¡Ah!, por cierto ...

WORD TIP *recordarle a alguien que* is followed by the subjunctive.

remote control *noun*
el **mando a distancia**

to **remove** *verb*
quitar [17]
He removed his jacket. Se quitó la chaqueta.
The chairs had all been removed. Habían quitado todas las sillas.

to **renew** *verb*
(a licence, etc) **renovar [24]**

ᶴ to **rent** *verb* ▷ see **rent** *noun*
alquilar [17]
Simon's rented a flat. Simon ha alquilado un piso.

ᶴ **rent** *noun* ▷ see **rent** *verb*
el **alquiler** *masc*

ᶴ **rental** *noun*
el **alquiler** *masc*

to **repair** *verb* ▷ see **repair** *noun*
arreglar [17]
to get something repaired arreglar algo
We've had the television repaired. Hemos arreglado la televisión.

repair *noun* ▷ see **repair** *verb*
la **reparación** *fem*

to **repay** *verb*
devolver [45]
He repaid me the money he owed me. Me devolvió el dinero que me debía.

ᶴ **repeat** *noun* ▷ see **repeat** *verb*
(of a programme) la **repetición** *fem*

ᶴ to **repeat** *verb* ▷ see **repeat** *noun*
repetir [57]
Could you repeat the question? **¿Podría repetir la pregunta?**

replacement *noun*
1 *(person)* el **sustituto** *masc*, la **sustituta** *fem*
2 *(thing)* **When can you find me a replacement?** ¿Para cuándo me puedes encontrar otro?

ᶴ to **reply** *verb* ▷ see **reply** *noun*
contestar [17]
He replied that he hadn't seen me. Contestó que no me había visto.
to reply to something contestar a algo
I still haven't replied to the letter. Aún no he contestado a la carta.

reply *noun* ▷ see **reply** *verb*
la **contestación** *fem*
I didn't get a reply to my letter. No recibí contestación a mi carta.
I phoned her but there was no reply. La llamé pero nadie cogió el teléfono.

ᶴ to **report** *verb* ▷ see **report** *noun*
1 *(a problem, accident)* **informar [17] sobre**
2 *(a crime)* **denunciar [17]**
We've reported the theft. Hemos denunciado el robo.
3 *(to present yourself)* **presentarse [17]**
I had to report to reception. Tuve que presentarme en recepción.

ᶴ **report** *noun* ▷ see **report** *verb*
1 *(piece of news)* la **noticia** *fem*
Reports are coming in of an accident. Están llegando noticias de un accidente.
2 *(newspaper article)* el **reportaje** *masc*
3 *(account of an event)* el **informe** *masc*
an official report un informe oficial
4 *(school report)* el **boletín de notas**

reporter *noun*
el & la **periodista** *masc & fem*

representative *noun*
el & la **representante** *masc & fem*

a b c d e f g h i j k l m n o p q r s t u v w x y z

republic *noun*
la **república** *fem*

reputation *noun*
la **reputación** *fem*
a good reputation una buena reputación
to have a reputation for something tener [9] fama de algo
She has a reputation for honesty. Tiene fama de honesta.

to **request** *verb* ▷ see **request** *noun*
pedir [57]

request *noun* ▷ see **request** *verb*
la **petición** *fem*
on request a solicitud

to **rescue** *verb* ▷ see **rescue** *noun*
rescatar [17]
They rescued the dog. Rescataron al perro.

rescue *noun* ▷ see **rescue** *verb*
el **rescate** *masc*
to come to somebody's rescue acudir [19] en auxilio de alguien
- **rescue party** el equipo de rescate
- **rescue worker** el & la socorrista

to **research** *verb* ▷ see **research** *noun*
(*the causes, a problem*) **investigar** [28]
to research into something investigar sobre algo
a well-researched programme un programa bien documentado

research *noun* ▷ see **research** *verb*
la **investigación** *fem*
research into Aids la investigación sobre el sida
to do research investigar [28]

to **resemble** *verb*
parecerse [35] **a**
She resembles her aunt. Se parece a su tía.

♪ **reservation** *noun*
(*booking*) la **reserva** *fem*
to make a reservation hacer [7] una reserva

♪ to **reserve** *verb* ▷ see **reserve** *noun*
reservar [17]
This table is reserved. Esta mesa está reservada.

reserve *noun* ▷ see **reserve** *verb*
1 (*stock*) la **reserva** *fem*
We have some in reserve. Tenemos algo de reserva.
2 (*special area*) **a nature reserve** una reserva natural
3 (*substitute player*) el & la **reserva** *masc & fem*

resident *noun*
el & la **residente** *masc & fem*

residential *adjective*
residencial *masc & fem*
a residential area un área residencial

to **resign** *verb*
dimitir [19]
to resign from something dimitir algo
She resigned from the committee. Dimitió su cargo en la comisión.

resignation *noun*
(*from a post*) la **dimisión** *fem*

to **resist** *verb*
(*an offer, temptation*) **resistir** [19]
I can't resist! ¡No puedo resistirlo!

to **resit** *verb*
to resit an exam volver [45] a presentarse a un examen

♪ **resort** *noun*
1 (*for holidays*) **a holiday resort** un centro turístico
a ski resort una estación de esquí
a seaside resort un centro turístico costero
2 (*recourse*) **as a last resort** como último recurso

to **respect** *verb* ▷ see **respect** *noun*
respetar [17]

respect *noun* ▷ see **respect** *verb*
el **respeto** *masc*

respectable *adjective*
respetable *masc & fem*

respectful *adjective*
respetuoso *masc*, **respetuosa** *fem*

responsibility *noun*
la **responsabilidad** *fem*

responsible *adjective*
responsable *masc & fem*
He's not very responsible. No es muy responsable.
to be responsible for something ser [1] responsable de algo
I'm responsible for booking the rooms. Soy responsable de reservar las habitaciones.
He's responsible for the delay. Él es el responsable del retraso.

♪ to **rest** *verb* ▷ see **rest** *noun*
(*to relax*) **descansar** [17]
Don't disturb him, he's resting. No lo molestes, que está descansando.

English-Spanish
a b c d e f g h i j k l m n o p q r s t u v w x y z

♪ **rest** *noun* ▷ see **rest** *verb*
1 (*relaxation*) el **descanso** *masc*
ten days' complete rest diez días de completo descanso
2 (*short break*) **to have a rest** descansar [17]
to stop for a rest parar [17] para descansar
3 (*remainder*) **the rest** el resto
the rest of the day el resto del día
the rest of the world el resto del mundo
The rest of the money is mine. El resto del dinero es mío.
4 (*others*) **the rest** los otros
The rest have gone home. Los otros se han ido a casa.

♪ **restaurant** *noun*
el **restaurante** *masc*
- **restaurant car** el coche-comedor

to **restore** *verb*
restaurar [17]

♪ **result** *noun*
el **resultado** *masc*
the exam results los resultados del examen
as a result como consecuencia de ello
As a result we missed the ferry. Como consecuencia de ello perdimos el ferry.

to **retire** *verb* ▷ see **retired** *adj*
(*from work*) **jubilarse** [17]
She retires in June. Se jubila en junio.

retired *adjective* ▷ see **retire** *verb*
(*from work*) **jubilado** *masc*, **jubilada** *fem*
a retired couple una pareja de jubilados

retirement *noun*
la **jubilación** *fem*

♪ to **return** *verb* ▷ see **return** *noun*
1 (*to come back, get home*) **volver** [45]
to return from holiday volver de vacaciones
He returned ten minutes later. Volvió diez minutos más tarde.
I'll ask her to phone as soon as she returns. Le diré que te llame en cuanto vuelva.
2 (*to give back*) **devolver** [45]
Gemma never returned the video. Gemma no devolvió nunca el vídeo.

♪ **return** *noun* ▷ see **return** *verb*
1 (*to a place*) la **vuelta** *fem*
on his return a su vuelta
the return journey el viaje de vuelta
2 (*ticket*) el **billete de ida y vuelta**
3 (*birthday greeting*) **Many happy returns of the day!** ¡Feliz cumpleaños!
4 (*in expressions*) **by return of post** a vuelta de correo
in return a cambio
in return for his help a cambio de su ayuda
- **return fare** el precio del billete de ida y vuelta
- **return ticket** el billete de ida y vuelta

reunion *noun*
la **reunión** *fem*
a class reunion una reunión de ex compañeros de clase

revenge *noun*
la **venganza** *fem*
to get one's revenge on someone vengarse [28] de alguien

to **reverse** *verb* ▷ see **reverse** *noun*
1 (*in a car*) **dar** [4] **marcha atrás**
She reversed her car into the garage. Entró en el garaje dando marcha atrás.
2 (*when making a phone call*) **to reverse the charges** llamar [17] a cobro revertido

reverse *noun* ▷ see **reverse** *verb*
1 (*of a coin*) el **reverso** *masc*
2 (*gear*) la **marcha atrás**
3 (*of a page*) el **dorso** *masc*
4 (*opposite*) **The reverse is true.** Es al contrario.

to **review** *verb* ▷ see **review** *noun*
escribir [52] **la crítica de**
The film was well reviewed. La película recibió buenas críticas.

review *noun* ▷ see **review** *verb*
(*of a book, play, film*) la **crítica** *fem*

to **revise** *verb*
repasar [17]
Tessa's busy revising for her exams. Tessa está muy ocupada repasando para los exámenes.

revision *noun*
el **repaso** *masc*

revolting *adjective*
asqueroso *masc*, **asquerosa** *fem*
The sausages are revolting. Las salchichas están asquerosas.

revolution *noun*
la **revolución** *fem*
the French Revolution la Revolución Francesa

♪ to **reward** *verb* ▷ see **reward** *noun*
recompensar [17]
He was rewarded for handing it in. Lo recompensaron por haberlo entregado.

⚷ **reward** *noun* ▷ see **reward** *verb*
la **recompensa** *fem*
a £100 reward una recompensa de cien libras

rewarding *adjective*
gratificante *masc & fem*

to **rewind** *verb*
rebobinar [17]

rhubarb *noun*
el **ruibarbo** *masc*

rhyme *noun*
la **rima** *fem*

rhythm *noun*
el **ritmo** *masc*

rib *noun*
la **costilla** *fem*

ribbon *noun*
la **cinta** *fem*

⚷ **rice** *noun*
el **arroz** *masc*
chicken and rice pollo y arroz
• **rice pudding** el arroz con leche

⚷ **rich** *adjective*
1 (*person, country*) **rico** *masc*, **rica** *fem*
the rich and the poor los ricos y los pobres
We're not very rich. No somos muy ricos.
2 (*food*) **con alto contenido de grasas, huevos, azúcar, etc**
Avoid rich foods Evite las comidas pesadas.

rid *adjective*
to get rid of something deshacerse [7] de algo
We got rid of the car. Nos deshicimos del coche.

riddle *noun*
la **adivinanza** *fem*

⚷ to **ride** *verb* ▷ see **ride** *noun*
1 (*a bicycle*) **He learned to ride a bike.** Aprendió a montar en bicicleta.
Can you ride a bike? ¿Sabes montar en bicicleta?
2 (*a horse*) **I am learning to ride.** Estoy aprendiendo a montar a caballo.
I've never ridden a horse. Nunca he montado a caballo.

⚷ **ride** *noun* ▷ see **ride** *verb*
1 (*on a bicycle*) **to go for a ride** ir [8] a montar en bicicleta
2 (*on a horse*) **to go for a ride** ir [8] a montar a caballo

rider *noun*
1 (*of a horse*) el & la **jinete** *masc & fem*
2 (*of a bicycle*) el & la **ciclista** *masc & fem*
3 (*of a motorbike*) el & la **motorista** *masc & fem*

ridiculous *adjective*
ridículo *masc*, **ridícula** *fem*

⚷ **riding** *noun*
la **equitación** *fem*
to go riding hacer [7] equitación
• **riding school** la escuela de equitación

rifle *noun*
el **rifle** *masc*

⚷ **right** *adjective* ▷ see **right** *adv, noun*
1 (*not left*) **derecho** *masc*, **derecha** *fem*
my right hand mi mano derecha
2 (*correct*) **correcto** *masc*, **correcta** *fem*
the right answer la respuesta correcta
the right telephone number el teléfono correcto
Is this the right address? ¿Son éstas las señas?
3 (*person*) **to be right** tener [9] razón
You see, I was right. ¿Ves? tenía yo razón.
4 **You were right to stay at home.** Hiciste bien en quedarte en casa.
He was right not to say anything. Hizo bien en no decir nada.
5 (*just, morally correct*) **to be right** ser [1] justo
What they did wasn't right Lo que hicieron no fue justo.
It's not right to talk like that. No está bien hablar así.

right *adverb* ▷ see **right** *adj, noun*
1 (*to turn, look*) **a la derecha**
Turn right at the lights. Gira a la derecha en el semáforo.
2 (*correctly*) **bien**
You're not doing it right. No lo estás haciendo bien.
3 (*completely*) **right at the bottom** al fondo del todo
right now ahora mismo
right at the beginning justo al principio
right in the middle justo en medio
4 (*okay*) **vale**
Right, let's go. Vale, vamos.

⚷ **right** *noun* ▷ see **right** *adj, adv*
1 (*direction*) la **derecha** *fem*
the second street on the right la segunda calle a la derecha
on my right a mi derecha
It's on the right. Está a la derecha.
to drive on the right conducir [60] por la derecha ⏩

English-Spanish

2 (*entitlement*) el **derecho** *masc*
the right to strike el derecho a hacer huelga
You have no right to say that. No tienes derecho a decir eso.

right-click *noun* ▷ see **right-click** *verb*
el **clic con el botón derecho**

to **right-click** *verb* ▷ see **right-click** *noun*
hacer [7] clic con el botón derecho
Right-click the icon. Haz clic en el icono con el botón derecho.

right-hand *adjective*
on the right-hand side a mano derecha

right-handed *adjective*
diestro *masc*, **diestra** *fem*

to **ring** *verb* ▷ see **ring** *noun*
1 (*bells, phones*) **sonar [24]**
The phone rang. Sonó el teléfono.
2 (*somebody*) **llamar [17]**
I'll ring you tomorrow. Te llamaré mañana.
Could you ring for a taxi? ¿Podrías llamar un taxi?
- **to ring back**
volver [45] a llamar
I'll ring you back later. Te volveré a llamar más tarde.
- **to ring off**
colgar [23]

ring *noun* ▷ see **ring** *verb*
1 (*on the phone*) to give somebody a ring llamar [17] a alguien
2 (*for your finger*) el **anillo** *masc*
3 (*circle*) el **círculo** *masc*
4 (*on a doorbell*) There was a ring at the door. Llamaron a la puerta.
- **ring tone** el tono de llamada

to **rinse** *verb*
enjuagar [28]

ripe *adjective*
maduro *masc*, **madura** *fem*
Are the tomatoes ripe? ¿Están maduros los tomates?

rip-off *noun*
It's a rip-off! ¡Es una estafa!

to **rise** *verb* ▷ see **rise** *noun*
1 (*sun*) **salir [63]**
when the sun rose cuando salió el sol
2 (*prices*) **subir [19]**
The price has risen by $200. El precio ha subido dos cientos dólares.

rise *noun* ▷ see **rise** *verb*
la **subida** *fem*
a rise in price una subida de precio
a pay rise un aumento de sueldo

to **risk** *verb* ▷ see **risk** *noun*
(*your life, reputation*) **arriesgar [28]**
She risked her life. Arriesgó su vida.

risk *noun* ▷ see **risk** *verb*
el **riesgo** *masc*
to take risks arriesgarse [28]

rival *noun*
el & la **rival** *masc & fem*

river *noun*
el **río** *masc*
the River Plate el Río de la Plata

road *noun*
1 (*out of a town*) la **carretera** *fem*
the road to London la carretera de Londres
2 (*in a town*) la **calle** *fem*
on the other side of the road al otro lado de la calle
3 (*in expressions*) across the road enfrente
They live across the road from us. Viven enfrente de nosotros.
- **road accident** el accidente de carretera
- **road map** el mapa de carreteras

mini-info: roads
The world's longest road, the Pan-American Highway (25,750 km), runs from Alaska to Argentina with less than 100 km between Panama and Colombia still to be completed.

roadside *noun*
el **borde de la carretera**
by the roadside al borde de la carretera

road sign *noun*
la **señal de tráfico**

roadworks *plural noun*
las **obras** *plural fem*

to **roast** *verb* ▷ see **roast** *noun, adj*
asar [17]
I've roasted the potatoes. He asado las patatas.

roast *noun* ▷ see **roast** *adj*
el **asado** *masc*

roast *adjective* ▷ see **roast** *noun*
asado *masc*, **asada** *fem*
- **roast beef** el rosbif
- **roast potatoes** las patatas asadas

to **rob** *verb*
1 (*person*) **robar [17]**
2 (*a bank*) **atracar [31]**

robber *noun*
el **ladrón** *masc*, la **ladrona** *fem*
a bank robber un atracador

robbery *noun*
el **robo** *masc*
a bank robbery un atraco a un banco

rock *noun*
1 (*big stone*) la **roca** *fem*
She was sitting on a rock. Estaba sentada en una roca.
2 (*the material*) la **piedra** *fem*
3 (*music*) el **rock** *masc*
a rock band un grupo de rock
to dance rock and roll bailar [17] rock and roll

rock climbing *noun*
la **escalada en roca**
to go rock climbing hacer [7] escalada

rock star *noun*
la **estrella de rock**

rocket *noun*
el **cohete** *masc*

rocking horse *noun*
el **caballito de balancín**

rocky *adjective*
rocoso *masc*, **rocosa** *fem*

rod *noun*
1 (*bar*) la **varilla** *fem*
2 (*fishing rod*) la **caña de pescar**

role *noun*
el **papel** *masc*
He played the role of the king. Interpretó el papel del rey.

♪ **roll** *noun*
1 (*of material*) el **rollo** *masc*
a roll of fabric un rollo de tela
a toilet roll un rollo de papel higiénico
2 (*of bread*) a bread roll un panecillo
• **to roll something up**
(*a carpet*) **enrollar** [17] **algo**
He rolled up his sleeves. Se remangó las mangas.

rollerblades *plural noun*
los **patines en línea**

rollercoaster *noun*
la **montaña rusa**

roller skates *plural noun*
los **patines de ruedas**

Roman Catholic *adjective & noun*
1 **católico** *masc*, **católica** *fem*
2 el **católico** *masc*, la **católica** *fem*

WORD TIP Adjectives and nouns for religion do not have capital letters in Spanish.

♪ **romantic** *adjective*
romántico *masc*, **romántica** *fem*

roof *noun*
el **tejado** *masc*
• **roof rack** la baca

rook *noun*
1 (*in chess*) la **torre** *fem*
2 (*the bird*) el **grajo** *masc*

♪ **room** *noun*
1 (*part of a building*) la **habitación** *fem*
a three-room flat un piso de tres habitaciones
She's in the other room. Está en la otra habitación.
It's the biggest room in the house. Es la habitación más grande de la casa.
2 (*bedroom*) la **habitación** *fem*
Lola's in her room. Lola está en su habitación.
3 (*space*) el **sitio** *masc*
There is enough room for two. Hay sitio suficiente para dos.
There was very little room. Había muy poco espacio.

root *noun*
la **raíz** *fem*

rope *noun*
la **cuerda** *fem*

♪ **rose** *noun*
la **rosa** *fem*
• **rosebush** el rosal

♪ **rosé wine** *noun*
el **vino rosado**

to **rot** *verb*
pudrirse [59]

rota *noun*
la **lista de turnos**

rotten *adjective*
podrido *masc*, **podrida** *fem*

rough *adjective* ▷ see **rough** *adv*
1 (*scratchy*) **áspero** *masc*, **áspera** *fem*
2 (*vague*) **aproximado** *masc*, **aproximada** *fem*
a rough idea una idea aproximada
3 (*stormy*) a rough sea un mar agitado
4 (*difficult*) to have a rough time pasarlo [17] mal
5 (*ill*) He feels a bit rough today. Hoy no está muy bien.

rough *adverb* ▷ see **rough** *adj*
to sleep rough dormir [51] a la intemperie

roughly *adverb*
(approximately) **aproximadamente**
roughly ten per cent aproximadamente el diez por ciento
It takes roughly three hours. Lleva aproximadamente tres horas.

round *adjective* ▷ see **round** *adv, prep, noun*
redondo *masc*, **redonda** *fem*
a round table una mesa redonda

round *adverb* ▷ see **round** *adj, prep, noun*
1 *(in a circle)* **all the year round** todo el año
They ran round and round. Dieron vueltas y vueltas corriendo.
2 *(to a place)* **to go round to somebody's house** ir [8] a casa de alguien
We invited Sally round for lunch. Invitamos a Sally a comer.

round *preposition* ▷ see **round** *adj, adv, noun*
1 *(encircling)* **alrededor de**
round the city alrededor de la ciudad
round my arm alrededor de mi brazo
They were sitting round the table. Estaban sentados alrededor de la mesa.
It's just round the corner. Está a la vuelta de la esquina.
2 *(through)* **to go round the shops** ir [8] de tiendas
to go round a museum visitar [17] un museo

round *noun* ▷ see **round** *adj, adv, prep*
1 *(in a competition)* la **vuelta** *fem*
2 *(of cards)* la **partida** *fem*
3 *(of drinks)* la **ronda** *fem*
It's my round. Esta ronda la pago yo.

roundabout *noun*
1 *(for traffic)* la **rotonda** *fem*
2 *(in a fairground)* el **tiovivo** *masc*

route *noun*
la **ruta** *fem*
The best route is via Leeds. La mejor ruta es pasando por Leeds.
a bus route el recorrido de un autobús

to **row** *verb* ▷ see **row** *noun*
1 *(in a boat)* **remar** [17]
It's your turn to row. Te toca remar.
We rowed across the lake. Cruzamos el lago remando.
2 *(to argue)* **reñir** [65]

row *noun* ▷ see **row** *verb*
1 *(of seats)* la **fila** *fem*
in the front row en la primera fila
in the back row en la última fila
2 *(line)* la **hilera** *fem*
a row of huts una hilera de cabañas
3 *(succession)* **four times in a row** cuatro veces seguidas
4 *(quarrel)* la **pelea** *fem*
to have a row pelearse [17]
They've had a row. Se han peleado.
I had a row with my parents. Me peleé con mis padres.
5 *(noise)* el **ruido** *masc*
They are making a terrible row! ¡Están haciendo un ruido terrible!

rowing *noun*
el **remo** *masc*
to go rowing practicar [31] el remo
• **rowing boat** el bote de remos

royal *adjective*
real *masc & fem*
the royal family la familia real

to **rub** *verb*
frotar [17]
to rub your eyes frotarse los ojos
• **to rub something out**
borrar [17] **algo**

rubber *noun*
1 *(eraser)* la **goma de borrar**
2 *(the material)* la **goma** *fem*
rubber soles suelas de goma
• **rubber band** la goma elástica

rubbish *adjective* ▷ see **rubbish** *noun*
The film was rubbish. La película fue una porquería.
They're a rubbish band. Es una porquería de grupo.

rubbish *noun* ▷ see **rubbish** *adj*
1 *(for the bin)* la **basura** *fem*
2 *(nonsense)* las **estupideces** *plural fem*
You're talking rubbish! ¡Estás diciendo estupideces!
• **rubbish bin** el cubo de la basura

rucksack *noun*
la **mochila** *fem*

rude *adjective*
1 *(person)* **maleducado** *masc*, **maleducada** *fem*
2 *(words, behaviour)* **That's rude.** Eso es de mala educación.
3 **a rude joke** una broma grosera
a rude word una palabrota

rug *noun*
1 (*on the floor*) la **alfombra** *fem*
2 (*to keep someone warm*) la **manta de viaje**

rugby *noun*
el **rugby** *masc*
to play rugby jugar [27] al rugby
a rugby match un partido de rugby

to **ruin** *verb* ▷ see **ruin** *noun*
1 (*an outfit, a toy, a carpet*) **estropear** [17]
You'll ruin your jacket. Vas a estropear tu chaqueta.
2 (*a day, holiday*) **fastidiar** [17] (*informal*)
It ruined my holiday. Me fastidió las vacaciones.

ruin *noun* ▷ see **ruin** *verb*
la **ruina** *fem*
in ruins en ruinas

rule *noun*
la **regla** *fem*
the rules of the game las reglas del juego
the school rules el reglamento del colegio
as a rule como norma

ruler *noun*
la **regla** *fem*
I've lost my ruler. He perdido mi regla.

rumour *noun*
el **rumor** *masc*

♪ **run** *noun* ▷ see **run** *verb*
1 (*jog*) **to go for a run** ir [8] a correr
2 (*in cricket*) la **carrera** *fem*
3 (*period of time*) **in the long run** a la larga

♪ to **run** *verb* ▷ see **run** *noun*
1 (*to move quickly*) **correr** [18]
I ran ten kilometres. Corrí diez kilómetros.
Kitty ran for the bus. Kitty corrió para coger el autobús.
He ran across the pitch. Cruzó el campo corriendo.
2 (*to organize*) **organizar** [22]
Who's running this concert? ¿Quién organiza el concierto?
3 (*a business*) **dirigir** [49]
He ran the firm for forty years. Dirigió la compañía durante cuarenta años.
4 (*trains, buses*) **circular** [17]
The buses don't run on Sundays. Los autobuses no circulan los domingos.
The trains run every half hour. Hay trenes cada media hora.
They run extra trains on Saturdays. Los sábados ponen más trenes.
5 (*an engine*) **hacer** [7] **funcionar**, (*a computer program*) **pasar** [17]
(*a bath*) **to run a bath** preparar [17] un baño
6 (*to flow*) **correr** [18]
Drops of sweat ran down his face. Le corrían gotas de sudor por la cara.
The water ran cold. Empezó a salir agua fría.
The river runs through the town. El río pasa por la ciudad.
• **to run away**
huir [54]
• **to run into**
chocar [31] **con**
The car ran into a tree. El coche chocó con un árbol.
• **to run out of something**
I'm running out of money. Se me está acabando el dinero.
• **to run somebody over**
atropellar [17] **a alguien**
You'll get run over! ¡Te van a atropellar!

runner-up *noun*
el **segundo** *masc*, la **segunda** *fem*

running *noun*
Running is good exercise. Correr es un buen ejercicio.

runway *noun*
la **pista** *fem*

to **rush** *verb* ▷ see **rush** *noun*
1 (*to hurry*) **darse** [4] **prisa**
I must rush! ¡Tengo que darme prisa!
Louise was rushed to hospital. Llevaron a Louise corriendo al hospital.
2 (*to run*) **She rushed into the street.** Salió corriendo a la calle.
I rushed into the room. Entré corriendo en la habitación.

rush *noun* ▷ see **rush** *verb*
to be in a rush tener [9] prisa
Sorry, I'm in a rush. Perdona, tengo prisa.

rush hour *noun*
la **hora punta**
in the rush hour a la hora punta

Russia *noun*
Rusia *fem*

Russian *adjective & noun*
1 **ruso** *masc*, **rusa** *fem*
2 (*person*) un **ruso** *masc*, una **rusa** *fem*
the Russians los rusos
3 (*the language*) el **ruso** *masc*

WORD TIP Adjectives and nouns for nationality, regional origin, and language do not have capital letters in Spanish.

rusty *adjective*
oxidado *masc*, **oxidada** *fem*

rye *noun*
el **centeno** *masc*

English–Spanish
a b c d e f g h i j k l m n o p q r s t u v w x y z

English-Spanish

S s

Sabbath *noun*
1 (*Jewish*) el **sábado** *masc*
2 (*Christian*) el **domingo** *masc*

WORD TIP Months of the year and days of the week start with small letters in Spanish.

sack *noun* ▷ see **sack** *verb*
1 (*container*) el **saco** *masc*
2 (*for dismissal*) **to give somebody the sack** despedir **[57]** a alguien
He got the sack. Le despidieron.

to **sack** *verb* ▷ see **sack** *noun*
to sack somebody despedir **[57]** a alguien

sacred *adjective*
sagrado *masc*, **sagrada** *fem*

sacrifice *noun*
el **sacrificio** *masc*

sad *adjective*
triste *masc & fem*
to feel sad sentirse **[14]** triste

saddle *noun*
1 (*for a horse*) la **silla de montar**
2 (*for a bike*) el **sillín**
- **saddlebag** la alforja

safe *adjective*
1 (*out of danger*) **seguro** *masc*, **segura** *fem*
to feel safe sentirse **[14]** seguro, *fem* segura
2 **to be safe from something** estar **[2]** a salvo de algo
We'll be safe from the storm in here. Aquí dentro estaremos a salvo de la tormenta.
3 (*not dangerous*) **seguro** *masc*, **segura** *fem*
The path is safe. El camino es seguro.
This ladder's not safe. Esta escalera no es segura.
4 **to be safe and sound** estar **[2]** sano y salvo
The girls were safe and sound. La niñas estaban sanas y salvas.

safety *noun*
la **seguridad** *fem*
- **safety belt** el cinturón de seguridad
- **safety pin** el imperdible

Sagittarius *noun*
el **Sagitario** *masc*
Kylie's Sagittarius. Kylie es sagitario.

WORD TIP Use a small letter in Spanish to say *I am* ... etc with star signs. Star signs in Spanish are used without *el, un, la, una*

sail *noun*
la **vela** *fem*

sailing *noun*
la **vela** *fem*
to go sailing ir **[8]** a hacer vela
She does a lot of sailing. Practica mucho la vela.
- **sailing boat** el bote de vela
- **sailing ship** el barco de velero

sailor *noun*
el **marinero** *masc*

saint *noun*
el **santo** *masc*, la **santa** *fem*

sake *noun*
for your mother's sake por tu madre
For heaven's sake! ¡Por el amor de Dios!

salad *noun*
la **ensalada** *fem*
a tomato salad una ensalada de tomate
- **salad dressing** el aliño para la ensalada

salami *noun*
el **salchichón** *masc*

salary *noun*
el **sueldo** *masc*

sale *noun*
1 (*selling*) la **venta** *fem*
the sale of the house la venta de la casa
These items are for sale. Estos artículos están en venta.
'For sale' 'Se vende'
2 **the sales** las rebajas
I bought it in the sales. Lo compré en las rebajas.

sales assistant *noun*
el **dependiente** *masc*, la **dependienta** *fem*

salesman *noun*
el **representante** *masc*
He's a salesman. Es representante.

saleswoman *noun*
la **representante** *fem*

saliva *noun*
la **saliva** *fem*

salmon *noun*
el **salmón** *masc*
smoked salmon salmón ahumado

a b c d e f g h i j k l m n o p q r s t u v w x y z

salt *noun*
la **sal** *fem*
Le has echado demasiada sal. You've put too much salt on it.
- **salt cellar** el salero

salty *adjective*
salado *masc*, **salada** *fem*

to **salute** *verb*
saludar [17]

Salvadorean *adjective & noun*
1 **salvadoreño** *masc*, **salvadoreña** *fem*
2 el **salvadoreño** *masc*, la **salvadoreña** *fem*
the Salvadoreans los salvadoreños

WORD TIP Adjectives and nouns for nationality and regional origin do not have capital letters in Spanish.

Salvation Army *noun*
el **Ejército de Salvación**

same *adjective* ▷ see **same** *pron*
1 *(with a singular noun)* **mismo** *masc*, **misma** *fem*
at the same time al mismo tiempo
She said the same thing. Ella dijo lo mismo.
It's the same girl as yesterday. Es la misma chica que ayer.
Their car's the same as ours. Su coche es el mismo que el nuestro.
Her birthday's the same day as mine. Su cumpleaños es el mismo día que el mío.
2 *(with a plural noun)* **mismos** *plural masc*, **mismas** *plural fem*
They were wearing the same shoes. Llevaban los mismos zapatos.
She always sings the same songs. Siempre canta las mismas canciones.
3 **to look the same** parecer [35] iguales
They all look the same to me. Todos me parecen iguales.

same *pronoun* ▷ see **same** *adj*
1 **the same** lo mismo
It's not the same. No es lo mismo.
It's always the same. Es lo mismo que siempre.
He said the same as yesterday. Dijo lo mismo que ayer.
2 *(replying to greetings)* **The same to you!** ¡Igualmente!
'Happy New Year!'— 'The same to you!' 'Feliz Año Nuevo!'— '¡Igualmente!'

sample *noun*
la **muestra** *fem*
a free sample una muestra gratuita

sand *noun*
la **arena** *fem*

sandal *noun*
la **sandalia** *fem*
a pair of sandals un par de sandalias

sand castle *noun*
el **castillo de arena**

sandpaper *noun*
el **papel de lija**

sandwich *noun*
el **sándwich** *masc*
a ham sandwich un sándwich de jamón
a toasted cheese sandwich un tostado de queso

sanitary towel *noun*
la **compresa** *fem*

Santa Claus *noun*
Papá Noel *masc*

sarcasm *noun*
el **sarcasmo** *masc*

sarcastic *adjective*
sarcástico *masc*, **sarcástica** *fem*

sardine *noun*
la **sardina** *fem*

satchel *noun*
la **cartera** *fem*

satellite *noun*
el **satélite** *masc*
- **satellite dish** la antena parabólica
- **satellite television** la televisión por vía satélite

satisfactory *adjective*
satisfactorio *masc*, **satisfactoria** *fem*

satisfied *adjective*
satisfecho *masc*, **satisfecha** *fem*
to be satisfied with something estar [2] satisfecho con algo
He's very satisfied with the results. Está muy satisfecho con el resultado.

to **satisfy** *verb*
satisfacer [7]

satisfying *adjective*
1 *(pleasing)* **satisfactorio** *masc*, **satisfactoria** *fem*
2 *(filling)* **a satisfying meal** una comida que llena

Saturday *noun*
el **sábado** *masc*
on Saturday el sábado
every Saturday todos los sábados
next Saturday el próximo sábado
last Saturday el sábado pasado
on Saturdays los sábados ▸▸

I'm going out on Saturday. Voy a salir el sábado.
See you on Saturday! ¡Te veo el sábado!
The museum is closed on Saturdays. El museo cierra los sábados.
to have a Saturday job trabajar **[17]** los sábados

WORD TIP Months of the year and days of the week start with small letters in Spanish.

sauce *noun*
la **salsa** *fem*
tomato sauce salsa de tomate

saucepan *noun*
el **cazo** *masc*
to wash the saucepans lavar **[17]** los cazos

saucer *noun*
el **platillo** *masc*
flying saucers platillos volantes

sausage *noun*
1 la **salchicha** *fem*
pork sausages salchichas de cerdo
2 (*salami*) el **salchichón** *masc*

savage *noun*
el & la **salvaje** *masc & fem*

to **save** *verb*
1 (*to rescue*) **salvar [17]**
to save somebody's life salvarle la vida a alguien
The doctors saved his life. Los médicos le salvaron la vida.
2 (*money, energy, time, etc*) **ahorrar [17]**
I've saved £60. He ahorrado sesenta libras.
Try to save electricity. Intenta ahorrar electricidad.
We took a taxi to save time. Tomamos un taxi para ahorrar tiempo.
I walk to school to save money. Voy al colegio a pie para ahorrar dinero.
3 (*to put aside*) **guardar [17]**
Save the cake for later. Guarda el pastel para luego.
4 (*Computers*) **guardar [17]**
You must save your files. Hay que guardar tus ficheros.
5 (*a goal*) **parar [17]**
• **to save up**
ahorrar [17]
I'm saving up to go to Spain. Estoy ahorrando para ir a España.

savings *plural noun*
los **ahorros** *plural masc*
to spend your savings gastar **[1]** los ahorros

savoury *adjective*
salado *masc*, **salada** *fem*
a savoury pancake un crepe salado
I prefer savoury things to sweet things. Prefiero lo salado a lo dulce.

saw *noun*
la **sierra** *fem*

saxophone *noun*
el **saxofón** *masc*
to play the saxophone tocar **[31]** el saxofón

to **say** *verb* ▷ see **saying** *noun*
1 (*in general*) **decir [5]**
She says she's tired. Dice que está cansada.
What did you say to him? ¿Qué le has dicho?
The letter doesn't say how much I have to pay. La carta no dice cuánto hay que pagar.
He said to wait for him here. Dijo que lo esperásemos aquí.
2 (*to repeat*) **to say something again** repetir **[57]** algo
3 (*in expressions*) **... as they say** ... como dicen
He hasn't arrived. That is to say, he won't make it. No ha llegado. Es decir, no va a llegar a tiempo.
That goes without saying. Eso no hace falta ni decirlo.

saying *noun* ▷ see **say** *verb*
el **dicho** *masc*
as the saying goes ... como dice el dicho ...

scab *noun*
la **costra** *fem*

scale *noun*
1 (*size*) la **escala** *fem*
on a large scale en gran escala
the scale of the disaster la escala del desastre
2 (*in music*) la **escala** *fem*
3 (*of a fish*) la **escama** *fem*

scales *plural noun*
la **balanza** *fem*
kitchen scales una balanza de cocina
bathroom scales una báscula de baño

scalp *noun*
el **cuero cabelludo**

scandal *noun*
1 (*disgraceful event*) el **escándalo** *masc*
2 (*gossip*) el **chismorreo** *masc*

Scandinavia *noun*
Escandinavia *fem*

Scandinavian *adjective & noun*
1 **escandinavo** *masc*, **escandinava** *fem*
2 el **escandinavo** *masc*, la **escandinava** *fem*
the Scandinavians los escandinavos

WORD TIP Adjectives and nouns for nationality and regional origin do not have capital letters in Spanish.

scanner *noun*
el **escáner** *masc*

scar *noun*
la **cicatriz** *fem*

scarce *adjective*
escaso *masc*, **escasa** *fem*

scarcely *adverb*
apenas
I could scarcely see it. Apenas lo veía.

scare *noun* ▷ see **scare** *verb*
1 el **susto** *masc*
to give somebody a scare darle [4] un susto a alguien
2 **a bomb scare** una amenaza de bomba
• **scarecrow** el espantapájaros

WORD TIP *espantapájaros* does not change in the plural.

to **scare** *verb* ▷ see **scare** *noun*
to scare somebody asustar [17] a alguien
You scared me! ¡Me has asustado!

scared *adjective* ▷ see **scare** *noun, verb*
asustado *masc*, **asustada** *fem*
to be scared estar [2] asustado *masc*, asustada *fem*
I'm scared! ¡Estoy asustado!
to be scared of something tenerle [9] miedo a algo
He's scared of dogs. Les tiene miedo a los perros.

scarf *noun*
1 (*for warmth*) la **bufanda** *fem*
2 (*of silk, etc*) el **foulard** *masc*

scary *adjective*
de miedo
a scary film una película de miedo

scene *noun*
1 (*of an accident, a crime*) la **escena** *fem*
the scene of the crime la escena del crimen
2 (*world*) el **mundo** *masc*
the music scene el mundo de la música
3 (*sight*) **scenes of violence** escenas violentas
4 (*fuss*) **to make a scene** montar [17] un número (*informal*)

scenery *noun*
1 (*landscape*) el **paisaje** *masc*
2 (*in a theatre*) el **decorado** *masc*

♪ **schedule** *noun*
el **programa** *masc*
We have a very busy schedule. Tenemos un programa muy apretado.
The repairs are behind schedule. Las reparaciones van atrasadas.

scheduled flight *noun*
el **vuelo regular**

scheme *noun*
el **plan** *masc*

scholarship *noun*
la **beca** *fem*

♪ **school** *noun*
1 (*primary*) la **escuela**
2 (*secondary*) el **colegio** *masc*
to go to school ir [8] al colegio
She's still at school. Todavía va al colegio.
When I leave school, I'll go to ... Cuando termino el colegio, iré a ...
• **schoolbook** el libro de texto
• **schoolboy** el colegial
• **schoolchildren** los colegiales
• **schoolfriend** el compañero del colegio, la compañera del colegio
• **schoolgirl** la colegiala
• **school uniform** el uniforme escolar
• **school year** el año escolar

♪ **science** *noun*
la **ciencia** *fem*
a science teacher un profesor de ciencias
I like science. Me gustan las ciencias.
• **science fiction** la ciencia ficción

scientific *adjective*
científico *masc*, **científica** *fem*

scientist *noun*
el **científico** *masc*, la **científica** *fem*

scissors *plural noun*
las **tijeras** *plural fem*
a pair of scissors unas tijeras

scoop *noun*
1 (*of ice-cream*) la **bola** *fem*
How many scoops would you like? ¿Cuántas bolas quieres?
2 (*in a newspaper*) la **primicia** *fem*

score *noun* ▷ see **score** *verb*
1 (*Sport*) el **resultado** *masc*
The score was three two. El resultado fue tres a dos.
What's the score? ¿A cómo van?
2 (*in a test, card game*) la **puntuación** *fem*

English–Spanish
a b c d e f g h i j k l m n o p q r s t u v w x y z

to score *verb* ▷ see **score** *noun*
1 *(a goal)* **marcar [31]**
Lenny scored a goal. Lenny marcó un gol.
2 *(points)* **conseguir [64]**
I scored three points. Conseguí tres puntos.
3 *(to keep score)* **llevar [17] la puntuación**

Scorpio *noun*
1 *(the star sign)* el **Scorpio** *masc*
2 *(person)* **un & una scorpio** *masc & fem*
Jess is Scorpio. Jess es escorpio.

WORD TIP Use a small letter in Spanish to say *I am ...* etc with star signs. Star signs in Spanish are used without *el, un, la, una.*

Scot *noun*
el **escocés** *masc*, la **escocesa** *fem*
the Scots los escoceses

WORD TIP Adjectives and nouns for nationality and regional origin do not have capital letters in Spanish.

Scotland *noun*
Escocia *fem*
in Scotland en Escocia
We're from Scotland. Somos de Escocia.

Scots *adjective*
escocés *masc*, **escocesa** *fem*
a Scots accent un acento escocés

Scotsman *noun*
un **escocés** *masc*

Scotswoman *noun*
una **escocesa** *fem*

Scottish *adjective*
escocés *masc*, **escocesa** *fem*
a Scottish accent un acento escocés

WORD TIP Adjectives and nouns for nationality and regional origin do not have capital letters in Spanish.

scout *noun*
el **explorador** *masc*

scrambled eggs *noun*
los **huevos revueltos**

scrap *noun*
a scrap of paper un trocito de papel

to scrape *verb*
rayar [17]

scratch *noun* ▷ see **scratch** *verb*
1 *(on your skin)* el **arañazo** *masc*
2 *(in paint, wood)* el **rayón** *masc*

to scratch *verb* ▷ see **scratch** *noun*
(with nails, claws) **arañar [1]**
to scratch yourself rascarse **[31]**
to scratch your head rascarse **[31]** la cabeza

scream *noun* ▷ see **scream** *verb*
el **grito** *masc*
a scream of terror un grito de terror

to scream *verb* ▷ see **scream** *noun*
gritar [17]
He screamed with pain. Gritó de dolor.
They screamed for help. Gritaron pidiendo ayuda.

screen *noun*
la **pantalla** *fem*
on the screen en la pantalla
a flat screen TV un televisor de pantalla plana

screw *noun* ▷ see **screw** *verb*
el **tornillo** *masc*

to screw *verb* ▷ see **screw** *noun*
to screw something down ajustar **[17]** algo con tornillos
to screw a lid on enroscar **[30]** una tapa
• **screwdriver** el destornillador

to scribble *verb*
garabatear [17]

to scrub *verb*
cepillar [17]
to scrub your nails cepillarse las uñas

scuba diving *noun*
el **submarinismo** *masc*

sculpture *noun*
la **escultura** *fem*

sculptor *noun*
el **escultor** *masc*, la **escultora** *fem*
She's a sculptor. Es escultora.

sea *noun*
el **mar** *masc*
a village by the sea un pueblo a orillas del mar
• **seafood** el marisco
• **seagull** la gaviota

seal *noun* ▷ see **seal** *verb*
(the animal) la **foca** *fem*

to seal *verb* ▷ see **seal** *noun*
(an envelope) **cerrar [29]**

seaman *noun*
el **marinero** *masc*

search *noun* ▷ see **search** *verb*
la **búsqueda** *fem*
the search for the treasure la búsqueda del tesoro
• **search engine** el buscador

to search *verb* ▷ see **search** *noun*
1 (*to look for*) **buscar [31]**
I've searched my desk but I can't find the letter. He buscado en mi escritorio pero no encuentro la carta.
to search for something buscar **[31]** algo
I've been searching everywhere for the scissors. He buscado las tijeras por todas partes.
I searched the room for the money. Revisé la habitación buscando el dinero.
2 (*a building, person*) **registrar [17]**
The police searched the house. La policía registró la casa.

seashell *noun*
la **concha de mar**

seasick *adjective*
to be seasick estar **[2]** mareado, *fem* mareada
to get seasick marearse **[17]**

seaside *noun*
la **costa** *fem*
at the seaside en la costa

♪ **season** *noun*
1 (*for sport, fruit*) la **temporada** *fem*
the rugby season la temporada de rugby
the high season la temporada alta
the low season la temporada baja
Strawberries are not in season at the moment. Ahora no es temporada de fresas.
2 (*time of year*) **the four seasons of the year** las cuatro estaciones del año
• **season ticket** el abono de temporada

♪ **seat** *noun*
1 (*in general*) el **asiento** *masc*
Take a seat. Toma asiento.
the front seat el asiento delantero
the back seat el asiento trasero
Can you keep my seat? ¿Puedes guardarme el sitio?
2 (*in a cinema, theatre*) la **localidad** *fem*
to book seats reservar **[17]** localidades
• **seatbelt** el cinturón de seguridad

♪ **second** *adjective* ▷ see **second** *noun*
segundo *masc*, **segunda** *fem*
for the second time por segunda vez
on the second floor en la segunda planta
He comes every second Friday. Viene cada dos viernes.

♪ **second** *noun* ▷ see **second** *adj*
1 (*unit of time*) el **segundo** *masc*
Just a second. Un segundo, por favor.
2 (*to talk about the date*) **the second of July** el dos de julio
We leave on the second. Nos vamos el día dos.

second class *adjective*
(*ticket, hotel*) **de segunda clase**
a second class team un equipo de segunda clase

♪ **secondary school** *noun*
el **colegio de enseñanza secundaria**

♪ **second-hand** *adjective, adverb*
de segunda mano
a second-hand bike una bicicleta de segunda mano
I bought it second hand. Lo compré de segunda mano.

secondly *adverb*
en segundo lugar

secret *adjective* ▷ see **secret** *noun*
secreto *masc*, **secreta** *fem*
a secret plan un plan secreto

secret *noun* ▷ see **secret** *adj*
el **secreto** *masc*
in secret en secreto
to keep a secret guardar **[17]** un secreto

secretarial college *noun*
la **escuela de secretariado**

♪ **secretary** *noun*
el **secretario** *masc*, la **secretaria** *fem*
the secretary's office la secretaría
She's a secretary. Es secretaria.

secretly *adverb*
en secreto

sect *noun*
la **secta** *fem*

♪ **section** *noun*
la **sección** *fem*

security *noun*
la **seguridad** *fem*

security guard *noun*
el **guarda jurado**, la **guarda jurada**
He's a security guard. Es guarda jurado.

♪ **to see** *verb*
1 (*in general*) **ver [16]**
I saw Lindy yesterday. Vi a Lindy ayer.
Have you seen the film? ¿Has visto la película?
We saw him leave ten minutes ago. Lo vimos salir hace diez minutos.
They see each other every day. Se ven todos los días. ⏩

You must see a doctor. Tienes que ver al médico.
Let's see. A ver.

2 (*to make out*) **to be able to see something** ver **[16]** algo
I can't see anything. No veo nada.

3 (*to say good-bye*) **See you!** ¡Hasta luego!
See you on Saturday! ¡Hasta el sábado!
See you soon! ¡Hasta pronto!
See you tomorrow! ¡Hasta mañana!

4 (*to accompany*) **to see somebody home** acompañar **[17]** a alguien a casa

- **to see to something**
  ocuparse [17] de algo
  Joe's seeing to the drinks. Joe se ocupa de las bebidas.

seed *noun*
la **semilla** *fem*
to plant seeds plantar **[17]** semillas

to seem *verb*
parecer [35]
It seems she's left. Parece que se ha ido.
He seems quite shy. Parece bastante tímido.
It seems odd to me. Me parece raro.
They seem to be out. Parece que no están.
The museum seemed to be closed. Parecía que el museo estaba cerrado.

seesaw *noun*
el **balancín** *masc*

to select *verb*
seleccionar [17]

selection *noun*
la **selección** *fem*

self-confidence *noun*
la **confianza en sí mismo**
She has a lot of self-confidence. Tiene mucha confianza en sí misma.

self-confident *adjective*
seguro de sí mismo *masc*, **segura de sí misma** *fem*

self-conscious *adjective*
cohibido *masc*, **cohibida** *fem*

self-employed *adjective*
autónomo *masc*, **autónoma** *fem*
My father's self-employed. Mi padre es autónomo.
the self-employed los autónomos

selfish *adjective*
egoísta *masc & fem*

self-service *adjective*
de auto servicio
a self-service restaurant un autoservicio

to sell *verb*
vender [18]
to sell something to somebody venderle algo a alguien
I sold him my bike. Le vendí mi bici.
They don't sell bread. No venden pan.
The house has been sold. La casa se ha vendido.
The concert's sold out. No quedan localidades para el concierto.

sell-by date *noun*
la **fecha límite de venta**

seller *noun*
el **vendedor** *masc*, la **vendedora** *fem*

Sellotape® *noun*
el **celo** *masc*

semi *noun*
la **casa adosada**
We live in a semi. Vivimos en una casa adosada.

- **semicircle** el semicírculo
- **semicolon** el punto y coma
- **semi-detached house** la casa adosada
- **semi-final** la semifinal
- **semi-skimmed milk** la leche semidesnatada

to send *verb*
mandar [17]
to send something to somebody mandarle algo a alguien
I sent her a text on her birthday. Le mandé un SMS el día de su cumpleaños.

- **to send somebody back**
  hacer [7] volver a alguien
- **to send something back**
  devolver [45] algo
- **to send for somebody**
  hacer [7] llamar a alguien
  The headmistress sent for us. La directora nos hizo llamar.
  Send for the doctor! ¡Llama al médico!
- **to send for something**
  pedir [57] algo
  I sent for a brochure. Les escribí para pedir un folleto.

senior citizen *noun*
la **persona de la tercera edad**

sensation *noun*

1 (*feeling*) la **sensibilidad** *fem*
She had no sensation in her fingers. No tenía sensibilidad en los dedos.

2 (*impact*) la **sensación** *fem*
She caused a sensation. Causó sensación.

sensational *adjective*
sensacional *masc & fem*
a sensational goal un gol sensacional

sense *noun*
1 *(being sensible)* el **sentido** *masc*
common sense sentido común
It makes a lot of sense. Tiene mucho sentido.
It doesn't make much sense to buy it. No tiene mucho sentido comprarlo.
2 **to have a sense of humour** tener [9] sentido del humor
She has no sense of humour. No tiene sentido del humor.
3 *(meaning)* el **significado**
4 *(ability)* **the sense of smell** el olfato
the sense of touch el tacto

⚷ **sensible** *adjective*
sensato *masc*, **sensata** *fem*
She's very sensible. Es muy sensata.
It's a sensible decision. Es una decisión sensata.
Tell him to be sensible and come home. Dile que sea razonable y vuelva a casa.

sensitive *adjective*
sensible *masc & fem*
for sensitive skin para pieles sensibles

⚷ **sentence** *noun* ▷ see **sentence** *verb*
1 *(Grammar)* la **oración** *fem*
Write two sentences in Spanish. Escribe dos oraciones en español.
2 *(in law)* la **sentencia** *fem*

⚷ to **sentence** *verb* ▷ see **sentence** *noun*
condenar [17]
to sentence somebody to something condenar a alguien a algo
She was sentenced to five years' imprisonment. Fue condenada a cinco años de prisión.

sentimental *adjective*
sentimental *masc & fem*

separate *adjective* ▷ see **separate** *verb*
1 *(holidays, accounts)* **separado** *masc*, **separada** *fem*
They have separate rooms. Tienen habitaciones separadas.
2 *(away from each other)* **aparte** *masc & fem*
in a separate pile en un montón aparte
on a separate sheet of paper en una hoja de papel aparte
3 *(meaning, problem)* **distinto** *masc*, **distinta** *fem*
That's a separate issue. Ése es un asunto distinto.

to **separate** *verb* ▷ see **separate** *adj*
1 **separar** [17]
to separate the good from the bad separar lo bueno de lo malo
2 *(couples, partners)* **separarse** [17]
Her parents have separated. Sus padres se han separado.

separately *adverb*
por separado

separation *noun*
la **separación** *fem*

⚷ **September** *noun*
el **septiembre** *masc*
in September en septiembre
Term starts on the fifth of September. El trimestre empieza el cinco de septiembre.

WORD TIP Names of months and days start with small letters in Spanish.

sequel *noun*
la **continuación** *fem*

⚷ **serial** *noun*
la **serie** *fem*
the last episode of the serial el último episodio de la serie

series *noun*
la **serie** *fem*
a television series una serie de televisión

⚷ **serious** *adjective*
1 *(not funny)* **serio** *masc*, **seria** *fem*
I'm serious about it. Estoy hablando en serio.
She's not serious about it. No se lo toma en serio.
2 *(injury, mistake, condition, etc)* **grave** *masc & fem*
We have a serious problem. Tenemos un problema grave.
His condition is serious. Está grave.

seriously *adverb*
1 *(not joking)* **en serio**
Seriously, I have to go now. En serio, tengo que irme.
Seriously? ¿En serio?
2 **to take somebody seriously** tomarse [17] en serio a alguien
3 *(ill, injured)* **gravemente**
She's seriously injured. Está gravemente herida.

servant *noun*
el **criado** *masc*, la **criada** *fem*

English-Spanish

serve *noun* ▷ see **serve** *verb*
(*in tennis*) el **saque** *masc*
It's your serve. Te toca sacar.

to **serve** *verb* ▷ see **serve** *noun*
1 (*in general*) **servir** [57]
to serve the soup servir la sopa
2 (*in a shop*) atender [36]
Are you being served? ¿Le atienden?
3 (*in tennis*) **sacar** [31]

service *noun* ▷ see **service** *verb*
1 (*in restaurants, shops, etc*) el **servicio** *masc*
The service is very slow. El servicio es muy lento.
Service is included. El servicio está incluido.
the emergency services los servicios de emergencia
2 (*in a church*) el **oficio religioso**
3 (*of a car, machine*) la **revisión** *fem*

to **service** *verb* ▷ see **service** *noun*
(*a car, machine*) **revisar** [1]

service charge *noun*
el **servicio** *masc*
What's the service charge? ¿Cuánto se cobra por el servicio?

service station *noun*
la **estación de servicio**

serviette *noun*
la **servilleta** *fem*

session *noun*
la **sesión** *fem*
a recording session una sesión de grabación

set *adjective* ▷ see **set** *noun, verb*
at a set time a una hora determinada
a set menu un menú del día
a set price un precio fijo

set *noun* ▷ see **set** *adj, verb*
1 (*for games*) el **juego** *masc*
a chess set un juego de ajedrez
a train set un tren de juguete
2 (*of keys, tools*) el **juego** *masc*
a set of spanners un juego de llaves inglesas
3 (*in tennis*) el **set** *masc*

to **set** *verb* ▷ see **set** *adj, noun*
1 (*a date, time*) **fijar** [17]
2 (*a record*) **establecer** [35]
3 (*the table*) **to set the table** poner [11] la mesa
4 (*a watch, alarm clock, etc*) **poner** [11]
to set a watch poner [11] el reloj en hora
I've set my alarm for seven. He puesto el despertador para las siete.
5 (*a film, play*) **ambientar** [1]
The novel is set in Majorca. La novela está ambientada en Mallorca.
6 (*sun*) **ponerse** [11]
• **to set off**
salir [63]
We're setting off at ten. Salimos a las diez.
They set off for Barcelona tomorrow. Salen para Barcelona mañana.
• **to set off something**
1 (*fireworks*) **tirar** [17]
2 (*an alarm*) **hacer** [7] **sonar**
• **to set out**
salir [63]
They set out for Seville yesterday. Salieron ayer para Sevilla.

settee *noun*
el **sofá** *masc*

to **settle** *verb*
1 (*a bill*) **pagar** [28]
2 (*a problem*) **solucionar** [17]

seven *number*
siete *invariable number*
Khalil's seven. Khalil tiene siete años.
It's seven o'clock. Son las siete.

seventeen *number*
diecisiete *invariable number*
Jason's seventeen. Jason tiene diecisiete años.

seventh *adjective* ▷ see **seventh** *noun*
séptimo *masc*, **séptima** *fem*
on the seventh floor en la séptima planta

seventh *noun* ▷ see **seventh** *adj*
1 (*fraction*) **a seventh** una séptima parte
2 (*in dates*) **the seventh of April** el siete de abril
She came on the seventh. Vino el día siete.

seventies *plural noun*
the seventies los años setenta
in the seventies en los años setenta

seventy *number*
setenta *invariable number*
seventy-five setenta y cinco
He's seventy. Tiene setenta años.

several *adjective, pronoun*
varios *plural masc*, **varias** *plural fem*
He took several. Tomó varios.
I've seen her several times. La he visto varias veces.
I've seen several of his films. He visto varias películas suyas.

severe *adjective*
1 *(person)* **severo** *masc*, **severa** *fem*
2 *(weather)* **malo** *masc*, **mala** *fem*
3 *(injury)* **grave** *masc & fem*

Seville *noun*
Sevilla *fem*

to **sew** *verb*
coser [18]

sewer *noun*
la **alcantarilla** *fem*

sewing *noun*
la **costura** *fem*
I like sewing. Me gusta la costura.
• **sewing machine** la máquina de coser

sex *noun*
1 *(gender)* el **sexo** *masc*
the opposite sex el sexo opuesto
2 *(intercourse)* las **relaciones sexuales**
to have sex with someone tener [9] relaciones sexuales con alguien
• **sex education** la educación sexual

sexism *noun*
el **sexismo** *masc*

sexist *adjective*
sexista *masc & fem*
sexist remarks comentarios sexistas

sexual *adjective*
sexual *masc & fem*
• **sexual harassment** el acoso sexual

sexuality *noun*
la **sexualidad** *fem*

sexy *adjective*
sexy *invariable adjective*

shabby *adjective*
gastado *masc*, **gastada** *fem*

shade *noun*
1 *(from the sun)* la **sombra**
in the shade en la sombra
2 *(of a colour)* el **tono** *masc*
a shade of green un tono verde

shadow *noun*
la **sombra** *fem*

to **shake** *verb*
1 *(to tremble)* **temblar** [29]
Her hands are shaking. Le tiemblan las manos.
The ground was shaking. Temblaba la tierra.
2 *(a bottle, medicine)* **agitar** [17]
Shake before use. Agitar antes de abrir.
3 *(a cloth, building)* **sacudir** [19]
The explosion shook the building. La explosión sacudió el edificio.
4 *(someone's hand)* **to shake hands with somebody** darle [17] la mano a alguien
She shook hands with me. Me dio la mano.
We shook hands. Nos estrechamos la mano.
5 *(meaning no)* **to shake your head** negar [30] con la cabeza

shall *verb*
Shall I come with you? ¿Voy contigo?
Shall we stop now? ¿Paramos ya?

shallow *adjective*
(water, river) **poco profundo** *masc*, **poco profunda** *fem*
the shallow end of the pool la parte poco profunda de la piscina
The water's very shallow here. El agua es muy poco profunda aquí.

shambles *noun*
el **caos** *masc*
It was a total shambles! ¡Fue un caos total!

shame *noun*
1 *(feeling)* la **vergüenza** *fem*
Shame on you! ¡Debería darte vergüenza!
2 *(pity)* **What a shame!** ¡Qué pena!
It's a shame she can't come. Qué pena que no pueda venir.

ℰ **shampoo** *noun*
el **champú** *masc*
I bought a herbal shampoo. Compré un champú de hierbas.

shamrock *noun*
el **trébol** *masc*

shandy *noun*
la **clara** *fem*
a shandy una clara

shape *noun*
la **forma** *fem*
What shape is it? ¿Qué forma tiene?
to be in good shape estar [2] en buena forma

share *noun* ▷ see **share** *verb*
1 *(portion)* la **parte** *fem*
your share of the money tu parte del dinero
my share of the bill lo que me corresponde de la cuenta
2 *(in a company)* la **acción** *fem*

English-Spanish

to **share** *verb* ▷ see **share** *noun*
compartir [19]
to share the costs compartir los costes
I'm sharing a room with Emma. Comparto una habitación con Emma.
• **to share out**
repartir [19]

shark *noun*
el **tiburón** *masc*

sharp *adjective*
1 (*knife, blade*) **afilado** *masc*, **afilada** *fem*
a sharp pencil un lápiz con mucha punta
a sharp bend una curva cerrada
This knife isn't very sharp. Este cuchillo no está muy afilado.
2 (*clever*) **listo** *masc*, **lista** *fem*

to **sharpen** *verb*
1 (*a knife, blade*) **afilar** [17]
2 (*a pencil*) **sacarle** [31] **punta a**

sharpener *noun*
el **sacapuntas** *masc, pl:* los **sacapuntas**

to **shave** *verb*
afeitarse [17]
He's shaving. Se está afeitando.
to shave off your beard afeitarse [17] la barba
to shave your legs afeitarse [17] las piernas
• **shaving cream** la crema de afeitar
• **shaving foam** la espuma de afeitar

she *pronoun*
1 **ella** (*see Word Tip*)
She's in her room. Está en su cuarto.
She's a student. Es estudiante.
She's a very good teacher. Es muy buena profesora.
Here she is! ¡Aquí está!
2 (*for emphasis*) **ella**
She did it. Lo hizo ella.

WORD TIP *she*, like other subject pronouns *he*, *you*, *we* etc, is generally not translated in Spanish; the form of the verb tells you whether the subject of the verb is *I*, *we*, *they*, etc, so *she* is translated only for emphasis or for clarity.

shed *noun*
1 (*in a garden*) el **cobertizo** *masc*
2 (*industrial*) la **nave** *fem*

sheep *noun*
la **oveja** *fem*
a flock of sheep un rebaño de ovejas
• **sheepdog** el perro pastor

sheet *noun*
1 (*for a bed*) la **sábana** *fem*
2 (*of paper*) la **hoja de papel**
a blank sheet una hoja en blanco
3 (*of glass, metal*) la **plancha** *fem*

shelf *noun*
1 (*at home*) el **estante** *masc*
a set of shelves una estantería
2 (*in a shop, fridge*) la **balda** *fem*

shell *noun*
1 (*of an egg, a nut*) la **cáscara** *fem*
2 (*seashell*) la **concha** *fem*
3 (*explosive*) el **proyectil** *masc*
• **shellfish** el marisco

shelter *noun*
el **refugio** *masc*
in the shelter of the tree al abrigo del árbol
to take shelter from the rain refugiarse [17] de la lluvia

sherry *noun*
el **jerez** *masc*

Shetland Islands *noun*
las **islas Shetland**

shield *noun*
el **escudo** *masc*

shift *noun* ▷ see **shift** *verb*
el **turno** *masc*
the day shift el turno de día
to be on night shift hacer [7] el turno de noche

to **shift** *verb* ▷ see **shift** *noun*
to shift something mover [38] algo

shin *noun*
la **espinilla** *fem*

to **shine** *verb*
brillar [17]
The sun's shining. Brilla el sol.

shiny *adjective*
brillante *masc & fem*

ship *noun*
el **barco** *masc*
a passenger ship un barco de pasajeros

shirt *noun*
la **camisa** *fem*

to **shiver** *verb*
temblar [29]

shock *noun* ▷ see **shock** *verb*
1 (*mental*) el **shock** *masc*
in a state of shock en estado de shock
It was a shock. Fue un shock.
It gave me a shock. Me llevé un shock.
2 (*electric*) la descarga eléctrica
I got an electric shock. Me dio una descarga eléctrica.

a b c d e f g h i j k l m n o p q r s t u v w x y z

to **shock** *verb* ▷ see **shock** *noun*
horrorizar [22]

shocked *adjective*
horrorizado *masc*, **horrorizada** *fem*
We were shocked. Nos quedamos horrorizados.

shocking *adjective*
1 (*news*) **horroroso** *masc*, **horrorosa** *fem*
2 (*behaviour*) **vergonzoso** *masc*, **vergonzosa** *fem*

shoe *noun*
el **zapato** *masc*
a pair of shoes un par de zapatos
What size shoes do you wear? ¿Qué numero calzas?
• **shoelace** el cordón de zapato
• **shoe polish** el betún
• **shoe shop** la zapatería

to **shoot** *verb*
1 (*to fire*) **disparar** [17]
to shoot at somebody disparar a alguien
She shot him in the leg. Le disparó en la pierna.
He was shot in the arm. Le dispararon en el brazo.
2 (*to kill*) **matar** [17] **a tiros**
He was shot by terrorists. Los terroristas lo mataron a tiros.
3 (*to execute*) **fusilar** [17]
4 (*in football, hockey*) **chutar** [1]
5 (*a film*) rodar [24]

shooting *noun*
1 (*shots*) el **tiroteo** *masc*
2 (*hunting*) la **caza** *fem*
target shooting tiro al blanco
3 (*murder*) el **asesinato** *masc*

shop *noun* ▷ see **shop** *verb*
la **tienda** *fem*
a record shop una tienda de discos
a shoe shop una zapatería
to go round the shops ir [8] de tiendas

to **shop** *verb* ▷ see **shop** *noun*
1 **hacer** [7] **compras**
She spent the whole day shopping. Pasó el día entero haciendo compras.
I always shop at the market. Compro siempre en el mercado.
2 **to go shopping** ir [8] de compras
On Saturdays I always go shopping. Los sábados siempre voy de compas.

shop assistant *noun*
el **dependiente** *masc*, la **dependienta** *fem*
Brad's a shop assistant. Brad trabaja de dependiente.

shopkeeper *noun*
el **tendero** *masc*, la **tendera** *fem*

shoplifter *noun*
el **ladrón** *masc*, la **ladrona** *fem*

shoplifting *noun*
el **hurto en las tiendas**

shopping *noun*
las **compras** *plural fem*
Can you put the shopping away? ¿Puedes guardar las compras?
I've got a lot of shopping to do. Tengo muchas cosas que comprar.
• **shopping centre**, **shopping mall** el centro comercial
• **shopping trolley** el carrito

shop window *noun*
el **escaparate** *masc*

shore *noun*
la **orilla del mar**

short *adjective*
1 (*in general*) **corto** *masc*, **corta** *fem*
a short dress un vestido corto
a short break un descanso corto
a short visit una visita corta
a short time ago hace poco tiempo
She has short hair. Tiene el pelo corto.
It's a short walk from the station. Queda bastante cerca de la estación.
2 (*person*) **bajo** *masc*, **baja** *fem*
He's quite short. Es bastante bajo.
3 **to be short of something** andar [21] escaso de algo
We're a bit short of money at the moment. De momento andamos escasos de dinero.
We're getting short of time. Se nos está acabando el tiempo.

shortage *noun*
la **escasez** *fem*

shortbread *noun*
la **galleta de mantequilla**

shortcrust pastry *noun*
la **pasta quebrada**

short cut *noun*
el **atajo** *masc*
to take a short cut tomar [1] un atajo

to **shorten** *verb*
acortar [17]

shortly *adverb*
dentro de poco

English–Spanish

a b c d e f g h i j k l m n o p q r s t u v w x y z

shorts *plural noun*
los **shorts** *plural masc*
a pair of shorts unos shorts
my red shorts mis shorts rojos

short-sighted *adjective*
miope *masc & fem*
I'm short-sighted. Soy miope.

short-sleeved *adjective*
de manga corta
a short-sleeved shirt una camisa de manga corta

shotgun *noun*
la **escopeta** *fem*

should *verb*
1 (*should + verb*) **You should ask Simon.** Deberías preguntárselo a Simon.
The potatoes should be cooked now. Las patatas deberían estar hechas ya.
2 (*should + have*) **You should have told me.** Deberías habérmelo dicho.
You shouldn't have stayed. No deberías haberte quedado.

WORD TIP *should* is translated by *debería*, etc. *should have* is translated by *debería, etc + haber*.

3 (*in expressions*) **I should forget it if I were you.** Yo en tu lugar me olvidaría del asunto.
I should think he's forgotten. Yo diría que se ha olvidado.

shoulder *noun*
el **hombro** *masc*
• **shoulder bag** el bolso

shout *noun* ▷ see **shout** *verb*
el **grito** *masc*
to give a shout dar [4] un grito
He gave a a shout of pain. Dio un grito de dolor.

to shout *verb* ▷ see **shout** *noun*
gritar [17]
Stop shouting! ¡Deja de gritar!
They shouted at us to come back. Nos gritaron que volviésemos.

shovel *noun*
la **pala** *fem*

show *noun* ▷ see **show** *verb*
1 (*on stage*) el **espectáculo** *masc*
We went to see a show. Fuimos a ver un espectáculo.
2 (*on TV*) el **programa** *masc*
He has a TV show. Tiene un programa en la tele.
3 (*exhibition*) el **salón** *masc*
the motor show el salón del automóvil

to show *verb* ▷ see **show** *noun*
1 (*in general*) **enseñar** [17]
to show something to somebody enseñar algo a alguien
I'll show you my photos. Te enseño mis fotos.
to show somebody how to do something enseñarle a alguien cómo hacer algo
He showed me how to make paella. Me enseñó cómo hacer paella.
2 (*to demonstrate*) **demostrar** [1]
You must show that you understand how it works. Tienes que demostrar que entiendes cómo funciona.
• **to show off**
presumir [19]
She's always showing off. Siempre está presumiendo.

shower *noun*
1 (*in a bathroom*) la **ducha** *fem*
I have a shower every day. Me ducho todos los días.
2 (*of rain*) el **chaparrón** *masc*

showing *noun*
(*of a film*) la **proyección** *fem*

show-off *noun*
el **fanfarrón** *masc*, la **fanfarrona** *fem*

to shriek *verb*
gritar [17]
He shrieked with pain. Gritó de dolor.

shrimp *noun*
el **camarón** *masc*

shrine *noun*
el **santuario** *masc*

to shrink *verb*
encoger [3]

Shrove Tuesday *noun*
el **martes de Carnaval**

to shrug *verb*
to shrug your shoulders encogerse [3] de hombros

to shuffle *verb*
to shuffle the cards barajar [17] las cartas

shut *adjective* ▷ see **shut** *verb*
cerrado *masc*, **cerrada** *fem*
The doors are shut. Las puertas están cerradas.

to shut *verb* ▷ see **shut** *adj*
cerrar [29]
Shut the door, please. Cierra la puerta, por favor.

The shops shut at six. Las tiendas cierran a las seis.

- **to shut up**

callarse [17]
Shut up! ¡Cállate! (*to one person*), ¡Cállaos! (*to more than one person*)

shuttlecock *noun*
el **volante** *masc*

⚷ **shy** *adjective*
tímido *masc*, **tímida** *fem*

shyness *noun*
la **timidez** *fem*

Sicily *noun*
Sicilia *fem*

⚷ **sick** *adjective*
1 (*ill*) **enfermo** *masc*, **enferma** *fem*
Amy's off sick today. Amy está enferma hoy y no ha venido.
2 (*when you vomit*) **to be sick** devolver **[45]**
I was sick several times. Devolví varias veces.
to feel sick tener **[9]** ganas de devolver
3 (*bored*) **to be sick of something** estar **[2]** harto, *fem* harta de algo
I'm sick of that song. Estoy harto de esa canción.
4 **a sick joke** una broma de mal gusto

sickness *noun*
la **enfermedad** *fem*

⚷ **side** *noun*
1 (*of the street, room, etc*) el **lado** *masc*
on the other side of the street al otro lado de la calle
on the wrong side en el lado equivocado
They were sitting side by side. Estaban sentados juntos.
2 (*edge*) el **borde** *masc*
by the side of the pool al borde de la piscina
at the side of the road al borde de la carretera
by the side of the river a la orilla del río
3 (*team*) el **equipo** *masc*
She plays on our side. Juega en nuestro equipo.
4 (*in an argument*) **to take sides** tomar **[17]** partido
I'm on your side. (*I agree with you*) Estoy de tu lado.

⚷ **sideboard** *noun*
el **aparador** *masc*

siege *noun*
el **sitio** *masc*

sieve *noun*
el **tamiz** *masc*

sigh *noun* ▷ see **sigh** *verb*
el **suspiro** *masc*

to **sigh** *verb* ▷ see **sigh** *noun*
suspirar [17]

⚷ **sight** *noun*
1 (*something seen*) el **espectáculo** *masc*
It was a marvellous sight. Era un espectáculo maravilloso.
2 (*eyesight*) la **vista** *fem*
to have poor sight tener **[9]** mala vista
to know somebody by sight conocer **[35]** a alguien de vista
I know her by sight. La conozco de vista.
I'd lost sight of them. Los había perdido de vista.
3 (*when you see*) **She faints at the sight of blood.** Se desmaya a la vista de sangre.
It was love at first sight. Fue amor a primera vista.
4 (*place worth seeing*) **the sights** los lugares de interés
to see the sights of Barcelona visitar **[17]** los lugares de interés de Barcelona

sightseeing *noun*
to do some sightseeing hacer **[7]** turismo

sign *noun* ▷ see **sign** *verb*
1 (*notice*) el **letrero** *masc*
There's a sign on the door. Hay un letrero en la puerta.
2 (*of improvement, life, etc*) la **señal** *fem*
3 (*of the Zodiac*) el **signo** *masc*
What sign are you? ¿De qué signo eres?

to **sign** *verb* ▷ see **sign** *noun*
1 (*a document, etc*) **firmar [17]**
to sign a cheque firmar un cheque
2 (*using sign language*) **comunicarse [31] por señas**

- **to sign on**

(*as unemployed*) **inscribirse [17] al paro**

signal *noun*
la **señal** *fem*

signature *noun*
la **firma** *fem*

significance *noun*
la **importancia** *fem*

significant *adjective*
importante *masc & fem*

sign language *noun*
el **lenguaje de gestos**

signpost *noun*
la **señal** *fem*

silence *noun*
el **silencio** *masc*

silent *adjective*
silencioso *masc*, **silenciosa** *fem*

silk *adjective* ▷ see **silk** *noun*
de seda
a silk shirt una camisa de seda

silk *noun* ▷ see **silk** *adj*
la **seda** *fem*

silky *adjective*
sedoso *masc*, **sedosa** *fem*

silly *adjective*
tonto *masc*, **tonta** *fem*
It was a silly thing to do. Hacer eso fue una tontería.

silver *adjective* ▷ see **silver** *noun*
de plata
a silver spoon una cuchara de plata

silver *noun* ▷ see **silver** *adj*
la **plata** *fem*

SIM card *noun*
la **tarjeta SIM**

similar *adjective*
parecido *masc*, **parecida** *fem*
Their essays are very similar. Sus trabajos son muy parecidos.

similarity *noun*
el **parecido** *masc*

simple *adjective*
sencillo *masc*, **sencilla** *fem*

to **simplify** *verb*
simplificar [31]

simply *adverb*
sencillamente

sin *noun*
el **pecado** *masc*

since *adverb, conjunction, preposition*
1 **desde**
I've been in Madrid since Saturday. Estoy en Madrid desde el sábado.
I've been learning Spanish since last year. Estoy aprendiendo español desde el año pasado.
I haven't seen her since. No la he visto desde entonces.
I haven't seen her since Monday. No la he visto desde el lunes.
Since when? ¿Desde cuándo?
2 **desde que**
since I have known her desde que la conozco
since I've been learning Spanish desde que aprendo español
3 (*because*) **como**
Since it was raining, the match was cancelled. Como estaba lloviendo, cancelaron el partido.

WORD TIP Spanish uses the present tense where English uses *have done* or *have been doing*.

sincere *adjective*
sincero *masc*, **sincera** *fem*

sincerely *adverb*
Yours sincerely, ... Atentamente, ...

to **sing** *verb*
cantar [17]

singer *noun*
el & la **cantante** *masc & fem*

singing *noun*
el **canto** *masc*
a singing lesson una lección de canto
I like singing. Me gusta cantar.

single *adjective* ▷ see **single** *noun*
1 (*not married*) **soltero** *masc*, **soltera** *fem*
a single man un soltero
a group of single women un grupo de solteras
2 (*only one*) **a single room** una habitación individual
a single bed una cama individual
3 (*in expressions*) **not a single ...** ni un solo ..., *fem* ni una sola ...
I haven't had a single reply. No he tenido ni una sola respuesta.
every single ... todos los, *fem* todas las ...
every single day todos los días
every single girl todas las chicas

single *noun* ▷ see **single** *adj*
(*ticket*) el **billete de ida**
a single to Valencia un billete de ida para Valencia

single parent *noun*
a single-parent family una familia monoparental
She's a single parent. Es madre soltera.

singular *noun*
(*Grammar*) el **singular** *masc*
in the singular en singular

sink *noun* ▷ see **sink** *verb*
1 (*in a kitchen*) el **fregadero** *masc*
2 (*in a bathroom*) el **lavabo** *masc*

🔑 to **sink** *verb* ▷ see **sink** *noun*
hundirse [19]

🔑 **sir** *noun*
el **señor** *masc*
Yes, sir. Sí, señor.

🔑 **sister** *noun*
la **hermana** *fem*
my little siser mi hermanita
My sister's ten. Mi hermana tiene diez años.
• **sister-in-law** la cuñada

🔑 to **sit** *verb*
1 **sentarse** [29]
You can sit on the sofa. Puedes sentarte en el sofá.
I can sit on the floor. Me puedo sentar en el suelo.
2 **to be sitting** estar [2] sentado
Leila was sitting on the sofa. Leila estaba sentada en el sofá.
3 **to sit an exam** presentarse [17] a un examen
She's sitting her driving test on Thursday. Se presenta al examen de conducir el jueves.
• **to sit down**
sentarse [29]
He sat down on a chair. Se sentó en una silla.
Do sit down. Siéntate (*informal form*)., Siéntese (*polite form*).

🔑 **site** *noun*
a building site una obra
1 **a camp site** un camping

🔑 **sitting room** *noun*
el **salón** *masc*, la **sala de estar**

situation *noun*
la **situación** *fem*

🔑 **six** *number*
seis *invariable number*
Tom's six. Tom tiene seis años.
It's six o'clock. Son las seis.

🔑 **sixteen** *number*
dieciséis *invariable number*
Hannah's sixteen. Hannah tiene dieciséis años.

🔑 **sixth** *adjective* ▷ see **sixth** *noun*
sexto *masc*, **sexta** *fem*
on the sixth floor en el sexto piso

🔑 **sixth** *noun* ▷ see **sixth** *adj*
1 (*fraction*) **a sixth** una sexta parte
2 (*in dates*) **the sixth of June** el seis de junio
He called me on the sixth. Me llamó el día seis.

sixties *plural noun*
the sixties los años sesenta
in the sixties en los años sesenta

🔑 **sixty** *number*
sesenta *invariable number*
sixty-five sesenta y cinco
She's sixty. Tiene sesenta años.

🔑 **size** *noun*
1 el **tamaño** *masc*
the size of the house el tamaño de la casa
What size is it? ¿De qué tamaño es?
2 (*of clothes*) la **talla** *fem*
What size do you take? ¿Qué talla usas?
3 (*of shoes*) el **número** *masc*
I take a size thirty-eight. Calzo el número treinta y ocho.
4 (*in measurements*) las **medidas** *plural fem*
What size is the window? ¿Qué medidas tiene la ventana?

skate *noun* ▷ see **skate** *verb*
el **patín** *masc*
an ice skate un patín de hielo
a roller skate un patín de ruedas

to **skate** *verb* ▷ see **skate** *noun*
1 (*on ice*) **hacer** [7] **patinaje sobre hielo**
2 (*on the ground*) **hacer** [7] **patinaje sobre ruedas**

skateboard *noun*
el **monopatín** *masc*

skateboarding *noun*
to go skateboarding patinar [17] con el monopatín

skater *noun*
el **patinador** *masc*, la **patinadora** *fem*

skating *noun*
el **patinaje**
to go skating (*on the ground*) ir [8] a patinar, (*on ice*) ir a patinar sobre hielo
• **skating rink** la pista de patinaje

skeleton *noun*
el **esqueleto** *masc*

sketch *noun*
1 (*drawing*) el **boceto** *masc*
2 (*in comedy*) el **sketch** *masc*

to **ski** *verb* ▷ see **ski** *noun*
esquiar [32]

English-Spanish
a b c d e f g h i j k l m n o p q r s t u v w x y z

ski *noun* ▷ see **ski** *verb*
el **esquí** *masc*
- **ski boot** la bota de esquí
- **ski lift** el telesquí
- **ski pants** los pantalones de esquí
- **ski resort** la estación de esquí
- **ski suit** el traje de esquí

to **skid** *verb*
1 (*car*) **patinar** [8]
The car skidded. El coche patinó.
2 (*person*) **resbalarse** [17]
I skidded. Me resbalé.

skier *noun*
el **esquiador** *masc*, la **esquiadora** *fem*

skiing *noun*
el **esquí** *masc*
to go skiing ir [8] a esquiar

skilful *adjective*
habilidoso *masc*, **habilidosa** *fem*

skill *noun*
la **habilidad** *fem*
It's not one of my skills. No es una de mis habilidades.

skimmed milk *noun*
la **leche desnatada**

skin *noun*
la **piel** *fem*
- **skinhead** el & la cabeza rapada

skinny *adjective*
flaco *masc*, **flaca** *fem*

skip *noun* ▷ see **skip** *verb*
el **contenedor** *masc*

to **skip** *verb* ▷ see **skip** *noun*
1 (*a meal, chapter*) **saltarse** [17]
I skipped the third chapter. Me salté el tercer capítulo.
2 **to skip a lesson** faltar [17] a clase

skipping rope *noun*
la **comba** *fem*

skirt *noun*
la **falda** *fem*
a long skirt una falda larga
a straight skirt una falda de tubo
a mini-skirt una minifalda

sky *noun*
el **cielo** *masc*

skyscraper *noun*
el **rascacielos** *invariable masc*
a fifty-storey skyscraper un rascacielos de cincuenta pisos

WORD TIP *rascacielos* never changes.

to **slam** *verb*
cerrar [29] **de un portazo**
She slammed the door. Cerró la puerta de un portazo.

slang *noun*
el **argot** *masc*

slap *noun* ▷ see **slap** *verb*
1 (*on the face*) la **bofetada** *fem*
2 (*on the bottom*) el **azote** *masc*

to **slap** *verb* ▷ see **slap** *noun*
to slap somebody (*in the face*) dar [4] una bofetada a alguien, (*on the bottom*) dar [4] un azote a alguien

slate *noun*
la **pizarra** *fem*

slave *noun*
el **esclavo** *masc*, la **esclava** *fem*

sledge *noun*
el **trineo** *masc*

sledging *noun*
to go sledging ir [8] en trineo

sleep *noun* ▷ see **sleep** *verb*
el **sueño** *masc*
six hours' sleep seis horas de sueño
I had a good sleep. Dormí bien.
She couldn't get to sleep. No pudo conciliar el sueño.
The film sent me to sleep. La película me hizo dormir.
to go to sleep dormirse [51]

to **sleep** *verb* ▷ see **sleep** *noun*
dormir [51]
She's sleeping. Está durmiendo.
Sleep well. Que duermas bien.

sleeping bag *noun*
el **saco de dormir**

sleeping pill *noun*
el **somnífero** *masc*

sleepy *adjective*
to be sleepy tener [9] sueño
I feel sleepy. Tengo sueño.
I was getting sleepy. Me estaba entrando sueño.

sleeve *noun*
la **manga** *fem*
to roll up your sleeves arremangarse [28]

slice *noun* ▷ see **slice** *verb*
1 (*of bread, cheese*) la **rebanada** *fem*
a slice of bread and butter una rebanada de pan con mantequilla

2 (*of meat*) la **loncha** *fem*
a slice of ham una loncha de jamón
3 (*of cake*) el **trozo** *masc*
4 (*of salami, tomato*) la **rodaja** *fem*

♪ to **slice** *verb* ▷ see **slice** *noun*
to slice something cortar **[17]** algo en rebanadas (*or* ***lonchas, trozos,*** *etc*) ▷ **slice**

♪ **slide** *noun*
1 (*in a playground*) el **tobogán** *masc*
2 (*photo*) la **diapositiva** *fem*
3 (*for hair*) el **pasador** *masc*

slight *adjective*
ligero *masc*, **ligera** *fem*
There's a slight problem. Hay un pequeño problema.

slightly *adverb*
ligeramente

slim *adjective* ▷ see **slim** *verb*
delgado *masc*, **delgada** *fem*

to **slim** *verb* ▷ see **slim** *adj*
adelgazar [22]
I'm slimming. Estoy adelgazando.

♪ **slip** *noun* ▷ see **slip** *verb*
1 (*mistake*) el **error** *masc*
2 (*female underwear*) la **combinación** *fem*

♪ to **slip** *verb* ▷ see **slip** *noun*
resbalarse [17]
The jar slipped out of my hand. El frasco se me resbaló de la mano.

slipper *noun*
la **zapatilla** *fem*

slippery *adjective*
resbaladizo *masc*, **resbaladiza** *fem*

slope *noun*
la **cuesta** *fem*
a gentle slope una cuesta poco pronunciada

slot *noun*
la **ranura** *fem*
• **slot machine** la máquina tragaperras

♪ **slow** *adjective*
1 **lento** *masc*, **lenta** *fem*
The service is very slow. El servicio es muy lento.
2 (*clock, watch*) **My watch is slow.** Mi reloj está atrasado.
• **to slow down**
reducir [60] la velocidad

♪ **slowly** *adverb*
despacio
He got up slowly. Se levantó despacio.
Can you speak more slowly? ¿Puede hablar más despacio? (*polite form*)

slum *noun*
el **barrio bajo**

smack *noun* ▷ see **smack** *verb*
1 (*on the face*) la **bofetada** *fem*
2 (*on the leg, bottom*) el **azote** *masc*

to **smack** *verb* ▷ see **smack** *noun*
to smack somebody (*in the face*) dar **[4]** una bofetada a alguien, (*on the leg, the bottom*) dar **[4]** un azote a alguien

♪ **small** *adjective*
pequeño *masc*, **pequeña** *fem*
a small dog un perro pequeño

smart *adjective*
1 (*posh*) **elegante** *masc & fem*
a smart restaurant un restaurante elegante
2 (*clever*) **listo** *masc*, **lista** *fem*

to **smash** *verb*
romper [40]
They smashed the window. Rompieron la ventana.

smashing *adjective*
fantástico *masc*, **fantástica** *fem*

smell *noun* ▷ see **smell** *verb*
el **olor** *masc*
a nasty smell un mal olor
There's a smell of burning. Huele a quemado.

to **smell** *verb* ▷ see **smell** *noun*
1 **oler [39]**
I can't smell anything. No huelo nada.
I can smell lavender. Huele a lavanda.
2 (*to smell bad*) **oler [39] mal**
The drains smell. Las alcantarillas huelen mal.

smelly *adjective*
apestoso *masc*, **apestosa** *fem*

smile *noun* ▷ see **smile** *verb*
la **sonrisa** *fem*

to **smile** *verb* ▷ see **smile** *noun*
sonreír [61]
She smiled at me. Me sonrió.
He was smiling. Estaba sonriendo.

♪ **smoke** *noun* ▷ see **smoke** *verb*
el **humo** *masc*

to smoke *verb* ▷ see **smoke** *noun*
fumar [17]
I don't smoke. No fumo.
Do you smoke? ¿Fumas?
She smokes. Es fumadora.
He smokes a pipe. Fuma en pipa.

smoked *adjective*
ahumado *masc*, **ahumada** *fem*
smoked salmon salmón ahumado

smoker *noun*
el **fumador** *masc*, la **fumadora** *fem*

smoking *noun*
'No smoking' 'Prohibido fumar'
to give up smoking dejar **[17]** de fumar
to take up smoking empezar **[25]** a fumar

smooth *adjective*
1 (*stone, surface*) **liso** *masc*, **lisa** *fem*
a smooth surface una superficie lisa
2 (*skin*) **suave** *masc & fem*

SMS *noun*
(*= Short Message Service*) el **SMS** *masc*
an SMS message un mensaje SMS

to smuggle *verb*
to smuggle something pasar **[17]** algo de contrabando
to smuggle something out sacar **[31]** algo clandestinamente

smuggler *noun*
1 (*of goods*) el & la **contrabandista** *masc & fem*
2 (*of drugs*) el & la **narcotraficante** *masc & fem*

smuggling *noun*
el **contrabando** *masc*
drugs smuggling el narcotráfico
arms smuggling el tráfico de armas

snack *noun*
el **tentempié** *masc*
- **snack bar** la cafetería, la bocatería

snail *noun*
el **caracol** *masc*

snake *noun*
la **serpiente** *fem*

to snap *verb*
1 (*to break*) **romperse [40]**
2 (*to make a noise*) **to snap your fingers** chasquear **[17]** los dedos

to snatch *verb*
1 (*to grab*) **arrebatar [17]**
to snatch something from somebody arrebatar algo a alguien
He snatched my glasses. Me arrebató las gafas.
2 (*to steal*) **robar [17]**
She had her bag snatched. Le robaron el bolso.

to sneak *verb*
to sneak in entrar **[17]** a escondidas
to sneak out salir **[63]** a escondidas
He sneaked up on me. Se acercó a mí sin que yo me diese cuenta.

sneeze *noun* ▷ see **sneeze** *verb*
el **estornudo** *masc*

to sneeze *verb* ▷ see **sneeze** *noun*
estornudar [17]

to sniff *verb*
olisquear [17]

snob *noun*
el & la **esnob** *masc & fem*

snobbery *noun*
el **esnobismo** *masc*

snooker *noun*
el **snooker** *masc*
to play snooker jugar **[27]** al snooker

to snore *verb*
roncar [31]

to snow *verb* ▷ see **snow** *noun*
nevar [29]
It's snowing. Está nevando.
It's going to snow. Va a nevar.

snow *noun* ▷ see **snow** *verb*
la **nieve** *fem*
- **snowball** la bola de nieve
- **snow drift** el montón de nieve
- **snowman** el muñeco de nieve

snowy *adjective*
It was very snowy. Hubo mucha nieve.

so *conjunction, adverb*
1 **tan**
He's so lazy. Es tan perezoso.
This coffee's so hot that I can't drink it. Este café está tan caliente que no puedo beberlo.
2 **not so ...** no tan ...
Our house is like yours, but not so big. Nuestra casa es parecida a la tuya pero no tan grande.
3 **verb + so much** tanto
I hate it so much! ¡Lo odio tanto!
4 **so much + noun** tanto, tanta
I have so much work to do. Tengo tanto trabajo que hacer.
5 **so many + plural noun** tantos, tantas
She has so many hats. Tiene tantos sombreros.

6 (*therefore*) **así que**
He woke up late so he missed his bus. Se despertó tarde así que perdió el bus.
7 (*for emphasis*) **So what's your name?** ¿Y cómo te llamas?
So what shall we do? ¿Y entonces qué hacemos?
So what? ¿Y qué?
8 **so do I, so did I, so am I, so was I** yo también
'I work in Truro.'— 'So do I.' 'Trabajo en Truro.'— 'Yo también.'
'I have a headache.'— 'So do I.' 'Me duele la cabeza.'— 'A mí también.'
'I like Green Day.'— 'So do I.' 'Me gusta Green Day.'— 'A mí tambien.'
'I used to live in Leeds.'— 'So did I.' 'Vivía antes en Leeds.'— 'Yo también.'
'We're Irish.'— 'So are we.' 'Somos irlandeses.'— 'Nosotros tambien.'
9 **so do we, so did we** nosotros también
10 (*with 'think', 'hope', 'expect', etc*) **I think so.** Creo que sí.
I hope so. Espero que sí.

soaked *adjective*
empapado *masc*, **empapada** *fem*
to be soaked to the skin estar [2] empapado hasta los huesos

soap *noun*
1 (*for washing*) el **jabón** *masc*
a bar of soap una pastilla de jabón
2 (*on TV*) la **telenovela** *fem*
• **soap powder** el jabón en polvo

sober *adjective*
to be sober estar [2] sobrio, *fem* sobria

soccer *noun*
el **fútbol** *masc*
to play soccer jugar [27] al fútbol

social *adjective*
social *masc & fem*

socialism *noun*
el **socialismo** *masc*

socialist *adjective* ▷ see **socialist** *noun*
socialista *masc & fem*

socialist *noun* ▷ see **socialist** *adj*
el & la **socialista** *masc & fem*

social security *noun*
1 (*benefit*) la **asistencia social**
to be on social security recibir [19] asistencia social
2 (*the system*) **social security** la seguridad social

social worker *noun*
el & la **asistente social**
She's a social worker. Es asistente social.

society *noun*
la **sociedad** *fem*

sociology *noun*
la **sociología** *fem*

sock *noun*
el **calcetín** *masc*
a pair of socks un par de calcetines

socket *noun*
el **enchufe** *masc*

sofa *noun*
el **sofá** *masc*
• **sofa bed** el sofá-cama

soft *adjective*
blando *masc* , **blanda** *fem*
• **soft drink** el refresco
• **soft toy** el muñeco de peluche
• **software** el software

softly *adverb*
1 (*to touch*) **suavemente**
I softly touched her arm. Le toqué suavemente el brazo.
2 (*to speak*) **bajito**

soil *noun*
la **tierra** *fem*

solar energy *noun*
la **energía solar**

soldier *noun*
el & la **soldado** *masc & fem*

solicitor *noun*
el **abogado** *masc*, la **abogada** *fem*
She's a solicitor. Es abogada.

solid *adjective*
1 (*pure*) **macizo** *masc*, **maciza** *fem*
a table made of solid pine una mesa de pino macizo
a solid gold ring un anillo de oro macizo
solid silver plata maciza
2 (*not flimsy*) **sólido** *masc*, **sólida** *fem*
a solid house una casa sólida

solo *adjective, adverb* ▷ see **solo** *noun*
en solitario
a solo album un álbum en solitario
to play solo tocar [31] en solitario

solo *noun* ▷ see **solo** *adj, adv*
el **solo** *masc*
a guitar solo un solo de guitarra

soloist *noun*
el & la **solista** *masc & fem*

English–Spanish

some *adjective, adverb*
1 (*with a singular noun*) **algún,** *fem* **alguna**
in some way de alguna manera
Some day he'll come. Algún día vendrá.
2 (*with a plural noun*) **unos,** *fem* **unas**
I've bought some eggs. He comprado unos huevos., He comprado huevos.
We picked some flowers. Cogimos unas flores., Cogimos flores.
3 (*certain*) **algunos,** *fem* **algunas**
Some people think he's wrong. Algunas personas piensan que no tiene razón.
4 (*with a mass noun*) **algo de**
some sugar algo de azúcar
We need some bread. Necesitamos pan.
Would you like some butter? ¿Quieres mantequilla?'
Can you lend me some money? ¿Puedes prestarme dinero?
He's eaten some of it. Ya ha comido un poco.

WORD TIP With words like *sugar, bread, butter,* and plural nouns, *some* is often not translated.

somebody, **someone** *pronoun*
alguien
There's somebody at the door. Hay alguien en la puerta.

WORD TIP *alguien* never changes.

somehow *adverb*
1 **de alguna manera**
I've got to finish it somehow. Tengo que terminarlo de alguna manera.
2 **I somehow think they will come.** No sé por qué, pero creo que vendrán.

somersault *noun*
la **voltereta** *fem*

something *pronoun*
algo (*invariable*)
something pretty algo bonito
something interesting algo interesante
There's something wrong. Algo va mal.
I've got something to tell you. Tengo algo que decirte.
This CD is really something! ¡Este CD sí que es genial!
a guy called Pete something or other un tipo llamado Pete no sé cuánto.

sometime *adverb*
un día de estos
Give me a ring sometime. Llámame un día de estos.
I'll ring you sometime next week. Te llamaré un día de la semana que viene.

sometimes *adverb*
a veces
I sometimes go by train. A veces voy en tren.

somewhere *adverb*
to go somewhere ir [8] a algún sitio
I've left my bag somewhere. He dejado mi bolso en algún sitio.
I've met you somewhere before. Te he conocido antes en algún sitio.

son *noun*
el **hijo** *masc*
her youngest son su hijo menor

song *noun*
la **canción** *fem*
They sang my favourite song. Cantaron mi canción favorita.

son-in-law *noun*
el **yerno** *masc*

soon *adverb*
1 **pronto**
It will soon be the holidays. Pronto llegarán las vacaciones.
See you soon! ¡Hasta pronto!, ¡Hasta ahora!
It's too soon. Es demasiado pronto.
How soon will they be here? ¿Cuándo llegarán?
2 **as soon as ...** tan pronto como ...
as soon as possible tan pronto como sea posible
As soon as she arrives. Tan pronto como llegue.

WORD TIP *tan pronto que* is followed by the subjunctive.

sooner *adverb*
1 (*earlier*) **antes**
She arrived sooner than us. Llegó antes que nosotros.
2 (*showing preference*) **I would sooner ...** preferiría ...
I'd sooner wait. Preferiría esperar.

soprano *noun*
el & la **soprano** *masc & fem*

sore *adjective* ▷ see **sore** *noun*
He has a sore throat. Le duele la garganta.
My legs are sore. Me duelen las piernas.

sore *noun* ▷ see **sore** *adj*
la **llaga** *fem*

sorry *adjective*
1 (*showing regret*) **to be sorry** sentirlo [14]
I'm really sorry. Lo siento mucho.
to be sorry about something sentir [14] algo

a b c d e f g h i j k l m n o p q r s t u v w x y z

I'm sorry I forgot your birthday. Siento haberme olvidado de tu cumpleaños.

WORD TIP *sentir* + *lo* is used to say you're sorry, but when you say *what* you are sorry about, don't use *lo*.

2 (*when interrupting*) **Sorry to disturb you.** Perdona que te moleste (*informal form*)., Perdone que le moleste (*polite form*).
3 (*to get past*) **Sorry!** ¡Perdón!
4 (*asking someone to repeat*) **Sorry?** ¿Perdón?
5 (*showing sympathy*) **to feel sorry for somebody** compadecer **[35]** a alguien
I feel sorry for her. La compadezco.
6 (*when apologizing*) **to say you're sorry** pedir **[57]** perdón
He said he was sorry for what he had done. Pidió perdón por lo que había hecho.

sort *noun*
el **tipo** *masc*
What sort of music do you like? ¿Qué tipo de música te gusta?
all sorts of ... todo tipo de ...
for all sorts of reasons por todo tipo de razones
• **to sort something out**
1 (*a room, papers, etc*) **ordenar [17] algo**
I must sort out my things. Tengo que ordenar mi cosas.
2 (*a problem, etc*) **solucionar [17]**
Liz is sorting it out. Liz lo está solucionando.

soul *noun*
1 (*spirit*) el **alma** *fem*
the soul el alma
2 (*music*) el **soul** *masc*

WORD TIP *alma* takes *el* and *un* in the singular even though it is fem.

♪ to **sound** *verb* ▷ see **sound** *noun*
sonar
Her name sounds Italian. Su nombre suena italiano.
You sound surprised. Suenas sorprendida.
He sounded tired. Sonó cansado.
It sounds easy. Parece fácil.
It sounds great! ¡Parece buena idea!

♪ **sound** *noun* ▷ see **sound** *verb*
1 (*noise*) el **ruido** *masc*
the sound of voices el ruido de voces
2 (*volume*) el **volumen** *masc*
to turn down the sound bajar **[17]** el volumen
• **sound asleep** profundamente dormido *masc*, profundamente dormida *fem*
• **sound card** la tarjeta de sonido
• **sound effect** el efecto sonoro
• **sound system** el equipo de sonido
• **soundtrack** la banda sonora

♪ **soup** *noun*
1 (*clear*) el **consomé** *masc*
2 (*thick*) la **sopa** *fem*
3 (*puréed*) la **crema** *fem*
mushroom soup la crema de champiñones
• **soup plate** el plato de sopa
• **soup spoon** la cuchara sopera

sour *adjective*
(*taste*) **agrio** *masc*, **agria** *fem*
sour cream nata agria
a sweet and sour sauce una salsa agridulce
to go sour cortarse **[1]**
The milk's gone sour. La leche se ha cortado.

♪ **south** *adjective, adverb* ▷ see **south** *noun*
sur *invariable adj*
the south side la parte sur
a south wind un viento del sur
south of Burgos al sur de Burgos
to travel south viajar **[17]** hacia el sur

WORD TIP *sur* never changes.

♪ **south** *noun* ▷ see **south** *adj, adv*
el **sur** *masc*
in the south of Scotland en el sur de Escocia

South Africa *noun*
Sudáfrica *fem*

South African *adjective & noun*
1 **sudafricano** *masc*, **sudafricana** *fem*
2 el **sudafricano** *masc*, la **sudafricana** *fem*
the South Africans los sudafricanos

WORD TIP Adjectives and nouns for nationality and regional origin do not have capital letters in Spanish.

♪ **South America** *noun*
Sudamérica *fem*

♪ **South American** *adjective & noun*
1 **suramericano** *masc*, **suramericana** *fem*
2 (*person*) el **suramericano** *masc*, la **suramericana** *fem*
the South Americans los suramericanos

WORD TIP Adjectives and nouns for nationality and regional origin do not have capital letters in Spanish.

southeast *adjective, adverb* ▷ see **southeast** *noun*
sureste *invariable adj*
in southeast England en el sureste de Inglaterra

WORD TIP *sureste* never changes.

southeast *noun* ▷ see **southeast** *adj, adv*
el **sureste** *masc*

South Pole *noun*
el **Polo Sur**

southwest *adjective, adverb*
▷ see **southwest** *noun*
suroeste *invariable adj*
in southwest Scotland en el suroeste de Escocia

WORD TIP *suroeste* never changes.

southwest *noun* ▷ see **southwest** *adj, adv*
el **suroeste** *masc*

souvenir *noun*
el **recuerdo** *masc*

soya *noun*
la **soja** *fem*
soya milk leche de soja

space *noun*
1 (*room*) el **sitio** *masc*
Is there enough space? ¿Hay suficiente sitio?
There's enough space for two. Hay suficiente sitio para dos.
2 (*gap*) el **espacio** *masc*
Leave a space. Deja un espacio.
3 (*Astronomy*) el **espacio** *masc*
in space en el espacio
• **spacecraft** la nave espacial
• **space shuttle** el transbordador espacial

spade *noun*
1 (*tool*) la **pala** *fem*
2 (*in cards*) la **pica** *fem*
the queen of spades la reina de picas

spaghetti *noun*
los **espaguetis** *plural masc*

Spain *noun*
España *fem*
He's from Spain. Es español.
She's from Spain. Es española.

Spaniard *noun*
el **español** *masc*, la **española** *fem*
the Spaniards los españoles *plural masc*

WORD TIP Adjectives and nouns for nationality and regional origin do not have capital letters in Spanish.

spaniel *noun*
el **spaniel** *masc*

Spanish *adjective* ▷ see **Spanish** *noun*
1 **español** *masc*, **española** *fem*
Pedro's Spanish. Pedro es español.
Lola's Spanish. Lola es española.
2 (*teacher, lesson*) **de español**
the Spanish class la clase de español

Spanish *noun* ▷ see **Spanish** *adj*
1 (*the language*) el **español** *masc*
our Spanish teacher nuestro profesor de español
to speak Spanish hablar [17] español
I'm learning Spanish. Estoy aprendiendo español.
Say it in Spanish. Dilo en español.
2 (*the people*) **the Spanish** los españoles

WORD TIP Adjectives and nouns for nationality, regional origin and language do not have capital letters in Spanish.

spanner *noun*
la **llave inglesa**

to **spare** *verb* ▷ see **spare** *adj*
Can you spare a moment? ¿Tienes un momento libre?
I can't spare the time. No tengo tiempo para eso.
We have eggs to spare. Nos sobran huevos.

spare *adjective* ▷ see **spare** *verb*
1 (*part, battery*) **de repuesto**
a spare battery una batería de repuesto
2 (*extra*) **de más**
We have a spare ticket. Tenemos una entrada de más.
• **spare room** la habitación de invitados
• **spare wheel** la rueda de repuesto

spare time *noun*
el **tiempo libre**
in my spare time en mi tiempo libre

sparrow *noun*
el **gorrión** *masc*

to **speak** *verb*
1 **hablar** [17]
She speaks two languages. Habla dos idiomas.
Do you speak Spanish? ¿Hablas español?
'Spanish spoken here' 'Se habla español'
spoken Spanish el español hablado
2 **to speak to somebody** hablar [17] con alguien
She's speaking to Rashid. Está hablando con Rashid.
We've never spoken to her. Nunca hemos hablado con ella.
I'll speak to him about it. Hablaré sobre ello con él.
3 (*on the phone*) **Who's speaking?** ¿Quién es?
Jane speaking. Soy Jane.

speaker *noun*
1 (*of a language*) **a Spanish speaker** un hablante de español
an English speaker un hablante de inglés
2 (*on a music system*) el **altavoz** *masc*

3 (*giving a speech, etc*) el & la **conferenciante** *masc & fem*

spear *noun*
la **lanza** *fem*

⚷ **special** *adjective*
especial *masc & fem*
a special offer una oferta especial
today's special la especialidad del día

specialist *noun*
el & la **especialista** *masc & fem*

⚷ **speciality** *noun*
la **especialidad** *fem*
the chef's speciality la especialidad del día
the house speciality la especialidad de la casa

to **specialize** *verb*
to specialize in something especializarse [22] en algo

specially *adverb*
especialmente
I came specially in order to see you. Vine especialmente para verte.
They are specially for you. Son especialmente para ti.
not specially no especialmente

spectacles *noun*
las **gafas** *plural fem*

spectacular *adjective*
espectacular *masc & fem*

⚷ **spectator** *noun*
el **espectador** *masc*, la **espectadora** *fem*

speech *noun*
el **discurso** *masc*
to make a speech dar [4] un discurso

speechless *adjective*
1 **sin habla**
I was speechless. Me quedé sin habla.
2 **to be speechless with rage** quedarse [17] mudo de cólera

speed *noun*
la **velocidad** *fem*
What speed was he doing? ¿A qué velocidad iba?
a twelve-speed bike una bici de doce marchas
• **to speed up**
acelerar [17]

speed camera *noun*
el **radar (de control de velocidad)**

speeding *noun*
He was fined for speeding. Le multaron por exceso de velocidad.

speed limit *noun*
el **límite de velocidad**

⚷ **spell** *noun* ▷ see **spell** *verb*
1 (*of time*) el **periodo** *masc*
a busy spell un periodo de mucho trabajo
2 (*of weather*) **a cold spell** una ola de frio
sunny spells intervalos de sol

⚷ to **spell** *verb* ▷ see **spell** *noun*
1 (*in writing*) **escribirse** [52]
How do you spell it? ¿Cómo se escribe?
How do you spell your surname? ¿Cómo se escribe tu apellido?
2 (*out loud*) **deletrear** [17]
Shall I spell it for you? ¿Te lo deletreo?
• **spell checker** el corrector ortográfico

spelling *noun*
la **ortografía** *fem*
a spelling mistake una falta de ortografía
• **spelling checker** el corrector ortográfico

⚷ to **spend** *verb*
1 (*money*) **gastar** [17]
I've spent all my money. Me he gastado todo el dinero.
2 (*time*) **pasar** [17]
We spent three days in Barcelona. Pasamos tres días en Barcelona.
She spends her time surfing the web. Pasa el tiempo navegando la web.

spice *noun*
la **especia** *fem*

spicy *adjective*
picante *masc & fem*
I don't like spicy food. No me gustan los platos picantes.

spider *noun*
la **araña** *fem*

to **spill** *verb*
derramar [17]
I've spilled beer on the table. He derramado cerveza en la mesa.

spinach *noun*
las **espinacas** *plural fem*
Do you like spinach? ¿Te gustan las espinacas?

spire *noun*
la **aguja** *fem*

spirit *noun*
to get into the spirit of the occasion entrar [17] en el ambiente

spirits *plural noun*
1 *(alcohol)* las **bebidas alcohólicas**
2 *(showing mood)* **to be in good spirits** estar **[2]** de buen humor

to **spit** *verb*
escupir [19]
to spit something out escupir algo

spite *noun*
1 **in spite of something** *(despite)* a pesar de algo
In spite of everything, we went. A pesar de todo, fuimos.
2 *(nastiness)* la **maldad** *fem*
to do something out of spite hacer **[7]** algo por maldad

spiteful *adjective*
1 *(person)* **malo** *masc*, **mala** *fem*
2 *(comment)* **malicioso** *masc*, **maliciosa** *fem*

splash *noun* ▷ see **splash** *verb*
1 *(in the water)* **He fell in the water with a splash.** Hizo plaf al caer al agua.
2 *(of colour)* **a splash of colour** un toque de color

to **splash** *verb* ▷ see **splash** *noun*
salpicar [31]

splendid *adjective*
espléndido *masc*, **espléndida** *fem*
They made us a splendid meal. Nos prepararon una comida espléndida.

splinter *noun*
la **astilla** *fem*

to **split** *verb*
1 *(with an axe, a knife)* **partir [19]**
to split a piece of wood partir un trozo de madera
2 *(to come apart)* **rajarse [17]**
The lining has split. El forro se ha rajado.
3 *(to divide up)* **dividirse [19]**
They split the money between them. Se dividieron el dinero entre ellos.
• **to split up**
1 *(married couple, group)* **separarse [17]**
2 **She's split up with her boyfriend.** Ha roto con su novio.

to **spoil** *verb*
1 **arruinar [17]**
It completely spoiled the evening. Arruinó la tarde completamente.
to spoil the surprise arruinar la sorpresa
2 *(food)* **estropear [17]**
3 *(a child)* **malcriar [32]**

spoiled *adjective*
malcriado *masc*, **malcriada** *fem*
a spoiled child un niño malcriado

spoilsport *noun*
el & la **aguafiestas** *masc & fem* (*pl:* **aguafiestas**)

spokesperson *noun*
el & la **portavoz** *masc & fem*, *fem pl:* las **portavoces**

sponge *noun*
la **esponja** *fem*
• **sponge cake** el bizcocho

sponsor *noun* ▷ see **sponsor** *verb*
el **patrocinador** *masc*, la **patrocinadora** *fem*

to **sponsor** *verb* ▷ see **sponsor** *noun*
patrocinar [17]

spooky *adjective*
espeluznante *masc & fem*

spoon *noun*
la **cuchara** *fem*
a soup spoon una cuchara sopera
a teaspoon una cucharilla

spoonful *noun*
1 *(large)* la **cucharada** *fem*
2 *(small)* la **cucharadita** *fem*

sport *noun*
el **deporte** *masc*
my favourite sport mi deporte favorito
to be good at sport tener **[9]** facilidad para los deportes
Do you do any sports? ¿Practicas algún deporte?

sports bag *noun*
la **bolsa de deportes**

sports car *noun*
el **coche deportivo**

sports centre *noun*
el **polideportivo** *masc*

sports club *noun*
el **club deportivo**

sportsman *noun*
el **deportista** *masc*
amateur sportsmen deportistas amateurs

sportswear *noun*
la **ropa de deporte**

sportswoman *noun*
la **deportista** *fem*
She's a professional sportswoman. Es deportista profesional.

spot *noun* ▷ see **spot** *verb*
1 (*in fabric*) el **lunar** *masc*
a red tie with black spots una corbata roja con lunares negros
2 (*on your skin*) el **grano** *masc*
I've got spots. Tengo granos.
to be covered in spots estar [2] cubierto de granos
3 (*stain*) la **mancha** *fem*
4 (*place*) el **sitio** *masc*
a beautiful spot un sitio precioso
5 (*spotlight*) el **foco** *masc*, (*in the home*) la **luz direccional**

to **spot** *verb* ▷ see **spot** *noun*
1 (*a person, an object*) **divisar** [17]
I spotted her in the crowd. La divisé entre la multitud.
2 (*an error*) **encontrar** [24]

spotlight *noun*
1 (*in a theatre, etc*) el **foco** *masc*
2 (*in the home*) la **luz direccional**

spotty *adjective*
(*pimply*) **lleno de granos** *masc*, **llena de granos** *fem*

sprain *noun* ▷ see **sprain** *verb*
el **esguince** *masc*

to **sprain** *verb* ▷ see **sprain** *noun*
to sprain your ankle hacerse [7] un esguince en el tobillo

spray *noun*
1 (*of seawater*) la **espuma** *fem*
2 (*spray can*) el **espray** *masc*

to **spread** *verb*
1 (*news, diseases*) **propagarse** [28]
2 (*jam, cement, glue*) **extender** [36]

spring *noun*
1 (*the season*) la **primavera** *fem*
in the spring en primavera
spring flowers flores de primavera
2 (*in a chair, etc*) el **muelle** *masc*
3 (*giving water*) el **manantial** *masc*

springtime *noun*
la **primavera** *fem*
in springtime en primavera

spring water *noun*
el **agua de manantial**

WORD TIP *agua* takes *el* or *un* in the singular even though it is *fem*.

sprint *noun* ▷ see **sprint** *verb*
el **esprint** *masc*

to **sprint** *verb* ▷ see **sprint** *noun*
correr [18] **a toda velocidad**
She sprinted after the thief. Salió corriendo a toda velocidad tras el ladrón.

sprout *noun*
(*Brussels sprout*) el **col de Bruselas**

spy *noun* ▷ see **spy** *verb*
el & la **espía** *masc & fem*

to **spy** *verb* ▷ see **spy** *noun*
to spy on somebody espiar [32] a alguien

spying *noun*
el **espionaje** *masc*

🔑 **square** *adjective* ▷ see **square** *noun*
cuadrado *masc*, **cuadrada** *fem*
a square box una caja cuadrada
three square metres tres metros cuadrados
The room is five metres square. La habitación tiene cinco metros cuadrados.

🔑 **square** *noun* ▷ see **square** *adj*
1 (*shape*) el **cuadrado** *masc*
2 (*in a town*) la **plaza** *fem*
the main square la plaza mayor
in the village square en la plaza del pueblo

squash *noun*
1 (*drink*) **lemon squash** la limonada
orange squash la naranjada
2 (*sport*) el **squash** *masc*
to play squash jugar [27] al squash

to **squeak** *verb*
1 (*doors, hinges*) **chirriar** [32]
2 (*people, animals*) **chillar** [17]

to **squeeze** *verb*
1 (*someone's hand, a tube*) **apretar** [29]
2 (*a lemon, an orange*) **exprimir** [19]

squid *noun*
el **calamar** *masc*

squirrel *noun*
la **ardilla** *fem*

to **stab** *verb*
apuñalar [17]

stable *adjective* ▷ see **stable** *noun*
estable *masc & fem*

stable *noun* ▷ see **stable** *adj*
la **cuadra** *fem*

stack *noun*
(*pile*) el **montón** *masc*
stacks of something montones de algo
She's got stacks of CDs. Tiene montones de compactos.

stadium *noun*
el **estadio** *masc*
a football stadium un estadio de fútbol

staff *noun*
1 (*of a company*) el **personal** *masc*
2 (*in a school*) el **profesorado** *masc*

stage *noun*
1 (*in a theatre, etc*) el **escenario** *masc*
to come on stage salir [63] al escenario
2 (*phase*) la **etapa** *fem*
the first stage of the project la primera etapa del proyecto
3 **At this stage it's hard to know.** A estas alturas es difícil saberlo.

stain *noun* ▷ see **stain** *verb*
la **mancha** *fem*

to **stain** *verb* ▷ see **stain** *noun*
manchar [17]

stainless steel *noun*
el **acero inoxidable**
a stainless steel knife un cuchillo de acero inoxidable

stair *noun*
1 (*step*) el **escalón** *masc*
2 **stairs** las escaleras
I met her on the stairs. Me la encontré en las escaleras.

staircase *noun*
las **escaleras** *plural fem*
a spiral staircase una escalera de caracol

stale *adjective*
1 (*bread*) **duro** *masc*, **dura** *fem*
2 (*news*) **añejo** *masc*, **añeja** *fem*

stalemate *noun*
(*in chess*) las **tablas** *plural fem*

stall *noun*
1 (*at markets, fairs*) el **puesto** *masc*
2 (*in a theatre*) **the stalls** el patio de butacas

to **stamp** *verb* ▷ see **stamp** *noun*
1 (*a letter*) **poner** [11] **sello(s) a**
2 (*a ticket, passport*) **sellar** [17]
3 **to stamp your foot** dar [4] una patada en el suelo

stamp *noun* ▷ see **stamp** *verb*
el **sello** *masc*
- **stamp album** el álbum de sellos
- **stamp collection** la colección de sellos

to **stand** *verb*
1 **estar** [2] **de pie**
They were standing. Estaban de pie.
We were standing outside the cinema. Estabamos delante del cine.
I'm standing here waiting for you. Estoy aquí esperándote.
2 **to stand on something** pisar [17] algo
You're standing on my foot. Me estás pisando.
3 (*to bear*) **soportar** [17]
I can't stand her. No la soporto.
I can't stand waiting. No soporto esperar.
- **to stand for something**
significar [31]
What does 'plc' stand for? ¿Qué significa 'plc'?
- **stand up**
ponerse [11] **de pie**
Everybody stood up. Todo el mundo se puso de pie.

standard *adjective* ▷ see **standard** *noun*
estándar *masc & fem*
the standard price el precio estándar

standard *noun* ▷ see **standard** *adj*
el **nivel** *masc*
the standard of living el nivel de vida

Standard grades *plural noun*
(*Exámenes escoceses que se realizan alrededor de los 16 años y que pueden abarcar hasta 7 asignaturas. Se califican desde 1 (nota máxima) hasta 7 (por haber terminado el curso). Muchos alumnos continúan estudiando para los Highers y Advanced Highers después de hacer los Standard grades.*)
▷ **Highers**

stands *noun*
(*in stadiums*) la **tribuna** *fem*

staple *noun* ▷ see **staple** *verb*
la **grapa** *fem*

to **staple** *verb* ▷ see **staple** *noun*
grapar [17]
to staple the pages together grapar las hojas

stapler *noun*
la **grapadora** *fem*

star *noun* ▷ see **star** *verb*
la **estrella** *fem*
She's our star pupil. Es nuestra alumna estrella.
a star performance una actuación estelar
He's a film star. Es una estrella de cine.

to **star** *verb* ▷ see **star** *noun*
to star in a film protagonizar [22] una película

to **stare** *verb*
mirar [17] **fijamente**
He was staring at me. Me estaba mirando fijamente.
What are you staring at? ¿Qué miras?

star sign *noun*
el **signo del zodíaco**
What star sign are you? ¿De qué signo eres?

start *noun* ▷ see **start** *verb*
1 (*in general*) el **principio** *masc*
at the start al principio
at the start of the film al principio de la película
from the start desde el principio
We knew from the start that it was going to be difficult. Sabíamos desde el principio que iba a ser difícil.
2 **to make a start on something** empezar [25] algo
I've made a start on my essay. He empezado mi trabajo.
3 (*of a race*) la **salida** *fem*

to **start** *verb* ▷ see **start** *noun*
1 (*in general*) **empezar [25]**
The film starts at eight. La película empieza a las ocho.
I've started the book. He empezado el libro.
2 **to start doing something** empezar [25] a hacer algo
I've started learning Spanish. He empezado a aprender español.
3 **to start a business** montar [17] un negocio
4 (*cars*) **arrancar [31]**
She started the car. Arrancó el coche.
The car wouldn't start. El coche no arrancaba.

starter *noun*
(*for a meal*) el **entrante** *masc*
What would you like as a starter? ¿Qué quieres de entrante?

to **starve** *verb*
morirse [55] de hambre
Thousands are starving. Miles de personas se están muriendo de hambre!
I'm starving! ¡Me muero de hambre!

state *noun* ▷ see **state** *verb*
1 (*condition*) el **estado** *masc*
The house is in a very bad state. La casa está en muy mal estado.
2 (*administrative*) el **estado** *masc*
the state el estado
3 (*USA*) **the States** (los) Estados Unidos
They live in the States. Viven en Estados Unidos.

to **state** *verb* ▷ see **state** *noun*
1 (*your intention, an opinion*) **declarar [17]**
2 (*your address, income, occupation, a reason*) **indicar [31]**

statement *noun*
la **declaración** *fem*

station *noun*
1 (*for buses, trains*) la **estación** *fem*
the railway station la estación de trenes
the bus station la estación de autobuses
2 **the police station** la comisaría
3 **a radio station** una emisora de radio
a TV station un canal de televisión

stationary *adjective*
estacionario *masc*, **estacionaria** *fem*

stationer's *noun*
la **papelería** *fem*

stationery *noun*
los **artículos de papelería**

statistics *noun*
1 (*subject*) la **estadística** *fem*
2 (*figures*) **the statistics** las estadísticas

statue *noun*
la **estatua** *fem*

status *noun*
el **estatus** *masc*

stay *noun* ▷ see **stay** *verb*
la **estancia** *fem*
our stay in Alicante nuestra estancia en Alicante
Enjoy your stay! ¡Que disfruten de su estancia!

to **stay** *verb* ▷ see **stay** *noun*
1 **quedarse [17]**
I'll stay here. Me quedaré aquí.
How long are you staying? ¿Cuánto tiempo te quedas?
to stay with somebody quedarse [17] con alguien
I'm going to stay with my sister this weekend. Me voy a quedar con mi hermana este fin de semana.
Can you stay the night? ¿Podéis quedaros a dormir?
2 (*to spend time*) **We're going to stay in Málaga for three days.** Vamos a pasar tres días en Málaga.
3 (*temporarily*) **hospedarse [17]**
Where are you staying? ¿Dónde te hospedas?
• **to stay in**
no salir [63]
I'm staying in tonight. Esta noche no salgo.

English–Spanish

steady *adjective*
1 **estable** *masc & fem*
a steady job un trabajo estable
2 **constante**
a steady increase un incremento constante
3 (*hand, voice*) **firme** *masc & fem*
4 **to hold something steady** sostener [9] algo firmemente

steak *noun*
el **filete** *masc*, el **bistec** *masc*
steak and chips bistec con patatas fritas

to **steal** *verb*
robar [17]
He stole them from me. Me los robó.

steam *noun*
el **vapor** *masc*
• **steam engine** la locomotora de vapor
• **steam iron** la plancha a vapor

steel *noun*
el **acero** *masc*

steep *adjective*
empinado *masc*, **empinada** *fem*
a steep slope una cuesta empinada

steeple *noun*
1 (*spire*) la **aguja** *fem*
2 (*tower*) el **campanario** *masc*

steering wheel *noun*
el **volante** *masc*

step *noun*
1 (*footstep*) el **paso** *masc*
to take a step forwards dar [4] un paso hacia adelante
2 (*stair*) el **escalón** *masc*
'Mind the step.' 'Cuidado con el escalón.'
• **to step back**
retroceder [18]
• **to step forward**
avanzar [22]
• **to step into**
(*a lift*) **entrar** [17] **en**

stepbrother *noun*
el **hermanastro** *masc*

stepdaughter *noun*
la **hijastra** *fem*

stepfather *noun*
el **padrastro** *masc*

stepladder *noun*
la **escalera de mano**

stepmother *noun*
la **madrastra** *fem*

stepsister *noun*
la **hermanastra** *fem*

stepson *noun*
el **hijastro** *masc*

stereo *noun*
el **estéreo** *masc*
• **stereo system** el equipo de música

sterling *noun*
la **libra esterlina**
We paid in sterling. Pagamos en libras esterlinas.

stew *noun*
el **estofado** *masc*

steward *noun*
el **camarero** *masc*

stewardess *noun*
la **camarera** *fem*

stick *noun* ▷ see **stick** *verb*
el **palo** *masc*
a walking stick un bastón

to **stick** *verb* ▷ see **stick** *noun*
1 (*with glue*) **pegar** [28]
I stuck it in my note book. Lo pegué en mi cuaderno.
2 (*to put*) **poner** [11]
Stick them on my desk. Ponlos en mi mesa.

sticker *noun*
la **pegatina** *fem*

sticky *adjective*
1 (*covered with glue*) **pegajoso** *masc*, **pegajosa** *fem*
My hands are sticky. Tengo las manos pegajosas.
2 (*adhesive*) **adhesivo** *masc*, **adhesiva** *fem*
sticky paper papel adhesivo
• **sticky tape** la cinta adhesiva

stiff *adjective*
to feel stiff estar [2] entumecido
to have stiff legs tener [9] las piernas entumecidas
to have a stiff neck tener [9] tortícolis

still *adjective* ▷ see **still** *adv*
1 **quieto** *masc*, **quieta** *fem*
Sit still! ¡Siéntate quieto!
Keep still! ¡Estate quieto!
Keep it still. No lo muevas.
2 (*mineral water*) sin gas

still *adverb* ▷ see **still** *adj*
todavía, **aún**
He's still sleeping. T odavía está durmiendo.
There's still a lot of beer left. Todavía queda

a b c d e f g h i j k l m n o p q r s t u v w x y z

mucha cerveza.
Do you still live in London? ¿Vives todavía en Londres?, ¿Vives aún en Londres?
I've still not finished. Todavía no he terminado, Aún no he terminado.

sting *noun* ▷ see **sting** *verb*
la **picadura** *fem*
wasp stings picaduras de avispa

to **sting** *verb* ▷ see **sting** *noun*
picar [31]
I was stung by a bee. Me picó una abeja.

stink *noun* ▷ see **stink** *verb*
la **peste** *fem*
What a stink! ¡Qué peste!

to **stink** *verb* ▷ see **stink** *noun*
apestar [17]
It stinks of cigarette smoke in here. Aquí apesta a tabaco.

to **stir** *verb*
remover [38]

stitch *noun*
1 (*in sewing*) la **puntada** *fem*
2 (*in knitting*) el **punto** *masc*
3 (*surgical*) el **punto de sutura**

to **stock** *verb* ▷ see **stock** *noun*
(*in a shop*) **vender** [18]
They don't stock dictionaries. No venden diccionarios.

stock *noun* ▷ see **stock** *verb*
1 (*in a shop*) el **estock** *masc*
to have something in stock tener [9] algo en estock
2 (*supply*) la **reserva** *fem*
I always have a stock of pencils. Siempre tengo una reserva de lápices.
3 (*for cooking*) el **caldo** *masc*
chicken stock caldo de pollo
• **stock cube** la pastilla de caldo
• **stock exchange** la bolsa de valores

stocking *noun*
la **media (de liguero)**

⚷ **stomach** *noun*
el **estómago** *masc*
The fish upset my stomach. El pescado me sentó mal al estómago.

⚷ **stomachache** *noun*
el **dolor de estómago**
to have stomachache tener [9] dolor de estómago
Dominic had stomachache. Dominic tenía dolor de estómago.

stone *noun*
1 la **piedra** *fem*
a stone wall una pared de piedra
to throw a stone tirar [17] una piedra
2 (*in fruit*) el **hueso** *masc*

stool *noun*
el **taburete** *masc*

⚷ **stop** *noun* ▷ see **stop** *verb*
la **parada** *fem*
the bus stop la parada de autobús
He gets off at the next stop. Se baja en la próxima parada.

⚷ to **stop** *verb* ▷ see **stop** *noun*
1 (*people, vehicles*) **parar** [17]
He stopped in front of the shop. Paró enfrente de la tienda.
Does the train stop in Cordoba? ¿Para el tren en Córdoba?
The music stopped. La música paró.
2 (*to stop working*) **pararse** [17]
The engine stopped. El motor se paró.
3 **to stop something, somebody** parar [17] algo, a alguien
Stop the engine. Para el motor.
She stopped me in the street. Me paró en la calle.
4 **to stop doing something** dejar [17] de hacer algo
He's stopped smoking. Ha dejado de fumar.
She never stops asking questions. Nunca deja de hacer preguntas.
5 **to stop somebody doing something** impedir [57] a alguien hacer algo
There's nothing to stop you going on your own. Nada te impide ir solo.

stopwatch *noun*
el **cronómetro** *masc*

store *noun* ▷ see **store** *verb*
(*shop*) la **tienda** *fem*

to **store** *verb* ▷ see **store** *noun*
1 (*to keep*) **guardar** [17]
2 (*on a computer*) **almacenar** [17]

storey *noun*
el **piso** *masc*
a three-storey house una casa de tres pisos

stork *noun*
la **cigüeña** *fem*

⚷ **storm** *noun*
la **tormenta** *fem*
a snowstorm una tormenta de nieve
a rainstorm una tormenta de lluvia

stormy *adjective*
tormentoso *masc*, **tormentosa** *fem*

♪ **story** *noun*
1 la **historia** *fem*
to tell a story contar [24] una historia
the story of her life la historia de su vida
2 (*tale*) el **cuento** *masc*

stove *noun*
1 (*cooker*) la **cocina** *fem*
2 (*heater*) la **estufa** *fem*

♪ **straight** *adjective* ▷ see **straight** *adv*
1 **recto** *masc*, **recta** *fem*
a straight line una línea recta
2 to have straight hair tener [9] el pelo liso
3 (*not crooked*) **derecho** *masc*, **derecha** *fem*
Put it straight. Ponlo derecho.

♪ **straight** *adverb* ▷ see **straight** *adj*
1 (*in direction*) **recto**
Go straight ahead. Sigue todo recto.
2 (*in time*) **directamente**
He went straight to the doctor's. Fue directamente al médico.
Come straight home after the film. Vuelve enseguida a casa cuando termine la película.
straight away en seguida

strain *noun* ▷ see **strain** *verb*
la **tensión** *fem*

to **strain** *verb* ▷ see **strain** *noun*
1 (*the vegetables, rice*) **colar** [17]
2 (*a muscle*) **hacerse** [7] **un esguince en**

strange *adjective*
extraño *masc*, **extraña** *fem*
a strange situation una situación extraña

♪ **stranger** *noun*
el **desconocido** *masc*, la **desconocida** *fem*
Don't speak to strangers. No hables con desconocidos.

to **strangle** *verb*
estrangular [17]

strap *noun*
1 (*on a handbag, a watch*) la **correa** *fem*
a watchstrap una correa de reloj
2 (*on a shoe*) la **tira** *fem*
3 (*for clothing*) el **tirante** *masc*

straw *noun*
1 la **paja** *fem*
a straw hat un sombrero de paja
2 a drinking straw una pajita

♪ **strawberry** *noun*
la **fresa** *fem*
strawberry jam mermelada de fresa
a strawberry milkshake un batido de fresa

stream *noun*
el **arroyo** *masc*

♪ **street** *noun*
la **calle** *fem*
I met Simon in the street. Me encontré con Simon en la calle.
- **streetlamp** el farol
- **street map** el plano de la ciudad
- **streetwise** avispado *masc*, avispada *fem*

strength *noun*
la **fuerza** *fem*

stress *noun* ▷ see **stress** *verb*
1 (*in general*) la **tensión** *fem*
2 (*Grammar*) el **acento** *masc*

to **stress** *verb* ▷ see **stress** *noun*
recalcar [31]
to stress the importance of something recalcar la importancia de algo

to **stretch** *verb*
(*clothes, shoes*) **dar** [4] **de sí**
This jumper has stretched. Este jersey ha dado de sí.

stretcher *noun*
la **camilla**

strict *adjective*
estricto *masc*, **estricta** *fem*

strike *noun* ▷ see **strike** *verb*
la **huelga** *fem*
to go on strike ponerse [11] en huelga
to be on strike estar [2] en huelga

to **strike** *verb* ▷ see **strike** *noun*
1 (*to hit*) **golpear** [17]
2 (*clocks*) **dar** [4]
The clock struck six. El reloj dio las seis.
3 (*to go on strike*) **ponerse** [11] **en huelga**

striker *noun*
1 (*in football*) el **delantero** *masc*, la **delantera** *fem*
2 (*striking worker*) el & la **huelguista** *masc & fem*

string *noun*
1 (*for parcels, etc*) el **cordel** *masc*
2 (*for a musical instrument*) la **cuerda** *fem*

to **strip** *verb* ▷ see **strip** *noun*
(*to undress*) **desnudarse** [17]

strip *noun* ▷ see **strip** *verb*
la **tira** *fem*
- **strip cartoon** la tira cómica

stripe *noun*
la **raya** *fem*

striped *adjective*
de rayas
a striped shirt una camisa de rayas

stroke *noun* ▷ see **stroke** *verb*
1 (*in swimming*) la **brazada** *fem*
2 (*Medicine*) el **derrame cerebral**
to have a stroke sufrir [19] un derrame cerebral

to **stroke** *verb* ▷ see **stroke** *noun*
acariciar [17]

strong *adjective*
1 (*in general*) **fuerte** *masc & fem*
2 (*material*) **resistente** *masc & fem*
3 (*accent*) **marcado** *masc*, **marcada** *fem*
a strong Welsh accent un marcado acento galés

struggle *noun* ▷ see **struggle** *verb*
1 (*fight*) la **lucha** *fem*
a power struggle una lucha por el poder
the struggle for independence la lucha por la independencia
2 (*difficult time*) **It's been a struggle.** Ha sido muy difícil.

to **struggle** *verb* ▷ see **struggle** *noun*
1 (*violently*) **forcejear** [17]
She struggled with the two robbers. Forcejeó con los dos ladrones.
2 (*to do something*) **luchar** [17]
They have struggled to survive. Han luchado para sobrevivir.
3 (*to find it difficult*) **I'm struggling to finish my homework.** Me cuesta terminar mis deberes.

stubborn *adjective*
terco *masc*, **terca** *fem*

stuck *adjective*
(*jammed*) **atascado** *masc*, **atascada** *fem*
The drawer's stuck. El cajón está atascado.

stud *noun*
1 (*on a belt, jacket*) la **tachuela** *fem*
2 (*on a boot*) el **taco** *masc*
3 (*earring*) el **pendiente de bolita**

student *noun*
el & la **estudiante** *masc & fem*
She's a medical student. Es estudiante de medicina.

studio *noun*
el **estudio** *masc*
• **studio flat** el estudio

to **study** *verb*
estudiar [17]
He's studying for his exams. Está estudiando para los exámenes.
She's studying medicine. Estudia medicina.

stuff *noun* ▷ see **stuff** *verb*
1 (*things*) las **cosas** *plural fem*
We can put all this stuff in the attic. Podemos poner todas estas cosas en el desván.
You can leave your stuff at my house. Puedes dejar tus cosas en mi casa.
2 (*substance*) la **cosa** *fem*

to **stuff** *verb* ▷ see **stuff** *noun*
1 (*to shove*) **meter** [18]
She stuffed her things into her backpack. Metió sus cosas en su mochila.
2 (*Cooking*) **rellenar** [17]
stuffed aubergines berenjenas rellenas

stuffing *noun*
(*Cooking*) el **relleno** *masc*

stuffy *adjective*
(*atmosphere*) **viciado** *masc*, **viciada** *fem*
It's very stuffy in here. Aquí dentro falta aire.

stunned *adjective*
1 (*dazed*) **aturdido** *masc*, **aturdida** *fem*
2 (*amazed*) **atónito** *masc*, **atónita** *fem*

stunning *adjective*
sensacional *masc & fem*

stunt *noun*
(*in films*) la **escena peligrosa**

stupid *adjective*
estúpido *masc*, **estúpida** *fem*
a stupid man un hombre estúpido
That was really stupid. Eso fue una verdadera estupidez.
to do something stupid hacer [7] una estupidez
He did something stupid and deleted it. Hizo una estupidez y lo borró.
Stop acting stupid. Deja de hacerte el tonto.
Don't be stupid! ¡No seas tonto!

stutter *noun* ▷ see **stutter** *verb*
to have a stutter tartamudear [17]

to **stutter** *verb* ▷ see **stutter** *noun*
tartamudear [17]

style *noun*
1 (*way*) el **estilo** *masc*
a style of living un estilo de vida
He has his own style. Tiene su propio estilo.
2 (*fashion*) la **moda** *fem*
It's the latest style. Es la última moda.

♪ **subject** *noun*
1 *(of a conversation, etc)* el **tema** *masc*
the subject of my talk el tema de mi charla
2 *(at school)* la **asignatura** *fem*
My favourite subject is biology. Mi asignatura favorita es la biología.

submarine *noun*
el **submarino** *masc*

subscription *noun*
la **suscripción** *fem*
to take out a subscription to something suscribirse **[52]** a algo

subsidy *noun*
la **subvención** *fem*

substance *noun*
la **sustancia** *fem*

substitute *noun* ▷ see **substitute** *verb*
1 *(person)* el **sustituto** *masc*, la **sustituta** *fem*
2 *(ingredient)* el **sucedáneo** *masc*

to **substitute** *verb* ▷ see **substitute** *noun*
sustituir [54]

♪ **subtitled** *adjective*
(film) **subtitulado** *masc*, **subtitulada** *fem*

♪ **subtitles** *plural noun*
los **subtítulos** *plural masc*

to **subtract** *verb*
restar [17]

♪ **suburb** *noun*
el **barrio residencial de las afueras**
a suburb of Edinburgh un barrio residencial de las afueras de Edimburgo
in the suburbs of London en los barrios residenciales de las afueras de Londres

subway *noun*
1 *(underpass)* el **paso subterráneo**
2 *(underground railway)* el **métro**

to **succeed** *verb*
1 *(to manage)* **lograr [17]**
to succeed in doing something lograr hacer algo
We've succeeded in contacting her. Hemos logrado contactar con ella.
2 *(to be successful)* **tener [9] éxito**
to succeed in life tener éxito en la vida

success *noun*
el **éxito** *masc*
a great success un gran éxito

successful *adjective*
1 **de éxito**
He's a successful singer. Es un cantante de mucho éxito.
2 **to be successful in doing something** lograr **[17]** hacer algo

successfully *adverb*
satisfactoriamente

such *adjective, adverb*
1 **tan**
I've had such a busy day! ¡He tenido un día tan ocupado!
It's such a long way. Queda tan lejos.
It's such a pity. Es una verdadera lástima.
They're such nice people! ¡Son gente tan simpática!
How could he say such a thing? ¿Cómo pudo decir tal cosa?
There's no such thing. No hay tal cosa.
2 **such a lot of** tantos, *fem* tantas
I've got such a lot of things to tell you! ¡Tengo tantas cosas que contarte!
3 **such as** como
in big cities such as Glasgow en grandes ciudades como Glasgow

to **suck** *verb*
chupar [17]

♪ **sudden** *adjective*
repentino *masc*, **repentina** *fem*
a sudden death una muerte repentina
all of a sudden de repente

♪ **suddenly** *adverb*
de repente
to die suddenly morir **[55]** de repente
He suddenly started to laugh. De repente empezó a reír.
Suddenly the light went out. De repente se apagó la luz.

suede *noun*
el **ante** *masc*
a suede jacket una chaqueta de ante

to **suffer** *verb*
sufrir [19]

♪ **sugar** *noun*
el & la **azúcar** *masc or fem*
brown sugar azúcar morena
Would you like sugar? ¿Quieres azúcar?

to **suggest** *verb*
sugerir [14]
I suggest you go. Sugiero que vayas tú.

suggestion *noun*
la **sugerencia** *fem*
to make a suggestion hacer **[7]** una sugerencia

suicide *noun*
el **suicidio** *masc*
to commit suicide suicidarse **[17]**

suit *noun*
1 (*man's*) el **traje** *masc*
2 (*woman's*) el **traje de chaqueta**

suitable *adjective*
1 **adecuado** *masc*, **adecuada** *fem*
a suitable hotel un hotel adecuado
to be suitable for someone, something ser [1] adecuado para alguien, algo
It's not suitable for minors. No es adecuado para los menores de edad.
It's suitable for dry-cleaning. Es adecuado para el lavado en seco.
2 (*clothing*) **apropiado** *masc*, **apropiada** *fem*
I don't have any suitable shoes. No tengo zapatos apropiados.

suitcase *noun*
la **maleta** *fem*

to **sulk** *verb*
enfurruñarse [17]

sum *noun*
la **suma** *fem*
a large sum of money una suma importante de dinero
- **to sum up**
resumir [19]

to **summarize** *verb*
resumir [19]

summary *noun*
el **resumen** *masc*

summer *noun*
el **verano** *masc*
in summer en verano
summer clothes la ropa de verano
the summer holidays las vacaciones de verano
We spent the summer holidays in Mallorca. Pasamos las vacaciones de verano en Mallorca.

summertime *noun*
el **verano** *masc*
in summertime en verano

summit *noun*
la **cumbre** *fem*

sun *noun*
el **sol** *masc*
to sit in the sun sentarse [29] al sol
The sun's in my eyes. Me da el sol en los ojos.
- **sunbathe** tomar [17] el sol
- **sunblock** el filtro solar
- **sunburn** la quemadura solar

sunburned *adjective*
1 (*tanned*) **moreno** *masc*, **morena** *fem*
2 (*Medicine*) **to get sunburned** quemarse [17]

Sunday *noun*
el **domingo** *masc*
on Sunday el domingo
I'm going out on Sunday. Voy a salir el domingo.
See you on Sunday! ¡Hasta el domingo!
on Sundays los domingos
The museum is closed on Sundays. El museo cierra los domingos.
every Sunday todos los domingos
last Sunday el domingo pasado
next Sunday el próximo domingo

WORD TIP Months of the year and days of the week start with small letters in Spanish.

sunflower *noun*
el **girasol** *masc*
sunflower oil el aceite de girasol

sunglasses *plural noun*
las **gafas de sol**

sunlight *noun*
la **luz del sol**

sunny *adjective*
1 (*day*) **a sunny day** un día de sol
It's going to be sunny. Va a hacer sol.
2 (*place*) **soleado** *masc*, **soleada** *fem*
in a sunny room en una habitación soleada
There will be sunny intervals and scattered showers. Habrá intervalos soleados y chubascos aislados.

sunrise *noun*
la **salida del sol**
at sunrise al amanecer

sunroof *noun*
el **techo solar**

sunset *noun*
la **puesta de sol**
at sunset al atardecer

sunshine *noun*
el **sol** *masc*
in the sunshine al sol

sunstroke *noun*
la **insolación** *fem*
to get sunstroke coger [3] una insolación

suntan *noun*
el **bronceado** *masc*
to get a suntan broncearse [17]
- **suntan lotion** la loción bronceadora
- **suntan oil** el aceite bronceador

English–Spanish
a b c d e f g h i j k l m n o p q r s t u v w x y z

English–Spanish

super *adjective*
genial *masc & fem*
We had a super time! ¡Lo pasamos genial!

supermarket *noun*
el **supermercado** *masc*
an all-night supermarket un supermercado que está abierto toda la noche

supernatural *adjective*
supernatural *masc & fem*

superstitious *adjective*
supersticioso *masc*, **supersticiosa** *fem*

to **supervise** *verb*
supervisar [17]

supervisor *noun*
el **supervisor** *masc*, la **supervisora** *fem*

supper *noun*
la **cena** *fem*
I had supper at Sandy's. Cené en casa de Sandy.
We had eggs and bacon for supper. Cenamos huevos y tocino.

supplement *noun*
el **suplemento** *masc*

supplies *plural noun*
(*of food*) las **provisiones** *plural fem*

to **supply** *verb*
suministrar [17]
The school supplies the books. El colegio suministra los libros.
to supply somebody with something suministrar algo a alguien
The farm supplies us with eggs and milk. La granja nos suministra huevos y leche.

supply *noun* ▷ see **supply** *verb*
1 las **reservas** *plural fem*
We have a good supply of coal. Tenemos reservas abundantes de carbón.
2 **to be in short supply** escasear [17]
Oil is in short supply. Escasea el petróleo.
• **supply teacher** el profesor suplente, la profesora suplente

support *noun* ▷ see **support** *verb*
el **apoyo** *masc*
He has a lot of support. Tiene mucho apoyo.

to **support** *verb* ▷ see **support** *noun*
1 (*to back up*) **apoyar** [17]
Her parents have really supported her. Sus padres la han apoyado mucho.
2 (*a team*) **ser** [1] **hincha de**
Graeme supports Manchester. Graeme es hincha del Manchester.
3 (*with money*) **to support a family** mantener [9] una familia

supporter *noun*
el & la **hincha** *masc & fem*
a Chelsea supporter un hincha del Chelsea

to **suppose** *verb*
suponer [11]
I suppose she is coming. Supongo que sí viene.

supposed *adjective*
to be supposed to do something tener [9] que hacer algo
You're supposed to wear a helmet. Tienes que usar casco.
He was supposed to be here at six. Tenía que estar aquí a las seis.

sure *adjective*
1 **seguro** *masc*, **segura** *fem*
I'm sure she'll come soon. Estoy seguro de que vendrá pronto.
Are you sure? ¿Estás seguro?
Are you sure you have enough money? ¿Seguro que tienes suficiente dinero?
Are you sure you saw her? ¿Estás seguro de que la viste?
2 **Sure!** ¡Claro!
'Can you shut the door?'—"Sure!' '¿Puedes cerrar la puerta?'—"¡Por supuesto!'

surely *adverb*
Surely she couldn't have forgotten! ¡No es posible que se haya olvidado!

WORD TIP *no es posible que* is followed by a verb in the subjunctive.

surf *noun* ▷ see **surf** *verb*
la **espuma** *fem*

to **surf** *verb* ▷ see **surf** *noun*
1 (*in the sea*) **hacer** [7] **surfing**
2 (*on the Net*) **navegar** [28]

surface *noun*
la **superficie** *fem*

surfboard *noun*
la **tabla de surf**

surfer *noun*
1 (*in the sea*) el & la **surfista** *masc & fem*
2 (*on the Net*) el & la **internauta** *masc & fem*

a b c d e f g h i j k l m n o p q r s t u v w x y z

surfing *noun*
el **surfing** *masc*
to go surfing hacer [7] surfing

surgeon *noun*
el **cirujano** *masc*, la **cirujana** *fem*
She's a surgeon. Es cirujana.

surgery *noun*
1 (*treatment*) la **cirugía** *fem*
laser surgery cirugía láser
to have surgery operarse [17]
2 (*doctors' offices*) el **consultorio** *masc*
the dentist's surgery la consulta del dentista

ℰ **surname** *noun*
el **apellido** *masc*
Her second surname is López. Su segundo apellido es López.

surprise *noun*
la **sorpresa** *fem*
What a surprise! ¡Qué sorpresa!

surprised *adjective*
sorprendido *masc*, **sorprendida** *fem*
We were surprised to see her. Nos sorprendió verla.
I'm surprised they arrived so early. Me sorprende que hayan llegado tan temprano.

ℰ **surprising** *adjective*
sorprendente *masc & fem*

surrender *noun* ▷ see **surrender** *verb*
la **rendición** *fem*

to **surrender** *verb* ▷ see **surrender** *noun*
1 **to surrender to somebody** entregarse [28] a alguien
They surrendered to the police. Se entregaron a la policía.
2 (*a castle, town*) **entregar** [28]

ℰ to **surround** *verb*
1 **rodear** [17]
2 **to be surrounded by something** estar [2] rodeado de algo
The town is surrounded by hills. La ciudad está rodeada de colinas.

ℰ **survey** *noun*
1 (*of opinion*) la **encuesta** *fem*
2 (*of a house, building site, etc*) la **inspección** *fem*

to **survive** *verb*
sobrevivir [19]

survivor *noun*
el & la **superviviente** *masc & fem*

suspect *adjective* ▷ see **suspect** *noun, verb*
sospechoso *masc*, **sospechosa** *fem*
a suspect package un paquete sospechoso

suspect *noun* ▷ see **suspect** *adj, verb*
el **sospechoso** *masc*, la **sospechosa** *fem*

to **suspect** *verb* ▷ see **suspect** *adj, noun*
sospechar [17]

to **suspend** *verb*
to be suspended ser [1] expulsado

suspense *noun*
el **suspense** *masc*

suspicious *adjective*
sospechoso *masc*, **sospechosa** *fem*
to be suspicious of someone, something sospechar [17] de alguien, algo
a suspicious parcel un paquete sospechoso
a suspicious-looking individual un individuo de apariencia sospechosa

swallow *noun* ▷ see **swallow** *verb*
(*bird*) la **golondrina** *fem*

to **swallow** *verb* ▷ see **swallow** *noun*
tragar [28]

swamp *noun*
el **pantano** *masc*

swan *noun*
el **cisne** *masc*

to **swap** *verb*
cambiar [17]
Do you want to swap? ¿Quieres que cambiemos?
He's swapped his bike for a computer. Ha cambiado su bici por un ordenador.
to swap seats with somebody cambiarse [17] de sitio con alguien

to **swear** *verb*
decir [5] **palabrotas**
He swears a lot. Dice muchas palabrotas.

swearword *noun*
la **palabrota** *fem*

sweat *noun* ▷ see **sweat** *verb*
el **sudor** *masc*

to **sweat** *verb* ▷ see **sweat** *noun*
sudar [17]

sweater *noun*
el **suéter** *masc*

sweatshirt *noun*
la **sudadera** *fem*

Swede *noun*
un **sueco** *masc*, una **sueca** *fem*

WORD TIP Adjectives and nouns for nationality and regional origin do not have capital letters in Spanish.

Sweden *noun*
Suecia *fem*

Swedish *adjective & noun*
1 **sueco** *masc*, **sueca** *fem*
2 (*the language*) el **sueco** *masc*

WORD TIP Adjectives and nouns for nationality, regional origin and language do not have capital letters in Spanish.

to **sweep** *verb*
barrer [18]

sweet *adjective* ▷ see **sweet** *noun*
1 (*food, smile*) **dulce** *masc & fem*
I try not to eat sweet things. Intento no comer cosas dulces.
2 (*kind*) **encantador** *masc*, **encantadora** *fem*
She's a sweet person. Es realmente encantadora.
It was really sweet of him. Ha sido un detalle encantador.
3 (*cute*) **rico** *masc*, **rica** *fem*
He looks really sweet in that hat! ¡Está muy rico con ese sombrero!
• **sweetcorn** el maíz tierno

sweet *noun* ▷ see **sweet** *adj*
1 (*wrapped*) el **caramelo** *masc*
She loves sweets. Le encantan los caramelos.
2 (*dessert*) el **postre** *masc*
For sweet there's caramel custard. De postre hay flan.
• **sweetshop** la tienda de golosinas

swelling *noun*
la **hinchazón** *fem*

to **swerve** *verb*
virar [17] bruscamente
The car swerved to avoid the cyclist. El coche viró para esquivar al ciclista.

swim *noun* ▷ see **swim** *verb*
to go for a swim ir **[8]** a nadar

to **swim** *verb* ▷ see **swim** *noun*
nadar [17]
I swam ten lengths today. Hoy nadé diez largos.
She swam to the boat. Nadó hasta la barca.
Can you swim? ¿Sabes nadar?
to swim across the river cruzar **[22]** el río a nado

swimmer *noun*
el **nadador** *masc*, la **nadadora** *fem*
She's a strong swimmer. Es muy buena nadadora.

swimming *noun*
la **natación** *fem*
to go swimming ir **[8]** a nadar
• **swimming cap** el gorro de baño
• **swimming pool** la piscina
• **swimming trunks** el bañador

swimsuit *noun*
el **traje de baño**

swindle *noun*
la **estafa** *fem*
What a swindle! ¡Qué estafa!

swing *noun*
el **columpio** *masc*

Swiss *adjective & noun*
1 **suizo** *masc*, **suiza** *fem*
2 (*person*) el **suizo** *masc*, la **suiza** *fem*
the Swiss los suizos

WORD TIP Adjectives and nouns for nationality and regional origin do not have capital letters in Spanish.

switch *noun* ▷ see **switch** *verb*
el **interruptor** *masc*
I can't find the light switch. No encuentro el interruptor de la luz.

to **switch** *verb* ▷ see **switch** *noun*
(*to change*) **cambiar [17]**
to switch places cambiar de sitio
• **to switch something off**
apagar [28] algo
Switch it off! ¡Apágalo!
• **to switch something on**
encender [36] algo
He switched the light on. Encendió la luz.

Switzerland *noun*
Suiza *fem*

swollen *adjective*
hinchado *masc*, **hinchada** *fem*

to **swop** *verb* ▷ **swap**

sword *noun*
la **espada** *fem*
• **swordfish** el pez espada

syllabus *noun*
el **programa** *masc*
to be on the syllabus estar **[2]** en el programa

sympathetic *adjective*
comprensivo *masc*, **comprensiva** *fem*

to **sympathize** *verb*
to sympathize with somebody
compadecer **[35]** a alguien
I sympathize with you. Te compadezco.

sympathy *noun*
la **compasión** *fem*

symphony *noun*
la **sinfonía** *fem*
- **symphony orchestra** la orquesta sinfónica

symptom *noun*
el **síntoma** *masc*

synagogue *noun*
(*Religion*) la **sinagoga** *fem*

synthesizer *noun*
el **sintetizador** *masc*

synthetic *adjective*
sintético *masc*, **sintética** *fem*

syringe *noun*
la **jeringa** *fem*

syrup *noun*
el **jarabe** *fem*
cough syrup el jarabe para la tos

system *noun*
el **sistema** *masc*

T t

table *noun*
1 (*piece of furniture*) la **mesa** *fem*
on the table en la mesa
to be sitting at the table estar **[2]** sentado a la mesa
2 (*list*) la **tabla** *fem*
the ten-times table la tabla del cuatro
multiplication tables las tablas de multiplicar
- **tablecloth** el mantel
- **table football** el futbolín
- **table mat** el salvamanteles, *pl:* los **salvamanteles**

tablespoon *noun*
la **cuchara de servir**
a tablespoon of flour una cucharada grande de harina

tablet *noun*
la **pastilla** *fem*
Take the tablets twice a day. Tómese las pastillas dos veces al día.

table tennis *noun*
el **ping-pong** *masc*
to play table tennis jugar **[27]** al ping-pong

tackle *noun* ▷ see **tackle** *verb*
1 (*in football*) la **entrada** *fem*
2 (*in rugby*) el **placaje** *masc*
3 (*equipment*) **fishing tackle** aparejos de pesca

to **tackle** *verb* ▷ see **tackle** *noun*
1 (*in football*) **entrarle [17] a**
2 (*in rugby*) **placar [31]**
3 (*a job, problem*) **abordar [17]**

tact *noun*
el **tacto** *masc*

tactful *adjective*
diplomático *masc*, **diplomática** *fem*
That wasn't very tactful. Eso no fue muy diplomático.

tactic *noun*
la **táctica** *fem*

tadpole *noun*
el **renacuajo** *masc*

tail *noun*
1 (*dog's, cat's*) el **rabo** *masc*
2 (*horse's, fish's, bird's*) la **cola** *fem*
3 (*when tossing a coin*) **'Heads or tails?'—"Tails.'** '¿Cara o cruz?'—"Cruz.'

tailor *noun*
el **sastre** *masc*

to **take** *verb*
1 (*to carry*) **llevar [17]**
Take this to your mother. Lleva esto a tu madre.
I'll take my camera with me. Me llevaré la cámara.
2 (*to drive, transport*) **llevar [17]**
to take somebody somewhere llevar a alguien a un lugar
We took him to the station. Lo llevamos a la estación.
This bus takes you into the centre. Este autobús te lleva al centro.
I'll take you in the car. Te llevo en el coche.
I must take the car to the garage. Tengo que llevar el coche al garaje.
3 (*to lead*) **llevar [17]**
He took them upstairs Los llevó arriba.
This path takes you to the main road. Este camino te lleva a la carretera.
4 (*a train, plane, bus*) **coger [3]**, **tomar [17]**
I took the bus. Cogí el autobús.
We had to take a taxi. Tuvimos que coger un taxi.
5 (*to hold*) **coger [3]**, **tomar [17]**
Take my hand. Cógeme la mano.
6 (*to remove, steal*) **llevarse [17]**
Somebody's taken my purse! ¡Alguien se me ha llevado el monedero!
7 (*talking about time*) **llevar [17]**
It takes two hours. Lleva dos horas.
How long does it take to make? ¿Cuánto tiempo lleva hacerlo?
Don't take too long! ¡No tardes demasiado!
8 **tomar [17]**, (*a sweet, food, medicine*) **tomar [17]**
He took a chocolate. Tomó un bombón.
Do you take sugar? ¿Tomas azúcar?
Have you taken your tablets? ¿Te has tomado las pastillas?
9 (*to accept*) **aceptar [17]**
Do you take cheques? ¿Aceptan cheques?
He wouldn't take the money. No quiso aceptar el dinero.
Take his advice. Sigue sus consejos.
10 (*an exam, a test, a course*) **hacer [7]**
She's taking her driving test. Va a hacer el examen de conducir.

I'm taking a Russian course. Estoy haciendo un curso de ruso.

11 (*with clothes, shoes*) **What size do you take?** ¿Qué talla usas?
What size shoes do you take? ¿Qué número calzas?

12 (*notes, etc*) **tomar [17]**
He took my name and address. Me tomó el nombre y la dirección.
He took my temperature. Me tomó la temperatura.

13 (*to need*) **Going there takes courage.** Hay que tener valor para ir allí.
It took four men to lift it. Se necesitaron cuatro hombres para levantarlo.

14 (*to tolerate*) **aguantar [17]**
I won't take any more nonsense from you. No pienso aguantarte más tonterías.
I can't take it any longer! ¡No puedo más!

15 (*to interpret*) **tomarse [17]**
I don't know how to take that remark. Ese comentario no sé cómo tomármelo.
She took it the wrong way. Se lo tomó a mal.

WORD TIP See the **Word Tip** at *coger* in the Spanish-English section about the differences in regional use between *coger* and *tomar*.

• **to take something apart**
desmontar [17] algo

• **to take something away**
llevarse [17] algo
He took the dirty dishes away. Se llevó los platos sucios.

• **to take something back**
devolver [45] algo
I took the book back to the library. Devolví el libro a la biblioteca.

• **to take down**
1 **bajar [17]**
Cheryl's taken the cups down. Cheryl ha bajado las tazas.
2 (*curtains, decorations, etc*) **quitar [17]**
3 (*notes*) **apuntar [17]**

• **to take off**
1 (*clothes, shoes*) **quitarse [17]**
He took off his shirt. Se quitó la camisa.
Take your feet off the sofa. Quita los pies del sofá.
2 (*from a price*) **rebajar [17]**
He took five pounds off the price. Rebajó cinco libras del precio.
3 (*planes*) **despegar [28]**

• **to take out**
1 (*a pen, wallet*) **sacar [31]**
Eric took out his wallet. Eric sacó su cartera.
I took the toy out of the box. Saqué el juguete de la caja.
2 (*a friend*) **He's taking me out to lunch.** Me ha invitado a comer fuera.
She took me out to the theatre. Me invitó a ir al teatro.

• **to take up**
1 (*to carry*) **subir [19]**
Could you take these towels up? ¿Puedes subir estas toallas?
2 (*a hobby*) **He's taken up badminton.** Ha empezado a jugar al badminton.
3 (*time*) **llevar [17]**
My homework took up most of the afternoon. Hacer los deberes me llevó la mayor parte de la tarde.

takeaway *noun*
1 (*meal*) la **comida para llevar**
an Indian takeaway una comida india para llevar
2 (*the outlet*) el **restaurante que hace comida para llevar**

tale *noun*
la **historia** *fem*

talent *noun*
el **talento** *masc*
to have a talent for something estar [2] dotado *masc*, dotada *fem* para algo

talented *adjective*
He's really talented. Tiene mucho talento.

⚷ **talk** *noun* ▷ see **talk** *verb*
1 (*conversation*) la **conversación** *fem*
after our talk después de nuestra conversación
I had a talk with Rob about it. Hablé con Rob acerca de ello.
2 (*lecture*) la **charla** *fem*
She's giving a talk on Hungary. Va a dar una charla sobre Hungría.

⚷ to **talk** *verb* ▷ see **talk** *noun*
hablar [17]
I was talking to Jason about football. Estuve hablando con Jason sobre fútbol.
What's he talking about? ¿De qué está hablando?
We'll talk about it later. Hablaremos de ello más tarde.

talkative *adjective*
hablador *masc*, **habladora** *fem*
He's very talkative! ¡Es muy hablador!

⚷ **tall** *adjective*
alto *masc*, **alta** *fem*
the tallest buildings in the city los edificios más altos de la ciudad
She's very tall. Es muy alta.
I'm 1.7 metres tall. Mido un metro setenta.
How tall are you? ¿Cuánto mides?

English–Spanish

tambourine *noun*
la **pandereta** *fem*

tame *adjective*
(*animal*) **domesticado** *masc*, **domesticada** *fem*

tampon *noun*
el **tampón** *masc*

♂ to **tan** *verb* ▷ see **tan** *noun*
broncearse [17]
I tan easily. Me bronceo fácilmente.

♂ **tan** *noun* ▷ see **tan** *verb*
el **bronceado** *masc*
to get a tan broncearse **[17]**

tangerine *noun*
la **mandarina** *fem*

tank *noun*
1 (*for petrol, water*) el **depósito** *masc*
a fish tank una pecera
2 (*military vehicle*) el **tanque** *masc*

tanker *noun*
1 (*ship*) el **petrolero** *masc*
2 (*truck*) el **camión cisterna**

tanned *adjective*
bronceado *masc*, **bronceada** *fem*

♂ to **tap** *verb* ▷ see **tap** *noun*
dar [4] un golpecito en
He tapped her on the shoulder. Le dio un golpecito en el hombro.

♂ **tap** *noun* ▷ see **tap** *verb*
1 (*for water*) el **grifo** *masc*
the hot tap el grifo del agua caliente
the cold tap el grifo del agua fría
to leave the taps running dejar **[17]** los grifos abiertos
2 (*light blow*) el **golpecito** *masc*
She gave me a tap on the shoulder. Me dio un golpecito en el hombro.

tap-dancing *noun*
el **claqué** *masc*
to do tap-dancing hacer **[7]** claqué

to **tape** *verb* ▷ see **tape** *noun*
grabar [17]
I want to tape the film. Quiero grabar la película.

tape *noun* ▷ see **tape** *verb*
1 (*for recording*) la **cinta** *fem*
a blank tape una cinta virgen
my tape of the Stones mi cinta de los Stones
I've got it on tape. Lo tengo en cinta.
2 (*adhesive*) la **cinta** *fem*
sticky tape la cinta adhesiva
- **tape measure** la cinta métrica
- **tape recorder** el magnetofón

tar *noun*
el **alquitrán** *masc*

target *noun*
el **objetivo** *masc*

♂ **tart** *noun*
la **tarta** *fem*
a raspberry tart una tarta de frambuesas

tartan *adjective*
de tela escocesa
a tartan skirt una falda de tela escocesa

task *noun*
la **tarea** *fem*

♂ to **taste** *verb* ▷ see **taste** *noun*
1 (*foods*) **saber [13]**
The soup tastes horrible. La sopa sabe fatal.
to taste of something saber a algo
It tastes of strawberries. Sabe a fresas.
2 (*to try*) **probar [24]**
Taste this. Prueba esto.
Do you want to taste it? ¿Quieres probarlo?

♂ **taste** *noun* ▷ see **taste** *verb*
1 (*flavour*) el **sabor** *masc*
the taste of onions el sabor a cebolla
2 (*for clothes, decor, etc*) el **gusto** *masc*
in bad taste de mal gusto
She has good taste. Tiene buen gusto.

tasty *adjective*
sabroso *masc*, **sabrosa** *fem*

tattoo *noun*
el **tatuaje** *masc*
He's got a tattoo on his arm. Tiene un tatuaje en el brazo.

Taurus *noun*
1 (*the star sign*) el **Tauro** *masc*
2 (*person*) **un & una tauro** *masc & fem*
Jo's Taurus. Jo es tauro.

WORD TIP Use a small letter in Spanish to say *I am* ... etc with star signs. Star signs in Spanish are used without *el, un, la, una.*

tax *noun*
el **impuesto** *masc*

taxi *noun*
el **taxi** *masc*
by taxi en taxi
to take a taxi tomar **[17]** un taxi
- **taxi driver** el & la taxista
- **taxi rank** la parada de taxis

TB *noun*
la **tuberculosis** *fem*

a b c d e f g h i j k l m n o p q r s t u v w x y z

tea *noun*
1 (*the drink*) el **té** *masc*
a cup of tea una taza de té
a herbal tea una infusión
to have a cup of tea tomar [17] una taza de té
Two teas, please. Dos tés, por favor.
2 (*afternoon snack*) la **merienda** *fem*
to have tea merendar [29]
3 (*evening meal*) la **cena** *fem*
to have tea cenar [17]
• **teabag** la bolsita de té

to **teach** *verb*
1 (*a subject*) **enseñar** [17]
She's teaching me Italian. Me está enseñando italiano.
to teach yourself something aprender [18] algo por su cuenta
Anne taught herself Italian. Anne ha aprendido italiano por su cuenta.
2 (*to work as a teacher*) **dar** [4] **clases de**
Her mum teaches maths. Su madre da clases de matemáticas.
She's been teaching for five years. Es profesora desde hace cinco años.

teacher *noun*
1 (*in a secondary school*) el **profesor** *masc*, la **profesora** *fem*
our biology teacher nuestra profesora de biología
My father's a teacher. Mi padre es profesor.
2 (*in a primary school*) el **maestro** *masc*, la **maestra** *fem*
She's a primary school teacher. Es maestra.

teaching *noun*
la **enseñanza** *fem*

team *noun*
el **equipo** *masc*
a football team un equipo de fútbol
Our team won. Nuestro equipo ganó.

teapot *noun*
la **tetera** *fem*

to **tear** *verb* ▷ see **tear** *noun*
1 (*clothes*) **romper** [40]
You've torn your shirt. Te has roto la camisa.
2 (*by itself*) **romperse** [40]
It tears easily. Se rompe fácilmente.
• **to tear off**
1 (*carefully*) **recortar** [17]
2 (*roughly*) **arrancar** [31]
• **to tear open**
1 (*carefully*) **abrir** [46]
2 (*roughly*) **rasgar** [28]
• **to tear up**
romper [40]
She tore up the letter. Rompió la carta.

tear *noun* ▷ see **tear** *verb*
1 (*when you cry*) la **lágrima** *fem*
to be in tears estar [2] llorando
2 (*in clothing*) el **roto** *masc*
I've got a tear in my jeans. Tengo un roto en los vaqueros.

teaspoon *noun*
la **cucharita** *fem*
a teaspoonful of ... una cucharadita de ...

teatime *noun*
la **hora de merendar**

tea towel *noun*
el **paño de cocina**

technical *adjective*
técnico *masc*, **técnica** *fem*
• **technical college** la escuela politécnica

technician *noun*
el **técnico** *masc*, la **técnica** *fem*

technological *adjective*
tecnológico *masc*, **tecnológica** *fem*

technology *noun*
la **tecnología** *fem*
information technology la informática *fem*

teddy bear *noun*
el **osito de peluche**

teenage *adjective*
1 (*girl, boy*) **adolescente** *masc & fem*
They have a teenage son. Tienen un hijo adolescente.
2 (*films, magazines*) **para adolescentes**
a teenage magazine una revista para adolescentes

teenager *noun*
el & la **adolescente** *masc & fem*
a group of teenagers un grupo de adolescentes

teens *plural noun*
to be in your teens ser [1] un, una adolescente
He's in his teens. Es un adolescente.

tee-shirt *noun*
la **camiseta** *fem*

telegram *noun*
el **telegrama** *masc*

telegraph pole *noun*
el **poste telegráfico**

to **telephone** *verb* ▷ see **telephone** *noun*
llamar [17] por teléfono
I'll telephone the doctor. Llamaré al médico.

telephone *noun* ▷ see **telephone** *verb*
el **teléfono** *masc*
She's on the telephone. Está hablando por teléfono.
- **telephone box** la cabina telefónica
- **telephone call** la llamada telefónica
- **telephone card** la carta telefónica
- **telephone directory** la guía teléfonica
- **telephone kiosk** la cabina telefónica
- **telephone number** el número de teléfono

television *noun*
1 (*the medium*) la **televisión** *fem*
She's watching television. Está viendo la televisión.
I saw it on television. Lo vi en televisión.
2 (*TV set*) el **televisor** *masc*
to turn the television on poner [11] el televisor
- **television news** las telenoticias, el telediario
- **television programme** el programa de televisión
- **television set** el televisor

to **tell** *verb*
1 (*to inform*) **decir [5]**
I told her straight away. Le dije enseguida.
Have you told Jack? ¿Se lo has dicho a Jack?
I didn't tell anyone. No se lo dije a nadie.
as I was telling you como te decía
to tell somebody something decirle [5] algo a alguien
I told him it was true. Le dije que era verdad.
That's what she told me. Eso es lo que me dijo.
I told myself that it wasn't true. Me dije a mi mismo que no era verdad.
2 (*to instruct*) **to tell somebody to do something** decirle [5] a alguien que haga algo
Do as you're told. Haz lo que se te dice.
He told me to do it myself. Me dijo que lo hiciera yo mismo.
She told me not to wait. Me dijo que no esperara.

WORD TIP *decirle a alguien que* is followed by the subjunctive when it means *to tell somebody to do something.*

3 (*to explain*) **decir**
Tell me how to do it. Dime cómo hacerlo.
4 (*a story*) **contar [24]**
She told me about Frank. Me contó lo de Frank.
Tell me about your holiday. Cuéntame qué tal tus vacaciones.
5 (*the difference, etc*) **notar [17]**
to tell the difference notar la diferencia
you can tell ... se nota ...
You can tell it's old. Se nota que es viejo.
You can tell she's cross. Se nota que está enfadada.
I can't tell them apart. No puedo distinguirlos.
- **to tell off**
  regañar [17]

telly *noun*
(*informal*) la **tele** *fem*
to watch telly ver [16] la tele
I like watching telly. Me gusta ver la tele.

temper *noun*
el **humor** *masc*
to be in a bad temper estar [2] de mal humor
to be in a good temper estar [2] de buen humor
to lose your temper perder [36] los estribos

temperature *noun*
la **temperatura** *fem*
the water temperature la temperatura del agua
to have a temperature tener [9] fiebre

temporary *adjective*
1 (*in general*) **temporal** *masc & fem*
2 (*worker*) **eventual** *masc & fem*

temptation *noun*
la **tentación** *fem*

tempted *adjective*
tentado *masc*, **tentada** *fem*
I'm tempted to go. Estoy tentado de ir.

tempting *adjective*
tentador *masc*, **tentadora** *fem*

ten *number*
diez *invariable number*
Harry's ten. Harry tiene diez años.
It's ten o'clock. Son las diez.

to **tend** *verb*
to tend to do something tender [36] a hacer algo
He tends to talk a lot. Tiende a hablar mucho.

tendency *noun*
la **tendencia** *fem*

tennis *noun*
el **tenis** *masc*
to play tennis jugar **[27]** al tenis
- **tennis ball** la pelota de tenis
- **tennis court** la cancha de tenis
- **tennis player** el jugador de tenis, la jugadora de tenis
- **tennis racket** la raqueta de tenis

tenor *noun*
el **tenor** *masc*

tenpin bowling *noun*
los **bolos** *plural masc*
to go tenpin bowling jugar **[27]** a los bolos

tense *adjective* ▷ see **tense** *noun*
tenso *masc*, **tensa** *fem*

tense *noun* ▷ see **tense** *adj*
(*Grammar*) el **tiempo** *masc*
the present tense el presente
in the future tense en futuro

⚷ **tent** *noun*
la **tienda** *fem*

⚷ **tenth** *adjective* ▷ see **tenth** *noun*
décimo *masc*, **décima** *fem*
on the tenth floor en la décima planta

⚷ **tenth** *noun* ▷ see **tenth** *adj*
1 (*fraction*) **a tenth** una décima parte
2 (*in dates*) **the tenth of April** el diez de abril

⚷ **term** *noun*
1 (*in school*) el **trimestre** *masc*
2 (*word*) el **término** *masc*
technical terms términos técnicos
3 (*period*) el **periodo** *masc*
a five-year term un periodo de cinco años
in the short term a corto plazo
in the long term a largo plazo
4 (*relations*) **to be on good terms with somebody** llevarse **[17]** bien con alguien
to be on bad terms with somebody llevarse **[17]** mal con alguien
We're on bad terms. No nos llevamos bien.

terminal *noun*
la **terminal** *fem*
terminal two la terminal dos
a computer terminal una terminal de ordenador

terrace *noun*
1 (*of a cafe*) la **terraza** *fem*
2 (*row of houses*) la **hilera de casas adosadas**
3 (*in a stadium*) **the terraces** las gradas

⚷ **terrible** *adjective*
espantoso *masc*, **espantosa** *fem*
The weather was terrible. El tiempo fue espantoso.

terribly *adverb*
1 (*very*) **muy**
not terribly clean no muy limpio que digamos
2 (*badly*) **fatal**
I played terribly. Jugué fatal.

terrific *adjective*
1 **increíble** *masc & fem*
at a terrific speed a una velocidad increíble
a terrific amount una cantidad increíble
2 **Terrific!** ¡Fenomenal!

terrified *adjective*
aterrorizado *masc*, **aterrorizada** *fem*

to **terrify** *verb*
aterrar [17]

territory *noun*
el **territorio** *masc*

terrorism *noun*
el **terrorismo** *masc*

terrorist *noun*
el & la **terrorista** *masc & fem*

⚷ to **test** *verb* ▷ see **test** *noun*
1 (*a student*) **examinar [17]**
to test somebody on something examinar a alguien sobre algo
What are we going to be tested on? ¿Sobre qué nos van a examinar?
2 (*knowledge, skills*) **evaluar [20]**
3 (*a product*) **probar [24] algo**
He tested the recipe on me. Probó la receta conmigo.
These cosmetics have not been tested on animals. No se han utilizado animales en las pruebas de laboratorio de estos cosméticos.
4 (*blood, urine*) **analizar [22]**
5 (*vision, hearing*) **examinar [17]**
You need your eyes tested. Tienes que hacerte examinar la vista.

⚷ **test** *noun* ▷ see **test** *verb*
1 (*of knowledge, skills, etc*) la **prueba** *fem*
a maths test una prueba de matemáticas
to put something to the test poner **[11]** algo a prueba
2 (*of a product, bomb*) la **prueba** *fem*
nuclear tests pruebas nucleares
3 (*Medicine*) el **análisis** *masc*
a blood test un análisis de sangre
an eye test un examen de la vista

to **text** *verb* ▷ see **text** *noun*
mandar [17] un mensaje de texto a
I'll text you tomorrow. Te mandaré un mensaje (de texto) mañana.

English-Spanish

text *noun* ▷ see **text** *verb*
el **texto** *masc*
- **textbook** el libro de texto
- **text message** el mensaje de texto, el SMS

Thames *noun*
the Thames el Támesis

than *preposition, conjunction*
1 (*in comparisons*) **que**
His house is bigger than mine. Su casa es más grande que la mía.
She can swim better than me. Sabe nadar mejor que yo.
They have less money than we do. Tienen menos dinero que nosotros.
2 (*in comparisons with numbers*) **de**
more than forty más de cuarenta
less than thirty years menos de treinta años
more than once más de una vez

to **thank** *verb*
dar [4] las gracias a

thanks *plural noun*
las **gracias** *plural fem*
No thanks. No gracias.
Thanks a lot. Muchas gracias.
Thanks for your letter. Gracias por tu carta.
thanks to gracias a
It was thanks to Micky. Fue gracias a Micky.

thank you *exclamation*
gracias
Thank you very much for the cheque. Muchas gracias por el cheque.
No thank you. No, gracias.
a thank-you letter una carta de agradecimiento

that *conjunction* ▷ see **that** *adv, adj, pron*
que
I knew that he was wrong. Sabía que no tenía razón.

WORD TIP *that* can be omitted in English, but *que* must always be used in Spanish.

that *adverb* ▷ see **that** *conj, adj, pron*
tan
It's not that funny. No es tan divertido.
Their house isn't that big. Su casa no es tan grande.

that *adjective* ▷ see **that** *conj, adv, pron*
1 (*in general*) **ese** *masc*, **esa** *fem*
that dog ese perro
that blue car ese coche azul
that woman esa mujer
that one ese *masc*, esa *fem*
'Which cake would you like?'— 'That one, please.' '¿Qué pastel quieres?'—'Ese, por favor.'
2 (*for something further away*) **aquel** *masc*, **aquella** *fem*
from that day on desde aquel día
Of all the skirts I like that one best. De todas las faldas me gusta más aquella.

that *pronoun* ▷ see **that** *adj, adv, conj*
1 (*in general*) **ese** *masc*, **esa** *fem*, **eso** *no gender* (*see Word Tip*)
That's not his car. Ese no es su coche.
That's my bedroom. Esa es mi habitación.
That's not what you told me. Eso no es lo que tú me dijiste.
That's not true. Eso no es cierto.
Did you see that? ¿Has visto eso?
What's that? ¿Qué es eso?
Who's that? ¿Quién es?
Where's that? ¿Dónde está?
2 (*for something further away*) **aquel** *masc*, **aquella** *fem*, **aquello** *no gender*
Not this one, that one. Este no, aquel.
What's that? ¿Qué es aquello?
3 (*as a relative pronoun*) **que**
the book that's on the table el libro que está en la mesa
the girl that I saw la chica que vi
4 (*with a verb + preposition*) **el que** *masc*, **la que** *fem*
the drawer that I put it in el cajón en el que lo metí
5 (*in expressions*) **that is** es decir
We all go, all the students, that is. Vamos todos, es decir, todos los estudiantes.

WORD TIP *eso* and *aquello* are used for things that are not obviously either masc or fem.

to **thaw** *verb* ▷ see **thaw** *noun*
1 (*snow, ice*) **derretirse [57]**
2 (*frozen food*) **descongelarse [17]**

thaw *noun* ▷ see **thaw** *verb*
el **deshielo** *masc*

the *determiner*
1 (*before a masc noun*) **el**
the cat el gato
the boy el chico
the branches of the tree las ramas del árbol
We went to the park. Fuimos al parque.
2 (*before a fem noun*) **la**
the table la mesa
the girl la chica
3 (*before masc plural nouns*) **los**
the plates los platos
the men los hombres

a b c d e f g h i j k l m n o p q r s t u v w x y z

4 (*before fem plural nouns*) **las**
the windows las ventanas
the women las mujeres

WORD TIP *de* + *el* becomes *del*; *a* + *el* become *al*.

theatre *noun*
el **teatro** *masc*
to go to the theatre ir [8] al teatro

theft *noun*
el **robo** *masc*
He was charged with theft. Lo acusaron de robo.

their *adjective*
1 (*before nouns*) **su** *masc & fem*, **sus** *plural masc & fem*
their flat su piso
their mother su madre
their presents sus regalos
2 (*with parts of the body, clothes*) **el**, **la**, **los**, **las**
They are brushing their hair. Se están cepillando el pelo.
They're washing their hands. Se están lavando las manos.
They got their shoes dirty. Se ensuciaron los zapatos.

WORD TIP Spanish uses *el, la, los, las* for *their* with parts of the body and clothes.

theirs *pronoun*
el suyo *masc*, **la suya** *fem*
Our garden's smaller than theirs. Nuestro jardín es más pequeño que el suyo.
Our house is bigger than theirs. Nuestra casa es más grande que la suya.
Our shoes were newer than theirs. Nuestros zapatos eran más nuevos que los suyos.
Our photos were better than theirs. Nuestras fotos eran mejores que las suyas.

them *pronoun*
1 (*as a direct object*) **los** *masc*, **las** *fem* (*see Word Tip*)
I like your shoes. Where did you buy them? Me gustan tus zapatos. ¿Dónde los compraste?
She has two brothers, but I don't know them. Tiene dos hermanos, pero no los conozco.
Remember Ann and Lisa? I saw them last week. ¿Te acuerdas de Ann y Lisa? Las vi la semana pasada.
He has a son and a daughter, do you know them? Tiene un hijo y una hija ¿los conoces?
I don't want to see them. No quiero verlos.
Listen to them! ¡Escúchalos!
Don't push them! ¡No los empujes!
2 (*as an indirect object*) **les**
I gave them my address. Les di mis señas.
I lent it to them. Se lo dejé.
Give it back to them. ¡Devuélveselo!
3 (*after prepositions, in comparisons, after the verb to be*) **ellos** *masc*, **ellas** *fem*
I'll go with them. Iré con ellos (*two boys; a boy and a girl, etc*)., Iré con ellas (*only girls*).
She's older than them. Es mayor que ellos (*two boys; a boy and a girl, etc*)., Es mayor que ellas (*only girls*).
without them sin ellos (*two boys; a boy and a girl, etc*), sin ellas (*only girls*)
It's them! ¡Son ellos (*two boys; a boy and a girl, etc*)!, ¡Son ellas (*only girls*)!

WORD TIP With a mixed masc and fem group, Spanish uses the masc form. *le* and *les* + *lo* or *la* become *se*.

theme park *noun*
el **parque temático**

themselves *pronoun*
1 (*reflexive*) **se**
They've hurt themselves. Se han hecho daño.
They helped themselves. Se sirvieron.
2 (*for emphasis*) **ellos mismos** *plural masc*, **ellas mismas** *plural fem*
The boys can do it themselves. Los chicos pueden hacerlo ellos mismos.
The girls will tell you themselves. Las chicas te lo dirán ellas mismas.
3 (*on their own*) **by themselves** ellos solos *plural masc*, ellas solas *plural fem*
They did it by themselves. Lo hicieron ellos solos (*talking about some boys, or boys and girls*).
They did it by themselves. Lo hicieron ellas solas (*talking about some girls*).

WORD TIP With a mixed masc and fem group, Spanish uses the masc form *ellos*.

then *adverb*
1 (*next*) **luego**
Have a shower and then make your bed. Dúchate y luego haz la cama.
I went to the post office and then the bank. Fui a Correos y luego al banco.
2 (*at that time*) **entonces**
We were living in York then. Entonces vivíamos en York.
3 (*in that case*) **entonces**
Then why worry? Entonces ¿para qué preocuparse?
That's all right then. Entonces vale.
4 (*in expressions*) **by then** para entonces
By then it was too late. Para entonces era demasiado tarde.

theory *noun*
la **teoría** *fem*
in theory en teoría

there *adverb*
1 (*in general*) **ahí**
Put it there. Ponlo ahí.
Stand there. Ponte ahí.
They're in there. Están ahí dentro.
over there ahí
She's over there talking to Mark. Está ahí hablando con Mark.
down there ahí abajo
up there ahí arriba
Look up there! ¡Mira ahí arriba!
2 (*for somewhere further away*) **allí**
Put it there. Ponlo allí.
Stand there. Ponte allí.
over there allí
She's over there talking to Mark. Está allí hablando con Mark.
down there allí abajo
up there ahí arriba, (*further away*) allí arriba
3 (*for somewhere even further away*) **allá**
over there, across the river allá, al otro lado del río
'Do you mean here?' - 'No, further over there.' '¿Dices aquí?' - 'No, más allá.'
4 (*standing for something already mentioned*)
I've seen photos of London but I've never been there. He visto fotos de Londres, pero nunca he estado.
Yes, I'm going there on Tuesday. Sí, voy a ir el martes.
Lots of his friends were there. Estaban muchos de sus amigos.
5 (*to indicate something*) **there is** hay
there are hay
There's a cat in the garden. Hay un gato en el jardín.
There was no bread. No había pan.
Yes, there's enough. Sí, hay suficiente.
There are three seats. Hay tres asientos.
6 (*in exclamations*) **ahí**
There they are! ¡Ahí están!
There she is! ¡Ahí está!
There's the bus coming! ¡Ahí viene el autobús!

therefore *adverb*
por lo tanto
He had lived in Madrid and therefore spoke Spanish well. Había vivido en Madrid y por lo tanto hablaba español bien.

thermometer *noun*
el **termómetro** *masc*

these *adjective, pronoun*
estos *masc*, **estas** *fem*
these envelopes estos sobres
these postcards estas postales
one of these days un día de estos
These are the best. Estos son los mejores. ▷ **this**

they *pronoun*
1 **ellos** *masc*, **ellas** *fen* (*see Word Tip*)
'The knives?'— 'They're in the drawer.' '¿Los cuchillos?'— 'Están en el cajón.'
I bought some apples but they're not very nice. Compré unas manzanas pero no están muy buenas.
They are teachers. Son profesores.
Here they are! ¡Aquí están!
2 (*for emphasis*) **ellos** *masc*, **ellas** *fem*
They did it. Lo hicieron ellos (*two boys; a boy and a girl, etc*)., Lo hicieron ellas (*only girls*).

WORD TIP *they*, like other subject pronouns, is generally not translated in Spanish; the form of the verb tells you whether the subject of the verb is *I*, *we*, *they*, etc, so *they* is translated only for emphasis or for clarity. With a mixed group, Spanish uses the masc form *ellos*.

thick *adjective*
1 (*in general*) **grueso** *masc*, **gruesa** *fem*
a thick layer of stones una capa gruesa de piedras
2 (*fog, fumes*) **denso** *masc*, **densa** *fem*
3 (*stupid*) **burro** *masc*, **burra** *fem*

thickness *noun*
1 (*of a wall, paper*) el **espesor** *masc*
2 (*of fog*) la **densidad** *fem*

thief *noun*
el **ladrón** *masc*, la **ladrona** *fem*

thigh *noun*
el **muslo** *masc*

thin *adjective*
1 (*in general*) **delgado** *masc*, **delgada** *fem*
to get thin adelgazar **[22]**
2 (*skinny*) **flaco** *masc*, **flaca** *fem*
She's very thin. Es muy flaca.
3 (*slice*) **fino** *masc*, **fina** *fem*
4 (*soup, sauce*) **poco espeso** *masc*, **poco espesa** *fem*

thing *noun*
1 (*object*) la **cosa** *fem*
shops full of pretty things tiendas llenas de cosas preciosas
There's no such thing. No hay tal cosa.
2 (*situation, event, act*) la **cosa** *fem*
A very strange thing happened. Pasó algo muy raro..

How could you do such a thing? ¿Cómo pudiste hacer una cosa así?
The things you say! ¡Qué cosas dices!
The best thing to do is ... Lo mejor que se puede hacer es ...
I want to do the right thing. Quiero hacer lo correcto.
The same thing happened to me. Me pasó lo mismo

3 (*thingamajig, gadget*) el **chisme** *masc* (*informal*)
Use that thing to open it. Usa ese chisme para abrirlo.

4 (*matter*) el **asunto** *masc*
I'm fed up with the whole thing. Estoy harto del asunto.

5 **things** (*belongings, equipment*) las cosas
You can put your things in my room. Puedes poner tus cosas en mi habitación.
He washed the breakfast things. Lavó las cosas del desayuno.
Bring your swimming things. Traigan traje de baño y toalla, etcétera.

6 (*important point*) **The thing is, I've lost her address.** Lo que pasa es que he perdido sus señas.

7 (*unfortunate person*) **You poor thing!** ¡Pobrecito!
He didn't know what to do, poor thing! El pobre no sabía qué hacer.

to think *verb*

1 (*to go over in your mind*) **pensar** **[29]**
He thought for a moment. Pensó un momento.
to think about somebody, something pensar en alguien, algo.
I'm thinking about you. Estoy pensando en ti.
He's always thinking about money. Siempre piensa en dinero.
She's thinking of studying medicine. Está pensando estudiar medicina.

2 (*to have an opinion*) **pensar** **[29]**
Tony thinks it's silly. Tony piensa que es una tontería.
What do you think of my new jacket? ¿Qué piensas de mi chaqueta nueva?
What do you think of that? ¿Qué piensas de eso?
What do you think of it? ¿Qué te parece?

3 (*to believe*) **creer** **[37]**
Do you think they'll come? ¿Crees que vendrán?
No, I don't think so. No, creo que no.
I think he's already left. Creo que ya se ha ido.

4 (*to imagine*) **imaginar** **[17]**
I never thought it would be like this! ¡Nunca me imaginé que sería así!
Just think! We'll soon be in Spain! ¡Imagínate! ¡Pronto estaremos en España!

third *adjective* ▷ see **third** *noun*
tercero *masc*, **tercera** *fem*
on the third floor en la tercera planta

third *noun* ▷ see **third** *adj*
1 (*fraction*) **a third** un tercio
2 (*in dates*) **the third of March** el tres de marzo

thirdly *adverb*
en tercer lugar

Third World *noun*
the Third World el Tercer Mundo

thirst *noun*
la **sed** *fem*

thirsty *adjective*
to be thirsty tener **[9]** sed
I'm thirsty. Tengo sed.
We were all thirsty. Todos teníamos sed.

thirteen *number*
trece *invariable number*
Ahmed's thirteen. Ahmed tiene trece años.

thirty *number*
treinta *invariable number*
thirty-five treinta y cinco
She's thirty. Tiene treinta años.

this *adjective* ▷ see **this** *pron*
1 (*with a masc noun*) **este**
this paintbrush este pincel
this tree este árbol
2 (*with a fem noun*) **esta**
this cup esta taza
this morning esta mañana
3 **this one** este (*for a masc noun*), esta (*for a fem noun*)
If you need a pen, use this one. Si necesitas un boli, usa este.
If you want a lamp, take this one. Si quieres una lámpara, toma esta. ▷ **these**

this *pronoun* ▷ see **this** *adj*
1 (*for a masc noun*) **este**
This is my car. Este es mi coche.
Who is this? ¿Quién es este?
2 (*for a fem noun*) **esta**
This is the best photo. Esta es la mejor foto.
Who is this? ¿Quién es esta?
3 (*without gender*) **esto**
Can you hold this for a moment? ¿Puedes sostener esto un momento?
What's this? ¿Qué es esto? ⏩

4 (*on the phone*) **This is Tracy.** Soy Tracy.
5 (*in introductions*) **This is my sister Carla.** Te presento a mi hermana Carla.
▷ **these**

thistle *noun*
el **cardo** *masc*

thorough *adjective*
1 (*search*) **a fondo**
2 (*person*) **concienzudo** *masc*, **concienzuda** *fem*

those *adjective* ▷ see **those** *pron*
1 (*with a masc pl noun*) **esos**, (*with a fem pl noun*) **esas**
those books esos libros
those cups esas tazas
2 (*for things further away*) **aquellos** *plural masc*, **aquellas** *plural fem*
those trees aquellos árboles
those houses aquellas casas

those *pronoun* ▷ see **those** *adj*
1 (*for a masc pl noun*) **esos**, (*for a fem pl noun*) **esas**
Knives? Take those. ¿Cuchillos? Toma esos.
If you need cups, take those. Si necesitas tazas, toma esas.
2 (*for things further away*) **aquellos** *pl masc*, **aquellas** *pl fem*
Not these ones, those ones. Estos no, aquellos.
What are those? ¿Qué son aquellos?

though *conjunction*
1 (*although*) **aunque**
though it's cold aunque hace calor
though he's older than she is aunque es mayor que ella
2 (*however*) **It was a good idea, though.** Aun así era una buena idea.

thought *noun*
el **pensamiento** *masc*

thoughtful *adjective*
1 (*considerate*) **amable**
It was really thoughtful of you. Fue muy amable de tu parte.
2 (*deep in thought*) **pensativo** *masc*, **pensativa** *fem*

thoughtless *adjective*
desconsiderado *masc*, **desconsiderada** *fem*

thousand *number*
mil *masc & fem*
a thousand mil
about a thousand people unas mil personas
a thousand euros mil euros
three thousand tres mil
two thousand and seven dos mil siete
Thousands of tourists come every year. Miles de turistas vienen cada año.

thread *noun* ▷ see **thread** *verb*
el **hilo** *masc*

to **thread** *verb* ▷ see **thread** *noun*
(*a needle*) **enhebrar [17]**

threat *noun*
la **amenaza** *fem*

to **threaten** *verb*
amenazar [22]
to threaten to do something amenazar con hacer algo

three *number*
tres *invariable number*
Lily's three. Lily tiene tres años.

three-quarters *plural noun*
tres cuartos *plural masc*

thrilled *adjective*
encantado *masc*, **encantada** *fem*
I was thrilled to hear from you. Me encantó tener noticias tuyas.

thriller *noun*
1 (*book*) la **novela de suspense**
2 (*film*) la **película de suspense**

thrilling *adjective*
emocionante *masc & fem*

throat *noun*
la **garganta** *fem*
to have a sore throat tener **[9]** dolor de garganta

through *preposition, adjective*
1 (*across*) **a través de**
a path through the forest un camino a través del bosque
to go through something atravesar **[29]** algo
We went through the park. Atravesamos el parque.
2 (*by way of*) **por**
through the window por la ventana
a through train un tren directo
The train went through Leeds. El tren fue por Leeds.
to go through customs pasar **[17]** la aduana

throughout *preposition*
throughout the match durante todo el partido
throughout the world por todo el mundo

♪ to **throw** *verb*
tirar [17]
Throw me the ball! ¡Tírame la pelota!
I threw the letter into the bin. Tiré la carta a la basura.
He threw the book on the floor. Tiró el libro al suelo.
We were throwing snowballs. Estábamos tirando bolas de nieve.
• **to throw something away**
tirar [17] algo
I've thrown away the old newspapers. He tirado los periódicos viejos.
• **to throw somebody out**
echar [17] a alguien
• **to throw something out**
tirar [17] algo a la basura
• **to throw up**
devolver [45]

thumb *noun*
el **pulgar** *masc*

thunder *noun*
los **truenos** *plural masc*
a peal of thunder un trueno
• **thunderstorm** la tormenta eléctrica

♪ **Thursday** *noun*
el **jueves** *masc*
on Thursday el jueves
I'm going out on Thursday. Voy a salir el jueves.
See you on Thursday! ¡Hasta el jueves!
on Thursdays los jueves
The museum is closed on Thursdays. El museo cierra los jueves.
every Thursday todos los jueves
last Thursday el jueves pasado
next Thursday el próximo jueves

WORD TIP Months of the year and days of the week start with small letters in Spanish.

to **tick** *verb*
1 (*clocks*) **hacer [7] tictac**
2 (*on paper*) **marcar [31]**

♪ **ticket** *noun*
1 (*for a film, an exhibition, etc*) la **entrada** *fem*
two tickets for the concert dos entradas para el concierto
2 (*for a plane, a train, etc*) el **billete** *masc*
a bus ticket un billete de autobús
3 (*from a machine*) el **ticket** *masc*
4 (*fine*) **a parking ticket** una multa
• **ticket inspector** el revisor, la revisora

♪ **ticket office** *noun*
1 (*at a station*) el **mostrador de venta de billetes**
2 (*at a cinema, etc*) la **taquilla** *fem*

to **tickle** *verb*
hacerle [7] cosquillas a

♪ **tide** *noun*
la **marea** *fem*
at high tide cuando la marea está alta
The tide is out. La marea está baja.

♪ **tidy** *adjective* ▷ see **tidy** *verb*
1 (*room, person*) **ordenado** *masc*, **ordenada** *fem*
My flat mate is very tidy. Mi compañero de piso es muy ordenado.
2 (*homework*) **bien presentado** *masc*, **bien presentada** *fem*
3 (*in appearance*) **bien arreglado** *masc*, **bien arreglada** *fem*
She always looks tidy. Siempre va bien arreglada.

♪ to **tidy** *verb* ▷ see **tidy** *adj*
ordenar [17]

♪ **tie** *noun* ▷ see **tie** *verb*
1 (*that you wear*) la **corbata** *fem*
a red tie una corbata roja
2 (*in a match*) el **empate** *masc*

♪ to **tie** *verb* ▷ see **tie** *noun*
1 (*a knot, a bow*) **atar [17]**
to tie your shoelaces atarse los zapatos
2 **to tie a knot in something** hacer **[7]** un nudo en algo
3 (*in a match*) **empatar [17]**
We tied two all. Empatamos a dos.

tiger *noun*
el **tigre** *masc*

tight *adjective*
1 (*too small*) **to be tight** apretar **[29]**
The skirt's a bit tight. La falda me aprieta un poco.
These shoes are too tight. Estos zapatos me aprietan mucho.
2 (*close-fitting*) **ceñido** *masc*, **ceñida** *fem*
She was wearing a tight dress. Llevaba un vestido ceñido.

to **tighten** *verb*
apretar [29]

tightly *adverb*
fuerte
Hold it tightly. Agárralo fuerte.

♪ **tights** *plural noun*
las **medias** *plural fem*
a pair of tights un par de medias

tile *noun*
1 (*for floors, walls*) el **azulejo** *masc*
2 (*for roofs*) la **teja** *fem*

English–Spanish

♪ **till** *noun* ▷ see **till** *prep*
la **caja** *fem*
Pay at the till. Pase a pagar por caja.

♪ **till** *preposition* ▷ see **till** *noun*
hasta
till then hasta entonces
till now hasta ahora
They're here till Sunday. Están aquí hasta el domingo.
She won't be back till ten. No volverá hasta las diez.

♪ **time** *noun*
1 (*on the clock*) la **hora** *fem*
ten o'clock Spanish time las diez hora española
on time a la hora
What time is it? ¿Qué hora es?
It's time for lunch. Es hora de comer.
2 (*an amount of time*) el **tiempo** *masc*
We've got lots of time. Tenemos mucho tiempo.
I don't have the time to drink coffee. No tengo tiempo para tomar café.
He talked for a long time. Habló durante mucho tiempo.
She hasn't called me for a long time. Hace mucho que no me llama.
3 (*moment*) el **momento** *masc*
at any time en cualquier momento
Is this a good time to phone? ¿Es buen momento para llamar?
4 (*in expressions*) **from time to time** de vez en cuando
at times a veces
for the time being por ahora
in time a tiempo
I arrived just in time. Llegué justo a tiempo.
5 (*in a series*) la **vez** *fem*, *fem pl:* las **veces**
the first time la primera vez
six times seis veces
the first time I saw you la primera vez que te vi
three times a year tres veces al año
6 **to have a good time** pasarlo [17] bien
We had a really good time. Lo pasamos muy bien.
Have a good time! ¡Que lo pases bien!
7 (*Maths*) **Three times two is six.** Tres por dos son seis.

time off *noun*
1 (*free time*) el **tiempo libre**
2 (*leave*) los **días libres**

♪ **timetable** *noun*
el **horario** *masc*
the bus timetable el horario de los autobuses
the school timetable el horario de clases

♪ **tin** *noun*
la **lata** *fem*
a tin of tomatoes una lata de tomates
• **tin foil** el papel aluminio

tinned *adjective*
en lata
tinned peas guisantes en lata

tin opener *noun*
el **abrelatas** *masc*, *pl:* los **abrelatas**

tiny *adjective*
diminuto *masc*, **diminuta** *fem*

♪ **tip** *noun* ▷ see **tip** *verb*
1 (*the end*) la **punta** *fem*
the tip of my finger la punta de mi dedo
2 (*money*) la **propina** *fem*
Give the waiter a tip. Dale una propina al camarero.
3 (*useful hint*) el **consejo** *masc*

♪ to **tip** *verb* ▷ see **tip** *noun*
(*a waiter, etc*) **darle** [4] **una propina a**

tiptoe *noun*
on tiptoe de puntillas

♪ **tired** *adjective*
1 **cansado** *masc*, **cansada** *fem*
I'm tired. Estoy cansado.
You look tired. Pareces cansado.
2 **to be tired of something** estar [2] harto *masc*, harta *fem* de algo
He's tired of London. Está harto de Londres.
I'm tired of watching TV. Estoy harta de ver la tele.

tiring *adjective*
cansado *masc*, **cansada** *fem*

tissue *noun*
el **pañuelo de papel**
Do you have a tissue? ¿Tienes un pañuelo de papel?

title *noun*
el **título** *masc*

to *preposition*
1 (*showing movement*) **a**
to London a Londres
to Spain a España
to Paul's house a casa de Paul
the road to London la carretera de Londres.
She's gone to the office. Se ha ido a la oficina.
I'm going to school. Voy al colegio.

I'm going to the dentist's tomorrow. Voy al dentista mañana.
2 (*until*) **hasta**
from beginning to end desde el principio hasta el final
from Monday to Friday de lunes a viernes
3 (*to a person*) **a**
Give the book to Leila. Dale el libro a Leila.
Who did you give it to? ¿A quién se lo diste?
to talk to somebody hablar [17] con alguien
He didn't talk to me. No habló conmigo.
I was nice to them. Fui amable con ellos.
4 (*in order to*) **para**
I went out to help her. Salí para ayudarla.
5 (*in time expressions*) **It's ten to nine.** Son las nueve menos diez.
It's twenty to. Son menos veinte.
6 (*in infinitives*) **We're ready to go.** Estamos listos para irnos.
It's easy to do. Es fácil de hacer.
I have nothing to do. No tengo nada que hacer.
I have a lot of homework to do. Tengo muchos deberes que hacer.

toast *noun*
1 (*made from bread*) el **pan tostado**
a piece of toast una tostada
two slices of toast dos tostadas
2 (*to your health*) el **brindis** *masc*
to drink a toast to the future brindar [17] por el futuro

toaster *noun*
el **tostador** *masc*

tobacco *noun*
el **tabaco** *masc*

tobacconist's *noun*
el **estanco** *masc*

today *adverb, noun*
hoy
She arrives today. Llega hoy.
Today's her birthday. Hoy es su cumpleaños.

toe *noun*
el **dedo del pie**
my big toe el dedo gordo del pie
• **toenail** la uña de un dedo del pie

toffee *noun*
el **toffee** *masc*

together *adverb*
juntos *plural masc*, **juntas** *plural fem*
Kate and Lindy arrived together. Kate y Lindy llegaron juntas.
They all left together. Se fueron todos juntos.

toilet *noun*
1 (*in a house*) el **baño** *masc*
She's gone to the toilet. Ha ido al baño.
2 (*in a public place*) el **servicio** *masc*
Where's the toilet? ¿Dónde está el servicio?
Where are the toilets? ¿Dónde están los servicios
• **toilet paper** el papel higiénico
• **toilet roll** el rollo de papel higiénico

token *noun*
1 (*for a machine, game*) la **ficha** *fem*
2 (*as a present*) el **cheque regalo**
a CD token un cheque regalo para un CD

toll *noun*
1 (*on a motorway*) el **peaje** *masc*
2 (*number*) el **número** *masc*
The death toll is 25. El número de víctimas mortales asciende a 25.

tomato *noun*
el **tomate** *masc*
a tomato salad una ensalada de tomate
tomato sauce salsa de tomate

tomorrow *adverb*
mañana
tomorrow afternoon mañana por la tarde
tomorrow morning mañana por la mañana
tomorrow night mañana por la noche
the day after tomorrow pasado mañana
I'll do it tomorrow. Lo haré mañana.

ton *noun*
la **tonelada** *fem*
She gets tons of letters. Recibe montones de cartas.

tongue *noun*
la **lengua** *fem*
to stick your tongue out sacar [31] la lengua

tonic *noun*
la **tónica** *fem*
a gin and tonic un gin tonic

tonight *adverb*
esta noche
I'm going out tonight. Voy a salir esta noche.

tonsillitis *noun*
las **anginas** *plural fem*

too *adverb*
1 **demasiado**
too often demasiado a menudo
It's too expensive. Es demasiado caro.
The tickets are too expensive. Las entradas son demasiado caras. ▸▸

2 **too much** demasiado
He eats too much. Come demasiado.
3 (*before nouns*) **too much** demasiado *masc*, demasiada *fem*
It takes too much time. Lleva demasiado tiempo.
I watch too much TV veo demasiada televisión
4 **too many** demasiados *masc pl*, demasiadas *fem pl*
too many beers demasiadas cervezas
There are too many accidents. Hay demasiados accidentes.
5 (*as well*) **también**
Karen's coming too. Karen también viene.
Me too! ¡Yo también!
6 (*very*) **muy**
I'm not too convinced. No estoy muy convencida.

WORD TIP Only when *demasiado* comes before a noun, can it become *demasiada, demasiados, demasiadas*.

tool *noun*
la **herramienta** *fem*
• **tool kit** el juego de herramientas

tooth *noun*
1 el **diente** *masc*
to brush your teeth cepillarse **[17]** los dientes
2 (*back tooth*) la **muela** *fem*

toothache *noun*
el **dolor de muelas**
to have toothache tener **[9]** dolor de muelas

toothbrush *noun*
el **cepillo de dientes**

toothpaste *noun*
la **pasta de dientes**

top *adjective* ▷ see **top** *noun*
1 (*step, floor*) **último** *masc*, **última** *fem*
It's on the top floor. Está en el último piso.
2 (*bunk, drawer, shelf*) **de arriba**
3 **in the top left-hand corner** en la esquina superior izquierda

top *noun* ▷ see **top** *adj*
1 (*of a ladder, stairs*) lo **alto** *masc*
the top of ... lo alto de ...
at the top of the stairs en lo alto de las escaleras
to be at the top of the list encabezar **[22]** una lista
2 (*of a page, container, box*) la **parte superior**
The top of the box is red. La parte superior de la caja es roja.
3 **on top of something** (*a table, wardrobe*) encima de algo
It's on top of the chest-of-drawers. Está encima de la cómoda.
4 (*of a mountain*) la **cima** *fem*
5 (*of a bottle*) el **tapón** *masc*
6 (*of a pen*) el **capuchón** *masc*
7 (*of a jar*) la **tapa** *fem*

topic *noun*
el **tema** *masc*

topping *noun*
la **guarnición** *fem*
Which topping do you want? ¿Qué guarnición quieres?

torch *noun*
la **linterna** *fem*

torn *adjective*
roto *masc*, **rota** *fem*

tornado *noun*
el **tornado** *masc*

tortoise *noun*
la **tortuga** *fem*

torture *noun* ▷ see **torture** *verb*
la **tortura** *fem*

to **torture** *verb* ▷ see **torture** *noun*
torturar [17]

Tory *noun*
el **conservador** *masc*, la **conservadora** *fem*

total *adjective* ▷ see **total** *noun*
total *masc & fem*

total *noun* ▷ see **total** *adj*
el **total** *masc*

totally *adverb*
totalmente

touch *noun* ▷ see **touch** *verb*
1 (*contact*) **to be in touch** estar **[2]** en contacto
to get in touch with somebody contactarse **[17]** con alguien
to stay in touch with somebody mantenerse **[9]** en contacto con alguien
We've lost touch. Hemos perdido el contacto.
We ought to get in touch. Deberíamos ponernos en contacto.
He's out of touch with fashion. No está al corriente de la moda.
2 (*a little bit*) un **poco** *masc*
a touch of vanilla un poco de vainilla
It was a touch embarrassing. Fue un poco embarazoso.

♪ to **touch** *verb* ▷ see **touch** *noun*
1 **tocar** [31]
He touched her hand. Le tocó la mano.
Don't touch! ¡No toques!
2 (*emotionally*) **conmover** [38]
I was touched. Me conmoví.

tough *adjective*
1 (*meat, climate, person*) **duro** *masc*, **dura** *fem*
a tough guy un tipo duro
The meat's tough. La carne está dura.
Fortunately, she's tough. Afortunadamente, es fuerte.
2 (*measure, discipline, teacher*) **severo** *masc*, **severa** *fem*
3 (*fabric*) **resistente** *masc & fem*
4 (*question, decision, job*) **difícil** *masc & fem*
Things are tough at the moment. Las cosas están difíciles en este momento.
Tough luck! ¡Mala suerte!

tour *noun*
1 la **visita** *fem*
a tour of the city una visita a la ciudad
a package tour un viaje organizado
We did the tour of the castle. Hicimos la visita al castillo.
2 (*by a band, group*) la **gira** *fem*
to go on tour ir [8] de gira

tourism *noun*
el **turismo** *masc*

♪ **tourist** *noun*
el & la **turista** *masc & fem*
• **tourist information office** la oficina de información y turismo

♪ **towards** *adverb*
hacia
towards the door hacia la puerta
towards the end of the concert casi al final del concierto

♪ **towel** *noun*
la **toalla** *fem*

tower *noun*
la **torre** *fem*
the Tower of London la Torre de Londres
• **tower block** el bloque de apartamentos

♪ **town** *noun*
la **ciudad** *fem*
to go into town ir [8] a la ciudad
• **town centre** el centro de la ciudad
• **town hall** el ayuntamiento

toxic *adjective*
tóxico *masc*, **tóxica** *fem*

♪ **toy** *noun*
el **juguete** *masc*

trace *noun* ▷ see **trace** *verb*
el **rastro** *masc*
There is no trace of it. No hay rastro de ello.

to **trace** *verb* ▷ see **trace** *noun*
1 (*a missing person*) **localizar** [22]
2 (*with tracing paper*) **calcar** [31]

tracing paper *noun*
el **papel de calco**

♪ **track** *noun*
1 (*for sport*) la **pista** *fem*
a track event una prueba de atletismo
2 (*path*) el **sendero** *masc*
3 (*song*) el **tema** *masc*
This is my favourite track. Es mi tema favorito.
4 (*for cars*) **a racing track** un circuito
• **track suit** el chandal

tractor *noun*
el **tractor** *masc*

trade *noun*
(*profession*) el **oficio** *masc*

trade mark *noun*
la **marca comercial**
a registered trade mark una marca registrada

trade union *noun*
el **sindicato** *masc*

tradition *noun*
la **tradición** *fem*

traditional *adjective*
tradicional *masc & fem*

♪ **traffic** *noun*
el **tráfico** *masc*
• **traffic jam** el embotellamiento
• **traffic lights** el semáforo
• **traffic warden** el & la guardia municipal

tragedy *noun*
la **tragedia** *fem*

tragic *adjective*
trágico *masc*, **trágica** *fem*

trail *noun*
(*path*) el **sendero** *masc*
a nature trail un sendero ecológico

trailer *noun*
1 (*on a car*) el **remolque** *masc*
2 (*of a film*) el **trailer** *masc*

English-Spanish

to train *verb* ▷ see **train** *noun*
1 (*for a profession*) **estudiar** [17]
He's training to be a nurse. Está estudiando para ser enfermero.
2 (*professionals*) **formar** [17]
They train people to use computers. Enseñan informática.
3 (*in sport*) **entrenar** [17]
The team trains on Saturdays. El equipo entrena los sábados.

train *noun* ▷ see **train** *verb*
el **tren** *masc*
the train to York el tren para York
He's coming by train. Viene en tren.
• **train ticket** el billete de tren
• **train timetable** el horario de trenes

trainer *noun*
1 (*of an athlete, a horse*) el **entrenador** *masc*, la **entrenadora** *fem*
2 (*shoe*) la **zapatilla de deporte**
my new trainers mis zapatillas de deporte nuevas

training *noun*
1 (*for a career*) la **formación** *fem*
2 (*for sport*) el **entrenamiento** *masc*

tram *noun*
el **tranvía** *masc*

trampoline *noun*
la **cama elástica**

transfer *noun*
1 (*of money*) la **transferencia** *fem*
2 (*to a new post*) el **traslado** *masc*
3 (*sticker*) la **calcomanía** *fem*

to translate *verb*
traducir [60]
to translate something into Spanish traducir algo al español

translation *noun*
la **traducción** *fem*

translator *noun*
el **traductor** *masc*, la **traductora** *fem*
I'd like to be a translator. Me gustaría ser traductora.

transparent *adjective*
transparente *masc & fem*

transplant *noun*
el **trasplante** *masc*

transport *noun*
el **transporte** *masc*
air transport el transporte aéreo
public transport transporte público

trap *noun*
la **trampa** *fem*

to travel *verb* ▷ see **travel** *noun*
viajar [17]
to travel by train viajar en tren
I want to travel. Quiero viajar.

travel *noun* ▷ see **travel** *verb*
los **viajes** *plural masc*
foreign travel los viajes al extranjero
a travel brochure un folleto de viajes
• **travel agency** la agencia de viajes
• **travel agent** el & la agente de viajes

traveller *noun*
1 (*for business, pleasure*) el **viajero** *masc*, la **viajera** *fem*
2 (*as a lifestyle*) **to be a traveller** llevar [17] una vida nómada
• **traveller's cheque** el cheque de viaje

travelling *noun*
el **viajar**
I like travelling. Me gusta viajar.

travel-sick *adj*
to be travel-sick, to get travel-sick marearse [17] en los viajes

tray *noun*
la **bandeja** *fem*

to tread *verb*
to tread on something pisar [17] algo

treasure *noun*
el **tesoro** *masc*

treat *noun* ▷ see **treat** *verb*
el **capricho** *masc*
to give yourself a treat darse [4] un capricho
It's a little treat. Es un caprichito.
I took them to the pool as a treat. Les llevé a la piscina como algo especial.

to treat *verb* ▷ see **treat** *noun*
1 **tratar** [17]
the doctor who treated me el médico que me trató
He treats his dog well. Trata bien a su perro.
2 **to treat somebody to something** invitar [17] a alguien a algo
I'll treat you to an ice cream. Te invito a un helado.
3 **to treat yourself** darse [4] un capricho
I treated myself to a new dress. Me compré un vestido para darme un capricho.

treatment *noun*
1 (*medical*) el **tratamiento** *masc*
2 (*of a person, an object, etc*) el **trato** *masc*

a b c d e f g h i j k l m n o p q r s t u v w x y z

treaty *noun*
el **tratado** *masc*

ʃ **tree** *noun*
el **árbol** *masc*
• **tree trunk** el tronco

tremendous *adjective*
tremendo *masc*, **tremenda** *fem*
a tremendous victory una tremenda victoria
a tremendous athlete un atleta formidable

trend *noun*
1 (*fashion*) la **moda** *fem*
2 (*tendency*) la **tendencia** *fem*

trendy *adjective*
de moda

trial *noun*
(*legal*) el **juicio** *masc*

triangle *noun*
el **triángulo** *masc*

tribe *noun*
la **tribu** *fem*

tribute *noun*
el **homenaje** *masc*

trick *noun* ▷ see **trick** *verb*
1 (*in cards, etc*) el **truco** *masc*
a card trick un truco con las cartas
It doesn't work, there must be a trick to it. No funciona, debe tener truco.
2 (*a joke*) la **broma** *fem*
to play a trick on somebody gastarle [17] una broma a alguien

to **trick** *verb* ▷ see **trick** *noun*
engañar [17]
He tricked me! ¡Me engañó!

tricky *adjective*
1 (*sensitive*) **delicado** *masc*, **delicada** *fem*
a tricky situation una situación delicada
2 (*difficult*) **difícil** *masc & fem*

tricycle *noun*
el **triciclo** *masc*

Trinidad *noun*
Trinidad *fem*

Trinidadian *adjective & noun*
1 **trinitense** *masc & fem*
2 un & una **trinitense** *masc & fem*
the Trinidadians los trinitenses

WORD TIP Adjectives and nouns for nationality and regional origin do not have capital letters in Spanish.

ʃ **trip** *noun* ▷ see **trip** *verb*
el **viaje** *masc*
a trip to Florida un viaje a Florida
a day trip to Bristol un viaje de un día a Bristol
to go on a trip hacer [7] un viaje
He's on a business trip. Está en viaje de negocios.

ʃ to **trip** *verb* ▷ see **trip** *noun*
tropezar [25]
Nicky tripped over a stone. Nicky tropezó con una piedra.

to **triple** *verb*
triplicar [31]
The price has tripled. El precio se ha triplicado.

ʃ **trolley** *noun*
el **carro** *masc*

trombone *noun*
el **trombón** *masc*
to play the trombone tocar [31] el trombón

trophy *noun*
el **trofeo** *masc*

trouble *noun*
1 los **problemas** *plural masc*
We had trouble with the car. Tuvimos problemas con el coche.
Steve's in trouble. Steve tiene problemas.
What's the trouble? ¿Cuál es el problema?
to get into trouble meterse [18] en problemas
2 (*difficulty*) **I had trouble finding a seat.** Me costó encontrar un sitio.
It's not worth the trouble. No vale la pena.
The trouble is, I've forgotten the number. El problema es que he olvidado el número.
It's no trouble! ¡No es ningún problema!

ʃ **trousers** *plural noun*
los **pantalones** *plural masc*
a pair of trousers unos pantalones, un par de pantalones

ʃ **trout** *noun*
la **trucha** *fem*

truant *noun*
to play truant hacer [7] novillos.
She's playing truant. Está haciendo novillos.

ʃ **truck** *noun*
el **camión** *masc*

ʃ **true** *adjective*
a true story una historia verídica
to be true ser [1] verdad
Is that true? ¿Es eso verdad?
It's true she's absent-minded. Es verdad que es despistada.

truly *adverb*
de veras

trump *noun*
el **triunfo** *masc*
Spades are trumps. Las picas son triunfo.

trumpet *noun*
la **trompeta** *fem*
to play the trumpet tocar [31] la trompeta

trunk *noun*
1 (*of a tree*) el **tronco** *masc*
2 (*of an elephant*) la **trompa** *fem*
3 (*for clothes*) el **baúl** *masc*

trunks *plural noun*
swimming trunks el bañador *masc*

trust *noun* ▷ see **trust** *verb*
la **confianza** *fem*

to **trust** *verb* ▷ see **trust** *noun*
confiar [32]
I trust her. Confío en ella.

truth *noun*
la **verdad** *fem*
To tell the truth, I'd completely forgottten. Si quieres que te diga la verdad, me había olvidado completamente.

try *noun* ▷ see **try** *verb*
el **intento** *masc*
It's my first try. Es mi primer intento.
You should have a try. Deberías intentarlo.
to have a try intentarlo [17]

to **try** *verb* ▷ see **try** *noun*
1 **intentar** [17]
to try to do something intentar hacer algo
I'm trying to open it. Estoy intentando abrirlo.
to try hard to do something esforzarse [26] por hacer algo
She's trying hard to learn Arabic. Se está esforzando por aprender árabe.
2 (*to taste*) **probar** [24]
Try this sauce. Prueba esta salsa.
• **to try something on**
(*clothes*) **probarse** [26] **algo**
Can I try it on? ¿Me lo puedo probar?

T-shirt *noun*
la **camiseta** *fem*

tub *noun*
1 (*for food*) la **tarrina** *fem*
2 (*bath*) la **bañera** *fem*

tube *noun*
1 el **tubo** *masc*
2 (*London underground*) **the tube** el metro

tuberculosis *noun*
la **tuberculosis** *fem*

Tuesday *noun*
el **martes** *masc*
on Tuesday el martes
I'm going out on Tuesday. Voy a salir el martes.
See you on Tuesday! ¡Hasta el martes!
on Tuesdays los martes
The museum is closed on Tuesdays. El museo cierra los martes.
every Tuesday todos los martes
last Tuesday el martes pasado
next Tuesday el próximo martes

WORD TIP Months of the year and days of the week start with small letters in Spanish.

tuition *noun*
las **clases** *plural fem*
piano tuition clases de piano
private tuition clases particulares

tulip *noun*
el **tulipán** *masc*

tumble-drier *noun*
la **secadora** *fem*

tummy *noun*
la **barriga** *fem*

tuna *noun*
el **atún** *masc*

tune *noun*
la **melodía** *fem*

tunnel *noun*
el **túnel** *masc*
the Channel Tunnel el Eurotúnel

turban *noun*
el **turbante** *masc*

Turk *noun*
un **turco** *masc*, una **turca** *fem*
the Turks los turcos

WORD TIP Adjectives and nouns for nationality and regional origin do not have capital letters in Spanish.

turkey *noun*
el **pavo** *masc*

Turkey *noun*
Turquía *fem*

Turkish *adjective & noun*
1 **turco** *masc*, **turca** *fem*
2 (*the language*) el **turco** *masc*

WORD TIP Adjectives and nouns for nationality, regional origin and language do not have capital letters in Spanish.

turn *noun* ▷ see **turn** *verb*
1 (*in a game*) el **turno** *masc*
It's your turn. Es tu turno.
Whose turn is it? ¿A quién le toca?
It's Jane's turn to play. Es el turno de Jane.
to take turns driving turnarse [17] para conducir
2 (*in a road*) la **curva** *fem*

to **turn** *verb* ▷ see **turn** *noun*
1 **girar** [17]
Turn your chair round. Gira la silla.
Turn left at the next set of lights. Gira a la izquierda en el próximo semáforo.
2 (*a page, mattress*) **dar** [4] **la vuelta a**
3 (*to become*) **ponerse** [11]
She turned red. Se puso roja.
• **to turn back**
volverse [45]
We turned back. Nos volvimos.
• **to turn off**
1 (*road*) **girar** [17]
2 (*a light, TV, etc*) **apagar** [28]
3 (*the gas, a tap, etc*) **cerrar** [29]
• **to turn on**
1 (*a light, TV, etc*) **encender** [36]
2 (*a tap*) **abrir** [46]
• **to turn out**
1 **to turn out well** salir [63] bien
to turn out badly salir [63] mal
It all turned out well in the end. Todo salió bien al final.
The holiday turned out badly. Las vacaciones salieron mal.
2 **It turned out that I was wrong.** Resultó que estaba equivocado.
• **to turn over**
1 (*in bed*) **darse** [4] **la vuelta**
2 (*a page*) **dar** [4] **la vuelta a**
• **to turn up**
1 (*to arrive*) **presentarse** [17]
They turned up an hour late. Se presentaron con una hora de retraso.
2 (*the gas*) **abrir** [46] **más**
3 (*the heating, volume*) **subir** [19]
Can you turn up the volume? ¿Puedes subir el volumen?

turning *noun*
la **bocacalle** *fem*
Take the first turning on the right. Toma la primera bocacalle a la derecha.
Take the first turning on the left. Toma la primera bocacalle a la izquierda.

turnip *noun*
el **nabo** *masc*

turquoise *adjective*
turquesa *masc & fem*

turtle *noun*
la **tortuga** *fem*

TV *noun*
la **tele** *fem*
I saw her on TV. La vi en la tele.

tweezers *plural noun*
las **pinzas** *plural fem*

twelfth *adjective* ▷ see **twelfth** *noun*
doceavo *masc*, **doceava** *fem*
on the twelfth floor en la duodécima planta

twelfth *noun* ▷ see **twelfth** *adj*
(*in dates*) **the twelfth of May** el doce de mayo

twelve *number*
doce *invariable number*
Tara's twelve. Tara tiene doce años.
It's twelve o'clock. Son las doce de la mañana (*midday*)., Son las doce de la noche (*midnight*).

twenty *number*
veinte *invariable number*
twenty-one veintiuno
twenty-five veinticinco
Marie's twenty. Marie tiene veinte años.

twice *adverb*
1 (*two times*) **dos veces**
I've asked him twice. Le he preguntado dos veces.
2 (*double the amount, number*) **twice as much sugar** el doble de azúcar
twice as many tourists dos veces más turistas

twig *noun*
la **ramita** *fem*

twilight *noun*
el **anochecer** *masc*

twin *noun* ▷ see **twin** *verb*
el **gemelo** *masc*, la **gemela** *fem*
her twin sister su hermana gemela
Helen and Tim are twins. Helen y Tim son gemelos.

to **twin** *verb* ▷ see **twin** *noun*
Oxford is twinned with León. Oxford está hermanado con León.

to **twist** *verb*
girar [17]

a b c d e f g h i j k l m n o p q r s t u v w x y z

two *number*
dos *invariable number*
two by two dos por dos
Ben's two. Ben tiene dos años.

type *noun* ▷ see **type** *verb*
el **tipo** *masc*
What type of computer is it? ¿Qué tipo de ordenador es?

to **type** *verb* ▷ see **type** *noun*
(*on a typewriter*) **escribir [52] a máquina**
I'm learning to type. Estoy aprendiendo a escribir a máquina.
I was busy typing some letters. Estaba ocupada escribiendo unas cartas a máquina.

typewriter *noun*
la **máquina de escribir**

typical *adjective*
típico *masc*, **típica** *fem*

typing *noun*
la **mecanografía** *fem*
Her typing is awful. Escribe muy mal a máquina.

typist *noun*
el **mecanógrafo** *masc*, la **mecanógrafa** *fem*

tyre *noun*
el **neumático** *masc*

U u

UFO *noun*
(*= Unidentified Flying Object*) el **ovni** *masc* (*= Objeto Volador No Identificado*)

♪ **ugly** *adjective*
feo *masc*, **fea** *fem*
What an ugly dog! ¡Qué perro más feo!

UK *noun*
el **Reino Unido**

Ulster *noun*
el **Ulster**

ulcer *noun*
la **úlcera** *fem*

♪ **umbrella** *noun*
el **paraguas** *invariable masc*
She forgot her umbrella. Se le olvidó el paraguas.

WORD TIP *paraguas* never changes.

umpire *noun*
el **árbitro** *masc*, la **árbitra** *fem*

UN *noun*
(*= United Nations*) la **ONU** *fem* (*= Organización de las Naciones Unidas*)

unable *adjective*
to be unable to do something no poder [10] hacer algo
He's unable to come. No puede venir.

unavoidable *adjective*
inevitable *masc & fem*

unbearable *adjective*
insoportable *masc & fem*

unbelievable *adjective*
increíble *masc & fem*

uncertain *adjective*
incierto *masc*, **incierta** *fem*
I'm uncertain whether they are coming. No estoy seguro si vienen o no.

♪ **uncle** *noun*
el **tío** *masc*
my Uncle Tom mi tío Tom
our uncle and aunt from Dublin nuestros tíos de Dublín

♪ **uncomfortable** *adjective*
incómodo *masc*, **incómoda** *fem*
This bed's very uncomfortable. Esta cama es muy incómoda.
Are you uncomfortable? ¿Estás incómodo?

unconscious *adjective*
inconsciente
Tessa's unconscious. Tessa está inconsciente.

♪ **under** *preposition*
1 (*underneath*) **debajo de**
under the bed debajo de la cama
It's under there. Está ahí debajo.
to go under something pasar [17] por debajo de algo
2 (*less than*) **menos de**
under £20 menos de veinte libras
children under five niños menores de cinco años

under-age *adjective*
to be under-age ser [1] menor de edad

♪ **underground** *adjective*
▷ see **underground** *noun*
subterráneo *masc*, **subterránea** *fem*
an underground car park un parking subterráneo

♪ **underground** *noun*
▷ see **underground** *adj*
(*railway*) el **metro** *masc*
We went on the underground. Fuimos en metro.

to **underline** *verb*
subrayar [17]

♪ **underneath** *adverb, preposition*
1 **debajo**
Look underneath. Mira debajo.
It's painted green underneath. Está pintado de verde por debajo.
2 (*+ noun, pronoun*) **debajo de**
It's underneath these papers. Está debajo de esos papeles.

♪ **underpants** *plural noun*
los **calzoncillos** *plural masc*
my underpants mis calzoncillos
a pair of underpants unos calzoncillos

underpass *noun*
1 (*for pedestrians*) el **paso subterráneo**
2 (*for traffic*) el **paso inferior**

♪ to **understand** *verb*
entender [36]
Do you understand? ¿Entiendes?
I don't understand. No entiendo.
They understand Portuguese. Entienden portugués.
I can't understand what he's saying. No entiendo lo que dice.

understandable *adjective*
comprensible *masc & fem*
That's understandable. Eso se entiende.

underwear *noun*
la **ropa interior**

to **undo** *verb*
1 (*a button, garment*) **desabrochar** [17]
2 (*your shoelaces*) **desatar** [17]
3 (*a parcel, knot*) **deshacer** [7]

undone *adjective*
1 (*buttons*) **to come undone** desabrocharse [17]
2 (*shoelaces*) **to come undone** desatarse [17]

to **undress** *verb*
to get undressed desvestirse [57]
I got undressed. Me desvestí.

unemployed *adjective*
▷ see **unemployed** *noun*
parado *masc*, **parada** *fem*
She's unemployed. Está parada.

unemployed *noun*
▷ see **unemployed** *adj*
the unemployed los parados
There are two million unemployed. Hay dos millones de parados.

unemployment *noun*
el **paro** *masc*

uneven *adjective*
irregular *masc & fem*

unexpected *adjective*
inesperado *masc*, **inesperada** *fem*

unexpectedly *adverb*
de improviso

unfair *adjective*
injusto *masc*, **injusta** *fem*
It's unfair to young people. Es injusto para la gente joven.

to **unfasten** *verb*
desabrochar [17]

to **unfold** *verb*
desdoblar [17]

unforgettable *adjective*
inolvidable *masc & fem*

unfortunate *adjective*
desgraciado *masc*, **desgraciada** *fem*
They were unfortunate enough to miss the plane. Tuvieron la desgracia de perder el avión.

unfortunately *adverb*
desgraciadamente
Unfortunately I've forgotten his address. Desgraciadamente he perdido su dirección.

unfriendly *adjective*
antipático *masc*, **antipática** *fem*

ungrateful *adjective*
desagradecido *masc*, **desagradecida** *fem*

unhappy *adjective*
1 (*miserable*) **infeliz** *masc & fem*
an unhappy childhood una infancia infeliz
2 (*discontented*) **to be unhappy** no estar [2] contento

unhurt *adjective*
ileso *masc*, **ilesa** *fem*
They were unhurt in the crash. Salieron ilesos del accidente.

uniform *noun*
el **uniforme** *masc*
in school uniform con el uniforme del colegio

uninhabited *adjective*
desierto *masc*, **desierta** *fem*

union *noun*
1 (*in general*) la **unión** *fem*
2 (*trade union*) el **sindicato** *masc*
• **Union Jack** la bandera del Reino Unido

unique *adjective*
único *masc*, **única** *fem*

unit *noun*
1 (*of measurement*) la **unidad** *fem*
2 (*in a kitchen*) el **módulo** *masc*
3 (*in hospitals, etc*) el **servicio** *masc*

United Kingdom *noun*
el **Reino Unido**

United Nations *noun*
las **Naciones Unidas**

United States *plural noun*
los **Estados Unidos**
the United States of America los Estados Unidos de América

WORD TIP Often referred to only as *Estados Unidos* without *los*.

universe *noun*
el **universo** *masc*

university *noun*
la **universidad** *fem*
university life la vida universitaria
He's a university lecturer. Es profesor universitario.
I want to go to university. Quiero ir a la universidad.

unjust *adjective*
injusto *masc*, **injusta** *fem*

unkind *adjective*
poco amable *masc & fem*

unknown *adjective*
desconocido *masc*, **desconocida** *fem*

⚷ **unleaded petrol** *noun*
la **gasolina sin plomo**

⚷ **unless** *conjunction*
a no ser que
... unless he does it ... a no ser que lo haga
... unless you tell her ... a no ser que se lo digas

WORD TIP *a no ser que* is followed by a verb in the subjunctive.

unlikely *adjective*
poco probable *masc & fem*
It's unlikely. Es poco probable.
It's unlikely they'll come. Es poco probable que vengan.

to **unload** *verb*
descargar [28]

to **unlock** *verb*
to unlock a door abrir [46] una puerta
The car's unlocked. El coche está abierto.
The door was unlocked. La puerta no estaba cerrada con llave.

unlucky *adjective*
(*person*) **de poca suerte**
to be unlucky no tener [9] suerte
I was unlucky, she'd gone. No tuve suerte, ya se había ido.
Thirteen is an unlucky number. El trece trae mala suerte.

unmarried *adjective*
soltero *masc*, **soltera** *fem*

unnatural *adjective*
poco natural *masc & fem*

unnecessary *adjective*
no necesario *masc*, **no necesaria** *fem*
It's unnecessary to book. No es necesario reservar.

to **unpack** *verb*
(*a suitcase, etc*) **deshacer** [7]
I unpacked my rucksack. Saqué las cosas de mi mochila.
We'll unpack and then come down. Deshacemos las maletas y bajamos.

unpaid *adjective*
1 (*bill*) **sin pagar**
2 (*work*) **no remunerado**

unpleasant *adjective*
desagradable *masc & fem*

unpopular *adjective*
poco popular *masc & fem*

unrealistic *adjective*
poco realista *masc & fem*

unreasonable *adjective*
poco razonable *masc & fem*
He's being unreasonable. No está siendo nada razonable.

unreliable *adjective*
poco fidedigno *masc*, **poco fidedigna** *fem*
unreliable data datos poco fidedignos
This computer is unreliable. No te puedes fiar de este ordenador.
He's unreliable. Es muy informal.

to **unroll** *verb*
desenrrollar [17]

unsafe *adjective*
peligroso *masc*, **peligrosa** *fem*

unsatisfactory *adjective*
insatisfactorio *masc*, **insatisfactoria** *fem*

to **unscrew** *verb*
1 (*a screw*) **destornillar** [17]
2 (*a lid*) **desenroscar** [31]

unsuccessful *adjective*
fallido *masc*, **fallida** *fem*
to be unsuccessful fracasar [17]
I tried, but I was unsuccessful. Lo intenté pero fracasé.

untidy *adjective*
desordenado *masc*, **desordenada** *fem*
The house is always untidy. La casa siempre está desordenada.

to **untie** *verb*
desatar [17]

⚷ **until** *preposition*
1 **hasta**
until now hasta ahora
until then hasta entonces
until the tenth hasta el diez
until Monday hasta el lunes
2 **not until ...** no hasta ...
not until September no hasta septiembre
It won't be finished until Friday. No estará terminado hasta el viernes.

unusual *adjective*
poco corriente *masc & fem*
an unusual beetle un escarabajo poco corriente
Storms are unusual in June. Las tormentas son poco corrientes en junio.

unwell *adjective*
to feel unwell sentirse [14] mal
She's feeling unwell. Se siente mal.
You look unwell. Tienes mala cara.

unwilling *adjective*
to be unwilling to do something no querer [12] hacer algo
She's unwilling to wait. No quiere esperar.

to **unwrap** *verb*
desenvolver [45]

up *adverb, preposition*
1 (*in a higher place*) **arriba**
up here aquí arriba
up there ahí arriba
up on the roof en el tejado
up in Glasgow en Glasgow
Hands up! ¡Manos arriba!
2 (*showing movement*) **to go up** subir [19]
We went up the street. Subimos la calle.
I ran up the stairs. Subí la escalera corriendo.
I'll go up to Bristol this weekend. Iré a Bristol este fin de semana.
It's just up the road. Está en esta calle un poco más arriba.
She came up to me. Se acercó a mí.
3 (*not in bed*) **to be up** estar [2] levantado
Liz isn't up yet. Liz aún no está levantada.
to get up levantarse [17]
We got up at six. Nos levantamos a las seis.
I was up late last night. Me acosté tarde anoche.
She was up all night. No se acostó en toda la noche.
4 **up to ...** hasta ...
up to here hasta aquí
up to fifty people hasta cincuenta personas
5 (*in expressions*) **What's up?** ¿Qué pasa?
What's up with him? ¿Qué le pasa?
What's she up to? ¿Qué está haciendo?
It's up to you to decide. Tú tienes que decidir.

uphill *adverb*
cuesta arriba

upright *adjective*
derecho *masc*, **derecha** *fem*
to stand upright estar [2] derecho, *fem* derecha
Put it upright. Ponlo derecho.

upset *adjective* ▷ see **upset** *noun, verb*
disgustado *masc*, **disgustada** *fem*
He's upset. Está disgustado.

upset *noun* ▷ see **upset** *adj, verb*
1 (*in sport, etc*) la **sorpresa**
2 **to have a stomach upset** estar [2] mal del estómago

to **upset** *verb* ▷ see **upset** *adj, noun*
to upset somebody disgustar [17] a alguien

upside down *adjective*
boca abajo
I turned them upside down. Los puse boca abajo.

upstairs *adverb*
arriba
Mum's upstairs. Mamá está arriba.
to go upstairs subir [19]
Don't go upstairs, he's asleep. No subas, está dormido.

up-to-date *adjective*
1 (*in fashion*) **moderno** *masc*, **moderna** *fem*
2 (*data*) **actualizado** *masc*, **actualizada** *fem*

urgent *adjective*
urgente *masc & fem*
She's in urgent need of help. Necesita ayuda urgentemente.

urgently *adverb*
urgentemente
She wants to see you urgently. Quiere verte urgentemente.

us *pronoun*
1 (*as direct and indirect object*) **nos**
She knows us. Nos conoce.
They saw us. Nos vieron.
He gave us a cheque. Nos dio un cheque.
They lent it to us. Nos lo dejaron.
Can you help us, please? ¿Puedes ayudarnos por favor?
Listen to us! ¡Escúchanos!
Wait for us! ¡Espéranos!
Don't push us! ¡No nos empujes!
2 (*in comparisons*) **nosotros** *masc*, **nosotras** *fem*
She's older than us. Es mayor que nosotros.
3 (*with prepositions*) **nosotros** *masc*, **nosotras** *fem*
behind us detrás de nosotros
They left without us. Se fueron sin nosotros
with us con nosotros, *fem* nosotras
4 (*with to be*) **It's us!** ¡Somos nosotros! (*all boys; boys and girls*), ¡Somos nosotras! (*all girls*)

US, USA *noun*
(*= United States, United States of America*) **los EE.UU.** *plural masc* (*Estados Unidos*)

♪ **use** *noun* ▷ see **use** *verb*

1 el **uso** *masc*
It has many uses. Tiene muchas aplicaciones
to make use of something hacer [7] uso de algo
'Instructions for use' 'Instrucciones de uso'

2 **to be no use: It's no use.** Es inútil.
It's no use phoning. Es inútil llamar.

♪ to **use** *verb* ▷ see **use** *noun*

usar [17]
We use nails. Usamos clavos.
It's easy to use. Es fácil de usar .
I used scissors to open the parcel. Usé tijeras para abrir el paquete.

- **to use up**

1 (*food*) **consumir** [19] **todo**
2 (*money, petrol*) **gastar** [17] **todo**

used *adjective, verb*

1 **to be used to something** estar [2] acostumbrado a algo
I'm used to getting up early. Estoy acostumbrado a levantarme temprano.
She's not used to it. No está acostumbrada.
We're not used to eating in restaurants. No estamos acostumbrados a comer en restaurantes.

2 **to get used to something** acostumbrarse [17] a algo
I've got used to living here. Me he acostumbrado a vivir aquí.
I'm not used to it yet. Todavía no me he acostumbrado.

3 (*about a past activity*) **She used to smoke.** Antes fumaba.
They used to live in the country. Vivían en el campo.

used *verb* ▷ see **used** *adj*

She used to smoke. Antes fumaba.
They used to live in the country. Vivían en el campo.

♪ **useful** *adjective*

útil *masc & fem*
It's very useful to me. Me es muy útil.
She finds the mixer very useful. La batidora le parece muy útil.

♪ **useless** *adjective*

inútil *masc & fem*
You're useless! ¡Eres un inútil!
I'm useless at football. Soy negado para el fútbol.
This knife is useless. Este cuchillo no sirve para nada.

user *noun*

el **usuario** *masc*, la **usuaria** *fem*

- **user-friendly** fácil de usar

♪ **usual** *adjective, adverb*

1 (*time, place, problem*) **de siempre**
It's the usual problem. Es el problema de siempre.
2 (*method*) **habitual** *masc & fem*
3 (*in expressions*) **as usual** como siempre
It's colder than usual. Hace más frío de lo normal.

♪ **usually** *adverb*

normalmente
I usually leave at eight. Normalmente salgo a las ocho.

utensil *noun*

el **utensilio** *masc*

U-turn *noun*

el **cambio de sentido**
to do a U-turn cambiar [17] de sentido

V v

vacancy *noun*
1 (*in a small hotel*) **'Vacancies'** 'Habitaciones libres'
'No vacancies' 'Completo'
2 (*for a job*) la **vacante**
a job vacancy una oferta de trabajo

vacant *adjective*
(*room, seat*) **libre** *masc & fem*

to **vaccinate** *verb*
vacunar [17]
to vaccinate somebody against something vacunar a alguien contra algo

vaccination *noun*
la **vacuna** *fem*
to have a vaccination vacunarse **[17]**

vacuum *noun* ▷ see **vacuum** *verb*
el **vacío** *masc*
• **vacuum cleaner** la aspiradora

to **vacuum** *verb* ▷ see **vacuum** *noun*
pasar [17] la aspiradora
I'm going to vacuum the living room. Voy a pasar la aspiradora por el salón.

vagina *noun*
la **vagina** *fem*

vague *adjective*
poco preciso *masc*, **poco precisa** *fem*

vaguely *adverb*
vagamente

vain *adjective*
1 (*attempt*) **vano** *masc*, **vana** *fem*
in vain en vano
2 (*person*) **vanidoso** *masc*, **vanidosa** *fem*

valentine card *noun*
la **tarjeta del día de San Valentín**

Valentine's Day *noun*
el **día de San Valentín**

valid *adjective*
válido *masc*, **válida** *fem*

valley *noun*
el **valle** *masc*

valuable *adjective*
valioso *masc*, **valiosa** *fem*
to be valuable ser **[1]** valioso
That watch is very valuable. Este reloj es muy valioso.
He gave us some valuable information. Nos dio información muy valiosa.

to **value** *verb* ▷ see **value** *noun*
valorar [17]

value *noun* ▷ see **value** *verb*
el **valor** *masc*

van *noun*
la **furgoneta** *fem*

vandal *noun*
el **vándalo** *masc*, la **vándala** *fem*

vandalism *noun*
el **vandalismo** *masc*

to **vandalize** *verb*
destrozar [22]

🔑 **vanilla** *noun*
la **vainilla** *fem*
a vanilla ice cream un helado de vainilla

to **vanish** *verb*
desaparecer [35]

🔑 **varied** *adjective*
variado *masc*, **variada** *fem*
She has had a varied career. Ha tenido una carrera variada.

variety *noun*
la **variedad** *fem*

🔑 **various** *adjective*
varios *plural masc*, **varias** *plural fem*
There are various ways of doing it. Hay varias formas de hacerlo.

WORD TIP *varios* always goes before the noun.

to **vary** *verb*
variar [32]
It varies a lot. Varía mucho.

vase *noun*
el **jarrón** *masc*

vast *adjective*
enorme *masc & fem*

VAT *noun*
(*= Value Added Tax*) el **IVA** *masc* (*Impuesto al Valor Añadido*)

VCR *noun*
(*= Videocassette Recorder*) la **cámara de vídeo**

VDU *noun*
(*= Visual Display Unit*) el **monitor** *masc*

🔑 **veal** *noun*
la **ternera** *fem*

vegetable *noun*
la **verdura** *fem*
vegetable soup sopa de verduras
We grow our own vegetables. Cultivamos nuestras propias verduras.

vegetarian *adjective*
▷ see **vegetarian** *noun*
vegetariano *masc*, **vegetariana** *fem*
vegetarian food comida vegetariana
He's vegetarian. Es vegetariano.

vegetarian *noun* ▷ see **vegetarian** *adj*
el **vegetariano** *masc*, la **vegetariana** *fem*

vehicle *noun*
el **vehículo** *masc*

vein *noun*
la **vena** *fem*

velvet *noun*
el **terciopelo** *masc*

vending machine *noun*
la **máquina expendedora**

Venezuela *noun*
Venezuela *fem*

Venezuelan *adjective & noun*
1 **venezolano** *masc*, **venezolana** *fem*
2 un **venezolano** *masc*, una **venezolana** *fem*
the Venezuelans los venezolanos

WORD TIP Adjectives and nouns for nationality and regional origin do not have capital letters in Spanish.

ventilation *noun*
la **ventilación** *fem*

verb *noun*
el **verbo** *masc*

verdict *noun*
el **veredicto** *masc*

verge *noun*
1 (*roadside*) el **arcén** *masc*
2 **to be on the verge of doing something** estar [2] a punto de hacer algo
I was on the verge of leaving. Estaba a punto de irme.

version *noun*
la **versión** *fem*
There are several versions of what happened. Hay varias versiones de lo que pasó.

versus *preposition*
contra
Arsenal versus Chelsea Arsenal contra Chelsea

vertical *adjective*
vertical *masc & fem*

vertigo *noun*
el **vértigo** *masc*

very *adjective* ▷ see **very** *adv*
1 (*just*) **It was the very thing he was looking for.** Era justo lo que buscaba.
The very person I need! ¡Justo la persona que necesito!
2 (*in expressions*) **in the very middle** justo en medio
at the very end justo al final
at the very front justo delante

very *adverb* ▷ see **very** *adj*
muy
very well muy bien
It's very difficult. Es muy difícil.
very much mucho
I like it very much. Me gusta mucho.

vest *noun*
la **camiseta** *fem*

vet *noun*
el **veterinario** *masc*, la **veterinaria** *fem*
She's a vet. Es veterinaria.

via *preposition*
por
to go via somewhere ir [8] por un lugar
We're going via Dover. Vamos por Dover.
We'll go via the bank. Pasaremos por el banco.

vicar *noun*
el **párroco** *masc*

vicious *adjective*
1 (*dog*) **fiero** *masc*, **fiera** *fem*
2 (*attack*) **feroz** *masc & fem*

victim *noun*
la **víctima** *fem*

victory *noun*
la **victoria** *fem*

to video *verb* ▷ see **video** *noun*
grabar [17]
I'll video it for you. Yo te lo grabo.

video *noun* ▷ see **video** *verb*
1 (*film*) el **vídeo** *masc*
to watch a video ver [16] un vídeo
I've got it on video. Lo tengo en vídeo.
2 (*cassette*) la **cinta de vídeo**
I bought a video. He comprado una cinta de vídeo.
3 (*video recorder*) el **vídeo** *masc*
- **video camera** la cámara vídeo
- **video game** el videojuego
- **video recorder** el vídeo
- **video shop** la tienda de vídeos

English–Spanish
a b c d e f g h i j k l m n o p q r s t u v w x y z

English–Spanish

view *noun*
1 (*outlook*) la **vista** *fem*
a room with a view of the lake una habitación con vista al lago
2 (*sight*) la **vista** *fem*
to disappear from view perderse [36] de vista
The hotel came into view. El hotel apareció ante nuestra vista.
3 (*opinion*) la **opinión** *fem*
in my view en mi opinión
her views on the plan su opinión sobre el plan

viewer *noun*
(*Television*) el & la **televidente** *masc & fem*

viewpoint *noun*
el **punto de vista**

vile *adjective*
horrible *masc & fem*

villa *noun*
el **chalet** *masc*

village *noun*
el **pueblo** *masc*

villager *noun*
el & la **habitante de un pueblo**

vine *noun*
la **vid** *fem*

vinegar *noun*
el **vinagre** *masc*

vineyard *noun*
el **viñedo** *masc*

violence *noun*
la **violencia** *fem*

violent *adjective*
violento *masc*, **violenta** *fem*

violin *noun*
el **violín** *masc*
to play the violin tocar [31] el violín

violinist *noun*
el & la **violinista** *masc & fem*

virgin *noun*
la **virgen** *fem*

Virgo *noun*
1 (*the star sign*) el **Virgo** *masc*
2 (*a person*) un & una **virgo** *masc & fem*
Robert's Virgo. Robert es virgo.

WORD TIP Use a small letter in Spanish to say *I am* ... etc with star signs. Star signs in Spanish are used without *el, un, la, una*.

virtual reality *noun*
la **realidad virtual**

virus *noun*
(*Computers, Medicine*) el **virus** *masc, pl:* los **virus**
anti-virus software software anti virus

visa *noun*
el **visado** *masc*

visible *adjective*
visible *masc & fem*

to visit *verb* ▷ see **visit** *noun*
visitar [17]
We visited Auntie Pat at Christmas. Visitamos a la tía Pat en Navidad.
We visited the castle. Visitamos el castillo.

visit *noun* ▷ see **visit** *verb*
la **visita** *fem*
This is my first visit to Vigo. Esta es la primera vez que visito Vigo.
to pay a visit to somebody hacerle [7] una visita a alguien
My father paid us a visit. Mi padre nos hizo una visita.

visitor *noun*
1 (*guest*) la **visita** *fem*
We've got visitors this evening. Esta tarde tenemos visita.
2 (*tourist*) el & la **visitante** *masc & fem*

visual *adjective*
visual *masc & fem*

vital *adjective*
importantísimo *masc*, **importantísima** *fem*
It's vital to book. Es importantísimo reservar.

vitamin *noun*
la **vitamina** *fem*

vivid *adjective*
1 (*colour, imagination*) **vivo** *masc*, **viva** *fem*
to have a vivid imagination tener [9] una imaginación muy viva
2 (*memory, dream*) **vívido** *masc*, **vívida** *fem*

vocabulary *noun*
el **vocabulario** *masc*

vocational *adjective*
vocacional *masc & fem*

vodka *noun*
el **vodka** *masc*

a b c d e f g h i j k l m n o p q r s t u v w x y z

voice *noun* (key word)
la **voz** *fem, fem pl:* las **voces**
to raise your voice levantar [17] la voz
to lower your voice bajar [17] la voz
Keep your voice down! ¡No levantes la voz!
She spoke in a low voice. Habló en voz baja
• **voice mail** el buzón de voz

volcano *noun*
el **volcán** *masc*

volleyball *noun*
el **vóleibol** *masc*
to play volleyball jugar [27] al vóleibol

volume *noun*
el **volumen** *masc*
the volume of letters el volumen de cartas
to turn down the volume bajar el volumen
What is the volume of this bottle? ¿Qué capacidad tiene esta botella?

voluntary *adjective*
voluntario *masc*, **voluntaria** *fem*
to do voluntary work trabajar [17] de voluntario *masc*, voluntaria *fem*

to **volunteer** *verb* ▷ see **volunteer** *noun*
to volunteer to do something ofrecerse [35] a hacer algo
She volunteered to cook dinner. Se ofreció a hacer la cena.

volunteer *noun* ▷ see **volunteer** *verb*
el **voluntario** *masc*, la **voluntaria** *fem*
• **volunteer aid worker** el & la cooperante

to **vomit** *verb* (key word)
vomitar [17]

vote *noun* ▷ see **vote** *verb* (key word)
el **voto** *masc*
We won by two votes. Ganamos por dos votos.

to **vote** *verb* ▷ see **vote** *noun* (key word)
votar [17]
to vote for somebody votar a alguien
She always votes for the Greens. Siempre vota a los verdes.

voucher *noun*
el **vale** *masc*

vowel *noun*
(*Grammar*) la **vocal** *fem*

voyage *noun*
el **viaje** *masc*

vulgar *adjective*
grosero *masc*, **grosera** *fem*

W w

waffle *noun*
(*for eating*) el **gofre** *masc*

wage *noun*, **wages** *plural noun*
el **sueldo** *masc*

wagon *noun*
el **vagón** *masc*

waist *noun*
la **cintura** *fem*
- **waistband** la pretina
- **waistcoat** el chaleco
- **waist measurement** la medida de cintura

wait *noun* ▷ see **wait** *verb*
la **espera** *fem*
an hour's wait una espera de una hora
You're going to have a long wait. Tendrás que esperar un buen rato.

to wait *verb* ▷ see **wait** *noun*
1 **esperar [17]**
They're waiting in the car. Están esperando en el coche.
She kept me waiting. Me tuvo esperando.
I'm waiting to see the nurse. Estoy esperando para ver a la enfermera.
2 **to wait for something** esperar algo
Wait for the signal. Espera la señal.
Wait for me! ¡Espérame!
1 (*in excitement*) **I can't wait to open it!** ¡Estoy deseando abrirlo!

waiter *noun*
el **camarero** *masc*
I'm a waiter. Soy camarero.
We left the waiter a tip. Le dejamos una propina al camarero.

waiting list *noun*
la **lista de espera**

waiting room *noun*
la **sala de espera**

waitress *noun*
la **camarera** *fem*
I work as a waitress. Trabajo de camarera.

to wake *verb*
1 (*somebody else*) **despertar [29]**
Jess woke me at six. Jess me despertó a las seis.
Don't wake the baby. No despiertes al bebé.
2 (*yourself*) **despertarse [29]**
I woke up at six. Me desperté a las seis.
Wake up! ¡Despiértate!

Wales *noun*
el **País de Gales**
I'm from Wales. Soy galés (*boy speaking*)., Soy galesa (*girl speaking*.)

WORD TIP Adjectives and nouns for nationality and regional origin do not have capital letters in Spanish.

walk *noun* ▷ see **walk** *verb*
el **paseo** *masc*
to go for a walk ir **[8]** a dar un paseo
We went for a walk in the woods. Fuimos a dar un paseo por el bosque.
We'll go for a little walk round the village. Daremos un paseo por el pueblo.
It's about five minutes' walk from here. Está a unos cinco minutos de aquí a pie.
to take the dog for a walk sacar **[31]** a pasear al perro

to walk *verb* ▷ see **walk** *noun*
1 **andar [21]**
I like walking on sand. Me gusta andar sobre la arena.
2 (*on foot*) **ir [8] andando**
It's not far, we can walk. No está lejos, podemos ir andando.
- **to walk around**
dar [4] una vuelta por
We walked around the old town. Dimos una vuelta por la parte vieja de la ciudad.
- **to walk with somebody**
acompañar a alguien
I'll walk to the bus stop with you. Te acompaño hasta la parada del autobús.

walking *noun*
1 **hacer [7] senderismo**
We're going walking in Scotland. Vamos a hacer senderismo en Escocia.
2 **It's within walking distance of the sea.** Se puede ir andando hasta la playa.

walking stick *noun*
el **bastón** *masc*

walkman® *noun*
el **walkman**® *masc*

wall *noun*
1 (*of a house*) la **pared** *fem*
2 (*of a garden*) el **muro** *masc*
She jumped off the wall. Saltó del muro.

3 (*of a city*) la **muralla** *fem*
the Great Wall of China la Gran Muralla de China

𝄞 **wallet** *noun*
la **cartera** *fem*

wallpaper *noun*
el **papel pintado**

walnut *noun*
la **nuez** *fem, fem pl:* las **nueces**

to **wander** *verb*
to wander around town pasear **[17]** por la ciudad
to wander off alejarse **[17]**

𝄞 **want** *noun* ▷ see **want** *verb*
all our wants todo lo que necesitamos

to **want** *verb* ▷ see **want** *noun*
1 **querer [12]**
Do you want some coffee? ¿Quieres café?
What do you want to do? ¿Qué quieres hacer?
I want to go to the beach. Quiero ir a la playa.
He wants to be a pilot. Quiere ser piloto.
We don't want to go with them. No queremos ir con ellos.
2 **to want someone to do something** querer que alguien haga algo
What do you want me to do? ¿Qué quieres que haga?
I want them to help me. Quiero que me ayuden.

WORD TIP *querer que* is followed by the subjunctive.

war *noun*
la **guerra** *fem*

ward *noun*
(*Medicine*) la **sala** *fem*

𝄞 **wardrobe** *noun*
el **armario** *masc*
Why don't you hang your shirts in the wardrobe? ¿Por qué no cuelgas las camisas en el armario?

warehouse *noun*
el **almacén** *masc*

warm *adjective* ▷ see **warm** *verb*
1 (*climate, water*) **templado** *masc*, **templada** *fem*
2 (*breeze, voice*) **cálido** *masc*, **cálida** *fem*
3 (*food, drink, bath*) **caliente** *masc & fem*
I'll keep your dinner warm. Te tendré la comida caliente.
4 (*day, person*) **It's warm today.** Hoy hace calor.
I'm warm. Tengo calor.
Are you warm enough? ¿Tienes frío?
5 (*friendly*) **caluroso** *masc*, **calurosa** *fem*
a warm welcome una bienvenida calurosa

to **warm** *verb* ▷ see **warm** *adj*
calentar [29]
to warm the plates calentar los platos
• **to warm up**
1 (*weather*) **It's warming up.** Está empezando a hacer más calor.
2 (*athlete*) **entrar [17] en calor**
3 **calentar [29]**
I'll warm up some soup for you. Te calentaré un poco de sopa.

warmth *noun*
el **calor** *masc*

to **warn** *verb*
advertir [14]
I warn you, it's expensive. Te lo advierto, es caro.
to warn somebody to do something advertir a alguien que haga algo
He warned me to lock the car. Me advirtió que cerrase el coche.

warning *noun*
la **advertencia** *fem*

wart *noun*
la **verruga** *fem*

𝄞 to **wash** *verb* ▷ see **wash** *noun*
lavar [17]
to wash the dishes lavar los platos
I've washed your jeans. He lavado tus vaqueros.
to wash your hands lavarse las manos
I've washed my hands. Me he lavado las manos.
to wash your hair lavarse la cabeza
You have to wash your hair. Tienes que lavarte la cabeza.
to get washed lavarse **[17]**
• **to wash up**
lavar los platos

𝄞 **wash** *noun* ▷ see **wash** *verb*
to give something a wash lavar **[17]** algo
to have a wash lavarse **[17]**
• **washbasin** el lavabo

𝄞 **washing** *noun*
1 (*dirty*) la **ropa sucia**
2 (*clean*) la **ropa limpia**
• **washing machine** la lavadora
• **washing powder** el detergente

English–Spanish

washing-up *noun*
los **platos sucios**
to do the washing-up lavar **[17]** los platos
• **washing-up liquid** el lavavajillas

wasn't *short for* **was not** ▷ **to be**

wasp *noun*
la **avispa** *fem*

waste *noun* ▷ **see waste** *verb*
1 (*of food, money, paper*) el **desperdicio** *masc*
2 (*of time*) **It's a waste of time.** Es una pérdida de tiempo.

to **waste** *verb* ▷ **see waste** *noun*
1 (*food, money, paper*) **desperdiciar [17]**
2 (*time*) **perder [36]**
You're wasting your time. Estás perdiendo el tiempo.

waste-bin *noun*
el **cubo de la basura**

wastepaper-basket *noun*
la **papelera** *fem*

watch *noun* ▷ **see watch** *verb*
el **reloj** *masc*
My watch is fast. Mi reloj está adelantado.
Your watch is slow. Tu reloj está atrasado.

to **watch** *verb* ▷ **see watch** *noun*
1 (*to look at*) **mirar [17]**
I'm watching a blackbird in the garden. Estoy mirando un mirlo en el jardín.
2 (*films, TV*) **ver [16]**
He was watching TV. Estaba viendo la televisión.
3 (*to keep a check on*) **Watch the time.** Estate atento al reloj.
Could you watch the baby for a while? ¿Puedes cuidar al niño un rato?
4 (*suspicious person*) **vigilar [17]**
5 (*to be careful*) **Watch you don't spill it.** Ten cuidado de no tirarlo.
• **to watch out**
Watch out! ¡Cuidado!
Watch out for wasps. Cuidado con las avispas.

water *noun* ▷ **see water** *verb*
el **agua** *fem*
drinking water el agua potable
a glass of water un vaso de agua

WORD TIP *agua* takes *el* and *un* in the singular even though it is fem.

to **water** *verb* ▷ **see water** *noun*
regar [30]
to water the plants regar las plantas

watercolours *plural noun*
las **acuarelas** *plural fem*

waterfall *noun*
la **cascada** *fem*

watering can *noun*
la **regadera** *fem*

watermelon *noun*
la **sandía** *fem*

waterproof *adjective*
impermeable *masc & fem*

water-skiing *noun*
el **esquí acuático**
to go water-skiing hacer **[7]** esquí acuático

water sports *plural noun*
los **deportes naúticos**

wave *noun* ▷ **see wave** *verb*
1 (*in the sea*) la **ola** *fem*
2 (*saying hello*) el **saludo** *masc*
3 (*saying goodbye*) el **adiós** *masc*
She gave him a wave from the bus. (*to say hello*) Le saludó con la mano desde el autobús., (*to say goodbye*) Le dijo adiós con la mano desde el autobús.

to **wave** *verb* ▷ **see wave** *noun*
1 (*to say hello*) **saludar [17]**, (*to say goodbye*) **decir [5] adiós**
2 (*a flag, newspaper*) **agitar [17]**

wax *noun*
la **cera** *fem*

way *noun*
1 (*road, route*) el **camino** *masc*
on the way en camino
the way to town el camino a la ciudad
We asked the way to the station. Preguntamos el camino a la estación.
Do you know the way to Caernarfon? ¿Sabes cómo se llega a Caernarfon?
on the way back en el camino de vuelta
'Give Way' 'Ceda el Paso'
2 (*direction*) la **dirección** *fem*
Which way did he go? ¿En qué dirección se fue?
Come this way. Ven por aquí.
to be in the way estorbar **[17]**
3 (*position*) **Put it the right way up.** Ponlo bien.
the wrong way up boca abajo
Your jumper is the wrong way round. Tu jersey está al revés.
4 (*distance*) **It's a long way.** Está muy lejos.
Terry went all the way to York. Terry fue hasta York.
5 (*manner*) la **manera** *fem*
a way of talking una manera de hablar
Do it this way. Hazlo de esta manera.
He does it his way. Lo hace a su manera.

a b c d e f g h i j k l m n o p q r s t u v w x y z

I did it the wrong way. Lo hice mal.
That's not the way to do it. No se hace así.
Either way, she's wrong. Sea como sea, está equivocada.
6 (*in expressions*) **No way!** ¡Ni hablar!
by the way por cierto
- **way in** la entrada
- **way out** la salida

we *pronoun*
1 **nosotros** *masc*, **nosotras** *fem* (*see Word Tip*)
We live in Carlisle. Vivimos en Carlisle.
We're going to the cinema tonight. Vamos a ir al cine esta noche.
2 (*for emphasis*) **nosotros** *masc*, **nosotras** *fem*
We did it. Lo hicimos nosotros.

WORD TIP *we*, like other subject pronouns *he*, *you*, *they*, is generally not translated in Spanish; the form of the verb tells you whether the subject of the verb is *I*, *she*, *it*, etc, so *we* is translated only for emphasis or for clarity.

weak *adjective*
1 (*feeble*) **débil** *masc & fem*
Her voice was weak. Su voz era débil.
2 (*coffee, tea*) **poco cargado** *masc*, **poco cargada** *fem*

wealth *noun*
la **riqueza** *fem*

wealthy *adjective*
rico *masc*, **rica** *fem*

weapon *noun*
el **arma** *fem*

WORD TIP *arma* takes *el* and *un* in the singular even though it is feminine.

wear *noun* ▷ see **wear** *verb*
1 (*clothing*) **children's wear** ropa de niños
sports wear ropa de deporte
2 (*use*) **I bought some shoes for everyday wear.** Compré unos zapatos para todos los días.

to wear *verb* ▷ see **wear** *noun*
llevar [17]
to wear make-up llevar maquillaje
Tamsin's wearing her trainers. Tamsin lleva sus zapatillas de deporte.
He was wearing black trousers. Llevaba pantalones negros.
She often wears red. A menudo viste de rojo.
Wear your new dress. Ponte el vestido nuevo.
What are you going to wear? ¿Qué te vas a poner?

weather *noun*
el **tiempo** *masc*
in bad weather cuando hace mal tiempo
The weather was hot Hacía calor.
What's the weather like? ¿Qué tiempo hace?
The weather is fine. Aquí hace buen tiempo.

weather forecast *noun*
el **pronóstico del tiempo**
The weather forecast is rain. El pronóstico del tiempo dice que va a llover.

web *noun*
1 (*of a spider*) la **telaraña** *fem*
2 (*Internet*) **the Web** la Web
- **website** el sitio web

wedding *noun*
la **boda** *fem*
The wedding was held in Wigan. Se celebró la boda en Wigan.

Wednesday *noun*
el **miércoles** *masc*
on Wednesday el miércoles
I'm going out on Wednesday. Voy a salir el miércoles.
See you on Wednesday! ¡Hasta el miércoles!
on Wednesdays los miércoles
The museum is closed on Wednesdays. El museo cierra los miércoles.
every Wednesday cada miércoles
last Wednesday el miércoles pasado
next Wednesday el próximo miércoles

WORD TIP Months of the year and days of the week start with small letters in Spanish.

weed *noun*
la **mala hierba**

week *noun*
la **semana** *fem*
last week la semana pasada
next week la próxima semana
this week esta semana
for weeks durante semanas
a week today una semana a partir de hoy

weekday *noun*
on weekdays entre semana

weekend *noun*
el **fin de semana**
last weekend el fin de semana pasado
next weekend el próximo fin de semana
every weekend cada fin de semana
They're coming for the weekend. Vienen a pasar el fin de semana.
I'll do it at the weekend. Lo haré durante el fin de semana.
Have a nice weekend! ¡Que pases un buen fin de semana!

English–Spanish
a b c d e f g h i j k l m n o p q r s t u v w x y z

weekly *adjective, adverb*
1 *(paper, magazine)* **semanal** *masc & fem*
a weekly magazine una revista semanal
2 *(to visit, to deliver)* **semanalmente**, **cada semana**
I see her weekly. La veo cada semana.

to **weigh** *verb*
pesar **[17]**
to weigh something pesar algo
How much do you weigh? ¿Cuánto pesas?
I weigh 50 kilos. Peso cincuenta kilos.
to weigh yourself pesarse **[17]**

weight *noun*
el **peso** *masc*
to put on weight engordar **[17]**
to lose weight adelgazar **[22]**

weird *adjective*
estrafalario *masc*, **estrafalaria** *fem*

welcome *adjective* ▷ see **welcome** *noun, verb*
1 *(to a place)* **bienvenido** *masc*, **bienvenida** *fem*
You're welcome any time. Siempre eres bienvenido.
Welcome to Leeds! ¡Bienvenidos a Leeds! *(to several people)*
2 *(as an answer)* **'Thank you!'— 'You're welcome!'** 'Gracias.'—'De nada.'

welcome *noun* ▷ see **welcome** *adj, verb*
la **bienvenida** *fem*
They gave us a warm welcome. Nos dieron una calurosa bienvenida.

to **welcome** *verb* ▷ see **welcome** *adj, noun*
dar [4] la bienvenida a
We welcomed our Italian guests. Dimos la bienvenida a nuestros invitados italianos.

well *adverb* ▷ see **well** *noun*
1 **bien**
to feel well sentirse **[14]** bien
Terry played well. Terry jugó bien.
The operation went well. La operación salió bien.
I'm very well, thank you. Estoy muy bien, gracias.
Well done! ¡Bien hecho!
2 *(in expressions)* **as well** también
Kevin's coming as well. Kevin también viene.
as well as además de
He has a broken arm as well as flu. Además de una gripe, tiene un brazo roto.
3 *(in questions, statements)* **Well, what's the problem?** Entonces, ¿cuál es el problema?
Well, well! Look who it is! ¡Anda! Mira quién es!
Very well then, you can go. Muy bien, entonces ya puedes irte.

well *noun* ▷ see **well** *adv*
(for water) el **pozo** *masc*

well-behaved *adjective*
a well-behaved child un niño que se porta bien
Be well behaved. Pórtate bien.

well-done *adjective*
(Cooking) **muy hecho** *masc*, **muy hecha** *fem*

well-dressed *adjective*
bien vestido *masc*, **bien vestida** *fem*
a well-dressed old lady una anciana bien vestida

wellington (boot) *noun*
la **bota de goma**

well-known *adjective*
conocido *masc*, **conocida** *fem*
a well-known singer un conocido cantante

well-off *adjective*
acomodado *masc*, **acomodada** *fem*
the well-off residents of Knightsbridge los vecinos acomodados de Knightsbridge

Welsh *adjective* ▷ see **Welsh** *noun*
galés *masc*, **galesa** *fem*
a Welsh recipe una receta galesa
My grandparents are Welsh. Mis abuelos son galeses.

Welsh *noun* ▷ see **Welsh** *adj*
1 *(the people)* **the Welsh** los galeses
2 *(the language)* el **galés** *masc*
Everybody here speaks Welsh. Aquí todo el mundo habla galés.

WORD TIP Adjectives and nouns for nationality, regional origin and language do not have capital letters in Spanish.

Welshman *noun*
un **galés** *masc*

Welshwoman *noun*
una **galesa** *fem*

weren't *short for* **were not** ▷ **to be**

west *adjective, adverb* ▷ see **west** *noun*
oeste
the west side la parte oeste
a west wind un viento del oeste
west of Toledo al oeste de Toledo
to travel west viajar **[17]** hacia el oeste
West Africa África Occidental

WORD TIP *oeste* never changes.

♪ **west** *noun* ▷ see **west** *adj, adv*
el **oeste** *masc*
in the west of Ireland en el oeste de Irlanda

♪ **western** *adjective* ▷ see **western** *noun*
oeste *masc & fem invariable*, **occidental** *masc & fem*
Western Europe Europa Occidental

♪ **western** *noun* ▷ see **western** *adj*
(*film*) la **película de vaqueros**

West Indian *adjective & noun*
1 **afroantillano** *masc*, **afroantillana** *fem*
2 (*person*) un **afroantillano** *masc*, una **afroantillana** *fem*
the West Indians los afroantillanos

WORD TIP Adjectives and nouns for nationality and regional origin do not have capital letters in Spanish.

West Indies *plural noun*
las **Antillas** *fem*
in the West Indies en las Antillas

♪ **wet** *adjective*
1 (*in general*) **mojado** *masc*, **mojada** *fem*
The grass is wet. La hierba está mojada.
My shirt is wet. Tengo la camisa mojada.
to get wet mojarse **[17]**
We got wet. Nos mojamos.
2 (*weather*) **lluvioso** *masc*, **lluviosa** *fem*
a wet day un día lluvioso

whale *noun*
la **ballena** *fem*

♪ **what** *adjective, pronoun*
1 (*asking questions: in general*) **qué** (*see Word tip*)
What is it? ¿Qué es?
What's the matter? ¿Qué pasa?
What did you say? ¿Qué has dicho?
What's she doing? ¿Qué está haciendo?
What did you buy? ¿Qué has comprado?
What's happening? ¿Qué pasa?
What time is it? ¿Qué hora es?
2 (*asking for precise information*) **¿cuál?**
What's your address? ¿Cuál es su dirección?
What's the problem? ¿Cuál es el problema?
3 (*in surprise*) **What?** ¿Cómo?
4 (*asking for a description*) **What's it like?** ¿Cómo es?
What's her name? ¿Cómo se llama?
5 (*after Spanish prepositions*) **What for?** ¿Para qué?
What colour is it? ¿De qué color es?
What make is it? ¿De qué marca es?
What's it for? ¿Para qué sirve?
What did you buy it for? ¿Para qué lo has comprado?
What country is it in? ¿En qué país está?
6 (*without a question*) **lo que**
Tell me what you bought. Dime lo que has comprado.
She told me what had happened. Me dijo lo que había pasado.
What I want is a car. Lo que quiero es un coche.

WORD TIP When *qué, cuál* and *cómo* are used in questions, they always have an accent.

wheat *noun*
el **trigo** *masc*

wheel *noun*
la **rueda** *fem*
the spare wheel la rueda de repuesto
the steering wheel el volante
- **wheelbarrow** la carretilla
- **wheelchair** la silla de ruedas

♪ **when** *adverb, conjunction*
1 (*in questions*) **cuándo**
When's she arriving? ¿Cuándo llega?
When's your birthday? ¿Cuándo es tu cumpleaños?
Ask when the next train is leaving. Pregunta cuándo sale el próximo tren.
2 (*in statements*) **cuando**
It was raining when I went out. Estaba lloviendo cuando salí.
Call me when he arrives. Llámame cuando llegue.

WORD TIP When *cuándo* is used in a question, it always has an accent.

whenever *adverb*
1 (*any time*) **cuando**
Come whenever you like. Ven cuando quieras.
2 (*each time*) **siempre que**
Whenever we go out, we lock the door. Siempre que salimos, cerramos la puerta con llave.

♪ **where** *adverb, conjunction, pronoun*
1 (*in questions*) **dónde**
Where are the plates? ¿Dónde están los platos?
Where do you live? ¿Dónde vives?
Where are you going? ¿Dónde vas?
I don't know where they live. No sé dónde viven.
2 (*in statements*) **donde**
the place where I live el lugar donde vivo
This is where I left it. Ahí es donde lo dejé.

WORD TIP When *dónde* is used in a question, it always has an accent.

a b c d e f g h i j k l m n o p q r s t u v w x y z

English–Spanish

whether *conjunction*
si
I don't know whether he's back or not. No sé si ha vuelto o no.

which *adjective, pronoun*
1 (*in questions*) **qué**
Which CD did you buy? ¿Qué compacto compraste?
Which drawer did she put it in? ¿En qué cajón lo metió?
2 **which one** cuál
Which one do you prefer? ¿Cuál de ellos prefieres?
'I saw your sister.'— 'Which one?' 'Vi a tu hermana.'— '¿A cuál?'
3 (*relative pronoun*) **que**
the lamp which is on the table la lámpara que está en la mesa
the book which you chose el libro que escogiste
the DVD which I told you about el DVD del que te hablé
the office in which she works la oficina en la que trabaja

WORD TIP When *qué*, *cuál* are used in a question, they always have an accent.

whichever *adjective, pronoun*
1 (*any + noun*) **Whichever watch you choose, make sure it has a guarantee.** Cualquiera que sea el reloj que escojas, asegúrate que tenga garantía.
It takes three hours, whichever way you go. Te lleva tres horas sea cual sea el camino que elijas.
Whichever way you look at it, it's difficult. De todos puntos de vista, es difícil.
2 (*any one*) **Take whichever you want.** Toma el que quieras.
Whichever you take, keep it safe. Cualquiera que tomes, guárdalo bien.

while *noun, conjunction*
1 (*long time*) **for a while** durante un tiempo
She worked here for a while. Trabajó aquí durante un tiempo.
after a while después de un tiempo
every once in a while cada de vez en cuando
2 (*short time*) **for a while** durante un rato
I read for a while. Leí durante un rato.
after a while después de un rato
in a little while dentro de un ratito
3 (*at the same time as*) **mientras**
Make some coffee while I finish my homework. Haz un café mientras termino los deberes.
Shoe repairs while you wait. Reparaciones de calzado al minuto.
4 (*but*) **mientras que**
I'm Catholic, while Debbie's Jewish. Soy católica, mientras que Debbie es judía.

whip *noun* ▷ see **whip** *verb*
el **látigo** *masc*

to **whip** *verb* ▷ see **whip** *noun*
(*cream*) **montar [17]**
whipped cream la nata montada

whirlpool *noun*
el **remolino** *masc*

whiskers *plural noun*
los **bigotes** *plural masc*

whisky *noun*
el **whisky** *masc*

whisper *noun* ▷ see **whisper** *verb*
el **susurro** *masc*
to speak in a whisper hablar **[17]** en susurros

to **whisper** *verb* ▷ see **whisper** *noun*
susurrar [17]

whistle *noun* ▷ see **whistle** *verb*
1 (*sound*) el **silbido** *masc*
2 (*instrument*) el **silbato** *masc*

to **whistle** *verb* ▷ see **whistle** *noun*
silbar [17]

white *adjective* ▷ see **white** *noun*
blanco *masc*, **blanca** *fem*
white wine vino blanco
a white shirt una camisa blanca

white *noun* ▷ see **white** *adj*
1 (*colour*) el **blanco** *masc*
2 (*of an egg*) **an egg white** una clara de huevo
• **white coffee** el café con leche

Whitsun *noun*
el **Pentecostés** *masc*

who *pronoun*
1 (*in questions*) **quién** *masc & fem*
Who wants a sweet? ¿Quién quiere un caramelo?
Who are they? ¿Quiénes son?
2 (*relative, as the subject*) **que** *masc & fem*
my friend who lives in Madrid mi amigo que vive en Madrid
the girl who lives next door la chica que vive al lado
3 (*relative, as the object: for one person*) **el que** *masc*, **la que** *fem*
the girl who I sent it to la chica a la que se lo envié
4 (*relative, as the object: more than one person*) **los que** *plural masc*, **las que** *plural fem*

a b c d e f g h i j k l m n o p q r s t u v w x y z

the friends who we've invited los amigos a los que hemos invitado
the girls who we've invited las chicas a las que hemos invitado

WORD TIP When *quién* is used in a question, it always has an accent.

whole *adjective, noun*
todo *masc*, **toda** *fem*
the whole time todo el tiempo
the whole morning toda la mañana
the whole world todo el mundo
our whole family toda la familia
They took the whole lot. Se lo llevaron todo.
the whole of the class toda la clase
on the whole en general
On the whole we like it here. En general estamos a gusto aquí.

♪ **wholemeal bread** *noun*
el **pan integral**

whom *pronoun*
1 (*in questions*) **quién** *masc & fem*
Whom did you see? ¿A quién viste?
2 (*as a relative pronoun*) **que**
the person whom I saw la persona que vi
the teacher whom I saw el profesor que vi
the people whom I saw las personas que vi
3 (*after a preposition: for one person*) **el que** *masc*, **la que** *fem*
the person to whom I wrote la persona a la que escribí
the manager to whom I wrote el gerente al que escribí
4 (*after a preposition: for more than one person*) **los que** *plural masc*, **las que** *plural fem*
the people to whom I wrote las personas a las que escribí
the teachers to whom we wrote los profesores a los que escribimos

WORD TIP When *quién* is used in a question, it always has an accent.

whose *pronoun, adjective*
1 (*in questions*) **de quién**
Whose is it? ¿De quién es?
Whose is this jacket? ¿De quién es esta chaqueta?
Whose shoes are they? ¿De quién son estos zapatos?
I know whose it is. Sé de quién es.
2 (*as a relative: before a singular noun*) **cuyo** *masc*, **cuya** *fem*
the man whose wallet has disappeared el hombre cuya cartera ha desaparecido
the woman whose car has disappeared la mujer cuyo coche ha desaparecido
3 (*as a relative; before a plural noun*) **cuyos** *pl masc*, **cuyas** *pl fem*
the people whose names are on the list las personas cuyos nombres están en la lista
a friend whose daughters I give lessons to un amigo a cuyas hijas doy clases

WORD TIP *cuyo* and *cuya* agree with the noun that follows, not the person who 'owns.'

why *adverb*
por qué
Why did she phone? ¿Por qué llamó?
Nobody knows why he did it. Nadie sabe por qué lo hizo.

wicked *adjective*
1 (*bad*) **malvado** *masc*, **malvada** *fem*
2 (*brilliant*) **genial** *masc & fem*

♪ **wide** *adjective* ▷ see **wide** *adv*
ancho *masc*, **ancha** *fem*
a piece of paper 20 cm wide un trozo de papel de veinte centímetros de ancho
a wide range una amplia gama
The river is very wide here. El río es muy ancho aquí.
How wide is it? ¿Cuánto mide de ancho?

♪ **wide** *adverb* ▷ see **wide** *adj*
to be wide awake estar [2] completamente despierto
to be wide open estar [2] abierto de par en par

♪ **wide-screen television** *noun*
el **televisor de pantalla grande**

to **widen** *verb*
ensanchar [17]

♪ **widow** *noun*
la **viuda** *fem*
war widows viudas de guerra

♪ **widower** *noun*
el **viudo** *masc*
a widower who lived on his own un viudo que vivía solo

width *noun*
el **ancho** *masc*

♪ **wife** *noun*
la **mujer** *fem*
This is my wife. Te presento a mi mujer.

wig *noun*
la **peluca** *fem*

wild *adjective*
1 (*animal*) **salvaje** *masc & fem*
2 (*plant*) **silvestre** *masc & fem*
3 (*party*) **desenfrenado** *masc*, **desenfrenada** *fem*
4 (*idea*) **disparatado** *masc*, **disparatada** *fem*
5 (*person*) **to be wild about something** estar [2] loco por algo

English–Spanish

wildlife *noun*

a programme on wildlife in Africa un programa sobre la flora y la fauna de África

- **wildlife park** la reserva natural

will *verb*

1 (*using future tenses in Spanish*) **I will see you soon., I'll see you soon.** Te veré pronto.
He'll be pleased to see you. Estará contento de verte.
Will he come today? ¿Vendrá hoy?
It won't rain. No lloverá.
He'll be pleased to see you. Estará contento de verte.
There won't be a problem. No habrá problemas.
You won't forget it, will you? No lo olvidarás ¿verdad?

2 (*using the present tense in Spanish*) **I'll call them right now.** Los llamo ahora mismo.
Will you give me a lift to the station? ¿Me llevas a la estación?
Will you have a drink? ¿Quieres beber algo?
Will you help me? ¿Me ayudas?
The car won't start. El coche no arranca.
He won't open the door. No quiere abrir la puerta.

3 (*for future plans*) **ir [8] a hacer**
I'll see them this evening. Voy a verlos esta tarde.
What will they do? ¿Qué van a hacer?

willing *adjective*

to be willing to do something estar [2] dispuesto *masc*, dispuesta *fem* a hacer algo
I'm willing to pay for it. Estoy dispuesto a pagarlo.

willingly *adverb*

de buena gana

willow *noun*

el **sauce** *masc*
a weeping willow un sauce llorón

win *noun* ▷ see **win** *verb*

la **victoria** *fem*
our win over Everton nuestra victoria sobre Everton

to win *verb* ▷ see **win** *noun*

ganar [17]
We won! ¡Hemos ganado!
Granada won by two goals. El Granada ganó por dos goles.
I've won the lottery! ¡Me ha tocado la lotería!

to wind *verb* ▷ see **wind** *noun*

1 (*a wire, rope*) **enrollar [17]**
2 (*a clock*) **dar [4] cuerda a**

wind *noun* ▷ see **wind** *verb*

el **viento** *masc*
the North wind el viento del norte

- **wind farm** el parque eólico
- **wind instrument** el instrumento de viento

> mini-info **wind power**
>
> Spain is the second largest producer of wind-powered electricity in the world after Germany.

window *noun*

1 (*in a building*) la **ventana** *fem*
to look out of the window mirar [17] por la ventana
2 (*in a car, bus, train*) la **ventanilla** *fem*

windscreen *noun*

el **parabrisas** *masc, pl:* los **parabrisas**

- **windscreen wipers** los limpiaparabrisas

windsurfing *noun*

el **windsurf** *masc*
to go windsurfing hacer [7] windsurf

- **windsurfing board** la tabla de windsurf

windy *adjective*

1 (*place*) **con mucho viento**
2 (*day*) **de viento**
It's windy today. Hoy hace viento.

wine *noun*

el **vino** *masc*
a glass of white wine una copa de vino blanco
a bottle of red wine una botella de vino tinto

wing *noun*

1 (*of a bird*) el **ala** *fem*
the wing el ala
2 (*in sport*) el & la **alero** *masc & fem*

WORD TIP *ala* takes *el* and *un* in the singular even though it is fem.

to wink *verb*

to wink at somebody guiñar [17] el ojo a alguien

winner *noun*

el **ganador** *masc*, la **ganadora** *fem*

winning *adjective*

(*team*) **ganador** *masc*, **ganadora** *fem*

winnings *plural noun*

las **ganancias** *plural fem*

a b c d e f g h i j k l m n o p q r s t u v w x y z

℘ **winter** *noun*
el **invierno** *masc*
in winter en invierno
winter sports los deportes de invierno

℘ to **wipe** *verb*
limpiar [17]
I'll just wipe the table. Voy a limpiar la mesa.
to wipe your nose limpiarse [17] la nariz
- **to wipe up**
(*dishes*) **secar** [17]

wire *noun*
el **alambre** *masc*
an electric wire un cable
- **wire netting** la red de alambre

℘ **wireless** *adjective*
inalámbrico *masc*, **inalámbrica** *fem*

℘ **wise** *adjective*
sabio *masc*, **sabia** *fem*
a wise man un sabio

wish *noun* ▷ see **wish** *verb*
1 (*something hoped for*) el **deseo** *masc*
Make a wish! ¡Piensa un deseo!
2 (*in letters*) **Best wishes, Ann** Saludos de Ann.

to **wish** *verb* ▷ see **wish** *noun*
1 (*in greetings*) **I wished him a happy birthday.** Le deseé un feliz cumpleaños.
2 (*saying what you want*) **I wish you were here.** Ojalá estuvieses aquí.

WORD TIP *ojalá* is followed by a verb in the subjunctive.

wit *noun*
el **ingenio** *masc*

witch *noun*
la **bruja** *fem*

℘ **with** *preposition*
1 **con**
with James con James
with me conmigo
with you contigo
with them con ellos
with pleasure con gusto
Beat the eggs with a fork. Bate los huevos con un tenedor.
He took his umbrella with him. Se llevó el paraguas.
2 (*in descriptions*) **a girl with blue eyes** una chica de ojos azules
the man with the red shirt el hombre de la camisa roja
the boy with the broken arm el chico con el brazo roto
3 (*at the house of*) **We're staying the night with Frank.** Nos quedamos a dormir en casa de Frank.
4 (*after past participles*) **de**
filled with water lleno de agua
covered with mud cubierto de barro
red with rage rojo de ira

℘ **without** *preposition*
sin
without you sin ti
without sugar sin azúcar
without a sweater sin un jersey
without looking sin mirar

witness *noun*
el & la **testigo** *masc & fem*

witty *adjective*
ingenioso *masc*, **ingeniosa** *fem*

wizard *noun*
el **brujo** *masc*

wolf *noun*
el **lobo** *masc*

℘ **woman** *noun*
la **mujer** *fem*
a woman friend una amiga
a woman lawyer una abogada
a young woman una joven

wonder *noun* ▷ see **wonder** *verb*
la **maravilla** *fem*
No wonder you're tired. No es extraño que estés cansado.

to **wonder** *verb* ▷ see **wonder** *noun*
preguntarse [17]
I wonder why he did it. Me pregunto por qué lo hizo.
I wonder where Jack is. Me pregunto dónde está Jack.

wonderful *adjective*
maravilloso *masc*, **maravillosa** *fem*

℘ **won't** *short for* **will not** ▷ **will**

℘ **wood** *noun*
1 (*material*) la **madera** *fem*
The lamp is made of wood. La lámpara está hecha de madera.
2 (*trees*) el **bosque** *masc*
a walk through the wood un paseo por el bosque

wooden *adjective*
de madera

woodwork *noun*
la **carpintería** *fem*

English-Spanish

wool *noun*
la **lana** *fem*

woollen *adjective*
de lana
woollen gloves guantes de lana.

word *noun*
1 la **palabra** *fem*
a long word una palabra larga
in other words en otras palabras
What's the French word for 'window'? ¿Cómo se dice 'ventana' en francés?
to have a word with somebody hablar **[17]** con alguien
2 **to give somebody your word** prometer **[18]** algo a alguien
He broke his word. Rompió su promesa.
3 (*lyrics*) **the words of a song** la letra de una canción
- **word processing** el tratamiento de textos
- **word processor** el procesador de textos

work *noun* ▷ see **work** *verb*
1 (*your job*) el **trabajo** *masc*
She's at work. Está en el trabajo.
He's out of work. Está sin trabajo.
I've got some work to do. Tengo trabajo que hacer.
Ben's off work. Ben no ha ido a trabajar porque está enfermo.
2 **to be hard work** ser **[1]** difícil
It's hard work to understand it. Es difícil entenderlo.

to **work** *verb* ▷ see **work** *noun*
1 (*at your job*) **trabajar [17]**
She works in an office. Trabaja en una oficina.
Dad works at home. Papá trabaja en la casa.
Ruth works in accounts. Ruth trabaja en contabilidad.
He works nights. Trabaja por las noches.
I've worked hard for the exam. He estudiado mucho para el examen.
2 (*to operate*) **hacer [7] funcionar**
Can you work the DVD recorder? ¿Sabes hacer funcionar la grabadora de DVD?
3 (*to function*) **funcionar [17]**
The dishwasher's not working. El lavavajillas no funciona.
That worked really well! ¡Eso ha funcionado muy bien!
- **to work out**
1 **entender [36]**
I can't work it out. No lo entiendo.
2 (*to calculate*) **calcular [17]**
I'll work out how much it would cost. Calcularé cuánto puede costar.
3 (*to exercise*) **hacer [7] ejercicio**
4 (*to go well*) **salir [63] bien**

worked up *adjective*
to get worked up ponerse **[11]** nervioso, *fem* nerviosa

worker *noun*
1 (*in a factory*) el **trabajador** *masc*, la **trabajadora** *fem*
2 (*in an office, a bank*) el **empleado** *masc*, la **empleada** *fem*

work experience *noun*
las **prácticas de trabajo**
to do work experience hacer **[7]** prácticas
I did work experience in a hospital. Hice prácticas en un hospital.
to be on work experience estar **[2]** haciendo prácticas

working-class *adjective*
de clase obrera
a working-class background un ambiente de clase obrera
a working-class district un barrio obrero

work of art *noun*
la **obra de arte**

workbook *noun*
el **cuaderno** *masc*, (*Latin America*) el **quaderno** *masc*

workshop *noun*
el **taller** *masc*

workstation *noun*
(*Computers*) el **terminal de trabajo**

world *noun*
el **mundo** *masc*
the longest river in the world el río más largo del mundo
the western world el mundo occidental

World Cup *noun*
the World Cup la Copa del Mundo

world war *noun*
la **guerra mundial**
the Second World War la segunda Guerra Mundial

worm *noun*
el **gusano** *masc*

worn out *adjective*
1 (*person*) **agotado** *masc*, **agotada** *fem*
2 (*clothes, shoes*) **gastado** *masc*, **gastada** *fem*

worried *adjective*
preocupado *masc*, **preocupada** *fem*
They're worried. Están preocupados.

a b c d e f g h i j k l m n o p q r s t u v w x y z

We're worried about Susan. Estamos preocupados por Susan.
I'm worried about the delay. Me preocupa el retraso.

⚷ **worry** *noun* ▷ see **worry** *verb*
la **preocupación** *fem*
My biggest worry is the cost. Mi mayor preocupación es el coste.

⚷ to **worry** *verb* ▷ see **worry** *noun*
preocuparse [17]
She worries about the slightest thing. Se preocupa por la menor tontería.
Don't worry! ¡No te preocupes!
There's nothing to worry about. No hay razón para preocuparse.

worrying *adjective*
preocupante *masc & fem*

worse *adjective*
peor *masc & fem*
It was even worse this time. Fue aún peor esta vez.
to get worse empeorar [17]
The weather's getting worse. El tiempo está empeorando.
Things are getting worse and worse. Las cosas van cada vez peor.

worst *adjective*
the worst el peor
It was the worst day of my life. Fue el peor día de mi vida.
if the worst comes to the worst en el peor de los casos

worth *adjective*
1 **to be worth** valer [43]
How much is it worth? ¿Cuánto vale?
2 **to be worth doing something** valer la pena hacer algo
It's worth trying. Vale la pena intentarlo.
It's not worth it. No vale la pena.

to **would** *verb*
1 *(using the Spanish conditional tense)* **That would be a good idea.** Eso sería una buena idea.
If we asked her she would help us. Si le preguntásemos, nos ayudaría.
2 *(expressing wishes)* **I would like to go to the cinema.** Me gustaría ir al cine.
We would like to do that. Nos gustaría hacer eso.
3 *(in polite requests)* **Would you mind ...?** ¿Te importa ...?
Would you mind closing the window? ¿Te importa cerrar la ventana?
I would like an omelette. Quisiera una tortilla.
I would like four tickets. Quería cuatro entradas.
4 *(offering things)* **Would you like ...?** ¿Quieres ...?
Would you like something to eat? ¿Quieres comer algo?
Would you like a lift to the station? ¿Quieres que te lleve a la estación?
5 *(in refusals)* **He wouldn't answer.** No contestaba.
The car wouldn't start. El coche no arrancaba.

⚷ **wouldn't** *short for* **would not** (*See:* **would**)

wound *noun* ▷ see **wound** *verb*
la **herida** *fem*

to **wound** *verb* ▷ see **wound** *noun*
herir [14]

to **wrap** *verb*
envolver [45]
I'm going to wrap (up) my presents. Voy a envolver mis regalos.
Could you wrap it for me please? ¿Me lo envuelve, por favor?
Shall I gift-wrap it for you? ¿Se lo envuelvo para regalo?

wrapping paper *noun*
el **papel de envolver**

wreck *noun* ▷ see **wreck** *verb*
(of a train, car, etc) **los restos**
I feel a wreck! ¡Estoy hecho polvo!

to **wreck** *verb* ▷ see **wreck** *noun*
1 *(an object, a car)* **destrozar** [22]
2 *(a plan, an occasion)* **arruinar** [17]
It's wrecked my evening! ¡Me ha arruinado la tarde!

wrestler *noun*
el **luchador** *masc*, la **luchadora** *fem*

wrestling *noun*
la **lucha** *fem*

wrinkle *noun*
la **arruga** *fem*

wrinkled *adjective*
arrugado *masc*, **arrugada** *fem*

wrist *noun*
la **muñeca** *fem*

♂ to **write** *verb*

1 (*a letter, story*) **escribir [52]**
I'll write her a letter. Le escribiré una carta.
to write to somebody escribirle a alguien
I wrote to Jean yesterday. Ayer le escribí a Jean.
We write to each other a lot. Nos escribimos mucho.
to write an essay redactar **[17]** un ensayo

2 **to write somebody a cheque** extenderle **[36]** un cheque a alguien

• **to write down**
anotar [17]
I wrote down her telephone number. Anoté su número.

writer *noun*
el **escritor** *masc*, la **escritora** *fem*

writing *noun*
la **escritura** *fem*

♂ **wrong** *adjective*

1 (*factually*) **the wrong answer** la respuesta equivocada
I've brought the wrong CD. He traído el CD equivocado.
It's the wrong address. No son las señas correctas.
The information was wrong. La información era incorrecta.

2 (*mistaken*) **to be wrong** equivocarse **[31]**
I was wrong. Me equivoqué.
You're wrong. Te has equivocado

3 (*not as it should be*) **Something's wrong.** Pasa algo.
What's wrong? ¿Qué pasa?
What's wrong with her? ¿Qué le pasa?

X x

xerox *noun* ▷ see **xerox** *verb*
la **fotocopia** *fem*

to **xerox** *verb* ▷ see **xerox** *noun*
fotocopiar [17]

⚷ **X-ray** *noun* ▷ see **X-ray** *verb*
la **radiografía** *fem*
She had an X-ray. Le hicieron una radiografía.
I saw the X-rays. Vi las radiografías.

⚷ to **X-ray** *verb* ▷ see **X-ray** *noun*
hacer [7] **una radiografía de**
They X-rayed his knee. Le hicieron una radiografía de la rodilla.

Y y

yacht *noun*
1 (*sailing boat*) el **velero** *masc*
2 (*luxury boat*) el **yate** *masc*

to **yawn** *verb*
bostezar [22]

year *noun*
1 el **año** *masc*
last year el año pasado
six years ago hace seis años
the whole year todo el año
year after year año tras año
Happy New Year! ¡Feliz Año Nuevo!
They lived in Murcia for years. Vivieron en Murcia durante años.
He's seventeen years old. Tiene diecisiete años.
2 (*at school*) el **año scolar**
I'm in year eleven. Estoy en quinto de ESO (*the equivalent in the Spanish system.*)

yearly *adjective, adverb*
anual *masc & fem*, **cada año**
a yearly event un acontecimiento anual

to **yell** *verb*
gritar [17]

yellow *adjective*
amarillo *masc*, **amarilla** *fem*

yes *adverb*
sí
Yes, I know. Sí, ya lo sé.
'Is Tom there?'— 'Yes, he is.' '¿Está Tom ahí?'— 'Sí.'

yesterday *adverb*
ayer
yesterday afternoon ayer por la tarde
yesterday morning ayer por la mañana
the day before yesterday anteayer
I saw her yesterday. La vi ayer.

yet *adverb*
1 (*with a negative*) **aún**
not yet aún no
It's not ready yet. No está listo aún.
2 (*in a question*) **ya**
Have you finished yet? ¿Has terminado ya?

yoga *noun*
la **yoga** *fem*

yoghurt *noun*
el **yogur** *masc*
a banana yoghurt un yogur de plátano
a plain yoghurt un yogur natural

yolk *noun*
la **yema** *fem*

you *pronoun*
1 (*as the subject: informal*) **tú,** (*pl*) **vosotros, vosotras;** (*polite*) **usted,** (*pl*) **ustedes** (*see Word Tip*)
Do you want to go to the cinema? ¿Quieres ir al cine? (*one person*)., ¿Queréis ir al cine? (*more than one person*).
2 (*for emphasis: to one person*) **tú**, (*pl*) **vosotros** *plural masc*, **vosotras** *plural fem*
You said it! ¡Tú lo dijiste!
But you all saw it! ¡Pero todos vosotros lo visteis!
3 (*polite form: to one person*) **usted**, (*pl*) **ustedes**
Are you our new teacher? ¿Es usted nuestro nuevo profesor?
Are you Mr and Mrs Atkins? ¿Son ustedes los señores Atkins?
4 (*as direct and indirect object: to one person*) **te**, (*to one more than one person*) **os**
I'll write to you. Te escribiré.
I'll write to you. Os escribiré.
5 (*as direct and indirect object polite form: to one person*) **le**, (*pl*) **les**
I saw you. Le vi.
I saw you. Les vi (*more than one*).
I shall send you the document. Le mandaré el documento.
Dear Mr and Mrs Jones, I am sending you the information ... Estimados señor y señora Jones: Les mando la información ...
I shall send it to you on Monday. Se lo mandaré el lunes.

WORD TIP When used with another pronoun, *le* and *les* become *se*.

6 (*in comparisons*) **tú**, (*pl*) **vosotros** *masc*, **vosotras** *fem*
He's older than you. Es mayor que tú., Es mayor que vosotros.
7 (*with prepositions*) **for you** para ti, (*pl*) para vosotros *masc* vosotras *fem*
in front of you delante de ti, delante de vosotros
with you contigo, con vosotros
8 (*polite form: with prepositions and in comparisons*) **usted**, (*pl*) **ustedes**
for you para usted, para ustedes

She's older than you. Es mayor que usted., Es mayor que ustedes.

WORD TIP *you*, like *I*, *he*, *they* etc, is generally not translated into Spanish; the ending of the verb tells you if the subject of the verb is *tú*, *vosotros*, *usted*, etc, so *you* is translated only for emphasis or clarity.

young *adjective*
joven *masc & fem*
a young woman una joven
a couple of young men un par de jóvenes
young people la gente joven
He's younger than me. Es más joven que yo.
Tessa's two years younger than me. Tessa tiene dos años menos que yo.
I'm the youngest in the team. Soy el más joven del equipo.

your *adjective*
1 (*to one person*) **tu**
I like your skirt. Me gusta tu falda.
You've forgotten your CDs! ¡Te has olvidado tus compactos!
2 (*to more than one person*) **vuestro** *masc*, **vuestra** *fem*
Your Spanish exam is on Friday. Vuestro examen de español es el viernes.
Your rucksacks are in the car. Vuestras mochilas están en el coche.
3 (*formal form*) **su**
Thank you for your hospitality. Gracias por su hospitalidad.
Your letters have arrived. Han llegado sus cartas.
4 (*with parts of the body, clothes*) **el**, **la**, **los**, **las**
Show me your hand. Muéstrame la mano.
Take your shoes off. Quítate los zapatos.
You've cut your hand. Se ha cortado la mano (*polite form*).
Do you want to take your coat off? ¿Quiere quitarse el abrigo? (*polite form*)

WORD TIP Spanish uses *el*, *la*, *los*, *las* for *your* with parts of the body and clothes.

yours *pronoun*
1 (*to one person*) **el tuyo** *masc*, **la tuya** *fem*
a friend of yours un amigo tuyo, una amiga tuya
My brother's younger than yours. Mi hermano es más joven que el tuyo.
These aren't my glasses, are they yours? Estas gafas no son mías, ¿son tuyas?
Yours are better. Los tuyos son mejores.
2 (*to more than one person*) **el vuestro** *masc*, **la vuestra** *fem*
a friend of yours un amigo vuestro, una amiga vuestra
Our house is smaller than yours. Nuestra casa es más pequeña que la vuestra.
Our car is smaller than yours. Nuestro coche es más pequeño que el vuestro.
Our children are older than yours. Nuestros hijos son mayores que los vuestros.
3 (*formal form*) **el suyo** *masc*, **la suya** *fem*
Excuse me, is this book yours? ¿Perdone, es suyo este libro?
Excuse me, are these books yours? ¿Perdone, son suyos estos libros?

WORD TIP The form of *tuyo*, *vuestro* or *suyo* to choose depends on whether the thing owned is *masc*, *fem*, *singular* or *plural*.

yourself *pronoun*
1 (*reflexive*) **te**
You'll hurt yourself. Vas a hacerte daño.
2 (*for emphasis*) **tú mismo** *masc*, **tú misma** *fem*
Did you do it yourself? ¿Lo hiciste tú mismo?, ¿Lo hiciste tú misma?
by yourself solo *masc*, sola *fem*
3 (*polite form: reflexive*) **se** *masc & fem*
You've hurt yourself. Se ha hecho daño.
4 (*polite form: for emphasis*) **usted mismo** *masc*, **usted misma** *fem*
as you yourself will understand como usted mismo comprenderá

yourselves *pronoun*
1 (*reflexive*) **os**
when you have washed yourselves cuando os hayáis lavado
Help yourselves. Servidos.
by yourselves solos *masc*, solas *fem*
2 (*for emphasis*) **vosotros mismos** *plural masc*, **vosotras mismas** *plural fem*
Did you do it yourselves? ¿Lo hicisteis vosotros mismos?, ¿Lo hicisteis vosotras mismas?
3 (*polite form: reflexive*) **se**
Please, help yourselves. Sírvanse, por favor.
4 (*polite form: for emphasis*) **ustedes mismos** *plural masc*, **ustedes mismas** *plural fem*
Did you do it yourselves? ¿Lo hicieron ustedes mismos?, ¿Lo hicieron ustedes mismas?

youth *noun*
1 (*stage of life*) la **juventud** *fem*
2 (*young people*) la **juventud** *fem*
today's youth la juventud de hoy, los jóvenes de hoy
3 (*young male*) el **joven** *masc*
about ten youths unos diez jóvenes
• **youth club** el club juvenil
• **youth hostel** el albergue juvenil

indicates key words

Z z

zany *adjective*
chiflado *masc*, **chiflada** *fem*

zebra *noun*
la **cebra** *fem*
- **zebra crossing** el paso de cebra

zero *noun*
el **cero** *masc*

to **zigzag** *verb*
zigzaguear [17]

zip *noun*
la **cremallera** *fem*

zodiac *noun*
el **zodiaco** *masc*
the signs of the zodiac los signos del zodiaco

zone *noun*
la **zona** *fem*

zoo *noun*
el **zoo** *masc*

zoom lens *noun*
la **lente de zoom**

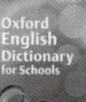